Environmental Law Handbook

Twenty-third Edition

Thomas F. P. Sullivan
Editor Emeritus

authors

Richard Alonso
Christopher L. Bell
Michael Boucher
F. William Brownell
Ronald E. Cardwell
Andrew N. Davis
Jason B. Hutt
Jessica O. King
Stanley W. Landfair
Duke K. McCall, III
Marshall Lee Miller

Karen J. Nardi
Austin P. Olney
Peggy Otum
Thomas Richichi
John M. Scagnelli
James W. Spensley
Daniel M. Steinway
Rolf R. von
Oppenfeld
Michael Weller

 **Bernan** Press

Lanham • Boulder • New York • Toronto • Plymouth, UK

Published by Bernan Press
A wholly owned subsidiary of Rowman & Littlefield
4501 Forbes Boulevard, Suite 200, Lanham, Maryland 20706
www.rowman.com
800-865-3457; info@bernan.com

10 Thornbury Road, Plymouth PL6 7PP, United Kingdom

ISSN: 0147-7714
ISBN: 978-1-59888-865-2
eISBN: 978-1-59888-866-9

♾ ™ The paper used in this publication meets the minimum requirements
of American National Standard for Information Sciences—Permanence
of Paper for Printed Library Materials, ANSI/NISO Z39.48-1992.

Printed in the United States of America

Summary Contents

Contents

Chapter 9   **Comprehensive Environmental Response,
Compensation, and Liability Act** **585**

Chapter 15 Emergency Planning and Community Right-to-Know Act 963

Preface

Upon release, each of the previous 22 editions of the *Environmental Law Handbook* has been the most up-to-date and comprehensive resource for critical information on important environmental regulations. The 23rd edition is no different. With major updates to several chapters, this edition will be your go-to reference for a multitude of topics related to environmental law.

This edition has many new authors joining the project. As always, these authors are at once among the top experts in their respective fields and practicing lawyers who are keenly aware of the regulatory issues that businesses and individuals must face. And, as always, these authors present the most critical and actionable content in plain English while avoiding legal jargon, so that you get the guidance and information you need quickly and easily.

The 23rd edition of the *Environmental Law Handbook* once again begins with an introduction to the form, structure, procedures, and implications of environmental laws in general, followed by an overview of enforcement and liability issues, before looking at specific regulations in greater detail. The many chapters to see significant updates in this edition include the chapters on the Clean Water Act, the Oil Pollution Act, the Toxic Substances Control Act, climate change, and pesticides, along with several others.

This book should once again serve as one of the first stops in any search for authoritative and actionable information on the most important environmental laws and issues. Its timeliness, comprehensiveness, insightfulness, accuracy, and accessibility make it an indispensible reference for students, scholars, business owners, and practicing lawyers alike. Keep it within reach.

About the Authors

Richard Alonso

Richard Alonso is a partner in Bracewell LLP's Environmental Strategies Group in Washington, D.C. He advises manufacturers and energy companies on environmental, permitting, compliance and enforcement issues before state and federal agencies. His practice focuses on Clean Air Act issues such as complex New Source Review applicability and permitting, mobile source regulations, EPA rulemaking efforts, legal challenges to EPA actions, and Clean Air Act enforcement defense and compliance counseling. He also advises companies on multi-media enforcement matters, including Clean Water Act compliance issues. Rich's environmental enforcement defense docket includes cases with EPA, states, and national environmental groups. He is called upon by various industrial clients for his knowledge of EPA federal enforcement and how EPA's enforcement office interacts with the rest of the Agency and with national environmental groups. Rich has nearly 10 years of service with EPA's enforcement office, principally with the Clean Air Act, Clean Water Act, and Safe Drinking Water Act programs.

E-mail
richard.alonso@
bracewelllaw.com

Website
www.bracewelllaw.com

Christopher L. Bell

Mr. Bell is a partner in the international law firm of Greenberg Traurig LLP. He counsels clients and defends in civil and criminal enforcement cases on a wide range of issues, including compliance with water, waste, air, chemical, transportation, pollution prevention, cleanup, product stewardship, and safety requirements as well as international issues such as the EU's ROHS Directive and REACH Regulation, and issues such as climate change, sustainable development, nanotechnology, and social responsibility. He participates in legislative and regulatory advocacy involving most of the major environmental laws. He has extensive experience designing, implementing, and auditing environmental management and compliance assurance systems, including systems based on ISO 14001, RC 14001, and the Sentencing Guidelines. He was a lead U.S. international negotiator on ISO 14001 for a decade and also served as a negotiator in the development of the ISO 37001:2016 standard on anti-bribery management systems. He is currently serving as an independent monitor overseeing compliance with complex Federal debarment and probation agreements arising from the resolution of a major criminal environmental case.

E-mail
bellc@gtlaw.com

Website
www.gtlaw.com

Michael Boucher

Michael Boucher is a member of Dentons US LLP's environment practice and leads the firm's chemical, pesticide, and consumer product regulation team. Mr. Boucher advises and represents manufacturers, distributors, and retailers with respect to federal and state regulation of basic and specialty chemicals and agricultural, institutional, and household pesticides; federal and state inspections and enforcement actions under chemical and pesticide laws; voluntary auditing of compliance with, including voluntary disclosures of non-compliance with, federal and state chemical and pesticide laws; development and implementation of systems for managing compliance with federal and state chemical and pesticide laws; federal agency rulemaking and litigation; environmental marketing claims; pre- and post-acquisition chemical and pesticide regulatory due diligence; chemical and pesticide data task force formation and administration; and international chemical and pesticide regulation and enforcement. He also counsels consumer product manufacturers about voluntary and mandatory consumer product recalls; consumer product take-back and recycling; consumer product hazard, defect, and incident reporting; consumer product safety standards; classification, packaging, and labeling requirements for consumer products; federal and state regulation of advertising and claims for consumer products; and consumer product warranties. In addition, Mr. Boucher lectures regularly on pesticide, chemical, and consumer product regulation and enforcement.

E-mail
michael.boucher@
dentons.com

Website
www.dentons.com

F. William Brownell

E-mail
bbrownell@hunton.com

Website
www.hunton.com

William Brownell is the head of the Hunton & Williams law firm's Regulatory and Environmental Law Team in Washington, D.C. His practice covers a broad range of environmental law issues in proceedings before federal agencies, state and federal courts, and Congress. He has represented clients in many of the major rulemakings and judicial review proceedings under the Clean Air Act as well as in citizen suits and enforcement actions. Mr. Brownell's practice also extends to issues arising under other environmental statutes. He is a member of the American Bar Association's sections on Administrative Law and Natural Resources Law. He speaks and writes frequently on environmental and administrative law issues and is an author of the *Clean Air Handbook*.

Ronald E. Cardwell

Ronald Cardwell is a shareholder with McNair Law Firm, P.A., in Greenville, South Carolina. He is a former assistant group counsel with a Fortune 500 manufacturing company, where his responsibilities covered all environmental issues. His practice embraces environmental challenges related to solid and hazardous wastes, groundwater, and real estate transactions. He has been involved extensively in environmental and toxic tort litigation at trial and appellate levels in state and federal courts relating to property damage, personal injury, and cost recovery under Superfund. His diverse environmental practice has led him to counsel clients in the sale, purchase, and development of properties with actual or perceived environmental liabilities. He is a member of the North Carolina, South Carolina, and Tennessee Bars and served as chairperson of the Environment and Natural Resources Section of the South Carolina Bar. He is a frequent lecturer and writer on environmental law topics.

E-mail
rcardwell@mcnair.net

Website
www.mcnair.net

Andrew N. Davis

E-mail
adavis@goodwin.com

Website
www.shipmangoodwin
.com

Andrew N. Davis is a partner and leads the national environmental practice at Shipman & Goodwin LLP. He counsels clients in transactional, permitting, compliance, and enforcement matters under health and safety, hazardous waste, air and water pollution, site development, and property transfer laws. With his advanced degrees in marine science, he has developed an international reputation in the area of oil and chemical spills and the assessment and restoration of natural resource damages, representing some of the world's largest shipping companies and their insurers in several high-profile marine casualty events throughout the United States, including most recently in the Gulf of Mexico, northern Atlantic (Buzzards Bay) and Pacific (Puget Sound) Oceans. Andrew is a member of several national and international environmental organizations, a frequent speaker on a variety of environmental/health and safety topics, and the author of several articles, chapters, and books on environmental issues, including oil pollution. He is an adjunct professor of environmental studies/law and policy at Connecticut College and a Fellow at the Goodwin-Niering Center for the Environment. Andrew earned his J.D. from George Washington University Law School, his M.S. and Ph.D. from the University of Massachusetts at Amherst, and his B.S. from Trinity College.

Jason B. Hutt

Jason Hutt, head of Bracewell LLP's Environmental and Natural Resources practice, advises and defends clients in administrative, civil and criminal enforcement actions (and internal investigations) related to the federal and state agencies, including EPA, DOI, DOE, CFPB and DOJ. He also counsels energy companies, manufacturers, project developers, investor groups and financial institutions about environmental risks and liabilities associated with incident response, regulatory compliance, project development, congressional hearings and corporate transactions, including current and upcoming regulatory and policy developments at the nexus of environment and energy policy. Within the energy sector, Jason's experience includes oil and gas development and transportation, petroleum refineries, liquefied natural gas (LNG) terminals, renewable energy projects (e.g., wind, biofuels and geothermal), natural gas processing plants, and propane retailers. Representative work in other sectors involves operations and industries such as chemical and other industrial manufacturers, oil field services companies, and hazardous waste management facilities.

E-mail
jason.hutt@bracewelllaw
.com

Website
www.bracewelllaw.com

Jessica O. King

E-mail
JKing@mcnair.net

Website
www.mcnair.net

Jessica O. King has practiced environmental law in South Carolina for almost twenty years. A graduate of the University of South Carolina School of Law in 1996, Jessie is a former staff attorney and head counsel for the Environmental Quality Control Division of the South Carolina Department of Health and Environmental Control (SCDHEC). While at SCDHEC, Jessie was the primary attorney for all cost recovery actions in federal court to recover costs for cleanup of state Superfund sites and advised the agency on hazardous waste, solid waste, air, and water issues. Since leaving SCDHEC, Jessie has worked for industry as a private-sector attorney. She is currently special counsel at McNair Law Firm, P.A., a firm with an established environmental practice with offices in South Carolina, North Carolina, and Kentucky. At McNair, Jessie represents potentially responsible parties at state and federal Superfund sites and advises industry on environmental permitting and compliance issues. In addition to complex litigation and regulatory issues, Jessie counsels her clients on brownfields, lending, foreclosure, bankruptcy, and inheritance. Jessie is a member of the South Carolina Bar and admitted to practice in the U.S. District Courts for the District of South Carolina and the U.S. Court of Appeals for the Fourth Circuit.

Stanley W. Landfair

Stan Landfair is a partner in the international law firm of Dentons US LLP (McKenna Long & Aldridge, LLP). He has been with the firm for several years and practices in the firm's San Francisco office. Mr. Landfair specializes in environmental law, administrative law, and state and federal litigation. He provides TSCA compliance counseling to many companies in the chemical, aerospace, and electronics industries. He has defended numerous TSCA enforcement actions, assisted many companies in self-disclosing TSCA violations under the EPA Audit Policy, and supervised and conducted numerous TSCA audits.

E-mail
stan.landfair@dentons
.com

Website
www.dentons.com

Duke K. McCall, III

Mr. McCall is a partner in the Washington, D.C., office of Morgan, Lewis & Bockius LLP, where he focuses his practice on environmental law and complex litigation. He represents clients in enforcement proceedings, cost recovery and contribution actions, citizens' suits, toxic tort litigation, and regulatory matters, including actions brought under the Comprehensive Environmental Response, Compensation, and Liability Act (Superfund), the Clean Water Act, the Clean Air Act, RCRA, and analogous state laws. He holds a B.A. degree from Furman University and a J.D. degree from Vanderbilt University.

E-mail
duke.mccall@morgan
lewis.com

Website
www.morganlewis.com

Marshall Lee Miller

Marshall Miller is a partner in the Washington, D.C., office of the law firm Baise & Miller, where he specializes in the areas of environmental law, occupational health and safety, and international transactions. Mr. Miller was previously special assistant to the first administrator of the U.S. Environmental Protection Agency, chief EPA judicial officer, associate deputy attorney general in the U.S. Department of Justice, and deputy administrator and acting head of the Occupational Safety and Health Administration. He was educated at Harvard, Oxford, Heidelberg, and Yale.

E-mail
miller@baisemiller.com

Karen J. Nardi

Karen Nardi is a partner in the environmental group of the firm Arnold & Porter LLP. She focuses her practice on a wide range of environmental and health and safety laws, and works with companies to manage their liabilities in business transactions. She also represents clients in enforcement actions. A poll published by *GC California* named Ms. Nardi the top environmental compliance attorney in California. Ms. Nardi has also been selected for inclusion in the *Super Lawyers* list of Northern California's top attorneys four years in a row, and she twice ranked among the top fifty females. In 2007 and 2008, she was listed in *The Best Lawyers in America* for her environmental experience. Ms. Nardi holds a master's degree in public policy from the University of California, Berkeley, and a law degree from its School of Law (Boalt Hall). She served as a law clerk to Judge William Schwarzer of the U.S. District Court in San Francisco. She has been a legislative analyst for the California State Assembly and an intern at the Congressional Budget Office in Washington, D.C. She is the coauthor of several books.

E-mail
Karen.Nardi@aporter.com

Website
www.arnoldporter.com/

E-mail
apojgo@gmail.com

Austin P. Olney

Austin P. Olney is a consulting counsel to Shipman & Goodwin LLP on environmental and maritime matters. Before retiring from full-time practice, he was a partner in the Boston office of Holland & Knight LLP. Prior to joining Holland & Knight LLP, he was the managing partner of the Boston, Massachusetts, office of Dewey & LeBoeuf LLP. Over his thirty-five-year career in private practice, he represented domestic and foreign clients in corporate, environmental, marine safety, and pollution matters. He has testified before the U.S. Congress on oil pollution legislation and has served as lead counsel, representing shipowners and their marine insurers, in connection with numerous high-profile oil spill incidents on the East, Gulf, and West Coasts. He has lectured extensively on oil pollution issues in the United States, Europe, and Asia. Previously, Mr. Olney served as the Secretary of Natural Resources and Environmental Control for the State of Delaware. He also served as counsel to the U.S. House of Representatives Merchant Marine and Fisheries Committee. He graduated with a B.A. cum laude from Harvard College and a J.D. from Georgetown University Law Center.

Peggy Otum

Peggy Otum has represented clients on complex environmental issues at the federal and state level for well over a decade. Her practice focuses on advising corporate clients on a broad range of environmental enforcement, litigation, and transactional matters, primarily involving hazardous waste requirements, natural resources, and real estate issues under the major federal environmental statutes and state analogs, with a particular focus on RCRA and CERCLA. Ms. Otum counsels companies in a variety of sectors, including chemicals, energy, pharmaceutical, electronics, real estate development and private equity. Her litigation experience includes toxic tort defense in addition to routinely representing clients in enforcement actions brought by federal and state regulators for violations of RCRA, CERCLA, EPCRA, TSCA, and the Clean Air Act, as well as state extended producer responsibility and product stewardship laws. Her transactional experience includes counseling clients with respect to M&A and real estate environmental due diligence for large scale and single parcel transactions, insurance and risk mitigation counseling, and post-sale indemnity disputes. Ms. Otum is a member of the Leadership Advisory Committee of the National Women's Law Center (NWLC) and an ardent supporter of women leaders in business and law. In addition to her work with NWLC, Ms. Otum has helped cultivate Arnold & Porter's San Francisco WomenConnect program, which provides a forum for San Francisco Bay Area women lawyers and senior-level clients to network and learn from each other. She was recently featured on *Working Mother* magazine's list of "The 2015 Working Mothers of the Year."

E-mail
peggy.otum@aporter.com

Website
www.arnoldporter.com

Thomas Richichi

E-mail
trichichi@bdlaw.com

Website
www.bdlaw.com

Tom Richichi is a principal in the Washington, D.C., office of Beveridge & Diamond, P.C. His practice has involved the representation of industry associations, corporations, and municipalities in regulatory compliance, enforcement, and litigation matters for more than twenty-five years. He has previously served as the chair of the firm's litigation practice and currently heads its practice relating to the Safe Drinking Water Act (SDWA). In that capacity, he has worked extensively on drinking water rulemakings, compliance issues, and matters involving risk assessment related to the establishment of enforceable drinking water standards. He has also successfully challenged major SDWA rulemakings, defended drinking water enforcement actions, and negotiated administrative orders on consent. His experience extends to underground injection control (UIC) programs and related matters, including hydraulic fracturing and carbon sequestration. Prior to joining the firm, he served as law clerk to the Hon. John J. Sirica on the United States District Court in Washington, D.C. He is a member of the bar of the United States Supreme Court and numerous trial and appellate courts, and regularly appears before regulatory agencies including the U.S. Environmental Protection Agency and its state counterparts.

John M. Scagnelli

John M. Scagnelli is a partner in the Lyndhurst, New Jersey, office of Scarinci Hollenbeck. During the past twenty years, he has represented domestic and foreign public and private clients in all aspects of environmental and corporate and commercial law. Prior to joining Scarinci Hollenbeck, Mr. Scagnelli was a partner and headed the Environmental Law Departments of Whitman Breed Abbott & Morgan, LLP, and Clapp & Eisenberg. He has served as a commissioner on the Interstate Sanitation Commission, a tristate environmental agency; as vice president and general counsel of Allied Maintenance Corporation, a subsidiary of the Ogden Corporation; and as legal counsel with Chesebrough-Ponds, Inc. Mr. Scagnelli has lectured and published widely in the environmental law field on topics that include brownfields development, natural resource damages, environmental issues in corporate transactions, and international environmental legal issues.

E-mail
jscagnelli@njlegalink.com

Website
www.njlegalink.com

James W. Spensley

E-mail
jwspensley@aol.com

James W. "Skip" Spensley is one of the nation's experts on the National Environmental Policy Act of 1969 (NEPA) working with its requirements from numerous perspectives, including administrative, legislative, judicial, and project development. Mr. Spensley served as an intern to the President's Council on Environmental Quality (CEQ) in 1970 after NEPA was first enacted. He assisted in preparing the first CEQ guidelines on environmental impact statement (EIS) preparation. In 1975, Mr. Spensley was hired by the U.S. House of Representatives to act as legal counsel to the subcommittee responsible for NEPA. During his tenure there, he was responsible for writing the first and only amendment to NEPA in 1975. Mr. Spensley has lectured on environmental law and NEPA at both the University of Colorado and the University of Denver Law Schools since 1982. He also serves as an adjunct professor in the Environmental Policy and Management graduate program at the University of Denver, where he teaches the NEPA course. He is the author of the *NEPA Compliance Manual* for federal managers and author of the NEPA chapter in the *Environmental Law Handbook* (editions 12–21) for Government Institutes. He conducts regular annual national workshops on NEPA and the EIS process.

Daniel M. Steinway

Daniel M. Steinway is a partner with Baker Botts, LLP's national environmental law practice, which advises corporate entities, trade associations, and business organizations on civil and criminal environmental matters. Mr. Steinway's practice includes all aspects of environmental counseling and litigation, including representation in governmental enforcement actions and litigation involving corporate entities and counseling on environmental regulatory matters and business transactions. Mr. Steinway previously served as minority (Republican) counsel responsible for environmental matters on the Committee on Science and Technology of the U.S. House of Representatives and as an attorney/adviser with the Office of Enforcement of the U.S. Environmental Protection Agency. Mr. Steinway received a B.S.E. (engineering science, cum laude) from the University of Michigan and a J.D. (with honors) from the George Washington University National Law Center.

E-mail
daniel.steinway@
bakerbotts.com

Website
www.bakerbotts.com

E-mail
rvo@testlaw.com

Website
www.testlaw.com

Rolf R. von Oppenfeld

Rolf R. von Oppenfeld is an environmental attorney with the Team for Environmental Science and Technology Law (TESTLaw) Practice Group, Rolf R. von Oppenfeld, P.C., in Phoenix, Arizona. Mr. von Oppenfeld received his B.S. in chemistry and biology and worked as a chemist and in the enforcement and Superfund offices at EPA headquarters. He received his J.D. (summa cum laude) in 1982 from George Washington University. He has published numerous articles, including "South Carolina Release Prevention, Reporting and Liability: A Primer on the Legal Requirements Imposed to Avoid and, if Necessary, to Respond to 'Environmental Accidents,'" 11 *Southeastern Envtl. L. J.* 223 (2003), and "The Federal Title V Air Quality Permit Program for Operating a Major Source of Air Pollution: A Primer on the Substantive and Procedural Requirements Imposed on Industrial Facilities by the 1990 Clean Air Act Amendments, Applicable Regulations, and Key EPA Guidance Documents," 33 *Envtl. L. Rptr.* 10815 (2003).

Michael Weller

E-mail
michael.weller@
bracewelllaw.com

Website
www.bracewelllaw.com

Michael Weller is an associate in Bracewell LLP's Environmental Strategies Group. He advises clients in the context of government investigations and enforcement actions, regulatory compliance and advocacy, litigation, permitting, and in quantifying and allocating liabilities during business transactions. He represents clients in the energy sector, including upstream oil and gas companies and pipelines, as well as industry trade associations, manufacturers, importers, and financial institutions in a wide range of environmental law and business matters. Mike regularly advises and advocates for clients in the face of new regulatory initiatives undertaken by the EPA, the Department of Interior, the Bureau of Land Management, the Federal Aviation Administration (FAA), the U.S. Customs and Border Protection, the Department of Transportation, the Pipeline and Hazardous Materials Safety Administration (PHMSA) and the Federal Motor Carrier Safety Administration (FMCSA).

About the Editor Emeritus

Thomas F. P. Sullivan

Thomas Sullivan has been at the forefront of the environmental field since the 1960s. He used his scientific and legal degrees in industry before practicing law and representing clients in the environmental field. He founded Government Institutes in 1973 and has authored and edited more than one hundred books, including *The Greening of American Business, Environmental Health and Safety Manager's Handbook*, and *Directory of Environmental Information Sources*. He has lectured extensively on environmental topics and served as president of Government Institutes until his retirement in 1998.

Environmental Law Handbook

Twenty-third Edition

Chapter 1

Fundamentals of Environmental Law

Daniel M. Steinway
Baker Botts LLP[1]

1.0 Environmental Law as a System

Over the past four decades, "Environmental Law" has evolved into a legal system of statutes, regulations, guidelines, requirements, policies, and case-specific judicial and administrative interpretations that address a wide-ranging set of environmental issues and concerns. These laws and requirements address not only the natural environment, including the air, water, and land, but also how humans interact with that natural environment and ecological systems. In addition, this system of environmental laws involves multiple layers of regulatory controls, since not only the federal government, but also state and local levels of government, have imposed interrelated and sometimes overlapping environmental requirements. This legal system is complex in itself and is made even more challenging by the difficulty of the interdisciplinary subject matter to be regulated (health, safety, and environment) and the quickly evolving scientific and technical issues typically presented in environmental cases.

Understanding the U.S. environmental law system, its principles and the ways in which the individual elements work together to achieve the legal system's objectives, is a challenge for those who try to comply with environmental laws. In fact, one of the key issues emerging in the environmental arena in the new millennium is the proper role of federal and state governments. At the federal level, there has been emphasis on "reinventing" environmental regulations and developing effective regulatory programs that may not always rely on old "command-and-control" concepts. The traditional "command-and-control" system has usually involved the establishment of environmental standards, permit enforcement procedures, liability assignment, and penalties (civil and/or criminal) for noncompliance, giving the governmental regulators wide powers to "authorize" or "prohibit" activities or pollution. As part of this approach, the regulatory authorities typically issue permits (or licenses) to parties to authorize various forms of emissions or discharges, and any breach of the terms of the permit or license would constitute an offense subject to prosecution and the full range of penalties provided for by statute. Moreover, the regulatory authorities generally retain associated powers to require environmental audits, cleanup, the cessation of work, the disclosure of information, and financial assurances and to specify that companies conduct activities pursuant to an environmental management plan or pollution reduction plan as part of a traditional "command-and-control" regulatory approach.

Although "command-and-control" strategies have made substantial progress in reducing pollution, this approach has sometimes been criticized for not achieving various legislative mandates and deadlines in a relatively timely manner and for being economically inefficient and difficult to enforce. In addition, many standards are often attacked on the ground that they are unrealistic and infeasible or do not focus on high-priority concerns. These strategies also are quite burdensome for regulatory agencies to administer, since these agencies must obtain detailed information concerning production processes and the suitability of various pollution control devices in order to develop a realistic and effective "command-and-control" program. With diverse industries, it is extremely expensive and time-consuming to obtain the necessary information and expertise on each industry. Other problems with this approach are the high costs for pollution control that leave little opportunity to take advantage of economies of scale.

In recent years, the federal government has adopted various economic instruments, such as market-based trading programs for the emissions of air pollutants and wastewater constituents, to introduce more flexibility, efficiency, and cost-effectiveness into pollution control measures. Most of these instruments operate as incentives to polluters who can determine the most efficient and cost-effective means for achieving environmental targets. To various degrees, these measures incorporate the "polluter pays" principle, whereby the polluter pays a financial penalty for higher levels of pollution and pays a smaller penalty or receives a financial reward for lower levels of pollution, or the "user pays" principle, whereby the user of a resource pays the full social cost of supplying the resource, such as for water and related services including treatment costs.

At the same time, many states are implementing or pursuing new programs to gain more control over their environmental affairs and increasingly are being viewed as "laboratories" for the development of new and innovative approaches to environmental regulation. Consistent with this trend, many state legislatures and environmental agencies have recently been developing proposals to address the potential risks of climate change through programs to control and/or reduce the production of greenhouse gases such as carbon dioxide. Leading this effort have been states in the northeastern United States and California. In the Northeast, the states have banded together to form the "Regional Greenhouse Gas Initiative," which relies on a multi-state cap-and-trade program with a market-based emissions trading system. This program requires electric power generators in participating states to reduce carbon dioxide emissions. Other states have begun to use so-called "product stewardship" approaches to environmental regulation. "Product stewardship" is based on the regulatory principle that industrial processes and manufactured goods should be designed to minimize their environmental impacts, and that products should be appropriately managed after their useful life. For example, several states have adopted product stewardship initiatives, passing stringent new laws that would impose specific environmental labeling and/or notice requirements for products that contain allegedly harmful components such as mercury.

While this and subsequent chapters of the *Environmental Law Handbook* focus on the environmental law system established in the United States, environmental law also plays an increasingly important role at the international level. International environmental law is derived in large part from a collection of international environmental conventions that have been adopted through the auspices of the United Nations and/or by international treaty. Examples of these conventions include the 1972 Stockholm Declaration that set forth a 109-point statement of environmental principles and led to the creation of the United Nations Environment Program; the 1987 Montreal Protocol, under which the production of certain substances that deplete the ozone layer has been prohibited; and the Kyoto Protocol on Climate Change that seeks to establish a framework for future reductions in the global emissions of greenhouse gases such as carbon dioxide and ozone. Most of these international environmental conventions are not directly enforceable but call for all nations that have subscribed to a particular convention to implement an appropriate national legislative program within their respective countries that may impose specific restrictions or requirements for affected businesses or facility activities. Thus, for example, the U.S. Congress has previously adopted amendments to the federal Clean Air Act (CAA) in order to implement the phase-out requirements for certain ozone-depleting chemicals established under the 1987 Montreal Protocol. A complete discussion and analysis of international environmental law principles is provided in *International Environmental Auditing*, published by Government Institutes.

The following chapters of this book are intended to provide assistance in meeting the challenge of understanding and complying with the environmental law system implemented in the United States.

2.0 Defining the Subject Matter: What Is Environmental Law?

The key to understanding a legal system as complex as environmental law is the definition of the subject. The best definition, we believe, is as follows:

> The environmental law system is an organized way of using all of the laws in our legal system to minimize, prevent, punish, or remedy the consequences of actions which damage or threaten the environment, public health, and safety.

This definition illustrates how the environmental law system is now often interpreted to encompass the protection of public health and workers' safety in addition to the environment. By this definition, what makes a law or regulation a part of the environmental law system is not its label or original function but the purpose for which it is used. For example, a compilation of the federal environmental statutes does not include the entire body of environmental law; in fact, the criminal code and the federal Administrative Procedure Act also play important roles in the environmental law system.

Based on this understanding, the environmental law system should be viewed as including all aspects of our legal system—the U.S. Constitution, statutes, regulations, rules of evidence, rules of procedure, judicial interpretations, the common law, and, indeed, the criminal law—to the extent that these elements are being applied toward environmental ends. Environmental law is best defined not as a book or compilation of certain laws but instead as a system for using all of the laws for environmental, public health, and safety purposes.[2]

In summary, environmental law encompasses all the protections for our environment that emanate from the following sources:

(1) laws: federal and state statutes and local ordinances;

(2) regulations promulgated by federal, state, and local agencies;

(3) court decisions interpreting these laws and regulations;

(4) the common law, including tort concepts of liability such as nuisance; and

(5) the U.S. Constitution and state constitutions, and even treaties.

In order to best comprehend this system, we should start at the beginning with a brief review of how the laws and regulations are made.

2.1 How a Federal or State Environmental Law Is Adopted[3]

Both the federal and state legislative processes follow similar procedures in enacting new laws; since that is the case, the federal procedure is used here for illustration purposes. First, as part of the federal legislative process, a bill is introduced in either the U.S. House of Representatives or the U.S. Senate. Bills are subsequently referred to the appropriate congressional committees for further consideration. The committee(s), in considering a bill, may hold hearings, study, investigate, and issue a report and a recommendation on whether or not the particular bill should pass. When a bill is voted on and then reported out of committee, it is placed on a legislative calendar in the respective house, considered, debated, and then voted on.

In the environmental field, both bodies of Congress—the House and Senate—generally pass different bills, and a congressional conference of House and Senate representatives is needed to resolve the differences. After passage in both the House of Representatives and the Senate, the act is sent to the president of the United States. The act will become law if it is signed by the president of the United States or if the act is not vetoed within ten days. Overall, this legislative process is often long and arduous, resulting in the adoption of sometimes confusing language which reflects the compromises necessary to obtain agreement among all the differing factions and the approval of the president.

2.2 How Environmental Regulations Are Issued[4]

Environmental statutes generally empower a governmental administrative agency, like the U.S. Environmental Protection Agency (EPA), to develop and promulgate regulations. The president may also empower an executive agency to promulgate regulations through an executive order.

Rulemaking is a process of adopting regulations in accordance with the federal Administrative Procedure Act (APA). This process involves publishing proposed regulations in the *Federal Register*; subsequently providing opportunity for the public to comment either through submission of written comments or through public hearings that concern the regulations; and publishing the final regulations in the *Federal Register*, which have the full force and effect of law when they become effective. The regulations are annually combined into the Code of Federal Regulations (CFR).

As regulatory systems have become more complex, there has been a trend by governmental agencies, and particularly EPA, to try to supplement their administrative actions by issuing "regulatory guidance" which has been aimed at clarifying and removing uncertainties that may exist in implementing regulatory obligations imposed under federal statutes. This form of regulatory action does not follow the strict requirements of the APA and is generally viewed as discretionary in nature and not having the full force and effect of law. In these cases, these guidances may often be modified or changed by subsequent presidential administrations. However, when agencies have attempted to essentially "legislate" new obligations by issuing informal guidance, the courts have required that such guidance be rescinded and instead be adopted through APA rulemaking procedures.

3.0 Laws That Establish Compliance Obligations

In the United States, the federal environmental laws cover two broad areas of law—natural resource development and protection matters and other environmental laws including those relating to the air, water, land, chemicals, and general environmental policy matters. The natural resource laws such as the Endangered Species Act and those related to fish, wildlife, oil and gas exploration, forests, and mining are covered in the *Natural Resources Law Handbook* published by Government Institutes. Although these laws are important for the protection of the natural environment, we have elected to approach them from the natural resource perspective so that we do not overwhelm our readers with too much information to comprehend in a reasonable time period. On the other hand, we focus in this *Environmental Law Handbook* on environmental laws, specifically those intended to protect the human environment, health, and safety.

3.1 Major Environmental Laws

In general, our major federal environmental statutes define most of the substantive compliance obligations of the environmental law system. The major federal environmental statutes do not, however, operate alone. There are other components of environmental laws that supplement or complement the programs that the federal environmental statutes establish, such as regulations which may clearly specify the regulatory obligations of the regulated industry. As noted above, these "other components" of environmental law include various international treaties and obligations.[5] While many international environmental treaties have not been formally ratified by the United States,[6] they still have important legal ramifications for U.S. citizens as many U.S.-based companies either conduct business abroad or have assets located in foreign countries. Conflicts arising under international environmental law have been addressed in U.S. courts,[7] foreign courts, and a growing number of international legal venues as well.[8]

3.2 State Statutes and Regulations Implementing the Federal Statutes

Many of the federal statutes, such as the CAA or Clean Water Act (CWA), establish federal/state regulatory programs in which the states are given the opportunity to enact and enforce laws (which meet federal minimum criteria) to achieve the regulatory objectives which Congress has established. In most instances where the states have had the opportunity to take over regulatory programs in their jurisdictions, they have enacted the appropriate laws and regulations and have acted to enforce these regulatory programs. The states are typically the primary permitting and enforcement authorities and are subject to federal intervention only if they do not enforce effectively or rigorously enough.

Generally, the states are given considerable leeway to follow enforcement interpretations that may not be fully consistent with those applied at the federal level and are not precluded from enforcing criteria more stringent than those required by the federal laws, although the federal government may retain the ability to "overfile" and bring an enforcement action even if the state has acted previously. Thus, the laws and interpretations used to apply and enforce the federal laws may vary considerably from state to state, and these variations may not be readily apparent. Government Institutes has published broad, comprehensive environmental law handbooks for most states, and reference should be made to these respective handbooks to fully understand all the environmental obligations in a specific jurisdiction.

3.3 State Laws Independent of the Federal Requirements

Many states provide their citizens and their environment with protection beyond that generally available under the federal statutes. Most state constitutions address environmental protection or natural resources in some way. Five—the constitutions of Hawaii, Illinois, Massachusetts, Montana, and Pennsylvania—guarantee a substantive right to a clean environment. These state constitutional environmental protections have generally had little practical effect. However, a 2013 Pennsylvania Supreme Court decision demonstrates that these state constitutional provisions can constitute an independent source of environmental protection. In *Robinson Township v. Commonwealth of Pennsylvania,*[9] a group of Pennsylvania municipalities and residents petitioned for review of a state statute ("Act 13") that aimed to facilitate natural gas extraction. Act 13, among other things, imposed limits on the ability of local governments to regulate oil and gas development activities in order to promote uniform development of the state's oil and gas resources, leaving regulation of oil and gas operations primarily to the state Department of Environmental Protection. A plurality of the court held that these provisions of Act 13 violated Pennsylvania's Environmental Rights Amendment, which provides that:

> The people have a right to clean air, pure water, and to the preservation of the natural, scenic, historic and esthetic values of the environment. Pennsylvania's public natural resources are the common property of all the people, including generations yet to come. As trustee of these

resources, the Commonwealth shall conserve and maintain them for the benefit of all the people.[10]

The plurality concluded that this language imposes an obligation on the government to refrain from unduly infringing upon or violating the right to clean air or pure water, including by legislative enactment or executive action. Thus, the plurality explained, Act 13 violated the state constitution by preventing Pennsylvania's municipalities from carrying out their constitutional responsibilities to protect the environment within their respective jurisdictions.

States have also adopted a wide variety of statutes related to environmental protection that operate independently of federal environmental laws. Such state laws include the following:

- Toxic waste minimization laws, such as one in Massachusetts[11] which imposes mandatory waste reduction objectives on companies that use or generate toxic or hazardous wastes.

- Environmental full disclosure laws, such as California Proposition 65,[12] which requires extraordinary efforts to make the public aware of health risks associated with products or environments to which they are exposed.

- Property transfer environmental laws such as the New Jersey Industrial Site Recovery Act,[13] which requires extensive investigation and cleanup of contaminated industrial sites before they are sold or transferred.

- "Product stewardship" laws, such as the Vermont statute that requires the labeling of certain mercury-containing products, including batteries and electric lamps, that are sold in Vermont and imposes a ban on the disposal of such products in Vermont landfills.[14]

- Laws regulating emissions of "greenhouse gases" (carbon dioxide and other emissions related to global warming and climate change). In 2006, California became the first state in the United States to enact a comprehensive law requiring mandatory industry-wide reductions in greenhouse gas emissions by 2020.[15] Other states have adopted similar laws, such as those that are participating in the Regional Greenhouse Gas Initiative in the northeastern United States.[16]

- Measures to encourage recycling of electronic wastes, particularly cathode ray tubes (often found in television screens and computer monitors). California has adopted a system allowing manufacturers to impose a fee on the sale of equipment to finance such recycling efforts, and Maine has enacted legislation to require recycling of used televisions and computer monitors.[17]

- State groundwater protection laws, including detailed permit programs. Many, if not most, of the states have adopted these laws, although the federal government has not yet adopted comprehensive groundwater protection legislation.[18]

Additional environmental protection measures adopted by some states include state citizens' action laws, laws compelling response at hazardous substance sites not on the federal Superfund list, facility siting laws, laws governing the operation of publicly owned treatment works and landfills, asbestos abatement laws, state auditing provisions, and so on. State laws in many states may be a more important factor in dictating the focus of compliance programs than the laws that exist at the federal level, and therefore, it is very important to give considerable attention to the particular jurisdiction in which the activities are being undertaken in order to ensure that the appropriate regulatory requirements are properly considered.

3.4 Tax Laws

In addition to specific environmental regulatory programs, the federal government and many state governments have enacted tax law provisions that create incentives toward the manufacture and use of environmentally benign products and activities and disincentives against products and activities considered to be environmentally detrimental. Gas-guzzler taxes, recycling tax credits, taxes on use of virgin materials, taxes on hazardous waste generation, and excise taxes on various products are among the approaches that have been adopted or seriously discussed. These approaches and other economic incentive–oriented strategies are expected to be promoted in the future.

3.5 Business Regulatory Laws

Numerous other federal administrative agencies have authorities that may be used to address impacts to human health and the environment. For example, the Federal Trade Commission and a number of state attorneys general have taken initiatives to use their ordinary business regulatory authorities to police environmental claims made for products. In addition, the U.S. Securities and Exchange Commission (SEC) has for some time required the full disclosure of environmental liabilities in statements and reports falling under its jurisdiction. The Sarbanes-Oxley Act of 2002[19] enhanced and broadened these disclosure requirements, and also imposed new standards for corporate governance. These requirements include a duty to provide information about a company's internal system of accounting controls; obligations that officers of a company provide specific written certifications, subject to the threat of potential civil or criminal liability, concerning the accuracy of filed financial statements; and other measures to ensure that corporations provide full and accurate financial disclosures. While the SEC and Congress are considering modifications to these broadened disclosure requirements to address concerns raised by various segments of the business community, the essential features of the expanded disclosure regime established by the Sarbanes-Oxley Act are likely to remain in place for the foreseeable future.

The innovative abilities of both state and federal officials will continue to be applied to effective use of all the laws in their arsenal in an effort to enforce increasingly stringent standards of protection for health, safety, and the environment. The limits on this kind of creativity are yet to be seen and are unlikely to be reached in the immediate future because sound and appropriate environmental protection has long been an acknowledged political goal.

3.6 Local and Municipal Laws

In addition to the federal and state levels of government, the local and municipal authorities also have great powers to control the location and operation of facilities within their jurisdictions and are often able to effectively use this authority. Active community involvement and participation in the consideration and/or adoption of local ordinances are, for a number of businesses, essential to their continued ability to operate profitably. While it is difficult to generalize, some of the key issues that often warrant particularly careful attention in the local/ municipal legislative process include the operation of the local waterworks and waste treatment plants, local recycling initiatives and associated product initiatives, zoning and noise control ordinances, nuisance laws, air emission requirements, landfill restrictions or closures, local community right-to-know and emergency planning, and initiatives relating to waste site cleanup. In every instance, the impact of this kind of local action can be as immediate and severe as that of any taken at the state or federal level. From the perspective of an environmental law compliance program, local certainly does not mean trivial but rather suggests immediate, important, largely unreviewable, and deserving of considerable attention. Effective environmental compliance requires acceptance of these facts of life.

3.7 Environmental Law and Judicial Decisions

As the courts interpret the environmental laws and regulations and apply them to specific factual situations, they are continually determining what the law actually means in specific cases or factual situations. In order to gain the proper understanding of court decisions, a basic knowledge of the U.S. court system is therefore needed. The courts and their role are described later in this chapter (see 6.2).

3.8 Common Law

Underlying the development of legal theory in the United States is a body of rules and principles relating to the government and security of persons and property which had its origin, development, and formulation in England. Brought to the American colonies by people of Anglo-Saxon heritage, these basic rules were formally adopted in the states in which they were in force after the American Revolution. Known as the common law, these principles are derived from the application of natural reason, an innate sense of justice, and the dictates of conscience. The common law is not the result of legislative enactment. Rather, its authority is derived solely from the usages and customs which have been recognized, affirmed, and enforced by the courts through judicial decisions over many years.

At the same time, it is important to realize that common law is not a fixed or absolute set of written rules in the same sense as statutory or legislatively enacted law. The unwritten principles of common law are flexible and adaptable to the changes that occur in a growing society. New institutions and public policies; modifications of usage and practice; changes in values, trade, and commerce; inventions; and increasing knowledge all generate new factual situations which require the application and reinterpretation of the fundamental principles of common law by the courts.

As the courts examine each new set of facts in the light of past precedents, an orderly development of common law occurs through a slow and naturally evolving process. Thus, the basic principles underlying American jurisprudence remain fundamentally constant, evolving slowly and progressively over time.

The common law, so far as it has not been expressly abrogated, is recognized as an organic part of the jurisprudence of most of the states. The major exception is Louisiana jurisprudence, which is based on the Roman law, a relic of French rule prior to the Louisiana Purchase. However, since the state court systems have functioned independently of each other, subject only to federal review in cases of national importance, the common law varies slightly from state to state.

The common law actions that we will discuss in subsequent sections are civil suits in which the plaintiff (the party bringing the lawsuit) generally seeks to remedy a violation of a right relating to an environmental matter. We also distinguish civil actions from criminal proceedings, in which the state seeks to redress a breach of public or collective rights that are established in codified penal law. Subsequent sections of this chapter review the four most frequently used types of common law actions that can be the basis of a lawsuit in the pollution control field.

4.0 Common Law Environmental Requirements: Torts

Tort is the word used to denote a common law civil wrong for which a court will provide a remedy. This legal cause of action arises from the existence of a generalized duty to avoid causing harm to others through acts of omission as well as commission. Every adult person is obliged to fulfill a duty of care for the personal and property rights of others while engaged in daily life. Carelessness in exercising this responsibility may give rise to a cause of action (a lawsuit) by means of which the injured party may seek restitution or the recovery of damages. This duty is noncontractual; that is, this action does not arise specifically from an explicit promissory agreement between the parties to the action. Thus, a tort action is further distinguished from a contract right, which is dependent upon the nature of the contract itself.

Tens of thousands of tort lawsuits have been filed over the years involving environmental issues such as the adverse health effects of asbestos and other toxic chemicals.[20] It is clear that tort law is of major interest in the environmental field as more and more tort lawsuits are filed. The four types of torts most commonly encountered in the environmental field are nuisance, trespass, negligence, and strict liability. Each of these common law torts is described in the following sections.

4.1 Nuisance

Nuisance is defined as "that activity which arises from the unreasonable, unwarrantable, or unlawful use by a person of his own property, working an obstruction or injury to the right of another or to the public, and producing such material annoyance, inconvenience, and discomfort that the law will presume resulting damage."[21] There are two types of common law nuisance claims: those based on a "public" nuisance and those based on a "private" one.

The general rule is that a person may use his land or personal property in any manner he sees fit. However, this rule is subject to a limitation: The owner must use his property in a reasonable manner. A nuisance arises whenever a person uses his property to cause material injury or annoyance to a reasonable neighbor.

In determining whether a given act constitutes a nuisance, the court considers the nature of the act itself. The courts have generally acknowledged that any discomfort from a nuisance must amount to a material injury or annoyance; an act must tangibly affect the physical or mental health of ordinary people under normal circumstances or conditions in order to be considered a nuisance.

4.1.1 Noise Nuisance

Noise produced by human activities may often result in an environmental problem. In order to constitute a nuisance in the legal sense, noise must generally be of such a magnitude and intensity as to cause actual or psychological discomfort to persons of ordinary sensibilities. For example, noise from the operation of an industrial plant typically constitutes an actionable nuisance if it injures the health or comfort of ordinary people in the plant's vicinity to an unreasonable extent. However, the courts and legislatures have often had difficulty in setting objective standards of general applicability for determining when noise constitutes a nuisance, so rulings in particular cases are based on the specific circumstances of each case.

O'Neill v. Carolina Freight Carriers Corp.[22] is a good example of a noise nuisance case in which a homeowner was awarded both injunctive relief and damages from the operators of a nearby business. In this case the plaintiffs showed that they were ordinary people and that the noise from the trucks and loading operations at a terminal located immediately adjacent to their home was unreasonable. In fact, this noise actually caused them loss of sleep and prevented the general enjoyment of their home. After considering these facts, the court ruled that the truck terminal noises between 11:00 P.M. and 6:00 A.M. were unreasonable and that every property owner must make reasonable use of his land so as not to cause unnecessary annoyance to his neighbors.

The case of *Rose v. Chaikin*[23] presents another interesting situation in which noise constituted a nuisance. On the New Jersey Shore just north of Atlantic City, the energy conservation–minded and environmentally conscious Joseph Chaikin erected a windmill on his residence. However, when it began to produce offensive noise exceeding levels permissible under the controlling city ordinance, Joel Rose and other neighbors initiated a suit to enjoin the operation of the windmill. Due to the unreasonable character, volume, frequency, duration, time, and locality of the noise, the court subsequently issued an injunction prohibiting any further operation of the windmill. In reaching this decision, the court announced the following standard: "The essence of a private nuisance is an unreasonable interference with the use and enjoyment of land. The elements are myriad. . . . The utility of the defendant's conduct must be weighed against the quantum of harm to the plaintiff. The question is not simply whether a person is annoyed or disturbed, but whether the annoyance or disturbance arises from an unreasonable use of the neighbor's land. . . . Unreasonableness is judged not according to exceptionally refined, uncommon, or luxurious habits of living, but according to the simple tastes and unaffected notions generally prevailing among plain people."[24]

There is no fixed standard as to what degree or kind of noise constitutes a nuisance; in essence, the circumstances of each case must be considered independently. Generally, the key determination is whether the noise is unreasonable and causes some physical or psychological harm. This determination varies from one community to another and from one period of time to another depending on local attitudes and customs.

4.1.2 Other Nuisances

A number of other elements—such as odors, dust, smoke and other airborne pollutants, water pollutants, and hazardous substances—have also been held to be nuisances, as the following cases illustrate.

In one case, a federal trial court found that two industrial manufacturers were liable under a nuisance theory of liability to the City of Portland, Oregon, for contaminating several of the municipality's potable drinking-water supply wells.[25] The court determined that historical spills and releases of an industrial solvent—trichloroethylene—at these manufacturers' facilities had contaminated the local groundwater aquifer in the vicinity of several of the city's water supply wells. Due to this contamination, the city had been required to curtail its use of the affected wells and also had incurred various environmental investigation and response costs. The court concluded that the defendants' contamination of the groundwater supply qualified as a nuisance for which the city could recover its damages.

An Illinois court has applied similar reasoning to hold the owner of a gasoline service station liable under an Illinois common law nuisance claim for the migration of petroleum contaminants from its property to a nearby facility.[26] In reaching its conclusion, the court noted that the petroleum-related contamination in that case specifically qualified as a "public nuisance" because the contamination had created a direct injury to the plaintiff and posed a threat to the safety and health of the public. Thus, the court found the defendant was liable for the plaintiff's property damages caused by the migrating petroleum constituents.

The case of *Washington Suburban Sanitary Commission v. CAE-Link Corp. et al.*[27] provides an example of an odor being classified as a nuisance. In this 1993 case, the Washington, D.C., area faced a health and safety emergency because sewage was increasingly being discharged into the Potomac River in violation of the Clean Water Act. As a result, the U.S. District Court for the District of Columbia ordered the Washington Suburban Sanitary Commission to build a sewage-sludge composting facility next to the Montgomery Industrial Park. However, when the facility began operating, it emitted noxious odors. Companies in the Montgomery Industrial Park, such as the Washington Post Company, AT&T Resource Management Corporation, and CAE-Link Corporation, claimed these odors were a nuisance, and the parties went to court.

In holding that these odors constituted a nuisance, the Maryland Court of Appeals established that, "To prove the existence of a nuisance, therefore, the complained of interference must cause actual physical discomfort and annoyance to those of ordinary sensibilities, tastes, and habits; it must interfere seriously with the ordinary comfort and enjoyment of the property . . . [I]n Maryland, nuisance is a matter of strict liability and . . . 'liability for nuisance may arise even where there is compliance with applicable laws and regulations or where the offending instrumentality is authorized or permitted . . . by state statute.'" Following these established principles, the court reasoned that, like the purchase of the property for the sewage treatment facility, the elimination of odors or the compensation of those affected was a cost of the new facility. Thus, the court ruled that the Washington Suburban Sanitary Commission was strictly liable for the odors as a nuisance, demonstrating Maryland's adherence to the traditional formulation of the law of nuisance.

Similarly, in 1993, a federal court in Kentucky ruled for the plaintiff on a nuisance claim in *Fletcher v. Tenneco, Inc.*[28] In this case, the three-generation Fletcher family had lived on two farms in Powell County, Kentucky, next to a natural gas pipeline station owned by a nearby company. Polychlorinated biphenyls (PCBs)—toxic chemicals that were an ingredient in a lubricant used at the pipeline station—leaked into the ground beneath the station and migrated in the soil and drainage water to the Fletchers' parcels of land. The PCBs found their way into the Fletchers' beef cattle as well as into the blood of at least two of the Fletchers themselves.

Notwithstanding the company's scientific affidavit to the contrary, the court ruled in this case that PCBs were indeed hazardous, as Congress concluded when it passed the Toxic Substances Control Act (TSCA), the CWA, and the Comprehensive Environmental Response, Compensation, and Liability Act (CERCLA). Thus "the lack of any genuine issue of material fact as to the company's (1) unreasonable use of its land, and (2) the resultant grave harm to the plaintiffs required that [the company] be deemed liable as a matter of law for the creation of a nuisance."[29] Note that the two criteria for nuisance liability in Kentucky— (1) the reasonableness of the defendant's use of his property and (2) the gravity of harm to the plaintiff[30]—also have placed Kentucky in the group of states that follows the traditional formulation of the law of private nuisance.

In contrast to the foregoing cases, the court in *Chicago v. Commonwealth Edison*[31] declined to find that air pollution from an electric company's facilities was actionable as a nuisance. In this case the court found that although the public had a right to clean air, the notion of "pure" air has come to mean clean air consistent with the character of the locality and the attending circumstances. Based on this standard, the court ruled that the city had failed to answer the threshold question of whether Commonwealth Edison's Indiana facility caused substantial harm so as to constitute an actionable invasion of a public right.

Consequently, this case represents a situation where the court used a strict interpretation of the law of nuisance, possibly because the plaintiff sought injunctive relief to stop an operation that would have had a broad impact on employment and local economies. In contrast, if the action had sought legal relief or damages, the court may have approached it differently and not followed a strict interpretation of the law of nuisance.

In *Harrison v. Indiana Auto Shredders*[32] the U.S. Court of Appeals for the Seventh Circuit also refused to permanently enjoin operation of an automobile shredding and recycling plant based on a nuisance action. The court held that under the evidence presented and in the absence of an imminent hazard to health or welfare—none of which was established—the defendant could not be prevented from continuing to engage in its operation. In addition, the court believed that the operation should be allowed a reasonable time to correct any defects not posing threats of imminent or substantial harm.

In essence, the courts were not convinced by the evidence presented in these last two cases that the harm caused by the alleged nuisance was so great as to justify forcing the defendant to cease its operation. If these facilities had been shut down, many families would have been injured by the forced unemployment. Thus, the weighing of equities by the courts in these cases resulted in a determination based on all the evidence presented in favor of allowing continued operations. This approach is generally called balancing the equities.

In another case, the environmental group Greenpeace had pursued a nuisance claim[33] to block the operation of a hazardous waste incinerator in East Liverpool, Ohio. In applying Ohio common law, the court found that where a facility has obtained from the state the required authority to operate, the facility could not be deemed a nuisance. Thus, the court determined that while the hazardous waste incinerator may omit offensive odors and toxic dioxins, the incinerator's owner could not be held liable in a cause of action for nuisance because it had a permit.

More recently, nuisance law has been used to seek relief from various harms allegedly caused by climate change.[34] For example, in 2006 the State of California brought suit against several auto manufacturers alleging that the trucks and cars they sold in the United States emitted excessive greenhouse gases, thereby creating a public nuisance under federal common law by contributing to global warming and directly injuring the citizens of California.[35] In 2007, a federal judge dismissed the case in favor of the automakers because the case required reliance on as-then unmade policy decisions best left for legislatures, not for the courts. Although the California attorney general initially appealed the case the attorney general ultimately withdrew the appeal in 2010 in light of actions taken by the Obama Administration involving greenhouse gas emission controls.

On June 6, 2011, the U.S. Supreme Court issued its decision in *American Electric Power Co. v. Connecticut.*[36] This case involved the appeal of a Second Circuit decision that reinstated a public nuisance case filed against electric utilities for greenhouse gas emissions from their coal-fired power plants. The district court had initially dismissed the case, but the Second Circuit reinstated the action, finding that the plaintiffs had standing to bring the suit based on federal common law nuisance claims and because those claims did not present nonjusticiable questions of policy. The Supreme Court reversed the appellate decision, finding that the federal Clean Air Act displaces federal common law and barring plaintiffs' common law nuisance claims.

4.1.3 Key Defenses to Nuisance Actions

Nuisance actions have often been decided by balancing the equities (weighing the impact of the injuries to respective parties involved in litigation) as noted above. In any balancing of the equities, the good faith efforts of the polluter, while not absolving him, would be a factor considered by the court in determining whether to grant relief.[37]

The availability of pollution control devices is, of course, another significant factor that can be considered by the court. For example, in *Renkin v. Harvey Aluminum*[38] the court noted Harvey Aluminum's failure to keep pace with technological advances in pollution controls and thus ordered the defendant company to use such controls.

In general, the courts are moving to strict liability for environmental nuisances so that, practically speaking, there are few good defenses to liability. The solution is clear: Do not create nuisances. If you have an existing nuisance, you are best advised to abate it.

4.1.4 Coming to a Nuisance

Coming to a nuisance is the phrase used to describe a defense that the complainant or plaintiff affected by the nuisance moved into the area where the "complained about activity" had already been in existence. An example of coming to a nuisance occurs when someone moves onto property near an airport or industrial complex and then complains of the nuisance that existed prior to his moving there. Generally, the fact that an individual purchases property with the knowledge of the existence of a nuisance or that he came to the nuisance will not defeat his right to the abatement of the nuisance or recovery of damages,[39] nor will his right to recovery be affected if the property is sold to another while the lawsuit is pending.[40]

However, some cases have recognized a defense to a nuisance lawsuit in situations where the complainant came to a nuisance. This view is probably a result of an old axiom of law that one who voluntarily places himself in a situation whereby he suffers an injury will not prevail.[41] The test of liability in these cases is often the knowledge of the plaintiff regarding the consequences of his conduct.

The majority rule, however, is that the fact that a person moved into the vicinity of a nuisance by purchasing or leasing property in the area does not in and of itself bar him from complaining in an action against the continued operation or maintenance of the nuisance.[42] This rule is based on the theory that the right to "pure" air and the comfortable enjoyment of property belongs to persons as much as does the right of possession and occupancy. If people take up residence in formerly vacant areas and thereby approach a nuisance, it is the duty of those who are responsible for the offending activity to put an end to it.

4.2 Trespass

An action in trespass is distinguished from a nuisance claim in that trespass is categorized as an interference with the possession of property, whereas a nuisance claim is based on an interference with the use and enjoyment of property.[43] Trespass is commonly divided into two types:

- Trespass to chattels is an injury to or interference with the possession of personal property, with or without the exercise of personal force. This trespass involves the destruction of personal property, taking from the possession of another, or a refusal to surrender possession.

- Trespass to land is an unlawful, forcible entry on another's realty. An injury to the realty of another or an interference with the possession, above or below ground, is a trespass, regardless of the condition of the land and regardless of negligence.

Both types of trespass are categorized as intentional interferences with property. In the environmental context, parties which have been held liable under trespass theories would have, for example, caused contamination which has migrated, or trespassed onto other property, causing damage and interfering with the neighbor's exclusive possession. However, the concept of intent in trespass is subtle and tricky. In order to support a lawsuit under the theory of trespass to land, the Second Restatement of Torts, § 163, Comment b, indicates that the intent necessary is simply an intent to be at the place on the land where the trespass allegedly occurred. As long as the defendant voluntarily interfered with the personal property, trespass to chattels will be appropriate. For both types of trespass, the "intent" requires no wrongful motive. For example, it is no defense that the defendant thought the land or chattels were his own. The property right is protected at the expense even of an innocent mistake.[44]

Trespass to land is the type of trespass action that is generally used in pollution control cases. In an action for trespass to land, an entry upon another's land need not be in person; it may, in fact, be made by causing or permitting a thing to cross the boundary of the premises. The trespass may be committed by casting material upon another's land; by discharging water, soot, or carbon; or by allowing gas or oil to flow underground into someone else's land, but not by mere vibrations or light, which are generally classed as nuisances.

In the environmental context, the parties which have been held liable under trespass theories usually have neither personally entered upon adjacent property nor taken anything from the property but rather have caused contamination that has migrated or trespassed onto other property, causing damage and interfering with the neighbor's exclusive possession. Thus, consistent with this theory of liability, the court in *Sterling v. Velsicol Chemical Corp.*[45] held a chemical company liable in trespass for contamination emanating from its chemical landfill that affected a nearby water supply well.

Oftentimes, trespass claims brought in the environmental context are faced with statute-of-limitations concerns if the contamination at issue occurred several years prior to discovery or to the initiation of legal action. However, courts generally toll the applicable statute of limitations until the contamination is discovered, or at least until it reasonably should have been discovered. In some cases the courts have held that the statute of limitations is simply inapplicable to certain types of trespass. For example, in *Degussa Construction Chemical Operations Inc. v. Berwind Corp.*,[46] a court held that under Pennsylvania law, contamination that effects a permanent change in the condition of the property constitutes a permanent trespass, not a continuing trespass, and that therefore the statute of limitations did not bar a trespass claim.

The line between trespass and nuisance is sometimes difficult to determine. Similarly, the concepts of negligence and trespass have sometimes been used interchangeably, as seen in the case of *Stacy v. VEPCO*.[47] In this case the court ruled that there was "negligence and/or trespass on the part of VEPCO" because of damage caused to Stacy's trees by the emissions from VEPCO's Mount Storm power plant. It is interesting to note that the court in this case was convinced by the expert meteorologist's testimony that the emissions could travel the 22-mile distance from the plant to damage the trees. The important point to remember is that courts can and do minimize the importance of the form of the action—namely, whether it is a nuisance, trespass, or negligence—but endeavor to make a relatively just decision based on all of the evidence presented.

4.3 Negligence

Negligence is "the omission to do something which a reasonable man, guided by those ordinary considerations which ordinarily regulate human affairs, would do, or the doing of something which a reasonable and prudent man would not do."[48] Negligence is that part of the law of torts which deals with acts not intended to inflict injury.

In order to recover under a negligence theory, the plaintiff must establish that the defendant owed the plaintiff a duty of care, that the duty was breached, and that the breach was the proximate cause of the plaintiff's injury.[49] Proximate cause is that which in the natural and continuous sequence, if unbroken by an efficient intervening act, produces injury and without which the result would not have happened. A negligence claim may be asserted by a plaintiff who alleges that the party has suffered property damage or personal injury as a result of a defendant's breach of a lawful duty. In addressing the defendant's duty of care, the courts have acknowledged that the standard of care required by law is that degree of care which would be exercised by a person of ordinary prudence under the same circumstances. This is often called the reasonable man rule, what a reasonable person would do under all the circumstances.

There are a number of important defenses that may be asserted in a negligence action. For example, depending on when the activity occurred, a defendant may be able to assert a "state-of-the-art" defense in a negligence case involving exposure to toxic chemicals. This defense is based on the notion that in determining whether a defendant is liable for negligence, the defendant's conduct should be examined in light of the circumstances at the time of the alleged conduct. In applying this type of defense, a defendant in a negligence action would assert that conduct that currently may be found to be negligent would not have been negligent in the past based on scientific and/or technological advances that have raised the legal standard of care involved with a particular activity. For example, changes in scientific knowledge about the potentially harmful effects associated with human exposure to a particular chemical substance may only necessitate increased care now—as opposed to the past—when handling the substance to reduce the risks of exposure.

The court's decision in *Nissan Motor Corp. v. Maryland Shipbuilding & Drydock Co.*[50] provides an illustrative example of a negligence action involving environmental claims. In this case the shipbuilding company's employees failed to follow company regulations when painting ships, allowing spray paint to be carried by the wind onto Nissan's cars. While the shipbuilders had knowledge of the likely danger of spray painting, under these circumstances, the company nevertheless failed to exercise due care in conducting the painting operations in question. Consequently, the court determined in this case that this failure to exercise due care amounted to negligence.

Persons harmed as a result of careless and improper disposal or handling of hazardous waste can recover for their losses under a negligence cause of action.

Indeed, state and federal courts have long recognized this common law theory of recovery against defendants who engage in the negligent disposal of pollutants such as hazardous waste.[51] Where negligence can be established, it is no defense that the negligent action was in full compliance with all government regulations[52] and permit conditions.[53] On the other hand, noncompliance with environmental regulations or applicable statutory requirements may be prima facie evidence (proof without any more evidence) of liability in some states pursuant to a "negligence per se" theory of liability.[54]

4.4 Strict Liability and Dangerous Substances

Strict liability in tort is another common law theory often applied by the courts in environmental cases to remedy environmental harm. Under this theory, liability for damages to persons or property can be imposed without requiring a showing of negligence. In the environmental context, a common example of an action based on strict liability might involve an ultrahazardous activity such as a landowner keeping a potentially dangerous substance on his land which, if permitted to escape, is certain to injure others. Under the doctrine of strict liability, the landowner in such situations must make good the damage caused by the escape of the substance, regardless of negligence on his part.

This strict liability theory is based on long-standing legal principles. More than a century ago, an English court in *Rylands v. Fletcher*[55] determined that a defendant could be liable without regard to fault for property damage resulting from the flooding of a neighboring property when a dam failed on the defendant's property. The court justified its decision by declaring that a party must bear the costs of damages resulting from a dangerous and "unnatural" use of land, regardless of whether the party exercised due care in attempting to control the risks associated with such use.

The reasoning for this strict liability standard is that when persons suffer loss, no good reason can be found to charge the loss against anyone who did not contribute to it. However, if someone is engaged in an ultrahazardous or dangerous activity for profit, that party should bear the burden of compensating others who are harmed by its activities. In determining what kinds of conduct will constitute an ultrahazardous or dangerous activity, the courts will look at a number of factors, such as the degree of risk associated with the activity, the defendant's ability to eliminate the risk, and the degree to which the value of the activity is outweighed by its risk.

Not surprisingly, courts have applied strict liability theories in cases involving the disposal of hazardous waste and hazardous materials management. For example, in *Crawford v. National Lead Co.*,[56] Ohio residents who lived near a federally owned uranium metals production plant alleged that the defendants failed to prevent the emission of uranium and other harmful materials from the plant and that this failure caused emotional distress and diminished property values. Based on its review of the particular facts in this case, the court determined that the provision of uranium in various forms to nuclear facilities throughout the country is an abnormally dangerous activity.[57] The court therefore ruled in favor of the residents, holding that emotional distress and property damage would support a claim of strict liability in Ohio.

In another important strict liability case involving environmental contamination, the New Jersey Supreme Court has even concluded that the current owner of a contaminated property could maintain an action in strict liability against a prior owner of the same property.[58] In *T&E Industries v. Safety-Light Corp.*, the court held the prior owner of a radium processing facility strictly liable for the improper disposal of radium at the site. While some courts have declined to allow parties to assert common law causes of action in nuisance, trespass, or strict liability against prior owners of the same property,[59] the court in *T&E Industries* nevertheless concluded that there were important policy justifications for imposing strict liability in such cases, including the desire to impose liability on enterprises that are responsible for pollution and/or have engaged in abnormally dangerous activities.

Strict liability principles also form a key element of many of the federal environmental laws. In fact, the U.S. Environmental Protection Agency itself has acknowledged that "[m]ost of the statutes which the EPA administers are [based on] strict liability."[60] For example, the liability of current owners and operators of contaminated properties under section 107(a) of CERCLA for the costs of cleaning up those properties is strict, joint, and several.[61] As a result, in CERCLA cases a party can be held strictly liable for the cleanup of contamination even if that party did not determine where its contaminating waste was placed for disposal. An example of the imposition of such liability is found in *United States v. ASARCO Inc.*,[62] in which a mining company was held liable for contamination resulting from its mine waste. In that case, mine tailings produced as a result of the company's operations had been used by other parties as fill material in the construction of roads and for similar purposes. The court held that if the mining company had allowed the removal of the contaminated tailings from the mine site by a third party and the tailings were used as ballast for roads and other urbanization projects, the mining company could be liable for the cleanup of the contamination resulting from the tailings wherever the tailings came to be located.

In addition, the federal courts have recognized the application of strict liability to facilities regulated under the Federal Water Pollution Control Act, which is commonly referred to as the Clean Water Act (CWA). In one case, the court in *United States v. Allegheny Ludlum Corp.*[63] held the owner of a steel manufacturing facility strictly liable under the CWA for its wastewater discharges that failed to comply with the applicable terms and conditions of the facility's National Pollutant Discharge Elimination System permit. Based on the CWA's strict liability scheme, the court specifically rejected claims by the steel company that certain of the alleged permit violations had resulted from improper handling of wastewater samples at the steel company's laboratory. In reaching this conclusion, the court noted that "[g]iven the Act's scheme of strict liability, and the importance placed on self-monitoring and self-reporting, we are unlikely to adopt a new defense in this litigation, especially since the Act can be interpreted as creating an obligation to ensure that the self-monitoring of pollutants is accurate, assigning the risk of inaccuracy to the company."[64]

The courts have recognized limits to the application of strict liability principles. For example, in addressing strict liability in even another context in 1993, a federal bankruptcy court in Washington State addressed the specific question of "whether receivers or trustees personally are strictly liable for acts done in the course of their official duties."[65] This case involved some of Washington State's renowned apples, specifically a bankrupt apple orchard in receivership, the trees of which needed to be staked to prevent wind damage. However, hazardous substances that had been used at the site to treat the wooden stakes to prevent their deterioration when stuck in the soil, as well as other hazardous materials used as pesticides and stored in various spots around the orchard, had dripped into the ground. Nevertheless, based on various policy factors, the court in this case decided not to apply the principle of strict liability, noting that "if a receiver was personally liable for any damage that results from an abnormally dangerous activity despite the lack of showing of a negligent or knowingly wrongful act, courts would be unable to obtain the services of a receiver for any site where abnormally dangerous acts are a routine part of business."[66]

Even so, the courts have continued to narrowly apply statutory defenses and exceptions to the strict liability scheme established under federal environmental laws. For example, the U.S. Court of Appeals for the Fourth Circuit recently affirmed the District of South Carolina's judgment that a brownfields redeveloper—Ashley II—did not meet the statutory requirements for *bona fide* prospective purchaser (BFPP) liability protection under the Small Business Liability Relief and Brownfields Revitalization Act;[67] this statutory protection can effectively shield a landowner from all CERCLA liability for conducting and paying for a waste site cleanup.[68] Ashley II, the purchaser and current owner of a contaminated property where fertilizer production wastes had been previously disposed, brought suit to recover response costs it incurred at the site. According to the court, Ashley II's management of the site "clearly show[s] that it failed to exercise 'appropriate care.'" At trial, the district court found that Ashley II failed to remediate and fill in contaminated sumps that were discovered when related aboveground structures were demolished, and did not adequately manage pre-existing soil contamination (*e.g.*, debris piles and limestone crush and run cover) by preventing the cross-contamination of nearby areas. Based on these findings, the Court of Appeals affirmed the district court's determination that Ashley II was strictly liable for environmental response costs as the current owner of a site where hazardous substances had been released.

5.0 Laws That Enforce Permits, Prohibitions, and Penalties

Although the environmental law's mechanisms for enforcing its mandates are essentially the same as those available in other legal disciplines, there are several distinctive aspects to the overall enforcement of environmental laws and regulations. In essence, this area of law involves the use of a broad range of mechanisms to compel effective enforcement of environmental regulatory obligations.

5.1 Permits

Perhaps the most distinctive aspect of environmental enforcement is its extensive and effective use of permitting mechanisms. Particularly with laws as complex and technical as most of the environmental statutes, it is critical that there be an effective mechanism for bridging from generalities like "Effluents shall be treated in compliance with best available technology" to specifics like

> [T]he Permittee is authorized to discharge from outfall number 001 "x" pounds per day of pollutant "y," subject to the condition that the discharge be monitored in accordance with specified protocols and that periodic reports be provided.

The permit fulfills this need by, in effect, establishing the "law" for a particular discharge or activity. The granting or withholding of permits, licenses, or other authorizations is an important tool for controlling pollution. The requirement to obtain a permit and operate in compliance with its terms and conditions is an individualized and highly effective way of ensuring that regulators are notified of releases or activities of which they need to be aware. It is also an effective way of ensuring and demonstrating that the person required to comply is on notice of obligations. These permits or licenses are generally tied to an air or water quality standard and may be subject to the fulfillment of specific conditions, such as compliance with a code of practice, selection of the location that minimizes environmental and economic impacts, installation of a treatment system or pollution control equipment within a certain time period, or adoption of other environmentally protective measures. One major advantage of permits and licenses is that they facilitate the enforcement of environmental procedures by including in one document all of a facility's pollution control obligations with respect to one environmental medium such as air or water. Other advantages are that they may be withdrawn or suspended according to the needs of the national economy or other social interests, and they often require a fee that can be used to help defray the costs of the government's pollution control program. The use of permits and licenses normally involves regular monitoring and facility reporting. The role of permits in bridging the substantive requirements of the environmental laws—notification, discharge controls, and so forth—and the other enforcement mechanisms is discussed below. Permitting requirements, however, are by no means the only weapon in environmental law's enforcement arsenal.

5.2 Enforcement Provisions of the Federal and State Environmental Statutes

Each of the major federal environmental statutes provides an array of enforcement sanctions to compel compliance with its mandates. Generally, these enforcement provisions include the following:

- Administrative penalties imposed by agencies for various violations.

- Administrative orders to respond to or abate violations, enforceable by civil and criminal sanctions.

- Civil actions for relief, including prohibitions or mandatory injunction enforced by judicial decree.

- Civil penalties assessed per violation or day of violation, with maximum penalties varying by statute and adjusted annually for inflation.[69]

- Citizens' civil actions to compel compliance with or collect damages for violation of the statute.

- Criminal sanctions against organizations and responsible individuals for misrepresentation or knowing or negligent violation of the statutes.

There is no doubt that the federal environmental statutes and the regulations under them present a formidable set of reasons for a business or other organization to institute programs for aggressive compliance with the environmental laws. They are supported and complemented by similar enforcement provisions in the state environmental statutes as well as in local laws and ordinances.

Criminal enforcement of the federal environmental laws has become an increasingly important element of the government's enforcement agenda. Environmental crimes are those that involve negligent, knowing, or willful violations of federal environmental requirements. Generally speaking, knowing violations are those that are deliberate and not the product of accident or mistake. Knowledge of the specific statutes or regulations that prohibit the wrongful conduct is not required. When a violator is aware that the wrongful conduct is prohibited by law, the violation is said to be "willful." For criminal law violations, the requisite intent element can be as low as simple negligence. For instance, at least two federal circuit courts have held that, under the CWA, simple negligence triggers criminal liability.[70] Such a low threshold for criminal liability is alien to most other statutory schemes because it creates criminal liability for failure to exercise reasonable care; most statutes only attach criminal liability to gross negligence. In recent years, the lower simple negligence threshold has come under fire as prone to abuse and failing to serve justice on the parties involved.

5.3 General Purpose Criminal Laws

The last major category of "environmental laws that enforce" are laws from the criminal code, originally enacted to punish more traditional crimes and which have now been adapted to the prosecution of crimes which are essentially environmental in nature. The criminal code provisions which have proven particularly useful in this connection include the following:

- Prohibition against False Statements to the Federal Government—18 U.S.C. § 1001.

- Mail Fraud Statutes—18 U.S.C. §§ 1341, 1343.

- Conspiracy Laws—18 U.S.C. § 371.

- Criminal Aiding and Abetting—18 U.S.C. § 2.

Even more traditional criminal laws, such as the murder statutes, have sometimes been used, at least at the state level, to successfully prosecute environmental offenses. These nonenvironmental laws have become almost as important as the environmental statutes in defining the liability of violators.

Various actions illustrate the government's widening use of sophisticated methods to address alleged environmental crimes. During 2001 the Justice Department announced that it had targeted several individuals and an environmental consulting firm for prosecution under the federal "Racketeering Influenced and Corrupt Organizations," or "RICO," statute for illegal conduct and related violations of federal environmental requirements. In this case, several officials of an environmental consulting firm, Hi-Po, Inc., pleaded guilty to violating the federal RICO law by, among other things, illegally discharging diesel fuel and other contaminants in violation of the federal CWA in order to generate cleanup work for their firm; the firm itself admitted that it committed two felony violations of the CWA due to these illegal discharges. The RICO statute provides that a person may not, through a pattern of racketeering activity, acquire or maintain any interest in or control of an enterprise engaged in interstate commerce, or conspire with others to commit such acts. This law previously had been used expansively by federal prosecutors to target a wide range of illegal conduct such as mail and wire fraud.

In their plea agreement with federal prosecutors, the two Hi-Po officials admitted that their firm had violated the federal CWA by intentionally dumping various pollutants into waters of the United States in order to generate cleanup work for their firm, and they had engaged in two acts of money laundering as part of that scheme. In particular, these individuals admitted that they had intentionally dumped diesel fuel and certain industrial chemicals into a pond and storm water drain and then subsequently been paid to clean up the resulting contamination. They further acknowledged that through their improper conduct and several acts of alleged mail fraud, they had operated their consulting firm as an organized crime enterprise in violation of the RICO law. The plea agreements in this case resulted in several years of imprisonment for each defendant and criminal fines of $250,000 apiece.

In other cases, the courts have even broadly applied the federal environmental laws to impose criminal sanctions on persons for the acts of third parties. In one notable case, the owner of a commercial laundry service was convicted of causing, and aiding and abetting, the illegal disposal of hazardous wastes without a permit based on his hiring of an unlicensed contractor to dispose of his surplus inventory of dry cleaning chemicals and other hazardous wastes at a non-hazardous waste landfill.[71] At trial, the laundry owner initially was convicted by the jury on this criminal count, but the court reversed the jury's decision since the trial court was of the view that a person who merely arranges for the disposal of a waste cannot be convicted of illegally disposing of such waste. The government appealed this acquittal to the U.S. Court of Appeals for the Third Circuit, where the appellate court ultimately sided with the government and reversed the laundry owner's acquittal. The Third Circuit ruled that a generator of wastes can be convicted of improper disposal, despite the use of contractors or other intermediaries, if the defendant has enough actual knowledge of the disposal activities and the relevant legal requirements to have had a duty to be aware of, and ensure compliance with, the applicable environmental rules.[72]

As illustrated by the foregoing, the environmental law enforcement system is a carefully structured combination of methods—environmental and general purpose, traditional and newly conceived—which work together to bring significant consequences to those who fail to fulfill their environmental compliance obligations. This interaction has been effective and will become even more formidable as the environmental law system continues to mature.

6.0 Laws That Define the Environmental Law Framework

Having discussed the substantive mandates of the environmental laws and the enforcement methods which make compliance mandatory, it is also important to examine the laws that establish the framework within which the system operates. The fact is that many of the questions which are most critical to successful compliance efforts and most difficult to answer fall within this category:

- What level of government has authority to regulate?

- What protections are available to the regulated?

- How do questions of scientific fact get answered?

- Who can go to court and who pays for it?

Answers to these and similar questions critical to the resolution of environmental cases are sometimes found not in the environmental statutes or regulations, but in organic laws such as constitutions—federal and state—and city charters, and procedural laws such as the APA and state analogs, judicial codes, and rules of evidence. These determine how our overall legal system works in environmental contexts as well as in others. It is, of course, impossible in one chapter of a handbook to do more than highlight some important requirements which are particularly germane to the subject at hand.

6.1 The Organic Laws: Constitutions and Charters

In the federal system of government, the powers of government and the rights of individuals are defined primarily in the organic acts by which governments are created—constitutions in the case of federal and state governments and, generally, charters in the case of local governmental units like cities and counties. These laws provide the foundation for the environmental law system just as they do for the legal system in general. We look to this foundation to give us answers to the most basic and often most important questions encountered.

6.1.1 Federal, State, and Local Roles

A question which arises in the development of environmental regulatory programs revolves around which level of government—state, federal, or local—is to play the primary role in regulating particular activities affecting the environment. The federal government is a government of limited authority, which may act only through the exercise of the enumerated powers granted to it under the Constitution. In practice, the enumerated powers—particularly the power to regulate interstate and foreign commerce found in Article I, Section 8 of the U.S. Constitution, commonly known as the Commerce Clause—have generally been broadly construed, and there are few, if any, instances where federal laws enacted to protect public health and welfare have been held to be in excess of constitutional authority.

However, the U.S. Supreme Court has made clear that congressional authority under the Commerce Clause is not unlimited. For example, in *Solid Waste Agency of Northern Cook County v. U.S. Army Corps of Engineers* ("*SWANCC*"),[73] the Court considered the extent to which the U.S. Army Corps of Engineers (Corps) could assert jurisdiction over isolated waters under the CWA based on the use of such waters by migratory birds. The petitioners argued that the Commerce Clause did not provide the Corps with the authority to regulate isolated ponds which had no hydrological connection with interstate waters. While the Court ultimately did not decide the case on constitutional grounds, the Court's interpretation of the CWA to preclude the Corps' assertion of jurisdiction over isolated waters based on their use by migratory birds was based in large part on the Court's concern that the Corps' arguments in favor of its assertion of jurisdiction raised "significant constitutional questions."[74] Thus, concerns about the extent of federal regulatory authority under the Constitution can affect the interpretation of environmental laws and regulations even where the laws and regulations themselves are not overturned on constitutional grounds.

Once federal authority has been exercised and a federal system of regulation has been established, important questions arise about the continuing ability of state and local governments to operate in that same area. While state and local governments have broad police powers to do what is necessary to protect the health and safety of their citizens, their authorities may be displaced where a scheme of federal regulation, pursuant to enumerated authority, preempts the field of regulation and precludes the further exercise of state and local authority. The judicial trend in these preemption cases is toward upholding continued state authority except where the U.S. Congress has explicitly expressed a clear intention to fully occupy the field and displace state authority to regulate. The trend in the Congress is to explicitly preserve the states' continuing authority to regulate. Similar issues arise in terms of the relationship between state and local regulations. Under certain circumstances state laws can preempt local regulation of activities. A prominent recent example of disputes regarding the appropriate interaction between state and local authority concerns the regulation of oil and gas exploration and production, including the regulation of hydraulic fracturing. In cases such as *Northeast Natural Energy, LLC v. The City of Morgantown, West Virginia*,[75] courts have held that state statutes that give state regulatory authorities the responsibility for overseeing oil and gas development preempt local ordinances that seek to ban oil and gas activity or otherwise control where such activities can take place, limiting local authority to matters such as road use and noise. These cases typically find that local regulation of oil and gas development would impede the goal of orderly development of a state's oil and gas resources. At the same time, courts in other states have found that oil and gas laws do not preempt local bans of exploration and production activity. For example, in *Norse Energy Corp. v. Town of Dryden*,[76] a New York appellate court held that the state's Oil, Gas and Solution Mining Law did not preempt a town's zoning ordinance that banned all activities related to oil and gas exploration and production activities. The court found that the language and legislative history of the state law evidenced an intent to establish uniform state-wide regulation of the technical aspects of exploration and production activities but did not demonstrate an intent to preempt traditional local zoning authority to establish permitted uses of land.

6.1.2 Commerce Clause as a Limit on State Authority

One line of constitutional cases dealing with this question of who can regulate involves the issue of whether, even in the absence of preemptive federal action, a state or local law may be unconstitutional because it improperly restrains interstate or foreign commerce. The Commerce Clause grants to Congress the authority "to regulate Commerce with foreign Nations, and among the several States, and with the Indian Tribes." If the courts find that state statutes or regulations impermissibly burden interstate commerce, then they are unconstitutional and unenforceable.

It is well settled that a state regulation validly based on police power does not impermissibly burden interstate commerce if the regulations neither discriminate against interstate commerce nor operate to disrupt its required uniformity.[77] Where there is a reasonable basis to protect the social welfare of a community, as distinguished from economic welfare, the courts will not deny this exercise of sovereign power and hold it to violate the Commerce Clause.

There have been numerous environmental cases involving the application of the Commerce Clause as a limit on state authority. For example, the U.S. Supreme Court considered a Commerce Clause case involving Alabama's Emelle facility, the nation's largest commercial hazardous waste landfill and one of the oldest. For disposal of hazardous waste at the Emelle facility, Alabama charged $72 more per ton for waste generated outside Alabama than it did for waste generated inside Alabama. However, in striking down this practice, the Supreme Court ruled that the additional fee discriminated against hazardous waste generated in states other than Alabama and that such burdensome taxes on interstate commerce were forbidden.[78]

Another Commerce Clause case involved a Chicago ordinance banning the sale of detergents containing phosphates.[79] The U.S. Court of Appeals for the Seventh Circuit held that the ordinance did not violate the Commerce Clause because, although it had some minor effect on interstate commerce, the benefits of the ordinance far outweighed these effects, and the ordinance was a reasonable method of achieving the legitimate goal of improving water quality in Lake Michigan.

Many municipal solid-waste management cases also have involved challenges under the Commerce Clause. For example, a number of states have enacted so-called "flow control" laws, affecting the municipal solid waste generated by counties and municipalities, which have withstood constitutional challenges. In *United Waste Systems of Iowa, Inc. v. Wilson,*[80] the U.S. Court of Appeals for the Eighth Circuit upheld an Iowa law that requires all Iowa counties and cities to submit a comprehensive plan to the Iowa Department of Natural Resources detailing how they will dispose of their municipal solid waste. This law forbids garbage haulers from transporting a county's or city's waste to a facility not designated in that county's or city's comprehensive waste management plan. In finding that the law did not violate the Commerce Clause, the court noted that the law provides each municipality and county government "complete discretion" to contract with any landfill operator or hauler when preparing its disposal plan, including sending part or all of its waste to an out-of-state facility.

In contrast to these cases, the courts have applied the Commerce Clause to overturn several state environmental laws. For example, in *Waste Management Holdings Inc. v. Gilmore,*[81] a federal appeals court affirmed a lower court ruling that found a Virginia state solid waste law had discriminated against interstate commerce in solid waste. In taking this action, the court applied a two-tier test, asking first whether the Virginia law on its face discriminated against interstate commerce law in practical effect or in its purpose, or alternatively, if the law only indirectly affected interstate commerce in evenhandedly regulating a given subject. Applying this test, the court concluded that several of the law's provisions violated the Commerce Clause since they were designed, at least in part, to control the amount of out-of-state waste that was being shipped to several Virginia landfills, and the state had failed to demonstrate that it had selected the least burdensome alternative for imposing its regulatory program. Consequently, the court affirmed the lower court's decision striking down the following provisions: a 2,000-ton-per-day cap on the amount of wastes that Virginia landfills could accept; a ban on the shipping of wastes by barge on three Virginia rivers; a truck cargo certification requirement; and a truck regulatory requirement that applied only to commercial solid-waste transporters with four or more axles.

6.1.3 Equal Protection

Another category of cases of relevance to the environmental field are those limiting the ability of federal and state governments to regulate conduct under the constitutional mandate of equal protection.

Section One of the Fourteenth Amendment to the Constitution prohibits governments from denying to any person the equal protection of the laws. This provision has been applied, essentially, to prevent inappropriate discrimination and has been invoked by plaintiffs in various cases in the environmental context. The courts generally hold that for a classification to violate the constitutional guarantee of equal protection, there must be a showing that there is no reasonable basis for the distinction. A law is presumptively valid; thus, unless clear and convincing proof demonstrates that a particular law is arbitrary or unreasonable, the law must be upheld.

Given these strictures, few environmental laws have been held to violate the equal protection clause. For example, in Hawaii several environmental groups sought to stop an interstate highway project known as H-3,[82] but Congress thwarted their efforts in 1986 when it passed Public Law No. 99-591. Section 114 of this law provided for the specific exemption of the H-3 project from federal statutes requiring that no public parks, wildlife refuges, or historical sites be used for any project unless "no feasible and prudent alternative" exists and unless harm to the area is minimized.

Following that congressional action, several environmental groups asked the court to hold that section 114 violated the equal protection provision of the U.S. Constitution. These groups claimed that the right to a healthy environment is an important individual right and that Congress violated constitutional principles of federalism in enacting a provision which discriminates against the citizens of Hawaii. To support their claims, these groups further argued that section 114 "creates an arbitrary classification [based on state citizenship] by denying residents of Hawaii the environmental protections provided by the 4(f) statutes."

The U.S. Court of Appeals for the Ninth Circuit ruled against the Hawaiian environmental groups, remarking that no court had yet found a constitutional right to a healthy environment to exist. The court held that Congress had the power to exempt specific projects from certain federal laws, and that exempting this particular project did not amount to arbitrarily or categorically discriminating against Hawaii.

Equal protection claims also have been raised unsuccessfully in other environmental cases, such as in the Superfund context. For example, in *United States v. Iron Mountain Mines, Inc.*,[83] a potentially responsible party that had been sued by the United States and the state of California to contribute financially to the cleanup of contamination at a mining site argued that the imposition of joint and several liability under CERCLA[84] violated the Equal Protection Clause because it encouraged "selective prosecution," that is, it encouraged suits against those that were least able to reimburse the federal government for cleanup costs it had incurred. The court followed prior judicial decisions in rejecting the argument, holding that Congress had a rational basis for enacting the liability scheme.

6.2 The Courts' Role

The organic laws that form the U.S. environmental law system define the authorities of the executive and legislative branches of the federal government with respect to environmental regulation. These laws, as well as the U.S. Constitution, also vest certain powers in the judicial branch of government, including the power to interpret the laws and hear actions seeking to enforce their requirements on certain regulated parties. To understand these environmental laws as they are applied in practice, one must certainly understand the courts' role in interpreting these laws in the environmental context.

6.2.1 Federal and State Court Systems

There are two primary judicial systems in the United States: (1) the state and local courts, established in each state under the authority of the state government; and (2) the federal courts, set up under the authority of the U.S. Constitution by the Congress of the United States.

The state courts have general, unlimited power to decide almost every type of case, subject only to the limitation of state law. State and local courts are located in every town and county and are the tribunals with which citizens most often have contact. The great bulk of legal business, such as divorce, probate of estates, traffic accidents, and all other matters except those assigned to the federal courts, is handled by these state and local courts.

The federal courts, on the other hand, have the authority to hear and decide only selected types of cases, which are specifically enumerated in the U.S. Constitution and federal statutes. These courts are located principally in the larger cities, while state and local courts are found throughout the country.

6.2.2 Federal Court System

The structure and scope of the federal court system in the United States has evolved over the course of the nation's history. The essential elements of the federal judiciary are defined in the U.S. Constitution, which provides that "[t]he Judicial Power of the United States shall be vested in one Supreme Court, and in such inferior Courts as the Congress may from time to time ordain and establish." Thus, the only court that is constitutionally mandated is the U.S. Supreme Court; all other federal courts have been created through an act of Congress.

The federal court system currently involves three distinct tiers of courts, with the two lower tiers subject to the final authority and precedential rulings of the Supreme Court of the United States, the highest court in the land. Immediately below the Supreme Court are the 13 U.S. circuit courts of appeal, most of which have jurisdiction over federal appellate cases within a distinct geographic area, usually covering several states.[85] At the lowest tier are the 94 U.S. district courts as well as certain other specialized trial courts, such as the U.S. Court of Federal Claims. These are the federal courts where complaints are initially filed and trials held.

A lawsuit that is commenced in the federal court system may proceed sequentially through each of the three levels of the federal judiciary. Generally, the case will first be heard and decided by one of the courts at the district court level. If the plaintiff or the defendant is dissatisfied with the court's decision, the losing party will usually have the right to seek review of the district court decision by the federal appeals court with jurisdiction over the state in which the action was originally commenced; for example, actions tried in federal district courts located in Virginia may be appealed to the U.S. Court of Appeals for the Fourth Circuit. If still dissatisfied by the final appeals court decision, a party may seek review by the Supreme Court of the United States by filing what is known as a petition for certiorari. However, review is generally granted by the Supreme Court only in cases involving matters of national importance or where different courts of appeals have reached conflicting results on an issue.

This three-tiered organizational structure of the federal courts serves two purposes. First, the U.S. Supreme Court and the federal appeals courts can correct errors that have been made in the decisions of the trial courts. Second, the higher courts can ensure uniformity of decision by reviewing cases in which two or more lower courts have issued conflicting interpretations of law or contrary rulings on a particular legal issue.

State courts generally have a similar tiered structure, with a basic trial court or similar court of original jurisdiction, an appellate court, and then a final supreme court. In some jurisdictions, however, the state courts may be known by somewhat different names; for example, the highest court in the state of New York is the State Court of Appeals, while the New York trial courts are known as supreme courts. Thus, at the state level the nomenclature may be somewhat confusing, but the system of a lower court initially deciding a case with the subsequent opportunity for review of the decision by appellate courts is similar to the federal system.

6.2.3 Courts in Practical Perspective

Under the federal and state court systems, the significance of a particular court decision may vary depending on the unique attributes of the case and whether the decision was rendered merely by a trial court or a higher appeals court. Thus, for example, a decision by the U.S. Supreme Court would have precedential value throughout the entire country. In contrast, if a state or municipal court issues a ruling in a case, the decision typically will have limited interest nationally but may have substantial effects within the local jurisdiction.

It is important to bear in mind that the interpretation and application of law is not an exact science; there are many examples of two lower courts reaching conflicting opinions on a point of law. The potential variability in the decisions rendered by different courts has led to considerable litigation, particularly in the area of environmental law. Courts asked to consider claims involving environmental issues often must confront not only complex legal issues, but also difficult factual and technical questions, such as those involving the movement of contamination within groundwater, that may be the subject of considerable debate within the scientific community. Thus, the field of environmental law may involve a somewhat higher degree of uncertainty than other areas of law because of its extensive regulatory regime, the complex technical issues involved, and the continued evolution of federal and state environmental requirements. As a result, the regulated community would be well advised to become informed about the environmental laws, regulations, and court opinions that may be applicable within a particular jurisdiction. These legal requirements, as well as the practical implications of ensuring compliance, should be taken into consideration when making decisions in this arena.

In addition, it is important to keep in mind that the court system, although hailed as one of the fairest systems ever developed by mankind, is subject to human frailties. Human interactions, such as those that occur between judges, lawyers, plaintiffs, defendants, and jurors, are another source of uncertainties.

6.2.4 Court Jurisdiction and Forum Shopping

When considering possible legal claims, a party should carefully evaluate which court may have jurisdiction in a particular case. In fact, the selection of the court in which to file a claim can play a significant role in the overall strategy for winning a lawsuit. This practice of considering which of several courts should be selected as the court in which to file the claim is sometimes called forum shopping. When initiating a lawsuit, a good lawyer will evaluate which court is more inclined toward the client's position. For example, the judges of the U.S. Courts of Appeals for the Ninth Circuit and certain other federal courts of appeal have historically been known for their pro-environmental record. Consequently, organizations such as the Environmental Defense Fund and the Sierra Club historically have been inclined to initiate their lawsuits in the federal courts in the Ninth Circuit. In contrast, regulated entities may be more inclined to file a lawsuit in a district court where they have business operations or in jurisdictions that have a conservative judicial record.

In addition, parties may need to consider whether they prefer to litigate claims in federal court or state court. Many kinds of cases that can be filed in federal court can also be filed and heard in state court. However, in such cases many defendants will prefer to litigate the claims in federal court; if the case is originally filed by the plaintiff in state court a defendant will "remove" the case—that is, have it transferred—to federal court. If a case is removed from state court to federal court, the plaintiff may seek to have the federal court decline jurisdiction on a variety of grounds and send the case back to state court.

6.2.5 When Courts Can Act

According to Article III, Section 2, Clause 1 of the United States Constitution, federal courts have limited jurisdiction. These courts may act only on actual "cases" or "controversies," which means:

(1) moot questions cannot be decided;

(2) advisory opinions cannot be issued;

(3) cases must be "ripe for decision," such that the issues to be tried must be concrete and focused, and must not be premature and abstract;

(4) the executive and/or legislative branches must have issued a final decision on the matter at issue;

(5) collusive and feigned cases will be dismissed; and

(6) parties must have standing to sue.

A number of cases help illustrate the practical application of the U.S. Constitution's "case or controversy" requirement. For example, in *Woodland Private Study Group v. New Jersey Department of Environmental Protection*,[86] the U.S. Court of Appeals for the Third Circuit ordered a complaint dismissed as moot when two industrial companies challenged the New Jersey Spill Compensation and Control Act as unconstitutional. Before their case was decided, however, the New Jersey Supreme Court in two different cases performed what the court called judicial surgery on the New Jersey Spill Act, bringing it into conformity with the federal constitution. Both of these companies subsequently agreed in letters to the court that this action rendered their case moot, and it was eventually dismissed.

In another case, *TJ Baker, Inc. v. Aetna Casualty & Surety Co.*,[87] the court declined to hear the plaintiff's claims because the plaintiff in effect sought an advisory opinion from the court. In this case the plaintiff (Baker) was named as a potentially responsible party (PRP) for environmental pollution at several sites. Aetna Casualty and Surety Co. had issued comprehensive general liability (CGL) insurance policies to Baker, and Baker sought "partial summary judgment on the legal interpretation, under New Jersey law, of a provision contained in the CGL policies which defined an occurrence—the event which triggers coverage under each policy." The court determined that the plaintiff could not maintain its claims, stating that "[w]hat the plaintiff seeks, in essence, is an advisory opinion on the state of New Jersey law regarding the widely used occurrence definition in CGL policies. This requested ruling would not require an examination of any of the facts, disputed or otherwise, involved in this matter, nor would this determination dispose of any claim or any part of any claim asserted by plaintiff."[88] Consequently, the court dismissed the case for failing to involve an actual "case" or "controversy" that was ripe for decision.

In another example, the court in *In re Combustion Equipment Associates, Inc.*[89] dismissed a party's complaint on ripeness grounds. In this case EPA had sent the appellant a letter naming it as a PRP for groundwater contamination at two landfill sites. In response to EPA's claims, the appellant sought judgment that any CERCLA liability it may have had was discharged by its subsequent Chapter 11 bankruptcy reorganization. Rejecting this claim, the court ruled that there was no finality to the EPA's action of naming the appellant a PRP; since there was not yet any determination that the appellant was actually responsible, the court could not properly be asked to assess the effect of the bankruptcy reorganization on such responsibility. The court therefore dismissed the action as not ready or ripe for determination.

In a 1993 decision the U.S. Court of Appeals for the Third Circuit also addressed challenges to a plaintiff's claims due to ripeness concerns. In this case, *New Hanover Township v. Army Department*,[90] New Hanover Corporation (NHC) sought to use land located within New Hanover Township as a municipal waste landfill. Under the federal CWA, the secretary of the Army through the Army Corps of Engineers has the authority to issue permits to persons who want to discharge dredged or fill material into waters of the United States. New Hanover Township objected to the Corps' issuance of a permit to NHC to discharge dredged or fill material in connection with the operation of the municipal waste landfill. The court in this case described the following standard for ripeness:

> In determining whether this case involves an abstract disagreement or a dispute which requires judicial intervention, the court should examine (1) whether the issues are fit for judicial resolution and (2) whether withholding judicial resolution will result in hardship to the parties.[91]

The court pointed out that although the Corps had made a decision on the permit application submitted by NHC, the company still needed to obtain a water quality permit from the Pennsylvania Department of Environmental Resources (PADER). The court also noted "not all decisions that represent an agency's last word on an issue are final for purposes of review. . . . Rather, finality is to be interpreted in a pragmatic way."[92] In essence, the court found that PADER had a veto over the Corps' proposed decision. Consequently, the court concluded that "a pragmatic view of the facts mandates a decision that this case is not ripe for review."[93]

In *Sackett v. Environmental Protection Agency*,[94] the U.S. Supreme Court addressed the requirement that an agency action be "final" before it can be subject to judicial review. EPA issued a compliance order that directed the Sacketts to restore filled wetlands at a residential home site in Idaho. When the Sacketts tried to challenge EPA's jurisdiction over the wetlands, EPA denied the Sacketts' request for a hearing. The U.S. District Court for the District of Idaho granted EPA's motion to dismiss the suit that was subsequently filed by the Sacketts on the ground that the CWA does not provide for review of compliance orders prior to the time EPA seeks to enforce the order against a party for failure to comply with its terms. The Supreme Court, however, unanimously found that EPA's compliance order amounted to final agency action and that it was subject to challenge. The Court found that in issuing the order EPA had determined rights or obligations of the Sacketts. The Court expressed discomfort with the notion that if the compliance order was not subject to judicial review the Sacketts would either have had to comply with EPA's expensive compliance order, apply for a wetland-fill permit that the Corps of Engineers was unlikely to grant, or wait—while allowing up to $75,000 of fines per day to accrue—until EPA sought to enforce the compliance order in order to mount a legal challenge to EPA's jurisdiction over the wetlands.

The Supreme Court returned to the issue of finality in *U.S. Army Corps of Engineers v. Hawkes Co., Inc.*,[95] in which a company was challenging a Corps "jurisdictional determination," i.e., a Corps determination that the land the company wanted to use for peat mining included "waters of the United States" that were subject to the Corps' jurisdiction under the CWA. The Corps' determination left the company with the option of applying for a permit to conduct work in the jurisdictional areas—a process the Court noted could be "arduous, expensive and long"—or proceeding without a permit based on its belief that the Corps' determination was erroneous and risking significant penalties for violations of the CWA if the company was later determined to be wrong. A unanimous Court found that the Corps' determination was a final agency action subject to judicial review because it represented the Corps' final word on the presence of "waters of the United States" on the property and had direct and appreciable legal consequences and because the company had no adequate alternative to court review.

In addition to constitutional limitations on the ability of federal courts to hear a particular claim, the federal courts have also established certain "prudential" limits that in some circumstances will lead courts to decline to hear a case. One such prudential limit is the requirement that a plaintiff has "exhausted" all available administrative remedies before proceeding to challenge an agency's decision in federal court. The rationale underlying this requirement is that agencies should be allowed to consider and respond in the first instance to issues raised by applicants or others involved in a particular agency process, particularly in light of the fact that through such proceedings the agency may be able to resolve issues and thereby eliminate the need for the intervention of the courts. Requiring a plaintiff to exhaust administrative remedies also helps to ensure that the agency will have made a final, definitive decision on a matter before that decision is reviewed by the courts and that the agency will have created an adequate record for judicial review.

An example of the application of the exhaustion doctrine is *Kleissler v. U.S. Forest Service*,[96] in which plaintiffs alleged that the Forest Service had violated the National Environmental Policy Act (NEPA) and the National Forest Management Act (NFMA) in approving two timber-cutting projects in the Allegheny National Forest. The plaintiffs filed administrative appeals for both projects, and the project approvals were affirmed in final administrative determinations. The plaintiffs then challenged the projects in the U.S. District Court for the Western District of Pennsylvania, where their claims were dismissed for failure to exhaust the available administrative remedies, despite having filed their complaint after the conclusion of both administrative appeals. Affirming the district court, the U.S. Court of Appeals for the Third Circuit found that the claims plaintiffs made in their complaint differed from the issues they had raised in their administrative appeals. Because the administrative appeals had not sufficiently put the Forest Service on notice of the allegations in the plaintiffs' complaint, the agency had no opportunity to address those allegations through the administrative process or develop a record before the suit was brought in federal court. Thus, the court found that the plaintiffs had failed to exhaust their administrative remedies with respect to the particular claims asserted in the complaint because they had not raised those claims in their administrative appeals.

It is also important to note that there are some instances in which a plaintiff is able to demonstrate that there is a case or controversy, but the court is nevertheless effectively barred from ruling on the merits of a claim because the defendant is immune from suit. Such situations typically arise when the defendant is a governmental entity that is able to claim sovereign immunity. Most of the federal environmental statutes contain "citizen suit" provisions that waive the federal government's sovereign immunity to specific types of claims. However, where a claim against a federal agency does not fall within the parameters of one of the statutory provisions waiving sovereign immunity, the agency may still assert immunity from suit.[97]

Finally, statutes themselves may authorize some types of lawsuits challenging agency actions but prohibit others, or may specify which courts are authorized to hear specified categories of cases. For example, CERCLA prohibits challenges to determinations by EPA regarding the appropriate cleanup remedy for a contaminated site except in specified circumstances.[98] The CWA provides that lawsuits challenging specified types of EPA actions must be filed in the appropriate U.S. Court of Appeals rather than a federal district court.[99] Similar provisions are found in other federal environmental statutes.

6.2.6 Who May Sue

As noted above, the courts have found that parties may commence lawsuits only under certain conditions. Among other things, the courts have held that the U.S. Constitution requires that a party as an initial matter have standing or an appropriate individual interest in the outcome of the case in order to proceed with its claims. In order to have standing to sue in federal court, the courts have held that the Constitution requires that a party demonstrate that it has suffered an injury in fact, that the action being challenged caused the injury, and that a decision by the court could redress the injury. For example, in the 1989 case of *McCormick v. Anschutz Mining Corp.*,[100] the plaintiff, Walter McCormick, alleged that Anschutz Mining had violated CERCLA. However, McCormick testified at his deposition that he had not been injured in any way by alleged discharges of pollution from a mine owned by Anschutz Mining. While McCormick was worried that he might be exposed to future liability because he had been in charge of the refinery at the mine until it was closed, "[t]he mere possibility of future injury is not enough." Hence, the court dismissed McCormick's case for lack of standing.

The U.S. Supreme Court has further held that, when a cause of action arises under a statute such as an environmental law, a court must also consider whether Congress intended for the plaintiff to have standing to bring a claim under the statute. In determining whether a plaintiff has statutory standing, a court will generally consider whether the plaintiff's injury is to an interest "arguably within the zone of interests to be protected" by the statute in question.

Many of the leading environmental cases addressing whether a plaintiff possesses sufficient injury in fact to have standing to assert its claims are cases involving the National Environmental Policy Act (NEPA) and the preparation of environmental impact statements under this Act. The seminal case involving NEPA standing is the U.S. Supreme Court decision in *Sierra Club v. Morton*.[101] This case involved the recreational development of the Mineral King Valley in California. The question in *Sierra v. Morton* was this: How does a plaintiff demonstrate its standing to claim injury of a noneconomic nature to widely shared public interests? The court recognized that environmental well-being, like economic well-being, is an important public policy objective for our society. The fact that environmental interests are shared by many individuals, rather than the few, does not make them less deserving of legal protection. But the injury in fact test, according to the Court, requires that the party seeking review be itself among the injured. The Sierra Club did not show that it or its members would be affected in any of their activities or pastimes by the development. Thus, the Court found that the organization lacked standing to pursue its claims in court.

Nevertheless, despite this adverse ruling, many plaintiffs in subsequent environmental cases have found it easy to demonstrate their standing by alleging that an aesthetic or other noneconomic interest was injured. For example, in *United States v. Students Challenging Regulatory Agency Procedures (SCRAP)*,[102] the U.S. Supreme Court ruled that certain law students had standing to sue the Interstate Commerce Commission (ICC) in a rate increase case involving recyclables. The Supreme Court found that the students possessed standing to assert their claims based on their showing that they used the forests and streams in the Washington, D.C., area for camping and hiking and that this use would be impaired by the adverse environmental impact that was caused by the nonuse of recyclable goods brought on by the ICC rate increase on recyclable commodities.

In more recent cases, the U.S. Supreme Court has required plaintiffs in environmental cases to make specific allegations of particularized injuries. For example, in *Lujan v. National Wildlife Federation*,[103] the Supreme Court reversed a decision that held that two affidavits filed on behalf of the National Wildlife Federation had satisfactorily alleged injury in fact to establish the Federation's standing in this case, even though the affidavits were not specific as to the actual injury. In finding that the affidavits failed to adequately demonstrate the Federation's standing, the Court stated that "whether one of respondent's members has been, or is threatened to be, 'adversely affected or aggrieved' by Government action—Rule 56(e) is assuredly not satisfied by pleadings which state only that one of respondent's members uses unspecified portions of an immense tract of territory, on some portions of which mining activity has occurred or probably will occur by virtue of the governmental action."[104]

The 1992 case of *Lujan v. Defenders of Wildlife*[105] further illustrates the requirement that plaintiffs allege an injury in fact that is concrete and specific. This lawsuit challenged the view that U.S. agencies' funding of development projects overseas does not have to comply with the Endangered Species Act. The court did not rule on the question of whether the law's provisions extend to overseas projects, but rather dismissed the case on the legal ground that the plaintiffs lacked standing to sue. One of the plaintiffs in this lawsuit, Joyce Kelly, had asserted that she would suffer harm because the Bureau of Reclamation's project to rebuild the Aswan Dam in Egypt threatened the endangered Nile crocodile. Another plaintiff, Amy Skilbred, said she would be harmed by the Mahaweli water resource project in Sri Lanka, funded by U.S. AID, which threatened the endangered Asian elephant and leopard. Justice Scalia, writing for the Court majority, said that although both women had visited the area of the projects and alleged their intention to return, such claims did not demonstrate that they were in immediate danger of suffering harm. He indicated that plaintiffs, to have standing to sue, must prove they suffer individual, concrete harm as a result of the government's actions.

At the same time, the Court has loosened the requirements for the zone of interest test that has at times been used by the courts to deny standing to plaintiffs in environmental cases, particularly where the plaintiffs allege only economic injuries. In *Bennett v. Spear*,[106] the Court held that local irrigation districts in Oregon that faced the prospect of reduced water supplies had standing to challenge the determination of the U.S. Fish and Wildlife Service that withdrawals of water from the Klamath Project for irrigation or other purposes would cause a taking of endangered fish species. The Court held that the citizen suit provision of the Endangered Species Act, which authorizes "any person" to commence a civil suit to enforce the requirements of the act,[107] reflected an intent by Congress that the zone of interest test not apply to citizen suits under the act. The Court further held that, where the "zone of interest" test does apply, as in suits under the APA, a plaintiff need not be directly regulated by a statute nor seek to further the overall good of an environmental statute in order to be within the zone of interest of the statute for purposes of establishing standing.

The U.S. Supreme Court has recognized two important exceptions to the general requirements of standing, both of which result in the application of a relaxed standing requirement in some cases. The first applies to litigants "to whom Congress has accorded a procedural right to protect his concrete interests."[108] Such litigants are entitled to "assert that [procedural] right without meeting all the normal standards for redressability and immediacy [of harm]."[109] In other words, "when a litigant is vested with a procedural right, that litigant has standing if there is some possibility that the requested relief will prompt the injury-causing party to reconsider the decision that allegedly harmed the litigant."[110] A second exception to the general standing requirements involves "a suit by a State for an injury to it in its capacity of quasi-sovereign."[111] In such circumstances the states "are not normal litigants for the purposes of invoking federal jurisdiction."[112] Instead, their quasi-sovereign interests entitle them to the application of a relaxed standing requirement.[113] In the Supreme Court's decision of *Massachusetts v. EPA*, both of these exceptions to the normal standing requirements were applicable to Massachusetts. In a decision involving EPA's denial of a petition for rulemaking to regulate greenhouse gas emissions from automobiles, the Court concluded that Massachusetts was "entitled to special solicitude in our standing analysis" because Congress had accorded it a procedural right to protect its concrete interests and because it had a quasi-sovereign interest in the outcome of the litigation.[114]

More recently, growing attention—both in the courts and the U.S. Congress—has been given to questions of whether private parties possess standing to contest certain types of judicial settlements involving EPA. These settlements result from the increasing use of a so-called "sue and settle" strategy by environmental organizations and citizens' groups that file actions in federal district and/or appellate courts seeking to compel the Agency to adopt new or revised regulatory standards. Once such an action is filed, the citizens' group and EPA will often enter into negotiations that ultimately result in a consent decree being filed with the court, under which the Agency agrees to implement a rulemaking with specified time deadlines to address particular provisions of the federal environmental laws. If approved by the court, this decree then becomes a binding obligation on EPA, and carries the potential threat of judicial sanctions should the Agency fail to adhere to the settlement terms and time-frames. Industry groups and some Members of Congress have raised concerns about these types of settlements, because (a) in many instances the public receives no notice or information about the EPA-citizens' group negotiations until the consent decree is filed with the court, and (b) several courts have found that parties who did not participate in the negotiations with EPA lack standing to judicially challenge the resulting consent decree. During the 113th Congress, federal legislation was introduced to curtail the use of "sue and settle" consent decrees, banning them unless the parties affected by the proposed regulations are allowed to participate in the settlement negotiations and the proposed settlement is released for notice and comment.[115] Nevertheless, in the absence of such legislation being enacted, the courts have generally found that such parties lack standing to contest a "sue and settle" consent decree, on the grounds that such parties have not suffered a sufficient injury-in-fact because the decree usually merely specifies that EPA undertake a rulemaking process and does not mandate particular provisions of a new or revised rule.[116]

6.3 Defining the Limits of Governmental Authority

The environmental law system in the United States is premised on the same constitutional rights and limitations on governmental action that are applicable to other areas of law. Consequently, the courts in a number of cases have been called upon to interpret the scope and availability of certain constitutional rights in the environmental context. The courts' consideration of these important constitutional issues is briefly summarized below.

6.3.1 Search Warrants and the Fourth Amendment

Several of the key constitutional protections for individual rights have been established under the Fourth Amendment to the U.S. Constitution. This amendment provides as follows:

> The right of the people to be secure in their persons, houses, papers, and effects, against unreasonable searches and seizures shall not be violated, and no warrants shall issue, but upon probable cause, supported by oath or affirmation and particularly describing the place to be searched and the persons or things to be seized.

Cases interpreting the Fourth Amendment's warrant requirement arise most frequently in connection with the collection or obtaining of evidence by the government. Evidence is necessary for any civil or criminal environmental enforcement program. However, federal and state evidence collection is limited by Fourth Amendment prohibitions. Thus, while warrants may sometimes be required to obtain necessary information, government investigators generally will seek a warrant in facility inspection cases only after entry to a particular facility has been refused, because there is no need for a search warrant when the owner or operator has given his consent.

The courts have held that the Fourth Amendment applies to corporate entities as well as to private citizens. In addition, the Supreme Court has held that the requirement for a search warrant even applies to routine inspections.[117] For example, in the *Camara* case, the Supreme Court held that the warrant requirement applied to a municipal health inspector's search of a private residence. A similar conclusion was reached with respect to a fire inspector's attempted search of a commercial warehouse.[118] In these cases, the Supreme Court indicated that a lesser degree of probable cause would be required for an administrative search warrant than for the typical criminal search warrant. Based on these rulings, routine periodic searches of all structures in a given area may be permissible under the U.S. Constitution when justified based on an appraisal of conditions in the area as a whole rather than on a knowledge of conditions in a particular building. The reasonableness of such inspections must be weighed against the invasion of rights that the search entails.

Some courts have held that the lessened expectation of privacy that corporations have justifies warrantless searches of corporate facilities. For example, in November 1989 the Supreme Court of Pennsylvania upheld the warrantless, unannounced inspection provisions of Pennsylvania's Solid Waste Management Act.[119] The court in this case found that the act authorized a Department of Environmental Resources (DER) employee to obtain access to a transfer station where trash was compacted, since the employee entered the transfer station "to ascertain the compliance or noncompliance by any person or municipality with the provisions of this act." The DER employee had seen one of the appellant's loaded trash trucks enter the transfer station, which the appellant had not been issued a permit to operate. The court reasoned that the *Colonnade-Biswell* exception[120] to the warrant requirement of the Fourth Amendment allows greater latitude to conduct warrantless inspections of commercial property because "the expectation of privacy that the owner of commercial property enjoys in such property differs significantly from the sanctity accorded an individual's home."[121]

Following the rationale of such cases, the U.S. Congress has amended several federal laws to authorize government inspectors and investigators to conduct warrantless searches in an effort to minimize the need for search warrants under certain circumstances. In *Marshall v. Barlow's, Inc.*,[122] the Court held that Section 8 of the federal Occupational Safety and Health Act (OSH Act), which authorized warrantless inspections, violated the Fourth Amendment prohibition against warrantless searches and was therefore unconstitutional. Notwithstanding this ruling, as a practical matter few businesses challenge governmental inspections without warrants under the federal environmental laws because to do so could be construed by government officials as indicating that a facility may have a problem or be hiding improper conduct. Nevertheless, the Fourth Amendment's warrant requirement does impose some minimal restraints on the federal government's ability to conduct repetitive or needless inspections.

Several of the federal environmental laws specifically authorize EPA to conduct warrantless searches of regulated facilities. However, EPA has avoided any test of the constitutionality of these provisions, including those set forth under the Resource Conservation and Recovery Act (RCRA), by not seeking to enforce its statutory authority. In fact, if an EPA inspector is refused admission, EPA, as standard procedure, will typically simply obtain a search warrant and not even try to use the Agency's warrantless search authority under RCRA. This approach has allowed the Agency to avoid many serious challenges to its information-gathering powers under the federal environmental laws.

While Congress may not have the power to authorize warrantless searches in all cases, the courts have identified several exceptions to the constitutional obligation of the government to obtain a warrant in order to inspect private property. One example of such an exception is the so-called open fields exception described in the U.S. Supreme Court case *Air Pollution Variance Board v. Western Alfalfa*.[123] In this case, an inspector from the Colorado Department of Health entered the premises of Western Alfalfa Corporation without its knowledge or consent to make a Ringelmann reading of plumes of smoke being emitted from the company's chimneys. Western Alfalfa Corporation claimed that the inspector violated the Fourth Amendment by entering its property to collect evidence without a search warrant. In response, the Supreme Court ruled that the inspector's actions fell under an exception to the Fourth Amendment and had not violated the rights of Western Alfalfa Corporation. The Court noted in general that the act of conducting tests on a defendant's premises without either a warrant or the consent of defendant would constitute an unreasonable search prohibited by the Fourth Amendment. However, in this case the inspector did not enter the company's building or offices. Instead, he merely observed what anyone in the area near the plant could see. He was on the defendant's property, but there was no showing that he was on premises from which the public was excluded. Thus, the Court held that there is an open fields exception to the constitutional requirement for a search warrant which was applicable in this case.

In a similar case, *Dow Chemical Co. v. United States*,[124] Dow challenged EPA's warrantless aerial photography of a Dow manufacturing site. In this case, Dow argued that EPA had performed an illegal search under the Fourth Amendment by employing a commercial aerial photographer to photograph Dow's facility. Rejecting Dow's claim, the Supreme Court found that Dow's industrial complex, with numerous structures spread over 2,000 acres, was comparable to an open field, and was therefore open to aircraft surveillance. The Court held that "the taking of aerial photographs of an industrial plant complex from navigable air-space is not a search prohibited by the Fourth Amendment."[125]

Another case describing the open fields exception is the interesting case of *Forsythe v. Commonwealth of Pennsylvania*.[126] After various discussions with appellant Barb Forsythe about the condition of her property, Larry Smith, Franklin Township's code enforcement officer, periodically inspected her premises. Smith observed "numerous junked cars, piles of trash, washers, mailboxes, wheel rims, water heaters, concrete blocks, and miscellaneous car parts on her property."[127] Ms. Forsythe claimed she was operating a "recycling center" and admitted she had a business sign with the designation "Jay's Auto Parts" erected at the entrance to her yard. Forsythe was convicted of operating a junkyard without a license. Forsythe appealed her conviction by arguing that because enforcement officer Smith had entered her property without a warrant, her conviction should be overturned. The appellate court disagreed, however, concluding that "[t]he condition of [appellant's] land was easily ascertainable from a public road. She could have no expectation of privacy in an open field."[128] Since the only evidence used in her conviction was easily ascertainable from a public road, the open fields exception applied and Forsythe's conviction was upheld by the court.

As a practical matter, many companies and individuals who face inspections of their facilities under the federal environmental laws will often consent to these inspections. Thus, absent a compelling basis for refusing entry to a governmental inspector, most organizations will choose to cooperate with their regulators. In these cases, consent to enter a facility's premises may be given either verbally or in writing and is commonly given by employees simply by admitting the inspectors to the company premises or giving answers to oral or written questions by government employees.

One method that is sometimes used by the government to avoid the necessity of obtaining a search warrant is to require the owner or operator of the pollution source to obtain an environmental permit or license that specifically authorizes governmental inspections without warrants. The U.S. Supreme Court has not yet ruled on the constitutionality of this method. Since permit systems are now being used more and more by federal, state, and local agencies to control pollution, the use of environmental permit provisions by the government to obtain desired information may be an important trend and could provide the government with the necessary consent to satisfy Fourth Amendment concerns.

6.3.2 Prohibition against Self-Incrimination: The Fifth Amendment

The Fifth Amendment to the U.S. Constitution prohibits compulsory self-incrimination and typically is invoked in criminal cases. If the government agency seeking information intends to use it only for civil enforcement purposes, such as fines or injunctions, the courts have concluded that the Fifth Amendment generally is not applicable. In addition, many courts have clarified that the Fifth Amendment applies only to persons and not to corporations or partnerships.

In *Braswell v. United States*,[129] the Supreme Court summarized many of the Fifth Amendment's key protections against self-incrimination. In this case, the petitioner Randy Braswell had purchased and sold timber, land, equipment, and oil and gas interests through his two corporations. When a federal grand jury subpoenaed Braswell, as president of both corporations, to produce the corporations' books and records, Braswell claimed that according to the Fifth Amendment he should not be compelled in any criminal case to be a witness against himself.[130] In the Court's decision, Chief Justice Rehnquist explained that the Fifth Amendment neither applies to collective entities such as corporations, unions, or partnerships, nor to people acting as agents of collective entities. Rather, the Fifth Amendment applies to people in personal capacities and protects individuals' private papers. Notably, the Court found that a sole proprietorship—unlike corporations—is considered to be a "personal" entity and is protected by the Fifth Amendment. Despite these findings, the Supreme Court ultimately upheld Braswell's conviction. Because the subpoena identified Braswell as an agent of collective entities—specifically, he was the president of certain targeted corporations—the Fifth Amendment's protections did not apply. If, on the other hand, Braswell had been operating sole proprietorships as he had in the past, he would have been protected by the Fifth Amendment.

Most environmental statutes provide penalties for both individuals and corporations. Therefore, in a case where the evidence or samples taken might be used in a criminal action, the person in authority at the place where evidence is to be taken should be advised of his rights to remain silent, to have an attorney, and to be made aware that any evidence taken may be used against him in a subsequent criminal action. If these rights are not formally observed, the evidence so collected potentially may not be admissible in a criminal action based on the constitutional protections provided under the Fifth Amendment. (See section 6.5.6 of this chapter, "Your Own Reports as Evidence against You.")

6.3.3 Due Process: The Fifth and Fourteenth Amendments

Another important constitutional restraint on the government's enforcement powers is the requirement that government entities provide due process of law. This "due process" obligation is established under the Fifth and Fourteenth Amendments to the U.S. Constitution. The Fifth Amendment provides that "No person shall . . . be deprived of life, liberty, or property, without due process of law; nor shall private property be taken for public use, without just compensation." Similarly, the Fourteenth Amendment to the U.S. Constitution states: "No State shall make or enforce any law which shall abridge the privileges or immunities of citizens of the United States; nor shall any State deprive any person of life, liberty, or property without due process of law; nor deny to any person within its jurisdiction the equal protection of the law." Courts recognize two types of due process rights: substantive and procedural. As the U.S. Supreme Court has stated, the " 'touchstone of due process is protection of the individual against arbitrary action of government' . . . whether the fault lies on the denial of fundamental procedural fairness . . . or in the exercise of power without any reasonable justification in the service of a legitimate governmental objective."[131] Substantive due process bars "certain government actions regardless of the fairness of the procedures used to implement them," including actions that are arbitrary or "shock the conscience."[132] Procedural due process, on the other hand, refers to the procedures, such as giving notice and allowing a hearing, that the government must follow before depriving someone of either their rights or property.

When interpreting these provisions, the courts have ruled that the Fifth Amendment prohibition applies to the federal government and the Fourteenth Amendment applies to the state and local governments. For example, a court determined that the Fourteenth Amendment's substantive due process requirements applied to certain actions by a municipality in *Construction Industry Ass'n. v. Petaluma*.[133] In this case the court held that a city ordinance that limits issuance of new building permits to achieve a goal of preserving "small-town" character, open spaces, and low-density population did not violate the due process clause of the Fourteenth Amendment. The court's opinion explained that to satisfy the due process mandate, particular zoning regulations must be justified by the government's need to protect the public welfare. The court subsequently found that the concept of the public welfare is sufficiently broad to uphold Petaluma's desire to preserve its small-town character, open spaces, and low-density population.

In another case, a due process challenge was used to contest a beverage container ordinance adopted by the city of Bowie, Maryland.[134] In this case the court ruled that there was no violation of procedural due process requirements since there was not a showing that the government's police power had been exercised arbitrarily, oppressively, or unreasonably. The court also held that a law should not be held void if any considerations of public welfare can support it.

The court in *Massachusetts v. Blackstone Valley Electric Co.*[135] applied the Constitution's due process protections to the federal CERCLA law. According to CERCLA, a Remedial Investigation/Feasibility Study (RI/FS) must be conducted once a hazardous waste site has been identified. CERCLA further requires that the alleged generators of a site's hazardous waste be notified of cleanup efforts, be allowed access to the RI/FS, and have a chance to comment on the work plan and data. This input becomes important because it establishes the administrative record from which the cleanup costs owed by the individual hazardous waste generators can eventually be calculated. In this case the Massachusetts Department of Environmental Protection did not notify Blackstone Valley Electric Company of the cleanup until approximately one year after it had begun. Blackstone Valley Electric Company argued that its procedural due process rights would be violated if it were forced to pay for cleanup efforts about which it knew nothing and over which it had no input or control. The court agreed with these claims and ordered the Massachusetts Department of Environmental Protection to supplement the administrative record with comments submitted by Blackstone, to hold meetings for Blackstone to comment on the selected cleanup actions, to accept written submissions by Blackstone for 30 days following the date of the last of these meetings, and to certify to the court a supplemented administrative record including any decreases in the cleanup costs it sought from the defendants. Thereby, defendant Blackstone Valley Electric Company had its important Fourteenth Amendment due process rights protected.

Another example of the importance of due process concerns in the environmental context, and specifically the CERCLA context, can be seen in litigation between General Electric and EPA. General Electric has claimed that the CERCLA provisions that limit pre-enforcement judicial review of EPA-issued remedial orders violate Constitutional due process requirements. General Electric alleges that these due process concerns are heightened by the harsh penalties imposed for failure to comply with the remedial orders issued by EPA. In *General Electric Co. v. EPA*, the trial court initially ruled on summary judgment in favor of EPA, but General Electric nevertheless sought to appeal the decision based on its procedural claims.[136] On appeal, the D.C. Circuit affirmed the district court's summary judgment ruling, holding that EPA's unilateral administrative orders (UAOs) did not violate due process requirements because "[t]o the extent the UAO regime implicates constitutionally protected property interests by imposing compliance costs and threatening fines and punitive damages, it satisfies due process because UAO recipients may obtain a pre-deprivation hearing by refusing to comply and forcing EPA to sue in federal court."[137]

6.3.4 Police Power and Due Process

As noted above, the courts have found that the due process requirements of the Fifth and Fourteenth Amendments of the U.S. Constitution impose certain restraints on a state government's inherent "police power." The "police power" of the state has been generally construed as the power to pass laws for the protection of the health, welfare, morals, and property of the people within its jurisdiction. This power extends to all public needs and may be asserted in support of government actions deemed to be greatly or immediately necessary for the protection of the public welfare. By exercise of reasonable police power, states—and through the exercise of delegated authority local governments—may regulate the conduct of individuals and the use of their property and, in some instances, take property without compensation.

Although the police power of a state and its instrumentalities is very broad, it is not without limitation. It is always within the power of the court to declare a law void which, although enacted pursuant to the governmental police power, is not justified as such. In other words, a law enacted as a police regulation must be reasonable. If a law is found to be unreasonable or exercised in an arbitrary manner, it can be constitutionally overturned for taking life, liberty, or property without due process of law.

The federal court decision in *Browning-Ferris Industries (BFI) of Alabama, Inc. v. Alabama Department of Environmental Management (ADEM)*[138] illustrates the interplay between the government's police power and a corporation's due process rights. BFI was trying to open a hazardous waste facility when the Alabama legislature passed the Minus Act prohibiting hazardous waste facilities from opening without prior legislative approval. BFI challenged the statute as violative of the Fourteenth Amendment's Due Process Clause. In response to BFI's claim, the court first determined that the storage of hazardous waste is an appropriate area for control by the Alabama legislature under its police power, noting that "The Court emphasizes that the Constitution does not foreclose legislative restrictions on hazardous waste facilities. Such restrictions appear to this Court to be essential for the protection of the health and safety of Alabama citizens."[139] However, the federal court found that the specific statute being challenged by BFI provided absolutely no standards by which to approve hazardous waste facilities. The court stated that "the guarantee of due process . . . demands only that the law shall not be unreasonable, arbitrary and capricious and that the means selected shall have some real and substantial relationship to the object sought to be obtained. . . ."[140] Thus, while the statute addressed an area appropriate for police power protection, the pertinent provision of the Minus Act was held an unconstitutional violation of due process.

An example of the valid exercise of police power which did not violate the due process principle is provided by the U.S. Supreme Court case *Village of Belle Terre v. Borass*.[141] In this case a New York village ordinance restricted land use to one-family houses and precluded occupancy by more than two unrelated persons. The Court held that this ordinance was a valid exercise of the city's police power, stating:

> A quiet place where yards are wide, people few, and motor vehicles restricted are legitimate guidelines in a land use project addressed to family needs. The police power is not confined to elimination of filth, stench, and unhealthy places. It is ample to lay out zones where family values, youth values, and the blessings of quiet seclusion and clean air make the area a sanctuary for people.

6.3.5 Prohibition against Taking Property without Compensation

The Fifth Amendment to the U.S. Constitution further limits the government's regulatory and enforcement powers by prohibiting unjust takings of private property. The Fifth Amendment provides, in part, that ". . . private property [shall not] be taken for public use, without just compensation."

Takings come in various forms. The most common and most easily recognized form of taking historically has been the exercise by governmental authorities of the power of eminent domain, through which the government explicitly acknowledges that it is taking private property for a public purpose such as building a public highway or a railroad, or promoting economic development within a targeted area.[142] However, the government can also take private property for which it is required to pay compensation even where the government authority does not acknowledge that property is being taken. Such takings can occur when a government authority or someone acting as its agent physically "invades" private property and thereby takes from the property owner one of the "sticks" in the "bundle of rights" that are historically recognized as being part of property ownership, in this case the right to exclude others from the property.

One example of such a physical invasion constituting a taking under the Fifth Amendment has arisen in the context of cleanups of contaminated property. In *Hendler v. United States*,[143] individuals who owned property near a contaminated site received an order from the state of California, acting as an agent for EPA, requiring the landowners to allow government contractors to enter their property for the purpose of installing monitoring and extraction wells as part of the remediation of contaminated groundwater. The court held that the actions of EPA through its agents and contractors in entering onto private property with heavy equipment to install and sample wells, and other equipment, constituted a taking of private property because the landowners had been deprived of their right to exclude others from the property.

In contrast, in another case Southview Associates Ltd. had purchased 88 acres with the intent to build a residential subdivision. When it became known that this land was a winter habitat for white-tailed deer, the Vermont Department of Fish and Wildlife opposed the development project. Southview's land use permit application was then turned down by the state District III Environmental Commission, as was its appeal to the Vermont Environmental Board. In *Southview Associates Ltd. v. Bongartz*,[144] the court ruled that Southview had not lost the rights to possess the allegedly occupied land that forms part of the deeryard and to exclude people and even deer therefrom, and that Southview retained substantial control over the property, including the rights to build on up to 10 acres for any purpose and to camp, walk, ski, or even hunt deer—regardless of whether these activities caused the deer to abandon the deeryard, consequently holding that Southview's right to sell the land was by no means worthless. The court ruled that no absolute, exclusive physical occupation existed. The property was not "emptied . . . of any value"[145] by the permit denial. "Indeed, the deer activity displaces only a few sticks in the bundle of rights that constitute ownership."[146] The court therefore dismissed Southview's physical taking claim, finding that "denial of the . . . permit—foreclosing one configuration of a development plan—represents a regulation of the use of Southview's property, rather than a per se physical taking."[147]

Instances of physical invasion that constitute takings under the Fifth Amendment are not limited to physical occupation of land. For example, a series of cases has held that airport noise can constitute a taking of property rights. In the landmark case *United States v. Causby*,[148] the Supreme Court held that frequent low flights over the Causbys' land by military aircraft landing at a nearby airport operated by the United States constituted a taking of the Causbys' property without compensation in violation of the Fifth Amendment. The noise from the aircraft rendered it impossible to continue the use of the property as a commercial chicken farm. Although the flights did not completely destroy the enjoyment and use of the land, they were held to be so low and frequent as to constitute a direct and immediate interference with the full enjoyment of the land, limiting the utility of the land and causing a diminution in its value, therefore constituting a taking under the Fifth Amendment.

In another major Supreme Court decision on this issue, *Griggs v. Allegheny County*,[149] the Court held that Allegheny County, which owned and operated the Greater Pittsburgh Airport, was liable for a taking of property under the Fifth Amendment because the noise from takeoffs and landings at the airport on flight paths over the Griggs' property rendered the property undesirable and unbearable for residential use. The Court saw no difference between the county's responsibility to pay for land on which runways were built and its responsibility for air easements necessary for airport operation. The Court observed that the glide path for the northwest runway was as necessary for the operation of the airport as a surface right-of-way. Several states have interpreted their own constitutions to require compensation under less strict circumstances, when noise from aircraft has diminished the market value of a homeowner's property. Interference must be substantial and sufficiently direct to require compensation in the majority of jurisdictions.

Corporate trade secrets also have been the subject of constitutional takings claims. In *Ruckelshaus v. Monsanto Company*,[150] Monsanto objected to the data-disclosure and data-consideration provisions of the Federal Insecticide, Fungicide, and Rodenticide Act (FIFRA), alleging that these provisions amounted to a taking without just compensation in violation of the Fifth Amendment. The Supreme Court held that to the extent Monsanto, as an applicant for the registration of pesticides, had an interest in its health, safety, and environmental data recognizable as a trade-secret property right under Missouri law, its property right was protected by the taking clause of the Fifth Amendment.

In addition to these physical invasions, occupations or appropriations of property, a government can take private property within the meaning of the Fifth Amendment simply by regulating the uses of property.[151] The U.S. Supreme Court long ago recognized that governments must be allowed to regulate the use of private property to some extent without being required to pay for any incidental impacts on the value of the property being regulated. However, the Court stated that "while property may be regulated to a certain extent, if regulation goes too far it will be considered a taking."[152] The Court has made clear that there is no bright line test for determining when a regulation goes too far in restricting the use of property and will result in a taking; a determination as to whether a taking has occurred requires a consideration of the facts of each case. In any event, the courts have provided some guidance, indicating that if the impact of governmental conduct is felt by many persons similarly situated and is in the nature of a restriction that ought to be borne by the individual as a member of society for the good of the public, it is generally viewed as a reasonable exercise of police power not requiring compensation. In contrast, if the impact on the property owner is so great that he ought not to bear it under generally accepted standards, then courts are inclined to treat it as a taking, or an unreasonable exercise of police power requiring compensation.

In addition to this general guidance, the U.S. Supreme Court has identified three factors that a court should consider in determining whether a regulatory taking has occurred, including the regulation's economic impact on the property owner, the extent to which the regulation interferes with reasonable, investment-backed expectations, and the character of the government action.[153] The Court has further indicated in *Lucas v. South Carolina Coastal Council (Lucas)*[154] that if the analysis of the first prong of this three-part test concludes that a regulatory action categorically prohibits all economically viable use of the land at issue, the only remaining issue is whether regulation would be permitted under the common law nuisance doctrine. Thus, where an owner of beachfront property was precluded by state statute from engaging in any development activity on his property and was forced to leave the property economically idle, a categorical taking was found on that basis alone.[155]

The Supreme Court has also provided guidance for applying the "character of the government action" criterion, which involves determining when a governmental restriction on the use of private property will be considered a reasonable and necessary exercise of the police power that is intended to prevent harm rather than a taking of private property that requires compensation. In *Lucas*, the Court explained that the Fifth Amendment is designed to protect uses of property that an owner would be entitled to engage in by virtue of his or her ownership. However, there are some uses of property—such as those that constitute nuisances—that no landowner is entitled to engage in, so a governmental action restricting such a use does not deprive the landowner of any right the owner otherwise had. Thus, if a government agency restricts a use of property that would be considered a nuisance under state law, that restriction does not result in a taking.

The decision in *Bowles v. United States*[156] illustrates the circumstances under which a regulatory taking can be proven. In Bowles, the owner of several lots in a residential subdivision was denied a CWA Section 404 permit to fill wetlands in connection with preparation of one of the lots for construction. The permit denial left the owner without any economically viable use for the lot. The Court held that the landowner had a reasonable expectation that he would be able to develop the lot despite the presence of wetlands on the property because owners of other lots in the subdivision that also contained wetlands had not been required to obtain Section 404 permits from the Corps of Engineers prior to development. Consequently, the Court concluded that the plaintiff's property had been taken and that the United States was required to pay the plaintiff just compensation for the taking.

The Supreme Court has indicated that a regulatory taking may also occur as a result of the imposition of conditions on a regulatory approval. Thus, in *Nollan v. California Coastal Commission (Nollan)*,[157] the Supreme Court held that a taking had occurred where the defendant conditioned its approval of a building permit for a beachfront home on an agreement by the property owners to allow the public to walk across their property along the beach, in effect requiring the property owners to grant a public easement along the beach in exchange for the building permit. The Court held that the imposition of this condition did not "substantially advance a legitimate state interest" and therefore constituted a taking for which compensation was required.[158] Similarly, in *Dolan v. City of Tigard (Dolan)*,[159] the Court held that certain conditions that a municipality attached to a building permit for the expansion of a plumbing supply store—including a requirement that the landowner dedicate a portion of her property to the city to be used for a storm drainage system and for a bike path—resulted in a taking. The Court found that the city had made no finding that the dedications of property it required in exchange for the building permit were related both in nature and extent to the impacts expected from the proposed development.

The Supreme Court recently expanded its regulatory takings doctrine to allow petitioners to challenge conditions included in permit denials on the grounds that they constitute a taking. In *Koontz v. St. Johns River Water Management District*,[160] the Court expressed concern that regulatory authorities may circumvent restrictions on permit conditions by rejecting permits and then providing compliance alternatives that would constitute impermissible takings if the conditions had been required as part of an approved permit. The Court also expressed discomfort with the magnitude of monetary exactions a land-use authority could induce from property owners. The Court held that "the government's demand for property from a land-use permit applicant must satisfy the requirements of *Nollan* and *Dolan* even when the government denies the permit and even when its demand is for money."

In sum, the courts have required the federal government and state and local governments to pay compensation for takings of private property as a result of a variety of regulatory actions. While the constitutional rights of individuals and organizations may be more difficult to uphold in contexts where these private rights arguably conflict with public rights to a safe and healthy environment, the courts have nevertheless determined that these important constitutional rights must be upheld in order to provide effective restraints on governmental actions, including those taken pursuant to the federal environmental statutes.

6.3.6 The Constitution as an Action-Forcing Mechanism

In contrast to the action-limiting aspects of the U.S. Constitution described above, a possible trend is emerging in which plaintiffs are asserting an action-forcing role for the Constitution in the environmental law context. In *Juliana v. United States*,[161] a group of youth plaintiffs allege that the federal government's actions (i.e., approval of fossil fuel development) and omissions (i.e., failure to "take necessary action to curtail fossil fuel emissions") have destabilized the climate and, in turn, violated the plaintiffs' constitutional rights. Specifically, the plaintiffs claim that (1) increased carbon dioxide emissions "shock the conscience" and violate the plaintiffs' substantive due process rights to life and liberty, (2) denying youth the protections afforded to prior generations and favoring the short-term economic interests of present-day adults violates the youth plaintiffs' Fifth Amendment equal protection rights, (3) the government has violated plaintiffs' implicit Ninth Amendment right to a stable climate, and (4) denying future generations essential natural resources violates the public trust doctrine, as secured by the Ninth Amendment. The plaintiffs seek declaratory and injunctive relief aimed at compelling the U.S. government to phase out fossil fuels and stabilize the climate. A magistrate judge for the U.S. District Court for the District of Oregon found the allegations plausible and recommended that the court deny the motions to dismiss the suit.

Thus, the U.S. Constitution is, and will continue to be, a major aspect of environmental law, primarily as a limitation on the scope of federal and state legislation and the actions of federal and state regulators, but perhaps also as a means of forcing legislators and regulators to take additional steps to protect the environment.

6.4 Administrative Law and Procedure

As with most areas of law, the environmental law system has been implemented through a complex set of administrative rules and procedures. While the substantive and organic environmental laws outlined above establish the legal framework for many of the environmental requirements imposed on the regulated community, the agencies charged with administering these laws—such as EPA—have considerable authority over how specific regulatory requirements are established, implemented, and applied. Thus, the administrative process used by EPA to develop these requirements can be a key factor in determining the outcome of cases involving challenges to particular environmental rules.

The courts in a number of cases have established guidelines for determining whether a particular EPA environmental rule has been adopted within the agency's authority, consistent with required procedures, and is otherwise in accordance with law. For example, the U.S. Court of Appeals for the Eighth Circuit examined EPA's interpretation of the Superfund Amendments and Reauthorization Act of 1986 (SARA) in the case *Dico v. Diamond (Dico)*.[162] When SARA became effective on October 17, 1986, it created a new right of a nonliable party who "receives and complies with the terms of any administrative order . . ."[163] to be reimbursed for cleanup costs. However, EPA sought to deny reimbursement to anyone who was unfortunate enough to have received a cleanup order before Congress made provision for reimbursement.[164] Dico felt not only unfortunate to have received a cleanup order less than three months before Congress made provision for reimbursement, but positively wronged, and so filed suit. In considering EPA's interpretation of the federal environmental statutes, courts have observed that EPA's interpretation of a statute it administers should be accorded substantial deference.[165] The U.S. Supreme Court pointed out in *Chevron U.S.A., Inc. v. Natural Resources Defense Council, Inc.*[166] that the questions for the court are these: (1) whether Congress has directly addressed the precise issue at question; and (2) if not, whether the agency's answer is based on a permissible construction of the statute. In *Dico*, however, the Eighth Circuit concluded that EPA was not entitled to substantial deference in interpreting CERCLA's reimbursement provision and, in fact, found that Dico could pursue its reimbursement claim.[167]

The critical questions of environmental law—the cutting-edge issues of science, risk assessment, application of technology, and analytical methods—are often resolved not through the scientific and engineering disciplines but through argument and procedural determinations. Any detailed discussion of the rules for those determinations is well beyond the scope of this text. However, the following brief illustrative examples may help clarify some of the key legal principles of the federal administrative law system:

(1) In general, the courts have found that administrative agencies have no inherent or residual authority but can act only pursuant to authority delegated to them in the statutes enacted by Congress. Thus, if an agency acts beyond the scope of its delegated authority, its action is illegal and void.

(2) An agency's interpretation of its own regulations and the statutes it administers will, particularly if consistently held over a substantial period of time, be granted deference by the courts.

(3) Agencies must act in accordance with the procedures specified in their enabling legislation, or, if no other procedures are specified, in accordance with the Administrative Procedure Act. These procedures normally entail publication of proposed rules in the *Federal Register*, opportunity for public comment, sometimes a public hearing, response to public comment, and publication of a final rule.

(4) Agencies must act in accordance with their own rules and regulations. Failure to follow those rules may cause administrative actions to be subject to legal challenge.

(5) Agencies must maintain a docket or record in support of their actions, and there must be evidence in that record to support the agency action. The record must be open for public examination throughout the period when public comments are being received.

(6) Agency actions may not be arbitrary and capricious. Thus, there must be at least some evidence in the agency's administrative record to support the agency decision. In some cases a statute specifically requires agencies to support their decisions with substantial evidence. Although the difference between some evidence and substantial evidence is somewhat obscure, agencies disfavor substantial evidence requirements.

(7) Agency decisions may be appealed to the courts under either specific judicial review provisions in the enabling statutes or the general judicial review provision of the Administrative Procedure Act. A plaintiff will not have a justifiable claim, however, unless it has standing, the issue is ripe, it has exhausted the available administrative remedies, and a final agency decision has been issued.

(8) On appeal, administrative agency actions are generally upheld in the absence of some glaring procedural defect or a clearly inadequate record. However, these circumstances occur frequently, and successful appeals, while not the rule, are far from a rarity.

President Obama's time in office provided an interesting test case for administrative action in the context of his Administration's efforts to address greenhouse gases and climate change. Congress has struggled over whether and how to address greenhouse gas emissions, with some in Congress seeking to bar the executive branch from construing its own powers in a manner that allows the Administration to regulate, limit, tax, or otherwise control greenhouse gases. In the meantime, the Obama Administration promulgated greenhouse gas and fuel economy standards for cars and trucks,[168] and regulations for carbon pollution under the Clean Air Act for new[169] and existing[170] power plants. Both power plant rules have been challenged in court.

In addition to the traditional tools of administrative power, the Obama Administration's Climate Action Plan set out a variety of "soft" administrative tools it planned to use to address climate change.[171] These include—among other approaches—a "presidential memorandum" to speed interagency cooperation on electric-transmission siting,[172] expanded financing under existing loan and loan-guarantee programs for renewable energy and energy efficiency projects,[173] an executive order requiring federally funded projects to meet flood risk standards that account for impacts of climate change,[174] and coordination and information sharing with foreign partners, including several bilateral and multilateral commitments to reduce emissions and shift to "clean power."[175] While such approaches may have limited reach and durability, they may influence future regulations or regulatory guidance, and they often channel agency resources in ways that affect a variety of public and private interests.

6.5 Rules of Evidence

When environmental claims are litigated, the court may consider questions of responsibility, liability sharing, and contribution. Each of these matters can involve detailed fact-finding by a court and specific testimony or other evidence necessary to support a party's claims. The following discussion provides a summary of some of the key concepts associated with the potential evidentiary issues that may arise in the environmental context.

6.5.1 Burden of Proof and Presumptions

In cases in which the scientific facts of a controversy are being hotly debated in the scientific community or the facts are otherwise unclear, a court's decision may be influenced by whether the plaintiff or the defendant has the burden of proof and which party has the obligation of going forward with the evidence. In our legal system, plaintiffs in civil cases normally have the burden of proving their cases. They typically must do so by a preponderance of the evidence. Thus, the government in a civil enforcement action would have the burden of proving by a preponderance of the evidence that the defendant had violated a particular statute or regulation. Since the party with the evidentiary burden will often face greater obstacles in proving its claim, the question of who bears the burden of proof is one of the most contentious issues in civil litigation in the environmental context.

In contrast to these rules for civil actions, the prosecutor in a criminal case has the burden of proving guilt beyond a reasonable doubt, and defendants are presumed innocent until proven guilty. This evidentiary burden for criminal prosecutions is a more difficult standard to achieve than is required for civil enforcement proceedings. Finally, a different evidentiary standard applies to cases involving challenges to a particular agency regulation or other action. In such cases, the courts have determined that an agency rule or action has a presumption of validity and the contesting party has the obligation of proving conclusively that the action is arbitrary and capricious, unsupported by the evidence, or otherwise not in accordance with law.

6.5.2 Hearsay

When courts weigh the evidence in a particular case, they may be called upon to consider so-called "hearsay" evidence. Hearsay is evidence that depends for its truth or falsity solely upon statements of a person other than the witness. Hearsay, in itself, has no evidentiary value. The witness cannot be cross-examined regarding hearsay, because the statements were made by another party. Generally, the courts will find that hearsay is inadmissible, but there are numerous exceptions to this general rule. For example, in the case of documents, many federal and state evidentiary rules allow an official custodian or witness to certify to the authenticity or validity of particular documents in order to overcome the hearsay objection.

6.5.3 Opinion Evidence and Expert Witnesses

Generally, the testimony of a witness will be confined to a statement of concrete facts based upon his own observation or knowledge. However, expert opinion evidence, though often based largely on hearsay, opinions, or conclusions not normally admissible into evidence, is admissible when it concerns scientific or technical matters and is presented by an appropriately qualified expert.

In a significant case involving evidentiary matters, the U.S. Supreme Court in *Daubert v. Merrell Dow Pharmaceuticals, Inc.* (*Daubert*)[176] identified several important principles that courts should follow to determine whether scientific expert testimony can be used as admissible evidence in court. First, the Supreme Court indicated that a trial judge should act as a gatekeeper and make a decision about whether the methodology of the expert testimony is scientifically valid. If not, the judge can strike the evidence even before the case goes to trial, so that it is never presented to a jury. The Court in *Daubert* also identified a set of criteria, based on the Federal Rules of Evidence, that should be used as the standard criteria for evaluating the reliability of and evidentiary weight to be afforded expert testimony. The criteria identified by the court in its *Daubert* decision include the following:

(1) Has the expert's theory or technique been adequately tested and can the results be replicated?

(2) Has the theory or technique been subjected to peer review and publication?

(3) Have scientifically accepted protocols or standards been followed in the research that the expert is using as a basis for his or her opinion?

6.5.4 Witnesses

With respect to nonexpert testimony, the courts have generally concluded that all persons with knowledge about a particular case or event may be competent to testify but have indicated that a witness's credibility can be attacked. When challenging the credibility of a witness at trial, an attorney may use leading questions (ones which suggest an answer) but only when dealing with unwilling witnesses or adverse parties. A testifying witness must answer all questions asked which will provide information on the issue under investigation—unless this testimony may subject the witness to criminal prosecution. In addition, the opposing party has a right to cross-examine the witness. If the witness refuses to answer on cross-examination, his entire testimony may be expunged from the record. However, cross-examinations are limited to facts on which a witness testified during direct examination.

6.5.5 Privileged Communication and Environmental Audits

The courts have established a number of extremely important evidentiary "privileges" in order to protect certain categories of information and communications from disclosure in litigation or other adversarial contexts. A legal privilege is an exception to the rule that the public has the right to know every man's evidence. The courts have created these exceptions in part based on public policy concerns. These legal protections can be applicable to a wide range of communications, including communications between an attorney and her client. In addition, evidentiary privileges can be asserted not only in lawsuits but also to protect legal advice that has been provided to a client in connection with environmental audits and assessments. Thus, though there is no absolute assurance that the privilege can be maintained, it may be useful to have a lawyer supervise the information-gathering process during an environmental audit and establish procedures for controlling access to all documents generated during the audit. Several states also have now passed laws to protect against the disclosure of audit report findings.

There have been various cases interpreting the scope of privileged communications in the context of environmental audits. For example, in *Andritz Sprout-Bauer, Inc. v. Beazer East, Inc.*,[177] the court found that drafts of environmental studies and audit-related reports circulated among environmental consultants and attorneys for comment and review were protected under the attorney-client privilege because the drafts contained comments or notations of counsel. The court in this case also held that documents provided by the environmental consultants to counsel for the specific purpose of explaining or interpreting technical data so as to allow counsel to provide legal advice to the client were protected under the attorney-client privilege.

6.5.6 Your Own Reports as Evidence against You

Many of the federal environmental laws and regulations specifically require companies to file reports and/or data with EPA and various state or local environmental agencies. However, while a considerable amount of information must be affirmatively supplied to these agencies under federal law, many corporations may wish to protect other key information from disclosure in litigation. For example, a company may wish to protect the results of an internal corporate audit or environmental investigation. In order to protect these reports and other types of communications from disclosure, a corporation may assert a claim of legal privilege based on the attorney-client privilege,[178] the attorney work product doctrine,[179] and/or the privilege of self-evaluation.[180]

6.5.7 Samples or Physical Evidence

One of the common evidentiary problems raised in many cases involves disputes over the reliability of physical evidence. In environmental cases, this evidence often involves a sample of an environmental medium such as soil or groundwater or technical data relating to such samples. Some of the key evidentiary questions that may be raised with respect to physical evidence include:

- Has the evidence or data been altered or contaminated?

- Was the equipment used in evidence collection properly calibrated?

- Were scientifically acceptable and standard methods of analysis used in evaluation?

- Who has handled the evidence (chain of custody)?

In order to address these questions, the applicable federal evidentiary rules require a party to lay a proper foundation for the admission of particular evidence in court. For example, an attorney should be able to present the individuals identified in the chain of custody for environmental samples and/or technical data to testify about their involvement in collecting the sample and obtaining the data and their proper handling of this evidence. However, in some cases, the courts will allow the parties to stipulate to the authenticity of the evidence to avoid this tedious form of proof. In legal terminology, to stipulate is to agree initially on conduct or evidence for the purpose of shortening the legal proceedings.

6.5.8 Evidence Collection and Constitutional Rights

As noted above, the U.S. Constitution creates a number of important limitations on the government's authority to gain access to corporate or other private party facilities and information. For example, the Fourth Amendment to the U.S. Constitution prohibits all unreasonable searches and requires a warrant in some cases in order to obtain access to private property. However, the courts have determined that no search warrant is needed in at least three situations: (1) when the government demonstrates the existence of an emergency, (2) when the owner or operator of a facility gives its consent, or (3) when samples of soil or groundwater could be taken from outside the property boundaries (open fields exception). (See the previous discussion in section 6.3.1.)

In addition, the Fifth Amendment to the U.S. Constitution protects parties against self-incrimination. Thus, in cases involving criminal charges against private parties, this Fifth Amendment right must be properly observed or the courts will not allow evidence to be introduced in the case. However, these Fifth Amendment protections apply only to private persons and not to corporations or partnerships.

7.0 Joint and Several Liability, Indemnity, and Contribution

In cases involving disputes over environmental cleanup costs, the courts often are asked to apply certain key legal theories of environmental liability, such as joint and several liability, indemnity, and contribution. Depending on the legal claims asserted in a particular case, these liability theories can be used to assign all, or only a portion, of a contaminated property's cleanup costs to a single party. For example, contribution is an equitable concept that dictates that parties share the loss incurred based on their respective responsibility for the costs or loss in a particular case. The right of contribution assumes joint fault and partial reimbursement. The courts have considered contribution claims in numerous cases involving environmental cleanup sites, such as the 1994 case *Akzo Coatings, Inc. v. Aigner Corp.*[181] In that case, after Akzo Coatings, Inc., was ordered to perform an initial emergency cleanup at a Superfund site (at a cost of more than $1.2 million), the company later sought a pro rata payment from Aigner Corp. for Aigner's share of the total cleanup costs incurred by Akzo. The court ruled that Akzo had a right to a contribution from Aigner for the emergency cleanup of the polluted site, though not for other costs incurred in attempting to anticipate future claims.

Several courts have determined that in addition to paying their fair share of site cleanup costs, responsible parties in contribution cases also can be required to pay so-called orphan share costs (i.e., remediation costs attributable to parties that are insolvent or cannot be located or identified).[182] These orphan share costs are typically apportioned according to a party's relative equitable share of overall site cleanup costs.[183] In addition, most courts have found that parties that bear partial responsibility for site contamination cannot seek to hold other responsible parties jointly and severally liable for all site cleanup costs but are limited to actions for contribution.[184]

Recent decisions by the U.S. Supreme Court have brought to the fore the issue of whether liable parties may recover costs incurred in investigating and cleaning up contaminated sites from other potentially responsible parties (PRPs) under CERCLA. In *Cooper Industries, Inc. v. Aviall Services, Inc.* (*Cooper Industries*),[185] the Supreme Court held that a plaintiff cannot maintain a contribution claim under Section 113(f)(1) of CERCLA for the recovery of cleanup costs from other responsible parties unless the plaintiff first has been the subject of a prior government order under Section 106 of CERCLA to perform cleanup work or has been sued for recovery of costs under Section 107 of CERCLA. While foreclosing recovery of voluntary cleanup costs under Section 113 of CERCLA, the Court's decision in *Cooper Industries* failed at the same time to address other potential cost recovery options that might be available, causing much confusion. As a result, some parties who voluntarily incurred cleanup costs sought to recover such costs from other PRPs by asserting an "implied" right to contribution under CERCLA Section 107, or alternative theories of recovery pursuant to other federal and/or state statutes or common law. Moreover, some courts ruled that CERCLA Section 107 contained an implied right to contribution and allowed parties who voluntarily performed cleanups to obtain contribution from other PRPs pursuant to this provision.[186] In contrast, other courts rejected this interpretation of CERCLA Section 107, and instead suggested that voluntarily incurred cleanup costs may be recouped only through alternative legal theories.[187] In *United States v. Atlantic Research Corp.*,[188] the Court resolved this confusion by holding that a PRP is entitled to bring a claim against other PRPs under Section 107 of CERCLA in order to recover cleanup costs that it has voluntarily incurred.[189] However, such claims are limited to costs incurred by the PRP itself in cleaning up a site, and any payments made by the PRP to satisfy a settlement agreement or a court judgment, or to reimburse EPA or another federal or state agency for cleanup costs incurred by that agency, are not recoverable under Section 107 and may only be recovered through an action for contribution under Section 113 of CERCLA.[190]

In addition to contribution claims, many plaintiffs in environmental cleanup cases seek to recover their cleanup costs through contractual indemnity claims. Under an indemnity claim, one party typically is seeking to shift the entire loss to another party who bears sole responsibility for the loss. The right of indemnity assumes derivative fault or a special contractual relationship between the parties and total reimbursement. For example, an indemnity obligation may arise when a potentially responsible party has previously contracted with an insurance company for complete coverage of an environmental accident. The insurance company thus indemnifies the insured party and bears the entire loss.

The federal government and private party plaintiffs in some of these cases have filed environmental cost recovery claims based on joint and several liability. Joint and several liability is a concept which dictates that a party that tortiously contributes to a site's pollution is individually liable for all of the damages at a site. Under this concept any one party can be held liable (by EPA, for example) for all of the costs of a remedial action. In such a case, this one party may be responsible for identifying others to share the liability (i.e., to contribute to the cost of the cleanup). However, in *Burlington Northern & Santa Fe Railway Co. v. United States*, the U.S. Supreme Court recently held that under CERCLA joint and several liability should not be imposed on a party where the harm at the particular site is capable of apportionment.[191] In this case the Court found that apportionment of liability is proper whenever a party raises a divisibility defense which establishes that "There is a reasonable basis for determining the contribution of each cause to a single harm."[192] In fact, the Court specifically mentioned that "divisibility may be established by volumetric, chronological, or other types of evidence, including appropriate geographic considerations."[193] In another example, one court held that natural resource damages that resulted from several decades of mining operations were divisible based on the amount of waste discharged by each of the defendants during their similar mining operations.[194] There, the court noted that divisibility based on volume "may not be the perfect method of divisibility, but it certainly is reasonable based on the historical facts available in this particular case."[195]

8.0 Environmental Compliance Principles

Once a basic understanding of the environmental law system and its requirements is achieved, the next step is to apply that knowledge to maintain an acceptable compliance posture in the organization you work for or advise. The development of an effective compliance program rests on the basic premise that full compliance is the most effective protection. Numerous books have been published that describe the elements of an appropriate corporate environmental compliance program. The following principles derived from these works may be instructive:

(1) All functions and levels within a corporation or similar organization may have some role in enabling the organization to achieve environmental compliance. Thus, to protect against liability, all partners and employees should continually demonstrate due concern and diligent efforts to comply.

(2) Providing appropriate education and training as well as sufficient informational resources is a good demonstration of concern for compliance and an important key to a successful environmental management program.

(3) The development of an appropriate corporate culture or management structure may help ensure that objectives are achieved.

(4) An effective environmental management program will provide the organization's officers and employees with the knowledge, resources, and motivation required to meet and exceed environmental requirements.

(5) After an organization has implemented an environmental compliance program, periodic audits to verify compliance and identify areas where compliance can be improved may be useful.

Building on the foregoing principles, over the past two decades increasing numbers of businesses and corporations have established comprehensive programs—commonly referred to as environmental management systems (EMSs)—to help assure that they effectively manage not only their environmental compliance obligations but also the environmental aspects and impacts associated with their particular products and services. Many of these EMS programs have been modeled after the standards specified under ISO 14001:2015, *Environmental Management Systems—Requirements with Guidance for Use*, which incorporates the four-step "Plan, Do, Check, Act" process for achieving continual improvement in business management. In essence, EMS programs embody a systematic approach for managing all of the environmental concerns and responsibilities of a particular business or organization, and have proven effective over the years in helping companies achieve beneficial improvements in their environmental operations.

9.0 Importance of Knowledge of Environmental Law

Given the importance of environmental issues to contemporary society, many organizations now need a working understanding of the environmental law system. Our actions and inactions, what we know and—perhaps most importantly—what we ought to know about this legal system, can have dramatic effects on the financial well-being of organizations, as well as their officers and employees. The failure to know or be aware of particular environmental requirements that are applicable to your organization will not typically be a legitimate defense to possible liability. In fact, under the legal theory of constructive knowledge, the senior or responsible corporate officers of an organization may be presumed to possess knowledge of the acts of the organization under many of the federal environmental laws' criminal liability provisions.

Based on these principles, many organizations are compelled to have a thorough knowledge of, and strict adherence to, the mandates of the environmental laws. We hope that this chapter and this *Environmental Law Handbook* will help motivate you to aggressively seek both the information and the understanding needed to achieve full compliance with the letter and spirit of the environmental laws.

10.0 Research Sources

There is a wide range of sources available for research regarding environmental law in the United States. We have provided below a number of references to research and general informational materials that are readily available on the Internet, as well as those that can be obtained from certain well-recognized publishers.

- American Bar Association—Section of Environment, Energy, and Resources: http://www.americanbar.org/groups/environment_energy_re sources.html

- Bureau of National Affairs—Environment Reporter: http://www.bna .com/environment-reporter-p4885/ (subscription required)

- CleanupLevels.com—A compendium of federal, state, and international cleanup standards: http://www.cleanuplevels.com/

- Duke Environmental Law & Policy Forum: http://www.law.duke.edu/ journals/delpf/

- ELI—The Environmental Law Institute: http://www.eli.org/

- Elizabeth G. Geltman, *Modern Environmental Law: Policy and Practice* (American Casebook Series) (1997)

- Inside Washington Publishers—Inside EPA Daily and Weekly Reports: http://insideepa.com/ (subscription required)

- Law 360, Portfolio Media, Inc.—Environmental Law: http://www.law 360.com/environmental/ (subscription required)

- Legal Information Institute—Environmental Law: http://www.law.cor nell.edu/wex/Environmental_law

- Regulations.gov—Source of pending rulemakings and *Federal Register* notices by EPA and other federal agencies: http://www.regulations.gov/

- William A. Rodgers, *Environmental Law* (Hornbook Series) (2nd ed. 1994)

- United Nations Environment Programme: http://www.unep.org/

- U.S. Department of Justice, Environment and Natural Resources Division: http://www.justice.gov/enrd/

- U.S. EPA, Office of Compliance and Enforcement: http://www.epa.gov/ enforcement/

- U.S. EPA, Office of Compliance and Enforcement—Compliance Incentives and Auditing: http://www.epa.gov/compliance/how-we-monitor -compliance

- U.S. EPA—Envirofacts Multisystem Query: http://www.epa.gov/enviro/ facts/multisystem.html

- U.S. EPA—Federal Environmental Laws and Regulations: http://www .epa.gov/lawsregs/index.html

Notes

[1] The author wishes to thank J. Barton Seitz, Thomas C. Jackson, and Jennifer Golinsky of Baker Botts LLP, for their assistance in writing this chapter, in addition to Thomas F. P. Sullivan, who contributed to previous editions of this chapter.

[2] An article by Robert G. Schwartz titled "Criminalizing Occupational Safety Violations: The Use of Knowing Endangerment Statutes to Punish Employers Who Maintain Toxic Working Conditions" illustrates both the expansion of the term *environmental law* and the utilization of seemingly nonenvironmental statutes toward environmental ends. 14 *Harvard Environmental Law Review* 487 (1990).

[3] The reader is encouraged to read *The ABCs of Environmental Regulation* by Joel Goldsteen (Government Institutes, 2002). In addition, the parliamentarian of the U.S. House of Representatives, in consultation with the U.S. Senate Office of the Parliamentarian, has prepared a well-renowned treatise that describes the federal legislative review and approval process. *See* Johnson, Charles W., *How Our Laws Are Made* (U.S. Government Printing Office, 2003).

[4] *Id.*

[5] Examples of international treaties with environmental ramifications include the North American Free Trade Agreement; the United Nations Convention on the Law of the Sea; the Kyoto Protocol; the Montreal Protocol on Substances That Deplete the Ozone Layer; the Basel Convention on the Control

of Transboundary Movements of Hazardous Wastes and Their Disposal; the Joint Convention on the Safety of Spent Fuel Management and on the Safety of Radioactive Waste Management; and many others.

6   Treaties can be binding on the United States even if they are not formally ratified (*e.g.*, the United Nations Convention on the Law of the Sea). *See* Maureen O'C. Walker, United States Department of State, Office of Oceans Affairs, Acting Deputy Director, Opening U.S. Statement to the United Nations Open-ended Informal Consultative Process on Oceans and Law of the Sea, May 7, 2001 ("The U.N. Convention on the Law of the Sea provides the fundamental legal framework for all uses of the oceans").

7   *See, e.g., Pakootas v. Teck Cominco Metals, Ltd.,* 452 F.3d 1066 (9th Cir. 2006).

8   Some of the international tribunals available to resolve environmental conflicts include the International Court of Justice, the Permanent Court of Arbitration, and the International Court of Environmental Arbitration and Conciliation. While the decisions of these tribunals can be binding on the participants, such decisions typically carry no precedential value. However, an exception to this rule is the Trail Smelter Arbitral Decisions, which established the customary international law principle that "no State has the right to use or permit the use of its territory in such a manner as to cause [environmental] injury . . . in or to the territory of another." *See* 33 *American Journal of International Law* 182 (1939); 35 *American Journal of International Law* 684 (1941).

9   83 A. 3d 901 (Pa. 2013).

10 PA. CONST. art. I, § 27.

11 Massachusetts Toxics Use Reduction Act, added by Stat. 1989, c. 265, § 3, approved July 24, 1989.

12 California Safe Drinking Water and Toxic Enforcement Act, adopted as Prop. 65 in 1986, Cal. Health and Safety Code §§ 25249.5-25249.13.

13 N.J. Stat. Ann. 13:1K-6 *et seq.*, Industrial Site Recovery Act, L. 1993, c. 139, § 1.

14 10 Vt. Stat. Ann. §§ 6621a and 6621d. The U.S. Court of Appeals for the Second Circuit has specifically rejected industry claims that Vermont's law violated the Commerce Clause of the U.S. Constitution. *National Electrical Manufacturers Ass'n v. Sorrell,* 272 F.3d 104, 53 ERC 1385 (2d Cir. 2001).

15 California Global Warming Solutions Act of 2006, adopted as A.B. 32, Cal. Health & Safety Code, §§ 38500 *et seq.*

16 *See* Memorandum of Understanding among Connecticut, Delaware, Maine, New Hampshire, New Jersey, New York, and Vermont, Regional Greenhouse Gas Initiative (Dec. 20, 2005) (http://www.rggi.org/docs/mou_12_20_05.pdf).

17 Cal. Pub. Res. Code § 42464; Maine Public Law 661, An Act to Protect Public Health and the Environment by Providing for a System of Shared Responsibility for the Safe Collection and Recycling of Electronic Waste, 38 Maine Rev. Stat. Ann. § 1610.

18 *See, e.g.,* Municipal and Rural Domestic Ground Water Transfers Permit Act, Neb. Rev. Stat. 46-638 *et seq.*; Ground Water Exploration and Protection Act, Kan. Stat. Ann. 82a-1201 *et seq.*; Ground Water Basin Protection Act (Porter-Dolwig), Cal. Water Code § 12920 *et seq.*

19 18 U.S.C. § 1514A *et seq.*

20 Tort claims involving injuries that are alleged to be the result of exposure to toxic substances are often referred to as "toxic torts." Toxic tort lawsuits have become increasingly prevalent and often take the form of class action suits in which groups of individuals—such as those living in proximity to an industrial facility which has released hazardous substances into the environment—file claims relating to common exposures to substances. *See, e.g., Adams v. Star Enterprise,* 51 F.3d 517 (4th Cir. 1995) (suit for property damage and other injuries by several hundred homeowners against the operator of an oil distribution facility from which there had been a release of oil resulting in groundwater contamination).

21 *Black's Law Dictionary* 1065 (6th ed. 1990).

22 156 Conn. 613, 244 A.2d 372 (1968).

23 187 N.J. Super. 210 (N.J. Super. Ch. Div. 1982).

24 *Id.* at 216.

[25] *Portland v. Boeing Co.*, 179 F. Supp. 2d 1190 (D. Or. 2001).

[26] *Mondry v. Speedway SuperAmerica LLC*, 1999 U.S. Dist. LEXIS 9095 (N.D. Ill. May 12, 1999).

[27] 330 Md. 115, 622 A. 2d 745, 37 ERC 1863 (1993).

[28] 37 ERC 1237 (E.D. Ky. 1993).

[29] *Id.* at 1241.

[30] *Id.* at 1239.

[31] 24 Ill. App. 3d 624, 321 N.E. 2d 412, 7 ERC 1480 (Ill. App. Ct. 1974).

[32] 528 F.2d 1107, 8 ERC 1569 (7th Cir. 1975).

[33] *Greenpeace, Inc. v. Waste Technologies Industries*, 9 F.3d 1174 (6th Cir. 1993).

[34] *See Connecticut v. American Electric Power Co.*, 406 F. Supp. 2d 265 (S.D.N.Y. 2005) (lack of justiciability barred suit brought by various states against several electric utilities claiming that global warming will cause irreparable harm to property and the health, safety, and well-being of citizens); *rev'd & remanded*, 582 F.3d 309 (2d Cir. 2009) (finding justiciable controversy does exist); *rev'd & remanded, American Electric Power Co. v. Connecticut*, ___ U.S. ___, 131 S. Ct. 2527 (2011); *Comer v. Murphy Oil USA Inc.*, No. 05-CV-436LG (S.D. Miss. 2005) (dismissing based on lack of standing a class action lawsuit alleging that the greenhouse gas emissions from coal and other energy companies contributed to powerful and more frequent storms such as Hurricane Katrina), *rev'd*, 585 F.3d 855 (5th Cir. 2009), *reh'g granted*, 598 F.3d 208 (5th Cir. 2010), *reh'g denied*, 607 F.3d 1049 (5th Cir. 2010) (holding that the court lacked the necessary quorum to transact business after disqualification and recusal of one of the nine judges who had properly vacated the panel judgment and opinion), *mandamus denied sub nom. In re Comer*, ___ U.S. ___, 131 S. Ct. 902 (2011), *refiled*, 839 F. Supp. 2d 849 (S.D. Miss. 2012) (holding that doctrines of res judicata and collateral estoppel barred the action, while finding lack of standing and other grounds for dismissal), *aff'd*, ___F.3d ___, 2013 WL 1975849 (5th Cir. 2013) (holding that, despite convoluted procedural history, the district court's 2005 judgment was never disturbed). *See also Native Village of Kivalina v. ExxonMobil Corp.*, 663 F. Supp. 2d 863, 883 (N.D. Cal. 2009) (dismissing for lack of subject matter jurisdiction claims by a village of 400 people alleging that greenhouse gas emissions from 24 major oil and energy companies are to blame for rising sea levels and seeking $400 million in damages [the cost of relocating the entire village]), *aff'd*, 696 F.3d 849 (9th Cir. 2012) (affirming the district court's dismissal, but on grounds that the Clean Air Act and the agency actions it authorizes displaced federal common-law nuisance claims related to greenhouse gases), *cert. denied*, ___ U.S. ___, 133 S. Ct. 2390 (2013).

[35] *California v. General Motors Corp.*, 2007 WL 2726871 (N.D. Cal. 2007) (dismissed because the court "cannot adjudicate Plaintiff's federal common law global warming nuisance tort claim without making an initial policy determination of a kind clearly for non-judicial discretion").

[36] *American Electric Power Co. v. Connecticut*, ___ U.S. ___, 131 S. Ct. 2527 (2011).

[37] *McElwain v. Georgia Pacific*, 245 Or. 247, 421 P.2d 957 (1986).

[38] 226 F. Supp. 169 (D. Or. 1963).

[39] *See, e.g., Fertilizing Co. v. Hyde Park*, 97 U.S. 659 (1987).

[40] *Abbott v. City of Princeton, Texas*, 721 S.W.2d 872 (Tex. App. 1986)

[41] *See, e.g., Carriker Ford, Inc. v. Clow Corp.*, 21 ERC 1419, 1423-24 (D. Iowa 1984).

[42] *See, e.g., Jacque v. Pioneer Plastics, Inc.*, 676 A.2d 504, 508 (Me. 1996) ("as a rule, it is no justification for maintaining the nuisance that the party complaining of it came voluntarily within its reach, and the doctrine of 'coming to the nuisance' is not a complete defense in an action based upon nuisance"). A comprehensive article addressing the "coming to a nuisance" defense is found in 42 A.L.R. 3rd 344 (1972). That article includes a listing of the jurisdictions and relevant cases that recognize the majority rule.

[43] Prosser and Keeton on the Law of Torts 622 (5th ed. 1984).

[44] Prosser and Keeton on the Law of Torts 87 (5th ed. 1984).

45 647 F. Supp. 303, 317-19 (W.D. Tenn. 1986); *see also Castles Auto & Truck Serv. v. Exxon Corp.*, 16 Fed. Appx. 163 (4th Cir. 2001) (affirming lower court's determination that plaintiff could recover its property damages from Exxon pursuant to a North Carolina common law trespass claim based on the migration of petroleum to the plaintiff's property).

46 280 F. Supp. 2d 393 (E.D. Pa. 2003).

47 7 ERC 1443 (E.D. Va. 1975).

48 *Black's Law Dictionary* 1032 (6th ed. 1990).

49 *See* Restatement (Second) of Torts § 281 (1977).

50 544 F. Supp. 1104 (D. Md. 1982).

51 *See, e.g., Howell v. City of Lumberton*, 144 N.C. App. 695, 548 S.E.2d 835 (2001); *Knabe v. National Supply Div. of Armco Steel Corp.*, 592 F.2d 841 (5th Cir. 1979).

52 *Friends of H Street v. City of Sacramento*, 20 Cal. App. 4th 152, 160, 24 Cal. Rptr. 2d 607, 611 (1993).

53 *Brown v. Petroland, Inc.*, 102 Cal. App. 3d 720, 162 Cal. Rptr. 551 (Cal. Ct. App. 1980).

54 *See, e.g., Andritz Sprout-Bauer Inc. v. Beazer East Inc.*, 174 F.R.D. 609 (M.D. Pa. 1997) (finding that former property owner's alleged violation of the Virginia state Water Control Law provides basis for negligence *per se* claim); *VEPCO v. Savoy Constr. Co., Inc.*, 294 S.E. 2d 811, 817 (Va. 1982) (establishing liability under negligence *per se* claim based on violation of a state building code).

55 L.R. 3 H.L. 330 (1868).

56 784 F. Supp. 439 (S.D. Ohio 1989).

57 *Id.* at 442 (citing Restatement (Second) of Torts §§ 519, 520 (1977)).

58 *T&E Industries v. Safety-Light Corp.*, 123 N.J. 371, 587 A.2d 1249 (1991). However, the courts in a number of other jurisdictions have specifically declined to so broadly apply strict liability theories and have rejected claims by current owners of contaminated properties that seek to make prior owners or tenants of the same parcel strictly liable for contamination that occurred during their prior ownership or tenancy. *See, e.g., Kennedy Building Assocs. v. Viacom, Inc.*, 375 F.3d 731, 741-42 (8th Cir. 2004); *Rosenblatt v. Exxon Co.*, 642 A.2d 180, 185-88 (Md. 1994); *Hicks v. Humble Oil & Refining Co.*, 970 S.W.2d 90, 97 (Tex. Civ. App. 1998); *Hydro-Mfg., Inc. v. Kayser-Roth Corp.*, 640 A.2d 950, 958 (R.I. 1994); *Futura Realty v. Lone Star Bldg. Ctrs.*, 578 So.2d 363, 365 (Fla. Dist. Ct. App. 1991); *Andritz Sprout-Bauer, Inc. v. Beaser East, Inc.*, 174 F.R.D. 609, 623-26 (M.D. Pa. 1997); *Cross Oil Co. v. Phillips Petroleum Co.*, 944 F. Supp. 787, 789-90 (E.D. Mo. 1996); *325-343 E. 56th St. Corp. v. Mobil Oil Corp.*, 906 F. Supp. 669, 677-678 (D.D.C. 1995); *Dartron Corp. v. Uniroyal Chem. Co.*, 893 F. Supp. 730, 740 (N.D. Ohio 1995); *55 Motor Ave. Co. v. Liberty Indus. Finishing Corp.*, 885 F. Supp. 410, 423 (E.D.N.Y. 1994); *Wellesley Hills Realty Trust v. Mobil Oil Corp.*, 747 F. Supp. 93, 101-02 (D. Mass. 1990).

59 *See, e.g., Philadelphia Elec. Co. v. Hercules, Inc.*, 762 F.2d 303, 314 (3d Cir. 1985) (the duty owed by a former landowner under nuisance law is to its neighbors, and not to the buyer or subsequent purchasers of the affected parcel).

60 U.S. Environmental Protection Agency, *A Framework for Statute-Specific Approaches to Penalty Assessments: Implementing EPA's Policy on Civil Penalties at 24* (Feb. 16, 1984).

61 42 U.S.C. § 9607(a); *see also Nurad, Inc. v. William E. Hooper & Sons Co.*, 966 F.2d 837 (4th Cir. 1992).

62 392 F. Supp. 2d 1197 (D. Idaho 2005).

63 118 F. Supp. 2d 615 (W.D. Pa. 2000), *aff'd in part, vacated in part on other grounds*, 366 F.3d 164 (3d Cir. 2004).

64 *Id.* at 618.

65 *In re: Sundance Corp.*, 149 B.R. 641, 36 ERC 1470, 1476 (Bankr. E.D. Wash. 1993).

66 *Id.*, 36 ERC at 1477.

67 *PCS Nitrogen Inc. v. Ashley II of Charleston LLC*, 714 F.3d 161, 178–81 (4th Cir. 2013).

68 42 U.S.C. §§ 9601(40), 9607(r)(1).

69   Under the Federal Civil Penalties Inflation Adjustment Act Improvements Act of 2015 (the 2015 Act), Pub. L. 114–74 § 701, EPA is required to adjust statutory civil penalties annually to account for inflation. Penalties vary between and within each environmental statute, depending on which section of a statute has been allegedly violated. For example, pursuant to EPA's initial inflation adjustment under the 2015 Act—a one-time "catch-up" adjustment which took effect on August 1, 2016—the owner or operator of a stationary source that violates the Clean Air Act can face a maximum penalty of $93,750 per day, while the manufacturer or dealer of a mobile source that violates the Clean Air Act can face a maximum penalty of $44,539 per day. *See* 81 Fed. Reg. 43,091, at 43,095 (July 1, 2016).

70   *See United States v. Ortiz,* 427 F.3d 1278, 1283 (10th Cir. 2005); *United States v. Hanousek,* 176 F.3d 1116, 118-20 (9th Cir. 1999).

71   *United States v. Wasserson,* 418 F.3d 225 (3d Cir. 2005) (*Wasserson*). The laundry owner had been charged with violations of the federal Resource Conservation and Recovery Act, 42 U.S.C. § 6928(d)(2), and 18 U.S.C. § 2 (criminal aiding and abetting).

72   *Wasserson,* 418 F.3d at 237-39.

73   531 U.S. 159 (2001).

74   *Id.* at 174. Subsequent to the Court's decision in *SWANCC,* the Supreme Court was asked to revisit the scope of the Corps' wetlands regulatory jurisdiction under the CWA, and again the Court chose to rely in its decision on the statutory interpretation of the CWA rather than the Commerce Clause. *Rapanos, et al. v. United States,* 547 U.S. 715 (2006). A plurality of the Court held that the Corps and EPA have jurisdiction over tributaries of waters that are navigable in fact and adjacent wetlands only if the tributaries have continuously flowing or permanent standing water. The plurality stated—as in *SWANCC*—that a broad interpretation of CWA jurisdiction such as that advocated by the Corps would raise constitutional concerns. In his concurrence, Justice Kennedy found that the Corps could assert jurisdiction over tributaries that are intermittent or ephemeral streams or drainage features if they can demonstrate that those tributaries have a significant nexus to navigable-in-fact waters. *Id.* (Kennedy, J., *concurring*).

75   Civil Action No. 11-C-411 (Circuit Ct. Monongahela Co. Aug. 12, 2011).

76   964 N.Y.S.2d 714 (3d Dept. 2013).

77   *See, e.g., National Electrical Manufacturers Ass'n v. Sorrell,* 272 F.3d 104, 53 ERC 1385 (2d Cir. 2001), *cert. denied,* 536 U.S. 905 (2002). In *National Electrical Manufacturers Ass'n,* the court concluded that Vermont's mercury-labeling law did not impose improper burdens in violation of the Commerce Clause of the U.S. Constitution or otherwise establish unconstitutional requirements on the manufacturers of electric lamps, batteries, and certain other mercury-containing products.

78   *Chemical Waste Management, Inc. v. Hunt,* 504 U.S. 334 (1992); *see also Fort Gratiot Sanitary Landfill, Inc. v. Michigan Dept. of Nat. Res.,* 504 U.S. 353 (1992).

79   *Procter & Gamble Co. v. Chicago,* 509 F.2d 69, 7 ERC 1328 (7th Cir.), *cert. denied,* 421 U.S. 978 (1975).

80   189 F.3d 762 (8th Cir. 1999).

81   252 F.3d 316, 52 ERC 1818 (4th Cir. 2001).

82   *Stop H-3 Ass'n v. Transportation Department,* 870 F.2d 1419, 29 ERC 1390 (9th Cir. 1989).

83   812 F. Supp. 1528 (E.D. Cal. 1992).

84   42 U.S.C. §§ 9601-9675.

85   The U.S. Court of Appeals for the Federal Circuit does not have a defined geographic jurisdiction but rather hears appeals from specialized courts such as the U.S. Court of Federal Claims.

86   846 F.2d 921, 27 ERC 1911 (3d Cir. 1988).

87   28 ERC 1237 (D.N.J. 1988).

88   *Id.* at 1239.

89   838 F.2d 35, 27 ERC 1227 (2d Cir. 1988).

90   992 F.2d 470, 37 ERC 1189 (3d Cir. 1993).

91   *Id.* at 1191.

92 *Id.*

93 *Id.*

94 _____ U.S. _____, 132 S. Ct. 1367 (2012).

95 136 S. Ct. 615 (2016).

96 183 F.3d 196 (3d Cir. 1999).

97 *See, e.g., Marina Bay Realty Trust L.L.C. v. United States,* 407 F.3d 418 (1st Cir. 2005) (federal government was immune from suit brought by developer under the Federal Tort Claims Act, state law, and common law to recover costs of cleaning up contamination from leaking oil at a former Navy base).

98 42 U.S.C. § 9613(h).

99 33 U.S.C. § 1369(b)(1).

100 29 ERC 1707 (E.D. Mo. 1989).

101 405 U.S. 727 (1972).

102 412 U.S. 669 (1973).

103 497 U.S. 871 (1990).

104 *Id.* at 889.

105 504 U.S. 555 (1992).

106 520 U.S. 154 (1997).

107 16 U.S.C. § 1540 (g).

108 *Mass. v. EPA,* 549 U.S. 497, 517 (2007).

109 *Id.* at 517–18.

110 *Id.* at 518.

111 *Id.* at 518–19 (quoting *Georgia v. Tennessee Copper Co.,* 206 U.S. 230, 237 [1907]).

112 *Id.* at 518.

113 *Id.* at 519 ("Just as Georgia's independent interest in all the earth and air within its domain supported federal jurisdiction a century ago, so too does Massachusetts' well-founded desire to preserve its sovereign territory") (citing *Georgia v. Tennessee Copper Co.,* 206 U.S. 230, 237 [1907]).

114 *Id.* at 520. Not only was Massachusetts entitled to relaxed standing requirements, but the Court held that the commonwealth satisfied the traditional standing requirements as well. *Id.* at 1455.

115 *See* H.R. 1493 (Sunshine for Regulatory Decrees and Settlements Act of 2013, Rep. D. Collins (R-GA)); S. 714 (Sunshine for Regulatory Decrees and Settlements Act of 2013, Sen. C. Grassley (R-IA)).

116 *See, e.g., Defenders of Wildlife v. Perciasepe,* 714 F.3d 1317 (D.C. Cir. 2013).

117 *Camara v. Municipal Court of San Francisco,* 387 U.S. 523 (1967) (*Camara*).

118 *See v. City of Seattle,* 387 U.S. 541 (1967).

119 *Com., DER v. Blosenski Disposal Serv.,* 523 Pa. 274, 566 A.2d 845, 30 ERC 1835 (1989).

120 *Colonnade Catering Corp. v. United States,* 397 U.S. 72 (1970); *United States v. Biswell,* 406 U.S. 311 (1972). In these cases, the U.S. Supreme Court effectively determined that owners of commercial property are entitled to a lesser expectation of privacy than residential home owners.

121 *Com., DER v. Blosenski Disposal Serv.,* 566 A.2d 845, 848 (Pa. 1989).

122 436 U.S. 307 (1978).

123 416 U.S. 861 (1974).

124 476 U.S. 227 (1986).

125 *Id.* at 239.

126 601 A.2d 864 (Pa. Commw. Ct. 1992).

127 *Id.* at 865.

128 *Id.* at 866.

129 487 U.S. 11 (1988).

130 U.S. Const. amend. V.

131 *County of Sacramento v. Lewis,* 523 U.S. 833, 845-46 (1998) (citations omitted).

132 *Id.* at 840, 846.

133 522 F.2d 897, 8 ERC 1001 (9th Cir. 1975), *cert. denied,* 424 U.S. 924 (1976).

134 *Bowie Inn v. City of Bowie,* 274 Md. 230, 335 A.2d 679, 7 ERC 2083 (1975).

135 808 F. Supp. 912, 37 ERC 1380 (D. Mass. 1992).

136 595 F. Supp. 2d 8 (D.D.C. 2009). Initially in 2005, the district court granted EPA's motion for summary judgment against GE's facial challenge to the text of CERCLA but allowed GE's "pattern and practice" claim to proceed (i.e., that EPA administers CERCLA "in a manner that denies PRPs the necessary protection of procedural due process"). *General Electric Co. v. EPA,* 362 F. Supp. 2d 327, 333 (D.D.C. 2005). However, after the parties conducted discovery regarding this latter claim the court granted a subsequent motion for summary judgment filed by EPA with respect to this claim. 595 F. Supp. 2d 8 (D.D.C. 2009).

137 *General Elec. Co. v. Jackson,* 610 F.3d 110, 113-114 (D.C. Cir. 2010), *cert. denied,* 563 U.S. 1032 (2011).

138 710 F. Supp. 313, 30 ERC 1166 (M.D. Ala. 1987).

139 *Id.* at 1169.

140 *Id.* at 1168.

141 416 U.S. 1 (1974).

142 *Kelo v. City of New London, Connecticut,* 545 U.S. 469 (2005).

143 952 F.2d 1364 (Fed. Cir. 1991).

144 980 F.2d 84, 36 ERC 1024 (2d Cir. 1992).

145 *Id.* at 1032.

146 *Id.*

147 *Id.* at 1033.

148 328 U.S. 256 (1946).

149 369 U.S. 84 (1962).

150 467 U.S. 986 (1984).

151 Such takings are sometimes referred to as "inverse condemnation."

152 *Pennsylvania Coal Co. v. Mahon,* 260 U.S. 393, 416 (1922).

153 *Penn Central Transp. Co. v. City of New York,* 438 U.S. 104, 124 (1978).

154 *Lucas v. South Carolina Coastal Council,* 505 U.S. 1003 (1992).

155 *Id.*

156 31 Fed. Cl. 37, 38 ERC 1607 (1994).

157 483 U.S. 470 (1987).

158 While the Supreme Court held in 1980 that the regulation of private property could result in a taking if it did not substantially advance a legitimate state interest, *Agins v. Tiburon,* 447 U.S. 260 (1980) (application of zoning ordinance to particular property did not result in a taking where the application of the ordinance substantially advanced a legitimate state interest), the Court has recently held that the "substantial advancement test" is not a proper standard for determining whether a taking has occurred. *Lingle v. Chevron USA Inc.,* 125 S. Ct. 2074 (2005). However, the Court in *Lingle* reaffirmed its holdings in *Nollan* and *Dolan,* explaining that while the Court in *Nollan* and *Dolan* quoted the "substantial advancement" test of *Agins,* those cases did not actually apply the test and are more properly understood as involving a special application of the doctrine of "unconstitutional conditions" whereby a government cannot require a person to give up a constitutional right such as the right to receive just compensation when property is taken for a public use in exchange for a discretionary benefit conferred by the government that has little or no relation to the property.

159 512 U.S. 374 (1994).

160 _____U.S._____, 133 S. Ct. 2586 (2013).

161 No. 15-1517-TC, Doc. 68 (D. Or. Apr. 8, 2016).

162 35 F.3d 348 (8th Cir. 1994).

163 CERCLA § 106(b)(2), 42 U.S.C. § 9606(b)(2).

164 *Wagner Seed Co. v. Bush*, 946 F.2d 918, 920, 33 ERC 1897 (D.C. Cir. 1991), *cert. denied*, 503 U.S. 970 (1992).

165 *See, e.g., Bethlehem Steel Corp. v. Bush*, 918 F.2d 1323, 1328 (7th Cir. 1990).

166 467 U.S. 837 (1984).

167 *Dico*, 35 F.3d at 351, 353.

168 Light-Duty Vehicle Greenhouse Gas Emission Standards and Corporate Average Fuel Economy Standards; Final Rule, 75 Fed. Reg. 25,324 (May 7, 2010) (codified at 40 C.F.R. pts. 85, 86, 600) (for light-duty cars and trucks in model years 2012–2016; 2017 and Later Model Year Light-Duty Vehicle Greenhouse Gas Emissions and Corporate Average Fuel Economy Standards, 77 Fed. Reg. 62,624 (Oct. 15, 2012) (codified at 40 C.F.R. pts. 85, 86, 600) (for light-duty cars and trucks in model years 2017–2025).

169 Standards of Performance for Greenhouse Gas Emissions From New, Modified, and Reconstructed Stationary Sources: Electric Utility Generating Units, 80 Fed. Reg. 64,510 (Oct. 23, 2015) (codified at 40 C.F.R. pts. 60, 70, 71, 98).

170 Carbon Pollution Emission Guidelines for Existing Stationary Sources: Electric Utility Generating Units, 80 Fed. Reg. 64,662 (Oct. 23, 2015) (codified at 40 C.F.R. pt. 60) (this rule is often called "the Clean Power Plan"). Its effectiveness is currently stayed as a result of litigation.

171 Executive Office of the President, *The President's Climate Action Plan* (June 2013), available at https://www.whitehouse.gov/sites/default/files/image/president27sclimateaction plan.pdf.

172 Transforming Our Nation's Electric Grid Through Improved Siting, Permitting, and Review; Memorandum for the Heads of Executive Departments and Agencies, 78 Fed. Reg. 35, 539 (June 12, 2013).

173 Press Release, U.S. Dept. of Energy Loan Programs Office, DOE Finalizes $1 Billion in New Loan Guarantee Authority and Announces New Application Dates (Oct. 21, 2015), available at http://energy.gov/lpo/articles/doe-finalizes-1-billion-new-loan-guarantee-authority-and-announces-new -application.

174 Establishing a Federal Flood Risk Management Standard and a Process for Further Soliciting and Considering Stakeholder Input, Exec. Order No. 1390, 80 Fed. Reg. 6,425 (Feb. 4, 2015).

175 *See, e.g.,* Press Release, White House Office of the Press Secretary, North American Climate, Clean Energy, and Environment Partnership Action Plan (June 29, 2016), *available at* https://whitehouse.gov/the-press-office/2016/06/29/north-american-climate-clean-energy-and-environment-partnership-action (announcing trilateral partnership between the United States, Canada, and Mexico).

176 509 U.S. 579 (1993).

177 174 F.R.D. 609, 633 (M.D. Pa. 1997) (*Andritz*). *See also Olen Properties, Inc. v. Sheldahl, Inc.*, 1994 WL 212135 (C.D. Cal. 1994) (audits that were prepared on behalf of attorneys "to assist [them] in evaluating compliance with relevant laws and regulations" were protected under the attorney-client privilege).

178 *See, e.g., Andritz*, 174 F.R.D. at 633 (discussing scope and limits of attorney-client privilege).

179 *See, e.g., Burlington Indus., Inc. v. Exxon Corp.*, 65 F.R.D. 26, 42 (D. Md. 1974) (analyzing scope of protection provided by work product doctrine to documents and investigative reports compiled by a non-attorney for an attorney); *Bituminous Casualty Corp. v. Tonka Corp.*, 140 F.R.D. 381, 388 (D. Minn. 1992) (same).

180 *See, e.g., Reichhold Chems., Inc. v. Textron, Inc.*, 157 F.R.D. 522, 524 (N.D. Fla. 1994) (finding that self-evaluative privilege applies to certain environmental reports); *Bredice v. Doctors Hospital, Inc.*, 50 F.R.D. 249 (D.D.C. 1970) (concluding that self-evaluation privilege protects certain hospital records from discovery in medical malpractice suits), *aff'd mem.*, 479 U.S. 920 (D.C. Cir. 1973).

181 30 F.3d 761 (7th Cir. 1994).

182 *See Sun Co. v. Browning-Ferris, Inc.,* 124 F.3d 1187, 1193 (10th Cir. 1997); *Pinal Creek Group v. Newmont Mining Corp.,* 118 F.3d 1298, 1303 (9th Cir. 1997).

183 *Id.*

184 *See, e.g., Prisco v. A&D Carting Corp.,* 168 F.3d 593 (2d Cir. 1999).

185 543 U.S. 157.

186 *See, e.g., Consolidated Edison Co. v. UGI Utilities Inc.,* 423 F.3d 90 (2d Cir. 2005); *Atlantic Research Corp. v. UGI Utilities Inc.,* 459 F.3d 827 (8th Cir. 2006).

187 *See, e.g., E.I. DuPont de Nemours & Co. v. United States,* 460 F.3d 515 (3d Cir. 2006) remanded to 508 F.3d 126 (3d Cir. 2007).

188 551 U.S. 128, 127 S. Ct. 2331 (2007).

189 See *Kotrous v. Goss-Jewett Co. of Northern California,* 523 F.3d 924 (9th Cir. 2008).

190 *United States v. Atlantic Research Corp.,* 551 U.S. 128, 139 (2008).

191 556 U.S. 599, 613-14 (2009).

192 *Id.* at 614 (quoting Restatement (Second) of Torts § 433A(1)(b), p. 434 (1963–64)).

193 556 U.S. at 617–18.

194 *Coeur D'Alene Tribe v. ASARCO Inc.,* 280 F. Supp. 2d 1094 (D. Idaho 2003).

195 *Id.* at 1120.

Chapter 2

Enforcement and Liability

Jason B. Hutt and Michael Weller[1]
Bracewell LLP

1.0 Introduction

The preceding chapter offered an essential overview of what environmental law is and how it is structured, and the chapters that follow each address a specific federal statute or regulatory initiative (or, in the case of the final chapter, a specific international standard for environmental management). Our task in this chapter is to focus on the enforcement of the environmental laws generally, with specific references to particular statutes to illustrate the general principles and challenges of enforcement.

We approach our task with an overview of federal enforcement trends in order to give scale to our subject. We then introduce the governing precepts, purposes, and methods of enforcement and liability in our federalized system of environmental law. Next we turn to civil enforcement specifically, analyzing the features that distinguish it from criminal enforcement and providing a guide to the major issues involved in initiating and pursuing civil enforcement by the government and by private parties. A similar analysis of criminal enforcement follows. Having described in some detail how civil and criminal enforcement arises, and what its consequences may be, we then offer some observations about how the regulated community can manage its affairs to avoid or mitigate the risk of environmental enforcement and liability. Thereafter, we review some of the more recent trends in enforcement and liability, such as EPA's Next Generation Compliance Initiative and EPA's methane enforcement initiative. Finally, we offer a scattershot of big-picture observations about the nature and direction of environmental enforcement.

2.0 Enforcement Trends

The landscape of environmental enforcement is continuously changing. New laws passed by Congress, new regulations promulgated by EPA, judicial decisions, changes in presidential administrations, and actions taken by task forces and special prosecutors, among other factors, shift the intensity and focus of federal enforcement programs from year to year. Each presidential administration brings unique priorities to the foreground, implemented by handpicked senior officials at EPA and, indirectly, through the appointment of federal judges.

The Bush Administration focused its enforcement philosophy on compliance assistance for the regulated community, reducing the amount of pollutants, and mandating environmental cleanup projects.[2] The Bush administration was criticized by nongovernmental groups that claim EPA softened the enforcement of environmental laws. The Environmental Integrity Project, for example, released a study in 2007 that documented a general steep decline in the number of enforcement actions when comparing the first five years of the Bush administration to the last five years of the Clinton administration.[3]

Under the Obama Administration, the number of environmental cases referred to the Department of Justice (DOJ) has not swelled. However, a distinctly different set of priorities and tactics has emerged over the past eight years. EPA's 2014–2018 Strategic Plan enumerates five strategic goals to guide the agency's work through 2018, including (1) Addressing Climate Change and Improving Air Quality; (2) Protecting America's Waters; (3) Cleaning Up Communities and Advancing Sustainable Development; (4)Ensuring the Safety of Chemicals and Preventing Pollution; and (5) Protecting Human Health and the Environment by Enforcing Laws and Assuring Compliance.[4] To carry out this goal, EPA has indicated it will be taking a targeted approach focused on "the most serious water, air, and chemical hazards in communities to achieve compliance."[5]

EPA's Office of Enforcement Compliance and Assurance (OECA) is tasked with carrying out the agency's enforcement goals. OECA spearheads the agency's environmental compliance and enforcement activities and sets multiyear national priorities for environmental enforcement. Otherwise referred to as the "National Enforcement and Compliance Assurance Priorities" (NECAP), the multiyear national priorities are set by OECA taking into consideration patterns of noncompliance as well as areas where enforcement could lead to significant environmental benefits or a reduction in the risk to human health or the environment.[6] Through the NECAP, OECA characterizes the problems in the world of environmental enforcement and establishes goals for addressing those problems. When OECA accomplishes its goals, a priority enforcement area may be dropped from the next NECAP.

The NECAP offers insight into EPA's strategic plan for future enforcement, and there is often a strong correlation between problems that are designated national priorities and the pollutant reductions and injunctive relief achieved.[7] Looking forward, OECA has laid out its list of priority enforcement areas for FY

2017–2019.[8] A few national enforcement priorities from prior years remain a key focus for EPA for FY 2017–2019, including (1) Keeping raw sewage and contaminated stormwater out of federal waters; (2) Preventing animal waste from contaminating surface and ground water; (3) Reducing air pollution from the largest sources; and (4) Ensuring that the energy extraction sector complies with environmental laws.[9]

EPA has added two new enforcement initiatives for FY 2017–2019, including (1) Reducing risks of accidental releases at industrial and chemical facilities; and (2) Keeping industrial pollutants out of the nation's waters.[10] EPA has also expanded an initiative focused on cutting hazardous air pollutants, targeting leaks, flares, and excess emissions from refineries, chemical plants and other industries that emit hazardous air pollutants.[11] It is evident that environmental priorities of the White House, such as combatting climate change or addressing risks at large industrial facilities—topics often discussed by President Obama and given substantial focus in the proposed 2017 Federal Budget—see their practical implementation in the NECAP.[12]

In addition to setting national enforcement priorities, on a yearly basis OECA provides a statistical analysis of the expenses incurred to investigate, defend, and settle the cases that are brought. OECA's yearly report also lays out the number of civil and criminal cases EPA refers to DOJ on an annual basis. In FY15 EPA referred 141 civil cases while charging 185 criminal defendants.[13] According to OECA, in FY15, administrative civil and criminal penalties totaled more than $242 million, not to mention $7.3 billion in injunctive relief and $39 million in supplemental environmental projects (SEPs).[14]

The numbers provided by OECA are presented, as one might expect, with public relations in mind: they help establish or support executive branch claims of being tough on crime, being strict about environmental performance, being innovative, or serving the political leanings of the sitting administration. In addition, OECA may report enforcement statistics in a specific way to serve as a deterrent to polluters fearing steep penalties.

EPA is not alone in adopting this strategy. Over the past several years, DOJ has also used press releases to take a hard stance when proposing criminal fines for environmental violations. For instance, in 2007, DOJ took a hard-line position regarding the possible penalties that might be imposed on CITGO Refining and Chemical Co. after the company was found guilty of committing violations of the Migratory Bird Treaty Act. CITGO failed to install roofs on two tanks at its Corpus Christi refinery, and a 2007 press release issued by DOJ indicated that CITGO could face a penalty ranging anywhere from $500,000 to two times the profit obtained through the company's illegal action.[15] Then, in late 2012,

DOJ recommended that CITGO be sentenced to pay $44,000,000 in "community service obligations" *in lieu* of performing community service as a condition of probation pursuant to 18 U.S.C. § 3563(b)(12) and (22), in addition to a statutory fine of $2,090,00 for Clean Air Act and Migratory Bird Treaty Act violations.[16]

However, the government's request for fines for community service obligations was denied because the court believed a fine above the statutory maximum could not be imposed when the facts supporting that fine had not been proved to a jury beyond a reasonable doubt.[17] In February 2014, CITGO was sentenced to pay a $2 million in fines for Clean Air Act violations and $45,000 in fines for misdemeanor violations of the Migratory Bird Treaty Act.[18]

Regardless of whether it is for public relations reasons or to create a deterrent effect, year-to-year and report-to-report comparisons are often difficult to make because the enforcement data are presented in different formats. Variations in the presentation of enforcement data are also likely driven by the goals EPA outlines for a particular period, so that OECA can best demonstrate its fulfillment of those goals.

In 2009, Lisa Jackson became the EPA Administrator during the first Obama administration.[19] During Jackson's tenure, EPA continued the Bush Administration's practice of bringing New Source Review (NSR) enforcement cases against large coal-fired power plants.[20] The agency also brought NSR enforcement action against other priority industries, such as the cement and glass manufacturing sectors.[21] Aside from these NSR enforcement cases, much of EPA Headquarters' enforcement resources were dedicated to responding to the Deepwater Horizon incident.[22] As a result, more enforcement originated from the EPA regional offices than EPA Headquarters such that EPA was more focused on regional priorities than bringing national priority cases. One notable facet of Jackson's tenure was that the enforcement program failed to build momentum in its initiative to focus on bringing enforcement against oil and gas exploration and development companies.[23] EPA ultimately conducted few inspections and filed little enforcement action under this initiative. Overall, EPA's enforcement was not as aggressive under Administrator Jackson as it had been during the Bush Administration; rather, her tenure at EPA was dedicated primarily to the agency's aggressive regulatory agenda, which included issuing the finding that greenhouse gas emissions endanger human health.[24] Jackson stepped down from office on February 14, 2013.[25]

On July 18, 2013, after a 136-day wait—the longest for any EPA administrator nominee[26]—the former head of EPA's Office of Air and Radiation, Gina McCarthy, was confirmed to fill the role vacated by Jackson.[27] Industry members and environmentalist groups alike are hopeful that during McCarthy's tenure she will clarify many pending regulatory matters.[28] Under McCarthy's watch, EPA has released several notable rulemakings, including the "Waters of the United States" rule, which clarifies (and expands) the federal governments' jurisdiction under the Clean Water Act[29] and the "Clean Power Plan," the centerpiece of President Obama's climate change initiative, a rule focused on regulating GHG emissions from electric utility generating units.[30] Both rules have been controversial, and both rules have been challenged in federal court by industry and states, resulting in delays in implementation. With the Obama administration winding down, the EPA rulemakings have slowed and the government has shifted focus to defending its bold regulatory push in court. Gina McCarthy's ultimate legacy as EPA Administrator is thus inextricably tied to the success or failure of these major rulemakings in federal court.

Overall, deciphering enforcement and compliance trends requires a bit of speculation. Bearing that in mind, set out below are a few observations. Please note, however, that these observations are based solely on the numbers reported by OECA and others, without potentially important insights into how the underlying statistics were compiled. Moreover, the observations do not reflect other enforcement mechanisms touched on in this chapter, such as enforcement by state environmental agencies, citizen suits, toxic tort litigation, and natural resource damage recovery. To the extent enforcement trends are used to guide how a compliance program is designed or how environmental risk is managed, these other mechanisms should be accounted for.

2.1 Remedy Preferences

Changes in enforcement are also driven by the evolution of regulatory philosophies. The "command-and-control" approach forged in the 1970s and premised on fines and penalties has yielded somewhat to market-driven schemes like "cap-and-trade" and reliance on compliance incentives like voluntary audit disclosures and environmental management systems.

Injunctive relief, i.e., actions or equipment to control pollution, continues to be a significant factor in EPA's settlements, averaging over $10.5 billion annually between FY11 and FY15.[31] Gauging the true value of injunctive relief and SEP remedies is different from the "bean counting" involved in tracking how many penalty dollars EPA receives in a given year. According to OECA, the injunctive relief numbers include efforts to "correct violations and take additional steps to protect the environment."[32] This rather vague description is believed to include actions compelling compliance with law (i.e., the costs to take actions that might otherwise already be required). The compelled action also may be on a faster timetable or be required to meet more stringent standards, thus costing more to implement under direction from EPA. However, the compliance component and any additional components are not meaningfully differentiated in OECA's reports. Separately, injunctions may be liability-related (not compliance-related). For example, CERCLA Section 106 orders may effectively impose liability on a party by ordering them to respond to a release, without a meaningful right of appeal or contest.[33] Like compliance-related injunctions, a portion of the value "recovered" by the public in a liability-related injunction includes expenditures that the liable party would already have been on the hook for.

SEPs are essentially leveraged investments that the defendant in an enforcement action can voluntarily choose to perform in lieu of paying a portion of the penalties owed. Expenditures for the SEP are a multiple of the penalty amount, not dollar-for-dollar. Companies accept or reject SEPs based on many factors, including public relations, the amount of the assessed penalty versus SEC disclosure thresholds, bank relationships, tax consequences, and perceived negotiation value. EPA encourages SEPs in many cases because investment is typically geared toward the environmental community that suffered harm pursuant to the violation, and SEPs often take a practical, tangible form. SEPs also provide a larger raw number for EPA to publicize than what the agency might have obtained from a pure penalty.

2.2 Statute-by-Statute Enforcement

It is also instructive to note the level of enforcement under each federal statute. The fact that the Clean Water Act is near the top of the charts for enforcement dollars, while the Emergency Planning and Community Right-to-Know Act is toward the bottom, will come as no surprise. What is more interesting is how EPA uses different mechanisms to enforce different statutes and the results obtained from the different methods. For example, the Clean Air Act and the Clean Water Act typically yield a high dollar value from civil penalties, while the dollar amount of administrative penalties is far less significant.[34] A statute like TSCA, however, will yield the vast majority of its penalties in the administrative forum, while civil penalties are almost nonexistent.[35] The largest numbers, however, often come from the *estimated* value of injunctive relief.[36] In comparing enforcement between statutes, keep in mind that the settlement of major enforcement cases from one year to the next can skew the analysis.

3.0 General Concepts of Enforcement and Liability

A cardinal component of the environmental regulatory system in the United States is the enforcement mechanism. The enforcement mechanism must reflect the broad nature and scope of the regulated activities, the potential impact of violations of environmental law on health and the environment, and the limited resources of the regulatory agencies. The goal is an integrated set of regulatory requirements and enforcement vehicles designed to maximize enforcement impact at reasonable effort and cost.

This section discusses selected concepts of enforcement and liability that are somewhat peculiar to the environmental regulatory system. The section focuses, in turn, on the purposes of enforcement activity, the applicable law that may give rise to enforcement exposure, the mechanisms available to the government to identify violations, the remedies available under environmental law, and the agencies that may act on the violations. By any measure, the enforcement exposure under environmental law is broad, the enforcement reach is wide-ranging, and the impact on a person or entity can be significant. The system works effectively, if at times not efficiently.

3.1 Enforcement Purposes

Environmental laws and regulations are designed to protect human health and the environment.[37] Thus, the level of air emissions that may be allowed in a particular situation, or the water discharges that may be permitted from a discrete facility, for example, ideally would be those that are not expected to undermine ambient air or water quality standards. Conversely, violation of the allowable or permitted limits could have an adverse effect on health and the environment. The primary purpose of enforcement actions under environmental law is to prevent or minimize adverse impacts from violations on health and the environment, and to assure a prompt return to compliance.[38]

A secondary purpose of enforcement activity is to deter further violations by the alleged wrongdoer and by others.[39] Environmental law typically includes a substantial penalty component that is applied over and above the costs that may need to be spent to return the regulated activity to compliance promptly.[40] To further ensure that the violator does not benefit economically from the noncompliant activity, sanctions under environmental law normally include recovery of some or all of the economic benefit that the violator may have enjoyed by operating in violation of applicable requirements.[41] This economic-benefit component may well exceed the amount of a penalty.

The Alternative Fines Act allows a court to impose a fine that is significantly more likely to have a deterrent effect. Under 18 U.S.C. § 3571, an offender may be fined under one of two sentencing schemes: up to $500,000 per offense per entity under § 3571(c); or twice the gross pecuniary gain the defendant obtained or twice the gross loss the defendant caused to a third party by the violation under § 3571(d). However, in 2012 the Supreme Court held in a criminal case that an alternative fine above the statutory maximum can only be imposed if the facts supporting the fine have been presented to a jury and proven beyond a reasonable doubt.[42] As such, alternative fines are difficult to obtain in the context of environmental enforcement.[43]

To encourage others to maintain compliance, and to alert them to the significant risks of noncompliance, regulatory agencies regularly publicize enforcement actions, including details of the alleged violations, the activities and costs required to return to compliance, and the applicable sanctions. At both the federal and state levels, agencies routinely publish news releases that are easily accessible through agency websites.[44] At least at the federal level, the EPA also publishes information on enforcement accomplishments on an annual basis.[45]

3.2 Applicable Law

The basic foundations of enforcement exposure are the legal requirements themselves. In the context of environmental law, the operative requirements may arise from a multitude of sources. Apart from understanding the law, identifying all relevant sources of applicable law may present a challenge in itself.

Requirements may arise from self-implementing prohibitions in federal and state statutes and regulations; from limitations and conditions in permits, licenses, or other construction or operating authorizations issued by federal or state agencies; and from the terms of administrative orders or judicial decrees entered at the federal or state levels, by consent or otherwise. In addition, while in certain situations a federally approved state requirement may take the place of federal law, both federal and state requirements may, and typically do, apply to a particular activity. Depending on the location of the regulated activity, municipal or other local ordinances also may apply.

Environmental requirements often are comprehensive and complex, and they are normally adopted after public notice and comment pursuant to the federal Administrative Procedure Act[46] or the corresponding state statute. Agency descriptions and explanations of the meaning and scope of a proposed or promulgated rule are published in the *Federal Register* or a similar state publication and often are critical components of compliance activity and, necessarily, enforcement exposure.[47] Likewise, federal and state agencies publish notices, policies, guidance and directives that may narrow or expand the scope of environmental requirements or otherwise explain the agency's probable response and approach to specific types of violations, and the corresponding assessment of penalties.[48] In brief, the law applicable to a regulated activity may not be found simply in the relevant statute or regulations; other components of environmental law are likely to affect the agency's enforcement discretion and the regulated party's enforcement exposure.

3.3 Compliance Monitoring

An essential prerequisite to enforcement activity is the agency's discovery of apparent violations. Another key piece of the enforcement framework deals with the mechanisms available to the agency to monitor compliance and identify violations. The agencies certainly enjoy the statutory right to enter and inspect regulated facilities, and to request, even from the probable violator itself, information that may identify a violation.[49] Because agency resources are limited, however, enforcement activity under environmental law depends in large measure upon a system of self-monitoring and self-reporting.

Regulated entities are required to monitor specific activities on a periodic basis and to record and/or report the results of the monitoring to the relevant government authority.[50] The scope and frequency of the required monitoring and reporting varies from program to program, and from state to state. Because the self-monitoring cannot be continuous, though, any periodic monitoring needs to be representative of the monitored activity, and the reported information must be accurate (thus, one may not cherry-pick the moment to take a sample with an eye on assuring compliance). The reporting method also normally requires an affirmative statement by a responsible individual at the regulated entity to the effect that the information submitted is true, accurate, and complete.[51] Certain programs also require a periodic certification of compliance.[52]

The monitoring reports provide the agency ready access to compliance data. The certifications of accuracy, or of compliance, also essentially operate as admissions of violations that may be evident from reported data, and they make the defense of an alleged violation difficult without challenging the regulated entity's own reports.

3.4 Enforcement Remedies

Agency enforcement remedies include administrative, civil and criminal actions. The criminal component carries significant sanctions, and the criminal provisions in the environmental statutes capture much more than just the typical criminal conduct. Even so, the administrative and civil components are widely regarded as a more realistic threat to the average party involved with regulated activities. While a regulated party will rarely if ever be subjected to a criminal action, it can almost be assured of an administrative or civil enforcement proceeding, at some level, at some point.

Criminal provisions in environmental law challenge traditional notions of criminal conduct. Criminal activity in other contexts typically involves only intentional or deliberate acts. In the environmental context, however, "willful" and "reckless" violations may be prosecuted under criminal provisions, but "negligent" and "knowing" violations may be considered criminal actions as well.[53] In addition, while the government must establish guilt "beyond a reasonable doubt," as in normal criminal cases, it has been effective in developing some options as to its burden of proof on some elements of the criminal activity. For example, a person may be convicted simply with a showing of general (and not specific) intent to violate the law.[54] A person also may be held criminally responsible for his own conduct, and for that of others under his supervision.[55] The requisite "knowledge" of the violation may be knowledge imputed to the individual, and does not have to be actual knowledge.[56]

Most regulated entities operate as good corporate citizens, develop and implement environmental compliance programs, and intend to comply with applicable law. Even so, violations do occur from time to time, and administrative or civil enforcement often follows.

In the civil context, the government's path to applying sanctions can be relatively simple. Decisions to initiate enforcement action, especially informal administrative action, usually are delegated to low levels at the agency, and, in the first instance, the sanction may be imposed by the enforcement arm of the agency alone. Review by an independent trier of fact, such as an administrative law judge, may occur only upon specific request by the affected entity.[57] Even at that level, the government does not need to show intent to violate the law, but only show, by a preponderance of the evidence, that the violation occurred.[58]

3.5 Enforcement Authority

The structure of the environmental regulatory system significantly affects the scope of enforcement authority and, necessarily, the enforcement exposure to the regulated community. Major environmental programs typically provide for the states to adopt their own regulatory programs.[59] The state program can then take the place of the federal program, by delegation of the federal regulatory authority, if it is at least as stringent as the federal program.[60] If a program is adopted at the state level, but not approved at the federal level, both programs would apply, subject to prevailing laws of federal preemption. If a state program is approved at the federal level, it takes the place of the federal program and the state is given primary enforcement authority, subject to federal oversight.[61]

The net result is that federal enforcement may occur in either situation, and generally may occur whether or not the state has taken some enforcement action.[62] For example, in *United States v. Smithfield Foods, Inc.*, the owner and operator of two pork-processing plants argued that EPA's civil enforcement action was precluded by a preexisting settlement with the state of Virginia. The

Court of Appeals for the Fourth Circuit concurred with the lower court's finding that Virginia's enforcement scheme was not "sufficiently comparable" to EPA's Clean Water Act authority to bar EPA from bringing its own "independent penalty action."[63] In practice, federal enforcement is not expected to occur in reference to a delegated program unless the federal agency determines that the state agency has not taken adequate or sufficient action to meet the enforcement goals of the federal program.

4.0 Civil Enforcement and Liability

4.1 Introduction

In this section we review the important civil aspects of enforcement and liability under federal environmental law.[64] But before doing so, we acknowledge that not all federal environmental liability arises under statutes covered in this handbook or enforced by EPA. Federal environmental enforcement authority also lies with agencies such as the Department of Interior's Bureau of Safety and Environmental Enforcement (enforcement of violations arising under the Outer Continental Shelf Lands Act, 43 U.S.C. § 1331 *et seq.*), the U.S. Coast Guard (enforcement authority for violations occurring on waters of the United States), the U.S. Army Corps of Engineers (enforcement of wetlands violations shared with EPA), the Bureau of Land Management (enforcement authority over violations occurring on federal lands), and the National Oceanic and Atmospheric Administration (enforcement of the Magnuson–Stevens Fishery Conservation and Management Act 16 U.S.C. § 1801 *et seq.*). The discussion that follows is focused on enforcement of the various statutes discussed in this handbook—authority that is primarily held by EPA.

We start with a grounding in the statutory standards of liability and defense. We turn then to agreed-upon (as opposed to legislated or promulgated) principles of liability and enforcement, such as permits and consent orders. Next we summarize EPA's executive policies and practices with regard to civil enforcement, and we conclude by sketching the trajectory of a civil enforcement proceeding from beginning to end, noting the various roles of the participants.

At the outset we can usefully distinguish between principles of enforcement and liability that derive from unilateral acts of the legislature (i.e., statutes), on the one hand, and principles that are mutually agreed with the government (like permits and consent orders), on the other hand. Both sources of law establish binding legal responsibilities and set consequences for failing to carry out these responsibilities, but the agreed documents have special attributes that tailor them to a particular entity in a manner that the legislature cannot duplicate without skirting the constitutional prohibition against bills of attainder. We consider each separately.

4.2 Statute-Specific Principles of Liability and Defense

Statutory standards are the backbone of modern environmental law. Unlike traditional—and still valid—principles of common law, statutes reflect the deliberate will of the legislature to govern the conduct of the regulated community for the benefit of human health and the environment. The federal environmental statutes vary considerably in the clarity of their exposition and the level of technical detail that is left to the discretion of the implementing agency (EPA, in most instances). In part the variation reflects the evolution in environmental policy between the earliest statutes and the latecomers, and in part it reflects specific enforcement needs that became evident with experience. No one who reads the Clean Air Act in all its chaotic detail can fail to marvel at the simple directness of the Clean Water Act.[65]

Despite their variation, statutes share several important features, two worth noting here. First, they set the outer parameters of responsibility and, to a greater or lesser degree, leave it to the executive branch to stimulate and enforce the responsibility within those parameters. For example, the Clean Water Act prohibits the discharge of pollutants to navigable waters from a point source absent a permit, but the regulatory scheme by which the permit is to be applied for and granted is left largely to the executive agencies. Second, and for present purposes more important, the environmental statutes lay the basic groundwork for enforcement by stating the elements of legal responsibility. The detailed blueprint for enforcement in the event of dereliction, however, is left to the executive branch.

4.3 Statutory Standard of Conduct

Administrative and civil enforcement of the environmental laws are not limited to circumstances where the legal transgression was intended. By and large, the liability provisions contained in federal statutory environmental laws are "strict liability" provisions that disregard the intention and motive of the entity charged with a duty to comply.[66] This means, in essence, that if a party does not follow the requirements of a statute (e.g., fails to file an import certification as required under TSCA) the administrator of EPA may bring an enforcement action against that party based solely on its failure to obey the requirements of the statute, regardless of the reason for the failure and regardless of the entity's good intentions to comply. There is generally no requirement that the party have a certain level of knowledge or intent in order for a violation to exist.[67] Thus, under most federal statutory environmental laws, one only need act or fail to act in a way prohibited by the statute in order to be exposed to potential civil enforcement and liability.

4.4 Statutory Defenses

While most federal statutory environmental laws share a "strict liability" approach, the statutes vary in the specific defenses that they recognize. For example, the Clean Water Act prohibits the discharge of pollutants from a point source to waters of the United States unless the discharge is done in compliance with a permit issued by EPA or a state with authority delegated from EPA.[68] Violation of the permit constitutes an enforceable violation of the act.[69] In certain circumstances, however, the permittee may assert a defense that excuses the violation. The Clean Water Act provides that "an upset constitutes an affirmative defense to an action brought for noncompliance."[70] Upset means "an exceptional incident in which there is an unintentional and temporary noncompliance with technology based permit effluent limitations because of factors beyond the reasonable control of the permittee."[71] If a facility experiences this type of event, it can, subject to certain conditions, assert the "upset" defense.[72] Likewise, the statute excuses noncompliance in the event of "bypass," provided certain circumstances are present. A bypass is an "intentional diversion of waste streams from any portion of a treatment facility."[73] Under the Clean Water Act, a facility may cause its wastewater stream to bypass the treatment process if: (1) the bypass was unavoidable to prevent loss of life, personal injury, or severe property damage; (2) there were no feasible alternatives to bypass; and (3) proper notice was given.[74]

A facility may also avoid liability under the Clean Water Act by asserting the so-called "permit shield."[75] If a facility is in compliance with its discharge permit (federal or state-delegated), the facility is deemed to be in material compliance with the Clean Water Act. The logic behind this is that, once the government and the facility have agreed upon a set of permit conditions, it would be incongruous for the government to assert that the facility is in violation of the Clean Water Act if the facility is obeying the terms of its permit. Thus, compliance with a permit can act as a "shield" against liability.[76] The Clean Air Act also provides for a "permit shield" defense, but it is narrower in scope than the "shield" provided under the Clean Water Act.[77] Compliance with a Clean Air Act permit only shows: (1) compliance with the permit; (2) compliance with provisions above and beyond the ordinary permit requirements if those provisions were included in the permit; and (3) compliance with a provision that the permitting authority determines is not applicable to the permittee and so states in the permit.[78]

Statutory and regulatory definitions can also be used as defenses to enforcement actions. In *United States v. Self*, a defendant was accused of illegally disposing of a hazardous waste when he sold natural gas condensate intended for disposal at a waste treatment facility as automotive fuel.[79] The Court of Appeals for the Tenth Circuit overturned the defendant's conviction by agreeing with the defendant's position that "so long as natural gas condensate is burned for energy recovery, it is not a byproduct and, therefore, not a discarded material by virtue of being recycled, and, therefore, not a solid waste, and, therefore, not a hazardous waste under RCRA."[80] Thus, even though the natural gas condensate exhibited the statutory characteristics of a hazardous waste, the court found that, through an interpretation of RCRA's statutory definitions, the natural gas condensate could not be considered a hazardous waste.[81]

Under CERCLA, a party can avoid liability if the party can show that the release was caused solely by: (1) an act of God; (2) an act of war; or (3) an act or omission of a third party, other than an employee or agent of the defendant or party with whom there is a contractual relationship, as long as the defendant exercised due care and took precautions against foreseeable acts of the third party.[82] While the "act of God" and "act of war" defenses are rarely used successfully,[83] the so-called "third-party" defense is used with greater frequency and success.[84]

Three well-known versions of the third-party defense are: (1) the Innocent Purchaser defense; (2) the Bona Fide Prospective Purchaser defense; and (3) the Contiguous Property Owner defense. These defenses are intended to encourage the purchase of contaminated or potentially contaminated land. In the past, CERCLA served (unintentionally) to discourage the purchase of such land by holding innocent purchasers and neighbors liable for contamination that they did not cause and were not aware of. These three defenses provide some protection to purchasers of contaminated or potentially contaminated land provided that certain criteria are met. While each of these defenses has its own specific requirements, EPA has issued general guidance on "common elements" that must be met in order to claim one of the defenses.[85] The elements are:

- One must perform "all appropriate inquiries" into the property.[86]
- One must have no affiliation with the person liable for cleanup at the site.
- One must comply with land use restrictions and institutional controls going forward.
- One must take reasonable steps to stop continuing releases, prevent future releases, and prevent or limit human, environmental, or natural resource exposure to earlier hazardous substance releases.
- One must cooperate with, assist, and provide access to persons authorized to conduct response actions at the site.
- One must comply with information requests and administrative subpoenas.
- One must provide legally required notices.

Effective October 6, 2015, parties wishing to undertake "all appropriate inquiries" can adhere to ASTM International's E1527–13 "Standard Practice for Environmental Site Assessments: Phase I Environmental Site Assessment Process."[87] A Phase I Environmental Site Assessment must be performed by an environmental professional who meets all of the qualifications for licensing, education, and relevant work experience required by ASTM.

In sum, the environmental statutes generally establish strict-liability regimes that permit civil enforcement when the bare facts of a transgression are present, without regard for motive, intent, or, for that matter, cause. Nevertheless, several statutes, including those noted briefly above, recognize defenses against enforcement, in certain circumstances. Permit shields, intervening acts of third parties, regulatory definitions, and the like all play a substantial role in the civil enforcement context. As we will explore next, however, the regulated entity can always bargain away its defenses (or add to its affirmative responsibilities) by concluding an agreement with the government.

4.5 Agreed-Upon Principles of Enforcement and Defense

4.5.1 Permits

The concept of statutory standards of liability and defense (discussed above) is a familiar one. The idea that a law exists, after being passed by the legislature, and that the citizenry is expected to obey that law is a fundamental concept universally recognized. Just as intuitive is the concept of an agreed-upon standard (e.g., a contract). Agreed-upon standards have become a leading source of responsibility and enforcement under the federal environmental laws. As opposed to a statutory standard, which is imposed on the public by the government, an agreed-upon standard is the product of negotiation between the government and an affected entity. As such, an agreed-upon standard is subject to different considerations and has different implications for the parties involved.

The classic agreed-upon standard in federal environmental law is a permit. Permits play a decisive role by providing an approval that overcomes a generally applicable prohibition (consider the Endangered Species Act's prohibition against a taking). By the same token, they allow the government to tailor environmental requirements to a particular geographical location and a particular permittee in order to achieve a desired result for all involved. Such flexibility allows state and federal agencies to meet certain minimum standards (as required by statute), while also meeting local, site-specific, and private needs. As discussed above (and below), the permit approach also creates new enforcement and liability benefits and concerns.

The Clean Water Act's National Pollution Discharge Elimination System (NPDES) permit is a good example of how this concept works in action. In general, a party must obtain an NPDES permit if it wishes to discharge a pollutant from a point source to waters of the United States.[88] The permit is issued either by EPA or by a state to which EPA has delegated its authority.[89] The permitting authority must, at a minimum, require the facility to meet the federal statutory standards,[90] although a state permitting authority may impose standards that exceed the federal requirements.[91] Typically, a facility will apply for a permit, the governmental authority will issue a draft permit, the facility (and the public) will comment on the permit, and, if agreement can be reached, a final permit will issue. To be sure, the permitting process is not as flexible as private contractual negotiations, and the government has the upper hand, but in practice permittees in good standing have room to negotiate acceptable terms.

An issue of key significance with regard to an agreed-upon standard such as a permit is that failure to abide by the terms of the permit is "de facto" noncompliance.[92] The specificity of the permit's terms, its tailoring to the permittee's circumstances, and the permit's detailed enforcement provisions (which supplement the general enforcement terms of the statute) put the permittee in a weak position from which to defend itself against enforcement. For example, the applicability and meaning of the permit's requirements cannot easily be disputed because the permittee countersigned the permit. Moreover, the permit may require the permittee to keep detailed records of its regulated operations, thereby ensuring the availability of the information necessary for strong enforcement. That said, the permittee may still assert whatever statutory defenses (e.g., upset) have not been waived or revised in the permit.

4.5.2 Consent Orders

Another type of agreed-upon standard is the consent order, in which a regulated entity voluntarily agrees to an agency order. The Section 5(e) consent order under TSCA is a useful example.[93] Suppose an importer submits an application to EPA in order to import a new chemical substance into the United States. During its review, EPA determines that there is insufficient information to evaluate the risk posed by the chemical substance, but it concludes that the chemical substance is unlikely to pose a threat to human health and the environment if the circumstances of its importation and use can be controlled. For these circumstances, rather than prohibiting the importation pending further scientific analysis, EPA has developed the practice of issuing consensual orders under Section 5(e) of TSCA. The consent orders follow a predetermined format, typically limiting the volume and use of the imported substance and sometimes regulating the final disposal of all materials associated with the imported substance.

TSCA grants EPA considerable authority to issue unilateral orders to protect human health and the environment, but the very absence of complete risk information would undermine the use of such authority and invite legal challenge. In a word, the unilateral order is too blunt an instrument and is, therefore, rarely used.[94] EPA and the regulated community prefer to use consent orders because they provide flexibility and reliability and because they reduce the chance that the issue will be litigated.[95]

4.6 Agency Principles and Policies

4.6.1 Penalty Policies

EPA has developed penalty policies to provide guidance to EPA personnel in determining an appropriate penalty to assess against an alleged violator.[96] These policies were developed both to clarify or make more concrete the statutory language and to provide guidance to agency officials in the application of permissible statutory discretion in enforcement. A federal environmental statute typically defines the maximum amount that a party can be fined for a particular violation, but ultimately it is up to the agency to develop its own protocol for deciding when and how to enforce the law.

The starting point for the penalty policies is the list of factors identified in the statute as relevant to enforcement.[97] The Clean Water Act, for example, states, "In determining the amount of a civil penalty the court shall consider the seriousness of the violation or violations, the economic benefit (if any) resulting from the violation, any history of such violations, any good-faith efforts to comply with the applicable requirements, the economic impact of the penalty on the violator, and such other matters as justice may require."[98]

Though helpful, a bare list of factors does not amount to a clear, informative, and concrete policy. How much weight should be accorded each factor? How much should a penalty be increased or decreased given a particular set of facts? The text of the statute provides no guidance and, therefore, no predictability. Predictability is not only in the interest of the regulated community: EPA must avoid claims that its enforcement actions are arbitrary and capricious. The approximately twenty-five sets of penalty guidelines developed by EPA help to address these issues by expanding on and clarifying the statutory language. EPA has created some overarching penalty policies[99] as well as some statute-specific penalty policies.[100]

4.6.2 Statute-Specific Penalty Policies

While EPA has general civil penalty policies, the statute-specific policies can be of greater help when dealing with a particular statute. The RCRA penalty policy provides a useful example.

When assessing a penalty amount, RCRA requires that EPA "take into account the seriousness of the violation and any good faith efforts to comply with applicable requirements."[101] EPA has expanded upon this language in its penalty policy, which enumerates a sequence of four steps that EPA personnel are to take when assessing a penalty under RCRA: (1) determine a gravity-based penalty based on a penalty matrix (shown below); (2) add a "multi-day" component, as appropriate; (3) adjust the gravity-based and multi-day components, up or down, for case-specific circumstances; and (4) factor in any economic benefit gained from noncompliance.[102]

Under RCRA, the gravity component is based on two factors: (1) the potential for harm, and (2) the extent of deviation from a statutory or regulatory requirement.[103] In order to determine the appropriate gravity-based penalty, EPA provides the following matrix:

Gravity-based penalty matrix to supplement the RCRA Civil Penalty Policy for violations that occur after January 12, 2009		

Extent of Deviation from Requirement

		MAJOR	MODERATE	MINOR
Potential for Harm	MAJOR	$37,500 to $28,330	$28,3300 to $21,250	$21,250 to $15,580
	MODERATE	$15,580 to $11,330	$11,330 to $7,090	$7,090 to $4,250
	MINOR	$4,250 to $2,130	$2,130 to $710	$710 to $150

Note: After calculating the gravity-based penalty for each count, the total applicable gravity-based penalty for all counts in a particular case/matter should be rounded to the nearest unit of $100 as required by the memorandum from Granta Nakayama, dated December 29, 2008.

As the matrix makes clear, a RCRA gravity-based penalty can range from $150 to $37,500 per violation per day.[104] The penalty policy provides examples of what is major, moderate, and minor for both "potential for harm" and "extent of deviation."[105] As an example, a major potential for harm is described as a "violation that poses or may pose a substantial risk of exposure of humans or other environmental receptors to hazardous waste or constituents," while a minor potential for harm is described as a "violation that poses or may pose a relatively low risk of exposure."[106] Once the agency has determined the level of both the "potential for harm" and the "extent of deviation," it can select the gravity-based penalty it intends to use according to the table above.

Some RCRA violations qualify for a multi-day penalty. If EPA determines that a violation has continued for more than one day, the penalty policy provides further guidance and a separate matrix (ranging from $150 to $7,090) to assist the agency in calculating the penalty.[107] In order to determine which "box" of the matrix applies, EPA first determines whether multi-day penalties for the alleged violation are mandatory, presumed, or discretionary.[108] These distinctions are somewhat similar to the major, moderate, and minor distinctions. The RCRA penalty policy discusses this in detail, but also states that the "analysis should be conducted in the context of the Penalty Policy's broad goals (discussed below)."[109] Once the per-day penalty is determined, that number is simply multiplied by the number of days constituting the duration of the violation and then added to the gravity-based penalty.

After a penalty has been calculated with regard to the gravity-based and multi-day components, various adjustment factors are considered. These facts may increase or decrease a penalty assessment. Some factors that are considered include: (1) good faith efforts to comply; (2) degree of willfulness or negligence; (3) history of noncompliance; (4) ability to pay; and (5) other factors. Typically, each adjustment may result in a change up or down of up to 25 percent (or in unusual circumstances 40 percent). These factors reflect the goals of the agency's penalty policy: (1) deterrence; (2) fair and equitable treatment of the regulated community; and (3) swift resolution of environmental problems.[110]

In the end, even with guidance on such fine distinctions as "major" vs. "minor," "substantial risk" vs. "low risk," and so forth, the agency enjoys considerable latitude in interpreting the facts according to its tastes. Practiced EPA agents will seek out precedents within the agency for handling certain circumstances to help ensure uniformity, but the guidance does not compel uniformity, relational fairness or even rationality.

EPA has a general policy goal to prevent a violator from gaining economic benefit from noncompliance.[111] If a violator gained "significant"[112] economic benefit through noncompliance, an economic benefit component is factored in. Economic benefits may come from delayed or avoided costs.[113] EPA uses two methods to determine the amount of such economic benefits. EPA either uses a "rule of thumb" approach or it uses a computer model named "BEN."[114] The methodology used for either approach will not be discussed in detail here,[115] but suffice it to say that EPA's calculations deserve close scrutiny for inappropriate assumptions that may be built into the model used.

4.6.3 Counting Violations

Although the maximum penalty for a violation varies from law to law and violation to violation, many of the federal statutory environmental laws were enacted with a statutory maximum of $20,000 per violation *per day*.[116] Aware that over time a static penalty amount would become less and less of a deterrent, Congress passed the Federal Civil Penalties Inflation Adjustment Act of 1990 to prompt federal agencies to periodically review and adjust their statutory civil penalty amounts for inflation.[117] Most recently, on July 1, 2016, EPA released an interim final rule adjusting the level of statutory civil monetary penalty amounts for the statutes that the agency administers.[118] The civil penalty adjustment in the 2016 interim final rule is based on the Consumer Price Index for all Urban Consumers (CPI–U) for the month of October 2015. Some changes are significant, with enacted maximum penalties of $25,000 moving up to $93,750 adjusted in the case of certain Clean Air Act and RCRA penalties.[119] One can see how an ongoing violation can subject one to a significant cumulative penalty. For instance, an excursion from the discharge limit in a permit under the Clean Water Act can result in a "continuing violation" penalty that reflects the entire period between the initial discharge violation and the final proof that the discharge is again in compliance—depending on the testing schedule, the period may easily last a month. That said, EPA can choose to use this cumulative total as a starting point and adjust the penalty using an applicable penalty policy as guidance (or adjust it in negotiations). The "continuing violation" theory has also been used by the agency under certain circumstances to extend the applicable statute of limitations.[120] Some federal courts and the Environmental Appeals Board have declined to follow EPA's continuing violations theory under the Clean Water Act.[121] Others have limited its application under the Clean Air Act.[122] Also, the statute of limitations applied to many environmental laws can be found at 28 U.S.C. § 2462. In a key non-environmental decision, the Supreme Court concluded in *Gabelli v. S.E.C.* that the "discovery rule"—a tort law theory that has been used by EPA and adopted by some federal courts to toll the statute of limitations until the underlying violation is discovered or should have been discovered—does not apply to the statute of limitations under 28 U.S.C. § 2462.[123] Just as important is the observation that a single act can result in more than one violation of applicable law. For instance, suppose a party imports a chemical substance into the United States that it incorrectly believes is on the TSCA Inventory. The single importation could result in a violation of the requirement to file a Premanufacture Notice (PMN), a failure to file a Notice of Commencement (which follows a PMN filing), and a failure to file a correct TSCA § 13 Import Certification.[124] Each violation is separately calculated as though separate acts caused the transgressions. The penalty policies are structured to favor such leveraging of a single error into multiple violations and penalties.

4.6.4 Enforcement Discretion

As discussed above, the statutory language of many of the environmental laws provides a considerable amount of discretion with regard to enforcement. Every year EPA and related federal and state agencies are faced with a number of situations that might merit enforcement action. EPA pursues some vigorously and declines to enforce others, while others it settles or drops. Different elements factor into such discretionary decisions. Earlier we discussed how the "strict liability" aspect of civil liability in most of the federal statutory environmental laws obviates the need for a showing of intent or knowledge in order for liability to attach. While this is true, EPA can use its enforcement discretion to recognize the presence or absence of an element of intent. If a party was culpable, acted in bad faith, acted with knowledge, was a repeat offender, or something similar, EPA is more likely to initiate an enforcement action. If the violator is a first-time offender, who acted in good faith, and without knowledge, EPA may be less likely to enforce. That said, there are numerous examples of first-time offenders being enforced against.[125] EPA may also consider the deterrence value of the case, the severity of the violation, what resources are available, and the likelihood that EPA will prevail in the case.[126]

4.6.5 Voluntary Audit Disclosures

EPA's compliance incentive approach is reflected in its voluntary audit policy, which first took shape in 1986 when EPA touted the benefits of institutionalizing audit practices.[127] The regulated community remained apprehensive, however, out of fear that their own audit findings could be used by enforcement officials as a basis to pursue enforcement actions and assess penalties. To further encourage voluntary auditing, EPA released a revised voluntary audit policy in December 1995 and a final policy statement in May 2000 that called for reducing the gravity component of civil penalties when regulated entities voluntarily discover, promptly disclose, and expeditiously correct noncompliance.[128] Gravity-based penalties are that portion of the penalty that satisfies punishment objectives separate from any recovery of the economic benefit of noncompliance.[129]

To qualify for the benefits of EPA's policy, systematic discovery of the violation is required through a voluntary environmental audit or a compliance management system. Legally required monitoring, sampling, or auditing procedures cannot be treated as "audits" under the policy since they do not satisfy the requirement to be voluntary. Disclosure to the agency must also be prompt, cooperative, and in writing, and the violation must be corrected immediately, with steps taken to prevent recurrence. Repeat violations and violations that could have given rise to imminent and substantial harm do not qualify for penalty relief. Likewise, violations of specific terms of an administrative or judicial order or consent agreement do not qualify.

In an effort to modernize the audit process and to make it more efficient for both regulated entities and EPA, in December 2015 EPA launched eDisclosure, an online reporting system for self-disclosed violations.[130] All self-disclosed civil violations (other than new owner disclosures) must now be made through eDisclosure.[131] For some limited types of violations, regulated entities submitting disclosures will receive an electronic Notice of Determination stating that the violations are resolved without issuance of civil penalties.[132] For most types of violations, however, the regulated entity will only receive an Acknowledgment Letter stating that EPA will make a determination as to eligibility for penalty mitigation if and when an enforcement action is contemplated. Within 60 days of disclosure, the entity must certify that it has corrected the identified violation(s).[133] EPA cautions that confidential business information should not be submitted through the eDisclosure portal.[134]

4.6.6 Enforcement Forums and Referral

When EPA decides to pursue an enforcement action against a party, it has several options about how to pursue such an action. EPA can initiate an internal administrative action against an alleged violator or it can refer the case to the DOJ so that the DOJ can enforce against the alleged violator in federal court. EPA enjoys substantial benefits by pursuing an action internally. Notably, an internal administrative action is subject to EPA's rules of procedure, and the EPA official prosecuting the case is likely to be more familiar with the internal workings of EPA's administrative processes than the alleged violator. On the flip side, there are some results that only the DOJ can obtain through judicial action. If the situation calls for injunctive action, recovery of response costs, or enforcement of an administrative order, EPA must refer the case to the DOJ so that it may pursue the matter in federal court on behalf of its client, EPA.[135] EPA may also wish to refer cases that are overly complex so that the issue can be resolved in federal court, thereby helping to establish precedent or, ironically, helping to limit the applicability of the precedent to the jurisdiction of the court.[136] While the referral option is always available, the majority of cases EPA brings each year are dealt with in the administrative forum.[137]

EPA also coordinates with other federal agencies in enforcement, such as the Occupational Safety and Health Administration ("OSHA") of the Department of Labor. In 1990, EPA entered into an interagency Memorandum of Understanding ("MOU") with OSHA "to improve the combined efforts of the agencies to achieve protection of workers, the public, and the environment at facilities subject to EPA and OSHA jurisdiction; to delineate the general areas of responsibility of each agency; to provide guidelines for coordination of interface activities between the two agencies with the overall goal of identifying and minimizing environmental or workplace hazards."[138] More recently, the Department of Justice announced a plan in December 2015 to more effectively prosecute those that put workers in danger. Under the new "Worker Endangerment Initiative," Deputy Attorney General Sally Quillian Yates encouraged federal prosecutors to work with the DOJ's Environmental Crimes Section in pursuing worker endangerment violations.[139] This latest initiative encourages federal attorneys to consider utilizing Title 18 and environmental offenses, "which often occur in conjunction with worker safety crimes, to enhance penalties and increase deterrence," because worker safety statutes generally provide for only misdemeanor penalties.[140] The U.S. DOJ entered into a MOU with the Department of Labor to facilitate coordination on prosecuting worker safety violations.[141] The MOU focuses on criminal referrals to DOJ, information and data sharing, as well as enhancement of cross-training.[142]

4.7 Progression of a Civil Enforcement Proceeding

The progression of a civil enforcement proceeding is not always the same, but it usually follows a general pattern. Typically, an enforcement proceeding starts with an investigation by the government that is triggered by a routine inspection, a formal request for information, a call from an anonymous tipster, reports filed by the company in the ordinary course (such as discharge monitoring reports), or the company's voluntary disclosure of a release.

If the matter merits investigation, EPA must decide what the initial scope of the inquiry will be. EPA may choose to pursue its investigations through a written request for information, civil interrogatories, or a site visit (announced or unannounced). An on-site inspection may come as an informal, consensual inspection, or it could be backed with a search warrant and armed officers. The more aggressive on-site investigations involve the sudden arrival of a multimedia enforcement team trained in locking down a facility, sequestering employees, debriefing employees in parallel, securing computer records (e.g., ripping out or copying hard drives), confiscating files of all kinds, and taking physical samples. To embark on such an inspection, the agency need not have concluded in advance that criminal, as opposed to civil, enforcement is ultimately required.

During an on-site investigation, the party being investigated faces competing interests. On the one hand, there is a desire to be completely open and cooperative with the government agency in an attempt to foster good relations, encourage a mutually beneficial outcome, and show a willingness to cooperate. On the other hand, there is a competing need to protect privileged information, some of which may be trade secrets or material that was prepared with the assistance of legal counsel. Also, site inspectors often seek to understand and gather information by questioning individuals. There is typically no obligation for the individuals to cooperate and a misunderstood statement can give rise to personal liability.

The party investigated often is forced to make these decisions in an atmosphere that is not conducive to level-headed thinking and in any event may not be afforded the opportunity to object or to defer agency action until counsel arrives by phone or in person to assist.

4.7.1 Initiation of a Legal Proceeding and Rules of Process

If the investigation yields sufficient evidence of a violation, the agency may choose to initiate a legal proceeding. As discussed above, how and in what forum the legal proceeding is initiated can have a significant impact on how the proceeding will progress. If EPA decides to pursue the action in an administrative setting, the regulations set out the rules of practice.[143] Once EPA has decided to pursue an administrative action, EPA will file a complaint with EPA's regional hearing clerk at the commencement of the proceeding.[144]

Once the proceeding has begun, the alleged violator has several choices. First, the respondent may choose to admit to the allegations contained in the complaint and pay the penalty asserted in the complaint. Second, the respondent may choose to negotiate with the agency in an attempt to come to a mutual understanding as to the needs of both parties and in an attempt to resolve the case through mutual agreement. Lastly, the respondent may choose to litigate the case. Regardless of whether the respondent wishes to settle or litigate, the respondent must submit an answer to the complaint. Failure to answer an allegation within the time provided "constitutes an admission of the allegation" and effectively terminates any settlement discussions.[145]

4.7.2 Settlement Negotiations

Settlement negotiations may proceed through a formal arbitration process, or the parties may elect to negotiate informally, which is the more customary method.[146] EPA's regulations encourage settlement talks between the government and the alleged violator, provided that "the settlement is consistent with the provisions and objectives of the Act and applicable regulations."[147] The fact that settlement talks are underway does not relieve either side from its obligations (e.g., for the defendant to file an answer to the complaint).[148] That said, if both sides are making progress toward a settlement that is in accordance with the applicable statute, the presiding judge is likely to grant the extensions necessary to complete negotiations, in effect staying the litigation phases of discovery and trial pending resolution of settlement discussions. If the parties cannot come to a negotiated settlement in a reasonable amount of time, the discovery phase of the proceeding will begin, followed ultimately by presentation of the evidence to the court (or presiding administrative law judge).

4.7.3 Consent Agreements and Final Orders

If EPA and the respondent can come to an agreement that settles the claims in the complaint, the parties may submit a consent agreement to the court for its consideration.[149] If the presiding officer determines that the consent agreement is acceptable, the parties must obtain a final order from the regional judicial officer, the regional administrator, or the Environmental Appeals Board (EAB) in order for the settlement to take effect.[150] If a settlement cannot be reached, the administrative law judge will decide the matter through litigation. EPA's Environmental Appeals Board hears appeals from initial administrative decisions.[151] Decisions of the EAB may be appealed in federal court as provided for in the individual statutes.[152]

5.0 Private Civil Enforcement by Citizen Suits

Apart from civil enforcement actions by the government agencies, a fundamental component of the environmental enforcement framework is the availability of a statutory right for citizens to enforce environmental law in certain circumstances. The major environmental statutes generally allow a citizen who is or may be adversely affected by violations to bring a civil action in federal court (i) against an entity that is in violation of an environmental requirement and (ii) against EPA if the agency has failed to perform a nondiscretionary duty.[153] This enforcement vehicle at times may present a more compelling deterrent to the regulated community than government enforcement. This section discusses, in turn, the practical enforcement impact of citizen suits, the general terms and requirements of citizen suit provisions, and some recent developments as to selected issues in this area.

Because of the broad scope of compliance information that the agencies make available to the public, either as a matter of course or upon specific request, a concerned citizen could quickly garner basic compliance data sufficient to allege violations at a relevant facility.[154] As a private citizen, the potential plaintiff is not bound by any standards of prosecutorial discretion that an agency would apply in deciding whether an enforcement action is appropriate in that situation, or whether the appropriate remedy is to bring an action in court. Likewise, the citizen plaintiff would not be bound by any agency enforcement or penalty policies that may suggest, for example, some leniency as to first-time offenders, as to violations that are minor or may not have had a significant impact on the environment, or as to violators that may not have the financial capability to pay a significant penalty. In brief, the citizen may well have little incentive but to seek to apply, across the board, the maximum penalty for each and every identified violation. Under a system that ascribes civil penalties of up to $37,500 per day per violation, the total amount of the penalty sought to be assessed in a citizen suit can quickly rise to extraordinary levels. Even if the outcome of the citizen suit ultimately may be somewhat more reasonable, the damage to the regulated entity's public profile may be significant simply from the filing of the lawsuit.

The possibility of a citizen suit further effectively prevents the regulated community from deriving any comfort from an agency's failure to take enforcement action as to violations identified in the public records. The regulated entity effectively has little control over who may see or act upon that information. Consider that, unlike with agency staff, the regulated entity cannot seek to develop a working relationship with every citizen potentially affected by its violations, and that the potential citizen plaintiff could be anyone, including someone with access to internal company data.

Once the compliance data exists, and apart from the regulated entity's corporate commitment to maintaining compliance, the entity should consider, and should act as appropriate, to resolve violations that present a realistic threat of a citizen suit. Those actions may include prompt, curative compliance activity to resolve the cause of the violation, possible affirmative disclosure of the violation to the government, and resolution of the enforcement exposure. Under the typical statutory provisions governing citizen suits, such curative and other actions by the alleged wrongdoer may operate to bar a citizen suit.

Citizen suits provisions generally establish certain prerequisites to filing suit.[155] Once those are met, the federal district courts have jurisdiction to enforce applicable law, apply appropriate civil penalties, and award litigation costs (including attorney fees).[156] The statutes also seek to protect the interests of the United States by requiring notice of the suit to EPA and, in some cases, to the attorney general of the United States, and by allowing EPA to intervene in the cases as a matter of right.[157]

The prerequisites to suit primarily involve advance notice of the intended lawsuit to EPA, the state, and the alleged violator.[158] The primary purpose of the citizen suit provision is to supplement and not supplant government enforcement action;[159] the advance-notice requirement thus provides the government an opportunity to enforce, and the violators an opportunity to remedy, the violation.[160] Where the federal or state government has commenced and is diligently prosecuting an action to require compliance with the applicable environmental requirement, the suit by the citizen is precluded.[161]

Litigation involving citizen suits often focuses on whether the citizen suit is precluded (i) by prior government action or (ii) by the compliance status of the alleged violator at the time of the lawsuit. Each issue is discussed below.

The citizen suits provisions generally defer to government enforcement action and preclude citizen action if the government has commenced and is prosecuting an action in a federal or state court. The Clean Water Act also precludes a citizen suit if EPA has commenced and is prosecuting a similar action in the administrative context, or if the state has done the same under a state law "comparable" to the Clean Water Act.[162] The courts have found that the requirement for action under "comparable" state law should be interpreted broadly.[163] For the state law to be considered comparable, the public participation and judicial review provisions must be roughly comparable to those in the Clean Water Act.[164]

The citizen suit provisions in the Clean Water Act and RCRA authorize actions against a person alleged to be in violation of certain applicable environmental requirements.[165] The courts have found that, for the suit to proceed, the private plaintiff must show "ongoing violations," including violations that continue at the time of filing of the complaint, and/or the reasonable likelihood of recurrence of those violations.[166] Wholly past violations will not support liability.[167]

The citizen suit provisions in the environmental statutes also contain a "savings clause" providing that they are not intended to restrict any right that a person may have under any statute or common law to seek enforcement of applicable law, or any other relief.[168] Persons adversely affected by violations of regulated entities thus are not prohibited from pursuing, and often do pursue, causes of action under common law.[169] Frequent actions involve claims of nuisance or trespass under state law.[170]

Whether proceeding under the statutory citizen suits provisions, or under state common law claims, citizen actions effectively complement government enforcement.

Citizen suits are often used by environmental groups to achieve a broader agenda, for example, opposing local development or seeking information and leverage related to a broader policy objective, e.g., opposition to the oil and gas industry. In one recent instance, plaintiffs brought a citizen suit under RCRA against oil and gas companies, alleging an increased incidence of earthquakes in Oklahoma associated with the disposal of oil and gas wastewater had caused an "imminent and substantial endangerment."

6.0 Criminal Enforcement and Liability

Early instances of criminal environmental enforcement focused on "midnight dumpers," but today's federal, state, and even local officials devote even more time and resources to the criminal prosecution of individuals and companies that run afoul of complex regulatory requirements. The expanded role of criminal environmental enforcement has, in part, led to the government's contemporaneous investigation and enforcement of alleged environmental wrongs in both the civil and criminal realms. For study purposes, each realm is often compartmentalized, perhaps largely because the procedures and potentially dire consequences of jail time are readily distinguished. Nevertheless, civil and criminal enforcement often occur in parallel, requiring the practitioner to navigate the intricacies of both.

In the criminal realm, the major environmental statutes focus on the culpability of the individual or company. The prosecution of environmental crimes generally can proceed independent of traditional "corporate veil" limitations on individual liability.[171] Likewise, individual liability for officers and directors is not limited to exceptional circumstances such as failure to observe corporate formalities or use of the corporation for an illegal purpose. For management, culpability is largely a measure of whether they actively participated in or countenanced the environmental misconduct. Federal environmental law reflects these broader limits on criminal liability, in part, through statutory definitions of terms such as "person," "person in charge," "owner," and "operator," which are read expansively to include not only employees, but also officers and directors.[172]

6.1 Approaches and Defenses to Criminal Liability

With the exception of NEPA, each of the major environmental statutes provides for criminal sanctions in addition to the civil penalties already discussed. Consistent with the precepts of criminal law generally, distinguishing criminal conduct—that is, determining whether the acts or omissions of a party warrant the stigma of criminal liability and potential imprisonment—hinges on the state of mind of the accused. This added element of *mens rea* (also called the *scienter* or knowledge requirement) is a subject of intense debate within the courts and among environmental practitioners. A brief analysis of the salient issues, along with illustrative examples, is provided below, followed by a discussion of key exceptions and defenses used in the criminal setting.

6.1.1 Satisfying *Mens Rea*

The *mens rea* element requires a demonstration that the accused wrongdoer exhibited an "evil-meaning mind."[173] Under the major environmental statutes, two categories of intent or states-of-mind are generally used to satisfy this element—specific intent and general intent.

Specific intent, the more stringent of these categories, must generally be mandated in the statute itself and typically requires the government to prove both that the defendant intended to act, and that the defendant knew the consequences of his or her acts would be illegal. For example, RCRA Sections

3008(d)(2)(B) and (C) impose fines of up to $50,000 per day of violation or imprisonment of up to two years, or both, on a person who *"knowingly* treats, stores or disposes of any hazardous waste [i.e., knowledge of the act] . . . in *knowing* violation of any material condition or requirement of such permit; or in *knowing* violation of any material condition or requirement of any applicable interim status regulations or standards [i.e., knowledge of the violation]."[174]

Another form of specific intent under criminal environmental law, "knowing endangerment," requires the government to prove both that the defendant intended to act, and had knowledge of the imminent danger of death or serious bodily injury posed by such acts. For "knowing endangerment" offenses, the Clean Air Act,[175] the Clean Water Act,[176] and RCRA[177] carry stiff fines (up to $1 million per violation for organizations), up to fifteen years imprisonment, or both. Each of these statutes instructs that, in determining whether an individual defendant held the requisite knowledge of imminent danger of death or serious bodily injury, the defendant is responsible only for actual awareness or belief possessed, and not for the knowledge of others.[178] However, in proving a defendant's actual knowledge, "circumstantial evidence may be used, including evidence that the defendant took affirmative steps to be shielded from relevant information."[179]

General intent offenses require the government to prove that the defendant knew or was conscious of his actions, and not that the act or omission violated a statutory, regulatory, or permit requirement.[180] Although not set in the context of environmental law, the Supreme Court's decisions in *Morissette,*[181] *Staples,*[182] and *X-Citement Video, Inc.*[183] provide useful guideposts as to how the knowledge elements of a crime are distilled, particularly because the analysis is driven by statutory construction.

In brief, the *scienter* requirement will be applied "to each of the statutory elements which criminalize otherwise innocent conduct."[184] Looking again at RCRA Section 3008, a general intent crime gives rise to a fine or imprisonment when "any person . . . *knowingly* treats, stores or disposes of any hazardous waste identified or listed under this subchapter—(A) without a permit under this subchapter."[185] Here, most courts have agreed that Congress specified a *scienter* requirement for the act of treatment, storage, or disposal, but not for the absence of a permit.[186]

Nevertheless, the critical fact that renders a person's acts or omissions illegal is often difficult to discern. For example, environmental statutes such as the Clean Air Act and the Clean Water Act generally require a permit in order to release pollutants or hazardous substances into the environment. In order for prosecutors to impose criminal liability for violating these permitting requirements, courts have required the government to prove that the defendant knew both that the substances being discharged were hazardous[187] and that a permit violation ultimately would result from the defendant's conduct.[188] In addition, the government must demonstrate a sufficient nexus between the defendant and the criminal conduct, often through the defendant's ability to control or prevent the culpable acts or omissions.

Notably, the federal government takes the position that a company can manifest a specified *scienter* even if no individuals are charged with the same felony. In 2016, in the aftermath of the San Bruno pipeline explosion that killed eight people, the federal government charged Pacific Gas & Electric (PG&E) with twelve safety-related felonies and one count of corruptly obstructing a government investigation.[189] Absent from the indictment are any allegations against individuals for these specific crimes.[190] The trial started in June 2016, and PG&E noted the lack of charges against any individuals during its opening statement. The government has a high burden of demonstrating how a company knowingly and willfully violated safety statutes through circumstantial evidence of alleged guilt. Combining the safety counts with the obstruction count does give the government one advantage—it provides more latitude for presenting evidence on the San Bruno explosion. Although this case is not about the explosion, the government wants to have witnesses discuss the explosion and likely wants jury members to infer that lax attitudes may lead to catastrophic consequences. The case is at trial as this goes to publication.

6.1.2 Eroding *Mens Rea*

It is important to bear in mind that not all environmental crimes require proof of an "evil-meaning mind." Some major environmental statutes include strict liability offenses that require no proof of intent at all, and others like the Clean Air Act and the Clean Water Act include misdemeanors for negligent behavior. Likewise, practitioners and the judiciary have extended the reach of criminal environmental provisions by applying other legal doctrines such as the public welfare offense doctrine and the responsible corporate officer doctrine.

6.1.2.1 Criminal Negligence

Under the Clean Water Act and the Clean Air Act, Congress allowed for misdemeanors against any person who negligently violates certain provisions of each statute. Clean Water Act Section 309(c)(1) gives rise to criminal liability for any person who *negligently*: (A) violates any of eight specific sections of the statute, any permit condition or limitation implementing such sections, or any requirement imposed in an approved pretreatment program; or (B) introduces into a sewer system or into a publicly owned treatment works any pollutant or hazardous substance which such person knew or reasonably should have known could cause personal injury or property damage or, other than in compliance with applicable law, which causes such treatment works to violate any effluent limitation or condition in any permit issued to the treatment works.[191] Similarly, Clean Air Act Section 113(c)(4) gives rise to criminal liability for any person who *negligently*: releases any hazardous air pollutant or extremely hazardous substance into the ambient air, and who at the time negligently places another person in imminent danger of death or serious bodily injury.[192]

Convictions carry up to a year in prison on a first conviction, and double that for a subsequent offense, even though a "guilty" individual may lack both knowledge of the underlying act and an "evil" state of mind. Neither statute defines the term "negligently," and their legislative histories provide very little clarification.

Case law is also scarce.[193] In *United States v. Hanousek*, the Ninth Circuit provided a *de novo* review of Clean Water Act Section 309(c)(1)(A), affirming the lower court's use of an ordinary negligence standard.[194] The defendant, the supervisor at a railroad construction project, was convicted of negligently discharging an estimated 1,000 to 5,000 gallons of oil into the Skagway River after a backhoe operator ruptured a high-pressure pipeline.[195] The lower court rejected Hanousek's contention that criminal negligence required "a gross deviation from the standard of care that the reasonable person would observe in that situation," and required the government to prove only that Hanousek acted negligently— that is, the "failure to use reasonable care."[196] Relying in part on *Hanousek*, the Fifth Circuit held likewise in a separate case, finding that Clean Water Act Section 309(c)(1)(A) "requires only proof of ordinary negligence."[197]

Despite the lack of abundant case law addressing these negligence standards, their potential value as a plea-bargaining tool for prosecutors and defendants should not be overlooked. For prosecutors, the negligence standard allows for a conviction even if their ability to prove knowledge at trial is on shaky ground. For defendants, settlement of a negligence violation offers reduced sentencing and penalty consequences, lessens the stigma associated with the violation from a felony to a misdemeanor, and avoids any admission of knowingly violating the underlying environmental law.

6.1.2.2 Public Welfare Offenses

Public welfare offenses are those that do not involve moral delinquency and that are "prohibited only to secure the effective regulation of conduct in the interest of the community."[198] For environmental crimes that do not prescribe a *scienter* requirement, courts have used this doctrine to hold that proof of intent is not required in order for the government to obtain a conviction (in other words, courts determined that Congress intended a strict liability offense).

Without regard to knowledge, the Refuse Act prohibits the discharge or deposit, from any ship or from the shore, of "any refuse matter . . . into navigable waters of the United States, or into any tributary," other than that flowing from streets and sewers.[199] Any person who violates that prohibition is guilty of a misdemeanor punishable by a fine, imprisonment, or both.[200] Courts have refused to read a *scienter* requirement into this statute.[201] In turn, prosecutors have used the prohibition as a strict liability enforcement tool, adding to charges that might otherwise be brought under the Clean Water Act with proof of intent or negligence.[202]

6.1.2.3 Responsible Corporate Officer Doctrine

The responsible corporate officer doctrine provides that an officer of a corporation, such as a CEO, may be prosecuted for environmental crimes based on his or her "position in the corporation [and] responsibility and authority either to prevent the first instance, or promptly to correct, the violation complained of, and that he [or she] failed to do so."[203] Essentially, the doctrine expands the list of potentially culpable parties to include those in positions to address the criminal behavior, even if those people are not directly involved in carrying out the alleged action. Determinations of guilt or innocence are not based on whether the individuals were "personally present at the time or place of the commission of" the acts or omissions.[204]

The two seminal decisions outlining the responsible corporate officer doctrine are *United States v. Dotterweich*[205] and *United States v. Park*.[206] In 1938, *Dotterweich* involved the misdemeanor conviction of a pharmaceutical company president for shipping misbranded and adulterated drugs in violation of the Federal Food, Drug, and Cosmetic Act of 1938 (FDCA).[207] The Supreme Court affirmed the conviction by concluding that a public welfare statute like the FDCA levied criminal liability on anyone who bears "a responsible share in the furtherance of the transaction which the statute outlaws."[208] In 1975, *Park* involved the conviction of a national food chain president for causing contamination of food stored in a rodent-infested warehouse in violation of the FDCA.[209] The Supreme Court rejected the executive's argument that his responsibility for sanitation had been delegated to "dependable subordinates," finding that the analysis was based on whether the defendant: (i) was in a responsible position, and (ii) had the responsibility and authority to prevent or correct the violation.[210]

The responsible corporate officer doctrine is also expressly written into the Clean Air Act and the Clean Water Act using the definition of "person." Clean Water Act Section 309(c)(6) states that for purposes of the subsection on enforcement, "the term 'person' means, in addition to the definition contained in section [502(5)] of the title, any responsible corporate officer."[211] A similar approach is taken under Clean Air Act Section 113(c)(6). The method of incorporation in these statutes—that is, via the definition of "person"—highlights an important limitation of the responsible corporate officer doctrine, namely that while the doctrine allows the government to pursue company officers for criminal responsibility, the doctrine does not negate any statutory requirement that the defendant have a prescribed level of knowledge.

Nevertheless, since direct involvement is not a prerequisite, courts have allowed circumstantial evidence to be used to prove the knowledge component. In *United States v. MacDonald & Watson Waste Oil Co.*, the Court of Appeals for the First Circuit stated that "a mere showing of corporate responsibility under *Dotterwiech* and *Park* is not an adequate substitute for direct or circumstantial proof of knowledge."[212] Conscious avoidance of the underlying act may also suffice.[213] Thus far, the responsible corporate officer doctrine has been used predominantly against officers who held more than a passive role in the criminal activities. Bear in mind that plant managers and other corporate officials are increasingly "active" in environmental matters of a company by fulfilling record-keeping and reporting requirements such as annual compliance certifications. It is not yet clear how willing courts may be to impute knowledge from subordinates to officers in the absence of any such role.

6.1.3 Defenses

Environmental criminal defenses are frequently rooted in the elements of an alleged crime, which the prosecution must prove beyond a reasonable doubt. As with the civil provisions, other defenses may be found in the complex regulatory schemes. For example, a company's EHS manager may not fall within a particular statutory definition of "person," since he or she is not involved in day-to-day operations at any particular facility, and he or she is not an officer of the company. In some instances, a good faith, but erroneous, belief in a material fact may be used as a defense.[214] Ignorance or mistake-of-law are generally not valid defenses, except perhaps for a specific intent crime that requires a knowing violation.[215]

6.1.4 Selected Non-Environmental Offenses

The charging authority of environmental prosecutors is by no means limited to offenses outlined under the major environmental statutes. According to the United States Attorneys' Manual, "experience has shown that cases involving violations of federal environmental laws . . . also may involve violations of certain other federal statutes."[216] DOJ's Environmental Crimes Section is, therefore, "empowered to investigate and prosecute violations of additional criminal statutes when such violations arise within the context of environmental crimes."[217]

Examples may include the following conventional crimes: aiding and abetting (18 U.S.C. § 2); false claims (18 U.S.C. § 287); conspiracy (18 U.S.C. § 371); theft or conversion of public property or money (18 U.S.C. § 641); false statements (18 U.S.C. § 1001); mail fraud (18 U.S.C. § 1341); wire fraud (18 U.S.C. § 1343); obstruction of administrative proceedings (18 U.S.C. § 1505); and perjury (18 U.S.C. §§ 1621 to 1623).[218]

A few of the more commonly used examples are briefly touched on below. Practitioners should keep in mind that the penalties for conventional criminal offenses have historically been harsher than those applied to environmental crimes. Moreover, the Sarbanes-Oxley Act of 2002, largely an attempt to bolster securities laws after a series of corporate scandals, also significantly increased jail time for mail and wire fraud (now up to twenty years) and directed the U.S. Sentencing Commission to strengthen the federal sentencing guidelines to reflect the get-tougher approach on corporate malfeasance.[219] Subject to constitutional questions swirling around the sentencing guidelines (discussed in section 6.3.5 below), stiffening consequences behind these conventional offenses are likely to increase their use by prosecutors in the environmental realm.

6.1.4.1 False Statements—18 U.S.C. § 1001

Section 1001, among other things, prohibits any person from knowingly and willfully making a materially false statement regarding any matter within the jurisdiction of the federal government.[220] Convictions are punishable by up to $10,000, two years imprisonment, or both.[221] In the environmental context, Section 1001 might be used for false statements made during any commonplace interaction between a company and the regulatory authorities such as a permit application process, periodic compliance certifications, or discharge monitoring reports.[222]

6.1.4.2 Mail and Wire Fraud—18 U.S.C. §§ 1341 and 1343

In relevant part, Section 1341 prohibits the use of the mails in furtherance of "any scheme or artifices to defraud or for obtaining money or property by means of false or fraudulent pretenses, representations, or promises."[223] Like the false statements crime, commonplace correspondence between a company and government officials can give rise to allegations.[224] For mail fraud, however, specific intent to defraud must be demonstrated (i.e., reckless disregard for the truth and knowingly making false representations are insufficient to establish the prima facie case).

The wire fraud statute is quite similar to the mail fraud statute. It prohibits similar activities over wire, radio, or television communication. The wire fraud statute, however, is becoming a more powerful tool for federal prosecutors. In many instances, federal prosecutors are able to assert a violation of the wire fraud statute when an environmental crime might be more difficult to prove.[225] In an age when wire fraud can encompass not only telephone calls but also e-mail traffic, the wire fraud statute is an increasingly essential part of a prosecutor's tool kit.

6.1.4.3 Conspiracy—18 U.S.C. § 371

The federal conspiracy statute prohibits two or more persons from conspiring to commit any offense against the United States.[226] Like mail fraud, conspiracy requires proof of a specific intent—here, an intent to achieve the objectives of the conspiracy. Also, proof of a conspiracy to violate a federal criminal statute requires the prosecution to prove whatever degree of *scienter* is specified in the substantive offense.[227]

Conspiracy is a very common charge in federal environmental prosecutions, particularly because environmental crimes rarely involve a single individual. Conspiracy charges also offer several tactical advantages to prosecutors enforcing environmental crimes. Perhaps foremost is the opportunity to join defendants and offenses in a single action, which allows the government to paint a more detailed picture of the alleged crime (and often to introduce evidence that might otherwise be inadmissible).

6.2 Agency Principles and Policies

The erosion of *mens rea* as a critical component of criminal liability and the use of conventional criminal statutes in the environmental realm place heightened importance on the discretion of prosecutors. A handful of policies were developed in the early 1990s to assist federal prosecutors with their decision-making, some of which are discussed below. While the nuances of these policies and the evolution of their implementation are too numerous to detail here, keep in mind that they generally serve as nonbinding guidelines, subject to outside factors such as the prevailing political environment and the individual approach of prosecutors. What emerges is an inconsistent system that promises unpredictability in determining whether a particular environmental violation will give rise to a civil action, a criminal action, or both.

6.2.1 Enforcement Referral

EPA's Office of Criminal Enforcement exercises considerable influence over the prosecution of criminal violations through its investigation function as well as its decisions on whether to refer a matter to DOJ for consideration of criminal charges. In 1994, the general principles guiding EPA's selection for cases for the criminal enforcement program were set out to focus on circumstances where significant environmental harm and culpable conduct exist.[228] Significant environmental harm includes the presence of actual harm (e.g., an illegal discharge, release, or emission), as well as the threat of significant harm (e.g., threat of an illegal discharge, release, or emission), to the environment or human health.[229] Significance is, in part, a measure of whether the illegal conduct appears to represent a trend or common attitude within the regulated community for which a criminal investigation may provide a deterrent effect on others. "Criminal prosecutions are also important in those instances where those who are required by law to provide sampling results, scientific data, or other information to governmental agencies fail to do so in an accurate and timely manner, thereby impeding the ability of those agencies to fulfill their obligations."[230]

According to EPA's guidance, culpable conduct is not solely a measure of intent and may be indicated by the following factors: (a) a history of repeat violations; (b) direct or circumstantial evidence of deliberate misconduct resulting in violation; (c) concealment of misconduct or falsification of required records; (d) tampering with monitoring or control equipment; and (e) operations without a required permit, license, manifest, or other required documentation.[231] EPA's culpability assessment also includes whether the violation was reported voluntarily and whether an effective compliance program was in place. EPA's self-disclosure policy provides that the agency will not refer a voluntarily disclosed violation to DOJ for prosecution, provided that the disclosure meets certain other conditions.[232]

6.2.2 Prosecutorial Discretion

For decisions on whether to prosecute an environmental violation criminally, a DOJ attorney's primary reference is the Principles of Federal Prosecution. Cast in general terms, these principles call for commencement of criminal prosecution if the prosecutor believes that the conduct of the person in question "constitutes a Federal offense and that the admissible evidence will probably be sufficient to obtain and sustain a conviction, unless, in his/her judgment, prosecution should be declined because: (1) no substantial Federal interest would be served by prosecution; (2) the person is subject to effective prosecution in another jurisdiction; or (3) there exists an adequate non-criminal alternative to prosecution."[233]

Except in the context of self-disclosed violations, DOJ has not published formal policies specific to the decision on whether to prosecute an environmental violation. Nevertheless, public comments from DOJ officials suggest that DOJ's emphasis will be similar to that of EPA—that is, first on the "midnight dumpers" and others operating totally outside the requirements of environmental law, and second on those who take deliberate actions to thwart environmental law.[234] For self-disclosed violations, DOJ has set out the following factors for determining whether to prosecute criminally: (1) whether the regulated entity voluntarily discloses its violation or cooperates with authorities; (2) whether the regulated entity has a pervasive level of noncompliance; (3) whether the regulated entity establishes preventative measures and compliance programs; and (4) whether the regulated entity promulgates its own internal disciplinary action and produces subsequent compliance.[235]

6.3 Progression of an Enforcement Proceeding

Criminal enforcement proceedings for environmental matters require unique and specialized legal expertise. Similar to the decision of whether to charge a person criminally, prosecutors are provided with guidelines and, to a greater extent, rules that govern how a person will be prosecuted.[236] Defense counsel must, in turn, navigate these rules while balancing other factors at play. In the environmental realm, these factors often include: multiple potential defendants (represented by multiple lawyers); the potential for a parallel civil proceeding that can give rise to hefty fines; internal investigations by the organization; media inquiries; disclosure of a criminal investigation to shareholders; privileges against self-incrimination; responding (and potentially objecting) to grand jury subpoenas and discovery requests; and the negotiation of immunities and settlements.

What follows is a thumbnail sketch of selected milestones in the progression of an enforcement proceeding. For additional detail on criminal proceedings, refer to section 11 for further readings.

6.3.1 Initiating Criminal Investigations

Investigation of a particular person or company can develop in several different ways. Violations may be brought to the government's attention pursuant to the self-reporting obligations found in one of the federal environmental statutes,[237] or through the so-called "whistle-blower" employee. In some cases, corporations voluntarily disclose a violation in order to take advantage of penalty mitigation policies and leniency from prosecution.

In other cases, investigations arise out of a scheduled or surprise inspection by an administrative inspector, or a criminal search conducted by federal agents. Most major environmental statutes authorize administrative inspections, so that agencies can monitor compliance. Although some prescribe a minimal frequency for administrative inspections (e.g., RCRA requires them every two years[238]), agencies are typically authorized to exercise their inspection authority at "reasonable times."[239] Unless exigent circumstances exist or evidence is in plain view, the government first must obtain consent from the company to conduct an inspection, obtain an administrative warrant, or obtain a criminal search warrant.[240] To obtain an administrative warrant, probable cause must show either

(1) specific evidence of an existing violation, or (2) a showing that the inspection is being conducted pursuant to a "general neutral administrative plan."[241] To obtain a criminal search warrant, probable cause must show that the search is likely to reveal evidence of a crime.[242]

Federal agents may also use informal interviews of an organization's employees to gather initial information. As a general rule, government lawyers cannot contact represented parties without consent of counsel, subject to certain exceptions that include persons who have not yet been named as parties, current employees who are not the "controlling" individuals, and former employees.[243] However, if these parties are individually represented, then government communication without the consent of counsel is generally prohibited.[244]

6.3.2 Role of the Grand Jury

A grand jury may serve both a screening function (i.e., evaluating evidence supporting possible charges to determine whether an indictment should be returned based on probable cause) and an investigative function (i.e., developing information that is of value to determining whether grounds for a charge exist).[245] For environmental criminal cases, prosecutors often use the latter to prompt the compulsory disclosure of a company's records via *subpoenas duces tecum*. Although subpoenas must specify with some reasonable degree of specificity the records covered, prosecutors are allowed broad latitude before courts are willing to quash these investigative efforts, particularly when the government is looking into corporate affairs.[246]

The investigative function of a grand jury also allows for the testimony of witnesses, with key distinctions between someone who is a "target" or a "subject" of an investigation. A "target" is "a person as to whom the prosecutor or the grand jury has substantial evidence linking him or her to the commission of a crime and who, in the judgment of the prosecutor, is a putative defendant."[247] Notably, officers or employees of a company are not automatically considered a target, even if their conduct contributed to the commission of a crime by the target company.[248] A "subject" of an investigation is "a person whose conduct is within the scope of the grand jury's investigation."[249] In determining whether to approve a subpoena for a "target," the following factors are considered: (1) the importance to the successful conduct of the grand jury's investigation of the testimony or other information sought; (2) whether the substance of the testimony or other information sought could be provided by other witnesses; and (3) whether the questions the prosecutor and the grand jurors intend to ask or the other information sought would be protected by a valid claim of privilege.[250]

6.3.3 Discovery and Proof

Unlike federal civil discovery, which allows for inquiries regarding "any matter, not privileged, that is relevant to the claim or defense of any party,"[251] federal criminal discovery is more limited. "Exceptional circumstances" must warrant the taking of a deposition or production of a document.[252] Otherwise, criminal discovery is premised on reciprocal access, allowing the government to discover documents and reports that the defendant intends to use as evidence, but only if the defendant has requested and received similar access from the government.[253] Practitioners should be wary of parallel civil and criminal proceedings throughout the discovery process, particularly because the information obtained under the more liberal structure of civil discovery generally can be used in pursuing criminal actions (absent bad faith in conducting the civil proceeding).[254]

Separately, while the burden of proof for environmental crimes parallels criminal law in general (i.e., the prosecution must prove its case beyond a reasonable doubt), the recordkeeping and reporting requirements of environmental law materially aid development of the case. In a non-environmental prosecution, investigators set out to prove every single element of a crime by cobbling together facts and data gleaned from eyewitnesses and documents. In an environmental case, on the other hand, significant portions of the prosecution's case are already laid out in databases, files, and reports that companies prepare as part of their day-to-day effort to comply with environmental law. For example, criminal violation of the CWA for unpermitted discharges to waters of the United States would require proof regarding the amount discharged, the source of the discharge, and the pollutants contained in the discharge, all of which is set forth in an organization's permit application materials and discharge monitoring records.

6.3.4 Plea Bargaining

Most criminal environmental enforcement cases are resolved through negotiated settlement, rather than trial. Specific sentencing guidelines for environmental crimes, which are discussed below, have reduced the latitude that prosecutors have during the negotiation process. Also, a plea bargain with the federal government forecloses the defendant's right of appeal, and does not preclude other sovereigns (i.e., state or tribal governments) from prosecuting an organization or person whose conduct also violated the laws of their jurisdiction. Likewise, settlement of a criminal proceeding does not necessarily resolve a defendant's liability for civil enforcement, keeping in mind that a guilty plea may serve largely to satisfy the government's prima facie case in a civil proceeding.

For individuals, one form of a plea bargain is to seek immunity in exchange for testimony. Federal immunity is available in two forms: statutory immunity (conferred pursuant to 18 U.S.C. §§ 6001–6005) and "letter" immunity (typically formalized in a letter agreement between the prosecution and the witness). "Letter" immunity does not bind federal or state prosecutors in other jurisdictions.

6.3.5 Sentencing

Criminal prosecution of an organization or an individual can lead to fines as well as imprisonment. As periodically noted above, many of the major environmental statutes prescribe maximum penalties for violation of their criminal provisions. For conventional crimes (and, to some extent, for the environmental statutes), sentences are governed by the United States Sentencing Commission (USSC) Guidelines, which include a specific section for environmental crimes.

Environmental crimes are divided into six categories: (1) knowing endangerment resulting from mishandling hazardous or toxic substances, pesticides, or other pollutants; (2) mishandling of hazardous or toxic substances or pesticides; recordkeeping, tampering, and falsification; unlawfully transporting hazardous materials in commerce; (3) mishandling of other environmental pollutants; recordkeeping, tampering, and falsification; (4) tampering or attempted tampering with a public water system; threatening to tamper with a public water system; (5) hazardous or injurious devices on federal lands; and (6) offenses involving fish, wildlife, and plants.[255] Subject to judicial and prosecutorial discretion, factors for adjustment or departure from these categories are also provided.[256]

On November 1, 2008, a new set of federal sentencing guidelines became effective.[257] The USSC often wrestles with controversial issues and considers amendments to the guidelines.[258] In 2006, the USSC voted unanimously to reverse a 2004 amendment to the sentencing guidelines that allowed federal prosecutors to pressure entities to waive their attorney-client and work product protections as a condition for receiving credit for cooperation during investigations.[259] As previously discussed, further sentencing developments may arise in response to the Sarbanes-Oxley Act of 2002, which directs the USSC to strengthen the federal sentencing guidelines to reflect the get-tougher approach on corporate malfeasance.[260]

In the mid-2000s, the constitutionality of entire sentencing guideline schemes was brought under serious fire, premised on the grounds that judges are allowed to consider sentence-enhancing factors about a crime that were not admitted by the defendant and not shown to a jury at trial. In *Blakely v. Washington*,[261] the Supreme Court held that sentencing guidelines used in the state of Washington violated the Sixth Amendment because evidence used for sentencing was not proven beyond a reasonable doubt to a jury. In *United States v. Booker*, the Supreme Court then applied its reasoning in *Blakely* to the federal sentencing guidelines and held that statutory language making the guidelines mandatory must be invalidated.[262] Even before the *Booker* decision was released, USSC was already exploring alternative approaches to attaining the goal of diminishing sentencing disparity.[263] At least one study evaluating data between 2004 and

2007 has shown that environmental defendants received prison terms less frequently than other federal defendants (a little over one-third of the time versus more than 80 percent).[264] Of those environmental defendants who were sentenced to prison, more than half received below-range sentences.[265]

7.0 Avoidance and Mitigation of Environmental Enforcement and Liability

As we have seen, the federal environmental laws form a web of requirements that may entangle a company in legal enforcement and liability of various kinds. Given the potential consequences (in terms of potential fines, negative publicity, jail terms, capital investments, etc.), companies have developed specialized corporate systems designed to help them avoid such responsibility or, if avoidance fails, to help them mitigate the repercussions. Two widely used systems relate to assessment through auditing and improvement through better management. Both are pertinent to ongoing operations of the business. Assessment programs are also useful when evaluating the acquisition of new operations or the divestiture of existing ones; we consider such transactions-related issues separately, under "Corporate Transactions."

7.1 Corporate Systems for Environmental Assessment

Environmental laws are complex technical and legal documents. They invite both misunderstanding and disagreement. Moreover, environmental laws vary according to the EPA region and the individual state in which they are applied, and they may differ in important respects from internal corporate policies that seek to establish uniformity across a multistate or multinational set of operations. In the face of such complexity, a company might wish to avoid the topic of environmental law altogether, but by now most established companies in the United States have learned that cultivating ignorance of environmental issues does nothing to protect the company against legal responsibility, often causes the issues to fester, and may spur the government to consider more severe punishments than it otherwise would.

With prudence as their guide, many companies have instead created auditing programs to help ensure that the company is aware of its status in relation to applicable law and is in a position to correct concerns and avoid or mitigate any liability. Company audit programs vary widely in their scope, sophistication, and evolution, but they tend to share five key attributes:

- they are periodic (e.g., all facilities are audited on a multiyear cycle);

- they are comprehensive as to subject matter (tackling air, water, waste, permitting, recordkeeping, and many other compliance topics);

- they are implemented by trained auditors, often outside experts paired with in-house personnel from facilities other than the facility being audited;

- they result in a written report that is used as the basis for subsequent checkups on the status of issues identified in the report; and

- they are prepared at the direction and with the involvement of legal counsel, in order to support the legal work of the company and, derivatively, to help secure the audit report against unwanted discovery in legal proceedings.

For example, a corporate auditing program at a large manufacturing company might require an audit of the company's major manufacturing facilities every three years and of its warehouse and other less heavily regulated facilities every six years. The audit might cover compliance with laws, regulations, permits, policies, and procedures in all of the major program areas as well as a basic field-level review of on-site conditions, relevant historical uses of the audited site, and other uses and environmental issues in the area surrounding the site. The audit team might include an environmental lawyer, an outside technical consultant trained in auditing, and an in-house environmental engineer conversant with corporate policy. Before arriving at the facility, the audit team might review prior audit reports, be briefed on the nature of the operations at the facility, and send to the facility a pre-audit checklist of documents that should be available for on-site review. Once on site, the auditors would review these documents (permits and permit applications, release reports, waste manifests, corporate policy documents, etc.) and interview relevant personnel. The field review would include a guided walk-through of the entire property (facility, storage areas, parking areas, unimproved land, etc.), with follow-up interviews as necessary to complete the picture.

The resulting audit report would typically not be given to the facility either orally or in writing until it had passed through outside counsel and/or the company's corporate legal and environmental departments for review and comment. On occasion, such review prompts follow-up interviews to clarify an issue, fill a perceived gap, or correct a misunderstanding. The lawyer who directs the audit then typically sends the final audit report to the facility's management for review and corrective action. Check-up efforts in subsequent weeks and months track the facility's progress on the issues identified in the audit.

The benefits of auditing are numerous. First and foremost, audits identify latent environmental compliance concerns (and, depending upon the audit's scope, also conditions of contamination) that require attention by the company if it is to avoid or mitigate responsibility under environmental law. Beyond this elemental purpose, audits serve several other useful functions:

- they stimulate environmental awareness and stewardship at the facility level;

- they document regulatory status in a manner consistent across a company, thereby allowing comparisons to be drawn and systemic issues grasped;

- they can spread innovative environmental ideas from one facility to another;

- they propound and inculcate corporate environmental policies; and

- they prepare a historical record for use in avoiding or defending legal proceedings.

That said, audits can be severely misused or so misdesigned that they fail to achieve their purpose or even invite environmental liability. Classic errors include the application of premature or improperly absolute conclusions respecting compliance status, using outdated protocols or legal references, preventing the auditors from using common sense in assessing the severity of an issue or the credibility of an interviewee, unnecessarily using legally loaded language to describe findings, insisting that auditors follow a script to the exclusion of following their instincts, and accepting the resolution of an issue on the basis of a promise that it will be done. Audits can also be a detriment when a company considers the audit itself to be the goal, rather than a precursor to improvement: audit findings that are not addressed are now documented and may be viewed as knowing or willful in the absence of prompt, appropriate, and effective corrective measures.

What to do with audit results is a perennial question. Companies often perform triage to rank the severity of the audit findings according to (a) their potential for harm to human health or the environment, (b) the potential for penalties or other financial harm, and (c) the likelihood of becoming more severe absent countermeasures. With priorities in hand, the company sets about planning and implementing corrective measures, which generally are noted in the audit files.

Internal corrective efforts, onerous as they sometimes seem, are often easier to decide upon than whether the audit findings demand or otherwise merit self-disclosure to the government. For example, if an audit turns up a significant discrepancy between actual air emissions output and what was stated in the air permit application, what communications with their permitting authority are required, and how does one initiate such a communication? In these matters the practices of U.S. companies still vary widely. Some have gathered enough experience in self-disclosure that they have developed a clear statement of factors to be taken into account in considering when and how to self-disclose; others treat each circumstance separately without much regard for precedent within the company (perhaps because there is no precedent or the precedent no longer reflects the company's priorities).

7.2 Corporate Systems for Environmental Management

Corporate systems for improving environmental performance have developed in parallel with the trend toward systematic environmental auditing. The two are not the same, though they should interrelate in useful ways once properly implemented. Environmental management systems (EMSs), epitomized by the ISO 14001 standards, focus directly on the processes and infrastructure necessary for optimum environmental performance, rather than measuring the performance itself, on the theory that better processes and infrastructure lead to substantially greater improvements in performance than does a reactive cycle of audits, corrective measures, and more audits.

The guiding principles of EMS are not new: they derive from continuous-improvement ideas developed decades ago and applied in areas like production and finance. What is newer is the notion that these principles find legitimate and beneficial application to the complex world of environmental issues. EMS is not just the flavor of the month, any more than rigorous production methods are a fad. Doubtless, the particulars of EMS will continue to evolve, as they have in the past decade, but the core idea that environmental performance improves as a result of improved methods for managing environmental issues has found a permanent place in corporate America.

EMS varies according to the complexity, size, and objectives of the organization adopting it. It is, after all, a concept whose usefulness lies in tailoring general business-improvement principles to the particularities of the company. One size does not fit all. That said, two or three models for EMS have taken root internationally and within the United States, and among these the model developed by the International Standards Organization probably has the widest following. It is explored in detail in chapter 17 of this volume. For our purposes, it is sufficient to note that EMS is organized around certain requirements that establish the necessary infrastructure for systematic improvement. Key elements of the infrastructure include:

- publicizing a corporate policy of environmental compliance;

- assigning responsibility within the company's hierarchy;

- identifying significant environmental aspects of the company's business;

- setting reference standards (including, but not only, legal standards);
- establishing environmental goals and the metrics to measure progress toward them;
- developing operational controls that support the goals;
- implementing programs for training, monitoring, and communicating in relation to environmental matters;
- auditing and documenting the foregoing to identify gaps and appropriate improvements.

For companies new to EMS, these elements can be daunting. They entail nothing less than full corporate acceptance that environmental issues must be integrated into the daily management and operation of the company. Many first-timers are wise to start slowly, beginning with basic assessments of their operations, internal capabilities, and corporate objectives. Proceeding stepwise thereafter helps to ensure that environmental vision does not outstrip corporate reality. With the benefit of some years' experience, companies can work toward "shadow" certification and, later, true certification of adherence to the ISO standard for EMS (or another chosen standard). Such certifications, provided by recognized outside experts working in close coordination with the company, are valuable indicators to customers and government officials alike, although it must be remembered that ISO certification says nothing whatever about actual environmental impact or legal compliance.

7.3 Corporate Transactions

A company's current operations are not the only potential source of environmental responsibility and liability. A company may acquire problems directly through the acquisition of other companies and assets, and it may retain environmental problems despite the divestiture of the assets from which the problems originally arose. Accordingly, companies seeking to avoid or mitigate their environmental exposure approach corporate transactions with a rigorous program for identifying, assessing, and allocating environmental issues during the acquisition (or divestiture) phase, and for managing the issues after the deal has closed.

To start with, a company must understand how environmental responsibility and liability can move from one entity to another. Three pathways merit mention here.

7.3.1 Corporate Succession

The business law of each state establishes the legal principles that govern the combining of business entities by merger, acquisition of stock, acquisition of assets, and so forth. Such laws describe the circumstances under which the entity resulting from the combination is vested with all or some of the rights and obligations of the acquired (or merged) entity or assets. Since the purpose of combining businesses is, generally, to transfer one entity's business or assets to another, state business laws generally promote the idea that the resulting entity stands in the shoes of the entity it has acquired and therefore also inherits whatever liabilities the acquired entity had at the time of purchase.

The acquisition of the outstanding stock of a company will typically vest the surviving entity with all the environmental responsibilities of the target company. By contrast, the purchase of selected assets, rather than stock, may limit the transfer of liabilities because as a general rule only the liabilities attached to the assets are conveyed to the buyer. However, environmental law abhors stranded liabilities and therefore disfavors crafty efforts to split assets or businesses from their liabilities before the contemplated purchase.

7.3.2 Chain of Title or Possession

Environmental law does not always temper justice with mercy, in the sense that the entity that originally caused an environmental mishap may not be the only potential target for liability. Among others in the liability zone are those entities that own or operate the property where the environmental problem exists. By nature, corporate transactions broaden the class of owners and operators either by creating new entities that are owners and operators (say, by merger) or by vesting existing entities with new ownership or operational responsibility.

7.3.3 Private Agreement

Companies may agree by contract to share or reallocate environmental responsibility between them. Agreements for the purchase and sale of businesses or assets frequently accomplish such an allocation of environmental responsibility between buyer and seller. Allocations can range from the basic, in which the seller keeps pre-closing liabilities while the buyer accepts post-closing liabilities, to the baroque, in which the allocation depends upon many factors spelled out in the contract. Whether straightforward or complex, private agreements can effectively redistribute environmental liability, but they cannot alter the initial assignment of responsibility or liability under applicable law.

In other words, if statutory or common law imposes an obligation upon a specific entity, that entity typically remains responsible regardless of a private contractual allocation between that entity and another. The benefit of the private agreement is not so much to relieve a liable party from liability vis-à-vis the government (or an enforcing private party), as to secure financial or other protection against the effects of liability: the liable party can seek reimbursement (or assert other useful rights).[266]

Given these pathways by which environmental liability moves from one entity to another, businesses contemplating a corporate acquisition expend considerable effort in advance of the deal to assess the actual and potential liabilities of the business or assets to be acquired. The assessment effort typically includes a "due diligence" inquiry, in which the future acquirer investigates the environmental performance of the target entity, reviews pertinent documents and governmental databases, and conducts field inspections of the properties involved in the transaction. In addition to its own efforts, the acquiring company may force the target company (or the seller of assets, if it's an asset deal) to disclose pertinent environmental information to the acquirer pursuant to the contract for purchase and sale. Contractual disclosures come in the form of representations and warranties in the agreement, such as a representation that the company has for the last five years complied with applicable environmental law in all material respects, except as disclosed on a specified schedule to the agreement.

Guided by the results of its assessment efforts, the acquiring company adjusts its financial expectations (price, etc.) accordingly and negotiates appropriate substantive terms concerning the expected or feared environmental responsibilities and liabilities. In some transactions, the business leaders agree that the seller should be left largely without residual risk of environmental liabilities after the deal closes, even if it means the seller receives less favorable financial terms (to hedge the acquirer's risk). In other circumstances, the parties agree that the seller should have continuing responsibility for certain pre-closing matters and should be required (contractually) to reimburse the buyer after the closing for costs the buyer incurs as a result of specific classes of environmental risk or liability. Indemnities are a classic means for governing such reimbursement arrangements, and they are often at the heart of a transaction involving assets or businesses with significant environmental impairment.

A special case in the world of transactions is the loan transaction, in which a financial entity like a bank makes a monetary commitment to a business. The lender may take a secured interest in certain or all of the hard assets and receivables of the borrower in order to hedge the risk that the borrower will not fulfill its repayment obligations. Environmental law factors into the equation in at least two respects, from the lender's standpoint. First, to the extent the lender could be tainted with the environmental liabilities of the borrower, the lender must assess and allocate such liabilities much as would a buyer in a corporate transaction. Second, to the extent the borrower's ability to repay the lender could be impaired as a result of financial pressure from environmental responsibilities of the borrower, the lender has a vested interest in assessing the environmental liabilities of the borrower.

As to the first, which considers direct lender liability for the environmental ills of the borrower, environmental law has evolved toward the concept of a (relatively) safe harbor for lenders. The safe harbor concept, epitomized by CER-CLA § 101(20),[267] holds that a lender should by law be insulated from direct liability of the borrower so long as the lender acts only within the confines of its status as a lender and does not expand its role to include the management or operation of the business or the specific environmental issues giving rise to the borrower's liability. In short, the more the borrower looks and acts like a borrower, the easier it can insulate itself from direct environmental liability.[268]

As to the second point, which considers indirect effects upon the lender by virtue of the borrower's environmental liabilities, environmental law offers no protection. If the borrower becomes deeply committed to environmental expenditures (say, to pay for required remediation at third-party disposal sites) and can no longer repay the lender on the agreed terms, the risk is the lender's—hence the desire of lenders to secure debts with liquid or readily convertible assets. In the case of secured interests in contaminated property, however, a lender considering foreclosing on the property must bear in mind the strictures on its conduct, lest the lender find itself in the role of manager or operator of the contamination: that may trigger direct environmental liability of the lender.

7.3.4 Interim Approach for Applying EPA's Audit Policy

On August 1, 2008, the EPA formally announced a new "Interim Approach"[269] for applying its policy on "Incentives for Self-Policing: Discovery, Disclosure, Correction and Prevention of Violations," commonly referred to as the "Audit Policy."[270] The Interim Approach offers incentives to new owners of regulated facilities and companies if they assess, disclose, and correct environmental noncompliance at the newly acquired facilities or companies. Specific incentives include penalty mitigation over and above what is already provided in the Audit Policy and the modification of some of the Audit Policy conditions to better fit the transactional context.[271] EPA acknowledges that transactions can often give rise to the discovery of noncompliance and that new owners that audit, disclose, and correct should be eligible for penalty relief for violations that commenced before they took control of a noncompliant facility or company. The Interim Approach provides a clearer, streamlined path for audit disclosures in transactional contexts, and the EPA anticipates it will continue to increase the opportunities for using the Audit Policy and encourage the disclosure of more significant types of compliance findings. Although EPA has developed a new approach to E-Disclosure under the Audit Policy in most contexts, new owners can continue to pursue audit agreements and make written disclosures without following the E-Disclosure process.

8.0 New Trends in Enforcement and Liability

Various trends in enforcement and liability can be observed and deserve note. We address six trends, selected in part to show the variety of factors at work in reshaping environmental law on a daily basis.

8.1 SEC Compliance and Investor Relations

An ever larger dimension of climate change law and policy relates to the obligation of publicly traded companies to disclose material risks, trends, and liabilities to shareholders. For several years, shareholder activists have been pressing for more, as well as more detailed, corporate disclosures concerning climate change and the broader topic of sustainability and governance. The SEC is currently exploring a major modification of the existing regulatory framework for corporate disclosures under the Securities Act of 1933 and the Securities Exchange Act of 1934 (the '33 and '34 Acts, or the Acts). And the New York Attorney General has been pursuing highly visible investigations of certain energy companies to assess whether they deliberately misled the markets concerning climate change. Climate disclosure promises to be an important area of policy change and enforcement action in the coming years.

The number of companies providing climate disclosures has risen over the past ten years, and it continues to grow. By 2009, about 45 percent of S&P 500 companies were making climate-related disclosures in their annual reports on SEC Form 10-K; by 2013, the number was 60 percent, and rising.[272] Moreover, the number of investors signing on to investment principles relating to sustainability has also risen significantly. For example, in 2009, some 560 institutional investors with $18 trillion in assets had committed to the United Nations Principles for Responsible Investment (PRI). By 2014, the number was over 1,200 investors with $34 trillion in assets. The current number (2016) is in excess of 1,500 investors.[273]

The '33 and '34 Acts require disclosure of material information relating to the financial condition and business prospects of the publicly traded company. The '33 and '34 Acts were designed to respond to the crushing financial losses sustained during and after the 1929 stock market crash. Congress recognized that a well-functioning capital market relies on accurate, timely information concerning what is significant to the financial interests of investors and the financial condition and prospects of companies. The intent of the '33 and '34 Acts was to restore the public's confidence in capital markets and to enable investors to pursue and protect their financial interests.

For environmental matters, decisions on whether and how to disclose an enforcement risk or proceeding are most often wrapped into an analysis of the nonfinancial disclosure requirements set forth in Items 101, 103, and 303 of the SEC's Regulation S-K.[274] In particular, disclosure of pending legal proceedings under environmental law is often required (and may extend beyond what is financially material to the company).[275]

The prevailing belief, at least at EPA, has been that the practice of environmental disclosure is deficient. In 1998, an EPA study concluded that 10-K filings in 1996 and 1997 failed to report environmental legal proceedings 74 percent of the time.[276] As a result, officials are now instructed to distribute a notice concerning the potential applicability of corporate disclosure requirements as part of any enforcement actions.[277] In 2001, EPA also issued an Enforcement Alert notifying companies of the scope of their disclosure requirements.[278]

Corporate scandals like Enron, Arthur Andersen, and WorldCom intensified the focus of investors, lawmakers, regulators, lawyers, and others on disclosure. But comparatively few enforcement actions have been initiated by the SEC—the principal disclosure regulator—in relation to *environmental* disclosures. In part this is a reflection of the increasing amounts of environmental disclosure being made both formally in SEC filings and informally in corporate websites and sustainability reports.

Things took a turn September 2007, when the attorney general of New York subpoenaed five large energy companies seeking to determine whether their SEC disclosures adequately addressed the financial risks of global warming pollution.[279] Nearly one year later, two of the energy companies reached agreements under which the AG discontinued the inquiries and the companies agreed to disclose and discuss material financial risks posed by climate change, such as future regulation, climate change litigation, and the actual physical impacts of climate change.[280] These commitments did not take the companies beyond their existing disclosure obligations under the '33 and '34 Acts, but the agreements heralded a new front in potential environmental enforcement.

A few years later, on January 27, 2010, by a vote of three to two, the SEC itself adopted new interpretive guidance on how public companies should evaluate the impacts of climate change in their communications with shareholders.[281] This guidance[282] was long sought by certain pension funds, shareholder advocacy groups, and states, who were dissatisfied with the climate change disclosures of certain corporations. The guidance, however, did not modify the principal tenets of disclosure law. As the underlying laws and disclosure requirements remain the same, there has not been a noticeable change in the disclosures made by corporations.

In 2015, the New York Attorney General opened a new investigation, probing the disclosures of ExxonMobil Corporation and the company's decisions and assessments concerning climate change and the company's strategies for shaping the policy debate around climate legislation and regulation.[283] Although details are confidential, the investigation has garnered attention in Congress and among disclosure activists, while it has also drawn critical assessments of its legal premises and validity.[284]

In April 2016, the SEC published a "concept release" that invites public dialogue about whether to amend and expand the federal disclosure laws to mandate disclosure on social and environmental policy issues, including sustainability and climate change.[285] Since the disclosure laws already require disclosure for material issues (of all stripes, not only environmental), such a regulatory change would necessarily involve mandating disclosure *beyond* what is material to the company in order to respond to—or perhaps even drive—public disclosure on these policy issues. The concept release will be debated by shareholder activist groups, traditional investors, and companies for quite some time. If it ultimately results in regulatory change, enforcement interest is likely to rise with respect to environmental disclosure, even as companies are adapting to a new regulatory regime.

The SEC's disclosure requirements, the investigative power of the New York Martin Act, and investor opinion are likely to continue to influence how the regulated community navigates enforcement risk in relation to environmental disclosure issues and environmental enforcement actions, particularly as the regulatory framework for Sarbanes-Oxley takes shape and the investing public's access to environmental information continues to grow.[286]

8.2 Financial Accounting Standards

In 2008, the FASB proposed a new rule that would, in all but a few respects, replace the iconic FAS 5 standard, which was recodified in 2009 as the Accounting Standards Codification Topic 450 (ASC 450).[287] ASC 450 has for decades governed corporate accounting for loss contingencies.[288] ASC 450 holds that a charge to income must be accrued if (a) current information indicates that a loss contingency is *probable* and (b) the amount of loss can be *reasonably estimated*.[289] Even when an accrual is not mandated, disclosure of the loss contingency is required if there is at least a *reasonable possibility* that a loss or additional loss will occur.[290] Disclosure is not required if the loss contingency is an unasserted claim that the potential claimant appears to be unaware of, unless the loss contingency is probable and an unfavorable outcome is a reasonable possibility.[291] In practice, these requirements have led many companies to disclose limited information about environmental loss contingencies, given the uncertainties that often surround the probability and magnitude of environmental losses. Critics[292] have repeatedly argued for expanded environmental disclosure requirements, but without much success to date.

FASB proposed requiring expanded disclosure of certain loss contingencies, starting in fiscal years ending after December 15, 2008—thereby capturing Form 10-Ks filed for calendar year 2008. The proposal did not seek to rescind ASC 450, but suggested replacing "the disclosure requirements in Statement 5" for loss contingencies that are recognized under ASC 450, as well as for those that exist but currently would not need to be recognized under ASC 450. The proposal addressed only loss contingencies that are "liabilities," leaving unchanged the disclosure requirements under FAS 5 for loss contingencies arising from the impairment of assets.[293] Since environmental loss contingencies fall overwhelmingly into the category of "liabilities," the proposed rule—not FAS 5—was viewed as the latest disclosure standard for environmental loss contingencies.

Amid pressures and concerns that escalated during the comment period, FASB's proposal was withdrawn for the time being. Nevertheless, given the importance of ASC 450, the key elements of the board's proposal offer insight into aspects of the standard that some view as controversial:

- ASC 450 would no longer have been the standard governing the disclosure of loss contingencies that are liabilities. The new standard would have governed such disclosures while leaving ASC 450 as the governing standard for loss contingencies that are asset impairments.[294]

- Qualitative disclosure obligations would have been greatly extended to include, "at a minimum," a description of the contingency, how it arose, its legal basis, its current status, the most likely outcome, the timing of the outcome, the factors affecting the outcome, key assumptions in analyzing the outcome, and the qualitative and quantitative aspects of rights to recovery through insurance or indemnity.

- A tabular array of aggregated loss contingencies would need to have been provided with every statement of income to show the increase/decrease in loss contingencies, payouts, estimates, recoveries from insurance, and so on over the reporting period.

- Significant aspects of the tabular reconciliation would need to have been discussed, and companies would have been required to identify the line items in the statement of financial position in which loss contingencies were recognized.

- Disclosure would have been required even for a loss contingency liability that is not reasonably possible, if it is expected to be resolved "in the near term" (one year or less) and it "could" have a "severe" impact on the company.

- Even when disclosure would have been prejudicial to the outcome of the contingency itself (e.g., disclosure of unasserted claims against the company), the disclosure would have been required in an aggregated (higher level) format such as the tabular reconciliation unless, in a "rare" instance, even aggregated disclosure would be prejudicial, in which case only the specific information that would be prejudicial could have been withheld.

8.3 Natural Resource Damages

The commencement of an enforcement action after a release of hazardous substances or oil may also trigger parallel or future claims for natural resource damages. As discussed further in chapter 7, in the event that publicly owned natural resources are damaged or destroyed by a release of hazardous substances or oil, natural resource damage (NRD) claims are designed to compensate the public for the loss. Under CERCLA and OPA, federal agencies charged with responsibility for investigation and response (i.e., EPA or the Coast Guard) are required to notify and coordinate with the Natural Resource Trustees (NRTs).[295] The NRTs, who may include federal, state, and tribal officials, are then authorized to bring causes of action against potentially responsible parties based on an assessment of the injury to natural resources and the costs to return the natural resources to their baseline condition.[296]

NRD claims are often not resolved until after enforcement actions for the underlying release are concluded. In fact, for a site on the NPL (and not a federal facility), the statute of limitations for NRDs only requires that an action be filed within three years of completing all remedial action at the site.[297] For a site not on the NPL (and not a federal facility), the statute of limitations does not run until three years after the date that the loss and its connection to the release in question are discovered.[298] Since the nature and extent of injury may not be known for some time, let alone the connection of an injury to a specific release, the potential for NRD claims can linger for many years.

Insufficient federal and state financial resources have until recently hampered efforts to address the legal and technical complexities of NRD assessments. In the early 2000s, however, trustees became increasingly active in the pursuit of NRDs, particularly at the state level, in part fueled by the realization that NRDs are an untapped source of income for state coffers. In New Jersey, for example, NRD recoveries in 2003 exceeded the total for the six prior years combined, and the state's DEP commissioner announced plans to eventually pursue as many as 4,000 natural resource damage claims against responsible parties.[299] New Jersey has indicated an intent to rely on outside attorneys to process the state's claims for damages to natural resources, on a contingent fee basis.[300]

Resolution of an enforcement action involving a release of hazardous substances is often not the end of the road. Settlement terms, insurance policies, reserve analyses, property conveyance documents, and other risk management mechanisms will need to take into account potential NRD claims, particularly as the natural resource trustees refine their ability to calculate and pursue these types of claims.

8.4 EPA's Next Generation Enforcement

In 2014, EPA unveiled its "Next Generation Compliance: Strategic Plan for 2014–2017."[301] EPA describes its "NextGen" plan as "an integrated strategy, designed to bring together the best thinking from inside and outside EPA on how to structure regulations and permits combined with new monitoring and information technology, expanded transparency, and innovative enforcement." NextGen includes five interconnected components, focused on (1) More Effective Regulations and Permits; (2) Developing Advanced Monitoring; (3) Shifting to Electronic Reporting; (4) Increasing Transparency by Making Information More Accessible; and (5) Using the Next Generation Compliance Principles and Tools to Strengthen Enforcement.[302] While NextGen is perceived by many as a "branding" exercise more than anything, there are some tangible enforcement tools EPA hopes to develop. With respect to advanced monitoring, EPA wants to increase the use of cutting-edge technology—e.g., IR cameras and differential absorption LIDAR—and focus on real-time monitoring. Additionally, the increasing shift to electronic reporting means that the regulated community is providing more and more data directly to the agency in a searchable, electronic format. Easily searchable data allows the Agency to better understand the information and better evaluate patterns that might inform information requests, investigations and enforcement cases. For example, in 2015, EPA Region 6 issued RCRA Section 3007 information requests to permitted hazardous waste disposal facilities in order to identify waste generators that had shipped large quantities of hazardous waste to those facilities for disposal. EPA next would cross-check the records of the permitted waste disposal facilities against its own database of registered Large Quantity Generators (LQGs). Through this purely desktop exercise, and with no physical site inspections, EPA was able to identify parties that had shipped large quantities of hazardous waste but not registered as LQGs. EPA then would issue information requests—and potentially notices of violation—to the waste generators that failed to register.

Making data available to the public could also catalyze an increase in citizen suits as environmental groups and the public at large can focus in on regulated entities that might otherwise not gain the scrutiny of EPA. However, it is not just the average public that will utilize this data. Competitors will inevitably mine that data to see how they are performing compared to others in industry, which from EPA's point of view can lead to a "race to the top." The effects of the NextGen plan are already being felt by industry as EPA has incorporated advanced monitoring, electronic reporting, and increased transparency into civil and criminal case resolutions, e.g., requiring fence line monitors to report air pollution and making results available to the public or requiring third-party verification of compliance status.

8.5 Methane Enforcement Initiative

In support of the Obama Administration's Climate Action Plan, EPA is taking a multifaceted approach to reducing methane emissions in the oil and gas industry. That approach includes using next-generation monitoring to capture current violations, promulgating regulations to reduce methane emissions at new sources and collecting information from industry to better understand how additional regulations might further reduce methane emissions from existing sources.

With respect to enforcement, in April 2015, EPA reached a settlement with an oil and gas company regarding the alleged failure to control VOC emissions from multiple condensate storage tanks in Colorado. The company paid a $4.95 million civil penalty, committed to approximately $60 million in injunctive relief and $4.5 million in mitigation projects. The case arose after EPA and the state identified significant VOC emissions coming from the storage tanks. While the enforcement matter cites VOC emissions, it is widely understood that the reduction in VOCs has the co-benefit of reducing methane emissions.

On the regulatory front, on May 12, 2016, EPA issued regulations to control methane emissions from new oil and gas sources, along with a proposed information collection request seeking information regarding methane emissions from existing oil and gas sources to support future existing source regulations. These actions are part of the Obama Administration's Climate Action Plan to address climate change and fulfill the commitments the Administration made in 2015 to the international community in Paris.

8.6 State Attorneys General

While state-specific environmental enforcement is beyond the scope of this chapter, the growing national presence of state attorneys general in the environmental arena warrants mention. Over the past several years, various state attorneys general have banded together to file lawsuits against EPA with regard to its promulgation and implementation of environmental regulations. A portion of the litigation is rooted in statutory authority under environmental law. Section

126(b) of the Clean Air Act allows states to petition EPA for a finding that emissions from a major source or group of stationary sources in another state would interfere with the petitioning state's ability to implement its plan to attain certain air quality standards.[303]

State attorneys general have also found footing in rulemaking litigation under the Administrative Procedures Act. In October 1998, EPA finalized its ozone transport rule, also known as the "NOx SIP Call" (codified as 40 C.F.R. Part 96).[304] Several state attorneys general filed legal challenges and obtained a deferral of the rule and suspension of deadlines pending further review by the U.S. Court of Appeals for the District of Columbia.[305] The Court of Appeals upheld EPA's rule, although the lawsuits managed to delay implementation and three states (Georgia, South Carolina, and Wisconsin) were eventually removed from the rule.[306] As discussed above, similar rulemaking litigation was spawned in response to NSR rulemaking and EPA's enforcement initiative. More recently, twenty-nine state attorneys general filed suit against EPA regarding the Clean Power Plan, claiming that EPA lacks authority under the Clean Air Act to require states to cut carbon emissions from power plants by 32 percent from 2005 levels by 2030; eighteen other state AGs have vowed to help EPA defend the plan.[307] Implementation of the plan has been stayed pending judicial review.[308] The case will be reviewed by the D.C. Circuit *en banc* and oral arguments are set to begin on September 27, 2016.[309]

8.7 Utilizing Federal Enforcement to Increase Compliance

Another recent trend is that federal officials have been using criminal enforcement against large companies to increase compliance expectations. The most well-known example of this type of enforcement occurred in the aftermath of the April 2010 explosion that occurred on the Deepwater Horizon oil rig.[310] The Deepwater Horizon accident killed eleven workers[311] and released millions of barrels of oil into the Gulf of Mexico and onto the shorelines of coastal states.[312] Following the accident, the lessee, BP PLC, agreed to plead guilty to a dozen felony charges and two misdemeanors.[313] To settle the criminal charges arising from the incident, BP agreed to pay $4.0 billion in fines and penalties.[314] These penalties are in addition to the potential civil penalties BP may face for Clean Water Act violations, the cost of cleaning up the spill, and natural resource damages.[315] In addition, BP agreed to retain a process safety and risk management auditor to oversee its process safety, risk management and drilling equipment used for deepwater drilling in the Gulf of Mexico.[316] BP also agreed to retain an ethics monitor to ensure BP responds to the government with appropriate candor in the future.[317] Meanwhile, Transocean Ltd., the drilling contractor involved in the incident, agreed to pay $400 million in criminal fines and penalties for Clean Water Act violations and $1 billion in civil penalties for its role in the incident.[318] Under the terms of the agreement, Transocean is also required to improve its operational safety and emergency response capabilities at all drilling rigs operating in waters of the United States.[319] The incident spurred increased regulatory obligations for offshore drilling.[320] Attempts to hold BP employees responsible for their individual roles in the spill were largely unsuccessful. Of the five individuals charged, including a BP Vice President and two well site leaders, the majority of charges (including manslaughter) were dropped and no jail time was imposed.[321]

In a separate matter, DOJ brought three criminal cases against Wal-Mart Stores, Inc. for environmental violations related to improperly handling pesticides and hazardous wastes. Wal-Mart agreed to pay $81.6 million for negligently violating the Clean Water Act in California and violations of FIFRA in Missouri.[322] In conjunction with the criminal cases, Wal-Mart paid another $7.628 million in civil penalties and was required to implement a comprehensive, nationwide compliance plan to manage hazardous waste generated at its stores and to properly train personnel to handle such personnel.[323]

9.0 Final Thoughts

It is tempting, but misguided, to view the rules and practices of environmental enforcement as a static system. Much of the enforcement lexicon was indeed written ages ago (the *mens rea* requirement, for example, has ancient roots in European law), and revolutionary change is in any event rare in our American legal system. Nevertheless, enforcement principles do change from time to time because the world around them changes constantly. So in parting we offer a few thoughts on larger themes relevant to the environmental laws and their enforcement.

9.1 Cyclical Environmental Law

Environmental law is cyclical by nature, at various scales. Modern American environmental law was fledged in the early 1970s, took wing in the late 1970s and 1980s, flew to new (perhaps even oxygen-deprived) heights in the 1990s, settled into a long, irreversible decline toward the mundane or irrelevant, and regained prominence around 2010 in the wake of the Deepwater Horizon oil spill, the natural gas boom, and increasing public attention to global warming. On a small scale, environmental law renews itself regularly through new regulatory promulgations, new policies and guidelines, even new statutory pronouncements. On a larger scale, environmental law, like most bodies of law, is perpetually in a cycle of creation, interpretation, enforcement, and reinterpretation as the agencies, courts, and regulated communities accumulate wisdom (or at least shift their emphases).

Although relatively little new federal environmental legislation has been enacted in recent years, there has been an uptick in regulatory activity, as the executive branch's approach to environmental issues has changed from the Bush administration to the Obama administration, and now to the second Obama administration. This legislative gap has also been filled to some extent as environmental enforcement has increased by non-environmental agencies such as state attorneys general. Moreover, one must acknowledge the role that the regulated community plays in this cycle. Industry undertakes massive financial investments in order to comply with environmental law. Ironically, once such investments are made, the regulated community has an incentive to stabilize, rather than substantially diminish, the applicable environmental requirements.

9.2 Science Matters

Law does not invariably lead to justice, nor science to truth. Both are imperfect arts, but their interaction is an essential element of environmental law. Science is in many respects the first foundation for environmental law and enforcement, which are both directed toward the protection of human health and the environment (a matter of scientific inquiry). Under TSCA, for example, EPA must evaluate scientific information on a new chemical substance's risks in order to determine what legal actions are appropriate to regulate the substance (through outright prohibition, a Section 5(e) consent order, exclusion or exemption, etc.). Likewise, under the technology-forcing provisions of the Clean Air Act, the regulated community must invest in ever more effective (though not necessarily more efficient or cost-effective) technologies for reducing airborne pollutants, and these technologies evolve according to scientific study.

The reliance upon science is just as evident in the enforcement context. Wastewater discharge samples, continuous air emission measurements, toxicity studies, and so forth all lay the factual basis for specific claims and the subsequent proof of claims. EPA is increasingly making use of fenceline monitoring technology to detect fugitive emissions[324] and aerial cameras to remotely monitor releases.[325] Consequently, understanding the science involved in an enforcement proceeding can be critical to the success of either party. Is a "new" chemical substance actually already adequately described by a more general entry on the TSCA Inventory? Is a particular air control technology "demonstrated" technology, or is it still in prototype? What is the diluting effect of soil and surface water between the point of release and the alleged location of the fish kill—is the release really the culprit? These and scores more questions focus on the technical aspects of environmental law but go to the heart of the enforcement options available to the government and the defenses of the respondent.

9.3 Technology Brings Its Own Headaches

Low-tolerance engineering design is increasingly a feature of modern manufacturing and production facilities in many industry sectors. As engineering processes become more sophisticated and as financial pressure mounts to improve efficiencies throughout the production process, the technological margin for error can dwindle to near vanishing. Nevertheless, the temptation (sometimes the regulatory requirement) is to revise the facility's operating assumptions to account for the improved performance, without giving appropriate thought to the reduction in the margin for error that is so often the improved technology's correlative. The result can be substantially tighter permits, revised to reflect much lower discharge volumes, for example, but not revised to reflect the increased likelihood of an excursion and, therefore, enforcement. Managing enforcement risk well requires consideration of operational and technical issues that seem, at first glance, to be far removed from legal matters of enforcement.

9.4 Agency Discretion

The statutory origins of agency discretion have already been mentioned, but they deserve a further philosophical note. As a practical matter, one cannot eliminate agency discretion in enforcement, no matter how much ink is expended in drafting statutes, guidance documents, and policy statements: "significant," "substantial risk," and similar expressions remain at heart qualitative and subjective. Nor would the elimination of discretion provide much solace, since agency discretion is often essential to ensuring that the law is not nearly so often "a ass" as it might be, to paraphrase Mr. Bumble.[326] The difficulty lies in striking the balance. On the part of the enforcing agency, the difficulty is best addressed by senior leadership through the evolution of a commitment to *stare decisis* and to reasoned rather than rote application of the law. For its part, the regulated community is well advised to accord the respect due to enforcing agencies *and* their compliance-oriented brethren (such as permit writers), and to seek opportunities to build relationships rather than draw battle lines. It continues to surprise the authors how much misunderstanding and ill will needlessly fuel enforcement proceedings and inhibit swift, certain, and fair resolution of the underlying issues. The government is not nearly so obtuse, nor the corporate world so obstinate, as either claims.

9.5 Cross-Border Issues

Unlike medicine, which legitimately claims a measure of universality, environmental law remains geographically bounded even though its subject matter is not. Multistate and multinational companies experience the dilemma of conflicting (or at least differing) standards applying to similar operations in different locales. Can a company adopt a corporate standard that applies regardless of jurisdiction? How should a company address stringent foreign laws that are not generally enforced nor adhered to by indigenous competitors but nevertheless apply to its operations? Is the same environmental issue or responsibility necessarily as important in every community in which the company operates?

These and myriad similar questions resist easy answers, but they are part of the enforcement reality for companies with operations in multiple jurisdictions, even if confined to the United States (given the variability among the EPA regions and among the states). Managing enforcement risks appropriately across jurisdictions requires a patient and careful analysis of local legal principles and practices, as well as close study of the organizational needs of the company. Failing to undertake such analyses and to develop reasoned directives from them invites enforcement, especially now that enforcing agencies in one part of the country are apt to communicate with their counterparts elsewhere. By the same token, cross-border analyses have the substantial ancillary benefit of facilitating the communication of best practices through an organization, which itself helps to manage enforcement risk.

10.0 Conclusion

Environmental law in the United States relies heavily, though not exclusively, on enforcement to drive compliance and to propel environmental performance toward the objectives of safety and good environmental stewardship. The consequences of environmental enforcement are significant: penalties and other forms of mandatory investment easily reach into the hundreds of thousands or even millions of dollars in a given enforcement proceeding. Criminal sanctions, while arising less frequently, are a real threat even for those whose actions (or failures to act) were not intended to have the environmental consequences that resulted. Moreover, we know from following enforcement trends over many years that environmental law and environmental enforcement theories are constantly evolving and renewing themselves. Trends toward enforcement by non-environmental agencies and toward more public display of environmental performance lapses help to shape the overall enforcement landscape and augur more change in the years to come.

Nevertheless, the risks of enforcement and liability can be managed. More (and more sophisticated) tools are available to assist the regulated community to anticipate and protect against the operational failures that lead to enforcement and liability. Some of these tools, in particular audits and environmental management systems, have become widely accepted by businesses and governments alike as effective instruments for measuring and improving environmental performance. Understanding, adopting, and fully integrating such tools into the culture and decision-making of a business can lead to significant rewards in avoided costs and liabilities and may contribute indirectly to other substantial organizational improvements like better communication, diffusion of best practices, and the fostering of a culture of responsibility.

Federal and state environmental laws offer potent weapons for compelling compliance and imposing liability, and that will not change materially even if, here and there, the emphasis in enforcement priorities shifts. The chapters that follow offer detailed information and guidance on the specific laws that define our environmental system, and they should provide an excellent resource for managing your environmental affairs with success.

11.0 Research Sources

- Environmental Law Reporter, looseleaf (ELI 2006) (available by subscription as www.eli.org)

- Environment Reporter, multivolume series (BNA 2006) (available by subscription at http://www.bna.com/products/ens/ercr.htm)

- EPA Civil Penalty Policies: http://www.epa.gov/compliance/resources/policies/civil/

- EPA ECHO Database: http://www.epa.gov/echo

- EPA Enforcement and Compliance Docket and Information Center: http://www.epa.gov/compliance/resources/policies

- EPA OECA Compliance and Enforcement Reports: http://www.epa.gov/compliance/resources/reports/index.html

- Frank P. Grad, *Treatise on Environmental Law* (New York: Matthew Bender, 2006)

- Daniel Riesel, *Environmental Enforcement: Civil and Criminal* (Law Journal Press, 2006)

Notes

[1] The authors would like to thank Kevin A. Ewing for his assistance in updating and improving this year's chapter.

[2] *See, e.g.*, United States Environmental Protection Agency (U.S. EPA) press release, EPA Enforcement Cuts Pollution by 1 Billion Pounds; Requires $10 Billion to Be Spent Cleaning Up, Nov. 15, 2005.

[3] *See, e.g.*, Environmental Integrity Project, *Pollution Enforcement Efforts under Bush Administration's EPA Drop on Four Out of Five Key Fronts*, May 23, 2007.

[4] U.S. EPA, Fiscal Year 2014–2018 EPA Strategic Plan at 2 (Apr. 10, 2014), *available at* https://www.epa.gov/planandbudget/strategicplan (Jun. 30, 2016).

⁵ *Id.* at 3.

⁶ *See, e.g.,* the U.S. EPA website, *available at* https://www.epa.gov/enforcement/national-enforcement-initi atives (last visited on July 11, 2016).

⁷ For example, EPA noted that for FY 2006, the efforts under the national priorities were responsible for 74 percent of the total air and water pollutant reductions and 71 percent of the injunctive relief value achieved by OECA. *See* U.S. EPA, *FY2006 OECA Accomplishments Report* at 9 (Spring 2007).

⁸ U.S. EPA, National Enforcement Initiatives for Fiscal Years 2017–2019, https://www.epa.gov/enforce ment/national-enforcement-initiatives (last visited on July 12, 2016).

⁹ *Id.*

¹⁰ *Id.*

¹¹ *Id.*

¹² *See* Office of Management and Budget. Budget of the U.S. Government. Fiscal Year 2017. Available at https://www.whitehouse.gov/sites/default/files/omb/budget/fy2017/assets/budget.pdf. (last visited on July 12, 2016).

¹³ U.S. EPA, Enforcement Annual Results for Fiscal Year 2015. Available at https://www.epa.gov/enforce ment/enforcement-annual-results-numbers-glance-fiscal-year-fy-2015.http://www.epa.gov/enforcement/ data/eoy2012/eoy-data.html (last visited on July 12, 2016).

¹⁴ *Id.*

¹⁵ U.S. Department of Justice, press release, "CITGO Petroleum and Subsidiary Found Guilty of Environ-mental Crimes" (June 27, 2007).

¹⁶ *United States v. CITGO Petroleum Corp.,* No. 2:06-cr-00563 (S.D. Tex. Order filed Sept. 18, 2012).

¹⁷ *Id.*

¹⁸ U.S. Department of Justice press release, CITGO Sentenced to Pay More Than $2 Million for Environ-mental Crimes at Corpus Christi, Texas, Refinery, Feb. 5, 2014, https://www.justice.gov/opa/pr/citgo -sentenced-pay-more-2-million-environmental-crimes-corpus-christi-texas-refinery (last visited July 12, 2016).

¹⁹ *N.Y. Times,* The 44th President: The New Team, *available at* http://projects.nytimes.com/44th_ president/new_team/show/lisa-jackson (last visited July 12, 2016).

²⁰ *See* U.S. E.P.A., Reducing Air Pollution from the Largest Sources, https://www.epa.gov/enforcement/ national-enforcement-initiative-reducing-air-pollution-largest-sources (last visited July 12, 2016).

²¹ *Id.*

²² *See* Section 8.6 *infra.*

²³ *See* U.S. E.P.A., National Enforcement Initiatives, https://www.epa.gov/enforcement/national-enforce ment-initiatives (last visited July 12, 2016).

²⁴ John M. Broder, E.P.A. Chief Set to Leave; Term Fell Shy of Early Hope, *N.Y. Times,* Dec. 27, 2012, *available at* http://www.nytimes.com/2012/12/28/science/earth/lisa-p-jackson-of-epa-to-step-down.html ?pagewanted = all (last visited July 12, 2016).

²⁵ Environment & Energy Daily, Lisa Jackson Has Left the Building, Drawing Mixed Reviews on the Hill (Feb. 15, 2013), *available at* http://www.eenews.net (last visited July 12, 2016).

²⁶ Environment & Energy Daily, Deal-Making Past Will Serve McCarthy Well with Controversial Issues Ahead, Lawmakers and Interest Groups Agree (July 19, 2013), *available at* http://www.eenews.net (last visited July 12, 2016).

²⁷ *Washington Post,* Senate Confirms Gina McCarthy as EPA Administrator (July 18, 2013), available at https://www.washingtonpost.com/news/post-politics/wp/2013/07/18/senate-confirms-gina-mccarthy-as -next-epa-administrator-in-59-to-40-vote/ (last visited July 12, 2016).

²⁸ *Id.*

[29] EPA. Clean Water Rule: Definition of "Waters of the United States"; Final Rule. 80 Fed. Reg. 37,054 (Jun. 29, 2015).

[30] EPA. Carbon Pollution Emission Guidelines for Existing Stationary Sources: Electric Utility Generating Units; Final Rule. 80 Fed. Reg. 64,662 (Oct. 23, 2015).

[31] See EPA. FY 2015 Enforcement and Compliance Annual Results. Estimated Value of Administrative and Civil Judicial Complying Actions (Injunctive Relief) FY 2011–FY 2015 (Dec. 16, 2015). Available at https://www.epa.gov/sites/production/files/2015-12/documents/fy-2015-enforcement-annual-results-charts_0.pdf#page=3.

[32] U.S. EPA, *FY1999 Enforcement and Compliance Assurance Report* at 5, OECA, July 2000.

[33] 42 U.S.C. § 9606 (CERCLA).

[34] U.S. EPA, OECA, *Administrative and Civil Judicial Penalties FY 2000–FY 2011 Table* (Oct. 2011), *available at* http://www.epa.gov/compliance/resources/reports/nets/nets-f3-adminandjudpen.pdf (last visited on July 11, 2013).

[35] *Id.*

[36] U.S. EPA, Compliance and Enforcement Annual Results 2011 Fiscal Year, https://archive.epa.gov/enforcement/annual-results/web/pdf/eoy2011.pdf (last visited on July 12, 2016).

[37] See U.S. EPA, *2003–2008 EPA Strategic Plan: Direction for the Future*, Sept. 30, 2003.

[38] See generally U.S. EPA, *Principles of Environmental Enforcement*, July 15, 1992.

[39] *Id.*

[40] See, e.g., U.S. EPA, *RCRA Civil Penalty Policy*, June 2003.

[41] *Id.*

[42] *Southern Union Co. v. U.S.*, 567 U.S. _____ (2012).

[43] See, e.g., *U.S. v. Pacific Gas and Electric Company*, 3:14-cr-00175 (N.D. Ca. Apr. 1, 2014), and *U.S. v. CITGO Petroleum Corp.* (S.D. Tex. Nov. 6, 2012), where the government's requests for fines under the Alternative Fines Act were denied because the facts underlying the fines had not been proven beyond a reasonable doubt in front of a jury.

[44] See, e.g., the U.S. EPA website at www.epa.gov/newsroom/ (last visited on July 12, 2016); the website for Texas's environmental agency at http://www.tceq.state.tx.us/comm_exec/communication/media/ (last visited on July 12, 2016); and the website for New Jersey's environmental agency at http://www.state.nj.us/dep/newsrel/ (lasted visited on July 12, 2016).

[45] See supra (chapter 2, section 2).

[46] 5 U.S.C. §§ 701–706 (APA).

[47] The *Federal Register* is published daily (Monday through Friday excluding holidays), and includes rules, proposed rules, and other notices by EPA and other federal agencies. For copies of publications, see http://www.gpo.gov/fdsys/browse/collection.action?collectionCode; eqFR (last visited on July 12, 2016). For an example of a daily state publication of proposed and final rules, see http://www.sos.state.tx.us/texreg/index.shtml (last visited on July 12, 2016).

[48] See, e.g., U.S. EPA, *RCRA Civil Penalty Policy*, June 2003; U.S. EPA, *Revised Clean Water Act Section 404 Settlement Penalty Policy*, Dec. 2001.

[49] See, e.g., 42 U.S.C. §§ 6927 (RCRA), 7414 (CAA); 33 U.S.C. § 1318 (CWA).

[50] See, e.g., 40 C.F.R. § 403.12 and 40 C.F.R. Part 264, Subpart E. Examples include (i) baseline testing of wastewater discharges to assure compliance by a projected activity, (ii) monthly monitoring of wastewater discharges, (iii) periodic or continuous testing of air emissions from facility stacks, (iv) spill and release reporting, and (v) maintenance of operating records and recording of unusual events or conditions.

[51] See, e.g., 40 C.F.R. § 122.22(d) (NPDES Permits Program).

[52] See, e.g., 40 C.F.R. § 70.6(c)(5).

53 *See, e.g.,* 33 U.S.C. §§ 1319(c)(1) (CWA; negligent violations) and 1319(c)(2) (CWA; knowing violations); 42 U.S.C. §§ 7413(c)(4) (CAA; negligent releases into ambient air) and 7413(c)(1) (CAA; knowing violations).

54 *See infra* (chapter 2, section 6.1.2).

55 *See infra* (chapter 2, section 6.1.2.3).

56 *See United States v. Johnson & Towers, Inc.,* 741 F.2d 662 (3d Cir. 1984), *cert. denied sub nom. Angel v. United States,* 469 U.S. 1208 (1985) (stating that knowledge of individuals in responsible positions with corporate defendant may be inferred).

57 *See* discussion on the progression of a civil proceeding, *infra* (chapter 2, section 4.7).

58 *See* discussion on the "strict liability" nature of civil liability provisions in environmental law *infra* (chapter 2, section 4.3).

59 *See, e.g.,* 40 C.F.R. Part 52 (CAA), Part 123 (CWA), Parts 271-72 (RCRA).

60 *See, e.g.,* 42 U.S.C. § 6929 (RCRA).

61 *See, e.g.,* 33 U.S.C. § 1319(g)(6)(A)(ii) (CWA) (providing that so long as a state is diligently prosecuting an action under state law a comparable federal civil enforcement action shall not be commenced).

62 *See, e.g., United States v. Smithfield Foods, Inc.,* 191 F.3d 516 (4th Cir. 1999), *cert. denied,* 531 U.S. 813 (2000).

63 *Smithfield Foods, Inc.,* 191 F.3d at 526. *But see Harmon Industries v. Browner,* 191 F.3d 894, 904 (8th Cir. 1999) (holding that the state of Missouri's settlement with an alleged violator of RCRA precluded an EPA enforcement action based on res judicata); but *cf. United States v. Murphy Oil USA,* 143 F. Supp. 2d 1054, 1090-91 (W.D. Wis. 2001) (holding that *Harmon Industries* does not apply to the Clean Air Act).

64 Criminal enforcement principles are considered separately in chapter 2, section 6.

65 American environmental statutes also compare unfavorably in their prolixity with the environmental statutes promulgated in Germany, considered by many to be a leader in environmental thinking in Europe. The German statutes are lapidary by comparison.

66 While most civil liability provisions contained in federal statutory environmental laws are based in strict liability, some are not. *See, e.g.,* the Endangered Species Act, 16 U.S.C. § 1540.

67 The issue of knowledge (and its relation to negligent and willful conduct) is more important, however, in the criminal context and will be discussed later in the chapter. In addition, while most civil liability provisions in federal environmental laws are "strict liability," the degree of knowledge, willfulness, negligence, and other factors remains relevant in the civil enforcement context when EPA uses its discretion to determine whether to initiate enforcement and how much to penalize those it brings suit against. *See generally* U.S. EPA, *RCRA Civil Penalty Policy,* June 2003.

68 *See* 33 U.S.C. §§ 1311(a) and 1342(a) (CWA).

69 *See* 33 U.S.C. § 1319 (CWA).

70 40 C.F.R. § 122.41(n).

71 *Id.*

72 40 C.F.R. § 122.41(n)(3).

73 40 C.F.R. § 122.41(m)(1).

74 Depending on the nature of the bypass, notice may be required before or after the bypass. 40 C.F.R. § 122.41(m)(3).

75 33 U.S.C. § 1342(k) (CWA).

76 There are some limitations on the use of the permit shield. For example, if the permittee did not comply with the permit application requirements (e.g., notice), the shield will not apply. *See* U.S. EPA, *Policy Statement on Scope of Discharge Authorized and Shield Associated with NPDES Permits,* July 1, 1994. See further discussion of permits in chapter 2, section 4.5.1.

77 42 U.S.C. § 7661c(f) (CAA).

78 *Id.*

79 *United States v. Self,* 2 F.3d 1071, 1074 (10th Cir. 1993).

80 *Id.* at 1082.

81 *Id.* at 1076–82.

82 42 U.S.C. § 9607(b)(3) (CERCLA).

83 That said, several cases ruled that Hurricane Katrina was an "act of God." *See, e.g., Coex Coffee Int'l v. Depuy Storage & Forwarding LLC,* 2008 WL 1884041 (E.D. La. Apr. 28, 2008); *Dollar Thrifty Auto Group, Inc. v. Bohn-DC, L.L.C.,* 23 So.3d 301, 304 (La. Ct. App. 2008).

84 *See, e.g., United States v. 150 Acres of Land,* 49 ERC 1961 (BNA) (6th Cir. 2000); *New York v. Lashins Arcade Co.,* 91 F.3d 353 (2d Cir. 1996).

85 U.S. EPA, *Interim Guidance Regarding Criteria Landowners Must Meet in Order to Qualify for Bona Fide Prospective Purchaser, Contiguous Property Owner, or Innocent Landowner Limitations on CERCLA Liability ("Common Elements"),* Mar. 6, 2003

86 This element is discussed in greater detail below.

87 78 Fed. Reg. 79,319 (Dec. 30, 2013).

88 *See* 33 U.S.C. §§ 1311(a), and 1342(a) (CWA).

89 33 U.S.C. § 1342(a) and (b) (CWA).

90 33 U.S.C. § 1342(b) (CWA).

91 *See, e.g.,* 42 U.S.C. § 6929 (RCRA).

92 A permit also provides the permittee with certain defenses, *see supra* (chapter 2, sections 4.4.1 and 4.4.2).

93 Negotiated consent orders, in differing forms and for differing reasons, are also used in the following federal environmental statutes: CERCLA, RCRA, the Clean Water Act, and the Clean Air Act.

94 Carolyne R. Hathaway, David J. Hayes, and William K. Rawson, "A Practitioner's Guide to the Toxic Substances Control Act: Part II," *Environmental Law Reporter* 24, no. 6 at 10,286 (June 1994).

95 *See id.* for further discussion.

96 The penalty policies are not binding on EPA or the courts. "The penalty policies do not bind either the [administrative law judge] or the [Environmental Appeals] Board since these policies, not having been subjected to the rulemaking procedures of the Administrative Procedures Act, lack the force of law." *In re M.A. Bruder & Sons, Inc. D/B/A M.A.B. Paints, Inc.,* 10 E.A.D. 598, 610 (EAB 2002) (citing *In re City of Marshall,* 10 E.A.D. 173, 189 n.29 [EAB 2001]). Indeed, if the penalty policy would produce a result inconsistent with the statutory penalty factors, it should not be used. *See* Memorandum from Robert Van Heuvelen, director, Office of Regulatory Enforcement, *Guidance on Use of Penalty Policies in Administrative Litigation,* Dec. 15, 1995. Moreover, the penalty policies "cannot be relied upon to create rights, substantive or procedural, enforceable by any party in litigation with the United States." *See* U.S. EPA, *RCRA Civil Penalty Policy* at 6, June 2003.

97 *See, e.g.,* 33 U.S.C. § 1319(d) (CWA).

98 33 U.S.C. § 1319(d) (CWA).

99 *See, e.g.,* U.S. EPA, *A Framework for Statute-Specific Approaches to Penalty Assessments: Implementing EPA's Policy on Civil Penalties,* Feb. 14, 1984.

100 *See* U.S. EPA, *RCRA Civil Penalty Policy,* June 2003.

101 42 U.S.C. § 6928(a)(3) (RCRA).

102 *See* U.S. EPA, *RCRA Civil Penalty Policy,* June 2003. When EPA is pursuing an administrative case under RCRA, EPA performs two separate calculations under this policy: (1) EPA determines an appropriate penalty amount to seek in its complaint, and (2) it explains and documents the process by which it arrived at the penalty figure it agreed to accept in settlement. *Id.*

103 U.S. EPA, *RCRA Civil Penalty Policy,* June 2003.

[104] *See* U.S. EPA, *Revision to Adjusted Penalty Policy Matrices Package*, Nov. 16, 2009.

[105] *See* U.S. EPA, *RCRA Civil Penalty Policy* at 15, June 2003. While EPA's penalty policy provides more guidance than the statutory language, one might question the use of the major/moderate/minor categories and the penalty matrix. The limited matrix is somewhat inflexible in its approach and does not provide for discretion. That said, EPA is not required to follow the matrix and can always deviate from its recommendations, though it rarely does so at the outset of a proceeding.

[106] *See* U.S. EPA, *RCRA Civil Penalty Policy* at 15, June 2003.

[107] *Id.* at 23–26.

[108] *Id.* at 25–26.

[109] *Id.* at 27.

[110] U.S. EPA, *RCRA Civil Penalty Policy* at 6, June 2003.

[111] *Id.* at 28 (citing EPA's 1984 Policy on Civil Penalties). Note that this policy is not an absolute. Four exceptions are: (1) the economic benefit is insignificant; (2) taking the case to trial would not be in the public interest; (3) it is unlikely that EPA would benefit from taking the case to trial; and (4) the company has an inability to pay the proposed penalty. *Id.* at 29.

[112] *Id.* at 28. "Significant" is defined in relation to the gravity-based + multi-day penalty amount. For instance, if the GBP + MDP is $30,000 or less, an economic benefit of noncompliance component should be factored in if it totals at least $3,000. *Id.*

[113] *Id.* at 29–30.

[114] *Id.* at 30–31.

[115] For more information, *see id.* at 30–32.

[116] *See* 40 C.F.R. § 19.4 (*as amended by* 74 Fed. Reg. 627 (Jan. 7, 2009)).

[117] *See* The Federal Civil Penalties Inflation Adjustment Act of 1990, Public Law 101–410, 28 U.S.C. 2461.

[118] *See* U.S. EPA, *Civil Monetary Penalty Inflation Adjustment Rule.* 81 Fed. Reg. 43,091 (July 1, 2016).

[119] *Id.* at 43,095.

[120] *Sasser v. Adm'r, U.S. E.P.A.*, 990 F.2d 127, 129 (4th Cir. 1993) (concluding that EPA's action did not run afoul of the applicable Clean Water Act statute of limitations because "each day the pollutant remains in the wetlands without a permit constitutes an additional day of violation"); and *United States v. Reaves*, 923 F.Supp. 1530, 1533–34 (M.D.Fla. 1996) (holding that the five-year statute of limitations under 28 U.S.C. § 2462 had not begun to run because the unpermitted discharge of fill materials into a wetlands was a continuing violation for as long as the fill remained).

[121] *See United States v. Rutherford Oil Corp.*, 756 F. Supp. 2d 782, 793 (S.D. Tex. 2010) (concluding that under 33 U.S.C. § 1311(a) "[o]nce the violator ceases its discharging, its violation ends and the statute of limitations begins to run.") and *In the Matter of Robert G. Heser and Andrew Heser, Respondents*, CWA-05-2006-0002, 2007 WL 4618371 (Dec. 19, 2007) ("[f]inding a continuing violation . . . amounts to effectively legislating the statute of limitations out of the Clean Water Act, even though Congress did not do so and even though 28 U.S.C. § 2462 provides a five-year statute of limitations in such situations"); *United States v. Telluride Co.*, 884 F. Supp. 404, 408 (D. Colo. 1995), *reversed on other grounds*, 146 F.3d 1241 (10th Cir. 1998); and *Friends of Warm Mineral Springs, Inc. v. McCarthy*, No. 8:13-CV-3236-T-23TGW, 2015 WL 2169241, at *3 (M.D. Fla. May 8, 2015).

[122] *See Sierra Club v. Oklahoma Gas & Elec. Co.*, 816 F.3d 666 (10th Cir. 2016) (concluding that violations beyond the first day of an unpermitted modification under the Clean Air Act were "continuing violations," but that the statute of limitations began to run when the claim first accrued, i.e., when the boiler was initial modified, and thus EPA's action was time barred).

[123] *Gabelli v. S.E.C.*, 133 S. Ct. 1216 (2013).

[124] Even if an import certification was filed in the ordinary course, EPA will consider assessing a penalty for failure to file one, on the theory that the certification was, as it turned out, inaccurate.

[125] Indeed, EPA has taken the position that its penalty policy "is designed for first-time offenders." As such, EPA will not give credit to a first-time offender based on its lack of prior violations. Rather, EPA will only adjust upward on this factor if the party has a history of prior violations. *See, e.g., In the Matter of GCA Chemical Corporation*, 2002 EPA ALJ LEXIS 38 (June 18, 2002).

[126] *See* Edward E. Reich and Quinlan J. Shea, III, *A Survey of U.S. Environmental Enforcement Authorities, Tools and Remedies*, http://www.inece.org/1stvol1/reich-shea.htm (last visited on July 12, 2016).

[127] U.S. EPA, *Environmental Auditing Policy Statement*, 51 Fed. Reg. 25,004 (July 9, 1986).

[128] *See* U.S. EPA, *Incentives for Self-Policing: Discovery, Disclosure, Correction and Prevention of Violations*, 60 Fed. Reg. 66,706 (Dec. 22, 1995); U.S. EPA, *Incentives for Self-Policing: Discovery, Disclosure, Correction and Prevention of Violations*, 65 Fed. Reg. 19,618 (Apr. 11, 2000).

[129] *See* U.S. EPA's audit policy website at https://www.epa.gov/compliance/epas-audit-policy (last visited on July 12, 2016).

[130] *See* U.S. EPA, *Notice of eDisclosure Portal Launch: Modernizing Implementation of EPA's Self-Policing Incentive Policies*, 80 Fed. Reg. 76.476 (Dec. 9, 2015).

[131] *See* U.S. EPA's eDisclosure website at https://www.epa.gov/compliance/epas-edisclosure (last visited on July 12, 2016).

[132] *Id.*

[133] *Id.*

[134] *Id.*

[135] In 2004, DOJ accumulated a backlog of more than 300 referred cases. *BNA Daily Environment*, "DOJ Has Backlog of 301 Cases Referred By EPA But Not Acted Upon," Dec. 6, 2004.

[136] EPA has an internal policy that automatically refers certain types of cases to DOJ rather than deal with them internally. Memorandum from Thomas L. Adams, Jr., EPA assistant administrator, *Expansion of Direct Referral Cases to the Department of Justice*, OECM, OSWER Directive #9891.5A.

[137] *See, e.g.*, U.S. EPA, *Compliance and Enforcement Annual Results 2011 Fiscal Year*, *available at* https://archive.epa.gov/enforcement/annual-results/web/pdf/eoy2011.pdf (last visited on July 12, 2016).

[138] *See* EPA and OSHA MOU (Nov. 23, 1990).

[139] Memo from Sally Quillian Yates, Deputy Attorney General to All U.S. Attorneys, Prosecution of Worker Safety Violations. (Dec. 17, 2016).

[140] *See* U.S. DOJ. Worker Endangerment Initiative. Available https://www.justice.gov/enrd/worker-endangerment/about.

[141] *See* Memorandum of Understanding Between the U.S. Departments of Labor and Justice on Criminal Prosecution of Worker Safety Laws. (Dec. 17, 2015).

[142] *Id.*

[143] *See* 40 C.F.R. Part 22 (Consolidated Rules of Practice Governing the Administrative Assessment of Civil Penalties and the Revocation/Termination or Suspension of Permits).

[144] 40 C.F.R. § 22.13.

[145] 40 C.F.R. § 22.15(d).

[146] 40 C.F.R. § 22.18.

[147] 40 C.F.R. § 22.18(b).

[148] *Id.*

[149] 40 C.F.R. § 22.18(b)(2).

[150] 40 C.F.R. § 22.18(b)(3).

[151] 40 C.F.R. § 22.30.

[152] *See, e.g.*, 33 U.S.C. § 1319(g)(8) (CWA).

[153] *See, e.g.*, 42 U.S.C. § 7604 (CAA); 33 U.S.C. § 1365 (CWA); 42 U.S.C. § 6972 (RCRA). Because the focus of this section is enforcement, it highlights citizen suits against the regulated community and not those against EPA.

[154] Permits and compliance monitoring reports submitted to the agencies by the regulated community generally are available to the public for review under both federal and state law. Agency online databases also provide compliance information as to specific regulated facilities. *See, e.g.*, the EPA website designated as Enforcement and Compliance History Online (ECHO) at www.epa.gov/echo.com.

[155] *See, e.g.*, 42 U.S.C. § 7604(b) (CAA); 33 U.S.C. § 1365(b) (CWA); 42 U.S.C. § 6972(b) (RCRA).

[156] *See, e.g.*, 42 U.S.C. § 7604(a) and (b) (CAA); 33 U.S.C. § 1365(a) and (b) (CWA); 42 U.S.C. § 6972(a) and (e) (RCRA).

[157] *See, e.g.*, 42 U.S.C. § 7604(c) (CAA); 33 U.S.C. § 1365(c) (CWA); 42 U.S.C. § 6972(d); *see also* 40 C.F.R. Parts 54, 135, and 254. Other persons are allowed to intervene in cases involving violations if the government precludes the citizen suit by taking enforcement action. Under RCRA, a person with an interest related to the action may be allowed to intervene in a case involving allegations of imminent hazard. *See* 42 U.S.C. § 6972(b)(1)(B) and (E) (RCRA).

[158] *See, e.g.*, 42 U.S.C. § 7604(b) (CAA); 33 U.S.C. § 1365(b) (CWA); 42 U.S.C. § 6972(b) (RCRA). The notice period generally is sixty days, except that RCRA requires ninety days for actions involving imminent and substantial endangerment to health or the environment. *See* 42 U.S.C. § 6972(b)(2) (RCRA). A citizen suit nevertheless may be commenced immediately after the notification in certain situations. *See, e.g.*, 42 U.S.C. § 7604(b)(2) (CAA) (involving, for example, hazardous air pollutants); 33 U.S.C. § 1365(b)(2) (CWA) (involving, for example, toxic pollutants).

[159] *See Lockett v. EPA*, 319 F.3d 678, 684 (5th Cir. 2003).

[160] *See Swartz v. Beach*, 229 F. Supp. 2d 1239 (D. Wyo. 2002).

[161] *See, e.g.*, 42 U.S.C. § 7604(b)(1)(B) (CAA); 33 U.S.C. § 1365(b)(1)(B) (CWA); 42 U.S.C. § 6972(b)(1)(B) (RCRA).

[162] *See Lockett*, 319 F.3d at 684.

[163] *See McAbee v. City of Fort Payne*, 318 F.3d 1248, 1256 (11th Cir. 2003), *reh'g denied*, 65 Fed. Appx. 716 (2003).

[164] *Id.* at 1251.

[165] *See* 33 U.S.C. § 1365(a)(1) (CWA); 42 U.S.C. § 6972(a)(1)(A) (RCRA).

[166] *See Hiebenthal v. Meduri Farms*, 242 F. Supp. 2d 885 (D. Or. 2002).

[167] *See Aiello v. Town of Brookhaven*, 136 F. Supp. 2d 81 (E.D.N.Y. 2001) (CWA); *Lutz v. Chromatex*, 718 F. Supp. 413 (M.D. Pa. 1988) (RCRA).

[168] *See, e.g.*, 42 U.S.C. § 7604(e) (CAA); 33 U.S.C. § 1365(e) (CWA); 42 U.S.C. § 6972(f) (RCRA).

[169] *See Int'l Paper Co. v. Ouellette*, 479 U.S. 481 (1987).

[170] *See, e.g.*, *City of Tulsa v. Tyson Foods, Inc.*, 258 F. Supp. 2d 1263, 1288 (N.D. Okla. 2003), *vacated, City of Tulsa v. Tyson Foods, Inc.*, 2003 Dist. LEXIS 23416 (N.D. Okla. 2003) (vacated following settlement between the parties). Trespass generally involves a physical invasion of another's property, while nuisance protects the use and enjoyment of property. *Id. See also* discussion in chapter 2, section 8.5.

[171] *See United States v. Bestfoods*, 524 U.S. 51 (1998).

[172] For example, CERCLA includes a detailed notification system so that the government immediately learns about the release of a hazardous substance in a reportable quantity, which allows for a response to reduce harm to the environment and the public. *See generally* 42 U.S.C. § 9603 (CERCLA); *see also* chapter 9. This notification system is backed by criminal sanctions that can be applied to three categories of persons: (1) a "person in charge" of a facility; (2) a "person" who fails to report a release; and (3) the "owner or operator" of the facility. 42 U.S.C. § 9603 (CERCLA).

[173] *United States v. Bailey*, 444 U.S. 394, 402 (1980) (quoting *Morissette v. United States*, 342 U.S. 246 (1952)).

[174] 42 U.S.C. § 6928 (RCRA) (emphasis added). *See also* 42 U.S.C. § 6928(d)(7)(a) and (b) (RCRA).

[175] 42 U.S.C. § 7413(c)(5) (CAA).

[176] 33 U.S.C. § 1319(c)(3) (CWA).

[177] 42 U.S.C. § 6928(e) (RCRA).

[178] 42 U.S.C. § 7413(c)(5)(B) (CAA); 33 U.S.C. § 1319(c)(3)(B) (CWA); 42 U.S.C. § 6928(f)(2) (RCRA).

[179] 42 U.S.C. § 7413(c)(5)(B) (CAA); 33 U.S.C. § 1319(c)(3)(B) (CWA); 42 U.S.C. § 6928(f)(2) (RCRA).

[180] *See, e.g., United States v. Weitzenhoff,* 1 F.3d 1523, amended 35 F.3d 1275, 1284 (9th Cir. 1994), *cert. denied sub nom. Mariani v. United States,* 513 U.S. 1128 (1995) (rejecting the assertion that convictions under the Clean Water Act required proof that the defendants were cognizant of "the requirements or even the existence of the permit").

[181] *Morissette v. United States,* 342 U.S. 246 (1952).

[182] *Staples v. United States,* 511 U.S. 600 (1994).

[183] *United States v. X-Citement Video, Inc.,* 513 U.S. 64 (1994).

[184] *Id.* at 469.

[185] 42 U.S.C. § 6928(d) (RCRA) (emphasis added).

[186] Nevertheless, in *United States v. Johnson & Towers, Inc.,* the Court of Appeals for the Third Circuit held that the government was required to prove that the defendants knew that they did not possess a permit for their pumping of hazardous waste chemicals into a tributary of the Delaware River. 741 F.2d 662 (3d Cir. 1984). Analyzing the same provision, the Second, Seventh, and Ninth Circuits later declined to require the government to prove knowledge of a permit. *United States v. Laughlin,* 10 F.3d 961, 965–66 (2d Cir. 1993), *cert. denied sub nom. Goldman v. United States,* 511 U.S. 1071 (1994); *United States v. Wagner,* 29 F.3d 264 (7th Cir. 1994); *Weitzenhoff,* 35 F.3d 1275 (9th Cir. 1994).

[187] *United States v. Ahmad,* 101 F.3d 386 (5th Cir. 1996).

[188] *United States v. Sinskey,* 119 F.3d 712 (8th Cir. 1997).

[189] Associated Press, Pacific Gas and Electric Charged with 12 Felonies in Explosion, *New York Times,* Apr. 1, 2014, available at http://www.nytimes.com/2014/04/02/us/pacific-gas-and-electric-charged-with-12 -felonies-in-explosion.html?_r = 0 (last viewed July 6, 2016).

[190] *U.S. v. Pacific Gas and Electric Company,* 3:14-cr-00175-TEH (N.D. Ca., filed July 30, 2014).

[191] 33 U.S.C. § 1319(c)(1) (CWA). Notably, the 1987 amendments to the Clean Water Act inserted the negligent and knowing standards as replacements for a willful or negligent standard.

[192] 42 U.S.C. § 7413(c)(4) (CAA).

[193] *See, e.g., United States v. Hanousek,* 176 F.3d 1116 (9th Cir. 1999), *cert. denied,* 528 U.S. 1102 (2000); *United States v. Pruett,* 681 F.3d 232 (5th Cir. 2012); *United States v. Atlantic States Cast Iron Pipe Co.,* 2007 WL 2282514 (D.N.J. Aug. 2, 2007).

[194] *Hanousek,* 176 F.3d at 1120–21; *see also United States v. Baytank (Houston), Inc.,* 934 F.2d 599 (5th Cir. 1991) (finding that failure to require specific intent in the jury instructions on alleged violations of Clean Water Act Section 309(c)(1) was not error because at the time of the events in question, the statute expressly penalized negligent as well as willful violations).

[195] *Hanousek,* 176 F.3d at 1120.

[196] *Id.* (citing American Law Institute, Modal Penal Code § 2.02(2)(d) (1985) for *Hanousek*'s definition of "negligence" and *Black's Law Dictionary* for the prosecution's definition of "negligence").

[197] *Pruett,* 681 F.3d at 243.

[198] *Black's Law Dictionary,* 8th ed. (2004).

[199] 33 U.S.C. § 407.

[200] 33 U.S.C. § 411.

[201] *See United States v. White Fuel Corp.,* 498 F.2d 619 (1st Cir. 1974) (finding that "no court to our knowledge has held that there must be proof of scienter; to the contrary, the Refuse Act has commonly been termed a strict liability statute").

[202] *See, e.g., United States v. Exxon Corp.,* No. A90-0015-CR, 1990 U.S. Dist. Lexis 1821 (D. Alaska) (Feb. 27, 1990) (presenting the grand jury's indictment); 3 Oil Spill Litig. News 3190, 3191 (D. Alaska) (Mar.

1991) (imposing sentence). Notably, the term "refuse" has been read broadly to include materials such as commercially valuable gasoline and discolored water from coal operations, items that may not initially come to mind when considering the ordinary meaning of "refuse," particularly under a statute that imposes criminal liability without intent. *See United States v. Standard Oil Co.*, 384 U.S. 224, 229–30 (1966) (commercially valuable gasoline); *United States v. Kentland-Elkhorn Coal Corp.*, 353 F. Supp. 451, 456 (E.D. Ky. 1973) (discolored water from coal operations).

203 *United States v. Park*, 421 U.S. 658, 673–74 (1975).

204 *United States v. Iverson*, 162 F.3d 1015, 1023 (9th Cir. 1998) (citations omitted).

205 *Dotterweich*, 320 U.S. 277 (1943).

206 *Park*, 421 U.S. 658 (1975).

207 *Dotterweich*, 320 U.S. 277 (1943).

208 *Id.* at 284.

209 *Park*, 421 U.S. 658 (1975).

210 *Id.* at 673–74.

211 33 U.S.C. § 1319(c)(6) (CWA).

212 *United States v. MacDonald & Watson Waste Oil Co.*, 933 F.2d 35, 55 (1st Cir. 1991) (affirming conviction of a company president under RCRA for knowingly transporting hazardous waste to a facility that did not have a permit).

213 *United States v. Heredia*, 483 F.3d 913 (9th Cir. 2007); *United States v. Jewell*, 532 F.2d 697, 700 (9th Cir. 1976), *cert. denied*, 426 U.S. 951 (1976) (approving a jury instruction that allowed knowledge to be proven by a demonstration of the defendant's "conscious purpose to avoid learning" that the car he was driving into the United States contained 110 pounds of marijuana).

214 *United States v. Int'l Mineral & Chem. Corp.*, 402 U.S. 558, 559, 563-64 (1971) (stating that a "person thinking in good faith that he was shipping distilled water when in fact he was shipping some dangerous acid" could not be said to knowingly violate regulations pertaining to shipment of corrosive liquids); *United States v. Kelly*, 167 F.3d 1176, 1180 (7th Cir. 1999).

215 *United States v. Hopkins*, 53 F.3d 533, 538 (2d Cir. 1995), *cert. denied*, 516 U.S. 1072 (1996) (citing *Int'l Mineral & Chem. Corp.*, 402 U.S. at 563).

216 United States Attorneys' Manual, § 5–11.102 (2004).

217 *Id.*

218 *Id.*; *see also*, the Racketeer Influenced and Corrupt Organization Act (RICO), 18 USC §§ 1961–1965.

219 Sarbanes-Oxley Act of 2002, §§ 902, 905, and 1107; Pub. L. No. 107-204, 116 Stat. 745.

220 18 U.S.C. § 1001. *See also United States v. Daily*, 921 F.2d 994 (10th Cir. 1990). The Court of Appeals for the Second Circuit rejected the materiality requirement in *United States v. Bilzerian*, 926 F.2d 1285, 1299 (2d Cir. 1991).

221 18 U.S.C. § 1001.

222 *See, e.g., United States v. Brittain*, 931 F.2d 1413 (10th Cir. 1991) (upholding defendant's conviction under 18 U.S.C. § 1001 for submitting false discharge monitoring reports).

223 18 U.S.C. § 1341.

224 *See, e.g., United States v. Paccione*, 749 F. Supp. 478 (S.D.N.Y. 1990) (upholding mail and wire fraud convictions of defendants who failed to report the correct amount of fill placement in order to avoid city licensing fees).

225 *See generally United States v. Henry*, 136 F.3d 12 (1st Cir. 1998).

226 18 U.S.C. § 371.

227 *United States v. Feola*, 420 U.S. 671, 686 (1975).

228 *See* Memorandum from Earl E. Devaney, director, EPA's Office of Criminal Enforcement, to EPA Criminal Enforcement Employees, *The Exercise of Investigative Discretion*, Jan. 12, 1994 (hereinafter the "Devaney Memorandum"). *See also* Memorandum from Robert Perry, EPA's associate administrator, to EPA regional counsels, *Criminal Enforcement Priorities for the Environmental Protection Agency*, Oct. 12, 1982.

229 *See* Devaney Memorandum.

230 Memorandum from Steve Herman, assistant administrator to regional and OECA personnel, *Operating Principles for an Integrated Enforcement and Compliance Assurance Program* (Nov. 27, 1996).

231 *See* Devaney Memorandum.

232 U.S. EPA, *Incentives for Self-Policing: Discovery, Disclosure, Correction and Prevention of Violations*, 60 Fed. Reg. 66,706, 66,708-66,710 (Dec. 22, 1995).

233 United States Attorneys' Manual, § 9-27.220(A) (2004).

234 *See, e.g.*, Interview with Judson W. Starr, chief of ECS, 1 Corp. Crime Rep. 5, 7 (May 4, 1987); Donald A. Carr, *Environmental Criminal Liability: Avoiding and Defending Enforcement Actions*, 24–27 (1995) (citing remarks by: Judson W. Starr, chief of ECS; George W. Van Cleve, deputy assistant attorney general for the environment; and Richard Thornburgh, attorney general).

235 U.S. DOJ, *Factors in Decisions on Criminal Prosecutions for Environmental Violations in the Context of Significant Voluntary Compliance or Disclosure Efforts by the Violator*, July 1, 1991.

236 *See, e.g.*, DOJ's Criminal Resources Manual § 9-11.100 *et seq.*

237 *See, e.g.*, 42 U.S.C. § 9603(b) and (c) (CERCLA); 15 U.S.C. § 2607(e) (TSCA); and 42 U.S.C. § 7414 (CAA).

238 42 U.S.C. § 6927(e)(1) (RCRA).

239 *See, e.g.*, 42 U.S.C. § 6927(a)(1) (RCRA) and 42 U.S.C. § 9604(e)(3) (CERCLA).

240 *See Marshall v. Barlow's, Inc.*, 436 U.S. 307 (1978) (holding that the Fourth Amendment safeguarded against administrative inspections under OSHA without a warrant).

241 *Nat'l-Standard Co. v. Adamkus*, 881 F.2d 352, 361 (7th Cir. 1989) (addressing whether EPA's administrative warrant was issued with probable cause for a RCRA inspection) (citing *Barlow's, Inc.*, 436 U.S. at 320–21).

242 *Illinois v. Gates*, 462 U.S. 213, 238 (1983) (requiring a "fair probability that contraband or evidence of a crime will be found in a particular place" in order for a magistrate to issue a criminal search warrant).

243 *See* 28 C.F.R. § 77.10.

244 *See* 28 C.F.R. §§ 77.6 and 77.10(c) and (d).

245 *Black's Law Dictionary*, 8th ed. (2004). The grand jury is composed of 16 to 23 people, and can return an indictment if 12 or more jurors vote affirmatively. 18 U.S.C. Fed. R. Crim. P. 6(a)(1) and (f).

246 *See* George S. Gulick, Annotation, *Form, Particularity, and Manner of Designation Required in a Subpoena Duces Tecum for Production of Corporate Books, Records, and Documents*, 23 A.L.R.2d 862, § 3 (1952) and § 4 (1996, supplement).

247 DOJ Criminal Resources Manual § 9–11.151.

248 *Id.*

249 *Id.*

250 DOJ Criminal Resources Manual § 9-11.150.

251 28 U.S.C. Fed. R. Civ. P. 26(b)(1) (2004). *See also* 28 U.S.C. Fed. R. Civ. P. 26(a)(1) (requiring certain mandatory disclosures without awaiting a discovery request, including "all documents, data compilations, and tangible things that are in the possession, custody, or control of the party that the disclosing party may use to support its claims or defenses").

252 28 U.S.C. Fed. R. Civ. P. 15.

253 28 U.S.C. Fed. R. Civ. P. 16(b)(1).

254 For a discussion on parallel civil and criminal proceedings, see chapter 5 of Donald A. Carr, *Environmental Criminal Liability: Avoiding and Defending Enforcement Actions* (1995).

255 United States Sentencing Commission, *Guidelines Manual*, § 2Q1.1–2Q2.1 (Nov. 2008).

256 *See, e.g.*, United States Sentencing Commission, *Guidelines Manual*, § 2Q1.2(b)(2) (Nov. 2008) (increasing the level by nine if a mishandling of hazardous materials involves a "substantial likelihood" of death

or serious bodily injury); United States Sentencing Commission, *Guidelines Manual,* § 2Q1.2(b)(4) (Nov. 2008) (increasing the level by four if a mishandling of hazardous materials is done without a permit).

[257] United States Sentencing Commission, *Guidelines Manual* (Nov. 2008).

[258] *See, e.g.,* 71 Fed. Reg. 56,578 (Sept. 27, 2006).

[259] *See* 71 Fed. Reg. 28,063 (May 15, 2006).

[260] Sarbanes-Oxley Act of 2002, §§ 902, 905, and 1107; Pub. L. No. 107-204, 116 Stat. 745.

[261] *Blakely v. Washington,* 542 U.S. 296 (2004) (5–4 decision) (O'Connor, J., Rehnquist, C.J., Kennedy, J., and Breyer, J., dissenting).

[262] *United States v. Booker,* 543 U.S. 220 (2005) (5–4 decision) (different majorities support different aspects of the Court's holdings).

[263] Emily Parker, "Awaiting Sentence: The Constitutional Bottleneck," Medill School of Journalism—On the Docket, Dec. 15, 2004.

[264] Michael M. O'Hear, Bark and Bite: The Environmental Sentencing Guidelines after *Booker,* 2009, *Utah L. Rev.* 1151, 1156 (2009).

[265] *Id.* at 1159.

[266] *See* 42 U.S.C. § 9607(e)(1) (CERCLA).

[267] 42 U.S.C. § 9601(20) (CERCLA).

[268] *See also Bestfoods,* 524 U.S. 51 (1998).

[269] U.S. EPA, *Interim Approach to Applying the Audit Policy to New Owners,* 73 Fed. Reg. 44,991 (Aug. 1, 2008).

[270] 65 Fed. Reg. 19,618 (Apr. 11, 2000).

[271] 73 Fed. Reg. 44,992 (Aug. 1, 2008).

[272] See https://www.ceres.org/resources/reports/cool-response-the-sec-corporate-climate-change-reporting/ at 12.

[273] See https://www.unpri.org/signatory-directory/?co = &sta = &sti = &sts = &sa = join&si = join&ss = join&q = .

[274] For further discussion, *see* Kevin A. Ewing, Jason B. Hutt, and Erik E. Petersen, "Corporate Environmental Disclosures: Old Complaints, New Expectations," *Business Law International* 5, no. 3, p. 459 (Sept. 2004).

[275] *See* 17 C.F.R. § 229.103 (2003).

[276] The unreleased study is discussed in "Corporate Environmental Disclosure: Opportunities to Harness Market Forces to Improve Corporate Environmental Performance," a paper presented by Nicholas C. Franco to the ABA Conference on Environmental Law in Keystone, Colorado (Mar. 2001). *See also* GAO, *Environmental Disclosure: SEC Should Explore Ways to Improve Tracking and Transparency of Information,* July 2004 (discussing 27 studies and papers conducted between 1995 and 2003 on the topic of corporate environmental disclosure).

[277] Memorandum from Mary Kay Lynch and Eric V. Schaeffer to EPA's regional offices and enforcement coordinators, *Guidance on Distributing the Notice of SEC Registrants' Duty to Disclose Environmental Legal Proceedings in EPA Administrative Enforcement Actions,* Jan. 19, 2001.

[278] EPA Enforcement Alert, *Notifying Defendants of Securities and Exchange Commission's Environmental Disclosure Requirements,* EPA 300-N-01-008 at 3 (Oct. 2001).

[279] Felicity Barringer and Danny Hakim, "New York Subpoenas 5 Energy Companies," *New York Times,* Sept. 16, 2007, http://www.nytimes.com/2007/09/16/nyregion/16greenhouse.html (last visited on July 12, 2016).

[280] New York Office of the Attorney General press release, "First-Ever Binding and Enforceable Agreement Requiring a Company to Detail Financial Liabilities Related to Climate Change," Aug. 27, 2008; New

York Office of the Attorney General press release, "Second Major Agreement in Cuomo Initiative Requires Dynegy to Detail Financial Liabilities Related to Climate Change," Oct. 23, 2008.

[281] U.S. Securities and Exchange Commission, SEC Issues Interpretive Guidance on Disclosure Related to Business or Legal Developments Regarding Climate Change (Jan. 27, 2010), http://www.sec.gov/news/press/2010/2010-15.htm (last visited on July 12, 2016).

[282] U.S. Securities and Exchange Commission, Commission Guidance Regarding Disclosure Related to Climate Change, Exchange Act Release (Feb. 2, 2012), *available at* www.sec.gov/rules/interp/2010/33-9106.pdf (last visited July 12, 2016).

[283] Justin Gillis & Clifford Krauss, Exxon Mobil Investigated for Possible Climate Change Lies by New York Attorney General, *N.Y. Times,* Nov. 5, 2015, *available at* http://www.nytimes.com/2015/11/06/science/exxon-mobil-under-investigation-in-new-york-over-climate-statements.html (last visited July 12, 2016).

[284] Terry Wade, *U.S. States, Rockefellers Clash with U.S. House Panel on Exxon Climate Probes,* Reuters, Jun 24, 2016, *available at* http://www.reuters.com/article/us-exxon-mobil-climatechange-idUSKCN0ZA3KX (last visited July 12, 2016) (discussing Republican inquiries into several state attorney general investigations). Letter from Ted W. Lieu & Mark DeSaulnier, Members of House Oversight and Government Reform Committee, to Loretta E. Lynch, Attorney General (Oct. 14, 2015), *available at* https://lieu .house.gov/sites/lieu.house.gov/files/documents/2015.10.15%20Rep.%20Ted%20Lieu_DOJ_Exxon Mobil.pdf (requesting DOJ to investigate ExxonMobil). John Schwartz, Climate Change Activists Either Prod Exxon Mobil or Dump It, *N.Y. Times,* May 25, 2016, *available at* http://www.nytimes.com/2016/05/26/science/exxon-mobil-annual-meeting.html (last visited July 12, 2016) (describing differences in activist approaches). John C. Coffee, Jr., On Thin Ice: Climate Change, Exxon, the NYAG and the Martin Act, *The CLS Blue Sky Blog,* Nov. 23, 2015, *available at* http://clsbluesky.law.columbia.edu/2015/11/23/on-thin-ice-climate-change-exxon-the-nyag-and-the-martin-act/ (last visited July 12, 2016).

[285] Concept Release, No. 33-10064, *Business and Financial Disclosure Required by Regulation S-K,* Securities and Exchange Commission (Apr. 13, 2016), *available at* https://www.sec.gov/rules/concept/2016/33 -10064.pdf.

[286] *See, e.g.,* EPA's Enforcement and Compliance History Online (ECHO) Database, www.epa.gov/echo; and EPA's Envirofacts Data Warehouse, www.epa.gov/enviro. Corporate Environmental Reports (CERs) also inform the public about a company's environmental profile; in 2002, over half of the Global Fortune 250 prepared CERs. *See* KPMG, *International Survey of Corporate Sustainability Reporting* at 4 (2005).

[287] Financial Accounting Standards Board, News Release FASB Accounting Standards Codification Launches Today (July 1, 2009), http://www.fasb.org/cs/ContentServer?c_FASBContent_C&pagename _FASB %2FFAS BContent_C%2FNewsPage&cid_1176156318458 (last visited July 31, 2013).

[288] Financial Accounting Standards Board, Disclosure of Certain Loss Contingencies, http://www.fasb.org/jsp/FASB/FASBContent_C/ProjectUpdatePage&cid_900000011071 (last visited July 31, 2013).

[289] FAS 5, para. 8.

[290] FAS 5, para. 10.

[291] *Id.*

[292] For example, the Rose Foundation (www.rosefdn.org) and CERES (www.ceres.org).

[293] For most practical purposes, environmental liabilities will be governed by the new standard, not FAS 5.

[294] A few specified liabilities would have still been governed by FAS 5, notably guarantees and certain insurance and employment-related matters.

[295] 42 U.S.C. § 9607(a)(4)(C) (CERCLA); 33 U.S.C. § 2702(b)(2)(A) (OPA). *See also* 33 U.S.C. § 1321(b)(3) and (f)(4) (CWA) and the National Park System Resource Protection Act, 16 U.S.C. § 19jj.

[296] 42 U.S.C. § 9607(f)(1) (CERCLA), 33 U.S.C. § 2712(a)(2) (OPA), and 33 U.S.C. § 1321(f)(5) (CWA). "Natural Resources" is broadly defined under both CERCLA and OPA to include "land, fish, wildlife, biota, air, water, ground water, drinking water supplies, and other such resources," limited to

such resources held in trust for the public. 42 U.S.C. § 9601(16) (CERCLA) and 33 U.S.C. § 2701(20) (OPA). NRDs are compensation for injury to, destruction of, or loss of natural resources, including the reasonable costs of a damage assessment. 42 U.S.C. §§ 9601(6) and 9607(a)(4)(C) (CERCLA); 33 U.S.C. §§ 2701(5) and 2702(b)(2) (OPA). The measure of damages is the cost of restoring injured resources to their baseline condition, compensation for the interim loss of injured resources pending recovery, and the reasonable cost of a damage assessment. 43 C.F.R. Part 11; 15 C.F.R. Part 990.

[297] 42 U.S.C. § 9613(g)(1) (CERCLA).

[298] *Id.* Under OPA, an NRD claim must be brought within three years of when "the loss or connection of the loss with the discharge in question are reasonably discoverable with the exercise of due care," or when the NRD assessment is completed. 33 U.S.C. § 2717(f) (OPA).

[299] New Jersey Department of Environmental Protection's Policy Directive 2003–07, *Subject: Natural Resource Damages*, Sept. 24, 2003. The "first wave" of litigation was commenced about eight months later when the state filed NRD claims against 10 companies for 12 polluted sites. *BNA Daily Environment*, "State Seeks Compensation from 10 Firms for Alleged Natural Resource Damages," at A-9, May 24, 2004.

[300] E. Lynn Grayson, Industry Files Litigation against New Jersey Opposing Aggressive Natural Resource Initiatives, 34 ELR 10,566 (June 2004). Notably, an industry coalition has filed suit in opposition of the state's use of private law firms for NRD recovery. *Id.*

[301] EPA. Next Generation Compliance: Strategic Plan 2014–2017. (Oct. 2014).

[302] *Id.* at 6.

[303] 42 U.S.C. § 7426(b) (CAA).

[304] *See generally NOx Budget Trading Program (SIP Call) 2003 Progress Report* (Aug. 2004). The rule recommended that 22 states located predominantly in the eastern half of the United States develop state implementation plans (SIPs) to reduce nitrogen oxide (NOx) emissions to prescribed levels and on a prescribed time frame. *Id.* at 4–5. If the states failed to revise their SIPs, then EPA would implement a federal plan to accomplish equivalent reductions. *Id.*

[305] *Michigan v. EPA*, 213 F.3d 663 (D.C. Cir. 2000), *cert. denied*, 121 S. Ct. 1225 (2001).

[306] *Id.*

[307] *State of West Virginia, et al. v. U.S. EPA, et al.*, No. 15-1363 (D.C. Cir., Oct. 23, 2015).

[308] *Id.*

[309] *Id.*

[310] BP, Deepwater Horizon Accident and Responses, http://www.bp.com/en/global/corporate/gulf-of-mexico-restoration/deepwater-horizon-accident-and-response.html (last visited July 12, 2016).

[311] *Id.*

[312] National Oceanic and Atmospheric Administration, BP Oil Spill, http://www.gulfspillrestoration.noaa.gov/oil-spill/ (last visited July 12, 2016).

[313] In re: Oil Spill by the Oil Rig "Deepwater Horizon" in the Gulf of Mexico, on April 20, 2010, No. 2:10-md-02179 (E.D. La) (Consent Decree filed Nov. 25, 2012).

[314] *Id.*

[315] Department of Justice, Press Release, BP Exploration and Production Inc. Agrees to Plead Guilty to Felony Manslaughter, Environmental Crimes and Obstruction of Congress Surrounding Deepwater Horizon Incident (Nov. 15, 2012), http://www.justice.gov/opa/pr/2012/November/12-ag-1369.html (last visited July 12, 2016).

[316] *Id.*

[317] *Id.*

[318] *Id.* (Partial Consent Decree signed Jan. 3, 2013).

[319] Department of Justice, Press Release, Transocean Agrees to Plead Guilty to Environmental Crime and Enter Civil Settlement to Resolve U.S. Clean Water Act Penalty Claims from Deepwater Horizon Incident (Jan. 3, 2013), http://www.justice.gov/opa/pr/2013/January/13-ag-004.html (last visited July 12, 2016).

[320] *See, e.g.,* Bureau of Safety and Environmental Enforcement, Press Release, Finalizes Important, Achievable Safety Standards Put in Place Following Deepwater Horizon (Aug. 25, 2012), http://www.bsee.gov/BSEE-Newsroom/Press-Releases/2012/BSEE-Releases-Offshore-Drilling-Safety-Rule (last visited July 12, 2016).

[321] Aruna Viswanatha, U.S. Bid to Prosecute BP Staff in Gulf Oil Spill Falls Flat, *Wall St. J.,* Feb. 27, 2016, available at http://www.wsj.com/articles/u-s-bid-to-prosecute-bp-staff-in-gulf-oil-spill-falls-flat-1456 532116; *U.S. v. Kaluza et al.,* No. 2:12-cr-00265 (E.D. La., filed Nov. 11, 2014).

[322] *United States v. Wal-Mart Stores, Inc.,* No. 3:13-00334 (N.D. Cal.) (plea filed May 28, 2013); *United States v. Wal-Mart Stores, Inc.,* No. 4:13-cr-00135 (W.C. Mo.) (plea filed May 28, 2013).

[323] EPA, News Release, Wal-Mart Pleads Guilty to Federal Environmental Crimes and Civil Violations And Will Pay More Than $81 Million / Retailer Admits Violating Criminal and Civil Laws Designed to Protect Water Quality and to Ensure Proper Handling of Hazardous Wastes and Pesticides (May 28, 2013), http://yosemite.epa.gov/opa/admpress.nsf/d0cf6618525a9efb85257359003fb69d/d4628253b5e 27cab85257b79007349aa!OpenDocument (last visited July 12, 2016).

[324] *See* EPA, *Petroleum Refinery Sector Risk and Technology Review and New Source Performance Standards,* 80 Fed. Reg. 75178 (Dec. 1, 2015), establishing fenceline monitoring work practice standard to improve the management of fugitive emissions; EPA, *Consolidated Petroleum Refinery Rulemaking Repository—Webinars for Petroleum Refinery Fenceline Monitoring Data,* available at https://www3.epa.gov/ttn/atw/petref.html (last visited July 12, 2016).

[325] *See* U.S. EPA's Airborne Spectral Photometric Environmental Collection Technology (ASPECT), available at https://www.epa.gov/emergency-response/aspect (last visited July 12, 2016).

[326] Charles Dickens, *Oliver Twist* (1838) ("'If the law supposes that,' said Mr. Bumble, squeezing his hat emphatically in both hands, 'the law is a ass—a idiot.'").

Chapter 3

Resource Conservation and Recovery Act

Peggy Otum[1]
Arnold & Porter LLP
San Francisco, CA

1.0 Introduction and Overview

The United States has developed a comprehensive regulatory program for the management of hazardous wastes. The old adage "out of sight, out of mind" has given way to a national program that seeks to encourage resource recovery, high-technology treatment, and secure long-term disposal of hazardous wastes. Congress enacted a national mandate to minimize the threat from hazardous waste to human health and the environment in passing the Resource Conservation and Recovery Act of 1976 (RCRA).[2] The U.S. Environmental Protection Agency (EPA) and the states have implemented this mandate in extensive regulations issued under RCRA and the Hazardous and Solid Waste Amendments of 1984 (HSWA).[3]

RCRA is designed to provide "cradle-to-grave" management of hazardous wastes by imposing strict management requirements on the owners and operators of treatment, storage, and disposal (TSD) facilities. RCRA mainly applies to operating facilities that generate and manage hazardous wastes. Congress imposed liabilities and created remedies to address problems at abandoned and inactive sites in the Comprehensive Environmental Response, Compensation, and Liability Act of 1980, commonly known as Superfund,[4] which is discussed in detail in another chapter. RCRA has been amended periodically since its enactment, most importantly by the HSWA. The HSWA mandated far-reaching changes to the RCRA program, such as requiring waste minimization and introducing a national land disposal ban program, discussed below.

RCRA is divided into 10 subtitles, A through J. Subtitle A of RCRA declares that, as a matter of national policy, the generation of hazardous waste is to be reduced or eliminated as expeditiously as possible, and land disposal should be the least favored method for managing hazardous wastes. In addition, all waste that is generated must be handled so as to minimize the present and future threat to human health and the environment.[5] Subtitle A also describes a series of national objectives designed to achieve these goals, including proper management of hazardous waste in the first instance, minimizing the generation and land disposal of hazardous waste, a prohibition on open dumping, state assumption of RCRA programs, promoting research and development activities for waste management, and encouraging recovery, recycling, and treatment as alternatives to land disposal.[6] These goals and objectives give direction to EPA's regulatory efforts and are important to an informed understanding of the Subtitle C hazardous waste management program.

Subtitle C, which establishes the national hazardous waste management program, is perhaps the most important of the RCRA subtitles. Sections 3001–3023 in Subtitle C, 42 U.S.C. §§ 6921-6939g, establish the basic structure for the RCRA program. Under Section 3001, EPA was required to promulgate regulations identifying hazardous wastes, either by listing specific hazardous wastes or establishing characteristics of hazardous wastes. Persons managing such wastes are required to notify the EPA of their hazardous waste activities.[7]

Section 3002 authorizes a set of standards with which persons who generate or produce hazardous wastes (generators) must comply, including handling hazardous wastes properly and preparing manifests to track the shipment of the waste. Section 3003 provides another set of regulations regarding manifests, labeling, and the delivery of hazardous waste shipments to designated TSD facilities for persons who transport hazardous waste (transporters). Transporters must also comply with applicable U.S. Department of Transportation (DOT) rules relating to containers, labeling, placarding of vehicles, and spill response.

Section 3004 requires TSD facilities to comply with certain performance standards, including statutory minimum technology requirements, groundwater monitoring, air emission controls, corrective actions, and prohibitions on the land disposal of untreated hazardous wastes. Section 3005 requires owners and operators of TSD facilities to obtain permits that set the conditions under which they may operate. Section 3005(e) establishes the "interim status" provision for existing TSD facilities, which allows them to remain in operation until a site-specific permit is issued.

Section 3006 of RCRA authorizes states to assume responsibility for carrying out the RCRA program in lieu of the federal program. Pursuant to Section 3006, the state must administer and enforce a program that is consistent with and equivalent to the federal program. States can adopt more stringent requirements, but the state program may be no less stringent than the federal program. Sections 3007 and 3008 authorize site inspections, requests for information, and federal enforcement of RCRA and its implementing regulations.

Other sections of Subtitle C include provisions for compiling a state-by-state hazardous waste site inventory, monitoring and enforcement authority against previous owners of TSD facilities, EPA regulation of recycled oil, controls on the export of hazardous waste, Department of Energy planning for development of treatment technologies and capacity for mixed (hazardous and radioactive) wastes, and provisions for federally owned treatment works.[8]

The HSWA extensively amended RCRA by expanding both the scope of coverage and the detailed requirements of RCRA. For example, they required EPA to expand its regulation of an estimated 200,000 companies that produce only small quantities of hazardous waste (less than 1,000 kilograms per month). A regulatory program was created in Subtitle I ("eye") for underground storage tanks containing hazardous substances or petroleum that affected hundreds of thousands of facilities for the first time.[9] The numerous constraints imposed on those who treat, store, or dispose of hazardous wastes in land-based facilities, including restrictions on the disposal of liquid wastes and other common hazardous wastes in landfills, have dramatically changed the way that such wastes are managed. There were 72 major provisions in the 1984 HSWA, and these requirements have had a substantial impact on every U.S. business that produces hazardous waste.

During recent years, the RCRA program has matured. EPA and states have moved forward with program reforms and innovations, and U.S. business has successfully implemented new waste minimization, recycling, and compliance strategies. The U.S. private sector has made an enormous capital investment in hazardous waste management, largely as a result of the goals and requirements of RCRA. The days of Love Canal and Valley of the Drums are now in the past, and the focus in the future will be on implementing the waste management hierarchy of prevention, reuse and recycling, treatment, and secure disposal.

Major topics in the Subtitle C program are discussed below, as are the requirements of other important subtitles of RCRA.

2.0 Defining Solid and Hazardous Wastes

RCRA regulates both solid and hazardous waste. As "hazardous waste" is a subset of "solid waste," the first step in determining whether RCRA applies to a particular material is to identify whether the material is a solid waste.

2.1 Definition of Solid Waste

The starting point for determining the full scope of RCRA's coverage is the statute's definition of "solid waste." Section 1004(27), 42 U.S.C. § 6903(27), states,

> The term "solid waste" means any garbage, refuse, sludge from a waste treatment plant, water supply treatment plant, or air pollution control facility and other discarded material, including solid, liquid, semisolid, or contained gaseous material resulting from industrial, commercial, mining, and agriculture operations, and from community activities, but does not include solid or dissolved material in domestic sewage, or solid or dissolved materials in irrigation return flows or industrial discharges which are point sources subject to permits under section [402 of the Federal Water Pollution Control Act, as amended], or source, special nuclear, or byproduct material as defined by the Atomic Energy Act of 1954, as amended (68 Stat. 923).

The statute therefore applies to potentially any waste regardless of its physical form.

EPA has defined solid waste to include any discarded material, provided a regulatory exclusion or specific variance granted by EPA or an authorized state does not apply.[10] "Discarded material" is defined as any material that is abandoned, recycled, considered "inherently waste-like," or a military munition.[11] A material is abandoned if it is disposed of, burned or incinerated, accumulated, stored, or treated prior to or in lieu of abandonment. A material is inherently waste-like if EPA so defines it by regulation.[12] A material can be a solid waste if it is recycled in any of the following ways:

1. Applied to or placed on the land in a manner constituting disposal

2. Burned for energy recovery or used to produce a fuel

3. Reclaimed by being processed to recover a usable product or by being regenerated

4. Accumulated speculatively by not recycling at least 75 percent by weight or volume of the material accumulated at the beginning of the calendar year.

2.1.1 Exclusions from the Definition of Solid Waste

EPA has further defined "solid waste" by regulation, establishing important exemptions and detailed definitions of key terms in the statute. The exclusions from the definition of "solid waste" include the following:

1. Domestic sewage or any mixture of domestic sewage and other wastes that passes through a sewer system to a publicly owned treatment works

2. Industrial wastewater discharges that are point source discharges under the Clean Water Act

3. Irrigation return flows

4. Source, special nuclear, or by-product material under the Atomic Energy Act

5. In-situ mining materials

6. Reclaimed pulping liquors that are reused in the pulping process

7. Spent sulfuric acid used to produce new sulfuric acid

8. Certain reclaimed secondary materials that are returned to and reused in the original processes in which they were generated

9. Reclaimed and reused spent wood preserving solutions and wood preserving process wastewaters

10. Coke by-products processes wastes that exhibit the toxicity characteristic

11. Nonwastewater splash condenser dross residue

12. Recovered oil from petroleum exploration, production, or refining that is reinserted into the refining process

13. Certain scrap metal and shredded circuit boards that are recycled

14. Condensates derived from the overhead gases from kraft mill steam strippers

15. Hazardous materials used to produce fuels or syngas that are comparable to fossil fuels

16. Primary mineral processing industry spent materials from which minerals or other values are recovered by mineral processing or beneficiation

17. Petrochemical recovered oil from an associated organic chemical manufacturing facility

18. Spent caustic solutions from petroleum refining liquid treating processes used to produce cresylic or naphthenic acid

19. Hazardous secondary materials used to make zinc fertilizers and zinc fertilizers made from hazardous wastes

20. Used cathode ray tubes

21. Certain hazardous secondary material generated and reclaimed within the United States or its territories and managed in land-based units

22. Certain hazardous secondary material that is generated then transferred for the purpose of reclamation

23. Exported hazardous secondary material that is reclaimed at a foreign reclamation facility

2.1.2 Recycled Materials

Materials are not solid wastes when recycled if they are directly used or reused as ingredients or feedstocks in a production process, or as effective substitutes for commercial products, or are recycled in a closed-loop production process. Of course, materials that are never discarded, but are used or reused in an ongoing production process by the generating industry itself, are not solid wastes and therefore cannot be hazardous wastes.[13]

The interlocking definitions of solid and hazardous waste result in EPA regulating a universe of materials that may not commonly be understood to be "wastes" for a particular industry or company. In particular, discarded materials that will be reclaimed or recycled may still be solid wastes subject to RCRA unless a regulatory exclusion applies. In January 2015, EPA promulgated the long-awaited "Definition of Solid Waste" (DSW) Final Rule that revised the definition of solid waste to clarify what recycling activities are considered "legitimate recycling" in response to concern over the growth of "sham recycling." The DSW Final Rule bolsters the objective of RCRA to protect human health and the environment by ensuring that the hazardous secondary materials recycling regulations are implemented in a way that encourages reclamation that does not result in increased risk to human health and the environment from discarded hazardous secondary material.[14] The DSW Final Rule clarifies the distinction between genuine and sham recycling by establishing a clear and uniform legitimate recycling standard for all hazardous secondary materials and by revising the regulatory exclusions for hazardous secondary materials. Thus, EPA's revisions clarified which hazardous materials are not considered "discarded" for RCRA regulatory purposes. This regulatory step is critical because only discarded material is solid waste, and only "solid waste" can be "hazardous waste."

If a material meets the definition of solid waste but does not meet the definition of hazardous waste as described below, then it is subject to regulation under Subtitle D as a nonhazardous solid waste. Subtitle D regulates municipal solid waste, refuse, sludge from treatment plants or pollution control facilities, industrial wastes, and other discarded materials from industrial and commercial activities. Under Subtitle D, state and local governments are tasked with permitting and monitoring municipal and nonhazardous waste landfills. Subtitle D sets out minimal national requirements for location, operation, design, groundwater monitoring, corrective action, closure and post-closure care, and financial assurance responsibility.

2.2 Definition of Hazardous Waste

The Subtitle C regulatory program of RCRA covers those solid wastes that are deemed hazardous. As defined in Section 1004(5), the term "hazardous waste" means a solid waste, or combination of solid wastes, which because of its quantity, concentration, or physical, chemical, or infectious characteristics may

A. Cause, or significantly contribute to an increase in mortality or an increase in serious irreversible, or incapacitating reversible illness; or

B. Pose a substantial present or potential hazard to human health or the environment when improperly treated, stored, transported, or disposed of, or otherwise managed.

EPA's regulations automatically exempt certain solid wastes from consideration as hazardous wastes. These solid wastes are thus regulated under Subtitle D as nonhazardous wastes. The list of materials that are exempted by regulation is long and detailed and should be carefully consulted. Generally, these regulatory exemptions include the following:

- Household waste
- Agricultural wastes which are returned to the ground as fertilizer
- Mining overburden returned to the mine site
- Fly ash waste, bottom ash waste, slag waste, and flue gas emission control waste generated from coal or other fossil fuel combustion[15]
- Crude oil and natural gas exploration, development, or production drilling waste
- Certain chromium-bearing wastes that fail the test for the toxicity characteristic
- Wastes from the extraction, beneficiation, and processing of ores and minerals, including coal
- Cement kiln dust wastes
- Arsenical-treated wood wastes generated by end users of such wood
- Petroleum-contaminated media and debris that fail the test for the toxicity characteristic and that are subject to corrective action requirements[16]

- Carbon Dioxide streams injected into Underground Injection Control Class VI wells for purposes of geologic sequestration (i.e., carbon capture)[17]

- Used chlorofluorocarbon refrigerants from enclosed heat transfer equipment

- Non-terne plated used oil filters

- Used oil re-refining distillation bottoms used to manufacture asphalt products

- Leachate or gas condensate from landfills

EPA has also provided some regulatory exemptions under narrowly defined circumstances, such as for hazardous waste that is generated in a product or raw material storage tank, transport vehicle, pipeline, or manufacturing process unit prior to removal for disposal. Moreover, EPA has also adopted conditional exemptions for waste samples collected for testing to determine their characteristics or composition or to conduct treatability tests.[18]

Finally, certain "universal wastes" are exempted from the Subtitle C program and have special promulgated standards, discussed below.[19] Currently, nickel cadmium batteries, recalled pesticides, mercury-containing equipment including thermostats, and fluorescent lamps are eligible for these special standards.

3.0 Subtitle C: Hazardous Waste Management Program

3.1 Identification of Hazardous Wastes[20]

If a solid waste does not qualify for an exemption, it will be deemed a hazardous waste if it is listed by EPA in 40 C.F.R. Part 261, Subpart D, or if it exhibits any of the four hazardous waste characteristics in 40 C.F.R. Part 261, Subpart C. EPA's hazardous waste lists and the four hazardous waste characteristics are discussed in detail below.

3.1.1 Hazardous Waste Lists

EPA has established three hazardous wastes lists. A hazardous waste code is assigned to each listed waste and can be used to identify the waste on manifests, biennial reports, and other documents and for purposes of the land disposal ban program. The first list contains hazardous wastes from nonspecific sources (e.g., spent nonhalogenated solvents, such as toluene or methyl ethyl ketone).[21] The hazardous wastes on this nonspecific source list are assigned an "F" code (e.g., F001 assigned to various spent solvents).

The second list identifies hazardous wastes from specific sources (e.g., bottom sediment sludge from the treatment of wastewaters by the wood preserving industry).[22] The hazardous wastes on this source list are assigned a "K" code (e.g., K048 to K052 are certain petroleum refining wastes). These first two hazardous waste lists are fairly self-explanatory. EPA has largely concluded its efforts to develop the F and K lists of hazardous wastes from specific industries. The final listing actions have included carbamate production wastes, petroleum refinery wastes, inorganic chemical production wastes, dye and pigment wastes, and chlorinated aliphatics production wastes.[23] A company should compare its solid waste to the nonspecific source and specific source lists to determine if it manages a hazardous waste.

The third list sets forth commercial chemical products, including off-specification variants, containers, and spill residues, which, when discarded, must be treated as hazardous wastes.[24] This hazardous waste list consists of two distinct sublists. One sublist sets forth chemicals deemed "acutely" hazardous when discarded (40 C.F.R. 261.33[e]). These are assigned a "P" number and are subject to more rigorous management requirements (e.g., P076 is nitric oxide). A second sublist contains "U" listed chemicals that are deemed toxic and, therefore, hazardous when discarded (40 C.F.R. 261.33[f]) and that are regulated like other listed hazardous wastes (e.g., U002 is acetone).

Hazardous waste regulation under the commercial chemical list can be triggered when a company decides to reduce inventory or otherwise discards a listed commercial chemical product in its pure form. An accidental spill of the chemical may also trigger regulation.[25] If a listed commercial chemical is spilled, the spilled chemical and any contaminated material, such as dirt and other residue, are likely to be discarded and thus become a hazardous waste. Therefore, even companies that generally do not discard or intend to discard any of the commercial chemical products on the list must be prepared to comply with the RCRA hazardous waste regulations in the event of an accidental spill.[26] This may involve, as discussed below, obtaining an EPA identification number and complying, at a minimum, with applicable generator standards. For disposal of small amounts of chemicals or spill materials, a company may qualify as a conditionally exempt "small quantity generator."[27]

Since the RCRA program became effective in 1980, many companies have filed "delisting petitions" with EPA to remove wastes generated at their facilities from the RCRA hazardous waste lists at 40 C.F.R. Part 261.[28] The granting of a delisting petition exempts the waste generated at a particular facility from the RCRA hazardous waste program. A company seeking a delisting must demonstrate that its particular waste does not contain the hazardous constituents for which EPA listed the waste or any other constituents that could cause the waste to be hazardous.[29] For example, a company seeking to delist a waste which would otherwise be included under F006 (wastewater treatment sludge from electroplating operations) must show that the concentrations of chromium, nickel, and cyanide for which the waste was listed are below levels of regulatory concern, and also that no other heavy metals or other constituents are present that may cause the waste to be hazardous.

EPA or an authorized state must act on a delisting petition within two years of receiving a complete petition. EPA often will "condition" a delisting on disposal of the waste in a land disposal facility that has a liner and groundwater monitoring system. EPA regions and many states that have been delegated authority for delistings use the Delisting Risk Assessment Software (DRAS) developed by EPA Region 6. The DRAS is a computer program that calculates the potential risks to human health and the environment associated with disposing of a waste stream into a landfill or surface impoundment. For a given waste, the DRAS calculates both the waste's aggregate risks and also back-calculates each waste constituent's maximum allowable for delisting.[30]

3.1.2 Hazardous Waste Characteristics

If a waste is not listed as hazardous, the waste may still be subject to regulation under RCRA Subtitle C if it exhibits one of four characteristics: ignitability, corrosivity, reactivity, or toxicity.[31]

The hazardous waste characteristic of ignitability was established to identify solid wastes capable during routine handling of causing a fire or exacerbating a fire once started.[32] A solid waste is deemed to exhibit the characteristic of ignitability if it satisfies one of the following four descriptions: (1) It is a liquid, other than an aqueous solution containing less than 24 percent alcohol by volume, that has a flash point of less than 140 degrees Fahrenheit (60 degrees Celsius); (2) it is a nonliquid that under normal conditions can cause a fire through friction, absorption of moisture, or spontaneous chemical changes and burns so vigorously when ignited that it creates a hazard; (3) it is an ignitable compressed gas as defined by the DOT regulations at 49 C.F.R. 173.300; or (4) it is an oxidizer as defined by the DOT regulations at 49 C.F.R. 173.151. An ignitable hazardous waste has the EPA code of D001.

The hazardous waste characteristic of corrosivity was established to identify wastes capable of corroding metal, escaping their containers, and liberating other wastes.[33] In addition, wastes with a pH at either the high or the low end of the scale can harm human tissue and aquatic life and may react dangerously with other wastes. Therefore, EPA determined that any solid waste is deemed to exhibit the characteristic of corrosivity if it is (1) aqueous and has a pH of less than or equal to 2.0 or greater than or equal to 12.5 or (2) a liquid and corrodes steel at a rate greater than 6.35 millimeters (.250 inches) per year under specified testing procedures. A waste that exhibits the hazardous characteristic of corrosivity has the EPA code of D002.

The hazardous waste characteristic of reactivity was established to identify wastes that are extremely unstable and have a tendency to react violently or explode during management.[34] The regulation lists a number of situations where this may happen that warrant specific consideration (e.g., when the waste is mixed with water, when heated, etc.). Since test protocols for measuring reactivity are largely unavailable, EPA has promulgated a narrative definition of the reactivity characteristic that must be used. A waste that exhibits reactivity has EPA code D003.

The hazardous waste characteristic of toxicity was established to identify wastes that are likely to leach hazardous concentrations of specific toxic constituents into groundwater if mismanaged.[35] This characteristic is determined using a mandatory testing procedure called the Toxicity Characteristic Leaching Procedure (TCLP) that extracts the toxic constituents from a waste in a manner that EPA believes simulates the leaching action that occurs in municipal landfills.[36] A solid waste exhibits the characteristic of toxicity if the test methods prescribed by EPA show that the extract from a representative sample of the waste contains contaminants at levels of regulatory concern. The TCLP tests for 25 organic chemicals, 8 inorganic compounds, and 6 insecticides/herbicides. The levels that trigger the toxicity characteristic reflect health-based concentration thresholds and a factor for dilution and attenuation that was developed using modeling of the subsurface fate and transport of contaminants in groundwater. These hazardous wastes are given EPA codes D004 to D043, depending on the toxic constituent that causes the waste to be hazardous.

3.1.3 Empty Containers and Residues

A barrel, drum, or other container and any hazardous waste remaining in the container is subject to regulation until the container is considered empty.[37] A container is "empty" if all wastes have been removed using commonly employed practices, such as pouring, pumping, or aspirating the wastes, and no more than one inch (2.5 cm) of residue remains on the bottom of the container. Alternatively, for containers that are 119 gallons or smaller, the container is empty if no more than 3 percent by weight of the total capacity remains in the container, and for containers larger than 119 gallons, no more than 0.3 percent by weight can remain in the container after normal emptying.

A container that has held an "acutely" hazardous waste (e.g., a P-listed waste) is empty if the container or inner liner has been triple rinsed using an appropriate solvent or cleaned by an equivalent method. In such cases, the rinsate will be a hazardous waste. EPA does not have a formal approval process if an "equivalent" cleaning method is used to empty a container, but the generator should document the method and keep the record as part of the facility's operating record.

3.1.4 Mixtures of Hazardous Wastes and Solid Wastes

RCRA may also be applied to cover mixtures of hazardous and nonhazardous solid waste. Under what is known as the "mixture rule," a mixture of a listed hazardous waste and a solid waste is considered a hazardous waste, unless the mixture qualifies for an exemption.[38] The exemptions apply if, for example, (1) the listed hazardous waste in the mixture was listed solely because it exhibits a hazardous characteristic and the mixture does not exhibit that characteristic; (2) the mixture consists of wastewater and certain specified hazardous wastes in dilute concentrations, the discharge of which is subject to regulation under the Clean Water Act; or (3) the mixture consists of a discarded commercial chemical product resulting from de minimis losses during manufacturing operations. On the other hand, a mixture of a characteristic hazardous waste and a solid waste will be deemed hazardous only if the entire mixture continues to exhibit a hazardous characteristic. Note that these exemptions apply only when the hazardous waste becomes mixed with other wastes as part of the normal production or waste management process, and not when wastes are intentionally mixed to achieve dilution. Such mixing may constitute treatment and could require a RCRA permit.

3.1.5 Derived-From Hazardous Wastes

Of equal importance is EPA's so-called "derived-from rule." Under this rule, a waste that is generated from the treatment, storage, or disposal of a hazardous waste (e.g., ash, leachate, or emission control dust) is also a hazardous waste unless exempted.[39] If the waste is derived from a listed hazardous waste, it is considered a hazardous waste unless delisted. If the waste is derived from a characteristic hazardous waste, it is not hazardous if it does not exhibit that characteristic. Materials that are reclaimed from solid wastes for beneficial use are no longer wastes, unless the reclaimed material is burned as a fuel or used in a manner constituting disposal (i.e., applied to the ground).

3.1.6 Hazardous Contaminated Soils and Debris

Another relevant rule is embodied in the "contained-in principle." EPA has long taken the view that soil, groundwater, surface water, and debris that are contaminated with listed hazardous waste must be regulated under RCRA Subtitle C.[40] The contaminated media and debris are said to contain the listed hazardous waste and thus to require proper management. EPA has now codified this rule, along with the corollary that debris that is treated so that it no longer contains a listed hazardous waste will no longer be subject to Subtitle C regulation.[41]

3.1.7 Conditional Exclusion for Hazardous Secondary Materials That Are Reclaimed

In a major 2008 rulemaking, EPA established a new regulatory framework for recycling of hazardous secondary materials that would otherwise be solid and hazardous wastes if discarded.[42] The program is based on a conditional exclusion from the definition of solid waste for materials that are reclaimed under the control of the generator. This concept of control ensures that the generator remains responsible for legitimate and safe recycling, and therefore the material is not discarded and does not become a solid waste. EPA's January 2015 revision to the definition of solid waste, effective July 13, 2015, intends to more effectively accomplish the goal of excluding legitimately recycled hazardous secondary materials from the definition of solid waste.

The 2008 conditional exclusion is still available when the generator reclaims its own hazardous materials on-site ("generator-controlled exclusion"), but the 2015 rule replaces the 2008 "transfer-based exclusion" for generators that sent their materials to a third-party reclaimer with a "verified recycler exclusion."[43] Much of the substance of the 2008 rule was reaffirmed in the 2015 final rule. The major revisions were made to tailor the provisions to their original objective. Key comparisons between the 2008 and 2015 rules are discussed below.

The 2008 rule indicated that a generator must handle the material in units, such as containers, tanks, and surface impoundments, that meet a performance standard that requires the material to be contained in such units, without significant leakage or loss of material.[44] The 2015 generator-controlled exclusion clarified the definition of "contained" to mean that the unit in which hazardous secondary material is placed controls its movement out of the unit and into the environment. Hazardous secondary materials that are not contained but are instead released into the environment are not destined for recycling and are thus "discarded."

To qualify for the on-site exclusion under the 2008 framework, a generator must send a notification to EPA that includes the ID number of the facility, a list of the hazardous secondary materials that will be recycled, and the annual quantity of recycled materials.[45] This notification must be filed every two years to maintain the exclusion. When fully implemented, the notification scheme will provide the first accurate census of hazardous materials recycling in the United States. The 2015 rule largely retains the 2008 notification procedures but makes notification a condition, rather than a requirement, of exclusion. Therefore, failure to notify would result in the loss of exclusion for the hazardous secondary material as opposed to a violation of the notification regulations.

In addition, the generator must not engage in speculative accumulation, which means that at least 75 percent of the hazardous secondary materials must actually be recycled each calendar year.[46] The 2015 rule additionally requires placement in a storage unit and labeling with the first date of accumulation or documentation in an inventory log. Further recordkeeping of shipments sent or received under the exclusion and documentation of legitimacy factor determinations are required. Finally, EPA's 2015 revisions add a condition that generators must follow emergency preparedness and response regulations.

Under the verified recycler exclusion, generators must send the materials they want to recycle that would otherwise be regulated as hazardous waste to either a RCRA-permitted reclamation facility or to a verified recycler of hazardous secondary materials who has obtained a solid waste variance from EPA or an authorized state. The solid waste variance determines ex ante if a facility will properly manage hazardous secondary materials and legitimately recycle them based on the same criteria considered under the 2008 reasonable efforts analysis for transfer-based exclusions. EPA's 2008 rule lists five specific questions that the generator must affirmatively answer as part of the reasonable efforts inquiry relating to such matters as the compliance status of the reclaimer. In making this inquiry, the generator may rely on any credible evidence, including information provided by the reclaimer or a third party such as an audit company.

Additionally, the verified recycler exclusion is conditioned on a prohibition of speculative accumulation, a notice requirement (same as for the generator-controlled exclusion), a requirement that the hazardous secondary materials be contained, and emergency preparedness and response regulations. Other provisions are specifically applicable to generators, transporters, or reclamation facilities. For example, reclaimers and intermediate facilities are required to maintain records of received shipments for three years and to send documentation of receipt to the generator.

In addition, the reclaimer must have financial assurance for closing the facility and disposing of any hazardous secondary materials.[47] Financial assurance may take the form of a trust fund, surety bond, letter of credit, insurance, or satisfaction of a financial test and corporate guarantee. The amount of financial assurance is based on a closure cost estimate maintained at the facility that must be adjusted each year for inflation and changes to the facility.

The reclaimer must manage the hazardous secondary material in a manner that is at least as protective as that employed for analogous raw materials, and must meet a performance standard that the material is contained. Any residuals from the recycling process must be handled in a protective manner, and any residuals that exhibit a hazardous characteristic or are listed as a hazardous waste must be managed as a RCRA waste.

When shipping hazardous secondary materials to a reclaimer, generators may find it necessary to use a transfer facility or intermediate facility during transportation.[48] A transfer facility is generally a loading dock, parking lot, or storage area where shipments are held for up to 10 days during the normal course of transportation. An intermediate facility is a location where hazardous secondary materials are stored for more than 10 days. Generators must send their secondary materials directly to a reclaimer, with intervening storage at transfer facilities or intermediate facilities as necessary, but no other person or facility (such as a broker) may handle the material.

The generator must maintain records for at least three years of all shipments, including the names of the transporters and reclaimers, types and quantity of material, and confirmation of receipt from each reclaimer.[49] Special requirements apply to hazardous secondary materials that are exported to a reclaimer in a foreign country.[50]

Most importantly, the generator must be able to demonstrate that the recycling is legitimate.[51] EPA's 2015 final rule clarifies the factors that determine whether a particular recycling activity is legitimate or sham recycling, which is considered treatment or disposal of hazardous waste that requires a RCRA permit, and prohibits sham recycling (40 C.F.R § 261.2(g)). The generator is required to demonstrate that the recycling process is legitimate based on four legitimacy factors that all must be met: (1) the recycled hazardous secondary material provides a useful contribution to the recycling process or to a product or intermediate of the recycling process, (2) the recycling process produces a valuable product or intermediate, (3) the generator and recycler manage the hazardous secondary material as a valuable commodity, and (4) the product of the recycling process is comparable to a legitimate product or intermediate.

EPA also provides a petition process for case-by-case determinations that recycled materials are not solid wastes.[52] The petitioner must apply to EPA for a formal ruling, after public notice and opportunity for comment, that the hazardous secondary material is not discarded based on either of two criteria. The first criterion is that the hazardous secondary material is reclaimed in a continuous industrial process, considering whether management of the material is part of production and not waste treatment, whether the capacity of the production process is sufficient to use the material, and whether hazardous constituents in the material are recovered rather than released to the environment. Alternatively, the second criterion is that the hazardous secondary material is indistinguishable in all relevant aspects from a product or intermediate, considering whether market participants treat the material as a valuable material or a waste, whether the chemical and physical identity of the material is comparable to commercial products, and whether hazardous constituents in the material are recovered rather than released to the environment.

Exempted from hazardous waste definition (regulated by RCRA Subtitle D)	Exempted from solid waste definition (not regulated by RCRA)
Household wastes	Domestic sewage and any mixture of domestic sewage and other wastes going to a publicly owned treatment works
Agricultural wastes used as fertilizer	Industrial point source wastewater discharges under the Clean Water Act
Mining overburden returned to mine site	Irrigation return flows
Coal and fossil fuel combustion wastes	Source, special nuclear, or by-product material under the Atomic Energy Act
Crude oil and natural gas exploration, development, and production drilling waste	In-situ mining wastes
Certain chromium-bearing wastes	Reclaimed and reused pulping liquors
Ore and mineral extraction, beneficiation, and processing wastes	Spent sulfuric acid used to produce new sulfuric acid
Cement kiln dust	Certain reclaimed secondary materials that are returned to and reused in the original process in which they were generated
Arsenic-treated wood wastes	Reclaimed and reused spent wood preserving solutions and wastewater
Petroleum-contaminated media and debris	Certain coke by-products

Carbon-dioxide streams in geologic sequestration activities	Nonwastewater splash condenser dross residue
Used chlorofluorocarbon refrigerants	Oil-bearing hazardous secondary materials and recovered oil generated at a petroleum refinery
Used oil filters	Recycled scrap metal
Use oil re-refining distillation bottoms	Certain shredded circuit boards
Leachate or gas condensate from landfills	Kraft mill steam overhead gas-derived condensates Certain comparable fuels or comparable syngas fuels Primary mineral processing industry spent materials Petrochemical recovered oil Spent caustic solutions Hazardous secondary materials used to make zinc fertilizers and zinc fertilizers made from hazardous waste Used cathode ray tubes Certain U.S.-generated and reclaimed hazardous secondary material managed in land-based units Certain hazardous secondary material that is transferred for the purpose of reclamation Reclaimed exported hazardous secondary material

3.1.8 Electronic Waste (E-Waste)

The rapidly increasing use of computers, smart phones, tablets, video games, and similar devices both in businesses and households has resulted in a deluge of electronic waste. Each American household owns approximately 24 electronic products, and waste streams from these electronics are growing at 2–3 times that of other household wastes.[53] Many components of this e-waste contain hazardous materials, such as lead, mercury, and hexavalent chromium in circuit boards, batteries, and cathode ray tubes (CRTs); cadmium in chip resisters, infrared detectors, and semiconductors; and brominated flame retardants in plastic covers and cables. Computer monitors and older TV picture tubes contain an average of four pounds of lead and require special disposal.

E-waste can often be donated to an appropriate charity for reuse or repair. Otherwise, used electronics may be sent for recycling.[54] Fifty percent of the materials in a personal computer can be recycled. Many municipalities offer computer and electronics collections as part of household hazardous waste collection days or special events. In addition, county recycling drop-off centers, TV repair shops, electronics recycling companies, and even local electronics retailers may accept computers and other electronics for recycling.

When e-waste is disposed, regulatory requirements under the federal or state hazardous waste program may apply. Generators who send e-waste for disposal must make a hazardous waste determination, and if the e-waste exhibits a hazardous characteristic, then it must be manifested and disposed in a permitted RCRA landfill. For example, CRTs in color computer monitors and televisions are considered hazardous when discarded because of the presence of lead in the CRT. There has been a proliferation of state and local laws regulating e-waste recycling, which has prompted calls for regulation of e-waste on the federal level.

3.2 Notification of Hazardous Waste Management Activities

RCRA Section 3010(a) requires that any person who manages a hazardous waste (i.e., generators, transporters, and owners and operators of TSD facilities) must file a notification with EPA within 90 days after regulations are promulgated identifying the waste as hazardous. EPA has published Form 8700-12 as the Section 3010(a) notification form. The reporting company must identify itself, its location, and the EPA identification numbers for the listed and characteristic hazardous wastes it manages. Notifications must be filed for each site (e.g., plant) at which hazardous waste is managed.

3.3 Generators of Hazardous Waste

Generators play a crucial role in the overall RCRA hazardous waste regulatory scheme. The failure of a generator to properly identify and initiate the management of a hazardous waste may mean that the waste never enters the "cradle to grave" hazardous waste program. Thus, the requirements imposed on generators under RCRA Section 3002 and EPA's implementing regulations at 40 C.F.R. Part 262 are of key concern.

EPA's regulations define the term "generator" as "any person, by site, whose act or process produces hazardous waste identified or listed in Part 261 of this chapter or whose act first causes hazardous waste to become subject to regulation."[55] This definition refers explicitly to the particular site of generation. A corporation with several plants must evaluate and comply with the generator requirements at each facility site. In addition, any person who imports hazardous waste into the United States must comply with the standards applicable to generators.

A generator is initially required to determine whether any of its solid waste is a "hazardous waste" under the criteria described above.[56] The analytical methods for RCRA-related testing are contained in "Test Methods for Evaluating Solid Waste, Physical/Chemical Methods" (SW-846).[57] The records of any test results, waste analyses, or determinations that a waste is hazardous must be kept for at least three years from the date the waste was last sent to a TSD facility. Most generators retain such records indefinitely. The generator must then obtain an EPA identification number before any hazardous waste can be transported, treated, stored, or disposed of, and only transporters and TSD facilities that have obtained their EPA identification numbers can be used.[58]

The generator is responsible for preparing the Uniform Hazardous Waste Manifest, a control and transport document that accompanies the hazardous waste at all times.[59] The generator must specify the name and EPA identification numbers of each authorized transporter and the TSD facility or other designated facility that will receive the waste, describe the waste as required by DOT regulations, certify that it is properly packaged and labeled, provide an emergency response phone number, and sign the manifest certifications by hand. In 2012, President Obama authorized EPA to implement a national electronic waste manifest system, "e-Manifest," both for convenience to users and cost savings estimated to exceed $75 million per year.[60] EPA is under a statutory deadline of October 2015 to operationalize the new e-Manifest system, which, though not mandatory for users, is expected to be widely utilized.

All transporters and the designated TSD facility must sign and receive copies of the manifest, and a final copy must also be returned to the generator by the TSD facility. EPA is developing a comparable process for the e-Manifest system as for the current paper submissions. A copy of the final signed manifest must be kept for at least three years, although most generators retain copies for a longer period.[61]

If the manifest is not received back by the generator in a timely or properly executed manner, the generator must file an "exception report" with EPA or the state. The regulations specifically provide that a generator must contact the transporter and/or the TSD facility to determine what happened to the manifest and the hazardous waste. If, after 45 days from shipping the waste, the generator has not received a manifest with the proper signatures back from the TSD facility, the generator must submit an exception report that consists of a copy of the manifest for which the generator does not have confirmation of delivery and a cover letter that describes the efforts taken to locate the waste or manifest and the result of those efforts.[62]

A generator, in addition, must properly prepare the waste for transportation off-site. EPA has adopted the DOT regulations issued under the Hazardous Materials Transportation Act, 49 U.S.C. §§ 1802 et seq., with respect to the packaging, labeling, marking, and placarding of hazardous waste shipments.[63] In addition to the DOT regulations, EPA requires that any container of 119 gallons or less must be specifically marked with the generator's name, address, manifest tracking number, and the words "HAZARDOUS WASTE: Federal Law Prohibits Improper Disposal. If found contact the nearest police or public safety authority or the U.S. Environmental Protection Agency."

A generator is allowed to accumulate his own hazardous wastes on-site without a RCRA storage permit in two related circumstances. First, the generator can accumulate up to 55 gallons of hazardous wastes at or near the point of generation in "satellite accumulation areas."[64] The containers must be properly marked and maintained in good condition, and the waste must be moved into storage once the 55-gallon limit is reached. Second, a generator is also allowed to store hazardous waste on-site prior to shipment for a period of up to 90 days in tanks, containers, and containment buildings provided certain standards are met.[65] The generator must comply with the Part 265 interim status standards for the type of storage units used (e.g., operating standards, inspections, and air emission controls) and the requirements for personnel training, contingency planning, and emergency preparedness and response.

Generators who conduct "treatment" of their hazardous wastes must obtain a permit or interim status as a TSD facility or qualify for a treatment exemption. For example, generators may neutralize wastes that are hazardous due solely to corrosivity in a tank, container, or transport vehicle that qualifies as an "elementary neutralization unit" without a RCRA permit.[66] Similarly, generators may treat wastewaters as part of compliance with the Clean Water Act without a RCRA permit.

A generator must file biennial reports with EPA or an authorized state (some states require annual reports).[67] The reports, submitted using EPA's Form 8700 13A, contain standard information, such as the EPA identification number of the generator, and must also include information on the "waste minimization" efforts undertaken to reduce the volume and toxicity of the hazardous wastes and the results actually achieved in comparison with previous years. As a recordkeeping requirement, the generator must maintain copies of the biennial reports (and any exception reports filed) for at least three years. As a practical matter, in view of the liability imposed by Superfund, discussed in the Superfund chapter, generators should seriously consider maintaining RCRA waste determinations, test results, manifests, and reports for a lengthy period of time.

Special rules have been issued for persons who export or import hazardous wastes.[68] A generator who intends to export hazardous waste to a foreign country must first notify EPA in writing at least 60 days before the initial shipment and then use a special manifest form that includes a copy of the EPA Acknowledgement of Consent to the shipment. He must require the foreign consignee to confirm delivery of the waste, such as by returning a signed manifest. If the generator does not receive a manifest signed by the transporter stating the date and place of departure from the United States within 45 days or written confirmation of receipt from the foreign consignee within 90 days, an exception report must be filed. Annual reports of all exports must be submitted to EPA. A person who imports hazardous waste into the United States must initiate the manifest procedures as the generator.

3.3.1 Small Quantity Generators

EPA has promulgated special regulations for small-quantity generators that produce hazardous wastes in a total monthly quantity of less than 1,000 kilograms (2,200 pounds).[69] The regulations vary somewhat from the standards that apply to hazardous wastes of larger quantity generators. For example, small-quantity generators of between 100 and 1,000 kilograms may accumulate up to 6,000 kilograms (13,200 pounds) of hazardous waste on-site for up to 180 days without a permit. If the waste must be shipped more than 200 miles, the waste may be stored for up to 270 days.

Besides using a manifest, small-quantity generators must have their waste treated, stored (except short-term accumulation on-site), and disposed of at an interim status or permitted TSD facility and no longer at a state or municipally licensed landfill. The manifest contains a modified certification of waste minimization for such generators. In almost all other respects, however, small-quantity generators of between 100 and 1,000 kilograms per month are regulated the same as large generators.

Very small generators of less than 100 kilograms per month are still conditionally exempt from RCRA, but they are subject to certain minimum standards.[70]

3.4 Transporters of Hazardous Wastes

A transporter is any person engaged in the off-site movement of hazardous waste by air, rail, highway, or water.[71] Off-site transportation includes both interstate and intrastate commerce.[72] Thus, the reach of RCRA includes not only shippers and common carriers of hazardous wastes but also the company that occasionally transports hazardous wastes on its own trucks solely within its home state.

Anyone who moves a hazardous waste that is required to be manifested off the site where it is generated or the site where it is being treated, stored, and disposed of will be subject to the transporter standards. The only persons not covered are generators or operators of TSD facilities who engage in on-site transportation of their hazardous waste. Once a generator or a TSD facility operator moves its hazardous waste off-site, however, he is then considered a transporter and must comply with the regulations.[73]

EPA has promulgated standards for all transporters of hazardous wastes at 40 C.F.R. Part 263. These standards are closely coordinated with the standards issued by the DOT under the Hazardous Materials Transportation Act for the shipment of hazardous materials.[74] For the most part, EPA's regulations incorporate and require compliance with the DOT provisions on labeling, marking, placarding, using proper containers, and responding to spills. Of course, all transporters must obtain an EPA identification number prior to transporting any hazardous waste, and they may accept only hazardous waste that is accompanied by a manifest signed by the generator.[75] The transporter must sign and date the manifest acknowledging acceptance of the waste and return one copy to the generator before leaving the generator's property.

The transporter must keep the manifest with the hazardous waste at all times. When the transporter delivers the waste to another transporter or to the designated TSD facility, he must (1) date the manifest and obtain the signature of the next transporter or the TSD facility operator, (2) retain one copy of the manifest for his own records, and (3) give the remaining copies to the person receiving the waste.[76] If the transporter is unable to deliver the waste in accordance with the manifest, he must contact the generator for further instructions and revise the manifest accordingly.[77] The transporter must keep the executed copy of the manifest for a period of three years.[78]

The transporter may hold hazardous waste for up to 10 days at a transfer facility without obtaining a RCRA storage permit.[79] A transfer facility generally includes a loading dock, storage building, and similar areas where shipments of hazardous wastes are held during the normal course of transportation.

Transporters of hazardous wastes may become subject to the Part 262 requirements for generators if, for example, the transporter mixes hazardous wastes of different DOT descriptions by placing them into a single container or if he imports hazardous waste from a foreign country.[80] Also, a hazardous waste that accumulates in a transport vehicle or vessel will trigger the generator standards when the waste is removed.

If an accidental spill or other discharge of a hazardous waste occurs during transportation, the transporter is responsible for its cleanup.[81] The transporter must take immediate response action to protect human health and the environment. Such action includes treatment or containment of the spill and notification of local police and fire departments. The DOT's discharge-reporting requirements are incorporated into the RCRA regulations.[82] They identify the situations in which telephone reporting of the discharge to the National Response Center and the filing of a written report are required. Transporters are subject to both DOT and EPA enforcement.[83]

EPA has also established requirements for the transportation of hazardous waste–derived fuels.[84] In addition, railroads are shielded from the RCRA "citizen suit" and "imminent hazard" enforcement provisions (discussed below) if the railroad merely transports the hazardous waste under a sole contractual agreement and exercises due care.

3.5 Treatment, Storage, and Disposal (TSD) Facilities

The term "TSD" is commonly used to refer to the three management activities, treatment, storage, and disposal of hazardous wastes, that are regulated under RCRA Section 3004 and that thus require a permit under RCRA Section 3005. Section 3004 directed EPA to establish a comprehensive set of regulations governing all aspects of TSD facilities, including location, design, operation, and closure.

In 1984, Congress added a number of important provisions to Section 3004. These establish, among other things, a ban on the disposal of liquids in landfills, minimum technological requirements (e.g., double liners) for surface impoundments and landfills, corrective action for continuing releases at permitted TSD facilities, and controls on the marketing and burning of hazardous wastes used as fuels. Under its regulatory authority, EPA implemented a land disposal ban of all untreated hazardous wastes and established pretreatment standards for land disposal of all hazardous wastes. These requirements are discussed further below.

A facility will be regulated as a "treatment facility" if the operator uses any method, technique, or process designed to change the physical, chemical, or biological character or composition of any hazardous waste so as to neutralize such waste, to recover energy or material resources from the waste, or to render the waste nonhazardous or less hazardous, safer to transport, store or dispose of, or amenable for recovery, amenable for storage, or reduced in volume.[85] There is very little that can be done to a hazardous waste that would not qualify as treatment.

A "storage facility" is one which temporarily holds hazardous waste for a period of time, at the end of which the hazardous waste is treated, disposed of, or stored elsewhere.[86] A "disposal facility" is one at which hazardous waste is intentionally placed into or on any land or water and at which waste will remain after closure.[87] The term "facility" is separately defined to include "[a]ll contiguous land, and structures, other appurtenances, and improvements on the land."[88] Clarification of the foregoing definitions can be sought during the permitting process.

A number of different types of TSD facilities and hazardous waste activities are currently exempted from EPA regulation altogether. The list of exclusion includes the following:[89]

1. Facilities that dispose of hazardous waste by means of ocean disposal pursuant to a permit issued under the Marine Protection, Research, and Sanctuaries Act (except as provided in a RCRA permit-by-rule)

2. The disposal of hazardous waste by underground injection pursuant to a permit issued under the Safe Drinking Water Act (except as provided in a RCRA permit-by-rule)

3. A Publicly Owned Treatment Works (POTW) that treats or stores hazardous wastes that are delivered to the POTW by a transport vehicle or vessel or through a pipe

4. TSD facilities that operate under a state hazardous waste program authorized pursuant to RCRA Section 3006 and that are therefore subject to regulation under the state program

5. Facilities authorized by a state to manage industrial or municipal solid waste, if the only hazardous waste handled by such a facility is otherwise excluded from regulation pursuant to the special requirements for conditionally exempt small quantity generators of less than 100 kilograms

6. A facility that is subject to the special exemptions for certain recyclable materials, except as provided in Part 266

7. Temporary on-site accumulation of hazardous waste by generators in compliance with 40 C.F.R. § 262.34

8. Farmers who dispose of waste pesticides from their own use in compliance with 40 C.F.R. § 262.51

9. Owners or operators of a "totally enclosed treatment facility"

10. Owners and operators of "elementary neutralization units" and "wastewater treatment units," as defined in the regulations

11. Persons taking immediate action to treat and contain spills

12. Transporters storing manifested wastes in approved containers at a transfer facility for 10 days or less

13. The act of adding absorbent material to hazardous waste in a container to reduce the amount of free liquids in the container, if the materials are added when wastes are first placed in the container

The regulations should be consulted for the precise scope of these exemptions.

The adopted regulations include standards of general applicability (e.g., personnel training, security, financial responsibility),[90] as well as specific design and operating standards for each different type of TSD facility (e.g., storage tanks, landfills, incinerators). The standards of general applicability will be discussed first.

3.5.1 Standards of General Applicability

As discussed more fully in the permits section below, two categories of TSD facilities currently exist—interim status facilities and permitted facilities. Interim status facilities are those that are currently operating without final RCRA permits based upon a legislative decision to allow continued operation of existing facilities until RCRA permits can be issued. These facilities had to meet a three-part statutory test:

1. Exist as of November 19, 1980, or the effective date of statutory or regulatory changes that render the facility subject to the need for a RCRA permit

2. Notify EPA pursuant to RCRA Section 3010(a) of its hazardous waste management activities

3. File a preliminary permit application[91]

A facility's interim status ends when the facility receives a final RCRA permit. This in turn is based upon technical standards issued by EPA or a state with an approved program that are incorporated into the permit. As discussed in the next section on permits, the 1984 HSWA specified timetables for issuance of final permits to all interim status TSD facilities. All other TSD facilities must obtain an individual RCRA permit before commencing construction. Separate standards have been issued for interim status facilities[92] and permitted facilities.[93]

An operator of a TSD facility is required to obtain an EPA identification number.[94] The operator must also obtain or conduct a detailed chemical and physical analysis of a representative sample of a hazardous waste before the waste is treated, stored, or disposed of at the facility.[95] This is to ensure that the operator has sufficient knowledge of the particular waste being handled to properly manage it. The facility's waste analysis plan deals with such matters as representative samples, frequency of testing, and compliance with land disposal verifications.

Special precautions must be taken to prevent accidental ignition or reaction of ignitable, reactive, or incompatible wastes. While many of the handling requirements are largely commonsense practices, specific steps to protect against mixing of such wastes are included in the regulations. Compliance with the regulations concerning safe management of ignitable, reactive, or incompatible wastes must be documented.[96] Additionally, regulations for preparedness and prevention, requiring alarm systems and spill control equipment, are intended to minimize the possibility or consequences of an explosion, spill, or fire at a TSD facility.[97] The TSD facility must also be covered by liability insurance or other financial instruments for claims arising out of injuries to persons or property that result from hazardous waste management operations.[98]

Important recordkeeping requirements apply to TSD facilities.[99] Upon receipt of a manifested shipment of hazardous waste, the operator of a TSD facility must immediately sign, date, and give to the transporter a copy of the manifest prepared by the generator. The operator must return a completed copy of the manifest to the generator within 30 days and retain a copy of all manifests at the facility for at least three years from the date of delivery. All TSD facilities must maintain a complete operating record until closure.[100] The operating record must include a description and the quantity of each hazardous waste received and the method and date of its treatment, storage, and disposal; the location of each waste within the facility; and the results of waste analyses, trial tests, and inspections.

The TSD facility operator is also obligated to file basic reports with the EPA regional administrator or an authorized state. These include a biennial report of waste management activities for the previous calendar year,[101] an "unmanifested waste" report that the operator must file within 15 days of accepting any hazardous waste that is not accompanied by a manifest,[102] and certain specialized reports, such as an incident report in the event of a hazardous waste release, fire, or explosion.

There are general closure requirements applicable to all TSD facilities and additional requirements for each specific type of facility.[103] "Closure" is the period after which hazardous wastes are no longer accepted by a TSD facility and during which time the operator must complete treatment, storage, or disposal operations. "Postclosure" is the 30-year period after closure when operators of land disposal facilities, such as landfills, must perform certain monitoring and maintenance activities. Generally, the TSD facility must have a detailed written closure plan and schedule and a cost estimate for closure. The plan must be approved by EPA or the state. It must be amended when any changes in waste management operations affect its terms, and the cost estimate must be adjusted annually for inflation. The closure plan must be followed when the TSD facility ceases operations at the covered unit(s). Postclosure care must continue for 30 years after the date of completing closure and includes groundwater monitoring and the maintenance of monitoring and waste containment systems.

Financial responsibility requirements have been established to ensure that funds for closure and postclosure care are adequate and available.[104] TSD facilities must use one of the specified financial instruments, such as a corporate guarantee, to provide the closure and postclosure funds.

3.5.2 Standards for Specific Types of TSD Facilities

The standards discussed above are generally applicable to all TSD facilities, from the small drum storage area to the most complex commercial landfill or incinerator. EPA has also promulgated specific design, construction, and operating standards for each different type of TSD facility regulated under RCRA. The types of TSD facilities include containers; tanks; surface impoundments; waste piles; drip pads; land treatment units; landfills; incinerators; thermal treatment units; chemical, physical, and biological treatment units; underground injection wells; containment buildings; and "miscellaneous units."[105] In the years ahead, additional classes of facilities may also be addressed by distinct sets of standards.

Discussion of the detailed regulatory requirements for all of these types of facilities is beyond the scope of this chapter.[106] The following is an overview of the more significant standards that apply to containers and tanks; surface impoundments, waste piles, and landfills; and incinerators and industrial furnaces used for hazardous waste burning.

The RCRA standards for containers and tanks are basically good housekeeping practices.[107] A container is any portable device for storing or handling hazardous waste, including drums, pails, and boxes. Tank systems are stationary devices constructed primarily of nonearthen materials that provide structural support and any ancillary piping.[108] Drums must be maintained in good condition and handled so as to avoid ruptures or leaks. Containers must always be kept closed, except when adding waste. Tanks must be operated using controls and practices to prevent overflows and spills. Tank systems must be constructed of suitable materials and operated so as to contain the hazardous waste during the tank's intended useful life. Container storage areas must be inspected at least weekly and tank systems at least daily for leaks, corrosion, and other problems. More important, almost all container and tank storage areas must be constructed or retrofitted with a secondary containment system to collect spills and accumulated rainfall. EPA has also issued standards for air emission controls at TSD facilities, particularly for tanks and containers. The standards require controls on process vents,[109] controls related to leaks from equipment, such as pumps and compressors,[110] and control systems on tanks, containers, and surface impoundments that manage hazardous wastes with VO concentrations greater than 500 ppmw.[111] These standards also apply to 90-day containers and tanks at generator facilities.

A surface impoundment is any natural or man-made excavation or diked area designed to hold hazardous wastes containing free liquids, such as pits, ponds, or lagoons. A waste pile is any noncontainerized accumulation of solid, nonflowing hazardous waste. A landfill is a disposal facility where hazardous waste is placed in or on the land.[112] The most important performance standards for these land-based facilities are the "minimum technology requirements" (MTRs) enacted in the 1984 HSWA. All new, replacement, and expansion units at surface impoundments and landfills must have double liners, leachate collection systems, leak detection, and groundwater monitoring systems.[113]

Incinerators use controlled flame combustion to destroy hazardous wastes. For waste feeds it intends to handle, an incinerator must conduct a detailed waste analysis and trial burn to establish steady-state conditions and demonstrate sufficient destruction of hazardous constituents in the waste. EPA has also promulgated stringent emission standards under the joint authority of RCRA and the Clean Air Act.[114] The incinerator must have continuous monitoring and automatic controls to shut off the waste feed when operating requirements are exceeded.

EPA has also promulgated standards for industrial furnaces, such as cement kilns and boilers, that burn hazardous wastes.[115] All persons who produce, distribute, market, or burn hazardous wastes as fuel must notify EPA. The invoice or bill of sale for the fuel must bear the legend "Warning—This Fuel Contains Hazardous Waste" (followed by a list of the hazardous wastes). Such fuels cannot be burned except in qualified utility boilers and industrial furnaces, such as cement kilns. Generators, transporters, marketers, and burners of hazardous waste fuels are subject to storage standards for containers and tanks and to other specific RCRA standards. The owners and operators of boilers and industrial furnaces must comply with detailed technical standards similar to incineration standards and obtain RCRA permits.

3.6 The Land Disposal Restrictions Program

Perhaps the most significant provision of RCRA is the prohibition on the land disposal of hazardous wastes. This prohibition is intended to minimize reliance on land disposal of untreated hazardous wastes and to require advanced treatment and recycling of wastes. In the 1984 HSWA, Congress began by banning the disposal of bulk or noncontainerized liquid hazardous wastes and hazardous wastes containing free liquids in landfills.[116]

Next, Congress required EPA to determine whether to prohibit, in whole or in part, the disposal of all RCRA hazardous wastes in land disposal facilities. These include landfills, surface impoundments, waste piles, injection wells, salt domes, and the like. At the same time, EPA was told to promulgate regulations that establish levels or methods of treatment that minimize threats posed by the hazardous waste. If the waste is first treated in accordance with these treatment standards, the treated waste or residue can then be land disposed. In effect, the so-called "land ban" program is really a waste pretreatment program.

First, EPA banned the land disposal of dioxin and solvent containing hazardous wastes unless the wastes are pretreated.[117] EPA set treatment levels based on incineration of nonwastewater solvents and based on chemical/physical treatment for dilute solvent wastewaters.

Second, EPA banned the land disposal of certain hazardous wastes (which California had already banned) unless the wastes are pretreated. The "California list" includes liquid hazardous wastes, including free liquids associated with any sludge, that (1) contain free cyanides greater than 100 mg/L, (2) contain specified concentrations of heavy metals (arsenic, cadmium, chromium, lead, mercury, nickel, selenium, and thallium), (3) are acids below a pH of 2, (4) contain more than 50 ppm PCBs, and (5) are solid or liquid hazardous wastes containing halogenated organic compounds at concentrations greater than 1,000 ppm.[118]

Third, EPA published a ranking of all other hazardous wastes based on their intrinsic hazard and volume with a schedule for determining whether to ban the land disposal of such wastes. EPA restricted land disposal one-third of the ranking list at a time.[119] The first third of the ranking list covered the highest-priority hazardous wastes. EPA set treatment levels for many of the F and K listed wastes in this first third. EPA then extended the ban to the second third of the ranked hazardous wastes, and finally, EPA imposed the land ban restrictions on the final third of wastes, which included all characteristic hazardous wastes.

Congress wanted to promote treatment and recycling of hazardous wastes in lieu of or prior to land disposal. Therefore, at the same time that EPA promulgated these land disposal restrictions, EPA also promulgated regulations specifying the methods or levels of treatment that substantially diminish the toxicity or reduce the likelihood of migration of the waste from land disposal facilities. Generally, the treatment standards are based on the levels that can be achieved by the Best Demonstrated Available Technologies.[120] In most instances, the treatment standards are expressed as concentrations of constituents in the treated waste. Any treatment technology that meets the concentration-based standard can then be used. If EPA prescribes a specific technology, however, then that method must be used. A company that treats its hazardous waste in accordance with these pretreatment standards will not have the treated waste or residue subject to the land disposal ban.

After several years' experience with the land ban program, EPA revamped the format of the treatment standards in 1994. To supplement the waste-by-waste standards, EPA set "universal treatment standards" for hazardous constituents in certain hazardous wastes.[121] In addition, EPA set treatment standards for characteristic hazardous wastes that require removal of the characteristic and treatment of underlying hazardous constituents in the waste to levels that are more stringent than the characteristic itself.[122] Newly listed or identified wastes are brought under the land ban program in subsequent rule makings.

EPA has limited authority to grant a two-year grace period for hazardous wastes that become newly subject to the prohibition if adequate alternative treatment, recovery, or disposal capacity is not available. EPA can also grant a one-year grace period, renewable only once, to a company that demonstrates on a case-by-case basis that a binding contractual commitment has been made to construct or otherwise provide alternative treatment, recovery, or disposal capacity but because of circumstances beyond its control the alternative capacity cannot reasonably be made available by the ban deadline.

Finally, land disposal facilities may submit petitions to EPA which demonstrate, to a reasonable degree of certainty, that there will be no migration of hazardous constituents from a particular disposal unit or injection well for as long as the waste remains hazardous. EPA has granted a number of these so-called "no migration" petitions for deep injection wells.

3.7 Used Oil

In the 1984 HSWA, Congress directed EPA to decide whether to identify used automobile and truck crankcase oil or other used oil as hazardous waste.[123] Used oil is defined as any waste oil derived from crude or synthetic oil that has become contaminated with physical or chemical impurities due to use, such as transmission fluid, laminating oils, electrical insulating oil, and industrial process oil. EPA finally decided not to list used oil that is destined for recycling as a hazardous waste but instead to promulgate management standards for used oil collection and recycling.[124] These include general facility standards for used oil processors and re-refiners. In addition, EPA decided not to list used oil that is destined for disposal as a hazardous waste, but the hazardous waste characteristics do apply to such used oil.[125]

Under EPA's bifurcated approach, the RCRA management standards that apply to used oil depend on whether the used oil is recycled or disposed. EPA allows generators to presume that their used oil will be recycled, and therefore the Part 279 standards apply, unless a person in fact decides to dispose of the used oil or sends it off-site for disposal. Used oil that is burned as fuel must meet certain specifications for hazardous constituent content if burned in commercial, residential, or institutional boilers. Alternatively, so-called "off-spec" used oil must be burned in industrial furnaces or industrial/utility boilers to ensure adequate combustion. Used oil that contains greater than 1,000 ppm total halogens is presumed to have been mixed with listed chlorinated hazardous waste and therefore must be managed as hazardous waste unless the presumption can be rebutted. Marketers and burners of off-spec used oil are also subject to management standards in the regulations.

3.8 Universal Wastes

EPA has established a separate regulatory program that governs the collection and management of certain widely generated wastes.[126] At the present time, these "universal wastes" include nickel cadmium batteries, returned pesticides, mercury-containing equipment including thermostats, and fluorescent lamps. EPA may add to this list in the future.[127] Small-quantity handlers of these universal wastes (less than 5,000 kilograms) must comply with streamlined management standards related to preventing releases, employee training, proper packaging and labeling, limiting accumulation time, and tracking off-site shipments. Large-quantity handlers must also notify EPA and obtain an identification number. Handlers and transporters must take universal wastes to a qualified destination facility that treats, disposes, or recycles the waste in accordance with regulatory standards, including tracking and recordkeeping.

3.9 RCRA Permits

RCRA requires every owner and operator of a TSD facility to obtain a permit.[128] A TSD facility that was in existence before November 19, 1980, or on the date of any statutory or regulatory change that makes the facility subject to RCRA need only notify EPA of its hazardous waste management activity and file a Part A application to obtain interim status and continue operations.[129] However, a new TSD facility or an existing facility that did not qualify for interim status must obtain a full RCRA permit before commencing construction. EPA has developed a standardized permit for facilities that generate and then store or nonthermally treat hazardous waste on-site in tanks, containers, and containment buildings.[130]

States authorized under RCRA to administer their own programs are responsible mainly for reviewing applications and issuing permits. EPA regions perform this task in nonauthorized states. After a complete RCRA permit application is filed, the rules in 40 C.F.R. Part 124 establish the procedures for processing the application and issuing the permit. These include preparation of draft permits, public comment and hearing, and the issuance of final decisions. Permit issuance must be based on a determination that the TSD facility will comply with all requirements of RCRA. In HSWA, Congress enacted the RCRA permit "omnibus" provision directing that all permits contain "such terms and conditions as the Administrator (or the State) determines necessary to protect human health and the environment."[131] EPA has relied on this omnibus authority to develop facility-specific permit conditions that supplement the regulatory standards.

Permits for land disposal facilities, storage facilities, incinerators, and other treatment facilities can be issued only for a fixed term not to exceed 10 years.[132] While permits may be reviewed and modified at any time during their terms, permits for land disposal facilities must be reviewed every five years. At such time, the terms of a permit may be modified to ensure that the permit continues to incorporate the standards then applicable to land disposal facilities.

3.9.1 Standardized Permits

A standardized permit is available to generators who store their own hazardous wastes on-site in containers, tanks, or containment buildings.[133] The permit may authorize physical and chemical treatment of the wastes in those units but cannot authorize thermal treatment methods. Facilities that receive hazardous waste generated off-site by a facility under the same ownership are also eligible for the standardized permit.

The standardized permit consists of two parts: a uniform portion used for all qualified facilities and a supplemental portion that can be included at the discretion of the permitting agency. The standards in 40 C.F.R. Part 267 provide the basis for the uniform portion of the permit, including waste analysis, security, inspections, employee training, security, emergency response, unit management standards, closure, and financial assurance. The supplemental portion can include additional standards deemed necessary to be protective of human health and the environment, including any corrective action, and is based on site-specific factors at the facility.

EPA has adopted a streamlined process for a facility to obtain a standardized permit. The facility begins by filing a Notice of Intent (NOI) with the permitting agency requesting coverage under a standardized permit. Prior to submitting the NOI, the facility must conduct a meeting with the neighboring community and include a summary of the meeting with the NOI. The facility must also conduct an audit and submit a certification of compliance with the Part 267 standards based on the audit with its NOI. Other information required with the NOI includes a closure plan, closure cost estimate, documentation of financial assurance, and a waste analysis plan for facilities receiving waste from off-site.

The permit process should proceed relatively quickly. The agency will issue a draft permit decision within 120 days, which can be extended once for 30 days. The draft permit is then subject to public comment and opportunity for a hearing. A final standardized permit and response to comments is then issued, or the permit is denied. A permit can be denied for a number of reasons, including a poor compliance history.

3.10 RCRA Corrective Action

RCRA permits require the owner or operator of a TSD facility to take corrective action for all releases of hazardous waste and hazardous constituents from solid waste management units (SWMUs) at the facility, regardless of when the waste was placed in the unit or whether the unit is currently active.[134] An SWMU can be any tank, lagoon, waste pile, or other unit where any solid waste was placed and from which hazardous constituents are being released. RCRA permits must contain schedules of compliance for any required corrective action and assurances of financial responsibility for completing such action. If necessary, the operator of the TSD facility may have to take corrective action beyond the facility boundary. This type of authority for cleanup is analogous to Superfund and has had a substantial impact on many TSD facilities that need RCRA permits to continue operations.

EPA has codified the basic framework of the corrective action program in regulations, but much of the program is subject to guidance documents.[135] The corrective action process typically begins when a TSD facility applies for a RCRA permit. The application must identify any SWMUs at the facility so that EPA can conduct a facility assessment to determine if a release is likely to have occurred. If so, EPA can require the facility to conduct a RCRA facility investigation (RFI). The scope of the RFI, including the evaluation of existing site documentation, visual inspection, and site sampling, is specified in a compliance schedule that becomes part of the facility's permit. The RFI may be conducted in phases to address leaking SWMUs first and may include interim measures to stabilize the site and control any contaminant migration. A corrective measures study is then conducted to identify and evaluate potential cleanup alternatives. After EPA selects the appropriate cleanup measure, considering such factors as performance, cost, time requirements, and institutional concerns, the remedy and a compliance schedule are added to the permit as a modification. The final step involves the design, construction, and operation of the selected corrective action.

EPA's regulations include provisions for corrective action management units (CAMUs). A CAMU is an area within a facility that is designated by the regional administrator for the management of remediation wastes.[136] Placement of remediation waste into a CAMU does not trigger the land disposal prohibitions or minimum technology requirements for as-generated wastes. EPA has established standards, however, governing (1) the types of wastes that are eligible for CAMUs, (2) treatment requirements for wastes placed into CAMUs, (3) design standards for waste disposal in CAMUs, (4) information required for applications to use a CAMU, and (5) public participation in CAMU decisions.[137]

EPA has also promulgated requirements for hazardous contaminated media that are generated during cleanups.[138] These provisions allow such remediation wastes to be accumulated in staging piles, which are not subject to the minimum technology requirements for land disposal units. In addition, the treatment, storage, and disposal of remediation wastes can be authorized by a Remedial Action Plan (RAP) instead of a RCRA permit.[139] A RAP is used to address a specific cleanup action and does not subject the owner and operator to facility-wide corrective action. The treatment requirements that otherwise would apply to hazardous contaminated soils, by operation of the contained-in principle, were also modified to reflect the performance of remedial technologies.[140]

Under its corrective action guidance, EPA has tried to take near-term actions to control or abate threats at a greater number of facilities rather than undertaking comprehensive cleanups at a more limited number of sites. As a result, much corrective action work remains to be completed. EPA has also sought to use environmental indicators and facility-specific performance goals for site cleanups; innovative technical approaches, including voluntary accelerated cleanups; expanded public participation, such as the use of citizen advisory boards; and coordination with state cleanup programs.

EPA has also taken steps to coordinate the RCRA corrective action program with its other remediation authorities under Superfund and similar laws. The goal of the One Cleanup Program is to improve the coordination, speed, and effectiveness of cleanups at the nation's contaminated sites, including RCRA corrective action sites.[141] EPA's implementation plan includes pilot projects to demonstrate cross-program coordination and consistency at co-located or similarly contaminated sites; task forces to support new policies on groundwater cleanup, site assessment decisions, and long-term site stewardship; an integrated network of information systems on cleanup actions and technologies; and better performance measures to demonstrate the overall effectiveness and benefits of cleanups.

4.0 Enforcement

4.1 State Hazardous Waste Programs

States are authorized by RCRA to develop and carry out their own hazardous waste programs in lieu of the federal program administered by EPA.[142] To obtain EPA approval, the state program must be "equivalent" to and "consistent" with the federal program and other authorized state programs, and must provide adequate enforcement of compliance with the requirements of RCRA Subtitle C.[143]

Ordinarily, states have at least one year to make regulatory changes consistent with the federal program and two years if statutory changes are necessary. EPA allows states to consolidate program revisions for EPA review and approval on a periodic basis and has streamlined the approval process. Congress believed the 1984 HSWA provisions were important to implement quickly, however. Therefore, EPA regulations that implement the 1984 HSWA take effect in authorized states on the same day that they take effect under the federal program. EPA is responsible for implementing HSWA provisions until the state takes over authority. Authorized states can then apply for final authorization for the new requirement after promulgating an equivalent regulation.

This dual administration of the RCRA program means that joint permitting is often necessary, with EPA imposing the HSWA provisions and the state taking responsibility for the rest of the permitting.

4.2 Hazardous Waste Inspections

RCRA provides that any officer, employee, or representative of EPA or a state with an authorized hazardous waste program may inspect the premises and records of any person who generates, stores, treats, transports, disposes of, or otherwise handles hazardous waste.[144] EPA's inspection authority extends to persons and sites that have handled hazardous wastes in the past but no longer do so. The owner/operator must provide government officials access to records and property relating to the wastes for inspection purposes. Copying and sampling are also authorized.

EPA and the states must conduct inspections of all privately operated TSD facilities at least once every two years. Federally operated TSD facilities must be inspected on an annual basis. Similarly, EPA must conduct annual inspections of TSD facilities that are operated by a state or local government to ensure compliance with the requirements of RCRA.[145]

All organizations should have an established policy and procedure for handling RCRA inspections, including consideration of whether a search warrant should be required.

4.3 Civil and Criminal Enforcement Actions

EPA can bring several types of enforcement actions under RCRA. These include administrative orders and civil and criminal penalties.[146] Whenever EPA determines that any person is violating Subtitle C of RCRA (including any regulation or permit issued thereunder), it may either issue an order requiring compliance immediately or within a specified time period or seek injunctive relief against the alleged violator through a civil action filed in a U.S. district court.[147] Any person who violates any requirement of Subtitle C is liable for a civil penalty of up to $37,500 for each day of violation, regardless of whether the person had been served with a compliance order. A person subject to RCRA cannot rely on EPA to tell him when he is in violation, then take the required corrective action and thus avoid a penalty. Failure to comply with an administrative order may also result in suspension or revocation of a permit.

RCRA also imposes criminal penalties of up to $50,000, five years' imprisonment, or both for persons who "knowingly" commit certain violations. Fines and imprisonment can be imposed on generators for knowingly allowing hazardous waste to be transported to an unpermitted facility; for knowing violations of federal interim status standards or counterpart state requirements; for knowing material omissions or the knowing failure to file reports required under RCRA by generators, transporters, and TSD facility operators; and for knowing transport of hazardous waste without a manifest.

The "knowing" element of an environmental crime usually requires only that the defendant was aware of his or her own activities, not that the defendant had actual knowledge of EPA regulations or permit requirements. For example, in *United States v. Hayes International Corp.,* 786 F.2d 1499 (11th Cir. 1986), the court upheld a conviction for illegally transporting hazardous wastes in violation of RCRA, rejecting the proposed affirmative defense that the defendants did not know the wastes were classified as hazardous under EPA's regulations. Likewise, in *United States v. Laughlin,* 10 F.3d 961 (2d Cir. 1993), the court held that the defendants were guilty of illegal disposal under RCRA without proof that they had actual knowledge of the lack of a permit or RCRA's permit requirement. Under the Responsible Corporate Officer doctrine, individuals can be criminally liable if they are directly responsible within management for the conduct of subordinate employees and they knew that the type of improper activity allegedly committed by the subordinate was occurring. See *United States v. MacDonald & Watson Waste Oil Co.,* 933 F.2d 35 (1st Cir. 1991).

The statute also creates a crime of "knowing endangerment." The purpose of this sanction is to provide more substantial felony penalties for any person who commits the acts described above and "who knows at that time that he thereby places another person in imminent danger of death or serious bodily injury." Upon conviction, an individual faces a fine of up to $250,000 and/or up to 15 years' imprisonment. An organizational defendant is subject to a maximum fine of $1 million.[148]

The U.S. Department of Justice (DOJ) and EPA have aggressively applied the "knowing endangerment" provisions of RCRA. For example, in *United States v. Hansen,* 262 F.3d 1217 (11th Cir. 2001), the government secured convictions against three corporate officers who worked at the company's headquarters and oversaw operations at six chemical plants across the United States, including the plant where the violations occurred. The court held that EPA can establish that a defendant acted "knowingly" merely by showing that the defendant had knowledge of the "general hazardous character" of the chemical and knew that the chemical had the "potential to be harmful" to others. The testimony of former employees was sufficient to demonstrate that the defendants knew that the chemical plant did not comply with RCRA standards and also knew that this failure to comply posed a danger to the plant's employees.

4.4 Imminent Hazard Actions

In addition, EPA is authorized to bring suits to restrain an imminent and substantial endangerment to health or the environment.[149] EPA construes "imminent and substantial endangerment" to mean posing a "risk of harm" or "potential harm" but not requiring proof of actual harm.[150]

In response to conflicting federal court decisions, Congress reworded the "imminent hazard" provision in 1984 to clarify that actions that took place prior to the enactment of RCRA are covered by this provision. Thus, a nonnegligent generator whose wastes are no longer being deposited at a particular site may still be ordered to abate the hazard resulting from the leaking of previously deposited wastes.

EPA must provide for public notice and comment and the opportunity for a public meeting in the affected area prior to entering into a settlement or covenant not to sue in an imminent hazard action.

4.5 Citizen Suits

The RCRA citizen suit provision allows any person to bring a civil action against any alleged violator of RCRA requirements or against the EPA administrator for a failure to perform a nondiscretionary duty. Any person may also petition the EPA administrator for promulgation, amendment, or repeal of any regulation. Courts have recognized the citizen suit provision[151] and are authorized to award costs, including attorneys' fees, to a substantially prevailing party.[152]

The citizen suit provision authorizes suits in cases where past or present management or disposal of hazardous wastes has contributed to a situation that may present an imminent or substantial endangerment. However, citizen suits are prohibited with respect to the siting and permitting of hazardous waste facilities (except by a state or local government), where EPA is prosecuting an action under RCRA or Superfund, while EPA or the state is engaged in a removal action under Superfund or has incurred costs to engage in a remedial action, or where the responsible party is conducting a removal or remedial action pursuant to an order obtained from EPA. Affected parties may be allowed to intervene in ongoing suits. Plaintiffs must notify EPA, the state, and affected parties 90 days prior to commencement of a citizen suit.

5.0 State Solid Waste Programs under Subtitle D

Subtitle D of RCRA gives states the responsibility of regulating nonhazardous waste. Federal involvement is limited to establishing minimum criteria that prescribe the best practicable controls and monitoring requirements for solid waste disposal facilities.

EPA has established criteria for solid waste facilities that receive hazardous waste from households or from small generators to enable detection of groundwater contamination, provide for corrective action as necessary, and determine acceptable facility siting.[153] Disposal of solid waste in "open dumps" (i.e., those facilities not meeting the criteria) is prohibited. Existing dumps were allowed to make modifications that will permit them to meet the requirements, and it is the state's responsibility to ensure that such upgrading occurs or that the open dumps are closed.

EPA was not given any enforcement authority, however, for the ban on open dumps. Since EPA's enforcement authority under RCRA covers only hazardous wastes, EPA cannot take action against a person disposing of nonhazardous wastes in an open dump or against the state for failing to close open dumps, other than terminating certain grant funds available to the state under RCRA.

RCRA also envisions that the state, with the help of federal grant funds, will develop regional solid waste management plans. The program is patterned on Section 208 of the Clean Water Act and relies upon a comprehensive regional planning approach to solving solid waste problems. The state is responsible for identifying appropriate management areas, developing regional plans through the use of local and regional authorities, compiling inventories and closing or upgrading existing open dumps, and generally assessing the need for additional solid waste disposal capacity in the area.

Of particular significance is a requirement that states not have any bans on the importation of waste for storage, treatment, or disposal or have requirements that are substantially dissimilar from other disposal practices that would discourage the free movement of wastes across state lines. Although enforcement of this requirement may be difficult in light of the limited enforcement authority available to EPA, it does evidence a congressional policy for a national approach to solid waste disposal.[154]

6.0 The Federal Facility Compliance Act

The Federal Facility Compliance Act of 1992 (FFCA)[155] amended the enforcement of RCRA at federal facilities. The act includes provisions clarifying the waiver of sovereign immunity for civil fines and penalties and the personal liability of federal employees for environmental violations. The act also details RCRA's application to public vessels, waste munitions, radioactive mixed wastes, and federally owned wastewater treatment works. The principal provisions are discussed below.

6.1 Waiver of Sovereign Immunity

Prior to the FFCA, many state environmental regulatory agencies were concerned that RCRA unfairly "shielded" federal facilities from monetary fines and penalties. Sovereign immunity was a roadblock to the complete use of a state's traditional enforcement tools, and states could not reach the federal treasury unless Congress specifically authorized a waiver of sovereign immunity that would permit civil fines and penalties to be paid.

For example, in 1986 the state of Ohio sued the Department of Energy (DOE) for violating state and federal hazardous waste laws at its uranium processing plant in Fernald, Ohio. The lawsuit was eventually settled through a consent decree, except for the issue of civil penalties. The DOE insisted that it was not required to pay civil penalties; indeed, it could not pay because there was no waiver of federal sovereign immunity in RCRA with regard to such payments.[156] Following various appeals, the Supreme Court eventually held that RCRA did not clearly allow the states to directly impose civil penalties.[157]

Congress enacted Section 102 of the FFCA, 42 U.S.C. § 6961(a), to make a clear waiver of sovereign immunity under RCRA:

> The United States hereby expressly waives any immunity otherwise applicable to the United States with respect to any such substantive or procedural requirement (including, but not limited to, any injunctive relief, administrative order or civil or administrative penalty or fine referred to in the preceding sentence, or reasonable service charge).

Now states and the federal EPA are empowered to use the same full range of enforcement tools against federal facilities that were available in cases involving private and corporate entities.

6.2 EPA Administrative Orders

The FFCA provides that EPA has explicit authority to issue administrative compliance orders to other federal agencies that are in violation of RCRA. Previously, the discovery of environmental deficiencies at federal facilities was resolved by the negotiation of a consent agreement, wherein the facility would commit to correcting the problem within a certain period of time and according to a specified schedule. The FFCA's legislative history also makes clear that Congress intended for EPA to issue RCRA 3008(a) administrative complaints to federal facilities for violations similar to those found during private enforcement situations.[158]

7.0 Conclusion

As the foregoing discussion amply demonstrates, the RCRA program is incredibly complex. Compliance with its requirements demands careful study and attention to detail. The 1984 HWSA added many new requirements that posed a challenge to the will and imagination of the regulated community. Industry has been challenged to find new ways to minimize, treat, recycle, and dispose of hazardous waste. These include the use of innovative and emerging treatment technologies as well as modifications to production processes and raw materials. Never before has the incentive been greater to reuse or reclaim wastes or to identify new production processes and raw materials that do not result in the generation of hazardous waste in the first place.

8.0 Research Sources

To learn more about RCRA, here are some additional resources:

- Resource Conservation and Recovery Act (RCRA) Laws and Regulations: https://www.epa.gov/rcra

- Hazardous Waste—RCRA Subtitle C: https://www3.epa.gov/region02/waste/csummary.htm

- RCRA Online—Search Topics: https://yosemite.epa.gov/osw/rcra.nsf/topics?OpenView&count=5000

- RCRA FAQs Database: https://yosemite.epa.gov/osw%5Crcra.nsf/how+to+use

- Summary of RCRA: https://www.epa.gov/laws-regulations/summary -resource-conservation-and-recovery-act

- RCRA Subtitle C—Managing Wastes From Cradle to Grave: https://www.epa.gov/hw/learn-basics-hazardous-waste#cradle

- Resource Conservation Challenge: http://webapp1.dlib.indiana.edu/ virtual_disk_library/index.cgi/6825758/FID3536/partners/rcc.htm

- Hazardous Waste Management Facilities and Hazardous Waste Management Units: https://www.epa.gov/hwpermitting/hazardous-waste-man agement-facilities-and-hazardous-waste-management-units

- Land Disposal Restrictions for Hazardous Waste: https://www.epa.gov/ hw/land-disposal-restrictions-hazardous-waste

- Corrective Action—Guidance Documents: https://www.epa.gov/rcra/ policies-and-guidance-documents-resource-conservation-and-recovery -act-rcra-state-authorization#corrective action guidance

- Hazardous Waste Clean-Up Information: http://www.clu-in.org

- National Compliance Assistance Centers: http://www.assistancecenters .net

Notes

1. The author gratefully acknowledges the contributions of Sarah Greer and Rachael Shen.
2. Resource Conservation and Recovery Act, 42 U.S.C. §§ 6901–6992k (1988) (also known as the Solid Waste Disposal Act). Citations throughout this chapter are to sections of the Act, with parallel citations to the U.S. Code. See national policy in § 1003(b), 42 U.S.C. § 6903(b).
3. Pub. L. No. 94-550, 90 Stat. 2796 (1976), as amended, Pub. L. No. 96-482, 94 Stat. 2334 (1980); Hazardous and Solid Waste Amendments of 1984, Pub. L. No. 98-616, 98 Stat. 3221.
4. 42 U.S.C. §§ 9601 et seq.
5. Sections 1003(b), 1002(b). 42 U.S.C. §§ 6902(b), 6901(b).
6. Section 1003(a). 42 U.S.C. § 6902(a).
7. Section 3010(a). 42 U.S.C. § 6930(a).
8. Sections 3012, 3013, 3014, 3017, 3021, 3022. 42 U.S.C. §§ 6933, 6934, 6935, 6938, 6939c, and 6939d.
9. Sections 9001–9010. 42 U.S.C. §§ 6991–6991i. The underground storage tank program is discussed in a separate chapter.
10. 40 C.F.R. § 261.2(a). See 50 Fed. Reg. 664 (1985). The full list of regulatory exclusions in § 261.4(a) should be consulted for additional materials that are excluded from the regulatory definition of solid wastes.
11. 40 C.F.R. § 261.2(a)(2). In addition, certain military munitions, such as propellants, explosives, and chemical agents, are defined as solid wastes, but such waste munitions are regulated under a separate part of the RCRA regulatory program found at 40 C.F.R. Part 266, Subpart M. See Military Munitions Rule,

62 Fed. Reg. 6654 (1997). The court upheld the rule in *Military Toxics Project v. EPA*, 146 F.3d 948 (D.C. Cir. 1998).

[12] 40 C.F.R. § 261.2(d). For example, EPA has designated dioxin wastes as inherently waste-like in the regulations.

[13] In a series of important cases, the U.S. Court of Appeals for the District of Columbia Circuit has construed the definition of solid waste to exclude secondary and residual materials that are recycled as part of a continuous production or manufacturing process. *See American Mining Congress v. EPA*, 824 F.2d 1177 (D.C. Cir. 1987) (AMC I); *American Mining Congress v. EPA*, 907 F.2d 1179 (D.C. Cir. 1990) (AMC II); *Association of Battery Recyclers, Inc. v. EPA*, 208 F.3d 1047 (D.C. Cir. 2000); *American Petroleum Inst. v. EPA*, 216 F.3d 50 (D.C. Cir. 2000); and *Safe Food & Fertilizer v. EPA*, 350 F.3d 1263 (D.C. Cir. 2003). *See also Safe Air For Everyone v. Meyer*, 373 F.3d 1035 (9th Cir. 2004). The reader should consult these court decisions, as well as EPA's 2015 "Definition of Solid Waste" Rule, discussed herein on recycling.

[14] 80 Fed. Reg. 1694 (January 13, 2015). The Final DSW Rule retains the historic generator-controlled exclusion for onsite recycling or recycling within the same company, but requires notice of such recycling to the regulatory authority as a condition of the exclusion; requires documentation of the practices that support the legitimacy of the recycling; and places conditions on containment of hazardous secondary materials in the recycling process. The Rule also codifies the definition of "legitimate recycling" to allow for in-process recycling and commodity-grade materials, as well as finalizes the manufacturing exclusion for certain higher-value spent solvents that are remanufactured into commercial-grade products. *See* Overview of the 2015 Definition of Solid Waste Final Rule, EPA Presentation, https://www.epa.gov/sites/production/files/2015-08/documents/dsw_fnl_rul_brfng_012215.pdf. EPA estimates that the Final DSW Rule will affect over 5,000 industrial facilities in 634 industries.

[15] EPA published its determination that fossil fuel combustion wastes do not warrant regulation under Subtitle C. However, EPA determined that national regulations under Subtitle D are warranted when such wastes are disposed in landfills, surface impoundments, or mines. 65 Fed. Reg. 32214 (2000). In 2014, EPA established regulations under Subtitle D applicable to coal combustion residuals (commonly referred to as "coal ash") in response to a 2008 Tennessee Valley Authority discharge of 1 billion gallons of coal ash slurry into the Emory River and nearby town. *See* Final Rule *available at* https://www.gpo.gov/fdsys/pkg/FR-2015-04-17/pdf/2015-00257.pdf. The final rule includes structural integrity requirements for coal ash impoundments; groundwater monitoring and impoundment siting requirements; operating criteria; as well as a recordkeeping and notice requirements. *See* Fact Sheet: Final Rule on Coal Combustion Residuals Generated by Electric Utilities (December 2014), http://www2.epa.gov/sites/production/files/2014-12/documents/factsheet_ccrfinal_2.pdf.

[16] 40 C.F.R. § 261.4(b)(10).

[17] In 2014, EPA finalized a rule conditionally excluding carbon dioxide streams associated with carbon capture and sequestration (CCS) technologies from hazardous waste regulations. *See* 79 Fed. Reg. 350 (January 3, 2014).

[18] 40 C.F.R. § 261.4(c)–(f).

[19] 40 C.F.R. Part 273.

[20] For a more comprehensive description of the regulatory provisions of RCRA, the reader is referred to *RCRA Hazardous Wastes Handbook*, 12th ed., Hall, Ridgway M., Jr., *et al.*, softcover, 637 pages, 2001, Government Institutes 0-86587-833-1; and *Managing Your Hazardous Wastes: A Step-by-Step RCRA Compliance Guide*, 2nd ed., Voyles, J.K., softcover, 170 pages, 2002, Government Institutes 0-86587-936-2.

[21] 40 C.F.R. § 261.31.

[22] 40 C.F.R. § 261.32.

[23] For a discussion of EPA's listing decision policy, *see* 59 Fed. Reg. 66073 (1994) (proposed dye and pigment industry wastes). A number of the carbamate waste listings were vacated by the court in *Dithiocarbamate Task Force v. EPA*, 98 F.3d 1394 (D.C. Cir. 1996). EPA's listing of petroleum refining wastes

was largely upheld by the court in *American Petroleum Institute v. EPA*, 216 F.3d 50 (2000). For dye and pigment wastes, EPA developed a more flexible approach to listing that considered the total quantities of hazardous constituents in the waste that are annually disposed rather than simply hazardous constituent concentrations in the waste as done for prior listing decisions. *See* 70 Fed. Reg. 9138 (2005).

24 40 C.F.R. § 261.33.

25 40 C.F.R. § 261.33(d).

26 *See* 45 Fed. Reg. 76629 (1980).

27 40 C.F.R. § 261.5. Alternatively, a small spill may qualify as a de minimis loss exempt from the definition of hazardous waste in § 261.3(a)(2)(iv)(D).

28 During the first 20 years of the RCRA program from 1980 through 1999, EPA granted delisting petitions for a total of 136 different waste streams from 115 separate facilities, representing a cumulative total of 45 million tons of waste (mainly wastewaters). EPA estimates that the net cost savings to generators from the delisting program has been in the range of $1.2 to $2.4 billion. *RCRA Hazardous Waste Delisting: The First 20 Years*, U.S. EPA Office of Solid Waste (June 2002), *available at* https://www.epa.gov/sites/production/files/2016-01/documents/delistingreport.pdf.

29 40 C.F.R. § 260.22.

30 The DRAS model and Users Guide can be downloaded from the EPA website: https://www.epa.gov/sites/production/files/2016-01/documents/dras-uguide-200810.pdf.

31 40 C.F.R. § 261.3, § 261.20.

32 40 C.F.R. § 261.21.

33 41 C.F.R. § 261.22.

34 41 C.F.R. § 261.23.

35 40 C.F.R. § 261.24, as amended, 55 Fed. Reg. 11862 (1990).

36 40 C.F.R. Part 261, Appendix II. The court has rejected EPA's use of the TCLP test when disposal in an unlined municipal landfill was not applicable to particular wastes. *Edison Electric Institute v. EPA*, 2 F.3d 438 (D.C. Cir. 1993) (mineral processing and manufactured gas plant wastes); *Columbia Falls Aluminum Co. v. EPA*, 139 F.3d 914 (D.C. Cir. 1998) (aluminum potliner).

37 40 C.F.R. § 261.7.

38 40 C.F.R. § 261.3(a)(2).

39 40 C.F.R. § 261.3(b).

40 EPA's position that the contained-in policy was an interpretive gloss on the mixture and derived-from rules was upheld by the court. *Chemical Manufacturers Ass'n v. EPA*, 869 F.2d 1526 (D.C. Cir. 1989).

41 40 C.F.R. § 261.3(f).

42 73 Fed. Reg. 64668 (2008) to be codified in 40 C.F.R. Parts 260, 261, and 270. A "hazardous secondary material" means a spent material, by-product, or sludge that, when discarded, would be a hazardous waste. The conditional exclusion is not available for materials that are subject to specific management conditions under § 261.4(a) (e.g., fertilizer), spent lead acid batteries, burned to recover energy, or used to produce a fuel.

43 The generator on-site exclusion for non-land-based units is provided in 40 C.F.R. § 261.2(a)(2)(ii). The generator on-site exclusion for land-based units is set forth in 40 C.F.R. § 261.4(a)(23). The off-site reclaimer exclusion is set forth in 40 C.F.R. § 261.4(a)(24).

44 40 C.F.R. § 261.2(a)(2)(ii) and § 261.4(a)(23)(i).

45 40 C.F.R. § 260.42.

46 40 C.F.R. § 261.2(a)(2)(ii) and § 261.1(c)(8).

47 40 C.F.R. § 261.4(a)(24)(vi)(F) and 40 C.F.R. Part 261 Subpart H.

48 *See* 40 C.F.R. § 260.10. Definitions of "Intermediate facility" and "Transfer facility" and § 261.4(a)(24)(ii).

[49] 40 C.F.R. § 261.4(a)(24)(v)(D) & (E).

[50] 40 C.F.R. § 261.4(a)(25).

[51] 40 C.F.R. § 260.43.

[52] 40 C.F.R. § 260.30(d) & (e) and § 260.34.

[53] Consumer Electronics Association. Market Research Report: Trends in CE Reuse, Recycle and Removal. April 2008.

[54] *See* Electronics Donation and Recycling, U.S. EPA, https://www.epa.gov/recycle/electronics-donation -and-recycling.

[55] 40 C.F.R. § 260.10.

[56] 40 C.F.R. § 262.11.

[57] The SW-846 Manual is *available at* https://www.epa.gov/hw-sw846/sw-846-compendium. In addition, EPA issued the Methods Innovation Rule, which allows the use of other test methods that are equivalent to SW-846 methods, except where the RCRA regulatory requirement is defined by the test method (e.g., the Toxicity Characteristic Leaching Procedure). 70 Fed. Reg. 34538 (2005).

[58] 40 C.F.R. § 262.12(c).

[59] 40 C.F.R. §§ 262.20–262.23. *See* Uniform Manifest and Instructions, 40 C.F.R. Part 262, Appendix. EPA issued a final rule that revised and standardized the manifest, preempting state versions and simplify- ing the form, in early 2005. 70 Fed. Reg. 10776 and 70 Fed. Reg. 35034 (2005). The new rule standard- ized the content and appearance of the manifest form, allows companies to print their own forms with EPA approval, and adopts new procedures for tracking rejected loads, residues from nonempty hazardous waste containers, and wastes entering or leaving the United States. Use of the form was mandatory in all states after Sept. 5, 2006.

[60] "e-Manifest Frequent Questions," U.S. EPA, http://www.epa.gov/waste/hazard/transportation/manifest/ e-man-faqs.htm.

[61] 40 C.F.R. § 262.40.

[62] 40 C.F.R. § 262.42.

[63] 40 C.F.R. §§ 262.30–33.

[64] 40 C.F.R. § 262.34(c).

[65] 40 C.F.R. § 262.34(a). A small-quantity generator can store wastes for a longer time period, as discussed below. *See* 40 C.F.R. § 262.34(d)–(f). EPA allows generators of F006 electroplating wastewater treatment sludges to accumulate such waste for up to 180 days (or 270 days if the waste must be shipped more than 200 miles) without a permit or interim status, provided the waste is recycled through metals recovery and other conditions are met. Id.

[66] 40 C.F.R. §§ 264.1(g), 265.1(c), and 270.1(c).

[67] 40 C.F.R. § 262.41.

[68] 40 C.F.R. §§ 262.50–262.58.

[69] 40 C.F.R. § 261.5, § 262.34(d)–(f).

[70] 40 C.F.R. § 261.5.

[71] 40 C.F.R. § 260.10.

[72] Section 3003. 42 U.S.C. § 6923.

[73] *See* the definition of "on-site" in § 260.10, which could be read to define transportation off-site as any distance along, as opposed to simply going across, a public or private right-of-way. This definition is modified, however, by § 262.20(f), which provides that the transporter requirements do not apply to the transport of hazardous wastes on a public or private right-of-way within or along the border of contiguous property under the control of the same person, even if the property is divided by a public or private right- of-way.

[74] 49 U.S.C. §§ 1801 *et seq.*, 49 C.F.R. Parts 171–179.

75 40 C.F.R. § 263.11, § 263.20.

76 40 C.F.R. § 263.20. Special requirements apply to rail or water transport of hazardous waste and to persons who transport hazardous waste outside of the United States. 40 C.F.R. § 263.20(e)–(g), § 263.22(b)–(d).

77 40 C.F.R. § 263.21(b).

78 40 C.F.R. § 263.22.

79 40 C.F.R. § 263.12.

80 40 C.F.R. § 263.10(c).

81 40 C.F.R. § 263.30.

82 *See* 49 C.F.R. § 171.15 and § 171.16.

83 45 Fed. Reg. 51645 (1980).

84 40 C.F.R. § 266.33, discussed below.

85 40 C.F.R. § 260.10. This definition was upheld by the court in *Shell Oil Co. v. EPA*, 950 F.2d 741 (D.C. Cir. 1991).

86 *Id.*

87 *Id.*

88 *Id.*

89 See 40 C.F.R. § 264.1 and § 265.1(c).

90 See 40 C.F.R. Parts 264 and 265, discussed *infra*.

91 Section 3005(e). 42 U.S.C. § 6925(e).

92 40 C.F.R. Part 265.

93 40 C.F.R. Part 264.

94 40 C.F.R. § 265.11, § 264.11.

95 40 C.F.R. § 265.13, § 264.13.

96 40 C.F.R. § 265.17, § 264.17.

97 *See generally* 40 C.F.R. §§ 265.30–.37, §§ 264.30–.37.

98 40 C.F.R. § 265.143(e), § 264.143(f).

99 *See generally* 40 C.F.R. §§ 265.71–.72, §§ 264.71–.72.

100 40 C.F.R. § 265.73, §264.73.

101 40 C.F.R. § 265.75, § 264.75.

102 40 C.F.R. § 265.76, § 264.76.

103 *See generally* 40 C.F.R. §§ 265.110-.120, §§ 264.110–.120.

104 *See generally* 40 C.F.R. §§ 265.140-.150, §§ 264.140–.150.

105 40 C.F.R. Parts 264 and 265, Subparts J *et seq.*

106 These requirements are discussed in detail in Hall, *RCRA Hazardous Wastes Handbook* (Government Institutes), and in Voyles, *Managing Your Hazardous Wastes: A Step-by-Step RCRA Compliance Guide* (Government Institutes).

107 *See generally* 40 C.F.R. §§ 265.170–265.202, §§ 264.170–264.200.

108 40 C.F.R. § 260.10.

109 *See generally* 40 C.F.R. §§ 264.1030–264.1036, §§ 265.1030–265.1035.

110 *See generally* 40 C.F.R. §§ 264.1050–264.1065, §§ 265.1050–265.1064.

111 *See generally* 40 C.F.R. §§ 264.1080–264.1090, §§ 265.1080–265.1090.

112 40 C.F.R. § 260.10.

113 *See generally* 40 C.F.R. §§ 265.220–265.231, §§ 265.300–265.316, §§ 264.220–264.232, §§ 264.300–264.317.

114 40 C.F.R. Part 63.

[115] Section 3004(q)–(s); 40 C.F.R. 266, Subpart D.

[116] Congress also directed EPA to minimize the disposal of containerized liquid hazardous wastes in landfills. In order to discourage the use of absorbent materials (*e.g.,* kitty litter) to reduce free liquids in containerized wastes, EPA's regulations prohibit the landfilling of liquids that have been absorbed in materials that biodegrade or that release liquids when depressed during routine landfill operations. 40 C.F.R. §§ 264.314–.316.

[117] 40 C.F.R. Part 268. The dioxin-containing wastes are those chlorinated dioxins, -dibenzofurans, and -phenols listed as F020, F021, F022, F023, F026, F027, and F028. The solvent wastes are those listed as F001-F005 at 40 C.F.R. 261.31. *See generally* § 3004(d)–(m). 42 U.S.C. § 6924(d)–(m).

[118] Disposal by deep well injection is subject to special provisions and a different schedule for implementing the ban.

[119] The ranking and schedule are published at 40 C.F.R. 268.

[120] EPA's decision to use technology-based standards, rather than risk-based standards, was upheld by the court. *Hazardous Waste Treatment Council v. EPA*, 886 F.2d 355 (1989).

[121] 40 C.F.R. § 268.48. 59 Fed. Reg. 47982 (1994).

[122] EPA's authority to set treatment levels below the hazardous characteristic was upheld in *Chemical Waste Management, Inc. v. EPA*, 976 F.2d 2 (D.C. Cir. 1992). The court also ruled that EPA must ensure that hazardous wastes managed in Clean Water Act lagoon systems receive equivalent treatment to that mandated under RCRA. However, Congress then enacted the Land Disposal Program Flexibility Act of 1996, which exempts hazardous wastes managed in Clean Water Act impoundments from the LDR program. Pub. L. No. 104-119, 110 Stat. 830.

[123] *See* Section 3014(b). EPA had proposed listing used oil from motor vehicles and industrial manufacturing processes based on a determination that this used oil typically and frequently contains hazardous contaminants at levels of regulatory concern. 50 Fed. Reg. 49258 (1985). The final decision was published at 51 Fed. Reg. 41900 (1986).

[124] 40 C.F.R. Part 279.

[125] 57 Fed. Reg. 21524 (1992).

[126] 40 C.F.R. Part 273.

[127] EPA's proposal to add pharmaceutical wastes to the Universal Waste Rule was met with concerns associated with the lack of tracking requirements for this type of waste. *See generally* 73 Fed. Reg. 73520 (2008); "Management of Pharmaceutical Hazardous Waste," EPA website, https://www.epa.gov/hwgenerators/management-pharmaceutical-hazardous-waste. In lieu of finalizing the 2008 proposal, EPA developed a new proposal for management and disposal of hazardous pharmaceutical wastes in early 2015. *See id.*

[128] Section 3005. 42 U.S.C. § 6925.

[129] Section 3005(e). *See* the interim status standards for TSD facilities in 40 C.F.R. Part 265, discussed above.

[130] 70 Fed. Reg. 53420 (2005) (to be codified in 40 C.F.R. Part 267).

[131] Section 3005(c)(3). 42 U.S.C. § 6925(c)(3).

[132] Section 3005(c)(3).

[133] 40 C.F.R. Part 124 Subpart G, Part 267, and Part 270 Subpart J.

[134] Section 3004(u)–(v). 42 U.S.C. § 6924(u)–(v).

[135] 40 C.F.R. 264 Subparts F and S.

[136] 40 C.F.R. 264.552.

[137] 40 C.F.R. §§ 264.550–.555.

[138] 40 C.F.R. Part 264, Subpart S; 63 Fed. Reg. 65874 (1998).

[139] 40 C.F.R. Part 270, Subpart H.

140 In *Louisiana Environmental Action Network v. EPA*, 172 F.3d 65 (D.C. Cir. 1999), the court upheld a regulation that allows variances from the treatment requirements for wastes excavated from remediation sites and redeposited in a Subtitle C landfill.

141 One Cleanup Program, https://www3.epa.gov/reg3wcmd/ca/pgm_reforms.htm.

142 Section 3006, 42 U.S.C. § 6926; *see generally* 40 C.F.R. Part 271.

143 EPA has issued guidance on the degree of flexibility states may exercise under a RCRA authorized program. *See* Memorandum on Determining Equivalency of State RCRA Hazardous Waste Programs (Sept. 7, 2005), *available at* https://archive.epa.gov/epawaste/laws-regs/web/pdf/fe-9-7-05.pdf. The guidance discusses EPA approval of state requirements that do not exactly match the federal rules but that have an equal regulatory effect and provides guidelines to EPA regions for approval of state proposals that seek such flexibility.

144 Section 3007. EPA's inspection activities under RCRA Section 3007 are subject to the Fourth Amendment's protection against unreasonable searches or seizures, which the Supreme Court has applied in holding that a warrant is generally required for an inspection by an administrative agency. *See Marshall v. Barlow's, Inc.*, 436 U.S. 307 (1978), which involved the inspection provisions of the Occupational Safety and Health Act.

145 Section 3007(c)–(e). 42 U.S.C. § 6927(c)–(e).

146 Section 3008. 42 U.S.C. § 6928.

147 The U.S. Court of Appeals for the Eighth Circuit has held that the federal government cannot bring a civil action when the state program has been approved by EPA and the state has brought an enforcement action against the defendant for the same alleged violation. *Harmon Industries, Inc. v. Browner*, 191 F.3d 894 (8th Cir. 1999). Other courts have not agreed with this ruling, however, and have allowed EPA to "overfile" a state action. *See, e.g., United States v. Murphy Oil USA, Inc.*, 143 F. Supp. 2d 1054 (W.D. Wis. 2001).

148 The first major conviction for knowing endangerment under RCRA was *United States v. Protex Industries, Inc.*, 874 F.2d 740 (10th Cir. 1989) (drum recycling plant endangered employees exposed to toxic chemicals).

149 Section 7003. 42 U.S.C. § 6973.

150 *United States v. Vertac Chemical Corp.*, 489 F. Supp. 870 (E.D. Ark. 1980).

151 *See, e.g., City of Hurricane, W.V. v. Disposal Service Inc.*, 36 F. Supp. 3d 692 (S.D.W.Va. 2014); *Citizens Coal Council v. Matt Canestrale Contracting, Inc.*, 51 F. Supp. 3d 593 (W.D.Pa. 2014).

152 Section 7002. 42 U.S.C. § 6972.

153 Section 4010. 42 U.S.C. § 6949a.

154 In *C & A Carbone, Inc. v. Town of Clarkstown, New York*, 114 S. Ct. 1677 (1994), the Supreme Court held that a New York town's flow control ordinance violated the Commerce Clause because it favored a local operator to the detriment of out-of-state businesses.

155 Pub. L. 102-386, 106 Stat. 1505.

156 The DOE conceded that federal agencies might be liable for fines imposed to induce them to comply with judicial orders designed to modify future behavior, that is, coercive fines. But the DOE rejected the argument that RCRA waived sovereign immunity for fines imposed to punish past violations, that is, punitive fines.

157 *U.S. Department of Energy v. Ohio*, 503 U.S. 607 (1992).

158 H.R. No. 886, 102nd Cong., 2nd Sess. 19 (1992).

Chapter 4

Underground Storage Tanks

Karen J. Nardi[1]
Arnold & Porter LLP

1.0 Overview

Underground storage tanks (USTs) are widely recognized as a major environmental problem. They are the most significant source of soil and groundwater contamination in the United States, affecting hundreds of thousands of sites across the country. Studies have shown that there are many reasons why USTs cause contamination. Some tanks and associated piping simply corrode or structurally fail during years of use. In other cases, poor practices result in spills when tanks are emptied or when they overflow during filling.

Since 1984, the U.S. Environmental Protection Agency (EPA) has had authority to regulate USTs under the Resource Conservation and Recovery Act (RCRA).[2] Federal and state regulations have improved UST operating practices, cut back on the number of spills, and resulted in the cleanup of many contaminated sites. Nonetheless, progress on UST spills and remediation slowed in recent years, leading EPA to embark on an ambitious initiative to tighten federal regulations. This initiative concluded in 2015 with the first major revision of federal UST regulations since the program's inception.

EPA published its first comprehensive rule on USTs in 1988.[3] At the time, the agency estimated that there were more than 2 million UST systems (which include both the underground storage tank and the piping connected to it) located at more than 700,000 facilities nationwide.[4] EPA judged that roughly 75 percent of such systems posed the greatest potential for leakage and environmental harm because the UST systems were made of steel without any form of corrosion protection.[5] These numbers are now significantly reduced: In March 2015, EPA estimated that there were approximately 569,000 active federally regulated USTs at some 205,000 sites.[6] Of these, the overwhelming majority contain petroleum, with fewer than 10,000 holding hazardous substances.[7] EPA estimates that approximately 72 percent of active USTs are now in full compliance with leak prevention and detection requirements.[8]

Since 1984, tremendous resources have been devoted to cleaning up soil and groundwater contamination at UST sites. By March 2015, EPA had confirmed 525,095 releases from USTs in the fifty states and the District of Columbia since 1985.[9] EPA estimates that federal and state governments combined spend approximately $1 billion each year on soil and groundwater cleanup resulting from leaking USTs.[10] Nonetheless, there remain over 70,000 pending or incomplete UST cleanups,[11] and it is estimated that it would take an additional $11 billion to eliminate this backlog.[12]

In the mid-1990s, some experts asserted that we were spending too much to clean up USTs relative to the magnitude of the environmental problems they create, at least in the case of petroleum releases.[13] Consequently, a movement arose to develop a risk-based approach to cleanup,[14] including monitored natural attenuation (also called passive bioremediation, the natural degradation of contaminants without active remediation).[15] This movement toward less aggressive cleanups was later modified by the discovery that a new substance of concern—methyl tertiary-butyl ether (MTBE), a gasoline additive designed to reduce emissions and raise octane—was appearing in surface and groundwater. A study released in 1998 concluded that passive bioremediation was not very effective on MTBE plumes.[16] More recent research has revealed that bioremediation may be effective under certain conditions,[17] and there is ongoing research by both governmental and nongovernmental entities into other MTBE cleanup methodologies.[18] Many states continue to pursue risk-based investigation and remediation techniques by focusing on site-specific circumstances.

To mark the twentieth anniversary of the federal UST program, EPA's Office of Underground Storage Tanks (OUST) issued a report in March 2004 reflecting on the past twenty years and discussing continuing challenges, including (1) improving operational compliance, (2) completing cleanups, (3) minimizing leaks from new and upgraded tanks, and (4) cleaning up and reusing abandoned gas stations and other petroleum Brownfields.[19]

On August 8, 2005, President Bush signed the Energy Policy Act of 2005, which contained the Underground Storage Tank Compliance Act of 2005.[20] This law was aimed at addressing some of the challenges identified in EPA's 2004 report, including further reducing UST releases to the environment. In particular, the law expanded the eligible uses of the Leaking Underground Storage Tank (LUST) Trust Fund, and it made program grants to the states conditional on tighter regulations for UST inspection, operator training, delivery prohibition, secondary containment, financial responsibility, and cleanup.[21] Notably, however, the grant conditions did not apply to Indian tribes.

To implement the changes mandated in the Energy Policy Act, EPA has worked closely with states, other federal agencies, tank owners and operators, and other stakeholders.[22] All states have grant agreements in place to implement the act's provisions, and by 2011, most states had satisfied the act's major requirements, including additional measures to protect groundwater, delivery prohibition, compliance reporting, initial two-year inspections, and posting of public records.[23]

In the fall of 2011, EPA moved to consolidate and expand on the changes effected under the Energy Policy Act. The agency initiated rulemaking that would formalize the act's grant conditions, converting them into universal regulatory requirements. EPA also proposed changes that would modernize and strengthen regulations for UST spill prevention, monitoring, reporting, training, inspection, and recordkeeping.

After a lengthy process of public comment and internal review, EPA unveiled its final rule in June 2015. The rule was published in the Federal Register on July 15, 2015, and took effect October 15, 2015.[24] The 2015 UST Rule eliminated certain exceptions, raised operational standards, and capitalized on improvements in UST engineering and technology. In adopting this stricter approach, EPA made a decision to curtail the flexibility of UST owners and operators in favor of public safety. For example, in converting the grant conditions of the Energy Policy Act into regulatory requirements, the 2015 UST Rule equalized standards on Indian lands with those of the states. EPA also eliminated certain regulatory deferrals, and it sought to hasten compliance with modern methods of UST leak prevention and detection. Now, for example, if 50 percent or more of a piping system is replaced, the entire piping system must be replaced. If a tank's internal lining fails and cannot be properly repaired, the tank can no longer be upgraded for continued use, but must be taken out of service. If a UST system stores more than 10 percent ethanol or 20 percent biodiesel, it must affirmatively demonstrate its ability to safely contain such materials.[25] Finally, states implementing their own UST program under a federal delegation are given three years to modify their regulations to incorporate the stricter federal standards. Although some states will continue to exceed EPA's requirements, the federal government has significantly raised the regulatory floor.

Also in June 2015, EPA released its guidance for addressing petroleum vapor intrusion at leaking USTs.[26] This marks EPA's first formal guidance in this area.

1.1 Objectives of the UST Program

In enacting the UST provisions of RCRA in 1984, Congress had several basic public policy objectives. The statute addresses the problem of existing tanks that may have caused environmental damage and the problem of new tanks that should be designed and operated in accordance with the best modern engineering practices and technology.

One objective of the UST program is to identify existing tanks and require that they either be brought up to certain design and operating standards or be closed. Another purpose is to determine whether existing tanks have leaked, causing an environmental problem. If so, the law requires tank owners and/or operators to take corrective action to address the environmental damage.

For new tanks, the law requires that tanks meet strict design and operating standards and that the government be notified when they are installed. Any tanks that continue to be used must be operated in a way that will minimize the possibility of leaks or spills due to filling or emptying.

The RCRA program also requires the reporting, investigation, and cleanup of spills and other releases from USTs. Finally, federal law sets standards for closure of USTs and financial responsibility requirements for persons who own and operate USTs. Thus, the regulations, while detailed, were designed to accomplish the basic objectives of (1) leak prevention, (2) leak detection, and (3) leak cleanup.[27]

In 2000, EPA announced four program initiatives aimed at fulfilling its mission to protect human health and the environment from leaking USTs: (1) improve compliance with UST requirements; (2) achieve faster cleanups; (3) evaluate UST system performance; and (4) launch the "USTfields Initiative" to clean up petroleum contamination at abandoned industrial or commercial properties.[28] In 2002, the USTfields Initiative was complemented by passage of the Small Business Liability Relief and Brownfields Revitalization Act. It revised the definition of "brownfield" to include petroleum-contaminated sites. It also authorized EPA to give grants of up to $250 million annually to states and communities to assess, clean up, and reuse petroleum Brownfields.[29] OUST will work with EPA's regional offices and the states to further develop and carry out these initiatives.[30]

The RCRA UST program, like many federal laws, is a delegated program. States are given an opportunity to adopt laws and regulations that meet the minimum federal standards. EPA has delegated authority to certain states that have adequate UST programs. In such cases, states (not EPA) are the primary permitting and enforcement authorities for USTs. While states may enforce federal law regarding USTs, state and local laws may be stricter than federal law. Thus, it is very important to check whether more stringent state and local laws apply. As of March 2015, thirty-eight states, the District of Columbia, and Puerto Rico had all been granted state program approval.[31]

This chapter describes the various federal requirements that apply to owners and operators of new and existing UST systems. Many state and local authorities have adopted requirements that apply to UST systems. The reader is strongly encouraged to verify compliance with such requirements to the extent applicable. The following aspects are discussed in this chapter.

1.1.1 Basic Terminology

This section describes which UST systems and owners and operators are subject to the RCRA Subtitle I requirements.

1.1.2 Implementation and Enforcement

This section describes which regulatory agencies are responsible for implementation of the RCRA Subtitle I regulations and the mechanisms available for enforcement.

1.1.3 Summary of Reporting and Recordkeeping Requirements

This section provides a brief summary of the many reporting and recordkeeping obligations with which owners and operators of UST systems must comply.

1.1.4 New UST Systems

This section further describes the notification requirements for owners and operators of new UST systems. A summary of performance standards for new UST systems is also provided.

1.1.5 Existing UST Systems

This section further describes the notification requirements for owners and operators of existing UST systems. A summary of upgrading requirements for existing UST systems is also provided.

1.1.6 General Operating Requirements

This section describes the various operating requirements covering spill and overfill control, operation and maintenance of corrosion protection systems, substance compatibility, and UST system repairs.

1.1.7 Testing and Inspections

This section describes the testing and inspection requirements for UST systems and equipment.

1.1.8 Release Detection

This section summarizes the various release detection requirements and methods for USTs.

1.1.9 Release Reporting, Investigation, and Response

This section describes the various procedures for reporting, investigating, confirming, and cleaning up releases from UST systems.

1.1.10 Closure of UST Systems

This section summarizes the requirements for temporary and permanent closure and change-in-service of UST systems.

1.1.11 Financial Responsibility Requirements

This section briefly summarizes the various financial responsibility obligations facing UST owners and operators.

2.0 Basic Terminology

2.1 Underground Storage Tank Systems

By legal definition, a UST is more than just a tank that is buried underground. Tanks and piping systems that are partially below the ground surface may be subject to the UST regulations. To be specific, a UST is defined as follows:

[A]ny one or combination of tanks (including underground pipes connected thereto) that is used to contain an accumulation of regulated substances, and the volume of which (including the volume of underground pipes connected thereto) is [ten] percent or more beneath the surface of the ground.[32]

Several systems are specifically excluded from the definition of UST under RCRA Subtitle I, including the following:[33]

a. Farm or residential tanks of 1,100 gallons or less capacity that are used noncommercially for storage of motor fuel;

b. Heating oil storage tanks that are used on the premises where the tank is stored;

c. Septic tanks;

    d. Pipeline facilities (including gathering lines) that are regulated under
- Natural Gas Pipeline Safety Act of 1968 or Hazardous Liquid Pipeline Safety Act of 1979,[34] or
- Comparable state laws that regulate natural gas or hazardous liquid pipelines;

    e. Surface impoundments, pits, ponds, or lagoons;

    f. Stormwater or wastewater collection systems;

    g. Flow-through process tanks;

    h. Liquid traps or associated gathering lines directly related to oil or gas production and gathering operations;

    i. Storage tanks that are situated in an underground area (e.g., basement) if the tank is situated upon or above the surface of the floor in that area;

    j. Pipes connected to any of the tanks which are described in subparagraphs (a) through (i) above.

In addition to the above, several systems are specifically excluded from regulation under RCRA Subtitle I, including the following:[35]

    a. UST systems holding hazardous wastes listed or identified under Subtitle C of RCRA or a mixture of such hazardous wastes and other regulated substances. Such UST systems would be subject to the hazardous waste requirements of RCRA Subtitle C;

    b. Wastewater treatment tank systems that are part of a wastewater treatment facility regulated under Section 402 or 307(b) of the Clean Water Act;[36]

    c. Equipment or machinery that contains regulated substances for operational purposes (e.g., hydraulic lift tanks and electrical equipment tanks);

    d. UST systems with capacities of 110 gallons or less;

    e. UST systems that contain a de minimis concentration of regulated substances;[37]

    f. Emergency spill or overflow containment UST systems that are expeditiously emptied after use.

In addition to those systems fully excluded from the UST regulations, EPA has chosen to partially exclude several other UST systems from much of its regulation. These partially excluded UST systems include the following:

    a. Wastewater treatment tank systems that do not fall under Section 402 or 307(b) of the Clean Water Act;

    b. UST systems containing radioactive material that are regulated under the Atomic Energy Act of 1954;[38]

    c. UST systems that are part of an emergency generator system at nuclear power generation facilities licensed and regulated by the Nuclear Regulatory Commission.

Partially excluded UST systems are not subject to UST regulations governing construction, installation, operations, release detection, release reporting, system closure, or operator training. They are, however, subject to the UST regulations governing release response and remediation.[39]

No person may install a partially excluded UST system that stores regulated substances unless the system meets the following criteria:[40]

    a. Capable of preventing releases due to corrosion or structural failure throughout the system's operational life;

    b. Cathodically protected against corrosion, constructed of non-corrodible material, or otherwise designed or constructed in a manner to prevent the release or threatened release of any stored substance;

    c. Constructed or lined with a material that is compatible with the stored substance.

Partially excluded UST systems may be installed without corrosion protection provided a corrosion expert determines that the soil is not corrosive enough to cause a release due to corrosion during the operating life of the UST system. For the operating life of the tanks, owners and operators of those systems must maintain records that reflect such a determination.[41]

Until 2015, EPA also deferred several other categories of UST systems from regulation because the agency was uncertain whether the technology to monitor and detect releases was readily available.[42] These previously deferred UST systems include the following:

    a. UST systems storing fuel solely for use by emergency power generators;

    b. Airport hydrant fuel distribution systems;

    c. UST systems with field-constructed tanks.

Citing advances in technology over the past several decades, EPA eliminated these deferral categories in its 2015 UST Rule.[43] Now, UST systems storing fuel for emergency power generators must fully comply with UST regulations by October 15, 2018.[44] Airport hydrant fuel distribution systems and UST systems with field-constructed tanks must comply with their own, more flexible set of regulatory standards, generally also by October 15, 2018.[45]

2.2 Regulated Substances

The RCRA UST program applies to tanks that contain regulated substances. Any hazardous substance as defined in Section 101(14) of the Comprehensive Environmental Response, Compensation, and Liability Act (CERCLA) of 1980[46] is regulated under RCRA Subtitle I. Petroleum and petroleum-based substances, such as motor fuels, jet fuels, distillate fuel oils, residual fuel oils, lubricants, petroleum solvents, and used oils, are also subject to regulation under RCRA Subtitle I.[47] RCRA Subtitle I regulations do not apply to hazardous wastes because they are regulated under RCRA Subtitle C.

EPA has recognized that the increasing production and use of alternative fuels, such as biodiesel and ethanol, pose significant technical and regulatory issues.[48] EPA reports that UST components such as linings and seals may degrade or corrode when alcohol or biodiesel is present and that ethanol may complicate cleanups.[49] In 2010 EPA passed the Renewable Fuel Standard rulemaking ("RFS2"), requiring 36 billion gallons per year of biofuels to be used by 2022.[50] As the use of biofuels increases, EPA has grown more concerned about the compatibility of UST system materials, the functionality of leak detection, and the effects of biofuel releases.[51] EPA has broadened the scope of its regulations accordingly. In its 2015 UST Rule, EPA redefined "motor fuel" to include any complex blend of hydrocarbons used as fuel, and it modified "regulated substance" to eliminate the definition's specific reference to crude oil.[52]

2.3 Owners and Operators

Owners and operators of USTs have certain responsibilities under RCRA Subtitle I. An owner is any person who owns a UST that is used for the storage, use, or dispensing of regulated substances on or after November 8, 1984.[53] In addition, any person who owned a UST immediately before the discontinuation of its use prior to November 8, 1984, is considered an owner.[54] Thus, a person who acquires property containing USTs that were abandoned before acquisition of the property and before November 8, 1984, would not be an owner for purposes of the UST program. Also excluded from the definition of owner is any person who, "without participating in the management of an underground storage tank and otherwise not engaged in petroleum production, refining, or marketing, holds indicia of ownership primarily to protect the person's security interest [in the tank]."[55] This provision is intended to protect lenders or other persons holding security interests in petroleum UST systems that otherwise do not actively participate in the operation of such UST systems.[56]

RCRA Subtitle I defines operator as "any person in control of, or having responsibility for, the daily operation of the underground storage tank."[57] Unlike regulations for owners, which focus on both current and former owners, these regulations, although not entirely clear, appear to focus only on current operators of UST systems.

3.0 Implementation and Enforcement

3.1 Implementation

EPA has primary responsibility for implementation and enforcement of RCRA Subtitle I. However, the UST program allows for delegation of this authority to states. Subject to EPA approval, states may implement their own UST programs in place of the federal program if the state's requirements are "no less stringent" than the federal requirements and provide for adequate enforcement.[58] This remains the case under the 2015 UST Rule, which gives states with approved programs three years to update their regulations to comply with the new federal standards.[59] In addition to the federal program, many states and local authorities have adopted their own UST laws and regulations. Such requirements can, in fact, be more stringent than those provided under the federal regime. Thus, it is important for owners and operators of UST systems to verify compliance not only with federal requirements but also with state and local requirements.

Federally recognized Native American tribal governments collaborate with the UST program to oversee the approximately 2,500 active, federally regulated USTs on their lands.[60] As of 2007, 171 tribes had at least one active UST.[61] Over time, EPA has worked with tribal representatives and provided financial and technical assistance to prevent and clean up releases from USTs. EPA has also assisted in developing tribal UST programs and has directly implemented the UST program in Indian Country.[62] Under the Energy Policy Act of 2005, tribal governments were effectively subject to a less stringent regulatory regime than the states, whose program grants were made conditional on stricter state UST regulations. This two-tier approach ended with the 2015 UST Rule, which largely shifted the grant conditions of the Energy Policy Act into the Code of Federal Regulations and made them explicitly applicable to Indian tribes.

3.2 Enforcement

EPA has authority under RCRA Section 9006 to issue a compliance order to any person in violation of RCRA Subtitle I.[63] Alternatively, EPA may also commence a civil action in the U.S. district court for appropriate relief, including the issuance of a temporary or permanent injunction.[64] Failure to comply with an order issued by EPA may result in civil penalties of not more than $37,500 for each day of continued noncompliance.[65] Persons named on an order may request a public hearing to challenge the order within thirty days after the order is served.[66]

EPA may also assess civil penalties against owners and operators who do not comply with UST requirements. An owner who knowingly fails to notify or who submits false information pursuant to the RCRA Subtitle I initial notification requirements shall be subject to a civil penalty not to exceed $16,000 for each tank for which notification is not given or false information is submitted.[67] Owners or operators of USTs may also be subject to civil penalties, not to exceed $16,000 per tank per day of violation, for failing to comply with UST requirements relating to leak detection, recordkeeping, reporting, corrective action, closure, and financial responsibility.[68] Similar penalties may be assessed for violations of such requirements in any EPA-approved state UST program.

EPA has authority to order owners and operators of USTs to take corrective action for any releases of petroleum when EPA (or the state) determines that such corrective action will be done properly and promptly by the owner or operator.[69] Under RCRA Section 9003(h), EPA or the state (for EPA-approved state UST programs) may undertake corrective action itself only if such action is necessary to protect human health and the environment and one or more of the following situations exists:[70]

a. No owner or operator can be found to carry out such corrective action within 90 days or such shorter period as may be necessary to protect human health and the environment.

b. The situation is such that it requires prompt action by EPA or the state to protect human health and the environment.

c. Corrective action costs exceed the amount of coverage required by the RCRA Subtitle I financial responsibility requirements.

d. The owner or operator of the UST has failed or refused to comply with a compliance order of EPA under RCRA Section 9006 or with an order of the state to comply with corrective action regulations.

In 1991, EPA issued a final rule establishing procedures relating to the issuance of RCRA Section 9003(h) corrective action orders.[71] The final rule amends regulations provided in 40 C.F.R. Part 24 regarding the issuance of, and administrative hearings on, corrective action orders. Generally speaking, the rule provides that the same administrative procedures employed for issuance of RCRA Section 3008(h) corrective action orders are to be used for the issuance of RCRA Section 9003(h) orders. Such procedures are less formal and resource intensive than proceedings that would be required for RCRA Section 9006 compliance orders.[72]

4.0 Summary of Reporting and Recordkeeping Requirements

Owners and operators of USTs are subject to myriad reporting and recordkeeping requirements under RCRA Subtitle I. The following is a brief overview of the numerous reporting and recordkeeping obligations. Later sections of this chapter discuss how these requirements apply to new tanks as opposed to existing tanks.

4.1 Reporting Requirements

4.1.1 Initial Notification

Owners and operators of existing and new UST systems are required to notify the appropriate designated agency of the use of such systems or any change in ownership.[73] Typically, the state or local regulatory agency is designated to receive such initial notification.[74] Owners and operators also must certify compliance with requirements governing UST system installation, cathodic protection, financial responsibility, and release detection.[75]

Under the 2015 UST Rule, the owners of previously deferred airport hydrant systems and field-constructed tank systems have three years to notify the designated agency of the systems' existence. Owners must demonstrate financial responsibility at the same time.[76]

4.1.2 Suspected Releases

Owners and operators of USTs must report any suspected releases or unusual operating conditions to the implementing agency.[77] Unusual operating conditions include the unexplained presence of water in the storage tank, liquid in the interstitial space of secondarily contained systems, or sudden loss of product.[78]

4.1.3 Spills and Overfills

Owners and operators of USTs must report any spills and overfills from UST systems to the implementing agency.[79]

4.1.4 Confirmed Releases

Upon confirmation of any release, owners and operators of USTs must report such release to the implementing agency within twenty-four hours or within another reasonable period of time determined by the agency.[80] Release of a hazardous substance equal to or in excess of its reportable quantity must also be reported immediately to the National Response Center and appropriate state and local authorities pursuant to CERCLA and the Superfund Amendments and Reauthorization Act (SARA) of 1986.[81]

4.1.5 Corrective Action

Owners and operators of USTs have several reporting obligations when undertaking corrective action involving USTs, including the reporting of initial abatement measures,[82] initial site characterization,[83] removal of free product,[84] results of investigations for soil and groundwater cleanups,[85] and, if required by the implementing agency, submittal of corrective action plans.[86]

4.1.6 Permanent Closure/Change-in-Service

Owners and operators of USTs are required to provide advance notice of the permanent closure or change-in-service of any UST, unless such action is in response to corrective action.[87]

4.1.7 Financial Responsibility

Owners and operators of USTs are required to submit various forms demonstrating financial responsibility for taking corrective action and for compensating third parties for bodily injury and property damage caused by accidental releases arising from the operation of USTs.[88]

4.2 Recordkeeping Requirements

RCRA Section 9005(b), 42 U.S.C. § 6991d(b), provides that any records, reports, or information that are provided to implementing agencies shall be made available to the public, except information that has been designated as confidential by the agency.[89] Confidential records, reports, or information must be designated as confidential and submitted separately from other records that are otherwise submitted to the regulatory agencies.[90]

4.2.1 Site Corrosion Potential Analysis

Owners and operators of metal USTs and piping that are installed in soil without corrosion protection must maintain records demonstrating that the soil is not corrosive enough to cause release during the component's operating life.[91]

4.2.2 Operation of Corrosion Protection Equipment

Owners and operators of USTs must maintain records of inspections and testing of cathodic protection systems where used.[92]

4.2.3 Materials Compatibility

Owners and operators must maintain documentation of a UST system's compatibility with its contents as long as the system contains that material.[93]

4.2.4 UST Repairs

Repairs include any actions restoring UST system components to their proper operating condition after a release or other failure to properly function.[94] Owners and operators of USTs must maintain records of all UST system repairs until the UST system is permanently closed or undergoes a change-in-service.[95]

4.2.5 Spill Prevention Testing and Overfill Prevention Inspection

Owners and operators must maintain documentation of all testing and inspections performed on spill prevention equipment, overfill prevention equipment, and containment sumps used for interstitial monitoring of piping. All records must be maintained for three years.[96] Additionally, if spill prevention equipment or containment sumps are periodically monitored—meaning at least once every 30 days[97]—records must be maintained as long as periodic monitoring continues.[98]

4.2.6 Walkthrough Inspections

Owners and operators must maintain records of walkthrough inspections for one year. These records must include, at a minimum, a list of areas checked, whether each area was compliant, and a description of any actions taken to rectify noncompliance.[99]

4.2.7 Operator Training

Owners and operators must maintain a list of all currently designated Class A, B, and C operators, including names, classes, dates of designation, training, and retraining certification. Training records must be maintained as long as the operator is designated at the site, and must include the name of the trainer and training program.[100]

4.2.8 Release Detection

Owners and operators of USTs must maintain for five years all records that document performance claims made by manufacturers of release detection equipment; the results of any sampling, testing, and monitoring for releases; and records relating to the calibration, maintenance, and repair of release detection equipment.[101] Records of vapor and groundwater monitoring site assessments must be maintained for as long as such methods of release detection are used.[102]

Records of interstitial monitoring and annual operations tests must be maintained for three years.[103] Records of tank and line tightness testing must be maintained until the next test is conducted.[104] Records of all remaining sampling, testing, and monitoring must be maintained for one year.[105]

4.2.9 Permanent Closure

Owners and operators of USTs are required to maintain records of permanent closure or change-in-service of UST systems for at least three years after completion of the closure or change-in-service.[106]

4.2.10 Financial Responsibility

Owners or operators of USTs must maintain evidence of all financial assurance mechanisms used to demonstrate financial responsibility under the RCRA Subtitle I regulations.[107] Owners and operators of USTs must maintain their records either at the UST site or at a readily available alternative site. If a UST is permanently closed, owners and operators may mail closure records to the implementing agency if they cannot be kept at the site or at an alternative site.[108]

4.2.11 Requirements Under the Energy Policy Act of 2005

Under the Energy Policy Act, states receiving federal funds to support their UST programs[109] were required to develop a program to maintain and update UST records and make them available to the public.[110] The purpose of this "public record" requirement was to help EPA evaluate state UST programs and give the public information on the status of USTs within the state.

To the maximum extent practicable, the public record of a state must include the following:[111]

- The number, sources, and causes of UST releases in the state;
- The record of compliance by USTs in the state; and
- Data on the number of UST equipment failures in the state.

EPA has established guidelines for the states to meet the public record requirements.[112]

5.0 New UST Systems

5.1 Notification Requirements

Any owner who brings a UST system into use must notify the designated regulatory agency of the existence of such a tank system within thirty days of bringing the UST into use. A standard notification form is usually used. Owners and operators of new UST systems must certify in the notification form that they have complied with various UST requirements, including, for example, requirements for installation of tanks and piping, cathodic protection, financial responsibility, and release detection.[113]

The installer of the UST system must also certify in the notification form that the methods used to install the tank system comply with industry codes of practice developed by a nationally recognized association or independent testing laboratory in accordance with the manufacturer's instructions. The UST regulations refer to several industry codes of practice that may be used by installers to comply with these requirements.[114]

Finally, any person who sells a tank intended to be used as a UST must notify the purchaser of the various notification obligations for owners of USTs under the UST regulations.[115] Companies that sell property with underground storage tanks should be sure that they advise the buyer of the UST notice requirements. Typically this is done in the purchase and sale documentation.

5.2 Performance Standards

Owners and operators of new UST systems are required to meet several performance standards in order to prevent releases of regulated substances from the systems resulting from structural failure, corrosion, or spills and overfills. The following sections describe these performance standards.

5.2.1 Tanks

Under the 2015 UST Rule, secondary containment and interstitial monitoring are now required for all tanks installed or replaced after April 12, 2016.[116] The grant conditions of the Energy Policy Act already contained similar requirements.[117] However, the 2015 UST Rule extended secondary containment to Indian land, and it eliminated an exception for tanks installed more than 1,000 feet from an existing community water system or potable drinking water well.[118]

USTs must be properly designed, constructed, and protected from corrosion in accordance with appropriate industry codes of practice.[119] An owner may install a UST and corrosion protection system not specified by the regulations as long as the implementing agency determines that the system is capable of preventing the release or threatened release of any stored regulated substance in a manner that is no less protective of human health and the environment than other prescribed UST systems.[120]

Owners and operators wishing to install tanks constructed of metal without corrosion protection must have a corrosion expert determine that the site is not sufficiently corrosive to cause a release due to corrosion from the UST during its operating life. In addition, for the remaining life of the tank, owners and operators of such USTs must maintain records demonstrating such compliance.[121]

5.2.2 Piping

As with tanks, secondary containment is now required for all piping installed or replaced after April 12, 2016.[122] Additionally, when 50 percent of more of a piping run is replaced, the entire piping run must be replaced with secondarily contained piping.[123] Secondary containment of piping is common in most recent UST systems, as it was required as a grant condition of the Energy Policy Act.

UST regulations provide guidelines and industry codes of practice to follow in the design, construction, and corrosion protection of new piping systems. The regulations provide standards for new piping constructed of fiberglass-reinforced plastic and steel with cathodic protection.[124] Similar regulations are provided for piping constructed of metal without cathodic protection. They require the owner and operator to have a corrosion expert determine that the site is not corrosive and to maintain records that demonstrate that the site will remain noncorrosive for the remaining life of the UST piping.[125]

Piping other than that specifically described by the regulations may be constructed if the regulatory agency determines that it is as capable of preventing the release or threatened release of regulated substances as EPA-approved systems.[126]

5.2.3 Spill and Overfill Prevention Equipment

Owners and operators of new USTs must employ spill and overflow prevention equipment to prevent releases that may occur during the filling or emptying of such USTs. Overfill prevention equipment must be capable of one of the following:[127]

a. Automatically shutting off flow into the tank when the tank is no more than 95 percent full;

b. Alerting the transfer operator when the tank is more than 90 percent full by restricting the flow into the tank or triggering a high-level alarm;

c. Restricting flow thirty minutes prior to overfilling and alerting the transfer operator with a high-level alarm one minute before overfilling; or

d. Automatically shutting off the flow into the tank so that none of the fittings located on top of the tank are exposed to the product due to overfilling.

Spill prevention equipment must be capable of preventing the release of regulated substances into the environment when the transfer hose is detached from the tank's fill pipe.[128] Alternative spill and overflow prevention equipment can be used if owners and operators can satisfactorily demonstrate to the implementing agency that the equipment is no less protective of human health and the environment. However, flow restrictors used in vent lines can never be used as an overfill prevention method.[129]

No spill and overfill prevention equipment is required if transfers of regulated substances to and from the UST system involve no more than twenty-five gallons at one time.[130]

5.2.4 Installation

All new tanks and pipes must be properly installed in accordance with appropriate industry codes of practice. Owners and operators must certify, test, or inspect such installation to demonstrate compliance with such industry codes of practice.[131]

5.2.5 Dispenser Systems

Under the 2015 UST Rule, under-dispenser containment is required for all new dispenser systems installed after April 12, 2016. Dispenser systems include both the dispenser and the equipment connecting it to the UST.[132] Under-dispenser containment is common in most recent dispenser systems, as it was required as a grant condition of the Energy Policy Act.

6.0 Existing UST Systems

6.1 Notification Requirements

Owners of UST systems that were in the ground on or after May 8, 1986, were required to notify the designated regulatory agency of the existence of such tank systems, unless the owner knew that the tank system was subsequently removed from the ground.[133] No notification, however, was required if the UST systems were taken out of operation on or before January 1, 1974. The notice should specify, to the extent known by the owner, the date the tank was taken out of operation; the age of the tank on the date taken out of operation; the size, type, and location of the tank; and the type and quantity of substances left in the tank on the date the tank was taken out of operation.[134]

Although existing tanks should have been registered by May 1986, states continue to find previously unknown tanks at former gas stations and other businesses. One study estimated that as of July 2000, there were 190,000 unregistered USTs, approximately 38,000 of which are believed to be "active."[135] The remainder are considered "abandoned," but may still be subject to regulation depending on the date the UST was taken out of service.[136]

Companies that are considering the purchase of real property typically con-duct a due diligence review to learn whether the property has environmental liabilities that the owner will acquire. One item in an environmental due dili-gence checklist is underground tanks.[137] A prospective buyer can check agency records to see if the property has any registered tanks. Sometimes unregistered tanks are discovered by a prospective purchaser or his consultant during a site inspection.

Any person who assumes ownership of an existing UST system must inform the implementing agency of the change in ownership within thirty days.[138] Under the 2015 UST Rule, owners of existing airport hydrant systems and field-constructed tank systems have three years to notify the implementing agency of the systems' existence and to demonstrate financial responsibility.[139]

6.2 Upgrading of Existing UST Systems

All existing UST systems were required, by no later than December 22, 1998, to meet one of the following requirements:

    a. New UST system performance standards;[140]

    b. Tank upgrading requirements;[141] or

    c. Closure and corrective action requirements.[142]

Existing metal piping systems must also be upgraded to meet the performance standards for new piping systems.[143] Existing UST systems must also comply with new UST system requirements for spill and overfill prevention.[144]

As of March 2015, EPA estimated that 84.8 percent of the 569,000 regu-lated UST systems nationwide were in compliance with upgrade requirements for spill, overfill, and corrosion protection; 79.1 percent were in compliance with the leak detection requirements that were phased in from 1989 through 1993; and 71.8 percent were in compliance with both the leak detection and release prevention requirements.[145] In 2001, the General Accounting Office estimated that of the universe of tanks regulated by the states, nearly 90 percent met the upgrade requirements.[146]

USTs that were not upgraded to meet these requirements by December 22, 1998, should have been temporarily or permanently closed in accordance with the regulations.[147] Substandard USTs that continued to operate after the deadline are subject to fines of up to $16,000 per day.[148]

The 2015 UST Rule established special upgrade requirements for airport hydrant systems and UST systems with field-constructed tanks, both of which were previously deferred from regulation. These UST systems must be closed by no later than October 15, 2018, unless they satisfy requirements for corrosion protection, spill and overfill prevention, and release detection.[149]

6.3 Enforcement of Upgrade Requirements

In order to leverage compliance by the UST owner, many states have implemented some type of "delivery prohibition" to prevent fuel delivery to substandard USTs.[150] Federal law now includes a delivery prohibition requirement.[151] States receiving federal funds for their UST programs were required to implement delivery prohibition requirements by August 8, 2007.[152]

In August 2006, EPA issued final guidelines to states for implementing this delivery prohibition provision.[153] The guidelines describe the procedures that states must use in prohibiting fuel delivery to "ineligible" underground storage tanks. The guidance requires that a state classify USTs as ineligible for delivery, deposit, or acceptance of product if:[154]

- required spill prevention equipment is not installed;

- required overfill protection equipment is not installed;

- required leak detection equipment is not installed;

- required corrosion protection equipment is not installed; or

- other conditions a state deems inappropriate are evident.

The guidelines also provide that a state should classify a UST as ineligible if the owner/operator of the tank has been issued a written warning or citation under any of the following circumstances (and the owner/operator has failed to take corrective action after a reasonable time frame that is determined by the state):[155]

- Failure to properly operate and/or maintain leak detection equipment;

- Failure to properly operate and/or maintain spill, overfill, or corrosion protection equipment;

- Failure to maintain financial responsibility;

- Failure to protect a buried metal flex connector from corrosion; or

- Other conditions a state deems inappropriate exist.

In July 2012, EPA Headquarters issued guidelines to its regional offices for enforcing the delivery prohibition provision of the Energy Policy Act of 2005.[156] As with all other elements of the UST program, states may choose to be more stringent than the minimum requirements in the Energy Policy Act. EPA provides information on state law provisions at its web page "State Delivery Prohibition Programs."[157]

7.0 General Operating Requirements

7.1 Spill and Overfill Control

Owners and operators of USTs must ensure that the volume of the tank is greater than the volume of the regulated substance to be transferred into the tank before the transfer is made and that the transfer operation is monitored constantly to prevent overfilling and spilling.[158] The owner and operator must report, investigate, and clean up any spills and overflows that occur during transfer operations.[159]

7.2 Operation of Corrosion Protection Systems

All owners and operators of metal UST systems that employ corrosion protection must ensure that the corrosion protection systems are operated and maintained to continuously protect those metal components of the UST system that are in contact with the ground.[160]

7.3 Substance Compatibility

Regulations require owners and operators to use UST systems that are made of or lined with materials that are compatible with the regulated substances that are stored in the UST systems.[161] As EPA has grown more concerned about UST systems' compatibility with alternative fuels, it has moved to require advance notice and affirmative evidence of compatibility for UST systems storing these materials. Under the 2015 UST Rule, if a UST system will contain more than 10 percent ethanol or 20 percent biodiesel, the system must demonstrate compatibility with these contents with at least 30 days' notice to the implementing agency.[162]

7.4 UST System Repairs

Any repairs made to UST systems must be performed in a manner that will prevent releases due to structural failure or corrosion as long as the UST system is used to store regulated substances. Regulations specify that repairs to UST systems must be properly conducted in accordance with appropriate industry codes of practice.[163] Metal pipe sections and fittings that have released regulated substances as a result of corrosion or other damage must be replaced.[164] Repaired tanks, piping, and related secondary containment areas and containment sumps must be tightness tested within thirty days following the date of completion of the repair, except if alternative methods are used to verify the sufficiency of the repair.[165] Cathodic protection systems must be tested within six months following the repair of any cathodically protected UST system.[166] Spill prevention equipment must be tested and overfill prevention equipment inspected within thirty days following any repair.[167] UST regulations require owners and operators to maintain records of each repair until the UST system is permanently closed or undergoes a change-in-service.[168]

7.5 Operator Training

The 2015 UST Rule standardizes operator training requirements and for the first time extends them to Indian land.[169] Under these new requirements, operators are divided into three classes. Class A operators are trained on release prevention and detection, corrosion protection, emergency response, product and equipment compatibility, financial responsibility, notification and registration, system closure, reporting and recordkeeping, consequences of release, and the roles of Class B and C operators.[170] These are typically the site's environmental managers, who are responsible for system-wide decision-making.

Class B operators are trained on operation and maintenance, release prevention and detection, release reporting, corrosion protection and testing, emergency response, product and equipment compatibility, reporting and recordkeeping, consequences of release, and the role of Class C operators.[171] These are typically the site's day-to-day operators, who are responsible for ensuring regulatory compliance on the ground.

Class C operators are trained to respond to emergencies and release alarms. This includes notifying the appropriate authorities when necessary.[172]

Owners and operators of UST systems must designate at least one Class A and one Class B operator for each UST system.[173] The operators must be trained in accordance with the UST regulations, must pass an examination, and must be retrained and reexamined if the system they supervise is found to be out of compliance.[174] Responding to stakeholder concerns about the inflexibility of its draft operator training regulations, EPA clarified in its 2015 UST Rule that Class A and Class B operators may be designated for multiple USTs at once.[175] In addition, operators need not be trained by an independent organization, but may complete any in-house program that satisfies the regulatory requirements.[176]

8.0 Testing and Inspections

8.1 Equipment Testing and Inspection

All UST systems equipped with cathodic protection systems must be inspected for proper operation by a qualified cathodic protection tester in accordance with specific regulatory requirements.[177] Owners and operators of UST systems using cathodic protection must keep and maintain records of the operation of the cathodic protection systems.[178]

Under the 2015 UST Rule, owners and operators must comply with additional testing and inspection requirements for release prevention and detection equipment. Under the new rule, spill prevention equipment and the containment sumps used for interstitial monitoring of piping must be either tested every three years or double-walled with interstitial monitoring at least every thirty days.[179] Overfill prevention equipment must be inspected at least once every three years to ensure its proper functioning.[180] Release detection equipment must be tested annually.[181] Owners and operators of UST systems have until October 15, 2018, to comply with these requirements.[182]

8.2 Site Inspections Under the Energy Policy Act

The Energy Policy Act of 2005 required states receiving federal funding under the RCRA UST Program to conduct on-site inspections of certain UST systems to determine compliance with UST requirements.[183] USTs that had not been inspected since December 22, 1998, were required to have an on-site inspection conducted not later than August 8, 2007.[184] States were largely successful in meeting the 2007 inspection deadline, and almost all states completed the inspection requirement by the August 2010 deadline.[185]

8.3 Walkthroughs Under the 2015 UST Rule

The 2015 UST Rule requires owners and operators to conduct walkthrough inspections of each UST system.[186] Spill prevention equipment must be visually checked at least every thirty days, liquid and debris must be removed, and obstructions in the fill pipe must be removed.[187] Release detection equipment must also be checked at least every thirty days.[188]

Containment sumps must be checked annually for damages, leaks, and releases, and any debris or unexpected liquid must be removed.[189] Handheld release detection equipment must also be checked annually.[190]

Walkthroughs conducted according to an accepted industry code of practice will satisfy the UST regulation if they are "comparable" to the walkthroughs described in EPA regulations.[191] UST owners and operators must comply with the new walkthrough requirements by October 15, 2018.[192]

9.0 Release Detection

9.1 General Release Detection Requirements

Owners and operators of new and existing UST systems must provide a method or combination of methods of release detection that can detect a release from any portion of the tank and connected underground piping that routinely contains regulated substances. All new and existing UST systems must comply with release detection requirements.[193] Any existing UST system that cannot comply with release detection requirements must be closed.[194]

9.2 Methods of Release Detection for Tanks and Piping

UST regulations set standards for several methods of release detection that may be used for tanks and piping. Such methods for tanks include product inventory control, manual tank gauging, automatic tank gauging, vapor monitoring, groundwater monitoring, or any other approved method of release detection.[195] Release detection methods for piping include automatic line leak detectors, line tightness testing, vapor monitoring, groundwater monitoring, or any other approved method designed to detect a release from any portion of the underground piping that routinely contains regulated substances.[196] Release detection methods must be capable of detecting a leak rate specified in the regulations for each method with a probability of detection of 95 percent and a probability of false alarm of 5 percent.[197] Release detection equipment must be tested annually to ensure proper functioning.[198]

9.3 Specific Requirements for Petroleum USTs

Under the 2015 UST Rule, all USTs installed after April 12, 2016, must use secondary containment and interstitial monitoring.[199] Interstitial monitoring must be conducted at least every thirty days, and records retained for three years.[200] This applies to both tanks and piping.[201] Pressurized piping must be equipped with an automatic line leak detector.[202]

For older USTs, tank monitoring is required every thirty days unless the system meets the performance standards for new and upgraded tank systems.[203] Owners and operators of tanks with larger capacities and diameters may use manual tank gauging.[204]

For older USTs, pressurized piping must be equipped with an automatic line leak detector and have annual line tightness testing or monthly monitoring.[205] Underground piping that conveys regulated substances under suction must either have line tightness testing conducted at least every three years or use monthly monitoring. Suction piping may be exempt from release detection requirements if it meets specific design and construction standards.[206]

9.4 Specific Requirements for Hazardous Substance UST Systems

UST regulations have always required hazardous substance UST systems to have secondary containment and to be checked for evidence of a release at least every thirty days.[207] Similarly, the regulations have always required that underground piping for hazardous substance UST systems use secondary containment, and that pressurized piping be equipped with an automatic line leak detector system.[208]

For hazardous substance USTs installed before October 15, 2015, other methods of release detection for hazardous substance USTs may be used if approved by the implementing agency. Owners and operators, however, must demonstrate to the implementing agency that the alternative method can effectively detect a release of the stored hazardous substance. Owners and operators must provide information to the implementing agency on effective corrective action technologies, health risks, chemical and physical properties of the stored substances, and the characteristics of the UST site and must obtain agency approval to use the alternative release detection method before installation and operation of the new hazardous substance UST system.[209]

10.0 Release Reporting, Investigation, and Response

10.1 Overview

As of March 2015, some 525,095 releases had been confirmed from UST systems.[210] After a decade of improvement the number of contaminated sites with reported releases has gradually increased since 2012, when reported releases hit a low of 5,674.[211] Reported releases in 2014 reached 6,847, their highest number in five years.[212]

By March 2015, 501,766 cleanups had been initiated nationwide, with a reported 452,847 reaching completion.[213] This leaves 23,329 cleanups uninitiated and another 48,919 initiated but incomplete—a total backlog of 72,248, or 13.8 percent of all releases.[214] Although this figure may seem high, this marks a substantial improvement over the past decade. In 2004, there were 129,827 cleanups remaining—29 percent of all releases at that time.[215]

Cleanups typically involve excavation of contaminated soil and testing to see whether underlying groundwater has been affected. If groundwater has been contaminated, the cost of a cleanup can escalate rapidly. In many cases, on-site methods of soil treatment, such as soil vapor extraction, are needed to remove contaminants from areas such as those beneath buildings where excavation is impractical.

Studies suggest that the costs of cleaning up petroleum releases from USTs may outweigh the benefits because fuel hydrocarbons have limited impact on human health or the environment, as they readily biodegrade.[216] As a result, many states have moved toward a risk-based approach to corrective action. The discovery of MTBE as a contaminant in water may change the willingness of regulatory agencies to rely on natural attenuation, at least for those sites with more recent spills. MTBE was put in gasoline beginning in the 1970s as an oxygenate to reduce vehicle emissions. It is a chemical that moves quickly in water and does not readily biodegrade.[217] The same types of treatment technologies are used for the treatment of petroleum and MTBE, but the design and operating conditions for treatment of groundwater plumes with MTBE may differ.[218]

In 2009, EPA published Principles for Greener Cleanups, stating that reducing the environmental impact of cleanups is an EPA priority.[219] In assessing cleanup efforts, EPA focuses on the following five factors: total energy use and renewable energy use, air pollutants and greenhouse gas emissions, water use and impact to water resources, materials management and waste reduction, and land management and ecosystem protection.[220] EPA's UST program is considering the best way to work with state and territorial tank programs to reduce the environmental impact of cleanup efforts. In 2010, EPA conducted an analysis of cleanup backlog in these areas.[221]

This section discusses the legal requirements for reporting, investigating, and cleaning up releases from USTs.

10.2 Reporting of Suspected Releases

Owners and operators of UST systems must report any suspected release to the implementing agency within twenty-four hours or another reasonable time period specified by the implementing agency.[222] UST regulations identify several conditions which would require reporting:

a. The discovery of regulated substances released at the UST site or in the surrounding area;[223]

b. Unusual operating conditions observed by owners and operators, including, for example, the erratic behavior of product dispensing equipment, the sudden loss of product from the UST system, the unexplained presence of water in the UST, or the presence of liquid in interstitial spaces. Regulations note that the reporting of such unusual conditions is not required if the UST system equipment is found to be defective but not leaking, any unexpected liquid in the system's interstitial space is immediately removed, and the defective component is immediately repaired or replaced;[224] and

c. Monitoring results from any required release detection method that indicate that a release may have occurred, including investigation of alarms. Reporting is unnecessary if it is determined that a non-release event triggered the alarm. Reporting is also unnecessary if the release detection monitoring device is found to be defective; if the device is immediately repaired, recalibrated, or replaced; and if additional monitoring does not confirm the initial result.[225]

10.3 Release Investigation and Confirmation

UST regulations require all owners and operators to immediately investigate and confirm suspected releases of regulated substances within seven days or another reasonable time period as specified by the implementing agency.[226] Unless another procedure is approved by the implementing agency, owners and operators are required to take additional steps as described in the sections below.

10.3.1 System Test

Owners and operators must conduct tightness testing of the UST and associated piping to determine whether a leak exists or a wall has been breached. Should such testing indicate the presence of a leak, owners and operators must repair, replace, upgrade, or close the UST system and begin corrective action to remedy any release. No further investigation is required if testing results do not indicate the presence of a release and if environmental contamination was not the basis for suspecting a release. Owners and operators must conduct a site check, as described below, if environmental contamination has been observed at the site, even though testing results do not indicate the presence of a leak.[227]

10.3.2 Site Check

If environmental contamination is observed at the UST site, owners and operators must evaluate whether a release has occurred from the UST system. If test results indicate that a release has occurred, owners and operators must begin corrective action in accordance with UST regulations. If test results do not indicate that a release has occurred, further investigation is not required.[228]

10.4 Initial Release Response

Once a release from a UST system is confirmed, owners and operators must comply with various corrective action requirements. Owners and operators must perform certain initial response actions within twenty-four hours of a release or within another reasonable period of time determined by the implementing agency. Those actions include reporting the release to the implementing agency, taking immediate action to prevent any further release of the regulated substance into the environment, and identifying and mitigating any fire, explosion, and vapor hazards that may be associated with the release.[229]

10.5 Initial Abatement Measures

Following release confirmation, owners and operators of UST systems must also perform certain abatement measures. Those measures include the following actions:[230]

a. Removal of as much of the regulated substance from the UST system as is necessary to prevent further release to the environment;

b. Visual inspection of any above-ground or exposed below-ground releases and prevention of any further migration of such releases into surrounding soils and groundwater;

c. Continued monitoring and mitigation of any additional fire and safety hazards posed by vapors or free product in subsurface structures;

d. Remediation of any hazards posed by contaminated soils that are excavated or exposed as a result of release confirmation, site investigation, abatement, or corrective action activities;

e. If not already determined, investigation for the presence of a release where contamination is most likely to be present at the UST site; and

f. Investigation to determine the possible presence of free product and removal of free product as soon as practicable.

UST regulations require owners and operators to submit to the implementing agency a report summarizing the initial abatement steps taken and any resulting information or data within twenty days of release confirmation or within another reasonable time period specified by the implementing agency.[231]

10.6 Initial Site Characterization

Owners and operators must also assemble information about the site and the nature of the release, including information gained while confirming the release or completing the initial abatement measures. Such information must include at least:[232]

a. Data on the nature and estimated quantity of release;

b. Data from available sources and/or site investigations concerning surrounding populations, water quality, use and approximate locations of wells potentially affected by the release, subsurface soil conditions, locations of subsurface sewers, climatological conditions, and land use;

c. Results of the site check; and

d. Results of the free product investigations.

Owners and operators must submit this initial site characterization to the implementing agency within forty-five days of release confirmation or according to a schedule required by the implementing agency.

10.7 Free Product Removal

Where investigation has indicated the presence of free product, owners and operators must remove free product to the maximum extent practicable as determined by the implementing agency.[233] Owners and operators must prepare and submit to the implementing agency a free product removal report that describes conditions and the measures taken to abate the presence of free product.[234]

10.8 Investigations for Soil and Groundwater Cleanup

Owners and operators must also conduct investigations of soil and groundwater at the area of release, the release site, and the surrounding area possibly affected by the release if any of the following conditions exist:[235]

a. Groundwater wells have been affected by the release;

b. Free product is found to need recovery;

c. Contaminated soils may be in contact with groundwater; and

d. The implementing agency requests an investigation, based on the potential effects of contaminated soil or groundwater on nearby surface water and groundwater resources.

Owners and operators are required to submit information collected from such investigations as soon as practicable or in accordance with a schedule established by the implementing agency.

10.9 Reporting and Cleanup of Spills and Overfills

Spills and overfills must be contained and immediately cleaned up. Owners and operators must report any spill and overfill incident to the implementing agency within twenty-four hours or other reasonable time period specified by the implementing agency and begin corrective action if there are:[236]

a. Spills or overfills of petroleum that exceed twenty-five gallons or another reasonable amount specified by the implementing agency, or that cause a sheen on nearby surface water; or

b. Spills or overfills of hazardous substances that equal or exceed its reportable quantity under CERCLA.

Owners and operators are required to contain and immediately clean up spills and overfills of amounts less than those described above, but they are not required to report such incidents. However, the regulations provide that if such cleanup cannot be accomplished within twenty-four hours or another reasonable time period as specified by the implementing agency, owners and operators must immediately report such incidents.[237]

10.10 Corrective Action Plan

The implementing agency may require owners and operators to submit a corrective action plan for contaminated soils and groundwater.[238] In such instances, owners and operators typically will prepare the plan according to a schedule and format established by the implementing agency. In some instances, owners and operators may choose to voluntarily submit a corrective action plan for contaminated soil and groundwater. The corrective action plan must provide for adequate protection of human health and the environment as determined by the implementing agency. Upon approval of the corrective action plan by the implementing agency, owners and operators must implement the plan and monitor, evaluate, and report the results of such implementation in accordance with a schedule and format typically established by the implementing agency.[239]

Owners and operators may begin cleanup of soil and groundwater before a corrective action plan is approved by the implementing agency. However, owners and operators must first notify the implementing agency of their intention to begin cleanup, and they must comply with any conditions imposed by the implementing agency. Owners and operators must then incorporate those self-initiated cleanup measures into the corrective action plan that is submitted to the implementing agency for approval.[240]

The American Society for Testing and Materials (ASTM) has worked to develop a standard using risk-based corrective action (RBCA) techniques at petroleum-release sites.[241] EPA supports the use of risk-based approaches that seek to protect human health and the environment while considering site-specific circumstances.[242] As a result, many states have implemented risk-based corrective action programs for the management of petroleum releases.

The Lawrence Livermore National Laboratory (LLNL), commissioned by the California State Water Resources Control Board to study California's program for remediating leaking underground storage tanks, endorsed the use of risk-based approaches in a 1995 report.[243] After studying the fate and transport characteristics of petroleum leaks in California, LLNL announced several findings and conclusions:

   a. The public water supply is not threatened with high levels of benzene. Of the 12,150 public water supply wells tested statewide, the LLNL determined that only forty-eight had measurable benzene concentrations. The report concluded that money spent to remediate low-risk sites over the past decade had not been cost-effective.[244]

b. Passive bioremediation acts to naturally complete the cleanup process once the source of petroleum contamination is removed. Passive bioremediation should be used as a remediation alternative "whenever possible."[245]

c. A modified ASTM risk-based approach that incorporates tiered decision-making should be implemented at the majority of leaking petroleum UST sites in California.[246]

These conclusions were accepted by California regulatory agencies,[247] but the growing momentum toward passive approaches to remediation came into question for newer spills when regulators became aware that another substance of concern—MTBE—was increasingly showing up in the state's surface and groundwaters. MTBE is an octane-enhancing gasoline additive widely used throughout the country since the 1970s in order to meet the 1990 Clean Air Act requirements for reducing emissions of carbon monoxide. Effective May 6, 2006, the oxygenate mandate was removed from the Clean Air Act.[248] MTBE has also been banned in many states.[249] Taken together, MTBE is effectively being phased out from the nation's gasoline supply.[250]

In June 1998, the LLNL released a report on the impacts of MTBE in groundwater.[251] This report concluded that passive bioremediation is not very effective on MTBE because MTBE plumes are more mobile than BTEX compounds and travel at a much higher rate of speed than BTEX. Thus, the Lawrence Livermore Report II suggests that more aggressive approaches to remediation are needed for more recent spills from fuel tanks in use since MTBE was added to gasoline. Since issuance of the report, however, other research has shown that biodegradation may be an effective remediation option under specific conditions.[252] According to several states, discovery of MTBE has not typically altered the cleanup method at a given site, although detection of MTBE often increases the time and costs of remediation.[253]

In 1999, EPA initiated the MTBE Demonstration Project, assembling a work group to conduct field evaluations of technologies and processes to treat drinking water and groundwater contaminated with MTBE.[254] Three technologies were selected, and the onsite field demonstration began in 2001 at the Naval Construction Battalion Center, Port Hueneme, California.[255] Other entities—such as the American Petroleum Institute and the University of California, Davis—are also studying and developing MTBE remediation techniques.[256] In March 2000, the California State Water Resources Control Board issued guidelines for the investigation and cleanup of MTBE and other ether-based oxygenates.[257] Although the guidelines are based on the premise that the standard approach for dealing with petroleum releases will not suffice for MTBE, the guidelines operate within the RBCA framework by focusing on site-specific factors in determining appropriate investigative and remedial action.[258] To address the additional costs associated with MTBE contamination, in 2005 Congress authorized $200 million from the LUST Trust Fund (for each of the fiscal years from 2006 through 2011) to be used for cleanup of oxygenated fuel releases.[259]

Even with the issues arising from MTBE and other ether-based oxygenates, RBCA techniques have dramatically changed the approach to cleanup at a number of UST sites where the selected remedy is now passive bioremediation. Some sites with groundwater contamination that previously would have required the installation of pump-and-treat technology have received approval for regulatory closure without any form of active remediation.

10.11 USTfields Initiative and Recycling Abandoned Gas Stations (RAGS)

EPA states that of the estimated 450,000 Brownfields sites in the United States, approximately one-half, or more than 200,000, are thought to be impacted by underground storage tanks (USTs) or some type of petroleum contamination.[260] In 2000, EPA launched the USTfields Initiative to address cleanup and revitalization of abandoned UST sites, initially designating ten pilot programs.[261] The USTfields program was necessary because petroleum contamination generally could not be cleaned up through EPA's then existing Brownfields program because of the petroleum exclusion in CERCLA. In July 2002, EPA announced an additional forty pilot grants totaling $3.8 million to be used to clean up contamination from abandoned USTs in twenty-six states.[262] In all, EPA granted almost $5 million to fund these fifty USTfields projects.

To complement and expand on the USTfields Initiative, Congress passed the Small Business Liability Relief and Brownfields Revitalization Act in 2002.[263] The 2002 Brownfields law revised the definition of "brownfield" to include petroleum-contaminated sites and authorized EPA to give grants of up to $250 million annually to states and communities to assess, clean up, and reuse petroleum Brownfields.[264] By law, EPA must make available 25 percent of the total Brownfields grant funds each year for the assessment and/or cleanup of relatively low-risk petroleum-contaminated sites for which there is no viable responsible party.[265] During the 2003–2007 grant cycles, EPA received more than 800 applications for petroleum Brownfields project grants and awarded 390 grants.[266] In 2013, EPA implemented a pilot petroleum Brownfields multi-purpose grant program to provide up to $550,000 for assessment and cleanup under one grant award.[267]

11.0 Closure of UST Systems

11.1 Temporary Closure

Occasionally, owners and operators will discontinue the use of USTs for an extended period. However, owners and operators must continue to comply with requirements governing the operation and maintenance of corrosion protection and release detection systems, as well as requirements for release reporting, investigation, confirmation, and corrective action if a release is suspected or confirmed during the period of temporary closure. Compliance with release detection requirements is not necessary as long as the UST is empty.[268]

If a UST system is temporarily closed for three months or more, in addition to the above requirements, owners and operators must leave vent lines open and functioning and must cap and secure all other lines, pumps, man-ways, and ancillary equipment.[269] If a UST system is temporarily closed for more than twelve months and does not meet either performance standards for new UST systems or the upgrading requirements for existing systems (excluding spill and overfill requirements), then owners and operators must permanently close the UST system, unless the implementing agency provides an extension of the twelve-month temporary closure period.[270] Owners and operators must complete a site assessment in accordance with 40 C.F.R. § 280.72 before applying for such an extension.

As of February 1999, states reported 73,700 UST systems in temporary closure.[271] EPA estimated that this number was significantly less by June 2000 because some of these systems have since been upgraded or permanently closed.[272]

11.2 Permanent Closure/Change-in-Service

Before beginning either permanent closure or a change-in-service[273] of a UST system, owners and operators must notify the implementing agency, at least thirty days before beginning such activities, of their intent to undertake such activities, unless such action is in response to corrective action associated with any release from the UST system.[274] For permanent closure, tanks must be emptied, cleaned, and either removed from the ground or filled with inert solid material.[275] Before permanent closure or a change-in-service is completed, owners and operators must conduct a site assessment to evaluate whether releases have occurred at the UST site. Corrective action must be undertaken if contamination is encountered during the site assessment.[276]

For UST systems that were permanently closed before December 22, 1988, the implementing agency may direct owners and operators to assess the area involved in the UST closure and may close the UST system in accordance with UST regulations if releases from the UST are determined to pose a current or potential threat to human health and the environment.[277]

Owners and operators must maintain records of closure or change-in-service that are capable of demonstrating compliance with the regulatory requirements. The results of any site assessment must be maintained for at least three years after completion of permanent closure or change-in-service by the owners and operators who took the UST system out of service, by the current owners and operators of the UST system site, or by the implementing agency if the records cannot be maintained at the closed facility.[278]

As of March 2015, more than 1.8 million substandard USTs have been permanently closed.[279] Closure is an increasingly common requirement under state regulations governing single-walled UST systems. As EPA and the states have moved to require secondary containment for all new USTs, some jurisdictions have grown concerned about the threat posed by older, single-walled systems that remain active. For example, Massachusetts requires removal of most single-walled tanks by August 2017.[280] California requires all single-walled USTs to be permanently closed no later than December 2025.[281]

12.0 Financial Responsibility Requirements

12.1 Applicability and Compliance

Owners and operators of all petroleum UST systems that are subject to the UST regulations must demonstrate an ability to pay for cleanups and to compensate third parties for bodily injury and property damage caused by accidental releases arising from the operation of petroleum USTs.[282] These financial responsibility requirements were phased in over time. Under the 2015 UST Rule, the financial responsibility requirements were extended to the previously deferred UST systems.[283]

An owner or operator is no longer required to maintain financial responsibility after the UST has been permanently closed or, if corrective action is required, after corrective action has been completed and the tank has been properly closed.[284]

12.2 Amount and Scope of Financial Responsibility Required

Owners or operators of petroleum USTs must demonstrate financial responsibility in at least the following per occurrence amounts:[285]

   a. $1 million for owners or operators of petroleum USTs that are located at petroleum marketing facilities or that handle an average of more than

10,000 gallons of petroleum per month based on annual throughput for the previous calendar year;

b. $500,000 for all other owners or operators of petroleum USTs; and

c. Owners or operators of petroleum USTs must also demonstrate financial responsibility in at least the following annual aggregate amounts:
• $1 million for owners or operators of 1 to 100 petroleum USTs, and
• $2 million for owners or operators of 101 or more petroleum USTs.

12.3 Allowable Financial Responsibility Mechanisms

There are several ways owners and operators of UST systems can demonstrate compliance with the financial responsibility requirements. Large companies may self-insure if they meet certain self-insurance requirements.[286] Subsidiaries of large companies may obtain guaranties[287] or letters of credit[288] from a parent company. Other methods of compliance include surety bonds,[289] trust agreements,[290] and EPA-approved state-assurance funds.[291] Local governments may also use a bond rating test, a local government financial test, a government guarantee, or maintenance of a fund balance to comply with the requirements.[292] EPA also publishes a list of known insurance providers who may be able to assist UST owners with their financial responsibility requirements.[293]

12.4 Available State UST Cleanup Funds

Congress provides money to EPA to fund cleanups where no responsible party can be found and to assist states with overseeing corrective actions through the LUST Trust Fund.[294] Through assistance agreements, EPA distributes approximately 90 percent of its disbursements from the LUST Trust Fund to states, territories, and tribes for cleanup and prevention programs.[295] In February 2009, Congress passed the American Recovery and Reinvestment Act of 2009, providing $200 million appropriation from the LUST Trust Fund for cleaning up petroleum releases.[296] In fiscal year 2013, Congress appropriated another $67.2 million from the LUST Trust Fund for corrective action activities, $58.6 million of which is for assessing and cleaning up UST releases.[297] As of April 2015, the LUST Trust Fund was valued at roughly $500 million.[298]

The LUST Trust Fund faces a number of future revenue challenges. It is financed by a 0.1-cent excise tax on each gallon of motor fuel sold.[299] This excise tax is not indexed to inflation and has not been raised since 1993.[300] As a result, inflation has gradually reduced the relative value of funding flowing to the Trust Fund. Improvements in fuel economy have had a similar effect in recent years. Furthermore, the other accounts of the Highway Trust Fund are also funded by excise taxes on motor fuel, and they face similar difficulties as a result of inflation.

Twice in the past five years, this has led Congress to transfer money from the LUST Trust Fund to cover shortfalls in the Highway Account.[301]

In addition to the LUST Trust Fund, forty states have set up UST cleanup funds to help private parties pay for UST cleanup work.[302] It is estimated that these state funds are collecting nearly $1 billion a year through gasoline taxes and other sources.[303] Over the past ten years, these state funds have expended approximately $7 billion to clean up leaking UST sites.[304] These state funds have been an important factor in speeding the investigation and cleanup of the thousands of UST sites throughout the country. Prior to conducting a cleanup, the responsible party should investigate whether it is eligible to tap into the applicable state's UST cleanup fund and whether there are any specific state funding requirements or priorities.[305] Some states' UST cleanup funds (e.g., Texas's and Arizona's) have already sunset, while other states' funds will sunset in the coming years (e.g., California's fund will sunset at the end of 2025).[306]

12.5 Reporting and Recordkeeping Requirements

Owners or operators must maintain evidence of all financial assurance mechanisms used to demonstrate compliance with financial responsibility requirements until released from the requirements. The type of evidence to be maintained by the owner or operator depends on the financial assurance mechanism used.[307] An owner or operator must maintain an updated copy of a certification of financial responsibility that follows the wording provided in the regulations. Owners or operators must also submit evidence of financial responsibility to the implementing agency under certain conditions.[308]

13.0 Conclusion

Finding and cleaning up existing spills from leaking underground storage tanks and enforcing strict standards for new tanks present a serious challenge to the government and to private companies (and other entities) responsible for USTs. The regulations facing owners and operators of UST systems are numerous and can be confusing.

The basic purpose of the federal UST program is fivefold:

1. To identify existing tanks and require that they be removed or upgraded;

2. To clean up past problems caused by USTs;

3. To require new tanks to meet strict new standards;

4. To require that all tanks be operated to minimize the possibility of leaks and be properly closed; and

5. To require the reporting, investigation, and cleanup of UST spills and releases.

This chapter has described only the federal requirements for underground storage tanks. More information may be obtained from the nearest regional office of EPA, and EPA's website.[309] States and local governments may have additional, stricter requirements for USTs. States may also have tank cleanup funds to reimburse companies for the cost of cleaning up UST sites.

14.0 Research Sources

To learn more about USTs, here are some additional resources:

- U.S. EPA Office of Underground Storage Tanks website: http://www.epa.gov/oust

- Overview of the Federal UST Program: http://www.epa.gov/swerust1/overview.htm

- UST Program Facts: http://www.epa.gov/oust/pubs/ustfacts.htm

- UST Program Performance Measures: http://www.epa.gov/oust/cat/camarchv.htm

- Meeting UST System Requirements: http://www.epa.gov/swerust1/ustsystm/index.htm

- EPA's "Musts for USTs" (2015 Draft): http://www.epa.gov/oust/fedlaws/regs2015-musts.pdf

- Summary of 2015 Revised UST Regulations: http://www.epa.gov/oust/fedlaws/revregs.html

- Major Changes Enacted Under the 2015 UST Rule: http://www.epa.gov/oust/fedlaws/regs2015-crosswalk.pdf

- UST Regulations: http://www.gpo.gov/fdsys/pkg/FR-2015-07-15/pdf/2015-15914.pdf

- Leaking Underground Storage Tank (LUST) Trust Fund: http://www.epa.gov/swerust1/ltffacts.htm

- U.S. EPA Office of Underground Storage Tanks Program Contacts: http://www.epa.gov/swerust1/oustcont.htm

- U.S. EPA Office of Underground Storage Tanks Publications: http://www.epa.gov/swerust1/pubs/index.htm

- MTBE and Underground Storage Tanks: http://www.epa.gov/swerust1/mtbe/index.htm

- Frequent Questions about USTs: http://www.epa.gov/swerust1/faqs/index.htm

- UST Docket: http://www.epa.gov/swerust1/resource/docket.htm

- Links to More Information on USTs: http://www.epa.gov/swerust1/resource/index.htm

- UST Compliance Help: http://www.epa.gov/swerust1/cmplastc/index.htm

- Petroleum Brownfields Information: http://www.epa.gov/oust/petroleumbrownfields/index.htm

- USTfields Initiative: http://www.epa.gov/swerust1/rags/ustfield.htm

- Internet Addresses for State UST, LUST, and Financial Assurance Programs: http://www.epa.gov/swerust1/states/fndstatus.htm

- Index of State, Local, and Tribal UST Programs: http://www.epa.gov/swerust1/states/index.htm

- Links to Laws, Regulations, and Policies Related to USTs: http://www.epa.gov/swerust1/fedlaws/index.htm

- Underground Storage Tank Provisions of the Energy Policy Act of 2005: http://www.epa.gov/swerust1/fedlaws/epact_05.htm

- Community Engagement and the Underground Storage Tank Program: http://www.epa.gov/oust/communityengagement/index.htm

Notes

[1] The author gratefully acknowledges the contributions of John J. Gregory and Niall Mackay Roberts.

[2] In an attempt to address the widespread problems with USTs, Congress enacted the Hazardous and Solid Waste Amendments of 1984, which established, in Subtitle I to the Resource Conservation and Recovery Act (RCRA) of 1976, a regulatory program for both new and existing USTs. See 42 U.S.C. §§ 6991–6991h.

[3] EPA adopted regulations pursuant to RCRA Subtitle I in 1988. See 53 Fed. Reg. 37082 et seq. (Sept. 23, 1988) (codified at 40 C.F.R. Part 280). Since 1988, EPA has issued several amendments to its UST regulations. See, e.g., 54 Fed. Reg. 5451 (Feb. 3, 1989); 54 Fed. Reg. 47077 (Nov. 9, 1989); 55 Fed. Reg. 17753 (Apr. 27, 1990); 55 Fed. Reg. 17767 (Apr. 27, 1990); 55 Fed. Reg. 18566 (May 2, 1990); 55 Fed. Reg. 23737 (June 12, 1990); 55 Fed. Reg. 24692 (June 18, 1990); 55 Fed. Reg. 27837 (July 6, 1990); 55 Fed. Reg. 32647 (Aug. 10, 1990); 55 Fed. Reg. 33430 (Aug. 15, 1990); 55 Fed. Reg. 36840 (Sept. 7, 1990); 55 Fed. Reg. 46022 (Oct. 31, 1990); 56 Fed. Reg. 24 (Jan. 2, 1991); 56 Fed. Reg. 38342 (Aug. 13, 1991); 56 Fed. Reg. 40292 (Aug. 14, 1991); 56 Fed. Reg. 49376 (Sept. 27, 1991); 56 Fed.

Reg. 66369 (Dec. 23, 1991); 58 Fed. Reg. 9026 (Feb. 18, 1993); 59 Fed. Reg. 9604 (Feb. 28, 1994); 59 Fed. Reg. 29958 (June 10, 1994); 60 Fed. Reg. 46692 (Sept. 7, 1995); and 60 Fed. Reg. 57747 (Nov. 20, 1995). In 2005, Congress amended the RCRA UST Program as part of the Energy Policy Act of 2005, which is discussed below. For a general overview of the RCRA UST Program, see EPA, Underground Storage Tanks Cleanup under the Resource Conservation and Recovery Act, http://www.epa.gov/oecaerth/cleanup/rcra/tanks.

[4]   53 Fed. Reg. 37095 (Sept. 23, 1988).

[5]   *Id.*

[6]   U.S. Environmental Protection Agency (EPA), Office of Underground Storage Tanks (OUST), Semiannual Report of UST Performance Measures (Mid Fiscal Year 2015) i, available at http://www.epa.gov/oust/cat/ca-15-12.pdf [hereinafter Mid-2015 Semiannual UST Report].

[7]   *Id.* at 8. Petroleum is the most common agent of groundwater contamination. EPA, OUST, UST Program Facts 2 (May 2015), *available at* http://epa.gov/oust/pubs/ustfacts.pdf.

[8]   EPA, EPA-510-R-12-001, FY 2011 Annual Report on the Underground Storage Tank Program 1 (Mar. 2012), available at http://www.epa.gov/oust/pubs/fy11_annual_ust_report_3-12.pdf [hereinafter EPA 2011 Annual UST Report].

[9]   EPA, OUST, Mid-2015 Semiannual UST Report 5.

[10] EPA, OUST, Pay for Performance Toolbox, http://www.epa.gov/swerust1/pfp/toolbox1.htm.

[11] EPA, OUST, Mid-2015 Semiannual UST Report 5.

[12] Association of State and Territorial Solid Waste Management Officials (ASTSWMO), Leaking Underground Storage Tank (LUST) Trust Fund Fact Sheet (August 2014) 2, *available at* http://www.astswmo.org/Files/Policies_and_Publications/Tanks/2014-08-ASTSWMO-LUSTTrustFundFSv2.pdf.

[13] See Lawrence Livermore National Laboratory, Recommendations to Improve the Cleanup Process for California's Leaking Underground Fuel Tanks (LUFTS) 16 (Oct. 16, 1995), available at http://www-erd.llnl.gov/library/121762.pdf [hereinafter Lawrence Livermore Report I].

[14] *Id.* at 17–18; see also EPA, Risk-Based Decision-Making and Underground Storage Tanks, http://www.epa.gov/oswer/riskassessment/oust_rbdm.htm [hereinafter EPA, Risk-Based Decision-Making].

[15] Lawrence Livermore Report I, supra note 13, at 10–11, 19; see also EPA, Risk-Based Decision-Making, supra note 14.

[16] Lawrence Livermore National Laboratory, An Evaluation of MTBE Impacts to California Groundwater Resources (June 11, 1998), available at http://cluin.info/download/contaminantfocus/mtbe/mtbe.pdf [hereinafter Lawrence Livermore Report II].

[17] See, e.g., EPA, EPA-510-F-97-015, MTBE Fact Sheet #2, Remediation of MTBE Contaminated Soil and Groundwater (Jan. 1998), available at http://www.epa.gov/oust/mtbe/Mtbefs2.pdf; EPA, MTBE Clean Up and Treatment, http://www.epa.gov/mtbe/clean.htm; EPA, MTBE Remediation and Treatment, http://www.epa.gov/oust/mtbe/mtberem.htm (citing additional sources).

[18] For example, EPA launched the MTBE Demonstration Project in 1999; the Western States Petroleum Association, Oxygenated Fuels Association, and the Association of California Water Agencies formed the California MTBE Research Partnership in 1997; the American Petroleum Institute has sponsored various MTBE studies; and many oil companies have undertaken their own research, often in conjunction with universities.

[19] EPA, EPA-510-R-04-001, Underground Storage Tanks: Building on the Past to Protect the Future (Mar. 2004), available at http://www.epa.gov/oust/pubs/20annrpt.pdf [hereinafter Building on the Past].

[20] Energy Policy Act of 2005 Title XV, Subtitle B, Pub. L. No. 109-58 (Aug. 8, 2005).

[21] EPA, OUST, Legislation Requires Changes to the Underground Storage Tank Program, http://www.epa.gov/swerust1/fedlaws/nrg05_01.htm.

[22] EPA, OUST, Legislation Requires Changes to the Underground Storage Tank Program, http://www.epa.gov/swerust1/fedlaws/nrg05_01.htm.

23 EPA 2011 Annual UST Report, *supra* note 8, at 2.

24 Revising Underground Storage Tank Regulations—Revisions to Existing Requirements and New Requirements for Secondary Containment and Operator Training, 80 Fed. Reg. 41,566 (July 15, 2015) (codified at 40 C.F.R. Parts 280 and 281).

25 In July 2011, EPA published final guidance on the compatibility of underground storage tanks with biofuel blends.

26 EPA, OUST, Technical Guide for Addressing Petroleum Vapor Intrusion at Leaking Underground Storage Tank Sites, *available at* http://www.epa.gov/oust/cat/pvi/pvi-guide-final-6-10-15.pdf; Peggy Otum, Karen J. Nardi, & Jonathan L. Koenig, EPA Guidance Brings Consistency, Preserves Flexibility, *Daily Journal,* July 8, 2015, at 3; *see also* EPA, OUST, Petroleum Vapor Intrusion (PVI) Compendium, http://www.epa.gov/oust/cat/pvi/index.htm.

27 Building on the Past, supra note 19, at 9.

28 EPA, memorandum, Underground Storage Tank Program Initiatives (Oct. 23, 2000).

29 Pub. L. No. 107-118 (2002); see also EPA, OUST, Assessing and Cleaning Up Petroleum Brownfield Sites, http://www.epa.gov/oust/petroleumbrownfields/pbassess.htm.

30 *Id.*

31 EPA, OUST, UST Program Facts, *supra* note 7, at 1. The states with approved programs are Alabama, Arkansas, Colorado, Connecticut, Delaware, Georgia, Hawaii, Idaho, Indiana, Iowa, Kansas, Louisiana, Maine, Maryland, Massachusetts, Minnesota, Mississippi, Missouri, Montana, Nebraska, Nevada, New Hampshire, New Mexico, North Carolina, North Dakota, Oklahoma, Oregon, Pennsylvania, Rhode Island, South Carolina, South Dakota, Tennessee, Texas, Utah, Vermont, Virginia, Washington, and West Virginia. EPA, OUST, List of States With Approved UST Programs and Respective Federal Register Notices, http://www.epa.gov/oust/fedlaws/spa_frs.htm.

32 40 C.F.R. § 280.12; 42 U.S.C. § 6991(10). Regulated substances are described in section 2.2 below.

33 42 U.S.C. § 6991(10); 40 C.F.R. § 280.12.

34 49 U.S.C. §§ 60101–140.

35 40 C.F.R. § 280.10(b).

36 Pub. L. No. 95-217; 33 U.S.C. §§ 1342, 1317(b).

37 In its preamble to the final UST regulations, EPA does not define what a de minimis concentration is but states that the implementing agency shall determine on a case-by-case basis if tanks that hold very low or de minimis concentrations of regulated substances are to be excluded from the UST regulations. 53 Fed. Reg. at 37108 (Sept. 23, 1988).

38 42 U.S.C. §§ 2011–2286i.

39 Under the 1988 UST Rule, these UST systems were categorized as "deferred." The 2015 UST Rule has reclassified these systems as "partially excluded," but the regulatory burdens on these systems remain unchanged. *See* EPA, OUST, Comparison of 1988 UST Regulations and New 2015 UST Regulations 5 (June 2015), *available at* http://www.epa.gov/oust/fedlaws/regs2015-crosswalk.pdf [hereinafter Comparison of Regulations].

40 40 C.F.R. § 280.11(a).

41 40 C.F.R. § 280.11(b).

42 EPA, OUST, Comparison of Regulations, *supra* note 39, at 4–5.

43 *Id.*; EPA, Summary of Comments and EPA's Response to the November 2011 Proposed UST Rule 95 (June 2015), *available at* http://www.epa.gov/oust/fedlaws/regs2015-rtc.pdf [hereinafter Response to Comments].

44 EPA, OUST, Comparison of Regulations, *supra* note 39, at 4.

45 *Id.* at 5; EPA, Response to Comments, *supra* note 43, at 88–90, 97–98.

46 42 U.S.C. § 9601(14).

47 40 C.F.R. § 280.12 (definition of regulated substance).

48 EPA 2011 Annual UST Report, supra note 8, at 3.

49 EPA, Biofuels Compendium, http://www.epa.gov/oust/altfuels/bfcompend.htm; EPA, Biofuels Compendium—State Information, http://www.epa.gov/oust/altfuels/states.htm.

50 EPA, Renewable Fuels: Regulations & Standards, http://www.epa.gov/otaq/fuels/renewablefuels/regulations.htm.

51 EPA, EPA-510-R-11-001, FY 2010 Annual Report on the Underground Storage Tank Program 2 (Mar. 2011), available at http://www.epa.gov/oust/pubs/fy10_annual_ust_report_3-11.pdf [hereinafter EPA 2010 Annual UST Report].

52 40 C.F.R. § 280.12.

53 42 U.S.C. § 6991(4); 40 C.F.R. § 280.12.

54 40 C.F.R. § 280.12.

55 42 U.S.C. § 6991b(h)(9). This definition appears to apply only to owners of USTs that contain petroleum as opposed to any regulated substance.

56 Holders of security interests are permitted to satisfy regulatory obligations as operators prior to foreclosure by undertaking specified "minimally burdensome" and "environmentally protective" actions to secure and protect the UST or UST system while remaining exempt from RCRA's corrective action requirements. 60 Fed. Reg. 46692, 46695 (Sept. 7, 1995); see also 40 C.F.R. § 280.230.

57 42 U.S.C. § 6991(3); 40 C.F.R. § 280.12.

58 42 U.S.C. § 6991c(a), (b)(1). As of 2015, thirty-eight states and the District of Columbia and the Commonwealth of Puerto Rico had approved "state" programs. See supra note 31. This chapter shall refer to the agency responsible for implementing the federal UST requirements (i.e., either EPA or the state agency with an EPA-approved UST program) as the implementing agency.

59 In the meantime, state program approval remains in effect unless EPA revokes it for other reasons. EPA, Revising Underground Storage Tank Regulations 194–210 (June 2015), available at http://www.epa.gov/oust/fedlaws/regs2015-finalrule.pdf; EPA, OUST, Comparison of Regulations, supra note 39, at 10. Despite the breadth of changes in the 2015 UST Rule, a wholesale revision of state regulations is unlikely to be necessary, as much of the 2015 UST Rule simply formalizes changes the states had already implemented under the Energy Policy Act. See EPA, Response to Comments, supra note 43, at 160–62.

60 EPA, EPA-510-R-06-005, Strategy for an EPA/Tribal Partnership to Implement Section 1529 of the Energy Policy Act of 2005 3 (Aug. 2006), available at http://www.epa.gov/oust/fedlaws/tribal-strat-080706r.pdf [hereinafter Strategy for an EPA/Tribal Partnership]; EPA, OUST, Mid-2015 Semiannual UST Report, supra note 6, at 5.

61 EPA, OUST, Report to Congress on Implementing and Enforcing the Underground Storage Tank Program in Indian Country 5 (Aug. 2007), available at http://www.epa.gov/oust/fedlaws/rtc_final blnkpgs.pdf.

62 The RCRA UST Program does not provide the authority to treat Native American Indian tribes as states. Therefore, EPA is charged with implementing the federal UST program in Indian Country. Some tribal governments have developed their own UST programs with assistance from EPA. EPA, Strategy for an EPA/Tribal Partnership, supra note 60, at 3.

63 42 U.S.C. § 6991e(a)(1).

64 For those states with UST programs that have been approved by the EPA, EPA is required to give notice to the state prior to issuing any order or commencing any civil action. 42 U.S.C. § 6991e(a)(2).

65 40 C.F.R. § 19.4; 42 U.S.C. § 6991e(a)(3).

66 42 U.S.C. § 6991e(b).

67 40 C.F.R. § 19.4; 42 U.S.C. § 6991e(d).

68 40 C.F.R. § 19.4; 42 U.S.C. §§ 6991b(c), 6991e(d).

69 42 U.S.C. § 6991b(h)(1)(A).

[70] 42 U.S.C. § 6991b(h)(2).

[71] See 56 Fed. Reg. 49376 (Sept. 27, 1991).

[72] *Id.* at 49378.

[73] 40 C.F.R. § 280.22. Notification of change of ownership was a requirement of the 2015 UST Rule. However, most states already had such a requirement. EPA, Response to Comments, *supra* note 43, at 122.

[74] Owners and operators should contact the nearest EPA regional office to determine which agency has been designated for submittal of such notification.

[75] 40 C.F.R. § 280.22.

[76] 40 C.F.R. § 280.251(b).

[77] 40 C.F.R. § 280.50.

[78] 40 C.F.R. § 280.50(b).

[79] 40 C.F.R. §§ 280.30(b), 280.53.

[80] 40 C.F.R. § 280.61.

[81] 40 C.F.R. § 280.53, note.

[82] 40 C.F.R. § 280.62.

[83] 40 C.F.R. § 280.63.

[84] 40 C.F.R. § 280.64(d).

[85] 40 C.F.R. § 280.65.

[86] 40 C.F.R. § 280.66.

[87] 40 C.F.R. § 280.71(a).

[88] 40 C.F.R. § 280.93.

[89] See 18 U.S.C. § 1905.

[90] 42 U.S.C. § 6991d(b)(3).

[91] 40 C.F.R. § 280.20(a)(4), (b)(3).

[92] 40 C.F.R. § 280.31(d).

[93] 40 C.F.R. § 280.32(c).

[94] 40 C.F.R. § 280.12.

[95] 40 C.F.R. § 280.33(g).

[96] *Id.*

[97] EPA, Response to Comments, *supra* note 43, at 39.

[98] 40 C.F.R. § 280.35(c).

[99] 40 C.F.R. § 280.36(b).

[100] 40 C.F.R. § 280.245.

[101] 40 C.F.R. § 280.45(a), (c).

[102] 40 C.F.R. § 280.45(a).

[103] 40 C.F.R. § 280.45(b); EPA, Response to Comments, *supra* note 43, at 47.

[104] 40 C.F.R. § 280.45(b).

[105] *Id.*

[106] 40 C.F.R. § 280.74.

[107] 40 C.F.R. § 280.111.

[108] 40 C.F.R. § 280.34(c).

[109] In order to receive funding under the RCRA UST Program (Subtitle I of the Solid Waste Disposal Act), states must comply with this requirement.

[110] Energy Policy Act of 2005, Section 1526; 42 U.S.C. § 6991a(d). EPA, EPA-510-R-07-001, Grant Guidelines to States for Implementing the Public Record Provision of the Energy Policy Act of 2005 (Jan.

2007), available at http://www.epa.gov/oust/fedlaws/final-pub-rec-gls-011907.pdf [hereinafter EPA, Public Record Grant Guidelines].

111 Energy Policy Act of 2005, Section 1526; 42 U.S.C. § 6991a(d).

112 EPA, Public Record Grant Guidelines, supra note 110.

113 40 C.F.R. § 280.22.

114 40 C.F.R. §§ 280.20(d), 280.22(f).

115 40 C.F.R. § 280.22(g).

116 40 C.F.R. § 280.20.

117 The Energy Policy Act allowed states to comply with grant conditions either by adopting secondary containment and under-dispenser containment requirements or by adopting financial responsibility and installer certification requirements. Almost all states opted for secondary containment.

118 EPA, Response to Comments, supra note 43, at 22–23.

119 40 C.F.R. § 280.20(a)(1)–(3) (addressing tanks constructed of fiberglass-reinforced plastic, steel with cathodic protection, and steel-fiberglass-reinforced-plastic composite).

120 40 C.F.R. § 280.20(a)(5).

121 40 C.F.R. § 280.20(a)(4).

122 40 C.F.R. § 280.20. Secondary containment is not required for safe suction piping or piping for airport hydrant systems or field-constructed tanks greater than 50,000 gallons. EPA, OUST, Comparison of Regulations, supra note 39, at 2.

123 40 C.F.R. § 280.20; EPA, OUST, Comparison of Regulations, supra note 39, at 2.

124 40 C.F.R. § 280.20(b)(1)–(2).

125 40 C.F.R. § 280.20(b)(3).

126 40 C.F.R. § 280.20(b)(4).

127 40 C.F.R. § 280.20(c)(1)(ii).

128 40 C.F.R. § 280.20(c)(1)(i).

129 40 C.F.R. § 280.20(c)(3).

130 40 C.F.R. § 280.20(c)(2).

131 40 C.F.R. § 280.20(d), (e).

132 40 C.F.R. § 280.20(f).

133 42 U.S.C. § 6991a(a); 40 C.F.R. § 280.22(a).

134 42 U.S.C. § 6991a(a)(2)(B).

135 EPA, EPA-510-R-00-001, Report to Congress on a Compliance Plan for the Underground Storage Tank Program 11–12 (June 2000), available at http://www.epa.gov/swerust1/pubs/rtc.htm [hereinafter EPA 2000 Report to Congress]. This number is slightly less than the estimated 220,000 unregistered USTs in 1995. See Environmental Information, Ltd., Underground Storage Tank Cleanup: Status and Outlook (1995).

136 EPA 2000 Report to Congress, supra note 135, at 11–12. In 2005, the Government Accountability Office issued a report recommending that EPA require states to provide all known information on the location and status of abandoned tanks within their state. The report concluded that "the lack of specific and complete data on known abandoned tanks limits EPA's program oversight and its ability to efficiently and effectively allocate LUST Trust Fund resources." U.S. Government Accountability Office, GAO-06-45, Report to Congress, Environmental Protection—More Complete Data and Continued Emphasis on Leak Prevention Could Improve EPA's Underground Storage Tank Program 28 (Nov. 2005), available at http://www.gao.gov/new.items/d0645.pdf.

137 See, e.g., Standard Practice for Environmental Site Assessments: Phase I Environmental Site Assessment Process, ASTM E1527-05, available at http://www.astm.org/Standards/E1527.htm. On November 1,

2005, EPA published a final rule establishing specific regulatory requirements and standards for conducting all appropriate inquiries into the previous ownership, uses, and environmental conditions of a property. 70 Fed. Reg. 66069 (Nov. 1, 2005) (codified at 40 C.F.R. part 312). The final rule establishes specific requirements for conducting "all appropriate inquiries" into the previous ownership, uses, and environmental conditions of a property for the purposes of qualifying for certain landowner liability protections under CERCLA. The final rule took effect on November 1, 2006. To obtain liability protection under CERCLA, parties must comply with the requirements of the All Appropriate Inquiries final rule or follow the standards set forth in the ASTM E1527-05 Phase I Environmental Site Assessment Process. All environmental due diligence must be conducted in compliance with either of these standards to obtain protection from potential liability under CERCLA as an innocent landowner, a contiguous property owner, or a bona fide prospective purchaser. See EPA, All Appropriate Inquiries, http://www.epa.gov/swerosps/bf/aai/index.htm.

138 40 C.F.R. § 280.22.

139 40 C.F.R. § 280.251(b).

140 40 C.F.R. § 280.21(a)(1). 40 C.F.R. § 280.20 details the standards.

141 40 C.F.R. § 280.21(a)(2). 40 C.F.R. § 280.21(b) provides upgrading requirements for steel tanks, including requirements relating to the upgrading of the interior lining of the tanks and cathodic protection. Specific industry codes of practice are referenced. Under the 2015 UST Rule, if a tank's internal lining ceases to properly perform and cannot be repaired in accordance with an accepted industry code of practice, the tank must be permanently closed. 40 C.F.R. § 280.21(b)(1)(ii).

142 40 C.F.R. § 280.21(a)(3). 40 C.F.R. § 280 Subparts F and G describe the requirements.

143 40 C.F.R. § 280.21(c) notes that the industry codes of practice and standards listed in 40 C.F.R. § 280.20(b)(2) may be used to comply with the upgrading requirements.

144 40 C.F.R. § 280.21(d) specifies that the requirements in 40 C.F.R. § 280.20(c) are to be followed.

145 EPA, OUST, Mid-2015 Semiannual UST Report, *supra* note 6, at 7.

146 U.S. General Accounting Office, GAO-01-464, Report to Congressional Requesters, Environmental Protection: Improved Inspections and Enforcement Would Better Ensure the Safety of Underground Storage Tanks 2 (May 2001), available at http://www.gao.gov/products/GAO-01-464; see also U.S. General Accounting Office, GAO-03-529T, Testimony before the Sub-Committee on Environment and Hazardous Materials, Environmental Protection: Recommendations for Improving the Underground Storage Tank Program 3 (Mar. 2003), available at http://www.gao.gov/products/GAO-03-529T [hereinafter 2003 GAO Testimony].

147 40 C.F.R. § 280.21(a)(3). 40 C.F.R. § 280 subpart G addresses the requirements for temporary and permanent closure. See infra section 11.0.

148 40 C.F.R. § 19.4; 42 U.S.C. § 6991e(d)(2).

149 40 C.F.R. 280.252(b).

150 See EPA 2000 Report to Congress, supra note 135, at 15–16. The "delivery prohibition" programs use a wide variety of methods—from tagging the fill pipe of a UST found to be out of compliance during an inspection (indicating to the driver not to deliver gasoline) to requiring the posting of a compliance certificate or permit (without which gasoline cannot be delivered). *Id.*; see also 2003 GAO Testimony, supra note 146, at 9 (as of 2003, twenty-three states had the authority to impose delivery prohibitions).

151 42 U.S.C. § 6991k.

152 42 U.S.C. § 6991k(a)(1).

153 EPA, EPA-510-R-06-003, Grant Guidelines to States for Implementing the Delivery Prohibition Provision of the Energy Policy Act of 2005 (Aug. 2006), available at http://www.epa.gov/oust/fedlaws/delvproh-080706.pdf.

154 *Id.*

155 *Id.*

156 EPA, EPA's Policy on Underground Storage Tanks Delivery Prohibition (June 2012), available at http://www.epa.gov/oust/fedlaws/ust_delv_proh_guid_6-25-12.pdf.

157 EPA, State Delivery Prohibition Programs, http://www.epa.gov/swerust1/dp/index.htm.

158 40 C.F.R. § 280.30.

159 See 40 C.F.R. § 280.53 for requirements regarding the reporting and cleanup of spills and overfills.

160 40 C.F.R. § 280.31(a).

161 40 C.F.R. § 280.32.

162 40 C.F.R. § 280.32(b).

163 40 C.F.R. § 280.33(a)–(b).

164 40 C.F.R. § 280.33(c).

165 40 C.F.R. § 280.33(d).

166 40 C.F.R. § 280.33(e).

167 40 C.F.R. § 280.33(f),

168 40 C.F.R. § 280.33(g)

169 See EPA, Response to Comments, supra note 43, at 12 (describing federal operator training requirements as "intended to provide training requirements in jurisdictions, such as in Indian country, not covered by requirements in the Energy Policy Act"). Section 1524 of the Energy Policy Act of 2005 required that EPA, in coordination with states, develop training guidelines for UST operators. In order to receive federal UST funding, states were required to develop state-specific training requirements consistent with EPA's guidelines by August 2009. State requirements continue to apply to the exclusion of the federal requirements in all jurisdictions with both state program approval and active state operator training programs.

170 40 C.F.R. § 280.242(a).

171 40 C.F.R. § 280.242(b).

172 40 C.F.R. § 280.242(c).

173 40 C.F.R. § 280.241(a).

174 40 C.F.R. §§ 280.242, 280.244.

175 EPA, Response to Comments, supra note 43, at 12 ("Although EPA thinks there is a natural limit to the number of facilities an individual can adequately address, we do not have a basis to provide a limit at this time").

176 Id. at 13.

177 40 C.F.R. § 280.31(b) and (c) provide frequency and inspection criteria.

178 40 C.F.R. § 280.31(d).

179 40 C.F.R. § 280.35(a). In its 2011 draft UST rule, EPA initially proposed periodic secondary containment testing of secondarily contained tanks and piping. As a result of heavy opposition in the comment period, EPA eliminated this requirement. EPA, Response to Comments, supra note 43, at 46. EPA expressed concern that the draft rule might give owners of older, single-walled systems a disincentive to replace those systems with secondarily contained systems. Id.

180 40 C.F.R. § 280.35(b).

181 40 C.F.R. § 280.40(a).

182 EPA, OUST, Comparison of Regulations, supra note 39, at 3.

183 Energy Policy Act of 2005, Section 1523; 42 U.S.C. § 6991d(c).

184 Id. On June 8, 2006, EPA issued a memorandum in order to identify which USTs needed to have an on-site inspection before August 8, 2007. EPA, memorandum, Inspection Requirements of the Energy Policy Act: Determining Which Underground Storage Tanks Have Undergone an Inspection since December 22, 1998 (June 2006), available at http://www.epa.gov/oust/fedlaws/inspection_final_gl_4-24-07.pdf.

185 "OUST Data Show States on Track to Meet Three-Year Inspection Cycle," 22 No. 8 Underground Storage Tank Guide Newsletter 7, May 2010; "Five Years of Progress Implementing The Energy Policy Act," EPA 2010 Annual UST Report, supra note 51, at 3.

186 40 C.F.R. § 280.36(a).

187 40 C.F.R. § 280.36(a)(1)

188 *Id.*

189 *Id.*

190 *Id.*

191 40 C.F.R. § 280.36(a)(2).

192 40 C.F.R. § 280.36(a).

193 See 40 C.F.R. § 280.40(a).

194 40 C.F.R. § 280.40(d).

195 See 40 C.F.R. § 280.43 (listing specifications on tank size and appropriate gauging methods).

196 40 C.F.R. § 280.44.

197 40 C.F.R. § 280.40(a)(4).

198 40 C.F.R. § 280.40(a)(3).

199 40 C.F.R. § 280.41(a)(2); 40 C.F.R. § 280.42; 40 C.F.R. § 280.43(g).

200 40 C.F.R. § 280.41(a)(2); 40 C.F.R. § 280.42; EPA, Response to Comments, *supra* note 43, at 46–47. Secondarily contained UST systems with periodic interstitial monitoring are markedly more secure than single-walled systems. Continuous interstitial monitoring may be even more secure. In California, secondary containment has been required for all new UST systems since 1998. Continuous interstitial monitoring using vacuum, pressure, or hydrostatic (VPH) monitoring has been required since July 2004. In that time, the State Water Resources Control Board is "unaware of a release occurring from any VPH system." Booz Allen Hamilton, Implementation of UST Provisions of the Energy Policy Act 2005 20, 39 (Sept. 2014), *available at* http://www.waterboards.ca.gov/ust/leak_prevention/epact/ca_ev alrpt_2014sept.pdf.

201 40 C.F.R. § 280.41(a)(2), (b)(2). Secondary containment and interstitial monitoring is not required for safe suction piping, piping associated with airport hydrant systems, or piping associated with field-constructed tanks over 50,000 gallons. 40 C.F.R. § 280.252; EPA, OUST, Comparison of Regulations, *supra* note 39, at 2.

202 40 C.F.R. § 280.41(b)(2)(i).

203 See 40 C.F.R. §§ 280.20–280.21.

204 40 C.F.R. § 280.41(a)(3).

205 40 C.F.R. § 280.41(b)(1).

206 40 C.F.R. § 280.41(b)(2).

207 40 C.F.R. § 280.42(b). The regulation notes that the provisions of 40 C.F.R. § 265.193 regarding containment and detection of releases for hazardous waste storage tanks may be used to comply with the release detection requirements for hazardous substance USTs.

208 40 C.F.R. § 280.42(b)(4).

209 40 C.F.R. § 280.42(b)(5).

210 EPA, OUST, Mid-2015 Semiannual UST Report, *supra* note 6, at 5.

211 *Id.*

212 *Id.*; EPA 2011 Annual UST Report, *supra* note 8, at 2.

213 EPA, OUST, Mid-2015 Semiannual UST Report, *supra* note 6, at 5.

214 *Id.*

215 *Id.*

216 See Lawrence Livermore Report I, supra note 13, at 15–16.

217 See generally Lawrence Livermore Report II, supra note 16.

218 EPA, Office of Superfund Remediation and Technology Innovation, Technologies for Treating MTBE and Other Fuel Oxygenates (May 2004), available at http://www.cluin.org/download/remed/542r04009/542r04009.pdf.

219 EPA, Office of Solid Waste and Emergency Response, Principles for Greener Cleanups (Aug. 2009), available at http://www.epa.gov/oswer/greenercleanups/pdfs/oswer_greencleanup_principles.pdf.

220 Id.

221 EPA 2010 Annual UST Report, supra note 51, at 4. The results of EPA's backlog analysis are available at http://www.epa.gov/oust/cat/backlog.html.

222 40 C.F.R. § 280.50.

223 40 C.F.R. § 280.50(a).

224 40 C.F.R. § 280.50(b).

225 40 C.F.R. § 280.50(c).

226 40 C.F.R. § 280.52.

227 40 C.F.R. § 280.52(a)(3).

228 40 C.F.R. § 280.52(b).

229 40 C.F.R. § 280.61.

230 40 C.F.R. § 280.62(a).

231 40 C.F.R. § 280.62(b).

232 40 C.F.R. § 280.63.

233 40 C.F.R. § 280.64.

234 40 C.F.R. § 280.64(d).

235 40 C.F.R. § 280.65.

236 40 C.F.R. § 280.53(a). For designation and reportable quantities of hazardous substances under CERCLA, see 40 C.F.R. Part 302.

237 40 C.F.R. § 280.53(b). UST regulations also note that pursuant to 40 C.F.R. §§ 302.6 and 355.40, a release of a hazardous substance equal to or in excess of its reportable quantity must also be reported immediately (rather than within twenty-four hours) to the National Response Center under Sections 102 and 103 of CERCLA and to appropriate state and local authorities under Title III of SARA.

238 40 C.F.R. § 280.66(a).

239 40 C.F.R. § 280.66(c); see also 40 C.F.R. § 280.67.

240 40 C.F.R. § 280.66(d).

241 See American Society for Testing Materials (ASTM), E1739-95, Standard Guide for Risk-Based Corrective Action Applied at Petroleum Release Sites (2010), available at http://www.astm.org/Standards/E1739.htm.

242 EPA, OSWER Directive 9610.17, Use of Risk-Based Decision-Making in UST Corrective Action Programs (Mar. 1995), available at http://epa.gov/swerust1/directiv/od961017.htm.

243 See generally Lawrence Livermore Report I, supra note 13.

244 Id. at 4, 16.

245 Id. at 19.

246 Id. at 18.

247 See, e.g., letter from Walt Pettit, Executive Director of the State Water Resources Control Board, to All Regional Water Board Chairpersons concerning the Lawrence Livermore Report (Dec. 8, 1995), available at http://www.waterboards.ca.gov/sanfranciscobay/docs/supp_inst_low_risk_fuel_sites.pdf.EPA. On the other hand, it took a more cautious approach and criticized several aspects of the Lawrence Livermore study, including its emphasis on passive bioremediation as a remedial alternative. EPA Region IX, Comments on LLNL Recommendations to Improve the Cleanup Process for California's Leaking Underground Fuel Tanks (June 6, 1996).

248 Energy Policy Act of 2005.

249 See generally Congressional Research Service Report for Congress, MTBE in Gasoline: Clean Air and Drinking Water Issues (Apr. 14, 2006), available at http://digitalcommons.unl.edu/cgi/viewcontent.cgi?article=1025&context=crsdocs.

250 Id.

251 See generally Lawrence Livermore Report II, supra note 16.

252 EPA, EPA-510-F-97-015, MTBE Fact Sheet #2, Remediation of MTBE Contaminated Soil and Groundwater 4 (Jan. 1998), available at http://www.epa.gov/oust/mtbe/Mtbefs2.pdf; see also EPA, MTBE Remediation and Treatment, http://www.epa.gov/swerust1/mtbe/mtberem.htm (citing additional sources).

253 U.S. General Accounting Office, GAO-02-753T, Testimony Before the Sub-Committee on Environment and Hazardous Materials, MTBE Contamination from Underground Storage Tanks 2, 9–10 (May 2002), available at http://www.gpo.gov/fdsys/pkg/GAOREPORTS-GAO-02-753T/html/GAOREPORTS-GAO-02-753T.htm.

254 EPA, EPA/625/F-00/003, MTBE Demonstration Project Fact Sheet (Apr. 2000), available at http://www.epa.gov/oust/mtbe/fctsheet.pdf.

255 The technologies selected were (1) E-beam technology using a beam of high-energy electrons to treat contaminated groundwater, (2) an advanced oxidation process using ozone and hydrogen to destroy organic compounds, and (3) in situ bioremediation using propane-oxidizing bacteria. Results from the field tests are available on EPA's MTBE Demonstration Project website, EPA, OUST, MTBE Demonstration Project, http://www.epa.gov/OUST/mtbe/mtbedemo.htm.

256 See, e.g., American Petroleum Institute, API Publication 4699, Strategies for Characterizing Subsurface Releases of MTBE (Feb. 2000), available at http://www.api.org/environment-health-and-safety/clean-water/ground-water/~/~/media/A0EDE318DCD9450A8D7120ED845AA5B9.ashx; American Petroleum Institute, Oxygenates, http://www.api.org/ehs/groundwater/oxygenates/index.cfm; University of California at Davis, New Sources for Research on MTBE Contamination, http://www.news.ucdavis.edu/news_releases/05.98/news_mtbesources.html.

257 California State Water Resources Control Board, Guidelines for Investigation and Cleanup of MTBE and Other Ether-Based Oxygenates (Mar. 2000), available at http://www.swrcb.ca.gov/ust/cleanup/docs/mtbe_finaldraft.pdf.

258 Id. at 1–2. American Petroleum Institute issued API Publication 4699, Strategies for Characterizing Subsurface Releases of Gasoline Containing MTBE (Feb. 2000), supra note 256, which applies the principles of risk-informed decision-making to MTBE-affected sites.

259 Energy Policy Act of 2005, Section 1525; 42 U.S.C. §§ 6991b(h)(12), 6991m(2)(B).

260 EPA, OUST, Basic Information on Petroleum Brownfields, http://www.epa.gov/oust/petroleumbrownfields/pbbasic.htm.

261 EPA, press release, EPA Making $1 Million in Grants Available to States under New Program to Cleanup Leaking Gas Tanks, Nov. 2, 2000, available at http://yosemite.epa.gov/opa/admpress.nsf/d0cf6618525a9efb85257359003fb69d/edf407bc3e4f60108525698b00654169!OpenDocument.

262 EPA, press release, EPA Announces $3.8 Million to Clean Up Petroleum from Underground Storage Tank Sites at Gas Stations in 26 States, July 1, 2002, available at http://yosemite.epa.gov/opa/admpress.nsf/2002+press+releases/915ded9bdedcae9185256be90055501b?opendocument.

263 Pub. L. No. 107-118 (2002).

264 Id.; see also EPA, OUST, Petroleum Brownfields, http://www.epa.gov/oust/petroleumbrownfields/index.htm/.

265 Id.

266 EPA, U.S. EPA's Petroleum Brownfields Action Plan: Promoting Revitalization and Sustainability (Oct. 2008), available at http://www.epa.gov/oust/pubs/petrobfactionplan.pdf.

267 EPA, Petroleum Brownfields 2013 Opportunities for Action (Feb. 2013), available at http://www.epa .gov/oust/pubs/petrobfactionplan2013.pdf.

268 See 40 C.F.R. § 280.70(a).

269 40 C.F.R. § 280.70(b).

270 40 C.F.R. § 280.70(c).

271 EPA 2000 Report to Congress, supra note 135, at 24.

272 *Id.*

273 A change-in-service is described as the continued use of a UST system to store a nonregulated substance. 40 C.F.R. § 280.71(c).

274 40 C.F.R. § 280.71(a).

275 40 C.F.R. § 280.71(b).

276 40 C.F.R. § 280.72.

277 40 C.F.R. § 280.73.

278 40 C.F.R. § 280.74.

279 UST Program Facts, *supra* note 7, at 1 [http://www.epa.gov/oust/pubs/ustfacts.pdf].

280 527 Mass. Code Regs. 9.05(G)(10).

281 Cal. Health & Safety Code §§ 25292.05(a), 25298.

282 Financial responsibility regulations state that if the owner and operator of a petroleum UST are separate persons, only one person is required to demonstrate financial responsibility. However, both parties are liable in the event of noncompliance with the financial responsibility regulations. 40 C.F.R. § 280.90(e).

283 EPA, OUST, Comparison of Regulations, *supra* note 39, at 5.

284 40 C.F.R. § 280.113.

285 40 C.F.R. § 280.93(a)–(b).

286 40 C.F.R. § 280.95.

287 40 C.F.R. § 280.96.

288 40 C.F.R. § 280.99.

289 40 C.F.R. § 280.98.

290 40 C.F.R. §§ 280.102, 280.103.

291 40 C.F.R. § 280.101. Thirty-five states have active State Financial Assurance Funds to provide tank owners and operators with a means of complying with the federal financial responsibility regulations. These states are Alabama, Arkansas, California, Colorado, Georgia, Idaho, Illinois, Indiana, Kansas, Kentucky, Louisiana, Maine, Massachusetts, Minnesota, Mississippi, Missouri, Montana, Nebraska, Nevada, New Hampshire, New Mexico, New York, North Carolina, North Dakota, Ohio, Oklahoma, Pennsylvania, Rhode Island, South Carolina, South Dakota, Tennessee, Utah, Vermont, Virginia, and Wyoming. EPA, OUST, State UST Financial Assurance Funds, http://www.epa.gov/swerust1/states/fndstatus.htm. Another five states have discontinued funds that provide assistance only for eligible past releases. These states are Arizona, Connecticut, Florida, Texas, and Wisconsin. *Id.* Many UST owners and operators look to these state funds to comply with the RCRA financial assurance requirements because of the difficulty in obtaining private insurance.

292 40 C.F.R. §§ 280.104–107.

293 EPA, EPA-510-B-12-002, List of Known Insurance Providers for Underground Storage Tank Owners and Operators (July 2012), available at http://www.epa.gov/swerust1/pubs/inslist.htm.

294 26 U.S.C. § 9508.

295 *Id.*

296 EPA, OUST, Leaking Underground Storage Tank (LUST) Trust Fund, http://www.epa.gov/swerust1/ ltffacts.htm.

297 EPA, OUST, UST Program Facts, supra note 7.

298 U.S. Department of the Treasury, Leaking Underground Storage Tank Trust Fund Balance Sheet 5 (Apr. 2015), *available at* ftp://ftp.publicdebt.treas.gov/dfi/tfmb/dfilu0415.pdf.

299 EPA, OUST, LUST Trust Fund, *supra* note 296.

300 Sean Lowry, Congressional Research Service, The Federal Excise Tax on Motor Fuels and the Highway Trust Fund: Current Law and Legislative History 1 (Feb. 6, 2014).

301 ASTSWMO, LUST Trust Fund Fact Sheet, *supra* note 12, at 2.

302 *See supra* note 291.

303 EPA, UST Program Facts, supra note 7.

304 EPA, State UST Financial Assurance Funds, supra note 291.

305 *See, e.g.*, California State Water Resources Control Board, Underground Storage Tank Focus on Groundwater Priorities and Funding (Jan. 2013), available at http://www.waterboards.ca.gov/water_issues/programs/ust/docs/gw_priorities_funding_jan2013.pdf.

306 *Id.* California's fund was originally set to expire in 2015. In late 2014, the Legislature passed SB 445, which funded a ten-year extension. California State Water Resources Control Board, Underground Storage Tank Cleanup Fund, Senate Bill 445, http://www.waterboards.ca.gov/water_issues/programs/ustcf/sb445.

307 *See* 40 C.F.R. § 280.111(b).

308 *See* 40 C.F.R. §§ 280.110–111(b).

309 *See* infra section 14.0.

Chapter 5

Clean Air Act

F. William Brownell[1]
Hunton & Williams LLP
Washington, D.C.

1.0 Overview

Since the 1960s, the Clean Air Act (hereafter CAA or Act) has evolved from a set of principles designed to guide states in controlling sources of air pollution (the 1967 Air Quality Act) to multiple levels of pollution control requirements (the 1970, 1977, and 1990 amendments to the Act) that the federal government implements by regulation and that the states administer and apply. This division of authority between federal and state governments is known as "cooperative federalism." While CAA emission standards traditionally reflected a command-and-control approach to pollution control, beginning in 1990, the focus of CAA regulation began to shift to market-based mechanisms.

The CAA regulatory programs fall into three categories. First, new and existing sources of air pollution are regulated to ensure attainment and maintenance of ambient air quality levels designed to protect public health and welfare. This ambient air quality program is implemented through source-specific emission limits contained in state implementation plans (SIPs). Second, new sources of pollution are subject to preconstruction review to ensure attainment of air quality standards and the application of up-to-date control technologies. Third, the Act addresses specific pollution problems, including acid deposition, hazardous air pollution, visibility impairment, and, beginning in 2007 with the Supreme Court's decision in *Massachusetts v. EPA*, greenhouse gases (GHGs). Apart from these substantive regulatory programs, Congress in 1990 added to the CAA an operating permit program to focus in one place all of the CAA requirements that apply to a given source of air pollution.

This chapter reviews briefly each of the CAA regulatory programs. Because CAA rules and guidance are invariably litigated, this chapter also reviews major litigation and judicial decisions under the Act. Legislative initiatives that could reform these programs are discussed at the end of this chapter.

2.0 CAA Regulatory Programs

2.1 Air Quality Regulation

The centerpiece of the CAA is the national ambient air quality standard (NAAQS) program, which addresses pervasive pollution that endangers public health and welfare. NAAQS have been established for six pollutants: sulfur dioxide (SO_2), nitrogen dioxide (NO_2), particulate matter (PM), carbon monoxide (CO), ozone (O_3), and lead (Pb).[2] For each of these pollutants, NAAQS are set at levels designed to protect public health with an adequate margin of safety (referred to as the primary NAAQS) and to protect public welfare against known or anticipated adverse effects (the secondary NAAQS).[3] Areas that do not meet one or more of the NAAQS are known as "nonattainment" areas and must comply with a number of special requirements (as described below in section 2.1.2).

NAAQS are to be reviewed and revised as appropriate at least every five years.[4] As a practical matter, the U.S. Environmental Protection Agency (EPA or Agency) has had difficulty meeting this schedule. Nevertheless, over the past fifteen years, and largely as a result of pressure from the courts, EPA has made a number of decisions regarding the NAAQS program that have important implications for regulation under the CAA. The experience with NAAQS decisions is an illustration of the challenges that EPA faces in implementing the CAA generally.

In 1994, EPA decided not to revise the NAAQS for CO, which were a primary eight-hour NAAQS of 9 parts per million (ppm) and a 1-hour NAAQS of 35 ppm.[5] After an abortive review that began in 1997, EPA, under a court order, determined in 2011 that the existing standards adequately protected the public health and that no secondary standard was warranted.[6] The decision was upheld on judicial review.[7]

EPA's quarterly NAAQS for Pb of 1.5 micrograms per cubic meter ($\mu g/m^3$) was reviewed in the early 1990s, but that review produced no proposal to revise or to reaffirm the NAAQS. In November 2008, however, acting pursuant to a court order,[8] EPA revised the NAAQS by lowering it to a quarterly maximum level of 0.15 $\mu g/m^3$.[9] Following a pattern of litigation at the end of final NAAQS decisions, the revised Pb NAAQS was challenged in court and was upheld in court in 2010.[10] In 2015, EPA proposed retention of the 2008 NAAQS.[11] The Agency has not yet taken final action on that proposal.

EPA had reviewed and reaffirmed its annual primary and secondary NAAQS for SO_2 and NO_2—primary and secondary annual NO_2 NAAQS of 0.053 ppm and, a primary annual NAAQS of 0.03 ppm, a 24-hour primary NAAQS of 0.14 ppm and a secondary NAAQS of 0.05 ppm for SO_2 in the 1990s.[12] In 2010, in compliance with a court-ordered schedule,[13] EPA revised the primary NAAQS for NO_2 by adding a 1-hour standard of 100 parts per billion (ppb),[14] and revised the primary SO_2 NAAQS by replacing the annual and 24-hour standards with a 75 ppb 1-hour standard.[15] On April 3, 2012, EPA decided not to revise the secondary NAAQS for NO_2 and SO_2.[16] Each of these actions was upheld following judicial review.[17]

The overall pattern of reaffirmation of NAAQS in the 1990s, followed by revision of the NAAQS in the past decade, does not hold for the NAAQS for PM and O_3. In 1997, EPA substantially tightened these NAAQS. EPA added new 24-hour average primary and secondary NAAQS for fine particles of 2.5 microns or less (i.e., $PM_{2.5}$) of 65 $\mu g/m^3$, and new annual primary and secondary $PM_{2.5}$ NAAQS of 15 $\mu g/m^3$ while making only minor adjustments to the preexisting 24-hour (150 $\mu g/m^3$) and annual (50 $\mu g/m^3$) NAAQS for PM-10 (particles of 10 microns or less).[18] At the same time, EPA promulgated a new, more stringent NAAQS for O_3 of 0.08 ppm, using an eight-hour average, with compliance based on the average fourth-highest reading over three calendar years.[19] The eight-hour NAAQS was designed to replace the existing one-hour O_3 NAAQS of 0.12 ppm.

The 1997 $PM_{2.5}$ and O_3 NAAQS and EPA's related implementation decisions were the subject of much controversy and litigation over the ensuing years. The revisions to the PM-10 NAAQS were vacated in 1999, and the new O_3 NAAQS were remanded for EPA to address evidence of beneficial effects associated with O_3 in the ambient air.[20] The $PM_{2.5}$ NAAQS were ultimately upheld,[21] and EPA subsequently reaffirmed the eight-hour 0.08 ppm standard.[22] Following these decisions, EPA promulgated several rules implementing them. Although, as discussed below in section 2.1.2.3, parts of these implementation rules were vacated or remanded by the D.C. Circuit, implementation of these NAAQS is well underway.

Since the 1997 revisions to the $PM_{2.5}$ and O_3 NAAQS, EPA has revised each of them twice. On October 17, 2006, the Agency published revisions to the PM NAAQS,[23] reducing the level of the primary and secondary 24-hour $PM_{2.5}$ NAAQS from 65 $\mu g/m^3$ to 35 $\mu g/m^3$ while retaining the present primary and secondary annual $PM_{2.5}$ NAAQS of 15 $\mu g/m^3$. EPA also revoked the 50-$\mu g/m^3$ annual standard for PM-10 but retained the 150-$\mu g/m^3$ 24-hour primary and secondary NAAQS as a means of controlling coarse particles. In 2009, the Agency's decisions not to set a separate secondary NAAQS and not to reduce the level of the annual standards were remanded to EPA, while other aspects of the rule were upheld.[24] EPA has since completed yet another review of the PM NAAQS and lowered the annual $PM_{2.5}$ standard to 12 $\mu g/m^3$ in a rule promulgated in January 2013, but again decided against a separate secondary NAAQS. EPA's rule has been upheld.[25]

On March 27, 2008, the Agency revised the O_3 NAAQS.[26] EPA tightened the eight-hour O_3 NAAQS from 0.08 ppm to 0.075 ppm. While judicial challenges to this NAAQS revision were pending in the D.C. Circuit,[27] EPA decided *sua sponte* to reconsider its 2008 decision and proposed to reduce the level of the eight-hour NAAQS from 0.075 to within the range of 0.070 to 0.060 ppm and to adopt a separate seasonal secondary standard.[28] Ultimately, EPA decided to wrap that reconsideration proceeding into the 5-year review of the ozone NAAQS. Thereafter, the 2008 NAAQS was upheld following judicial review.[29] EPA subsequently revised the O_3 NAAQS again in October 2015, lowering both the primary and secondary NAAQS from 0.075 ppm to 0.070 ppm.[30] The D.C. Circuit is currently considering challenges to the 2015 O_3 NAAQS by states, industry and environmental groups.[31]

2.1.1 State Implementation Plans

Sections 107 and 110 of the CAA give each state primary responsibility for ensuring that emissions from sources within its borders are maintained at a level consistent with the NAAQS. This is achieved through the establishment of source-specific emission limits and other requirements in SIPs addressing the primary and secondary air quality standards. The SIP is a constantly evolving regulatory document that must be updated as federal requirements and local conditions change.

States are responsible for developing SIPs and keeping them up to date. Before a SIP becomes enforceable as a matter of federal law, however, it must be submitted to EPA for review and approval. Until a SIP is approved by EPA, it is enforceable only as a matter of state law. The Act contains substantive and procedural requirements governing the development and approval of SIPs.[32]

2.1.1.1 Requirements regarding SIP Content

Section 110(a)(2) of the Act requires that all SIPs (regardless of whether an area attains or does not attain the level of air quality specified in the NAAQS) must be adopted after reasonable notice and public hearing. EPA refers to these as "Infrastructure SIPs." They include the following:

Enforceable emission limitations. A SIP must include enforceable emission limitations and other control measures, including economic incentives and timetables, as necessary to comply with the Act.[33]

Air quality data. A SIP must include provisions for developing data on ambient air quality—the concentrations of pollutants in the outside air that people breathe—to be made available to EPA.[34] These data are used to classify areas as attainment or nonattainment. EPA recently revised its requirements for the monitoring that states must do.[35]

Preconstruction review and notification requirements. A SIP must meet the requirements of Part C of Title I of the Act (i.e., the prevention of significant deterioration (PSD) program) requiring preconstruction review and approval of major[36] new stationary sources of air pollution in attainment areas.[37] Other stationary sources must undergo preconstruction review to the extent that the state finds such review is needed to ensure that construction of the source is consistent with attainment and maintenance of the NAAQS.[38]

Part D requirements. A SIP must meet the additional preconstruction permitting requirements of Part D of Title I of the Act (discussed below) relating to construction of new sources and the operation of existing sources in areas that do not attain the NAAQS.[39]

Air quality modeling. A SIP must provide for air quality modeling and submission of related data as prescribed by the EPA administrator. This modeling is used in predicting the effect of the emissions of regulated pollutants on ambient air quality to evaluate the adequacy of individual source emission limitations.[40]

Interstate air pollution. A SIP must prohibit emissions that significantly contribute to nonattainment or interfere with maintenance of the NAAQS or with visibility protection requirements in another state.[41] A SIP must also include provisions ensuring compliance with applicable requirements of the Act relating to interstate and international air pollution.[42]

Enforcement. A SIP must establish a program for enforcement of the emission limitations and control measures established by the state for individual sources.[43] Stationary sources[44] are also subject to enforcement under the operating permit program established by Title V of the 1990 amendments.

Monitoring and emission data. A SIP must require monitoring and periodic reporting of emissions by stationary sources for use in state enforcement and EPA oversight.[45]

Adequate personnel, funding, and authority. A SIP must provide assurances that the designated control authority has adequate resources and authority to carry out the SIP under state or local laws. The state also must retain ultimate responsibility for implementation and enforcement despite any delegation of authority to local agencies.[46]

Contingency plans. A SIP must provide authority for certain emergency powers similar to the provisions contained in Section 303 of the Act and for adequate contingency plans to restrict emissions of pollutants that present an imminent and substantial danger to the public.[47]

Revision of the SIP. A SIP must provide for revision as necessary to take into account any changes in the NAAQS, any improved methods of attainment, or any finding by EPA of substantial inadequacy of the current plan.[48]

Permit fees. A SIP must include provisions requiring the owner or operator of each major stationary source to pay, as a condition of any permit, fees to cover the reasonable costs of reviewing, acting on, and enforcing the permit, until superseded by a fee program under Title V of the 1990 amendments.[49]

Local consultation. A SIP must provide for consultation with and participation by local political subdivisions affected by the plan.[50]

The starting point for identifying the terms of the federally enforceable SIP is the catalog of state-specific SIP actions listed in 40 C.F.R. Part 52 and the related *Federal Register* notices containing the details of EPA's SIP actions. SIP identification has been addressed by states in the context of their Title V operating permit programs (discussed below), which require permits to contain all federally applicable requirements, including those state requirements that EPA has approved as part of the SIP. Many state environmental agencies and EPA regional offices have developed SIP compilations for use in preparing Title V permit applications.

2.1.1.2 Procedural Requirements Regarding SIP Development

To ensure that its SIP is adequate to attain and maintain the NAAQS, a state must revise that SIP within three years of issuance of any new or revised NAAQS (or such shorter period as is prescribed by EPA).[51] Section 110(k) of the Act outlines the requirements for EPA action on new and revised SIP submittals. Generally, within 60 days of receiving a plan or plan revision, the administrator will determine whether the submission is complete.[52] If, after six months, the administrator has failed to issue a completeness determination, the SIP submittal is automatically deemed complete.[53] If, however, the administrator thereafter determines that the plan or any portion of the plan is not complete, the state is treated as having not made the submission.[54]

Once a plan submission is deemed complete, the administrator is required to approve or to disapprove the plan within 12 months.[55] A plan that meets all of the applicable requirements of the Act will be approved in whole. The administrator may also approve a plan in part or approve a plan revision on condition that the state adopt specific enforceable measures within one year.[56] Whenever the EPA administrator finds that a SIP is substantially inadequate (1) to attain or to maintain a NAAQS, (2) to mitigate adequately interstate air pollution,[57] or (3) to comply with any other requirement of the Act, the EPA administrator must publicly notify the state (a "SIP Call") and establish reasonable deadlines (but no later than 18 months after the administrator's finding) for submitting SIP revisions to correct the EPA-identified inadequacy.[58]

If EPA makes a finding that a state failed to make a required submission or a complete submission as required or if EPA disapproves a SIP submission in whole or in part,[59] EPA must promulgate a federal implementation plan (FIP) for the state within two years after the date of the EPA finding or disapproval. A FIP is not required, however, if the state corrects the deficiency before EPA promulgates the FIP.[60]

2.1.1.3 Sanctions for Failure to Develop a SIP

If a SIP deficiency has not been corrected by the state within 18 months of EPA's finding of deficiency or its disapproval of a SIP, the EPA administrator must either cut off federal highway funds or require additional emissions offsets[61] in at least a two-for-one ratio for new or modified major stationary sources until the state has corrected the deficiency. These sanctions apply only in nonattainment areas in the state. The administrator also may withhold grants to the states for air pollution planning and control programs. Further, if the administrator finds "lack of good faith" on the part of the state or if the deficiency has not been corrected within six months after imposition of one of the above sanctions, both of the above sanctions will apply until the state has come into compliance.[62]

The administrator also has authority under Section 110(m) of the Act to apply the sanctions discussed above at any time before expiration of the 18-month period for state correction of the SIP deficiency. The administrator has issued regulations on how EPA will exercise this discretionary authority to apply sanctions prior to the date for mandatory application of sanctions.[63]

2.1.2 Additional SIP Requirements in Nonattainment Areas

The CAA contains general requirements (in addition to the requirements discussed above in section 2.1.1) governing development of SIPs in areas that do not attain the NAAQS. The general purpose of these requirements is to ensure that the states make reasonable progress toward attaining the NAAQS. Moreover, Title I of the 1990 amendments to the CAA includes additional, specific requirements addressing nonattainment areas for O_3 (e.g., the one-hour O_3 standard), CO, and PM (e.g., the PM-10 standards). The 1990 amendments set new deadlines for attainment—including longer deadlines for areas with more serious nonattainment and shorter deadlines for areas with more moderate nonattainment—but also impose more stringent control requirements on areas with more serious nonattainment problems. Specific nonattainment provisions are described below.

2.1.2.1 Substantive Requirements for Nonattainment SIPs

In addition to complying with the general requirements for SIPs discussed above, states' nonattainment area SIPs must include the following additional provisions:

Reasonably available control technology. SIPs must provide for application of all reasonably available control measures for stationary sources as expeditiously as practicable, with adoption, at a minimum, of reasonably available control technology (RACT) for existing sources.[64]

Reasonable further progress. SIPs must provide for such "annual incremental reductions" in emissions of nonattainment pollutants as are specifically required by Title I of the 1990 amendments or that are reasonably required by EPA to ensure reasonable further progress in attaining the NAAQS by the applicable attainment date.[65]

Inventory of current emissions. SIPs must include a current inventory of actual emissions from all sources of the nonattainment pollutant or pollutants, including periodic revisions as may be required by EPA.[66]

Quantification of new emissions. SIPs must identify and quantify emissions that will be allowed from construction and operation of new or modified major stationary sources in the nonattainment area and must demonstrate that such emissions will be consistent with the achievement of reasonable further progress and attainment of the NAAQS by the applicable attainment date.[67] In essence, for each nonattainment area, the SIP must include an emissions budget that will govern future environmental control strategies and limit economic growth in the area.

Permits for new and modified major stationary sources. SIPs must require permits for the construction and operation of new or modified major stationary sources in the nonattainment area.[68] New and modified major stationary sources in the nonattainment area must meet the "lowest achievable emission rate" (LAER), a very low rate that typically is more stringent than the rate represented by RACT limits applicable to existing sources in nonattainment areas.[69] New and modified major stationary sources in nonattainment areas must also obtain emission offsets for increased emissions of the air pollutant for which the area is nonattainment.[70]

Contingency measures. SIPs must provide for automatic implementation of specific additional emission control measures if the area fails to make reasonable further progress or to attain the NAAQS by the applicable date.[71]

Equivalent techniques. The EPA administrator may allow, upon application by the state, the use of modeling, emission inventory, and planning procedures equivalent to those prescribed by EPA unless EPA determines that they are, in the aggregate, less effective than the EPA-specified methods.[72]

2.1.2.2 Specific Nonattainment Pollutants

To address persistent nonattainment problems, Congress in 1990 wrote into the CAA detailed substantive requirements applicable to specific nonattainment pollutants. These requirements generally are more stringent for areas with more serious nonattainment problems.

Ozone.[73] Under the 1990 amendments, areas that were nonattainment for the one-hour O_3 NAAQS were classified as marginal, moderate, serious, severe, or extreme, depending on the severity of the nonattainment problem. Marginal areas were required to attain the O_3 NAAQS within 3 years of enactment of the 1990 amendments (i.e., by November 15, 1993); moderate areas within 6 years; serious areas within 9 years; severe areas within 15 or, in some cases, 17 years; and extreme areas (the greater Los Angeles metropolitan area being the only extreme area) within 20 years.

States with O_3 nonattainment areas were required to revise their SIPs to address various new requirements, including annual, incremental reductions in emissions of volatile organic compounds (VOCs) or, in some cases, a mixture of VOC and nitrogen oxide (NOx) reductions. In addition, states with moderate (and higher) O_3 nonattainment areas were required to include motor vehicle inspection and maintenance programs in their SIPs, with serious (and higher) areas subject to a requirement for "enhanced" vehicle inspection and maintenance programs. Moderate (and higher) areas also had to include gasoline vapor recovery requirements for service stations in their SIPs. A higher-than-thenormal 1-to-1 emission offset ratio is specified for new and modified major stationary sources in one-hour O_3 nonattainment areas, ranging from 1.1 to 1 in marginal areas to 1.5 to 1 in extreme areas. The size of sources that are deemed "major" and therefore subject to new-source permitting (including emission offset and LAER requirements) is reduced (from the normal criterion of 100 tons per year (tpy) or more of emissions) to 50 tpy in serious areas, to 25 tpy in severe areas, and to 10 tpy in extreme one-hour ozone nonattainment areas.

Because all the O_3 classifications and control measures of the 1990 CAA are based on the one-hour NAAQS that existed in 1990, EPA's adoption of a revised eight-hour NAAQS in 1997 required EPA to develop a regulatory scheme for implementation of that new standard. In addition, to avoid ongoing dual planning requirements for O_3 NAAQS, EPA revoked most designations for the one-hour O_3 NAAQS effective June 15, 2005.[74] In December 2006, however, the D.C. Circuit vacated parts of the Agency's implementation program for the eight-hour O_3 NAAQS.[75] EPA's efforts to develop an implementation program for the eight-hour NAAQS are discussed in section 2.1.2.3 below. According to the D.C. Circuit, this O_3 implementation program must provide that control requirements adopted in nonattainment SIPs for the one-hour O_3 standard be maintained even after revocation designations for that standard.[76]

Carbon monoxide.[77] CO nonattainment areas are classified as either moderate or serious, depending on the degree of the area's nonattainment problem. The

260 ❖ Environmental Law Handbook

Act required moderate areas to attain the CO NAAQS by December 31, 1995, and serious areas by December 31, 2000. Because the CO NAAQS has not been revised since 1990, EPA has not been required to adapt these provisions to a new standard.

The 1990 amendments require that states with CO nonattainment areas include in their plans specific emission control measures (e.g., enhanced vehicle inspection and maintenance requirements and oxygenated gasoline requirements for certain areas). Serious areas also are subject to requirements for interim "milestone" emission reductions.

PM-10.[78] Under the 1990 amendments, all PM-10 nonattainment areas initially were classified as moderate and were to be reclassified later as serious if it was not practicable for the area to attain the PM-10 NAAQS by December 31, 1994. Serious PM-10 nonattainment areas were given until December 31, 2001, to attain the NAAQS.

The 1990 amendments contain requirements for PM-10 nonattainment areas that generally resemble the requirements for O_3 and CO nonattainment areas. For example, states must implement reasonably available control measures (RACM) for sources contributing to nonattainment of the PM-10 standard and must establish periodic emission reduction milestones for reasonable further progress (RFP) that must be met until attainment is achieved. The statute also directs EPA to issue technical guidance on reasonably available control measures and best available control measures for certain categories of PM-10 emissions. In 2013, the D.C. Circuit found that the statutory procedures for implementing the PM_{10} NAAQS must also be used for $PM_{2.5}$.[79]

2.1.2.3 Implementation of the Eight-Hour Ozone and PM$_{2.5}$ NAAQS

Implementation of the NAAQS for O_3 and $PM_{2.5}$ has followed a tortuous path, in large part as a result of judicial decisions rejecting aspects of EPA's plans to implement them. As a result, EPA is now implementing several NAAQS for each pollutant simultaneously.

Ozone. On April 30, 2004, EPA designated 126 areas as nonattainment for the 1997 eight-hour O_3 NAAQS.[80] In an implementation rule published at the same time (called the "Phase I Ozone Implementation Rule" or the "Phase I Rule"), EPA subjected some of these areas—those with O_3 air quality that, at the time of eight-hour designation, exceeded the one-hour O_3 standard of 0.12 ppm—to a classification system based on the one enacted in the 1990 CAA amendments for the one-hour O_3 NAAQS, as described in section 2.1.2.2 above.[81] The Phase I Rule established attainment dates ranging from 2007 to 2021 and mandatory control measures for these areas in provisions designed to parallel the specific nonattainment requirements for the one-hour O_3 standard.

EPA did not provide classifications for areas with O_3 air quality equal to or below the one-hour NAAQS; these areas were subject only to the general provisions governing nonattainment SIPs described in section 2.1.2.1 above. Although these areas were required to attain the eight-hour O_3 NAAQS as expeditiously as practicable, EPA expected most of them to meet the standard within five years after the effective date of their designation as nonattainment, that is, by 2009. While EPA's Phase I Rule revoked the one-hour standard for most areas as of June 15, 2005, under "anti-backsliding" provisions, areas that were nonattainment for the one-hour NAAQS standard were generally required to continue implementing a range of one-hour control requirements.

The Phase I Ozone Implementation Rule was challenged by states, environmental groups, and industry in the U.S. Court of Appeals for the D.C. Circuit. As noted above, in a decision issued on December 22, 2006, and modified in June 2007, the court vacated parts of the rule, requiring EPA to revise how areas are classified under the revised eight-hour O_3 standard, and what one-hour O_3 requirements must continue to apply following revocation of the one-hour standard. [82]

In the meantime, on November 29, 2005, EPA published additional rules governing implementation of the eight-hour O_3 NAAQS (known as the "Phase II Ozone Implementation Rule" or "Phase II Rule").[83] The Phase II Rule interpreted requirements for RACT and RACM, RFP, nonattainment new source review (NSR), and provisions for reformulated gasoline. These regulations were also the subject of judicial challenges by states, industry, and environmental groups and, on certain issues, a petition for Agency reconsideration by an environmental group. In 2009, one provision of the rule was vacated as violating "anti-backsliding" provisions of the Act while two other provisions were remanded to EPA.[84] In addition, EPA undertook reconsideration of another aspect of the Phase II Rule—allowing compliance with the Clean Air Interstate Rule (CAIR) program (discussed below) to satisfy a requirement for RACT,[85] and that aspect of the Phase II Rule was partially vacated and remanded in a separate case.[86]

EPA has undertaken several additional regulatory actions resulting from the judicial decisions concerning the Phase I and Phase II Rules, some of which have themselves resulted in litigation. In 2010, EPA released a guidance memorandum interpreting a "penalty fees" provision in section 185 of the Act that the court had found subject to the Act's "anti-backsliding" requirements, but that memorandum was vacated upon judicial review.[87] In 2012, the Agency published a rule revising its approach to classification of nonattainment areas for the 1997 NAAQS.[88] In 2014, the Agency proposed to withdraw the 2012 rule.[89]

EPA has also proceeded to implement the O_3 NAAQS that it promulgated in 2008. On May 21, 2012, EPA published its designation of 46 areas as nonattainment for that standard.[90] Although states, counties, industry groups, and environmental organizations sought dismissal of several of these designations, all of them were upheld by the court.[91] On the same day that EPA promulgated these designations, the Agency also promulgated a rule that addressed certain other issues related to implementation of that standard.[92] This rule specified that, as was ultimately the case for the 1997 ozone NAAQS all nonattainment areas for the 2008 NAAQS would be classified under Subpart 2 of Part D of Title I of the Act and established how those classifications were made. It also determined that the applicable attainment deadlines for nonattainment areas would be the end of the calendar year by which attainment was required (e.g., by December 31, 2015, for marginal areas with three years to attain and December 31, 2018, for moderate areas with six years for attainment). The rule also revoked the 1997 ozone NAAQS for transportation conformity purposes as of July 20, 2013. The provisions establishing the end of the applicable year as the deadline for attainment and revoking the 1997 NAAQS for purposes of transportation conformity were subsequently vacated.[93]

In March 2015, EPA published rules establishing requirements for SIPs in areas designated nonattainment for the 2008 NAAQS.[94] These rules revoked the 1997 NAAQS for all purposes and established anti-backsliding requirements related to that revocation. It specified SIP submission deadlines and clarified that attainment was required on the anniversary of a nonattainment designation. It also addressed many other aspects of implementation, including attainment demonstrations, RFP, RACT and RACM, and NSR. Petitions for judicial review of the rule, which have not yet been resolved, were filed by one state agency and several environmental groups.[95]

PM₂.₅. Implementation of the 1997 $PM_{2.5}$ NAAQS lagged shortly behind implementation of the 1997 O_3 NAAQS. On January 5, 2005, EPA designated 47 areas, consisting of all or parts of 224 counties, as nonattainment.[96] On April 14, 2005, the Agency changed the designations for eight of those areas, including all or part of 17 counties, from nonattainment to attainment.[97] With one exception (Rockland County, New York), these designations were upheld by the D.C. Circuit.[98] In 2009, EPA designated 31 areas in 120 counties nonattainment for the 2006 $PM_{2.5}$ NAAQS,[99] and, in 2015, EPA designated 14 areas in six states nonattainment for the 2013 $PM_{2.5}$ NAAQS.[100]

On April 25, 2007, EPA promulgated a rule governing implementation of the 1997 $PM_{2.5}$ NAAQS.[101] This rule clarified that implementation of $PM_{2.5}$ would proceed under the general requirements for nonattainment SIPs and would not be subject to the special provisions for PM-10 nonattainment areas discussed in section 2.1.2.2 above. The rule required states to address certain $PM_{2.5}$ precursor emissions (SO_2 and NOx), but not others (VOCs and ammonia) in developing their attainment plans. It also explained that states could take into account national programs such as CAIR, discussed below, that address regional sources of $PM_{2.5}$ precursor emissions.

This rule was followed in May 2008 by rules on NSR for $PM_{2.5}$.[102] Under these rules, EPA required states to address primary emissions of $PM_{2.5}$ as well as emissions of the $PM_{2.5}$ precursors SO_2 and NOx, while not requiring that states address VOCs or ammonia. For purposes of transition, the NSR rule for $PM_{2.5}$ allowed states to continue to rely for a limited time on implementation of its PM-10 NSR program as a surrogate for $PM_{2.5}$ NSR. EPA subsequently proposed to end that transitional program early, however.[103] To the extent it had not already expired, that policy was repealed on May 18, 2011.[104] In addition, although the NSR rule did not specify PSD increments for $PM_{2.5}$, the Agency adopted such increments as well as a significant monitoring concentration (SMC) and significant impact levels (SILs) that served to exempt sources with de minimus impacts from PSD permitting requirements in October 2010.[105]

Multiple petitions were filed seeking judicial review of these rules. Some of these challenges have been stayed as EPA undertakes reconsideration.[106] Others have been resolved by two cases decided in January 2013. The first case held that, because $PM_{2.5}$ is a subset of PM-10, EPA was required to implement NAAQS for $PM_{2.5}$ under the statutory provisions applicable to PM-10 nonattainment areas.[107] These provisions are discussed in section 2.1.2.2, above. The second case vacated provisions on the SMC and SILs.[108]

In response to these decisions, EPA has promulgated rules classifying all nonattainment areas for the 1997 and 2006 $PM_{2.5}$ NAAQS as Moderate and requiring they submit SIPs consistent with that classification by the end of 2014.[109] Several environmental groups have sought judicial review of the rule, but the case has yet to be decided.[110] EPA has proposed rules that would implement $PM_{2.5}$ NAAQS under the statutory scheme for PM-10 NAAQS.[111] It has yet to propose further regulatory action on the PSD program for $PM_{2.5}$.

Regional Transport. EPA has also promulgated regionally applicable rules to implement the NAAQS for O_3 and $PM_{2.5}$. EPA's first foray into this arena came in October 1998. Using the SIP Call authority discussed in section 2.1.1.2, EPA promulgated a NOx SIP Call that imposed requirements on states in the eastern half of the country to reduce NOx emissions to address nonattainment of the one-hour O_3 NAAQS.[112] This rule was largely upheld on appeal.[113]

EPA also relied on its SIP Call authority on May 12, 2005, when it adopted CAIR to address what EPA determined was significant interstate transport contribution to nonattainment of the 1997 $PM_{2.5}$ and eight-hour O_3 NAAQS.[114]

CAIR was based on the Agency's interpretation and application of section 110(a)(2)(D)(i)(I) of the CAA. That provision requires, in relevant part, that each state's plan for attaining the NAAQS "contain adequate provisions . . . prohibiting . . . any source or other type of emissions activity within the State from emitting any air pollutant in amounts which will . . . contribute significantly to nonattainment in, or interfere with maintenance by, any other State with respect to any [NAAQS]."

CAIR imposed statewide emission budgets to reduce emissions of NOx, SO_2, or both, from electric-generating units, and applied to most of the states in the eastern half of the country. The required emission reductions were calculated on the basis of the emission controls EPA determined were "highly cost-effective" for electric-generating units. CAIR also established an EPA-administered interstate emission allowance trading program to achieve the required emission reductions. The states covered by CAIR were required to achieve Phase 1 of the CAIR NOx emission reductions by January 1, 2009, and Phase 1 of the CAIR SO_2 emission reductions by January 1, 2010. They were required to achieve the Phase 2 emission reductions for both NOx and SO_2 by January 1, 2015.

On July 11, 2008, the D.C. Circuit vacated CAIR and then, in a supplemental opinion issued on December 23, 2008, reinstated and remanded the rule.[115] As a result, CAIR was left in place pending additional rulemaking by EPA to address the problems identified by the D.C. Circuit, including whether a program that allows interstate trading of pollution credits can prevent significant contributions to nonattainment in neighboring states.

In response to the CAIR remand, on July 6, 2010, EPA issued its Cross-State Air Pollution Rule (CSAPR), which also addressed the 2006 $PM_{2.5}$ NAAQS.[116] Like CAIR, CSAPR primarily addressed emissions from electric generating units. In contrast to the NOx SIP Call and CAIR, however, CSAPR was structured as a FIP that would apply almost immediately, without opportunity for state implementation. In this rule, EPA (i) established new methods for determining which states should be subject to the program and for calculating statewide emission budgets and unit allowance allocations; (ii) abandoned CAIR's use of allowances under Title IV of the Act for compliance with SO_2 emissions reduction requirements; (iii) created new NOx allowance programs that do not involve fuel adjustment factors; and (iv) adopted an aggressive implementation schedule that involved an initial compliance date of January 1, 2012 (May 1, 2012, for the ozone season NOx program), and a further SO_2 reduction requirement at the beginning of 2014 for many states subject to the program. On August 21, 2012, the D.C. Circuit vacated CSAPR, but the Supreme Court reversed that decision in April 2014 and remanded it for further proceedings.[117]

On remand, the D.C. Circuit remanded without vacatur emissions budgets for SO$_2$ and NOx for several states.[118] In November 2015, EPA proposed an "update" to CSAPR to address the 2008 O$_3$ NAAQS.[119] This proposed rule also purports to respond to the D.C. Circuit's remand of certain NOx emissions budget.

2.1.2.4 Conformity Program

CAA Section 176 provides that no federal department may engage in, support in any way, provide financial assistance for, or license or approve any activity that does not conform to a SIP. The 1990 CAA amendments put teeth in this provision by expanding the conformity program from a simple check on the implementation of transportation control measures to a requirement that all relevant state actions (1) conform to the purpose of the SIP (i.e., to eliminate or reduce the severity and number of NAAQS violations) and (2) do not cause or contribute to new violations of an ambient standard, increase the severity or frequency of existing violations, or otherwise delay attainment.

The federal conformity provisions have been implemented through two detailed rules. For transportation plans, programs, and projects requiring funding or approval from the Federal Highway Administration or the Federal Transit Administration (agencies of the U.S. Department of Transportation), the conformity provision is implemented by the Transportation Conformity rule, which was issued in 1993,[120] substantially amended in 1997,[121] and most recently amended and restructured in 2012.[122] This rule establishes the process by which federal and state transportation agencies and metropolitan planning organizations determine that highway and other transportation projects conform to the applicable emission budget established by the state as part of the SIP development process. For all other federal actions (including EPA and Army Corps of Engineers licensing and permit actions), the conformity program is implemented by the General Conformity rule issued by EPA in 1993,[123] and revised in 2010.[124]

Failure to comply with the Transportation Conformity rule can result in a cutoff of federal highway funds. In this way, the conformity program can operate as a de facto sanction for failure to satisfy SIP planning requirements. The conformity program does not apply in areas that have never been designated nonattainment; once an area has been designated nonattainment, however, conformity requirements apply indefinitely, even if the area is redesignated to attainment. Implementation of the new eight-hour O$_3$ and PM$_{2.5}$ NAAQS will extend the geographic reach of the conformity program by creating more nonattainment areas. Under legislation enacted in 2000, a newly designated nonattainment area for a new or revised NAAQS has a grace period of one year to meet transportation conformity requirements.[125]

2.1.3 Compliance Monitoring

In recognition of the fact that many SIPs require only limited testing and monitoring to determine compliance with emission limitations, Congress required EPA under Section 114(a)(3) of the 1990 amendments to establish requirements for enhanced monitoring of industrial emissions. This rulemaking was later split into two separate proceedings—the so-called credible evidence and compliance assurance monitoring (CAM) rules. The credible evidence rule, promulgated in early 1997,[126] removed restrictions in certain federal rules on use of information beyond that specified in the applicable rule to make compliance determinations, and authorized states to do the same in their SIPs. Under the credible evidence rule, any measurement technique that is shown to generate emissions data comparable to (and of the same duration as) the specified testing method (typically EPA's reference methods found in Appendix A to 40 C.F.R. Part 60) can be used to determine compliance with an emission limitation.

As a practical matter, the credible evidence rule can have the effect of making existing emission standards that were based on data from periodic stack tests conducted under representative operating conditions more stringent. A standard based on periodic tests conducted under normal operating conditions is more likely to reflect average source emissions, whereas enforcement based on short-term average continuous emission monitor data is more likely to be driven by brief periods of high emissions. This effect of the credible evidence rule led numerous industry organizations to challenge both that rule as well as the various federal standards affected by that rule in the U.S. Court of Appeals for the D.C. Circuit. On August 14, 1998, the D.C. Circuit dismissed the basic challenges to the credible evidence rule, telling industry it should raise those challenges in the context of specific factual settings.[127] As a result, industrial sources faced with enforcement based on information under the credible evidence rule must pursue their challenges in the context of specific enforcement cases.

The CAM rule, which was promulgated in October 1997,[128] requires additional monitoring at certain large industrial facilities. Under the CAM rule, large industrial facilities that use control devices to meet emission limitations must develop monitoring plans that identify control parameter trigger levels below the level of applicable emission limitations and require corrective action when the trigger levels are exceeded. In 1999, the U.S. Court of Appeals for the D.C. Circuit upheld the CAM rule's approach to ensuring compliance as sufficient to meet the statutory requirement for enhanced monitoring, rejecting an environmental group's contention that the statute requires direct monitoring of emissions.[129] CAM plans are implemented through the Title V operating permit program, which may also authorize imposition of new emissions monitoring and testing requirements in some circumstances (discussed below in section 2.4).

2.2 New Source Control Programs

In enacting the 1970 and 1977 amendments to the Act, Congress concluded that it would be more cost-effective to require high levels of technological performance at new sources because they have more flexibility as to location and design of control equipment than do existing sources.[130] As a result, construction of a new source of emissions triggers the potential application of more stringent levels of control under the Act.

2.2.1 New Source Performance Standards

In Section 111 of the 1970 Act, Congress required the EPA administrator to identify categories of new and modified sources that contribute significantly to air pollution that endangers public health or welfare. To date, EPA has identified well over fifty such source categories, including most large industrial categories.[131]

For these source categories, EPA sets emission standards that reflect the "degree of emission limitation achievable" through the best technology that the Agency determines has been "adequately demonstrated," taking into consideration "nonair quality health and environmental impact[s] and energy requirements."[132] New Source Performance Standards (NSPS) may be promulgated as design, equipment, work practice, or operational standards where numerical emission limitations are not feasible.[133]

Each NSPS in 40 C.F.R. Part 60 identifies the types of facilities (e.g., in terms of size and process) to which the standards apply. NSPS generally apply to any facility so identified on which construction is begun after the date of proposal of the NSPS. Section 111 defines a "new" source to include existing sources that are modified. In addition, NSPS apply to any affected facility that is "reconstructed" after the date of proposal of the NSPS.

Once set, NSPS serve as the minimum level of control that must be achieved by new sources through the new source preconstruction permitting program (discussed below). NSPS are to be reviewed at least every eight years and, if appropriate, revised through notice and comment rulemaking.[134]

In 1990, Congress mandated several revisions to specific NSPS, for example, repealing Section 111(a)(1) of the Act (which included the percentage reduction requirement for large fossil fuel–fired boilers) and requiring revision of NSPS for SO_2 for this source category. The 1990 amendments also set a new regulatory schedule for source categories that were listed under Section 111 but not regulated prior to enactment of the amendments.[135] NSPS that EPA has developed or revised in response to the 1990 amendments include NSPS for fossil fuel–fired steam generating units for NOx[136] and SO_2,[137] and NSPS for municipal waste combustion units, municipal solid waste landfills, medical waste incinerators, commercial and industrial solid waste incineration units,[138] and stationary combustion turbines.[139]

2.2.2 New Source Review

Construction of a new source of air pollution, or the modification of an existing source, may trigger preconstruction review and permitting as discussed below. The nature of the preconstruction permitting requirements depends upon whether the source is to be located in an area that attains or has failed to attain the NAAQS for the pollutant in question. Sources located in attainment areas are subject to the PSD permit program; sources in nonattainment areas are subject to the nonattainment permit program.[140]

The NSR programs apply to "major" stationary sources. For the PSD program, a "major" source is one that has the potential to emit at least 250 tpy of a regulated pollutant or at least 100 tpy of a regulated pollutant if the source falls within one of 28 listed source categories.[141] The nonattainment program defines a "major" source as one that has the potential to emit at least 10 to 100 tpy of the nonattainment pollutant, depending upon the pollutant and the seriousness of the nonattainment problem in the area in which the source is located.[142]

Whether a source has the potential to emit at these levels is determined based on the maximum capacity of the source to emit under its physical and operational design, taking into account any enforceable regulatory limits on source operations (e.g., operating limits included in a SIP or new source permit).[143] In *National Mining Association v. EPA*, the D.C. Circuit set aside the requirement of the federal air toxics program that only federally enforceable operational limits could be considered in defining a source's potential to emit.[144] The D.C. Circuit subsequently applied this decision to vacate the federally enforceable requirement in the NSR and Title V potential to emit rules.[145] The court suggested that any limit that was "effective as a practical matter" should be considered in defining a source's potential to emit. EPA has issued several guidance documents addressing how potential to emit will be calculated in light of these judicial decisions.[146]

2.2.2.1 PSD Program

Under the CAA, a pre-construction permit under the PSD program must be obtained before one can construct a major (i.e., 100/250 tpy) new source or undertake a major modification of an existing major source (as discussed below), in an area that attains the NAAQS.[147] In order to receive a PSD permit, the owner or operator of the proposed major new source or major modification must show that the major source or modification (1) will comply with ambient air quality levels designed to prevent deterioration of air quality (the PSD increments), (2) will employ best available control technology (BACT) for each pollutant regulated under the Act that it will emit in significant amounts, and (3) will avoid adverse impacts on federal Class I areas (including national wilderness areas and parks in existence on August 7, 1977, and greater than 5,000 or 6,000 acres in size, respectively).[148] BACT is defined as the "maximum degree of [emission] reduction . . . achievable," taking into account economic, energy, and environmental factors.[149] BACT must be at least as stringent as any NSPS applicable to the facility.

Both the amount of PSD increment a new source is allowed to consume and the BACT determination are matters of state discretion. Regarding the BACT determination, EPA in December 1987 issued guidance (referred to as the top-down BACT guidance) that, as applied, substantially restricted state discretion in BACT determinations. In response to a judicial challenge, EPA agreed in 1991 to issue a *Federal Register* notice clarifying its position on BACT review. While no such notice has been issued, state discretion with respect to BACT was later confirmed by the Supreme Court in *Alaska Department of Environmental Conservation v. EPA*.[150]

The BACT determination is based on the state's balancing of the economic, energy, and environmental impacts of alternative control technologies.[151] EPA retains authority, however, to issue stop construction orders to the extent it determines that a state's preconstruction authorization does not comply with the requirements of the CAA.[152]

BACT review applies to a pollutant "subject to regulation under [the] Act" that a major new or modified source has the potential to emit in a significant amount (as defined by the PSD rules).[153] Prior to 1990, BACT review included both criteria pollutants (i.e., pollutants subject to NAAQS) and air toxics. The 1990 amendments to the Act, however, provided that substances listed under the air toxics program in Section 112 are not subject to the PSD program.[154] Since the air toxics list is extensive (189 substances and compounds are listed in the Act), this provision means that BACT review is not required for regulated hazardous air pollutants (HAPs) for states that have been delegated authority to implement the federal PSD program or that have revised their PSD programs in response to the 1990 amendments. However, states may also choose to continue to require such analyses under state law. Moreover, state permitting authorities may consider the implications of proposed technologies for the emission of air toxics as part of the BACT analysis for other regulated pollutants.

The permit applicant defines the facility it seeks to permit, and BACT review then focuses on the facility as defined in the permit application.[155] While some have argued that an applicant must consider alternative, lower-emitting facilities as part of the BACT review process, EPA has rejected this position, and the Seventh Circuit accepted EPA's position in *Sierra Club v. EPA*. EPA has observed, however, that apart from the BACT process, permitting agencies have an obligation under Section 165(a) to consider and to respond to comments on alternatives to a source.[156]

While the BACT determination is perhaps the most important aspect of PSD permitting, other issues must also be resolved in order to receive a PSD permit. As noted above, the applicant must show that the proposed source will not cause or contribute to exceedances of either NAAQS or PSD increments.[157] For sources proposed to be located near national parks or other Class I areas (as defined in Section 162), the applicant must address concerns of the federal land manager (FLM) of an area where the proposed source might impact air quality related values (AQRVs) such as visibility. Once an applicant shows that emissions from a proposed source would comply with PSD increments in a Class I area, however, the burden is on the FLM to show that the source's emissions would nonetheless adversely impact AQRVs.[158]

Although EPA has not adopted any formal regulations addressing impacts of new sources on AQRVs in Class I areas, the FLMs have developed guidance for addressing AQRVs. This guidance—commonly known as the FLAG Guidance or the FLAG Report—was issued by the FLM's Air Quality Related Values Workgroup in December 2000, and was updated in October 2010. It establishes highly protective definitions for adverse impacts on AQRVs and sets out procedures for assessing whether such adverse impacts might occur. Although the FLAG Report is only guidance, as a practical matter, applicants for new source permits located near Class I areas follow the procedures that it describes and provide that information to the relevant FLM. If the FLM concludes that an adverse impact is threatened by the project, the FLM may object to issuance of the permit or may indicate conditions that the FLM believes should be included in the permit if it is issued. Ultimately, the permitting authority (usually the state) must determine whether it concurs with the FLM's position that an adverse impact on an AQRV has been demonstrated and with the FLM recommendations for addressing any such impact.

2.2.2.2 Nonattainment Program

In areas that have not attained the NAAQS for a given pollutant (i.e., nonattainment areas), new major stationary sources, or major modifications of existing major sources, must receive a nonattainment permit before construction can begin. A major source for purposes of the nonattainment program is generally one that has the potential to emit in excess of 100 tpy of a nonattainment pollutant. The 1990 amendments lower this threshold for areas with more serious nonattainment problems (e.g., to 50 tpy for VOC and NOx in serious ozone nonattainment areas, to 25 tpy for severe areas, and to 10 tpy for extreme areas). In areas that are attainment for some regulated pollutants and nonattainment for others, both a PSD and a nonattainment permit may be required.

States are responsible for implementing the nonattainment permit program. State permit programs must include, among other things, a requirement that major new or modified sources meet an emission limitation for nonattainment pollutants that reflects the "lowest achievable emission rate" (LAER). LAER is defined as "the most stringent emission limitation" contained in any SIP or that is "achieved in practice" by the same or a similar source category, whichever is more stringent. If the owner or operator of the proposed facility can demonstrate that the most stringent technology is not feasible for the proposed facility, the next most stringent level of control is used to establish LAER.

In order to ensure progress toward attainment of the NAAQS, the state permit program must require that the proposed new or modified source offset increased emissions of the nonattainment pollutants by securing emission reductions from nearby facilities at a greater than one-to-one ratio. EPA rules provide guidance for determining the baseline against which emission offsets are to be credited.[159] The CAA amendments of 1990 define the offset ratios that apply in O_3, CO, and PM-10 nonattainment areas, and these ratios increase as the nonattainment problem becomes more severe. For example, the offset ratio in ozone nonattainment areas in which the one-hour ozone NAAQS applies varies between 1.1 and 1.5 to 1, according to the seriousness of the area's nonattainment problem.

Finally, the source owner or operator must certify that its other sources are in compliance (or on a schedule to comply) with all applicable air quality requirements and that the benefits of the proposed source outweigh its environmental and social costs.[160]

2.2.2.3 Other Issues

As permitting of major new industrial facilities has become more controversial, additional issues have been raised in new source permit proceedings. One of these issues concerns the need for consultation under Section 7 of the Endangered Species Act (ESA) and state counterparts to this federal legislation regarding possible impacts of a proposed project on threatened and endangered species and their critical habitat. Whether state or federal endangered species law applies to CAA permitting depends on whether the state is the new source permitting authority under an approved SIP or whether the state has been delegated authority to implement the federal program (so that EPA retains the ultimate authority to issue the permit). Unless the ESA "action" agency terminates the consultation process by making a "no adverse effect" determination, the consultation process can result in consideration of permit requirements to mitigate impacts on endangered species. The role of the ESA in new source permitting has been addressed on several occasions by EPA's Environmental Appeals Board (EAB).[161]

2.2.3 Reconstruction and Modification Rules

As noted above, new source requirements are triggered by the construction of new sources of emissions. An existing source that is reconstructed is treated as a new source of emissions for the NSPS program. CAA Section 111 defines a new source to include the modification of an existing source. Modifications are potentially subject to either the NSPS applicable to the source category or the new source permitting programs. The modification provision is perhaps the most controversial provision of the CAA and has given rise to a significant amount of litigation. The modification controversy is discussed briefly below in section 2.2.3.2.

2.2.3.1 Reconstruction

EPA promulgated the reconstruction rule in 1975 to address projects designed to extend the useful life of existing industrial facilities.[162] The rule defines when a project to rebuild an existing facility becomes so extensive that it is substantially equivalent to replacing the facility "at the end of its useful life."[163] The reconstruction rule appears only in the NSPS program and not the PSD or nonattainment permit programs. A reconstruction rule has also been adopted for the air toxics program (discussed below).

In general, the reconstruction rule requires a source owner or operator to notify EPA if work to rebuild an existing facility will involve expenditures that are 50 percent or more of the capital cost of a comparable new facility.[164] The rule then requires that EPA, upon receipt of this notice, determine whether the project would constitute "reconstruction." Recognizing that control technology standards developed for new facilities may not be appropriate for reconstructed, existing facilities, the rule provides that for there to be a "reconstruction," EPA must find that application of NSPS is technologically and economically feasible, based on consideration of costs, remaining useful life, and potential emission reductions associated with application of NSPS.[165]

When EPA promulgated the reconstruction rule, it stated that it did not anticipate that many facilities would trigger reconstruction review. EPA said that it would address more specific concerns, if any, with life extension of existing sources in rulemakings establishing NSPS for specific source categories.[166] It is important, therefore, to examine the NSPS rules applicable to individual source categories for further guidance on whether and when activity that is tantamount to replacing an existing facility at the end of its useful life might trigger NSPS.

2.2.3.2 Modification

Unlike the reconstruction rule, a modification of an existing major source may trigger application of the PSD and nonattainment permit programs as well as NSPS. In contrast to the reconstruction rule, which focuses on the size of a project and the feasibility of additional controls, the modification rule asks whether a project creates a new source of pollution. The modification provision has been the subject of a number of important regulatory and litigation developments over the past decade.

Regulatory developments—The 1970 CAA contained one definition of "modification" for both the NSPS and SIP preconstruction review programs: the definition of "modification" in Section 111 of the Act. Following enactment of the 1970 Act, EPA used this definition in Section 111 to promulgate rules defining "modification" for both NSPS (in 1971 and 1975) and for PSD (in 1974).[167] EPA's rules defined "modification" for both programs as activity that increases a facility's emission rate. The rules also provided that a modification shall not include specific activities (e.g., routine maintenance, repair and replacement, or an increase in production rate or hours of operation) that are consistent with a facility's operating design. These provisions implement a simple statutory concept: a "modification" is activity that creates a new source of emissions. As a result, "if a facility is expanded to create new pollution, then that facility and its new pollution must be reviewed and regulated."[168]

In 1976, EPA adopted a regulatory NSR program for nonattainment areas. In those rules, EPA provided that the more stringent nonattainment requirements of that rule would apply only to "modifications" that were "major." EPA defined "major" in terms of annual tonnage thresholds for increased emissions.[169] As a result of this rule, activity in a nonattainment area that created new pollution would be subject to NSPS and, if the NSPS modification was "major," to nonattainment NSR as well. By contrast, PSD review, like NSPS, applied under the 1974 PSD rules to all NSPS modifications (i.e., to all activity that creates new emissions), whether "major" or not.

Congress, in the 1977 amendments, defined "modification" for the statutory NSR programs (both PSD and nonattainment) by reference to the preexisting NSPS definition of modification. It is not surprising, then, that "modification" continued to have the same basic elements for each of these programs. For there to be a "modification" under the Act, there must be a "physical change" or "change in the method of operation" at an emissions unit that increases the "amount of a pollutant emitted" or that results in the emission of a regulated pollutant "not previously emitted."

In 1980, EPA promulgated a rule defining "major modification" for *both* the PSD and nonattainment NSR programs, while leaving unchanged its 1974

PSD definition of "modification." As the court explained in Chevron, "major modification" was intended to allow "an existing plant that contains several pollutant-emitting devices . . . [to] modify one piece of equipment . . . if the alteration will not increase the total emissions from the plant."[170] In other words, as in the 1976 nonattainment NSR rule, one could undertake a "modification" of an emitting unit as defined in EPA's rules (i.e., activity that creates new pollution) but still avoid NSR if the "modification" was not "major" for the source (i.e., did not increase source-wide annual emissions above specific tonnage thresholds).

In spite of this simple concept, application of the modification/major modification rules has been the subject of intense controversy over the past decades. In the Wisconsin Electric Power Company (WEPCo) determination issued by EPA in 1988, EPA introduced what it called an "activist" approach under which the Agency assumed that a modification for NSR programs included virtually any physical or operational change, by requiring that an "emissions increase" be determined by comparing an existing source's past actual and future potential emissions. In response to an industry challenge, the U.S. Court of Appeals for the Seventh Circuit rejected the key element of EPA's position, finding no basis for interpreting the PSD regulations to require a "past actual-to-future potential" emissions comparison for a facility that has begun normal operations.[171]

In 1990, Congress made several attempts to address and to clarify the modification provision through amendments to the CAA. The final legislation contained no general revisions to this provision, however, because EPA committed to clarify its modification rules along the lines of the administration's legislative proposal.[172] The first set of clarifications (the so-called WEPCo rule and preamble) was issued in July 1992.[173]

The 1992 WEPCo rule had two parts. First, the preamble to the rule contains the Agency's clarifications and interpretations of the existing major modification rules. This interpretive rule confirmed that the Agency would in most respects continue to apply its pre-WEPCo interpretations of these rules. For example, where an existing source had begun normal operations, the Agency confirmed that it would not calculate an emissions increase based on a comparison of past actual emissions and future potential to emit. According to the Agency, such an emissions comparison is "impermissible." Moreover, the Agency said that it would continue to exclude pollution control projects from new source permitting rules. Finally, the Agency said that whether repair or replacement activity is "routine" under the modification regulations, "while made on a case-by-case basis, must be based on the evaluation of whether that type of equipment has been repaired or replaced by sources within the relevant industrial category."[174] These interpretive rulings are important because they apply to all industrial sources, whereas the formal legislative rule discussed below applied only to large utility boilers.

Second, in a legislative rule, the Agency clarified and amended certain aspects of the major modification rules as applied to large utility boilers subject to the acid deposition program (Title IV) of the 1990 amendments.[175] Under this rule, a utility that could avoid application of PSD by projecting that the source's future utilization would decline sufficiently to offset the impact (on an annual basis) of any projected increase in hourly emissions rate. To take advantage of this rule, however, the facility would have to submit post-project emissions data for at least five years to show that annual emissions in fact decreased.[176] Facilities that did not submit such data would remain subject to EPA's prior (i.e., 1980) modification/major modification rules.

The WEPCo rule had several other provisions:

• The rule confirmed that pollution control projects would not trigger NSR even where the project caused some collateral increase in emissions.

• The rule confirmed that the test for NSR is whether a specific project results in (i.e., causes) an increase in emissions. As a result, where an emissions increase results from an increase in demand or from other market forces, NSR would not be required.

In 1992, EPA formed a New Source Review Workshop to discuss further changes to the modification/major modification rules. As a result of the discussions of that group, EPA in July 1994 issued a guidance memorandum discussing when pollution control projects at nonelectric utility sources would be excluded from NSR. This memorandum provided interim guidance pending promulgation of a formal regulatory exclusion for such projects in a future rulemaking.[177]

In July 1996, EPA published in the *Federal Register* a proposal to revise and to clarify further the modification rules.[178] Two years later, on July 24, 1998, EPA issued a supplemental notice in which it proposed to repeal portions of the WEPCo rule and the interpretations announced in the preamble to that rule.[179]

In 2002 and 2003, EPA attempted (with only partial success) to bring to a conclusion this decade-long NSR rulemaking. First, in December 2002, EPA issued a final rule concluding the rulemaking begun in 1996 to reform the NSR program.[180] Second, following up on the promise made in the 1992 WEPCo rule preamble to provide further guidance on the meaning of "routine maintenance, repair and replacement," EPA issued in December 2002 a proposed rule providing a safe harbor for certain "routine replacement" projects. This proposal was finalized in October 2003.[181]

The NSR reform rule promulgated in December 2002 had four components. First, it codified the pollution control project exclusion contained in earlier EPA guidance and revised it in certain respects. The rule provided, however, that emission reductions achieved by a project that took advantage of the pollution control exclusion could not be used in the future for NSR netting or emission reduction credits.[182]

Second, the rule addressed the methodology for computing an emissions increase, extending to all industry a test similar to the one made available to large electric utility boilers under the 1992 WEPCo rule.[183] Under this rule, a source could avoid triggering NSR if it projected that emissions would not increase due to the project, and then confirmed that projection through post-project monitoring and reporting. In contrast to the 1992 WEPCo rule, however, the new rule allowed facilities the option to use the actual-to-potential method rejected by the Seventh Circuit in WEPCo.

Third, the rule provided a "clean unit" exclusion from NSR.[184] Under this provision, a unit that met a BACT-equivalent level of emissions control for an NSR pollutant could avoid triggering NSR for ten years, provided that it did not undertake activity that caused an increase in the facility's maximum achievable hourly emission rate.

Fourth, the rule provided criteria and procedures for the development of "plantwide applicability limits" (PALs).[185] A PAL is a sourcewide bubble. Once a PAL is established for a source, emissions-increasing activities can be undertaken by an emitting unit at the source as long as the activity does not cause an exceedance of the PAL.

The October 2003 NSR rule, called the Equipment Replacement Provision (ERP) rule, provided a "safe harbor" for certain equipment replacement activity. According to EPA, Congress never intended that replacement of deteriorating or broken equipment that allowed a facility to continue to operate as it had always operated would constitute a modification.[186] Accordingly, the ERP rule provided that replacement of equipment with identical or functionally equivalent equipment that did not change a facility's operating capacity would not be a physical change. However, if the cost of the replacement project exceeded 20 percent of the cost of a comparable new facility, the project would have to be submitted to the permitting authority for review even if it met the other criteria of the rule. Replacement projects that did not automatically qualify under the ERP rule could still be found "routine" through a case-by-case evaluation by the permitting authority.

Both the December 2002 NSR rule and the October 2003 ERP rule were challenged by environmental groups and certain states in the D.C. Circuit. In

June 2005, the D.C. Circuit issued its decision regarding the 2002 rules, upholding them in large part but also vacating portions of the rule.[187] Specifically, the court upheld the approach for pre-project notice and post-project monitoring of whether emissions increases would be caused by a project and the PAL provisions, and it vacated the pollution control project exclusion and the clean unit provision. The court rejected other challenges to these rules, including challenges to the requirement that an increase in emissions must be "caused" by a project (the so-called "demand growth" provision), and to the NSPS emission rate test of the 1992 WEPCo rule.

The most controversial aspect of this decision is the vacatur of the NSR pollution control project exclusion of the 1992 WEPCo rule and the 2002 NSR reform rule. Pollution control projects that cause a secondary increase in a regulated pollutant may now have to undergo NSR permitting.

In March 2006, the D.C. Circuit vacated the ERP rule.[188] According to the court, because "Congress place[d] the word 'any' before [the] phrase ['physical change']" in the statutory definition of "modification," and because that phrase "physical change" has "several common meanings, the statutory phrase [must] encompass[] each of those meanings."[189] As a result, the court held that "the ERP violates section 111(a)(4) of the Clean Air Act" because it would allow equipment replacements that could result in non-de minimis emission increases.[190] At the same time, confirming the narrowness of this decision, the court said it "ha[d] no occasion to decide whether part replacements or repairs necessarily constitute a 'modification' under the definition taken as a whole."[191]

In addition to the 2002 and 2003 NSR rules, EPA initiated two other rulemakings to clarify aspects of the NSR program. On October 20, 2005, EPA proposed to make clear that NSR is triggered only by activity that increases a facility's achievable hourly emission rate.[192] This proposed rule would have made clear that the NSR modification test is consistent with NSPS, that is, focused on activity that creates new pollution. While EPA proposed this rule only for electric utilities, it requested comment on whether to apply it to other industries as well. EPA also requested comment on whether to retain the "major modification" emissions netting test for projects that are NSPS modifications. In December 2008, at the end of the Bush administration, EPA announced that it had decided to abandon this rulemaking.

On September 14, 2006, EPA proposed rules providing guidance on three topics: debottlenecking, project aggregation, and project netting.[193] The intent of these rulemakings was to clarify (i) when NSR is required as a result of activity that removes constraints on necessary inputs to or the output of an emissions unit; (ii) when individual projects must be aggregated for consideration of their emissions consequences; and (iii) when projects undertaken concurrently that each have an emissions impact are to be considered based on their combined impact or, alternatively, have to go through a sourcewide netting analysis. These rules were not finalized by the end of the Bush Administration, and it is now unclear whether they ever will be.

NSR enforcement developments—Rather than wait for the conclusion of the long-pending NSR clarification rulemakings begun in the early 1990s, EPA in the late 1990s began to file enforcement actions against industry. In these lawsuits, EPA alleged that companies had been violating the NSR program for decades by repairing and replacing broken or deteriorating equipment. NSR enforcement actions have been filed against refineries, paper companies, electric utilities, cement plants, and ethanol plants, among others.[194]

The most controversial of these NSR enforcement efforts has been directed against the electric utility industry. In November 1999, EPA instituted enforcement proceedings against seven utilities and the Tennessee Valley Authority (TVA) alleging that these companies had modified their facilities without necessary new source permits. The most complete statement of the EPA Enforcement Office's approach to NSR, as reflected in the utility NSR enforcement initiative, is contained in an order of EPA's EAB issued on September 15, 2000,[195] finding that TVA modified nine of its generating units without obtaining needed new source permits.

The EAB Order was challenged by TVA and others in the U.S. Court of Appeals for the 11th Circuit in November 2001.[196] On June 24, 2003, the 11th Circuit issued a decision finding that the CAA provision for development of administrative compliance orders that was the basis for the EAB Order to TVA violated constitutional due process and separation of powers principles. Because the CAA provides that violation of administrative compliance orders can subject affected persons to civil and criminal penalties, the court declared the CAA's enforcement regime for administrative compliance orders unconstitutional and the TVA order "legally inconsequential." Furthermore, the court found that EPA's attempt to create procedures for development and review of the EAB Order were inadequate and "ignored the rule of law." The Supreme Court then denied the solicitor general's petition for certiorari. Because the 11th Circuit has declared the EAB decision legally inconsequential, courts have since refused to rely on the EAB decision as having precedential value.[197]

Since the TVA decision was issued by the 11th Circuit, a number of district courts have addressed the substance of EPA's NSR enforcement arguments under the 1980 NSR rules. Many of these courts have agreed with industry (e.g., *Cinergy*[198], *Otter Tail*,[199] *TVA*,[200] *Duke Energy*,[201] *Alabama Power*,[202] *East Kentucky Power Coop.*,[203] *Allegheny Energy*[204]), some have agreed with EPA (e.g., *Ohio Edison*[205] and *SIGECo*[206]), and others have produced mixed results. In *United States v. Ohio Edison*, for example, the court deferred to EPA's NSR interpretations, finding (1) that whether activity is "routine maintenance, repair or replacement" must be determined based on the frequency with which an activity is undertaken at an individual unit, and (2) that an "emissions increase" can occur when annual emissions increase due to increased hours of operation within permit limits. The court noted, however, that EPA had not previously enforced the law in this manner and that EPA had in fact taken positions inconsistent with its enforcement positions. The court attributed this to an "abysmal breakdown" in the implementation and enforcement of NSR[207] and said it would take this "abysmal breakdown" into account in fashioning an appropriate remedy. In March 2005, however, Ohio Edison announced that it had settled its case with the government before the remedy trial began.

By contrast, in *United States v. Duke Energy Corp.*, the court refused to defer to EPA's enforcement positions, finding them inconsistent with the statute, the regulations, and EPA's previous positions.[208] According to the court, the CAA and EPA's regulations require (1) that "routine" be evaluated in terms of common industry practice, and (2) that a significant net increase in annual emissions could occur only when activity creates new pollution (i.e., where there is an increase in the maximum capacity of a facility to emit pollution, unaffected by variations in hours of operation).[209] The "emissions increase" portion of the *Duke Energy* decision was appealed by the Government to the U.S. Court of Appeals for the Fourth Circuit, and the Fourth Circuit upheld the district court decision in June 2005.[210] The Supreme Court granted certiorari to review the Fourth Circuit's decision on May 15, 2006.

On April 2, 2007, the Supreme Court reversed the decision of the Fourth Circuit in *Duke Energy*.[211] According to the Court, the Fourth Circuit was wrong in concluding that Congress's use of the same definition of "modification" for NSPS and NSR programs requires that the term be defined similarly for both programs:

> We hold that the Court of Appeals's reading of the 1980 PSD regulations, intended to align them with NSPS, was inconsistent with their terms and effectively invalidated them; any such result must be shown to comport with the Act's restrictions on judicial review of EPA regulation for validity.[212]

The Court, however, did not address the meaning of the 1980 NSR rules, observing that "[o]n its face . . . the PSD regulations specif[y] no rate at all. . . . What these provisions are getting at is a measure of actual operations averaged over time."[213] Nor did the Court address EPA's authority to define "modification" congruently for NSPS and PSD. Finally, the Court observed that it was not addressing "charges that the agency has taken inconsistent positions and is now 'retroactively targeting twenty years of accepted practice.' "[214]

Precisely what the 1980 PSD rules mean in the context of specific projects therefore is still an open issue in future enforcement cases. For example, the Seventh Circuit has suggested that all that is required for a project *not* to constitute a modification is a reasonable engineering projection that emissions will not increase as a result of the project: a company's duty is "not prescience, but merely a reasonable estimate of the amount of additional emissions the change will cause."[215] Reflecting this approach, the district court for the Western District of Pennsylvania observed that the PSD "regulations . . . did not put the utilities on notice that they were required to use . . . any particular methodology." As a result, the government's burden in an enforcement case, according to that court, is to demonstrate that "*all* reasonable methodologies *must* have projected a significant net increase."[216] And the Sixth Circuit has made clear that, at least under the 2002 NSR reform rules, EPA has no authority to "second guess" an operator's emission projections.[217]

Numerous other NSR enforcement cases are still pending, addressing issues and defenses not addressed or resolved by the Supreme Court in *Duke Energy*.[218] A number of other companies have entered settlements with EPA in order to avoid litigation.[219] Needless to say, this enforcement initiative has brought little clarity to the NSR program.

Conclusion—The modification provision was premised on a simple concept: If an industrial facility engages in activity that creates new pollution (e.g., a facility expands its fuel-burning capacity or exceeds an enforceable restriction on operations), that new pollution must be reviewed and regulated. Over the past two decades, there have been repeated efforts to transform this simple concept into an expansive program that imposes further regulation on most existing, regulated industrial sources of air pollution. At stake in this controversy is the very balance that Congress struck in the CAA regarding regulation of new and existing sources. This controversy will continue over the coming years before the courts addressing NSR enforcement, before EPA in additional NSR rulemaking, and before Congress as it addresses new legislative proposals concerning the CAA.

2.2.4 Minor New Source Review

Under Section 110(a)(2) of the 1970 Act, states must include in their SIPs programs for preconstruction review of the location of newly constructed and modified sources, as necessary to ensure attainment and maintenance of the NAAQS. States have substantial discretion as to the coverage, the substantive content, and the procedural format of these NSR programs, which extend to facilities that are not "major" sources or "major" modifications. (As a result, this program is often referred to as the "minor" NSR program.)

The minor NSR requirement received increased attention in the wake of the 1990 amendments to the CAA as a way of imposing federally enforceable operating limits on industrial facilities to avoid triggering the applicability of major NSR or the Title V operating permit program. Given the potentially broad coverage of the minor NSR program and the requirement for annual compliance certifications under the Title V operating permit program (discussed below), it is important that source owners/operators familiarize themselves with their state's program.

2.3 Specific Pollution Problems

Besides establishing generally applicable air quality and control technology requirements, the CAA addresses a number of specific pollution problems. The most important of these programs involve air toxics emissions, acid rain, visibility degradation, and stratospheric ozone-depleting substances. The Act also addresses the special concerns presented by mobile source emissions.

2.3.1 Air Toxics

Congress, in the 1990 amendments, altered the focus of the air toxics program under Section 112 of the CAA from health-based to technology-based regulation. The following discussion summarizes the key elements of this air toxics regulatory program, which appears at 40 C.F.R. Part 63.

2.3.1.1 Pollutants and Source Categories Subject to Regulation

Unlike the pre-1990 version, the current section 112 focuses on identifying source categories and regulating their HAP emissions rather than identifying and regulating individual HAPs. Section 112(b) establishes an initial list of 190 pollutants to be regulated as HAPs under section 112, including both hazardous organics and metals.[220] Substances can be added to or deleted from this list according to criteria specified in section 112(b)(2). Pursuant to timetables specified in the Act, Congress required EPA to identify all categories of sources of those listed HAPs and establish emission standards for each category.[221]

The Act provides that any stationary source having the potential to emit (a concept discussed under the NSR program) more than 10 tpy of any of the listed substances, or 25 tpy of any combination of the substances, is considered a "major source" and is subject to regulation under the major source program.[222] Whether a source is major for purposes of the air toxics program is defined by adding together the potential to emit of all emission units located at a common site and subject to common ownership, regardless of whether those emission units belong to the same industrial category or are otherwise functionally related.[223] EPA must examine all other sources (i.e., any isolated minor emission units) for regulation under an "area source" program. Specifically, EPA was required to identify the 30 HAPs emitted by area sources presenting the greatest threat to public health in urban areas and to identify and regulate the categories of area sources accounting for 90 percent of those emissions.[224] This program was to be developed within five years of enactment of the 1990 amendments (i.e., by November 15, 1995), but EPA was slow to promulgate area source standards. By the end of 2005, EPA had only promulgated standards for 15 area source categories. Under a court order from the U.S. District Court for the District of Columbia, EPA was required to complete regulatory action on 50 area source categories according to a staggered schedule.[225] EPA has since completed area source rulemakings for all of the source categories it identified.

In July 1992, EPA published an initial list of 174 major source categories of HAPs, such as oil refineries, chemical plants, and the like, that are to be regulated under Section 112.[226] In December 1993, EPA followed this list of source categories with a schedule for promulgation of emission standards that specifies when each of the listed source categories will be regulated.[227] EPA revised this list and its corresponding schedule on February 12, 2002.[228] To date, EPA has completed rulemakings for all of the source categories identified in its February 2002 list.[229]

2.3.1.2 Maximum Achievable Emission Limitations

For each listed category of major sources, EPA must promulgate emission standards—known as national emission standards for HAPs, or NESHAPs—requiring the application of measures that will result in the "maximum degree of reduction" that is achievable in light of economic, energy, and environmental considerations. This requirement has been referred to as the maximum achievable control technology, or MACT, standard. EPA is to base the standard on the best technology currently available for the source category in question, and these standards must be at least as stringent as the level achieved in practice by the best controlled source in the source category (for new source MACT standards) or by the best performing group of sources (for existing source MACT standards).[230] For existing source MACT standards, EPA defines the MACT floor (i.e., the minimum stringency level for existing source MACT) in terms of the central tendency (i.e., arithmetic mean or median) of the best performing 12 percent of sources in the source category (where there are 30 or more sources in the category) or the best performing five sources (where there are fewer than 30 sources in the category).

These NESHAPs were to be issued according to the schedule originally issued by EPA in December 1993. The first standards, referred to as the hazardous organic NESHAP, or HON, were finalized in March 1994. The HON addresses emissions of listed air toxics from approximately 370 synthetic and nonsynthetic organic chemical manufacturers and more than 940 chemical manufacturing processes. The standards require control of emissions from distillation, reactor and air oxidation process vents, wastewater operations, storage vessels, transfer operations, and equipment leaks.

Other source categories subject to NESHAPs include coke ovens, industrial cooling towers, halogenated solvent cleaning, magnetic tape manufacturing operations, gasoline terminals and pipeline breakout stations, petroleum refineries, aerospace manufacturing, wood furniture manufacturing, printing and publishing, and various aspects of polymer and resin production.[231] EPA updated its schedule for developing these standards several times, most recently on February 12, 2002.[232] EPA has issued standards for all of the source categories listed in the February 2002 list.

EPA has also issued regulations allowing exemptions from the NESHAPs for existing sources where the source demonstrates that it has achieved a voluntary reduction of 90 percent or more in emissions of a HAP before proposal of the NESHAP (95 percent for HAPs that are particulates). In this case, the source may be eligible for an extension of the standard's compliance deadline.[233] Final rules implementing this early reduction program were published in December 1992 and later amended in November 1993.[234] A final rule defining high-risk pollutants for purposes of this early reduction program (i.e., pollutants for which the use of offsets to establish program eligibility is limited) was issued in June 1994,[235] and a final rule providing a temporary permit mechanism to make early reductions enforceable was published in November 1994.[236]

Compliance with existing NESHAPs was complicated by the D.C. Circuit's 2008 decision in *Sierra Club v. EPA*, which vacated the exemption from complying with MACT standards during start-up, shutdown, and malfunction (SSM) events.[237] Under longstanding EPA policy, emissions during these SSM events were subject to a "general duty" to minimize emissions rather than a numeric emission limit. The court found that the CAA requires that a § 112 standard apply to a source's emissions on a continuous basis, and that the SSM exemption and its "general duty" to minimize emissions did not satisfy that requirement. As a result of this decision, facilities are now required to comply with MACT limits at all times, absent promulgation of alternative requirements that apply different limitations or work practice standards during SSM events.[238]

2.3.1.3 Source-Specific MACT and State Air Toxics Programs

Where EPA has missed the scheduled deadline for establishing a federal NESHAP for a source category, section 112(j) of the CAA requires that the Title V permit program be used to establish source-specific MACT standards. In June

1994, EPA promulgated rules providing guidance for establishment of source-specific MACT standards when EPA fails to promulgate a NESHAP.[239] In general, states with approved Title V programs must establish source-specific MACT standards through a Title V permit proceeding within 18 months of the missed regulatory deadline. On some occasions in the past, upon missing its regulatory deadlines, EPA has delayed the requirement for source-specific MACT standards by extending the effective date of the section 112(j) program.[240]

Questions have arisen about the applicability of § 112(j) in cases where EPA adopts a NESHAP for a source category, but the NESHAP is subsequently vacated upon judicial review by the D.C. Circuit. On March 30, 2010, EPA issued a proposed rule aimed at clarifying when § 112(j) applies and when facilities need to submit source-specific MACT applications.[241] In that rule, EPA proposed to interpret § 112(j) to require source-specific MACT standards where a NESHAP is completely vacated. EPA has yet to take final action on the proposal.

In addition, section 112(*l*) of the Act authorizes EPA to delegate implementation and enforcement of section 112 standards to states that meet certain criteria.[242] EPA has issued rules under section 112(*l*) providing guidance on the development of federally approvable state air toxics programs.[243] Under these rules, state air toxics programs may be substituted for the federal air toxics program where, *inter alia*, the state can demonstrate that its program is at least as stringent as the federal program.

2.3.1.4 Residual Risk and Technology Review

Because the MACT standards are technology based rather than health based, the 1990 amendments provide for a second phase of regulatory controls aimed at protecting public health with an "ample margin of safety." This health-based inquiry must take place for each source category no later than eight years after a MACT standard has been established for the source category. For known or suspected carcinogens, section 112(f) requires consideration of further control if the MACT standard does not reduce lifetime risk for the most exposed individual to a level of less than one in one million.[244] In addition, under section 112(f) EPA must assess whether the MACT standard sufficiently prevents adverse environmental effects.

In January 1997, EPA announced a Risk Identification Program to be used to set priorities for regulating HAPs, source categories, and geographic areas pursuant to the section 112(f) residual risk program. In March 1999, EPA submitted a Residual Risk Report to Congress addressing carcinogenic compounds.[245] This report describes the Agency's plans for implementation of section 112(f), in particular the "methods to be used to assess the risk remaining (i.e., the residual risk) after control technology standards applicable to emission sources of . . . HAPs have been promulgated and applied."[246]

In addition, the Act also provides for periodic review of section 112(d) standards to account for improvements over time in emission control technology. Under the technology review program, EPA must review its original section 112(d) standards for each source category every eight years and revise them "as necessary" to account for developments in practices, processes, and control technologies.[247]

EPA has developed a Risk and Technology Review (RTR) plan to evaluate both risk and technology as required by CAA § 112(d)(6) and (f) after the application of MACT standards. The Agency promulgated its first RTR rule in April 2005, and as of June 2016 had completed a total of 41 reviews.[248] EPA has generally lagged behind the eight-year deadline for conducting RTR rulemakings for each source category, prompting advocacy groups to file lawsuits seeking to compel the Agency to conduct RTR analyses for various source categories. EPA is currently subject to court orders and consent decrees requiring it to conduct RTR rulemakings for four different source categories,[249] and as of June 2016 several more lawsuits are pending that seek to impose timelines for RTR analysis of at least 43 additional source categories.[250]

EPA implements its § 112(f) residual risk obligations pursuant to a two-step analytical framework first outlined in its 1989 NESHAP rulemaking for benzene emissions.[251] Under this "Benzene" framework, EPA first determines whether the existing standard presents an acceptable level of risk based on health factors alone. Then, the Agency assesses whether the standard provides an "ample margin of safety," taking into account cost, feasibility, and other relevant factors in addition to health. EPA has determined that a health risk below 100 in one million is presumptively acceptable at the first step. Further, at the second step, a risk below one in one million presumptively affords an ample margin of safety. If the risk falls between one and 100 in one million, EPA must conduct the residual risk analysis, but has discretion to readopt its original MACT standards so long as EPA concludes they provide an ample margin of safety after considering the relevant factors.

In implementing § 112(d)(6), EPA is not required to recalculate the MACT floor each time it conducts a technology review: instead, the review is more akin to setting a "beyond-the-floor" standard under § 112(d)(2).[252] The Agency has taken a broad view of the "developments in practices, processes, and control technologies" that may justify more stringent emission standards. In addition to new control technologies, EPA has found that improvements in capture efficiency, reduced costs, or advancements in measurement technology may trigger new requirements under § 112(d)(6). The D.C. Circuit has also held that EPA is not required to tie changes in its standards adopted pursuant to the technology review to any specific "developments" in practices, processes, or control technologies. Instead, it is sufficient for EPA to "assess and discuss the collective impact of the developments it has identified, and to revise standards appropriately in light thereof."[253]

2.3.1.5 Industrial Boiler MACT

EPA's industrial boiler (IB) MACT rule is of great interest to the broad spectrum of industrial facilities that operate boilers. The rule has generated much controversy over the last decade because of the range of fuels these units burn and the wide variety of boiler types. A key issue that EPA has confronted in promulgating IB MACT limits is determining whether a unit is an IB subject to § 112(d) MACT standards or whether it is a commercial or industrial solid waste incineration (CISWI) unit subject to regulation exclusively under CAA § 129. EPA's initial IB MACT and CISWI rules were vacated by the D.C. Circuit in *Natural Resources Defense Council v. EPA* because EPA improperly defined IBs to include some units that meet the statutory definition of a CISWI unit.[254] In *NRDC*, the court found that a source is a CISWI unit if it "combusts any commercial or industrial solid waste material at all," subject only to the four exclusions listed in CAA § 129(g)(1).[255]

Following the *NRDC* decision, in March 2011 EPA issued revised IB MACT and CISWI rules and further clarified which units would be subject to each rule by issuing a new definition of defining the "non-hazardous secondary materials" that qualify as solid waste for the purposes of CAA § 129.[256] After receiving numerous petitions for reconsideration, EPA further modified its IB MACT standards and published final rules for major source and area source IBs on January 31, 2013, and February 1, 2013, respectively.[257] The 2013 IB MACT rule has been challenged by numerous industrial groups and environmental organizations.[258] Among the issues the petitioners raised are: (1) the subcategories of IBs chosen by EPA, (2) the approach EPA used to set MACT limits, (3) EPA's decision to require work practice standards for some HAPs, (4) EPA's choice of CO as a surrogate for some organic HAPs, (5) the provisions governing SSM events, and (6) EPA's failure to set alternative health based limits for HAPs such as hydrogen chloride (HCl). Oral argument was heard before the D.C. Circuit on December 3, 2015, but as of June 2016, no decision had been issued.

In January 2015, EPA issued a reconsideration proposal to provide an opportunity for public comment on certain requirements in the 2013 IB MACT rule.[259] The proposal was limited to: (1) the definitions of startup and shutdown periods; (2) alternative PM standards for low-sulfur oil boilers; (3) establishment of a subcategory for limited-use boilers and (4) the applicable standards for those units; and (5) provisions eliminating certain performance testing and fuel sampling requirements. The final reconsideration rule was published on November 20, 2015.[260] A number of environmental advocacy groups challenged the reconsidered IB MACT provisions, and the litigation is ongoing, with briefing scheduled to conclude in December 2016.[261] Among the issues expected to be raised in that case are EPA's CO emission limit and its adoption of work practice standards for periods of startup and shutdown.

2.3.1.6 HAP Emissions from Coal- and Oil-Fired Electric Utility Steam-Generating Units

Congress singled out electric utility steam generating units (EGUs) for special treatment under section 112 in the 1990 amendments. Recognizing that EGUs were already subject to numerous CAA programs regulating other pollutants (including the 1990 amendments' new Title IV acid rain program) that were likely to yield incidental reductions in HAP emissions, Congress declined to treat EGUs like other source categories. Instead, section 112(n)(1)(A) directs EPA to study the public health risks anticipated to remain after imposition of the CAA's other requirements that apply to EGUs. Then, based on the results of that study, EPA may only regulate EGUs under section 112 if it is "appropriate and necessary" to do so.

EPA's numerous attempts to implement this provision span multiple presidential administrations and reflect competing approaches as to how and whether to regulate EGUs under section 112. In December 2000, shortly before President Clinton left the White House, EPA issued a finding that it was "appropriate and necessary" to regulate coal- and oil-fired EGUs under section 112.[262] Consequently, EPA listed those units as a source category under section 112(c). The "appropriate and necessary" finding did not encompass natural gas-fired EGUs, which EPA concluded present negligible public health risks due to HAP emissions.

However, under the administration of President George W. Bush, EPA decided in 2005 to regulate mercury emissions from coal-fired EGUs under CAA section 111 rather than section 112. Accordingly, EPA withdrew the 2000 "appropriate and necessary" finding and issued the Clean Air Mercury Rule (CAMR), which established a cap-and-trade program for mercury emissions from both new and existing EGUs as well as standards of performance for new EGUs.[263] Under the cap-and-trade program, all sources had to hold allowances for their emissions, and were subject to a nationwide cap on the amount of mercury emissions actually emitted. Because allowances were freely tradable, utilities had incentives to reduce mercury emissions in the most cost-effective manner.

The D.C. Circuit vacated CAMR on February 8, 2008, in response to challenges from environmental groups and certain states.[264] The court did not reach the merits of the CAMR regulatory program; instead, it held that the rule violated the CAA because EPA failed to follow the proper procedures to remove EGUs from its list of source categories under section 112(c). According to the court, once EPA lists any source category—including EGUs—it cannot "delist" the category without following the specific procedures provided by Congress in section 112(c)(9). And because EGUs had not been properly removed from the section 112(c) source category list, then under EPA's own interpretation of the Act, it could not simultaneously regulate them under section 111. On remand, and pursuant to a consent decree, EPA proposed new MACT standards for new and existing EGUs under section 112 in March 2011, and published a final rule in February 2012.[265] The rule, known as the Mercury and Air Toxics Standards (MATS) Rule, sets emission limits for mercury, non-mercury metals (with filterable PM as a surrogate), and hydrochloric acid (with SO_2 as a surrogate), and establishes work practice standards for the control of organic HAPs. In promulgating the MATS Rule, EPA reaffirmed its 2000 finding that it is "appropriate and necessary" to regulate HAP emissions from EGUs under section 112. The Agency also rejected commenters' arguments that in assessing whether regulation is "appropriate," EPA must consider the cost of such regulation. By EPA's estimates, the MATS Rule was projected to cost $9.6 billion—the most expensive CAA rulemaking to date. While EPA also estimated that the Rule would provide $37 to $90 billion in total monetized benefits, only $4 to $6 million of that total was the result of reduced HAP emissions, with the remainder due to the co-benefits of reducing $PM_{2.5}$ exposure.[266]

Thirty petitions for review were filed challenging the MATS rule. Key issues raised in those challenges included: (1) EPA's legal interpretation of § 112(n)(1)(A), including its conclusion that the Agency is not required to consider cost when determining whether regulation is "appropriate"; (2) the factual bases for EPA's conclusion that regulation of EGUs under § 112 is "appropriate and necessary"; (3) EPA's decision not to distinguish between major and area sources in setting MACT limits; (4) the pool of best performing units EPA chose to set the mercury limits for existing units; and (5) the legality of the Rule's averaging and quarterly stack testing provisions. The D.C. Circuit denied the consolidated petitions for review of the MATS Rule in April 2014.[267] However, in a partial dissent, Judge Kavanaugh argued that it was unreasonable for EPA to exclude cost from its analysis of whether regulation was "appropriate."[268]

Several challengers successfully petitioned for a writ of certiorari to the Supreme Court on the question of whether EPA violated the CAA by failing to consider the MATS Rule's costs in its "appropriate and necessary" finding. In

June 2015, the Supreme Court held in *Michigan v. EPA* that "it was unreasonable for EPA to read [section 112(n)(1)(A)] to mean that cost is irrelevant to the initial decision to regulate power plants."[269] In its 5–4 decision, the Court found that "reasonable regulation ordinarily requires paying attention to the advantages *and* the disadvantages of agency decisions," and that "[n]o regulation is 'appropriate' if it does significantly more harm than good."[270] However, the Court noted that it would be up to EPA to determine how to go about considering costs, within the limits of reasonable interpretation. On remand, the D.C. Circuit remanded the MATS Rule for further proceedings consistent with the Supreme Court's decision, but declined to vacate the Rule.[271]

In response to the Supreme Court's decision in *Michigan*, in April 2015 EPA published a Supplemental Finding concluding that, even after considering the costs of the MATS Rule, it is "appropriate and necessary" under section 112(n)(1)(A) to regulate HAP emissions from EGUs.[272] EPA presented two alternative approaches for considering costs. Under its "preferred," qualitative approach, EPA assessed the MATS Rule's costs in light of: (1) the utility industry's annual revenue; (2) its annual capital and operating expenditures; (3) expected electricity price increases; and (4) the MATS Rule's effects on generating capacity and electric reliability. After finding that the Rule's costs are "reasonable" under each of these metrics, and noting the hazards that HAPs present generally, EPA determined that it was "appropriate" to regulate EGUs under section 112. In the alternative, EPA stated that its 2011 Regulatory Impact Analysis for the MATS Rule provides an independent, quantitative approach to the section 112(n)(1)(A) analysis. Because the Rule's benefits (when $PM_{2.5}$ co-benefits are included) outweigh its costs, EPA again found that regulation is "appropriate."

Industry groups and fifteen states filed petitions for review of the Supplemental Finding April through June 2016.[273] No briefing schedule has been set.

2.3.1.7 Prevention of Accidental Releases

The 1990 amendments require EPA to promulgate regulations to prevent accidental releases of certain hazardous substances.[274] Under EPA's risk management program (RMP) regulations, owners and operators of facilities at which such substances are present in more than a threshold quantity must prepare risk management plans for each substance used at the facility. EPA may also require annual audits and safety inspections to prevent leaks and other episodic releases. EPA promulgated its List of Regulated Substances under section 112(r) on January 31, 1994,[275] and issued regulations implementing the Accidental Release Prevention Program on June 20, 1996.[276] Sources were required to submit risk management plans for regulated chemicals by June 21, 1999, or the date on which a regulated substance first becomes present above a threshold quantity in a process, whichever is later.[277]

In March 2016, EPA proposed to revise its RMP regulations. The proposal is part of President Obama's efforts under Executive Order 13650 to improve chemical facility safety and security in response to a catastrophic explosion at a West, Texas, fertilizer facility in 2013.[278] The proposed revisions would generally increase regulated facilities' obligations with respect to investigating incidents, coordinating with first responders, and disclosing facility information. In particular, EPA proposes to: (1) redefine "catastrophic releases" triggering incident investigations to include releases that have on-site, as well as off-site, impacts; (2) require that compliance audits be performed by third parties, with strict prohibitions against hiring auditors with an "established relationship" with the facility owner or operator; (3) allow first responders to require that a facility prepare an emergency response program; and (4) require that facilities provide certain information about the facility's regulated substances, its accident history, and its emergency response procedures to the public through a website or other appropriate means. As of June 2016, EPA has not taken further action on the proposal.

2.3.2 Acid Rain

One of the most innovative regulatory programs established by the 1990 CAA amendments concerns the control of SO_2 and NOx, precursors of acid deposition. The centerpiece of Title IV of the 1990 amendments is the establishment of an emission allowance and trading program for electric-generating sources that emit SO_2. Through the allowance program, Title IV imposes a "cap" on total SO_2 emissions from these sources that represents about a 50 percent reduction from 1980 levels. The program also reduces NOx emissions from coal-fired electric-generating sources by directing EPA to impose NOx emission rate limitations on those sources.

On January 11, 1993, EPA published final rules addressing acid rain permits,[279] SO_2 emission allowance tracking and trading,[280] emission monitoring,[281] excess emissions penalties and offset plans,[282] and the administrative appeals process.[283] EPA also issued the standard forms needed for permit applications and compliance plans.

Sources subject to emission limitations under Title IV were assigned SO_2 allowances under tables and formulas in the statute.[284] An allowance is defined as an authorization to emit one ton of SO_2.[285] Final SO_2 allowance allocations were published in March 1993,[286] and adjustments of allowance allocations for a limited number of electric utility units were published in September 1998.[287]

A unit's SO_2 emissions during a given calendar year must not exceed the allowances held by that unit for that year. If they do, the unit's owner/operator is subject to penalties that are designed to be more costly than compliance. The 1990 amendments specify that allowances can be terminated or limited by the federal government.[288]

The Act makes specific SO_2 allowance allocations to Phase I units (i.e., electric-generating units that were required to comply with the Title IV program beginning January 1, 1995) and specifies formulas for allowances for 2000 and later years for both Phase I units and Phase II units (i.e., units that were required to comply with the Title IV program beginning January 1, 2000). Source owners and operators could submit compliance plans to pursue certain optional control strategies, particularly in Phase I (1995–2000).[289]

EPA's Title IV regulations set up an allowance auction to be held annually for a limited number of allowances established by statute.[290] Anyone may purchase allowances at the auction. All of the Phase I and Phase II allowances offered by EPA have been purchased each year because there is no minimum bid requirement.

In 1995, the Agency promulgated regulations addressing criteria and procedures for allowing owners and operators of industrial boilers, small electric-generating boilers, and other combustion sources not subject to the mandatory requirements of Title IV voluntarily to opt into the Title IV program.[291] The purpose of the opt-in program is to increase the number of allowances available, while expanding the scope of sources subject to the Title IV control requirements. Sources that opt into the program are subject to all of the program's permitting and monitoring requirements.

Title IV also addresses emissions of NOx. Under Section 407 of the Act, EPA established allowable emission rates for NOx emissions from certain categories of Phase I and Phase II coal-fired electric utility boilers. These allowable NOx emission rates, together with provisions permitting averaging of emission rates and alternative emission limitations under certain circumstances, are set out in 40 C.F.R. Part 76.

2.3.3 Visibility Protection and AQRVs

2.3.3.1 1977 CAA Amendments

In the 1977 CAA amendments, Congress established a national goal of preventing future and remedying existing man-made visibility impairment in "mandatory Class I areas"[292] and required that states make "reasonable progress" toward attaining that goal.[293] To make "reasonable progress" toward that goal, states are to develop requirements for best available retrofit technology (BART) and long-term strategies that address sources contributing to visibility impairment in Class I areas as part of the SIP process.[294]

In 1980, EPA adopted regulations addressing the criteria for SIPs for visibility impairment and directed states to focus regulatory attention on sources that cause plume blight (i.e., visible plumes in a Class I area readily traceable to a single source or a specific group of sources), also referred to as "reasonably attributable visibility impairment" (RAVI). The more technically complex and controversial issue of regulating sources that contribute to regional haze was specifically deferred.

During the 1980s, EPA found that, for all but one state and one Class I area, there were no sources to which plume blight was "reasonably attributable." Accordingly, in reviewing the adequacy of SIPs, EPA concluded that the 1980 visibility rules were satisfied by current SIP requirements except to the extent that the states needed to incorporate in their SIPs procedural requirements to ensure that visibility impairment would be addressed (e.g., through establishment of BART limits) if it were to occur.

In the early 1990s, EPA concluded (based on multi-million-dollar "tracer" technical studies and agreement among the parties) that visibility impairment in Grand Canyon National Park in Arizona could reasonably be attributed to the Navajo Generating Station (a coal-fired electric utility plant 10 miles from the park's boundary) and therefore initiated a regulatory program to address this issue. This finding was based on a National Park Service study in 1987 and a study by the owners of the Navajo Generating Station in 1990, both of which involved the release of artificial tracers from the Navajo Generating Station. Based on these studies and extensive public comment, EPA published a formal reasonable attribution rule in 1991 that called for 90 percent removal of SO_2 emissions from the Navajo Generating Station on a plantwide, annual average basis as BART for the facility.[295]

2.3.3.2 Visibility Impairment and the 1990 Amendments

The 1990 amendments to the Act addressed visibility in several respects. First, Congress authorized a $40 million, five-year research program to evaluate Class I area visibility impairment.[296] Second, Congress established a procedure for creating Visibility Transport Commissions made up of governors from states with sources that contribute significantly to interstate visibility impairment in Class I areas.[297] The 1990 amendments also established a visibility transport commission for the region affecting visibility in the Grand Canyon National Park.[298] These commissions are to make recommendations to EPA concerning what measures, if any, should be taken to remedy adverse visibility impacts from potential or projected growth in emissions from sources in the region.[299] Third, based on the commissions' recommendations, EPA must "carry out" its responsibility to facilitate development of a regional haze program.[300]

Pursuant to these provisions, EPA in 1999 developed a new regulatory program addressing regional haze in Class I areas.[301] This regional haze program will result in significant additional reductions in emissions of visibility-impairing pollutants such as SO_2 and NOx (which contribute to sulfate and nitrate concentrations) and PM. Under this rule, states are to require certain relatively large sources that contribute to haze in Class I areas to install BART, and states must also develop long-term strategies designed to achieve "reasonable progress" toward the goal of remedying man-made visibility impairment in Class I areas by 2064. States are to determine what rate of progress is reasonable for their Class I areas based on consideration of certain factors, including the costs of emission controls. States were required to submit their first "reasonable progress" and BART SIPs for regional haze by December 2007, although all but two states missed that deadline. On January 15, 2009, EPA published a finding of failure to submit regional haze SIPs (or, in some case, failure to submit complete regional haze SIPs) by 37 states, the District of Columbia, and the Virgin Islands.[302] Publication of this finding initiated a two-year "clock" for EPA's adoption of FIPs for those that have not submitted and received EPA approval of regional haze SIPs during that period.

In 2002, the U.S. Court of Appeals for the D.C. Circuit vacated in part and upheld in part EPA's 1999 regional haze regulations.[303] The D.C. Circuit ruled that the regulations' goal of achieving natural visibility conditions in Class I areas was permissible under the Act because the regulations do not "mandate" that the goal be achieved.[304] The court vacated the provisions relating to BART, however, concluding that they were "inconsistent with the Act's provisions giving the states broad authority over BART determinations"[305] because they required states to aggregate sources' emissions in analyzing their contribution to Class I area visibility impairment rather than allowing states to make an individual-source contribution determination. The court also held that the regulations unlawfully directed the states, in determining BART emission limits for an individual source, to consider the aggregate impact on visibility of controls on all sources in the region. The court held that states, in determining BART for a source, must consider only the visibility improvement from controls on that source individually.

In 2005, EPA published extensive revisions to the regional haze regulations in response to the D.C. Circuit's 2002 decision.[306] The 2005 rule revisions changed provisions of the 1999 rules that the court had vacated and, among other things, addressed the interaction of the BART requirements with the CAIR requirements as applied to electric-generating units. Certain provisions of the 2005 rule revisions were challenged by an environmental group and industry parties in the D.C. Circuit and were upheld by that court.[307]

On October 13, 2006, EPA published rules providing for alternatives to BART that states may opt to include in their SIPs.[308] These alternatives, which can include market-based emission trading programs, are subject to certain criteria designed to ensure that they produce greater reasonable progress toward improving visibility in Class I areas than would be achieved through traditional source-by-source BART.

EPA's actions to implement the regional haze program in recent years have proven controversial for a number of reasons. EPA action on state-specific implementation plans in the West, for instance, have frequently resulted in disagreements over the relationship between state and federal regulatory authority and how the BART factors must be weighed in reaching BART determinations. The Agency's 2011 final rulemaking actions on BART for Oklahoma[309] and New Mexico,[310] for example, rejected or wholly ignored state BART determinations contained in SIPs submitted for EPA approval and instead imposed FIPs with significantly different (and much more stringent) BART requirements. Both of those rules were challenged in the U.S. Court of Appeals for the Tenth Circuit by state officials and affected utilities. The Tenth Circuit issued a decision in *Oklahoma v. EPA* in July 2013, upholding EPAs disapproval of Oklahoma's regional haze SIP on the grounds that the state had improperly considered the cost factor in determining BART for two power plants.[311] The court also upheld EPA's FIP, deferring to EPA's assessment of the BART factors. The New Mexico litigation is in the process of being resolved through promulgation of a revised regional haze SIP, which EPA has proposed to approve.[312]

Environmental groups, on the other hand, have taken issue with the length of the compliance timeframes EPA has allowed for BART implementation (typically five years) and have, on occasion, challenged in federal court individual BART determinations as too lenient.[313] In 2013, the Eighth Circuit upheld EPA's partial approval of North Dakota's regional haze SIP for the Milton R. Young and Leland Olds Stations against such a challenge.[314]

In the East, regional haze-related controversy has centered primarily around EPA actions regarding reliance on other regulatory programs as BART alternatives for states subject to those programs. In conjunction with EPA's promulgation of CAIR, a NOx and SO_2 emission trading program applicable to 28 eastern states and the District of Columbia, EPA promulgated a rule declaring that states subject to CAIR's emission trading programs could rely on compliance with CAIR's requirements instead of requiring source-by-source BART for utilities within the CAIR states, i.e., the "CAIR = BART" rule.[315] Following EPA's promulgation of the CAIR = BART rule, the D.C. Circuit remanded CAIR to EPA, leaving it in place until EPA could promulgate a valid replacement rule for CAIR.[316]

On August 8, 2011, EPA promulgated CSAPR as a replacement for CAIR. CSAPR is also a NOx and SO_2 emissions trading program. After CSAPR's promulgation, EPA promulgated a "CSAPR = BART" rule to replace the CAIR = BART rule. That rule also disapproved all SIPs that relied on CAIR to satisfy BART requirements and promulgated FIPs replacing reliance on CAIR with reliance on CSAPR.[317] After EPA's promulgation of the CSAPR = BART rule, the D.C. Circuit vacated CSAPR and ordered that CAIR continue in effect until such time as EPA could promulgate a valid replacement rule.[318] The Supreme Court subsequently reversed that D.C. Circuit decision,[319] but, in subsequent "as-applied" challenges to CSAPR invited by the Supreme Court's decision, the D.C. Circuit remanded CSAPR budgets for a number of states,[320] creating uncertainty over the status of the CSAPR = BART rule and SIPs and FIPs related to that rule.

A number of parties have challenged various elements of the CSAPR = BART rule, and those cases have been consolidated and were held in abeyance by the U.S. Court of Appeals for the D.C. Circuit, pending resolution of much of the litigation over CSAPR. In May 2016, the D.C. Circuit issued an order establishing a briefing schedule in the CSAPR = BART litigation.[321] If that schedule remains in place, briefing would be completed in early 2017.

With the close of the first regional haze planning period approaching in 2018, EPA has also proposed new revisions to the regional haze rules that would govern implementation during the second planning period.[322] In addition to proposing to extend the deadline for submittal of new regional haze SIPs until July 31, 2021, the proposed rule includes new provisions related to reasonable progress and long-term strategies, and also includes extensive and possibly meaningful revisions to the RAVI provisions of EPA's visibility rules.

2.3.3.3 Visibility Impairment, AQRVs, and the NSR Program

Under the PSD permit program, before a permitting authority may issue a permit authorizing construction of a new or modified source, it must consider whether emissions from the proposed source "will have an adverse impact on the air quality-related values (including visibility)" of any Class I areas.[323] Based on this provision, FLMs have raised the issue of visibility impairment in a number of CAA permit proceedings. The U.S. Forest Service (Forest Service) has also developed a workbook to guide local FLMs in deciding whether proposed new sources would have an adverse impact on the AQRVs of Class I areas. This workbook indicates that the Forest Service is dissatisfied with the current air quality in many Class I areas and advises individual FLMs to challenge the licensing of new sources. The National Park Service has taken a similar approach, urging that proposed new facilities obtain offsetting emission reductions to ensure that those facilities add no contribution to atmospheric loadings of emissions that the FLMs regard as unacceptable. In 2010, an FLM workgroup released a revised guidance document addressing issues relevant to review of new sources' effects on visibility and other AQRVs in Class I areas.

2.3.4 Stratospheric Ozone Protection

In the mid-1970s, EPA expressed concern that certain chlorine-and bromine-containing chemicals were destroying stratospheric ozone—a thin, gaseous layer in the upper atmosphere that blocks ultraviolet radiation from the sun. At the time, these chemicals, known as ozone-depleting substances (ODSs), were used in thousands of everyday products, including refrigerators, air conditioners, industrial cleaning solvents, insulating foam-blowing agents, fire suppressants, and aerosol sprays.

Voluntary measures in the United States and elsewhere in the late 1970s helped curb ODS emissions temporarily, but in many cases adequate substitutes had not yet been developed and a surge in demand in the early 1980s ultimately swamped these efforts. In the mid-1980s, the international community responded to concerns about a "hole" in the stratospheric ozone layer over Antarctica by negotiating the Montreal Protocol on Substances That Deplete the Ozone Layer in 1987. The Montreal Protocol, which established binding commitments for both developed and developing countries to phase out ODS production, was signed by President Reagan and ratified by the Senate in a unanimous vote in 1988. It has since been signed and ratified by 191 countries.

Title VI of the CAA Amendments of 1990 established the regulatory regime that fulfills U.S. commitments under the Montreal Protocol, including any amendments or adjustments. Amendments, which require separate Senate ratification, have been used to establish the Montreal Protocol's financial mechanism and add new chemicals to its phase-out schedules. Adjustments, which have the force of amendments but do not require separate ratification, have been used to accelerate phase-out schedules. The Montreal Protocol has been amended four times and adjusted six times, most recently in 2007 to accelerate the phase-out of hydrochlorofluorocarbons (HCFCs).

Title VI establishes a phase-out program for ODS production that generally tracks Montreal Protocol requirements. The program relies on marketable allowances allocated by EPA to regulated entities to promote flexibility and cost-effectiveness. Like the Montreal Protocol, Title VI focuses on regulating production of ODSs, as opposed to emissions of ODSs, with production defined as production plus imports minus exports. This production-emissions distinction is important in two respects. First, unlike large stationary or mobile sources, ODS emissions can come from a wide variety of small applications, such as fire extinguishers, aerosol sprays, and foam-blowing agents, that are far too numerous to regulate directly. By contrast, there are a relatively small number of entities that produce ODSs. Second, while the use of fire extinguishers, aerosol sprays, foam-blowing agents, and other applications typically results in the immediate release of the ODSs they contain, refrigerators and air conditioners will still contain a significant amount of the ODS it used as a refrigerant at equipment end-of-life. Under its Title VI authority, EPA has targeted these emissions separately from its overall production phase-out by promulgating a variety of regulations on refrigerant recovery, recycling, and disposal.

Title VI creates two classes of ODSs. Class I substances include the most potent ODSs, such as chlorofluorocarbons (CFCs), halons, carbon tetrachloride, methyl chloroform, and methyl bromide. HCFCs, which generally are less potent than Class I substances, are listed as Class II substances. EPA is authorized to add chemicals to either list, but this authority is limited to substances that contribute to stratospheric ozone depletion. Title VI requires EPA to establish Ozone Depletion Potentials (ODPs) for Class I and Class II substances, which measure their relative impacts on the ozone layer. Title VI also requires manufacturers to label all products that contain or were made through the use of a Class I or Class II substance.

The production of virtually all Class I substances was phased out between 1994 and 1996. The remaining Class I substance, methyl bromide, was phased out in 2005. Title VI creates numerous exemptions for applications that rely on Class I substances and meet certain criteria, such as overriding social, economic, public health, or national security considerations, or if adequate substitutes are not widely available. These exemptions include: essential use exemptions for CFCs used as propellants in metered-dose inhalers that treat asthma and chronic obstructive pulmonary disease; critical use exemptions for methyl bromide for various agricultural uses; and quarantine and pre-shipment exemptions for methyl bromide used to fumigate shipping containers and wood pallets used in international commerce. Title VI provides for a broad de minimis exemption for laboratory and analytical uses and allows production of certain Class I substances for export to developing countries, which phase out ODSs later in time than developed countries. EPA also has promulgated a series of rules establishing outright bans on "nonessential" products containing Class I substances, such as plastic party streamers and noise horns that use CFC propellants and CFC-containing polyurethane foams used in packaging.

Class II substances include all HCFCs, many of which were introduced in the late 1980s and early 1990s as temporary substitutes for CFCs. Under Title VI, the production of all Class II substances will be completely phased out by 2030, with most Class II substances subject to earlier phase-out dates. This is more stringent than the Montreal Protocol, which does not differentiate between HCFCs. This differentiation, or "worst first" approach to the phase-out of HCFCs, first targets emissive uses of HCFCs that have the highest ODPs. For example, HCFC-141b, a Class II substance widely used as a foam-blowing agent, an emissive use, was phased out in 2003. Two widely used refrigerants with relatively high ODPs, HCFC-142b and HCFC-22, were to be phased out in 2010, with an exception, expiring in 2020, for use in equipment manufactured prior to 2010. All remaining HCFCs will be phased out by 2015, with an exception, expiring in 2030, for use in equipment manufactured prior to 2020. Exemptions similar to those available for Class I substances for essential and other uses may become available, but likely not until after the final phase-out in 2030. Under the Montreal Protocol, essential use and other exemptions are only available for substances that have been completely phased out.

Title VI also created the Significant New Alternatives Policy (SNAP), under which EPA reviews and approves ODS substitutes. The review process is based on a determination that the substitute in question does not present a greater risk than other available alternatives. To date, most ozone-depleting substances have been replaced with substitutes and alternatives that do not deplete the ozone layer. In particular, hydrofluorocarbons (HFCs) have replaced CFCs and HCFCs in virtually all applications and particularly in refrigeration and air conditioning appliances. Although HFCs do not deplete the ozone layer, they are considered GHGs, and their contribution to climate change has increased largely in tandem with their increasing use as ODS substitutes.

Looking forward, the success of the Montreal Protocol and Title VI in phasing out CFCs and HCFCs has prompted discussion of phasing out HFCs in a similar manner, perhaps even under the Montreal Protocol and Title VI. In its Advanced Notice of Proposed Rulemaking for Regulating Greenhouse Gases under the Clean Air Act, released in July 2008, EPA specifically asked for comment on how elements of the existing Title VI program could be used to provide further climate protection. A draft climate change bill released in October 2008 proposed separating HFCs from the five other primary GHGs and amending Title VI to provide for an HFC phase-down. And at the twentieth Meeting of the Parties to the Montreal Protocol in November 2008, the parties issued a decision calling for an open-ended dialogue to exchange views on how the experience of the Montreal Protocol can be used to address the impact of HFCs.

2.3.5 Climate Change

The scope of the CAA was dramatically expanded by the Supreme Court in *Massachusetts v. EPA*, 549 U.S. 497 (2007). Prior to *Massachusetts*, carbon dioxide (CO_2) and other so-called "greenhouse gases" (GHGs) were not considered by EPA to be air pollutants that could be regulated under the CAA. This position was based, in part, on the 1990 amendments to the CAA, in which Congress specifically considered but rejected proposals to amend the CAA to authorize regulation of CO_2 emissions.

In the regulatory proceeding that led to *Massachusetts*, EPA denied a petition for regulation of GHG emissions, including CO_2, from new light duty vehicles (LDVs) under § 202 of the Act. According to EPA, CO_2 did not fall within the general definition of "air pollutant" in § 302 of the Act. The Supreme Court disagreed. According to the Court, "[t]he statutory text forecloses EPA's reading. The Clean Air Act's sweeping definition of 'air pollutant' . . . embraces all airborne compounds of whatever stripe."[324]

The Court, however, did not direct EPA to regulate CO_2 under CAA § 202 or any other provision of the Act. Rather, the Court said that EPA must respond to the petition for rulemaking to set § 202 emission standards based on the criteria for regulation employed in that section of the Act: "Under the clear terms of the Clean Air Act, EPA can avoid taking further action only if it determines that greenhouse gases do not contribute to climate change or if it provides some reasonable explanation as to why it cannot or will not exercise its discretion to determine whether they do."[325]

In response to *Massachusetts*, EPA on July 30, 2008, issued an advance notice of proposed rulemaking (ANPR) addressing how CO_2 and other GHGs might be regulated under the CAA.[326] As EPA explained in the ANPR, CAA regulatory programs are not easily applied to a global pollutant like CO_2 which is emitted from millions of sources around the world, which mixes rapidly and disperses throughout the global atmosphere, and which has been accumulating in the atmosphere for centuries.[327] As a result, EPA in the ANPR asked for comment on a long list of issues regarding the practical, technical, and economic feasibility of using the CAA to regulate GHGs.

Furthermore, in the wake of *Massachusetts*, public interest groups began to argue in PSD permit proceedings that new and modified sources that emit CO_2 and other GHGs should be required to install BACT for those pollutants, because *Massachusetts* made CO_2 and other GHGs "subject to regulation" for purposes of PSD permitting. In response, EPA observed that it had historically taken the position that the phrase "subject to regulation" in the PSD program requires that a specific CAA emission limitation or standard apply to the pollutant before it becomes a candidate for PSD regulation. Because there were then no CO_2 emission limitations or standards under the CAA, EPA's position was that CO_2 was not "subject to regulation" under the Act. This position was addressed by EPA's EAB in *Deseret Power Elec. Coop.*, PSD Appeal No. 07-03, 2008 WL 5572891 (Nov. 13, 2008). According to the EAB, the language of the

CAA does not compel regulation of CO_2 or other GHGs under the PSD program in the absence of specific CAA emission standards governing those substances. At the same time, the EAB found that the evidence considered by the permitting authority in that case (EPA Region VIII) did not establish a formal EPA interpretation of "subject to regulation." On December 18, 2008, EPA responded to the EAB's decision by issuing a formal interpretive memorandum confirming its position that CO_2 is not "subject to regulation" under the Act.[328]

EPA's interpretive memorandum[329] was challenged in the D.C. Circuit by Sierra Club and others.[330] At the same time, Sierra Club asked for reconsideration of this interpretive memorandum first, in the Bush administration (reconsideration denied) and then in the Obama administration (reconsideration granted).[331] The change of administrations in 2009 brought a sea change to EPA's approach to regulation of GHGs under the CAA. Initially, the Obama administration held out CAA regulation as a threat to force Congress to act on climate change legislation. When Congress refused to act, the regulatory threat became the vehicle for regulating mobile and stationary source GHG emissions.

2.3.5.1 Regulation of New Light Duty Vehicles

In 2009, EPA proposed to find that the six GHGs targeted by the mobile source rulemaking petition addressed in *Massachusetts* "endangered" public health and welfare for purposes of CAA § 202 LDV regulation. On December 15, 2009, EPA published its final CAA § 202 "Endangerment Finding."[332]

Based on this finding, EPA proposed and then finalized CAA tailpipe emission standards for GHG emissions from new LDVs.[333] According to EPA, this LDV rulemaking made CO_2 and the other GHGs addressed in the rule "subject to regulation" for purposes of the stationary source PSD program.[334]

2.3.5.2 PSD Regulation of GHGs

After promulgating the LDV rules, EPA recognized that regulating stationary source GHG emissions under the CAA would have extraordinarily harsh impacts on the U.S. economy. For example, because CO_2 is emitted in quantities above the CAA definition of "major emitting facility" (i.e., 100 or 250 tpy depending on the source category) by small sources, EPA found that its interpretation of the CAA PSD program could result in the LDV rule triggering PSD and Title V permitting requirements for millions of commercial, residential, agricultural, and other facilities never before subject to the CAA.[335] EPA explained that the tens of thousands of PSD permits and millions of Title V permits potentially required by its actions could paralyze state and local permitting authorities and halt industrial activity.[336]

To address these problems, EPA promulgated two rules called the "timing rule"[337] and the "tailoring rule."[338] In the timing rule, EPA responded to the Sierra Club petition for reconsideration of its formal interpretive memorandum on when a pollutant is "subject to regulation" under the PSD program, by making clear that a pollutant does not become "subject to regulation" under the PSD program until an emission standard that limits emissions of a pollutant from a specific source or source category takes effect. For its LDV rule, EPA said, the "subject to regulation" date is January 2, 2011, when model year 2012 engines are first eligible for certification under that new rule.[339]

In the tailoring rule, EPA said that the impacts of CAA stationary source regulation of GHGs were so extreme that Congress could never have intended that result. According to EPA, in order to avoid this absurd result, it would rewrite the statutory thresholds for PSD regulation (i.e., 100 or 250 tpy) to a higher level (i.e., 100,000 tpy for new sources, and 75,000 tpy for major modifications).[340] In the tailoring rule, EPA codified these new regulatory thresholds by defining the term air pollutant "subject to regulation" to include only GHGs emitted above the higher regulatory thresholds. According to this rule, beginning on January 2, 2011, sources that trigger PSD for other pollutants would be reviewed for BACT for GHGs if the construction activity at issue increased GHG emissions by 75,000 tpy carbon dioxide equivalent (CO_2e) or more. Sources subject to Title V would have to address GHG requirements when they apply, renew, or revise their permits.[341] Starting on July 1, 2011, PSD review could be triggered based on GHG emissions alone, with 100,000 tpy CO_2e or more making a source "major" for PSD purposes, and GHG emissions of 75,000 tpy CO_2e as the threshold for triggering the major modification program. In addition, GHG emission sources that equal or exceed the 100,000 tpy CO_2e threshold would be required to obtain a Title V permit if they did not already have one.[342]

According to EPA, these higher permitting thresholds would ensure that PSD and Title V review would be triggered only for truly large sources. At the same time, EPA committed itself to a schedule to lower these thresholds over time to bring more stationary sources into the CAA GHG regulatory program, in accordance with its policy to secure substantial reductions in national GHGs emissions.[343]

EPA's efforts to regulate stationary source GHG emissions under the CAA led to more than 80 petitions for review by states, industry, public interest groups, and others challenging one or more of these climate change rules.[344] The D.C. Circuit held two days of oral argument in these cases on February 28 and 29, 2012, and issued a decision in August 2012 in which the Court rejected challenges to the endangerment and LDV rules, deferred to EPA's technical findings, and rejected legal arguments attacking EPA's failure to consider stationary source consequences. The court dismissed petitions to review the tailoring and timing rules, on the grounds that those rules relaxed a statutory mandate, thereby leaving petitioners without Article III standing to pursue their challenges.[345] Numerous petitions for certiorari were filed, and ultimately granted by the Supreme Court.

On June 23, 2014, the Supreme Court issued its decision rejecting in large part EPA's effort to regulate stationary source GHG emissions under the PSD and Title V programs.[346] According to the Court, the general definition of "air pollutant" addressed in *Massachusetts* defines the pollutants available for regulation under the various programs of the CAA generally; it does not compel regulation of every pollutant under every program. Applying the statutory language and purposes of the PSD program, the Court concluded that GHGs, and CO_2 in particular, are not pollutants that trigger PSD (or Title V) applicability. However, where PSD program applicability is triggered by *other* pollutants, EPA can require BACT review for GHGs.

In the wake of *UARG*, GHG emissions from stationary sources cannot themselves trigger PSD review. GHG emissions may be subject to BACT review under the PSD program, however, where PSD is triggered by *other* pollutants, and the project results in an increase in GHG emissions above the "significance" level (currently defined as 75,000 tpy CO_2e).

2.3.5.3 NSPS Regulation of GHGs

As discussed above, EPA is required to review and to revise NSPS for stationary sources on an 8 year cycle. During its latest review of the EGU and refinery source categories, EPA received comments that it should set GHG standards for these source categories. EPA's failure to do so was challenged in the D.C. Circuit[347] and, in response, EPA agreed to schedules for developing NSPS for these source categories.

On April 13, 2012, EPA proposed NSPS for GHG emissions from new fossil fuel-fired EGUs.[348] Because there is no "adequately demonstrated technology" for GHG emissions from coal-fired boilers, EPA proposed standards for those facilities based on the capabilities of gas-fired turbines. As EPA recognized, this would effectively ban the construction of any new coal-fired EGUs.[349] When EPA had not promulgated these standards by April 13, 2013, EPA received notices of intent to sue from several environmental non-governmental organizations and states attempting to force promulgation of those standards.

At the same time, EPA agreed to a schedule for promulgating performance standards under § 111(d) of the CAA for existing coal and gas-fired generating units.[350] After extended controversy and rulemaking delays, EPA published its rules for new and existing fossil fuel-fired electric generating units on October 23, 2015.[351] EPA established NSPS for newly constructed coal-fired boilers of 1400 lbs/MWh, based on EPA's conclusions regarding the consequences of partial carbon capture and sequestration in deep saline formations. For new gas-fired combined cycle turbines, EPA set NSPS of 1,000 and 1,100 lb/MWh, depending on turbine size. EPA also set separate NSPS for reconstructed and modified coal-fired boilers.

At the same time, EPA published rules establishing uniform national performance rates for existing coal-fired boilers (1305 lbs/MWh) and natural gas combined cycle units (771 lbs/MWh). EPA concluded that while these rates are *not* achievable with any system of emission control demonstrated for use at any individual unit, they can be met by shifting generation from fossil units to non-CO_2 emitting renewable generation and by reducing demand for electricity through demand-side efficiency programs. EPA's rule provides a number of options states might use in developing state plans to meet these rates, which focus in large measure on mechanisms for the creation and transfer of emission rate credits or allowances that reflect investment in renewable energy resources.

Both of these rules have been challenged by numerous state, labor, and industry petitioners in the D.C. Circuit. The challenges to the NSPS have been consolidated under the caption *North Dakota v. EPA,* Nos. 15-1381, et al. This case will likely be briefed in the second half of 2016, with a decision likely by mid-2017.

The challenges to the existing source rule have been consolidated before the caption *West Virginia v. EPA,* Nos. 15-1363, et al. In response to motions to stay the rule, on February 9, 2016, the Supreme Court issued an order staying the rule until all challenges to the rule are briefed and decided.[352] Briefing on the merits of the challenges to the rule was completed in April 2016, and argument before an en banc court is scheduled for September 27, 2016. The D.C. Circuit will likely decide the case by early 2017, and any decision will almost certainly be followed by petitions for certiorari to the Supreme Court.

EPA has not yet taken steps to regulate GHG emissions from other source categories, including refineries, under §111. EPA will likely wait for the conclusion of litigation over its EGU rulemakings before taking on other source categories.

Many have observed that CAA regulation is not an efficient method for addressing GHGs. The CAA, however, now appears to be the regulatory vehicle that EPA will pursue.

2.3.6 Mobile Sources, Fuels, and Fuel Additives

The 1990 CAA amendments substantially tightened mobile source emission standards. The amendments required automobile manufacturers to reduce tailpipe emissions of hydrocarbons (HC) and NOx by 35 percent and 60 percent from pre-amendment standards, respectively, beginning with 40 percent of the vehicles sold in 1994 and increasing to 100 percent of vehicles sold in 1996.[353] The amendments also required a further 50 percent reduction in mobile source emissions of these pollutants beginning with vehicles produced in 2003, unless EPA finds that these more stringent standards are not necessary, technologically feasible, or cost effective. In regulations promulgated in 2000, EPA determined that these more stringent standards are appropriate.[354] EPA also established a separate, voluntary program, known as the NLEV (National Low Emission Vehicle) program, which includes more stringent emission standards that apply prior to the 2004 model year.[355]

In addition to establishing new mobile source emission standards, the 1990 amendments established two new fuel-related programs designed to achieve emission reductions.[356] The first of these fuel programs—the reformulated fuel program—required the use of reformulated gasoline in certain CO and severe ozone nonattainment areas beginning in 1992 and 1995, respectively. Among other things, reformulated gasoline must be blended to achieve reductions in VOCs and toxic tailpipe emissions. EPA in 1994 published regulations implementing this provision.[357]

The second fuel program is the clean fuel vehicle program. Under this program, automobiles operating on clean alternative fuels (e.g., methanol, ethanol, natural gas, and reformulated gasoline) must meet even more stringent emission standards. The clean fuel vehicle program is implemented in two ways:

- By establishing a California pilot test program that requires the production and sale of 300,000 clean fuel vehicles annually by 1999.

- By requiring operators of centrally fueled fleets of 10 or more vehicles in certain CO and ozone nonattainment areas to purchase and use clean fuel vehicles beginning in 1998.

In addition, the Agency issued new rules on the registration of fuels and fuel additives in 1994.[358] Under these rules, a new fuel or fuel additive cannot be introduced into commerce until the manufacturer completes extensive test programs developed to assess the public health risks associated with use of the product. Existing fuels and fuel additives were given six years to comply with these testing requirements.

Finally, EPA now views vehicles and the fuels they operate on as an integrated system. This has prompted EPA to look beyond the continued use of traditional emission control technology to achieve the emission reductions required by the 1990 amendments. In particular, EPA has promulgated regulations that substantially reduce permissible sulfur levels in gasoline[359] and diesel fuel.[360] Viewing vehicles and fuels as an integrated system has also prompted the Agency to implement its responsibility to address mobile source air toxic emissions by focusing, at least initially, on fuel-based controls, including a limit on permissible benzene concentrations in gasoline.[361]

Reflecting the new integrated system for regulating fuels and vehicles, fuel and fuel additive manufacturers have shown greater interest in the program developed by EPA for evaluating motor vehicle compliance with CAA emission standards under the Section 206 "certification" provision of the CAA.[362] In 2002, the U.S. Court of Appeals for the D.C. Circuit reviewed regulations issued by EPA for the certification of motor vehicles (otherwise known as the CAP 2000 regulations) in a challenge initiated by fuel and fuel additive manufacturing interests. The petitioner challenged the regulations because they allowed automobile manufacturers to develop their own certification test procedures for verifying compliance with emission limits without disclosure of the test procedures to the public at large, including fuel and fuel additive manufacturers. The petitioner argued that EPA must establish test methods and procedures for the certification program by regulation. The D.C. Circuit agreed. The D.C. Circuit noted,

> First . . . a manufacturer of additives for motor vehicle fuels . . . has an interest in understanding the test methods and procedures by which the EPA certifies new motor vehicles. CAP 2000's provision for closed-door adoption of emission test procedures deprives [the manufacturer] of information that might well help it develop and improve its products with an eye to conformity to emissions needs.[363]

Because the regulations allowed vehicle manufacturers to develop certification test methods and procedures without rulemaking and public input, the court vacated the CAP 2000 program and ordered EPA to develop certification test methods and procedures by regulation. EPA proposed new certification regulations in April 2004.[364]

On May 7, 2010, EPA promulgated enhanced fuel economy standards for LDVs under CAA § 202.[365] Those rules were promulgated in response to the rulemaking petition addressed by the Supreme Court in *Massachusetts* to limit GHG emissions from new motor vehicles. Because the National Highway Traffic Safety Administration promulgated parallel standards at the same time under its independent statutory authority, the main impact of EPA's LDV standards will be on stationary sources, under EPA's interpretation of PSD applicability discussed in section 2.3.5 of this chapter.

2.4 Operating Permit Program

Prior to 1990, the only permit program contained in the CAA was the preconstruction permitting program for new and modified sources. While EPA issued guidance in the late 1980s addressing how a state, through its SIP, could create a federally enforceable operating permit program,[366] few states took advantage of this guidance. As a result, from the standpoint of federal law, existing sources were regulated almost exclusively through provisions established in SIPs and preconstruction permits rather than through source-specific operating permits.

Title V of the 1990 CAA amendments changed the basic approach to source-specific regulation under the Act by requiring each state to develop and implement a comprehensive operating permit program for most sources of air pollution. The purpose of this new permit program is to consolidate in a single document all of the federal regulations applicable to a source in order to facilitate source compliance and enforcement. With few exceptions, Title V does not authorize the creation of new substantive federal requirements. Permit programs are administered by the states, but EPA retains authority to review and to approve not only the overall permit program but also each individual permit issued by the state.

In July 1992, EPA issued final regulations addressing the minimum requirements for state operating permit programs.[367] Based on these minimum requirements, states have put in place Title V operating permit programs. Although some states did not initially receive full approval of their programs, EPA provided interim approval and allowed states additional time to correct any deficiencies.[368] When EPA attempted to extend those interim approvals beyond the time period allowed under the regulations,[369] the Agency's action was challenged. To settle that challenge, EPA agreed to accept comments from the public on perceived deficiencies in states' programs and, where EPA agreed that deficiencies existed, to issue notices of deficiency by specific deadlines.[370] Although EPA did issue some notices of deficiency, in other cases where EPA found deficiencies, the Agency reached agreements with states on terms to address those problems while still receiving full program approval. When EPA's refusal to issue notices of deficiency in the face of undisputed problems was challenged, the courts upheld EPA's action as a valid exercise of discretion.[371] If a state fails to implement an adequate Title V program of their own, a federal operating permit program will be applied, either by EPA or by the state under a delegation of authority from EPA. EPA issued rules governing this federal operating permit program on July 1, 1996.[372]

Immediately after promulgation of the July 1992 Title V regulations for state programs, several industry groups, environmental organizations, and states challenged the rules in the D.C. Circuit.[373] The parties jointly requested a stay in briefing for most issues in order to encourage settlement. A number of the issues raised in the litigation were the focus of rule-making proposals issued by EPA on August 29, 1994,[374] and August 31, 1995.[375] These proposals would have amended several elements of the existing Part 70 regulations, including those pertaining to when sources must seek revisions to their operating permits and the procedures applicable to each type of revision. When no final rule had been issued by the spring of 2004, several environmental organizations sought to move forward with the litigation. Although the parties reached an agreement to continue to hold the case in abeyance, EPA agreed to form a "task force" to gather information from stakeholders on the performance of the Title V program.[376] The task force issued its final report in April 2006.[377] The report included more than 100 recommendations for program improvement with varying degrees of support from task force members. In the summer of 2006, EPA began the process of considering those recommendations.

The following discussion summarizes the general features and status of the current program and, where possible, notes areas where change is likely.

2.4.1 Applicability

Section 70.3(a) of the Title V regulations requires a state program to provide for the permitting of at least the following sources:

I. Any major source, defined in Section 70.2 of the rules as any stationary source belonging to a single major industrial grouping that is
   A. A major source under Section 112 of the Act,
   B. A major source of air pollutants that directly emits or has the potential to emit 100 tpy or more of any air pollutant (including any major source of fugitive emissions of any such pollutant), or
   C. A major source as defined in Part D of Title I of the Act;

II. Any source subject to a standard, limitation, or other requirement under Section 111 of the Act;

III. Any source subject to a standard or other requirement under Section 112 of the Act (although a source is not required to obtain a permit solely because it is subject to regulation under Section 112(r) dealing with accidental release prevention);

IV. Any affected source under Title IV of the Act;

V. Any source in a source category designated by EPA.

Under Section 70.3(b), a state may defer permitting of any nonmajor sources pending further EPA rulemaking or as EPA specifically provides in rulemakings on new standards. EPA has provided deferrals for certain nonmajor sources of air toxics (referred to as area sources) in specific post-1990 Section 112 standards.[378] Section 70.5(c) also allows the states to develop exemptions for insignificant activities because of size, emission levels, or production rate. The rules preclude establishment of exemptions, however, if they would interfere with the determination or imposition of any applicable requirement or the calculation of fees.[379]

2.4.2 Permit Applications

A source subject to the Title V program must submit a complete permit application, including a compliance plan describing how the source plans to comply with all applicable requirements where there is noncompliance to the state permitting authority within one year after the permit program becomes effective.[380] Renewal applications must generally be filed at least six months (but not more than 18 months) prior to permit expiration (which generally occurs after a term of five years).[381]

The permitting authority must determine whether the application is complete within 60 days after receipt of an application. Unless the permitting authority requests additional information or otherwise notifies the applicant of incompleteness within this time period, the application is deemed complete.[382]

In general, if a source submits a timely and complete permit application, failure to have a permit is not considered a violation of the statutory requirement to operate with a permit, at least until the permitting authority takes final action on the application.[383] This protection is called the application shield.

A permit application must contain all information listed in Section 70.5(c), including the following details:

I.   All emissions of pollutants for which the source is major and all emissions of regulated air pollutants;

II.   Identification of all points of emissions;

III.   Emission rates in tons per year and in other terms necessary to establish compliance;

IV.   Description of air pollution control equipment;

V.   Identification of all federal air pollution control requirements;

VI.   Monitoring and measurement techniques used to demonstrate compliance with federal applicable requirements;

VII. A statement of current compliance status with respect to all federally applicable requirements, and a schedule for compliance in the event of noncompliance.

A responsible corporate official must certify the truth, accuracy, and completeness of the application.[384] States have developed standard application forms for use in satisfying the Title V permit application requirement.

2.4.3 Permit Issuance and Content

The permitting authority must take final action within 18 months after receiving a complete application.[385] However, anticipating the administrative burden of establishing the new permitting program, Congress, in Section 503(c) of the Act, provided for a phased schedule over three years for acting on initial Title V permit applications. The permitting authority was required to act on one-third of the permit applications received in the first year of the program in each year over a three-year period following program approval by EPA. EPA makes clear in the preamble to the Title V rules that "act on" means final action rather than initial review.[386] Most states did not meet this requirement as a result of numerous unanticipated questions and issues that have arisen during implementation of the program. In May 1999, EPA established a goal for states to issue all permits by January 2001.[387] By June of 2006, 98 percent of Title V permits had been issued.

The permitting authority must issue permits for a fixed term of no more than five years and include the following requirements:

I.   All applicable emission limitations and standards;

II. Monitoring and related recordkeeping and reporting requirements, including a requirement for "prompt" reporting of deviations from permit terms and conditions;

III. A permit condition prohibiting emissions of sulfur dioxide exceeding any allowances held under Title IV of the Act (for affected sources);

IV. A severability clause to ensure continued validity of remaining permit requirements if any provisions are challenged;

V.   A statement that the permit may be modified, revoked, reopened, and reissued or terminated for cause;

VI. A provision to ensure that a source pays fees consistent with an approved state permitting fee schedule.[388]

Insignificant emission units must be covered by the permit to the extent they are subject to applicable requirements.[389]

The permit also must contain the compliance requirements listed in Section 70.6(c), including (1) compliance certification, testing, monitoring, reporting, and recordkeeping requirements to assure compliance with the permit (including any terms needed to fill gaps in applicable compliance requirements); (2) inspection and entry requirements for permitting authority officials; and (3) a schedule of compliance and provisions for regular progress reports. Compliance certifications must be required at least annually and, like permit applications and other required reports, must include a certification of truth, accuracy, and completeness based on "reasonable inquiry."[390] In 1997, EPA revised the compliance certification provisions in Section 70.6(c) to address issues related to promulgation of the credible evidence and CAM rules (discussed above in section 2.1.3).[391] Those provisions were the subject of litigation that resulted in remand to the Agency for additional rulemaking[392] that EPA completed in 2003.[393]

One of the most contentious issues in Title V permitting has been specification of additional monitoring to satisfy EPA's requirement that permits include "periodic monitoring" sufficient to assure compliance.[394] Referred to as a gap-filling requirement, "periodic monitoring" applies to sources without existing requirements for periodic emissions monitoring that either have not yet implemented or are not subject to the CAM rule, in order to comply with the enhanced monitoring provisions of CAA Section 114(a)(3). To avoid further delaying the issuance of permits, EPA provided a phased implementation schedule for the CAM rule that delayed application to most sources until permit renewal. Significant permit revisions, however, could trigger CAM applicability earlier.[395]

In 1998, EPA issued "Periodic Monitoring Guidance" to inform state permitting authorities of the level of monitoring EPA would deem sufficient in its review of Title V permits. EPA's guidance, which urged states to conduct wide-ranging review of all compliance monitoring provisions and to impose new compliance methods that industry feared would make emission standards more stringent, was challenged by several industry groups as contrary to both EPA's regulations and Title V. In April 2000, the U.S. Court of Appeals for the D.C. Circuit, agreeing that EPA's guidance went well beyond the language of the regulation, invalidated the guidance as an unlawful amendment to the Title V rules.[396]

Although EPA initially responded to invalidation of its "Periodic Monitoring Guidance" by refraining from requiring states to supplement monitoring in Title V permits that already contained some monitoring, EPA later interpreted the general Part 70 requirement in Section 70.6(c) that permits include monitoring "sufficient to assure compliance" to once again require that states perform wide-ranging sufficiency review of all monitoring. When that interpretation was also challenged in the D.C. Circuit,[397] EPA responded by promulgating, under the "good cause" exception to the Administrative Procedure Act, an immediately effective Interim Final Rule designed to support its interpretation.[398] At the same time, EPA issued for comment a proposal to make the proposed revisions final.[399] In January 2004, EPA issued a final action declining to finalize its proposal and announcing a new interpretation of what it now calls the "umbrella monitoring" rules at Section 70.6(c)(1).[400] That action, which resolved a challenge to EPA's Interim Final Rule,[401] was vacated on procedural grounds in 2005.[402] In 2006, EPA conducted rulemaking to cure the procedural deficiency and adopt an interpretation under which permitting officials would not have authority to supplement existing monitoring in Title V permit proceedings, except as required under the "periodic monitoring rule" or the CAM rule.[403] That interpretation was vacated by the D.C. Circuit in 2008, which found that the interpretive rule contravened the statutory directive that each permit contain monitoring sufficient to assure compliance.[404] As noted in a dissenting opinion, the majority opinion appeared to turn on the factual twist that EPA had conceded that some monitoring was not adequate, but had itself taken no steps to fix it.[405]

Finally, pursuant to Section 70.6(b)(2), the permit must "specifically designate as not being federally enforceable . . . any terms and conditions included in the permit that are not required under the Act or under any of its applicable requirements" (e.g., state-only requirements). Such terms and conditions are not subject to Title V requirements regarding permit issuance, permit modification, and EPA and affected state review. Any terms not otherwise designated, however, are federally enforceable by either EPA or citizens under the citizen suit provisions of the Act.

Before permit issuance, the permitting authority must provide procedures for public notice, a comment period of at least 30 days, and the opportunity to request a public hearing on the draft permit.[406]

2.4.4 EPA and Affected State Review of Permit Applications

Section 70.8(a) requires the permitting authority to provide to EPA a copy of each permit application, draft permit, and final permit issued under Part 70. EPA may comment on a permit application or draft permit.

The permitting authority must also give notice of each draft permit to any affected state on or before the time public notice is provided.[407] An affected state is one whose air quality may be affected and that is contiguous to the state in which the source is located, or within 50 miles of the source.

If EPA objects to a proposed final permit within 45 days of receipt, the permitting authority may not issue the permit. Under Section 70.8(c), EPA must object to issuance of any proposed permit deemed not to be in compliance with the requirements of Part 70. If the permitting authority fails to revise and resubmit the proposed permit to EPA within 90 days of receipt of the objection notice, EPA must issue or deny the permit.[408]

If EPA does not object to the proposed permit, any person (including an affected state) may petition the Agency to object within 60 days after expiration of the 45-day EPA review period. The petition must be based on objections to the permit that were raised with reasonable specificity during the public comment period, unless the petitioner demonstrates that it was impracticable to raise such objections within that period or unless the grounds for the objection arose after that period. A petition for review does not stay the effectiveness of a permit if it was issued after EPA's original 45-day review period.[409] EPA has been asked to respond to more than 100 petitions for objection since the beginning of the program. Denial of a petition for objection is reviewable in the local U.S. Court of Appeals.[410]

2.4.5 Permit Shield

Section 504(f) of the Act provides that compliance with the permit shall be deemed compliance with applicable provisions of the Act. This permit shield is optional with the states, however. Section 70.6(f) of EPA's Title V rules provides that the permitting authority may include in a permit an express statement that compliance with the conditions of the permit shall be deemed compliance with any applicable requirements as of the date of issuance if (1) the applicable requirements are specifically identified in the permit or (2) the permitting authority determines in writing that other requirements specifically identified do not apply to the source and the permit includes that determination. If the permit does not expressly state that a permit shield applies, then no shield will be presumed.

2.4.6 Permit Revision and Operational Flexibility

The present Title V rules establish several categories of permit revisions. These requirements were the subject of intense debate throughout the rulemaking and the ensuing litigation, with industry and state agencies generally arguing for limited review of permit revisions during the five-year permit term and environmental groups in favor of more extensive interim review. At the heart of this debate is the issue of how much flexibility a source should have to change its operations without having to undertake a full-blown permit proceeding.

As a result of the judicial challenges to the final Title V rule, EPA proposed revisions to the flexibility provisions of 40 C.F.R. Part 70 in 1994[411] and then again in August 1995.[412] EPA's 1994 proposal would have provided for four revision tracks rather than the three that exist under the current rules. The complexity of this proposal, however, raised questions as to whether the proposed rule would in fact increase source flexibility to change operations in response to competition and other market conditions. Numerous parties, including states and regulated industries, criticized the proposal as too complex for both sources and permitting authorities.

In response to such criticism, EPA in August 1995 proposed a fundamental restructuring of the permit revision portions of the Title V rule. Under this proposed approach, during the five-year permit term, a source would have been able to undertake many changes in operations that require a permit revision simply by notifying the permitting authority at the time of the change and submitting a statement describing the revised permit term or new applicable requirements. This statement would have been attached to the permit itself. For environmentally significant changes (a term to be defined by the rule), this procedure would have been available for those changes for which a review process was afforded in conjunction with development or implementation of the applicable requirement if that review process was essentially equivalent to the Title V permit procedures. States would have had more flexibility as to the procedures afforded for less environmentally significant changes. Formal review under the Title V program would have occurred subsequently during the next permit renewal. EPA proposed additional revisions in 1997 but did not finalize any changes.

Below is a summary of the permit revision system as set forth in the current Title V rule.

2.4.6.1 Scope

Under the current Title V rule, a source must seek a permit revision only if the contemplated change could not be implemented without violating a term of the existing permit or if the change would trigger an applicable requirement to which the source had not previously been subject.

2.4.6.2 Administrative Permit Amendments

An administrative permit amendment is generally a simple revision that corrects typographical errors, identifies a change in name or similar information, requires more frequent monitoring, or incorporates requirements into the operating permit from a preconstruction review permit (if the state review also satisfies the procedural participation requirements of Title V). No public notice is required for administrative amendments. Administrative amendments may typically be implemented upon the filing of an application. No permit shield is available.

2.4.6.3 Minor Permit Revisions

Minor permit revisions are subject to limited review requirements and stream-lined procedures. The existing Title V rules do not require public review of such revisions but do require that EPA and affected states be notified of the application. To qualify for the minor permit revision procedure, the source may not be in violation of the permit term it seeks to change; further, the revision may not violate any requirement applicable to the source. The source may make the proposed change immediately, but once it makes the change, the source may be liable for violating its permit if the revision is ultimately denied (e.g., in response to EPA or affected state comments or a citizen suit challenging the state's failure to object to the proposed change).

2.4.6.4 Significant Permit Revisions

Significant permit revisions are those that would not qualify as administrative or minor revisions. They are subject to the procedural requirements applicable to permit issuance and renewal, including the requirements for public participation and review by affected states and EPA.

2.4.6.5 Operational Flexibility/Trading

Pursuant to Section 502(b)(10) of the Act, states must allow sources to engage in trading under a federally enforceable cap established in the permit and to make certain other changes that do not exceed emissions allowable under the permit provided at least seven days notice is provided.

2.4.6.6 Alternative Operating Scenarios

By far the best way to ensure operational flexibility is to write a permit that specifies operation under all of the reasonably anticipated operating scenarios of the facility. A source owner or operator would merely have to give notice of a change in operating scenarios, and no permit revision would be required. In the preamble to the final Title V rules, EPA also recognizes that an appropriate way to avoid the need for permit revisions is to base permit terms and conditions on reasonably conservative assumptions regarding source emissions and operations.

2.4.7 Permit Fees

Section 70.9(b) requires states to establish a fee schedule that results in collection of revenue sufficient to cover permit program costs. The costs to be covered by the fee schedule are listed in Section 70.9(b)(1). A state fee schedule may include emissions fees, application fees, service-based fees, or other types of fees.[413] EPA will assume that the fees are adequate to cover the costs of the state program if the fees are equal to $25 per year multiplied by the total tons of the actual emissions of each regulated pollutant emitted.[414] The fee schedule ultimately adopted by the state must be increased annually by the percentage increase in the Consumer Price Index in order to ensure adequate funding of the state program.[415]

3.0 Enforcement of the CAA

The 1990 amendments to the CAA gave EPA and the courts broader enforcement authority and significantly increased the civil and criminal penalties for violations. Moreover, the Title V operating permit program makes it easier to identify a source's applicable CAA requirements and compliance status. As a result, and as the substantive CAA programs have been implemented, CAA enforcement cases have increased. The following sections summarize the enforcement provisions of the Act.

3.1 Civil Enforcement

Section 113(b) of the Act authorizes EPA to bring civil actions for enforcement of an applicable implementation plan or permit and of other specified requirements of the Act. This section provides for civil penalties of $25,000 per day of violation to be adjusted periodically for inflation (the current penalty figure is $37,500 per day).

One of the most significant changes in civil enforcement under the 1990 amendments to the Act is the ability of the administrator to bring administrative enforcement actions against violators directly without going through the Department of Justice and the courts. The administrative enforcement provisions, modeled after similar provisions in the Clean Water Act, authorize the administrator to impose administrative penalties up to $200,000 or more (the current penalty adjusted for inflation is $295,000) if the administrator and the attorney general agree that a stiffer penalty is appropriate. The administrator must give written notice to the alleged violator. The alleged violator then has 30 days within which to request an adjudicatory hearing.[416] Administrative enforcement allows EPA to avoid having to coordinate first with the Department of Justice but also enables EPA to reach agreements with violators more quickly than would be possible through litigation.

The amendments also authorize a field citation program for minor violations.[417] The provision is intended to provide the Agency with a quick means to address minor violations by allowing Agency officials to inspect a facility and, if appropriate, to issue environmental traffic tickets with fines of up to $5,000 per day per violation. Alleged violators may request a hearing or simply pay the fine.

In addition to expanding the Agency's authority to enforce the Act, the 1990 CAA amendments authorized private citizens to seek civil penalties for violations of the Act. (Under the pre-1990 Act, when citizens brought suits against EPA for failure to perform a nondiscretionary act or against a particular source for violations of the statute, the court had authority only to order EPA to take action or to order the source to comply.) Plaintiffs must provide at least 60 days' notice of the action to the administrator, the state, and the alleged violator.[418] As might be anticipated, there has been a significant increase in citizen suit enforcement activity under the CAA in recent years.

To underscore how serious Congress is about enforcement of the CAA, it has authorized EPA to pay a bounty of up to $10,000 to anyone who provides information that leads to a criminal conviction or civil penalty.[419]

3.2 Criminal Penalties

The CAA imposes criminal liability in Section 113(c) on any person who knowingly violates the statute and makes a knowing violation of the Act a felony offense. The definition of person includes individuals as well as corporations and partnerships, and while some enforcement provisions can be enforced only against senior management personnel or corporate officers, the knowing violation provisions of the Act can be enforced against anyone involved in the violation. The 1990 amendments have increased fines to $250,000 per day per violation and up to five years in jail. Corporations are subject to even larger fines, up to $500,000 per violation.

The amendments have also expanded the penalties for crimes related to recordkeeping. Individuals are subject to fines up to $250,000 and two years in jail not only for making false statements to the Agency but also for failing to file or maintain records or reports required under the Act. Corporations face fines of up to $500,000 for the same violation. This provision is particularly important for Title V permittees because the CAA requires each permittee to certify at least once a year that the permitted facility "is in compliance with any applicable requirements of the permit, and to promptly report any deviations from permit requirements."[420]

Knowing failure to pay any fee owed to the government under the Act, such as permit fees, is a criminal act and is punishable by fines of up to $100,000 and one year in jail for individuals and fines of up to $500,000 for corporations. Penalties are doubled for repeat offenders.

Two sections of the 1990 CAA amendments impose criminal penalties for knowing or negligent release of air toxics that place another person in "imminent danger of death or serious bodily injury." An individual who knowingly releases any hazardous air pollutant or any extremely hazardous substance that places another person in "imminent danger of death or serious bodily injury" is subject to fines of up to $250,000 per day and up to a 15-year imprisonment. Corporations may be fined up to $1 million per day. This provision requires actual knowledge that the release placed others in imminent danger of death or serious bodily injury.[421]

An individual who negligently releases any air toxic which places another person in "imminent danger of death or serious bodily injury" is subject to fines of up to $100,000 and up to one year in jail. Corporations may be fined up to $200,000.[422] Because it criminalizes negligent behavior, this provision has serious implications for anyone with responsibility for environmental compliance and creates a particular need for effective environmental management programs that delineate responsibilities for ensuring compliance.

In addition to stiffer criminal penalties for violations of the CAA, Congress has required EPA to substantially increase the number of criminal investigators to enforce all environmental laws. The Pollution Prosecution Act of 1990 required EPA to have at least 200 trained criminal investigators by October 1995.

3.3 Sarbanes-Oxley Act of 2002

The Sarbanes-Oxley Act of 2002 dramatically expands the scope of conduct covered by federal criminal law and heightens concerns about a range of issues, including compliance programs and document retention.

For example, the Sarbanes-Oxley Act expands the obstruction of justice offense. Previously, 18 U.S.C. § 1512 imposed criminal liability on someone who causes another person to destroy evidence wanted for use in an "official proceeding." New Section 1519 covers an individual acting alone who, among other things, destroys, falsifies, or makes a false entry in a record. This individual can be prosecuted even if there is no "official proceeding" at the time of destruction of the evidence, as long as the person doing the act "contemplated" that there might be an "official proceeding" in the future. This crime is punishable by up to 20 years' imprisonment. This new provision has implications for record retention policies generally and for environmental records in particular.

The Sarbanes-Oxley legislation also adds a new Subsection (e) to 18 U.S.C. § 1513, which creates a felony offense for any person who retaliates (by "interference with the lawful employment or livelihood") against someone for providing information relating to the commission or possible commission of any federal offense. This provision provides for a 10-year term of imprisonment.

Section 805 of the Sarbanes-Oxley legislation requires the U.S. Sentencing Commission to review obstruction offenses and to consider additional penalty enhancements if there was destruction of a large number of documents, if there was a large number of participants, if the destruction was of particularly proba-tive or essential evidence, if there was more than minimal planning, or if the offense involved abuse of a special skill or a position of trust. In addition, Section 905 requires the Sentencing Commission to review sentencing guidelines for white-collar crime provisions generally to determine whether they provide "suf-ficient deterrence and punishment." The sentencing guidelines should be consid-ered in the development of environmental management and compliance programs.

3.4 Compliance Audits

In light of the expansion of criminal liability under the CAA and related develop-ments, including the Sarbanes-Oxley Act, companies are well advised to imple-ment an internal compliance program. Regular audits will reduce the chance of criminal actions against the company by enabling the company to detect and correct problems early. Such programs may also be considered a mitigating factor by a court imposing penalties.

Common concerns in connection with environmental audits are how to deal with violations once they are discovered and whether the company must report them to the Agency. Title V specifically requires permittees to report any devia-tion from a permit requirement to the Agency, and failure to do so carries civil and criminal penalties of its own. A comprehensive internal compliance program, however, can reduce a permittee's potential liability for violations.

In 1991, the Department of Justice released guidelines on factors the prose-cutor should consider in making criminal enforcement decisions under federal environmental statutes. The guidelines state that it is the policy of the Agency to encourage self-auditing and voluntary disclosure of environmental violations by the regulated community. To that end, the guidelines list several factors that will weigh against a criminal enforcement action, including the following:

- regular, comprehensive environmental audits;
- timely voluntary disclosure of violations;
- good-faith efforts to remedy noncompliance;
- an effective internal disciplinary system;
- prompt, good-faith efforts to reach compliance agreements with federal and state authorities.

Although the company may have an affirmative duty to report violations of the Act when it discovers them, voluntary disclosure and cooperation with enforcement authorities should help a company reduce its exposure to enforcement action based on those violations. These same themes are repeated in a guidance memorandum issued in January 1994 by EPA's director of criminal enforcement titled "The Exercise of Investigative Discretion."

In 1994, the Agency undertook a formal review of the environmental auditing guidelines it adopted in 1986.[423] Under the guidelines, the key audit elements are as follows:

- explicit top-management support;

- an environmental auditing function independent of audited activities;

- adequate staffing and training;

- prompt reporting of compliance problems to management;

- prompt corrective action.

In December 1995, EPA issued a notice concluding its review of the 1986 audit policy.[424] In this notice, EPA provided that it would generally seek lower civil penalties (by eliminating the gravity component) and not pursue criminal enforcement where a company discovered, voluntarily reported, and promptly corrected violations pursuant to a properly designed and implemented environmental audit program. The policy also restated EPA's long-standing policy of not requesting copies of regulated entities' voluntary audit reports. The 1995 policy on "Incentives for Self-Policing: Discovery, Disclosure, Correction and Prevention of Violations" was revised in April 2000 in response to comments from various interest groups with experience implementing the 1995 policy.[425] The revised policy clarifies some of the language in the 1995 policy, broadens its availability, and conforms the provisions to actual EPA practices.

Numerous states have adopted audit privilege and/or immunity legislation. EPA has generally opposed such legislation and has issued guidance describing circumstances in which such legislation will render a state's Title V program inadequate (based on the concern that such legislation could interfere with state enforcement of Title V permits).[426]

On August 1, 2008, EPA published in the *Federal Register* an "Interim Approach to Applying the Audit Policy to New Owners" which describes how EPA will apply the audit policy to new owners of regulated facilities.[427] The *Federal Register* notice states that EPA intends to tailor audit policy incentives for new owners that want to make a "clean start" at their recently acquired facilities by addressing environmental noncompliance that began prior to acquisition. Tailored incentives include penalty mitigation beyond what the audit policy offers and provides an expanded range of violations that may be eligible for audit policy consideration.

4.0 Legislative Proposals

4.1 CAA Reauthorization

During the George W. Bush administration, several proposals to amend the CAA were introduced in Congress, with most attention focused on competing proposals offered by the administration (H.R. 5266/S. 2815, called the "Clear Skies" legislation) and by Senator Jeffords (S. 566).[428] Owners and operators of power plants and other industrial facilities wanted clear regulatory requirements and a realistic planning horizon for implementing those requirements in a cost-effective manner. EPA and others wanted greater emission reductions. Congress never acted on these legislative proposals for a variety of reasons, including disagreement over the timing and amount of reductions of SO_2, NOx, and mercury emissions; over whether CO_2 emissions should be addressed in the legislation; and over whether a broader effort should be undertaken to reauthorize the CAA. Given the current legislative gridlock, it is unlikely that there will be any significant updating or refinement of the CAA any time soon.

4.2 Climate Change

Numerous proposals for climate change legislation were introduced early in the Obama administration. These legislative proposals generally provided for progressively declining caps on GHG emissions between now and 2050. Like the CAA Title IV cap-and-trade program on which these proposals are modeled, these legislative proposals would have required sources subject to the program to hold sufficient pollution allowances to cover their annual emissions, and these allowances could be freely traded among sources covered by the program.

Each of these proposals addressed the same basic issues, including (i) what sources and specific GHGs will be covered by the program; (ii) the stringency of the proposed cap, and the pace at which the cap will be reduced; (iii) how allowances will be distributed among covered sources (e.g., allocated to sources, or auctioned); (iv) how costs to industry and consumers will be contained (e.g., through a maximum price on allowances, or provisions for creation of domestic or international offsets and credits); and (v) how "leakage" of GHG emissions from the United States, caused by increased production in countries without climate change regulation, will be addressed.

The two leading legislative climate change proposals in the Obama administration were the Waxman-Markey bill in the House (which was approved by a narrow margin by the House in May 2009) and the Lieberman-Kerry bill in the Senate (which was never put to a vote). In the wake of the 2010 midterm election, however, President Obama observed that comprehensive climate legislation was unlikely, and the Administration shifted its focus to CAA regulation. As a result, any climate change program is likely to result from implementation of existing statutes, not congressional action.

5.0 Conclusion

Over the past two decades, EPA has faced implementation responsibilities under the CAA that far surpass those that have been assigned to virtually any other administrative agency. Interpretive rulings, policy guidance, negotiated rules, advisory committees, and enforcement actions have all been used extensively by EPA as statutory deadlines and an increasingly polarized environmental debate have made it difficult for the Agency to conduct rulemaking. As a practical matter, the scope and diversity of these regulatory efforts and the constantly changing nature of CAA regulatory requirements call on affected companies to monitor carefully EPA priorities and schedules, in order to anticipate compliance obligations.

As proceedings to implement the 1990 amendments have been completed and as source owners and operators confront the compliance monitoring and certification requirements of the Title V operating permit program, CAA enforcement actions have increased. With the difficulty of rulemaking, enforcement has become a key tool for policy making. Given the breadth of the Act and of EPA's new enforcement powers, comprehensive environmental planning is crucial to preserving a company's flexibility in the national and international marketplace.

The new frontier for CAA regulation is climate change. Regulation of GHGs under the Act could impose greater burdens and affect a wider range of commercial and institutional sources than any other environmental regulatory program. How to address the new climate change mandate given EPA by the Supreme Court will continue to present significant challenges for the current administration and the courts.

6.0 Research Sources

The following EPA web pages provide substantial additional information about the various programs of the CAA:

- Clean Air Markets Programs: https://www.epa.gov/airmarkets

- Office of Air and Radiation: https://www3.epa.gov/air

- Office of Air and Radiation, policy and guidance information: https://www3.epa.gov/ttn/oarpg

- Office of Air Quality Planning and Standards: https://www3.epa.gov/airquality

- Title V Petition Database: https://www.epa.gov/title-v-operating-permits/title-v-petition-database

- Title V Policy and Guidance Database: https://www.epa.gov/title-v-operating-permits/title-v-policy-and-guidance-database-and-petition-database-search

- Transportation Conformity: https://www3.epa.gov/otaq/stateresources/transconf/index.htm

Notes

1. The author acknowledges the support of colleagues at Hunton & Williams who assisted in updating this chapter, including Lauren Freeman, Cindy Langworthy, Aaron Flynn, Andrew Knudsen, and Sherry Fisher.
2. *See* 40 C.F.R. pt. 50.
3. CAA § 109. Public welfare consists of nonhuman health-related concerns such as vegetation and ecosystems. *See* CAA § 302(h).
4. *See* CAA § 109(d).
5. 59 Fed. Reg. 38906 (Aug. 1, 1994).
6. 76 Fed. Reg. 54294 (Aug. 31, 2011).
7. *Cmtys. for a Better Env't v. EPA*, 748 F.3d 333 (D.C. Cir. 2014).
8. *Missouri Coal. for the Env't v. EPA*, No. 04-0660, 2005 WL 2234579 (E.D. Mo. Sept. 14, 2005, *amended* July 1, 2008) (order granting mandatory injunction).
9. 73 Fed. Reg. 66964 (Nov. 12, 2008).
10. *Coal. of Battery Recyclers Ass'n v. EPA*, 604 F.3d 613 (D.C. Cir. 2010).
11. 80 Fed. Reg. 278 (Jan. 5, 2015).
12. 61 Fed. Reg. 52852 (Oct. 8, 1996); 61 Fed. Reg. 25566 (May 22, 1996); 58 Fed. Reg. 21351 (Apr. 21, 1993).
13. Consent Decree, *Ctr. for Biological Diversity v. Jackson*, No. 05-1814 (D.D.C. Nov. 19, 2007, *amended* Dec. 4, 2008, *amended* Oct. 22, 2009).
14. 75 Fed. Reg. 6474 (Feb. 9, 2010).
15. 75 Fed. Reg. 35520 (June 22, 2010).
16. 77 Fed. Reg. 20218 (Apr. 3, 2012).
17. *Ctr. for Biological Diversity v. EPA*, 749 F.3d 1079 (D.C. Cir. 2014) (secondary NAAQS); *Nat'l Envtl Dev. Ass'n's Clean Air Project v. EPA*, 686 F.3d 803 (D.C. Cir. 2012) (primary SO_2 NAAQS); *Am. Petroleum Inst. v. EPA*, 684 F.3d 1342 (D.C. Cir. 2012) (primary NO_2 NAAQS).
18. 62 Fed. Reg. 38652 (July 18, 1997).
19. 62 Fed. Reg. 38856 (July 18, 1997).

20 *Am. Trucking Ass'ns v. EPA*, 175 F.3d 1027 (D.C. Cir.), *modified in part on reh'g*, 195 F.3d 4 (D.C. Cir. 1999), *aff'd in part, rev'd in part on other grounds, and remanded sub nom. Whitman v. Am. Trucking Ass'ns*, 531 U.S. 457 (2001).

21 *Am. Trucking Ass'ns v. EPA*, 283 F.3d 355 (D.C. Cir. 2002).

22 68 Fed. Reg. 614 (Jan. 6, 2003).

23 71 Fed. Reg. 61144 (Oct. 17, 2006).

24 *Am. Farm Bureau Fed'n v. EPA*, 559 F.3d 512 (D.C. Cir. 2009).

25 *Nat'l Ass'n of Mfrs. v. EPA*, 750 F.3d 921 (D.C. Cir. 2014).

26 73 Fed. Reg. 16436 (Mar. 27, 2008).

27 *Mississippi v. EPA*, No. 08-1200 (D.C. Cir. filed May 23, 2008); *Am. Farm Bureau Fed'n v. EPA*, No. 06-1410 (D.C. Cir. filed Dec. 14, 2006).

28 75 Fed. Reg. 2938 (Jan. 19, 2010).

29 *Mississippi v. EPA*, 744 F.3d 1334 (D.C. Cir. 2013).

30 80 Fed. Reg. 65292 (Oct. 26, 2015).

31 *Murray Energy Corp. v. EPA*, No. 15-1385 (D.C. Cir. filed Oct. 26, 2015).

32 *See* CAA §§ 110, 172. As proceedings to enforce the CAA have multiplied, courts have increasingly been confronted with the question of whether the state or EPA receives deference regarding the meaning of the SIP. *See, e.g., Alaska Dep't of Envtl. Conservation v. EPA*, 540 U.S. 461, 490-91 (2004); *Sierra Club v. Leavitt*, 368 F.3d 1300, 1304 n.9 (11th Cir. 2004); *Fla. Power & Light Co. v. Costle*, 650 F.2d 579 (5th Cir. 1981); *United States v. Gen. Dynamics Corp.*, 755 F. Supp. 720, 722 (N.D. Tex. 1991); *United States v. Riverside Labs., Inc.*, 678 F. Supp. 1352, 1356 (N.D. Ill. 1988).

33 CAA § 110(a)(2)(A).

34 CAA § 110(a)(2)(B).

35 81 Fed. Reg. 17248 (Mar. 28, 2016). A petition for judicial review of these revisions is pending. *Sierra Club v. EPA*, No. 16-1158 (D.C. Cir. filed May 27, 2016).

36 A major stationary source is "any stationary facility or source of air pollutants which directly emits, or has the potential to emit, one hundred tons per year or more of any air pollutant." CAA § 302(j).

37 CAA § 110(a)(2)(J).

38 CAA § 110(a)(2)(C).

39 CAA § 110(a)(2)(I).

40 CAA § 110(a)(2)(K).

41 CAA § 110(a)(2)(D).

42 *See* CAA §§ 115, 126.

43 CAA § 110(a)(2)(C).

44 A stationary source generally is a fixed, unmovable source of air pollution such as a factory. Motor vehicles, for example, are not stationary sources. *See* CAA § 302(z).

45 CAA § 110(a)(2)(F).

46 *See* CAA § 110(a)(2)(E).

47 CAA § 110(a)(2)(G).

48 CAA § 110(a)(2)(H).

49 CAA § 110(a)(2)(L).

50 CAA § 110(a)(2)(M).

51 CAA § 110(a)(1).

52 CAA § 110(k)(1)(B); *see* 56 Fed. Reg. 42216 (Aug. 26, 1991) (completeness criteria).

53 CAA § 110(k)(1)(B).

54 CAA § 110(k)(1)(C).

55   CAA § 110(k)(2).

56   CAA § 110(k)(3), (4).

57   *See* CAA §§ 176A, 184.

58   CAA § 110(k)(5).

59   Numerous cases have been filed recently under section 304(b)(2) of the Act alleging that EPA has failed to take action with the 12 month period specified by the statute for EPA to approve, disapprove, or conditionally approve a SIP submittal or to make a timely finding that a state failed to make a required submittal. Many of these actions have resulted in a consent decree or consent judgment. *See, e.g.,* Consent Decree, *Sierra Club v. EPA,* No. 15-cv-3798 (C.D. Cal. Mar. 14, 2016); Judgment, *Sierra Club v. McCarthy,* No. 14-cv-5091 (N.D. Cal. May 15, 2015); Judgment, *Sierra Club v. McCarthy,* No. 14-cv-3198 (N.D. Cal. May 15, 2015); Consent Decree, *Sierra Club v. McCarthy,* No. 12-cv-6472 (N.D. Cal. Apr. 21, 2015).

60   CAA § 110(c)(1).

61   Prior to construction of a new major stationary source or modification of an existing major stationary source in a nonattainment area, emissions offsets must be obtained for any additional emissions that will result from the construction or modification, generally in a one-to-one ratio. For example, if the modification of a source in an area that is nonattainment for SO_2 will result in 200 tons of additional SO_2 emissions annually, then the owner of the source must obtain 200 tons of annual SO_2 emissions offsets. *See* CAA § 173(a), (b). As discussed in section 2.1.2.2, in most areas that were nonattainment for the one-hour ozone NAAQS, the emissions offset ratio was higher than one-to-one. CAA § 182.

62   CAA § 179. EPA has issued regulations on the sequence in which mandatory sanctions will be applied (imposing the increased-offset sanction first at the conclusion of the 18-month period, and then cutting off highway funds at 24 months). 59 Fed. Reg. 39832, 39859 (Aug. 4, 1994).

63   59 Fed. Reg. 1476, 1481 (Jan. 11, 1994).

64   CAA § 172(c)(1).

65   CAA §§ 171(1), 172(c)(2).

66   CAA § 172(c)(3).

67   CAA § 172(c)(4).

68   CAA §§ 172(c)(5), 173.

69   CAA § 173(a)(2).

70   CAA § 173(a)(1), (c).

71   CAA § 172(c)(9).

72   CAA § 172(c)(8).

73   *See* CAA §§ 181-185B.

74   70 Fed. Reg. 44470 (Aug. 3, 2005). The one-hour designations were not revoked for a few areas that entered into an "Early Action Compact" with EPA in an effort to avoid being designated as nonattainment for the eight-hour ozone NAAQS.

75   *S. Coast Air Quality Mgmt. Dist. v. EPA,* 472 F.3d 882 (D.C. Cir. 2006), *modified* 489 F.3d 1245 (D.C. Cir. 2007).

76   *S. Coast Air Quality Mgmt. Dist.,* 472 F.3d at 904.

77   *See* CAA §§ 186-187.

78   *See* CAA §§ 188-190.

79   *Natural* Res. Def. Council v. EPA, 706 F.3d 428 (D.C. Cir. 2013).

80   69 Fed. Reg. 23858 (Apr. 30, 2004).

81   69 Fed. Reg. 23951 (Apr. 30, 2004).

82   *S. Coast Air Quality Mgmt. Dist. v. EPA,* 472 F.3d 882 (D.C. Cir. 2006), *modified* 489 F.3d 1245 (D.C. Cir. 2007).

[83] 70 Fed. Reg. 71612 (Nov. 29, 2005).

[84] *Natural Res. Def. Council v. EPA*, 571 F.3d 1245 (D.C. Cir. 2009).

[85] 72 Fed Reg. 31727 (June 8, 2007).

[86] *Natural Res. Def. Council v. EPA,* No. 09-1198 (D.C. Cir. Aug. 30, 2013) (per curium order granting motion for remand and partial vacatur).

[87] *Natural Res. Def. Council v. EPA*, 643 F.3d 311 (D.C. Cir. 2011).

[88] 77 Fed. Reg. 28424 (May 14, 2012).

[89] 79 Fed. Reg. 32892 (June 9, 2014).

[90] 77 Fed. Reg. 30088 (May 21, 2012).

[91] *Mississippi Comm'n on Envtl. Quality v. EPA*, 790 F.3d 138 (D.C. Cir. 2015).

[92] 77 Fed. Reg. 30160 (May 21, 2012).

[93] *Natural Res. Def. Council v. EPA*, 777 F.3d 456 (D.C. Cir. 2014).

[94] 80 Fed. Reg. 12264 (Mar. 6, 2015).

[95] *S. Coast Air Quality Mgmt. Dist. v. EPA*, No. 15-1115 (D.C. Cir. filed Apr. 24, 2015).

[96] 70 Fed. Reg. 944 (Jan. 5, 2005).

[97] 70 Fed. Reg. 19844 (Apr. 14, 2005).

[98] *Catawba Cnty. v. EPA*, 571 F.3d 20 (D.C. Cir. 2009).

[99] 74 Fed. Reg. 58688 (Nov. 13, 2009).

[100] 80 Fed. Reg. 2206 (Jan. 15, 2015). EPA refers in this notice to designations for the "2012 NAAQS" because that was the date of signature on the rule establishing the NAAQS although the rule was not published until 2013.

[101] 72 Fed. Reg. 20586 (Apr. 25, 2007).

[102] 73 Fed. Reg. 28321 (May 16, 2008).

[103] 75 Fed. Reg. 6827 (Feb. 11, 2010).

[104] 76 Fed. Reg. 28646 (May 18, 2011).

[105] 75 Fed. Reg. 64864 (Oct. 20, 2010).

[106] *Nat'l Cattlemen's Beef Ass'n v. EPA*, No. 07-1227 (D.C. Cir. Feb. 12, 2008) (order granting motion to hold the case in abeyance).

[107] *Natural Res. Def. Council v. EPA*, 706 F.3d 428 (D.C. Cir. 2013).

[108] *Sierra Club v. EPA*, 705 F.3d 458 (D.C. Cir. 2013).

[109] 79 Fed. Reg. 31566 (June 2, 2014).

[110] *WildEarth Guardians v. EPA*, No. 14-1145 (D.C. Cir. filed July 31, 2014).

[111] 80 Fed. Reg. 15340 (Mar. 23, 2015).

[112] 63 Fed. Reg. 57356 (Oct. 27, 1998).

[113] *Michigan v. EPA*, 213 F.3d 663 (D.C. Cir. 2000).

[114] 70 Fed. Reg. 25162 (May 12, 2005).

[115] *See North Carolina v. EPA*, 531 F.3d 896 (D.C. Cir.), *modified*, 550 F.3d 1176 (D.C. Cir. 2008).

[116] 75 Fed. Reg. 45210 (Aug. 2, 2010).

[117] *EME Homer City Generation, L.P. v. EPA*, 696 F.3d 7 (D.C. Cir. 2012), *rev'd*, 134 S. Ct. 1854 (2014).

[118] *EME Homer City Generation, L.P. v. EPA*, 795 F.3d 118 (D.C. Cir. 2015).

[119] 80 Fed. Reg. 75706 (Dec. 3, 2015).

[120] 58 Fed. Reg. 62188 (Nov. 24, 1993).

[121] 40 C.F.R. §§ 93.100 *et seq.*; 62 Fed. Reg. 43780 (Aug. 15, 1997).

[122] 77 Fed. Reg. 14979 (Mar. 14, 2012).

[123] 40 C.F.R. §§ 51.850 *et seq.*; 58 Fed. Reg. 63214 (Nov. 30, 1993).

[124] 75 Fed. Reg. 17254, 17272 (Apr. 5, 2010).

[125] CAA § 176(c)(6) (enacted by Pub. L. No. 106-377 (2000)).

[126] 62 Fed. Reg. 8314 (Feb. 24, 1997).

[127] *Clean Air Implementation Project v. EPA*, 150 F.3d 1200 (D.C. Cir. 1998).

[128] 62 Fed. Reg. 54900 (Oct. 22, 1997), codified at 40 C.F.R. pt. 64.

[129] *Natural Res. Def. Council v. EPA*, 194 F.3d 130 (D.C. Cir. 1999).

[130] S. Rep. No. 91-1196 at 15-16 (1970).

[131] *See* 40 C.F.R. pt. 60.

[132] CAA § 111.

[133] CAA § 111(h)(1).

[134] CAA § 111(b)(1)(B).

[135] CAA § 111(f)(1); 40 C.F.R. § 60.16 (source category priority list).

[136] 63 Fed. Reg. 49442 (Sept. 16, 1998).

[137] 71 Fed. Reg. 9866 (Feb. 27, 2006).

[138] 40 C.F.R. pt. 60, subpts. Ea-EC, AAAA-DDDD.

[139] 71 Fed. Reg. 38482 (July 6, 2006).

[140] The PSD program is contained in Title I, Part C, of the CAA, and the nonattainment program is contained in Title I, Part D, of the Act.

[141] *See* 40 C.F.R. § 52.21(b)(1).

[142] *See, e.g.*, CAA § 182(b)-(e).

[143] *See* 40 C.F.R. § 52.21(b)(4).

[144] 59 F.3d 1351 (D.C. Cir. 1995).

[145] *Clean Air Implementation Project v. EPA*, No. 96-1224, 1996 WL 393118 (D.C. Cir. June 28, 1996); *Chem. Mfrs. Ass'n v. EPA*, 70 F.3d 637 (D.C. Cir. 1995).

[146] J. Seitz, director, EPA Office of Air Quality Planning and Standards (OAQPS), "Extension of January 25, 1995 PTE Transition Policy" (Aug. 27, 1996); J. Seitz, director, EPA OAQPS, "Release of Interim Policy an [*sic*] Federal Enforceability of Limitations on Potential to Emit" (Jan. 22, 1996); M. Nichols, EPA assistant administrator for Air and Radiation, and S. Herman, EPA assistant administrator for Enforcement, " 'Effective' Limits on Potential to Emit: Issues and Options" (Jan. 31, 1996).

[147] *See generally* 40 C.F.R. § 52.21.

[148] Significance levels are provided at 40 C.F.R. § 52.21(b)(23).

[149] 40 C.F.R. § 52.21(b)(12).

[150] *Alaska Dep't of Envtl. Conservation v. EPA*, 540 U.S. 461, 488 (2004) ("Congress entrusted state permitting authorities with initial responsibility to make BACT determinations"); *id.* at 487 ("[A]s to BACT, EPA will not intervene if the state has given a 'reasoned justification for the basis of its decision' ").

[151] *See, e.g.*, EPA, PSD Workshop Manual at I-B-2 (Oct. 1980); *see also Alaska Dep't of Envtl. Conservation*, 540 U.S. at 476 n.7.

[152] *Alaska Dep't of Envtl. Conservation*, 540 U.S. at 495.

[153] *See* 40 C.F.R. § 52.21(b)(12).

[154] CAA § 112(b)(6).

[155] *In re Prairie State Generating Co.*, PSD Appeal No. 05-05, 2006 WL 2847225, at *23-37 (EPA Envtl. Appeals Bd. Aug. 24, 2006), *aff'd sub. nom. Sierra Club v. EPA*, 499 F.3d 653 (7th Cir. 2007) (Prairie State Order of Aug. 24, 2006); Letter from S. Page, director, EPA OAQPS, to P. Plath, E3 Consulting LLC (Dec. 13, 2005).

[156] Prairie State Order of Aug. 24, 2006, at 37–44.

[157] *See* CAA §§ 163, 166.

[158] CAA § 165(d).

[159] CAA § 173(a)(1)(A).

160 *See* CAA § 173(a).

161 *In re Indeck-Elwood, LLC*, PSD Appeal No. 03-04, 2006 WL 3361087 at 104-119 (EPA Envtl. Appeals Bd. Sept. 27, 2006) (order denying review in part and remanding in part).

162 40 Fed. Reg. 58416 (Dec. 16, 1975); 40 C.F.R. § 60.15.

163 40 Fed. Reg. at 58417.

164 40 C.F.R. § 60.15(b)(1).

165 40 C.F.R. § 60.15(b)(2), (f).

166 39 Fed. Reg. 36946, 36948 (Oct. 15, 1974).

167 40 C.F.R. § 52.01(d).

168 *Alabama Power Co. v. Costle*, 636 F.2d 323, 401 (D.C. Cir. 1979) ("[T]he PSD provisions seek to assure that any decision to permit increased air pollution in any area to which this section applies is made only after careful evaluation of all the consequences"); 57 Fed. Reg. 32314, 32315 (July 21, 1992).

169 41 Fed. Reg. 55524 (Dec. 21, 1976).

170 *Chevron, U.S.A., Inc. v. Natural Res. Def. Council*, 467 U.S. 837, 840 (1984).

171 *Wisconsin Elec. Power Co. v. Reilly*, 893 F.2d 901 (7th Cir. 1990).

172 Letter from W. Reilly, EPA, to M. Boskin, Council of Economic Advisers (Oct. 26, 1990).

173 57 Fed. Reg. 32314 (July 21, 1992).

174 *Id.* at 32326.

175 *Id.* at 32333.

176 *Id.* at 32325.

177 Memorandum from J. Seitz, director, EPA OAQPS, to all regional directors, "Pollution Control Projects and New Source Review (NSR) Applicability" (July 1, 1994).

178 61 Fed. Reg. 38250 (July 23, 1996).

179 63 Fed. Reg. 39857 (July 24, 1998).

180 67 Fed. Reg. 80186 (Dec. 31, 2002).

181 68 Fed. Reg. 61248 (Oct. 27, 2003).

182 67 Fed. Reg. at 80232-39 (discussing pollution control project exclusion).

183 *Id.* at 80246-47, 80263, 80273.

184 *Id.* at 80249-51.

185 *Id.* at 80255-60.

186 *See, e.g.*, 68 Fed. Reg. at 61252-53 ("[M]ost identical and functionally equivalent replacements are necessary for the safe, efficient and reliable operations of virtually all industrial operations . . . [and] are not of regulatory concern").

187 *New York v. EPA*, 413 F.3d 3 (D.C. Cir. 2005) (*New York I*).

188 *New York v. EPA*, 443 F.3d 880 (D.C. Cir. 2006) (*New York II*).

189 *Id.* at 888.

190 *Id.* at 890.

191 *Id.* at 888 n.4.

192 70 Fed. Reg. 61081 (Oct. 20, 2005).

193 71 Fed. Reg. 54235 (Sept. 14, 2006).

194 *See* https://www.epa.gov/enforcement/air-enforcement#nsr.

195 *In re Tennessee Valley Auth.*, CAA Docket No. 00-6, 2000 WL 1358648 (EPA ALJ Sept. 15, 2000).

196 *Tennessee Valley Auth. v. Whitman*, 336 F.3d 1236 (11th Cir. 2003).

197 *See, e.g.*, *United States v. Duke Energy Corp.*, 278 F. Supp. 2d 619, 630 n.8 (M.D.N.C. 2003), *cert. granted sub nom. Envtl. Def. v. Duke Energy Corp.*, 547 U.S. 1127 (2006), *vacated* 549 U.S. 561 (2007).

198 *United States v. Cinergy Corp.*, 623 F.3d 455 (7th Cir. 2010).

199 *Sierra Club v. Otter Tail Power Co.*, 615 F.3d 1008 (8th Cir. 2010).

200 *Nat'l Parks Conservation Ass'n v. TVA*, No. 3:01-CV-71, 2010 WL 1291335 (E.D. Tenn. Mar. 31, 2010).

201 *United States v. Duke Energy Corp.*, 278 F. Supp. 2d 619 (M.D.N.C. 2003).

202 *United States v. Alabama Power Co.*, No. 2:01-CV-00152-VEH (N.D. Ala. Aug. 14, 2006) (Memorandum Opinion on Alabama Power Company's Motion for Summary Judgment and Entry of Rule 54(b) Judgment on Modification Claims).

203 *United States v. East Kentucky Power Coop., Inc.*, 498 F. Supp. 2d 976 (E.D. Ky. 2007).

204 *Pennsylvania Dep't of Envtl. Prot. v. Allegheny Energy, Inc.*, No. 02:05cv885, 2008 WL 4960090 (W.D. Pa. Nov. 18, 2008).

205 *United States v. Ohio Edison Co.*, 276 F. Supp. 2d 829 (S.D. Ohio 2003).

206 *United States v. Southern Indiana Gas & Elec. Co.*, 245 F. Supp. 2d 994 (S.D. Ind. 2003).

207 *Ohio Edison Co.*, 276 F. Supp. 2d at 832-33.

208 *United States v. Duke Energy Corp.*, 278 F. Supp. 2d 619 (M.D.N.C. 2003).

209 *Id.* at 637, 647.

210 *United States v. Duke Energy Corp.*, 411 F.3d 539 (4th Cir. 2005).

211 *Envtl. Def. v. Duke Energy Corp.*, 549 U.S. 561 (2007).

212 *Id.* at 566.

213 *Id.* at 577–78.

214 *Id.* at 581–82.

215 *See, e.g., United States v. Cinergy Corp.*, 458 F.3d 705, 709 (7th Cir. 2006).

216 *Pennsylvania Dep't of Envtl. Prot. v. Allegheny Energy, Inc.*, No. 02:05cv885, 2008 WL 4960090, at *6 (W.D. Pa. Nov. 18, 2008) (emphasis in original).

217 *United States v. DTE Energy Co.*, 711 F.3d 643 (6th Cir. 2013).

218 *Pennsylvania Dep't of Envtl. Prot. v. Allegheny Energy, Inc.*, No. 02:05cv885 (W.D. Pa. filed June 28, 2005); *United States v. DTE Energy*, No. 10-cv-13101 (E.D. Mich. filed Aug. 5, 2010).

219 The key aspects of these settlements involve (1) EPA's confirmation of the traditional understanding of the NSR emissions increase test (as described in *Duke Energy*) in return for (2) companies agreeing to install controls over the next 10 years that they were generally planning to install under other CAA programs. Makram B. Jaber, "Utility Settlements in New Source Review Lawsuits," 18 *Nat. Resources & Env't* 22 (Winter 2004).

220 There have been five delisting decisions since the original list of HAPs was established in 1990. Hydrogen sulfide was included improperly on the original HAP list because of a clerical error and was removed from the list by joint resolution of Congress signed into law on December 4, 1991. EPA then published a final rule delisting caprolactam on June 18, 1996. 61 Fed. Reg. 30816 (June 18, 1996). On August 2, 2000, EPA promulgated a final rule excluding surfactant alcohol ethoxylates and their derivatives from the CAA § 112(b)(1) category for glycol ethers. 65 Fed. Reg. 47342 (Aug. 2, 2000). On November 29, 2004, EPA promulgated a final rule removing the compound ethylene glycol monobutyl ether (EGBE) (2-butoxyethanol) from the group of glycol ethers. 69 Fed. Reg. 69320 (Nov. 29, 2004). Finally, on December 19, 2005, EPA promulgated a final rule removing methyl ethyl ketone (MEK) (2-butanone) from the list. 70 Fed. Reg. 75047 (Dec. 19, 2005).

221 CAA § 112(c)-(e).

222 CAA § 112(a)(1).

223 *Nat'l Mining Ass'n v. EPA*, 59 F.3d 1351 (D.C. Cir. 1995).

224 CAA § 112(k)(3)(B).

225 *Sierra Club v. Johnson*, 444 F. Supp. 2d 46 (D.D.C. 2006). The final deadline for promulgation under this schedule was originally June 15, 2009, but was extended numerous times.

226 57 Fed. Reg. 31576 (July 16, 1992); *see* CAA § 112(c).

[227] 57 Fed. Reg. 44147 (Sept. 24, 1992).

[228] 67 Fed. Reg. 6521 (Feb. 12, 2002).

[229] *See generally* 40 C.F.R. pt. 63. On December 19, 2003, EPA promulgated a final decision deleting the subcategory of the Chlorine Production Source category for facilities that do not use mercury cells to produce chlorine and caustic. 68 Fed. Reg. 70948 (Dec. 19, 2003).

[230] *See* CAA § 112(d)(3).

[231] *See generally* 40 C.F.R. pt. 63.

[232] 61 Fed. Reg. 28197 (June 4, 1996); 63 Fed. Reg. 7155 (Feb. 12, 1998); 64 Fed. Reg. 63025 (Nov. 18, 1999); 67 Fed. Reg. 6521 (Feb. 12, 2002).

[233] *See* CAA § 112(i)(5).

[234] 57 Fed. Reg. 61970 (Dec. 29, 1992); 58 Fed. Reg. 62539 (Nov. 29, 1993).

[235] 59 Fed. Reg. 32165 (June 22, 1994).

[236] 59 Fed. Reg. 59921 (Nov. 21, 1994).

[237] *Sierra Club v. EPA*, 551 F.3d 1019 (D.C. Cir. 2008), *cert. denied sub nom. Am. Chemistry Council v. Sierra Club*, 559 U.S. 991 (2010).

[238] *See* CAA § 112(h).

[239] 59 Fed. Reg. 26429 (May 20, 1994).

[240] 61 Fed. Reg. 21370 (May 10, 1996); 64 Fed. Reg. 26311 (May 14, 1999).

[241] 75 Fed. Reg. 15655 (Mar. 30, 2010).

[242] CAA § 112(*l*).

[243] 40 C.F.R. pt. 63, subpt. E.

[244] *See* CAA § 112(f)(2)(A).

[245] EPA, EPA-453/R-99-001, *Residual Risk Report to Congress* (Mar. 1999).

[246] *Id.* at ES-1.

[247] CAA § 112(d)(6).

[248] *See* https://www3.epa.gov/ttn/atw/rrisk/rtrpg.html.

[249] *Id.* (noting court-ordered deadlines for nutritional yeast manufacturing, pulp and paper combustion sources, publicly owned treatment works, and Portland cement source categories).

[250] *See California Communities Against Toxics v. McCarthy*, No. 1:15-cv-00512 (D.D.C. filed Apr. 8, 2015) (addressing 21 source categories); *Blue Ridge Envtl. Def. League v. McCarthy*, No. 1:16-cv-00364 (D.D.C. filed Feb. 24, 2016) (addressing 13 source categories); *Community In-Power & Dev. Ass'n v. McCarthy*, No. 1:16-cv-01074 (D.D.C. filed Jun. 8, 2016) (addressing 9 source categories).

[251] *NRDC v. EPA*, 529 F.3d 1077 (D.C. Cir. 2008); *see* 54 Fed. Reg. 38044 (Sept. 14, 1989) (Benzene NESHAP). In *NRDC*, the D.C. Circuit accepted EPA's interpretation that CAA § 112(f) incorporates the Benzene framework. *NRDC*, 529 F.3d at 1082–83.

[252] *NRDC*, 529 F.3d at 1084; *Ass'n of Battery Recyclers, Inc. v. EPA*, 716 F.3d 667, 673 (D.C. Cir. 2013).

[253] *Nat'l Ass'n for Surface Finishing v. EPA*, 795 F.3d 1, 11 (D.C. Cir. 2015).

[254] *Natural Res. Def. Council v. EPA*, 489 F.3d 1250 (D.C. Cir. 2007).

[255] *Id.* at 1257–58.

[256] 76 Fed. Reg. 15554 (Mar. 21, 2011) (area source IB MACT); 76 Fed. Reg. 15608 (Mar. 21, 2011) (major source IB MACT); 76 Fed. Reg. 15704 (Mar. 21, 2011) (CISWI rule).

[257] 78 Fed. Reg. 7138 (Jan. 31, 2013); 78 Fed. Reg. 7488 (Feb. 1, 2013).

[258] *U.S. Sugar Corp. v. EPA*, No. 11-1108 (D.C. Cir. filed Apr. 14, 2011).

[259] 80 Fed. Reg. 2871 (Jan. 21, 2015).

[260] 80 Fed. Reg. 72790 (Nov. 20, 2015).

[261] Order, *Sierra Club v. EPA*, No. 16-1021 (D.C. Cir. Mar. 24, 2016).

[262] 65 Fed. Reg. 79825 (Dec. 20, 2000).

[263] 70 Fed. Reg. 15994 (Mar. 29, 2005) (withdrawing "appropriate and necessary" finding); 70 Fed. Reg. 28606 (May 18, 2005) (promulgating CAMR).

[264] *New Jersey v. EPA*, 517 F.3d 574 (D.C. Cir. 2008), *cert. denied, sub nom. Utility Air Regulatory Grp. v. New Jersey*, 555 U.S. 1169 (2009).

[265] 76 Fed. Reg. 24976 (May 3, 2011); 77 Fed. Reg. 9304 (Feb. 16, 2012).

[266] *Id.* at 9306 Table 2.

[267] *White Stallion Energy Ctr., LLC v. EPA*, 748 F.3d 1222 (D.C. Cir. 2014).

[268] *Id.* at 1258 (Kavanaugh, J. concurring in part and dissenting in part).

[269] *Michigan v. EPA*, 135 S. Ct. 2699, 2711 (2015).

[270] *Id.* at 2707.

[271] Order, *White Stallion Energy Ctr., LLC v. EPA*, No. 12-1100, 2015 WL 11051103 (D.C. Cir. Dec. 15, 2015), *cert. denied sub nom. Michigan v. EPA*, No. 15-1152, 2016 WL 1046833 (June 13, 2016).

[272] 81 Fed. Reg. 24420 (Apr. 25, 2016).

[273] *Murray Energy Corp. v. EPA*, No. 16-1127 (D.C. Cir. filed Apr. 25, 2016).

[274] *See* CAA § 112(r).

[275] 59 Fed. Reg. 4478 (Jan. 31, 1994).

[276] 61 Fed. Reg. 31668 (June 20, 1996).

[277] 40 C.F.R. § 68.10(a).

[278] 81 Fed. Reg. 13638 (Mar. 14, 2016).

[279] 40 C.F.R. pt. 72.

[280] 40 C.F.R. pt. 73.

[281] 40 C.F.R. pt. 75.

[282] 40 C.F.R. pt. 77.

[283] 40 C.F.R. pt. 78.

[284] *See* CAA §§ 404, 405.

[285] CAA § 402(3).

[286] 58 Fed. Reg. 15634 (Mar. 23, 1993).

[287] 63 Fed. Reg. 51706 (Sept. 28, 1998).

[288] CAA § 403(f).

[289] CAA § 408.

[290] *See* CAA § 416.

[291] CAA § 410.

[292] Mandatory Class I areas include international parks, national wilderness areas, and national memorial parks that exceed 5,000 acres in size and national parks that exceed 6,000 acres in size if the areas were in existence on August 7, 1977. CAA § 162(a).

[293] CAA § 169A.

[294] CAA § 169A(b)(2).

[295] 56 Fed. Reg. 50172 (Oct. 3, 1991).

[296] CAA § 169B(a)(1).

[297] CAA § 169B(c).

[298] CAA § 169B(f).

[299] CAA § 169B(d).

[300] CAA § 169B(e)(1).

[301] 64 Fed. Reg. 35714 (July 1, 1999).

[302] 74 Fed. Reg. 2392 (Jan. 15, 2009).

303 *Am. Corn Growers Ass'n v. EPA*, 291 F.3d 1 (D.C. Cir. 2002).

304 *Id.* at 10.

305 *Id.* at 8.

306 70 Fed. Reg. 39104 (July 6, 2005).

307 *Utility Air Regulatory Grp. v. EPA*, 471 F.3d 1333 (D.C. Cir. 2006).

308 71 Fed. Reg. 60612 (Oct. 13, 2006).

309 76 Fed. Reg. 81728 (Dec. 28, 2011).

310 76 Fed. Reg. 52388 (Aug. 22, 2011).

311 *Oklahoma v. EPA*, 723 F.3d 1201 (10th Cir. 2013).

312 79 Fed. Reg. 60985 (Oct. 9, 2014).

313 *See, e.g.*, 77 Fed. Reg. 20894 (Apr. 6, 2012) (final rule for North Dakota allowing a higher-than-proposed NOx limit).

314 *North Dakota v. EPA*, 730 F.3d 750, 769-71 (8th Cir 2013).

315 70 Fed. Reg. 39104 (July 6, 2005).

316 *North Carolina v. EPA*, 531 F.3d 896 (D.C. Cir.); *modified by* 550 F.3d 1176 (D.C. Cir. 2008).

317 77 Fed. Reg. 33642 (June 7, 2012).

318 *EME Homer City Generation, L.P. v. EPA*, 696 F.3d 7 (D.C. Cir. 2012), *cert. granted*, 133 S. Ct. 2857 (2013).

319 *EPA v. EME Homer City Generation, L.P.*, 134 S. Ct. 1584 (2014).

320 *EME Homer City Generation, L.P. v. EPA*, 795 F.3d 118 (D.C. Cir. 2015).

321 Order, *Utility Air Regulatory Grp. v. EPA*, No. 12-1342 (D.C. Cir. May 17, 2016).

322 81 Fed. Reg. 26942 (May 4, 2016).

323 *See* CAA § 165(d)(2)(C)(ii).

324 *Massachusetts*, 549 U.S. at 528–29.

325 *Id.* at 533.

326 73 Fed. Reg. 44354 (July 30, 2008).

327 *See, e.g.*, CAA §§ 108(a), 111(b), 202(a).

328 73 Fed. Reg. 80300 (Dec. 31, 2008).

329 *See id.*

330 *Sierra Club v. EPA*, No. 09-1018 (D.C. Cir. filed Jan. 15, 2009).

331 *See* 75 Fed. Reg. 17004, 17005-06 (Apr. 2, 2010).

332 74 Fed. Reg. 66496 (Dec. 15, 2009).

333 75 Fed. Reg. 25324 (May 7, 2010).

334 *Id.* at 25401–02.

335 75 Fed. Reg. 31514, 31540, 31597 (June 3, 2010).

336 *Id.* at 31534–41.

337 75 Fed. Reg. 17004 (Apr. 2, 2010).

338 75 Fed. Reg. 31514 (June 3, 2010).

339 75 Fed. Reg. 25324 (May 7, 2010).

340 75 Fed. Reg. 31514 (June 3, 2010).

341 *Id.* at 31523.

342 *Id.* at 31523–24.

343 *Id.* at 31524–25.

344 *See Coal. for Responsible Regulation (CRR), et al. v. EPA*, No. 09-1322, *et al.* (D.C. Cir. filed Dec. 23, 2009) (endangerment finding and reconsideration challenges); *CRR, et al. v. EPA*, No. 10-1073, *et al.* (D.C. Cir. filed Apr. 2, 2010) (timing rule challenges); *CRR et al. v. EPA*, No. 10-1092, *et al.* (D.C. Cir.

filed May 7, 2010) (LDV rule challenges); *Southeastern Legal Found., et al. v. EPA*, No. 10-1131, *et al.* (D.C. Cir. filed June 3, 2010) (tailoring rule challenges).

345 *Coal. for Responsible Regulation v. EPA*, 684 F.3d 102 (D.C. Cir. 2012).

346 *UARG v. EPA*, 134 S. Ct. 2427 (2014).

347 *New York v. EPA*, No. 06-1322 (D.C. Cir. filed Sept. 13, 2006).

348 77 Fed. Reg. 22392 (Apr. 13, 2012).

349 EPA, EPA-452/R-12-001, Regulatory Impact Analysis for the Proposed Standards of Performance for Greenhouse Gas Emissions for New Stationary Sources: Electric Utility Generating Units at ES-3 (Mar. 2012), Doc. No. EPA-HQ-OAR-2011-0660-0024, available at http://www.regulations.gov.

350 75 Fed. Reg. 82392 (Dec. 30, 2010).

351 80 Fed. Reg. 64661 (Oct. 23, 2015) (existing source guidelines); 80 Fed. Reg. 64510 (Oct. 23, 2015) (new source standards).

352 *West Virginia v. EPA*, 136 S. Ct. 1000 (2016).

353 *See* CAA § 202.

354 65 Fed. Reg. 6698 (Feb. 10, 2000).

355 62 Fed. Reg. 31192, 31242 (June 6, 1997).

356 *See* CAA §§ 211(k), 241–50.

357 59 Fed. Reg. 7716 (Feb. 16, 1994).

358 59 Fed. Reg. 33042 (June 27, 1994).

359 65 Fed. Reg. 6698 (Feb. 10, 2000).

360 66 Fed. Reg. 5002 (Jan. 18, 2001).

361 66 Fed. Reg. 17230 (Mar. 29, 2001).

362 *See* CAA § 206.

363 *Ethyl Corp. v. EPA*, 306 F.3d 1144, 1147 (D.C. Cir. 2002).

364 69 Fed. Reg. 17532 (Apr. 2, 2004).

365 75 Fed. Reg. 25324 (May 7, 2010).

366 54 Fed. Reg. 27274 (June 28, 1989).

367 57 Fed. Reg. 32250 (July 21, 1992), codified at 40 C.F.R. pt. 70.

368 61 Fed. Reg. 56368 (Oct. 31, 1996).

369 65 Fed. Reg. 32035 (May 22, 2000).

370 65 Fed. Reg. 77376 (Dec. 11, 2000).

371 *See Ohio Pub. Interest Research Grp., Inc. v. Whitman*, 386 F.3d 792 (6th Cir. 2004); *Pub. Citizen, Inc. v. EPA*, 343 F.3d 449 (5th Cir. 2003); *New York Pub. Interest Research Grp. v. Whitman*, 321 F.3d 316 (2d Cir. 2003).

372 61 Fed. Reg. 34202 (July 1, 1996), codified at 40 C.F.R. pt. 71.

373 *Clean Air Implementation Project v. EPA*, No. 92-1303 (D.C. Cir. filed July 21, 1992).

374 59 Fed. Reg. 44460 (Aug. 29, 1994).

375 60 Fed. Reg. 45530 (Aug. 31, 1995).

376 69 Fed. Reg. 27921 (May 17, 2004).

377 Title V Task Force, "Final Report to the Clean Air Act Advisory Committee: Title V Implementation Experience" (Apr. 2006).

378 70 Fed. Reg. 75320 (Dec. 19, 2005).

379 57 Fed. Reg. 32250, 32273 (July 21, 1992).

380 40 C.F.R. § 70.5(a)(1); CAA § 503(a). However, 40 C.F.R. § 70.5(a)(1)(i) stipulates that the permitting authority may establish an earlier date for submission of a permit application.

381 40 C.F.R. §§ 70.5(a)(1)(iii), 70.6(a)(2).

382 40 C.F.R. § 70.7(a)(4).

383 40 C.F.R. § 70.7(b).

384 40 C.F.R. § 70.5(d).

385 40 C.F.R. § 70.7(a)(2).

386 57 Fed. Reg. 32250, 32266 (July 21, 1992).

387 Letter from J. Seitz, director, EPA OAQPS, to R. Hodanbosi, STAPPA/ALAPCO at 2 (May 20, 1999).

388 40 C.F.R. § 70.6(a).

389 *See, e.g.,* 61 Fed. Reg. 39335, 39337 (July 29, 1996).

390 40 C.F.R. § 70.5(d).

391 62 Fed. Reg. 54900 (Oct. 22, 1997).

392 *Natural Res. Def. Council v. EPA,* 194 F.3d 130 (D.C. Cir. 1999).

393 68 Fed. Reg. 38518 (June 27, 2003).

394 40 C.F.R. § 70.6(a)(3)(i)(B).

395 40 C.F.R. § 64.5.

396 *Appalachian Power Co. v. EPA,* 208 F.3d 1015 (D.C. Cir. 2000).

397 *Utility Air Regulatory Grp. v. EPA,* 320 F.3d 272 (D.C. Cir. 2003).

398 67 Fed. Reg. 58529 (Sept. 17, 2002).

399 67 Fed. Reg. 58561 (Sept. 17, 2002).

400 69 Fed. Reg. 3202 (Jan. 22, 2004).

401 *Utility Air Regulatory Grp. v. EPA,* No. 02-1290, 2004 WL 434073 (D.C. Cir. Mar. 3, 2004).

402 *Envtl. Integrity Project v. EPA,* 425 F.3d 992 (D.C. Cir. 2005).

403 71 Fed. Reg. 75422 (Dec. 15, 2006).

404 *Sierra Club v. EPA,* 536 F.3d 673 (D.C. Cir. 2008).

405 *Id.* at 682.

406 40 C.F.R. § 70.7(h).

407 40 C.F.R. § 70.8(b)(1).

408 40 C.F.R. § 70.8(c).

409 40 C.F.R. § 70.8(d).

410 CAA § 505(b)(2).

411 59 Fed. Reg. 44460 (Aug. 29, 1994).

412 60 Fed. Reg. 45530 (Aug. 31, 1995).

413 40 C.F.R. § 70.9(b)(3).

414 40 C.F.R. § 70.9(b)(2)(i).

415 40 C.F.R. § 70.9(b)(2)(iv).

416 CAA § 113(d)(1)-(2).

417 Although CAA § 113(d)(3) provides that the EPA administrator may implement "a field citation program through regulations," EPA has taken the position that the statutory field citation program is self-implementing. *See* 59 Fed. Reg. 22776, 22780 (May 3, 1994). Consequently, the Agency withdrew its 1994 proposed field citation rules in May 2002. *See* 67 Fed. Reg. 33724, 33734 (May 13, 2002) (Regulatory Agenda).

418 CAA § 304.

419 CAA § 113(f).

420 CAA § 503(b)(2).

421 CAA § 113(c)(5).

422 CAA § 113(c)(4).

423 59 Fed. Reg. 38455 (July 28, 1994).

[424] 60 Fed. Reg. 66706 (Dec. 22, 1995).

[425] 65 Fed. Reg. 19618 (Apr. 11, 2000).

[426] M. Nichols, EPA assistant administrator for Air Programs, and S. Herman, EPA assistant administrator for Enforcement and Compliance Assurance, "Effect of Audit Immunity/Privilege Laws on States' Ability to Enforce Title V Requirements" (Apr. 5, 1996).

[427] *See* 73 Fed. Reg. 44991 (Aug. 1, 2008).

[428] Clear Skies Act of 2002, H.R. 5266 and S. 2815, 107th Cong. (2002); The Clean Power Act of 2001, S. 556, 107th Congress § 132(c) (2001).

Chapter 6

Clean Water Act

Duke K. McCall, III[1]
Morgan, Lewis & Bockius LLP
Washington, D.C.

1.0 Overview

The Clean Water Act (hereafter CWA), 33 U.S.C. §§ 1251–1387, is the primary federal statute that addresses water pollution in the United States. It establishes a number of programs designed to restore and protect the quality of our nation's waters by eliminating the discharge of pollutants into surface waters. The programs established under the act include the National Pollutant Discharge Elimination System (NPDES) permit program, the dredge and fill permit program, and municipal wastewater treatment programs. The U.S. Environmental Protection Agency (EPA), together with other federal, state, and local agencies, administers these and the other programs established under the act.

2.0 Brief History of the CWA

Today's CWA traces its roots to the Federal Water Pollution Control Act (FWPCA) amendments of 1972.[2] The 1972 amendments to the FWPCA required, for the first time, that EPA set nationwide limits for discharges from industrial sources and publicly owned treatment works into the navigable waters of the United States. The 1972 amendments further required that EPA establish more stringent effluent limitations for specific sources or groups of sources where necessary to protect water quality in a specific portion of the nation's navigable waters. The 1972 amendments also established the NPDES permit program. These provisions—the effluent limitations, water quality requirements, and NPDES permit program—remain the foundation of the CWA.

In implementing the 1972 amendments, EPA initially focused on the control of conventional pollutants, such as biological oxygen demand and suspended solids, rather than toxic pollutants. Dissatisfied with EPA's progress toward reducing toxic water pollution, environmental groups sued the agency for its failure to meet the statutory deadlines for toxics controls. This lawsuit resulted in a consent decree, known as the Flannery Decree, in 1976.[3] The Flannery

Decree set out a detailed toxics strategy, requiring EPA to promulgate effluent guidelines, new source performance standards, and pretreatment standards for 65 toxic pollutants (the "priority pollutants") in each of 21 major industrial categories by December 31, 1979.[4] Congress endorsed the Flannery Decree's approach to toxics regulation in its 1977 amendments to the FWPCA, writing several portions of the decree into law. The 1977 amendments to the FWPCA also amended the short title of the statute, noting that it had become "commonly referred to as the Clean Water Act."[5]

The act was amended again in 1987. The 1987 amendments created new programs for toxics control, established a timetable for regulation of storm water, strengthened requirements related to water quality, tightened requirements for certain variances, established a revolving loan fund for construction of sewage treatment plants, and expanded EPA's enforcement tools.[6]

In response to the *Exxon Valdez* oil spill, Congress overhauled the oil spill provisions of the act in the Oil Pollution Act of 1990, sometimes referred to as OPA 90.[7] In addition to its amendments to the existing oil spill provisions in Section 311 of the CWA, the Oil Pollution Act also created a separate statutory program governing oil spill liability and compensation.[8] The Oil Pollution Act is discussed in detail in the next chapter of this book.

3.0 Clean Water Act Goals and Policies

Like many federal environmental statutes, the CWA contains a statement of objectives, goals, and policies. The act's stated objective is to "restore and maintain the chemical, physical, and biological integrity of the nation's waters."[9] To achieve this objective, the act declares an interim goal of attaining a level of water quality that "provides for the protection and propagation of fish, shellfish and wildlife and provides for recreation in and on the water."[10] The act further declares an ultimate goal of eliminating the discharge of pollutants into the nation's navigable waters.[11]

The stated policies sought to be advanced by the act include "that the discharge of toxic pollutants in toxic amounts be prohibited" and "that programs for the control of nonpoint sources of pollution be developed and implemented in an expeditious manner so as to enable the goals of [the act] to be met through the control of both point and nonpoint sources of pollution."[12]

While these objectives, goals, and policies are not legal mandates, EPA and the courts rely on them to determine what Congress intended when it enacted the CWA. Thus, for example, the act's stated policy of prohibiting the discharge of "toxic pollutants in toxic amounts" provided the foundation for the Flannery Decree and has been a primary focus of the act's implementation since 1977.

4.0 Elements of the CWA

The CWA contains a broad range of regulatory tools to attain its statutory objectives and goals and to implement its underlying policies. These tools include the following major elements:

- A prohibition on discharges, except as in compliance with the act (Section 301);

- A permit program to authorize and regulate discharges in compliance with the act (Section 402);

- A system for determining the limitations to be imposed on authorized and regulated discharges (Sections 301, 306, 307);

- A permit program governing the discharge or placement of dredged or fill material in the nation's waters (Section 404);

- A system for preventing, reporting, and responding to spills into the nation's waters (Section 311);

- A procedure for cooperative federal/state implementation of the act (Sections 401, 402); and

- Strong enforcement mechanisms (Sections 309, 505).

These elements and other aspects of the CWA program will be discussed in some detail in the rest of this chapter.

5.0 The Discharge Prohibition

Section 301 of the CWA establishes a broad prohibition against "the discharge of any pollutant by any person" except as in compliance with the act's permit requirements, effluent limitations, and other enumerated provisions.[13] The effect of the "except as in compliance" language is to shift the burden of proof in an enforcement action. This language requires the discharger to prove that the discharge was in compliance with the act rather than requiring the government to prove that a discharge was out of compliance.

Because the Section 301 prohibition establishes the act's scope, it is useful to dissect and examine its language. First, the discharge of a pollutant is defined to mean, in relevant part, "any addition of any pollutant to navigable waters from any point source."[14] Thus, the terms "addition," "pollutant," "navigable waters," and "point source" are all of critical importance.

5.1 Addition

EPA and the courts have interpreted the term "addition" broadly. Generally, almost any introduction of a pollutant into a body of water is an addition. The scope of the term has been limited only by the requirement that there must be an addition of a new material into an area or an increase in the amount or type of material that is already present.[15]

EPA's regulations make an exception to this principle for pollutants that are present in a discharge only by reason of their presence in the discharger's intake water if the intake water is drawn from the same body of water as the one into which the discharge is made and if the pollutants are not removed by the discharger as part of its normal operations.[16] The Supreme Court also has held that the transfer of polluted water from one part of a water body to another part of the same water body does not constitute an "addition" of pollutants.[17] In addition, discharges of water from dams, even if a dam's operations adversely affect the temperature or dissolved oxygen content of the water, have been determined not to be additions of pollutants.[18]

The EPA Environmental Appeals Board has held that a company can be held liable for exceedances of metals limitations that result from metals in rainfall and from leaching of metal building materials caused by acid rain.[19] Moreover, courts have held that the mere transfer of water from one body of water to another may be an addition of pollutants, even if the water bodies are of the same quality.[20]

5.2 Pollutant

Pollutant is defined in the act as "dredged spoil, solid waste, incinerator residue, sewage, garbage, sewage sludge, munitions, chemical wastes, biological materials, radioactive materials, heat, wrecked or discarded equipment, rock, sand, cellar dirt and industrial, municipal, and agricultural waste discharged into water."[21] Despite this seemingly specific definition, courts have broadly interpreted the term to include virtually any material, as well as such material characteristics as toxicity and acidity.[22]

5.3 Point Source

Point source is defined in the act as "any discernable, confined and discrete conveyance . . . from which pollutants are or may be discharged."[23] This definition has been interpreted to cover almost any natural or man-made conveyance from which a pollutant may be discharged, including pipes, ditches, erosion channels, and gullies.[24] Vehicles, such as bulldozers or tank trucks, have also been held to be point sources.[25] But human beings have been held not to be point sources, at least for purposes of criminal enforcement of the act.[26]

Point sources include sources from which pollutants "may be" discharged. Thus, the term includes not only sources from which pollutants are routinely discharged but also conveyances from which a pollutant may be discharged only in extreme conditions, such as during an unusual storm event.[27]

5.4 Navigable Waters ("Waters of the United States")

Navigable waters are defined by the act as "the waters of the United States, including the territorial seas."[28] This definition has proved difficult to apply to the myriad of different types of water bodies in the United States, resulting in numerous judicial and administrative efforts to determine the scope of the CWA. A joint rule promulgated by EPA and the Army Corps of Engineers in June 2015 defines the term "waters of the United States" to include:

1. All waters which are currently used, were used in the past, or may be susceptible to use in interstate or foreign commerce, including all waters which are subject to the ebb and flow of the tide;

2. All interstate waters, including interstate wetlands;

3. The territorial seas;

4. All impoundments of waters otherwise identified as waters of the United States;

5. All tributaries of waters identified in paragraphs 1–3;

6. All waters adjacent to a water identified in paragraphs 1–5, including wetlands, ponds, lakes, oxbows, impoundments, and similar waters;

7. All prairie potholes, Carolina bays and Delmarva bays, pocosins, Western vernal pools, and Texas coastal prairie wetlands, where they are determined, on a case-specific basis, to have a significant nexus to a water identified in paragraphs 1–3;

8. All waters located within the 100-year floodplain of a water identified in paragraphs 1–3, and all waters located within 4,000 feet of the high tide line or ordinary high water mark of a water identified in paragraphs 1–5, where they are determined on a case-specific basis to have a significant nexus to a water identified in paragraphs 1–3.[29]

A number of features are also specifically excluded from the definition of "waters of the United States" under the 2015 rule. Excluded features include prior converted cropland, certain ditches, stormwater control features, artificially irrigated areas, and artificial lakes or ponds.[30] Another notable feature that is explicitly excluded from the scope of the Clean Water Act under the 2015 rule is groundwater.[31] Groundwater is nonetheless included in many states' definitions of "waters of the state," and in these states, point-source discharges into groundwater may be covered by the state water permit program, even though they are not considered to be discharges to the "waters of the United States."[32]

The determination of whether relatively isolated, intrastate bodies of water fall within the definition of "waters of the United States" has long been controversial. EPA and the Corps of Engineers have generally supported the broadest possible interpretation of the act's coverage. But federal courts have not been willing to find that all waters are "waters of the United States." For example, in 2001, the U.S. Supreme Court invalidated a long-standing Corps of Engineers regulation that extended the act's dredge and fill permit program to intrastate waters used by migratory birds.[33]

In the Supreme Court's most recent case on the jurisdiction of the CWA, *Rapanos v. United States*, the Court reviewed consolidated cases in which the Sixth Circuit held that the CWA afforded federal regulatory jurisdiction over wetlands located some distance from navigable waters.[34] The Supreme Court issued a split decision overruling the Sixth Circuit.[35] The plurality concluded that the phrase "waters of the United States" includes only "relatively permanent, standing or continuously flowing bodies of water 'forming geographical features'" and that federal regulatory jurisdiction extended to "only those wetlands with a continuous surface connection to bodies that are 'waters of the United States' in their own right."[36] Justice Kennedy concurred in the judgment but rejected the plurality's reasoning. He concluded that federal regulatory jurisdiction under the CWA extends to wetlands that "possess a 'significant nexus' to waters that are or were navigable in fact or that could reasonably be so made."[37] He further concluded that wetlands "possess the requisite nexus" if "either alone or in combination with similarly situated lands in the region, [they] significantly affect the chemical, physical, and biological integrity of other covered waters more readily understood as 'navigable.'"[38]

Lower courts have struggled with how to apply the fractured reasoning of the Supreme Court in *Rapanos*. Some courts have concluded that Justice Kennedy's "significant nexus" test is controlling because it resolves the issue on the "narrowest grounds" or is the least restrictive of federal authority to regulate.[39] Other courts have concluded that jurisdiction should be found if either of the tests articulated by the plurality and Justice Kennedy are met.[40] EPA and the Corps of Engineers have applied the "significant nexus" test,[41] and some courts have been deferential to the agencies in determining what constitutes a significant nexus. For example, the Fourth Circuit has upheld a Corps of Engineers determination that a wetland connected by intermittent flow through man-made drainage ditches to a river approximately seven miles away had a significant nexus to the river.[42]

The 2015 rule promulgated by EPA and the Corp of Engineers sought to resolve some of the confusion over the scope of Clean Water Act jurisdiction.[43] Among other changes, the rule added for the first time two "bright-line" categories of waters that are always jurisdictional, "tributaries" and "adjacent waters," thus obviating the need to analyze jurisdiction over those waters on a case-by-case basis. The rule also added new categories of waters that are excluded from the definition of waters of the United States, such as stormwater control features and cooling ponds. The rule then expanded upon the definition of "significant nexus" articulated by Justice Kennedy in *Rapanos* by delineating the set of waters to which the significant nexus test applies and listing factors that may be considered when assessing whether a nexus is significant. While EPA and the Corps of Engineers have described the 2015 rule as a clarification of existing law, some industry members and property rights groups have viewed it as an expansion of the jurisdiction of the CWA that will result in increased permitting costs. Those stakeholders have brought a number of legal challenges to the rule, which have been consolidated for review by the Sixth Circuit.

A related issue courts have struggled with is when parties may obtain judicial review of determinations by the Corps of Engineers that specific waters are subject to the CWA. The Fifth Circuit held in 2014 that such jurisdictional determinations are not final agency actions subject to judicial review.[44] Under the Fifth Circuit's ruling, such jurisdictional determinations may only be challenged through applying for a permit and then appealing the jurisdictional determination or beginning work without a permit and challenging the government's jurisdiction after receiving a compliance order or civil enforcement action. The Eighth Circuit, in contrast, held in 2015 that jurisdictional determinations by the Corps are reviewable final agency actions, in part because of the prohibitive costs of the alternative methods of challenging whether waters are subject to the CWA.[45] The U.S. Supreme Court resolved this circuit split in May 2016 holding in *Army Corps of Engineers v. Hawkes Co.*, that determinations by the Corps of Engineers regarding whether a particular property is covered by the CWA are subject to immediate judicial review.[46] The Court found that the alternatives of: (1) applying for a permit and appealing the jurisdictional determination or (2) discharging without a permit and contending in any enforcement action that no permit was required did not provide adequate avenues for review due to their high costs and risk. The Court concluded that the lack of alternatives for review, combined with the significant implications of jurisdictional determinations, demonstrated that the determinations were final agency actions for which judicial review should be available. The Supreme Court's decision opens the door for a number of new challenges to jurisdictional determinations by landowners and project proponents, and it could also be used by environmental groups to challenge Corps of Engineers determinations that properties are not jurisdictional.

6.0 The NPDES Permit Program

6.1 What Is an NPDES Permit?

The NPDES permit program implements the CWA's prohibition on unauthorized discharges by requiring a permit for every discharge of pollutants from a point source to waters of the United States. NPDES permits give the permittee the right to discharge specified pollutants from specified outfalls, normally for a period of five years. The permit usually sets numerical limitations on the authorized discharges and imposes other conditions on the permittee.

6.2 What Discharges Require an NPDES Permit?

Generally, an NPDES permit is required for any discharge of a pollutant from a point source to waters of the United States. Discharges that require an NPDES permit include such waste streams as industrial process water, noncontact cooling water, and collected or channeled storm-water runoff. An NPDES permit is not required for sheet runoff (which is not a point-source discharge), discharges into wastewater treatment systems (which are excluded from the definition of "waters of the United States"), and certain exempted activities.[47]

6.3 State and Federal Roles

An NPDES permit is issued either by EPA or by a state, if the state has received permitting authority from EPA pursuant to Section 402(b) of the act.[48] Currently, 46 states have received permitting authority.[49] Upon EPA approval of a state program, EPA and the state enter into a memorandum of agreement (MOA) concerning the specific elements of the authorized state program.[50] In states that are not authorized to administer the NPDES program, permits are issued by EPA regional offices.

Permitting procedures for state-issued permits normally follow the EPA procedures described in section 6.4 below. EPA's regulations mandate that state permit programs include certain elements, such as signatory requirements, effluent limitations calculation methods, and issuance procedures.[51] It is not unusual, however, for aspects of state programs that are not mandated by EPA regulations, such as appeal procedures, to differ from federal procedures.

Substantively, state programs must be at least as stringent as the federal program. But states are free to implement requirements that are more stringent than the federal program.[52]

Permits issued by authorized states are subject to review by EPA.[53] If EPA objects to a state permit and the state does not change the permit to address EPA's concerns, EPA may issue its own permit for the facility.[54] EPA has the power to withdraw its approval of a state permit program and to take over the program if it finds that the state is not administering the program in accordance with the act's requirements.[55]

Where EPA is the permitting authority, the state in which the discharger is located must certify that the discharge authorized in the permit will comply with state water quality standards and other requirements.[56] If the state does not either certify the permit or deny certification within a reasonable time, it is deemed to have waived the certification requirement.[57] States often use the certification requirement as a means of persuading EPA to adopt more stringent conditions in a permit.

6.4 The Permit Process

6.4.1 The Permit Application

The NPDES permit application, whether for a new discharge or for an existing discharge, requires extensive information about the facility and the nature of its discharges. EPA application forms include Form 1 (general information), Form 2C (detailed information for existing industrial facilities), Form 2D (detailed information for new industrial facilities), Form 2E (for new and existing industrial facilities that discharge only nonprocess wastewater), Form 2F (for new and existing facilities whose discharge is composed entirely of storm water associated with industrial activity), and other forms for other specific types of discharges.[58] State application forms must, at a minimum, require the information required by EPA's forms.[59]

The permit application must be signed by a responsible corporate officer as defined in EPA's regulations.[60] The person signing the application must certify as follows:

> I certify under penalty of law that this document and all attachments were prepared under my direction or supervision in accordance with a system designed to assure that qualified personnel properly gather and evaluate the information submitted. Based on my inquiry of the person or persons who manage the system, or those persons directly responsible for gathering the information, the information submitted is, to the best of my knowledge and belief, true, accurate and complete. I am aware that there are significant penalties for submitting false information, including the possibility of fine and imprisonment for knowing violations.[61]

Because the person signing the application may have little direct knowledge of the application's contents, some companies have adopted the practice of having the application signed in a "signing ceremony" during which the responsible corporate officer may question those directly responsible for the application in order to ensure the correctness of its contents. This ceremony is then memorialized in a memorandum or other writing so that a record of this inquiry will exist if the accuracy of the application becomes an issue in the future.

If the discharger is located in a state authorized to issue NPDES permits, it must submit its permit application to the state permitting agency. If the discharger's state is not authorized to issue NPDES permits, the application must be submitted to the appropriate EPA regional office. Normally, the application must be submitted at least 180 days prior to the date a proposed discharge is to commence or 180 days prior to the expiration of an existing permit.[62]

If a complete application is filed at least 180 days prior to the expiration of an existing permit, the existing permit will be continued (i.e., will remain in effect) until a new permit is issued by the permitting authority.[63] Because it often takes up to a year for a state or EPA regional office to issue a renewed permit, it is essential that a permittee ensure that its renewal application is both timely and complete.

6.4.2 The Draft Permit and Comment Period

When a permit involves complicated or unusual features, EPA or the state typically will initiate early informal discussions with the permit applicant about the permit terms. Often the permitting agency will issue a predraft permit, sometimes accompanied by what is called a 14-day letter, upon which the permit applicant can submit comments, so that the draft permit, when it is issued for public comment, reflects the input of the permit applicant.

The draft permit, when it is issued, must be accompanied by a Fact Sheet or Statement of Basis explaining how the permit terms and conditions were calculated and developed.[64] The permitting agency must publish a notice of the issuance of the draft permit in a local newspaper and must accept comments from the public for at least 30 days.[65] If there is significant public interest in the draft permit, EPA or the state agency will hold a public hearing.[66]

All persons, including the permit applicant, must raise all reasonably ascertainable issues and submit all reasonably available arguments supporting its positions during the comment period on the draft permit.[67] If an issue is not raised during the comment period, the party loses its right to raise that issue during subsequent administrative or judicial challenges to the permit.[68]

6.4.3 Appealing the Final Permit Decision

After accepting comments, the permitting agency will issue a final permit decision, which becomes effective in thirty days, unless a later date is specified or review is requested.[69] Within thirty days after the final permit decision is issued, any person who filed comments on the draft permit or participated in the public hearing may directly petition the EPA Environmental Appeals Board (EAB) for review.[70]

A petition for review must include a statement of the reasons supporting review, including, as appropriate, that the permit condition in question is based on a clearly erroneous finding of fact or conclusion of law or that it is based on an exercise of discretion or important policy consideration which the EAB should review.[71] When the petition for review is denied or a decision on the merits of the appeal is rendered, the EPA regional administrator is required to issue a final permit decision, constituting the final agency action on the permit application.[72]

Where EPA is the permitting authority, the final agency action is subject to judicial review in the federal courts of appeal.[73] Where the state issues the permit, judicial review is in accordance with state procedures.[74] Normally, judicial review is a review of the agency's decision based solely on the administrative record. The court will review the record to determine whether the agency's decision was arbitrary and capricious, an abuse of discretion, contrary to a constitutional right, or otherwise not in accordance with law.[75]

6.5 NPDES Permit Conditions

The primary purpose of NPDES permits is to establish enforceable effluent limitations. In addition to effluent limitations, which are discussed in section 6.7 below, NPDES permits establish a number of other enforceable conditions, such as monitoring and reporting requirements (which are discussed in more detail in section 6.6 below), a duty to properly operate and maintain systems, upset and bypass provisions, recordkeeping, and inspection and entry requirements.[76]

Although these other conditions are often "boilerplate," some may be subject to a degree of negotiation with the permit writer and should not be accepted if they would impose an unreasonable burden upon a facility.[77] State boilerplate may be more stringent than EPA by, for example, omitting the upset defense provision or establishing more stringent standards for the use of the defense.[78]

In addition, NPDES permits may require the permittee to perform best management practices (BMPs).[79] BMPs are procedures designed to prevent or minimize the release of toxic pollutants. BMPs are often simple housekeeping measures such as requirements to store drums in specific locations or to clean up spills promptly. BMPs are especially appropriate for nontraditional NPDES permits, such as storm-water permits or permits for mining operations.

Where it is impossible for a permittee to immediately come into compliance with a permit, the permit may contain a schedule of compliance. Such a schedule may contain interim limitations and dates for the submittal of compliance plans designed to achieve full compliance by a certain date.

6.6 Monitoring Requirements

The implementation and enforcement of the NPDES program depend to a large extent on self-monitoring. Permits require dischargers to monitor their compliance with permit limitations on a regular basis and to report the results of this monitoring to the permitting authority on standardized discharge monitoring reports (DMRs).[80] EPA has revised the NPDES program to allow dischargers to obtain a waiver for sampling of pollutants that the discharger can certify are not part of its effluent (i.e., the effluent levels are no higher than background levels), although any permit limitation for the pollutant would remain in place.[81]

Monitoring must take place at the point of discharge into the receiving waters unless monitoring at that location is infeasible. For example, the permit may require the monitoring of internal waste streams where the final discharge point is inaccessible, where wastes at the point of discharge are so diluted as to make compliance monitoring impracticable, or where interference among pollutants at the point of discharge would prevent accurate detection or analysis.[82]

Permits normally contain requirements for the maintenance and proper installation of monitoring equipment and specify the monitoring and analytical methods that must be used.[83] Tampering with monitoring equipment or submitting false monitoring data to the permitting authority are criminal violations of the act.[84] The act gives the permitting authority the right to enter the premises of any permittee to inspect the facility's monitoring and other records, inspect monitoring equipment, and take samples to verify monitoring results.[85]

6.7 Effluent Limitations

The CWA mandates a two-part approach to establishing effluent limitations. First, all dischargers are required to meet treatment levels based on EPA's assessment of the capabilities of treatment technologies that are technologically and economically achievable in the discharger's particular industry. This technology-based treatment level is considered to be the baseline for dischargers. Second, more stringent treatment requirements must be met where they are found to be necessary to achieve water quality goals for the particular body of water into which a facility discharges. Water quality–based controls may be a combination of chemical-specific limitations, whole effluent toxicity control, and a biological criteria/bioassay and biosurvey approach.[86]

6.7.1 Forms of Permit Limitations

Permit limitations may be expressed in several ways. Most technology-based or water quality–based limitations are expressed either as a mass limitation (e.g., two pounds per day or two pounds per "X" units of production) or a concentration limitation (e.g., 50 parts per million). Other types of permit limitations include visual observations (e.g., no visible sheen, foam, or floating solids), monitor-only requirements, requirements to perform specified tests, limitations on indicator parameters (e.g., biological oxygen demand, total organic carbon), flow limitations, pH range limitations, and temperature limitations.

Most permits impose both maximum limitations (i.e., the discharge may not exceed the limit during any monitoring event during the permit term, known as a daily maximum limitation) and monthly average limitations (i.e., the average of discharge levels as revealed in daily, weekly, or monthly monitoring throughout the month may not exceed the limitation). For some parameters, particularly pH, a permit may require continuous monitoring and virtually continuous compliance.[87]

6.7.2 Technology-Based Limitations

EPA establishes national effluent guidelines (or effluent limitations guidelines) for industrial categories through notice and comment rulemakings.[88] These guidelines establish limitations for all types of dischargers within the industrial category (i.e., direct and indirect dischargers, existing and new sources) and for specific types of discharges (e.g., process water, cooling water, sanitary wastewater). The effluent guidelines are enforceable only through their incorporation into an NPDES permit.

EPA has issued effluent guidelines for more than 50 industrial categories.[89] In a 1992 consent decree,[90] EPA agreed to meet a schedule for issuing 19 additional effluent guidelines over an 11-year period. This schedule has been extended through several amendments to the 1992 agreement.[91]

Section 304(m) of the act requires EPA to issue biennial reports, or effluent limitations guideline plans, listing candidate sectors for new or revised effluent limits.[92] In 2006 one district court held that, although EPA historically has opted not to issue effluent limitations guidelines for all sectors identified for possible regulation, Section 304(m) requires EPA to issue effluent limitations guidelines for industry sectors identified for possible regulation in the plan.[93]

For dischargers in industrial categories for which EPA has not yet issued effluent guidelines and for types of discharges not covered by an applicable effluent guideline, permit writers will apply best professional judgment (BPJ) to establish permit limitations.[94] Normally, in applying BPJ, the permit writer will assess potentially applicable technologies applied to similar discharges in other industrial categories and may evaluate effluent treatability and analytical methods to develop limitations roughly equivalent to what an applicable effluent guideline would prescribe.[95]

Permit limitations based on BPJ are subject to EPA's antibacksliding policy. This policy, which was codified in the 1987 amendments to the act, prohibits, with a few exceptions, the relaxation of BPJ limitations in subsequent permits even if subsequently promulgated effluent guidelines would allow less stringent limitations.[96] The 1972 amendments to the act established a two-step program for the development of effluent limitations based on an application of technology-based controls. In the first phase, industrial dischargers were required by July 1, 1977, to meet a level of pollutant control based on the application of the best practicable control technology currently available (BPT).[97] In the second phase, to be achieved by July 1, 1983, industrial dischargers were required to meet differing standards depending on the type of pollutant at issue.[98] For toxic and nonconventional pollutants, industrial dischargers were required to meet a level of pollution control based on the application of best available technology economically achievable (BAT).[99] For conventional pollutants (biological oxygen demand, total suspended solids, fecal coliform, pH, oil, and grease), the act allows the application of a more lenient best conventional pollutant control technology (BCT).[100]

The BPT/BAT/BCT system of standards does not apply to new sources.[101] Direct discharges that are new sources must meet new source performance standards (NSPS), which are based on best available demonstrated control technology.[102]

Industrial dischargers that discharge into publicly owned treatment works (POTWs)—known as indirect dischargers—are not regulated by the standards applicable to direct dischargers. Instead, they are regulated under the Section 307(b) pretreatment program, which is discussed in section 7.

6.7.2.1 BPT

EPA sets BPT standards by surveying the particular industry to determine the types of treatment facilities typical of the industry and, with this information, determining the levels of pollution control achieved by the better-run facilities using the typical technologies. The agency then considers the category-wide or subcategory-wide cost of applying the technology in relation to the effluent reduction benefits.[103] This results in a control level reflecting the average of the best achieved by the industry.[104]

Although the 1977 deadline for meeting BPT limitations is long past, EPA has continued to promulgate or revise BPT standards for conventional pollutants.[105] It is EPA's position that Congress did not intend BCT standards to replace BPT standards for conventional pollutants. Instead, EPA has asserted that BCT, which places cost-effectiveness constraints on incremental technology requirements that exceed BPT, was intended only to supplement BPT.[106]

6.7.2.2 BAT

BAT controls are intended to represent the maximum feasible pollution reduction for an industry. In making this determination, EPA often looks beyond the technologies usually employed by an industry, basing its standards on technologies used in other industries or on pilot plant data. The act's requirement that BAT be the best technology does not mean that the chosen technology must be the one with the highest level of pollutant removal. The determination of best technology is based on numerous factors—for example, non-water-quality environmental impacts, energy requirements, and the cost of achieving effluent reduction—only one of which is pollution control.[107]

Although no cost-benefit analysis is required, the standards must be economically achievable. EPA generally considers BAT standards to be economically achievable if they would not force the closure of a large portion of the plants in an industrial category or subcategory.[108] In June 2002, EPA proposed to significantly pare back proposed effluent guidelines for the iron and steel manufacturing industry based on a finding that the industry was not financially equipped to comply with the broader proposed guidelines.[109]

6.7.2.3 BCT

Congress created the BCT category of controls because it was concerned that the costs of moving beyond BPT to BAT for conventional pollutants were likely to be unreasonable considering the nature of conventional pollutants. It therefore required BCT standards to meet a cost-reasonableness test.[110] In most industrial categories, the BCT limitations are no more stringent than those established for BPT.

6.7.2.4 NSPS

New sources are subject to NSPS. The question of whether a discharge is a new source is often disputed. New source is defined in the act as "any source, the construction of which is commenced after the publication of proposed regulations prescribing a standard of performance . . . which will be applicable to such source, if such standard is thereafter promulgated."[111] EPA regulations modify this definition somewhat, defining a new source as a facility for which construction begins after the promulgation of an applicable final NSPS or after proposal of such an NSPS, if the NSPS is finally promulgated within 120 days of its proposal.[112]

The determination of whether a facility is a new source can be far more complicated than suggested by the regulatory definition. For one thing, the U.S.

Courts of Appeals are in conflict regarding the validity of the 120-day provision.[113] Further, it is not always clear when construction has begun. EPA's regulations define commencement of construction to include the placement, assembly, or installation of facilities or equipment, or significant site preparation work, or the entering into of a binding contract for the purchase of facilities or equipment.[114] Controversy may also arise as to whether construction at an existing facility should be considered a new source or simply a facility modification. To answer this question, EPA uses a substantial independence test, which looks at the degree to which the new unit functions independently of the existing facility, the degree of integration, and the extent to which the new unit is engaged in the same general type of activity as the existing source.[115]

NSPS are intended to reflect "the greatest degree of effluent reduction . . . achievable through application of the best available demonstrated control technology, processes, operating methods, or other alternatives, including, where practicable, standards permitting no discharge of pollutants."[116] Although NSPS often are very similar to BAT standards, they can be more stringent than BAT, based on EPA's position that it can require the installation of state-of-the-art treatment technology in new facilities where requiring existing facilities to retrofit their processes and systems to include such technology would be economically unreasonable. In addition, because EPA must consider alternative production processes and operating methods, NSPS can also effectively dictate the choice of production processes used by a new source. For example, the NSPS for the steam electric category prohibit the discharge of fly ash transport water, effectively requiring new source plants in this category to use a dry-ash handling system.[117]

One benefit of being a new source is that any new source facility constructed to meet all applicable NSPS may not be subjected to any more stringent standards for 10 years after the date construction is completed or for the period of depreciation under the Internal Revenue Code, whichever is shorter. This 10-year protection, however, applies only to technology-based limitations; it does not prevent more stringent water quality–based limitations from being imposed on a new source. In addition, at the end of the 10-year period, immediate compliance with the standards in effect at that time will be required.[118]

6.7.3 Water Quality-Based Limitations

6.7.3.1 Water Quality Standards

Water quality standards are established by the states and consist of two elements: (1) use classifications and (2) criteria that, if not exceeded, will protect those uses.[119] The CWA requires all states to classify the waters within the state according to intended use (e.g., public drinking water supplies, propagation of fish and wildlife, recreational purposes, and industrial, agricultural, and other uses).[120]

Water quality criteria quantitatively describe the physical, chemical, and biological characteristics of waters necessary to support the designated uses. State water quality standards thus normally consist of a numeric level of a pollutant that cannot be exceeded in the ambient water in order to protect the designated use. For example, the standard may state that the level of arsenic in a stream designated for trout propagation may not exceed 0.2 milligrams per liter.[121]

The state water quality standards must attain the act's goal of fishable, swimmable waters wherever possible and, under EPA's antidegradation policy, must maintain both the uses designated in the standards and the current uses unless the state can demonstrate that the designated use is unattainable or infeasible for reasons specified in EPA's regulations.[122]

State criteria normally are based on federal water quality criteria, which have been published for more than 150 pollutants.[123] The federal criteria are not enforceable standards but are guidance that can be used by states in determining appropriate numerical criteria for water bodies within the state. A state may, however, choose to set site-specific criteria based on the characteristics of the local water body. For example, site-specific criteria may be appropriate in water bodies with species different from those used in the development of the federal criteria or where adaptive processes have enabled a viable, balanced aquatic community to exist with levels of pollutants that exceed the national criteria.[124]

Courts have held that both states and citizen groups may bring actions for violations of state water quality standards, even if those standards are not translated into permit limitations.[125]

6.7.3.2 Translating Standards into Chemical-Specific Permit Limitations

EPA's regulations require permits to include water quality–based limitations for all pollutants that "are or may be" discharged at levels that cause, have a "reasonable potential to cause, or contribute to an excursion above any State water quality standard."[126] In setting a permit limitation to meet a water quality standard, the permit writer will calculate how much of the pollutant the permittee may discharge without causing the ambient standard to be exceeded.

To calculate an appropriate permit limitation based on a numerical state standard, the permit writer will take into account the dilution provided by the receiving water. Where mixing with the receiving water occurs rapidly, the permit writer typically will consider the flow of the receiving stream (usually the 7Q10 low flow[127]) as compared to the flow of the outfall and will develop a dilution factor.[128] For example, an outfall that discharges 50,000 (0.05 million) gallons per day into a receiving stream with a low flow of 1.0 million gallons per day would be assigned a dilution factor of 20. The ambient water standards would then be multiplied by this dilution factor to determine the permit limitations.[129]

Where mixing occurs less rapidly, a permit writer typically will set permit limitations based on a mixing zone. A mixing zone is that portion of the receiving water that immediately receives an effluent discharge and in which the initial dilution of the discharge takes place.[130] Normally, permit writers will allow water quality standards to be exceeded within the mixing zone so long as acutely toxic conditions do not exist.[131] Some states will take mixing into account through the use of dynamic modeling which models the fate of a discharge in the receiving waters.

6.7.3.3 Total Maximum Daily Loads

Section 303(d) of the act requires that states identify and establish a priority ranking for water bodies for which technology-based effluent limitations required by Section 301 are not stringent enough to attain and maintain applicable water quality standards.[132] For these priority waters, the states must establish total maximum daily loads (TMDLs) for the pollutants causing the impairment in those water bodies and submit the list of impaired water bodies and TMDLs to EPA for approval.[133] If a state fails to do so, EPA will establish a list of impaired water bodies and TMDLs for the state.[134]

A TMDL is a quantitative assessment of pollutants that cause water quality impairments in a particular water body. A TMDL specifies the total amount of a particular pollutant that a segment of water may receive (from point, nonpoint, and natural background sources)[135] without exceeding applicable water quality criteria, allocates allowable pollutant loads among the sources contributing the pollutant to the water body, and provides the basis for attaining or maintaining water quality standards. Where a TMDL has been established for a water body, water quality–based effluent limits for point-source discharges to the water body are based on allocations of pollutants assigned to the point source through the TMDL.

Despite the long-standing statutory mandate, states have generally been slow to submit lists of impaired water bodies to EPA and even slower in developing TMDLs. To jump-start the TMDL program, EPA issued a final rule revising the federal TMDL regulations on July 13, 2000.[136] The rule expanded the program's reach to include the regulation of nonpoint sources of pollution as well as point sources and set rigid schedules for submitting impaired waters lists and TMDLs. The July 2000 rule was extremely controversial. The agency received more than 34,000 comments on the proposed TMDL rule. To counter congressional threats to eliminate funding for implementing the rule, EPA established the effective date of the final rule as October 1, 2001.

More than a dozen groups, including farm groups, environmental groups, municipal wastewater treatment officials, and state water pollution agencies, filed challenges to the revised TMDL rule.[137] On July 16, 2001, EPA filed a proposal to stay the litigation for 18 months to allow the agency to revise the TMDL rule. EPA issued a *Federal Register* notice in October 2001 that extended the effective date of the final rule to April 30, 2003.[138] Ultimately, however, EPA withdrew the July 2000 rule. As a result, the 1992 TMDL amendments establish the current program rules.

On December 5, 2013, EPA released a new "collaborative framework" for TMDL implementation.[139] This framework provides long-term goals for EPA and the states to work together to achieve. The chief goal is to, by 2020, have states identify and characterize the extent of healthy and impaired waters in priority watersheds or waters through site-specific assessments. The framework does not alter existing responsibilities or authorities under Section 303(d) or its regulations.

Apart from the challenges to the federal TMDL regulation, there have also been lawsuits filed in at least 38 states over the delay in issuance of TMDLs under the existing TMDL program. In most cases, courts have established mandated timetables for the establishment of TMDLs (generally five years).

A 2006 decision by the District of Columbia Court of Appeals has proved significant in this regard.[140] At issue in the case before the court was EPA's approval of TMDLs for the Anacostia River, an impaired waterway, that limited the annual discharge of oxygen-depleting substances and limited the seasonal discharge of pollutants contributing to turbidity. An environmental group petitioned for review of EPA's approval of the TMDLs, arguing that the CWA requires the establishment of "total maximum daily loads," not seasonal or annual loads.[141] The Court of Appeals agreed that the plain language of the act requires the establishment of daily limits and remanded the case to the district court with instructions to vacate EPA's approval of the TMDLs.[142] EPA published guidance in light of the court's decision, noting that load allocations should be expressed in daily time increments.[143]

EPA has considered an alternative approach known as the Watershed Rule, which contains many of the elements of the TMDL rule, but also varies in some important ways. For example, the Watershed Rule would include a pollutant trading program (see section below) and require states to submit a Continuing Planning Process program that would provide blueprints for implementing the states' clean water programs rather than TMDL implementation plans. A draft of the Watershed Rule was issued in 2003, but it has never been finalized.

6.7.3.4 Pollutant Trading

In June 1996, EPA introduced the concept of watershed-based trading of pollutants in effluents.[144] Under the proposed effluent trading approach, facilities that can reduce pollution to meet water quality standards at lower costs could accumulate credits by going beyond their permit requirements. Once these reductions are achieved, a trading program would allow companies to sell or barter credits to other facilities within the same watershed. Small dischargers are expected to be able to purchase these credits at a lower price than they would pay to install the technology needed to reduce pollution to meet water quality standards. A trade will not be approved if it would result in any violation of water quality standards. In addition, trades would require a net reduction in pollution. Pollutant trading may not be used to meet federal technology-based permit limitations (e.g., BPT, BAT, NSPS).[145]

State and local permitting authorities have included pollutant trading in their permit programs. Point/nonpoint trading programs were originally established for the Tar-Pamlico estuary in North Carolina, the Dillon Creek Reservoir in Colorado, and Cherry Creek in Colorado. More recently, planned or pilot trading programs have been developed for the state of Michigan, the Chesapeake Bay watershed, the Long Island Sound, the Lower Boise River in Idaho, and the Fox-Wolf, Rock River, and Red Cedar basins in Wisconsin. Other states are considering trading programs. EPA has published materials for permit writers and stakeholders to assist in determining whether trading programs are appropriate for specific watersheds and how such programs could be designed and implemented.[146]

On October 13, 2006, EPA and the Agriculture Department's Natural Resources Conservation Service (NRCS) entered into a partnership agreement intended to eliminate barriers to and to develop standards for water quality credit trading. In addition to coordinating programs and activities, the agreement provides for the development of a water quality credit trading pilot project (or related market-based project) in a watershed within the Chesapeake Bay basin. This partnership between EPA and the NRCS is intended to increase the use of market-based approaches to improve water quality.

6.7.3.5 Watershed Permits

In 2003, EPA adopted a new approach to NPDES permits that allows states to issue NPDES permits for an entire watershed instead of specific facilities. Such permits are intended, among other objectives, to facilitate pollutant trading and ease the significant backlog of permits to be issued. EPA issued guidance in 2003 and again in 2007 on the watershed-based approach, setting forth a number of case studies implementing the NPDES watershed framework, including some involving multisource water-shed based permits.[147]

6.7.4 Toxicity-Based Limitations

Because of the enormous difficulties associated with setting individual water quality–based permit limitations, EPA and the states rely extensively on limitations based on whole effluent toxicity (WET).[148] WET limitations are imposed in the form of a permit requirement to perform toxicity testing on the permittee's effluent. Effluent toxicity tests involve exposing selected species of aquatic life to one or more concentrations of an effluent in a laboratory setting to determine the short-term and/or long-term effects of exposure to the effluent.[149]

Most permits now require dischargers to conduct toxicity tests on a regular basis (normally monthly or quarterly).[150] For example, a permit may require the permittee to conduct a monthly 24-hour acute toxicity test on a species of water flea known as Daphnia magna using 100 percent effluent. In some cases, the permit may require longer-term chronic toxicity testing on a species of fish, such as the fathead minnow. This toxicity testing can be very expensive, in some cases more expensive than all of the other monitoring and testing required by a permit.

In addition, a permit may establish a limitation on the results of the testing, such as providing that the mortality rate in an acute toxicity test may be no more than 10 percent. With this type of permit, the failure of a toxicity test will be considered a violation of the permit and could subject the permittee to penalties. In other permits, the failure of a toxicity test is not a permit violation, but it triggers a requirement to perform a toxicity identification evaluation or toxicity reduction evaluation to identify and eliminate the source of the effluent toxicity.[151]

6.7.5 Biological Criteria

In the early 1990s, EPA began to focus on a third approach for controlling water pollution. In addition to chemical-specific and WET requirements, EPA turned its attention to biological assessments—that is, evaluating the integrity of receiving waters directly by comparing various in-stream characteristics, such as species diversity and number, to the characteristics representative of "unaffected" waters.[152] It is now EPA's policy that states must fully integrate chemical-specific limitations, toxicity testing, and biological criteria, or biocriteria, into their water quality programs.[153]

6.7.6 Nutrient Criteria

Eutrophication of water bodies has been a significant long-standing problem in the United States, causing fish kills, low dissolved oxygen, murky water, and depletion of desirable flora and fauna. In February 2002, EPA published nine nutrient water quality criteria documents for water bodies within certain geographical "ecoregions."[154] These criteria documents supplemented the 17 ecoregional nutrient criteria documents announced by EPA in January 2001.[155] The criteria documents present recommended criteria for causal parameters (total phosphorus and total nitrogen) and response variables (chlorophyll and turbidity). In 2008 EPA released a report describing progress made by states in the preceding decade in adopting numeric nutrient criteria.[156] Because states have been slow to adopt numeric nutrient criteria for all their waters, EPA has continued to offer guidance and technical assistance.[157]

6.7.7 Variances

The statutory mechanisms for obtaining a variance from a technology-based standard are very limited. One such variance is the fundamentally different factors (FDF) variance.[158] The FDF variance mechanism allows a discharger to obtain a variance from technology-based limitations (including pretreatment limitations) other than NSPS. The variance is not available for water quality–based limitations.

To obtain an FDF variance, a discharger must demonstrate that the factors applicable to its facility are fundamentally different from those considered in the development of the effluent limitations guidelines applicable to the facility. Factors that may be fundamentally different include the following:

1. The nature or quality of the pollutants contained in the discharge;

2. The volume of the discharge;

3. The non–water-quality environmental impacts of control and treatment of the discharge;

4. The energy requirements of the treatment technology; and

5. The age, size, land availability, and configuration as they relate to the discharger's equipment, facilities, and processes.

The variance is not available simply because the cost of compliance with the limitations would force plant closure.[159]

Under the 1987 amendments to the act, a permittee must file a request for an FDF variance within 180 days after the publication of the applicable effluent guideline or standard.[160] In addition, an applicant for an FDF variance must show that it raised the fundamentally different factors during the development of the effluent guideline or show why it did not have a reasonable opportunity to raise such issues. This requirement makes it imperative that affected industries monitor and participate in the development and revision of effluent guidelines.

Several other variances are available under the act, although they are rarely, if ever, granted. Under Section 301(c), EPA may modify BAT requirements or pretreatment requirements affecting nonconventional nontoxic pollutants if it can be shown that the economic capability of the discharger requires less stringent limitations. The modified limitation must be shown to result in further progress toward elimination of the discharge of pollutants. Under Section 301(g), EPA may grant a variance from BAT for several nonconventional nontoxic pollutants (ammonia, chlorine, color, iron, and total phenols) where the applicable BAT limits are unnecessarily stringent.

6.8 Storm-Water Discharges

6.8.1 Regulation of Storm-Water Discharges

The problem of how to regulate storm-water discharges has plagued EPA for decades. Although the CWA has prohibited unpermitted point-source discharges of any pollutant to navigable waters since 1972, EPA and the courts struggled long and hard to develop a feasible program to reconcile the statutory requirement with the practical problems of regulating possibly millions of diverse point-source discharges of storm water. At the same time, EPA continued to identify storm-water runoff as a significant source of water quality impairment. Ultimately, the storm-water program required congressional action.

In the 1987 amendments to the act, Congress established a schedule for the regulation of, and issuance of permits for, storm-water discharges. The amendments required EPA to issue regulations setting forth permit requirements for storm-water discharges "associated with industrial activity" and for discharges from municipal separate storm-water sewer systems serving populations of 250,000 or more by February 4, 1989; to issue regulations setting forth permit requirements for municipal separate storm-water sewer systems serving populations of 100,000 or more but less than 250,000 by February 4, 1991; and to issue regulations designating other storm-water discharges to be regulated to protect water quality by October 1, 1992.[161]

In the regulations EPA issued, storm water is defined as "storm water runoff, snow melt runoff, and surface runoff and drainage."[162] This definition does not include infiltration (water that enters a sewer system from below the surface of the ground through defective pipes, pipe joints, connections, or manholes) or street wash waters.

The definition of storm-water discharge associated with industrial activity in the regulations is long and complex and requires careful reading.[163] In general, the term is defined to include discharges from any point source used for collecting and conveying storm water that is directly related to manufacturing, processing, or materials storage areas at an industrial plant.[164] The definition excludes storm water discharged from areas that are separate from industrial activities, such as office buildings and parking lots, unless the drainage is combined with storm water drained from areas used for industrial activities.[165] The definition also excludes discharges from facilities engaged in wholesale, retail, service, or commercial activities.[166] EPA and permitting states retain the authority to require a permit for discharges falling outside this definition that contribute to water quality violations or are significant contributors of pollutants to water bodies.[167]

Industrial facilities with no exposure of industrial materials and activities to storm water may be able to obtain a conditional "no exposure" exemption from the storm-water permit requirement.[168] To obtain the exemption, the facility operator must submit a written certification that a condition of no exposure exists at the facility. The operator must provide a storm-resistant shelter to protect industrial materials and activities from exposure to rain, snow, snow melt, and runoff.[169]

The regulations define a municipal separate storm sewer as a conveyance or system of gutters, ditches, man-made channels, or storm drains that is owned by a state, county, municipality, or other public entity; is designed or used for conveying storm water; and is not a combined sewer or part of a publicly owned treatment works.[170] Discharges into municipal separate storm sewers are considered discharges to waters of the United States and require a permit to the same extent as direct discharges.

EPA may issue permits for municipal storm sewer systems either for a particular system or on a jurisdiction-wide basis. Permits for municipal storm sewer systems must control pollutants "to the maximum extent practicable."[171] Such permits must include a requirement to effectively prohibit non–storm-water discharges into the system's storm sewers. A federal appeals court has upheld EPA's policy that allows states to issue storm-water permits to municipal storm-water systems that rely on BMPs rather than numeric discharge limits.[172]

In 1999, EPA issued regulations requiring small municipalities (populations under 100,000) and construction sites of between one and five acres to obtain a discharge permit by March 10, 2003, and to implement BMPs to meet water quality standards.[173] The regulation was challenged in three separate actions and consolidated in the Ninth Circuit, which invalidated parts of the regulations that allowed small municipalities to obtain permits without typical regulatory review and public participation.[174] EPA has since issued guidance to update the permitting process for municipal separate storm sewer systems.[175]

6.8.2 The Storm-Water Permit Process

Dischargers initially had three options for obtaining coverage under a storm-water permit:

- Coverage under a general permit

- Application for a permit through a group application

- Obtaining an individual storm-water permit.[176]

Only the general permit and individual permit options remain.[177]

6.8.2.1 General Permits

A storm-water discharger may apply for an NPDES permit by filing a notice of intent to be covered by a general permit issued by EPA or an authorized state. EPA has issued several general permits for storm-water discharges associated with industrial activity and discharges associated with construction activity. Although EPA's general permits apply only in the states and territories where EPA is the permitting authority, most authorized states have adopted EPA's general permits or have developed general permits of their own.

In September 1995, EPA issued a multisector general storm-water permit (MSGP) that would apply to 11,000 facilities in 29 industrial segments in the unauthorized states and territories.[178] Under the multisector program, any facility that falls into one of the 29 industrial sectors, including facilities already covered by one of the baseline general permits, is allowed to apply for coverage under the five-year MSGP permit. Under the permit, storm-water dischargers are required to develop site-specific pollution prevention plans based on industry-specific BMPs specified in the permit. For most facilities, the requirements under the more tailored multisector permit are less stringent than those under the baseline general permit. Most authorized states have used the EPA multisector permit as a model for state-issued general permits.

6.8.2.2 Storm-Water Management Plans and Pollution Prevention Plans

EPA contends that pollution prevention is the most environmentally sound and cost-effective way to control the discharge of pollutants in storm-water runoff from industrial facilities.[179] Thus, a primary component of all state and federal general permits is the requirement to develop and implement a storm-water pollution prevention plan, also referred to as a storm-water management plan, to control the pollutants carried by storm-water discharges into surface waters. These plans generally contain various BMPs that may be general, industry specific, or site specific.

The major objectives of such plans are (1) to identify sources of pollution potentially affecting the quality of storm-water discharges associated with industrial activity from the facility and (2) to describe and ensure implementation of practices to minimize and control pollutants in storm-water discharges from the facility and to ensure compliance with the terms and conditions of the general permit.[180]

6.8.2.3 Individual Storm-Water Permits

If a facility cannot qualify for coverage under a general permit, it must submit an individual storm-water permit application. The preparation of the individual application is very burdensome, requiring not only detailed information about the facility but also quantitative data based on sampling of storm-water discharges collected during storm events.[181]

6.9 Combined Sewer Overflows and Sanitary Sewer Overflows

Two other wet weather problems that are largely the responsibility of municipalities are combined sewer overflows (CSOs) and sanitary sewer overflows (SSOs). CSOs usually occur when combined sanitary and storm sewer systems are overwhelmed during heavy rains. EPA estimates that approximately 770 communities, primarily in the Northeast and Great Lakes regions, still have combined sewer systems. EPA issued a CSO control strategy in April 1994 that requires municipalities to take several short-term and long-term measures to control CSOs.[182] SSOs occur when a separate sanitary sewer system is overwhelmed, generally as a result of increased flows or structural, operational, or maintenance problems.[183] EPA has identified CSOs and SSOs, particularly those occurring in dry weather, as top priorities for enforcement and has issued an enforcement policy to address such overflows.[184]

6.10 Thermal Discharges

Section 316 of the act establishes special criteria for the discharge of heat, which is defined as a pollutant under the act and is therefore subject to technology-based limitations.[185] Under Section 316(a), if a discharger can demonstrate that the applicable technology-based limitation is more stringent than necessary to ensure protection and propagation of a balanced, indigenous population of shellfish, fish, and wildlife in and on the receiving water, EPA or the state may adjust the limitation to a less stringent level. The Supreme Court has also held that EPA may utilize a cost-benefit analysis in setting Section 316(B) performance standards.[186] Section 316 is of particular importance to electric-generating facilities because heat is a significant part of their discharge.[187]

The Section 316 process is quite complex and requires the discharger to develop substantial amounts of scientific data. Today, most Section 316 applications are supported by extensive computer modeling of the effects of a thermal discharge on the receiving waters.

6.11 Ocean Discharges

No NPDES permit may be issued for a discharge into the territorial seas, the contiguous zone, or the oceans unless the permittee complies with special criteria.[188] The permitting authority may issue a permit for such a discharge only if it determines that the discharge is in the public interest and will not result in the unreasonable degradation of the marine environment. Unreasonable degradation of the marine environment is defined as any one of the following conditions:

- a significant adverse change in ecosystem diversity, productivity, and stability of the biological community within the discharge area and surrounding biological communities;

- a threat to human health through direct exposure to pollutants or through consumption of exposed aquatic organisms; or

- a loss of aesthetic, recreational, scientific, or economic values that is unreasonable in relation to the benefit to be derived from the discharge.[189]

Permit conditions may be imposed to ensure that such degradation does not occur.

The dumping of materials into the oceans (i.e., discharges that are not through outfalls) is regulated under the Marine Protection Research and Sanctuaries Act (MPRSA).[190] Under the MPRSA, transporting material from the United States for ocean dumping is prohibited except as authorized by a permit issued under the act.[191] The only ocean dumping activity of any significance that is currently permitted is the disposal of dredged spoil.[192] Under the MPRSA, the U.S. Army Corps of Engineers is authorized to issue permits for the transportation of dredged materials for ocean disposal.[193] EPA may designate ocean sites for dumping and may designate other sites as protected from ocean dumping. Approximately 100 dredged material disposal sites have been designated.[194]

The Ocean Dumping Ban Act of 1988, which amended the MPRSA, imposed strict prohibitions on the types of materials that can be dumped in the oceans. Under that act, it is unlawful to dump sewage sludge or industrial waste into ocean waters.[195]

Ocean dumping is also regulated by the Coast Guard under Annex V of the International Convention for the Prevention of Pollution from Ships, known as

MARPOL V. This treaty restricts the discharge of garbage and plastics into the ocean from ships of the signatory countries. Provisions of MARPOL V were codified as part of the Marine Plastic Pollution Research and Control Act of 1987.[196] In addition, the discharge of sewage from vessels is controlled under the Marine Sanitation Device Program.[197]

7.0 The Pretreatment Program

Industrial discharges that do not discharge directly into waters of the United States but instead discharge into a public sanitary sewer system are regulated under the CWA pretreatment program.[198] POTWs receive about 80 percent of the nation's wastewater flow (approximately 30 billion gallons per day). Under the pretreatment program, limitations are imposed on industrial users (IUs) of a POTW through a permit, order, or contract issued by the POTW or municipality rather than by the state or EPA.

The pretreatment program involves a three-part system for controlling the pollution caused by IUs of POTWs. This system includes (1) national general and specific discharge prohibitions, (2) national categorical standards, and (3) local limits developed by POTWs.

7.1 General Prohibitions

Discharges of pollutants that may interfere with a POTW's operations are regulated through the general pretreatment regulations found at 40 C.F.R. Part 403.[199] The regulations contain both general discharge prohibitions and specific prohibitions. The general prohibitions prohibit an IU from introducing into a POTW any pollutant that causes pass through or interference.[200] Pass through is defined as a discharge that exits the POTW into waters of the United States in quantities or concentrations that, alone or in conjunction with a discharge or discharges from other sources, cause a violation of any requirement of the POTW's NPDES permit (including an increase in the magnitude or duration of a violation).[201] Interference is defined as a discharge that, alone or in conjunction with a discharge or discharges from other sources, (1) inhibits or disrupts the POTW, its treatment processes or operations, or its sludge processes, use, or disposal and (2) causes a violation of any requirement of the POTW's NPDES permit (including an increase in the magnitude or duration of a violation) or prevents sewage sludge use or disposal in compliance with applicable statutory provisions and regulations.[202]

7.2 Specific Prohibitions

The regulations establish eight specific prohibitions that are generally intended to prevent interference with the POTW's operations. These prohibitions include prohibitions on the discharge of pollutants that may be fire or explosion hazards, pollutants that will cause corrosive structural damage to the POTW, solid or viscous pollutants that would cause an obstruction in flow, heat that would inhibit the biological activity at the POTW, and pollutants that could cause acute worker health and safety problems.[203]

7.3 National Categorical Standards

The prohibition on discharges that pass through POTWs is implemented through categorical effluent guidelines. Effluent guidelines for an industrial category will normally include pretreatment standards for existing sources and pretreatment standards for new sources (PSNS). The standards establish specific numerical limitations on pollutants considered incompatible pollutants—that is, pollutants other than biological oxygen demand, suspended solids, pH, and fecal coliform bacteria.

7.4 Removal Credits

The categorical standards are intended to result in the same level of treatment prior to discharge from the POTW as would have been required if the industrial facility had discharged those pollutants directly into the receiving waters. Thus, the user must meet the equivalent of BAT control unless the stringency of the standard is reduced through the mechanism of removal credits, which gives an industrial discharger credit for the actual level of removal of a pollutant consistently achieved by the POTW.[204] In other words, the industrial discharger may meet a less stringent limitation if treatment of the pollutant occurs at the POTW. Removal does not include dilution or volatilization that occurs at or on the way to the POTW.[205]

In 1986, the U.S. Court of Appeals for the Third Circuit interpreted the act to require EPA to promulgate comprehensive sewage sludge regulations before any removal credits could be authorized.[206] Congress codified this interpretation in the 1987 amendments to the act.[207] Removal credits were thus not available for several years because EPA had failed to promulgate final regulations governing the disposal and use of POTW sludge.

Regulations governing sludge that is codisposed in municipal solid waste landfills were promulgated in October 1991[208] and were upheld by the D.C. Circuit Court of Appeals in December 1993.[209] EPA promulgated Phase I of its comprehensive sludge use and disposal regulations in February 1993.[210] Phase I established numerical pollutant limits for certain metals when sewage sludge is applied to the land, disposed of at surface disposal sites, or incinerated.

Removal credits are thus now available for (1) pollutants sent to POTWs that codispose of their sludge in municipal landfills and (2) the pollutants listed in 40 C.F.R. § 403 Appendix G that are discharged to other POTWs that comply with the sludge regulations.[211] EPA has considered proposing a rule that would expand the universe of pollutants for which removal credits may be authorized.[212]

7.5 Local Limits

POTWs may establish local limits that are more stringent than the federal categorical standards.[213] For example, the local limits may impose more stringent limitations on pollutants regulated under the federal standards or may establish limits on pollutants that are not limited in the federal standards. Two factors that often require local limits are the prevention of fume toxicity to workers and the reduction of POTW air emissions. Where the local limit is more stringent than the federal standard, the local limit supersedes the federal standard. A local limit that is less stringent than a federal standard, however, does not relieve the IU of its obligation to meet the federal standard.

7.6 Pretreatment Program Enforcement

Although the pretreatment program is implemented primarily by the municipality operating the POTW, EPA and the states retain enforcement authority.[214] If EPA becomes aware of a pass through or interference at a POTW and sends notice of the incident to the POTW and the POTW does not take appropriate enforcement action within 30 days, EPA may bring an enforcement action for the violation.[215] Similarly, an authorized state has the power to bring an action for penalties even though a POTW has sought penalties for the same noncompliance, if the state determines that the penalty sought by the POTW is insufficient.[216]

POTWs with approved pretreatment programs may take enforcement action against violations of pretreatment permits, including violations of the national pretreatment standards.[217] POTWs, to be approved under the federal pretreatment program, must have the authority to seek injunctive relief for noncompliance and to seek or assess civil or criminal penalties of at least $1,000 per day for each violation of a pretreatment requirement.

8.0 Nonpoint-Source Discharges

Nonpoint sources of pollution (i.e., discharges other than those defined as point-source discharges) are a major source of pollution of our nation's waters. It is estimated that agricultural runoff alone is responsible for 70 percent of the nation's impaired rivers and streams. Siltation, salinity, pesticides, and nutrient discharges are the primary impacts on surface waters caused by nonpoint sources.

Several sections of the act establish various programs for controlling non-point sources of pollution. In addition, states and EPA have targeted nonpoint sources through the TMDL program, discussed above.

8.1 The Section 319 Program

The 1987 amendments to the act established a program for the control of non-point sources of water pollution, codified in Section 319 of the act, that depends primarily on state implementation. Section 319 requires states to submit to EPA for approval an assessment of waters within the state that, without additional action to control nonpoint sources of pollution, cannot reasonably be expected to attain or maintain applicable water quality standards.[218] Section 319 further requires states to obtain EPA approval of state management programs that identify the measures to be undertaken by the state to reduce the pollutant loadings resulting from nonpoint-source discharges, the state programs to achieve these measures, and a schedule for implementing the measures.[219] State programs must be developed in cooperation with local, substate regional, and interstate entities involved in the nonpoint-source issue. Congress authorized up to $400 million over four years to fund the state management programs.[220] This statutory provision has been greatly weakened, however, by Congress's failure to appropriate the money. Additionally, the statute provides no sanction against states for failing to submit an adequate plan.[221]

8.2 Coastal Zone Management Program

The Coastal Zone Management (CZM) program provides for the protection of coastal areas from nonpoint sources of pollution.[222] The CZM program is a voluntary partnership between the federal government and the 28 coastal states and five U.S. territories. Under the program, which is jointly administered by EPA and the National Oceanic and Atmospheric Administration, the participating states and territories must develop Coastal Nonpoint Pollution Control (CNPC) programs. The CNPC programs describe how the state will implement nonpoint-source pollution controls in accordance with technical guidance issued by EPA.[223] States were scheduled to implement the first phase of their approved programs by 2004 and, if necessary, the second phase by 2009.

8.3 National Estuary Program

The 1987 amendments to the CWA also created the National Estuary Program (NEP) to promote long-term planning and management for nationally significant estuaries threatened by pollution, development, or overuse.[224] This program is a major vehicle for the implementation of nonpoint-source controls. The NEP requires the preparation of Comprehensive Conservation and Management Plans

(CCMP), which recommend approaches for correcting and preventing problems for estuaries nominated by state governors or the EPA administrator. A CCMP is prepared through a Management Conference, to which federal, state, and local governments and representatives of industry and the general public may be invited. There are currently 28 estuaries included in the NEP.

9.0 Dredge and Fill Permits

The CWA's broad prohibition on the discharge of pollutants, except in compliance with the act, applies to dredged or fill material. Section 404 of the CWA provides for the issuance of permits for the discharge of dredge or fill material into the navigable water of the United States.[225] The Section 404 dredge and fill permit program is administered by the U.S. Army Corps of Engineers.

9.1 Waters within the Scope of the Program

Questions regarding the scope of the Section 404 program often arise with respect to the dredging and filling of wetlands. Wetlands may be jurisdictional waters if they are adjacent to or have a significant nexus with other waters of the U.S., or if they cross state lines. But it can be very difficult to determine whether certain areas are wetlands covered by the CWA, or if they are even wetlands at all. In 1987, the EPA, Corps of Engineers, Fish and Wildlife Service, and Soil Conservation Service therefore issued a guidance manual for identifying wetlands that constitute waters of the U.S.[226] This document describes technical criteria, field indicators, and other relevant information for identifying and delineating jurisdictional wetlands.

The 2015 CWA jurisdiction rule does not alter the definition of "wetlands" or the procedures for wetlands delineation set out in the 1987 manual.[227] The proposed rule does, however, modify the definition of adjacency, so that waters adjacent to other waters of the U.S. do not necessarily need to be wetlands to be jurisdictional. Prior to the proposed rule, only "adjacent wetlands" had been specifically recognized as jurisdictional;[228] under the 2015 rule, all waters adjacent to another water of the U.S. are jurisdictional.[229] Nonetheless, the 1987 manual will likely continue to be important in determining whether certain areas are wetlands or non-jurisdictional dry lands.

9.2 Covered Activities

The Section 404 permit program covers only the actual discharge or placement of dredged and fill material into waters of the United States. EPA's and the Corps' Section 404 jurisdiction does not extend to incidental fallback of dredged material during wetlands dredging operations.[230] However, regulations create a rebuttable presumption that all mechanized ditching, channelization, and excavation results in discharges greater than incidental fallback and is therefore within Section 404 jurisdiction.[231]

Redeposit of dredged materials into a wetland or water body is subject to the Section 404 program. For example, in one case, the court held that the rearrangement of indigenous materials in a riverbed, undertaken to cut off high water channels to protect riverbanks from erosion, required a Section 404 permit.[232] In another case, the court held that Section 404 applied to owners of a tugboat where the boat's propellers cut into a river bottom, uprooting and destroying sea grass and depositing bottom sediment on adjacent sea grass beds.[233] Some fill activities are exempted from Section 404 if specified effects on navigable waters are avoided. These exempted activities include maintenance of dams, dikes, and similar structures; the construction of temporary sedimentation basins and temporary farm, forest, and mining roads; and some agricultural activities.[234]

In *Southeast Alaska Conservation Council v. U.S. Army Corps of Engineers*, the Ninth Circuit ruled that Section 404 also does not apply to a discharge of material that meets the regulatory definition of "fill material" where EPA previously has adopted, under the NPDES permit program, a performance standard applicable to such discharges.[235] Conservation groups challenged the Corps' issuance of a Section 404 permit to Coeur Alaska, Inc. for the disposal of mine tailings.[236] Coeur Alaska planned to use a froth flotation system to remove gold fines from tailings, and then discharge the process wastewater, containing the residual tailings, into a nearby lake.[237] Because the discharge would raise the bottom of the lake by approximately fifty feet, the discharge met the regulatory definition of "fill material."[238] EPA, however, previously had promulgated a performance standard under Sections 301 and 306 of the CWA that prohibits discharges from froth-flotation mills into waters of the United States.[239] The plaintiffs argued that the Corps' issuance of the Section 404 permit and the proposed discharge of process wastewater thus violated Sections 301 and 306 of the CWA.[240]

The Ninth Circuit held that "[e]ven though the discharge . . . facially qualifies for the permitting scheme under § 404 of the Clean Water Act . . . the discharge is nevertheless prohibited by the clearly applicable and specific performance standard."[241] The court reasoned that the plain language of Sections 301 and 306 requires that all discharges comply with applicable effluent and performance standards, with no exceptions for discharges that would otherwise qualify for regulation under Section 404.[242] The court further reasoned that the regulatory history demonstrated that EPA and the Corps "intended for effluent limitations and performance standards to apply even to discharges that facially meet the definition of the term 'fill material.'"[243]

Coeur Alaska sought certiorari from the Ninth Circuit's decision, arguing that "[i]t changes the Section 404 permit program from a distinct permitting scheme . . . , into a secondary permitting scheme that has only residual application."[244] The Supreme Court reversed the Ninth Circuit, holding that the Corps acted in accordance with law in issuing the permit.[245]

9.3 Individual Permits

The Corps has issued national regulations governing the issuance of Section 404 permits.[246] Corps district engineers also develop and implement local policies and procedures. The local procedures must allow potential applicants to contact the local office for preapplication consultation for major projects.[247]

In reviewing an application for an individual Section 404 permit, the Corps will conduct a "Public Interest Review."[248] This review involves "evaluation of the probable impacts . . . of the proposed activity and its intended use on the public interest" and consideration and balancing of "conservation, economics, aesthetics, general environmental concerns, wetlands, historic properties, fish and wildlife values," flood damage prevention, water supply, water quality, energy, and other factors.[249] The Corps cannot deny a permit solely on the basis of economics unrelated to environmental impacts.[250]

In reviewing a permit application, the Corps must apply EPA's Section 404 guidelines.[251] Under EPA's guidelines, "no discharge of dredged or fill material shall be permitted if there is a practicable alternative to the proposed discharge which would have less adverse impact on the aquatic ecosystem."[252] An alternative is "practicable" if it is "capable of being done" taking into account "cost, existing technology, and logistics in light of overall project purposes."[253] There is a presumption that a permit will not be granted for work in a wetland unless there are no practicable, less environmentally damaging alternatives.[254] A heavy burden is placed on the applicant to overcome this presumption.[255] EPA's guidelines also contain a policy statement that a discharge may not cause or contribute to significant degradation of the aquatic ecosystem.[256]

No Section 404 permit may be granted by the Corps unless the affected state (or states) certifies that the permitted activities will not violate applicable laws and regulations.[257] The Corps must consult with EPA[258] and the federal Fish and Wildlife Service[259] before issuing a permit. Section 404(c) allows EPA to veto such activities. The D.C. Circuit has held that EPA can veto a permit years after issuance, even when the permittee is in full compliance with the permit.[260]

In addition, the requirements of the National Environmental Policy Act[261] apply to Section 404 permits.[262] Thus, if a project authorized by a Section 404 permit would result in significant effects on the human environment, the Corps of Engineers must prepare an environmental impact statement before issuing the permit.[263] This requirement can significantly delay development and construction projects.

The Corps' regulations require permit applications to be concurrently processed at federal, state, and local levels. Some states and Corps districts are working to streamline the permit application process. For example, the Pennsylvania Department of Conservation and Natural Resources (DCNR) and the Corps have created a general wetlands permit, called the Pennsylvania State Programmatic General Permit, for activities that have a limited environmental impact on wetlands less than one acre in size or on less than 250 linear feet of streams. This general permit will allow developers to submit only one application for authorization and will allow the DCNR to approve an activity without it undergoing extensive federal review.

9.4 The Mitigation Policy

The guidelines issued under Section 404(b)(1) require applicants to take all practicable steps to minimize the adverse effects of proposed filling activities. Once the amount of wetland damage has been reduced to its barest minimum, the remaining damage must be mitigated.

Under a February 1990 MOA between the EPA and the Corps of Engineers, the Corps committed to minimize the loss of wetlands resulting from its permit decisions.[264] This no-net-loss policy requires the Corps to determine first whether potential impacts have been avoided to the maximum extent practicable, then whether any remaining unavoidable impacts have been mitigated "to the extent appropriate and practicable," and then to compensate financially for aquatic values. Unavoidable wetlands impacts often may be offset by wetlands restoration or creation.[265]

Compensatory mitigation—for example, restoration of existing degraded wetlands or creation of man-made wetlands—can be accomplished by three methods: (i) permittee-responsible mitigation, where the permittee retains responsibility for the mitigation; (ii) mitigation banks, sites where a third party conducts mitigation activities and sells credits to permittees to satisfy their mitigation obligations; (iii) or in-lieu fee programs, where a governmental or nonprofit resource management entity conducts mitigation and provides credits to permittees.[266] On March 31, 2008, EPA and the Corps of Engineers issued a final rule setting forth performance standards for compensatory mitigation projects and establishing a preference for mitigation banks over in-lieu fee programs and permittee-responsible mitigation.[267] The rule also provides that all mitigation should be located in the same watershed as the impacted resource and must be sufficient to replace the lost aquatic resource functions.[268]

9.5 Nationwide Permits

The Corps is authorized to issue nationwide and general (state, regional, or nationwide) Section 404 permits for specific categories of activities involving the discharge of dredged or fill materials determined to have minimal adverse environmental effects.[269] An activity covered by a nationwide or general permit may be performed without an individual Section 404 permit so long as the general conditions[270] of the nationwide or general permit are observed.[271] The general and nationwide permits are intended to allow certain minor-impact activities to take place without delay or paperwork.[272]

Nationwide permits have been issued for approximately 50 activities, including some survey activities, backfilling of utility lines, minor road crossings, construction of outfall structures, bank stabilization, oil and gas structures, hydropower projects, and maintenance activities.[273] A number of the nationwide permits require that special notice be given to the Corps prior to proceeding with an activity. The remaining nationwide permits are self-executing,[274] although it is prudent to contact the Corps when planning an activity within a possible wetland area.[275]

9.6 Potential Liabilities under the Section 404 Program

Like violations of other parts of the act, violations of the Section 404 permit requirement may result in penalties of up to $37,500 per day.[276] In addition, the Corps may bring an action to compel the restoration of areas that have been filled without obtaining the required permit or dredged in violation of permit conditions. Extensive restoration, including replication of natural topography and hydrology, has been ordered in some cases.[277]

Discharging dredged or fill material without a Section 404 permit can also lead to criminal penalties. Criminal penalties will normally be imposed only for cases of extreme conduct, such as refusing to obey a cease and desist order or causing severe damage to a wetland.[278]

10.0 Preventing, Reporting, and Responding to Spills

10.1 Spill Prevention

Section 311 of the CWA establishes a national policy that "there should be no discharges of oil or hazardous substances into or upon the navigable waters of the United States, adjoining shorelines, or into or upon the waters of the contiguous zone" and creates a comprehensive scheme of prohibitions, reporting requirements, penalties, and cleanup obligations to implement this policy.[279]

The act requires many facilities to develop and maintain plans for preventing and responding to spills of oil and hazardous substances, called Spill Prevention Control and Countermeasure (SPCC) Plans. As amended by the Oil Pollution Act of 1990 (OPA), the act now also requires owners and operators of some facilities to prepare and submit a more extensive plan, called a Facility Response Plan, for responding to a worst-case spill of oil.

10.1.1 SPCC Plans

A facility must prepare an SPCC plan if it drills, produces, gathers, stores, processes, refines, transfers, distributes, or consumes oil and if, because of its location, it could reasonably be expected to discharge[280] oil in harmful quantities, as defined in Part 110 of the regulations, into or upon surface waters, adjoining shorelines, or the contiguous zone.[281] Exempted from this requirement are facilities where (1) the total underground storage capacity is 42,000 gallons or less of oil and (2) the aboveground storage capacity is 1,320 gallons or less of oil.[282] Also exempted are completely buried underground tanks already regulated under the Underground Storage Tank Program.[283]

The SPCC plan describes steps the facility will take to prevent spills and to minimize the risk of harm to surface waters in the event of a release of oil. The SPCC plan need not be submitted to the regulatory agency but must be maintained at the facility at all times and may be reviewed during state or federal inspections.[284] Owners or operators of new facilities must prepare and implement an SPCC plan within six months after the date the facility begins operations.[285]

The SPCC plan must be amended whenever there is a change in facility design, operation, or maintenance that materially affects the facility's potential to discharge oil. Notwithstanding this requirement, the plan must be reviewed and evaluated for adequacy at least once every five years.[286] Plans must be reviewed and certified by a registered professional engineer.[287]

If a facility discharges more than 1,000 gallons of oil into the waters of the United States or upon adjoining shorelines or discharges more than 42 gallons of oil to waters of the United States or adjoining shorelines twice within a 12-month period, the owner or operator of the facility must submit additional information to the EPA regional administrator within 60 days.[288] After reviewing this information, the regional administrator may require the facility to amend the SPCC plan if he or she finds that the existing plan does not meet the requirements of the regulations or that amendment of the plan is necessary to prevent or contain discharges from the facility.[289]

EPA's regulations set forth detailed guidelines for the preparation of SPCC plans.[290] The plan must contain a description of recent spill events and, in some circumstances, a prediction of the direction, rate of flow, and total quantity of oil that could be discharged from the facility as a result of a failure in containment.[291] The regulations specify the types of containment structures and other spill control mechanisms that may—or in some cases must—be included in the plan.[292]

The plan must also designate a person who will be accountable for oil spill prevention and who will report to facility management.[293] Owners and operators are responsible for properly instructing their personnel in the operation and maintenance of equipment to prevent oil discharges, and in applicable pollution control laws and regulations.[294]

10.1.2 Facility Response Plans

Under the OPA, a non-transportation-related onshore facility is required to prepare a Facility Response Plan if it handles, transports, or stores oil and if it, "because of its location, could reasonably be expected to cause substantial harm to the environment by discharging into or on the navigable waters, adjoining shorelines, or the exclusive economic zone."[295] Facilities that do not meet EPA's substantial harm criteria must complete and maintain a certification verifying that the criteria do not apply.[296]

EPA has established criteria for determining which facilities may cause substantial harm in the event of a discharge of oil.[297] Facility Response Plans must be prepared for two classes of facility:

1. Facilities that transfer oil over water to or from vessels that have a total oil storage capacity greater than or equal to 42,000 gallons, and

2. Facilities with total oil storage capacity of at least one million gallons, where one or more of the following is true:

   • The facility does not have secondary containment for each aboveground storage area sufficiently large to contain the capacity of the largest tank plus sufficient freeboard for precipitation,

   • The facility is located in the vicinity of fish and wildlife or sensitive environments such that a discharge could cause injury to them,

   • The facility is located in an area where a discharge would shut down operations at a public drinking water intake, or

   • The facility has had a reportable spill greater than or equal to 10,000 gallons within the past five years.[298]

The regional administrator may require facilities other than substantial harm facilities to prepare and submit a Facility Response Plan under certain circumstances.[299]

The Facility Response Plan is intended to be a plan for responding to a worst-case release of oil. EPA's regulations include a worksheet that is to be used to calculate what this worst-case event would be.[300] The regulations also set forth a model plan that is to be followed in developing facility plans.[301] The plan must, among other things, identify the person with authority to implement the plan, require immediate communication to appropriate federal officials, ensure that adequate private personnel and equipment will be available to respond to the discharge, describe the immediate measures that will be taken in the event of a spill to secure the source of the discharge and provide containment, contain plans for evacuation, and require training, drills, and equipment testing.[302] The plan must be consistent with the National Oil and Hazardous Substance Pollution Contingency Plan.[303]

Facilities that have not submitted such plans are not permitted to operate.[304] Facilities may operate for up to two years pending federal approval of submitted plans if the owner of the facility certifies that he or she has ensured by contract or other means the availability of private personnel and equipment necessary to respond to a worst-case discharge. If that period expires or if approval is denied, the facility must discontinue its storage, transportation, and handling of oil.[305]

10.2 Spill Notification

Section 311(b)(5) of the act requires persons in charge of facilities to immediately notify the National Response Center of discharges of harmful quantities of oil or a hazardous substance to navigable waters or adjoining shorelines.[306] It is a criminal offense to fail to make such a report, punishable by up to five years in prison.[307]

For spills of oil,[308] EPA has determined that a harmful quantity is any quantity causing a film or sheen on the receiving waters, any quantity causing a sludge or emulsion to be deposited beneath the surface of the water or upon adjoining shorelines, or any quantity that violates an applicable water quality standard.[309]

EPA has designated over 300 substances as hazardous substances subject to the Section 311 reporting requirement[310] and has identified the reportable quantity for each of these substances.[311] Any release of more than the reportable quantity of a hazardous substance within a 24-hour period must be reported to the National Response Center.[312] This reporting requirement is in addition to reporting requirements under the Comprehensive Environmental Response, Compensation, and Liability Act, the Emergency Planning and Community Right-to-Know Act, and other federal or state requirements.

Under certain conditions, an NPDES permit may insulate a permittee from the statutory notification requirement. For purposes of Section 311, discharge is defined to exclude the following:

- discharges in compliance with an NPDES permit;

- discharges resulting from circumstances identified, reviewed, and made a part of the public record with respect to an NPDES permit, and subject to a condition in such permit;

- continuous or anticipated intermittent discharges from a point source, identified in an NPDES permit or permit application, that are caused by events occurring within the scope of the relevant operating or treatment systems; and[313]

- discharges incidental to authorized mechanical removal.

10.3 Spill Response and Liability

The discharge of harmful quantities of oil or a hazardous substance into waters of the United States or onto adjoining shorelines or the contiguous zone is prohibited.[314] Owners and operators of facilities from which oil or a hazardous substance is discharged to navigable waters, to shorelines, or into the contiguous zone in quantities greater than the reportable quantity are strictly liable for (1) penalties, (2) the costs of cleaning up the spill, and (3) natural resource damages caused by the spill.[315] Liability is strict, although several limited defenses are available against a claim for liability for the costs of the cleanup of a spill.[316]

The OPA increased the penalties to which a discharger may be subject. Any owner, operator, or person in charge may be fined up to $37,500 per day for a discharge, or up to $2,100 per barrel of oil discharged.[317] Where a discharge results from gross negligence or willful misconduct, the minimum penalty is $150,000, and the maximum penalty is $5,300 per barrel of oil or unit of reportable quantity of hazardous substance discharged.[318]

11.0 Enforcement

11.1 Federal and State Roles

The CWA's enforcement mechanisms are structured to allow states (and local governments in the case of the pretreatment program) to assume an active role in the act's enforcement. To obtain approval of its NPDES permit program, a state must demonstrate that its environmental control agency has adequate powers of enforcement, roughly equivalent to those exercised by EPA under the act.[319] At a minimum, authorized states must have civil and criminal enforcement authority, and virtually all have some form of administrative enforcement authority.

State enforcement programs are not required to be identical to the federal program. For example, states may impose maximum civil penalties as low as

$5,000 per day per violation (compared to the daily maximum of $32,500 under the federal program) and may impose maximum criminal penalties as low as $10,000 per day per violation (compared to $50,000 per day under the federal program).[320] In addition, EPA currently does not require authorized states to provide a mechanism for citizen suits under the state program. States are required only to allow intervention of citizens in enforcement actions, to investigate and respond in writing to citizen complaints, and to provide notice and opportunity for comment on proposed settlements of state enforcement actions.[321]

In states with authorized permit programs, EPA retains the right to initiate an enforcement action even if the state determines that no action is warranted. EPA must first notify the alleged violator and the state of its intent to bring an enforcement action and must allow the state 30 days to commence a state enforcement action.[322]

Moreover, EPA may bring a federal enforcement action even though an authorized state has brought a parallel action.[323] Where a final judgment has been issued in a state judicial action, however, EPA is generally foreclosed from relitigating the factual issues decided in the state proceeding.[324]

In addition, if EPA finds that permit violations within a state are widespread and appear to result from the state's failure to enforce its permits, EPA must so notify the state. If the state's failure to enforce extends more than 30 days beyond the notice, EPA must assume responsibility for enforcing permits within the state. This period of federally assumed enforcement ends only after EPA determines that the state will adequately enforce its permit program.[325]

In states where EPA retains permitting authority, EPA (usually through the regional offices) is the primary enforcement authority. Nonauthorized states may enforce in state courts any state statutes and regulations that are not inconsistent with or duplicative of the federal scheme.

11.2 Enforcement Theories

The CWA is viewed by many as the easiest of the federal environmental statutes to enforce. This is because persons regulated under the act normally must report their own compliance and noncompliance to the regulating agency. For example, holders of NPDES permits must file periodic discharge monitoring reports (or DMRs), which must contain the results of all monitoring of discharges, and must indicate where those discharges exceeded permit limitations.[326] In addition, permittees must report any noncompliance that may endanger health or the environment within 24 hours of the time the permittee becomes aware of the circumstances.[327] Permittees are also required to report any anticipated noncompliance,[328] any noncompliance not required to be reported under any other specific provision,[329] and any noncompliance that the permittee failed to report as required elsewhere by the regulations or the permit.[330]

The most common substantive basis for a federal enforcement action is Section 301(a) of the act, the discharge prohibition discussed earlier in this chapter.[331] Because this provision effectively prohibits the discharge of any pollutant except as in compliance with the act, it imparts broad enforcement authority. For example, any discharge in excess of a permit limitation is not only a potential violation of Section 402 (which sets out the permit program) but also a violation of Section 301(a). Likewise, any discharge without a permit would potentially violate Section 301(a).

For civil enforcement purposes, and arguably for some criminal violations, the CWA is a strict liability statute. This means that the intent of the violator is irrelevant; once the violation is established, liability attaches. A person need not have acted negligently or with any intent to violate the statute to be found liable.[332] Thus, enforcement actions may be brought based on little, if anything, more than the DMRs and other reports submitted by the permittee itself. In addition, EPA or the state may generate additional evidence of violations through inspections of the permitted facility.

EPA often enforces in cycles, focusing its enforcement efforts on a particular issue or industrial group in a coordinated manner. For example, in October 1997, the EPA water enforcement program announced that it planned to focus its enforcement efforts on combined sewer overflows, storm water, NPDES permitting, deep well injection, and wetlands. That is not to say that when EPA is focusing on a particular type of activity, it will ignore all other types of violations. It is probably safe to say, however, that when the agency is targeting a certain type of activity, all entities participating in that activity should be aware that they are likely to be scrutinized. In 2009 EPA outlined its strategic goals for developing future enforcement priorities.[333]

11.3 Defenses

Because liability under the act is strict, there are few defenses available to a permittee accused of violating its permit. For example, good faith, the pendency of a permit modification request, and data errors have all been rejected as defenses to liability under the act.[334] Courts have differed on the question of whether impossibility may be a defense under the act.[335]

Two defenses that exist under EPA's regulations are theories of upset and bypass. A third defense, known as permit-as-a-shield, may also be available in some situations.

11.3.1 Upset

Several courts have ruled that, since the equipment underlying the technology-based permit limitations is inherently subject to failure for reasons beyond the control of the operator, EPA must allow for upsets in applying those standards.[336] EPA's regulations define an upset as "an exceptional incident in which there is unintentional and temporary noncompliance with technology-based permit effluent limitations because of factors beyond the reasonable control of the permittee."[337] The term does not include noncompliance "caused by operational error, improperly designed treatment facilities, inadequate treatment facilities, lack of preventive maintenance, or careless or improper operation."[338] An upset constitutes an affirmative defense in an enforcement action for violations of technology-based permit limitations.[339]

To claim upset as a defense, the permittee must submit notice of the upset within 24 hours of the event.[340] The permittee must be able to show, through properly signed contemporaneous operating logs or other relevant evidence, the cause of the upset, that the facility was being operated properly at the time of the upset, and that appropriate remedial measures were taken.[341] The permittee seeking to establish the upset defense has the burden of proving that the defense applies.[342]

The upset defense is available to a permittee only if it is incorporated into the permit expressly or by reference to the relevant regulatory provisions.[343] It is also important to note that, since state permit programs can be more stringent than the federal program, a state can choose not to allow the upset defense.[344]

11.3.2 Bypass

A more limited defense may be available through EPA's regulations governing bypasses. A bypass is defined as "the intentional diversion of waste streams from any portion of a treatment facility."[345] Bypasses are allowed only in very limited circumstances. Even a bypass that does not cause effluent limitations to be exceeded is allowed only for essential maintenance to ensure efficient operation.[346] Essential maintenance is not routine maintenance that can be performed during periods of nonprocess operations but includes only repairs and maintenance that cannot wait until the production process is not in operation to be performed; for example, if a seal on a valve malfunctions or a pipe bursts during production hours, the facility operator may bypass that particular process unit to perform corrective maintenance.[347]

Bypasses that cause effluent limitations to be exceeded are prohibited except in circumstances where they are necessary to avoid severe property damage, personal injury, or loss of life.[348] Under these circumstances, bypass is permitted only if there are no feasible alternatives, such as the use of auxiliary treatment facilities, retention of untreated wastewaters, or maintenance during normal periods of downtime.[349] In addition, if the permittee knows in advance of the need for a bypass, it must submit prior notice, if possible, at least 10 days before the date of the anticipated bypass.[350] The regulatory agency must be notified within 24 hours of any unanticipated bypass.[351] Where all of these conditions are met, bypass may be used as an affirmative defense in an enforcement action.[352]

11.3.3 Permit-as-a-Shield

Under Section 402(k) of the act, compliance with an NPDES permit acts as a shield against enforcement.[353] In other words, so long as a permittee is in compliance with the limitations and conditions in its NPDES permit, neither the state nor EPA can bring an enforcement action against it for violation of the act, such as for discharging pollutants not limited in the permit.[354] The Supreme Court has noted that the purpose of Section 402(k) "seems to be . . . to relieve [permit holders] of having to litigate in an enforcement action the question whether their permits are sufficiently strict."[355] The shield does not apply to violations of the act outside the scope of the NPDES program (e.g., spill reporting, Section 404 violations).

In *Atlantic States Legal Foundation, Inc. v. Eastman Kodak Co.*, 12 F.3d 353 (2d Cir.), *cert. denied*, 115 S. Ct. 62 (1994), a citizens group sued an NPDES discharger for discharging, over a four-year period, more than a million pounds of pollutants that were limited in the discharger's permit. The court held that Section 402(k) prohibited an enforcement action against the discharger since the discharger was in compliance with its permit at all relevant times. The court stated, "Viewing the regulatory scheme as a whole, . . . it is clear that the permit is intended to identify and limit the most harmful pollutants while leaving the control of the vast number of other pollutants to disclosure requirements. Once within the NPDES or SPDES scheme, therefore, polluters may discharge pollutants not specifically listed in their permits so long as they comply with the appropriate reporting requirements and abide by any new limitations when imposed on such pollutants."[356]

However, the permit shield defense is not absolute. A permittee must strictly comply with disclosure obligations; if a likely pollutant was not disclosed to and considered by the regulator, it can fall outside the scope of the permit.[357] And the 9th Circuit has held that the permit shield does not apply when the express terms of the permit prohibit discharges not explicitly authorized.[358]

11.4 Enforcement Options

Federal enforcement may take the form of (1) an administrative order requiring compliance and/or assessing an administrative penalty, (2) an action for civil penalties and/or an injunction, or (3) an action for criminal penalties. State enforcement schemes generally follow the federal system.

EPA typically will choose the least resource-consuming enforcement option that is appropriate for the violation, which in most cases will be an administrative order.[359] A civil judicial action may be appropriate when there is a need for a court order directing immediate or long-term compliance measures (i.e., a temporary restraining order or injunction), such as where the noncompliance is serious and continuing and the violator is uncooperative. In addition, civil judicial action is needed to assess a penalty of more than $187,500. Criminal enforcement actions will be brought for serious violations that are knowing or negligent.[360]

11.5 Administrative Order

The 1987 amendments to the act authorized EPA to issue administrative orders assessing penalties for CWA violations, including permit violations. Class I penalties may not exceed $16,000 per violation, up to a maximum of $37,500.[361] Before assessing a Class I penalty, EPA must give the alleged violator written notice of the proposed assessment and an opportunity to request an informal hearing.[362] A Class II penalty may not exceed $16,000 per day for each violation, up to a maximum of $187,500.[363] Class II penalties may be imposed only after notice and an opportunity for a full adjudicatory hearing.[364]

EPA may also issue an administrative order requiring compliance with the act.[365] Administrative orders for permit violations often include a compliance schedule and may also include interim limitations that must be met while the scheduled activities are being performed. Administrative compliance orders are administrative commands and do not impose any sanctions for the underlying violations or for a violation of the compliance order itself. Nevertheless, in *Sackett v. EPA* a unanimous Supreme Court held that a compliance order was a final agency action with respect to EPA's jurisdictional decision that certain property contained "navigable waters" and, therefore, the court granted pre-enforcement judicial review.[366] Failure to comply with an administrative order could also form the basis of a criminal prosecution for a knowing violation or of a civil action where a claim of bad faith is made.

11.6 Civil Judicial Enforcement

EPA, through its U.S. Department of Justice attorneys, may bring an action in federal district court seeking civil penalties for violations of the act.[367] Civil penalties may be imposed without a showing of negligence or fault on the part of the defendant and may be assessed at up to $37,500 per day for each violation.[368] An alleged violator is entitled to a jury trial to determine liability for civil penalties, and a citizen suit plaintiff can also insist on a jury determination of liability.[369] Once liability is established, however, the court retains the power to determine the amount of the penalty.[370]

EPA's CWA Penalty Policy[371] establishes a method for calculating an appropriate penalty as part of a settlement of a CWA enforcement action.[372] The penalty is to consist of an economic benefit component plus a gravity component, plus or minus adjustments. It is EPA's policy that penalties should recover the full economic benefit of noncompliance, calculated from the beginning of the noncompliance until the point when the facility was or will be in compliance. Under the Penalty Policy, EPA normally calculates this benefit using the BEN computer program.[373] The gravity component is based on four considerations:

1. The significance of the violation.

2. The actual or potential harm to human health or the environment.

3. The number of violations.

4. The duration of noncompliance.

Adjustments may be made for the following circumstances:

- a history of recalcitrance,

- ability to pay,

- litigation considerations (e.g., the potential for protracted litigation and the maximum penalty likely to be awarded by a court), and

- other equitable considerations.

EPA may also initiate a civil action to obtain an injunction. The district court has the power to enter preliminary and permanent injunctions to restrain and abate violations of the act, regulations, and permits, including state permits. If an injunction is violated, the violator is subject to the criminal and civil penalty provisions of the act as well as to the criminal and civil contempt powers of the court.

11.7 Criminal Enforcement

EPA may refer a matter to the Department of Justice for the institution of a criminal action against any discharger who knowingly or negligently violates the act.[374] The penalties for an initial conviction for a negligent violation include a fine of $2,500 to $25,000 per day, imprisonment for not more than one year, or both. The penalties for a knowing violation are a fine of $5,000 to $50,000 per day, imprisonment for not more than three years, or both.[375] In both cases, the maximum penalties for subsequent convictions are doubled.[376]

In an important case, the Ninth Circuit Court of Appeals held that the manager and assistant manager of a sewage treatment plant were criminally liable under the act for knowing violations even though the two men did not know that their discharges of sludge violated the facility's permit. The court held that criminal sanctions may be imposed on an individual who knowingly engages in conduct that results in a permit violation, regardless of whether he is cognizant of the requirements or even the existence of the permit.[377]

A person who knowingly violates a permit or other requirement of the act and knows at the time that he thereby places another person in imminent danger of death or serious bodily injury is subject to a fine of up to $250,000 ($1 million for an organization) and imprisonment for up to 15 years. The punishment, with respect to both fines and imprisonment, is doubled for second offenses.[378]

An action for such knowing endangerment may, for example, be brought if a person knowingly contaminates a water supply or deliberately dumps hazardous materials into sewers or waterways.[379]

Criminal penalties may also be imposed against any person who makes a false statement, representation, or certification to the government or any person who falsifies, tampers with, or knowingly renders inaccurate any monitoring device required under the act.[380] These violations may subject a violator to a fine of not more than $10,000, imprisonment for not more than two years, or both, with penalties doubled for a subsequent violation.

Criminal penalties may be imposed against corporations, persons directly involved in a violation, and responsible corporate officers.[381] Corporate officers who deliberately shield themselves from knowledge of violations are likely to be considered responsible under the act.

11.8 Citizen Suits

Section 505 of the act allows any person "having an interest which is or may be adversely affected"[382] to commence a civil action against any person for violation of any effluent standard, limitation, or order or against EPA for failure to perform a nondiscretionary duty.[383] Citizen groups have frequently used this citizen suit provision, particularly in actions against dischargers for violations of NPDES permits. These suits are often rather straightforward since NPDES permittees normally must report all exceedances of permit limitations to the permitting agency on a monthly or quarterly basis. A citizen group may therefore bring an action for a permit violation using the permittee's own reports as evidence. In a 2004 decision, the U.S. Court of Appeals for the Sixth Circuit allowed a citizen group to assume an even greater role in enforcement, holding that the group had standing to sue a water commission for failing to submit monitoring reports.[384] And numerous courts have allowed citizen suits even when a discharger was told by the regulator that it did not need a permit.[385]

A citizen suit may be brought only if neither EPA nor a state is "diligently prosecuting" the violation.[386] An EPA or state enforcement action that results in a compliance order and not a penalty assessment, however, has been held not to constitute a diligent prosecution that would foreclose a citizen suit.[387]

The plaintiff must give the alleged violator, EPA, and the state 60 days' notice prior to initiation of the lawsuit, unless the action involves a violation of Sections 306 or 307(a) of the act.[388] The notice must include a parameter-by-parameter description of the alleged violations[389] and must specify a time period in which the alleged violations occurred.[390]

Most citizen suits settle under a consent agreement providing for some combination of the following penalties and/or agreements:

- payment of a civil penalty,[391]
- payment of attorney's fees and costs to the plaintiffs,[392]
- a compliance schedule to bring the permittee into compliance,
- stipulated penalties for failure to meet the compliance schedule, and
- payment of money to support an environmental activity selected by the plaintiff.

EPA has the right to review and object to any consent agreement entered in a citizen suit.[393] A decision in the *Exxon Valdez* case held that, although the CWA does not specifically provide for punitive damages in citizen suits, Section 505 does not prohibit the award of such damages under common law.[394]

Citizen suits may be brought only for continuing or intermittent violations.[395] To meet this requirement, however, a plaintiff need only make a good-faith allegation of a continuous or intermittent violation at the time the statutory 60-day notice of intent to sue is given. A violation will be considered to be continuing for jurisdictional purposes unless it is "absolutely clear that the allegedly wrongful behavior could not reasonably be expected to recur."[396] A court has jurisdiction only over violations included in the plaintiff's 60-day notice letter and post-complaint continuing violations of the same type.[397]

12.0 Research Sources

The following EPA webpages provide substantial additional information about the various programs of the CWA:

- Combined Sewer Overflows: http://water.epa.gov/polwaste/npdes/cso/
- National Estuary Program: http://www.epa.gov/nep

- NPDES Program Home Page: http://cfpub.epa.gov/npdes/index.cfm
- Nonpoint-Source Program: http://www.epa.gov/owow/nps/index.html
- Oceans, Coasts, Estuaries & Beaches: http://water.epa.gov/type/oceb/
- Oil Spill Program: http://www.epa.gov/oilspill
- Office of Wastewater Management Home Page: http://www.epa.gov/owm
- Pretreatment Program: http://water.epa.gov/polwaste/npdes/pretreatment/index.cfm
- Sanitary Sewer Overflows: http://water.epa.gov/polwaste/npdes/sso/
- Storm-Water Program: http://water.epa.gov/polwaste/npdes/stormwater/index.cfm
- Total Maximum Daily Load Program: http://www.epa.gov/owow/tmdl/index.html
- Water Quality Standards for Surface Waters: http://water.epa.gov/scitech/swguidance/standards/index.cfm
- Watershed Management: http://www.epa.gov/owow/watershed/
- Wetlands Program: http://www.epa.gov/owow/wetlands/

Notes

[1] The author thanks David M. Halverson and Douglas A. Hastings for their invaluable assistance in updating this chapter for publication.

[2] Pub. L. No. 92–500, 86 Stat. 816 (1972).

[3] *NRDC v. Train,* 8 E.R.C. 2120 (D.D.C. 1976), *modified,* 12 E.R.C. 1833 (D.D.C. 1979), *aff'd, Environmental Defense Fund, Inc. v. Costle,* 636 F.2d 1229 (D.C. Cir. 1980).

[4] This date was subsequently postponed to June 30, 1984. EPA completed issuance of the effluent guidelines required by the decree in 1987.

[5] Pub. L. No. 95–217, 91 Stat. 1566 (1977).

[6] Pub. L No. 100–4, 101 Stat. 7 (1987).

[7] Pub. L. 101–380, 104 Stat. 484 (1990).

[8] 33 U.S.C. § 2701–2761.

[9] Section 101(a), 33 U.S.C. § 1251(a).

[10] Section 101(a)(2), 33 U.S.C. § 1251(a)(2).

[11] Section 101(a)(1), 33 U.S.C. § 1251(a)(1).

[12] Section 101(a)(3) & (7), 33 U.S.C. § 1251(a)(3) & (7).

[13] Section 301(a), 33 U.S.C. § 1311(a).

[14] Section 502(12), 33 U.S.C. § 1362(12).

[15] *United States v. Wilson,* 133 F.3d 251(4th Cir. 1997); *see also Catskill Mountains Chapter of Trout Unlimited, Inc. v. New York City,* 273 F.3d 481 (2d Cir. 2001) (transfer of turbid water from reservoir into

stream through tunnel requires NPDES permit); *Friends of Santa Fe County v. LAC Minerals, Inc.*, 892 F. Supp. 1333, 1354 (D.N.M. 1995) (migration of residual contamination resulting from previous release not an *addition*).

[16] 40 C.F.R. § 403.15. This credit for pollutants in uptake water, referred to as a *net/gross credit*, is available only for technology-based limitations.

[17] *L.A. Flood Control Dist. v. Natural Resources Def. Council, Inc.*, 133 S. Ct. 710 (2013).

[18] *National Wildlife Fed'n v. Consumers Power Co.*, 862 F.2d 580 (6th Cir. 1988); *National Wildlife Federation v. Gorsuch*, 693 F.2d 156 (D.C. Cir. 1982). *But see Comm. to Save the Mokelumne River v. East Bay Mun. Util. Dist.*, 13 F.3d 305 (9th Cir. 1993), *cert. denied*, 115 S. Ct. 198 (1994) (discharges from dam used to collect acid mine drainage from abandoned mine subject to CWA permit requirement).

[19] *In re General Motors Corp., CPC-Pontiac Fiero Plant*, 7 E.A.D. 465 (E.P.A. Dec. 24, 1997), *upheld, General Motors Corp. v. EPA*, 168 F.3d 1377 (D.C. Cir. 1999).

[20] *Catskill Mountain Chapter of Trout Unlimited v. City of New York*, 451 F.3d 77 (2d Cir. 2006); *DuBois v. U.S. Dept. of Agriculture*, 102 F.3d 1273 (1st Cir. 1996), *cert. denied*, 117 S. Ct. 2510 (1997). Effective August 12, 2008, EPA adopted the National Pollutant Discharge Elimination System Water Transfers Rule, which is intended to clarify that "water transfers," defined as "activit[ies] that convey[] or connect[] waters of the United States without subjecting the transferred water to intervening industrial, municipal, or commercial uses," are excluded from regulation under the CWA because there is no "addition" of a pollutant to the waters being transferred. 73 Fed. Reg. 33697 (June 13, 2008) (codified at 40 C.F.R. pt. 122). Environmental groups, municipal water providers, states, and others filed a number of lawsuits challenging the new rule. Although some consolidated cases were dismissed for lack of subject matter jurisdiction, *see Friends of the Everglades v. EPA*, 699 F.3d 1280 (11th Cir. 2012), the Southern District of New York reached a decision on the merits in *Catskill Mountains Chapter of Trout Unlimited, Inc. v. EPA*, 8 F.Supp.3d 500 (SDNY 2014). The court found the Water Transfer Rule to be arbitrary and capricious and remanded the Rule to EPA. Multiple parties subsequently appealed the decision to the 2nd Circuit.

[21] Section 502(6), 33 U.S.C. § 1362(6).

[22] *E.g., Natural Resources Defense Council v. EPA*, 859 F.2d 156 (D.C. Cir. 1988); *United States v. Hamel*, 551 F.2d 107, 110–12 (6th Cir. 1977); *see also United States v. Teixeira Foods Inc.*, C.R. 98–1015 (C.D. Cal. Jan. 13, 1999) (dumping of 100 ostrich carcasses into tributary constituted discharge of a "pollutant"); *United States v. West Indies Transp., Inc.*, 127 F.3d 299 (3d Cir. 1997), *cert. denied*, 118 S. Ct. 700 (1998) (dumping of 250-ton concrete and rebar block from barge was discharge of a pollutant).

[23] Section 502(14), 33 U.S.C. § 1362(14).

[24] In 2001, the Ninth Circuit held that the application of aquatic herbicides (e.g., to control weeds in irrigation ditches) required an NPDES permit. *Headwaters, Inc. v. Talent Irrigation District*, 243 F.3d 526 (9th Cir. 2001). In response to this decision, EPA issued a policy statement that the use of aquatic herbicides fell within the definition of return flows from irrigated agriculture, which are excluded from the "point source" definition. EPA thus takes the position that such herbicide use results in only nonpoint source discharges, which do not require an NPDES permit. U.S. EPA, "Interpretive Statement and Regional Guidance on the Clean Water Act's Exemption for Return Flows from Irrigated Agriculture" (March 2002).

[25] *E.g., Concerned Area Residents for Env't v. Southview Farm*, 34 F.3d 114 (2d Cir. 1994), *cert. denied*, 115 S. Ct. 1793 (1995); *see also United States v. West Indies Transp., Inc.*, 127 F.3d 299 (3d Cir. 1997), *cert. denied*, 118 S. Ct. 700 (1998) (concrete barge is point source).

[26] In other words, a person dumping pollutants into a water body, other than through a hose or pipe, for example, would not be in violation of the act's prohibition of discharges from point sources without a permit. The person may, however, be in violation of other laws and regulations. *United States v. Plaza Health Lab., Inc.*, 3 F.3d 643, 649 (2d Cir. 1993), *cert. denied*, 114 S. Ct. 2764 (1994) (dumping of vials of medical waste into Hudson River).

27 Although "point sources" are statutorily defined to include sources from which pollutants "may be discharged," EPA appears to have limited authority under the act to take regulatory action against "potential discharges" from a point source. In *Waterkeeper Alliance, Inc. v. EPA*, 399 F.3d 486 (2d Cir. 2005), environmental groups and farm groups brought multiple challenges to EPA-promulgated rules governing the emission of water pollutants from concentrated animal feeding operations (CAFOs). The court vacated various provisions of the CAFO rule, including a requirement that all CAFOs apply for an NPDES permit. *Id.* at 524. EPA argued that the provision requiring all CAFOs to apply for a permit or demonstrate that there is no potential to discharge was appropriate because all CAFOs presumptively present a "potential to discharge" pollutants. *Id.* at 505. The court found EPA's argument unavailing, concluding that the CWA gives EPA authority to regulate only "actual discharges" from point sources, not "potential discharges" or point sources themselves. *Id.* In response to the *Waterkeeper* decision, EPA adopted revised CAFO regulations, effective December 22, 2008. The revised regulations require only those CAFOs that "discharge" or "propose to discharge" wastewater to apply for NPDES permits. 73 Fed. Reg. 70418 (Nov. 20, 2008).

28 Section 502(7), 33 U.S.C. § 1362(7).

29 Clean Water Rule: Definition of "Waters of the United States," 80 Fed. Reg. 37054, 37104–05.

30 *Id.* at 37105.

31 *Id.*

32 EPA has developed the Comprehensive State Groundwater Protection Program (CSGWPP), a nonregulatory approach that seeks better coordination between federal and state groundwater activities and prioritization of protection efforts based on groundwater uses and values.

33 *Solid Waste Agency of Northern Cook County v. U.S. Army Corps of Engineers*, 531 U.S. 159, 121 S. Ct. 675 (2001). Legislation has been introduced in the House of Representatives multiple times that would overturn this decision by broadly defining "waters of the United States," but none of the legislation has garnered sufficient support to be enacted into law.

34 547 U.S. 715, 126 S. Ct. 2208 (2006).

35 *Id.* at 739.

36 *Id.* at 742 (emphasis in the original).

37 *Id.* at 759.

38 *Id.* at 779.

39 *United States v. Robison*, 505 F.3d 1208 (11th Cir. 2007) (holding that Justice Kennedy's test is controlling because it is the view of the member who concurred in the judgment on the narrowest grounds), *reh'g denied*, 521 F.3d 1319 (11th Cir. 2008); *United States v. Gerke Excavating, Inc.*, 464 F.3d 723 (7th Cir. 2006) (finding that Justice Kennedy's test is controlling in most cases because it is the least restrictive of federal authority to regulate); *Northern California River Watch v. City of Healdsburg*, 496 F.3d 993 (9th Cir. 2007) (stating that Justice Kennedy's test provides the controlling rule of law).

40 *See, e.g. United States v. Johnson*, 467 F.3d 56 (1st Cir. 2006); *United States v. Donovan*, 661 F.3d 174 (3rd Cir. 2011); *United States v. Cundiff*, 555 F.3d 200 (6th Cir. 2009); *United States v. Bailey*, 571 F.3d 791 (8th Cir. 2009).

41 *See* 80 Fed. Reg. 37054.

42 *Precon Dev. Corp. v. Army Corps of Engineers*, No. 13-2499, 2015 WL 1020693, at *5 (4th Cir. Mar. 10, 2015).

43 80 Fed. Reg. 37054.

44 *Belle Co. v. U.S. Army Corps of Engineers*, 761 F.3d 383, 394 (5th Cir. 2014).

45 *Hawkes Co. v. U.S. Army Corps of Engineers*, 782 F.3d 994, 1001–02 (8th Cir. 2015).

46 No. 15–290 (May 31, 2016).

47 Certain discharges of pollutants are exempted from the NPDES permit requirement. These include discharges from some agricultural and silvicultural activities, discharges into publicly owned treatment works,

and discharges in compliance with instructions from an on-scene coordinator responding to a spill incident. 40 C.F.R. § 122.3. Discharges incidental to the normal operation of vessels also enjoyed a decades-long exemption, but this was ultimately invalidated by the courts. *Northwest Envtl. Advocates v. EPA*, No. 03–05760 (N.D. Cal. Sept. 18, 2006), *aff'd*, 537 F.3d 1006 (9th Cir. 2008). In response, EPA created a NPDES Vessel General Permit to cover these discharges. 73 Fed. Reg. 79473 (Dec. 29, 2008). Congress also passed the Clean Boating Act of 2008, Pub. L. No. 110–288, which amended the Clean Water Act and exempts recreational vehicles from the requirement to obtain a NPDES permit. *See* Section 402(r), 33 U.S.C. § 1342(r).

48 State-issued permits are sometimes referred to as State Pollutant Discharge Elimination System (SPDES) permits. *See* 40 C.F.R. Part 123 for EPA's regulations regarding the approval process for state programs.

49 Currently, only the following do *not* have permitting authority: District of Columbia, Idaho, Massachusetts, New Hampshire, New Mexico, and six U.S. territories. Indian tribes are also considered to be "states" for CWA purposes and have authority under the act to apply their own water quality standards to the activities of nonmembers operating on tribal lands. *State of Montana v. EPA*, 941 F. Supp. 945 (D.Mont. 1996), *aff'd*, 137 F.3d 1135 (9th Cir. 1998).

50 40 C.F.R. § 123.24.

51 40 C.F.R. § 123.25.

52 40 C.F.R. § 123.1(i); *see also Atlantic States Legal Found., Inc. v. Eastman Kodak Co.*, 12 F.3d 353, 358–59 (2d Cir.), *cert. denied*, 115 S. Ct. 62 (1994) (state requirement more stringent than federal requirement may be enforced by the state or EPA but not through citizen suit provisions of act).

53 Section 402(d), 33 U.S.C. § 1342(d). EPA has 90 days in which to make its comments, objections, or recommendations to the state permitting agency. 40 C.F.R. § 123.44(a)(1).

54 Section 402(d)(4), 33 U.S.C. § 1342(d)(4).

55 Section 402(c)(3), 33 U.S.C. § 1342(c)(3). Citizens may also petition EPA to withdraw a state's authorization to issue NPDES permits. Although EPA has never withdrawn such state authorization in response to such a petition, the petitions have served as an effective aid in EPA's oversight of state programs.

56 Section 401(a), 33 U.S.C. § 1341(a); 40 C.F.R. Part 121. This state certification authority under § 401(a) also applies to licensing decisions made by other federal agencies, such as hydropower project licenses issued by the Federal Energy Regulatory Commission. *See PUD No. 1 of Jefferson County v. Washington Dept. of Ecology*, 511 U.S. 700, 114 S. Ct. 1900 (1994) (state certification may include requirement to maintain certain level of flow from hydropower facility); *American Rivers, Inc. v. FERC*, 129 F.3d 99 (2d Cir. 1997) (FERC may not exclude conditions in state certification from hydropower project license).

57 Section 401(a)(1), 33 U.S.C. § 1341(a)(1).

58 *See* 40 C.F.R. § 122.21 for a full discussion of the information required in NPDES permit application forms.

59 40 C.F.R. § 123.25(a)(4).

60 40 C.F.R. § 122.22(a).

61 40 C.F.R. § 122.22(d).

62 40 C.F.R. § 122.21(c) and (d).

63 This permit continuance policy is in effect for EPA-issued permits and in most authorized states. *See Natural Resources Defense Council v. EPA*, 859 F.2d 156, 213–14 (D.C. Cir. 1988) (upholding EPA policy to continue expired permits, reasoning that policy is necessary to prevent undue hardships on permittees).

64 40 C.F.R. §§ 124.7, 124.8, 124.56. In some states, this document is referred to as a "Rationale."

65 40 C.F.R. §§ 124.10(c), 124.11.

66 40 C.F.R. § 124.12. There must be at least 30 days' notice of a hearing on a draft permit. Thus, the grant of a hearing extends the comment period at least until the end of the hearing.

67 40 C.F.R. § 124.13.

68 *See, e.g., Mueller v. EPA*, 993 F.2d 1354, 1357 (8th Cir. 1993).

69 40 C.F.R. § 124.15(b). If no comments requesting a change in the permit are received during the public comment period, the final permit will become effective immediately upon issuance. 40 C.F.R. § 124.15(b)(3).

70 40 C.F.R. § 124.19(a).

71 *Id.*

72 40 C.F.R. § 124.19(l)(2).

73 Section 509(b)(1)(F), 33 U.S.C. § 1369(b)(1)(F).

74 States must allow citizens as well as permit applicants to challenge final permit decisions in court. 40 C.F.R. § 123.30, 61 Fed. Reg. 20972 (May 8, 1996).

75 5 U.S.C. § 706.

76 40 C.F.R. § 122.41.

77 The NPDES regulations were substantially revised in September 1984. The *Federal Register* preamble to that revision, found at 49 Fed. Reg. 37998 (Sept. 26, 1984), contains useful discussions of EPA policies concerning the NPDES program, including some boilerplate requirements. The D.C. Circuit Court of Appeals' discussion of these regulations also provides useful information about the permit program. *Natural Resources Defense Council, Inc. v. EPA*, 859 F.2d 156 (D.C. Cir. 1988).

78 40 C.F.R. § 123.25(a).

79 *See* Section 304(e), 33 U.S.C. § 1314(e).

80 EPA's regulations require that permits contain monitoring requirements that are sufficient to yield representative data. 40 C.F.R. § 122.48. The regulations, however, establish only minimal specific requirements for monitoring method and frequency, leaving most such decisions to the discretion of the permit writer. Regardless of monitoring frequency, monitoring results must be reported to the permitting agency at least once per year. 40 C.F.R. § 122.44(i)(2).

81 65 Fed. Reg. 30886 (May 15, 2000).

82 40 C.F.R. §§ 122.44(i)(1)(iii), 122.45(h). Note, however, that although EPA may require monitoring of an internal waste stream, it cannot impose effluent limitations on an internal stream. *American Iron and Steel Inst. v. EPA*, 115 F.3d 979, 995–96 (D.C. Cir. 1997).

83 EPA-approved analytical methods are contained in 40 C.F.R. Part 136.

84 Section 309(c)(4), 33 U.S.C. § 1319(c)(4). Such actions are frequently a target of enforcement action. For example, in 2007 a jury convicted a corporation and its president and principal owner of knowingly making false statements in required reports. *United States v. Hagerman*, 525 F. Supp. 2d 1058, 1060 (S.D. Ind. 2007) aff'd, 301 F. App'x 552 (7th Cir. 2008) published with modifications at 555 F.3d 553 (7th Cir. 2009).

85 Section 308(a), 33 U.S.C. § 1318(a).

86 40 C.F.R. § 122.44(d)(1)(iv). *See* U.S. EPA, *Technical Support Document for Water Quality-Based Toxics Control* at 1 (Mar. 1991).

87 Permittees measuring compliance with a pH limitation through the use of a continuous pH monitor are allowed to exceed the pH limitation on a limited basis. No individual pH excursion may exceed 60 minutes in length, and the total time of noncompliance during any calendar month may not exceed seven hours and 26 minutes. 40 C.F.R. § 401.17(a).

88 Despite the "guideline" nomenclature, the effluent guidelines are not merely guidance to permit writers in setting limitations in NPDES permits. The guidelines establish substantive requirements that must be met by facilities within the regulated industrial categories. *E.I. DuPont de Nemours & Co. v. Train*, 430 U.S. 112 (1977).

89 40 C.F.R. Parts 405–471.

90 *Natural Resources Defense Council v. EPA*, No. 89–2980 (D.D.C. Jan. 31, 1992).

91 *See* U.S. EPA, "Effluent Guidelines Program Plan," 67 Fed. Reg. 55012 (Aug. 27, 2002). EPA continues to develop effluent guidelines for various industrial categories.

92 33 U.S.C. § 1314(m).

93 *Natural Resource Defense Council v. EPA*, 437 F. Supp. 2d 1137 (C.D. Cal. 2006).

94 *See* 40 C.F.R. § 125.3(c).

95 A major difference between BPJ requirements and requirements based on effluent guidelines is that a permittee can challenge the propriety of a BPJ limitation when the permit is issued. Where a permit limitation is based on an effluent guideline, the validity of the guideline itself cannot be challenged in a permit appeal; rather, the permittee may challenge only the application of the guideline to the specific discharge and the permit writer's translation of the guideline into limitations.

96 Section 402(o), 33 U.S.C. § 1342(o); *see also Natural Resources Defense Council v. EPA*, 859 F.2d 156, 197–203 (D.C. Cir. 1988) (upholding EPA's pre-1987 nonstatutory antibacksliding policy).

97 Section 301(b)(1)(A), 33 U.S.C. § 1311(b)(1)(A).

98 The 1987 amendments to the act extended this deadline to March 31, 1989.

99 Section 301(b)(2)(A), 33 U.S.C. § 1311(b)(2)(A).

100 Section 301(b)(2)(E), 33 U.S.C. § 1311(b)(2)(E).

101 *See* discussion of *new source* in section 6.7.2.4 below.

102 Section 306, 33 U.S.C. § 1316.

103 *See, e.g.,* 52 Fed. Reg. 42522, 42525, 42533–38 (Nov. 5, 1987) (discussion of development of BPT limitations for OCPSF industrial category).

104 *BP Exploration & Oil, Inc. v. EPA*, 66 F.3d 784, 789 (6th Cir. 1995). EPA develops extensive supporting documentation for its categorical effluent guidelines. These "Development Documents" provide EPA's technical basis for the promulgated limitations and for its decision to regulate particular pollutants and waste streams under the guidelines. These Development Documents are often essential resources when challenging permit limitations.

105 *See, e.g.,* 40 C.F.R. Part 414; 79 Fed. Reg. 12661 (March 6, 2014).

106 *See Chemical Mfr. Ass'n v. EPA*, 870 F.2d 177, 207 (5th Cir. 1989), *cert. denied, PPG Indus. Inc. v. EPA*, 495 U.S. 910 (1990).

107 *BP Exploration & Oil v. EPA*, 66 F.3d at 796.

108 *See, e.g.,* 52 Fed. Reg. 42522, 42538–45 (Nov. 5, 1987) (discussion of development of BAT for OCPSF category).

109 67 Fed. Reg. 38752 (June 5, 2002).

110 This *cost-reasonableness* test is discussed in detail at 51 Fed. Reg. 24974 (July 9, 1986). *See also BP Exploration & Oil, Inc. v. EPA*, 66 F.3d at 798; *American Paper Inst. v. EPA*, 660 F.2d 954 (4th Cir. 1981).

111 Section 306(a)(2), 33 U.S.C. § 1316(a)(2).

112 40 C.F.R. § 122.2. It is almost impossible for EPA to issue a final NSPS within 120 days of its proposal. Thus, for practical purposes, new sources are sources for which construction begins after promulgation of the final NSPS.

113 *See Natural Resources Defense Council, Inc. v. EPA*, 822 F.2d 104, 114 (D.C. Cir. 1987) (120-day provision valid); *National Ass'n of Metal Finishers v. EPA*, 719 F.2d 624 (3d Cir. 1983), *rev'd on other grounds sub nom. Chemical Mfrs. Ass'n v. Natural Resources Defense Council*, 470 U.S. 116 (1985) (120-day provision not valid interpretation of congressional intent).

114 40 C.F.R. § 122.29(b)(4).

115 40 C.F.R. § 122.29(b)(1)(iii); 49 Fed. Reg. 37998, 38043–45 (Sept. 26, 1984); 45 Fed. Reg. 59343 (Sept. 9, 1980).

116 Section 306(a)(1), 33 U.S.C. § 1316(a)(1); *see also CPC Int'l, Inc. v. Train*, 540 F.2d 1329, 1341–42 (8th Cir. 1976), *cert. denied*, 430 U.S. 966 (1977) (setting NSPS does not require cost-benefit analysis;

"[w]hat is required . . . is a thorough study of initial and annual costs and an affirmative conclusion that these costs can be reasonably borne by the industry").

[117] *See* 40 C.F.R. § 423.15(g).

[118] Section 306(d), 33 U.S.C. § 1316(d).

[119] A federal court ruled in 1997 that state water quality standards cannot be effective until they are approved by EPA. *Alaska Clean Water Alliance v. Clarke*, 45 E.R.C. 1664, 1997 WL 446499 (W.D. Wash. 1997). EPA issued a final rule in April 2000 to bring the approval process in line with that decision. 65 Fed. Reg. 24641 (Apr. 27, 2000). The rule provides that new and revised state water quality standards are not effective until they are approved by EPA. Standards submitted to EPA before the effective date of the new rule, however, are considered effective whether or not they have been approved by EPA.

[120] Section 303(c)(2), 33 U.S.C. § 1313(c)(2); 40 C.F.R. § 131.10(a); *see also* U.S. EPA, "Strategy for Water Quality Standards and Criteria" (Aug. 2003).

[121] The 1987 amendments to the act require states to establish numerical criteria (rather than narrative criteria) for toxic pollutants. Pub. L. No. 100–4; *see also* Section 303(c)(2)(B), 33 U.S.C. § 1313(c)(2)(B). In December 1992, EPA issued what is referred to as the National Toxics Rule (NTR), which established numerical criteria for the 14 states that failed to meet the statutory deadline for developing their own numerical criteria. 57 Fed. Reg. 60848 (Dec. 22, 1992). The NTR was modified somewhat as the result of litigation challenging the rule. 60 Fed. Reg. 22229 (May 4, 1995) (rule modified to base criteria for metals on measurement of total dissolved metals rather than total recoverable metals).

[122] 40 C.F.R. §§ 131.10(g), 131.12.

[123] Section 304(a)(1), 33 U.S.C. § 1314(a)(1). EPA published a compilation of its criteria for 157 pollutants in December 1998, 63 Fed. Reg. 68354 (Dec. 10, 1998), and maintains a summary table of criteria on its web site. *See* http://water.epa.gov/scitech/swguidance/standards/criteria/current/index.cfm. Criteria are also updated periodically. *See, e.g.,* 79 Fed. Reg. 27303 (May 13, 2014) (draft revisions for criteria of 94 chemical pollutants).

[124] U.S. EPA, Water Quality Standards Handbook at 3.7 (1983, updated 1994 and 2014).

[125] *PUD No. 1 of Jefferson County v. Washington Dept. of Ecology*, 511 U.S. 700, 114 S. Ct. 1900 (1994); *Northwest Environmental Advocates v. City of Portland*, 56 F.3d 979 (9th Cir. 1995).

[126] 40 C.F.R. § 122.44(d)(1)(i); see also *American Iron and Steel Inst. v. EPA*, 115 F.3d 979, 999–1001 (D.C. Cir. 1997) (upholding EPA procedures for determining reasonable potential).

[127] The 7Q10 flow is the historical low flow for a period of seven days during a 10-year period, normally expressed as million gallons per day (MGD) or cubic feet per second (cfs). The 7Q10 flow may occur on nonconsecutive days during any one year.

[128] *See* U.S. EPA, "Compilation of EPA Mixing Zone Documents" (July 2006).

[129] This calculation is significantly more complicated for parameters such as pH, temperature, and biological oxygen demand. In these cases, permit limitations are often based on modeling of the effects of a discharge on the receiving waters.

[130] *See American Iron and Steel Inst. v. EPA*, 115 F.3d at 998 (upholding EPA policy to limit mixing zones to the *discharge-induced mixing area*, defined as "the immediate vicinity of the discharge where mixing occurs due to the turbulence created by the momentum of the discharge" and limited to a quantity of water equal to 10 times the quantity of effluent).

[131] *See* U.S. EPA, "Technical Support Document for Water Quality-Based Toxics Control" at 33–34 (Mar. 1991).

[132] 33 U.S.C. § 1313(d).

[133] The Ninth Circuit said in *dicta* that a state must implement TMDLs only to the extent that it seeks to avoid losing federal grant money, and that "there is no pertinent statutory provision otherwise requiring implementation of [Section] 303 plans or providing for their enforcement." *Pronsolino v. Nastri*, 291 F.3d 1123, 1140 (9th Cir. 2002).

[134] *See* 33 U.S.C. § 1313(d); 40 C.F.R. § 130.7. The Eleventh Circuit held that EPA is not required to develop a formal TMDL implementation plan if a state fails to do so. *Sierra Club v. Meiburg,* 296 F.3d 1021 (11th Cir. 2002).

[135] The Ninth Circuit held that waters contaminated exclusively by nonpoint sources of pollution must be included in state lists of impaired waters. *Pronsolino,* 291 F.3d at 1140–41.

[136] 65 Fed. Reg. 43586 (July 13, 2000).

[137] These cases were consolidated as *American Farm Bureau Fed. v. Whitman,* D.C. Cir. No. 00–1320.

[138] 66 Fed. Reg. 53044 (Oct. 18, 2001).

[139] U.S. EPA, "A Long-Term Vision for Assessment, Restoration, and Protection under the Clean Water Act Section 303(d) Program" (Dec. 2013).

[140] *Friends of the Earth, Inc. v. EPA,* 446 F.3d 140 (D.C. Cir. Apr. 25, 2006).

[141] *Id.* at 143.

[142] *Id.* at 148.

[143] Establishing TMDL "Daily" Loads in Light of the Decision by the U.S. Court of Appeals for the D.C. Circuit in *Friends of the Earth, Inc. v. EPA, et al.,* No. 05–5015 (April 25, 2006) and Implications for NPDES Permits (Nov. 15, 2006), available at http://water.epa.gov/lawsregs/lawsguidance/cwa/tmdl/dailyloadsguidance.cfm.

[144] 61 Fed. Reg. 29563 (June 11, 1996); *see also* EPA Proposed Water Quality Trading Policy, 67 Fed. Reg. 34709 (May 15, 2002).

[145] *See* U.S. EPA, "Sharing the Load: Effluent Trading for Indirect Dischargers" (1998).

[146] U.S. EPA, "Water Quality Trading Assessment Handbook" (Nov. 2004); U.S. EPA, "Water Quality Trading Toolkit for Permit Writers" (Aug. 2007, updated June 2009).

[147] Watershed-based National Pollution Discharge Elimination System (NPDES) Permitting Implementation Guidance (December 2003) available at http://www.epa.gov/npdes/pubs/watershedpermitting_finalguidance.pdf; Watershed-based National Pollution Discharge Elimination System (NPDES) Permitting Technical Guidance (August 2007) available at http://www.epa.gov/npdespub/pubs/watershed_techguidance.pdf.

[148] Toxicity-based permit limitations may also be imposed on a chemical-specific basis. This approach imposes concentration limitations on specific toxic pollutants based on established concentrations known to prevent toxic effects of the particular pollutants. In recent years, EPA and most states have concentrated their toxicity-based permitting on WET rather than chemical-specific limitations.

[149] EPA issued guidance for WET test methods in 2002. 67 Fed. Reg. 69952 (Nov. 19, 2002).

[150] EPA has issued guidance documents providing useful information on WET testing: "National Whole Effluent Toxicity (WET) Implementation Guidance Under the NPDES Program" (Nov. 2004); "Method Guidance and Recommendations for Whole Effluent Toxicity (WET) Testing (40 C.F.R. Part 136)," 65 Fed. Reg. 46457 (July 28, 2000); and "Understanding and Accounting for Method Variability in Whole Effluent Toxicity (WET) Applications under the NPDES Program," 65 Fed. Reg. 44528 (June 30, 2000).

[151] *See* 55 Fed. Reg. 30082, 30110 (July 24, 1990).

[152] *See* U.S. EPA, "Estuarine and Coastal Marine Waters: Bioassessment and Biocriteria Technical Guidance" (Dec. 2000); "Policy on the Use of Biological Assessments and Criteria in the Water Quality Program" (June 19, 1991); U.S. EPA, "Lake and Reservoir Bioassessment and Biocriteria" (Aug. 1998); U.S. EPA, "Notice of Availability: Biological Criteria: Technical Guidance for Streams and Small Rivers," 61 Fed. Reg. 42610 (Aug. 16, 1996).

[153] *TSD* at 41; *see also* 63 Fed. Reg. 36742 (July 7, 1998) (advance notice of proposed rulemaking regarding requirement to adopt biological criteria into state water quality standards).

[154] 67 Fed. Reg. 9269 (Feb. 28, 2002). This was finalized in January, 2003. 68 Fed. Reg. 557 (Jan. 6, 2003).

[155] 66 Fed. Reg. 1671 (Jan. 9, 2001).

156 U.S. EPA, "State Adoption of Numeric Nutrient Standards (1998–2008)" (Dec. 2008).

157 *See* U.S EPA, "Actions to Help States Address Barriers to Numeric Nutrient Criteria Implementation (2012–2014)" (Aug. 2013); U.S. EPA, "Working in Partnership with States to Address Phosphorus and Nitrogen Pollution through Use of a Framework for State Nutrient Reductions" (Mar. 16, 2011).

158 Section 301(n), 33 U.S.C. § 1311(n); 40 C.F.R. § 125.30–125.32. Only EPA may grant an FDF variance, even where the state is the permit-issuing authority.

159 *See* 40 C.F.R. § 125.31.

160 Section 301(n)(2), 33 U.S.C. § 1311(n)(2); 40 C.F.R. § 122.21(m)(1). For effluent guidelines promulgated before February 4, 1987, the request was required to be submitted by July 3, 1989. The statutory provisions regarding FDF variances apply only to variances from BAT limitations and pretreatment standards. FDF variances from BPT or BCT would presumably be handled under the regulatory provisions in 40 C.F.R. Part 125 Subpart D.

161 Pub. L. No. 100–4, 101 Stat. 7 (1987). The October 1, 1992, deadline was extended to October 1, 1993. *See* Section 402(p), 33 U.S.C. § 1342(p).

162 40 C.F.R. § 122.26(b)(13).

163 *See* 40 C.F.R. § 122.26(b)(14). The scope of "associated with industrial activity" is discussed at length at 55 Fed. Reg. 47990, 48007–15 (Nov. 16, 1990).

164 40 C.F.R. § 122.26(b)(14).

165 *Id.*

166 *See* 55 Fed. Reg. at 48007 (Nov. 16, 1990).

167 Section 402(p)(2)(E), 33 U.S.C. § 1342(p)(2)(E).

168 40 C.F.R. § 122.26(g).

169 *Id.*

170 40 C.F.R. § 122.26(b)(8).

171 Section 402(p)(3)(B)(iii), 33 U.S.C. § 1342(p)(3)(B)(iii).

172 *Defenders of Wildlife v. Browner*, 191 F.3d 1159 (9th Cir. 1999).

173 64 Fed. Reg. 68722, 68840 (Dec. 8, 1999); 40 C.F.R. § 122.26.

174 *Envtl. Defense Center, Inc. v. EPA*, 344 F.3d 832 (9th Cir. 2003).

175 U.S. EPA, Implementing the Partial Remand of the Stormwater Phase II Regulations Regarding Notices of Intent & NPDES General Permitting for Phase II MS4s (Apr. 16, 2004); U.S. EPA, MS4 Permit Improvement Guide (Apr. 2010).

176 55 Fed. Reg. 47990 (Nov. 16, 1990).

177 40 C.F.R. § 122.26(c).

178 60 Fed. Reg. 50804 (Sept. 29, 1995). The final modifications to this multisector permit were issued on September 30, 1998. 63 Fed. Reg. 52430. The revisions, among other things, require the notice of intent to be covered by the permit to include a certification that any endangered species in proximity to the storm-water discharge would not be adversely affected by the discharge. Facilities that cannot make this certification must obtain an individual permit. The multisector permit was reissued and expanded in October 2000. 65 Fed. Reg. 64746 (Oct. 30, 2000). The revised MSGP allows permitting authorities to apply the MSGP to facilities not covered by any of the 29 specific industrial sectors.

179 57 Fed. Reg. at 41243 (Sept. 9, 1992).

180 *Id.* at 41242.

181 EPA estimates that the individual storm-water permit application takes approximately 60 hours to complete. *See* EPA, *Guidance Manual for the Preparation of NPDES Permit Applications for Storm Water Discharges Associated with Industrial Activity* (April 1991).

182 59 Fed. Reg. 18688 (Apr. 19, 1994).

183 In January 2001, EPA proposed regulations that would clarify and expand permit requirements for municipal sanitary sewer systems in order to reduce SSOs, but the proposal was withdrawn. The proposed rules were designed to reduce the number of SSOs through increased recordkeeping; improvements in capacity, management, operation, and maintenance; and expanded permit coverage to satellite collection facilities. In June 2010, EPA announced "listening sessions" to seek input on potential revisions to the regulations. 75 Fed. Reg. 30395 (June 1, 2010).

184 U.S. EPA, "Compliance and Enforcement Strategy Addressing Combined Sewer Overflows and Sanitary Sewer Overflows" (Apr. 27, 2000). 175 33 U.S.C. § 1326.

185 Section 502(6), 33 U.S.C. § 1362(6).

186 *Entergy Corp. v. Riverkeeper, Inc.*, 556 U.S. 208 (2009).

187 Section 316(a) governs thermal discharges. Section 316(b) governs cooling water intake structures. In 2014, EPA finalized regulations under Section 316(b) that require new facilities with a design intake flow of more than 2 million gallons per day and which use at least 25% of water withdrawn exclusively for cooling to adopt certain design and location requirements to minimize adverse effects on aquatic life caused by cooling water intake. 79 Fed. Reg. 48300 (Aug. 15, 2014).

188 Section 403, 33 U.S.C. § 1343. *Territorial seas, contiguous zone,* and *ocean* are defined in CWA Section 502, 33 U.S.C. § 1362. On January 19, 2001, the EPA administrator signed a rulemaking that would have established minimum criteria for discharges; established a new designated use, Healthy Ocean Waters; and identified ocean areas as Special Ocean Sites. As part of the Bush administration transition, this proposed rule was withdrawn on January 20, 2001.

189 40 C.F.R. § 125.121(e). The permitting authority may not issue a permit if it is uncertain whether the discharge will result in an unreasonable degradation, unless the permittee (1) agrees to provide additional data, such as a chemical analysis of the discharge, bioassays, or a dilution analysis, at a later date; and (2) can demonstrate that there are no reasonable alternatives to the disposal and that the discharge will not result in irreparable harm to the marine environment while the data are being obtained. 40 C.F.R. §125.123(c).

190 33 U.S.C. § 1401–45.

191 33 U.S.C. § 1411(a). The standard for permit issuance is whether the dumping will "unreasonably degrade or endanger" human health, welfare, or the marine environment.

192 33 U.S.C. § 1413. No permit is required for dumping of fish wastes under the ocean dumping program, except for dumping in harbors or other areas where such wastes could endanger health, the environment, or ecological systems. 33 U.S.C. § 1412(d).

193 33 U.S.C. § 1413; 33 C.F.R. Part 324.

194 40 C.F.R. § 228.15.

195 33 U.S.C. § 1414b.

196 33 U.S.C. § 1901 *et seq.*

197 33 U.S.C. § 1322; 40 C.F.R. Part 140.

198 Section 307(b), 33 U.S.C. § 1317(b). Discharges *from* publicly owned treatment works must comply with NPDES permits for direct dischargers, including *secondary treatment standards* for biological oxygen demand (BOD5), suspended solids, and pH. 40 C.F.R. Part 133.

199 EPA substantially revised its general pretreatment regulations in 1988. The preamble to that regulatory revision, found at 53 Fed. Reg. 40562 (Oct. 17, 1988), provides extensive discussions of several important aspects of the pretreatment program. EPA issued a proposed rule to amend its general pretreatment regulations and to relax the regulatory burden they impose in July 1999. 64 Fed. Reg. 39564 (July 22, 1999). A final rule was issued in 2005. 70 Fed. Reg. 60134 (Oct. 14, 2005).

200 40 C.F.R. § 403.5(a)(1).

201 40 C.F.R. § 403.3(p).

202 40 C.F.R. § 403.3(k).

203   40 C.F.R. § 403.5(b).

204   40 C.F.R. § 403.7.

205   40 C.F.R. § 403.7(a)(i) (dilution); 52 Fed. Reg. 42522, 42547 (Nov. 5, 1987) (volatilization).

206   *Natural Resources Defense Council v. EPA*, 790 F.2d 289 (3d Cir. 1986), *cert. denied*, 479 U.S. 1084 (1987).

207   Pub. L. No. 100–4 § 402 (1987).

208   56 Fed. Reg. 50978 (Oct. 9, 1991).

209   *Sierra Club v. EPA*, 992 F.2d 337 (D.C. Cir. 1993).

210   40 C.F.R. Part 503; 58 Fed. Reg. 9248 (Feb. 19, 1993). Under the terms of a consent decree, *Gearhart v. Reilly*, Civil No. 89–6266-JO (D. Ore.), EPA was required to promulgate Phase II of the sludge regulations by December 15, 2001, although the deadline was later extended to October 17, 2003.

211   *See* 40 C.F.R. Part 403 App. G. In addition to the pollutants addressed in the Phase I sludge regulations, removal credits may be available for two additional metals and 14 organic pollutants when sludge is applied to the land, for seven additional metals and 14 organic pollutants when sludge is disposed in a surface disposal site, and for three other metals when sludge is incinerated, if the concentration of the pollutant in the sludge does not exceed levels established in Part 403.

212   *See* 70 Fed. Reg. 60199 (Oct. 14, 2005).

213   *See* Section 307(b)(4), 33 U.S.C. § 1317(b)(4); 40 C.F.R. § 403.4; *see also* U.S. EPA, "Local Limits Development Guidance" (July 2004).

214   Section 309, 33 U.S.C. § 1319; 40 C.F.R. § 403.10(f)(1).

215   Section 309(f), 33 U.S.C. § 1319(f); 40 C.F.R. § 403.5(e).

216   40 C.F.R. § 403.10(f)(iv).

217   *See* U.S. EPA, "Intro to the National Pretreatment Program" (June 2011).

218   Section 319(a)(1), 33 U.S.C. § 1329(a)(1).

219   Section 319(b), 33 U.S.C. § 1329(b).

220   Section 319(j), 33 U.S.C. § 1329(j).

221   In May 1996, EPA and the states issued an agreement titled "Nonpoint Source Program & Grants Guidance for Fiscal Year 1997 & Future Years." This agreement gives states more flexibility in administering their nonpoint-source control programs and streamlines the grants program. This guidance was updated most recently in 2013 and applies to 319-funded grant activities beginning in fiscal year 2014. U.S. EPA, "Nonpoint Source Program & Grants Guidelines for States and Territories" (April 12, 2013).

222   Coastal Zone Management Act, 16 U.S.C. § 1451–1466, as amended by the Coastal Zone Act Reauthorization Amendments of 1990 (Pub. L. 101–508); *see* 58 Fed. Reg. 5182 (Jan. 19, 1993).

223   U.S. EPA, Guidance Specifying Management Measures for Sources of Nonpoint Pollution in Coastal Waters (Jan. 1993).

224   Section 320, 33 U.S.C. § 1330; *see also* 54 Fed. Reg. 40798 (Oct. 3, 1989).

225   33 U.S.C. § 1344.

226   U.S. Army Corps of Engineers, Technical Rep. Y-87–1, *Corps of Engineers Wetlands Delineation Manual* (Jan. 1987), *available at* http://el.erdc.usace.army.mil/elpubs/pdf/wlman87.pdf.

227   *See* Clean Water Rule: Definition of "Waters of the United States," 80 Fed. Reg. 37054, 37088.

228   *See United States v. Riverside Bayview Homes*, 474 U.S. 121 (1985).

229   80 Fed. Reg. 37104.

230   *See* 40 C.F.R. §§ 232.2(1), (2)(iii); 33 C.F.R. § 323.2(d)(1), (2)(iii); *see also Am. Mining Cong. v. U.S. Army Corps of Eng'rs*, 951 F. Supp. 267 (D.D.C. 1997), *aff 'd sub nom. Nat'l Mining Ass'n v. U.S. Army Corps of Eng'rs*, 145 F.3d 1339 (D.C. 1998).

231   *See* 66 Fed. Reg. 4550 (Jan. 17, 2001); 33 C.F.R. § 323.2(d)(2)(i); 40 C.F.R. § 232.2(2)(i).

232   *United States v. Sinclair Oil Co.*, 767 F. Supp. 200, 203–05 (D. Mont. 1990).

233 *United States v. M.C.C. of Fla., Inc.*, 772 F.2d 1501, 1505–06 (11th Cir. 1985), *vacated and remanded on other grounds*, 107 S. Ct. 1968 (1987), *readopted in relevant part on remand*, 848 F.2d 1133 (11th Cir. 1988); *see also Avoyelles Sportsmen's League v. Marsh*, 715 F.2d 897, 923–24 (5th Cir. 1983).

234 *See* Section 404(f), 33 U.S.C. § 1344(f).

235 486 F.3d 638 (9th Cir. 2007).

236 *Id.* at 641–43.

237 *Id.* at 640–41.

238 *Id.* at 644.

239 *Id.*

240 *Id.* at 655.

241 *Id.* at 655.

242 *Id.* at 647.

243 *Id.* at 649.

244 Petition for Writ of Certiorari at 11–12, *Coeur Alaska Inc. v. S.E. Alaska Conservation Council*, No. 07–984, 2008 WL 244990 (Jan. 28, 2008).

245 *Coeur Alaska, Inc. v. S.E. Alaska Conservation Council*, 129 S. Ct. 2458 (2009).

246 33 C.F.R. § 325.1.

247 33 C.F.R. § 325.1(b).

248 33 C.F.R. § 320.4(a).

249 *Id.*

250 *Mall Properties Inc. v. Marsh*, 672 F. Supp. 561, 566 (D. Mass. 1987).

251 33 C.F.R. §§ 320.4(a)(1), 325.2(a)(6).

252 40 C.F.R. § 230.10(a).

253 40 C.F.R. § 230.3(q).

254 40 C.F.R. § 230.10(a)(3).

255 *Id.* ("[W]here a discharge is proposed for a special aquatic site, all practicable alternatives to the proposed discharge which do not involve a discharge into a special aquatic site are presumed to have less adverse impact on the aquatic ecosystem, unless *clearly demonstrated otherwise*") (emphasis added).

256 40 C.F.R. § 230.10(c); *see also* 40 C.F.R. §§ 230.1(c).

257 Section 401, 33 U.S.C. § 1341(a)(1); 33 C.F.R. § 325.2(b)(1)(ii); *see also United States v. Marathon Dev. Co.*, 867 F.2d 96, 98–99 (1st Cir. 1989). The certifying agency may be deemed to have waived its certification if it does not act within 60 days. 33 C.F.R. § 325.2(b)(1)(ii).

258 Section 404(c), 33 U.S.C. § 1344(c). EPA may veto a Section 404 permit if it determines that the discharge would have "an unacceptable adverse effect on municipal water supplies, shellfish beds and fishery areas . . . , wildlife, or recreation areas." *Id.*; *see also Alameda Water & Sanitation Dist. v. Reilly*, 930 F. Supp. 486 (D. Colo. 1996).

259 Section 404(m), 33 U.S.C. § 1344(m).

260 *Mingo Logan Coal Co. v. EPA*, 714 F.3d 608 (D.C. Cir. 2013).

261 42 U.S.C. §§ 4321–4370h.

262 33 C.F.R. § 325.1(b).

263 *But see Wetlands Action Network v. U.S. Army Corps of Eng'rs*, 222 F.3d 1105, 1122 (9th Cir. 2000) (Corps may conduct abbreviated environmental assessment rather than an environmental impact statement in some cases).

264 Memorandum of Agreement between the Environmental Protection Agency and the Department of the Army concerning the Determination of Mitigation under Clean Water Act Section 404(b)(1) Guidelines (Feb. 6, 1990); *see also* 67 Fed. Reg. 2020 (Jan. 15, 2002) (reissuance of nationwide permits, reinforcing commitment to "no net loss" policy).

265 The February 1990 MOA contains a controversial provision limiting mitigation requirements where a high proportion of the land is wetlands. The MOA also states that the sequencing set forth in the MOA (avoidance, minimization, compensation) may not be required where wetland alterations constitute "insignificant environmental losses."

266 *Compensatory Mitigation for Losses of Aquatic Resources*, 73 Fed. Reg. 19594, 19671–72 (Apr. 10, 2008).

267 *Id.*

268 *Id.* at 19673.

269 *See* Section 404(e)(1), 33 U.S.C. § 1344(e)(1).

270 *See* 67 Fed. Reg. at 2089–94 (Jan. 15, 2002).

271 *See* 33 C.F.R. §§ 330.1(c), 330.2(c).

272 *See* C.F.R. § 330.1(b).

273 *See* 77 Fed. Reg. 10184 (Feb. 21, 2012).

274 *See* 33 C.F.R. §§ 330.1(c), 330.2(c).

275 *See* 33 C.F.R. § 330.6(a) ("Nationwide permittees may, and in some cases must, request from a [district engineer] confirmation that an activity complies with the terms and conditions of an NWP").

276 Section 309(d), 33 U.S.C. § 1319(d); Section 404 (s), 33 U.S.C. § 1344(s); 40 C.F.R. § 19.4. EPA issued a Section 404 penalty policy in December 2001. "Clean Water Act Section 404 Settlement Penalty Policy" (Dec. 21, 2001).

277 *See, e.g., United States v. Cumberland Farms*, No. 91–10051-MLW (D. Mass. July 25, 1996), 61 Fed. Reg. 40248 (Aug. 1, 1996) (settlement under which company will establish 30-acre wildlife and wetlands corridor on site it allegedly damaged and will turn over additional 225 acres to state for permanent conservation); *United States v. Larkins*, 657 F. Supp. 76, 86 (W.D. Ky. 1987), *aff'd*, 852 F.2d 189 (6th Cir. 1988); *United States v. Bd. of Trs., Fla. Keys Cmty. Coll.*, 531 F. Supp. 267, 275–76 (S.D. Fla. 1981).

278 *See United States v. Ellen*, 961 F.2d 462, 467 (4th Cir. 1992), *cert. denied*, 506 U.S. 875 (1992); *United States v. Pozsgai*, 897 F.2d 524 (3d Cir.) (unpublished table decision), *cert. denied*, 498 U.S. 812 (1990).

279 Section 311(b)(1); 33 U.S.C. § 1321(b)(1).

280 In determining whether a facility could reasonably discharge oil into navigable waters or adjoining shorelines, an operator may not take into consideration man-made features such as dikes, equipment, or other structures. 40 C.F.R. § 112.1(d)(1).

281 40 C.F.R. § 112.1(b). Although the act requires EPA to issue regulations requiring SPCC plans for discharges of oil or hazardous substances, 33 U.S.C. § 1321(j)(5)(A), EPA has issued such regulations only for discharges of oil (40 C.F.R. Part 112). States, however, often require SPCC plans for hazardous substances under state programs.

282 40 C.F.R. § 112.1(d)(2). In calculating these totals, only containers of oil with a capacity of 55 gallons or greater are counted.

283 40 C.F.R. § 112.1(d)(4).

284 40 C.F.R. § 112.3(e). SPCC plans must be maintained at a facility if the facility is normally attended at least four hours a day. If the facility is normally attended fewer than eight hours a day, the plan may be maintained at a nearby field office. 40 C.F.R. § 112.3(e).

285 40 C.F.R. § 112.3(b).

286 40 C.F.R. § 112.5.

287 40 C.F.R. § 112.3(d). The engineer must certify that the plan has been prepared in accordance with good engineering practices.

288 40 C.F.R. § 112.4(a).

289 40 C.F.R. § 112.4(d). Section 112.4(e) and (f) set forth the procedures for appealing a decision by the regional administrator requiring amendment of an SPCC plan.

290 40 C.F.R. § 112.7.

291 40 C.F.R. § 112.7(a) and (b). This information is required if experience indicates that there is a reasonable potential for equipment failure (such as tank overflow, rupture, or leakage).

292 With the exception of secondary containment requirements, EPA's 2002 final rule allows deviations from most rule provisions when equivalent environmental protection is provided.

293 40 C.F.R. § 112.7(f)(2).

294 *Id.* at (f)(1).

295 Section 311(j)(5)(C)(iv), 33 U.S.C. § 1321(j)(5)(C)(iv).

296 40 C.F.R. § 112.20(e).

297 As in the SPCC program, EPA now exempts from the Facility Response Plan program completely buried underground tanks that are subject to the underground storage tank technical requirements and containers of oil with a capacity of less than 55 gallons.

298 40 C.F.R. § 112.20(f).

299 40 C.F.R. § 112.20(b), (f)(2).

300 40 C.F.R. Part 112, App. D.

301 40 C.F.R. Part 112, App. F.

302 Section 311(j)(5)(D), 33 U.S.C. § 1321(j)(5)(D).

303 40 C.F.R. Part 300.

304 Section 311(j)(5)(F), 33 U.S.C. § 1321(j)(5)(F).

305 Section 311(j)(5)(G), 33 U.S.C. § 1321(j)(5)(G).

306 Section 311(b)(5), 33 U.S.C. § 1321(b)(5). For purposes of the Section 311 program, *discharge* is defined as including, but not limited to, "any spilling, leaking, pumping, pouring, emitting, emptying or dumping." Section 311(a)(2), 33 U.S.C. § 1321(a)(2).

307 Section 311(b)(5), 33 U.S.C. § 1321(b)(5).

308 *Oil* is defined as "oil of any kind or in any form, including, but not limited to, petroleum, fuel oil, sludge, oil refuse, and oil mixed with other than dredged spoil." Section 311(a)(1), 33 U.S.C. § 1321(a)(1). This definition includes animal fats and vegetable oils. 62 Fed. Reg. 54508 (Oct. 20, 1997).

309 40 C.F.R. § 110.3; *see also Orgulf Transp. Co. v. United States*, 711 F. Supp. 344 (W.D. Ky. 1989) (EPA determination that any discharge of oil causing a sheen may be harmful is authorized by the act, even though all spills of oil create a sheen). The use of a dispersant or emulsifier to prevent a sheen to circumvent the notice requirement is prohibited. 40 C.F.R. § 110.4.

310 40 C.F.R. Part 116.

311 40 C.F.R. Part 117.

312 40 C.F.R. § 117.21.

313 Section 311(a)(2), 33 U.S.C. § 1321(a)(2); 52 Fed. Reg. 10712 (Apr. 2, 1987).

314 Section 311(b)(3), 33 U.S.C. § 1321(b)(3).

315 For example, in 2011 CITGO Petroleum Corporation was assessed a penalty of $9 million under the CWA and a state environmental statute for discharging over 2 million gallons of slop oil. *United States. v. CITGO Petroleum Corp.*, No. 08-cv-0893 (W.D. La. Sept. 29, 2011), 2011 WL 10723934.

316 Section 311(f)(2), 33 U.S.C. § 1321(f)(2). These defenses include: (1) an act of God, (2) an act of war, (3) negligence on the part of the U.S. government, and (4) an act or omission of a third party. *Id.*

317 For discharges of hazardous substances, the maximum quantity-based penalty is $1,000 per reportable quantity unit. In other words, if the reportable quantity for a substance is ten pounds, and 10,000 pounds are discharged, the maximum penalty would be $1 million. Section 311(b)(7)(A), 33 U.S.C. § 1321(b)(7)(A); 40 C.F.R. § 19.4.

318 Section 311(b)(7)(D), 33 U.S.C. § 1321(b)(7)(D); 40 C.F.R. § 19.4.

319 Section 402(b)(7), 33 U.S.C. § 1342(b)(7); 40 C.F.R. § 123.27(a).

320   40 C.F.R. § 123.27(a)(3); *see also Natural Resources Defense Council v. EPA*, 859 F.2d 156, 179–180 (D.C. Cir. 1988).

321   40 C.F.R. § 123.27(d).

322   Section 309(a), 33 U.S.C. § 1319(a).

323   A federal appeals court has held that EPA cannot *overfile* a RCRA enforcement case where a state environmental agency has resolved a violation through a consent decree. *Harmon Ind., Inc. v. Browner*, 191 F.3d 894 (8th Cir. 1999). In a CWA case raising the same issue, the Fourth Circuit held that EPA was *not* barred from bringing an action after the state had settled with a violator. *U.S. v. Smithfield Foods, Inc.*, 191 F.3d 516 (4th Cir. 1999), *cert. denied*, 531 U.S. 813 (2000).

324   *United States v. ITT Rayonier, Inc.*, 627 F.2d 996, 1001 (9th Cir. 1980).

325   Section 309(a)(2), 33 U.S.C. § 1319(a)(2).

326   40 C.F.R. § 122.41(l)(4) and (7).

327   40 C.F.R. § 122.41(l)(6).

328   40 C.F.R. § 122.41(l)(2).

329   40 C.F.R. § 122.41(l)(7).

330   40 C.F.R. § 122.41(l)(8).

331   33 U.S.C. § 1311(a).

332   *E.g., Am. Canoe Ass'n v. Murphy Farms*, 412 F.3d 536, 540 (4th Cir. 2005); United *States v. Texas Pipeline Co.*, 611 F.2d 345 (10th Cir. 1979); *United States v. Amoco Oil Co.*, 580 F. Supp. 1042 (W.D. Mo. 1984).

333   U.S. EPA, "Clean Water Act Action Plan" (Oct. 15, 2009).

334   *United States v. Amoco Oil Co.*, 580 F. Supp. 1042 (W.D. Mo. 1984) (good faith); *Student Public Interest Research Group of N.J. v. Monsanto*, 600 F. Supp. 1479 (D.N.J. 1985) (permit modification pendency); *Public Interest Research Group of N.J., Inc. v. Elf Atochem N.A., Inc.*, 817 F. Supp. 1164 (D. N.J. 1993) (where there was laboratory error, permittee will not be held liable for discharge violations but will be liable for each measurement proved to be erroneous). In 1998, a New Mexico hot sauce manufacturer pleaded guilty to a CWA violation for dumping hot pepper rinse water into a ditch that flowed into the Rio Grande. The manufacturer was charged with a criminal violation of the act although it had erroneously applied for and received a storm-water discharge permit rather than an NPDES permit. EPA officials had reviewed the issuance of the storm-water permit, and EPA had informed the company that its NPDES permit was a low priority and could not expect to be issued for about 15 years. *United States v. Cervantes Enterprises, Inc.* (D.N.M., plea filed Aug. 6, 1998).

335   Compare *Hughey v. JMS Dev. Corp.*, 78 F.3d 1523, 1530 (11th Cir.), *cert. denied*, 117 S. Ct. 482 (1996) (where storm-water permit not available under state's program, developer not liable for storm-water runoff from construction site despite act's strict prohibition on discharges without a permit; based on finding that "Congress could not have intended a strict application of the zero discharge standard in section 1311[a] when compliance is factually impossible") with *Driscoll v. Adams*, 181 F.3d 1285 (11th Cir. 1999), *cert. denied*, 120 S. Ct. 1961 (2000) (facility operator could be subject to a citizen suit for violation of storm-water requirements even though state agency was not prepared to issue storm-water permits).

336   See *Marathon Oil Co. v. EPA*, 564 F.2d 1253 (9th Cir. 1977); *FMC Corp. v. Train*, 539 F.2d 973 (4th Cir. 1976). These decisions extend only to federally issued NPDES permits. As discussed below, states are not required to include the upset defense in state-issued permits.

337   40 C.F.R. § 122.41(n)(1); *see also* 40 C.F.R. § 403.16(a); *Chesapeake Bay Found., Inc. v. Bethlehem Steel Corp.*, 652 F. Supp. 620 (D. Md. 1987) (violations of permit nearly every day during two-month period were not upsets).

338   40 C.F.R. § 122.41(n)(1).

339   40 C.F.R. § 122.41(n)(2). In 1988, the U.S. Court of Appeals for the D.C. Circuit ruled that EPA's refusal to extend the upset defense to water quality–based permit limits was arbitrary and capricious. *Natural Resources Defense Council v. EPA,* 859 F.2d 156, 209–10 (D.C. Cir. 1988). Upon remanding the regulation to the agency, the court specifically stated that it did not mean to imply that EPA must allow the defense for water quality–based limitations, only that if the agency decides not to extend the defense, it must provide a reasoned basis for its decision. EPA appears to have taken no action in response to the court's holding but appears to consider the issue on a case-by-case basis.

340   40 C.F.R. § 122.41(n)(3)(iii); *Public Interest Research Group of N.J., Inc. v. U.S. Metals Refining Co.,* 681 F. Supp. 237 (D.N.J. 1987).

341   40 C.F.R. § 122.41(n)(3).

342   40 C.F.R. § 122.41(n)(4).

343   *Sierra Club v. Union Oil Co. of Cal.,* 813 F.2d 1480, 1487 (9th Cir. 1987), *vacated on other grounds,* 485 U.S. 931, *reinstated on remand,* 853 F.2d 667 (9th Cir. 1988).

344   40 C.F.R. § 123.25(a).

345   40 C.F.R. § 122.41(m)(1)(i); see also 40 C.F.R. § 403.17(a).

346   40 C.F.R. § 122.41(m)(2); *see also Natural Resources Defense Council v. EPA,* 822 F.2d 104 (D.C. Cir. 1987) (upholding bypass prohibition even where limitations not exceeded).

347   49 Fed. Reg. 37998, 38037 (Sept. 26, 1984).

348   40 C.F.R. § 122.41(m)(4).

349   40 C.F.R. § 122.41(m)(4)(i)(B); *see also United States v. Municipality of Penn Hills,* 6 F. Supp. 2d 432 (W.D. Pa. 1998) (bypass was illegal where facility could have installed equalization tanks or other alternatives to bypassing).

350   40 C.F.R. § 122.41(m)(3)(i).

351   40 C.F.R. § 122.41(m)(3)(ii).

352   *See, e.g., United States v. CPS Chem. Co.,* 779 F. Supp. 437, 454 (E.D. Ark. 1991); *Student Public Interest Research Group of N.J., Inc. v. AT&T Bell Lab.,* 617 F. Supp. 1190, 1204 (D.N.J. 1985).

353   33 U.S.C. § 1342(k).

354   U.S. EPA, "Revised Policy Statement on Scope of Discharge Authorization and Shield Associated with NPDES Permits," Memorandum from Robert Perciasepe, Assistant Administrator for Water, et al., to Regional Administrators and Regional Counsels (April 11, 1995).

355   *E. I. du Pont de Nemours & Co. v. Train,* 430 U.S. 112, 138 n.28 (1977).

356   Atlantic States Legal Found., 12 F.3d at 357; *see also Piney Run Preservation Assn. v. County Commissioners of Carroll County, Maryland,* 268 F.3d 255 (4th Cir. 2001), *cert. denied,* 122 S. Ct. 1960 (2002); *In re Ketchikan Pulp Co.,* 7 E.A.D. 605 (1998) (EPA Appeals Board holding that permit shield covers all pollutants that have been adequately disclosed to the permitting agency during the application process, whether or not listed in the permit).

357   *S. Appalachian Mountain Stewards v. A&G Coal Corp.,* 758 F.3d 560 (4th Cir. 2014).

358   *Alaska Cmty. Action on Toxics v. Aurora Energy Servs., LLC,* 765 F.3d 1169 (9th Cir. 2014), *cert. denied,* 135 S. Ct. 2830 (2015).

359   U.S. EPA, "Guidance on Choosing Among Clean Water Act Administrative, Civil and Criminal Enforcement Remedies" (Aug. 28, 1987).

360   *Id.*

361   Section 309(g)(2)(A); 33 U.S.C. § 1319(g)(2)(A); 40 C.F.R. § 19.4.

362   For guidance on Class I penalty procedures, *see* 52 Fed. Reg. 30730 (Aug. 17, 1987).

363   Section 309(g)(2)(B), 33 U.S.C. § 1319(g)(2)(B); 40 C.F.R. § 19.4.

364   Section 309(g), 33 U.S.C. § 1319(g); 40 C.F.R. Part 22.

365   Section 309(a), 33 U.S.C. § 1319(a).

366 *Sackett v. EPA*, 132 S.Ct. 1367 (2012).

367 Section 309(a), 33 U.S.C. § 1319(a).

368 Section 309(d), 33 U.S.C. § 1319(d); 40 C.F.R. § 19.4.

369 *Tull v. United States*, 481 U.S. 412 (1987); *N. Carolina Envtl. Justice Network v. Taylor*, 2014 WL 7384970 (E.D.N.C. Dec. 29, 2014).

370 *United States v. Tull*, 481 U.S. 412 (1987).

371 U.S. EPA, "Interim Clean Water Act Settlement Penalty Policy" (March 1, 1995).

372 The Penalty Policy states that it is not to be used by a court in determining a penalty at trial.

373 EPA implemented changes to the BEN model in 2005. 70 Fed. Reg. 50326 (Aug. 26, 2005).

374 Section 309(c), 33 U.S.C. § 1319(c). A number of courts have held this standard only requires ordinary, rather than gross, negligence. *See, e.g., United States v. Pruett*, 681 F. 3d 232 (5th Cir. 2012).

375 Section 309(c), 33 U.S.C. § 1319(c). In 1991, the president of a drum reconditioning company in Florida was sentenced to 13 years in prison for intentionally and continuously dumping toxic waste into the Tampa sewer system. *United States v. Benkovitz*, Nos. 97–331, 98–349 (M.D. Fla. Aug. 16, 1999).

376 Section 309(c), 33 U.S.C. § 1319(c).

377 *United States v. Weitzenhoff*, 1 F.3d 1523 (9th Cir.), *amended and superseded on denial of reh'g en banc*, 35 F.3d 1275 (9th Cir. 1993), *cert. denied*, 513 U.S. 1128 (1995); *accord United States v. Sinskey*, 119 F.3d 712 (8th Cir. 1997) (government did not have to prove that defendants knew their conduct was illegal, only that they knew of their relevant conduct); *United States v. Hopkins*, 53 F.3d 533 (2d Cir. 1995) (defendant only had to know of the commission of the act, not that the act violated the company's discharge permit); *United States v. Wilson*, 133 F.3d 251 (4th Cir. 1997) (to prove felony violation of act, government must prove defendant's knowledge of facts meeting each essential element of offense but need not prove defendant knew conduct was illegal).

378 Section 309(c)(3), 33 U.S.C. § 1319(c)(3).

379 *See United States v. Borowski*, 977 F.2d 27 (1st Cir. 1992) (prosecution for knowing endangerment cannot be premised on danger that occurs before pollutant reaches water); *United States v. Villegas*, 784 F. Supp. 6 (E.D.N.Y. 1991), *rev'd in part and remanded, United States v. Plaza Health Lab., Inc.*, 3 F.3d 643 (2d Cir. 1993), *cert. denied*, 512 U.S. 1245 (1994) (defendant who placed vials of blood into river bulkhead could not be convicted of knowing endangerment because there was insufficient evidence that he knew there was a high probability that by placing the vials in the river he was placing another person in imminent danger).

380 Section 309(c)(4), 33 U.S.C. § 1319(c)(4); *see also United States v. Carnival Corp.* (S.D. Fla. Apr. 19, 2002) (cruise ship operator ordered to pay $18 million after pleading guilty to falsifying records on oil discharges at sea); *United States v. Warner-Lambert Inc.*, Crim. No. 97–2394 (D.P.R. Sept. 19, 1997) (company fined $3.6 million for filing false discharge reports, despite lack of evidence of environmental harm from violations); *United States v. Rettig* (D. Va. Jan. 16, 1997) (30-month prison sentence imposed for filing false water quality reports and discarding or destroying laboratory reports).

381 Section 309(c)(6), 33 U.S.C. § 1319(c)(6). A corporate officer may be criminally liable if he has authority to exercise control over the activity that is causing the illegal discharges, even if such responsibility is not expressly vested in him by the company. *United States v. Iverson*, 162 F.3d 1015 (9th Cir. 1998). Moreover, a corporate officer can be convicted of "knowing endangerment" to others even if he has no actual knowledge of the violation. *United States v. Hansen*, 262 F.3d 1217 (11th Cir. 2001), *cert. denied*, 122 S. Ct. 2326 and 122 S. Ct. 2327 (2002).

382 The standing requirement of this section has been broadly construed. Normally, a citizen group can demonstrate standing by showing that one or more of its members makes use of the water body that is affected by the discharge at issue. *See Natural Resources Defense Council v. Texaco Ref. and Mktg., Inc.*, 2 F.3d 493 (3d Cir. 1993); *Public Interest Research Group of N.J., Inc. v. Powell-Duffryn Terminals, Inc.*, 913 F.2d 64 (3d Cir. 1990), *cert. denied*, 498 U.S. 1109 (1991). *But see Public Interest Research Group of*

N.J., Inc. v. Magnesium Elektron, Inc., 123 F.3d 111 (3d Cir. 1997) (group had no standing where violation of permit did not cause actual or threatened injury to river, although group argued knowledge of violations caused them to reduce their use and enjoyment of the river); *Friends of the Earth Inc. v. Crown Central Petroleum Corp.*, 95 F.3d 358 (5th Cir. 1996) (citizen group does not have standing where members used waters three tributaries and 18 miles downstream from facility and no evidence that pollutants had migrated from facility to those waters).

383 Section 505(g), 33 U.S.C. § 1365(g).

384 *American Canoe Assoc., Inc. v. City of Louisa Water & Sewer Commission*, 389 F.3d 536 (6th Cir. 2004).

385 *See Soundkeeper, Inc. v. A & B Auto Salvage Inc.*, 19 F.Supp.3d 426 (D.Conn. 2014); *San Francisco Baykeeper v. Cargill Salt Div.*, 481 F.3d 700, 706 (9th Cir. 2007); *Sierra Club, Lone Star Chapter v. Cedar Point Oil Co. Inc.*, 73 F.3d 546 (5th Cir. 1996).

386 Section 505(b), 33 U.S.C. § 1365(b).

387 *Natural Resources Defense Council v. Fina Oil & Chem. Co.*, 806 F. Supp. 145 (E.D. Tex. 1992); *see also California Sportfishing Prot. Alliance v. Chico Scrap Metal, Inc.*, 728 F.3d 868 (9th Cir. 2013) (citizen suit barred only if federal or state action involves the same standard, limitation, or order as the citizen suit, not merely a comparable one); *Citizens for a Better Environment v. Union Oil Co. of Cal.*, 83 F.3d 1111 (9th Cir. 1996), *cert. denied*, 117 S. Ct. 789 (1997) (citizen suit not barred by company's settlement with state under which it paid $780,000 to push back a compliance date under state law not comparable to federal enforcement provisions); *Knee Deep Cattle Co. v. Bindana Inv. Co.*, 94 F.3d 514 (9th Cir. 1996), *cert. denied*, 117 S. Ct. 1027 (1997) (state prosecution for solely past violations did not constitute diligent prosecution for ongoing violations).

388 Section 505(b), 33 U.S.C. § 1365(b); *but see Black Warrior Riverkeeper, Inc. v. Black Warrior Minerals, Inc.*, 734 F.3d 1297 (11th Cir. 2013) (citizen suit cannot evade 60-day waiting period by asserting violations of new source performance standards and ignoring the NPDES permit which incorporates those standards).

389 *Natural Resources Defense Council v. Texaco Ref. and Mktg., Inc.*, 2 F.3d 493, 499 (3d Cir. 1993). The notice need not identify the specific outfall, however. *Atlantic States Legal Found., Inc. v. Stroh Die Casting Co.*, 116 F.3d 814 (7th Cir. 1997), *cert. denied*, 118 S. Ct. 442 (1997).

390 *Hudson Riverkeeper Fund Inc. v. Putnam Hosp. Ctr. Inc.*, 891 F. Supp. 152 (S.D.N.Y. 1995).

391 Any civil penalty recovered goes to the U.S. Treasury. *New Jersey Public Interest Research Group v. Powell-Duffryn Terminals, Inc.*, 913 F.2d 64 (3d Cir. 1990). If a suit is settled without a finding or admission of a violation of the act, the money recovered is not required to be paid to the Treasury, although it often will be. *Sierra Club v. Electronic Controls Design, Inc.*, 909 F.2d 1350 (9th Cir. 1990).

392 A 2001 Supreme Court case decided under the Americans with Disabilities Act suggests that attorney fee awards under CWA citizen suits may be limited to cases in which there is an official judicial ruling or court-sanctioned consent decree. *Buckhannon Board & Care Home v. West Virginia*, 532 U.S. 598, 121 S. Ct. 1835 (2001).

393 Section 505(c)(3), 33 U.S.C. § 1365(c)(3). Often, EPA or the U.S. Department of Justice will require that any environmental activity receiving settlement funds be related to the alleged violation (e.g., money paid in settlement of an alleged water permit violation would not be allowed to be designated for an air monitoring project).

394 *In re the Exxon Valdez*, 270 F.3d 1215 (9th Cir. 2001).

395 *Gwaltney of Smithfield Ltd. v. Chesapeake Bay Foundation, Inc.*, 484 U.S. 49 (1987).

396 *Id.* at 66, quoting *United States v. Phosphate Export Ass'n, Inc.*, 393 U.S. 199 (1968). The Fourth Circuit, on remand in the *Gwaltney* case, stated, "Intermittent or sporadic violations do not cease to be ongoing until the date when there is no real likelihood of repetition." *Gwaltney of Smithfield Ltd. v. Chesapeake Bay Foundation, Inc.*, 844 F.3d 170, 172 (4th Cir. 1988). *But see Allen County Citizens for the Environment v. BP Oil Co.*, 762 F. Supp. 733 (N.D. Ohio 1991), *aff'd*, 966 F. 2d 1451 (6th Cir. 1992) (violation

not "continuing" where no exceedances had occurred during the 42 months preceding the date the complaint was filed, even though two exceedances occurred after complaint was filed).

397 *Public Interest Research Group v. Hercules, Inc.*, 830 F. Supp. 1549, 1556 (D.N.J. 1993); *see also Paolino v. JF Realty, LLC,* 710 F.3d 31, 33 (1st Cir. 2013) (notice sufficient where "notice identifies the potential plaintiffs, provides basic contact information, and allows the putative defendants to identify and remedy the alleged violations").

Chapter 7

Oil Pollution Act

Andrew N. Davis[1] and Austin P. Olney
Shipman & Goodwin LLP
Hartford, Connecticut

1.0 Overview

The history of maritime commerce is punctuated with many popular names like *Titanic, Morro Castle, Herald of Free Enterprise, Torrey Canyon, Amoco Cadiz, Exxon Valdez, Deepwater Horizon,* and *Cabo Rojo.* They are synonymous with tragic and often cascading miscalculations by the designers, builders, owners or operators of ships. Public outrage at the magnitude of these tragedies has periodically driven important advances in international and domestic maritime safety and environmental laws. In the wake of the 1989 *Exxon Valdez* oil spill in Alaska, Congress enacted one of the most comprehensive and stringent environmental laws ever written—the Oil Pollution Act of 1990 (OPA or the Act)—ending years of deadlock over the adoption of a comprehensive oil spill regime.[2]

Vivid and fresh images of environmental devastation in Prince William Sound, Alaska, and the ensuing political backlash caused Congress, with uncharacteristic dispatch, to impose new strict liability standards and extensive operating requirements on the marine oil industry. Following the enactment of OPA, the industry scrambled to comply with the detailed regulations that emerged from the largest regulatory project ever conducted by the U.S. Coast Guard (USCG).[3] Although the commercial dislocations widely predicted by the industry during the OPA congressional debate did not materialize, many companies, including some major oil companies, either restructured their operations, sold tanker assets, or simply stopped trading to the United States.[4]

Since the enactment of OPA in 1990, the number and volume of marine oil spills has dropped markedly, more so than in other parts of the world where less stringent standards apply.[5] Many factors contribute to the improvement of the oil spill record in the United States. One obvious factor is more prompt and efficient oil spill containment and recovery brought about by the OPA-mandated spill response plans and the availability of prepositioned response resources. OPA also required the phase-out of older single-hull tankers by January 1, 2015, and the replacement of those tankers with double-hull tankers that are less susceptible to spills that result from collisions and groundings. Another explanation is that OPA has forced the industry to be more careful because the legal and financial consequences of spills, including the threat of criminal prosecution, are so severe.[6]

No spill in U.S. waters approached the magnitude of the *Exxon Valdez* until April 20, 2010, when the semi-submersible oil rig, the *Deepwater Horizon*, caught fire and exploded in the Gulf of Mexico, 41 miles southeast of the entrance to the Mississippi River. The explosion killed 11 workers. The blow-out preventer failed, releasing an estimated 4.9 million barrels of crude oil into the Gulf of Mexico before the so-called *Macondo* well was capped on July 15, 2010.

It is the largest oil spill in U.S. history. It tested every aspect of OPA, including the liability and compensation regime, the response system and the claims handling procedures. The response was unprecedented in its scale. At the height of the response more than 40,000 workers were employed daily. More than 7,000 vessels were involved in cleanup and recovery operations, and 12.7 million feet of containment boom were deployed along the coastline.

Because of the unprecedented level of claims and the limited funds available under the Oil Spill Liability Trust Fund (the Fund or OSLTF),[7] the claims process established under OPA was replaced by the Gulf Coast Claims Facility (GCCF), an independent claims facility established by BP. The GCCF was funded through BP's initial commitment of $20 billion to be paid on an installment basis. On August 23, 2010, the GCCF began processing claims from individuals and businesses for costs and damages incurred as a result of the *Deepwater Horizon* spill. During its one-and-a-half-year existence, the GCCF processed over one million claims and paid out approximately $6.2 billion to 220,000 individual and business claimants.[8]

In addition, hundreds of private third-party complaints were filed in different states. Some of the claims arose out of OPA, while many were based on federal and state statutes and common law that were outside the scope of OPA. Pursuant to 28 U.S.C. §1407, these claims were consolidated by the Judicial Panel on Multi-District Litigation (MDL) into one case, *In re: Spill by the Oil Rig "Deepwater Horizon" in the Gulf of Mexico on April 20, 2010*, in the federal court for the Eastern District of Louisiana and assigned to Judge Barbier.[9] That case was ongoing at the time of publication.[10]

While the unprecedented scale of the *Deepwater Horizon* spill did result in the establishment of an *ad hoc* claims process that superseded the statutory claims procedures, the balance of the OPA regime has remained intact, without material modification by Congress or significant departures by courts from prior decisions. Twenty-six years of judicial interpretation have resolved several ambiguities in the law, but the fundamental elements of OPA have not been challenged or changed. The most notable trends reflect the growing use of the provisions holding a responsible party (RP)[11] accountable to the public for natural resource damages and frequent use of criminal enforcement provisions of OPA and related statutes. These trends are not unique to OPA cases and reflect trends in related fields of environmental law enforcement.

The effectiveness of OPA can be attributed to the fact that it is more comprehensive and stringent than any previous U.S. or international oil pollution liability and prevention law. OPA is divided into nine titles, Title I of which created a new section on oil pollution liability and compensation in Title 33 of the U.S. Code.[12] In Title I, OPA imposes strict liability for a comprehensive list of damages, including natural resource damages, arising from an oil spill into the water from vessels and facilities.[13] The law contains limits on this liability, but the limits are far higher than under prior U.S. law or international law.[14] These limits are subject to important qualifications and exceptions.

OPA established a supplemental compensation fund for oil spills. The fund was originally established by imposing a five-cents-per-barrel tax on the receipt of imported crude oil and petroleum products.[15] The combined effect is to place the burden of paying cleanup costs and damages in the first instance on the owner or operator of the vessel or facility that is the source of the spill. If the costs and damages exceed the limit of liability for the vessel or facility, the OSLTF pays the balance, effectively placing the secondary responsibility to pay for oil spill cleanup and damages on the receivers of crude oil or petroleum products. The OSLTF is also available to pay for cleanup and damages when the spiller has a valid defense or when the source of a discharge cannot be identified.[16]

Title IV of OPA amended provisions of the Federal Water Pollution Control Act (also known as the Clean Water Act or CWA)[17] concerning oil spills. Title IV expanded the authority and capability of the federal government to direct and manage oil spill cleanup operations; this was a direct response to confusion over who was in charge during the pre-OPA *Exxon Valdez* spill response and cleanup. It requires vessel and facility operators to file detailed oil spill response plans evidencing the availability of private-sector cleanup and removal resources. Title IV contains amendments to Title 46 of the U.S. Code on shipping. OPA sets numerous operational requirements for vessels to prevent oil spills, including the phased replacement of single-hull oil tankers and barges with double-hull vessels. Title IV of OPA also substantially increases the civil and criminal penalties for causing spills and for violating many marine safety and environmental protection laws.

Of the seven other OPA titles, Title III concerns the implementation of international conventions. Title III does not require the United States to adopt any international conventions on oil spills. Titles II, VI and IX contain technical and conforming amendments to other laws. The remainder of the Act addresses subjects primarily concerned with Alaska and is beyond the scope of this chapter. Title V contains provisions on oil spill prevention and removal in Prince William Sound,[18] Title VII sets up an oil pollution research and development program[19] and Title VIII amends the Trans-Alaska Pipeline System Act.[20]

2.0 Background

While the grounding of the *Exxon Valdez* on March 24, 1989, and several subsequent accidents in 1989 and 1990, are generally viewed as the inspiration for the enactment of OPA, the law was actually the product of nearly 20 years of Congressional debate on oil pollution liability and tanker safety. This debate frequently centered on whether federal law should preempt state law and whether federal law should be circumscribed by international treaties.

In 1972, Congress responded to concern over water pollution by enacting the CWA. Section 311 addressed oil spills from vessels and facilities by imposing strict liability to the federal government for cleanup and removal costs.

In addition, three specialized statutes were subsequently enacted to address oil spills in specific circumstances: the Trans-Alaska Pipeline Authorization Act,[21] the Deepwater Port Act of 1974[22] and the Outer Continental Shelf Lands Act Amendments of 1978.[23] These statutes set up strict liability schemes and supplemental compensation funds for spills occurring in their respective areas. During the same time period, Congress also enacted laws to promote safer port operations and safer vessels, including the Ports and Waterways Safety Act of 1972 (PWSA),[24] which was later modified by the Port and Tanker Safety Act of 1978 (PTSA).[25]

Several U.S. states also adopted their own oil pollution laws. Although a few states—notably California, Florida and Maine—adopted oil pollution laws in the late 1970s, a majority of the 24 coastal states enacted special oil spill laws or amendments after 1986.

Roughly contemporaneous with these efforts in the United States, the International Convention on Civil Liability for Oil Pollution Damage (CLC) was signed in 1969 and came into force in 1975.[26] The CLC established a strict liability regime subject to limits on liability for tankers carrying persistent oil. Another multinational initiative, the International Convention on the Establishment of an International Fund for Compensation for Oil Pollution Damage (Fund Convention),[27] created a supplemental compensation fund financed by the cargo interests. The Fund Convention was signed in 1971 and came into force in 1978.

Although the United States participated in the diplomatic conferences for these two conventions, neither the CLC nor the Fund Convention was ratified by the United States for two reasons: the U.S. Senate considered the limits of liability to be too low, and the Senate opposed CLC and Fund Convention preemption of federal and state law.[28] In an effort to improve the prospects for Senate advice and consent, the executive branch strongly promoted amendments in the form of two protocols to the CLC and the Fund Convention that were adopted at a diplomatic conference held in 1984 (1984 Protocols).[29] The 1984 Protocols sought to increase the limits of liability, expand the scope of compensable damages and increase the size of the supplemental compensation fund.[30]

While the United States refrained from adopting either the CLC or the Fund Convention, even with the 1984 Protocols, legislative developments in the Congress, including the PTSA, provided many of the structural and operational requirements that were incorporated into the Protocol of 1978 Relating to the International Convention for the Prevention of Pollution from Ships, 1973.[31]

Thus, while the aftermath and public global outcry following the *Exxon Valdez* spill may have provided the final impetus for OPA, the Act evolved from a continuum of environmental legislation and heightened international efforts to address pollution from ships over two decades.

3.0 Title I: Oil Pollution Liability and Compensation

Title I[32] establishes the federal liability scheme for vessels and facilities that release oil in waters subject to United States jurisdiction. It sets out the scope of the Act: the waters, vessels and facilities to which OPA applies. It defines the standard of liability and enumerates compensable damages. The provisions of Title I also set up the claims procedures, financial responsibility requirements and the uses of the OSLTF.

3.1 Definitions

Section 1001 of OPA contains 37 definitions that are used throughout the Act.[33] OPA restates verbatim many of the definitions of the CWA.

Except where otherwise limited, OPA applies to all vessels, not just tankers. Consequently, a spill involving fuel from a pleasure craft or bunkers[34] from a general cargo vessel is subject to OPA liability, though many of the more stringent operational and construction requirements contained in Title IV apply only to tank vessels. Thus, OPA provisions need to be read with reference to the type of vessel involved. For example, OPA liability is imposed on all types of vessels which discharge oil (Section 1002), while double-hull requirements apply specifically to tank vessels (Section 4115).

Vessels are defined to include "every description of watercraft or other artificial contrivance used, or capable of being used, as a means of transportation on water, other than a public vessel."[35] Public vessels are noncommercial government vessels.

Tank vessels are vessels constructed or adapted to carry, or that do carry, oil or hazardous materials in bulk as cargo or cargo residue and that are U.S.-documented vessels, operate in U.S. waters, or transfer oil or hazardous material in a place subject to the jurisdiction of the United States. This definition of tank vessels is not limited to oil tankers and barges but also includes tankers and barges carrying hazardous materials such as explosives, liquefied petroleum gas and liquefied natural gas.[36]

Mobile offshore drilling units, like the *Deepwater Horizon*, are drilling units capable of use as an offshore facility; self-elevating lift vessels are not included in this definition.

Facility is any structure, group of structures, equipment or device (other than a vessel) that is used for any of the following purposes: exploring for, drilling for, producing, storing, handling, transferring, processing or transporting oil. The term also includes any motor vehicle, rolling stock or pipeline used for these purposes.[37] Facilities are further subdivided into onshore and offshore facilities.

Oil includes oil of any kind, including petroleum, fuel oil, sludge, oil refuse, and oil mixed with wastes, other than dredge spoils. The definition goes on to exclude petroleum, including crude oil or any fraction thereof, which is specifically listed as a hazardous substance under Section 9601(14)(A) through (F) of the Comprehensive Environmental Response, Compensation, and Liability Act (CERCLA).[38] Congress intended there to be no overlap between the liability provisions of OPA and those of CERCLA. Agencies charged with implementing OPA regulations have interpreted the definition of oil under OPA to include nonpetroleum oils, such as animal fat and vegetable oils. In response to industry concerns about overregulation of such "edible" oils, Congress, the USCG, and the U.S. Environmental Protection Agency (EPA) have engaged in a protracted dispute over the extent to which OPA regulations should differentiate between edible oils and petroleum oils.[39]

Person is defined broadly to include both natural persons and commercial and government entities, including states, municipalities, commissions, political subdivisions and interstate bodies.

Owner or operator is the person(s) who bears the burden for the substantive obligations of OPA. In the case of a vessel this means a person who owns, operates or demise (bareboat) charters a vessel. With respect to facilities, the definition covers those persons "owning or operating" the facility, a standard that is susceptible to flexible application depending upon the specific facts.[40] For an abandoned vessel or facility, it is the person who would have been the owner or operator immediately prior to abandonment. This definition was expanded in the U.S. Coast Guard and Maritime Transportation Act of 2004 (CGMT-04) to include any person who owned or operated or otherwise controlled a facility immediately before that person conveyed ownership to a state or local government due to bankruptcy, foreclosure or tax delinquency.[41] The CGMT-04 also identifies those lenders and persons who hold indicia of ownership to protect a security interest in a vessel or facility and who exercise decision-making control over environmental compliance or who exercise day-to-day managerial control as coming under the definition of owners or operators.[42]

Responsible party[43] is the person(s) liable for removal costs and damages under Section 1002. Generally, the term means the owner or operator whose vessel or facility is the source of an oil discharge or poses the substantial threat of a discharge.[44] For deepwater ports, the RP is the licensee and for offshore facilities the RP is the lessee or the permittee of the area in which the facility is located. Public entities are not considered RPs in connection with onshore facilities.

Discharge is any sort of emission or release into the navigable waters, the adjoining shoreline or the exclusive economic zone. A discharge of oil triggers OPA jurisdiction and potential liability thereunder. A discharge of CERCLA hazardous substances[45] triggers OPA containment and removal provisions.

Incident means one or more discharges from the same source.

Navigable waters indicates all water of the United States beginning with marshes and extending seaward 12 miles to the limits of the territorial sea. A discharge in these waters or on the adjoining shoreline is covered by OPA; the courts have recently started to address the "gray" areas, such as groundwater contamination and spills in inland waters that have a tenuous connection to navigability.[46]

Guarantor means any person who provides financial responsibility for an RP under OPA; it does not include the RP, however.

Exclusive economic zone includes those waters that extend seaward 200 nautical miles from the baseline that is used to measure the breadth of the territorial sea. Discharges in these waters are also covered by OPA.

Remove or removal means that under Title IV of OPA, public and private entities are to carry out the effective and immediate removal of a discharge and mitigate or prevent the substantial threat of a discharge. Remove or removal is defined as containment and removal of the oil or hazardous substance from the water and shorelines and other actions to minimize or mitigate damage.

In addition to modifying the definition for owners or operators, the CGMT-04 added several new definitions to the original legislation, including the term "participate in management." This term is defined as "actually participating in the management or operational affairs of a vessel or facility," with numerous exceptions for various financial arrangements and participation in removal actions.[47]

The CGMT-04 also added a lengthy definition for the term "contractual relationship."[48] The new definition, which focuses primarily on property relationships, has a significant impact on the availability of a defense based on the negligent act of a third party with whom there is no contractual relationship.[49]

4.0 Elements of Liability

OPA makes parties responsible for vessels and facilities liable for the results of oil spills without regard to fault, subject only to certain narrow defenses and limitations. While this is essentially the same liability that vessel and facility owners and operators had under the CWA before OPA, the damages that can be recovered from them after an oil spill are potentially much greater under OPA.[50]

4.1 Standard of Liability

Section 1002 states that liability under OPA exists "[n]otwithstanding any other provision or rule of law." This removes any prerequisite to liability and means no other law will affect the ability of a claimant to recover under OPA, such as the requirement that a claimant show physical damage to its property. This also means that a vessel owner is unable to limit its liability to the value of the vessel and its freight under the Limited Liability Act (Limitation Act).[51]

Litigation over the continued application of the Limitation Act has occupied significant court time in the years since OPA's enactment. Perhaps the most long-lived case is *Bouchard Transp. Co. v. Updegraff*,[52] which, as the court noted at the time of its July 31, 1998 ruling, "has been before the Eleventh Circuit several times already."[53] The case involved the 1993 collision in Tampa Bay between a freighter and two tugs pushing petroleum-carrying barges. The owners of the two tug-barge units initiated limitation proceedings pursuant to the Limitation Act, arguing that Rule F of the Limitation Act generally applies to all limitation statutes and that OPA, which limited an owner's liability to $1,200 per gross ton[54] for cleanup costs and damages, must be governed by Rule F.[55] The Eleventh Circuit rejected this contention, holding that "OPA 90 is not subject to Rule F for two reasons: (1) OPA 90 claimants do not face a limited fund necessitating a pro rata distribution; and (2) Congress has specifically set forth procedures to implement the strictures of OPA 90."[56]

OPA further states that each party responsible for a vessel or facility is liable for removal costs and damages.[57] This envisions that in some circumstances multiple RPs could be jointly and severally liable for the entire amount of removal costs and damages.[58]

4.2 Removal Costs and Spill Response

An RP is liable for all removal costs incurred by the federal government, state governments or federally recognized Indian tribes under the authority of either the CWA, as amended by OPA, or the Intervention on the High Seas Act,[59] which governs discharges in international waters that threaten the United States. OPA provides that removal costs can include expenses of actions taken by virtually any agency or department of federal, state and local governments to avert the threat of a discharge and to ensure the immediate and effective containment and removal of the oil or hazardous substance, including the government's costs of monitoring a spill response.[60] These costs and expenses could also include those resulting from whatever action is necessary to protect fish, shellfish, wildlife, public and private property, shorelines, beaches, and living and nonliving natural resources.[61]

An RP is also liable for any removal costs incurred under the authority of state law[62] and for any removal costs incurred by any person—that is, private individuals and organizations—for actions taken which are consistent with the National Contingency Plan (NCP).[63]

Typically, as a part of removal and spill response activities, an RP will have the opportunity to work cooperatively with the USCG, the National Oceanic and Atmospheric Administration (NOAA), and other federal and state governmental spill response personnel (which may include natural resource trustees) (see *infra* section 5.0). These cooperative removal and cleanup activities (such as shoreline cleanup assessment team [SCAT] work) can often be cost-effectively and strategically combined with data gathering for potential natural resource damages assessments.[64] Even in the case of what appears to be a "small" spill,[65] it is prudent and cost-effective for an RP to thoroughly document the spill response process and obtain timely and extensive data regarding the environmental conditions within (and upgradient and downgradient of) the area affected by a spill (for potential use in the natural resource damage process).[66]

4.3 Compensatory Damages

In addition to removal costs, OPA makes an RP liable for six categories of compensatory damages: (1) Natural Resources; (2) Real or Personal Property; (3) Subsistence Use; (4) Governmental Revenues; (5) Profits and Earning Capacity; and (6) Public Services.[67]

4.3.1 Natural Resources

The United States, states, federally recognized Indian tribes and foreign governments are entitled to recover from an RP for damages to, injury to, destruction of, loss of and loss of use of natural resources. Consequently, only governments or tribes acting in their trustee capacities may recover these types of damages. Private citizens do not have standing to bring such claims. However, private citizens, such as commercial fishermen, would have standing to bring claims for economic losses, such as lost earnings that are related to diminished fisheries stocks.[68] In contrast, recreational fishermen would not have standing for their loss of use of a fishery because they would not have suffered an economic loss; the public at large would have suffered lost enjoyment of using the natural resource which would be compensable to the natural resource trustees.[69] Natural resource damages also include the reasonable cost of conducting an assessment to determine if natural resources were lost or damaged and, if so, the extent of such damage.[70] The special procedures for assessing natural resource damages are discussed at section 5.0, *infra*.

4.3.2 Real or Personal Property

A property owner or lessee may recover for injury to, or economic losses resulting from destruction of, the property.[71] Compensable damages may include loss of goodwill or intangible assets.[72]

4.3.3 Subsistence Use

Any person who relies on natural resources for subsistence (as opposed to commercial reliance, which is covered under loss of profits and earnings) may recover damages for injury to natural resources regardless of who owns or manages those resources.[73] One court interpreting the term "subsistence" held that it relates to use of a natural resource, such as water, to obtain the minimum necessities for life.[74] Tribes are often subsistence users who bring claims to recover damages under this section.

4.3.4 Governmental Revenues

Federal, state and local governments are entitled to recover damages equal to the net loss of taxes, royalties, rents, fees or net profit shares resulting from the destruction or loss of real or personal property, or natural resources.[75]

4.3.5 Profits and Earning Capacity

Any claimant is entitled to loss of profits or impairment of earning capacity due to the injury, destruction, or loss of real or personal property or natural resources.[76] The claimant need not own, or have an interest in, the damaged property or resources.[77] General maritime law (i.e., non-OPA) tort claims, however, remain subject to the "economic loss rule" of *Robins Dry Dock & Repair Co. v. Flint*, 275 U.S. 303, 309 (1927), which preconditions recovery for economic losses on physical injury to the claimant's property.[78]

4.3.6 Public Services

State and local governments are entitled to recover damages for the net costs of providing increased or additional public services resulting from removal activities, including fire, safety and health protection.

4.4 Interest

An RP, or its insurer, may be liable to a claimant for interest on the amount to be paid in satisfaction of a claim.[79] The interest period begins 30 days after the claim is presented to the RP and continues until the claim is paid. An offer of the amount claimed can suspend the interest period, as will reasons beyond the control of the RP. Interest payments are not included in liability limit calculations.

5.0 Natural Resource Damages

Under OPA, an RP is liable to the federal government, state governments[80] and foreign governments, as well as to federally recognized Indian tribes,[81] for injury to, destruction of, or loss of natural resources.[82] Unlike other categories of compensatory damages, natural resource damages (NRDs) are assessed under a specific regime established by OPA that is patterned after parallel provisions in CERCLA.[83] Typical natural resources injured by oil spills may include the following:[84]

- marine, aquatic and terrestrial ecosystems and their services;
- birds including migratory, endangered and common species;
- shorelines and vegetation;
- marine, aquatic, and terrestrial mammals, reptiles, amphibians, finfish, lobsters[85] and shellfish;
- recreational lost use;[86] and
- cultural resources.[87]

OPA establishes standards for measuring the NRDs resulting from oil spills.[88] Federal agencies, such as NOAA and the Department of the Interior's U.S. Fish and Wildlife Service (FWS), state authorities and federally recognized tribes that serve as "trustees" are responsible for recovering damages from RPs for injuries to the natural resources under their respective jurisdiction.[89] Where there is joint jurisdiction, the trustees are to exercise joint management or control over the shared resources; no group of trustees can preempt another group. NOAA was directed to develop and issue regulations for assessing NRDs.[90]

The designated federal, state, foreign and Indian trustees are also directed to assess damages to their natural resources and to calculate the restoration costs.[91] OPA prohibits double recovery for NRDs, and the trustees are required to consolidate assessment and restoration activities.[92] The trustees must develop and implement plans for the restoration, rehabilitation and replacement of the natural resources damaged by the spill. The cost of developing and implementing these plans is the major component of a natural resource damages assessment (NRDA).[93]

Under 15 C.F.R. §990.14, the trustees are required to invite the RP to participate in the NRDA process. This cooperative NRDA approach affords the RP an opportunity to avoid the double burden of funding its own assessment and a parallel assessment undertaken by the trustees. The cooperative approach is designed to encourage an immediate dialogue between the RP and the trustees over using common data sources and assessment methodologies. The effect of this collaborative approach is to raise and address differences between the parties at the technical level, early in the process, thereby avoiding duplication of effort and the contentiousness that is inherent in a process whereby the RP and trustees conduct separate and independent damage assessments.

The trustee plans must provide the basis for calculating NRDs for which an RP is liable.[94] The plans may include provisions for the acquisition of equivalent resources—that is, resources comparable to the injured resources—to restore the injured ecosystem if the trustees determine that restoration, rehabilitation or replacement of the precise injured resource is not feasible.[95] The trustees are required to determine the cost of implementing these plans, as well as to calculate the diminution in value of the damaged resources pending restoration.

Trustees must take into account the following three factors when determining the standard measure of damages to natural resources that is to apply to any action brought under OPA:

1. The cost of restoring, rehabilitating, replacing or acquiring the equivalent of the damaged natural resources;

2. The diminution in value of those natural resources pending restoration; and

3. The reasonable cost of assessing the damage.[96]

Amounts recovered by the respective trustees for NRDs are to be retained by the trustees in their own trust accounts to be used, without further appropriation, exclusively for the costs of carrying out their restoration plans. Excess amounts are to be deposited in the OSLTF.[97] Any person can obtain judicial review of trustees' actions in federal court.[98]

The under secretary of commerce for oceans and the atmosphere (i.e., NOAA), in consultation with other affected federal agencies, was required to promulgate regulations for the assessment of NRDs.[99] Trustees' NRDAs made according to these regulations are treated legally as rebuttable presumptions.[100] This means that the trustees are presumed to be correct in any administrative or judicial proceeding under OPA; although this presumption can be overcome, anyone challenging the accuracy of the assessment will have the burden of proving that the trustees' assessment is incorrect.[101]

5.1 NRDA Regulations

NOAA published final NRDA regulations under OPA, effective February 5, 1996.[102] The regulations describe measures that may be taken by designated federal, state, foreign, and federally recognized Indian tribe trustees in assessing NRDs resulting from an oil spill.[103]

The regulations set forth three major components of a damage assessment:

1. Preassessment Phase;

2. Restoration Planning; and

3. Restoration Implementation.

As noted above, 15 C.F.R. §990.14 requires the trustees to invite the RP to participate in the NRDA process. The terms of engagement of the cooperative NRDA are sometimes set out in a Memorandum of Agreement (MOA) negotiated by the trustees and the RP.[104] While this cooperative process affords an RP significant opportunities to participate in the NRDA process, the "[f]inal authority to make determinations regarding injury and restoration rest [sic] solely with the trustees."[105] Trustees also have the authority to "end the participation" of the RP if they, in their sole discretion, determine that the RP is not being sufficiently cooperative.[106] Moreover, as noted above, while the RP may be engaged in a cooperative NRDA, to the extent disputes arise between the trustees and RP, "any determination or assessment of damages to natural resources made by the trustees shall have the force and effect of a rebuttable presumption on behalf of the trustees in any administrative or judicial proceeding" brought under OPA.[107]

In sum, the regulations grant trustees extensive latitude for conducting assessments and mean that an RP: (1) will fully fund the reasonable costs of a cooperative process;[108] (2) will not be provided with a "right" to vote; (3) will be disadvantaged by an evidentiary presumption in favor of the trustees' determinations, unless challenged in an administrative or judicial proceeding; and (4) will have to give the trustees the final word on all decisions.[109]

Under the regulations, trustees determine, in the Preassessment Phase, threshold criteria that establish their authority to begin a NRDA. Following assessment procedures that may include field and lab work, literature evaluation and modeling,[110] the trustees make a preliminary determination as to whether natural resources or natural resource services[111] have been injured or diminished. After this determination, the trustees then determine, in coordination with response agencies, whether further response actions will eliminate the threat of ongoing injury or loss of services.

The Restoration Planning phase has two basic components: (1) injury assessment; and (2) restoration selection. Injury is defined as an observable or measurable adverse change in a natural resource or impairment of a natural resource service. Once trustees have determined that an injury has occurred, they must quantify the degree and the spatial and temporal extent of the injury.[112]

In most oil spills, the critical data needed for realistic injury assessments are ephemeral. If the critical data are not captured from the outset (typically the first 24 to 48 hours) and collected with an appreciation for the ultimate role/use of the particular data in the NRDA, the trustees may default to computer models to quantify the nature and extent of injury to the impacted resources.[113] Trustees often use proprietary models to estimate the potential NRDs that can have significant adverse financial consequences for an RP.[114]

Upon completion of the injury assessment, the trustees must develop both a Draft and Final Restoration Plan that take into account a reasonable range of restoration alternatives. The Draft Restoration Plan must consider public comments.[115]

During Restoration Implementation, the restoration alternatives selected by the trustees, and often with the input of the RP, may be natural recovery (no human intervention);[116] active primary restoration, in which injured natural resources are returned to baseline on an accelerated time frame; compensatory restoration, which encompasses actions to compensate for interim losses of natural resources pending recovery; or a combination of the three. The regulations require that the identified restoration alternatives be evaluated based upon several factors:

1. The cost to carry out the alternative;

2. The extent to which each alternative is expected to meet the goals and objectives of the trustees in returning the injured resources or services to baseline and/or compensate for interim losses;

3. The likelihood of success of each alternative;

4. The extent to which each alternative will prevent future injury and avoid collateral injury as a result of implementing the alternative;

5. The extent to which each alternative benefits more than one natural resource and/or service; and/or

6. The effect of each alternative on public health and safety.

The regulations further provide that the trustees select the most cost-effective of two or more equally preferable alternatives.

NOAA's proposed regulations provided for a contingent valuation (CV) methodology in determining equivalent values for lost services. The final regulations allow for the use of CV or other valuation methodologies, but only where a resource-to-resource or service-to-service approach to scaling the restoration action is inappropriate.[117]

Finally, following public comment and, where appropriate, compliance with National Environmental Policy Act (NEPA)[118] requirements, the Final Restoration Plan is presented to the RPs to implement or to fund the trustees' costs of implementing the plan.

5.2 Application of NRDA Regulations

To provide perspective, below are brief summaries of six recent and major oil spills triggering the NRDA provisions of OPA and its regulations. More extensive information on the various NRDAs is maintained by NOAA online at http://www.darrp.noaa.gov.[119]

5.2.1 The *North Cape* Oil Spill

One of the early and most extensively documented tests of the OPA NRDA regulations involved the *North Cape* spill that occurred off the coast of Rhode Island. On January 19, 1996, the tug *Scandia* (with the tank barge *North Cape* in tow) caught fire, causing the crew to abandon ship in harsh conditions. Both vessels foundered, and the *North Cape* spilled approximately 828,000 gallons of No. 2 home heating oil. High winds dispersed the oil over a wide area, resulting in the temporary closure of several coastal ponds and of an approximately 250-square-mile area of Block Island Sound to fishing. Technical reports subsequent to the spill revealed losses sustained by multiple varieties of marine life, including lobsters, marine birds and fish.

On September 15, 1998, NOAA issued a Draft Restoration Plan and Environmental Assessment for the spill that had been developed under the newly adopted NRDA regulations.[120] The Draft Restoration Plan presented the NRDA and restoration plan that was developed by NOAA, the state of Rhode Island Department of Environmental Management and the U.S. Department of Interior (DOI) (collectively, "the Trustees"). Subsequent to the publication of the Draft Restoration Plan, the RP and the Trustees negotiated a consent decree that included a detailed "Statement of Work" committing the RPs, among other things, to a five-year lobster restoration project. On October 6, 2000, a consent decree between EW Holding Corp. and the United States for NRDs resulting from the *North Cape* spill was entered by the U.S. District Court for the District of Rhode Island.[121] In that consent decree, EW Holding agreed to pay approximately $12 million in NRDA costs, in addition to agreeing to restore the lobsters that were estimated to have died as a result of the spill through an RP-funded and implemented (with Trustee oversight) v-notching preservation plan for 1.248 million legal-sized female lobsters.[122] Of the $12 million, approximately $4 million covered past assessment costs incurred by the Trustees. The remaining $8 million was paid to the NRDA fund for distribution to the Trustees to implement and oversee other restoration projects.[123] These figures do not include some of the costs absorbed directly by the RPs and all of the costs to develop and manage the lobster restoration program.[124]

The restoration program, which began in 2000, was successful in achieving demonstrable recovery and restoration of affected species. In addition to the 1.248 million female lobsters that were required to be "notched" and returned into Rhode Island and southeastern Massachusetts coastal waters, the Trustees and RP: purchased a conservation easement and secured permanent protection for 60 acres of land adjacent to Ninigret Pond; contributed to the acquisition and protection of 1.5 million acres of land in Maine to protect over 125 loon nesting pairs and their habitat; and increased the number of piping plover nesting pairs on Rhode Island's South County beaches by 60 percent, among other various restoration techniques.[125]

5.2.2 The M/T *Athos I* Oil Spill

On November 26, 2004, while preparing to dock at the Citgo refinery in Paulsboro, New Jersey, the M/T *Athos I* struck submerged debris, including an 18,000-pound anchor. The anchor punctured the vessel's hull, releasing nearly 265,000 gallons of crude oil into the Delaware River and surrounding tributaries. The resulting NRDs identified by the trustees included 1,729 acres of shoreline and

1,899 acres of tributaries oiled, an estimated 11,869 dead birds, and an estimated $1,319,097 of recreational lost use for approximately 41,709 affected trips to the river for hunting, fishing, crabbing and/or pleasure boating.[126] The trustees' final restoration plan and environmental assessment proposed seven projects to compensate for the identified damages: (1) restore seven acres of freshwater tidal wetlands within a federal wildlife refuge in Pennsylvania; (2) create 78 acres of oyster reef in the Delaware River; (3) remove three dams from and restore ten acres of riparian habitat along a creek in southeastern Pennsylvania; (4) restore 59.6 acres of wetlands and create 35 acres of wet meadow and 100 acres of grassland on state-owned property in New Jersey; (5) restore 0.9 acres of shoreline in Pennsylvania; (6) convert 16 acres of existing agricultural land in Delaware to pond and pasture habitat for migratory geese; and (7) address lost recreational use, improve the Stow Creek (NJ) boat ramp, construct an additional breakwater at another boat ramp in Delaware and "enhance" the recreational trail on Little Tinicum Island (PA).[127]

5.2.3 The M/V *Cosco Busan* Oil Spill

On November 7, 2007, the container ship M/V *Cosco Busan* allided with the San Francisco-Oakland Bay Bridge, rupturing its fuel tank and releasing approximately 53,000 gallons of fuel oil. The oil spread into San Francisco Bay and the Pacific Ocean and onto approximately 90 miles of the adjacent shoreline.[128]

The NRDA trustees (California Dept. of Fish and Game, California State Lands Commission, DOI, National Park Service, Bureau of Land Management and NOAA) and the RP entered into a consent decree, which required the owners and operators of the M/V *Cosco Busan* to pay $44 million for NRDs and penalties and to reimburse the governmental entities for response costs incurred as a result of the spill. Of that $44 million, $18.8 million was apportioned to compensate for lost recreational uses of the shoreline and San Francisco Bay.[129]

The federal and state natural resource trustees estimated that the spill killed 6,849 birds, impacted 14 to 29 percent of the herring spawn that winter, oiled 3,367 acres of shoreline habitat and resulted in the loss of more than 1,000,000 recreational user-days.[130]

Approximately $32.3 million was set aside in the February 2012 Final Restoration Plan to be spent on a wide variety of restoration projects.[131] About $5 million was set aside for bird restoration, $4 million for habitat restoration, $2.5 million for fish and habitat (eelgrass) restoration and $18.8 million for recreational use improvements. An additional $2 million was dedicated to restoration planning and administration oversight, with any unused funds to be spent toward more restoration.[132]

5.2.4 The T/B *B 120* Oil Spill

The tank barge *B 120,* under tow by the tug *Evening Tide,* struck a shoal located outside the ship channel while entering the western end of Buzzards Bay, Massachusetts. The barge released an estimated 93,000 gallons of No. 6 oil, which eventually affected approximately 98 miles of coastline in Massachusetts and Rhode Island and killed approximately 450 birds, including loons, plovers and terns.

The trustees (NOAA, DOI/U.S. Fish and Wildlife Service (USFWS), the Executive Office of Energy and Environmental Affairs for the Commonwealth of Massachusetts and Rhode Island Department of Environmental Management[133]) conducted a cooperative NRD with the RP. The injury assessment covered the impact on the shoreline habitats, birds and wildlife, recreational uses and aquatic resources. The RP and the trustees reached an agreement which was set forth in a partial consent decree filed with U.S. District Court for the District of Massachusetts on November 15, 2010. The partial consent decree required the RP to pay $6,076,393 of which $1,522,000 was applied to injuries to aquatic and shoreline resources; $534,000 was applied to injury to Ram Island shoreline resources; $3,305,393 was applied to lost recreational resources; and $715,000 was applied to injury to piping plovers.[134] At the time of publication, the RP and the Trustees had not yet entered into a final consent decree to resolve the unsettled injured resource categories (loons, roseate and common terns, and other birds).

5.2.5 The BP/Deepwater Horizon Oil Spill

On April 20, 2010, the Deepwater Horizon Macondo oil well drilling platform exploded, ultimately releasing approximately 3.19 million barrels (134 million gallons) of oil into the Gulf of Mexico; 11 workers were killed and 17 workers were injured by the explosion and fire. Following the explosion and sinking of the Macondo platform, the oil well over which it was positioned continuously and uncontrollably flowed for about 87 days, until the well was capped on July 15, 2010.[135] To clean the oil that had dispersed over thousands of square miles of the Gulf of Mexico—from Texas to Florida—1.8 million gallons of dispersants[136] were pumped directly into the leak and applied aerially to the water.[137] The oil that had spread came into contact with numerous natural resources including deep-sea coral, productive wetlands habitats, birds and endangered sea turtles, among many others.[138] The spill also prevented people from fishing, going to the beach and enjoying other recreational activities along and around the Gulf of Mexico.[139]

The breadth of the spill required the largest NRDA ever taken.[140] On April 4, 2016, the District Court for the Eastern District of Louisiana entered a consent decree under which BP agreed to pay $7.1 billion in NRDs (not including the $1 billion already committed during early restoration) and up to an additional $700 million to respond to NRDs unknown at the time of the agreement.[141] Of the $7.1 billion directed at NRD payments, $5 billion was allocated to compensate Louisiana, $1.24 billion was allocated to restore "the open ocean," broadly defined as restoration of resources primarily in the ocean, but which also includes administrative and preliminary planning across restoration areas and $350 million was allocated to "region-wide" projects to benefit resources across the Gulf, but which also included funding for NRD research, monitoring, oversight and planning.[142]

5.2.6 Cost of NRDAs

At this stage in the history of OPA NRDAs, the debate continues about the cost of NRDAs compared to other classes of damages. Since the issuance of the NRDA regulations, several OPA consent decrees involving NRDs have been published in the *Federal Register*.[143] These consent decrees do not present a consistent pattern that could be used to predict future costs or to generalize about the magnitude of NRDA costs. Rather, each NRDA and restoration effort is suited to the particular circumstances of each individual case and may vary significantly. While some consent decrees require solely monetary compensation, others require action on the part of the RP. For example, some decrees require the settling defendants to acquire land on behalf of the trustees[144] or, as in the *North Cape* case, to undertake a very complex resource restoration project.[145] Adding to the difficulty of making comparisons, some payments provided in the consent decrees include civil penalties, while others do not.

The published information about oil-related NRDAs is limited.[146] Two NOAA[147] representatives (acting in their individual, unofficial capacities) analyzed past oil spill costs in order to put NRDA costs into perspective with respect to other spill costs.[148] Their study concluded that NRDA costs are assessed in less than 1 percent of all reported oil spills and that NRDA costs only constitute about 26 percent of the total costs associated with those spills.[149] Industry reports, however, indicate that this number is much higher.[150] Under either statistical interpretation, NRDA costs can make up a substantial portion of the total cost of an oil spill, depending upon the circumstances of a particular incident.[151]

6.0 Defenses to Liability

Strict liability is a legal doctrine that imposes on a person who engages in a particular activity the responsibility for compensating others for the harm he causes, regardless of fault. OPA makes an RP strictly liable for oil spill damages. There are only four defenses that exonerate an RP from liability: three complete defenses to liability and one defense to particular claimants.[152]

The complete defenses require showing the intervention of outside forces: an act of God;[153] an act of war; and an act or omission of a third party. If one or more of these events (or a combination of them) is the sole cause of the discharge or threat of a discharge of oil and the resulting damages or removal costs, then the RP is exculpated. However, the RP is able to avail itself of these defenses only if it fulfills its other obligations under OPA. It must report the spill, must cooperate and assist with removal efforts, and must comply with official removal orders.

An RP also has a defense to the claim of a particular claimant to the extent that the incident giving rise to the claim is caused by the gross negligence or willful misconduct of the claimant.[154]

In the event of terrorist acts, it appears that an RP would have to use the third-party defense rather than the act of war defense.[155] While there are no OPA cases interpreting the "act of war" defense, there is precedent under CERCLA confirming that acts of war are typically government-sponsored activities.[156] The term "act of war," while nowhere clearly defined in U.S. law, appears to be borrowed from international law, where it is defined as a " 'use of force or other action by one state against another' which 'the state acted against recognizes . . . as an act of war, either by use of retaliatory force or a declaration of war.' "[157]

6.1 Third-Party Liability

When an RP is able to establish that a discharge, or the substantial threat of a discharge, and resulting removal costs and damages were caused solely by the act or omission of one or more third parties, then the third parties are treated as the RPs instead of the original RP.[158]

However, a third party will be treated as the RP only in limited circumstances. The third party cannot be an employee or agent of the RP. Nor will the third party be treated as the RP if the third party's act or omission causing a discharge, or the substantial threat of a discharge, occurred in connection with a contract between the RP and the third party,[159] unless the contract only involves carriage of oil by a common carrier by rail. The RP must prove that it exercised due care in handling the oil and took precautions against foreseeable acts of the third party and any foreseeable consequences of those actions.[160]

Furthermore, the RP must first pay removal costs and damages to any claimant. Only at that point is the RP entitled to be subrogated to the claimants' rights and recover the amount for any claims paid from the third party or from the OSLTF. Although an RP is entitled to reimbursement from the OSLTF if a third party is found liable, the RP may only recoup those costs it incurred that result from the discharge or substantial threat of discharge of oil into navigable waters and not subsequent events that occur as a result of the spill or discharge.[161]

The defense of third-party liability being invoked successfully is relatively rare.[162] In a well-publicized case, Tsakos Shipping and Trading SA asserted the third-party defense following the M/T *Athos I* spill in the Delaware River on November 26, 2004.[163] Although the ship owner initially took responsibility for the cleanup, the ship owner and operator were not liable for damages because the vessel was within the channel, under the direction and control of a pilot, and the submerged debris, which punctured the vessel's hull and caused the spill, was unmarked and otherwise unknown to the maritime community.[164] The OSLTF reimbursed the owner/operator for $88 million of the $180 million the owner had spent in cleanup costs. Seeking to recoup the remaining costs for which it had not been reimbursed, the tanker owner/operator filed suit against the marine terminal owner, alleging claims in contract and tort. Specifically, the owner/operator alleged that the terminal owner had breached the safe port and safe berth warranties. The government, as a statutory subrogee, sought reimbursement from the terminal owner for the $88 million it had reimbursed to the owner/operator on the basis of the owner/operator's contractual claims only. The District Court for the Eastern District of Pennsylvania found that the terminal owner was not liable for the accident.[165]

On appeal, the Third Circuit, concluding that the safe berth warranty was an express assurance of safety, requiring more than just due diligence on the part of the charterer, held that it could not be sure whether the warranties were actually breached, as the District Court had made no findings as to the owner/operator's actual draft (the distance between the lowest point of the ship and the waterline) nor the amount of clearance that was actually provided.[166] The Court then remanded to the District Court for further findings on the scope of the warranties.[167]

7.0 Limits on Liability

The Act limits the liability of an RP for removal costs and damages to specified dollar amounts per gross tonnage depending on the type and size of vessel or facility involved in the spill.[168] However, egregious or aberrant behavior by an RP or its failure to fulfill its reporting and assistance obligations under OPA creates circumstances in which these limits do not apply. It is important to understand that the limit of liability is not a limitation on the rights of claimants to recover removal costs or damages. The limit of liability allows a facility or vessel owner/operator to shift the cost of paying removal costs or damages that exceed the statutory limit of liability to another party or to the OSLTF, which is financed by the receivers of crude oil and product.

7.1 Standard for Limiting OPA Liability

The right of a vessel or facility owner to limit its liability is a conditional right. The right to limit is lost if the incident was proximately caused by the gross negligence, willful misconduct, or violation of an applicable federal safety, construction, or operating regulation by the RP.[169] Similarly, the failure of an RP to fulfill its reporting, cooperation and compliance obligations under OPA will render the liability limits inapplicable.[170] The actions of an agent, employee or contracted party (not including rail common carriers) are considered to be the acts of the RP. These exceptions to the limits on liability are far broader and more numerous than the ones under prior law. Previously, under the CWA, only if the government could show that the discharge was the result of willful negligence or willful misconduct within the privity and knowledge of the owner or operator would the limits on liability not apply.[171]

7.2 Specific Liability Limits

OPA increased the liability limits for vessel and facility owners or operators from the limits that were set under the CWA. Furthermore, OPA limits are now the only limits available for vessel owners since other statutory limits have been abrogated.

OPA liability limits increased with the enactment of the Delaware River Protection Act of 2006 (DRPA), found in Title VI of the U.S. Coast Guard and Maritime Transportation Act of 2006 (CGMT-06).[172] DRPA also conditioned liability limits for tank vessels on whether they have a single or double hull and whether they are designed or used to carry oil or hazardous material.[173]

For single-hull, oil-cargo tank vessels, the limit is the greater of $3,500 per gross ton or either $7,048,800 for vessels 3,000 gross tons or smaller or $25,845,600 for vessels larger than 3,000 gross tons. For single-hull, hazardous-material-cargo tank vessels and for all double-hull tank vessels, the limit is the greater of $2,200 per gross ton or either $4,699,200 for vessels 3,000 gross tons or smaller or $18,796,800 for vessels larger than 3,000 gross tons. For other vessels, including nontank vessels, the limit is the greater of $1,100 per gross ton or $939,800.[174] For vessels that carry oil as cargo from outer continental shelf facilities, these limits apply only to liability for damages. The owners or operators of such vessels are liable for all removal costs, without limit, resulting from a discharge.

The limit for onshore facilities is $350 million, for deepwater ports it is $373.8 million[175] and for offshore facilities (except deepwater ports), the limit is $75 million plus the total of all removal costs.[176] For outer continental shelf facilities, these limits only apply to liability for damages. The owners or operators of such facilities are liable for all removal costs, without limit, resulting from a discharge. Liability limits for mobile offshore drilling units that operate as offshore facilities and are involved in a discharge or the threat of a discharge are the same as for tank vessels. However, if the removal costs and damages exceed the applicable tank vessel liability limits, then the facility liability limits (minus the tank vessel limits) apply.

These liability limits also apply to third parties. If the act or omission of a third party that causes an incident occurs in connection with a vessel or facility owned or operated by the third party, then its liability is subject to the limits under OPA. In other cases, the liability of a third party is restricted in amount to the limit of the RP for the vessel or facility from which the discharge occurred, as if the RP were liable.[177]

7.3 Adjustment of Liability Limits

The president is directed to report periodically to Congress on the desirability of adjusting the statutory limits of liability. Consistent with this authority, on July 11, 2006, President George W. Bush signed into law DRPA, which amended the liability limits for vessels.[178] The president also has the authority to adjust the limits of liability for onshore facilities and deepwater ports without an amendment to the statute.[179]

With respect to onshore facilities, the president may set by regulation specific limits of liability between $8 million and $350 million for any class or category of onshore facility. The secretary is also required to report on the relative risks associated with the use of deepwater ports as compared with the risks associated with other ports and is authorized to lower the limits of liability by regulation for deepwater ports to $50 million.

The president is also directed to amend the limits of liability by regulation, at least triennially, to reflect significant increases in the Consumer Price Index.[180] In 2009, the USCG issued inflation-adjusted limits for vessels and deepwater ports.[181]

8.0 Recovery by a Foreign Claimant

Section 1007 permits a foreign claimant (a person residing in a foreign country or a foreign government) to bring an OPA claim in the United States for a discharge in the territorial sea, internal waters or adjacent shoreline of a foreign country. Section 1007 is the only specific statutory authority for a foreign claimant to bring an OPA action in U.S. courts.[182]

There are a number of conditions that must be fulfilled for a foreign claimant to bring an OPA action in a U.S. court. These conditions essentially ascertain that the origin of the spill had a strong connection with the United States. The foreign claimant must demonstrate that it has not received compensation for removal costs and damages and, except for Trans-Alaska Pipeline oil spilled in

Canada, that recovery under OPA is provided for in a treaty or executive agreement or by reciprocal right. At present, there are no such agreements or rights.

9.0 Recovery by an RP

An RP entitled to a defense to liability under Section 1003 or entitled to limit its liability under Section 1004 can assert a claim to the OSLTF under Section 1013 for amounts paid.[183] The RP with a complete defense to liability can recover all payments of removal costs and damages. The RP entitled to limit its liability under Section 1004 can recover amounts paid that exceed the limit.

10.0 Contribution and Indemnification

Where multiple parties are involved in an oil spill, any person can bring a contribution action against any other person who is liable or potentially liable under OPA or another law.[184]

No RP may divest itself of OPA statutory liability by contract. However, any person potentially liable under OPA may agree to have others contractually assume the responsibility to pay for some or all of those liabilities through insurance contracts or indemnity agreements and hold harmless agreements.[185]

11.0 Oil Spill Liability Trust Fund (OSLTF)

The OSLTF is available to provide a source of liquidity to the states for initiating cleanup and response and to pay claims that would otherwise not be paid either because the RP declined to pay them or the RP was able to successfully assert a defense or limitation of liability or because the source of the spill and the identity of the RP is unknown. The OSLTF is administered by the National Pollution Funds Center (NPFC), which is part of the USCG.

Some of the principal sections applicable to the creation and operation of the OSLTF are the following:

- Section 1012, Use of Fund;
- Section 1013, Claims Procedure;
- Section 1014, Designation of Source and Advertisement;
- Section 1015, Subrogation; and
- Section 6002, Annual Appropriations.

Also relevant are Section 1007, Recovery by Foreign Claimants; Section 1008, Recovery by Responsible Party; and Section 9509 of the Internal Revenue Code.[186]

11.1 Principal Sections

Some of the principal sections applicable to the operation of the Fund are the instructions for claims procedures in Section 1013 and the guidelines for recovery by RPs and foreign claimants in Sections 1007 and 1008. Section 9001 of OPA makes significant alterations to the Internal Revenue Code (I.R.C. §9509) to reflect the changes in structure of the Fund.

11.2 Preservation of State Funds

Although the OPA abolished the existing special-purpose, federal funds dealing with oil pollution damages and cleanup costs, it preserves the right of the states to establish or continue any state oil pollution compensation fund or the right of the states to tax for the purpose of oil pollution compensation funds.[187]

11.3 Funding of the Fund

The OSLTF has several funding sources, including a barrel tax on domestic and imported oil, transfers from other pollution funds, interest on the Fund principal from U.S. Treasury investments and cost recoveries or civil penalties from RPs. The largest source of this income is the eight-cents-per-barrel tax on oil received at U.S. refineries and petroleum products entering the United States for consumption, use or warehousing. The original five-cents tax initially expired on December 31, 1994, but was reinstated on April 1, 2006, by the Energy Policy Act of 2005, and was subsequently increased to eight cents per barrel by the Energy Improvement and Extension Act of 2008.[188]

The second-largest funding source is the integration of legacy pollution funds into the OSLTF. Transfers from the Oil Pollution Fund, Offshore Oil Pollution Compensation Fund, Deepwater Port Liability Fund and Trans-Alaska Pipeline Liability Fund have deposited more than $550 million into the OSLTF since 1990.[189] At this time, however, no additional funds remain to be transferred to the OSLTF.

In addition to the interest on the Fund principal and cost recoveries from RPs, the OSLTF is replenished by civil penalties paid by RPs. Penalties from CWA §311 violations, Deepwater Port Act violations and Trans-Alaska Pipeline Authorization Act violations are paid into the OSLTF, along with excess money from natural resource damage settlements.

The attorney general of the United States is authorized to recover any compensation paid by the OSLTF and all administrative costs of the claim. The OSLTF is also authorized to borrow up to $1 billion from the U.S. Treasury.[190]

11.4 Uses of the Fund

The Internal Revenue Code sets a $1 billion per incident limit on government and private uses of the Fund.[191] For NRDAs and claims in connection with any single incident, the Internal Revenue Code sets a $500 million limit.[192]

11.4.1 Government Uses

Unlike the former Federal Water Pollution Control Act Fund, in which the availability of funds was subject to appropriation, the OSLTF provides an annual emergency fund of $50 million to be available at the disposal of removal projects as needed. This $50 million per fiscal year, including $250,000 at the request of a state, is made immediately available without further appropriation for federal and state removal and monitoring costs to provide a quick response to an incident.[193]

Up to $500 million per incident is provided for NRDs. Payment of removal costs and damages resulting from a discharge from a foreign offshore unit must be consistent with the NCP. OPA also provides for payment of administrative, operational and personnel costs and expenses for implementation, administration and enforcement. Certain of these expenditures are specifically authorized.

11.4.2 Private Uses

The Fund can be used for payment of uncompensated removal costs and damages consistent with the NCP for claims submitted according to the claims procedure. These amounts are available for payment without further appropriation by Congress. Uncompensated claims could result from defenses to liability and liability limits or the financial inability to pay claims.

Moreover, when there is no identified RP, the Fund is available to pay claims for the costs of assessing NRDs and for developing and implementing restoration plans.[194]

12.0 Claims

OPA sets up a notification and claims procedure to facilitate the prompt filing and payment of claims for damages from oil spills.[195] Procedures are also detailed for the processing of claims by the Fund. The Fund is available to satisfy claims that are not promptly or fully compensated by the RP. The USCG issued final regulations that address the presentation, processing, settlement and adjudication of claims against the Fund in 1992.[196]

12.1 Designation of the Source and Advertisement

OPA requires the person in charge of a vessel or a facility to report a spill to the National Response Center (NRC) of the USCG. If reporting directly to the NRC is not possible, reports can be made to the EPA regional office or the USCG Marine Safety Office in the area where the incident occurred.[197] Failure to notify the authorities is grounds for imposing penalties and abolishing defenses to, or limits on, liability. Under OPA, upon receiving information about a spill, federal authorities will designate the source and notify the RP and its insurer. If the spill does not involve damages or removal costs, no designation need be made.

Depending on whether the RP accepts liability, either the RP or the federal authorities will advertise the source of the spill and the claims procedure.[198]

12.1.1 Responsible Party Advertises

If the RP or its guarantor does not deny designation within five days, thus accepting liability for the spill, they must advertise the designation and the claims procedure within 15 days of the designation and continue to do so for 30 days.

12.1.2 Government Advertises

If the federal authorities are unable to designate the source, if the source is a government vessel or if the RP accepts the designation but fails to advertise, the government will advertise at the RP's expense. The implementing regulations were issued in final form on August 12, 1992.[199]

12.2 Procedure

Claims for removal costs and damages must be presented first to the designated RP or its guarantor. If the RP or guarantor denies liability for the claim, or if the claim is not settled within 90 days after it was presented or after the RP began advertising the claims procedure, whichever is later, the claimant has the option of bringing a lawsuit against the RP or its guarantor or presenting the claim to the OSLTF.[200]

Several courts have upheld the presentation requirement of Section 1013 of OPA,[201] holding that it creates a mandatory condition precedent such that a failure to first present all claims for removal costs and damages to the RP or guarantor precludes a claimant from bringing a court action under OPA.[202] OPA claims in these cases were dismissed without prejudice since the claimants had not first presented their claims under Section 1013.[203]

Claims can be presented first to the OSLTF if the RP denies the designation, if the authorities are unable to designate the source, if the RP has already reached its liability limits,[204] or if the source is a government vessel. Insufficiently compensated claims submitted according to the claims procedure can be presented directly to the Fund.[205]

Claims are also subject to a statute of limitations. The time limit for presentation of claims for recovery of removal costs from the Fund is six years after completion of the removal action. Claims for recovery of removal costs from the RP must be presented within three years after completion of the removal action.[206] Claims for damages (other than NRDs) must be submitted within three years of discovery of loss. Claims for damages to natural resources must be submitted within three years of completion of the NRDA.[207]

13.0 Financial Responsibility

OPA extended and expanded the CWA requirement that owners and operators of vessels and certain specified facilities demonstrate, through an approved form of guarantee, the financial capacity to pay claims up to their limits of liability. A Certificate of Financial Responsibility (COFR) commits the guarantor to stand in the shoes of the owner or operator if the owner or operator is unable or unwilling to pay for cleanup costs or damages.[208]

13.1 Calculation of Financial Responsibility Amounts

For vessels, the owner or operator must show financial responsibility sufficient to meet its limit of liability under 33 U.S.C. §2704(a).[209] The owner or operator of multiple vessels is only required to establish evidence of financial responsibility for the vessel having the greatest maximum liability.[210]

For offshore facilities other than deepwater ports, the general requirement is for $75 million of financial responsibility, plus the total of all removal costs. For any onshore facility and deepwater ports, the amount is $350 million.[211] The secretary may lower these limits.[212] Owners or operators of multiple facilities must establish evidence of financial responsibility only for the facility having the greatest financial responsibility requirement under OPA.[213]

13.2 Methods of Demonstrating Financial Responsibility

Financial responsibility may be evidenced by one or more of the following methods: insurance; surety bond; guarantee; letter of credit; self-insurance; or "other evidence of financial responsibility."[214] The president (in the case of facilities) and the secretary (in the case of vessels) may issue regulations that set standards for policy or contract defenses, conditions, and terms.[215] An entity other than the RP that provides evidence of financial responsibility is a guarantor.[216]

13.3 Role of the Guarantor

The stated purpose of having a guarantor of the owner's liability is to "provide claimants with a full range of options for pursuing their claims."[217] Consequently, OPA requires guarantors to be directly liable to claimants for removal costs and damages, subject to very limited defenses. Claimants are intended to have direct access to recovery, regardless of whether the RP is insolvent or otherwise unavailable to pay claims.

13.4 Vessels

The financial responsibility requirements apply to any tank vessel over 100 gross tons and any other vessel over 300 gross tons (except a non-self-propelled vessel that is not carrying oil on board, either as fuel or cargo). Consequently, all classes of vessels, passenger ships, ferries, tugboats, fishing boats, containerships and dry bulk cargo vessels, as well as tankers, must comply with the financial responsibility requirements.

The requirements also apply to any vessel, regardless of tonnage, that is either transshipping or lightering oil within the exclusive economic zone. The financial responsibility requirements do not apply to vessels in innocent passage or vessels transferring oil not destined for the United States.[218]

13.5 Financial Responsibility Regulations for Vessels

The USCG regulations relating to financial responsibility specify the types of instruments that vessel owners and operators must submit to the USCG to demonstrate ability to pay for damages and removal costs arising from an oil or hazardous substance spill.[219] The regulations mirror the requirements of the Act in allowing only insurance, surety bond, guarantee and self-insurance to serve as evidence of financial responsibility. The regulations also include the category of "other evidence of financial responsibility," which creates an opportunity for a vessel owner to suggest an alternative method of proving evidence of financial responsibility. Any vessel owner using this alternative route must obtain approval from the director of the NPFC by submitting an application describing the proposed method 45 days before the certificate is required.[220]

These regulations superseded the financial responsibility regulations issued prior to the enactment of OPA (principally the CWA, the Deepwater Port Act and the Trans-Alaska Pipeline Authorization Act) and consolidated financial responsibility requirements for both Section 1002 of OPA and Section 107(a)(1) of CERCLA in one rulemaking. The regulations require guarantors providing evidence of financial responsibility to agree to be sued directly for any damages or removal costs that could be obtained from the vessel owner or operator. The following defenses are available to guarantors who comply with the regulations:

- Guarantors are not liable for incidents caused by the willful misconduct of the vessel owner or operator;[221]

- Guarantors can invoke any defense available to the person for whom the COFR is issued;

- Guarantors are not liable for claims that exceed the amount of the guaranty they issued;

- Given that the regulations only address OPA and CERCLA coverage, guarantors are not liable for claims that are not brought under OPA or CERCLA; and

- Guarantors are not liable if the gross tonnage of the vessel at the time of the incident exceeds the amount entered on the vessel's International Tonnage Certificate or other official applicable certificate of measure, unless the guarantor knew or should have known that the applicable tonnage certificate was incorrect.[222]

In addition, the USCG regulations provide that, in instances where multiple guarantors issue a guarantee, such cosubscribing guarantors may limit liability to the extent of their participation in the guaranty. This alters somewhat the guarantors' joint and several liability in preexisting financial responsibility undertakings.[223]

For vessel owners providing evidence of self-insurance, the USCG requires demonstration of net worth[224] and working capital,[225] each in amounts equal to or greater than the amount needed to satisfy the COFR regulations.

13.6 Financial Responsibility Regulations for Facilities

The financial responsibility requirements apply to offshore facilities and deepwater ports but not to onshore facilities. The Bureau of Ocean Energy Management, Regulation, and Enforcement (BOEMRE), formerly the Minerals Management Service (MMS), of the DOI is charged with issuing financial responsibility regulations for offshore facilities. These regulations were issued August 11, 1998.[226] The regulations replace the regulations at 33 C.F.R. Part 135, which were written to implement the Outer Continental Shelf Lands Act. Those regulations were limited to facilities located in the outer continental shelf (OCS) and set the amount of oil spill financial responsibility (OSFR) that had to be demonstrated by RPs at $35 million. The replacement regulations cover both the OCS and certain state waters and require RPs to demonstrate as much as $150 million in OSFR if the BOEMRE determines that it is justified by the risks from potential oil spills from covered offshore facilities (COFs). The minimum amount of OSFR for COFs in the OCS is $35 million and $10 million for COFs located in state waters.[227]

14.0 Subrogation

Any person who compensates a claimant for removal costs or damages is subrogated to all the rights that the claimant may have under OPA and any other law.[228] The Fund is subrogated in respect to any claims it pays and can assume the claimant's rights under any law, including state law.[229] RPs entitled to a complete defense or limitation of liability, and who expect to recover their costs or damages from the Fund, must be careful to preserve all subrogation rights against other parties potentially liable for contribution.[230]

OPA does not expressly grant any presumption to the Fund and makes no reference to any standard of review for subrogated claims.[231] Moreover, as the language of OPA's subrogation clause indicates, OPA does not distinguish between claims brought by the Fund under subrogation and claims brought under subrogation by private parties: The Fund is treated as "any person" and, apparently, stands on the same ground as a private party.[232]

15.0 Litigation and Jurisdiction

Although OPA channels the resolution of claims first to the RP and its guarantor and then to the OSLTF, courts will consider claims for damages and can be petitioned to review OPA rules. Section 1017 sets out the rules for this litigation and defines the role of state courts.[233]

15.1 Jurisdiction

United States federal district courts have exclusive original jurisdiction over all OPA cases. However, petitions to review OPA regulations are filed with the United States Circuit Court of Appeals for the District of Columbia.[234] A state trial court with jurisdiction over removal costs and damages may consider OPA claims and state claims.

15.2 Limitations

Claims for removal costs must be brought within three years after the removal actions have been completed. Claims for damages must be brought within three years of the date of the discovery of the loss and, in the case of NRDs, within three years after the completion of the NRDA performed by the trustees. Contribution actions must be brought within three years after judgment on costs and damages or approval of settlement. Subrogation actions must be commenced within three years after the payment of a claim for removal costs or damages.[235]

16.0 Relationship to Other Laws

Congress structured OPA so that it would coexist with state laws. While it was clear that OPA preserved state liability regimes, it was less clear whether the state laws that touched upon vessel operations were still valid under OPA. It took almost a decade to settle this issue.

16.1 Preservation of State Oil Spill Liability Law

Congress rejected efforts to preempt state oil spill liability laws and to make OPA the exclusive remedy for oil spill liability and compensation. The "savings" clauses found in Title I of OPA specifically preserve the right of states and local governments to impose additional liability requirements or additional fines and penalties.[236] The effect of OPA on state efforts to regulate the design, operation and manning of vessels was unclear, however, until the Supreme Court unanimously decided to vacate certain Washington State tanker regulations that had been challenged by an international association of tanker owners.[237] The Court concluded in its *Locke* decision that "Congress intended to preserve state laws of a scope similar to the matters contained in Title I of OPA. . . . The evident purpose of the savings clauses is to preserve state laws which, rather than imposing substantive regulation of a vessel's primary conduct, establish liability rules and financial requirements relating to oil spills."[238] The decision limits the effect of the savings clauses and reaffirms traditional federal preeminence in the regulation of vessel design, construction, and operation.

States may also enforce federal financial responsibility requirements in state waters.[239]

16.2 Preservation of Federal Laws

OPA does not affect the Solid Waste Disposal Act.[240] Nothing in the OPA creates a cause of action against federal officials or employees.[241] In addition, OPA does not preclude federal officials from pursuing claims for cleanup costs or damages under any other applicable federal statutes.[242]

16.3 Federal Preemption under the *Locke* Case

The *Locke* decision is a significant qualification of the state prerogatives that OPA sought to preserve in the Title I savings clauses. The decision squares the explicit OPA decision to preserve state liability laws with an implicit decision to retain the traditional preemptive effect of federal marine safety and pollution prevention laws that predate OPA.

The U.S. Supreme Court, in the *Locke* decision, observed that "[w]e doubt that Congress will be surprised by our conclusion, for the Conference Report on OPA shared our view that the statute [OPA] 'does not disturb the [U.S.] Supreme Court decision in *Ray v. Atlantic Richfield Co.*'"[243] The congressional endorsement of the *Ray* decision in the OPA legislative history reinforced the Court's affirmation of historic federal preeminence in the field of tank vessel operation, design and manning.

The *Locke* case is really a continuation of the *Ray* dispute. After the *Exxon Valdez* incident, Washington State promulgated more marine safety regulations that duplicated—and in some cases exceeded—the federal pollution prevention and marine safety requirements.[244] The International Association of Independent Tanker Owners (Intertanko) challenged 16 of these state regulations on the basis that this area was preempted by the constitutional and federal occupation of the field. The District Court rejected Intertanko's arguments and upheld the Washington State regulations, citing the savings provisions in OPA.[245] On appeal, in which the United States joined as an appellant, the circuit court upheld the state regulations, except the regulation that required tankers to be equipped with global positioning systems, two radar systems and emergency towing equipment; it reasoned that comparable provisions had been struck down by the Court in the *Ray* decision.[246] Over the dissent of Judge Graber, the circuit court rested its decision in part on the two savings clauses in Title I of OPA, which reserved to the states the authority to impose "additional liability or requirements" relating to the discharge of oil.[247]

On March 6, 2000, a unanimous U.S. Supreme Court struck down Washington State's regulations establishing requirements for: (1) training and spill drills; (2) English-language proficiency for crews; (3) casualty reporting requirements; and (4) watch-standing standards, and remanded the balance of the regulations to the circuit court for review consistent with its opinion.[248] The Court found that the Title I savings clauses of OPA did not extend to vessel operation or manning requirements[249] and that these four requirements fell within the "field" preemption of Title II of the PWSA.[250] The Court remanded the balance of the regulations to determine whether certain of the other regulations, such as the watch requirements for restricted visibility, are sufficiently linked to local conditions to be compatible with the federal requirements.[251] The Court left open whether these remaining regulations would be subject to so-called "conflict preemption" under Title I of the PWSA,[252] or under the Title II "field preemption."[253]

The Washington State Department of Ecology subsequently repealed the tank vessel rules effective September 2, 2000, resolving that particular dispute but leaving for the future remaining questions about the precise line of demarcation between federal and state jurisdiction.[254] Although the Court's decision was ultimately based upon the preemptive effect of the PWSA, the Court did circumscribe the effect of the savings clauses of OPA.

The preemption debate resurfaced again in Massachusetts. On August 4, 2004, in response to the April 27, 2003 oil spill in Buzzards Bay, the Commonwealth of Massachusetts enacted the Act Relative to Oil Spill Prevention and Response in Buzzards Bay and Other Harbors and Bays of the Commonwealth, which featured provisions governing barge design and equipment, drug and alcohol testing, and pilotage, manning, navigation, tug escort and financial assurance requirements.[255] In response, the USCG announced that "[i]t is the view of the U.S. Coast Guard that several provisions of the Massachusetts Act touch categories of regulation reserved to the Federal Government and are preempted per the ruling in *Locke* and *Ray*."[256] Thus began a decade of litigation that "has ebbed and flowed as the matter passed from judicial officer to judicial officer" as one district judge recently lamented.[257] Throughout the course of litigation the District Court has been more inclined to defer to the federal government's authority to establish a preemptory regime for the regulation of tug and barge traffic in the Commonwealth's waters, whereas the First Circuit has consistently pressed the District Court and the federal government to present a more compelling justification for preemption of the Massachusetts Oil Spill Prevention Act ("MOSPA"). Like the *Locke* case, the MOSPA case reinforced the limits of the Title I savings clause of OPA and focused on the preemptive effect of Title I of the PWSA.[258]

The United States sued the Commonwealth in the U.S. District Court for the District of Massachusetts, alleging the provisions were preempted by federal law or regulations.[259] The District Court agreed and permanently enjoined the Commonwealth from enforcing the challenged provisions, reaffirming the preemptive effect of the federal legislation in the area of maritime safety, notwithstanding OPA's deference to parallel state liability and compensation regimes.[260]

On appeal to the First Circuit, the Commonwealth challenged the District Court's injunction of the vessel manning, tug escort and financial assurance requirements.[261] Concerned the District Court "acted prematurely," and without "adher[ing] to the analytical structure the Supreme Court has required to resolve federal-state conflicts in this area,"[262] the First Circuit vacated the injunction with respect to all three provisions and remanded the case for further development of the record.[263]

Following remand, the parties reached an agreement as to the financial assurance provision, and the USCG promulgated revised regulations expressly purporting to preempt the remaining provisions at issue.[264] Pointing to the new preemption language in the regulations, the District Court granted summary judgment for the United States and permanently enjoined enforcement of the vessel manning and tug escort provisions.[265] On appeal to the First Circuit, the Commonwealth challenged the validity of the USCG regulations because the agency had failed to prepare either an Environmental Impact Statement or and Environmental Assessment as required by the National Environmental Policy Act ("NEPA").[266] The First Circuit remanded the case to the District Court without reaching the ultimate issue of whether MOSPA was preempted by the USCG's rulemaking and vacated the injunction of the MOSPA regulations for manning of towing vessels and barges and for tug boat escorts in Buzzards Bay.[267] The District Court had not ruled at the time of publication, and MOSPA's provisions remain in effect.

17.0 Title II: Conforming Amendments

Title II contains conforming amendments transferring the balance of funds under the CWA,[268] the Deepwater Port Act[269] and the Outer Continental Shelf Lands Act[270] to the OSLTF. The secretary is also authorized to use the OSLTF for removal activities under the Intervention on the High Seas Act.[271]

18.0 Title III: International Oil Pollution Prevention and Removal

A contentious issue in the OPA debate was U.S. participation in international oil pollution liability and compensation conventions. Generally, the House of Representatives advocated participation in the international conventions for reasons of comity and international uniformity, while members of the Senate found that the international compensation levels were too low and that the preemption of federal and state laws by the conventions was unacceptable.[272]

The compromise proposed in Title III of OPA[273] stated the opinion of Congress that the interests of the United States would be best served by participation in an international prevention and compensation regime that was at least as effective as domestic law.[274]

Title III also contains provisions regarding cooperation between the United States and Canada on oil pollution matters.[275]

19.0 Title IV: Prevention and Removal

Title IV is divided into three subtitles. Subtitle A changes many of the laws governing the manning and operation of tank vessels to prevent oil spills. Subtitle B establishes a national planning and response system to ensure the prompt and effective removal of oil spills that do occur. Subtitle C substantially increases the severity of criminal and civil penalties that can be imposed on vessel and facility owners and operators for discharges of oil under OPA, the CWA and marine safety laws.

19.1 Subtitle A: Prevention

OPA contains stringent licensing and operating requirements designed to ensure the safe transportation and transfer of oil and hazardous substances.

19.1.1 Licensing Requirements and Drug and Alcohol Testing

Section 4101 states that the secretary is given the authority to require additional information on driving records, criminal records and results from mandatory drug and alcohol tests of applicants for new merchant mariners' papers, for renewal applicants and for current holders of licenses, certificates and merchant mariners' documents.[276] Current holders will be tested for drug and alcohol use on a random, periodic, reasonable cause and post-accident basis.

OPA adds grounds for suspension and revocation of current papers. Holders of licenses, certificates and merchant mariners' documents who perform safety sensitive functions may have their papers suspended for drug and alcohol violations. Holders also may have their papers suspended or revoked for a violation of safety or pollution laws and regulations, incompetence, misconduct or negligence.[277]

To ensure that all holders of current papers will be subjected periodically to background checks, the terms of all licenses, certificates and merchant mariners' documents are five years with five-year renewal periods.[278] Regulations establish a five-year term of validity and provide a schedule for the expiration of existing certificates and merchant mariners' documents that were issued in September 1994 and amended in 2009.[279]

The master or individual in charge of a vessel may be relieved of command if he is under the influence of alcohol or drugs and is incapable of commanding the vessel.[280]

19.1.2 Foreign Tank Vessel Manning Standards

The USCG is required to evaluate the manning, training, qualification and watch-keeping standards of a foreign country that issues vessel documentation to determine whether that country's standards are equivalent to U.S. or international standards and whether those standards are being enforced adequately. A rulemaking on this subject was withdrawn in 1995 and has not been reproposed;

however, the USCG published notice of a public meeting to discuss implementation of the 1995 amendments to the International Convention on Standards of Training, Certification and Watchkeeping for Seafarers (1978),[281] which, while not directly related to this evaluation, are anticipated to cover many aspects of foreign vessel manning, training, qualification and watch keeping.[282] The USCG also is required to conduct periodic review for each country as well as a post-casualty review.[283]

19.1.3 Tank Vessel Manning

The USCG was required to consider additional factors in formulating manning standards for tank vessels. These factors now include the navigation, cargo handling and maintenance functions of a tank vessel for protection of life, property and the environment.[284] The USCG initiated rulemaking on the operation of tank vessels in navigable waters under automatic pilot or with an unattended engine room. Regulations on the use of automatic pilot were issued in May 1993.[285] Unattended engine room regulations have yet to be proposed.

On self-propelled tank vessels, officers and crew members are restricted to working no more than 15 hours in any 24-hour period or no more than 36 hours in any 72-hour period. For these purposes, work includes administrative functions associated with the vessel, whether these functions are conducted on board the vessel or ashore.[286]

19.1.4 Marine Casualty Reporting

OPA expands existing marine casualty reporting requirements to include marine casualties involving "significant harm to the environment."[287] Casualty reporting requirements for foreign tank vessels are expanded to include casualties occurring in the exclusive economic zone.[288]

19.1.5 Pilotage and Tug Escort Requirements

Section 4116 of OPA directed the secretary to designate which tankers operating in U.S. waters over 1,600 gross tons would be required to have a licensed master or mate on the bridge in addition to the pilot. Also, the secretary was required to designate waters in the Northwest in which single-hull tankers would be required to be escorted by two tugs.[289] Final regulations, which were issued by the secretary in 1994, designate Prince William Sound, Alaska, and Puget Sound, Washington and certain associated waters, as waters where single-hull tankers over 5,000 gross tons must be escorted by at least two towing vessels.[290] OPA also tightened requirements for U.S.-registered and foreign-flag vessels operating in the Great Lakes by explicitly stating that such vessels must carry on board a U.S. or Canadian "registered" pilot. The clarifying provision was designed to eliminate the practice in which members of the ship's complement were operating under the authority of Canadian-issued pilotage "certificates" that did not meet the more stringent requirements for U.S. or Canadian registered pilots.[291] More stringent requirements are also imposed for Prince William Sound, Alaska.[292] On August 19, 2013, the USCG issued interim regulations to implement section 711 of the Coast Guard Authorization Act of 2010, which required two tug escorts for double-hull tankers over 5,000 gross tons transporting oil in bulk in Prince William Sound.[293] The final regulations were issued on June 13, 2014.[294]

19.1.6 Studies and Regulations (Sections 4107–4113)

These sections called for a number of studies and regulations on safety-related issues. Pursuant to Section 4107 of OPA, the secretary was required to conduct a study of vessel traffic systems and report the results to Congress.[295] USCG regulations establish requirements and procedures for Vessel Traffic Services (VTS) and make participation in all VTS mandatory.[296] The secretary was also required to issue regulations on minimum standards for plating thickness and periodic gauging of plating thickness, as well as minimum standards for, and use of, overfill devices and tank level or pressure monitoring devices.[297] The regulations establishing minimum plating thickness standards for tank vessels and requiring periodic gauging of vessels more than 30 years old were published on October 8, 1993. Additional regulations were published to reduce the likelihood of oil spills caused by overfilling of cargo tanks on oil tankers and barges.[298] These regulations apply to both U.S. and foreign tank vessels and went into effect on January 19, 1995. The secretary also was required to issue regulations on radio equipment for vessels subject to the Vessel Bridge-to-Bridge Radiotelephone Act.[299]

The secretary completed a comprehensive study to evaluate the adequacy of existing navigation laws and regulations for the safe operation of tankers.[300] The secretary evaluated crew size and qualifications, electronic navigation and position-reporting equipment, navigation procedures, inspection standards, and whether to impose tanker-free zones. The secretary also analyzed whether there are correlations among tanker size, cargo capacity, national origin and oil spills. The secretary further considered the use of computer simulators and remote alcohol testing.[301]

19.1.7 Double-Hull Requirements for Tank Vessels

The requirement that a tank vessel have a double hull went into effect upon enactment for a new vessel and according to a phase-out schedule for an existing vessel.[302] The phase-out schedule began on January 1, 1995, and ran until January

1, 2015. Older and larger vessels were retired first. An existing vessel is one for which a contract for construction or for a major conversion had been placed prior to June 30, 1990, and the vessel was delivered under that contract prior to January 1, 1994. Consequently, a future major conversion on an existing vessel could result in that vessel being treated as a new vessel for double-hull purposes. Major conversion means a substantial change in the type, carrying capacity, or dimensions of the vessel or a conversion that substantially prolongs the life of the vessel or makes it a new vessel.[303] A major reconstruction of the hull structure that enhances environmental compatibility also constitutes a major conversion.

While OPA does not define what constitutes a double hull, the USCG published regulations setting forth standards for double hulls.[304] The USCG specifically rejected design alternatives to double-hull construction. The regulations require tank vessels contracted for after September 12, 1992, to have a double-hull construction with dimensions consistent with International Maritime Organization (IMO) standards adopted in March 1992. The technical standards include the required clearances between the minor hull and the outer hull on the sides and on the bottom. Vessels for which construction was begun according to a contract awarded prior to September 11, 1992, and after June 30, 1990, must have a double-hull construction consistent with USCG standards adopted in Navigation and Vessel Inspection Circular (NVIC) No. 2-90.[305] The interim final regulation contains some additional mandates beyond NVIC No. 2-90:

- Piping requirements must be consistent with IMO Rules 13F and 13G;

- The vessel must have protected ballast tanks; and

- There must be clearance between framing on inland vessels.

NVIC No. 2-90 provides policy guidance on double-hull dimensions to assist in planning and designing tank vessels that must be fitted with double hulls under OPA. Vessels built under plans that are approved in accordance with NVIC No. 2-90 prior to the effective date of final regulations will be deemed to be in compliance with the double-hull requirement in Section 4115 of OPA.

19.1.7.1 Exceptions to the Requirements

New tank vessels are required to be built with a double hull. The only exceptions are vessels used only to respond to oil spills and newly constructed vessels less than 5,000 gross tons. The latter category must be equipped with a double containment system that has been determined to be as effective as a double hull.

The double-hull requirement did not go into effect until 2015 in three cases:

1. Vessels unloading at deepwater ports;

2. Vessels delivering to lightering vessels in established lightering zones at least 60 miles offshore;[306] and

3. Existing vessels less than 5,000 gross tons.

19.1.7.2 Effect of Double-Side or Double-Bottom Modifications

OPA provided extended service time for those tank vessels equipped with either double bottoms or double sides. Although OPA permits owners to extend the life of single-hull tank vessels by retrofitting a double hull, the statute and its implementing regulations were not clear whether retrofitting a double bottom or double sides would similarly extend the service of a reconfigured tank vessel that was otherwise scheduled for retirement. After several inquiries from owners, the USCG formally announced its determination that conversion of single-hull tank vessels adding only double sides or double bottoms after August 18, 1990, would not extend a vessel's retirement date under OPA.[307]

19.1.7.3 Additional or Alternative Requirements

Additionally, the secretary was directed to complete a rulemaking proceeding to determine whether any structural or operational requirements should be imposed on existing vessels subject to the double-hull requirements during the period before the requirement goes into effect.[308] In partial fulfillment of this mandate, the USCG issued a final rule consisting of requirements for lightering equipment and the reporting of a vessel's international IMO number prior to port entry that was published in August 1994.[309] The USCG also issued a final rule for single-hull tank vessels requiring all of the following:

- written bridge procedures;

- vessel-specific training measures;

- enhanced surveys;

- cargo and mooring system surveys;

- autopilot alarm systems, maneuvering tests; and

- calculation and notification of keel clearance prior to entering ports.[310]

The secretary was also required to conduct a study and issue a report, based on recommendations from the National Academy of Sciences, on whether other structural and operational requirements would provide equal or better protection than double hulls.[311] This report was submitted to Congress in January 1993. The secretary, also in conjunction with the National Academy of Sciences, is to review periodically the impact of double hulls on environmental safety and to consider other methods of increasing tank vessel safety.[312]

19.1.7.4 Title XI Loan Guarantees

The secretary can provide loan guarantees under the current provisions of Title XI of the Merchant Marine Act, 1936, for the construction of replacement vessels or reconstruction of vessels rendered inoperable by changes in the law.[313] The borrower must be already operating this type of vessel and must agree to use the newly constructed or reconstructed vessels as replacements. The new vessels must not be larger than the vessels they replace. These provisions essentially restate existing authority.

19.2 Subtitle B: Removal

Under OPA, federal authorities have the responsibility for averting threats of oil spills and cleaning up ones that happen. These activities are conducted according to the National Response System and the NCP.[314] Although the OPA oil spill response system uses governmental planning and direction, it relies primarily on private resources to mitigate or remove spills. To ensure the availability of private response personnel and equipment, OPA requires approved individual vessel and facility response plans for vessel and facility owners and operators. Private response efforts are encouraged by conferring immunity from liability for removal costs and damages on those rendering care, assistance or advice in response to a spill.

19.2.1 Federal Removal Authority

OPA emphasizes federal direction of public and private efforts both of the response to avert the threat of an oil spill and of the removal of oil that has been spilled.[315] Under the CWA, federal authorities were authorized to act at any time to remove oil in the event of a spill or the threat of a spill, but removal could be entrusted to the vessel or facility owner or operator. However, OPA states that federal authorities are to ensure the immediate removal of a discharge and mitigate and prevent the substantial threat of a discharge.[316] This authority applies to spills or threats in navigable waters, shorelines and the waters of the exclusive economic zone. It also applies to situations where natural resources are affected or threatened.

OPA is more explicit than the CWA about federal responsibility for responding to the threat of a spill and removing a spill, and it also provides the government with a wider range of authority to accomplish immediate removal. The federal authorities may merely direct or monitor federal, state and private removal and mitigation actions. More actively, the federal authorities may assume the responsibility and costs of the actions subject to reimbursement from the RP. This is referred to as "federalizing" the effort. They may go so far as to remove and destroy a discharging vessel, using any means available. At least in regard to emergency response measures, the federal government is exempted from contract and employment laws.

19.2.1.1 Discharges That Constitute a Substantial Threat to Public Welfare

The federal government has extensive authority over containment and removal of a particular class of spills: those that are deemed to pose a substantial threat to the public health or welfare of the United States. The public health or welfare of the United States includes fish, shellfish, wildlife and other natural resources, and public and private shorelines and beaches. Criteria for identification of these spills as well as procedures for responding to them are to be addressed in the NCP. The NCP gives the USCG the authority to designate a federal on-scene coordinator (FOSC) "for the removal of releases of hazardous substances, pollutants, or contaminants into or threatening the coastal zone."[317] The FOSC is tasked with investigating the spill, determining the threat to public safety, classifying the size of the spill and initiating removal efforts.[318]

In the case of spills such as the *Exxon Valdez* in Alaska, the *American Trader* in California, the *Mega Borg* in the Gulf of Mexico and the *Deepwater Horizon* in the Gulf of Mexico that are of such a size and character as to be a substantial threat to the public health or welfare, the Act states unequivocally that the federal government shall direct all federal, state and private actions to remove the discharge or to prevent a substantial threat of a discharge. This delineation of authority is intended to eliminate the confusion that allegedly impeded response efforts to these types of spills in the past.[319]

Spills that are classified as a substantial threat to the public health or welfare may be further classified as a "spill of national significance" (SONS), which means "a spill that due to its severity, size, location, actual or potential impact on the public health and welfare or the environment, or the necessary response effort, is so complex that it requires extraordinary coordination of federal, state, local, and responsible party resources to contain and clean up the discharge."[320] The authority to designate a discharge as a SONS rests, in the coastal zone, with the Commandant of the USCG.[321] Classifying an oil spill as a SONS provides additional support to the FOSC to manage national, political and policy level issues that result from a catastrophic oil spill of release.[322] Upon classifying a coastal zone discharge as a SONS, "the Commandant may name a National Incident Commander (NIC) who will assume the role of the [on-scene coordinator] in communicating with affected parties and the public, and coordinating federal, state, local, and international resources at the national level."[323]

On April 29, 2010, the *Deepwater Horizon* oil spill was classified as a SONS; two days later, USCG Commandant Thad Allen was named as the NIC.[324]

19.2.2 State and Local Removal Authority

The Act specifies federal preeminence in undertaking and directing response actions but preserves state authority over significant aspects of removal activities. State and local governments may impose additional requirements with respect to removal activities.[325] Further, in regard to the conclusion of removal activities, the federal government is required to consult with the governors of affected states before making a determination that removal with respect to any discharge is considered complete.[326]

19.2.3 Responder Immunity

To induce vessel operators, cleanup contractors and cleanup cooperatives to undertake prompt and effective measures in response to spills and threats of spills, OPA insulates them from liability.[327] When a person is rendering care, assistance or advice, he is not liable for removal costs or damages that result from his acts or omissions. However, his acts or omissions must be consistent with the NCP or be directed by the federal government. It was also recognized that the NCP and federal orders may not cover every detail or eventuality of a spill response. Consequently, responder immunity is extended to actions that are in keeping with the overall objectives of the NCP or federal directives.

This immunity does not, however, apply to an RP—that is, the owner or operator of the vessel or facility from which the discharge originates. It applies only to other individuals or entities that they retain. Furthermore, although the responder may be relieved of liability for removal costs and damages, that liability is borne by the RP.

Immunity does not apply in cases of personal injury or wrongful death or if the person is grossly negligent or engages in willful misconduct. It does not apply to CERCLA cleanups, nor does OPA immunity prevent states from imposing their own requirements for the liability of persons involved in the removal of oil.[328]

The U.S. District Court for the Eastern District of Louisiana in *Deepwater Horizon* recently examined the possibility of derivative immunity for responders to spills for claims that arose outside the scope of OPA responder immunity. The court granted a motion for summary judgment filed by one of the responder defendants which was sued by various plaintiffs allegedly injured by their exposure to oil and to dispersants used in the cleanup. The court granted summary judgment to the responder defendant, holding that the claims for personal injury brought under state law and general maritime law were preempted by the CWA and the NCP.[329]

More recently, the same court granted the motions for summary judgment filed by several other responder defendants, dismissing the majority of the negligence and gross negligence claims filed by the plaintiffs, who consisted of boat captains, crew and workers allegedly injured by their exposure to oil and dispersants used during the *Deepwater Horizon* cleanup efforts. Some of the plaintiffs also alleged that the defendants' failure to use "reasonably safe dispersant chemicals" further exacerbated the pollution of the Gulf of Mexico and the injury to the plaintiffs.[330] Judge Barbier found that the evidence submitted by the parties indicated that the defendants did not exceed or disobey the authority conferred by the CWA and that therefore, the defendants were entitled to CWA derivative immunity. The defendants were also entitled to discretionary function immunity under the Federal Tort Claims Act (FTCA).[331] In extending derivative immunity and discretionary function immunity under the FTCA to those defendants who used or manufactured dispersants, Judge Barbier noted that the use of dispersants was specifically authorized by the FOSC, which continuously monitored and evaluated their use throughout the cleanup efforts. The Court further noted that the evidence submitted by the defendants demonstrated that they complied with the FOSC dispersant authorizations.[332] These determinations, the Court held, "are precisely the types of governmental decisions that are afforded discretionary function immunity and shielded from 'second-guessing' via an action in tort."[333]

In analyzing the applicability of the Implied Conflict Preemption Doctrine, Judge Barbier held that permitting the plaintiffs' claims to proceed could cause private responders to think twice before participating in cleanup efforts. Moreover, because the defendants are required to obey the FOSC during a response effort, "it would be physically impossible for the [defendants] to comply with these federal directives, as well as state or maritime law, if the actions that are the subject of the [plaintiffs'] claims are deemed to be in violation of the directives."[334]

19.2.4 National Planning and Response System

OPA retained the NCP under the CWA,[335] which establishes the overall methodology for the containment, dispersal and removal of oil and hazardous substances. The NCP addresses the assignment of duties and responsibilities among federal departments and agencies, state and local agencies, and port authorities and sets up USCG strike teams manned by trained personnel and specially equipped to deal with oil spills. These teams can be called in by the FOSC to provide assistance and training. The NCP also creates a national surveillance and notice system intended to give immediate warning of threatened spills or actual spills to state and federal officials and a national center to coordinate and direct the implementation of the plan.

Pursuant to the CWA as amended by OPA,[336] the EPA (through authority delegated to it by the president) was required to revise and republish the NCP to ensure coordination among the various response organizations. These revisions were published by the EPA in September 1994.[337] Among other things, the regulations established the National Strike Force Coordination Center to coordinate spill responses, revised the list of acceptable dispersants and bio-remediation agents, and added a new appendix to the NCP with spill response procedures and assignment of responsibility among various federal and state agencies.[338]

The NCP provides that federal and state officials work jointly to formulate a schedule for the use of dispersants and other chemicals to mitigate or remove a spill and that the schedule detail both the waters in which it is deemed appropriate to use such chemicals and the amounts of the chemicals that can be used. The NCP must include provisions for the protection of fish and wildlife resources.[339]

The OPA also created a new National Planning and Response System under the CWA.[340] This system established a federal, state and local hierarchy for spill response. The elements of this system are the National Response Unit, USCG Strike Teams, USCG District Response Groups, Area Committees, Area Contingency Plans and vessel and facility response plans. One of the primary purposes of this system is to prevent duplication of federal and private response efforts. While much of the planning and organization is conducted by public agencies and officials, the objective of this system is to have response equipment and personnel provided primarily by private entities.[341]

Local Area Committees comprised of federal, state and local agencies are established to prepare and periodically update detailed local area contingency plans to respond to a worst-case oil discharge—or the threat of such a discharge—from a vessel, offshore facility or onshore facility in or near the area. These plans must be federally reviewed and approved. The plans must describe the area that they cover and identify any subareas of special economic and environmental importance. They are to integrate with the operating procedures of the National Response Unit, other area plans and individual vessel and facility response plans. The area plans are to list all available federal, state, local and private response equipment and personnel, as well as firefighting equipment, and are to delegate respective responsibilities among federal, state and local agencies and owners and operators. The plans are also to contain procedures for obtaining expedited decisions on the use of dispersants.

19.2.5 Vessel and Facility Response Plans

Owners and operators of vessels, offshore facilities and certain onshore facilities are required to have response plans to remove discharges of oil.[342] These plans must be consistent with the NCP and Area Contingency Plans. Vessel and facility response plans must identify the Qualified Individual having full authority to implement removal actions and must require immediate communications between federal officials and private removal contractors. The response plans must identify and ensure by contract or other approved means the availability of private personnel and equipment necessary to remove, to the maximum extent practicable, a worst-case discharge (including a discharge resulting from fire or explosion) and to mitigate or prevent a substantial threat of such a discharge. A worst-case discharge for a vessel is a discharge of its entire cargo in adverse weather conditions. For a facility, it is the largest foreseeable discharge in adverse weather conditions.

The vessel and facility response plans must also describe training, equipment testing, periodic unannounced drills and response actions of vessel and facility personnel to mitigate or prevent the discharge. The plans must be updated periodically and be resubmitted for approval of each significant change. It is not a defense to liability that an owner or operator was acting in accordance with an approved response plan.

19.2.5.1 Tank Vessel Response Plan Regulations for Oil

The requirements for vessel response plans became fully effective on August 18, 1993.[343] All owners and operators of vessels handling, storing or transporting oil in bulk as cargo in waters under U.S. jurisdiction must have on board a vessel response plan approved by the USCG in order to operate. The plan must include these elements:

- identification of the Qualified Individual and alternate;
- accurate representation of the quantity involved in a worst-case discharge;
- adequate descriptions of training and drills;
- identification of private resources ensured by contract or other approved means to respond to a worst-case discharge; and
- adequate notification procedures about a discharge.

The regulations establish two different planning standards: one for vessels carrying oil as primary cargo and one for vessels carrying oil as a secondary cargo.

The plan must address not only responses to worst-case spill scenarios but also responses to the average most probable discharge and maximum most probable discharge.

Plans must provide for mobilizing response resources within two hours of a spill's discovery and for resources to be in place within 12 hours in high-volume port areas; within 24 hours in river, inland, nearshore and offshore areas; and within 24 hours "plus travel time" for spills occurring in the open ocean more than 50 miles from shore.

The regulations provide for tiering of resources in responding to a worst-case spill. Tier 1 resources must arrive at the scene within 12 hours in high-volume port areas or 24 hours in other areas. Tier 2 and Tier 3 resources "must be capable of arriving in 24-hour increments thereafter." RPs must notify Tier 1 resources within 30 minutes of the spill's discovery.

On December 31, 2008, the USCG finalized its rules regarding salvage and marine firefighting services.[344] The regulations require plan holders to identify, in their plans, a salvage and marine firefighting resource provider(s) that performs specified salvage and marine firefighting services within specified response times (in hours).[345] The services specified by the rule include salvage assessment and survey, salvage stabilization, specialized salvage operations, marine firefighting assessment and planning, and fire suppression.[346] The intent of this rule is to require that the listed provider be contacted in the event of a marine incident; resource providers must provide a written statement that they are able to meet the required response times for each service they would provide.[347] Plan holders who are unable to obtain resource providers that can meet the specified response times may request a temporary waiver from the USCG.[348]

The USCG regulations also require vessels carrying oil in bulk as cargo to carry on board certain discharge removal equipment, to install spill prevention coamings and to install emergency towing arrangements.[349] The regulations detail specific requirements for vessels measuring 400 feet or more in length as well as for smaller vessels. There are also requirements for inland oil barges and vessels that carry oil as secondary cargo. Vessels measuring 400 feet or more in length must have equipment and supplies capable of containing and removing on-deck cargo spills of at least 12 barrels. Vessels under 400 feet must carry equipment and supplies capable of handling an on-deck spill of at least seven barrels. Inland oil barges must have equipment capable of handling an on-deck spill of at least one barrel, and vessels carrying oil as secondary cargo must be able to handle a spill of one-half barrel.[350]

In addition to the requirement for on-deck spill cleanup capacity, the USCG issued requirements for on-water oil recovery capacity (referred to as caps).[351]

The caps are based on the size of a vessel and the territory in which it operates. They take into account maximum possible discharge of a vessel and prescribe the appropriate amount of recovery measures needed based on that number.[352]

In 2009, the USCG added dispersants and aerial oil tracking as required response equipment for manned vessels and unmanned tank barges carrying groups I through IV petroleum oil as a primary cargo.[353] Under the revised regulations, vessels operating in areas where dispersant use is "pre-authorized" by the EPA[354] must identify and ensure the availability of dispersant response resources capable of commencing "dispersant-application operations" within seven hours of the FOSC's decision to use dispersants.[355] Vessels not operating exclusively on inland rivers must also identify and ensure aerial oil-tracking resources (including trained personnel) capable of arriving at the site of a discharge in advance of other response resources and supporting removal operations continuously for three ten-hour periods during the first seventy-two hours of a spill.[356]

19.2.5.2 Nontank Vessel Response Plan Regulations for Oil

The CGMT-04 amended the CWA to require response plans for nontank vessels, which the legislation defined as "a self-propelled vessel of 400 gross tons measured under [46 U.S.C. § 14302], or greater, other than a tank vessel, that carries oil of any kind as fuel for main propulsion and that is a vessel of the United States or operates on the navigable waters of the United States."[357] CGMT-04 also directed the president to promulgate nontank vessel response plan regulations within one year of the statute's enactment, or August 9, 2005.[358] Realizing it was unlikely to finalize its regulations in time, the USCG issued Navigation and Vessel Inspection Circular (NVIC) No. 01-05 on February 4, 2005; nontank vessels that comply with NVIC No. 01-05's requirements can obtain an interim authorization to operate for two years without an approved response plan.[359] In 2008, the USCG announced it would begin actively enforcing the response plan requirement for nontank vessels of 1,600 gross tons or greater.[360] A year later, the USCG noticed a proposed rulemaking for nontank vessel response plans. The proposed rules closely resembled the response plan regulations promulgated for tank vessels[361] and, until the rules were finalized, nontank vessels subject to enforcement were obligated to comply with NVIC No. 01-05's requirements.[362] On September 30, 2013, the USCG issued its final rules noting that, while they closely resemble the NVIC, several changes had been made including, for example, the addition of one-time port waivers and five-year approvals for approved response plans.[363]

19.2.5.3 Tank Vessel Response Plan Regulations for Hazardous Substances

The proposed rules for tank vessels carrying hazardous substances were published on March 22, 1999.[364] The preamble to the proposed rule acknowledges the differences between rules for responding to oil spills and hazardous substance spills. "A fundamental underpinning of these proposed regulations is that, for hazardous discharges, the availability of information and expertise is essential to support response decision-making, while mobilization of containment and collection equipment will be feasible only as conditions allow."[365] Facing the prospect that containment may be infeasible for certain types of chemicals, the proposed rules embrace a "quickly assess the risk and respond accordingly" approach rather than a "rush in to contain and collect" approach.[366]

The proposed rule would not apply to containerized or packaged hazardous substances. Like the oil spill counterpart regulations, the owner must ensure in advance the availability of response resources by contract and ensure the ability to activate the plan through the appointment of a Qualified Individual.[367] The format of the plans that must be filed with the USCG is very similar to that required for tank vessels carrying oil. The plan must identify the resources that are available to assist in an emergency; it must describe the roles and responsibilities of the RP in the command structure, the available response resources that are under contract, and the available public response organizations.[368] The actual response requirements for prepositioned equipment depend upon the nature of the hazardous substance; the "floaters" that can be collected and removed like oil are subject to the formula-driven approach used in the oil spill regulations.[369] Although the comment period was reopened in 2011,[370] a final rule has not been promulgated.

19.2.5.4 Facility Response Plan Regulations for Oil

The USCG published final regulations[371] requiring the development and submission of oil response plans by marine transportation–related facilities (MTRs), which took effect May 29, 1996.[372] Any facility transferring more than 250 barrels of oil to or from a vessel over water must develop a response plan. The regulations cover trucks and trains loading or unloading cargo at facilities as mobile facilities subject to OPA plan requirements.

Facilities that are determined to threaten either substantial harm or a significant and substantial harm in the event of a discharge must submit response plans. The criteria used to determine which facilities must submit plans include the following:

- type of facility;
- storage capacity and material stored;
- number of tanks, their age and the presence of secondary containment;
- proximity to navigable waters and public supply intakes or wells;
- proximity to sensitive environmental areas;

- spill history; and

- the likelihood of natural disasters, such as floods, hurricanes and earthquakes.

The USCG will also consider operational items, such as:

- the number of annual tank barge or tank vessel transfers;

- the type or quantity of petroleum product transferred each year;

- the ability of the facility to perform multiple transfers; and

- other unidentified risk factors.

Each facility plan must address a worst-case discharge as well as the substantial threat of a worst-case discharge, such as loss of the entire facility or loss of the single largest tank or battery of tanks within the same secondary containment system. The plan must also address an average most probable discharge and a maximum most probable discharge.[373]

For non-transportation-related facilities, EPA issued a final rule that requires these facilities to prepare and submit oil spill response plans called Spill Prevention Control and Countermeasure (SPCC) Plans.[374] In July 2002, EPA issued another final rule amending the original regulatory provisions.[375] Pursuant to this rule, which became effective August 16, 2002, non-transportation-related onshore and offshore facilities "engaged in drilling, producing, gathering, storing, processing, refining, transferring, distributing, using, or consuming oil or oil products" that could reasonably be expected to discharge harmful quantities of oil "into or upon the navigable waters of the United States or adjoining shorelines, or into or upon the waters of the contiguous zone, or in connection with activities under the Outer Continental Shelf Lands Act or the Deepwater Port Act of 1974, or that may affect natural resources belonging to, appertaining to, or under the exclusive management authority of the United States" are required to prepare an SPCC Plan.[376]

For onshore pipelines, the Research and Special Programs Administration (RSPA) of the Department of Transportation requires pipeline operators to compute worst-case discharges for response zones and prepare response plans that take into account the proximity of pipelines to navigable waters and environmentally sensitive areas.[377]

19.2.5.5 Facility Response Plan Regulations for Hazardous Substances

The rules for MTRs handling hazardous substances[378] differ from the rules relating to MTRs handling oil in that many of the covered substances[379] cannot be contained and removed from the environment if released. The rules share many common elements with the counterpart oil response regulations, including preparation of plans with detailed facility-specific information that will facilitate emergency response[380] and the appointment of a Qualified Individual who is available to implement all the necessary response actions on behalf of the owner or operator of the MTR.[381]

Hazardous substance spills, however, present a wide variety of hazards and containment strategies that cannot be standardized as in the case of oil spill response. In many cases, the substance can be neither contained nor collected. In those cases where the substances can be contained ("floaters"), the MTR response plan will resemble the plans developed for oil spills with a list of contractors and equipment that correlate to the worst-case event that is calculated in accordance with the regulatory formula. In those cases where the substances cannot be contained, the equipment and response requirements are more flexible and will be based upon a case-by-case analysis that produces the most effective control strategies.[382] Although the comment period was reopened in 2011, the final rule has not yet been issued.[383]

19.2.5.6 Facility Response Plans for Nonpetroleum Oils

When the USCG issued MTR regulations in 1993, the so-called Subpart F requirements did not distinguish between hydrocarbon-derived oils and those derived from animals and vegetables. The industry that handles the latter products believed that these products did not present a comparable risk to the environment, a position that has led to a protracted struggle between the USCG, EPA (which has responsibilities for the non-MTR facilities), and Congress.[384]

The end result was the publication of a final rule on June 30, 2000.[385] The primary effect of the rule was to downgrade the classification of the affected facilities handling nonpetroleum oils from "significant and substantial" to "substantial" and to downgrade the planning standard to an "average most probable" standard. These changes reduced some of the planning and equipment requirements relative to those standards applicable to facilities that handle petroleum products.

19.2.5.7 National Preparedness for Response Exercise Program

In order to meet the "Area Drills" requirement of 33 U.S.C. §1321(j)(7), the USCG, EPA, BOEMRE and RSPA have developed the Preparedness for Response Exercise Program (PREP). In April 2016, the USCG published a notice of availability of updated PREP Guidelines.[386] Participants in these exercises—the agencies, states and oil industry—are tested on their ability to respond effectively to oil spills. Guidelines for the PREP are published through notice and comment rulemaking procedures every five years.[387]

19.3 Subtitle C: Penalties[388]

OPA significantly increased the severity of criminal and civil penalties resulting from discharges of oil into navigable waters and other offenses contributing to a discharge of oil.

Under the OPA amendments to the CWA, a negligent violation of Section 311(b)(3) of the CWA may constitute a criminal offense, under Section 309, rather than a civil matter.[389] Previously, there was no criminal penalty for a simple negligent discharge of oil. Other existing criminal penalties for deficient operation of a tank vessel have been increased, about five times for individuals and about 10 times for organizations.[390]

19.3.1 CWA Criminal Penalties

Section 309(c)(1) of the CWA provides that any person who negligently violates Section 301 of the act is subject to criminal penalties and possible jail time.[391]

Section 309(c)(2) provides that any person who knowingly violates Section 301 of the act is subject to felony criminal prosecution.[392]

Section 309(c)(3) penalizes violations involving knowing endangerment.[393] This section is triggered when a person, at the time of committing a knowing violation, has actual knowledge that his actions pose a serious threat to human health and life.

OPA amended Section 309(c) to include within its coverage violations of Section 311(b)(3). Thus, an oil discharge in violation of Section 311(b)(3) can be treated as a criminal offense. Under Section 309(c)(1), a conviction for negligently discharging oil carries a criminal fine of $2,500 to $25,000 per day of violation, up to one year imprisonment, or both. A prior conviction doubles the fines and term of imprisonment. Under Section 309(c)(2), the crime of a knowing discharge of oil carries a criminal fine of $5,000 to $50,000 per day of violation and up to three years imprisonment. A prior conviction also doubles the penalties.

If a knowing discharge of oil is committed with the knowledge that another person is placed in imminent danger of death or serious bodily harm, Section 309(c)(3) provides a maximum criminal fine of $250,000 and up to 15 years' imprisonment. For an organization, knowing endangerment carries a maximum fine of $1 million.

An early example of enforcement of these provisions occurred following the grounding of the barge *Morris J. Berman*, which resulted in a 750,000-gallon spill of oil off the coast of Puerto Rico in January 1994. The captain and first mate of the tug *Emily S*, who were both involved in making an improper emergency repair of the tug's tow cables, pleaded guilty to violating the CWA. In the related criminal case against the corporate defendants, three corporations and several corporate officers were convicted by a jury of violating the CWA. Fines against the corporate defendants totaled $75 million.[394]

Over the past decade, a pattern has emerged in plea agreements that include OPA violations along with counts under the Migratory Bird Treaty Act (MBTA).[395] For example, in September 1997, Eklof Marine Corp. entered into a plea agreement with the United States and state of Rhode Island under both statutes wherein Eklof agreed to pay a total of $7 million in federal and state criminal fines, which encompassed a $3.5 million fine for Eklof's MBTA violation, and $1.5 million to the Nature Conservancy as a result of a 1996 incident in which the tug *Scandia* caught fire and the crew abandoned ship, allowing the barge *North Cape* to break free and run aground, resulting in an approximately 828,000-gallon spill of No. 2 home heating oil into Rhode Island's coastal waters.[396] Similarly, following the April 2003 Bouchard tank barge *B 120* oil spill in Buzzards Bay, Massachusetts, Bouchard Transportation Company was charged with OPA, CWA and MBTA violations. In the final plea agreement, Bouchard Transportation Company was assessed $2 million to be paid into the OSLTF for OPA violations, $7 million for MBTA violations to be paid to the DOI to fund wetlands conservation programs, and an additional $1 million that was suspended pending monitoring of implementation of special conditions placed on the company.[397] More recently, Fleet Management Ltd., the Hong Kong–based operator of the M/V *Cosco Busan*, pleaded guilty to violating the CWA, MBTA and other federal statutes for its role in the vessel's November 7, 2007 allision with a protective fender of the San Francisco–Oakland Bay Bridge, which released approximately 53,000 gallons of bunker fuel oil into San Francisco Bay. Pursuant to its plea agreement, Fleet was ordered to pay $8 million in criminal fines (with $7 million to be paid to the OSLTF) and $2 million to fund marine environment initiatives in San Francisco Bay. Fleet was also ordered to institute comprehensive compliance measures, including a series of training and voyage planning reforms subject to auditing by an outside firm and to supervision by the court.[398]

19.3.1.1 Criminal Penalties for Failure to Notify

OPA also increased the criminal penalty for failure to notify the appropriate federal official of a discharge of which a person is aware under Section 311(b)(5) of the CWA. The previous penalty was $10,000 and up to one year imprisonment. The penalty under OPA is a maximum $250,000 fine and up to five years' imprisonment for individuals and a maximum fine of $500,000 for organizations.[399]

19.3.1.2 Criminal Penalties for Violations of Vessel Inspection, Manning, and Operation Requirements

OPA increased criminal penalties for violations of the vessel inspection, manning and operation provisions of Title 46 of the U.S. Code.[400] For example, the negligent operation of a vessel, which previously called for a penalty of a $5,000 fine and up to one year imprisonment, was amended to constitute a Class A misdemeanor, which now carries with it a fine of up to $100,000 for an individual or $200,000 for an organization. Should the gross negligence result in death, the maximum penalty for an individual is $250,000 and up to one year imprisonment; the maximum penalty for an organization is $500,000. The criminal penalty for operating a vessel while intoxicated is identical. [401]

The maximum penalty for a willful and knowing violation of the bulk dangerous cargoes rules in 46 U.S.C. Chapter 37 has been increased from $50,000 and up to five years' imprisonment to a $250,000 fine and up to six years' imprisonment for an individual and a $500,000 fine for an organization. The bulk dangerous cargoes rules govern the design, construction, operation and manning of tank vessels.[402]

Section 4301(a) eliminates all use immunity for organizations arising from spill notification and eliminates personal derivative use immunity.[403]

Section 4302 strengthens penalties under a number of other marine transportation safety laws.[404]

The maximum penalty for a willful violation of a regulation, order or direction under the Intervention on the High Seas Act[405] or Deepwater Port Act of 1974[406] was increased from a fine of $10,000 to a fine of $100,000 for individuals and a fine of $200,000 for organizations.[407] If death occurs as a result of a violation, the penalty is a $250,000 fine and up to one year in prison for an individual and a $500,000 fine for an organization.[408] The maximum penalty for a willful violation of the PWSA, or regulation issued thereunder, is a fine of $250,000 for individuals and $500,000 for organizations and not more than six years' imprisonment.[409]

19.3.1.3 Criminal Penalties for Violations of the Migratory Bird Treaty Act and Refuse Act

The trend to bring charges for violations of the MBTA or the Refuse Act, 33 U.S.C. §§ 407, 411 (2008)[410] in conjunction with violations of OPA[411] has raised objections and criticism from the oil and shipping industries[412] because no showing of fault is required to find the RP guilty, in contrast to OPA, which requires a showing of simple negligence. Under the RA and the MBTA, prosecutors need only establish that a spill caused the death of a migratory bird in order to find the RP guilty even if there was no negligence on the part of the defendant. While bills have been introduced by members of both the Senate and the House to end this practice and make the criminal punishments available under OPA exclusive in response to an oil spill, no legislation has yet been passed that would achieve this goal.[413]

19.3.2 Civil Penalties[414]

In addition to the imposition of criminal penalties, OPA established new Class I and Class II penalties for discharges of oil in violation of Section 311(b)(3) of the CWA or for failure to comply with regulations under Section 311(j) of the CWA governing the NCP, Area Contingency Plans, and vessel and facility response plans. The maximum Class I penalty for a prohibited discharge or for a failure to comply with the contingency or response plan regulations is $16,000 per violation, not to exceed $37,500. This penalty may be assessed only after the liable party is given notice and a reasonable opportunity to be heard and to present evidence concerning the imposition of the penalty.

The maximum Class II penalty for a prohibited discharge or for a violation of a contingency or response plan regulation is $16,000 per day of violation, not to exceed $187,500. Procedural prerequisites for the imposition of a Class II penalty are notice and an opportunity for a hearing on the record comporting with the Administrative Procedure Act at which interested persons are afforded the opportunity to testify.[415] Judicial review of the assessment is available; otherwise, the penalty becomes final 30 days after issuance.

OPA provides an alternative civil penalty scheme for owners, operators and persons in charge of vessels or facilities. The penalty for discharges violating the CWA is up to $37,500 per day of violation or up to $2,100 per barrel of oil discharged. If the discharge results from gross negligence or willful misconduct, the penalty is not less than $150,000 and not more than $5,300 per barrel of oil discharged. The alternative civil penalties for failure to comply with presidential orders relating to discharges is up to $37,500 per day of violation or an amount of up to three times the costs incurred by the OSLTF resulting from the failure to comply. Failure to comply with contingency plan regulations carries a penalty of $37,500 per day of violation. This penalty can be assessed against any person who fails to comply with the contingency plan requirements and is not limited in applicability to the owner, operator or person in charge of the vessel or facility.[416] This penalty is imposed by the U.S. District Court. In order to expedite the processing of civil penalties for spills of 100 gallons or less or for violations of pollution prevention regulations involving penalties not more than $2,500, the USCG regulations for so-called fast-track resolution apply.[417]

OPA also sets out a number of criteria to be used in determining the level of civil penalties. The official imposing the penalty—the secretary, EPA administrator or judge—is to consider the seriousness of the violation, the possible economic benefit to the violator, the degree of culpability, prior violations, efforts of the violator to mitigate or minimize the effects of the discharge and the economic impact of the penalty on the violator.[418]

Assessment is by written notice.[419] Criteria to be used to determine the penalty amount are the nature, circumstances, extent and gravity of the violation, degree of culpability, prior violation and ability to pay. In addition to or in lieu of assessing a civil penalty, the president may request that the attorney general obtain a judicial order to ensure compliance, including such relief as terminating operations of the company or individual.

20.0 Title VII: Research and Development Program

OPA created the Interagency Coordinating Committee on Oil Pollution Research (ICCOPR) to develop a comprehensive program for oil pollution research and technology development.[420] The ICCOPR includes representatives from numerous federal agencies charged with establishing a program that fosters the development of improved technologies to prevent or mitigate oil discharges. The research program monitors and evaluates the environmental effects of oil spills and focuses on developing better models to predict spills and improved methods to assess NRDs.[421] The ICCOPR is also charged with coordinating regional research programs that offer grants to universities or research institutions to study regional aspects of oil pollution.

The Delaware River Protection Act of 2006 amended Title VII of OPA to include a submerged oil program.[422] As a result of the M/T *Athos I* spill in the Delaware River in 2004, the law creates a program that directs NOAA and the USCG to monitor the environmental effects of submerged oil in that region. These agencies are to report to Congress on the development of methods to remove, detect and monitor, and predict the environmental impact of submerged oil. The program also authorizes $2 million per year for the USCG to develop technologies and practices for the removal of submerged oil.

21.0 Research Sources

To learn more about OPA, here are some additional resources:

- USCG Home Page: http://www.uscg.mil

- USCG National Pollution Funds Center: http://www.uscg.mil/ccs/npfc

- USCG National Resource Damage Claims Division: http://www.uscg. mil/npfc/nrd/

- National Oceanic and Atmospheric Administration (NOAA) Home Page: http://www.noaa.gov

- NOAA Damage Assessment and Restoration Program (DARP): http:// www.darp.noaa.gov

- U.S. Department of Transportation Home Page: http://www.dot.gov

- U.S. Department of Transportation—National Transportation Library: http://ntl.bts.gov

- National Response Center: http://www.nrc.uscg.mil

- International Maritime Organization: http://www.imo.org

Notes

[1]   The authors thank Andrea Gomes, an associate in Shipman & Goodwin's Hartford office, for her valuable contributions to this update.

[2]   Pub. L. 101-380, 104 Stat. 484 (Aug. 18, 1990).

[3]   In Section 888 of the Homeland Security Act of 2002, the USCG was removed from the U.S. Department of Transportation and placed in the new Department of Homeland Security. Section 1704 of the Homeland Security Act substituted references to Homeland Security in place of Transportation in many sections of Titles 14, 10, 37 and 38 of the U.S. Code. See Pub. L. 107-380 (Nov. 25, 2002). There were no direct changes to Title 33 because OPA §1001(33) defined the term "Secretary" as "the Secretary of the department in which the U.S. Coast Guard is operating," 33 U.S.C. §2701(33), which is presently the U.S. Department of Homeland Security. Thus, unless otherwise noted, any reference to the secretary herein shall have the meaning in 33 U.S.C. §2701(33).

[4]   See Jeffrey D. Morgan, The Oil Pollution Act of 1990: A Look at Its Impact on the Oil Industry, 6 Fordham Envtl. Law J. 1 (Fall 1994), for one commentator's examination of the oil industry's pre-OPA predictions compared to post-OPA events.

[5]   The commandant of the USCG testified before Congress on the tenth anniversary of the Exxon Valdez oil spill that, since the enactment of OPA, the number of marine oil spills greater than 10,000 gallons has been cut by two-thirds and that there have been no spills over 1 million gallons in U.S. waters since 1990, although there have been several large spills in other parts of the world. Oil Pollution Act of 1990: Joint Hearings before the Subcomms. on U.S. Coast Guard and Maritime Transp. and on Water Resources and Env't of the House Comm. on Transp. and Infrastructure, 106th Cong. 7–11 (1999). See also U.S. Dep't of Homeland Sec., U.S. Coast Guard Report on the Implementation of the Oil Pollution Act of 1990 at 28–34 (2005) (OPA Report), illustrating graphically the downward trend in oil pollution incidents and associated volumes for 1992–2004.

[6]   See Dagmar Schmidt Etkin, Cutter Information Corp., Financial Costs of Oil Spills in the United States (1998) (Etkin 1998), for a historical survey of oil spills and the resulting financial and legal consequences; see also Dagmar Schmidt Etkin, Analysis of Oil Spill Trends in the United States and Worldwide, presented at the March 2001 International Oil Spill Conference, available at: http://www.environmental-research .com/publications/pdf/spill_costs/paper4.pdf. More recently, see Gail Tverberg, Research Reports on the Economic and Environmental Impact of Oil Spills, July 7, 2010, available at: http://oilprice.com/ The-Environment/Oil-Spills/Research-Reports-On-The-Economic-And-Environmental-Impact-Of-Oil-Spills.html.

7   The Fund was established by Section 9509 of the Internal Revenue Code of 1986, 26 U.S.C. §9509. Section 1012 of OPA authorized use of the Fund for the payment of spill removal costs, the payment of claims for uncompensated removal costs and other spill-related expenses. More information is available on the USCG website: http://www.uscg.mil/npfc/About_NPFC/osltf.asp.

8   Gulf Coast Claims Facility Report of Findings & Observations to the U.S. Department of Justice, BDO Consulting, June 5, 2012, at p. 59. "On March 2, 2012, BP reached an agreement-in-principle with plaintiffs in the class action law suit, *In Re: Spill by the Oil Rig "Deepwater Horizon" in the Gulf of Mexico on April 20, 2010,* pending in the U.S. District Court for the Eastern District of Louisiana . . . As part of that litigation, on March 8, 2012, U.S. District Court Judge Carl Barbier issued an order . . . creating a process . . . for transitioning from the GCCF claims process to the court-authorized claims process that would result from the settlement . . ." *Id.* at 56. The interaction between the GCCF and parallel class action proceedings is addressed in a note in the Stanford Law Review. Colin McDonell, *The Gulf Coast Claims Facility and the Deepwater Horizon Litigation, Judicial Regulation of Private Compensation Schemes,* 64 Stanford L. Rev. 765 (March 2012).

9   *See In re: Oil Spill by the Oil Rig Deepwater Horizon in the Gulf of Mexico, on April 20, 2010,* 731 F. Supp. 2d 1352 (U.S. Jud. Pan. Mult. Lit. 2010). Recent decisions reached by Judge Barbier in *Deepwater Horizon* relating to OPA are discussed *infra* Section 19.2.3.

10 Many of the actions brought pursuant to OPA in the wake of the spill have since been dismissed. Those claims range from a suit brought by companies involved in offshore drilling activities, which claimed economic losses that resulted from a moratorium on offshore drilling imposed by the federal government in the aftermath of the spill, *see In re: Oil Spill by the Oil Rig "Deepwater Horizon" in the Gulf of Mexico,* on April 20, 2010, No. MDL 2179, 2016 WL 915257 (U.S. Jud. Pan. Mult. Lit. 2016) (appeal dismissed, U.S. Fifth Cir. No. 16-30245) to personal injury claims for alleged toxic exposure to Corexit, a chemical dispersant used following the spill, *see In re Oil Spill by Oil Rig "DEEPWATER HORIZON" in the Gulf of Mexico, No. MDL 2179,* 2012 WL 5960192 (U.S. Jud. Pan. Mult. Lit. 2012).

11 The responsible party of an incident is the person, business or entity that has been identified as owning the vessel or facility that caused the spill. *See* 33 U.S.C. §2701(32).

12 OPA §§1001–1019; 33 U.S.C. §§2701–2719. Where feasible, dual citations are provided for ease of reference.

13 *See, infra* Part 5.0.

14 In 2006, Congress increased these limits for the first time since OPA was enacted in 1990. *See, infra* section 7.2, for a discussion of the amendment contained in the U.S. Coast Guard and Maritime Transportation Act of 2006 (CGMT-06), Pub. L. No. 109-241 (July 11, 2006), codified at 33 U.S.C. §1321(f)(1).

15 *See, infra* section 11.3; the Energy Improvement and Extension Act of 2008 extended the per-barrel excise tax through December 2017 and increased the per-barrel excise tax from 5 cents to 8 cents from 2009–2016 and to 9 cents in 2017.

16 *See* 26 U.S.C. §9509 for the OSLTF generally and 33 U.S.C. §2703 for defenses to liability.

17 33 U.S.C. §§1251–1387 (commonly referred to as the Clean Water Act). OPA Title IV, Subtitles B and C, make extensive amendments to Section 311 of the CWA (33 U.S.C. §1321).

18 OPA §§5001–5008; 33 U.S.C. §§2731–2738.

19 OPA §7001; 33 U.S.C. §2761.

20 OPA §§8001–8302; 16 U.S.C. §3145 and 43 U.S.C. §§1350, 1642, 1653 and 1656.

21 Pub. L. No. 93-153 (Nov. 16, 1973), codified at 43 U.S.C. §§1651–1656.

22 Pub. L. No. 93-627 (Jan. 3, 1975), codified at 33 U.S.C. §§1501–1524.

23 Pub. L. No. 95-372 (Sept. 18, 1978), codified at 43 U.S.C. §§1344–1355, 1801, 1802, 1841–1845 and 1862–1866.

24 Pub. L. No. 92-340 (July 10, 1972), codified at 33 U.S.C. §§1221–1232b.

25 Pub. L. No. 95-474 (Oct. 17, 1978), codified at 33 U.S.C. §§1221, *et seq.*

26 International Convention on Civil Liability for Oil Pollution Damage, 1969, 9 I.L.M. 40 (1970).

27 The International Convention on the Establishment of an International Fund for Compensation for Oil Pollution Damage, 1971, 11 I.L.M. 284 (1972).

28 Tyler J. Savage, *North American Oil Pollution: Who is Liable for a Canadian/American Catastrophe?*, 4 Roger Williams University L. Rev. 344-47 (Fall 1998).

29 Protocol of 1984 to the International Convention on Civil Liability for Oil Pollution Damage and the Protocol of 1984 to the International Convention on the Establishment of an International Fund for Compensation for Oil Pollution Damage.

30 The 1984 Protocols were superseded by two protocols adopted in London on November 27, 1992: The Protocol of 1992 to Amend the International Convention on Civil Liability for Oil Pollution Damage (1992 CLC), 1969; and the Protocol of 1992 to Amend the International Convention on the Establishment of an International Fund for Compensation for Oil Pollution Damage (IOPC Fund), 1971, 35 I.L.M. 1406 (1996). Both of the 1992 protocols entered into force on May 30, 1996, and amendments to the protocols, which raised the compensation limits by 50 percent, were adopted on October 18, 2000, and entered into force on November 1, 2003. The International Maritime Organization and IOPC Fund subsequently considered and developed a proposed International Supplementary Fund to provide compensation over and above the 1992 IOPC Fund Convention, at a diplomatic conference in May 2003. The Supplementary Fund Protocol entered into force on March 3, 2005, after eight nations ratified the new measures.

31 17 I.L.M. 546 (1979). Available at: https://treaties.un.org/doc/Publication/UNTS/Volume%201340/volume-1340-I-22484-English.pdf.

32 OPA §§1001–1019; 33 U.S.C. §§2701–2719.

33 OPA §1001; 33 U.S.C. §2701. Seven additional definitions were added by the CGMT-04, Pub. L. No. 108-293 (Aug. 9, 2004).

34 *See* 33 C.F.R. §158.120.

35 In *GMD Shipyard Corp. v. M/A Anthea Y*, 2004 U.S. Dist. LEXIS 20079 (S.D.N.Y. Oct. 8, 2004), Judge Sweet determined that a ship undergoing repairs at dry dock for a period of two months was still a vessel for the purpose of OPA.

36 These materials are listed at 49 C.F.R. §172.101.

37 *Facility* does not include locomotive fuel tanks. *See United States v. Southern Pac. Transp. Co.*, 1995 U.S. Dist. LEXIS 5247 (D. Or. Feb. 20, 1995).

38 42 U.S.C. §§9601–9675. CERCLA may not be applied to a release of virgin petroleum or petroleum product, although it may be applied to used oil or oil for recycling. Even though oil may exhibit characteristics of a hazardous waste, or be listed as a hazardous waste on the Resource Conservation and Recovery Act list (40 C.F.R. §§261.1 *et seq.*), courts distinguish between "waste" petroleum and reusable petroleum "product." In *United States v. Western Processing Co., Inc.*, 761 F. Supp. 713 (W.D. Wash. 1991), the court ruled that "tank bottoms," made up of petroleum residue contaminated with sand and rust from the tank, were *not* excluded from CERCLA. In *Wilshire Westwood Assoc. v. Atlantic Richfield Co.*, 881 F. 2d 801 (9th Cir. 1989), the court stated that refined gasoline containing a CERCLA hazardous substance is exempt from CERCLA jurisdiction under the CERCLA petroleum exclusion if the hazardous substance is "indigenous" to such products. Under similar analysis, the court in *State of Washington v. Time Oil Co.*, 687 F. Supp. 529 (W.D. Wash. 1988), ruled that the CERCLA petroleum exclusion is not applicable to hazardous substances that are found in oil products in *excess* of levels that are normally found in a refined product. *See also Mid Valley Bank v. N. Valley Bank*, 764 F. Supp. 1377, 1384 (E.D. Cal. 1991) ("waste oil containing CERCLA hazardous substances does not fall under the CERCLA petroleum exclusion").

39 In brief, Congress enacted the Edible Oil Regulatory Reform Act (EORRA), Pub. L. No. 104-55 (Jan. 4, 1995), which required federal agencies to recognize that nonpetroleum oils, such as vegetable and animal fats, were less harmful to the environment than petroleum-based oils and to reflect lower level of risk in the regulations. The USCG issued regulations in 1990 that, in theory, responded to the industry concerns; they created separate subparts (Subparts H and I to 33 C.F.R. Parts 154 and 157) with more flexible standards for the nonpetroleum products. *See* 55 Fed. Reg. 25428 (June 21, 1990) and 57 Fed. Reg. 36222 (Aug. 12, 1992). Reflecting continuing industry pressure, Congress added to the 1996 U.S. Coast Guard Authorization Act a requirement that the secretary report annually to the Congress on compliance with EORRA. On October 20, 1997, the EPA denied a petition filed by several agricultural organizations to modify the facility response plan regulations (40 C.F.R. §§112.20 *et seq.*) and treat edible oils differently from petroleum-based oils. *See* 62 Fed. Reg. 54508 (Oct. 20, 1997). The 1998 Department of Transportation Appropriations Act contained a restriction on the use of appropriated funds for enforcing any 33 C.F.R. Part 157 requirements that did not reflect the different levels of risk posed by nonpetroleum oils. Similar legislative directives followed in the 1999 Omnibus Consolidated and Emergency Supplemental Appropriations Act. On June 30, 2000, the USCG published a final rule (65 Fed. Reg. 40825 (June 30, 2000)) making several changes that responded to the congressional directive to further differentiate between its requirements for petroleum oil and those nonpetroleum oils governed by Subparts H and I.

40 The circular definition of operator finds its origins in the CWA, and that definition is replicated in both CERCLA and OPA. The first court to examine the scope of the OPA "operator" definition noted the "similarly tautological" construction of the CERCLA and OPA operator provisions. *Harris v. Oil Reclaiming Co.*, 94 F. Supp.2d 1210, 1213 (D. Kan. 2000). The *Harris* court cited with approval the Supreme Court's characterization in *United States v. Bestfoods*, 524 U.S. 51, 66–67 (1998) of what constituted a CERCLA operator: "an operator must manage, direct, or conduct operations specifically related to pollution, that is, operations having to do with leakage or disposal of hazardous waste, or decisions about compliance with environmental regulations." *Harris* at 1213. This view was endorsed in the United States District Court for the Middle District of Georgia in the 2003 case *United States v. Jones*, 267 F. Supp.2d 1349 (M.D. Ga. 2003), but criticized that same year in the District of Oregon case *Green Atlas Shipping SA v. United States*, 306 F. Supp.2d 974 (D. Or. 2003). In *Green Atlas*, Judge King stated that he was not persuaded by the dicta in *Harris* that CERCLA cases should inform OPA rulings. Focusing on the financial responsibility requirement of OPA, Judge King determined that Congress did not intend for vessel captains to be "within the liability net" of OPA. *Id.* at 981.

41 OPA §1001(26); 33 U.S.C. §2701(26), as amended by the CGMT-04, Pub. L. No. 108-293 (Aug. 9, 2004).

42 *Id.* Many of the new financial terms in this definition are given the meaning that they have under CERCLA. *See* 42 U.S.C. §9601.

43 OPA §1001(32); 33 U.S.C. §2701(32). In *United States v. Bois D'Arc Operating Corp.*, 1999 U.S. Dist. LEXIS 3199 (E.D. La. Mar. 10, 1999), the defendant claimed that it was not a "responsible party" under OPA because it fell under the provision for abandonment of an offshore facility in §2701(32)(F). In such a case, the RP is the person who would have been responsible prior to abandonment. The court ruled that the defendant was an RP under paragraph (C), which defines "responsible party" for offshore facilities. According to the court, the fact that another RP may be found under paragraph (F) comports with the legislative purpose to define those responsible "broadly." *See id.* at *9–*10.

44 The U.S. Coast Guard Authorization Act of 2010 amended the term to include "the owner of oil being transported in a tank vessel with a single hull after December 31, 2010 (other than a vessel described in [46 U.S.C. §3703a(b)(3)])." Pub. L. 111-281, Title VII, §713, 124 Stat. 2988 (Oct. 15, 2010). Albeit in few cases, the cargo interests are now exposed to direct liability under OPA.

45 *See* 43 Fed. Reg. 10474 (Mar. 13, 1978); 40 C.F.R. §§116.1 *et seq.*

[46] Courts interpreting the scope of "navigable waters" under OPA have taken various approaches, making it difficult to determine the outer limits of this definition. Some courts have simply applied the same interpretation of "navigable waters" as used in CWA cases. *See, e.g., D.E. Rice v. Harken Exploration Co.*, 250 F.3d 264, 269 (5th Cir. 2001). Others have rejected the CWA interpretation based on the legislative history and intent of OPA. *See Sun Pipe Line Co. v. Conewago Contractors, Inc.*, 1994 U.S. Dist. LEXIS 14070, at *17–18, 37 (M.D. Pa. Aug. 22, 1994) (the court stated that OPA was "enacted to address a problem of more limited geographic scope" and concluded that "some link, direct or indirect, to United States coastal or inland waterways must be demonstrated to invoke the protections of the OPA"). *See also Harris v. Oil Reclaiming Co.*, 94 F. Supp.2d 1210, 1214 (D. Kan. 2000) (where there was "no evidence that the oil had actually entered any stream, river, or *arroyo*, or other tributary of a navigable water," the court rejected the CWA interpretation and refused to adopt a broad definition of "navigable waters" for purposes of OPA). At that point in time, the meaning of "navigable waters" under the CWA was not any clearer than the meaning of "navigable waters" under OPA. In 2001 the Supreme Court attempted to clarify the meaning of "navigable waters" as used in the CWA. *Solid Waste Agency of Northern Cook County v. United States Army Corps of Engineers*, 531 U.S. 159 (2001) (*SWANCC*). In S*WANCC*, the Supreme Court held that the Army Corps of Engineers could not exercise regulatory authority over isolated bodies of water. *Id.* The Supreme Court's ruling in *SWANCC* led to disagreement over its application. Some courts, particularly the Fifth Circuit, concluded that *SWANCC* limited "navigable waters" under the CWA to waters that were "actually navigable" or "adjacent to an open body of navigable water." *D.E. Rice v. Harken Exploration Co.*, 250 F.3d 264, 269 (5th Cir. 2001). *See also United States v. Needham*, 354 F.3d 340 (5th Cir. 2003). Other courts followed the lead of the Ninth Circuit in *Headwaters, Inc. v. Talent Irrigation District*, 243 F.3d 526, 533 (9th Cir. 2001), and interpreted *SWANCC* to allow the application of the CWA when there is a significant nexus between the body of water and navigable waters. *See United States v. Lamplight Equestrian Center, Inc.*, 2002 U.S. Dist. LEXIS 3694 (N.D. Il. 2002); *Brace v. United States*, 51 Fed. Cl. 649 (Fed. Cl. 2002); *United States v. Rueth Development Co.*, 189 F. Supp.2d 874 (N.D. Ind. 2001). The Supreme Court recently ended any debate and clarified that "navigable waters" are not limited to waters that are actually navigable. *Rapanos v. United States*, 126 S. Ct. 2208, 2220 (2006). A plurality of the *Rapanos* Court attempted to clarify the meaning of "navigable waters," holding that "navigable waters" do not include "channels that sometimes host ephemeral flows of water." *Id.* at 2224. The plurality concluded that "navigable waters" are "bodies *forming geographical features* such as oceans, rivers, [and] lakes . . . [and] wetlands abutting such a 'hydro-graphic feature.'" *Id.* (emphasis in the original), citing *United States v. Riverside Bayview Homes, Inc.*, 474 U.S. 121, 131 (1985); Webster's Dictionary Second 2882. Justice Kennedy concurred in the opinion, but he rejected the plurality's rationale. Justice Kennedy believes jurisdiction extends to wetlands that "possess a 'significant nexus' *to waters that are or were navigable in fact or that could reasonably be so made.*" *Id.* at 2236 (emphasis added). Justice Kennedy further concluded that wetlands have the requisite nexus if "either alone or in combination with similarly situated lands in the region, [they] significantly affect the chemical, physical, and biological integrity of other covered waters more readily understood as 'navigable.'" *Id.* at 2248. The majority of courts considering the meaning of "navigable waters" in light of *Rapanos* adopted Justice Kennedy's "significant nexus" test. *United States v. Gerke Excavating, Inc.*, 464 F.3d 723, 725 (7th Cir. 2006); *No. Cal. River Watch v. City of Healdsburg*, 457 F.3d 1023, 1025 (9th Cir. 2006). *See also United States v. Chevron Pipe Line Co.*, 437 F. Supp.2d 605, 613 (N.D. Tex. 2006) (applying Justice Kennedy's "significant nexus test" but relying on Fifth Circuit precedent to do so because Justice Kennedy did not elaborate standards for the test). However, other courts held that CWA jurisdiction exists when either Justice Kennedy's test or the plurality's test are satisfied, as was suggested by the *Rapanos* dissenters. *United States v. Johnson*, 2006 WL 3072145, at *8-*10 (1st Cir. Oct. 31, 2006); *United States v. Evans*, 2006 WL 2221629, at *19 (M.D. Fla. Aug. 2, 2006). Largely in response to the *SWANCC* and *Rapanos* decisions, the EPA and the U.S. Army Corps of Engineers issued a final rule on June 29, 2015, effective August 28, 2015, expanding the scope of "waters of the United States."

80 Fed. Reg. 37054 (June 29, 2015). The new rule encompasses: (1) tributaries of navigable waters, interstate waters, and territorial seas; (2) waters adjacent to navigable waters, interstate waters, territorial seas, tributaries, and impoundments; (3) regional types of wetlands if they have a significant nexus to navigable waters, interstate waters, or territorial seas; and (4) waters in the 100-year floodplain or within 4,000 feet of impoundments, navigable waters, interstate waters, territorial seas, and tributaries, if they have a "significant nexus" to navigable waters, interstate waters, or territorial seas. Since publication of the new rule, various groups across the United States have challenged its provisions. *See, e.g., N. Dakota v. U.S. E.P.A.,* 81 ERC 1729, 2015 WL 5060744 (D. North Dakota, Aug. 27, 2015); *see also In re E.P.A.,* 803 F.3d 804 (6th Cir. 2015) (issuing a stay pending determination of the Court's jurisdiction to consider the validity of the rule) and *In re U.S. Dept. of Def., U.S. E.P.A. Final Rule: Clean Water Rule: Definition of "Waters of U.S.,"* No. 15-3839, 2016 WL 723241 (6th Cir., Feb. 22, 2016) (holding that the U.S. Court of Appeals for the 6th Circuit has jurisdiction to review challenges to the rule).

47 OPA §1001(38); 33 U.S.C. §2701(38). Other new definitions include (39) extension of credit, (40) financial or administrative function, (41) foreclosure and foreclose, (42) lender, (43) operational function, and (44) security interest. As spelled out in the text of these new sections, these terms and their definitions were imported from CERCLA, specifically 42 U.S.C. §9601(20)(G)(i)–(vi).

48 OPA §1003(d); 33 U.S.C. §2703(d), as amended by Pub. L. 108-293 §703(c) (Aug. 8, 2004).

49 *See, infra* section 6.0, for a more complete discussion.

50 *See* 33 U.S.C. §1321.

51 46 U.S.C. §§30501 *et seq.* As explained by the court in *In re Complaint of Metlife Capital Corp.,* 132 F. 3d 818 (1st Cir. 1998), the Limitation Act "was enacted . . . to promote shipbuilding and to induce investment in the growing American shipbuilding industry." To this end, "[t]he law permits the ship-owner to limit his or her liability as to certain claims for damages arising out of the voyage of his or her vessel to the post-accident value of the vessel plus pending freight." *Metlife,* 132 F.3d at 820.

52 147 F.3d 1344 (11th Cir. 1998), *cert. denied,* 525 U.S. 1171 (1999).

53 *Id.* at 1348 n.2.

54 The RP's liability has since been increased to $1,900 per gross ton. *See* 33 U.S.C. §2704. *See, infra* section 7.0.

55 As explained by the court, "Rule F evolved as a procedural device to implement the [Limitation Act]." *Id.* at 1347. "Rule F implements the provisions of the Limitation Act by providing a mechanism for the *pro rata* distribution among claimants of the fund created by the Limitation Act's liability limits." *Id.*

56 *Id.* at 1350. Further, "[s]ubjecting OPA 90 claims to Rule F effectively would allow ship owners to opt out of the Congressionally mandated procedures for resolving OPA 90 claims." *Id.* at 1351. *See also, e.g., In re Jahre Spray II K/S,* 1996 U.S. Dist. LEXIS 11594, 13–14 (D.N.J. Aug. 5, 1996) ("Not only does the specific language of the OPA indicate that it supersedes the Limited Liability Act, but also the existence of provisions in OPA such as §2703 creating specific defenses to OPA claims and §2704 establishing liability limitations suggests that the OPA governs oil spill claims because these provisions would otherwise be redundant"); *Van Schaeffer v. Tsakos Shipping and Trading, S.A.,* 2006 WL 1192939, at *1 (E.D. Pa. May 2, 2006) (noting that while "[g]eneral maritime and admiralty claims remain subject to the Limitation Act," OPA "excludes certain claims from the requirements of the Limitation Act"). One court has held also that the Limitation Act's protections do not apply to contribution actions under OPA. *See In re Alex C Corp.,* 2010 WL 4292328, at *13-14 (D. Mass. Nov. 1, 2010).

57 *See Complaint of Metlife Capital Corp.,* 132 F.3d at 820 (OPA "repealed the Limitation Act with respect to removal costs and damages claims against responsible parties").

58 *See In re Petition of Settoon Towing LLC,* 722 F. Supp.2d 710, 714 (E.D. La. 2010) ("When there is more than one responsible party under OPA, their liability is joint and several").

59 Pub. L. No. 93-248 (Feb. 5, 1974), codified at 33 U.S.C. §1471 *et seq.*

60 OPA §1002; 33 U.S.C. §2702. Several operators challenged the USCG's efforts to recover its *monitoring* costs when the agency stood by but did not actually direct cleanup and removal operations. *See United States v. Murphy Exploration and Production Co*, 939 F. Supp. 489 (E.D. La. 1996); *United States v. Conoco*, 916 F. Supp. 581 (E.D. La. 1996). Elaborating on its decision in *Conoco*, the District Court for the Eastern District of Louisiana ruled in *Murphy Exploration* that although "the statute is not 'a model of clarity,' [the] provisions sufficiently support the conclusion that 'removal' is more than actual containment and cleanup, and [33 U.S.C.] Section 2702's reference to Section 1321(c) is inclusive rather than exclusive of monitoring costs." *Murphy Exploration*, 939 F. Supp. at 491, citing *Conoco*, 916 F. Supp. at 583. The matter has probably been laid to rest for good by *United States v. Hyundai Merchant Marine Co. et al.*, 172 F.3d 1187 (9th Cir. 1999), *cert. denied*, 120 S. Ct. 397 (1999). In this case, the United States sued Hyundai to recover its costs for the USCG's response to a 1991 tanker spill off the coast of Alaska. While Hyundai actually contained the spill at its own cost, the USCG spent 11 days monitoring Hyundai's efforts. Hyundai appealed a District Court award of $1.7 million for the United States. It argued that the government should not be eligible to recoup its base costs. The court upheld the award to the government because the broad definition of "costs of removal" in §2701(32) includes prevention costs, which the court felt adequately described the USCG operations. *Id.* at 1190. Ultimately, unless its cleanup and removal actions are held to be arbitrary or capricious, the United States is likely to recover all costs associated with those actions. *See id.* at 1191. *See also In re Petition of Settoon Towing LLC*, 722 F. Supp.2d 706, at 709-10 (E.D. La. Dec. 4, 2009); *United States v. Kilroy & Assocs., Inc.*, 2009 WL 3633891, at *5 (W.D. Wash. Oct. 30, 2009); *United States v. Jones*, 267 F. Supp.2d 1349, 1362-63 (M.D. Ga. 2003).

61 33 U.S.C. §§2702(b)(2)(A), 2706. However, the costs incurred by a dock owner in mooring a disabled vessel are not compensable as removal costs. *See Alabama State Docks Dept. v. Compania Antares de Navegacion*, 1998 WL 1749264 (S.D. Ala. Aug. 27, 1998).

62 Many states also have enacted statutes and promulgated regulations that impose significant follow-on cleanup requirements independent of OPA, such as the Massachusetts Oil and Hazardous Material Release Prevention and Response Act, Mass. Gen. Laws Ann., Ch. 21E, §5, and its implementing regulations under the Massachusetts Contingency Plan, 310 C.M.R. 40.0000 *et seq.*, even after federal spill response agencies determine that an area impacted by an oil spill is "cleaned up." Likewise, the State of Washington's Sediment Management Standards, W.A.C. Ch. 173-204 *et seq.*, require stringent cleanup of contaminated sediments "to reduce and ultimately eliminate adverse effect on biological resources and significant health threats to humans from surface sediment contamination." W.A.C. Ch. 173-204-100(2).

63 OPA §1002; 33 U.S.C. §2702(b)(1)(B). In *Avitts v. Amoco Prod. Co.*, 840 F. Supp. 1116 (S.D. Tex. 1994) (later vacated on jurisdictional grounds), attorneys' fees incurred in compelling the operators of an oil field to conduct a study of the threat of oil being discharged from the defendant's facilities into navigable waters and the feasibility of remedial action were held to be consistent with the NCP and recoverable removal costs under OPA. Although the District Court's award of attorneys' fees was vacated on jurisdictional grounds, it is indicative of what a court might do under similar circumstances.

64 For example, in response to the 1997 M/V *Kuroshima* oil spill in Unalaska, Alaska, which released approximately 39,000 gallons of heavy oil, the trustees, RP and response agencies collected information to evaluate potential natural resource damages (NRDs) and identify the need for restoration actions or additional studies, including: (1) photo and video documentation; (2) oil trajectory and overflight information; (3) fingerprinting of oil contamination; (4) evaluation of oil fates and weathering; (5) collection of response information, baseline data, and literature; (6) SCAT surveys; (7) dive surveys; (8) documentation of wildlife recovery and rehabilitation; (9) vegetation surveys; (10) sediment and water quality studies; (11) invertebrate studies; and (12) salmonid enumeration. NOAA *et al.*, Final Restoration Plan and Environmental Assessment for the M/V *Kuroshima* Oil Spill, 22–25 (Apr. 2002) (*Kuroshima* Plan) available at: http://docs.lib.noaa.gov/noaa_documents/NOS/ORR/DARP/DARRP_Kuroshima.pdf.

[65] In many oil spills, the volume released is often grossly underestimated given that an RP is, by the very nature of being embroiled in an emergency incident, focused on recovery of the vessel and its cargo and must typically deal with significant inclement weather and other technical and emergency conditions that surround the spill, as well as the inability to measure with any precision the amount of oil spilled due to variations in the oil type (including its specific gravity) and the confounding and varying effects of ambient air and seawater temperature on the oil. Andrew N. Davis and Austin P. Olney, *Cooperative Natural Resource Damage Assessments: Lessons Learned from the Oil Pollution Act of 1990*, Harris Martin's Natural Resource Damages & Envtl. Claims Report 1, 4–9 at n.19 (Sept. 2006).

[66] For example, if an RP doesn't promptly collect water column and sediment samples to establish the concentrations of toxic constituents in and around a spill site, both during and after a spill, in the absence of real data, the trustees may impute very conservative toxicity levels and ecosystem/species recovery curves from the literature and/or models and apply very conservative assumptions about injury (which could have significant financial consequences for an RP). *See, infra* section 5.0. *See also* Davis and Olney, *supra* note 65, at n.20.

[67] OPA §1002; 33 U.S.C. §2702. The United States District Court for the Eastern District of Louisiana has held that OPA preempts general maritime law claims for these enumerated damages. *See In re Petition of Settoon Towing LLC*, 2009 WL 4730971, *3 (E.D. La. Dec. 4, 2009); *Gabarick v. Laurin Mar. (Am.) Inc.*, 623 F. Supp.2d 741, 750 (E.D. La. 2009). *See also Clausen v. M/V New Carissa*, 171 F. Supp.2d 1127, 1133 (D. Or. 2001) (OPA provides the exclusive federal remedy for property damage claims resulting from oil spills).

[68] *See, infra* section 4.3.5.

[69] Natural resources means land, fish, wildlife, biota, air, water, groundwater, drinking water supplies, and other such resources belonging to, managed by, held in trust by, appertaining to, or otherwise controlled by the United States (including the resources of the exclusive economic zone), any state or local government or Indian tribe, or any foreign government, as defined in OPA §1001(20), 33 U.S.C. §2701(20). 15 C.F.R. §990.30. *See, infra* section 5.0.

[70] Reasonable assessment costs are defined in 15 C.F.R. §990.30.

[71] OPA §1002; 33 U.S.C. §2702(b)(2)(B).

[72] *See South Port Marine, LLC v. Gulf Oil Ltd. P'ship*, 73 F. Supp.2d 17, 19 (D. Me. 1999). On appeal, the U.S. Court of Appeals for the First Circuit reversed the District Court in part and reinstated the jury award for lost revenues, finding sufficient evidence to support the award, and affirmed the District Court's vacature of the awards for loss of goodwill and for business stress because of insufficient evidence. The circuit court also held that an OPA claimant is entitled to a jury trial and affirmed that OPA does not provide for punitive damages. *South Port Marine, LLC v. Gulf Oil Ltd. P'ship*, 234 F.3d 58 (1st Cir. 2000). The issue of an OPA claimant's right to a jury trial resurfaced in *United States v. Viking Res., Inc.*, 607 F. Supp.2d 808 (S.D. Tex. 2009). There the court held that "at least one component of natural resource damages—the diminution in value of those natural resources pending restoration—is legal in nature" and, therefore, must be tried by a jury. *Id.*, 607 F. Supp.2d at 832 ("It amounts to compensating the plaintiff for injury to its property, much like damages recovered in nuisance or trespass—both classic *legal* causes of action." [Emphasis in original]). More significant, perhaps, is a corollary to the holding: the jury must also decide all underlying factual issues, including those related to liability. *See id.*

[73] OPA §1002; 33 U.S.C. §2702(b)(2)(C).

[74] *In re Petition of Cleveland Tankers, Inc.*, 791 F. Supp. 669, 678 (E.D. Mich. 1992).

[75] OPA §1002; 33 U.S.C. §2702(b)(2)(D).

[76] OPA §1002; 33 U.S.C. §2702(b)(2)(E).

[77] *See In re Taira Lynn Marine Ltd. No. 5, LLC*, 444 F.3d 371, 382 (5th Cir. 2006) ("§ 2702(b)(2)(E) allows a plaintiff to recover for economic losses resulting from damage to another's property"); *Ballard Shipping Co. v. Beach Shellfish*, 32 F.3d 623, 631 (1st Cir. 1994), citing H. R. Conf. Rep. No. 101-653,

101st Cong., 2d Sess. 103 (1990) ("The House Conference Report makes clear that, under section 2702(b)(2)(E), 'the claimant need not be the owner of the damaged property or resources to recover for lost profits or income.'"). *See also* 33 C.F.R. §136.231(a) (claims against the Fund). *Contra In re Petition of Cleveland Tankers, Inc.*, 791 F. Supp. at 678–79 ("injury, destruction, or loss" must be to claimant's property).

78 *See In re Taira Lynn*, 444 F.3d at 377-78. *See also Dunham-Price Group, LLC v. Citgo Petrol. Corp.*, 2010 WL 1285446 (W.D. La. Mar. 31, 2010) (comparing proprietary interest requirement, or lack thereof, under OPA and general maritime law). The Ninth Circuit has recognized an exception to the rule for commercial fishermen claiming lost profits due to a spill. *See Union Oil Co. v. Oppen*, 501 F.2d 558 (9th Cir. 1974).

79 OPA §1005; 33 U.S.C. §2705.

80 Many states also have enacted legislation granting independent authority to seek NRDs for oil and hazardous substance spills. In recent years, these states also have shown a willingness to pursue NRD claims under independent authority. For example, the state of New Jersey has embarked on an aggressive NRD recovery initiative. Further information is available at http://www.nj.gov/dep/nrr/. *See also* "State-by-State Guide to NRD Programs in All 50 States," Brian D. Israel, Arnold & Porter LLP (March 12, 2015), available at: http://www.arnoldporter.com/~/media/files/perspectives/publications/2015/03/state bystate-guide-to-nrd-programs-in-all-50-sta__/files/publication/fileattachment/nrd-statebystate-guide 1.pdf.

81 The Bureau of Indian Affairs publishes a list of federally recognized Indian tribes in the *Federal Register*. The latest publication was on January 14, 2015. *See* 80 Fed. Reg. 1942 (Jan. 14, 2015).

82 OPA §1006; 33 U.S.C. §2706(a).

83 *See* 42 U.S.C. §9607(f).

84 *See, infra* section 5.2, for specific examples of NRDs from recent incidents. In addition to being required to pay the trustees' direct costs related to the assessment of damages to natural resources, some trustees include charges for indirect costs related to the natural resource damages assessment (NRDA) process, including administrative costs and so-called "overhead" charges. Because these rate-based indirect charges can be significant, an RP should be diligent in its review of documentation of such indirect/overhead costs.

85 For example, as part of the compensation for NRDs related to the 1996 *North Cape* oil spill, the trustees required the implementation of a novel lobster-notching program that protected 1.248 million female lobsters in Rhode Island and southern Massachusetts waters to ensure sufficient reproduction to compensate for the loss of an estimated 9 million lobsters. Further information on the *North Cape* spill and the lobster restoration program is available at http://darrp.noaa.gov/northeast/north_cape/index.html. *See also, infra* section 5.2.1. Recovery for NRDs related to commercially important species like lobsters and shellfish raises interesting issues about double recovery (i.e., overlapping compensation for lost natural resources and lost earnings/profits), which is prohibited under OPA. OPA §1006; 33 U.S.C. §2706(d)(3). *See* 15 C.F.R. §990.22. *See also* Carol A. Jones *et al., Public and Private Claims in Natural Resource Damage Assessments*, 20 Harv. Envtl. L. Rev. 111–164 (1996).

86 Lost public uses, such as recreational shellfishing, beach and boating use, ferry boat rides, and whale watching tours, are also taken into account in damage assessments. *See United States v. Amity Products Carriers, Inc*, 65 Fed. Reg. 3738 (Jan. 24, 2000); 2000 EPA Consent LEXIS 18 (Jan. 7, 2000); *see also* Consent Decree 1, *United States of America v. Bouchard Transportation Company, Inc., Tug Evening Tide Corporation, and B. No. 120 Corporation*, May 17, 2011, U.S. District Court, District of Massachusetts, available at: http://www.gc.noaa.gov/gc-cd/051911-cb-bouchard.pdf (RP paid over $3.3 million as compensation for injury to recreational resources).

87 While not defined under OPA or its implementing regulations, NOAA guidance and precedents from prior NRDAs have established that natural resources include "cultural resources" that generally are the

archaeological and historic resources of an area as well as other related nonrecreational human uses. In the context of tribal claims for damage to natural resources, the term may also capture alleged damages to cultural, spiritual, and religious resources. *See generally* Kuroshima Plan at 16–17; NOAA, *Damage Assessment Restoration Program, Scaling Compensatory Restoration Actions*: Guidance Document for Natural Resource Damage Assessment under the Oil Pollution Act of 1990, 2-1–2-4 (Dec. 1997).

88 OPA §1006; 33 U.S.C. §2706(d). NRDs do not include fines, cost of prevention, response costs or cleanup costs.

89 *Id.* at §2706(b).

90 *Id.* at §2706(e).

91 *Id.* at §2706(c)(1)-(4).

92 *Id.* at §2706(d)(3).

93 *See, infra* section 5.1.

94 OPA §1006; 33 U.S.C. §2706(d)(2).

95 *Id.* at §2706(c)(1)–(4). Examples of projects undertaken using equivalent resources to compensate directly for lost resources include the construction of a disabled-accessible kayak/canoe launch, improvements to a boat ramp, and the implementation of other recreational projects to compensate for the loss of an estimated 125,000 recreational trips. NOAA *et al.*, Final Restoration Plan and Environmental Assessment for the April 7, 2000 Oil Spill at Chalk Point on the Patuxent River, Maryland, 63–74 (Nov. 2002) (Chalk Point Plan). *See also* "Deepwater Horizon Oil Spill: Final Programmatic Damage Assessment and Restoration Plan and Final Programmatic Environmental Impact Statement" February 2016, available at: http://www.gulfspillrestoration.noaa.gov/restoration-planning/gulf-plan/.

96 OPA §1006; 33 U.S.C. §2706(d)(1).

97 *Id.* at §2706(f). *See also* 15 C.F.R. §990.65.

98 OPA §1006; 33 U.S.C. §2706(g).

99 *Id.* at §2706(e)(1).

100 *Id.* at §2706(e)(2). *See also* 15 C.F.R. §990.13.

101 *See* 61 Fed. Reg. 440, 443 (Jan. 5, 1996).

102 61 Fed. Reg. 440 (Jan. 5, 1996); 15 C.F.R. §990.10 *et seq.*

103 Two groups of industry petitioners sued NOAA over the final rules. The industry objected in particular to the use of so-called contingent valuations in damage assessments and objected to the recovery of "passive" use or "nonuse" values for temporary losses of natural resources. Although the Court of Appeals substantially upheld the regulations in *General Electric Co. v. United States Dep't of Commerce*, 128 F.3d 767 (D.C. Cir. 1997), the ruling asked NOAA to clarify certain language discrepancies and to address the relationship between response and restoration authorities. NOAA published proposed amendments to the final regulations in the *Federal Register* on July 31, 2001, to address the issues remanded to NOAA by the Court of Appeals and to propose some clarifying and technical amendments. 66 Fed. Reg. 39464. On October 1, 2002, NOAA published a final rule addressing the remanded issues and comments received. *See* 67 Fed. Reg. 61483 (Oct. 1, 2002).

104 NOAA maintains online administrative records for each NRDA at http://www.darrp.noaa.gov/index .html. These administrative records typically include MOAs, press releases, technical NRDA documents, fact sheets and other documents. An example of a recent MOA can be found at http://www.darrp.noaa .gov/northeast/buzzard/relate.html. In other cases, where the time and effort often required for the drafting, negotiation and implementation of an MOA is not feasible, "Guiding Principles" may be used by the parties instead. *See* May 10, 2007 Letter and Attachment from Andrew N. Davis to Christopher J. Plaisted, NOAA Office of General Counsel, Re: K-Sea DBL-152 Cooperative Natural Resource Damage Assessment Guiding Principles, available at: https://casedocuments.darrp.noaa.gov/southeast/dbl152/pdf/ 2312%20 Davis%20%28RP%29%20Letter%205_10_07.pdf.

105 15 C.F.R. §990.14(c)(4).

106 15 C.F.R. §990.14(c)(5).

107 OPA §1006; 33 U.S.C. §2706(e)(2). *See generally* Davis and Olney, *supra* note 66, for further discussion of the implications of the cooperative NRDA process.

108 Under OPA §1006, NRDA trustees may recover their "reasonable assessment costs" as defined at 33 U.S.C. §2706(d)(1)(C) and 15 C.F.R. §990.30.

109 Davis and Olney, *supra* note 65, at 4. Notwithstanding the burdens placed on the RP throughout the cooperative NRDA process, a cooperative approach is typically preferred over litigation for various reasons. In the broadest sense, a cooperative NRDA allows the RP to have meaningful input into the assessment process, which input has the potential of ultimately benefitting both the trustees and the RP jointly. For example, blending SCAT work (*see, infra* §§4.2, 5.1) with the NRDA work where possible not only ensures that the RP and trustees will capture time-sensitive spill data, but also avoids duplication of the parties' efforts and helps mitigate costs. In addition, the joint trustee/RP retention of experienced subject-matter/"resource" experts and the use of technical working groups (TWGs) ensures higher-productivity, provides ample opportunity for collaborative discussions among the scientific experts, and, once again, can ensure reduced transaction costs. Despite the inherent benefits to a cooperative NRD, RPs should still be ready to challenge assumptions and hypothetical data projections based on the *real* data collected. A precise agreement on the extent of the NRDs and the restoration required to ameliorate that damage is unnecessary. Instead, both the RP and trustees should work together to determine the most cost-effective restoration solutions for the situation at hand. For a further discussion, *see* Andrew N. Davis, Austin P. Olney, & Aaron D. Levy, "Oil Spills And The Environment: Strategies For Natural Resource Damage Assessments Under The U.S. Oil Pollution Act Of 1990," CorporateLiveWire, August 5, 2011, available at: http://www.shipmangoodwin.com/files/13164_CorporateLiveWireOilSpills Article.pdf.

110 *See* 15 C.F.R. §990.27.

111 *Natural resource services* means the functions performed by a natural resource for the benefit of another natural resource and/or the public. 15 C.F.R. §990.30.

112 *See* 15 C.F.R. §990.51(f) for the 10 factors considered.

113 Blending data collected during Shoreline Cleanup and Assessment Team (SCAT) work, which involves the surveying of an affected shoreline after a spill, with the NRDA data collection process is one cost-effective way of avoiding duplication of efforts and potentially inconsistent results in the assessment of natural resource injuries.

114 In the absence of adequate or reliable data, trustees will often utilize various assumptions (e.g., rate of breakdown of oil into its toxic components in the water column) in proprietary models to generate estimated losses, which in effect become synthetic evidence used to develop and scale restoration projects. This can have particularly acute effects in the case of models used to estimate, for example, avian injury. *See also* Davis and Olney, *supra* note 65, at 6 (discussing the importance of gathering data immediately following a spill). Gathering ephemeral ("real") data immediately after a spill may help counter the sometimes speculative nature of the trustees' injury assumptions and provide a more accurate data set to permit more precise injury determinations and calibration of the same to further the restoration efforts.

115 15 C.F.R. §990.14(d).

116 The trustees must consider natural recovery according to 15 C.F.R. §990.53.

117 43 C.F.R. §11.83.

118 42 U.S.C. §§4321 *et seq.*

119 For a complete listing of OPA and CERCLA NRDA consent decrees, *see* http://www.gc.noaa.gov/natu ral-office1.html.

120 NOAA *et al.*, Restoration Plan and Environmental Assessment for the January 19, 1996, *North Cape* Oil Spill (Sept. 15, 1998) (Draft Restoration Plan) and Summary of Changes to the September 14, 1998 Draft Restoration Plan, available at: http://www.gc.noaa.gov/gc-rp/rptchooz.htm.

[121] Notice of Proposed Consent Decree was issued by the Department of Justice on July 19, 2000. 65 Fed. Reg. 44808 (July 19, 2000).

[122] The notching of these 1,248,000 lobsters ultimately cost in the range of $20 million, bringing the total NRDA costs to in excess of $32 million. *See United States, et al. v. EW Holding Corp.*, Consent Decree, noticed at 65 Fed. Reg. 44808 (July 19, 2000); 2000 EPA Consent LEXIS 202 (July 6, 2000).

[123] This $8 million included funds for (1) lobster monitoring and oversight ($600,000) by the Trustees; (2) shellfish restoration ($1.5 million); (3) salt pond land acquisition ($1.6 million); (4) loon restoration ($3 million); (5) seabird restoration ($400,000); (6) piping plover restoration ($140,000); (7) fish run project ($160,000); and (8) general oversight ($400,000). *Id.*

[124] *See, supra* note 85.

[125] *See* News Release, Rhode Island Department of Environmental Management, "*North Cape* Oil Spill Trustees and Industry Successfully Complete *North Cape* Lobster Restoration Program" (Aug. 10, 2006), available at: http://www.dem.ri.gov/news/2006/pr/0810061.htm.

[126] NOAA *et al.*, Final Restoration Plan and Environmental Assessment for the November 26, 2004, M/T *Athos I* Oil Spill on the Delaware River near the Citgo Refinery in Paulsboro, New Jersey (Sept. 2009) (*Athos I* Plan), at vii, 1, and 38, available at: https://darrp.noaa.gov/sites/default/files/case-documents/ AthosFinalRP_0.pdf. The RP and the Trustees did not formally participate in a cooperative assessment because the RP refused to pay the Trustees' assessment costs. *Id.* at 10. The RP refused because it believed (correctly) that it had a complete defense to liability. *Id. See, infra* section 6.1.

[127] *Athos I* Plan, at viii–ix. The estimated cost of the proposed restoration projects was $26,474,470. *Id.* at 7. Because the RP successfully invoked a third-party defense to liability, the final *Athos I* plan was submitted to the OSLTF as part of a claim for funds to implement the preferred restoration projects. *Id.* at ix.

[128] *United States of America vs. M/V Cosco Busan*—Civil Action No. C 07-6045(SC)- Consent Decree at 2-3.

[129] Press Release, Department of Justice, Ship Owners and Operators to Pay $44 Million in Damages and Penalties for 2007 Bay Bridge Crash and Oil Spill (Sept. 19, 2011), available at: https://casedocuments .darrp.noaa.gov/southwest/cosco/pdf/09-19-11_Cosco%20Busan_Overall_Consent_Decree_Press_Re lease%20FINAL.pdf.

[130] *Id.*

[131] *Cosco Busan* Oil Spill, Final Damage Assessment and Restoration Plan/Environmental Assessment (February 2012), available at https://nrm.dfg.ca.gov/FileHandler.ashx?DocumentID=42442&inline=true.

[132] *Cosco Busan* Final Restoration Plan Press Release (Mar. 1, 2012), available at https://www.wildlife.ca.gov/ OSPR/NRDA/cosco-busan.

[133] Originally, the Wampanoag "Aquinnah" Tribe of Gay Head was also a trustee but was settled out separately and privately early in the process.

[134] The settlement was memorialized in a partial consent decree, dated May 17, 2011. *See United States of America v. Bouchard Transportation Company, Inc., Tug Evening Tide Corporation, and B. No. 120 Corporation*, Docket No. 1:10-cv-11958-NMG (D. Mass. May 17, 2011). In that same Consent Decree, the RP agreed to pay over $1.5 million to the trustees in partial reimbursement of the trustees' costs of assessing the NRDs.

[135] *See* Deepwater Horizon oil spill: 2016 Final Programmatic Damage Assessment and Restoration Plan and Final Programmatic Environmental Impact Statement. Available at: http://www.gulfspillrestoration.noaa .gov/restoration-planning/gulf-plan.

[136] Dispersants, which are used in oil spill response operations to reduce the impact of the spill, "are chemical agents that emulsify, disperse, or solubilize oil into the water column or promote the surface spreading of oil slicks to facilitate dispersal of the oil into the water column." 40 C.F.R. §300.5.

[137] *Supra* note 135.

[138] *Id.*. During the oil spill response, over 600 sea turtles and 150 dolphins and whales were found dead. *See* http://www.nmfs.noaa.gov/pr/health/oilspill/gulf2010.htm. The long-term effects of the oil spill were far

greater, however, with an estimated 82,000 birds, 6,000 sea turtles, and 25,900 sea mammals affected by the spill. *See* Center for Biological Diversity Report, "A Deadly Toll: The Gulf Oil Spill and The Unfolding Wildlife Disaster" (April 2011), available at: http://www.biologicaldiversity.org/programs/public_lands/energy/dirty_energy_development/oil_and_gas/gulf_oil_spill/a_deadly_toll.html.

[139] *Id.*

[140] For more information, *see*: http://response.restoration.noaa.gov/oil-and-chemical-spills/significant-incidents/deepwater-horizon-oil-spill.

[141] *See* "Trustees Settle with BP for Natural Resource Injuries to the Gulf of Mexico" Press Release, available at: http://www.gulfspillrestoration.noaa.gov/2016/04/trustees-settle-with-bp-for-natural-resource-injuries-to-the-gulf-of-mexico/. For Consent Decree documents, *see*: https://www.justice.gov/enrd/deepwater-horizon.

[142] *See* Ocean Conservancy's Analysis of the Settlement Agreement with BP, available at: http://www.oceanconservancy.org/places/gulf-of-mexico/bp-settlement-fact-sheet.pdf.

[143] Some of the following Consent Decree descriptions included only general dollar amounts encompassing fines, NRDs, and other costs. Where NRDA costs were carved out from a lump sum and specifically identified, they are noted. *See, e.g., In re Oil Spill by the Oil Rig "Deepwater Horizon" in the Gulf of Mexico, on April 20, 2010*, Nos. 10-4536, 10-04182, 10-03059, 13-4677, 13-158, 13-00123 (E.D. La. Apr. 4, 2016) (BP agreed to pay $7.1 billion, plus any of the $1 billion previously agreed to plus accrued interest); *In re Oil Spill by the Oil Rig "Deepwater Horizon" in the Gulf of Mexico, on April 20, 2010*, No. 10-4536, 2013 EPA Consent LEXIS 6 (E.D. La. Jan. 3, 2013), 78 Fed. Reg. 1833-02 (Jan. 9, 2013) (Transocean agreed to pay $1 billion, 80% of which will go to the Gulf Coast Restoration Trust Fund, 20% of which will go to the OSLTF for NRDs resulting from the Deepwater Horizon Spill); *United States, et al. v. Bouchard Transp. Co., Inc., et al.*, No. 1:10-cv-11958 (D. Mass. Nov. 15, 2010), 75 Fed. Reg. 70947 (Nov. 19, 2010) ($1,573,529 to NOAA, U.S. Dept. of Interior, and other NRDA trustees for partial reimbursement of assessment costs and $6,076,393 for NRDs resulting from a 98,000-gallon heavy fuel oil spill in Buzzards Bay, off the shores of Massachusetts and Rhode Island); *United States and the Confederated Tribes of the Warm Springs Reservation of Oregon v. American Energy, Inc.*, 2006 EPA Consent LEXIS 22 (Mar. 22, 2006), 71 Fed. Reg. 17140 (Apr. 5, 2006) ($94,242 to NOAA and $15,533 to the U.S. Dept. of Interior for NRDA costs and $315,222.50 for NRDs resulting from a 5,000-gallon gasoline spill into a creek located on an Indian reservation); *United States and the State of Indiana v. Atlantic Richfield Co., et al.*, 69 Fed. Reg. 53736 (Sept. 2, 2004), 2004 EPA Consent LEXIS 86 (Aug. 20, 2004) (RPs to pay $56,353,000 toward restoration of natural resources in the Grand Calumet River and $2.7 million to DOI and the Indiana Department of Environmental Management for their costs of assessing NRDs); *United States and the Mississippi Comm'n on Env't Quality v. Genesis Energy, Inc. et al.*, 69 Fed. Reg. 39964 (July 1, 2004) (RP to perform a land acquisition and conservation supplemental environmental project at cost of at least $2 million and to pay at least $110,137.57 to trustees for associated costs of oversight, a wood duck nesting project and past NRDA costs); *United States v. Billabong II ANS*, 68 Fed. Reg. 42424 (July 17, 2003), 2003 EPA Consent LEXIS 205 (July 1, 2003) ($1,875,946 for NRDs after fuel oil spill off South Carolina coast on January 14, 1999); *United States v. BD Oil Gathering, Inc.*, 68 Fed. Reg. 17399 (Apr. 9, 2003), 2003 EPA Consent LEXIS 205 (July 1, 2003) ($11,000 civil penalty to OSLTF; $314,198.23 to federal trustees and $23,746.94 for release of 92 barrels of oil into the Big Sandy Creek, WV); *United States v. Potomac Elec. Power Co., et al.*, 67 Fed. Reg. 77804 (Dec. 19, 2002), 2002 EPA Consent LEXIS 576 (Dec. 11, 2002) ($2,710,498 for restoration projects from a rupture in an oil pipeline); *United States v. Torch Energy Co.*, 67 Fed. Reg. 37862 (May 30, 2002), 2002 EPA Consent LEXIS 214 (May 16, 2002) ($2,397,000 for NRDs arising from a 1997 spill of oil from the offshore drilling platform named "Irene"); *United States and State of Alaska v. Kuroshima Shipping, S.A. and Unique Trading Co., Ltd.*, 67 Fed. Reg. 17720 (Apr. 11, 2002), 2002 EPA Consent LEXIS 71 (Mar. 18, 2002) ($644,017 to trustees for restoring natural resources, $9,000 to the registry of the Court until the trustees determine whether it is necessary for the field component of the restoration plan or may be

returned, and in excess of $66,158.09 to the trustees for damage assessment costs); *United States v. Tesoro Hawaii Corp.*, 66 Fed. Reg. 46287 (Sept. 4, 2001), 2001 EPA Consent LEXIS 377 (Aug. 23, 2001) (defendants to carry out a net removal project and pay $580,000, which includes $500,000 for natural resource restoration projects for wildlife and habitat, $10,000 for restoration projects for lost human use, $15,000 penalty to the state, and $55,000 as a state supplemental environmental project); *United States v. Amity Products Carriers, Inc.*, 65 Fed. Reg. 3738 (Jan. 24, 2000), 2000 EPA Consent LEXIS 18 (Jan. 7, 2000) ($1.5 million for a 4,277 barrel spill); *United States v. Bulk Transport Ltd.*, 64 Fed. Reg. 66646 (Nov. 29, 1999), 1999 EPA Consent LEXIS 226 (Nov. 10, 1999) ($1.6 million for an 845 barrel spill); *United States v. Equilon Pipeline Co. LLC*, 64 Fed. Reg. 54643 (Oct. 7, 1999), 1999 EPA Consent LEXIS 202 (Sept. 28, 2002) ($480,000 for past costs and an unspecified amount for future costs for a 6,547-barrel spill); *United States v. Pearl Shipping Corp.*, 64 Fed. Reg. 54643 (Oct. 7, 1999), 1999 EPA Consent LEXIS 199 (Sept. 27, 1999) ($4,050,000 in NRDs, $196,200 for National Marine Sanctuaries Act violations, and $1,181,800 in civil penalties for a 3,000-gallon spill from the M/T *Command*); *United States v. Chevron Products Co.*, 64 Fed. Reg. 33,909 (June 24, 1999), 1999 EPA Consent LEXIS 99 (June 3, 1999) ($2,250,000 for a 928-barrel spill); *In re Complaint of United States*, 63 Fed. Reg. 40737 (July 30, 1998), 1998 EPA Consent LEXIS 127 (July 16, 1998) ($7,756,646 for settlement of state and federal claims for response costs, assessment costs and NRDs); *United States v. Texaco Refining and Marketing, Inc.*, 63 Fed. Reg. 17891 (Apr. 10, 1998), 1998 EPA Consent LEXIS 73 (Mar. 25, 1998) ($500,000 for a 5,000-barrel spill); *United States, Commonwealth of Virginia, and District of Columbia v. Colonial Pipeline Co.*, 62 Fed. Reg. 59371 (Nov. 3, 1997) (defendants to perform comprehensive projects to restore natural resources, reimburse all assessment costs of the natural resource trustees, including monitoring and oversight costs and pay $253,314 toward the construction of a fishway for Little Falls Dam on the Potomac River).

[144] The *Equilon Pipeline Co.* decree was amended on December 5, 2001 (66 Fed. Reg. 63256); 2001 EPA Consent LEXIS 719 (Sept. 17, 2001) (defendants must purchase 100 acres of replacement property and pay $250,000 to be used to construct estuarine and freshwater habitat); *United States v. Tsacaba Shipping Co.*, 64 Fed. Reg. 8121 (Feb. 18, 1999); 1999 EPA Consent LEXIS 58 (Jan. 28, 1999) ($8 million total monetary compensation, which includes $1,001,799 to provide compensation for ecological damages, including injuries to birds, sea turtles, sediments, water column and beach sand, and a $2.5 million fund to be administered by the trustees to compensate for recreational beach use losses. In addition to the monetary compensation, the defendants agreed to implement salt marsh restoration and purchased an 11-acre parcel of land to be deeded to public ownership, where defendants agreed to implement a mangrove restoration plan). *See also United States, et al. v. Enbridge Energy Ltd. P'ship*, No. 0:08-cv-5878 (Oct. 30, 2008), 73 Fed. Reg. 66921 (Nov. 12, 2008) (July 2002 subsurface pipeline discharge of 6,000 barrels of crude oil into a forested wetland within the watershed of a Mississippi River tributary; in addition to paying $128,300 for reimbursement of total assessment costs, Enbridge was required to remove part of a road and to restore wetlands within the Chippewa National Forest and to retrofit ten diesel school buses owned by the Ojibwe Indian tribe with diesel oxidation catalyst devices).

[145] *See, supra* section 5.2.1.

[146] *See, e.g.,* Etkin 1998, *supra* note 6, at 109–150, and Kevin R. Murray, Steven J. McCardell and Jonathan R. Schofield, "Natural Resource Damage Trustees: Whose Side Are They Really On?" 5 *Envtl. Law.* 407 (1999), for a critical analysis of the NRDA process under CERCLA and OPA. *See also* Marissa L. Curran, *The Wildlife Wildcard: Natural Resource Damages and Putting a Price on Nature,* 30 Nat. Resources & Envt'l 10 (Fall, 2015).

[147] *See* Douglas Helton and Tony Penn, *Putting Response and Natural Resource Damage Costs in Perspective* (1999 International Oil Spill Conference, Paper ID #114 1999), at n.1.

[148] *Id.* at 6, 15. *But cf.* Etkin 1998, *supra* note 6, at 131.

[149] Helton and Penn, *supra* note 147 at 6, 15.

150 Etkin, *supra* note 6 at 131. In a direct response to the 1999 paper of Helton and Penn, *supra* note 147, Dr. Etkin cites an example of NRDA costs being as high as 99 percent of the total costs of some spills.

151 For a more complete discussion of the statistics, *see* Helton and Penn, *supra* note 147, and Etkin 1998, *supra* note 6.

152 OPA §1003; 33 U.S.C. §2703.

153 *See Apex Oil Co., Inc. v. United States*, 208 F. Supp.2d 642 (E.D. La. 2002). Under an arbitrary and capricious standard, the District Court affirmed the findings of the NPFC that Apex was not entitled to an "act of God" defense for the June 16, 1995 allision of the Apex barges and the Vicksburg Highway 80 Bridge during a strong current and flood stage waters in the Mississippi River because the decision to proceed into the risky conditions contributed to the accident. Borrowing from CERCLA precedent, since the term "act of God" in OPA has the exact same definition, the court clarified that unlike the broader common law act of God defense, the statutory language of OPA requires that the claimant prove three elements: the natural phenomenon must be exceptional, inevitable and irresistible. *See Apex Oil Co., Inc.*, 208 F. Supp.2d at 653.

154 OPA §1003; 33 U.S.C. §2703(b). Interpreting identical language in OPA §1016, 33 U.S.C. §2716(f)(1)(C), the U.S. District Court for the District of Columbia held that a finding of willful misconduct could be based upon a series, or an "accumulation," of negligent acts creating a probability of harm so great that the failure to act in the face of that harm constitutes reckless disregard. *Water Quality Ins. Syndicate v. United States*, 522 F. Supp.2d 220, 228-30 (D.D.C. 2007), citing *In re Tug Ocean Prince*, 584 F.2d 1151 (2d Cir. 1978) (rejecting argument that "'willful misconduct' must be a single act 'intentionally done' and that a series of negligent acts can never constitute willful misconduct"). The NPFC defines gross negligence as "an extreme departure from the care required under the circumstances or a failure to exercise even slight care." *Kuroshima Shipping S.A. Act of God Defense and Limit of Liability Analysis*, 2003 AMC 1681, 1693 (2003).

155 The NPFC acknowledges that "[t]errorism or other criminal acts that cause an oil spill MAY present a liability defense" (emphasis in original). NPFC, *NPFC User Reference Guide (eURG)*, Appendix B, *FOSC Funding Information for Oil Spills and Hazardous Materials Releases* (April 2003) (available at http://uscg.mil/npfc/URG/default.asp). For a review of issues relating to terrorism, *see* 77 *Tul. Law Rev.* 2003, featuring the presentations from a symposium of the Admiralty Law Institute entitled *Confused Seas: Admiralty Law in the Wake of Terrorism*.

156 *United States v. Shell Oil Co.*, 841 F. Supp. 962, 971 (C.D. Cal. 1993), *aff'd*, 294 F.3d 1045 (9th Cir. 2002), *cert. denied*, 537 U.S. 1147 (2003).

157 *Id.* at 972 (internal citations omitted).

158 OPA §1002; 33 U.S.C. §2702(d).

159 *See Buffalo Marine Servs. Inc. v. United States*, 663 F.3d 750, 754-57, 759 (5th Cir. 2011) (the Coast Guard's determination that a contractual relationship existed between the party who caused the spill, a bunker supplier and the tanker was entitled to deference). *See also National Shipping Co. of Saudi Arabia v. Moran Mid-Atlantic Corp.*, 924 F. Supp. 1436, 1446, n.4 (E.D. Va. 1996), *aff'd*, 122 F.3d 1062 (4th Cir. 1997), *cert. denied*, 523 U.S. 1021 (1998) ("[defendant] Moran is not a responsible party, and, because it was operating under a contractual relationship with NSCSA, it may not be treated as a responsible party"). *See also In re Alex C Corp.*, 2003 AMC 256, 2003 WL 203078, *7 (D. Mass. Jan. 30, 2003) ("[§2702](d)(1) and (d)(2) refer to the same subset of third parties": those not in contractual privity with the RP).

160 In the case of a discharge, or the substantial threat of a discharge, of oil from a land-based facility, successfully invoking a third-party-liability defense also requires proving that before acquiring the real property on which the facility is located, the RP made *all appropriate inquiries* into the property's previous ownership and uses—in accordance with generally accepted good commercial and customary standards and practices—to determine the presence or likely presence of oil. *See* 33 U.S.C. §2703(d)(4)(A)(i). On

January 14, 2008, the USCG issued regulations prescribing standards and practices for conducting all appropriate inquiries. 73 Fed. Reg. 2146 (Jan. 14, 2008); 33 C.F.R. §§137.1 *et seq.* The regulations are consistent with those promulgated by the Environmental Protection Agency pursuant to nearly identical provisions in CERCLA. *See* 70 Fed. Reg. 66070 (Nov. 1, 2005); 40 C.F.R. §§312.1 *et seq.* Prospective landowners who have complied already with ASTM International E 1527-13 (2014), "Standard Practice for Environmental Site Assessments: Phase I Environmental Site Assessment Process"—the current industry standard defining good commercial and customary practice in the United States for conducting an environmental site assessment of a parcel of commercial real estate with respect to oil under OPA and hazardous substances under CERCLA—will be in compliance with the regulations.

[161] *See Gatlin Oil Co. v. U.S.*, 169 F.3d 207 (4th Cir. 1999). In *Gatlin*, the USCG had determined that Gatlin Oil, which was entitled to a complete defense because a vandal had caused the discharge, could recoup only $6,959 from the Fund. Gatlin Oil sought $850,000 in damages it incurred largely from a fire that erupted as a result of the spill. The court of appeals reversed the District Court and upheld the USCG's determination of the limited amount of damages to be awarded to Gatlin Oil.

[162] The USCG reported that between fiscal years 1992 and 2004, there were only seven instances of claims paid from the Fund in cases where affirmative defenses had been successfully asserted. OPA Report, *supra* note 5, at 12.

[163] *See, supra* section 5.2.2.

[164] *Delaware River Oil Spill: Hearing on the Delaware River Oil Spill Before the Subcommittee on U.S. Coast Guard and Maritime Transportation*, 109th Cong. (2005).

[165] *In re Frescati Shipping Co., Ltd.*, No. 05-CV-00305-JF, 2011 WL 1436878 (E.D. PA April 12, 2011).

[166] *In re Frescati Shipping Co., Ltd.*, 718 F.3d 184 (3d Cir. 2013), as amended (June 6, 2013), as amended (June 28, 2013), as amended on denial of reh'g and reh'g en banc (July 12, 2013).

[167] Which order on remand had not yet issued at the time of publication.

[168] OPA §1004; 33 U.S.C. §2704.

[169] OPA §1004; 33 U.S.C. §2704(c)(1). *See, supra* note 155. *See also, e.g., Bean Dredging, LLC v. United States*, 699 F. Supp.2d 118 (D.D.C. 2010) (reviewing the National Pollution Funds Center's determination that an RP was not entitled to limit its liability because it violated an applicable federal operating regulation); *Water Quality Ins. Syndicate v. United States*, 632 F. Supp.2d 108 (D. Mass. 2009) (reviewing NPFC's denial of limitation because an employee of an RP was grossly negligent).

[170] OPA §1004; 33 U.S.C. §2704(c)(2).

[171] Pub. L. No. 109-241 (July 11, 2006), codified at 33 U.S.C. §1321(f)(1).

[172] *Id.*

[173] Vessels with double sides only, or with a double bottom only, are considered single-hull vessels under the law. 33 U.S.C. §2704 (a)(1)(A).

[174] Pursuant to the president's delegated authority to adjust OPA's liability limits for inflation, *see, infra* section 7.3 and note 182, the USCG promulgated regulations that increase, for vessels and deepwater ports, the limits appearing in OPA §1004 (33 U.S.C. §2704). *See* 33 C.F.R. §138.230, as amended at 80 Fed. Reg. 72342 (Nov. 19, 2015). The regulations also "clarify" that OPA's single-hull liability limits apply only to a vessel "constructed or adapted to carry, or that carries, *oil* in bulk as cargo or cargo residue." 33 C.F.R. §138.220(b) (emphasis added). *See also* 74 Fed. Reg. 31357, 31364-65 (July 1, 2009) ("the single-hull category of OPA 90 is concerned with those vessels that were the focus of Congressional concern [in enacting DRPA], *i.e.*, oil cargo tank vessels"; "[i]t is this category of tank vessel that Congress was concerned with as presenting a greater threat of oil pollution, and thereby deserving of phase-out regulation [i.e., 46 U.S.C. §3703a and 33 C.F.R. Part 157] and higher limits of liability"). Thus, notwithstanding OPA's definition of "tank vessel," a single-hull tanker strictly designed and used for transporting hazardous material is entitled to the same liability limitation as a double-hull oil tanker. *See* OPA §1001(34); 33 U.S.C. §2701(34). Vessels carrying nonpetroleum, edible oils are considered *other vessels*,

subject to the lesser limits of liability and corresponding lesser requirements for demonstrating evidence of financial responsibility. *See* Edible Oil Regulatory Reform Act, Pub. L. No. 104-55 (Jan. 4, 1995), amending 33 U.S.C. §§2704(a)(1), 2716(a); *see also* 80 Fed. Reg. 72342 (Nov. 19, 2015) (clarifying applicability of the "other vessel" limits of liability to edible oil tank vessels and oil spill response vessels).

175 The USCG has concluded that only one deepwater port currently operating is subject to OPA—the Louisiana Offshore Oil Port (LOOP). *See* 74 Fed. Reg. 31357, 31365 (July 1, 2009). The USCG adjusted LOOP's facility-specific limit, which had not changed since it was established by regulation on August 4, 1995, from $62 million to $96,366,600. *See* 33 C.F.R. §138.230(b)(2)(i). *See also* 80 Fed. Reg. 72342 (Nov. 19, 2015).

176 BP waived this $75 million statutory limit in *Deepwater Horizon* stating that "BP consistently has said it would pay all legitimate claims, regardless of the OPA statutory limit of liability." *In re: Oil Spill by the Oil Rig "Deepwater Horizon" in the Gulf of Mexico, on April 20, 2010*, No. 2:10-md-02179-CJB-SS, Doc. No. 559 (E.D. La. Oct. 18, 2010).

177 OPA §1002; 33 U.S.C. §2702(d). It remains unsettled as to which third parties the liability limits apply. *Compare National Shipping Co. of Saudia Arabia, supra* note 159, at 1446–47 (§2702(d)(2)(A) applies to a third party in contractual privity with the RP), *with In re Alex C Corp.*, 2010 WL 4292328 (D. Mass. Nov. 1, 2010), at *10–13 ("subsections 2702(d)(1) and 2702(d)(2) are limited to non-contractual third parties").

178 *See, supra* section 7.2.

179 OPA §1004; 33 U.S.C. §2704(d). President Barack Obama issued an Executive Order delegating this authority to adjust the limits of liability to the Secretary of the department in which the Coast Guard is operating. *See, supra* note 3; *see also* Exec. Order—Amendments to Exec. Order No. 12,777 (March 15, 2013).

180 *Id.* at §2704(d)(4).

181 *See* 74 Fed. Reg. 31357 (July 1, 2009), as confirmed at 75 Fed. Reg. 750 (Jan. 6, 2010). *See also* 33 C.F.R. §138.240 ("Procedure for updating limits of liability to reflect significant increases in the Consumer Price Index (Annual CPI–U) and statutory changes").

182 OPA §1007; 33 U.S.C. §2707.

183 OPA §1008; 33 U.S.C. §§2708, 2713.

184 OPA §1009; 33 U.S.C. §2709. *See Texas Trading and Transp., Inc. v. Laine Construction Co., Inc.*, 1998 U.S. Dist. LEXIS 18669 (E.D. La. Nov. 18, 1998). In *Texas Trading*, the court found no right to contribution because the plaintiff never alleged that it was an RP, a premise to contribution under OPA.

185 OPA §1010; 33 U.S.C. §2710.

186 OPA §9001; 26 U.S.C. §9509.

187 33 U.S.C. §2718(b).

188 Pub. L. 110-343, Div. B, Title IV, §405, 122 Stat. 3860-61 (Oct. 3, 2008) ("Energy Improvement and Extension Act of 2008"); Pub. L. 109-58, Title XIII, §1361 (Aug. 8, 2005) ("Energy Policy Act of 2005"). The tax increases to nine cents a barrel after December 31, 2016. The OSLTF financing rate (i.e., the number of cents per barrel) will not apply after December 31, 2017 unless Congress renews or otherwise amends the financing rate. 26 U.S.C. §§4611(c)(2)(B)(ii) & 4611(f)(2). The Energy Improvement and Extension Act of 2008 also removed the Fund's ceiling, which was capped originally at $1 billion and increased to $2.7 billion by the Energy Policy Act of 2005.

189 *See* U.S. Dep't. of Homeland Sec., USCG Report on the Implementation of the Oil Pollution Act of 1990, at 28–34 (2005), illustrating graphically the downward trend in oil pollution incidents for 1992–2004.

190 33 U.S.C. §2715(c).

191 26 U.S.C. §9509(c)(2)(A)(i).

192 *Id.* at §9509(c)(2)(A)(ii).

193 OPA §1012; 33 U.S.C. §2712(d), (e). Interim final rules regarding access to the Fund by state officials were issued on November 13, 1992. *See* 57 Fed. Reg. 53969 (Nov. 13, 1992).

194 The OSLTF performed such a role after a mystery oil spill was discovered in Fort Lauderdale, Florida, on the morning of August 8, 2000. *See* 67 Fed. Reg. 59827 (Sept. 24, 2002).

195 OPA §1013; 33 U.S.C. §2713. A court denied a plaintiff insurance company's claim that its policy issued to a defendant oil company excluded recovery for costs incurred for the remediation of property following a spill. *See Celina Mutual Ins. Co. v. Marathon Oil Co.*, 2000 Ohio App. LEXIS 2453 (Ohio Ct. App. June 8, 2000). The insurance company asserted the recovery was not covered because its policy excluded recovery for any loss arising out of any "request, demand or order that any insured . . . test for, monitor, clean up, remove, contain, treat, detoxify or neutralize, or in any way respond to, or assess the effects of pollutants." *Id.* at *8–*9. The court declined to label the requirements pursuant to OPA as a " 'request, demand or order.' " *Id.* at *19. OPA "does not require a response it merely mandates a procedural framework for emergency response." *Id.* at *18.

196 57 Fed. Reg. 36316 (Aug. 12, 1992); 33 C.F.R. §§136.1 *et seq.*

197 *See* www.nrc.uscg.mil.

198 OPA §1014; 33 U.S.C. §2714.

199 57 Fed. Reg. 36316 (Aug. 12, 1992); 33 C.F.R. §§136.309 *et seq.*

200 The NPFC's website provides guidance on filing claims. *See* National Pollution Funds Center Oil Spill Claims page, available at http://www.uscg.mil/npfc/Claims/default.asp.

201 OPA §1013; 33 U.S.C. §2713.

202 *Boca Ciega Hotel, Inc. v. Bouchard Transp. Co., Inc.*, 51 F.3d 235 (11th Cir. 1995); *Russo v. M/T Dubai Star*, 2010 WL 1753187 (N.D. Cal. Apr. 29, 2010); *Gabarick v. Laurin Maritime (America) Inc.*, 2009 AMC 1004, 2009 WL 102549 (E.D. La. Jan. 12, 2009); *Abundiz v. Explorer Pipeline Co.*, 2003 WL 23096018 (N.D. Tex. Nov. 25, 2003); *LeBoeuf v. Texaco*, 9 F. Supp.2d 661 (E.D. La. 1998); *Johnson v. Colonial Pipeline Co.*, 830 F. Supp. 309 (E.D. Va. 1993). *But see Eastman v. Coffeyville Res. Ref. & Mktg.*, LLC, 2010 U.S. Dist. LEXIS 123366 (D. Kan. Nov. 19, 2010) (Plaintiffs properly presented their OPA claim by 1) faxing the defendant a "Notice of [OPA] Claim"; 2) filing, the following day, a complaint alleging only a nuisance claim but stating an intent to file an OPA claim after the 90-day period expired; and 3) moving to amend their complaint to add an OPA claim after the 90-day period expired without a response from the defendant); *United States v. M/V Cosco Busan*, 557 F. Supp.2d 1058 (N.D. Cal. 2008) (the United States, a state, or an Indian tribe is not required to present its claims for removal costs and damages to RPs before suing those parties); *Marathon Pipe Line Co. v. LaRoche Indus. Inc.*, 944 F. Supp. 476 (E.D. La. 1996) (§2713 presentation requirement does not apply to claims by an RP against allegedly sole-cause third party).

203 In *Targa Midstream Servs. LTD v. K-SEA Transp. Partners, L.P.*, 2006 U.S. Dist. LEXIS 64078 (S.D. Tex. Apr. 20, 2006) the District Court addressed the issue of whether the compulsory counterclaim requirements of Federal Rule of Civil Procedure 13(a) conflicted with the strict liability and compensation regimes of OPA in determining whether to grant the barge owner's, K-SEA, motion for leave or alternative motion to stay. In *Targa*, a barge hit unmarked submerged platform debris resulting from Hurricane Rita and discharged approximately 1 [*sic*—2] million gallons of oil into the Gulf of Mexico. *Targa*, 2006 U.S. Dist. LEXIS at *3. Targa, the platform owner, first sued K-SEA, the barge operator, for adding costs to its debris removal. Rule FRCP 13(a) required K-SEA to file its counter claim against the platform operators even though K-SEA was seeking to recover removal costs and damages from the OSLTF, asserting that the spill was caused by the failure of the platform owner to properly mark the platform debris. This created two problems. First, the pendency of the claim against *Targa* brought under compulsion of FRCP 13(a) could preclude recovery by K-SEA from the OSLTF under 33 U.S.C. §2713(b)(2). Second, the Fund was not party to the litigation, meaning that any rights the Fund might have under subrogation (by paying K-SEA for incurred removal costs and damages) would be extinguished by a

judicial resolution of the platform operator's liability to K-SEA. *Id.* at *6. The court denied K-SEA's motion because it failed to show that a stay was justified.

[204] For example, the owners of the M/T *Athos I* incurred cleanup costs over $100 million, which far exceeds their financial obligations under OPA. *See Athos I* Plan, *supra* note 126, at ix and 1. Any third-party claims were subsequently required to be submitted directly to the OSLTF. Press Release, National Pollution Funds Center, Delaware River Oil Spill Update #21 (Feb. 16, 2005) (available at https://casedocuments.darrp.noaa.gov/northeast/athos/pdf/USCG%202005a.pdf).

[205] 57 Fed. Reg. 36316 (Aug. 12, 1992); 33 C.F.R. §136.103.

[206] 33 U.S.C. §2717(f)(1). In *Nguyen v. Am. Commercial Lines L.L.C.*, 805 F.3d 134 (5th Cir. 2015), as revised (Nov. 13, 2015), the Fifth Circuit determined that OPA's 90-day waiting period for filing suit after the presentment of claims to the RP was independent of OPA's three-year limitations period. The Court noted that the "statutory language of the OPA clearly requires that the claimants comply with both the 90-day waiting period and the three-year period of limitations. Therefore, claimants may not ignore the 90-day waiting period simply because the period of limitations is about to expire." *Id.* at 144. Thus, a claimant must present its claims for damages to the RP at least 90 days before the end of OPA's three-year limitations period in order to satisfy both the 90-day presentment requirement and also be capable of satisfying the statute of limitations.

[207] OPA §1012; 33 U.S.C. §2712(h).

[208] *See* discussion of *Green Atlas Shipping SA v. United States*, 306 F. Supp.2d 974 (D. Or. 2003), *supra* note 40.

[209] OPA §1016; 33 U.S.C. §2716(a), as amended by Pub. L. 111-281, Title VII, §712, 124 Stat. 2988 (10/15/2010). *See also* 33 C.F.R. §138.80(f)(1) ("The applicable amount [of financial responsibility] under OPA 90 is equal to the applicable vessel limit of liability, which is determined as provided in [138.220(a)(1)] of this part"). On September 17, 2008, the USCG issued a final rule amending 33 C.F.R. Part 138. The new rule: (1) increased the amounts of financial responsibility that must be demonstrated to match increases in liability limits as part of the DRPA; and (2) divided Part 138 into two subparts—subpart A includes all of the former 33 C.F.R. Part 138 pertaining to vessel financial responsibility requirements; subpart B sets forth the limits of liability for vessels and deepwater ports. *See* 73 Fed. Reg. 53691 (Sept. 17, 2008). For an enumeration of limits of liability, *see supra* section 7.2. In *U.S. v. Inter-Bay Towing Co.*, 2005 U.S. Dist. LEXIS 41974 (S.D. Tex. Aug. 8, 2005) the Southern District of Texas held that, for purposes of liability as a guarantor, "a Certificate of Insurance is *not* a recognized guarantee of financial responsibility." 2005 U.S. Dist. LEXIS, at *17.

[210] 33 U.S.C. §2716(a).

[211] 33 U.S.C. §§2704 (a)(3)-(4).

[212] 33 U.S.C. §2704(d)(2)(C).

[213] 33 U.S.C. §2716(c)(1)(D).

[214] OPA §1016; 33 U.S.C. §2716(e).

[215] *Id.*

[216] OPA §1001; 33 U.S.C. §2701(13).

[217] HR. Conf. Rep. No. 101-653 at 119 (1990) (OPA Conf. Rep.).

[218] OPA §1016; 33 U.S.C. §2716(a).

[219] 61 Fed. Reg. 9264 (Mar. 7, 1996); 33 C.F.R. §§138.10 *et seq.*

[220] 33 C.F.R. §138.80.

[221] OPA §1016; 33 U.S.C. §2716(f)(1)(c). Guarantors successfully invoking this defense may claim directly against the Fund for removal costs and damages paid, but not insured, by them. *See Water Quality Ins. Syndicate, supra* note 169, at 230-32 (rejecting the government's argument that a guarantor may pursue only claims acquired by subrogation).

[222] 33 C.F.R. §138.80(d).

223 *Id.* at §138.80(c).

224 *Net worth* means the amount of all assets located in the United States minus all liabilities anywhere in the world. 33 C.F.R. §138.80(b)(3).

225 *Working capital* means the amount of current assets located in the United States less all current liabilities anywhere in the world. 33 C.F.R. §138.80(b)(3).

226 63 Fed. Reg. 42699 (Aug. 11, 1998); 30 C.F.R. §§253.1 *et seq.*

227 OPA §1016; 33 U.S.C. §2716(c)(1)(B).

228 OPA §1015; 33 U.S.C. §2715. *See Texas Trading and Transp., Inc. v. Laine Construction Co., Inc.*, 1998 U.S. Dist. LEXIS 18669 (E.D. La. Nov. 18, 1998). As with the plaintiff's claim for contribution, *see, supra* note 184, the court similarly found no right of subrogation, as there had been no allegation that the plaintiff had ever paid out money to any claimant. *See id.* at *14.

229 OPA §1012; 33 U.S.C. §2712(f).

230 A claimant seeking compensation from the Fund must be able to supply the government with *all* of its subrogation rights against an RP, not just those rights the claimant still possesses at the time of payment of the claim. *See Kenan Transp. Co. v. U.S. Coast Guard*, 2006 WL 1455658 (N.D. Ga. May 19, 2006) (upholding government's decision to refuse plaintiff's reimbursement claim where plaintiff assigned to an insurance company its rights to sue for property damages and other claims, including cleanup and removal costs, resulting from a land-based oil spill), *aff'd*, 2006 WL 3749570 (11th Cir. Dec. 21, 2006). *See also Rick Franklin Corp. v. U.S. Dept. of Homeland Sec.*, 2008 WL 337978 (D. Or. Feb. 4, 2008) (upholding government's decision to refuse plaintiff's reimbursement claim where plaintiff executed, as part of a settlement agreement, a covenant not to sue and enforce judgment against the RP).

231 OPA §1015; 33 U.S.C. §2715.

232 Where a distinction between the position of the government as a claimant and that of a private party is intended, OPA clearly provides for it. For example, in 33 U.S.C. §2702, which provides for the recovery of removal costs, private parties must show that their removal efforts are consistent with the NCP, whereas governmental claimants need not.

233 OPA §1017; 33 U.S.C. §2717.

234 *Id.* at §2717(a).

235 *Id.* at §2717(f). If the applicable statute of limitations has run, the federal government may resort to collecting removal costs owed by RPs using the administrative offset mechanism of the Debt Collection Improvement Act of 1996 (DCIA), 31 U.S.C. §§3701-33. *See, e.g., Red River Farms v. United States*, 2009 WL 2983195 (D. Ariz. Sept. 17, 2009).

236 OPA §1018; 33 U.S.C. §2718(c).

237 *United States v. Locke*, 529 U.S. 89, 120 S. Ct. 1135 (2000). *See, infra* section 16.3, for a more complete discussion.

238 *Id.* at 1146.

239 OPA §1019; 33 U.S.C. §2719.

240 42 U.S.C. §§6901-6992k.

241 OPA §1018; 33 U.S.C. §2718(d).

242 *Id.* at §2718(c). *See United States v. M/V Cosco Busan*, 557 F. Supp.2d 1058, 1063 (N.D. Cal. 2008) ("OPA contains an unambiguous savings clause that expressly preserves the authority of the United States to impose liability pursuant to statutes other than OPA"). *See also, e.g., United States v. Egan Marine Corp.*, 2009 AMC 1178, 2009 WL 855964 (N.D. Ill. Mar. 30, 2009) (United States could proceed against the RP for claims under the Rivers and Harbors Act [33 U.S.C. §403] and the Refuse Act [33 U.S.C. §407], in addition to its OPA claims).

243 *Locke*, 529 U.S. at 107, citing *Ray v. Atlantic Richfield Co.*, 435 U.S. 151, 98 S. Ct. 988 (1978), and OPA Conf. Rep., *supra* note 217, at 122 (1990). In the *Ray* case, the Court struck down Washington State's tanker construction regulations and found them preempted by the federal tanker safety regime.

[244] Wash. Rev. Code 88.46.040(3) (1994); the Washington State Office of Marine Safety issued the regulations—Wash. Admin. Code 317-21-130 *et seq.* (1999)—for tanker design, equipment, reporting and operating requirements that were challenged by Intertanko.

[245] *Int'l Ass'n of Indep. Tanker Owners (Intertanko) v. Lowry*, 947 F. Supp. 1484 (W.D. Wash. 1996), *aff'd in part and rev'd in part, remanded, International Ass'n of Indep. Tanker Owners v. Locke*, 148 F.3d 1053 (9th Cir. 1998).

[246] *Int'l Ass'n of Indep. Tanker Owners (Intertanko) v. Locke*, 159 F. 3d 1220 (9th Cir. 1998), *rev'd, remanded sub nom, United States v. Locke*, 529 U.S. 89 (2000).

[247] *Id.* at 1221.

[248] *Locke*, 529 U.S. at 116-117.

[249] *Id.* at 106.

[250] *Id.* at 111.

[251] *Id.* at 116.

[252] 33 U.S.C. §§1221 *et seq.*

[253] *Locke*, 529 U.S. at 116.

[254] *See Washington State Repeals Tank Vessel Rules*, Oil Spill Intelligence Report (Cutter Information Corp., Arlington, MA), Sept. 7, 2000, at 1.

[255] Mass. St. 2004, c. 251.

[256] 69 Fed. Reg. 206, 62430 (Oct. 26, 2004).

[257] *United States v. Massachusetts*, 724 F. Supp.2d 170, 173 (D. Mass. 2010).

[258] Ports & Waterways Safety Act, 33 U.S.C. §§1221-1232.

[259] *United States v. Massachusetts*, 440 F. Supp.2d 24 (D. Mass. 2006).

[260] *Id.* at 48.

[261] *United States v. Massachusetts*, 493 F.3d 1, 4 (1st Cir. 2007).

[262] *Id.* at 5.

[263] The First Circuit rejected the District Court's conclusion that the vessel manning provisions were preempted under Title II of the PWSA alone; the District Court should have considered whether the conflict preemption principles of Title I of the PWSA also control, in which case the court must analyze the five factors announced in *Locke* for conducting an inquiry into the "overlap" between Title I "conflict" preemption and Title II "field" preemption. *See id.* at 11–14. Concerning the tug escort provisions, the First Circuit vacated the injunction to give the parties an opportunity to address "the questions of whether the Coast Guard sufficiently expressed a clear intent to preempt the [provisions], and whether, if so, the Coast Guard's position is clearly inconsistent with congressional intent." *Id.* at 19 (citations omitted). With respect to the financial assurance requirements, the First Circuit held that the factual record had not been developed adequately to determine whether the requirements would have an effect significant enough to constitute the sort of indirect regulation that would "intrude impermissibly on the Coast Guard's exclusive authority under Title II [of the PWSA]." *Id.* at 24–25.

[264] *See United States v. Massachusetts*, 2010 WL 1345018, at *3 (D. Mass. Mar. 31, 2010). *See also* 72 Fed. Reg. 50052 (Aug. 30, 2007) (final rule).

[265] *United States v. Massachusetts*, 2010 WL 1345018, at *2 (D. Mass. Mar. 31, 2010) ("The decisive change in the tides controlling this litigation . . . was the enactment of the Final Rule by the Coast Guard, leaving no ambiguity regarding the intention to preempt [the Massachusetts statute]").

[266] 42 U.S.C. §§4321-4347.

[267] *United States v. Massachusetts*, 644 F.3d 26 (1st Cir. 2011).

[268] OPA §2002.

[269] *Id.* at §2003.

[270] *Id.* at §2004.

271 *Id.* at §2001.

272 *See, supra* section 2.0, for a full discussion.

273 OPA §3001.

274 For example, in February 2000, the United States notified the International Maritime Organization (IMO) that the revised Regulation 13G of the International Convention for the Prevention of Pollution from Ships (MARPOL 73/78) would not enter into force in the United States without the express approval of the U.S. government. Furthermore, in the *Federal Register* comments, the USCG stated that "the U.S. maintains that the Oil Pollution Act of 1990 (OPA 90) continues to be the more stringent requirement." 67 Fed. Reg. 7443 (Feb. 19, 2002).

275 OPA §§3002-3005.

276 OPA §4101; 46 U.S.C. §7101. Final rules were issued at 60 Fed. Reg. 65478 (Dec. 19, 1995). Additional regulations making drug and alcohol testing procedures more uniform in the transportation industry were promulgated by the secretary of the Department of Transportation on December 19, 2000, and went into effect on August 1, 2001. 65 Fed. Reg. 79462 (Dec. 19, 2000); 49 C.F.R. §§40.1 *et seq.*

277 OPA §4103; 46 U.S.C. §§7703, 7704. Final Rules were issued at 60 Fed. Reg. 4522 (Jan. 23, 1995).

278 OPA §4102(a)–(c); 46 U.S.C. §§7106, 7107, and 7302(f), as amended by Pub. L. 111-281, Title VI, §614(a)–(c), 124 Stat. 2970-71 (Oct. 15, 2010).

279 59 Fed. Reg. 49294 (Sept. 27, 1994); 46 C.F.R. §§10.101, as amended at 74 Fed. Reg. 11196 (Mar. 16, 2009) ("Consolidation of Merchant Mariner Qualification Credentials").

280 OPA §4104; 46 U.S.C. §8101.

281 *See* International Convention on Standards of Training, Certification and Watchkeeping for Seafarers, 1978, as amended in 1995, International Maritime Organization, London, 1996, available at: http://www .dma.dk/themes/LNGinfrastructureproject/Documents/IMO/STCW%20Convention.pdf. For more information, *see*: http://www.imo.org/en/OurWork/HumanElement/TrainingCertification/Pages/STCW -Convention.aspx.

282 *See* 59 Fed. Reg. 48845-02 (Sept. 23, 1994) for the notice of public meeting. No rules have been proposed since.

283 OPA §4106; 46 U.S.C. §9101(a).

284 OPA §4114; 46 U.S.C. §8101.

285 58 Fed. Reg. 27628 (May 10, 1993).

286 OPA §4114(b); 46 U.S.C. §8104.

287 The USCG amended its regulations governing marine casualty reporting requirements by adding "significant harm to the environment" as a reportable marine casualty and by requiring certain foreign flag vessels to report marine casualties that occur in waters subject to U.S. jurisdiction but beyond U.S. navigable waters when those casualties involve material damage affecting the seaworthiness or efficiency of the vessel, or significant harm to the environment. 70 Fed. Reg. 74669 (Dec. 16, 2005).

288 OPA §4106(b); 46 U.S.C. §6101.

289 OPA §4116; 46 U.S.C. §§8502 and 3703, as amended by Pub. L. 111-281, Title VII, §711(b), 124 Stat. 2981 (Oct. 15, 2010). The U.S. Circuit Court of Appeals for the District of Columbia rejected an effort by two environmental groups to compel the USCG to extend the dual-tug escort requirements for single-hull tank vessels to waters beyond the three areas that were specifically identified in the statute. *See In Re: Bluewater Network*, 234 F.3d 1305, 1310 (D.C. Cir. 2000). *See also, infra* note 297.

290 59 Fed. Reg. 42962 (Aug. 19, 1994); 33 C.F.R. §§168.01 *et seq.*

291 OPA §4108; 46 U.S.C. §9302. *See* OPA Conf. Rep., *supra* note 217, at 135–36.

292 The U.S. Court of Appeals for the Ninth Circuit ruled that Section 5007 of OPA (33 U.S.C. §2737), which bans from the waters of Prince William Sound any vessel that spilled more than 1 million gallons of oil into the marine environment after March 22, 1989, is constitutional. *SeaRiver Maritime Fin. Holdings v. Mineta*, 309 F.3d 662 (9th Cir. 2002).

293 78 Fed. Reg. 50335-02 (Aug. 19, 2013), amending 33 C.F.R. §§168.01, 168.05, and 168.50.

294 79 Fed. Reg. 33864 (June 13, 2014).

295 OPA §4107; 33 U.S.C. §1223.

296 59 Fed. Reg. 36316 (July 15, 1994); 33 C.F.R. Pts. 1, 26, 160, 161, 162, 164, and 165.

297 The U.S. Court of Appeals for the District of Columbia took the USCG to task for failing to issue regulations requiring tank vessels to install tank level and pressure monitoring devices and directed the agency to undertake a prompt rulemaking. *See In Re: Bluewater Network*, 234 F.3d 1305 (D.C. Cir. 2000). After much study, the USCG concluded that existing technology did not meet its internal standards for effective leak detection. In 1997, the USCG issued a temporary rule and deferred implementation until effective technology became available that would meet its standards. *Id.* at 1309. The temporary rule expired on April 29, 1999, without the technology coming into existence and without the issuance of standards. Two environmental groups petitioned the court of appeals to compel the USCG to issue the requirements. The court concluded that the agency was required to issue compliance standards and installation standards: "[T]he agency cannot avoid these commands simply by pointing to too-stringent compliance standards that have expired." *Id.* at 1315. On October 1, 2001, the USCG made a preliminary effort to comply with the court of appeals' decision by publishing a notice of proposed rulemaking in the *Federal Register*. *See* 66 Fed. Reg. 49877 (Oct. 1, 2001). The notice contained eight possible options depicting various vessel types and phase-in dates. The notice also contained a cost-benefit analysis contrasting the impact of the proposed rules with other rules promulgated by the USCG in accordance with the OPA. Between publication of the final rule and June 2005, no devices meeting the performance criteria had been submitted. As a result, Section 4110 of OPA was amended to allow the USCG discretion and to mandate that the USCG study leak detection alternatives. Therefore, the rules published in 33 C.F.R. Pts. 155 and 156 that contain requirements for the use of tank level and pressure monitoring devices were suspended for three years. 70 Fed. Reg. 41614 (July 20, 2005). On May 5, 2008, the USCG issued a final rule suspending the tank level and pressure monitoring devices regulations for an additional three years, until July 21, 2008. The extension was made necessary by a continuing lack of devices on the market capable of meeting the regulatory requirements. 73 Fed. Reg. 24497-02 (May 5, 2008). Then, on June 30, 2008, the USCG published notice of proposed rulemaking entitled "Tank Level or Pressure Monitoring Devices on Single-Hull Tank Ships and Single-Hull Tank Barges Carrying Oil or Oil Residue as Cargo." 73 Fed. Reg. 36825 (June 30, 2008). In response, the USCG received two letters commenting on the proposed rule, both of which supported the USCG's decision to remove the tank level or pressure monitoring device regulations because of a continuing lack of devices on the market. 73 Fed. Reg. 79314-01 (Dec. 29, 2008).

298 59 Fed. Reg. 53286 (Oct. 21, 1994); 33 C.F.R. Pts. 155 and 156.

299 OPA §4118; 33 U.S.C. §1203. *See* 33 C.F.R. §§26.01 *et seq.*

300 OPA §4111; 46 U.S.C. §3703.

301 In a related matter in 1998, the National Transportation Safety Board (NTSB) issued its annual report to Congress in which it recommended that the USCG develop mitigation regulations for tug-barge systems and also issue additional safety requirements for the vessel towing industry. *See* www.ntsb.gov/about/Documents/spc0002.pdf. The recommendations were the result of the NTSB's investigation of a 1996 fire aboard the tug *Scandia* and the subsequent grounding of the barge *North Cape*, which resulted in a spill of approximately 828,000 gallons of No. 2 home heating oil into Block Island Sound off the coast of Rhode Island (*see, supra* section 5.2.1). The NTSB found that a lack of adequate USCG and industry standards addressing towing vessel safety contributed to the accident. *See, supra* section 5.2.1.

302 OPA §4115; 46 U.S.C. §3703a. Maritrans Inc. challenged the constitutionality of the mandatory phase-out of its single-hull tank barges. In December 2001, the federal claims court evaluated the takings argument put forward by Maritrans and concluded that OPA did not result in a taking of property and that Maritrans was able to derive value from its single-hull vessels through the use, sale or retrofitting of others during the phase-out period. *Maritrans, Inc. v. U.S.*, 51 Fed. Cl. 277 (2001).

[303] In 1997, Congress fixed the tonnage of tank vessels effective July 1, 1997, effectively closing a loophole that allowed vessels to reduce their registered tonnage capacity in order to extend certain single-hull phase-out deadlines under OPA. *See* National Defense Authorization Act for Fiscal Year 1998, Pub. L. 105-85, §3606 (Nov. 18, 1997); 46 U.S.C. §3703a(e)(1) ("the gross tonnage of a vessel shall be the gross tonnage that *would have been* recognized by the Secretary on July 1, 1997, as the tonnage measured under [46 U.S.C. §14502], or as an alternate tonnage measured under [46 U.S.C. §14302] as prescribed by the Secretary under [46 U.S.C. §14104]") (emphasis added). In 2004, Hornbeck Offshore Transportation LLC brought suit, under the Administrative Procedure Act, to challenge the USCG's interpretation and application of §3703a(e)(1). *See Hornbeck Offshore Transp., LLC v. U.S. Coast Guard*, 424 F. Supp.2d 37 (D.D.C. 2006). Siding with Hornbeck, the court invalidated the USCG's interpretation of the statute as setting a vessel's gross tonnage at the gross tonnage that *was* in fact recognized by the secretary on July 1, 1997. Looking to the statute's plain language, particularly the phrase "would have been recognized," the court concluded that §3703a(e)(1) "fixes the determination of the tonnage on a hypothetical measurement of a particular vessel on the specified date—July 1, 1997—under the optional [46 U.S.C. §14502 or §14302] measurement systems. . . . Congress intended that either measurement system could be applied to [a vessel] as it existed on July 1, 1997." *Id.* at 51.

[304] 60 Fed. Reg. 13318 (Mar. 10, 1995); 33 C.F.R. Pts. 155 and 157; 46 C.F.R. Pts. 30, 32, 70, 90, and 172.

[305] NVIC No. 2-90, available at http://www.uscg.mil/hq/cg5/nvic/1990s.asp.

[306] The USCG established four such lightering zones in the Gulf of Mexico. *See* 60 Fed. Reg. 45,006 (Aug. 29, 1995); 33 C.F.R. §156.300.

[307] 65 Fed. Reg. 39260 (June 23, 2000).

[308] OPA §4115(b); 46 U.S.C. §3703a (note).

[309] 59 Fed. Reg. 40186 (Aug. 5, 1994).

[310] 61 Fed. Reg. 39770 (July 30, 1996). On November 27, 1996, the USCG announced the suspension of the portion of this rule which required owner notification of a vessel's under-keel clearance. *See* 61 Fed. Reg. 60189 (Nov. 27, 1996).

[311] OPA §4115(e); 46 U.S.C. §3703a (note). A final regulation regarding structural measures to prevent spills was promulgated on January 10, 1997. 62 Fed. Reg. 1622. No structural measures were imposed by the rule because the USCG determined that there were no interim structural measures that were both technologically and economically feasible for existing tank vessels without double hulls.

[312] In response to the *North Cape* spill off Rhode Island, the USCG issued a final rule that requires emergency measures for single-hull, non-self-propelled tank vessels or the vessel towing it. 65 Fed. Reg. 31806 (May 19, 2000). Additionally, the CGMT-04 amended OPA to establish an environmental equivalency evaluation index to assess overall outflow performance due to collisions and groundings for double-hull tank vessels and alternative hull designs. *See* 70 Fed. Reg. 41777 (July 20, 2005).

[313] OPA §4115(f); 46 U.S.C. §§53706, 53734.

[314] For more information, *see* https://www.epa.gov/emergency-response/national-response-system.

[315] A court denied a barge company's attempt to obtain a declaratory judgment that its property did not constitute a danger, thus preventing government officials from entering the company's property to conduct investigations of a release. *See Batture Fleet, Inc. v. Browner*, 2000 U.S. Dist. LEXIS 8309 (E.D. La. June 8, 2000). However, the court decided the case exclusively under CERCLA rather than OPA. *See id.* at n. 4.

[316] OPA §4201; 33 U.S.C. §1321.

[317] 40 C.F.R. §300.120(a)(1).

[318] 40 C.F.R. §300.320.

[319] *Id.*

[320] 40 C.F.R. §300.5.

321 40 C.F.R. §300.323(a).

322 USCG COMDTINST 16465.6 May 23, 2012, available at https://www.uscg.mil/directives/ci/16000-16999/CI_16456_6.pdf.

323 40 C.F.R. §300.323(c).

324 *See* Campbell Robertson, *White House Takes a Bigger Role in the Oil Spill Cleanup* (*New York Times*; Apr. 29, 2010); *Coast Guard Commandant Admiral Thad Allen Designated National Incident Commander for Continued Response to BP Oil Spill*, available at https://www.restorethegulf.gov/release/2015/07/01/coast-guard-commandant-admiral-thad-allen-designated-national-incident-commander.

325 OPA §1018; 33 U.S.C. §2718. In September 2000, the United States District Court for the District of Maryland reinforced the view that §2718 did not preempt state common law claims for negligence, trespass, strict liability and nuisance in the case of *Williams v. Potomac Electric Power Company*, 115 F. Supp.2d 561 (D. Md. 2000). Basing its reasoning on the then-recent U.S. Supreme Court decision in *United States v. Locke*, 529 U.S. 89 (2000), *supra* section 16.3, the District Court determined that, given the location of the savings clauses in Title I of OPA, OPA does not preempt "state laws of a scope similar to the matters contained in Title I of OPA." 115 F. Supp. 2d at 564, quoting *Locke*, 529 U.S. at 105.

326 OPA §1011; 33 U.S.C. §2711.

327 OPA §4201(a); 33 U.S.C. §1321(c)(4)(A).

328 *Id.* at §1321(c)(4)(B).

329 *In re: Oil Spill by the Oil Rig "Deepwater Horizon" in the Gulf of Mexico, on April 20, 2010*, No. 2:10-md-02179-CJB-SS, Doc. No. 8037, 2012 WL 5960192 (E.D. La. Nov. 28, 2012).

330 *In re: Oil Spill by the Oil Rig "Deepwater Horizon" in the Gulf of Mexico, on April 20, 2010*, No. MDL 2179, 2016 WL 614690, *2 (Feb. 16, 2016).

331 33 U.S.C. §2680(a).

332 *In re: Oil Spill by the Oil Rig "Deepwater Horizon" in the Gulf of Mexico, on April 20, 2010*, No. MDL 2179, 2016 WL 614690 at *10.

333 *Id.*

334 *Id.* at *11.

335 *See* OPA §4201.

336 *See* the CWA, 33 U.S.C. §1321(d), as amended by §4201 of the OPA, and pursuant to authority delegated by the President to the Administrator of the EPA in Executive Order No. 12777, 56 Fed. Reg 54757 (Oct. 18, 1991).

337 59 Fed. Reg. 47384 (Sept. 15, 1994); 40 C.F.R. §§300.1 *et seq.*

338 *Id.*

339 *See* 40 C.F.R. §§300.900 *et seq.*

340 OPA §4202(a); 33 U.S.C. §1321(j). This section also requires tank vessels to carry oil spill response equipment that is the best technology economically feasible and compatible with safe operation of the vessel. Interim Final Rules were published on December 22, 1993 (58 Fed. Reg. 67988), and amended on January 26, 1994 (59 Fed. Reg. 3749). *See* 33 C.F.R. §155.1050.

341 The USCG provides guidelines for oil spill removal organizations, available at: http://www.uscg.mil/hq/nsfweb/nsf/nsfcc/ops/ResponseSupport/RRAB/osroclassifiedguidelines.asp. These guidelines were revised on April 17, 2013.

342 OPA §4202(a)(6); 33 U.S.C. §1321(j)(5).

343 *See* 58 Fed. Reg. 7376 (Feb. 5, 1993), as confirmed at 61 Fed. Reg. 1052 (Jan. 12, 1996); 33 C.F.R. §§155.1010 *et seq.*

344 73 Fed. Reg. 80618 (Dec. 31, 2008); 33 C.F.R. §§155.4010 *et seq.*

345 33 C.F.R. §155.4030. *But see* 33 C.F.R. §155.4010(b) ("the response criteria specified in the regulations . . . are planning criteria, not performance standards, and are based on assumptions that may not exist

during an actual incident. . . . Failure to meet specified criteria during an actual spill response does not necessarily mean that the planning requirements . . . and regulations were not met. The Coast Guard will exercise its enforcement discretion in light of all facts and circumstances"); 73 Fed. Reg. 80618, 80619 (Dec. 31, 2008).

346 33 C.F.R. §155.4030(b).

347 33 C.F.R. §155.4045(b).

348 33 C.F.R. §155.4055(a).

349 *See* 33 C.F.R. §§155.200 *et seq.* Final regulations requiring vessels carrying oil as cargo to carry discharge removal equipment were issued on January 12, 1996. 61 Fed. Reg. 1052.

350 33 C.F.R. §§155.205–155.220.

351 *See* 61 Fed. Reg. 1052 (Jan. 12, 1996) (increasing the original 1993 cap by 25 percent to establish a 1998 cap). The caps were increased by 25 percent again in 2000. See 65 Fed. Reg. 710 (Jan. 6, 2000). In 2009, the USCG concluded that a further increase was "unjustified" because "oil spill volume [had] decreased significantly since the implementation of oil spill prevention regulations and innovative industry measures." 74 Fed. Reg. 45004, 45011 (Aug. 31, 2009).

352 *See* 33 C.F.R. Pt. 155, §155.1050(o) & App. B.

353 74 Fed. Reg. 45004 (Aug. 31, 2009); 33 C.F.R. §§155.1035(i)(10)–(11), 155.1040(j)(10)–(11), and 155.1050(k)–(l).

354 33 C.F.R. §155.1020 (defining "*[p]re-authorization for dispersant use*"). A list of "pre-authorization" areas is available at http://www.uscg.mil/vrp/reg/disperse.shtml.

355 33 C.F.R. §155.1050(k)(1). The dispersants must be of a type listed on the NCP Product Schedule (40 C.F.R. §300.905), and the response plan must provide for application of at least 50 percent of the dispersant by fixed-wing aircraft. *Id.* at (k)(2). The quantity and type of dispersant resources must be sufficient to treat a worst-case discharge or to meet the tiered requirements in Table 155.1050(k), whichever is less. *Id.* at (k)(3).

356 33 C.F.R. §155.1050(l).

357 Pub. L. 108-293, Title VII, §701(a)–(b), 118 Stat. 1067 (Aug. 9, 2004). The CGMT-06 amended the definition of "nontank vessel" to clarify that the triggering volume is "at least 400 gross tons as measured under [46 U.S.C. §14302], or, for vessels not measured under that section, as measured under [46 U.S.C. §14502]." Pub. L. 109-241, Title VI, §608, 120 Stat. 558 (July 11, 2006).

358 CGMT-04 §§701(b)(2) and (c), 118 Stat. 1067-68.

359 *See* 70 Fed. Reg. 36649 (June 24, 2005).

360 *See* 73 Fed. Reg. 35405 (June 23, 2008).

361 *See* 74 Fed. Reg. 44970 (Aug. 31, 2009).

362 *See* 73 Fed. Reg. 35405, 35406 (June 23, 2008).

363 78 Fed. Reg. 60100, 60112 (Sept. 30, 2013); *see also* 33 C.F.R. §155.5025 *and* 33 C.F.R. §151.27.

364 64 Fed. Reg. 13734 (Mar. 22, 1999).

365 64 Fed. Reg. 13735 (Mar. 22, 1999).

366 *Id.*

367 64 Fed. Reg. 13745 (Mar. 22, 1999); 33 C.F.R. §155.1026.

368 64 Fed. Reg. 13746 (Mar. 22, 1999); 33 C.F.R. §155.1035.

369 *See, e.g.,* 64 Fed. Reg. 13748–49 (Mar. 22, 1999); 33 C.F.R. §155.1035(h)(3)(i).

370 76 Fed. Reg. 9276 (Feb. 17, 2011).

371 The USCG proposed a rule to fill in perceived gaps in the hazardous spill response readiness of marine transport–related facilities. Proposed changes include eliminating the 250-barrel minimum vessel capacity threshold for compliance and redefining terms used in the response plan regulations to be more applicable and improve clarity. *See* 65 Fed. Reg. 17416 (Mar. 31, 2000).

372 *See* 61 Fed. Reg. 7890 (Feb. 29, 1996), finalizing the interim rule published at 58 Fed. Reg. 7330 (Feb. 5, 1993); 33 C.F.R. §§154.1010 *et seq.*

373 Nearly the same dispersant and aerial oil-tracking requirements that apply to vessel response plans, *see, supra* section 19.2.5.1, now also apply to MTRs that could reasonably be expected to cause significant and substantial harm to the environment. *See* 74 Fed. Reg. 45004 (Aug. 31, 2009); 33 C.F.R. §§154.1035(b)(3)(vi)–(vii) and 154.1045(i)–(j).

374 59 Fed. Reg. 34070 (July 1, 1994); 40 C.F.R. §112.3.

375 67 Fed. Reg. 47042 (July 17, 2002).

376 40 C.F.R. §112.1(b).

377 58 Fed. Reg. 244 (Jan. 5, 1993); 49 C.F.R. §§194.101 *et seq.*

378 65 Fed. Reg. 17416 (Mar. 31, 2000); 33 C.F.R. §§154.1010 *et seq.*

379 The OPA response plan requirements for oil and hazardous substances amended Section 311 of the CWA; the list of hazardous substances covered by this rule is found at 40 C.F.R. Table 116.4.

380 65 Fed. Reg. 17416, 17428–29 (Mar. 31, 2000); 33 C.F.R. §154.1026.

381 The Qualified Individual is required to meet the Occupational Safety and Health Administration standards for an "incident commander" found at 29 C.F.R. §1910.120(q)(6)(v). 33 C.F.R. §154.1050.

382 65 Fed. Reg. 17416, 17430 (Mar. 31, 2000); 76 Fed. Reg. 9276 (Feb. 17, 2011).

383 76 Fed. Reg. 9276 (Feb. 17, 2011).

384 *See* discussion of Edible Oil Regulatory Reform Act, *supra* note 39.

385 65 Fed. Reg. 40820 (June 30, 2000). The counterpart EPA regulations for the non-MTRs were published at 65 Fed. Reg. 40776 (June 30, 2000).

386 81 Fed. Reg. 21362 (Apr. 11, 2016).

387 *See, e.g.,* 80 Fed. Reg. 10704 (Feb. 27, 2015).

388 As of the date of this publication, several criminal penalties and two civil penalties have been assessed in *Deepwater Horizon.* BP paid $4.5 billion in criminal fines and pleaded guilty to eleven felony counts related to the deaths of eleven workers. Although two BP employees were also indicted on charges of manslaughter, those charges were dropped in late 2015. This settlement includes payments of $2.394 billion to the National Fish and Wildlife Foundation and $1.15 billion to the OSLTF, among others. Transocean, owner of the Deepwater Horizon rig, agreed to plead guilty to violations of the CWA and paid $1.4 billion in civil and criminal fines and penalties. *See In re Oil Spill by the Oil Rig "Deepwater Horizon" in the Gulf of Mexico, on April 20, 2010,* No. 10-4536 (E.D. La. Jan. 3, 2013), available at: https://www.justice.gov/iso/opa/resources/915201313122945254063.pdf. On October 5, 2015, BP settled all remaining federal and state claims arising from the Deepwater Horizon spill, for a total of $20.8 billion. The settlement agreement included: $5.5 billion to the United States for civil penalties under the CWA; $7.1 billion to the United States and the five Gulf Coast states (AL, FL, LA, MS, TX) for NRDs, plus any of the $1 billion BP had already committed for early restoration costs and accrued interest not yet paid; up to $700 million to be set aside to cover any NRD unknown at the time of settlement; $340 million for reimbursement of NRDA costs; $250 million to the United States for various costs including reimbursement of response or removal costs, in settlement of the False Claims Act, and others; $4.9 billion to settle economic and other claims made by the five Gulf Coast states; and up to $1 billion to resolve claims made by more than 400 local governmental entities.

389 OPA §4301(c); 33 U.S.C. §1319(c).

390 The USCG has issued internal guidance on the criminal prosecution of parties violating federal environmental laws for which the USCG has jurisdiction, including OPA, emphasizing the increasing tendency for environmental investigations to take on a criminal dimension. *See* Commandant Instruction M16201.1 (July 30, 1997), available at http://www.kattenlaw.com/files/upload/USCG-Commandant-instruction-M16201-1-July-30-1997.pdf.

391 33 U.S.C. §1319(c)(1).

392 *Id.* at §1319(c)(2).

393 *Id.* at §1319(c)(3).

394 *See U.S. Department of Justice Press Release*, 96-470 (Sept. 25, 1996), available at: https://www.justice.gov/archive/opa/pr/1996/Sept96/470enr.htm.

395 16 U.S.C. §§703 *et seq.* The MBTA makes it unlawful for any person, at any time, by any means or in any manner, to take or kill any migratory bird without a permit or as otherwise provided by regulation. 16 U.S.C. §§703, 707(a). The term "take" includes wounding. 50 C.F.R. §10.12.

396 *See United States v. Eklof Marine Corp. et al.*, 1:97-cr-75-ML, plea agreement filed September, 25, 1997 (#2) (D.R.I. Sept. 25, 1997). Specifically, Eklof agreed to pay the following federal fines: $100,000 for its OPA violation; $400,000 for violating the Refuse Act, 33 U.S.C. §§407, 411 (2008) (RA); and $3 million for its MBTA violations. In addition, Eklof agreed to pay $3.5 million to Rhode Island. Eklof also agreed to contribute $1.5 million to the Nature Conservancy to be used to purchase environmentally sensitive land around the site of the spill and to spend $1 million on safety improvements to its fleet of vessels. *Id.*

397 *See United States v. Bouchard Transportation Co.*, No. 04-10087 (D. Mass. Oct. 18, 2004).

398 *See United States v. Fleet Management Ltd.*, No. 08-0160 SI (N.D. Cal. Aug. 13, 2009); *U.S. Department of Justice Press Release*, 10-168 (Feb. 19, 2010).

399 Pub. Law. 101-380, Aug. 18, 1990, codified at 33 U.S.C. §1319(c).

400 OPA §4302; 46 U.S.C. §§2302, 3318, 3718, 5116, 8101, 8104, 8502, 8503, 8702.

401 46 U.S.C.A. §2302; *see also* 18 U.S.C. §§3571(b)(5), 3571(c)(5).

402 46 U.S.C.A. §3718; *see also* 18 U.S.C. §3571.

403 33 U.S.C. §1321.

404 *See* 46 U.S.C.A. §§2302, 3318, 3718, 5116, 8101, 8104, 8502, 8503, 8702; *see also* 33 U.S.C.A. §§1232, 1236, 1481, 1514, 1908.

405 OPA §4302; 33 U.S.C. §1481(a).

406 OPA §4302; 33 U.S.C. §1514(a).

407 *See* OPA §4302.

408 18 U.S.C.A. §3571.

409 OPA §4302; 33 U.S.C. §1232(b).

410 33 U.S.C. §§407, 411 (2008).

411 For example, Eklof Marine Corp. was fined $3 million for its violation of the MBTA and $400,000 for violation of the RA, in addition to other fines, in conjunction with the *North Cape* spill. *See, supra* note 396; *see also* Etkin 1998, *supra* note 6, at 307.

412 The oil and shipping industries have repeatedly voiced their strong objections to this form of prosecution in hearings before Congress. *See Criminal Liability For Oil Pollution: Hearing before the Subcommittee on U.S. Coast Guard and Maritime Transportation of the Committee on Transportation and Infrastructure House of Representatives*, 105th Cong. 80–81 (1998) (statement of Dennis L. Bryant); *Oil Pollution Act of 1990: Joint Hearing before the Subcommittees on U.S. Coast Guard and Maritime Transportation and Water Resources and Environment of the Committee on Transportation and Infrastructure House of Representatives*, 106th Cong. 321, 479 (1999) (statements of Thomas R. Moore, president of Chevron Shipping Co. and representing the American Petroleum Institute, and Howard McCormack, president of the Maritime Law Association of the United States).

413 *See, e.g.*, S. 2944 and H.R. 5100, 106th Cong. (2000).

414 Civil penalties under OPA and CWA for OPA violations were adjusted upward by 10 percent pursuant to the DCIA. *See* 61 Fed. Reg. 69360 (Dec. 31, 1996); 40 C.F.R. §19.4. The DCIA requires an inflationary adjustment to civil penalties every four years, with the most recent adjustment being issued in 78 Fed. Reg. 66643 (Nov. 6, 2013).

415 Final Regulations were issued in 59 Fed. Reg. 15020 (Mar. 30, 1994).

416 *See* 78 Fed. Reg. 66647 (Nov. 6, 2013).

417 *See* 59 Fed. Reg. 66477 (Dec. 27, 1994); 33 C.F.R. §1.07-11. *See also* 67 Fed. Reg. 38386 (June 2, 2002) (amending the procedure for a Notice of Violation in 33 C.F.R. §1.07-11 when the recipient fails to either accept or decline the notice within 45 days by treating a lack of response as a default and proceeding with the civil penalty).

418 In August 1998, the EPA's Office of Enforcement and Compliance Assurance issued a revised Civil Penalty Policy for Section 311(b)(3) and Section 311(j) of the CWA. *See* 33 U.S.C. §1321(b)(6)(B)(i). The revised policy, which addresses both civil and administrative penalty assessments under OPA, is available at: http://www.epa.gov/enforcement/civil-penalty-policy-section-311b3-and-section-311j-clean-water-act-cwa-august-1998.

419 33 U.S.C. §1321(b)(6)(B)(1).

420 OPA §7001; 33 U.S.C. §2761(a); *see also* http://www.uscg.mil/iccopr/.

421 *Id.* at §2761(c)(4).

422 OPA §7002; 33 U.S.C. §2762, added by Pub. L. 109-241, Title VI, §605(a)(2), 120 Stat. 555 (July 11, 2006). The Act also established the Delaware River and Bay Oil Spill Advisory Committee to provide advice and recommendations to relevant government agencies on measures to improve the prevention of and response to future oil spills in the Delaware River and Delaware Bay.

Chapter 8

Safe Drinking Water Act

Thomas Richichi
Beveridge & Diamond, P.C.
Washington, D.C.

1.0 Overview

The Centers for Disease Control and Prevention has identified drinking water treatment as among the most significant public health advancements of the twentieth century. As a result of such treatment, waterborne health epidemics such as typhoid and cholera are now issues of the past in the United States.[1] More recently, as health concerns have evolved to address exposures from chemical contaminants as well as biological pathogens, newer treatment techniques and risk reduction strategies are being introduced in conjunction with modern drinking water treatment and distribution technologies to move us into new realms of human health protection, driven by the Safe Drinking Water Act (SDWA or "the Act").[2] Indeed, for the more than 300 million Americans who consume water regulated by the provisions of the SDWA, the regulatory scheme it provides for protecting their health and preventing disease is an essential part of their well-being.

2.0 Background to U.S. Drinking Water Regulation

Many of the treatment techniques used today by drinking water plants include methods that have been used for more than a hundred years. Most large urban drinking water systems were first established in the early 1900s to provide treatment necessary to ensure the quality of water that they obtained from surface sources (rivers, lakes, and reservoirs), which were susceptible to pollution. State and local concerns regarding drinking water quality focused on acute health threats posed by disease-causing microbes and pathogens[3] in public water supplies which scientists associated with the turbidity of source water,[4] given that suspended solids were known to harbor such microorganisms. As a result, most of the early drinking water treatment systems built in the United States used sand filtration to reduce turbidity, thereby physically removing microbial contaminants that were the cause of waterborne epidemics.

However, while filtration was an effective treatment method for reducing turbidity, it was disinfectants like chlorine that played the largest role in reducing the number of waterborne disease outbreaks in the early 1900s.[5] As the distribution systems were extended to serve growing populations, disinfection was introduced to ensure the safety of water between the treatment plant and the consumer's tap, a treatment step which proved enormously effective in reducing health risks to the public.[6] Indeed, the foundation of the federal drinking water scheme that emerged in the 1970s and 1980s was premised in great part on the adoption of national treatment standards that required both filtration and disinfection of drinking water.

2.1 Drinking Water Regulation before the SDWA

Federal regulation of drinking water quality began in 1914, when the U.S. Public Health Service set standards for the bacteriological quality of drinking water. However, there was no national drinking water program at that time, and the standards applied only to water systems that provided drinking water to interstate carriers, such as ships and trains, and only covered contaminants capable of causing contagious disease. The Public Health Service revised and expanded these standards in 1925, 1946, and again in 1962. The 1962 Public Health Service standards regulated 28 substances, and, with minor modifications, all 50 states adopted them, either as regulations or as guidelines for all public water systems in those jurisdictions, previewing the national regulatory scheme that was to come. In this regard, drinking water regulation not only preceded other federal environmental regulatory regimes by decades, but also was implemented in the first instance at the state and local level, albeit applying adoptive federal standards.

2.2 The 1974 Safe Drinking Water Act

A number of environmental and health issues gained the attention of Congress and the public in the early 1970s, including chemical contamination of drinking water supplies. This increased awareness, which coincided with the creation of the Environmental Protection Agency (EPA or "the Agency"), led to the contemporaneous passage of several national environmental and health-related laws of consequence, one of which was the Safe Drinking Water Act of 1974.[7]

The basic objective to the 1974 Act was to establish a national drinking water program based on uniform drinking water standards applicable to the entire country that was to be administered at the state level, under the supervision of EPA. To that end, the Act authorized EPA to regulate contaminants in all drinking water systems that served the public, directing the Agency to establish national standards for levels of contaminants in public drinking water, as well as to regulate underground injection wells and sole-source aquifers.

2.3 The 1986 Amendments to the SDWA

The 1974 SDWA, while laying the predicate for a national drinking water program, fell short of congressional objectives, and, in an effort to further improve the nation's drinking water program, Congress significantly amended the Act in 1986.[8] The 1986 amendments incorporated a number of major new requirements and authorities, perhaps the most ambitious of which was a mandate directing EPA to establish maximum contaminant levels (MCLs) for 83 drinking water contaminants within three years, and to establish MCLs for 25 additional contaminants every three years thereafter.

Perhaps just as significantly, the 1986 SDWA amendments required all surface water treatment systems to undertake major infrastructure improvements to incorporate filtration into their water and treatment facilities, and to implement new disinfection standards and treatment techniques to address the removal or neutralization of the microbes, bacteria, and enteric viruses most commonly found in surface water sources. Complementing these new requirements and authorities, the 1986 amendments provided EPA stronger enforcement authority and established new requirements for groundwater protection and monitoring of unregulated contaminants.

2.4 The 1996 Amendments to the SDWA

The 1996 amendments to the SDWA[9] resulted in even more substantial changes to the national drinking water program for water utilities, states, and EPA by retooling the regulatory scheme of the original SDWA to focus on risk-based decision-making, sound science, transparency and consumer awareness. To that end, the 1996 amendments reformed the process for evaluating and adding regulated contaminants; mandated the use of the best available science in decision-making; strengthened EPA's scientific risk assessments and cost-benefit considerations in setting drinking water standards; required regular information disclosure to consumers; emphasized preventing contamination problems; and provided for new funding for states and communities through a Drinking Water State Revolving Fund. Because they provide the most important context for understanding the statutory framework that has resulted in the current SDWA regulatory scheme, these amendments are addressed briefly below and are more fully discussed in subsequent sections of this chapter.

Risk-Based Contaminant Monitoring and Selection. The 1996 SDWA amendments eliminated the requirement of the 1986 amendments that EPA regulate an additional 25 contaminants every three years. Instead, EPA was given the flexibility to create a contaminant candidate list (CCL) and the discretion to decide whether to regulate contaminants from the CCL, after completing a required review of a minimum of five contaminants on the list every five years. Further, the 1996 amendments directed that EPA conduct that review based on objective criteria that include the human health effects of a contaminant, its occurrence at levels of concern in drinking water supplies, and the opportunity for meaningful health risk reduction that could result from its regulation.[10] Such reviews are to be performed in consultation with the scientific community with an opportunity for public notice and comment.[11]

Cost-Benefit Analysis and Research for New Standards. As the result of another significant change brought about by the 1996 amendments, the SDWA now provides that EPA must conduct a thorough cost-benefit analysis for every new drinking water standard to determine whether the benefits of the standard justify its implementation costs.[12] After first identifying a drinking water maximum contaminant level or treatment technique[13] standard for a contaminant based on affordable technology, EPA must determine whether the costs of that standard would be justified by the benefits.

Consumer Information. A principal underlying philosophy of the SDWA is that consumers have a right to know what is in their drinking water, where it comes from, how it is treated, and how to help protect themselves in those instances where the water presents a potential health risk. Consistent with those statutory goals, the 1996 SDWA amendments established new requirements that all community water systems prepare and distribute annual "Consumer Confidence Reports" (CCRs) regarding the water they provide, including information on detected contaminants, possible health effects, and the source of the water.[14] In addition to the CCR, the 1996 amendments included provisions for improved disclosure of information to the public, most notably requiring that notice of any violation of a national drinking water standard "that has the potential to have serious adverse effects on human health as a result of short-term exposure" be made within 24 hours after the violation.[15]

Prevention of Contamination. The 1996 SDWA amendments also established a new emphasis on preventing contamination problems through source water protection and enhanced water system management. As a result, every state must now conduct an assessment of its sources of drinking water (rivers, lakes, reservoirs, springs, and groundwater wells) to identify significant potential sources of contamination and to determine how susceptible the sources are to these threats.[16]

Capacity Development. Capacity development is the process through which water systems acquire and maintain adequate technical, managerial, and financial capabilities to enable them to consistently provide safe drinking water. Recognizing the expansion of responsibilities that were being incorporated into the Act, the 1996 amendments required states to develop or revise state programs on capacity development to ensure that existing water systems needing improvements have the capacity and financial resources necessary to comply with drinking water standards.[17]

Operator Certification. Ensuring the knowledge and skills of public water system operators is one of the most important, cost-effective means to strengthen drinking water safety. To that end, the 1996 amendments required all states to carry out a program of operator certification. As a result, the SDWA now requires that each state must either: (a) implement a program that meets guidelines established by EPA, or (b) enforce an existing state program that meets the public health objectives of EPA's guidelines.[18]

Small system technologies, variances, and exemptions. Recognizing the scope and burden of the new requirements imposed on water suppliers by the 1996 SDWA amendments, Congress also included a number of provisions regarding variances to ease the burden of compliance for small water systems, both in terms of financial assistance and resort to alternative technology.[19]

Regulatory Development. The 1996 SDWA amendments also expanded efforts to strengthen protection from microbial contaminants, including Cryptosporidium,[20] while strengthening control over the by-products of chemical drinking water disinfection. Responding to a statutory mandate, EPA promulgated, in phases, the Stage 1/Stage 2 Disinfectants and Disinfection Byproducts Rules and the Interim/Long Term 1/Long Term 2 Enhanced Surface Water Treatment Rules to address these risks.[21] Congress also directed EPA to address standards and regulations for radon and arsenic in drinking water.[22] These rulemakings are discussed in greater detail later in this chapter.

Drinking Water State Revolving Fund (SRF). The 1996 SDWA amendments also established a Drinking Water State Revolving Fund to help address the cost to states and localities of its numerous mandates. Subject to Congressional funding, states can use the SRF to help water systems make infrastructure or management improvements, or to help systems assess and protect their source water.[23]

2.5 2002 Bioterrorism Act

The most recent major statutory revision of the SDWA occurred in 2002. After the events of 9/11, Congress took significant steps to improve the security of the U.S. drinking water supply and infrastructure. One of those steps was the enactment of the Public Health Security and Bioterrorism Preparedness and Response

Act of 2002 (Bioterrorism Act).[24] The Bioterrorism Act requires community drinking water systems and the EPA: (1) to work collaboratively to assess and reduce vulnerabilities of infrastructure to potential terrorist attacks; (2) to plan for and practice response to emergencies and incidents; and (3) to develop new security technologies to detect and monitor contaminants and prevent security breaches. The requirements of the act assign significant new responsibilities to both EPA and water utilities to enhance water system security and to develop response measures for potential threats to the nation's water supplies and systems.

2.5.1 Requirements for Community Drinking Water Systems under the Bioterrorism Act

The Bioterrorism Act requires every community water system serving more than 3,300 persons (1) to conduct assessments of their vulnerabilities to terrorist attack or other intentional acts; and (2) to prepare or revise an emergency response plan based on the results of the vulnerability assessment to defend against adversarial actions that might substantially disrupt the ability of a system to provide a safe and reliable supply of drinking water.

2.5.2 Responsibilities of EPA under the Bioterrorism Act

The Bioterrorism Act requires EPA to protect the vulnerability assessments submitted by drinking water systems while they are in EPA's possession; to provide guidance and information to community water systems on potential adversarial action that could threaten the water supply systems; and to provide potential strategies and responses to such incidents. EPA is also charged with conducting research studies in areas relevant to water security.

In response to these congressional mandates, through coordination with federal law enforcement and intelligence officials, EPA has completed an information protection protocol that protects water utilities' vulnerability assessments from unauthorized disclosure. The protocol includes restrictions on persons who are allowed access to the assessments, actions to ensure the security of the information, and security provisions regarding storage and handling of these documents. The security measures to be implemented include: (1) designating an EPA information security manager with "top secret" clearance to oversee the protection of information, manage protocol implementation, and conduct routine security checks; (2) restricting access to the vulnerability assessments and information derived from them; (3) designating a secure room for the review and processing of the documents; (4) using a document tracking system to trace security assessment documents at all times; and (5) prohibiting copying, faxing, and lending of the assessments, unless authorized by the director of the Office of Ground Water and Drinking Water.[25]

As noted, the Bioterrorism Act also requires EPA to provide information and guidance for conducting vulnerability assessments. In response, EPA has developed a threat information document, "Baseline Threat Information for Vulnerability Assessments of Community Water Systems," that outlines threats, methodologies, strategies, and responses for water utilities to consider when conducting vulnerability assessments.[26]

Finally, EPA conducts ongoing research regarding prevention and detection of, and actions in response to: (1) intentional introduction of contaminants to community water systems and source water, (2) methods by which terrorists could affect the supply of drinking water or threaten water system infrastructure and physical security, and (3) alternative supplies of safe drinking water in the event of destruction, impairment, or contamination of public water systems. For example, EPA's Office of Research and Development and Office of Water have developed a Water Security Research and Technical Support Action Plan[27] which identifies physical and cyber infrastructure protection projects, including: (1) contaminant identification; (2) monitoring and analysis; (3) treatment, decontamination, and disposal; (4) contingency planning; (5) infrastructure interdependencies; and (6) risk assessment and communication.

3.0 The SDWA Regulatory Scheme

The SDWA is unique among federal regulatory schemes in several respects. Unlike other federal regulatory programs, fundamental aspects of drinking water treatment and management were developed and widely implemented by states and municipalities long before a national drinking water program emerged. Moreover, unlike many other federal environmental programs that are primarily intended to regulate commercial or industrial entities whose activities may be potential sources of pollution, the SDWA is directed, in significant part, at entities that provide a public health service essential to consumers—the delivery of safe drinking water—and is primarily concerned with helping them to ensure that the delivery of that service minimizes risks to human health. Furthermore, the largest component of the regulated community in terms of affected consumers consists of public water authorities operating under state and local control.

The scheme is also unique in the extent to which it incorporates enforceable statutory mandates regarding the use of sound science, including express mandates regarding the appropriate use of science with respect to standard setting; data collection; and risk assessment, management, and communication.[28] In addition, the Act incorporates important regulatory cost-benefit and feasibility provisions relating to risk management. Finally, its reach is ubiquitous within the United States, covering large and small water suppliers, public and private owner-operators, and surface and groundwater sources.

3.1 Federal/State Relationship

The SDWA regulatory scheme has at its foundation a cooperative federal/state relationship that contemplates enforcement by the states in the first instance under the supervision of the federal government. Consistent with that scheme, states may apply for "primary enforcement responsibility" as "primacy agencies." The EPA may grant primacy authority if it determines that the state has adopted regulations "no less stringent" than the federal regulations and has appropriate enforcement mechanisms in place.[29] To date, 49 of the 50 states have been granted such authority.[30] If EPA believes a state regulatory program does not meet its stringency requirements, the Act creates procedures to require the state to revise or withdraw its program on pain of losing primary enforcement authority, and for payment of civil penalties.[31]

3.2 Primary and Secondary Standards

The SDWA provides for two basic types of regulations: (1) national primary drinking water regulations (NPDWRs) which specify certain enforceable requirements, including a maximum allowable contaminant level for chemicals and other substances in drinking water that "may have any adverse effect on the health of persons";[32] and (2) national secondary drinking water regulations, which address aesthetic considerations such as the odor, taste, and appearance of drinking water.[33] There are more than 80 NPDWRs, which establish federally enforceable drinking water standards (including treatment techniques) for contaminants and set forth monitoring, reporting, sampling, and recordkeeping requirements applicable to every public water system (PWS) for those respective contaminants.

Secondary drinking water regulations, by comparison, are not federally enforceable under the SDWA (although some contaminants are subject to both primary and secondary standards (e.g., fluoride).[34] For that reason, this chapter does not deal with them at any length. However, it is important to note that they address undesired aesthetic effects (e.g., odor, color, iron staining) that may nonetheless trigger public concern or even private legal actions for tort or nuisance. For example, the U.S. Second Circuit Court of Appeals upheld a $104 million jury verdict against a major petroleum company for contamination of New York City groundwater sources based, in part, on evidence that the contamination would affect the odor and taste of the water.[35]

Current federal secondary drinking water regulations address the following contaminants and water conditions:

- aluminum
- chloride

- color

- copper

- corrosivity

- fluoride

- foaming agents

- iron

- manganese

- odor

- pH

- silver

- sulfate

- total

- dissolved solids

- zinc

3.3 Who Is Regulated—Public Water Systems

The Safe Drinking Water Act was enacted to ensure that all members of the American public are provided with drinking water that meets minimum national standards for the protection of human health.[36] To that end, the SDWA and its implementing regulations provide EPA with regulatory jurisdiction to ensure the safety of any drinking water provided for human consumption by any "public water system."[37] In this regard, the regulation of public water systems serves as the functional centerpiece of the SDWA regulatory scheme. The Act governs all public water systems in the United States, comprising more than 155,000 regulated systems serving more than 300 million consumers. These range from large municipal water systems that serve major metropolitan areas with millions of water customers, such as New York City, to very small systems, such as rest stops or roadside restaurants that provide water to far fewer numbers of travelers or transient consumers.[38]

3.3.1 Definition of Public Water System (PWS)

The SDWA and its implementing regulations define what constitutes a PWS for regulatory purposes.[39] In particular, a water system that comprises at least 15 service connections *or* that provides water intended for human consumption to an average of at least 25 individuals daily at least 60 days a year (non-continuous) qualifies as a "public water system" potentially subject to the requirements of EPA's drinking water regulations.[40] "Human consumption" for regulatory purposes is broadly defined to include not only actual drinking of water, but its use for all residential and hygienic purposes involving human exposure, including hand washing, bathing, laundering, and food preparation.[41] Moreover, whether the system is publicly or privately owned is not a factor in the definition of a "public" water system, as the operative terms refer to who is *served* by a system (i.e., members of the public), rather than who owns or operates the water system.

3.3.2 Jurisdictional Coverage

With certain limited variances and exemptions, the Act requires that EPA's health-based drinking water regulations, the NPDWRs, "apply to each public water system in each State."[42] However, given that the potentially expansive scope of the PWS definition might be read so broadly as to include schools, businesses, office buildings, and the like, Congress drew a bright line to separate a *regulated* PWS from those entities that merely provide drinking water to the public by passing water through to consumers *from* a regulated PWS. More specifically, the SDWA provides that a PWS is *exempt* from compliance with the NPDWRs if it meets all four of the following conditions:

(1) it consists only of distribution and storage facilities (and does not have any collection and treatment facilities);

(2) it obtains all of its water from, but is not owned or operated by, a public water system to which such regulations apply;

(3) it does not sell water to any person; *and*

(4) it is not a common carrier which conveys passengers in interstate commerce.[43]

Thus, an entity that operates a water system that obtains its water from a regulated PWS *and* does not treat or sell that water is exempt from regulation, provided it is not a common carrier engaged in interstate commerce (e.g., commercial aircraft). The legislative history of the exemption confirms that the congressional intent was to "exempt businesses which merely store and distribute water provided by others," and which do not sell or bill water as a separate item, such as hotels, apartments and commercial office buildings.[44]

3.4 Classification of Public Water Systems

The frequency, nature, and scope of the regulatory requirements applicable to a PWS are largely a function of: (1) the size of population it serves, (2) the regularity with which it provides water to the same individuals, and (3) whether it is part of a network of water suppliers. PWSs are therefore classified based upon these considerations, which are discussed below.

3.4.1 System Classification by Size

The greater the population served and the more frequently the public water system provides drinking water to the same consumers, the broader and more rigorous are the regulatory requirements for monitoring, treatment, recordkeeping, and reporting that will apply. To this end, the EPA's drinking water regulations generally classify five categories of public water systems by size, according to the number of people they serve:

- very small water systems that serve 25–500 people;

- small water systems that serve 501–3,300 people;

- medium water systems that serve 3,301–10,000 people;

- large water systems that serve 10,001–100,000 people; and

- very large water systems that serve more than 100,000 people.[45]

As explained later in the chapter, certain exemptions and regulatory flexibilities apply with respect to systems that serve fewer than 10,000 people, particularly the small and very small systems. At the other end of the spectrum, very large systems may be subject to additional regulatory requirements, particularly with respect to monitoring and reporting, reflecting their size, resources, and potential impact on public health.

3.4.2 System Classification by Regularity of Service

The SDWA regulatory regime also distinguishes among public water systems on the basis of the regularity with which they serve the same consumers, a factor which has implications relating to whether the PWS serves a residential community or, a commercial or industrial facility. With respect to this distinction, it is important to note that the SDWA and NPDWRs regulate contaminants that have health impacts associated with both chronic long-term exposures (e.g., carcinogens), and acute, short-term exposure (e.g., infectious microorganisms). For municipal systems that serve large communities of residential customers over extended periods of time, both types of contaminants are of concern. For other systems that provide drinking water to transient consumers (e.g., rest stops, campgrounds, restaurants, aircraft) contaminants that present acute health threats are the principal concern.

3.4.2.1 Community Water Systems

Public water systems that sell water to residential populations are the most comprehensively regulated public water systems and fall under the regulatory rubric of "community water systems" (CWSs). They also serve most members of the public, with 54,000 community water systems serving more than 290 million people in the United States.[46] They are required to meet requirements of all NPDWRs. This includes both the contaminants that present chronic health threats from long-term exposure and the contaminants that present acute health threats that may arise from short-term exposure. Their systems are required to provide specific contaminant control and removal measures at their treatment facilities and within their distribution systems. Their contaminant monitoring similarly involves regular monitoring at treatment facilities and structured, periodic, representative sampling within the drinking water distribution system of the CWS.[47]

3.4.2.2 Noncommunity Water Systems

A noncommunity water system is a public water system that serves water to the public but does not serve the same people year-round. It is generally associated with public water systems that do not provide water to residential customers. There are two types of noncommunity systems: nontransient and transient.

Nontransient Noncommunity Water Systems. A nontransient noncommunity water system (NTNCWS) is a PWS that regularly supplies water to at least 25 of the same people at least 60 days per year but not year-round (which excludes nearly all residential systems). In order to be considered such a system, it is not necessary that the 60 days of service be continuous. Examples of NTNCWSs may include schools, factories, office buildings, and hospitals, *provided* they collect source water for their own water systems (e.g., wells), or they treat their own drinking water.[48] EPA estimates that there are approximately 20,000 NTNCWSs in the United States serving more than 6 million individuals, with groundwater serving as the source of water for nearly 90 percent of those systems.

Significantly, for many commercial and industrial facilities that purchase and treat finished water purchased from a municipal CWS for business or production-related purposes (e.g, a food processor, research facility, or brewery), the regulations present a potential coverage issue, if the owner/operators provide that same treated water to facility employees for drinking, hand washing, or hygienic purposes. Again, a facility may be exempt from regulation as long as it does not treat the water it provides.[49] When a facility treats water, however, even if that treatment involves purification or filtration, it may technically trigger an obligation to comply with the monitoring, reporting, and recordkeeping requirements of 40 C.F.R. Part 141 as an NTNCWS, if that treated water is also made available to employees at the facility. In such circumstances, the most practical solution is often to reroute the finished water that the facility receives from the CWS past any facility treatment equipment directly to employee areas.

Transient Water Systems. A transient noncommunity water system is one that serves water to members of the public for more than six months (noncontinuous) during the year, but not to the same individuals. For example, a highway rest area, gas station, or campground may be considered a transient water system, if it collects the source water that is served to the members of the public using that facility (e.g., from a well), rather than obtaining it from a regulated PWS. Transient noncommunity water systems are the most numerous in the country (there are approximately 85,000) and serve more than an estimated 13 million individuals, drawing their supplies in most instances from groundwater. However, they are generally subject only to the regulatory requirements associated with contaminants that present acute health risks, which are addressed more fully later in the chapter.[50]

3.4.3 Interstate Carrier Conveyances

Interstate Carrier Conveyances (ICCs) include vehicles, aircraft, and vessels that transport individuals in interstate travel, including crew members on board vessels transporting property. Consistent with SDWA regulations, aircraft, passenger vessels, trains, and buses whose water systems provide water to an average of at least 25 individuals daily (not necessarily the same individuals) at least 60 days a year (noncontinuous) are ICCs that qualify as "public water systems" subject to the requirements of EPA's NPDWRs.[51] ICCs are not regulated by the states but instead fall under the enforcement jurisdiction of the EPA regions and EPA headquarters.

With the adoption of the 1996 SDWA amendments and subsequent rulemakings, EPA has determined that its existing regulatory program for ICCs may not be fully in accord with the rest of the SDWA regulatory scheme. For that reason, it has suspended its prior compliance guidance for ICCs[52] and sought to address this issue through regulations specific to the health risk considerations presented by individual categories of ICCs. To that end, it has completed a rulemaking for aircraft drinking water, thus addressing one major ICC category.[53] At this writing, it appears that other ICCs also may soon be the subject of similar regulation.[54]

3.4.4 Consecutive Public Water Systems

In practice, several regulated public water systems may connect their systems to provide water service to consumers. In this type of network, water is treated by one system, which sells the water "downstream" to another system for further distribution or sale to end users. This is considered a "consecutive" water system. In such circumstances, EPA has discretionary authority to modify the strict monitoring requirements of the NPDWRs for public water systems that receive their water from an "upstream" PWS that meets all regulatory requirements, provided the "downstream" or "consecutive" PWS can demonstrate to the satisfaction of the Agency that there has been no subsequent reintroduction of contaminants or regrowth of regulated biological contaminants in its system.[55] EPA or the state primacy authority will generally require, however, that the downstream PWS provide meaningful verification that the derivative drinking water it is providing to the public remains protective of human health before it will relax any routine monitoring requirements for a consecutive system.

4.0 How Drinking Water Is Regulated—Standard Setting

4.1 Identification and Prioritization of Contaminants for Regulation

EPA was given a mandate in the 1986 SDWA amendments to establish NPDWRs for 83 specific contaminants,[56] and it has promulgated dozens of standards in response to that requirement. However, Congress subsequently recognized the wisdom of risk-based standard-setting and in the 1996 SDWA amendments introduced a new, more flexible risk-benefit approach to identifying contaminant candidates for regulation, and determining whether they should, in fact, be regulated. Under the current SDWA scheme, EPA's identification, prioritization, and final selection of contaminants for regulation is intended to be premised on objective criteria involving the seriousness of health effects and scientifically sound methods for determining occurrence and risk reduction benefits.

4.1.1 The Unregulated Contaminant Candidate List

As directed by the 1996 amendments, the selection of new contaminants for regulation is a two-step process, the first step of which is EPA's development of a Contaminant Candidate List (CCL) composed of contaminants (1) that are currently not regulated, (2) that are known or anticipated to occur in public water systems, and (3) which may require regulation under the SDWA.[57]

Development of the CCL is governed by SDWA Section 1412(b)(1), which provides that EPA is to consider a number of specific factors, to consult with the scientific community, including its own Science Advisory Board, as part of the listing process, and to publish the CCL for public notice and comment.[58] Among other factors, the Act directs EPA to consider for inclusion substances identified in Section 101(14) of the Comprehensive Environmental Response, Compensation, and Liability Act (CERCLA) and substances registered as pesticides under the Federal Insecticide, Fungicide, and Rodenticide Act (FIFRA).[59] The SDWA further requires the Agency to include in its selection determination data from the National Contaminant Occurrence Database established under Section 1445(g) of SDWA.[60]

In that regard, to help inform the Agency's efforts, the 1986 SDWA amendments required EPA to identify, on an ongoing basis, up to 30 unregulated contaminants for which monitoring would be required, and to develop a National Contaminant Occurrence Database covering regulated and unregulated contaminants, primarily using compliance monitoring detection data and information from that unregulated contaminant monitoring program. The principal use of the database is for EPA to make determinations whether to regulate a certain contaminant based upon its actual occurrence in public water supplies, but it also serves an ancillary function in the tailoring of system monitoring and source water protection.[61]

Finally, in developing the CCL, the Act directs the Agency to consider the health effects and occurrence information available for unregulated contaminants to identify those contaminants that present the greatest public health concern related to exposure from drinking water. This includes consideration of adverse health effects that may pose a greater risk to various life stages and other sensitive groups that represent a meaningful portion of the population.[62] For example, adverse health effects associated with infants, children, pregnant women, the elderly, and individuals with a history of serious illness are required to be considered by EPA in conjunction with the listing of a contaminant on the CCL.

Significantly, despite these directives, the SDWA expressly states that EPA's decision whether to select a contaminant for inclusion on the CCL is not subject to judicial review.[63] However, while this certainly would appear to foreclose a challenge to the merits of EPA's ultimate decision with respect to listing, it is still arguable that a procedural challenge to EPA's decision might be available, if the administrative record clearly demonstrated that it had not followed the selection procedures required by the Act (e.g., not making the list available for public notice and comment), or that it had not given any consideration to a factor prescribed by the Act.[64] Nonetheless, given the language of the Act, there appears to be little doubt that the merits of EPA's decision whether to include a contaminant on the CCL, upon consideration of those factors, would not be subject to judicial review.

EPA first published the first required CCL (CCL 1) in 1998, which was composed of 60 candidate contaminants.[65] Once that initial publication of the list was accomplished, EPA was then required by the Act to publish updated CCLs periodically, at intervals of not greater than 5 years, beginning August 6, 2001.[66] Consistent with that obligation, the second CCL (CCL 2) was published on February 24, 2005, and listed 51 contaminants which effectively were just carried over from CCL 1.[67] EPA's most recent final listing, representing CCL 3, was published on October 8, 2009, and comprised 116 contaminants.[68]

CCL 3 was of particular interest because it appears to have involved a far more robust review than the first two CCLs, listing 104 chemicals or chemical groups and 12 microbiological contaminants. The list included, among others, pesticides, biological toxins, disinfection by-products, chemicals, and waterborne pathogens. Moreover, the universe of potential candidate contaminants was quite extensive. The Agency considered data and information on health effects and occurrence to evaluate 7,500 unregulated substances and select the final 116 members of the CCL 3 that the Agency determined had the potential to present health risks through drinking water exposure.[69]

CCL 3 was also of interest inasmuch as EPA provided a detailed explanation of a multistep approach to the selection of contaminants for the expanded third list that the Agency had developed from the 7,500 contaminants it evaluated. That approach reflected a renewed Agency focus on chemical contaminants, particularly those associated with agricultural and industrial production. It included the following key steps and concepts:

(1) The identification of a broad universe of potential drinking water contaminants (the "CCL 3 Universe").

(2) A screening process that used screening criteria, ostensibly based on a contaminant's potential to occur in public water systems and thereby pose a potential public health concern, to narrow the broad universe of potential contaminants down to a Preliminary Candidate Contaminant List ("PCCL").[70]

(3) A structured classification process (e.g., a prototype classification algorithm model) that compared data and information as a tool and evaluated it in conjunction with expert opinions to develop a final CCL from the PCCL.[71]

The PCCL consisted of 561 chemicals that were screened from the CCL 3 Universe. To select contaminants for the CCL 3 from the PCCL, EPA used classification models in an effort to handle larger, more complex assortments of data in a consistent and reproducible manner. Drawing upon Agency experience, the classification models were trained based on past decisions that included input from outside experts. Algorithms were used to prioritize chemicals, which were then allowed to proceed to final expert evaluation and review.[71] In evaluating these criteria, EPA considered not only public water system monitoring data, but also data on concentrations in ambient surface and groundwaters, releases to the environment, and other factors.[72] Also, as required by the Act, the Agency considered adverse health effects that might pose a greater risk to life stages and other sensitive groups which represent a meaningful portion of the population. To that end, adverse health effects associated with infants, children, pregnant women, the elderly, and individuals with a history of serious illness were evaluated by EPA in conjunction with the development of the CCL.

EPA solicited public input on new CCL 4 "nominations" in a May 8, 2012 Federal Register Notice[73] and published its proposed CCL 4 list of contaminants for comment on February 4, 2015.[74] The proposed CCL 4 included 100 chemicals or chemical groups and 12 microbial contaminants known or anticipated to occur in public water systems. The list included, among others, chemicals used in commerce, pesticides, biological toxins, disinfection by-products, pharmaceuticals and waterborne pathogens.

Based on the proposed Agency's review of health effects and occurrence data, EPA made the following changes to the CCL 4 list from the previous CCL3 list:

- Two nominated contaminants, manganese and nonylphenol, were added.

- Perchlorate was removed because the Agency made a final Regulatory Determination in 2011 that was positive (see the subsequent discussion of the perchlorate determination in section 5.6.1 of this chapter).

- Five contaminants that had been the subject of preliminary Regulatory Determinations were removed from the list as part of the third Regulatory Determination process, which is discussed in the following section. More particularly, in October of 2014, EPA made preliminary determinations not to regulate four contaminants (1,3-dinitrobenzene; dimethoate; terbufos and terbufos sulfone) and to regulate one contaminant (strontium) listed on CCL 3. Accordingly, those five contaminants were removed from the draft CCL 4, pending publication of the final third Regulatory Determination.[75]

4.1.2 Selection of Candidate Contaminants for Regulation

The second step in the process of identifying new contaminants for regulation is EPA's actual selection of the candidates from the CCL. In this second step of the process, following the publication of a new CCL list, EPA is required to perform a periodic review of, and make a determination with respect to, at least five contaminants on that CCL regarding whether they should be regulated, i.e., a "Regulatory Determination." Every five years thereafter, EPA must repeat that process and determine whether to regulate at least five of the listed unregulated contaminants on the then current CCL.[76] The first Regulatory Determination under this scheme was published in the *Federal Register* on July 18, 2003, at which time EPA considered and decided not to regulate nine of the 60 CCL contaminants.[77] EPA's second Regulatory Determination was published five years later on July 30, 2008, at which time EPA announced its decision not to regulate 11 other contaminants it had selected for review.[78] As noted in the prior section, EPA published its draft third Regulatory Determination in the Federal Register in October of 2014, which included proposed negative determinations with respect to four contaminants and a positive determination with respect to strontium.[79] However, in its third Regulatory Determination published in January of 2016, although EPA made a final negative determination with respect to the four contaminants, it announced that it was delaying the final Regulatory Determination on strontium "in order to consider additional data and decide whether there is a meaningful opportunity for health risk reduction by regulating Strontium in drinking water."[80]

Looking to the criteria EPA is to employ in selecting contaminants from the CCL to regulate, the SDWA specifies that the Agency should regulate a contaminant if the EPA administrator determines that

(1) the contaminant may have an adverse effect on the health of persons;

(2) the contaminant is known to occur, or there is a substantial likelihood that the contaminant will occur in public water systems with a frequency and at levels of public health concern; and

(3) in the *sole* judgment of the administrator, regulation of such contaminant presents a meaningful opportunity for health risk reduction for persons served by public water systems.[81]

On their face, these provisions make risk prioritization a dominant factor in selecting contaminants to regulate. Furthermore, as might be expected, in the second step of the process, EPA evaluates the criteria with respect to the regulatory determination whether to actually regulate a contaminant more rigorously than the factors it considers in deciding which contaminants to place on the candidate list. EPA's stated goal is to work in partnership with the states and other stakeholders to identify and closely scrutinize unregulated contaminants that (1) are most prevalent in drinking water, (2) present the most serious threat to health, and (3) can be most productively and effectively controlled. In this process, sizable contaminant clusters (similar to the disinfection by-products/microbial cluster) may be reviewed and other contaminants added to the cluster for analysis—with only those that satisfy the three criteria above, however, qualifying for a positive determination to regulate.

It should also be noted that a fair reading of the last criterion is that the decision to *proceed* with the regulation of a contaminant involves a matter committed solely by Agency discretion that is not reviewable on the merits. While the first two criteria do not contain a similar expression of deference to the Agency, the determination to be made under the third criterion, which is entrusted to the "sole judgment of the administrator," appears to proceed from the assumption that the first two criteria are an integral part of that judgment. This is buttressed by the fact that the Act expressly provides that EPA decisions *not to proceed* with the regulation of a contaminant are final agency actions subject to judicial review.[82]

If EPA determines that all three of these statutory criteria are met, it is deemed to have made a final determination that an NPDWR is needed. In that case, Section 1412(b) of the Act provides that the Agency has 24 months following its determination to publish a *proposed* NPDWR.[83] Following publication of the proposed NPDWR, the Agency then has 18 months to promulgate a final NPDWR, reflecting an anticipated period of up to three and one-half years from the selection of a contaminant for regulation as part of a Regulatory Determination until the promulgation of an NPDWR accomplishing that purpose.[84]

4.2 NPDWR Standard Setting—MCLs and MCLGs

Once a determination is made that a contaminant on the CCL is to be regulated, that decision sets in motion the process of promulgating an NPDWR within the time frames provided under Section 1412(b) of the Act (above). With respect to the establishment of the drinking water standards for the contaminant that will be addressed by the new NPDWR,[85] the Act provides for a process that has two essential elements—establishment of an aspirational Maximum Contaminant Level Goal (MCLG) for the contaminant, and adoption of a corresponding enforceable standard designated as a Maximum Contaminant Level, or MCL. Once the rulemaking process has been set in motion, EPA is required to establish the MCLG and propose an MCL for the contaminant within the same 24 months that are provided for the development of a proposed NPDWR. The MCLG is to be "set at the level at which no known or anticipated adverse effects on the health of persons occur and which allows an adequate margin of safety."[86] A final MCL is then to be promulgated within 18 months thereafter as an enforceable standard set as close to the MCLG as is "feasible."[87]

Taken together, these provisions provide a straightforward, two-step process for the promulgation of drinking water standards.[88] The first step is the establishment of an MCLG through a scientific inquiry intended to identify the level below which no known or anticipated adverse effect on human health will occur, which must include "an adequate margin of safety."[89] As EPA has explained, the MCLG is to be "based upon the available evidence of carcinogenicity or noncancer adverse health effects from drinking water exposure using EPA's guidelines for risk assessment."[90] The establishment of the MCLG should therefore be a robust and objective scientific inquiry, devoid of nonscientific factors.[91] Risk must be assessed and quantified using the most current and best available scientific data and methods, but establishment of the MCLG does not include a determination whether it is affordable or achievable.

The MCL, on the other hand, is distinctly different from the MCLG, because setting an MCL is fundamentally a risk management exercise that incorporates a practical focus on economic and technological feasibility. After EPA identifies the aspirational, health-based goal, i.e., the MCLG, the Agency is then required to promulgate a corresponding MCL that is as close to the MCLG as practical feasibility and cost considerations will allow, based upon actual field conditions involving available technology. In sum, the MCLG serves as an objective benchmark against which the Agency can apply practical risk management considerations to set an enforceable MCL.[92] The MCL is the "real world" standard that reflects the statutory integration of the science-based MCLG with other nonscientific considerations, including feasibility, availability, and cost.

Judicial interpretations of the Act's standard-setting provisions confirm the MCLG as an objective, science-based goal, in contrast to the more policy-driven MCL. As explained in *Halogenated Solvents Indus Alliance v. Thomas*,[93] MCLs should closely track MCLGs.[94] However, unlike MCLGs, the enforceable MCLs are not based solely on the scientific evidence of a contaminant's health effects, but must take into consideration the reality of technological and economic factors in determining whether the MCL is feasible.[95]

To that end, EPA must determine whether the costs of the MCL, when implemented, would be justified by the benefits. If not, the Agency may adjust an MCL to a level that "maximizes health risk reduction benefits at a cost that is justified by the benefits." The authority to adjust the MCL is limited, however, and cannot be used to reduce the costs to large systems when the costs to such systems are justified by the benefits, unlike circumstances where smaller systems face issues of affordability. Congress reasoned that affordability problems for smaller systems should not affect the rationale for application of a broader national standard, because those systems would be eligible to receive a variance from that national standard on affordability grounds.[96]

4.3 Best Available Science—Risk Assessment, Management, and Communication

Significantly, the standard-setting process involving the identification of the MCLG and the establishment of the MCL is subject to a number of science mandates which are unique to the SDWA and whose provisions impose critical requirements upon the Agency regarding the use of sound science. In particular, the Act provides that, whenever the Agency employs science to make determinations involving standard setting under SDWA Section 1412, it *must* use "the best available, peer-reviewed science and supporting studies conducted in accordance with sound and objective scientific practices."[97] Moreover, the Agency must use "data collected by accepted methods or best available methods."[98] As the Agency has recognized, "[t]he use of the best available science is a core EPA principle as statutorily mandated by the SDWA amendments of 1996."

Furthermore, the Act not only requires use of the best available science and studies conducted in accordance with sound and objective practices for purposes of risk assessment and management, but also in terms of risk communication with respect to the promulgation of any new standard. Regarding the process of risk communication related to the promulgation of drinking water standards, the Act requires that, "in carrying out this section, the Administrator shall ensure that the *presentation* of information on public health effects is comprehensive, informative, and understandable."[99] Consistent with that requirement, EPA is required, "in a document made available to the public in support of a regulation promulgated under this section, to *specify*, to the extent practicable—

(i)   each population addressed by any estimate of public health effects;

(ii)   the expected risk or central estimate of risk for the specific populations;

(iii)   each appropriate upper-bound or lower-bound estimate of risk;

(iv)   each significant uncertainty identified in the process of the assessment of public health effects and studies that would assist in resolving the uncertainty; and

(v)   peer-reviewed studies known to the Administrator that support, are directly relevant to, or fail to support any estimate of public health effects and the methodology used to reconcile inconsistencies in the scientific data."[100]

Significantly, while these requirements are set forth in terms of *presentation*, they necessarily incorporate the substantive considerations addressed therein as essential aspects of the underlying risk assessment EPA must pursue. Taken as a whole, this science mandate with respect to standard-setting operates as an important check on EPA's rulemaking. While the Agency may exercise its discretion in weighing the scientific evidence, it must do so consistent with procedural and substantive commands of the Act and, in doing so, make a record that will withstand legal and scientific scrutiny.

In contrast to EPA's decision to include a contaminant on the CCL, or to proceed with the regulation of a contaminant, which are not subject to judicial review, Section 1448 of the Act expressly provides for judicial review of any rulemaking under the Act, including those related to standard-setting for MCLs. In pursuing any such challenge, the express science mandates set forth in the Act with respect to risk assessment, management, and communication serve as powerful legal constraints upon the Agency's authority to set drinking water standards. Indeed, this proved to be the case in a leading decision from the D.C. Circuit, *Chlorine Chemistry Council v. EPA*, 206 F.3d 1285 (D.C. Cir. 2000), where the U.S. Court of Appeals for the District of Columbia found that EPA had failed to follow the SDWA mandate regarding use of the best available science and reversed EPA's regulatory decision with respect to the standard it had adopted for disinfection by-products.[101]

4.4 Treatment Techniques

The SDWA establishes the legal framework under which EPA promulgates standards for the regulation of drinking water contaminants that "may have an adverse effect on the health of persons" and which are known or anticipated to occur in public water systems.[102] Such contaminants encompass a range of substances, including pathogens and microorganisms that threaten public health through the spread of disease and illness, and chemical contaminants and radio-nuclides that may pose other health risks.

Unfortunately the universe of contaminants is such that application of a numeric standard is not always practical. Therefore, the SDWA provides that EPA is authorized to list treatment techniques to achieve compliance with the maximum allowable contaminant levels and, in certain circumstances, to require particular treatment techniques to satisfy an MCL.[103] EPA generally may require a treatment technique for removing the contaminant if an MCL based on an absolute standard is neither economically or technologically feasible, or there is no accurate way to measure the level of the contaminant in water.[104]

For example, the Act generally contemplates that microbial contaminants may be controlled using approved treatment techniques (e.g., filtration and disinfection), while potentially harmful organic and inorganic chemical contaminants will be controlled through quantitative enforceable standards that limit the concentrations of such contaminants in drinking water. With respect to microorganisms, real-time sampling is not technically feasible, and such contaminants may be unevenly distributed in finished water[105] so as to render sample results, other than a simple positive or negative, uninformative with respect to the precise nature of the potential health risk. In such circumstances, treatment techniques, such as chlorination, can be administered at specific dosages that disperse uniformly in the treated water and serve as control measures that can be verified and accurately monitored by sampling throughout the systems. Thus, while the microorganism of concern cannot be quantified precisely in real time, disinfectant residuals techniques are measurable and, when used in conjunction with filtration, have proven to be reliable indicators of pathogen removal at levels sufficient to protect human health.[106] In addition, as reflected in EPA's Revised Total Coliform Rule,[107] treatment techniques can provide for the use of effective strategies and water management tools that protect human health by identifying pathways of contamination of distribution systems and corrective measures to address the risks they present.

4.5 Periodic Review of Existing NPDWRs

The 1996 SDWA amendments also established a requirement that EPA periodically review existing NPDWRs on a frequency of not less than every six years and revise them "as appropriate."[108] The Act provides that any revisions are to be accomplished in accordance with the requirements of Section 1412, which, at minimum, would include the science-based mandates relating to risk assessment, management, and communication, as well as the provision requiring data collected by accepted methods and studies conducted in accordance with sound and objective scientific practices. It is unclear from the Act, however, what time constraints, if any, apply to EPA's review, once the decision to revisit an NPDWR is made.

Significantly, EPA generally interprets the Act's requirement to "maintain or provide for greater protection of the health of persons" to incorporate an "antibacksliding" limitation on its review. As such, the Agency is averse to any revisions that would increase an MCL.[109] Notwithstanding that, EPA acknowledged during the second six-year review that the legislative history of the 1996 SDWA amendments indicates that Congress envisioned the possibility that a relaxed standard might be appropriate under circumstances in which it would not result in a lessening of the level of public health protection.[110]

As such, if the best available science and supporting data and studies conducted in accordance with sound and objective scientific practices demonstrate that a less stringent standard or revised treatment technique is equally or more protective of human health than one that is incorporated into an existing MCL, EPA would appear to have the discretion, consistent with its own interpretation of the limitations on "backsliding," to adopt such a relaxed standard or revised treatment technique. Indeed, the Revised Total Coliform Rule appears to do just that by doing away with the MCLG and MCL for Total Coliforms in favor of an MCLG and MCL focused on *E.coli* and a treatment technique intended to understand and address pathways for biological contaminants.[111]

As a result of prior rulemakings mandated by the Act and carried out by EPA, there are currently 87 NPDWRs that regulate contaminants.[112] In the intervening years since the 1996 amendments adopted the six-year review requirement, EPA has completed two such reviews with respect to these existing NPDWRs, the first in 2003 and a second in 2009.[113] EPA is currently conducting its third six-year review which began in September of 2015 and has not been completed as of this writing. It is worth noting that, while EPA solicits stakeholder input regarding the contaminants that will be the subjects of its review, it does not seek formal public comment regarding which candidates to review. Instead, it only seeks public comment with respect to how best to revisit the contaminants it has selected, once it has made its determination which ones to review.

Consistent with the Act, the primary goal of the six-year review is to identify, prioritize, and target candidates for regulatory revision that are most likely to result in a meaningful opportunity for health risk reduction and/or cost savings to public water systems and their customers while maintaining or providing for greater levels of public health protection.[114] To address this goal, and as part of the first six-year review that occurred in 2003,[115] EPA developed a protocol for performance of the review based on extensive inputs from the National Drinking Water Advisory Council (NDWAC) and the EPA Science Advisory Board (SAB).

For the second six-year review, EPA applied the same protocol with some refinements to improve the tracking of a contaminant through the decision process. The protocol focuses on several key elements that are intended to identify NPDWRs for which there is a health or technological basis for revising the NPDWR. The review is to rely upon an evaluation of relevant, new information for the most important technical elements, which include: (1) health effects, (2) analytical methods improvements, (3) treatment technology effectiveness, (4) occurrence and exposure analyses, and (5) potentially related regulatory changes.[116]

As a result of the 2003 review, the Agency determined that it would only be revisiting the Total Coliform Rule (discussed in section 5.2 of this chapter), and as a result of the 2009 review, it announced that four other existing NPDWRs were candidates for review: acrylamide, epichlorohydrin, tetrachloroethylene, and trichloroethylene. The 2009 review explained that review was not necessary with respect to 14 other NPDWRs, because they were the subject of recent or ongoing rulemaking activity. EPA also explained that 67 other existing NPDWRs were not considered candidates for review for one or more of four reasons:

- A health effects assessment was in process or the Agency was considering whether to initiate an assessment.

- The existing NPDWR was deemed to remain appropriate after review of new, relevant data/information.

- New, relevant information was available that indicated a potential change in the NPDWR, but no revision was recommended because it would have resulted in a negligible gain in public health protection and/or cost savings.

- Information gap(s) and/or emerging information were identified that warranted taking no further action at the time.[117]

4.6 Judicial Review

4.6.1 Review of Rulemakings

Section 1448(a)(1) of the Act[118] provides that a petition for review of actions pertaining to the establishment of NPDWRs (including specifically maximum contaminant level goals) may be filed only in the United States Court of Appeals for the District of Columbia Circuit. Section 1448(a)(2)[119] provides that a challenge to any other final Agency action may be filed in the United States Court of Appeals for the circuit in which the petitioner resides or transacts business which is directly affected by that action. Rulemakings may be challenged on grounds that they are arbitrary and capricious, or not otherwise in accordance with law.

Any such petition must be filed within the 45-day period beginning on the date of the promulgation of the regulations or any other final Agency action with respect to which review is sought or from the date of the determination with respect to which review is sought. The deadline is jurisdictional. Section 1448 does provide that certain actions may be filed *after* the expiration of such a 45-day period, but only if the petition is based solely on grounds arising after the expiration of that period. Furthermore, Agency rulemaking actions with respect to which review could have been pursued by a petition challenging that action within the 45-day time limit provided for under Section 1448(a)(1) are not thereafter subject to judicial review in a civil or criminal proceeding relating to enforcement, or in any subsequent civil action seeking to enjoin enforcement of the regulation.

4.6.2 Judicial Review of Administrative Fines and Penalties

Section 1448(a)(2) governs judicial review of actions involving appeals from administrative proceedings involving the assessment of fines and penalties for violations of the SDWA. (See also section 7.1.2.1 of this chapter.) In that regard, it provides that in any petition for review of an Agency action assessing of a civil penalty pursuant to SDWA Section 1414(g)(3)(B) jurisdiction rests with the U.S. Court of Appeals.[120] A petitioner challenging such an administrative penalty must simultaneously send copies of the complaint by certified mail to the EPA Administrator and the U.S. Attorney General. The Act provides that the Court of Appeals shall set aside and remand the penalty order if it finds that there is not substantial evidence in the record sufficient to support the finding of a violation, or that the assessment of the penalty by the Administrator was excessive and constituted an abuse of discretion.[121]

5.0 National Primary Drinking Water Regulations— Significant Regulations

While there are in excess of 80 NPDWRs, a number of NPDWRs are of particular significance given their broad applicability and their importance with respect to the protection of human health, and are summarized below.

5.1 Surface Water Treatment Rule

Treatment of drinking water drawn from surface sources has been a major aspect of the SDWA regulatory scheme since the 1986 amendments, and has involved a phased introduction of new requirements with respect to filtration and disinfection over a period of a dozen years through the promulgation of several major rulemakings. These rulemakings include: the 1989 Surface Water Treatment Rule (SWTR);[122] the 1998 Interim Enhanced Surface Water Treatment Rule (IESWTR);[123] the Long Term (1) Enhanced Surface Water Treatment Rule;[124] the Long Term (2) Enhanced Surface Water Treatment Rule; the Total Coliform Rule; and the Stage 1 and Stage 2 Disinfectants and Disinfection Byproducts Rules (DBPRs), all of which are addressed hereafter.

5.1.1 The 1989 Surface Water Treatment Rule

One of the most important regulations EPA has developed to counter the acute health risks posed by pathogens in drinking water is the 1989 Surface Water Treatment Rule (SWTR). Among its provisions, the SWTR requires that all surface water systems provide treatment sufficient to reduce the source water concentrations of *Giardia lamblia*[125] and viruses in finished water to levels that do not present a public health risk. To that end, the SWTR had as its key requirements:

- protecting against Giardia lamblia, viruses, and Legionella;

- achieving inactivation of 99.9 percent of Giardia and 99.99 percent of viruses;

- maintenance of appropriate disinfection residuals in the distribution system;

- filtration, unless avoidance criteria are met;[126]

- turbidity limits of 0.5 NTUs in 95 percent of monthly samples and no more than 5 NTUs in any given monthly sample;[127]

- watershed control programs; and

- water quality requirements for unfiltered systems.

In conjunction with the SWTR, EPA has identified four principal regulatory parameters associated with contaminants that present acute drinking water health threats that are addressed in the SWTR and corresponding NPDWRs. These parameters are total coliform, residual disinfectant, turbidity, and total nitrates. They are applicable to every non-ICC PWS, and are described below.

Total Coliform. Total coliform is an important testing parameter that provides a "snapshot" of coliform bacteria levels in drinking water.[128] Positive test results for coliform bacteria do not necessarily indicate the presence of harmful bacteria, but (1) may be an indicator that bacteria levels are sufficiently high to warrant further testing and (2) serve as a diagnostic tool for understanding potential pathways of contamination by harmful microbial pathogens that could represent vulnerabilities in a PWS distribution system. The current EPA regulations applicable to coliform require sampling by a PWS to confirm whether bacteria levels are, in fact, excessive and also whether harmful *Escherichia coli: (E coli) bacteria* are present.[129] An affirmative response in the latter situation will trigger the need for regulatory action on the part of a PWS, including prompt notice to the EPA and the public and the implementation of corrective measures (*see* discussion in section 5.2).

Residual Disinfectant. All water supplied by a PWS must be disinfected to reduce not only bacteria, but also harmful viruses and other pathogenic organisms that present acute health risks. This disinfection is usually accomplished by the source water provider (usually a CWS) at the treatment facility, most often through the addition of chlorine or another disinfectant (e.g., ozone, chlorine dioxide, chloramines) to the drinking water. In order to ensure that the introduction or regrowth of harmful bacteria, viruses, and pathogens is prevented, dosage levels of disinfectants are required to be sufficient to ensure the presence of a "detectable" chlorine residual (or its equivalent) in the distribution system up to the point of delivery to the consumer.[130]

Turbidity. Turbidity is a measurement of the presence of suspended solid material in drinking water using a metric based upon nephelometric turbidity units or NTUs. It is an important surrogate test for determining the presence of harmful pathogens, because they often are transported by attaching themselves to suspended solids in water. However, filtration of raw water, which is a general requirement for all CWSs, can remove nearly all such suspended material, and reintroduction of contamination following filtration is managed from a risk perspective by the use of disinfectants and other control strategies.[131]

Total Nitrates. The presence of nitrates and nitrites in drinking water is considered an indicator, among other things, of an environment favorable for the growth of bacteria and other microbial contaminants. Nitrates are often present as a result of urban or rural runoff containing fertilizers and/or human and animal wastes flowing into surface water supplies (e.g., a reservoir serving a CWS). Nitrates also can convert to nitrites in the human body with potential effects upon blood function, particularly in infants. A PWS must test for and take measures to ensure acceptable levels of nitrates in the finished water it provides.[132]

5.2 The Revised Total Coliform Rule

Total coliforms are a group of closely related bacteria that are generally not harmful to humans, but whose detection in drinking water may indicate the potential for more harmful bacteria to be present. For that reason, total coliforms testing can be used to help determine the efficacy of drinking water disinfection as well as identify pathways for contamination that may affect the integrity of the distribution system. Total coliforms react in a manner similar to most bacteria and many viral pathogens when exposed to chemical disinfectants. Thus, the absence of total coliforms in the distribution system decreases the likelihood that other, harmful pathogens are present. Accordingly, while the presence of total coliforms does not indicate that more harmful bacteria are, in fact, present, they are used to determine the *vulnerability* of a system to more serious bacterial and microbial contamination. This is true both with respect to finished water treatment and in post-treatment situations where cross-contamination may occur within the distribution system or in a consecutive system (*see* section 3.4.4).[133]

An NPDWR for total coliform, the Total Coliform Rule (TCR), was promulgated in 1989 and set maximum contaminant levels goals (MCLGs) and maximum contaminant levels (MCLs) for the presence of total coliform in drinking water.[134] However, as noted in section 4.5, the 1996 SDWA amendments require EPA to review each NPDWR, as appropriate, at least every six years to determine whether a revision is warranted. In its 2003 review, EPA announced its intent to revise the TCR in order to achieve greater public health protection. The outcome of the lengthy ensuing review of the TCR determined that there was an opportunity to reduce implementation burdens and to improve rule effectiveness, and that a revised TCR would offer an opportunity for greater public health protection against waterborne pathogens in the public drinking water distribution systems.

Thereafter, in February of 2013, EPA promulgated a revised TCR (the RTCR) based on recommendations of its federal advisory committees and in response to extensive comments received by the regulated community, public interest groups and a broad cross-section of other stakeholders.[135] Significantly, the RTCR, like the TCR before it, is the *only* microbial drinking water regulation that applies to *all* public water systems, including transient systems, with the exception of aircraft.[136]

In conjunction with that revision, the RTCR eliminated the previous MCLG and MCL for total coliform, replacing the latter with a treatment technique that requires a system assessment and corresponding corrective action.[137] Under the treatment technique for coliform in the RTCR, total coliform monitoring is still required and serves as an indicator of a potential pathway of contamination into the distribution system. Systems must monitor for the presence of total coliforms in the distribution system on a monthly basis employing a sample size that is based upon the number of people served and is statistically representative of the distribution system.[138] A PWS that exceeds the specified frequency of total coliform occurrence is required to conduct an assessment to determine if any sanitary defects exist in the distribution system and, if found, to correct them.

In place of the total coliform MCL, the RTCR establishes an MCLG and an MCL for *E. coli*, which is a more specific indicator of harmful contamination and potentially dangerous pathogens.[139] In the event of an *E. coli* violation, the treatment technique provisions require a PWS to conduct a similar, though more rigorous system assessment and correct any sanitary defects that are found.

As an incentive for improved water system operation, the RTCR establishes criteria for systems to qualify for and stay on reduced monitoring. Correspondingly, the rule also provides for increased monitoring for high-risk small systems with unacceptable compliance histories, and imposes new monitoring requirements for seasonal PWSs, such as state and national parks.

In view of these revisions, RTCR has also eliminated the previously required monthly public notification requirements based only on the presence of total coliforms. As explained in the regulatory history of the RTCR, total coliforms in the distribution system may indicate a potential pathway for contamination, but in and of themselves do not indicate a health threat. Instead, the RTCR requires public notification when an *E. coli* MCL violation occurs indicating a potential health threat, or when a PWS fails to conduct a required assessment and corrective action. In the event a positive *E. coli* result is obtained, a Tier 1 MCL violation has occurred and the PWS must (1) notify the primacy authority before the end of the next business day, (2) notify the public within 24 hours, and (3) initiate immediate corrective action.[140] A violation is triggered by any combination of an initial routine positive *E. coli* sample and a repeat sample that is positive,[141] and corrective measures may include discontinuation of water service, providing alternative water supplies, multimedia public education, and/or "boil water" warnings.

Because the RTCR contemplated a major transition for PWSs in terms of monitoring, compliance, reporting, risk assessment and corrective action and risk management, EPA adopted an effective date for compliance purposes that did not commence until April 1, 2016. Prior to that date, however, PWSs were allowed to implement the new requirements of the Revised Rule at their option.[142]

The PWSs directly affected by the RTCR are community water systems (systems that provide water and year-round residents in places likes homes or apartment buildings), non-community water systems (systems that provide water to people in locations such as schools, office buildings, restaurants, etc.), state primacy agencies, and local and tribal governments. As with the 1989 TCR, the RTCR will impact approximately 154,000 PWSs. EPA estimates that these water systems serve in excess of 300 million individuals.

5.2.1 The 1998 Interim Enhanced Surface Water Treatment Rule

The 1996 SDWA amendments recognized that the adoption and implementation of the new regulatory requirements was sufficiently complex and resource intensive as to require a phased approach to regulations, beginning with the largest surface water systems and proceeding on to the regulation of smaller systems and those systems served by groundwater.[143] Following that phased approach, in 1998, EPA promulgated the Interim Enhanced Surface Water Treatment Rule (IESWTR). The IESWTR amended the existing Surface Water Treatment Rule (SWTR) to strengthen microbial protection, including provisions specifically to address Cryptosporidium, and to address risk trade-offs associated with disinfection by-products for systems using surface water as a source.[144]

The IESWTR set an MCLG of zero for Cryptosporidium and strengthened combined filter effluent turbidity performance standards and individual filter turbidity provisions for filtered systems serving more than 10,000 people. For unfiltered systems, Cryptosporidium were required to be included in the watershed control requirements. In addition, the IESWTR built on the Total Coliform Rule by requiring sanitary surveys[145] for all public water systems using surface water and groundwater under the direct influence of surface water.[146] The IESWTR also requires covers for all new finished water storage facilities and includes disinfection benchmark provisions to ensure continued levels of microbial protection, while taking the necessary steps to comply with the disinfection by-product standards.[147]

5.2.2 Long Term 1 Enhanced Surface Water Treatment Rule

In 2002, in the next phase of surface water regulation mandated by the 1996 amendments, EPA finalized the Long Term 1 Enhanced Surface Water Treatment Rule (LT1ESWTR). It essentially extended the framework established for larger systems in the IESWTR to address small public water systems using surface waters serving fewer than 10,000 persons.[148] Similar to the IESWTR, the purpose of the LT1ESWTR was to improve control of microbial pathogens, specifically Cryptosporidium, in drinking water, and to address risk trade-offs associated with the increased potential for the generation of disinfection by-products. To that end, the rule requires these smaller public water systems to meet strengthened filtration requirements and to calculate levels of microbial inactivation to ensure that microbial protection would not be jeopardized if systems made changes to comply with requirements of the Stage 1 DBPR.[149]

5.2.3 Long Term 2 Enhanced Surface Water Treatment Rule

The Long Term 2 Enhanced Surface Water Treatment Rule (LT2ESWTR) continued to build upon the earlier IESWTR and LT1ESWTR and Stage 1 and 2 DBPRs by requiring additional Cryptosporidium treatment beyond that required in existing regulations for "higher risk" public water systems.[150] These higher risk systems include: (1) all PWSs that use surface water *or* groundwater under the direct influence of surface water that experience high levels of Cryptosporidium in their water sources, and (2) all unfiltered water systems that do not treat for Cryptosporidium.

Under the LT2ESWTR, systems must employ new monitoring approaches for their water sources to determine treatment requirements. Filtered water systems are classified in one of four treatment categories ("bins") based on their monitoring results. Systems classified in higher treatment bins must provide 90 to 99.7 percent (1.0 to 2.5-log removal) additional treatment for Cryptosporidium. Systems may select from a range of treatment and management strategies in the "microbial toolbox" to meet their additional treatment requirements. All *unfiltered* water systems must provide at least 99 or 99.9 percent (2 or 3-log) inactivation of Cryptosporidium, depending on the results of their monitoring.

This rule also contains provisions to reduce risks from uncovered finished water reservoirs by requiring these systems *to cover the reservoir*, or to treat the reservoir discharge to achieve 4-log virus inactivation, 3-log *Giardia lamblia* inactivation, and 2-log Cryptosporidium inactivation. In addition, systems must review their current level of microbial treatment before making any significant change in their disinfection practice. This review is intended to assist systems in maintaining protection against microbial pathogens as they take steps to reduce the formation of disinfection by-products under the Stage 2 DBPR, which EPA finalized along with the LT2ESWTR.[151]

5.3 Disinfection and Disinfection Byproducts Rule

The 1996 Safe Drinking Water Act amendments required EPA to introduce additional regulatory measures to reduce the threat from microbial contaminants, including Cryptosporidium, while strengthening control over the by-products of the chemical disinfection used to address those contaminants.[152] However, while chemical disinfectants provide effective treatment to reduce microorganisms in drinking water, excessive long-term exposure to those disinfectants or their by-products may present chronic health threats. Accordingly, EPA promulgated a set of interrelated regulations that address and attempt to balance risks from microbial pathogens and the by-products of drinking water disinfectants used to control them. They were promulgated in two steps as the Stage 1 and Stage 2 Disinfectants and Disinfection Byproducts Rules and are regulatory complements to the RTCR and various surface water treatment rules discussed above.

5.3.1 Stage 1 Disinfectants and Disinfection Byproducts Rule

The Stage 1 Disinfectants and Disinfection Byproduct Rule (Stage 1 DBPR) was the first of the two rules aimed at reducing the allowable levels of disinfectants, disinfection by-products (DBPs), and DBP precursors in drinking water.[153] Issued in 1998, the Stage 1 DBPR updated and superseded existing regulatory standards for total trihalomethane disinfection by-products (TTHMs) promulgated in 1979. The Stage 1 DBPR applies to all sizes of community water systems and nontransient noncommunity water systems that add a disinfectant to the drinking water during any part of the treatment process,[154] and to transient noncommunity water systems that use chlorine dioxide as a disinfectant.[155] The Stage 1 DBPR was promulgated simultaneously with the Interim Enhanced Surface Water Treatment Rule (IESWTR) to address concerns about potential risks that might result from implementation of the new control measures for pathogens required by the IESWTR.

The Stage 1 DBPR established seven new standards and treatment techniques to reduce human exposure to DBPs in finished drinking water. The rule established maximum residual disinfectant level goals (MRDLGs) and maximum residual disinfectant levels (MRDLs) for three chemical disinfectants—chlorine, chloramine, and chlorine dioxide.[156] It also established maximum contaminant level goals (MCLGs) and maximum contaminant levels (MCLs) for TTHMs, haloacetic acids (HAA5), chlorite, and bromate. As a result, conventional systems are now required to remove specified percentages of DBP precursors from their raw water through treatment techniques that include enhanced coagulation, enhanced softening, or alternative treatments.[157]

5.3.2 Stage 2 Disinfectants and Disinfection Byproducts Rule

In 2006, EPA promulgated the Stage 2 Disinfectants and Disinfection Byproducts Rule (Stage 2 DBPR), which built upon the Stage 1 DBPR to address higher risk public water systems and strengthen compliance monitoring requirements for two groups of DBPs—TTHMs and HAA5.[158] The rule applies to all community water systems and nontransient noncommunity water systems that add a primary or residual disinfectant other than ultraviolet (UV)[159] light, or deliver water that has been disinfected by a primary or residual disinfectant, other than UV. Like the Stage 1 DBPR and IESWTR, the Stage 2 DBPR was promulgated simultaneously with the Long Term 2 Enhanced Surface Water Treatment Rule to address concerns about risk trade-offs between pathogen control and DBPs that were presented by the regulatory requirements for disinfection.

Under the Stage 2 DBPR, systems must conduct an evaluation of their distribution systems, known as an Initial Distribution System Evaluation (IDSE), to identify the locations with high disinfection by-product concentrations. These locations are used by the systems as the sampling sites for Stage 2 DBPR compliance monitoring. Compliance with the maximum contaminant levels for TTHM and HAA5 is calculated for each monitoring location in the distribution system. This site-specific approach, referred to as the "locational running annual average," differs from previous requirements, which determined compliance by calculating the running annual average of samples from all monitoring locations across the system.

The Stage 2 DBPR also requires each system to determine if it has exceeded an operational evaluation level, which is identified using its compliance monitoring results. The operational evaluation level provides an early warning of possible future MCL violations, which allows the system to take proactive steps to remain in compliance. A system that exceeds an operational evaluation level is required to review its operational practices and submit a report to its state Primacy authority that identifies actions that may be taken to mitigate future high DBP levels, particularly those that may jeopardize its compliance with the DBP MCLs.[160]

5.4 Lead and Copper Rule

One of the most common sources of lead exposure for children is lead paint in older housing and the contaminated dust and soil it generates. Lead paint is primarily associated with housing built in the 1950s and homes with paint man-ufactured before 1973 that may contain lead. Dust from such paint may be ingested through the lungs and introduced there into the blood as an exposure pathway, and represents a potentially serious health threat, particularly to chil-dren. Several federal programs and surveillance and prevention programs at the state and local level are intended to reduce exposure to lead from such sources. In addition, EPA works with federal agencies such as the Departments of Hous-ing and Urban Development and Health and Human Services, pursuing a federal strategy whose objective is to eliminate childhood lead poisoning.

Although the greatest exposure risks are related to paint, lead in drinking water can also pose a risk to human health. As indicated in EPA's public educa-tion material for lead, up to 20 percent of a person's exposure to lead potentially can come from drinking water. Moreover, the level of exposure can be greater for children and infants, particularly if tap water is used to mix juices and formula.

Unlike most contaminants, however, lead is not generally introduced to drinking water supplies from source waters, because it seldom occurs naturally at levels of concern in water supplies like rivers and lakes. Rather, the primary sources of lead in drinking water are: (1) corrosion and/or wear on lead service lines that connect water distribution systems to older residential buildings, (2) lead-based solder used to connect pipe in older household plumbing systems, and (3) brass plumbing fixtures that contain lead. As such, simply setting a lead standard for water leaving the treatment plant will generally fail to capture the extent of lead leaching into drinking water from lead service lines and household plumbing.[161]

To address these corrosion-related sources, Congress and EPA have taken a number of regulatory actions over the past 20 years to reduce lead in drinking water.[162] An important first step occurred when the 1986 amendments to the SDWA effectively banned the use of lead solder and lead-containing pipes from public water supply systems and plumbing, and limited faucets and other brass plumbing components to no more than .8 percent lead.[163] Thereafter, Congress targeted lead exposure of children in schools in the Lead Contamination Control Act (LCCA) of 1988,[164] which forced the recall of drinking water coolers con-taining lead-lined water reservoir tanks and banned new drinking water coolers with lead parts. Furthermore, the 1986 SDWA amendments directed EPA to revise its regulations for lead in drinking water to reduce the "interim" standard for lead in drinking water of 50 parts per billion (ppb) that had been established in 1975. Accordingly, the Agency proposed revisions to the standard in 1988 and issued a new standard for lead as part of the 1991 Lead and Copper Rule (LCR).[165] The revised standard significantly changed the regulatory framework, setting an MCLG of zero for lead in drinking water.

However, the SDWA does not incorporate the authority to EPA to require homeowners to replace their plumbing systems if they contain lead.[166] Rather EPA can only require that a PWS meet regulatory standards for water quality entering the home. Accordingly, to reduce consumers' lead exposure from tap water, EPA decided to use its available authorities to require finished water to be as non-corrosive as possible to metals in the plumbing systems of PWS customers. The LCR therefore directs systems to optimize corrosion control to protect the integrity of household plumbing and prevent lead[167] from leaching into drinking water as a treatment technique. In order to achieve that objective, large systems serving more than 50,000 people were required to conduct studies of corrosion control and to install the state-approved optimal corrosion control treatment by January 1, 1997. Small and medium-sized systems are also required to optimize corrosion control if monitoring performed at the consumer taps shows action is necessary.

In order to ensure that corrosion control treatment technique requirements implemented by a PWS are effective in protecting public health, the LCR also established an "action level" of 15 ppb for lead in drinking water, measured at the customers' taps (with samples obtained by permission from the homeowner). CWSs are required to monitor a specific number of customer taps in a manner that is representative of the size and nature of the distribution system, taking into account high-risk homes. In the event a CWS exceeds the 15 ppb lead action level at more than 10 percent of the taps sampled,[168] it must initiate a broad-based and comprehensive action program commencing within 60 days of the exceedance. The essential requirements of the program are evaluation of source water and system water chemistry, enhanced monitoring and reporting, corrosion control treatment, and informational/educational outreach to the public.[169]

The informational aspects of the program are extensive and must address the nature of exceedance, the potential health risks it poses to the public, measures they can take to minimize any associated health risks, and what steps the CWS is taking to remedy the problem. This information is required to be provided to water consumers in multiple forms and through a variety of media, recognizing that all consumers are not necessarily residential customers. To that end, the LCR requires the insertion of mandatory warning language specific to the threats posed by lead in customer bills; in notices in major newspapers; in announcements on radio and television stations; and in brochures containing information and risk reduction measures with respect to lead that must be provided to health departments, schools, hospitals, clinics, pediatricians, family planning clinics, and welfare agencies that serve women, infants, and children.[170] These requirements include LCR revisions made in 2000 and 2007 to modify and enhance monitoring, reporting, and public education requirements, but the basic regulatory framework of the LCR, including the lead action level, was not changed.[171]

In sum, the LCR serves four main functions: (1) to determine tap water levels of lead and copper for customers who have lead service lines, lead plumbing, or lead-based solder in their plumbing system; (2) to require water suppliers to optimize their treatment system to control corrosion in customers' plumbing;[172] (3) to rule out the source water as a source of significant lead levels;[173] and, (4) if action levels are exceeded, to require the suppliers of finished water to initiate corrective measures and educate their customers about lead through public notices and public education programs identifying actions they can take to reduce their exposure to lead. Significantly, if a water system, after installing and optimizing corrosion control treatment, continues to fail to meet the lead action level, it must begin a multiyear program to replace the lead service lines under its ownership and, if necessary, provide alternative water treatment and/or supplies until it consistently demonstrates water quality below the action level at the tap.[174]

Finally, in addition to the general recordkeeping requirements applicable to all regulated contaminants, certain requirements specific to lead are imposed pursuant to 40 C.F.R. § 141.91. In particular, a PWS subject to the LCR must retain on its premises original records of all sampling data and analyses, reports, surveys, letters, evaluations, schedules, state determinations, and any other information required by the lead drinking water regulations (i.e., 40 C.F.R. §§ 141.81 through 141.88) for at least 12 years.

5.4.1 Lead Contamination Developments

Issues related to lead-contaminated drinking water have risen to national prominence recently as a result of events in Flint, Michigan. The water crisis there and the related litigation it has engendered have compelled EPA and public water supply systems across the country to reevaluate their lead control programs and look more closely at issues related to the corrosivity of their source water.[175]

The situation in Flint achieved national attention after a state-appointed "emergency manager" switched from the Detroit Water and Sewerage Department to the Flint River as the city's drinking water source. Although a corrosion control plan was proposed in the city's operating plan, it apparently was not implemented due to cost constraints. The corrosivity of the resulting water was problematic, causing elevated water lead levels in Flint homes with lead service lines or plumbing and fixtures with lead content. The seriousness of the situation and the national attention it has generated have led EPA to consider implementing a number of the recommendations of a blue-ribbon working group that would involve further revisions to the current Lead and Copper Rule.

The working group's recommendations, which were published in August of 2015, include: (1) implementation of more proactive lead service line replacement programs, (2) more robust public education requirements, including targeted outreach to at risk homeowners and vulnerable populations, (3) improved corrosion control treatment and monitoring, (4) implementation of a "household action level" that would trigger notice to the consumer and trigger health agency follow up, (5) separate corrosion control requirements for lead and copper, and (6) adoption of commensurate compliance and enforcement authorities.[176] As of this writing, EPA has not taken formal action on these recommendations, although it is facing significant political pressure to do so, particularly with respect to the "household action level."

In the wake of the Flint water situation, various plaintiffs have also initiated litigation seeking injunctive relief, penalties, and redress for damages, asserting violations of the LCR and tort claims under state laws. In *Gilcreast v. Lockwood*,[177] for example, a putative class is suing over a dozen defendants alleging numerous causes of action, including the government defendants' alleged failure to comply with the LCR's corrosion control and public notice requirements. At this writing, dozens of other cases asserting claims are pending in Michigan state courts.[178]

5.5 Inorganic Contaminants

In addition to NPDWRs for lead and arsenic, EPA has promulgated MCLs for 13 other inorganics, including antimony, asbestos, barium, beryllium, cadmium, chromium, cyanide, nickel, nitrate, nitrite, selenium, and thalium.[179] The regulations also set forth specific detection limits for these inorganic contaminants (except nitrate and nitrite), that are well below the MCL.[180] Every CWS and NCNTWS is required to monitor for all of these inorganics, though transient noncommunity water systems need only monitor for nitrate and nitrite. Routine monitoring is based upon a running average of samples taken at every entry point to the distribution system at a frequency determined on the basis of an initial compliance/monitoring period involving annual sampling.[181] In the event an MCL is exceeded, the monitoring frequency is increased to quarterly sampling, until such time as the PWS has a continuous record of compliance. Systems that do not exceed the MCL may seek a waiver based upon a record of continuous compliance.[182]

5.5.1 Fluoride

Section 1412(b)(11) of the Safe Drinking Water Act ("SDWA") generally provides that the national primary drinking water regulations may not require the addition of any substance for preventive health care purposes unrelated to contamination of drinking water.[183] However, while the EPA may not require the addition of fluoride, the legislative history and the standard-setting provisions of the SDWA make clear that states and local water authorities may voluntarily add fluoride up to EPA's enforceable limits as a public health measure for reducing the incidence of oral disease among treated population.[184] Approximately three-fourths of all community water systems in the United States, providing drinking water to nearly 200 million customers, choose to do so.[185]

Recognizing that fluoride may be added to drinking water or may be naturally present in raw source water, the SDWA nonetheless authorizes EPA to set both regulatory goals and enforceable limits for fluoride levels in drinking water. Consistent with the SDWA, EPA has established an MCLG of 4.0 mg/L or 4.0 parts per million ("ppm") for fluoride in drinking water.[186] As explained earlier in this chapter, MCLGs are aspirational health goals that EPA is required to establish using the best available science and supporting data. Pursuant to the SDWA, EPA must set an MCLG at the level at (1) which no known or anticipated adverse effects on the health of persons occur; and (2) which provides for an adequate margin of safety.[187]

EPA has also adopted an enforceable maximum contaminant level ("MCL") for fluoride in drinking water of 4.0 mg/L or 4.0 ppm.[188] Generally, the SDWA requires the MCL to be set as close to the corresponding MCLG as possible, taking into account health risk, benefits, and the ability of public water systems to detect and remove contaminants using suitable treatment technologies.[189] In the case of fluoride, EPA has set the enforceable MCL for fluoride at the same level as the MCLG, effectively ensuring that community water systems limit fluoridation to levels that EPA has determined present no known or anticipated adverse effects on human health, while allowing for an adequate margin of safety. This regulatory limit applies to all community water systems in the country.

EPA has also set a "secondary" standard for fluoride at 2.0 mg/L or 2.0 ppm.[190] As explained previously in section 3.2 of this chapter, secondary standards are non-enforceable guidelines that address potential cosmetic effects (such as skin or tooth discoloration) or aesthetic effects (such as taste, odor, or color) in drinking water. EPA recommends secondary standards for water systems, but the SDWA provides that the application of those secondary standards is a matter for state and local government determination.

Though not binding on state and local authorities, the U.S. Department of Health and Human Services ("HHS") recommends the fluoridation of drinking water and offers guidance regarding its use as a public health practice. On January 7, 2011, HHS issued a revised recommendation which identified an optimal level to 0.7 ppm of fluoride in drinking water to achieve the benefits of preventing tooth decay.[191] Additionally, EPA is involved in an ongoing process of updating its health and exposure assessments on fluoride as part of a broader SDWA requirement to review each National Primary Drinking Water Regulation at least once every six years.[192] Once EPA finalizes these assessments, it may review the existing MCL to determine whether any revisions are appropriate.

5.6 Synthetic Organic Contaminants

EPA has established MCLs for 33 synthetic organic contaminants (SOCs), which are comprised largely of pesticides.[193] As in the case of inorganic contaminants, in addition to establishing MCLs, the regulations set forth specific detection limits for each of the organic contaminants well below the MCL.[194] Routine monitoring is based upon a running average of samples taken at every entry point to the distribution system. If an SOC is found to be present above the detection limit during an initial compliance period, the system must monitor quarterly for the contaminant.[195] If the system remains reliably and consistently below the MCL, monitoring may be reduced. Systems that do not exceed the MCL may seek also a waiver based upon a record of continuous compliance and evidence that the systems' source water is not vulnerable to a contaminant.[196] Every CWS and NCNTWS is required to monitor for all of these organics, though transient noncommunity water systems are not. With respect to treatment of such contaminants, the regulations identify granulated activated carbon (GAC) or packed tower aeration /as the best technology treatment technique for achieving compliance with the SOC MCLs.[197]

5.6.1 Perchlorate

Perchlorates represent a group of naturally occurring and man-made salts that have been included on all three EPA Candidate Contaminant Lists.[198] Perchlorate salts are ingredients in fertilizer, fireworks, explosives and rocket propellants. In October of 2008, EPA published an initial regulatory determination in the Federal Register indicating that, consistent with Section 1412(b)(1)(A) of the SDWA, perchlorate did not occur with a frequency and at levels of public health concern such that its regulation would present a meaningful opportunity for health risk reduction relative to persons served by public water systems.[199] EPA received more than 33,000 comments on its initial determination and in February of 2011 reversed course and published a new determination in the Federal Register concluding that (1) perchlorate may have an adverse effect on human health, (2) that there is a substantial likelihood that it will occur in public water systems with a frequency and at levels of public health concern, and (3) that the regulation of perchlorate presents a meaningful opportunity to reduce health risk for persons served by public water systems.[200]

Having made that Regulatory Determination, EPA expressed its intent to adopt an MCLG for perchlorate and proposed an NPDWR with an MCL by

February, 2013, *i.e.*, within 24 months of its published determination, and finalize the NPDWR/MCL within 18 months thereafter as required by Section 1412(b)(1)(E) of the Act.[201]

Notwithstanding that regulatory deadline, EPA failed to propose an MCLG by February of 2013 or to propose an MCL. Significantly, the failure to adopt an MCLG and propose an MCL is the result of the recommendations set forth in a May 2013 report of the Science Advisory Board ("SAB") that EPA convened to address the human health risk assessment for perchlorate in drinking water.[202]

In a rather significant departure from prior Agency risk assessment methodology, the SAB recommended that EPA develop an MCLG (and MCL) not through the traditional resort to an algebraic application of a reference dose ("RfD") based on the greatest amount of perchlorate the Agency would estimate could be consumed on a daily basis without an adverse effect, but rather on the basis of a more refined physiological-based pharmaco-kinetic ("PBPK") model,[203] representing the best available science. A key aspect of the PBPK model is that it incorporates quantitative predictions of absorption, distribution, metabolism, and excretion of chemical substances in the body for purposes of health risk assessment.

Following up on the SAB recommendation, the Agency has delayed the adoption of an MCLG and taken steps that indicate its intent to apply a PBPK model in setting the MCLG for perchlorate. More specifically, in March of 2016, EPA published a Notice in the Federal Register seeking nominations of scientific experts to conduct "external peer review of the draft Biologically Based Dose-Response model for perchlorate in drinking water and a draft model support document.[204] As the Agency explained, "EPA scientists are collaborating with FDA scientists to develop appropriate PBPK models to inform the derivation of a maximum contaminant level goal (MCLG) for perchlorate in response to recommendations by EPA's Science Advisory Board (SAB). FDA scientists developed a model to relate perchlorate exposure to biological effects (*e.g.*, changes in thyroid hormones) in the late-stage fetus, one of the most sensitive lifestages. In response to SAB recommendations, FDA and EPA scientists are developing models to relate perchlorate exposure to biological effects in infants, another key lifestage. Scientists will use information from published models and literature to develop thyroid hormone models for the bottle-fed infant, breast-fed infant, and lactating mother."[205]

In a related development, in February of 2016, the Natural Resources Defense Council filed suit in federal district court to compel EPA to adopt a schedule to propose and finalize an NPDWR for perchlorate, and the parties have agreed to a consent decree providing deadlines of October 2018 and October 2019, respectively, for the proposed and final rules.[206]

5.7 Volatile Organic Compounds

The NPDWRs regulate 21 volatile organic chemicals (VOCs).[207] VOCs vaporize at relatively low temperatures and primarily include industrial and chemical solvents such as benzene and toluene that may have been discharged to the environment, including directly into surface water or in air injected into subsurface wells.[208] The VOC regulations also set forth specific detection limits for each of the organic contaminants well below the MCL.[209] Routine monitoring is based upon a running average of samples taken at every entry point to the distribution system. If a VOC is found to be present above the detection limit during an initial compliance period, the system must monitor quarterly for the contaminant.[210] If the system remains reliably and consistently below the MCL, monitoring may be reduced to annual sampling, and a waiver from sampling for up to six years may be granted by the primacy agency if no VOCs are detected in the initial compliance period.[211] Every CWS and NCNTWS is required to monitor for all of these VOCs, though transient noncommunity water systems are not.

5.8 Radionuclides

Radionuclides include the category of contaminants that emit radiation and are either naturally occurring or the result of oil and gas production and mining activities.[212] Radionuclides currently regulated in drinking water include (1) a combined radium-226 and radium-228 activity limit of no more than 5 picocuries per liter, (2) a gross alpha particle radioactivity (including radium, but not radon or uranium) limit which must be no more than 15 picocuries per liter of water, and (3) a limit on beta particle and photon radioactivity from man-made radionuclides of no more than that which would produce an annual dose equivalent to the total body or any internal organ of 4 millirems per year calculated on the basis of an intake of 2 liters of the water per day. However, if two or more beta or photon-emitting radionuclides are present, the sum of their annual dose equivalent to the total body or to any internal organ shall not exceed 4 millirems per year.[213]

5.9 Filter Backwash Recycling Rule

The 1996 amendments to the SDWA required EPA to promulgate a regulation governing the recycling of filter backwash water within the treatment process of a public water system.[214] The Filter Backwash Recycling Rule (FBRR) addresses filter backwash water and two additional recycle streams to reduce the risk of microbes such as Cryptosporidium passing through into finished drinking water.[215] The FBRR applies to all public water systems that: (1) use surface water or groundwater under the direct influence of surface water; (2) use direct or conventional filtration processes; and (3) recycle spent filter backwash water, sludge thickener supernatant, or liquids from dewatering processes.

The FBRR requires recycled filter backwash water, sludge thickener supernatant, and liquids from dewatering processes to be returned to a location such
that all processes of a public water system's conventional or direct filtration,
including coagulation, flocculation, sedimentation (conventional filtration only),
and filtration, are employed. The FBRR also requires that systems notify the
primacy agency in writing that they practice recycling of these fluids. Systems
must collect and maintain information regarding their recycling practices. The
primacy agency may, after evaluating the information, require a system to modify
its recycle location or recycle practices.[216]

6.0 Regulatory Compliance Requirements

While the most essential aspect of the NPDWRs are the drinking water standards
and/or treatment techniques prescribed for particular regulated contaminants,
the NPDWRs also address other critical requirements of the regulatory scheme,
including monitoring, sampling, reporting, notice to the public, recordkeeping, and actions to be taken in the event of a violation. With respect to the latter,
in addition to corrective action, the regulations generally require enhanced efforts
beyond routine monitoring, sampling, reporting, and notice requirements. This
is in keeping with the regulatory philosophy embodied in the SDWA that, when
a violation of an NPDWR occurs that may present a health risk to the public,
not only must diagnostic and corrective measures be taken to identify, characterize, and eliminate that risk, but (1) regulatory authorities must be promptly
advised so that they may provide oversight and ensure appropriate response and
compliance measures; and (2) the public must be provided with prompt, accurate, and complete information regarding the violation, its possible health implications, and options for addressing the same in order that they may take
appropriate actions to protect their health.

6.1 Monitoring/Sampling

The NPDWRs establish minimum monitoring requirements for PWSs applicable to biological, physical, and chemical contaminants. While specific monitoring and reporting requirements are best addressed in the context of the individual
contaminant at issue, a number of general regulatory considerations apply with
respect to all of the NPDWRs. In that regard, the frequency and extent of monitoring is premised on the nature and significance of the health risk posed by a
contaminant. The monitoring requirements with respect to biological and physical contaminants are generally more frequent and focus on water both in the
treatment facility and throughout the distribution system. Monitoring requirements associated with those risks (e.g., for total coliform and turbidity) must be
met by all PWSs, including CWSs, NCNTWSs, and transient systems.

With respect to organic and inorganic chemical contaminants, health risks from chronic exposures are the principal concern. Accordingly, monitoring can be less frequent and is generally focused on water entering the distribution system from a treatment facility (with the notable exceptions of lead and DBPs). In addition, unlike contaminants that present acute health threats, monitoring requirements for contaminants that present chronic health risks generally do not extend to transient water systems. With respect to chemicals, the monitoring requirements for inorganic, volatile organic, and synthetic organic contaminants regulated under the SDWA generally involve three categories of monitoring: (1) initial compliance monitoring to evaluate occurrence, (2) subsequent routine monitoring based upon the occurrence results, and (3) monitoring in the event of a sampling result above the maximum contaminant level.

With respect to chemical contaminants that pose chronic health risks, monitoring may be decreased over time, if occurrence data indicate an absence of the risk of public exposure. Similarly, in the event an MCL or an action level is exceeded, increased monitoring may be required, both to determine the nature and extent of the threat, and to determine when a return to routine monitoring may be warranted. In that regard, samples may be characterized as routine, confirmatory, or special purpose. Monitoring must be based on sampling representative of the system, and in some instances, may require consideration of seasonal or other factors. Monitoring is required for finished water entering the distribution system and, depending upon the contaminant, may be required within the distribution system and even at the customer's tap (e.g., lead). Monitoring results must be reported regularly to the primacy authority, and results that indicate a violation must be reported to the public, as appropriate to the health risk they seek to address. Such violations include not only exceeding of an MCL, but failure to monitor or report monitoring results. Finally, states may require additional monitoring if they administer their own drinking water program as "primacy agencies" authorized under the SDWA. The NPDWRs also establish sampling protocols and testing requirements specific to the contaminant of concern, the size of the PWS, and its classification (e.g., CWS or transient).

6.2 Reporting

The SDWA is premised on a regulatory approach that relies extensively on self-monitoring and reporting to ensure compliance and appropriate regulatory oversight of matters that may present human health risks from the consumption of drinking water. Indeed, given the number of regulated public water systems, the variety of consumers they serve, and the scope of the affected drinking water population, the regulatory scheme must necessarily rely on the monitoring and reporting efforts of PWSs in order to function. For those same reasons, failures to adhere to monitoring and reporting requirements are treated as serious violations of the NPDWRs, particularly with respect to acute health threats.

General reporting requirements applicable to every regulated PWS are set forth in the regulations at 40 C.F.R. § 141.31, though individual NPDWRs prescribe additional reporting requirements specific to particular drinking water contaminants.[217] General requirements include the following:

- Unless a shorter period is otherwise specified for a particular contaminant under an NPDWR, a PWS must report to the primacy agency[218] the results of any test or analysis required by the regulations part within (1) the first ten days following the end of the month in which the result were received, or (2) the first ten days following the end of any required monitoring period as adopted by the primacy authority, whichever is the shortest.[219]

- Unless a shorter period is otherwise specified for a particular contaminant under an NPDWR, a PWS must report to the primacy agency, within 48 hours, the failure to comply with any NPDWR, including failure to comply with monitoring requirements prescribed by the applicable regulation.[220]

- Within 10 days of completing the public notification requirements under the regulations (Subpart Q), a PWS must submit a certification to the primacy agency that it has fully complied with the public notification regulations with respect to any required initial public notice and repeat notices. The certification must include a representative copy of each type of notice distributed, published, posted, and made available to the persons served by the system and to the media.[221]

- SDWA Section 1445 provides that EPA or a state primacy agency may require a PWS to provide such monitoring data or other information as may be "reasonably" required for purposes of determining whether the PWS is in compliance with the requirements of the Act.[222] In the event of such a demand, the PWS must provide the information within the time stated in the request,[223] including copies of any records required to be maintained under the recordkeeping provisions of the regulations[224] or copies of any documents then in existence which the state or EPA is entitled to inspect pursuant to SDWA Section 1445, or the corresponding provisions of state law.[225]

6.3 Violations

The scope and significance of the national drinking water program dictates that all aspects of the NPDWRs must be enforced in order to protect the public health. Accordingly, the scope of regulatory violations includes: (1) exceeding an MCL or a maximum residual disinfectant level (MRDL), (2) failure to comply with a prescribed treatment technique, (3) monitoring violations, (4) sampling and testing violations, (5) reporting failures, (6) recordkeeping violations, (7) failure to provide required public notification, and (8) violations of variance and exemption requirements.[226] Violations are ranked on the basis of their seriousness and the risk they pose to public health. Those rankings consist of three tiers, which are discussed in greater detail in the context of the corresponding public notification requirements below. Violations may be subject to administrative or judicial enforcement, depending upon their nature and severity, as discussed in section 7 of this chapter, and primacy agencies may seek fines, penalties, and injunctive relief, as appropriate to the circumstances of the violation.

6.4 Public Notification

The SDWA recognizes that the public notification requirements of the NPD-WRs perform an essential role in carrying out the objectives of the regulatory scheme by alerting the public to potential health risks from violations of the drinking water standards, or other situations that may present a health risk. In view of this, and as required by the 1996 amendments, EPA published final regulations in the *Federal Register* on May 4, 2000,[227] significantly revising and expanding the general public notification requirements. The revised regulations are codified at 40 C.F.R. Part 141, Subpart Q, and became effective on June 5, 2000.[228]

The most important of the public notice requirements necessarily involve situations in which there has been a violation of an NPDRW. In that regard, the notice provisions of the regulations provide that, depending on the severity of the situation, water suppliers have from 24 hours to one year to notify their customers after a violation occurs. Public notification requirements are generally divided into three categories, or "tiers," to take into account the seriousness of the violation and any potential adverse health effects that may be involved.

6.4.1 Timing of Public Notice

Water systems have different amounts of time to distribute the notice and different ways to deliver the notice, depending upon the nature of violation:[229]

Tier 1—Immediate notice: Anytime a situation occurs in which there is the potential for human health to be immediately impacted, water suppliers have 24 hours to notify people who may drink the water of the situation. Water suppliers must use media outlets such as television, radio, and newspapers, post their notice in public places, and personally deliver notices to their customers in these situations.

Tier 2—Notice as soon as possible: Anytime a PWS provides water with levels of a contaminant that exceed EPA or state standards or that hasn't been treated properly, but that doesn't pose an immediate risk to human health, the water system must notify its customers as soon as possible, but within 30 days of the violation. Notice may be provided via the media, posting, or the mail.

Tier 3—Annual notice: When a water system violates a drinking water standard that does not have a direct impact on human health (e.g., failing to take a required sample on time) the system has up to a year to provide a notice of this situation to its customers. The extra time gives water suppliers the opportunity to consolidate these notices and send them with annual water quality reports (Consumer Confidence Reports).

6.4.2 Seriousness of Violations—Notice Requirements by Tier

Specific requirements apply with respect to the seriousness of the threat from particular MCL violations as summarized below.

Tier 1 Public Notice (Required within 24 Hours)

- *E. Coli* maximum contaminant level (MCL) violation or failure to conduct repeat test for contamination after a test that is positive.

- Nitrate/nitrite/combined nitrate and nitrite MCL violation, or failure to take confirmation sample.

- Chlorine dioxide maximum residual disinfectant level (MRDL) violation in the distribution system or failure to take repeat samples in the distribution system.

- Exceedance of maximum allowable turbidity level resulting in an MCL or treatment technique (TT) violation, when the primacy agency or EPA determines a Tier 1 notice is warranted.

- Special public notice for noncommunity water systems with nitrate exceedances between 10 mg/l and 20 mg/l, when allowed to exceed the MCL (10 mg/l) by the primacy agency.

- Waterborne disease outbreak or other waterborne emergency.

- Other high-risk situations as determined by the primacy agency.

Tier 2 Public Notice (Required within 30 Days)

- All other MCL, MRDL, and TT violations not identified as a Tier 1 notice.

- Monitoring and testing procedure violations, when the primacy agency requires a Tier 2 notice.

- Failure to comply with variance and exemption conditions.

Tier 3 Public Notice (Required within 1 Year)

- All other monitoring or testing procedure violations not already requiring a Tier 1 or Tier 2 notice.

- Operation under a variance or exemption.

- Special public notices (i.e., exceedance of the fluoride secondary maximum contaminant level; announcing the availability of unregulated contaminant monitoring results).

6.4.3 Content of Public Notices

40 C.F.R. § 141.205 sets forth general requirements for public notice that must be provided in the event of a violation of a regulatory requirement under the NPDWRs. Such notice must (1) be conspicuous; (2) not contain unduly technical language, small print, or similar characteristics that would frustrate its purpose; and (3) must be multilingual, as appropriate. In addition, it must include a clear and readily understandable description of the following:

- The violation or situation, including contaminant levels, if applicable.

- When the violation or situation occurred.

- Any potential adverse health effects (using standard health effects language from Appendix B of the public notification rule or standard monitoring language).

- The population at risk.

- Whether alternative water supplies should be used.

- What actions/preventative measures consumers should take.

- What the system is doing to correct the violation or situation.

- When the water system expects to return to compliance or resolve the situation.

- The name, business address, and phone number of the water system owner or operator.

- A statement encouraging distribution of the notice to others, where applicable.[230]

Persons served by a public water system must be given notice of any violation of a national drinking water standard "that has the potential to have serious adverse effects on human health as a result of short-term exposure" within 24 hours after violation by at least one effective means, and written notice of any other violation of a national standard or monitoring requirement within one year. States must "make readily available to the public" an annual report to the administrator on violations of national primary drinking water regulations by public water systems within the state.[231]

The regulations also set forth particularized informational requirements regarding health effects that must be included in the language of a notice,[232] including language specific to violations involving each of the more than 80 contaminants covered by the NPDWRs.[233] Additionally, EPA has issued detailed guidance regarding notification, and the regulations provide a summary table of notice and standard health effects language requirements.[234]

6.5 Recordkeeping

The NPDWRs generally provide that the owner or operator of a PWS must retain on or near its premises the following records:

(1) Records of bacteriological analyses required by the regulations, which must be kept for not less than 5 years.

(2) Records of chemical analyses made pursuant to the regulation, which must be kept for not less than 10 years.[235]

(3) Records of action taken by the system to correct violations of primary drinking water regulations, which must be kept for a period not less than 3 years after the last action taken with respect to the particular violation involved.

(4) Copies of any written reports, summaries, or communications relating to sanitary surveys of the system conducted by the system itself, by a private consultant, or by any local, state, or federal agency, which must be kept for a period not less than 10 years after completion of the sanitary survey involved.

(5) Records concerning a variance or exemption granted to the system, which must be kept for a period ending not less than 5 years following the expiration of such variance or exemption.

(6) Copies of public notices issued pursuant to Subpart Q of Part 141 and certifications made to the primacy agency pursuant to § 141.31, which must be kept for three years.[236]

6.6 Public Access

6.6.1 Public Availability of Reporting Data

Monitoring data and other information reported by a PWS and required to be kept as a record under 40 C.F.R. § 141.33 are considered to be in the public domain. EPA and the states make this information available through a variety of means including consumer confidence reports, notifications required by the Public Notification Rule, and user-friendly Internet resources. Such information may also be sought under the Freedom of Information Act (FOIA), including the specific SDWA regulations relating to FOIA disclosures.[237] Those regulations allow for broad public disclosure, providing that the Agency may not withhold any information in its possession that "deals with the existence, absence, or level of contaminants in drinking water."[238]

6.6.2 The Safe Drinking Water Information System

The SDWA recognizes that data management plays a critical role in helping states and EPA protect public health. Consistent with that view, EPA has established the Safe Drinking Water Information System (SDWIS) from federal and state databases. It contains information submitted by states, EPA regions, and public water systems in conformance with reporting requirements established by the SDWA and related regulations and guidance. This information, which is publicly available on the Internet,[239] includes the following:

- Basic information on each regulated PWS, including: name, ID number, city, county, number of people served, type of system (residential, transient, non-transient), whether it operates year-round or seasonally, and the characteristics of its sources of water.

- Violation information for each regulated PWS addressing whether it has followed established monitoring and reporting schedules, complied with mandated treatment techniques, violated any MCLs, or communicated vital information to its customers.

- Enforcement information setting forth actions primacy agencies have taken to ensure that drinking water systems return to compliance if they are in violation of a drinking water regulation.

- Sampling results for unregulated contaminants and for regulated contaminants when the monitoring results exceed the MCL.

EPA uses this information to determine if and when it needs to address noncompliant systems, to oversee state drinking water programs, to track contaminant levels, to respond to public inquiries, and to prepare national reports.

EPA also uses this information to evaluate the effectiveness of its programs and regulations, and to determine whether new regulations are needed to further protect public health.

6.7 Consumer Confidence Reports

The SDWA emphasizes that consumers have a right to know what is in their drinking water, where it comes from, how it is treated, and how to help protect it. The 1996 SDWA amendments expanded upon that "right-to-know" by requiring all community water systems to prepare and distribute annual consumer confidence reports about the water they provide, including information on detected contaminants, possible health effects, and the water's source.[240] In response to this statutory directive, EPA has promulgated the Consumer Confidence Rule,[241] which requires community water systems to provide consumer confidence reports (CCRs) to their customers annually on July 1.[242] The CCR summarizes information regarding drinking water sources used, any detected contaminants, compliance, potential health effects information, educational information, and contact information for additional sources of information.[243] The information in the CCRs does not diminish or replace any other public notification requirement under the NPDWRs, but instead supplements the public notification that water systems must provide to their customers upon discovering any violation of a contaminant standard.

Distribution of the CCRs depends on the size of the water system. Large water systems must mail the water quality reports to their customers, either with water bills or as a separate mailing, and take steps to get the information to people who do not receive water bills. The largest water systems must post their reports on the Internet, in addition to other delivery mechanisms, to make the reports easily accessible to all consumers.[244] Some smaller water systems (those serving fewer than 10,000 people) may be able to distribute the information through newspapers or by other means. For example, a state (acting through its governor) may allow systems serving between 500 and 10,000 people to publish the report in a newspaper rather than mail it. Systems serving fewer than 500 people, whose governor has not required mailing, may elect to give effective public notice that the report is available, rather than mail or publish it.[245]

As required by the Consumer Confidence Rule, EPA consults closely with the drinking water community, risk communication experts, environmental and public interest groups, and interested parties in developing these regulations. This consultation is intended to help ensure that the reports meet the aim of usefully informing the public, as well as the broader aim of encouraging an informed and engaged public to work with water suppliers and drinking water programs at all levels of government in the effort to secure safe drinking water.

6.8 Guidance Documents

Under the Administrative Procedure Act[246] and specific provisions of the 1996 SDWA amendments, EPA must publish and make all regulations and most guidance and information documents available for public notice and comment. Given the complexity of the drinking water regulations and the potential impacts upon public health associated with noncompliance, EPA works with a broad range of stakeholders to develop and publish comprehensive guidance documents to assist regulated PWSs in complying with the NPDWRs. The detailed guidance documents cover a wide range of regulatory matters, are an extremely valuable resource, and are generally available online.[247]

6.9 Operator Certification Guidance and Grants

Ensuring the knowledge and skills of public water system operators is widely considered one of the most important, cost-effective means to strengthen drinking water safety. Drinking water operator certification helps protect human health and the environment by establishing minimum professional standards for the operation and maintenance of public water systems.

To that end, the 1996 SDWA amendments required all states to carry out a program of operator certification. In 1999, EPA issued operator certification program guidelines specifying minimum standards for certification and recertification of the operators of community and nontransient noncommunity public water systems.[248] These guidelines are implemented through state operator certification programs which vary from state to state. Under the final guidelines, EPA withholds 20 percent of a state's Drinking Water State Revolving Fund (DWSRF) capitalization grant unless the state adopted and is implementing an operator certification program that meets the requirements of the final guidelines, or submits an existing program that is substantially equivalent to the guidelines. To facilitate the operator certification effort, EPA has implemented the Expense Reimbursement Grant (ERG) program for systems serving 3,300 persons or fewer. The ERG program provides grants to states to reimburse such systems for the costs of training and certification, including per diem for unsalaried operators.

Significantly, this program does not require that every water system operator be certified. EPA does not view that as necessary for proper system operation, nor is it a flexible or efficient approach. Rather, the objective of the program is to ensure every water system has, either directly, under contract, or in conjunction with other systems, an operator qualified to perform certain key compliance functions appropriate to the functions, facilities, and operations of that system.[249]

6.10 Variances and Exemptions

The SDWA provides states or EPA limited authority to grant (1) variances that allow public water systems to use less costly technology, and (2) exemptions to allow public water systems more time to comply with a new drinking water regulation. Variances allow eligible systems to provide drinking water that does not comply with an NPDWR on the condition that the system installs a certain technology and the quality of the drinking water is still protective of public health.[250] There are two types of variances: (1) general variances intended for systems that are not able to comply with an NPDWR due to their source water quality; and (2) small system variances intended for systems serving 3,300 persons or fewer that cannot afford to comply with an NPDWR, or systems serving up to 10,000 persons that cannot meet a compliance deadline.

The variance decision must include consideration of whether the system could comply with the standard through water treatment, alternative water supplies, or restructuring or consolidation. Members of the public may petition EPA to object to a variance proposed by a state, and EPA must respond to petitions within 60 days. If EPA objects to a variance, it cannot be granted until the state makes the requested changes or responds in writing to each objection.[251] The Act also authorizes "source water" variances from a standard for systems that have poor source water quality that prevent them from meeting the standard, even with treatment. However, these systems must agree to install affordable compliance technology to obtain a variance.

Exemptions, by comparison, allow eligible systems additional time to build capacity in order to achieve and maintain regulatory compliance with newly promulgated NPDWRs, while continuing to provide acceptable levels of public health protection. However, exemptions do not release a water system from its compliance obligations with respect to the NPDWRs. Rather, they are only intended to allow water systems additional time to comply with the NPDWRs. In order to obtain an exemption, a PWS must demonstrate that it is unable to comply with an NPDWR in a timely manner due to compelling factors (which may include economic factors), or is unable to implement measures to develop an alternative source of water to achieve compliance.[252] As is the case with a variance, an exemption may not be granted unless the primacy agency first provides notice and opportunity for a public hearing in the exemption schedule.[253] Systems that receive an exemption are generally not eligible for a variance.

6.10.1 Special Provisions for Small Systems

The 1996 SDWA amendments contained multiple provisions to ease the financial burden of compliance for small water systems. As part of every new drinking water standard, EPA is now required to identify technologies that comply with the standard and are specifically affordable for each of three groups of smaller systems. If such technologies do not exist for a certain group of smaller systems or quality of source water, a "variance" technology must be identified that need not meet the standard but must provide the maximum protection affordable for such groups of smaller systems and source waters.[254] States with primacy will make decisions on affordability variances for specific systems serving up to 3,300 persons, while EPA must also approve variances for systems between 3,300 and 10,000.

Most small systems whose source water quality does not meet a national standard should be able to comply, if they are allowed to use treatment specifically affordable for systems of their size. For those systems which cannot afford such treatment, the state (with EPA review, if applicable) will assess whether other changes—e.g., source water, restructuring, or connection to another system—could enable them to meet the standard. Only if such changes are not practicable can a system be given variances from a standard and be authorized to provide drinking water that does not fully meet a national standard.

Moreover, a system serving 3,300 or fewer persons may receive exemptions from a standard for up to nine years (three years were previously allowed) if it serves an economically disadvantaged community, is reasonably likely to get financial assistance to comply during the exemption term, and cannot comply by an alternative water source or by management or restructuring changes. Exemptions are meant to enable a system to avoid a continuing violation of a standard if it cannot now comply but will in the near future.[255]

6.10.2 Judicial Review of Variances and Exemptions

SDWA Section 1448(b)[256] provides the federal district court with jurisdiction to review petitions for relief in actions involving variances or exemptions, their filing periods, grounds arising after expiration of their filing periods, and exclusiveness of remedies under that section. Specifically, the United States District Courts have jurisdiction in actions brought to review: (1) the granting of, or the refusing to grant, a variance or exemption under SDWA Section 1415 or 1416;[257] or (2) the requirements of any *schedule* prescribed for a variance or exemption under such section, or the failure to prescribe such a schedule. Such an action may only be brought, however, upon a petition for judicial review filed (1) within the 45-day period beginning on the date the action sought to be reviewed is taken; or (2) in the case of a petition to review the *refusal* to grant a variance or exemption, or the failure to prescribe a schedule, within the 45-day period beginning on the date action is required to be taken on the variance, exemption, or schedule, at issue. Section 1448(b) does provide that petition for such review may be filed after the expiration of that period, however, if the petition is based solely on grounds arising after its expiration.

7.0 Enforcement

The NPDWRs are part of a regulatory scheme that places its most significant emphasis on preventative measures in order to ensure that contaminated water is kept from ever reaching the public. While EPA has the authority to encourage compliance through the imposition of penalties and the issuance of injunctions, in many circumstances, the protection of the public can be effectively addressed by carefully spelled out corrective measures, enhanced monitoring to verify their effectiveness, and reporting to the Agency regarding the implementation of those measures. Issuance of a detailed administrative order often accomplishes this objective from the Agency's perspective. Furthermore, the NPDWRs are complex and often confusing regulations that require interpretation or consideration of particularized practical considerations that may be best addressed by spelling them out in detail through an administrative enforcement mechanism explaining how compliance should be achieved.

7.1 EPA Enforcement

7.1.1 Administrative Orders

The SDWA generally does not provide for pre-enforcement review of regulatory violations. A regulated PWS may look to EPA guidance documents or seek informal interpretations and guidance from the Agency, but any formal litigation challenge must occur either (1) through a rulemaking challenge under SDWA Section 1448 within 45 days of the promulgation of a rule, or (2) on the basis of the factual record when the Agency seeks to enforce the regulations against a PWS. In part due to this lack of a pre-enforcement mechanism for exploring the boundaries of a potential regulatory violation, the Agency has been given authority to issue administrative orders that serve to further define the Agency's interpretative scope of the regulations and provide formal notice to a PWS of the specific circumstances under which EPA will consider a violation to have occurred.[258]

An Administrative Order on Consent (AOC) negotiated with EPA often takes this a step further by providing a more complete framework for discussion of possible violations and affording the PWS an opportunity to cure or seek further clarification of a potential violation scenario. Indeed, even when the Agency believes the terms and requirements of an administrative order have been violated in a manner serious enough to justify potential enforcement of the order in federal court, EPA may elect to proceed by issuing a follow-on administrative order directing compliance with the provision of the first order that has been violated. This serves to create the opportunity for correction and resolution short of litigation; to clarify the Agency's litigation position on the nature, scope, and gravity of the alleged violation; and, in certain circumstances, to provide a basis for negotiating stipulated penalties.

7.1.2 Enforcement Actions

7.1.2.1 Administrative Enforcement Action

Depending upon what penalties are sought, an administrative order may be enforced either (1) through the commencement of an enforcement action in federal district court, or (2) in an administrative hearing on the record, a decision on which is appealable to the appropriate United States Court of Appeals.[259] With respect to judicial enforcement, the Act establishes a threshold of $32,500 as a penalty demand by the government, above which the Agency must bring an enforcement action in federal district court.[260] Penalty demands less than $32,500 are to be resolved in an administrative hearing before the Agency on the record, as provided under the Administrative Procedure Act, 5 U.S.C. § 554.[261] A hearing on the record is a contested proceeding before an administrative law judge and may be appealed to the EPA Environmental Appeals Board.[262] Decisions in such administrative hearings are appealable to the U.S. Circuit Courts of Appeal and will be upheld if the Agency's exercise of its enforcement discretion is supported by substantial evidence in the record.[263] However, until EPA seeks to enforce an administrative order in federal court, a PWS may not challenge any provision of an order that has been issued to it.

7.1.2.2 Judicial Enforcement Actions

Alternatively, EPA may forgo the issuance of an administrative order and bring an action in federal court to remedy a violation.[264] Section 1414 (b) of that Act provides, "the Administrator may bring a civil action in the appropriate United States district court to require compliance with any applicable requirement with an order issued under subsection (g) of this section, *or* with any schedule or other requirement imposed pursuant to this title."[265] However, such an effort is resource-intensive and, in most circumstances, a PWS is primarily concerned with coming into compliance fully and promptly in order to protect human health and avoid litigation. Accordingly, compliance situations are often resolved simply by the issuance of an order and negotiation of the terms of compliance. EPA ordinarily prefers to proceed directly to federal court only in the more serious instances of a threat to human health, or when there have been recurring violations that justify significant penalties or injunctive relief.[266]

7.2 Fines, Penalties, and Injunctive Relief

With respect to specific remedies, SDWA Section 1414(b)[267] generally provides that, in an enforcement action brought by EPA, the court may enter such judgment as protection of public health may require, taking into consideration the time necessary to comply and the availability of alternative water supplies. Furthermore, if the court determines that there has been a violation of an NPDWR or other requirement with respect to which the action was brought (including an administrative order), it may impose a civil penalty of up to $53,907[268] for each day in which such violation occurs. That figure is subject to an upward adjustment periodically to account for inflation and larger fines may be imposed for other unlawful activities by individuals, such as tampering with water supplies.[269] The Agency may also seek injunctive relief. In evaluating the appropriateness of any penalty sought by the government, the Act provides that a reviewing court is to take into account (1) the seriousness of the violation, (2) the population at risk, and (3) other appropriate factors.[270]

7.2.1 Section 1431 Authority—Emergency Orders

Section 1431(a) of the SDWA also authorizes the EPA administrator to take action necessary "to protect the public's health from an imminent and substantial endangerment created by contaminants in a public water system."[271] Such action involves emergency powers that can be taken *notwithstanding any other provision of the Act*. The emergency powers granted in Section 1431 of the Act are available when EPA receives information and determines that

- a contaminant is present or likely to enter a public water system;

- the contaminant may present imminent and substantial endangerment to human health; and

- the appropriate state and local authorities have not acted to protect human health.[272]

Pursuant to Section 1431, EPA can issue administrative orders or initiate civil actions for appropriate relief, including restraining orders and injunctions, to protect the health of persons who use or may use the contaminated water supply. Significantly, under this section, EPA is given express authority to order responsible "persons" who "cause or contribute" to the endangerment to provide an alternate source of drinking water for those members of the public at risk. In this regard, EPA's emergency powers to protect the public in cases of imminent and substantial endangerment ostensibly extend beyond the regulation of public water systems to cover any responsible person or entity.[273] In this endeavor, to the extent practicable, EPA is required to "consult with local authorities in order to confirm the correctness of the information on which action proposed to be taken . . . is based and to ascertain the action such authorities are or will be taking."[274]

EPA invokes its authorities under Section 1431 not infrequently, and the courts have interpreted the Agency's discretion to act under this provision quite broadly, relying upon the legislative history of that provision.[275] In that regard, Congress stated that it intended to "confer completely adequate authority to deal promptly and effectively with emergency situations which jeopardize the health of persons" using public water systems.[276] Congress stressed that it "intends this language [to] be construed by the courts and the Administrator so as to give paramount importance to the objective of protection of the public health," and that "[a]dministrative and judicial implementation of this authority must occur early enough to prevent the potential hazard from materializing."[277] When reviewing EPA action under Section 1431, courts apply a "highly deferential" standard and will uphold EPA actions unless they are "arbitrary, capricious, an abuse of discretion, or otherwise not in accordance with law."[278]

However, EPA's emergency power is not without limitation. In *W.R. Grace & Co. v. United States EPA*, the Third Circuit recognized that "[t]he same House Report that expresses an intent to confer broad emergency authority on the EPA also explains that, '[i]n using the words "imminent and substantial endangerment" . . . the Committee intends that this broad administrative authority not to be used when the system of regulatory authorities provided elsewhere in the bill could be used adequately to protect the public health.' "[279]

More recently, when EPA issued an emergency administrative order to a company to cease natural gas "fracking" activities in order to prevent alleged private water well contamination based upon its Section 1431 authorities, the company was able to secure a stay of that order from the U.S. District Court,[280] following which EPA withdrew its emergency order during the pendency of the appeal in that case, leading to the dismissal of both the District Court and Appellate Court proceedings.[281] Significantly, EPA's March 30, 2012 decision to withdraw the emergency administrative order that it had issued pursuant to Section 1431 came only days after the Supreme Court's decision in *Sackett v. EPA*, 566 U.S. ___, 132. S. Ct. 1367 (2012) a case in which the Court held unanimously that an administrative order issued under the Clean Water Act was entitled to pre-enforcement review and a hearing on the merits in federal District Court under the Administrative Procedure Act. In the wake of *Sackett*, it therefore may be the case that EPA will approach the use of Section 1431 orders more cautiously as an enforcement tool in circumstances where an acute threat to human health is less certain.

7.3 State Primacy Authorities Related to Enforcement

Under the SDWA, states can request primary enforcement authority ("primacy") for their drinking water programs, which grants them the legal authority (1) to regulate drinking water in accordance with the SDWA within their borders, and (2) to enforce those regulations consistent with the Act. To obtain primacy, a state must (1) adopt regulations no less stringent than the national primary drinking water regulations promulgated by EPA; (2) have adequate procedures to enforce state regulations and conduct monitoring and inspections as required by federal regulations; (3) maintain records as required by EPA; (4) adopt appropriate administrative penalty authority; and (5) adopt and implement a sound plan to provide safe drinking water during emergencies.[282]

Forty-nine of the 50 states and the Navajo tribe have requested and obtained authority to administer their own drinking water programs. The remaining jurisdictions and sovereign tribal nations that do not have primacy authority are regulated by the appropriate EPA regional office. For example, EPA Region 8 administers the drinking water program in Wyoming, which does not have primacy, and EPA Region 3 administers the program in the District of Columbia, which does not have primacy.[283]

7.4 Citizen Suits

SDWA Section 1449 authorizes any person to commence a civil action to enforce the Act against an alleged violator of any requirement prescribed by or under the Act, or against the administrator for failure to perform any duty which is not discretionary under the Act.[284] No citizen suit may be commenced, however, without first giving sixty days' notice of the alleged violation to EPA, any alleged violator, *and* to the state primary agency. These notice requirements are a necessary precondition to bringing a citizen suit under the SDWA and vary depending upon the nature of the claim and the defendant(s), as summarized below.

7.4.1 Intent to Sue Requirements

Service of the 60-day notice of intent to file suit pursuant to Section 1449(a)(1) for an alleged violation of any requirement of the Act must be accomplished in one of three ways, depending upon who has been named as a defendant. They are as follows:

(1) *If the alleged violator is an individual or corporation*—Service of notice must be accomplished by certified mail, return receipt requested, addressed to, or by personal service upon, the individual or corporation. If a public water system or underground injection well is alleged to be in violation, service must be made upon the owner or operator of the well. A copy of the notice must also be sent by certified mail, return receipt requested, to the administrator of EPA, the regional EPA administrator for the region in which such violation is alleged to have occurred, the chief administrative officer of the responsible state agency (if any), and the attorney general for the state in which the violation is alleged to have occurred. If the alleged violator is a corporation, a copy of the

notice must also be sent by certified mail, return receipt requested, to the registered agent (if any) of the corporation in the state in which the violation is alleged to have occurred.

(2) *If the alleged violator is a state or local agency*—Service of notice must be accomplished by personal service or by certified mail, return receipt requested, addressed to the head of the agency. A copy of the notice must also be sent by certified mail, return receipt requested, to the administrator of EPA, the EPA regional administrator for the region in which the violation is alleged to have occurred, the chief administrative officer of the responsible state agency (if any), and the attorney general for the state in which the violation is alleged to have occurred.

(3) *If the alleged violator is a federal agency*—Service of notice must be accomplished by certified mail, return receipt requested, addressed to, or by personal service upon, the head of the agency. A copy of the notice must also be sent by certified mail, return receipt requested, to the administrator of EPA, the regional EPA administrator for the region in which the violation is alleged to have occurred, the attorney general of the United States, the chief administrative officer of the responsible state agency (if any), and the attorney general for the state in which the violation is alleged to have occurred. In the case of an intent to file suit pursuant to Section 1449(a)(2) of the Act for failure to perform a nondiscretionary duty, service must be accomplished by certified mail, return receipt requested, addressed to, or by personal service upon, the administrator of EPA. A copy of the notice must also be sent by certified mail to the attorney general of the United States.

7.4.2 Content of a Notice of a Violation of a Standard or Requirement

The actual notice regarding an alleged violation of any requirement prescribed by or under the Act must include sufficient information to permit the recipient to identify: (1) the specific requirement alleged to have been violated, (2) the activity alleged to constitute a violation, (3) the person or persons responsible for the alleged violation, (4) the location of the alleged violation, (5) the date or dates of the alleged violation, and (6) the full name, address, and telephone number of the person giving notice.

If the notice involves an alleged failure of the administrator to perform any act or duty under the Act which is not discretionary with the administrator it must: (1) identify the provision of the Act which requires the act or creates the duty, (2) describe with reasonable specificity the action taken or not taken by the administrator which is alleged to constitute a failure to perform such act or duty, and (3) state the full name, address, and telephone number of the person giving notice.

The notice provisions of Section 1445 are necessary prerequisites to bringing a citizen suit claim. That is to say, no action may be commenced under Section 1449(a)(1) or (a)(2) until the plaintiff has given each of the appropriate parties sixty days prior notice of intent to file such an action setting forth the information described above. This notice period is intended to allow the alleged violator an opportunity to correct the violation and to give EPA or the relevant state primacy agency the opportunity to bring an action to enforce compliance, thus making citizen enforcement unnecessary. Consistent with that provision, a citizen suit may be subject to dismissal if EPA or a state primacy authority is already diligently prosecuting a civil judicial action to enforce compliance.[285]

A court may grant injunctive relief and award attorney fees and costs to a prevailing party in circumstances in which it determines that such an award is warranted. Attorneys' fees and costs may also be awarded in circumstances in which the plaintiff only partially prevails. One issue yet to be expressly addressed by the courts, however, is whether citizen suits under the SDWA may lie for alleged violations that are entirely in the past. In this regard, the SDWA allows citizen suits against persons "alleged to be in violation of any requirements prescribed by or under this subchapter."[286] While it has not addressed the interpretation of this language in the context of the SDWA, the Supreme Court has construed the identical language in the Clean Water Act[287] as *not* authorizing citizen suits, absent a "continuous or intermittent violation," in *Gwaltney of Smithfield, Ltd. v. Chesapeake Bay Foundation, Inc.*,[288] holding that "the harm sought to be addressed by the citizen suit lies in the present or the future, not in the past."[289] As such, it is reasonable to assume that a similar interpretation would apply under the SDWA.

8.0 Private Tort and Nuisance Actions

The issue of whether an MCL establishes a standard of care in state common law torts has been addressed in several federal decisions, albeit obliquely, in the context of standing to sue. *Iberville Parish Waterworks District No. 3 v. Novartis Crop Protection, Inc.*,[290] for example, involved a situation in which the alleged contamination of a drinking water source by a private party had not exceeded, or even approached, the MCL as determined by the relevant drinking water regulations. In view of that, the court found that a plaintiff PWS had suffered no injury-in-fact and therefore concluded that there was no standing to sue in a federal forum. Similar outcomes occurred in *Brooks v. E.I. du Pont de Nemours & Co.*,[291] where plaintiffs who sued for damages to their private water supplies from sub-MCL MTBE contamination were found not to have standing, and *City of*

Moses Lake v. United States,[292] where, without addressing the standing issue, the court held that the municipal water supplier suffered no injury under circumstances in which there was no danger of contamination in excess of the MCL during the relevant time period.

However, in *In re MTBE Litigation*,[293] the court took a somewhat different approach to the question of "the extent to which an MCL defines what constitutes a legally cognizable harm." After a review of cases addressing the relationship between MCL and injury, including *Iberville Parish*, the court held that, while MCL levels can define injury to owners of contaminated property, they do not necessarily define injury if the property owner uses the property to satisfy a *further* duty to others to keep the property free from a certain level of contamination. The court found that the municipal water supplier plaintiffs in that case could have "a duty to take action—be it testing, monitoring, or treating contaminated wells—before that contamination reaches the applicable MCL."[294] The court thus concluded that CWS plaintiffs could be injured in circumstances where contamination affects raw water quality, even if the contamination does not exceed the MCL.[295] The court distinguished *Iberville Parish* on the grounds that (1) little of the remediation expense the plaintiffs sought to recover in that case was due to the alleged contamination, and (2) certain of the expenses claimed had not yet been incurred. In contrast, in the *In re: MTBE* case, the plaintiffs had already incurred costs to monitor, test, and treat contaminated raw water.

On appeal, the Second Circuit's affirmed the district court's decision,[296] upholding a $104 million jury verdict against the defendant oil company, based upon its alleged role in the contamination of New York City groundwater supplies. The opinion included a discussion of the legal standard for both Article III injury necessary to confer standing, and tort injury sufficient to confer liability in circumstances where injury is claimed with respect to contaminant levels that are below an applicable MCL.[297] The Court of Appeals discussed and distinguished the *Iberville Parish* case largely on the rationale advanced by the district court that a public water system may have an actionable injury based upon the need to avoid potentially exceeding an MCL in the future and to refrain from delivering water to customers that is of questionable aesthetic quality (taste and odor).

9.0 Preemption

In *Mattoon v. Pittsfield*,[298] the U.S. Court of Appeals for the First Circuit dismissed a variety of federal private common law claims brought by plaintiffs based upon allegations of drinking water contamination, holding that Congress "occupied the field of public drinking water regulation with its enactment of the

SDWA through the establishment of a comprehensive regulatory program supervised by an expert administrative agency."[299] Looking to that comprehensive regulatory program the court concluded that Congress meant to reserve the governance of public drinking water standards to federal administrative regulation, and held that the SDWA preempts all other forms of federal relief for violations of the SDWA that are based upon federal common law.[300] Other federal courts have generally followed the *Mattoon* holding.

10.0 Special Provisions Relating to the Sale of Drinking Water and Its Use in Food

10.1 Bottled Water

The 1996 SDWA amendments provided that regulation of bottled water was to be delegated to the federal Food and Drug Administration (FDA). In turn, FDA was directed to regulate the same contaminants that EPA regulates in public water supplies based upon standards "no less stringent" than the corresponding MCLs established by the NPDWRs for those contaminants, *unless* the FDA made a specific finding that a regulatory standard was not necessary to protect public health.[301]

Accordingly, while the SDWA vests authority to regulate drinking water in the EPA, in the 1996 amendments Congress reserved to FDA the authority to regulate bottled water. Consistent with that intent, Congress also enacted Section 410 of the Federal Food, Drug, and Cosmetic Act (FFDCA),[302] expressly conferring regulatory authority upon FDA to regulate bottled water under the FFDCA as a "food." Mirroring the directive of the 1996 SDWA amendments, Section 410 provides that FDA is to consult with the EPA within 180 days after the promulgation of an NPDWR and either promulgate amendments to its regulations applicable to bottled drinking water, or publish its reasons for not making such amendments in the *Federal Register.*

FDA's bottled water standards are set forth under its requirements for standardized beverages in its food regulations at 21 C.F.R. § 165.110. In that regard, FDA has adopted virtually all of the MCLs for inorganics, volatile organic, and synthetic organic contaminants set forth in the NPDWRs[303] as well as the standards for radionuclides.[304] In addition, the FDA regulations impose enforceable requirements with respect to certain substances that are designated secondary drinking water standards under the SDWA, such as iron and zinc.[305] With respect to biological health risks, the FDA standards adopt the MCLs for turbidity, nitrates, and disinfection by-products,[306] but do not require the use of disinfectants or filtration to ensure protection from microbial agents. Moreover, with respect to microorganisms, while the FDA regulations generally require bottled water to be safe for human consumption, they set a quantitative standard only as total coliform.[307]

The FDA regulatory scheme also presents somewhat different requirements with respect to enforcement of FDA standards. For example, violations of NPDWRs must be reported within certain time frames to EPA and/or the state primacy agency, while there is no comparable provision under the FFDCA.[308] Nonetheless, the FDA regulations do require that bottled water sources be tested using approved methods for regulated contaminants, and that companies maintain records for inspection and engage in good manufacturing practices with respect to source water protection, processing, bottling, storage, and transportation.

10.2 Drinking Water Used as a Food Ingredient

EPA and FDA also interpret the relevant statutory authorities to provide that any water used as ingredient in food is itself considered a food and subject to the provisions of the FFDCA. Thus, water used for food processing is also subject to applicable provisions of FFDCA.[309] To address the respective demarcation of regulatory authority in those circumstances in which finished water from a PWS is used in food processing, FDA and EPA have further agreed that the relevant statutory authorities should be interpreted to provide that a substance in water that is used in food shall be considered a food additive subject to the provisions of the FFDCA. However, a substance added to finished water provided by a PWS *before* such water enters a food processing establishment is not to be considered a food additive within the meaning of the FFDCA.[310]

10.3 Metered Water

The sale of water that triggers regulatory coverage under SDWA § 1411[311] generally does not include submetering (i.e., situations in which property owners meter and bill their tenants for water purchased by the owners, but distributed to and actually used by the tenants). In 2003, to encourage conservation of water, EPA reversed its long-held view with respect to apartment houses that submetering constituted the sale of water subject to regulation under the SDWA, and issued a regulation providing that it was not.[312] This reversal allows the owner of a property such as an apartment building to submeter tenants without triggering federal drinking-water regulations. However, EPA excluded manufactured housing, such as that found in mobile-home parks, from the scope of the regulatory change.[313]

11.0 Security Issues

As discussed earlier in the chapter, the federal government has enacted legislation and promulgated directives to protect the U.S. drinking water supply and utilities from terrorism and other hazards such as natural disasters. Specifically, the

Homeland Security Presidential Directives (HSPDs) and the Public Health Security and Bioterrorism Preparedness and Response Act (Bioterrorism Act) of 2002 (summarized in section 2.5) supplement existing legislation, such as the SDWA and the Clean Water Act, and affect the actions and obligations of EPA, its Water Security Division, and water utilities, as described below.

11.1 Homeland Security Presidential Directives

The Homeland Security Presidential Directives (HSPDs) disseminate presidential and Homeland Security decisions on national security matters. HSPDs 7, 8, 9, and 10 are of particular relevance to water security issues.[314] For example, under HSPD 7, EPA is designated as the sector-specific agency responsible for infrastructure protection activities for drinking water and wastewater systems from terrorist attacks. The Water Security Division developed a water sector specific plan (SSP), a water sector critical infrastructure protection implementation strategy developed under the Department of Homeland Security's National Infrastructure Protection Plan.[315] HSPD 8 establishes policies to strengthen the preparedness to prevent and respond to threatened or actual domestic terrorist attacks, major disasters, and other emergencies by establishing mechanisms for improved delivery of federal preparedness assistance to state and local governments.[316] Under HSPD 9, EPA is implementing a demonstration project program to design, deploy, and evaluate a model contamination warning system for drinking water security to provide early detection of water contamination. EPA has also developed the Water Laboratory Alliance (WLA). The purpose of the WLA is to provide the drinking water sector with an integrated nationwide network of laboratories with the analytical capabilities and capacity to support monitoring and surveillance, response, and remediation of intentional and unintentional drinking water supply contamination events involving chemical, biological, and radiochemical contaminants.[317] Finally, HSPD 10 provides directives to further strengthen the Biodefense Program through threat awareness, prevention and protection, surveillance and detection, and response and recovery.[318]

11.2 Security Enhancements, Research, and Technology

In addition to the legislatively mandated activities, EPA works with other federal agencies (e.g., the Centers for Disease Control and Prevention, the FBI, and the Department of Defense) and water sector organizations (e.g., the Water Environment Research Foundation) to improve information on technologies and conduct research for water sector security. These activities and tools help water utilities and other agencies to understand and use available scientific information and technologies to detect contaminants, improve physical facility security, develop and use monitoring protocols and techniques, and ensure treatment effectiveness. For example, EPA's Homeland Security Research Center, in conjunction with EPA's Laboratory and Capability Committee, has developed a list of Standardized Analytical Methods (SAMs) to be used by environmental laboratories in analyzing biological and chemical samples associated with threats to homeland security. In addition, EPA's Water Security Division is working with the Office of Research and Development to support verification of water security technologies for safe buildings.[319]

12.0 Funding and Grant Programs

Federal and state governments share responsibility for administering and funding drinking water programs. Funding for the federal drinking water program is determined by the president and Congress. Funding for state programs comes from the federal government, state general revenue funds, state fee programs, and other sources. Each year, Congress allocates Public Water System Supervision Grants to the 49 states with primacy as well as Indian tribes. States are required to match their grants by 25 percent. State general revenues and fees provide the majority of operational funding for state drinking water programs.[320] Historically, states on average have contributed around 65 percent of the costs of running the federal drinking water program while the federal government has contributed 35 percent. Beginning in 1976, EPA began providing grants to states in order to assist in implementation of both the Underground Injection Control (UIC) and Public Water System Supervision (PWSS) programs. In 2009, those amounts were $11 million and $99.1 million, respectively.[321]

Created by the 1996 SDWA amendments, the drinking water state revolving fund (SRF) assists public water systems in financing the costs of improvements. EPA provides the SRF grants to the states. In turn, the states lend money, at below-market interest rates, to drinking water systems to install, improve, or maintain treatment facilities to help meet standards for drinking water. Tribes, U.S. territories, and the District of Columbia receive direct grants for drinking water infrastructure improvements from EPA. In addition to the federal grants awarded, states are required to provide matching funds equal to 20 percent of the federal grant award received for the DWSRF program.

Some of the funds from the SRF can be directed into set-aside accounts by the states.[322] Each year, a state may set aside up to 31 percent of its federal grant award to fund certain specified components of the state's drinking water program activities. These set-aside funded activities can include administration of the DWSRF program, technical assistance to small drinking water systems, state drinking water program management, and local assistance or other state drinking water programs. Each state decides what percentage of set-aside to use, and how to use the set-aside funds based on public input and participation. However, the public must be provided with notice and an opportunity to comment on the annual priority list of projects eligible for SRF assistance that states will publish as a part of their SRF intended use plans.[323]

There are also national set-asides, which target funds from the overall DWSRF appropriation to address specific purposes. These national set-asides are used to fund drinking water projects for American Indian tribes and Alaska Native villages, to conduct monitoring of unregulated contaminants, and to reimburse drinking water operator certification training expenses. For example, in fiscal year (FY) 2004, national set-asides of $12.7 million were taken for American Indian tribes and Alaska Native villages, and $2 million was set aside for unregulated contaminant monitoring.[324]

Funding for drinking water systems is also available through the U.S. Department of Housing and Urban Development's Community Development Block Grants, bonds, and the Rural Utility Service of the U.S. Department of Agriculture, which provides funds for rural drinking water and wastewater systems.

13.0 International Regulation

In what is arguably a legislative oversight, the SDWA does not expressly address the reach of its provisions outside of the United States. While this may seem of limited significance in most instances, it does present difficult legal issues with respect to ICCs. That is because individual aircraft, trains, and passenger vessels can qualify as regulated public water systems under the SDWA. The Act does not, however, address the extent to which the NPDWRs apply once that PWS leaves the territorial limits of the United States. Just as significantly, the Act does not specifically address the regulatory requirements that apply when a foreign carrier (e.g., a passenger cruise ship) enters and operates within the United States.

14.0 Underground Injection Program

The SDWA required EPA to establish a federal-state system of regulation to assure that current and future underground sources of drinking water (USDWs) are not rendered unfit for such use by underground injection of contaminants.[325] By way of background, underground injection is the technology of placing fluids underground, in porous formations of rocks, through wells or other similar conveyance systems. Injection wells have a range of uses that include disposing of waste, enhancing oil production, mining, and preventing salt water intrusion. While rocks such as sandstone, shale, and limestone appear to be solid, they can contain significant voids or pores that allow water and other fluids to fill and move through them. Man-made or produced fluids (liquids, gases, or slurries) can move into the pores of rocks through the use of pumps or by gravity. These fluids may be water, wastewater, brine ("salt water"), or water mixed with chemicals.

Consistent with its statutory mandate, EPA has established minimum requirements for state, tribal, and federal Underground Injection Control (UIC) programs for regulating injection activities and provided mechanisms for implementation, authorization of and exercise primary enforcement authority by those respective entities. As with the SDWA drinking water programs, the Act contemplates that a state, territory, or tribe may seek primacy status to oversee and enforce the UIC regulations in the first instance for wells in Classes I–V. The SDWA authorizes primacy when a state submits a program submission to EPA showing that it can comply with the UIC program regulations.[326] Requirements differ, however, depending on the Class of injection well the state wishes to monitor.[327] Currently, thirty-four states and three territories have primacy programs for well Classes I–V; and six states and two tribes have primacy programs for Class II wells only. For those states without primacy, EPA implements the UIC requirements directly through its regional offices. Moreover, EPA directly implements the Class VI UIC program nationally.

The UIC program protects USDWs from endangerment by setting minimum requirements for injection wells, relying upon injection well technology to predict the capacity of rocks to contain fluids and provide the technical details required to do so safely. The scope of the UIC program extends to any injection well that fits within the definition of "a bored, drilled, or driven shaft, or a dug hole that is deeper than it is wide, an improved sinkhole, or a subsurface fluid distribution system."[328] All injection must be authorized under either general rules or specific permits. Injection well owners and operators may not site, construct, operate, maintain, convert, plug, or abandon the wells, or conduct any other injection activity that endangers USDWs. Pursuant to the UIC requirements, injected fluids must stay within the well and the intended injection zone, and fluids that are directly or indirectly injected into a USDW must not cause a public water system to violate drinking water standards or otherwise adversely affect public health.

14.1 Well Classes

EPA's UIC regulations group injection wells into six groups or "classes" based principally on potential for the type of injection to result in endangerment of an USDW. Each class includes wells with similar functions, construction, and operating features. The principal factor used to define each class is the type of activity and general nature of the fluids associated with that activity (except for Class V):

- Class I: injection of hazardous, industrial, and municipal waste;

- Class II: injection related to the production of oil and gas;

- Class III: injection related to the recovery of minerals;

- Class IV: other injection related to activities where data are insufficient to evaluate the threat to groundwater (where fluids are not hazardous, but may still pose a threat);

- Class V: all other wells not covered in Classes I–IV; and

- Class VI: injection of carbon dioxide (CO_2) for geologic sequestration (GS) purposes.

Class I, II, and III permitted wells have two major technical requirements that are similar: (1) a mechanical integrity testing requirement to assure that leaks do not result in significant movement of fluids into a USDW; and (2) an area of review requirement for new wells to assure that existing, improperly completed, and abandoned wells or transmissive faults or fractures within that area of endangering influence do not provide avenues for vertical migration into USDWs. The specific regulations which address each of the respective well classes are found in 40 C.F.R. Parts 146, 147, and 148. The most numerous categories of wells are Class II and Class V. In addition Class II wells have received a great deal of regulatory attention recently given their association with the oil and gas industry. Accordingly, a more comprehensive discussion of Class II and Class V wells is included herein.

14.1.1 Class II Wells

Class II wells are used only to inject fluids associated with oil and natural gas production. Class II fluids are primarily brines (salt water) that are brought to the surface while producing oil and gas. EPA estimates that over 2 billion gallons of brine are injected in the United States every day. Most oil and gas injection wells are in Texas, California, Oklahoma, and Kansas. The number of Class II wells varies from year to year based on fluctuations in oil and gas demand and production. At present, approximately 180,000 Class II wells are in operation in the United States.

Class II wells fall into one of three categories: (1) enhanced recovery wells, (2) disposal wells, and (3) hydrocarbon storage wells. The largest number of wells are those in the first category which are used for injecting waters and other fluids into a *producing* formation for secondary or tertiary recovery of oil or gas, and thus are referred to as enhanced oil recovery wells (EOR Wells). The bulk of the remainder, an estimated 30,000 wells, are used for disposal of production wastewaters into *non-producing* formations as saltwater disposal wells (Disposal Wells). As provided for in the Class II program, both EOR Wells and Disposal Wells generally inject regulated volumes on a regular basis over a period of years. A brief description of the key characteristics of the three well categories follows.

Disposal wells. During oil and gas extraction operations, salt water brines are also brought to the surface. Those brines are separated from hydrocarbons at the surface, at which point they may be treated or reinjected into the same or similar underground formations for disposal. Wastewater from hydraulic fracturing activities (see below) can also be injected into Class II wells.

Enhanced recovery wells. Fluids consisting of brine, freshwater, steam, polymers, or carbon dioxide are injected into oil-bearing formations to recover residual oil and in limited applications, natural gas. The injected fluids "thin" (*i.e.,* decrease the viscosity) or displace small amounts of extractable oil and gas. In the hydraulic fracturing scenario, the enhanced recovery activity is amplified by injecting the viscous fluid under high pressure until the desired fracturing is achieved, followed by the insertion of a "proppant" such as sand. The pressure is then released and the proppant holds the fractures open to allow fluid to return to the well. Oil and gas is then available for recovery in significant volumes. In a typical configuration, a single injection well is surrounded by multiple production wells that bring oil and gas to the surface. Significantly, the UIC program does not regulate EOR Wells that are solely used for production by virtue of a statutory exemption. (*See* section 15.0 below.) However, EPA does claim authority to regulate hydraulic fracturing when diesel fuels are used in fracking fluids or propping agents.

Hydrocarbon storage wells. Liquid hydrocarbons are injected into underground formations (such as salt caverns) where they are stored, generally, as part of the U.S. Strategic Petroleum Reserve. According to EPA, there are more than 100 liquid hydrocarbon storage wells in operation in the United States.

Protecting drinking water resources. As noted, extraction of oil and gas usually produces large amounts of brine. Brine is often saltier than seawater and may contain metals and radioactive substances. As such, brines are considered to be potentially damaging to the environment and public health, if discharged to surface waters or land. To address those concerns all state UIC programs have incorporated rules preventing disposal of brine in surface water bodies and soils. As the alternative, UIC programs have embraced deep underground injection of brines into formations isolated from underground sources of drinking water as the preferred way to dispose of such waste fluid and prevent soil and water contamination. In furtherance of that objective, all oil- and gas-producing states generally require the injection of brine into the *originating* or similar formations.

Seismicity. In addition to their potential impacts on USDW, a number of recent studies have focused on the relationship between Disposal Wells and the potential for induced or triggered seismicity, *i.e.,* earthquakes caused from human acts.[329] In that regard, the studies generally suggest that Disposal Wells present a greater potential for induced seismicity than EOR Wells or hydraulic fracking operations.

Those studies theorize that high injection volumes from Disposal Wells increase pore pressure which may result in a seismic event, if sufficient injection occurs in the proximity of a geological fault system associated with the granite basement rock. Although a large percentage of Disposal Wells throughout the United States operate for years without related seismic events, some study data suggest that a small percentage of such wells are associated with clusters of small to moderate earthquakes. These same studies also emphasize, however, that the science of induced seismicity is still evolving and any scientific assessment in that regard requires technical skills and collaboration of multiple experts, including seismologists, reservoir engineers, geotechnical engineers, geologists, hydrogeologists, and geophysicists.

Class II well requirements. States (including federally recognized tribes and U.S. territories) have the option of requesting primacy for Class II wells under either Section 1422 or 1425 of the SDWA. Under Section 1422 states must meet EPA's minimum requirements for UIC programs to obtain primacy. To that end, programs authorized under section 1422 must include well owner and operator requirements covering:

- Construction
- Operation
- Monitoring and testing
- Reporting, and
- Closure requirements

Under Section 1422 enhanced recovery wells may either be issued permits or be authorized by rule. Disposal wells, by comparison, must be issued permits by the primacy authority to operate. The owners or operators of the wells must meet all the above applicable requirements, including strict construction and conversion standards and regular testing and inspection requirements.

Under Section 1425 primacy states must also demonstrate that their existing standards are effective in preventing endangerment of USDWs. To meet that requirement, their regulatory programs must include provisions consistent with federal UIC regulations addressing:

- Permitting

- Inspections

- Monitoring

- Recordkeeping, and

- Reporting

14.1.2 Class V Wells

Of the six classes of wells regulated by EPA under the UIC program, Class V injection wells are the most numerous, with more than 650,000 across the 50 states. Class V wells are generally shallow disposal wells used to release non-hazardous fluids either directly into USDWs, or into the shallow subsurface formations adjacent to USDWs. There are over 20 sub-types of Class V wells, with those designed as low-tech systems, such as drywells or septic and leachfield combinations intended for sanitary waste disposal being the most familiar.

Under the federal UIC regulations, most Class V wells are "authorized by rule."[330] "Authorized by rule" means that well owners and operators are allowed to discharge fluids into such wells without specific prior approval from the regulatory authority, provided they comply with the general UIC program requirements.'[331] Because Class V wells are not presumptively considered to present a threat to human health or the environment, they are largely subject to informational regulatory requirements. More particularly, Class V wells that are authorized by rule may inject fluids as long as:

(1) They do not endanger USDWs,[332] and

(2) The well owners or operators have provided EPA or primacy state authorities with basic inventory information regarding the wells.[333]

The most important of the UIC requirements for Class V wells, and one that any owner or operator should be cognizant of, is that a well must not present an "endangerment" within the meaning of the regulations. To avoid endangerment, injection operations must avoid the migration of fluids containing contaminants into USDWs under circumstances which may result in a violation of an NPDWR, or otherwise adversely affect public health. To that end, Class V wells are authorized to inject only non-hazardous wastes.

Absent a properly documented inquiry by EPA or a state primacy authority, a well owner or operator is not required to make an affirmative showing to the Agency that the well does not endanger a USDW. At the same time, if the UIC Program Authority learns that a Class V well may violate an NPDWR, or adversely affect public health, it may take one or more of the following actions:

(1) Require the well owner or operator to obtain an individual permit;

(2) Order the owner to take actions (including well closure) to prevent the violation; and/or

(3) Take enforcement action[334]

Moreover, consistent with its authority under Section 1431 of the SDWA, EPA may take emergency action if the introduction of a contaminant into the USDWs could present "imminent and substantial endangerment to public health."[335]

For those wells that do not present an endangerment to a USDW, the Class V regulatory requirements are informational in nature and do not require ongoing sampling or reporting to UIC program authorities. From a compliance perspective, however, internal monitoring of well operations and associated recordkeeping are strongly recommended to establish a record of non-endangerment, particularly with respect to industrial and commercial facilities.

In order to receive authority "by rule" to inject, the owner or operator of a Class V well must submit general inventory information to the UIC program.[336] The following basic information must be provided:

(1) The facility name and location,

(2) The identity of the owner of the facility,

(3) Name and address of designated contact for the facility,

(4) The nature and type of injection wells at the facility, and

(5) The operating status of injection wells.

Significantly, if owners or operators have not provided such inventory information to the respective UIC program, they must cease injection and submit the required inventory information.[337] Similarly, the regulations indicate that a well owner or operator may not inject into a well that has not been inventoried. Moreover, upon submission of inventory information, a well owner or operator must wait 90 days before resuming injection, unless EPA notifies them that they can begin injection sooner.[338] Owners and operators of wells that fall into the exceptions to the rule are required to submit additional information under the inventory requirements.[339]

EPA may also require that the owner or operator of any well authorized by rule to submit information for review to determine if a well may be endangering a USDW in violation of 40 C.F.R. § 144.12. Be aware, though, that EPA must make its request in writing and include a statement of the reasons for requiring the information.[340] In such circumstances, the well operator is permitted to continue operation until such time as EPA either (1) issues an emergency order based on a finding of imminent and substantial endangerment to human health, or (2) notifies the owner/operator that a permit will be required for continued operation of the well.[341]

The UIC program authority may also require the owner or operator of any Class V well that is currently authorized by rule to apply for and obtain an individual or area UIC permit to operate the well in certain circumstances.[342] Criteria for requiring a permit include:

(1) The injection well is not in compliance with UIC requirements (e.g., presents an endangerment to a USDW),

(2) The injection well is not, or no longer is, within the category of wells and types of well operations authorized in the UIC regulation (e.g., it discharges hazardous wastes), or

(3) The protection of USDWs requires that the injection operation be regulated by requirements (e.g., corrective action, monitoring and reporting, or operation), which are not contained in the UIC regulation.[343]

In circumstances involving a Class V well authorized by rule, a permit will generally only be required where the well is believed to be endangering a USDW. Moreover, the Agency carries the burden, in the first instance, such that the primacy authority may only impose a permit requirement *after* it has (1) notified the owner/operator of the well in writing that a permit application is required, (2) provided the EPA's reasons for requiring a permit, and (3) included a copy of the application form and the time allowed for its submission.[344] Even under such circumstances, if previously authorized by rule, the Class V well will be allowed to continue to be operated until such time, if any, as the permit application is denied.[345]

If required, permits for Class V wells are generally issued for a fixed term not to exceed 10 years. As noted, a Class V well may be operated without additional conditions until such time as the permit issues. Correspondingly, a Class V well owner or operator is not allowed to inject into the well previously authorized by rule upon the effective date of permit denial, or upon failure by the owner or operator to submit an application in a timely manner as specified in the notice from the UIC program.[346]

In general, the best practice for a commercial or industrial owner or operator of a Class V well is (1) become familiar with the requirements for authorization by rule, (2) to make sure the well is inventoried, monitor and maintain records of the well's use.

14.2 Carbon Sequestration

On November 22, 2010, EPA issued the final rule, Federal Requirements under the Underground Injection Control (UIC) Program for Carbon Dioxide Geologic Sequestration Wells.[347] The final rule establishes new federal requirements for the underground injection of CO_2 for the purpose of long-term underground storage, or GS, and a new well class—Class VI—to ensure the protection of USDWs from injection-related activities.

While the elements of the final rule are based on the existing regulatory framework of EPA's UIC program,[348] the requirements are tailored to address the unique nature of CO_2 injection for GS. The corrosivity of CO_2 in the presence of water, the potential presence of impurities in captured CO_2, its potential mobility within subsurface formations, and large injection volumes anticipated at full-scale deployment are issues that are being assessed with respect to construction; testing and monitoring; and financial, implementation, and technical requirements tailored to this practice.

For the new regulations regarding Class VI GS wells, EPA will allow independent primacy, if states submit a complete primacy application that meets the requirements in 40 C.F.R. § 45.22 or § 145.32 within 270 days after the final rule is promulgated. If a state chooses not to submit a complete application during the 270-day period, or EPA has not approved a Class VI program, then EPA will establish a federal UIC Class VI program in that state after the 270-day application period closes. States may not issue Class VI permits until their Class VI UIC programs are approved. During the first 270 days and prior to EPA approval of a Class VI primacy application, states with existing SDWA UIC primacy programs may issue permits. States without existing Section 1422 primacy programs must direct all Class VI GS permit applications to the appropriate EPA region.

15.0 Hydraulic Fracturing

Hydraulic fracturing is used by gas producers to stimulate wells and recover natural gas from sources such as coal beds and shale gas formations. Fluids, commonly made up of water and chemical additives, are pumped into a geologic formation at high pressure during hydraulic fracturing. When the pressure exceeds the rock strength, the fluids open or enlarge fractures that can extend several hundred feet away from the well. After the fractures are created, a propping agent (*e.g.*, sand) is pumped into the fractures to keep them from closing when the pumping pressure is released. Conventional formations, by comparison, generally allow oil and natural gas to flow to the wellbore without hydraulic fracturing and typically contain trapped oil and natural gas that migrated from other subsurface locations. Hydraulic fracturing can be used to enhance oil and gas production from these formations. Moreover, in unconventional formations, hydraulic fracturing can serve to extract economical quantities of oil and gas.

Hydraulic fracturing has been used since the late 1940s and, for the first 50 years, was mostly used in vertical wells in conventional formations. Hydraulic fracturing is still used in these settings, but the process has evolved; technological developments (including horizontal and directional drilling) have led to the use of hydraulic fracturing in unconventional hydrocarbon formations that could not otherwise be profitably produced. These formations include:

- *Shales.* Organic-rich, black shales are the source rocks in which oil and gas form on geological timescales. Oil and gas are contained in the pore space of the shale. Some shales contain predominantly gas or oil, though many shale formations contain both.

- *Tight formations.* "Tight" formations are relatively low permeability, non-shale, sedimentary formations that can contain oil and gas. Like in shales, oil and gas are contained in the pore space of the formation. Tight formations can include, for example, sandstones, siltstone and carbonates.

- *Coalbeds.* In coalbeds, methane (the primary component of natural gas) is generally adsorbed to the coal rather than contained in the pore space or structurally trapped in the formation. Pumping the injected and native water out of the coalbeds after fracturing serves to depressurize the coal, thereby allowing the methane to desorb and flow into the well to the surface.

In the fracturing operation, the internal pressure in all of these types of geologic formations causes the injected fracturing fluids to rise to the surface where they may be stored in tanks or pits prior to disposal or recycling. Recovered fracturing fluids are referred to as flowback. Disposal options for flowback include discharge into surface water or underground injection. Surface water discharges of the flowback are regulated by the National Pollutant Discharge Elimination System (NPDES) program, which requires flowback to be treated prior to discharge into surface water or underground injection prior to discharge. Treatment is typically performed by wastewater treatment facilities. Underground injection of flowback is regulated by either an EPA UIC program or by a state with UIC enforcement primacy authority.

Congress has provided for certain exclusions to the UIC regulations, with the most recent language added as Section 1421(d)(1) of the SDWA via the Energy Policy Act of 2005. It provides that the term "underground injection" excludes the underground injection of natural gas for purposes of storage, and the underground injection of fluids or propping agents (other than diesel fuels) pursuant to hydraulic fracturing operations related to oil, gas, or geothermal production activities.[349]

While the SDWA specifically *excludes* hydraulic fracturing from UIC regulation under SDWA § 1421(d)(1), and the Agency's use of its Section 1431 emergency authorities to address hydraulic fracturing activities appear to be more open to question as a result of the *Range Resources* and *Sackett* decisions discussed in section 7.2 above, nonetheless the use of diesel fuel during hydraulic fracturing is still regulated by the UIC program. Any service company that performs hydraulic fracturing using diesel fuel must receive prior authorization from the UIC program. Injection wells receiving diesel fuel as a hydraulic fracturing additive will be considered Class II wells by the UIC program. Furthermore, state oil and gas agencies may impose additional regulations on hydraulic fracturing. In addition, states or EPA have authority under the Clean Water Act to regulate discharge of produced waters from hydraulic fracturing operations.

Most recently, in 2014, EPA released information clarifying UIC program requirements for underground injection of diesel fuels in hydraulic fracturing. The Agency also released guidance for EPA permit writers implementing UIC Class II requirements which:

- Explains that owners or operators must obtain a UIC Class II permit before injecting diesel fuels for hydraulic fracturing

- Explains EPA's interpretation of the SDWA term "diesel fuels" for permitting purposes

- Describes existing UIC Class II program requirements for permitting underground injection of diesel fuels in hydraulic fracturing, and

- Provide guidance for EPA's permit writers preparing UIC Class II permits for diesel fuels use in hydraulic fracturing[350]

15.1 Recent Developments

Over the past few years, several key technical, economic, and energy policy developments have spurred increased use of hydraulic fracturing for gas extraction over a wider diversity of geographic regions and geologic formations. The combined use of hydraulic fracturing with horizontal (or more generically, directional) drilling has led to an increase in oil and gas activities in areas of the country with historical oil and gas production, and an expansion of oil and gas activities to new regions of the country. EPA projects that shale gas will comprise more than 20 percent of the total U.S. gas supply by 2020. Along with the expansion of hydraulic fracturing, there has been increasing concern about its potential impacts on drinking water resources, public health, and the environment in the vicinity of these facilities.

In its FY 2010 budget report, the U.S. House of Representatives Appropriations Conference Committee identified the need for a focused study of hydraulic fracturing's potential impact on drinking water, human health, and the environment. In response thereto, EPA's Office of Research and Development (ORD) has been conducting a scientific study to investigate the possible relationships between hydraulic fracturing and drinking water and to help EPA identify potential risks associated with hydraulic fracturing. EPA initiated the study in 2011 and issued a progress report in December of 2012.[351] Thereafter, on June 5, 2015, EPA released for public comment and peer review by the SAB, its thousand-page "Draft Assessment on the Potential Impacts to Drinking Water Resources from Hydraulic Fracturing Activities."[352] EPA plans to issue a final report to the public in 2016.

Significantly, while the assessment concluded that "there are above and below ground mechanisms by which hydraulic fracturing activities have the potential to impact drinking water resources," EPA *did not find evidence that these mechanisms have led to widespread, systemic impacts on drinking water resources in the United States.*[353] The draft assessment went on to caution that the "rarity of effects on drinking water resources" in the United States might be due to limiting factors such as the availability of data and studies. However, the finding undercut arguments that hydraulic fracturing presents significant threats to USDWs in the United States. Needless to say, that conclusion will be subject to intense scrutiny and debate during the peer review and comment process and it will be interesting to see if the final assessment modifies those findings and conclusions.[354]

16.0 Source Water Protection

The Act requires states to submit a program for delineating source water areas of public water systems, and for assessing the susceptibility of such source waters to contamination.[355] States may use set-asides from the State Revolving Fund (SRF) to pay for source water assessments. Assessment programs may use data from other, related watershed-type survey activities, which will encourage the efficient use of funds and coordination among the varied programs to gather and analyze water resource–oriented data. Results of completed source water assessments must be made available to the public. These results are made a statutory prerequisite for state-tailored monitoring programs, because they provide a sound science basis for such tailoring.[356]

Additionally, under Section 1457 of the Act,[357] EPA may provide for a screening program to test for contaminants that may be endocrine disruptors if the Agency determines that such substances may be found in sources of drinking water and that "substantial populations" may be exposed to the substance. The Act and its legislative history do not explain what constitutes a "substantial population" in this context, although EPA appears to rely on its authorities with respect to CCL and the Agency's five-year review of unregulated contaminants to inform such screening programs.[358]

17.0 Research Sources

- Thomas Richichi can be reached at trichichi@bdlaw.com

- The Code of Federal Regulations, the *Federal Register*, and the United States Code can be accessed at www.gpo.gov/fdys/

- EPA's Safe Drinking Water Hotline can be accessed at 1-800-426-4791

- Most EPA SDWA guidance is available, organized by respective regulation, at http://water.epa.gov/lawsregs/guidance/sdwa/index.cfm. EPA also makes available a number of quick reference guides on the same site. Policy decisions related to implementation and compliance issues are also provided under the rubric of "Water Supply Guidance"

- USEPA, Understanding the Safe Drinking Water Act, EPA 816-F-04-030 (2004), available at http://water.epa.gov/lawsregs/guidance/sdwa/upload/2009_08_28_sdwa_fs_30ann_sdwa_web.pdf

- USEPA, Safe Drinking Water Act Amendments of 1996, available at http://water.epa.gov/lawsregs/guidance/sdwa/theme.cfm

- The Safe Drinking Water Information System (SDWIS) is available at http://water.epa.gov/scitech/datait/databases/drink/sdwisfed /index.cfm

- Revised Public Notification Handbook, EPA 816-R-09-013 (March 2010) (180 pages), available at http://water.epa.gov/lawsregs/rulesregs/sdwapublicnotif ication/compl iancehelp.cfm

- USEPA, "Public Notification Rule, Quick Reference Guide," EPA 816-F-00-023 (May 2000)

- USEPA, "Total Coliform Rule: A Quick Reference Guide," EPA 816-F-01-035 (Nov. 2001)

- USEPA, Total Coliform Rule, available at http://water.epa.gov/lawsregs/rulesregs/sdwa/tcr/regula tion.cfm

- USEPA, "Variances and Exemptions: A Quick Reference Guide," EPA 816-04-005 (Sept. 2004)

- An extensive history of U.S. drinking water treatment and regulations may be found in "The History of Drinking Water Treatment," EPA-816-F00-006 (Feb. 2000)

- The American Water Works Association is a source of many useful guides and resource materials and can be accessed at http://www.AWWA.org

- USEPA, Requirements of the Public Health Security and Bioterrorism Preparedness and Response Act of 2002, available at http://cfpub.epa .gov/safewater/watersecurity/bioterrori sm.cfm

- USEPA, Security Enhancements, Research and Technology, available at http://owpubauthor.epa.gov/infrastructure/watersecurity/secres/index .cfm

- Public Health Security and Bioterrorism Preparedness and Response Act of 2002 (Bioterrorism Act), Pub. L. No. 107–188 116 Stat. 682 (2002) (codified at 42 U.S.C. § 300i-2–300i-4), available at http://www.epa.gov/ safewater/watersecurity/pubs/security_act.pdf

- USEPA, Water Security Research and Technical Support Action Plan, available at www.epa.gov/safewater/watersecurity/pubs/action_plan_final .pdf

- USEPA, Interim Enhanced Surface Water Treatment Rule: What Does It Mean to You? EPA 816-R-01-014 (2001), available at http://water.epa .gov/lawsregs/rulesregs/sdwa/mdbp/upload/2001_10_23_mdbp_ieswtr whatdoesitmeantoyou.pdf

- USEPA, Fact Sheet: Interim Enhanced Surface Water Treatment Rule, EPA 815-F-98-009 (1998), available at http://www.epa.gov/ogwdw/ mdbp/ieswtrfr.pdf

- USEPA, Fact Sheet: Long Term 2 Enhanced Surface Water Treatment Rule, EPA 815-F-05-002 (2005), available at http://water.epa.gov/laws regs/rulesregs/sdwa/lt2/upload/2005_12_15_disinfection_lt2_fs_lt2_ finalrule.pdf

- USEPA, Long Term 2 Enhanced Surface Water Treatment Rule, available at http://water.epa.gov/lawsregs/rulesregs/sdwa/lt2/basicinformation.cfm

- USEPA, 2010 Fact Sheet, EPA 815-F-10-002 (2010), available at http:// www.epa.gov/safewater/disinfection/tcr/pdfs/RTCRpercent20draftper cent20factpercent20sheetpercent2061710.pdf

- USEPA, Fact Sheet on the *Federal Register* Notice for Stage 1 Disinfectants and Disinfection Byproducts Rule, EPA 815-F-98-010 (1998),

available at http://water.epa.gov/lawsregs/rulesregs/sdwa/mdbp/upload/
2001_10_23_mdbp_stage1dbprfactsheet.pdf

- USEPA, Complying with the Stage 1 Disinfectants and Disinfection
  Byproducts Rule, EPA 816-B-05-004 (2006), available at http://water
  .epa.gov/lawsregs/rulesregs/sdwa/mdbp/upload/2006_05_30_mdbp_
  guide_stage1_basic_final.pdf

- USEPA, Fact Sheet: Stage 2 Disinfectants and Disinfection Byproducts
  Rule, EPA 815-F-05-003 (2005), available at http://www.epa.gov/
  ogwdw/disinfection/stage2/pdfs/fs_st2_finalrule.pdf

- USEPA, Filter Backwash Recycling Rule: A Rule Summary for Systems,
  EPA-816-R-02-013 (2002), available at http://water.epa.gov/aboutow/
  ogwdw/upload/2002_09_05_fbrrstreamfinal08-26-02.pdf

- USEPA, Final Guidelines for the Certification and Recertification of
  Operators of Community and Nontransient Noncommunity Public
  Water Systems, 64 Fed. Reg. 5916 (Feb. 5, 1999)

- EPA Operator Certification Guidelines: Implementation Guidance
  (2000), available at http://water.epa.gov/infrastructure/drinkingwater/
  pws/dwoperatorcert/upload/2008_04_21_operatorcertification_guide_
  operatorcertification_implementationguidance.pdf

- USEPA, CCR, available at http://water.epa.gov/lawsregs/rulesregs/sdwa/
  ccr/index.cfm

- USEPA, Primacy, available at http://water.epa.gov/infrastructure/drink
  ingwater/pws/p rimacy.cfm

- USEPA, Water Security, available at http://water.epa.gov/infrastructure/
  watersecurity/index.cfm

- USEPA, Water Security: Legislation and Directives, available at http://
  cfpub.epa.gov/safewater/watersecurity/legislation.cfm

- USEPA, The Water Sector-Specific Plan, EPA 817-R-07-001 (2007),
  available at http://www.epa.gov/safewater/watersecurity/pubs/plan_se
  curity_wa tersectorspecificplan.pdf

- USEPA, Grants and Other Funding under the Safe Drinking Water Act
  (SDWA), available at http://water.epa.gov/grants_funding/sdwa/index
  .cfm

- USEPA, State and Territorial PWSS Program Allotments, available at
  http://water.epa.gov/grants_funding/pws/allotments_state-terr.cfm#2010

- USEPA, Technical Overview of the UIC Program, EPA 816-R-02-025 (2002), available at http://water.epa.gov/type/groundwater/uic/upload/2004_5_3_uicv_techguide_uic_tech_overview_uic_regs.pdf

- USEPA, Hydraulic Fracturing, available at http://water.epa.gov/type/groundwater/uic/class2/hydrau licfracturing /index.cfm

Notes

1. In the early twentieth century, the annual U.S. death rate from typhoid was approximately 30 per 100,000—that is, more people than now die in automobile accidents every year.
2. The SDWA comprises Title XIV of the U.S. Public Health Service Act and is codified at 42 U.S.C. §§ 300f through 300j-26.
3. Pathogens are microorganisms that can cause disease in other organisms or in humans, animals, and plants. They may be bacteria, viruses, or parasites and are found in sewage, in runoff from farms or rural areas populated with domestic and/or wild animals, or even in pristine waters, making their way into potential sources of drinking water.
4. Turbidity is a physical property of water that indicates its propensity to scatter light and thereby reduce its clarity. It is largely a function of suspended solids in the water.
5. Chlorine was used for the first time as a primary disinfectant of drinking water in Jersey City, New Jersey, in 1908. The use of other disinfectants such as ozone also began in Europe around that time, but they were not employed in the United States until several decades later.
6. A more extensive history of U.S. drinking water treatment and regulations may be found in "The History of Drinking Water Treatment," EPA-816-F00-006 (Feb. 2000).
7. Pub. L. No. 93-523 (1974). EPA regulations under the SDWA are found at 40 C.F.R. Parts 141 through 143.
8. Pub. L. No. 99-339 (1986).
9. Pub. L. No. 104-182, 110 Stat. 1613 (1996). The 1996 amendments are available at http://water.epa.gov/lawsregs/guidance/sdwa/theme.cfm.
10. SDWA § 1412(b)(1)(B)(i) and (ii); 42 U.S.C. § 300g-l(b)(1)(B)(i) and (ii).
11. Significantly, while the review of candidate contaminants is subject to public notice and comment, EPA's decision with respect to listing a contaminant on the CCL is not subject to judicial review. SDWA § 1412(b)(1)(i)(III); 42 U.S.C. § 300g-l(b)(1)(i)(III).
12. SDWA § 1412 (b)(3)(C)-(b)(4); 42 U.S.C. § 300g-l(b)(3)(C)-(b)(4).
13. In circumstances in which it is not technologically or economically "feasible" to adopt an MCL for a contaminant, the Act provides that EPA may adopt a treatment technique as a standard. For example, disinfection and filtration may be mandated as treatment techniques to achieve the desired protection from microorganisms, SDWA § 1412(b)(6)-(7); 42 U.S.C. § 300g-1(b)(6)-(7). The courts have upheld EPA's discretion to adopt a treatment technique based upon the Agency's determination of what is "feasible" in a particular case. *See American Water Works Association v. EPA*, 40 F.3d 1266 (D.C. Cir. 1994).
14. SDWA § 1414(c)(4); 42 U.S.C. § 300g-3(c)(4).
15. SDWA § 1414(c)(1)-(3); 42 U.S.C. § 300g-3(c)(1)-(3).
16. SDWA § 1453(a); 42 U.S.C. § 300j-13(a).
17. SDWA § 1420; 42 U.S.C. § 300g-9.
18. SDWA § 1419(a)-(c); 42 U.S.C. § 300g-8(a)-(c).
19. SDWA § 1412(b)(4)(E) and (b)(15); 42 U.S.C. § 300g-1(b)(4)(E) and (b)(15).

[20] Cryptosporidium is a microorganism that presents particular health risk concerns, given its persistence in the environment and resistance to treatment. It was associated with a particular serious health event in 1993 in Milwaukee prior to the 1996 amendments that led to increased focus on this microorganism.

[21] SDWA § 1412(b)(2)(C); 42 U.S.C. § 300g-1(b)(2)(C).

[22] SDWA § 1412(b)(12)(A) & (B); 42 U.S.C. § 300g-1(b)(12)(A) and (B).

[23] SDWA § 1452; 42 U.S.C. § 300j-12.

[24] Public Health Security and Bioterrorism Preparedness and Response Act of 2002 (Bioterrorism Act), Pub. L. No. 107-188 116 Stat. 682 (2002), codified at 42 U.S.C. § 300i-2-300i-4, available at http://www.epa.gov/safewater/watersecurity/pubs/security_act.pdf.

[25] USEPA, "Security Enhancements, Research and Technology," available at http://owpubauthor.epa.gov/infrastructure/watersecurity/secrets/i ndex.cfm.

[26] USEPA, "Requirements of the Public Health Security and Bioterrorism Preparedness and Response Act of 2002," available at http://cfpub.epa.gov/safewater/watersecurity/bioterrorism.cfm.

[27] USEPA, "Water Security Research and Technical Support Action Plan" (Action Plan), available at www.epa.gov/safewater/watersecurity/pubs/action_plan_final.pdf.

[28] Significantly, the language of the SDWA was used as the model for OMB's Information Quality Guidelines applicable to *all* federal regulatory programs, which are also adapted to become part of EPA's Information Quality Guidelines. *See* Office of Management and Budget, "Guidelines for Ensuring and Maximizing the Quality, Objectivity, Utility, and Integrity of Information Disseminated by Federal Agencies," 67 Fed. Reg. 8452 (Feb. 22, 2002); "EPA's Guidelines for Ensuring and Maximizing the Quality, Objectivity, Utility, and Integrity of Information Disseminated by the Environmental Protection Agency," EPA/260R-02-008 (Oct. 2002).

[29] SDWA § 1413(a)(1) and (2); 42 U.S.C. § 300g-2(a)(1) & (2). States thus are implicitly free to adopt more stringent regulations than those of EPA.

[30] Wyoming and the District of Columbia are notable among jurisdictions which have not obtained primacy authority. Primacy agency requirements are discussed in greater detail in section 7.3.

[31] SDWA § 1414; 42 U.S.C. § 300g-3; *see also* 40 C.F.R. §§ 142.12(a), 142.17(a). Individuals may also bring "citizen suits" under SDWA § 1449, 42 U.S.C. § 300j-8, to enforce such requirements. *See* discussion hereafter in section 7.2 relating to SDWA enforcement.

[32] SDWA §§ 1401 and 1412(b)(3); 42 U.S.C. §§ 300f(1) and 300g-1(b)(3).

[33] SDWA § 1401(2); 42 U.S.C. Sec. 300f(2).

[34] Certain secondary standards have been adopted, however, as enforceable standards for bottled water by the FDA. *See* discussion in section 10.1. Also, states may adopt their own primary standards for contaminants that are subject only to secondary standards by EPA.

[35] *See In re: Methyl Tertiary Butyl Ether ("MTBE") Products Liability Litigation,* 725 F.3d 65 (2d Cir. 2013). Interestingly, the Second Circuit opinion recounted expert testimony admitted at trial which asserted that MTBE would have detectable taste and odor for a substantial portion of the population at levels down to 1 part per billion ("ppb").

[36] *See* SDWA § 1401; 42 U.S.C. § 300f.

[37] The reference to a "public water system" is premised on the concept of a discrete and identifiable system of conveyances that provides water service to the public. While many public water systems are, in fact, publicly owned municipal systems, there is no requirement that a regulated water system be "publicly" owned or operated. Rather, both publicly and privately owned or operated water systems are covered by the Act. In fact, the greatest number of regulated systems (though much smaller in terms of persons served) are privately owned.

[38] *See* http://water.epa.gov.infrastructure/drinkingwater/pws/f actors.cfm. Rest stops and restaurants are not regulated, however, if they fall outside the jurisdictional coverage of the SDWA as described in Section 3.3.2 of this chapter.

[39]   SDWA §§ 1411 and 1401(4)(A); 42 U.S.C. §§ 300g and 300f(4)(A).

[40]   40 C.F.R. §§ 141.2, 141.3.

[41]   *See* 63 Fed. Reg. 53591 (Aug. 9, 1998).

[42]   SDWA § 1441; 42 U.S.C. § 300g. *See generally* 40 C.F.R. Part 141.

[43]   SDWA § 1411(1)–(4); 42 U.S.C. § 300g(1)-(4); 40 C.F.R. § 141.3.

[44]   H.R. Rep. No. 93-1185 (1974), as reprinted in 1974 U.S.C.C.A.N. 6454, 6470.

[45]   SDWA § 1412(b)(4)(E)(ii); 42 U.S.C. § 300g-l(b)(4)(E)(ii); 40 C.F.R. § 141.87.

[46]   Approximately one-third of that 290 million figure are people served by CWSs that rely on groundwater as a source (more than 40,000 systems).

[47]   With the exception of the Lead and Copper Rule, NPDWRs generally do not require monitoring at the customer's tap, due to the lack of legal authority over private residences and the practical limitation of securing representative sample sets from such locations on a regular basis.

[48]   Systems which do not collect, sell, or treat water are not regulated public water systems. Most large commercial and residential buildings fall into this category. Industrial enterprises that provide water to employees similarly are not regulated, *unless* they collect source water or sell or treat the water they provide. Water treatment that will trigger regulation is more likely with respect to such facilities, however, since they frequently provide the same treated water used in plant processes to employees for washing or drinking.

[49]   EPA has interpreted treatment to include any activity intended to change the physical or chemical characteristics of the finished water received by a facility.

[50]   Those requirements are set forth in the standards for total coliform, disinfection, turbidity, and nitrates.

[51]   40 C.F.R. §§ 141.2, 141.3.

[52]   *See* "EPA Water Supply Guidance 17" (1979) and "EPA Water Supply Guidance 29" (1986) for Interstate Carrier Conveyances.

[53]   74 Fed. Reg. 53590 (Oct. 19, 2009).

[54]   Like the airline industry before it, in April of 2012, Amtrak entered into an "Administrative Order for Compliance on Consent" with EPA which will presumably serve as a compliance and enforcement bridge to a rail passenger-specific rulemaking analogous to the Airline Drinking Water Rule promulgated in 2009. *See* EPA Docket No. SDWA-03-2012-0113-DS (April 26, 2012).

[55]   40 C.F.R. § 141.29. For example, a small municipal PWS may purchase finished water wholesale from a large municipal PWS for resale to the retail customers of the smaller PWS.

[56]   Section 1401(6) of the SDWA defines "contaminant" as any physical, chemical, biological or radiological substance or matter in water. 42 U.S.C. § 300f(6). As EPA notes, drinking water may reasonably be expected to contain at least small amounts of some contaminants. Moreover, some contaminants may be harmful if consumed at certain levels in drinking water, but the presence of contaminants does not necessarily indicate that the water poses a health risk.

[57]   SDWA § 1412(b)(1)(B)(i)(I); 42 U.S.C. § 300g-1(b)(1)(B)(i)(I).

[58]   *Id.*

[59]   SDWA § 1412(b)(1)(B)(i)(II); 42 U.S.C. § 300g-1(b)(1)(B)(i)(II).

[60]   42 U.S.C. § 300j-4. Prior to issuing a regulation, the Act provides that EPA may require systems to submit information for individual system compliance purposes, as well as to establish new regulations.

[61]   In the latter case, EPA must pay for any requirements to install treatment equipment or process changes, to test treatment technology, or to analyze or process monitoring samples. SDWA § 1445(a)(1); 42 U.S.C. § 300j-4.

[62]   SDWA § 1412(b)(1)(B); 42 U.S.C. § 300g-1(b)(1)(B).

[63]   SDWA § 1412(b)(1)(B)(i)(III); 42 U.S.C. § 300g-1(b)(1)(B)(i)(III).

[64] Any challenge would also have to overcome issues of standing, including whether actionable injury would flow from EPA simply including a contaminant on the candidate list.

[65] 63 Fed. Reg. 10273-10287 (Mar. 2, 1998).

[66] SDWA § 1412(b)(1)(B); 42 U.S.C.A. § 300g-1(b)(1)(B)(I).

[67] 70 Fed. Reg. 9071-9077 (Feb. 24, 2005). In the interim, EPA had reviewed 9 of the 60 contaminants from the first CCL and determined that they did not need to be regulated.

[68] 74 Fed. Reg. 51850 (Oct. 8, 2009).

[69] 74 Fed. Reg. at 51852.

[70] *See* "Final CCL 3 Chemicals: Identifying the Universe" (EPA, 2009a); and "Final CCL 3 Chemicals: Screening to a PCCL" (EPA, 2009b). The data and information used to evaluate contaminants on the PCCL is provided in Contaminant Information Sheets available in the CCL 3 docket (EPA-HQ-OW-2007-1189) at www.regulations.gov.

[71] "Final CCL 3 Chemicals: Identifying the Universe" (EPA, 2009a); and "Final CCL 3 Chemicals: Screening to a PCCL" (EPA, 2009b).

[72] 74 Fed. Reg. at 51852. For example, in evaluating the second criterion, EPA considered not only public water system monitoring data and data on concentrations in ambient surface and groundwaters, but also releases to the environment within the meaning of the EPCRA Toxics Release Inventory (TRI). *See* 74 Fed. Reg. at 51851. EPA has stated that while TRI data may not establish conclusively that contaminants occur in public water systems, the Agency believes these data are sufficient to anticipate that contaminants may occur in public water systems and support their inclusion on the CCL. *See* "Final CCL 3 Chemicals: Identifying the Universe" (EPA, 2009a); and "Final CCL 3 Chemicals: Screening to a PCCL" (EPA, 2009b). The logic of this is less than compelling and is arguably at odds with the SDWA's mandate in Section 1412 that, when the Agency employs science in the standard-setting process provided in Section 1412, it must use the "best available peer reviewed science" and data collected by the "best available methods."

[73] 77 Fed. Reg. 27057 (May 8, 2012).

[74] 80 Fed. Reg. 6076 (February 4, 2015).

[75] Those actions with respect to CCL 4 were taken based upon the *draft* third Regulatory Determination. As discussed in section 4.1.2, the final third Regulatory Determination that was published in the Federal Register on January 4, 2016 confirmed the negative determinations with respect to the four referenced contaminants, but delayed a final determination with respect to strontium.

[76] SDWA § 1412(b)(1)(B)(ii); 42 U.S.C. § 300g-l(b)(1)(B)(ii). The publication of a new CCL and the review of contaminants for regulation thus occur at similar intervals (at least every five years), but are staggered so that the CCL is available well in advance of EPA's decision regarding the selection of contaminants to regulate, ostensibly allowing for a thorough review.

[77] 68 Fed. Reg. 42897-42906 (July 18, 2003). EPA need not actually regulate at least five unregulated contaminants, but rather must undertake a determination whether *or not* to regulate with respect to at least five contaminants on the list.

[78] 73 Fed. Reg. 44251-44261 (July 30, 2008). The CCL 2 list consisted of the 51 contaminants that had not been acted upon from the CCL 1 list.

[79] 79 Fed. Reg. 62716 (October 20, 2014).

[80] 81 Fed. Reg. 13 (January 4, 2016).

[81] SDWA § 1412(b)(1)(A)(i)-(iii); 42 U.S.C. § 300g-1(b)(1)(A)(i)-(iii) (emphasis added).

[82] SDWA § 1412(b)(1)(B)(ii)(IV); 42 U.S.C. § 300g-1(b)(1)(B)(ii)(IV). In other words, the Act specifies those Agency actions with respect to selection of a contaminant that are subject to judicial review, and they do not include a challenge to the decision to regulate a substance, rather only a challenge to a decision *not* to regulate a contaminant.

[83] SDWA § 1412(b)(1)(E); 42 U.S.C. § 300g-1(b)(1)(E).

84 *Id.*

85 While the drinking water standard for a contaminant is the essential aspect of an NPDWR, its regulatory provisions also address monitoring, reporting, recordkeeping, public notifications, sampling procedures, and how violations are to be addressed.

86 SDWA § 1412(b)(4)(A); 42 U.S.C. § 300g-l(b)(4)(A).

87 *See* SDWA § 1412(b)(4)(B); 42 U.S.C. § 300g-l(b)(4)(B), which explains that feasible in this context means "feasible with the use of the best technology, treatment techniques and other means which the Administrator finds, after examination for efficacy under field conditions and not solely under laboratory conditions, are available (taking cost into consideration)."

88 56 Fed. Reg. at 3,534.

89 SDWA § 1412(b)(4)(A); 42 U.S.C. § 300g-l(b)(4)(A).

90 *See, e.g.,* 63 Fed. Reg. at 69,398.

91 56 Fed. Reg. at 3,536.

92 SDWA § 1412(b)(4)(C); 42 U.S.C. § 300g-l(b)(4)(C). As the *Halogenated Solvents* Court explained, MCLs involve practical and policy considerations while "[i]t is obvious that Congress intended that the MCLGs be based solely on scientific evidence."

93 783 F.2d 1262, 1264 (5th Cir. 1986).

94 The Court's opinion discussed MCLGs and their relationship to MCLs and the standard-setting process in the context of "recommended maximum contaminant levels" or RMCLs. The 1986 Safe Drinking Water Act amendments changed the Act's terminology to substitute the term MCLG for RMCL. *See* Section 101(a)(2) and (3) of the Safe Drinking Water Act amendments of 1986, Pub. L. No. 99 339 and H.R. Conf. Rep. No. 99-575, at 29 (1986), reprinted in 1986 U.S.C.C.A.N at 1593.

95 SDWA § 1412(b)(4)(C); 42 U.S.C. § 300g-l(b)(4)(C).

96 SDWA § 1412(b)(4)-(6); 42 U.S.C. § 300g-1(b)(4)-(6). *See* Section 6.10, *infra.*

97 SDWA § 1412(b)(3)(A); 42 U.S.C. § 300g-l(b)(3)(A).

98 *Id.* The complete language of 42 U.S.C. § 300g-1(b)(3)(A) provides that: in carrying out this section, and, to the degree that an Agency action is based on science, the administrator shall use (i) the best available, peer-reviewed science and supporting studies conducted in accordance with sound and objective scientific practices; and (ii) data collected by accepted methods or best available methods (if the reliability of the method and the nature of the decision justifies use of the data).

99 SDWA § 1412(b)(3)(B); 42 U.S.C. § 300g-l(b)(3)(B) (emphasis added).

100 SDWA § 1412(b)(3)(B)(i)-(v); 42 U.S.C. § 300g-l(b)(3)(B)(i)-(v).

101 The decision in *Chlorine Chemistry Council v. EPA* also is notable for confirming that, in conducting its risk assessment, EPA is not necessarily required to set the MCLG for carcinogens at zero, if the weight of the scientific evidence permits the identification of a mode of action and a threshold of exposure below which there will be no known or anticipated effects on human health, allowing for an adequate margin of safety. Furthermore, as indicated by the opinion, not only MCLs, but MCLGs may also be subject to judicial review.

102 SDWA § 1412(b)(1)(A); 42 U.S.C. § 300g-l(b)(1)(A).

103 SDWA § 1412(b)(6); 42 U.S.C. § 300g-1(b)(6)-(7). The courts have afforded EPA broad discretion to determine when a treatment technique is appropriate. See American Water Works Association v. EPA, 40 F.3d 1266, 1271 (D.C. Cir. 1994).

104 *Id.*

105 Finished water generally refers to water that is treated and distributed by a PWS and undergoes no further treatment other than maintenance of a disinfectant residual in the distribution system. 40 C.F.R. § 141.140.

106 Disinfectant residual levels have been proven to be reliable indicators of microorganism removal sufficient to ensure protection of human health.

[107] 78 Fed. Reg 10269 (February 13, 2013).

[108] SDWA § 1412(b)(9); 42 U.S.C. § 300g-1(b)(9), which provides that "[t]he Administrator shall, not less often than every 6 years, review and revise, as appropriate, each national primary drinking water regulation promulgated under this title. Any revision of a national primary drinking water regulation shall be promulgated in accordance with this section, except that each revision shall maintain, or provide for greater protection of the health of persons."

[109] If the best available science that had evolved during the six years since the original MCL was adopted demonstrated that the MCL could be increased without an adverse effect on human health, but while providing significant cost benefits, the Agency presumably would be within its discretion to revisit the MCL on that basis. On the other hand, whether a court could be persuaded that the Agency was required to do so in a particular circumstance is open to question.

[110] 75 Fed. Reg. 15500, 15504 n.2. (March 29, 2010), citing Senate Report No. 104-169, 104th Congress, 1st Session, 1995 at 38.

[111] Also, while the provisions of the SDWA § 1412 relating to the selection of contaminants for the CCL and the decision to regulate a previously unregulated substance are expressly exempted from judicial review, there is no specific language or corresponding provision carving out the decision to revisit an existing NPDWR from judicial review. However, principles of standing would suggest that until a revised MCL was promulgated, the existing standard would apply, and there might not be a redressable injury. The failure of EPA to conduct a review at least every six years, on the other hand, involves a nondiscretionary duty that would be judicially reviewable on procedural grounds.

[112] These include NPDWRs addressing microorganisms, disinfectants and disinfection by-products, organic and inorganic chemicals, and radionuclides. A complete list, including a breakdown by category, may be found at http://www.epa.gov/drink/contaminants/index.cfm#List and is also available in the publication EPA 816-F-09-0004 (May 2009).

[113] This review is to be distinguished from the review of *unregulated* contaminants under SDWA Section 1412(b)(1).

[114] SDWA § 1412(b)(9); 42 U.S.C. § 300g-l(b)(9).

[115] 68 Fed. Reg. 42908 (July 18, 2003).

[116] 75 Fed. Reg. 15500 (Mar. 29, 2010). As a practical matter, however, revisiting an existing NPDWR represents a significant effort and commitment of Agency resources that is not frequently undertaken, particularly given the mandate to periodically review *unregulated* contaminants and the amount of due diligence that is involved in promulgating the NPDWR in the first instance.

[117] 75 Fed. Reg. at 15562-03. An informative outline of the decision tree for evaluating candidates for review can be found in EPA 815–F-09-002 (Mar. 2010), available at www.epa.gov/safewater/review.html.

[118] 42 U.S.C. § 300j-7(a)(1).

[119] 42 U.S.C. § 300j-7(a)(2).

[120] 42 U.S.C. § 300g-3(g)(3)(B). As discussed later in this chapter in section 7.0 on enforcement, violations of the NPDWRs in which EPA seeks less than $32,500 in penalties are handled in the first instance by means of an administrative hearing "on the record," and the Agency's decision regarding such penalties may be challenged in the U.S. Court of Appeals.

[121] SDWA § 1448(a)(2); 42 U.S.C. § 300j-7(a)(2).

[122] 54 Fed. Reg. 27,486 (June 29, 1989).

[123] 63 Fed. Reg. 69,478 (Dec. 16, 1998).

[124] 67 Fed. Reg. 1811 (Jan. 14, 2002).

[125] *Giardia lamblia* is a parasitic microorganism that was first identified by regulators as a human pathogen capable of causing waterborne disease outbreaks in the late 1970s. Since then, it has become recognized as one of the most common causes of waterborne disease in the nation. It occurs in many water environments, from relatively pristine water to wastewater treatment plant effluent. This parasite is found in

every region of the United States, and is common in untreated surface waters. Disease outbreaks in Alaska and New York in 1995 were caused by *Giardia*. The outbreak of giardiasis in New York was of particular concern, because it is believed to have affected a significant number of people who had consumed water that was both chlorinated and filtered.

126 In limited circumstances, a PWS may avoid filtration requirements, provided it can satisfy strict requirements relating to the control of its watershed to minimize runoff and associated monitoring and disinfection requirements. 40 C.F.R. § 141.61.

127 40 C.F.R. § 141.22. *See* Standard Methods 2130A, 2130B. Turbidity of water is due to suspended solids (e.g., soil runoff, plankton, silt, finely divided organic matter, microscopic organisms, and similar materials). These solids will deflect (or scatter) light as it passes through a water sample. Turbidity is a measurement of that scattered light as compared to the amount of light scattered by a control standard. The more light that is deflected the higher the turbidity of the sample. The measuring device used in EPA-approved laboratories is a nephelometric meter. Such a meter does not measure all of the deflected light, but instead only that which is deflected at a right angle (90) from the sample and light source, which is a measurement that is considered accurate and consistent for testing purposes. Turbidity measured in this fashion is read as nephelometric turbidity units (NTU).

128 *See* 40 C.F.R. § 141.21. Total coliform is subject to one of the most important and extensive NPDWRs, which is addressed in greater detail later in the chapter.

129 40 C.F.R. § 141.21. Significantly, EPA has adopted a Revised Total Coliform Rule, 78 Fed. Reg. 10269 (February 13, 2013), which replaced the current Total Coliform Rule effective April 1, 2016, though PWSs were permitted to implement the Revised Rule in lieu of the existing rule before that date.

130 *See* 40 C.F.R. § 141.64(d)(2). At the same time, in order to maintain disinfectant by-products at levels that do not present a threat to human health, a PWS must also prevent residual levels of disinfectants from exceeding regulatory limits intended to reduce exposures to such by-products. 40 C.F.R. § 141.65.

131 *See* 40 C.F.R. § 141.22.

132 *See* 40 C.F.R. § 141.11. However, EPA may reduce the frequency of this monitoring requirement for a "downstream," or consecutive PWS. Such a waiver is ordinarily subject to initial water testing and diagnostics to establish that the nitrate levels being provided by the "upstream" PWS are well below regulatory limits.

133 Moreover, monitoring total coliform has practical benefits, because testing for *E. coli* can be performed in conjunction with testing for total coliforms.

134 National Primary Drinking Water Regulation: Total Coliforms (including Fecal Coliforms and *E. coli*) Final Rule, 54 Fed. Reg. 27544 (June 29, 1989).

135 National Primary Drinking Water Regulations: Revisions to the Total Coliform Rule, Final Rule, 78 Fed. Reg. 10269 (February 13, 2013); 79 Fed. Reg. 10665 (February 26, 2014).

136 Aircraft ICCs are now subject to their own stand-alone regulatory requirements for total coliform in light of the Aircraft Drinking Water Regulation, 74 Fed. Reg. 53590 (Oct. 19, 2009).

137 78 Fed. Reg. 10269 (February 13, 2013).

138 Monitoring may range from a single sample taken monthly for very small systems serving fewer than 1,000 persons, 40 C.F.R. §§ 141.854(b) and (e), 141.855(b), and 141.856(b), to up to 480 monthly samples taken throughout the distribution system of a very large CWS. 40 C.F.R. §§ 141.857(b).

139 *E. coli* is considered a more accurate indicator of a human health threat than fecal coliform and so the RTCR now also requires testing only for *E. coli*. 40 C.F.R. § 141.63(c).

140 *See generally* 40 C.F.R. § 141.859, 141.861, 141.202-203.

141 40 C.F.R. § 141.859.

142 SDWA § 1412(b)(2)(C); 42 U.S.C. § 300g-l(b)(2)(C).

143 *See* footnote 121 and accompanying text.

144 63 Fed. Reg. 69478 (Dec. 16, 1998).

[145] 40 C.F.R. § 141.21(d). The drinking water regulations define a sanitary survey as an on-site review of the water source, facilities, equipment, operation, and maintenance of a public water system conducted for the purpose of evaluating the adequacy of such source, facilities, equipment, operation, and maintenance for producing and distributing safe drinking water. 40 C.F.R. § 141.2.

[146] USEPA, "Interim Enhanced Surface Water Treatment Rule: What Does It Mean to You?" EPA 816R-01-014 (2001), available at http://water.epa.gov/lawsregs/rulesregs/sdwa/mdbp/upload/2001_10_23_mdbp_ieswtrwhatdoesitmeantoyou.pdf.

[147] 40 C.F.R. § 141.170. *See also* "USEPA, Interim Enhanced Surface Water Treatment Rule," EPA 815F-98-009 (1998), available at http://www.epa.gov/ogwdw/mdbp/ieswtrfr.pdf.

[148] 67 Fed. Reg. 1812 (January 14, 2002).

[149] USEPA, Long Term 1 Enhanced Surface Water Treatment Rule (LT1ESWTR) Implementation Guidance, EPA 816-R-04-008 (2004), available at http://water.epa.gov/lawsregs/rulesregs/sdwa/mdbp/upload/2004_11_22_mdbp_lt1eswtr_guidance_lt1_ig.pdf.

[150] 71 Fed. Reg. 654 (Jan. 5, 2006).

[151] *Id. See* 40 C.F.R. Part 141, Subparts H and M. *See also* USEPA, Long Term 2 Enhanced Surface Water Treatment Rule, EPA 815-F-05-002 (2005), available at http://water.epa.gov/lawsregs/rulesregs/sdwa/lt2/upload/2005_12_15_disinfection_lt2_fs_lt2_finalrule.pdf.

[152] Pub. L. No. 104-182, 110 Stat. 1613 (1996).

[153] 63 Fed. Reg. 69,390 (Dec. 16, 1998).

[154] USEPA, "Complying with the Stage 1 Disinfectants and Disinfection Byproducts Rule: Guide," EPA 816-B-05-004 (2006), available at http://water.epa.gov/lawsregs/rulesregs/sdwa/mdbp/upload/200 6_05_30_mdbp_guide_stage1_basic_final.pdf.

[155] 40 C.F.R. § 141.65(b)(2).

[156] 40 C.F.R. § 141.65(a).

[157] 40 C.F.R. § 141.135.

[158] Fed. Reg. 388 (Jan. 4, 2006).

[159] Residual disinfectants (e.g., chloramines) react over a more extended time frame and are used as an adjunct to primary disinfectants, such as chlorine, as a means of maintaining disinfection capabilities in finished water throughout the distribution system.

[160] USEPA, "Stage 2 Disinfectants and Disinfection Byproducts Rule," EPA 815-F-05-003 (2005), available at http://www.epa.gov/ogwdw/disinfection/stage2/pdfs/fs_st2_finalrule.pdf.

[161] Unfortunately, older homes that may contain lead paint are more likely to have lead in their plumbing.

[162] Congress accomplished this by providing incentives for states to amend their building codes accordingly.

[163] The Act created incentives compelling states to change their building codes for plumbing.

[164] Pub. L. 100-572 (1988).

[165] 56 Fed. Reg. 26478 (June 7, 1991).

[166] *See American Water Works Association v. EPA*, 40 F.3d 1266 (D.C. Cir. 1994), explaining that the limits of EPA legal authority do not allow it to impose regulatory requirements inside a private home.

[167] While copper is a secondary drinking water contaminant, its widespread use in plumbing led to its inclusion in the LCR to prevent corrosion in home plumbing systems. If an action level is exceeded under the LCR, a PWS is required to take corrective measures.

[168] 40 C.F.R. § 141.80(c). High-risk homes would include, for example, homes served by land service lines or those homes with plumbing that predates the ban on leaded solder.

[169] 40 C.F.R. § 141.80(d)-(j).

[170] 40 C.F.R. § 141.85. Because lead presents primarily a health threat due to chronic exposures and a CWS serves a much broader spectrum of the public, the notice/educational requirements for a NTNCWS are more limited. 40 C.F.R. § 141.85(a)(2).

[171] 65 Fed. Reg. 1950 (Jan. 12, 2000) and 72 Fed. Reg. 57781 (Oct. 10, 2007).

[172] 40 C.F.R. § 141.82.

[173] 40 C.F.R. § 141.83.

[174] 40 C.F.R. § 141.84. Replacement of lead lines is among the least preferable mitigation measure, not only because of its cost, but because (1) it only addresses the portion of a lead service line owned by the PWS, not that on the homeowner's property or in the home plumbing; (2) it requires years to accomplish, if a large number of homes are involved; and (3) severing lead lines exposes uncoated lead in the pipes and may disturb lead-containing sediments in the service connection to the home, exacerbating the problem. The latter consideration can be addressed by post-replacement monitoring measures provided for in the LCR, but also involves more difficult issues of homeowner participation in the sampling and the possibility of having to provide a temporary alternative water source.

[175] Media reports have contributed significantly to the heightened level of scrutiny. For example, a 2016 *USA Today* article reported that nearly 2,000 water systems in all 50 states recorded at least one drinking water sample that had exceeded the 15 ppb lead action level since 2012. Alison Young and Mark Nichols, Beyond Flint: Excessive Lead Levels Found in Almost 2,000 Water Systems Across All 50 States, *USA Today*, http://www.usatoday.com/story/news/2016/03/11/nearly-2000-water-systems-fail-lead-tests/81220466/.

[176] "*Report of the Lead and Copper Rule Working Group to the National Drinking Water Advisory Council*" (August 24, 2015).

[177] *Gilcreast v. Lockwood, Andrews & Newnam, P.C.*, 2:16-cv-11173-MAG-APP (E.D. Mich. March 31, 2016).

[178] However, in another class action seeking relief based on federal common law claims, the Court dismissed the action citing to *Mattoon v. Pittsfield*, 980 F.2d (1st Cir. 1992), a case which held that the SDWA has preempted the field of drinking water regulation and federal common law nuisance. *Boler v. Early*, No. 16-10323 (E.D. Mich. April 19, 2016). *See also* sections 8.0 and 9.0 of this chapter.

[179] 40 C.F.R. § 141.61(c).

[180] 40 C.F.R. § 141.23.

[181] 40 C.F.R. § 141.23(d). An exception applies with respect to nitrates and nitrites in systems served by surface water, which must be monitored quarterly.

[182] 40 C.F.R. § 141.23(c).

[183] 42 U.S.C. § 300g-l(b)(11).

[184] See 1974 Safe Drinking Water Act, H.R. Rep. No. 93-1185, at 6468 (1974).

[185] CDC, Fluoridation Basics, http://www.cdc.gov/fluoridation/benefits/background.htm.

[186] 40 C.F.R. § 141.51(b).

[187] 42 U.S.C. § 300g-l(b)(4)(A).

[188] 40 C.F.R. § 141.62(b)

[189] 42 U.S.C. §§300g-l(b)(3)(C) and (4)(B)

[190] 40 C.F.R. §143.3

[191] HHS, Proposed HHS Recommendation for Fluoride Concentration in Drinking Water for Prevention of Dental Caries, 76 Fed. Reg. 2383, 2384 (Jan. 13, 2011).

[192] 42 U.S.C. § 300g-l(b)(9). *See* section 4.5 of this chapter. *See also* News Release, HHS and EPA Announce New Scientific Assessments and Actions on Fluoride (Jan. 7, 2011), available at http://www.hhs.gov/news/press/2011pres/01/20110107a.htm.

[193] 40 C.F.R. § 141.61(c).

[194] 40 C.F.R. § 141.24(h)(18).

[195] 40 C.F.R. § 141.24(h).

[196] 40 C.F.R. §§ 141.24(h)(4) (monitoring frequency) and 141.24(h)(5) (waiver).

[197] 40 C.F.R. § 141.61(b).

[198] 63 Fed. Reg. 10273 (March 2, 1998); 70 Fed. Reg. 9071 (February 24, 2005); 74 Fed. Reg. 51850 (October 8, 2009). *See generally* discussion above at section 4.1.1.

[199] 73 Fed. Reg. 60262 (October 10, 2008).

[200] 76 Fed. Reg. 7762 (February 11, 2011).

[201] 42 U.S.C. § 300g-l(b)(1)(E).

[202] "SAB Advice on Approaches to Derive a Maximum Contaminant Level Goal for Perchlorate." May 29, 2013 Report to Bob Perciasepe, Acting Administrator from Dr. David T. Allen, Chair Science Advisory Board."

[203] A pharmaco-kinetic model is a mathematically based model used to make quantitative predictions of ADME, *i.e.*, absorption, distribution, metabolism and excretion of chemical substances in individuals for purposes of human health risk assessment. *See generally* "Characterization and Application of Physiologically-Based Pharmaco-Kinetic Models in Risk Assessment," World Health Organization (2010).

[204] 81 Fed. Reg. 10617 (March 1, 2016).

[205] United States Environmental Protection Agency Fiscal Year 2017 Justification of Appropriation Estimates for the Committee on Appropriations, EPA-190-K-16-001, February 2016. www.epa.gov/ocfo.

[206] *Natural Resources Defense Council v. Environmental Protection Agency*, No. 16-cv-1251 (S.D.N.Y. February 19, 2016).

[207] 40 C.F.R. § 141.61(a). They include benzene; carbon tetrachloride; chlorobenzene (monochlorobenzene); o-dichlorobenzene; p-dichlorobenzene; 1,2-dichloroethane; 1,1-dichloroethylene; trans-1,2-dichloroethylene; dichloromethane; 1,2-dichloropropane; ethylbenzene; styrene; tetrachloroethylene; toluene; 1,2,4-trichlorobenzene; 1,1,1-trichloroethane; 1,1,2-trichloroethane; trichloroethylene; vinyl chloride; and xylenes (total).

[208] 40 C.F.R. § 141.24(f).

[209] 40 C.F.R. § 141.24.(f)(7).

[210] 40 C.F.R. § 141.24(f)(4).

[211] 40 C.F.R. § 141.24(f)(5)-(7).

[212] 40 C.F.R. § 141.153(h)(l)(ii)(E).

[213] 40 C.F.R. 141.15. *See* 41 Fed. Reg. 28404 (July 9, 1976).

[214] 42 U.S.C. 300g-1(b)(14).

[215] 66 Fed. Reg. 31086 (June 8, 2001).

[216] USEPA, Filter Backwash Recycling Rule: A Rule Summary for Systems, EPA-816-R-02-013 (2002), available at http://water.epa.gov/aboutow/ogwdw/upload/2002_09_05_fbrrstreamfinal08-2 6-02.pdf.

[217] *See, e.g.*, 40 C.F.R. §§ 141.35 (unregulated contaminants), 141.75 (filtration and disinfection), 141.90 (lead), 141.134 (disinfection by-products and disinfectant residuals), and 141.175 (enhanced filtration).

[218] The drinking water regulations are directed at "states," but EPA interprets that term generally to encompass primacy agencies, including specifically those situations in which the Agency serves as the primacy authority.

[219] 40 C.F.R. §§ 141.31(a).

[220] 40 C.F.R. §§ 141.31(b).

[221] 40 C.F.R. §§ 141.31(d).

[222] 42 U.S.C. § 300j-4(a)(1)(B). If the state is the primacy agency, EPA is to consult with the state first.

[223] 40 C.F.R. §§ 141.31(e).

[224] 40 C.F.R. § 141.33, discussed hereafter in section 6.5 of this chapter.

[225] The Act contemplates that "reasonableness" will be determined on a case-by-case basis, SDWA § 300j-4(a)(1)(B), which the Agency and the courts will evaluate based upon the nature of the inquiry and the potential health risk that is implicated by the potential noncompliance.

226 40 C.F.R. § 141.201. The Act also establishes specific statutory violations for failure to comply with an emergency order, SDWA § 1431(b), 42 U.S.C. § 300i(b); and tampering or attempting to tamper with a PWS water supply with the intention of harming the public. SDWA § 1432; 42 U.S.C. § 300i-l.

227 65 Fed. Reg. 25981 (May 4, 2000).

228 However, they did not apply to public water systems in states with approved primacy programs until May 6, 2002, unless the primacy state chose to adopt the new requirements earlier. Public water systems where EPA directly implements the drinking water program (i.e., Wyoming, Washington, D.C., and tribal lands) were required to begin complying with the new regulations on October 31, 2000.

229 Specific notice requirements are identified by the tier of notice required and the nature of the violation (e.g., exceeding a standard or monitoring violations). They are fully indexed at 40 C.F.R. Subpart Q, Appendix A of the regulations.

230 40 C.F.R. § 141.32(d). The state primacy authority may provide the notice to the public required by the regulations, where appropriate, but the PWS remains legally responsible for ensuring that compliance with the notice provisions is met. 40 C.F.R. § 141.32(g).

231 SDWA § 1414(c)(1)-(3); 42 U.S.C. § 300g-3(c)(1)-(3).

232 40 C.F.R. § 141.32(d).

233 40 C.F.R. § 141.32(e)(1)-(81).

234 40 C.F.R. Subpart Q, Appendix B. *See* "Revised Public Notification Handbook," EPA 816-R-09-013 (March 2010) (180 pages), available at http://water.epa.gov/lawsregs/rulesregs/sdwapublicnotification/compliancehelp. cfm.

235 40 C.F.R. § 141.33. Actual laboratory reports may be kept, or data may be transferred to tabular summaries. Tabular summaries must include: (1) the date, place, and time of sampling, and the name of the person who collected the sample; (2) identification as to whether it was a routine distribution system sample, check sample, raw or process water sample, or other special purpose sample; (3) date of analysis; (4) laboratory and person responsible for performing analysis; (5) the analytical technique/method used; and (6) the analysis results. *Id.*

236 40 C.F.R. § 141.33.

237 40 C.F.R. § 2.304.

238 *Id. See also* U.S. EPA Freedom of Information Act Manual (1992).

239 EPA is also in the process of developing an application for use with mobile devices.

240 SDWA § 1414(c)(1)-(3); 42 U.S.C. § 300g-3(c)(1)-(3).

241 National Primary Drinking Water Regulation: Consumer Confidence Reports; Final Rule, 63 Fed. Reg. 44511 (Aug. 19, 1998). The CCR Regulations are codified at 40 C.F.R. Subpart O, §§ 141.151 through 141.155 and Appendix A.

242 40 C.F.R. § 141.152.

243 40 C.F.R. §§ 141.153 and 141.154.

244 http://water.epa.gov/drink/info/ccr/regulations.cfm.

245 SDWA § 1414(c)(4); 42 U.S.C. § 300g-3(c)(4).

246 5 U.S.C. § 552.

247 Most EPA SDWA Guidance is available, organized by respective regulation, at http://water.epa.gov/lawsregs/guidance/sdwa/index.cfm. EPA also makes available a number of quick reference guides on the same site. Policy decisions related to implementation and compliance issues are also provided under the rubric of "Water Supply Guidance."

248 "Final Guidelines for the Certification and Recertification of Operators of Community and Nontransient Noncommunity Public Water Systems," 64 Fed. Reg. 5916 (Feb. 5, 1999).

249 "EPA Operator Certification Guidelines: Implementation Guidance (2000)," available at http://water.epa.gov/infrastructure/drinkingwater/pws/dwoperatorcert/upload/2008_04_21_operatorcertification_guide_operatorcertification _implementationguidance.pdf.

250 63 Fed. Reg. 43833 (Aug. 14,1998).

251 SDWA § 1415(e); 42 U.S.C. § 300g-4(e).

252 SDWA § 1416(a)(1); 42 U.S.C. § 300g-5(a)(1); 40 C.F.R. § 142.50(a)(1).

253 SDWA § 1416(b)(1)(B); 42 U.S.C. § 300g-5(b)(1)(B); 40 C.F.R. § 142.54(a).

254 SDWA § 1412(b)(15); 42 U.S.C. § 300g-1(b)(15).

255 SDWA § 1416; 42 U.S.C. § 300g-5.

256 42 U.S.C. § 300j-7(b).

257 42 U.S.C. § 300g-4 and 300g-5.

258 SDWA § 1414(g); 42 U.S.C. § 300g-3(g).

259 SDWA §§ 1414(g) and 1448(a); 42 U.S.C. §§ 300g-3(g) and 300j-7(a); 73 Fed. Reg. 75345 (Dec. 11, 2008).

260 SDWA § 1414(g)(3)(B) and (C); 42 U.S.C. § 300g-3(g)(3)(B) and (C); 73 Fed. Reg. 75345 (Dec. 11, 2008).

261 *Id.* 40 C.F.R. § 19.4.

262 40 C.F.R. § 22.1(9). If the penalty sought by the Agency is less than $7,000, a hearing "on the record" will not be conducted, unless requested by the person against whom the penalty is sought. SDWA § 1414(g)(3)(A); 42 U.S.C. § 300g-3(g)(3)(A). Notice and the opportunity for a public hearing must be afforded, nonetheless.

263 SDWA 1448(a); 42 U.S.C. § 300j-7(a).

264 Subject to the $32,500 threshold of SDWA § 1414(g)(3)(B), if the Agency seeks only monetary penalties.

265 SDWA § 1414(b); 42 U.S.C. § 300g-3(b).

266 EPA has issued penalty guidance specific to the SDWA that sets forth the considerations it takes into account in assessing the seriousness of violations. *See* Water Supply Guidance 81, "Public Water System Supervision Program Settlement Penalty Policy" (May 25, 1994).

267 42 U.S.C. § 300g-3(b).

268 EPA's Enforcement Office has revised the per violation limit per day upward to $37,500 to take into account adjustment for inflation, as authorized by the Federal Civil Penalties Inflation Adjustment Act of 1990, 28 U.S.C. § 2461. *See* 81 Fed. Reg. 43091 (July 1, 2016) (setting forth basis and amount of the inflation adjustment under the respective environmental statutes and limits applicable to particular types of SDWA violations). EPA revised the respective penalty figures for specific violations set forth herein effective August 1, 2016.

269 Penalties in the case of a person who tampers or attempts to tamper with a PWS with the intent to harm the public are significantly higher. Tampering may incur a penalty of up to $1.31 million, and attempts to tamper may result in penalties of up to $131,185 per attempt. SDWA § 1432(c); 42 U.S.C. § 300i-l(c); 40 C.F.R. § 19.4.

270 SDWA § 1414(b)(2); 42 U.S.C. § 300g-3(b)(2).

271 42 U.S.C. § 300(a). Penalties of up to $22,537 per day may be imposed for violation of an emergency order under SDWA § 1431(b).

272 SDWA § 1431; 42 U.S.C. § 300i(a).

273 *Id.*

274 *Id.*

275 *See, e.g., Trinity American Corp. v. United States EPA*, 150 F.3d 389, 399 (4th Cir. 1998).

276 H.R. Rep. No. 93-1185 (1974) ("House Report"), reprinted in 1974 U.S.C.C.A.N. 6454, 6487.

277 *Trinity American Corp. v. United States EPA*, 150 F.3d at 399 (citing House Report at 6488).

278 *Trinity*, 150 F.3d at 395 (citations omitted).

279 *W.R. Grace & Co. v. United States EPA*, 261 F.3d 330, 339 (3rd Cir. 2991) (citing House Report at 6487-88).

280 *U.S. v. Range Resources*, et al., No. 11-CV-00116 (N.D. Tex 2011).

281 *Range Resources Corp. v. U.S. Environmental Protection Agency*, No. 11-60040 (5th Cir. 2011).

282 40 C.F.R. Part 142, Subpart B.

283 "Revisions to State Primacy Requirements to Implement Safe Drinking Water Act Amendments; Final Rule," 63 Fed. Reg. 23362 (Apr. 28, 1998). The definition of a PWS includes not only systems which provide water for human consumption through pipes, but also systems which provide water for human consumption through "other constructed conveyances."

284 42 U.S.C. § 300j-8.

285 In that regard, some courts have construed the same "diligent prosecution" precondition under the Resource Conservation and Recovery Act (RCRA) citizen suit provision, 42 U.S.C. § 6972(a)(1)(A), as a "claims processing" provision rather than a limitation on subject matter jurisdiction such that it must be raised in the context of a motion to dismiss under FRCP 12(b)(6), rather than as a challenge to subject matter jurisdiction under FRCP 12(b)(1), which may be brought at any time, including for the first time on appeal. *See*, e.g., *Adkins v. VIM Recycling, Inc.*, 644 F.3d 483 (7th Cir. 2011).

286 42 U.S.C. § 300j-8(a)(1).

287 33 U.S.C. § 1365(a).

288 484 U.S. 49, 64 (1987).

289 *Id.* at 59.

290 45 F. Supp. 2d 934,938 (S.D. Ala.), aff'd, 204 F.3d 1122 (11th Cir. 1999).

291 944 F. Supp. 448 (E.D.N.C. 1996).

292 430 F. Supp. 2d 1164, 1184 (E.D. Wash. 2006).

293 458 F. Supp. 2d 149 (S.D.N.Y. 2006).

294 *Id.* at 155-56.

295 *Id.*

296 *In re: Methyl Tertiary Butyl Ether ("MTBE") Products Liability Litigation*, 725 F.3d 65 (2nd Cir. 2013).

297 *Id.* at pp 64-72.

298 980 F.2d 1 (1st Cir. 1992).

299 *Id.*, citing *Milwaukee v. Illinois*, 451 U.S. 304, 317 (1981).

300 980 F.2d at 3-4.

301 Section 305 of the Safe Drinking Water Act Amendments of 1996, Pub. L. No. 104-82 (1996).

302 21 U.S.C. § 349.

303 21 C.F.R. § 165.110 (b)(4)(i)(A) and (b)(4)(iii)(A)-(C).

304 21 C.F.R. § 165.110 (b)(5).

305 21 C.F.R. § 165.110 (b)(4)(i)(A) and (b)(4)(iii)(D).

306 21 C.F.R. § 165.110 (b)(1)-(3).

307 It should also be noted that, while bottled water may be used by a PWS on a temporary basis to avoid health risks to the public, a PWS may not use bottled water to achieve compliance with an MCL under the NPDWRs. 40 C.F.R. § 141.101.

308 21 C.F.R. Part 129.

309 *See* Memorandum of Understanding between the Environmental Protection Agency and the Food and Drug Administration, MOU 225-79-2001.

310 *Id.*

311 42 U.S.C. § 300g.

312 68 Fed. Reg. 74233 (Dec. 23, 2003).

313 The exclusion was challenged and upheld by the U.S. Fourth Circuit Court of Appeals in *Manufactured Housing Institute v. EPA*, 467 F.3d 391 (4th Cir. 2006).

314 USEPA, "Water Security: Legislation and Directives," available at http://cfpub.epa.gov/safewater/water security/legislation.cfm.

315 "Homeland Security Presidential Directive 7: Critical Infrastructure Identification, Prioritization, and Protection," available at http://www.dhs.gov/xabout/laws/gc_1214597989952.shtm#1.

316 "Homeland Security Presidential Directive 8: Biodefense for the 21st Century," available at http://www .dhs.gov/xabout/laws/gc_1215444247124.shtm.

317 "Homeland Security Presidential Directive 9: Defense of United States Agriculture and Food," available at http://www.dhs.gov/xabout/laws/gc_1217449547663.shtm.

318 "Homeland Security Presidential Directive 10: Biodefense for the 21st Century," available at http:// www.dhs.gov/xabout/laws/gc_1217605824325.shtm.

319 USEPA, "The Water Sector-Specific Plan," EPA 817-R-07-001 (2007), available at http://www.epa.gov/ safewater/watersecurity/pubs/plan_securityew atersectorspecificplan.pdf.

320 "USEPA Drinking Water Costs & Federal Funding," EPA 816-F-04-038 (2004), available at http:// water.epa.gov/lawsregs/guidance/sdwa/upload/2009_08_28 _sdwa_fs_30ann_dwsrf_web.pdf.

321 "USEPA, Grants and Other Funding under the Safe Drinking Water Act (SDWA)," available at http:// water.epa.gov/grants_funding/sdwa/index.cfm.

322 Up to 10 percent of their capitalization grants may be used for source water protection, capacity development, and operator certification programs, as well as for the state's overall drinking water program, for which annual grants of $100 million are separately authorized elsewhere in the law. SDWA § 1443(a)(7); 42 U.S.C. § 300g-2(a)(7). Up to another 15 percent (no more than 10 percent for any one purpose) can be used for prevention projects in water systems, including source water protection loans, technical and financial aid for capacity development, source water assessments, and wellhead protection. SDWA § 1452(g)(2), (k); 42 U.S.C. § 300g-12(g)(2), (k). State set-asides have on average represented approximately 16 percent of federal DWSRF grants, cumulative from 1997 through 2003.

323 SDWA § 1452(b)(3)(B); 42 U.S.C. § 300j-12(b)(3)(B).

324 "USEPA, State and Territorial PWSS Program Allotments," available at http://water.epa.gov/grants _funding/pws/allotments_state-terr.cfm#2010.

325 SDWA § 1421(a)-(b); 42 U.S.C. § 300h(a)-(b). An underground source of drinking water (USDW) is an aquifer or a part of an aquifer that is currently used as a drinking water source or may be needed as a drinking water source in the future. See generally http://water.epa.gov/type/groundwater/uic/index.cfm.

326 40 C.F.R. Part 145.

327 40 C.F.R. Part 147.

328 40 C.F.R. § 144.3.

329 See, e.g., *Potential Injection-Induced Seismicity Associated with Oil & Gas Development: A Primer on Technical and Regulatory Considerations Informing Risk Management and Mitigation*, 2015, the Interstate Oil and Gas Compact Commission and the Ground Water Protection Council. The report incorporates numerous studies, models and references and provides a comprehensive overview of regulatory and technical issues with respect to potential induced seismicity.

330 40 C.F.R. 144.84(b)(2)

331 40 C.F.R. § 144.24.

332 40 C.F.R. §144.12

333 40 C.F.R. § 144.26.

334 40 C.F.R. § 144.12(c).

335 42 U.S.C. § 300i; 40 C.F.R. §144.12(e).

336 40 C.F.R. § 144.26.

337 40 C.F.R. § 144.83(a)(1)(ii).

338 40 C.F.R. § 144.83(a)(1)(ii).

[339] 40 C.F.R. § 144.26(b)(1)(iii)(F).

[340] 40 C.F.R. 144.27.

[341] *Id.*

[342] 40 C.F.R. 144.84.

[343] 40 C.F.R. § 144.25.

[344] 40 C.F.R. § 144.25(b).

[345] 40 C.F.R. § 144.25(b).

[346] 40 C.F.R. §§ 144.36, 144.25.

[347] 75 Fed. Reg. 77230 (Dec. 10, 2010), available at http://water.epa.gov/type/groundwater/uic/class6/gsreg ulation.cfm.

[348] "USEPA, Technical Overview of the UIC Program," EPA 816-R-02-025 (2002), available at http:// water.epa.gov/type/groundwater/uic/upload/2004_5_3_uicv_techguide_uic_tech_overview_uic_regs.pdf.

[349] SDWA §§ 1421(d)(1), 42 U.S.C. § 300h(d)(1).

[350] See https://www.epa.gov.uic/diesel-fuels-hydraulic-fracturing-dfhf.

[351] "The Potential Impacts of Hydraulic Fracturing on Drinking Water Resources: Progress Report, EPA 601/R-12/011 (December 2012), available at http://www2.epa.gov/hfstudy/potential-impacts-hydraulic -frac turing-drinki ng-water-resources-progress-report-december.

[352] Noticed at 80 Fed. Reg. 32111 (June 5, 2015) and available for download at https://www.epa.gov/ hfstudy under the title "Assessment of the Potential Impacts of Hydraulic Fracturing for Oil and Gas on Drinking Water Resources" (May 2015 External Revised Draft), EPA/600/R-15/047.

[353] *Id.* at ES-6 (emphasis added).

[354] As part of the Hydraulic Fracturing Study, EPA issued voluntary information requests to nine leading national and regional hydraulic fracturing service providers. The requests sought information on the chemical composition of fluids used in the hydraulic fracturing process, data on the impacts of the chemicals on human health and the environment, standard operating procedures at hydraulic fracturing sites, and the locations of sites where fracturing has been conducted.

[355] SDWA § 1453; 42 U.S.C. § 300j-13.

[356] SDWA §§ 1453, 1452(k)(1)(C); 42 U.S.C. §§ 300j-13, 300j-12(k)(1)(C).

[357] 42 U.S.C. § 300j-17.

[358] *See* "Endocrine Screening Program: Second List of Chemicals for Tier 1 Screening," 75 Fed. Reg. 70248, 70250-52 (Nov. 17, 2010).

Comprehensive Environmental Response, Compensation, and Liability Act

Ronald E. Cardwell and Jessica O. King
McNair Law Firm, P.A.
Columbia, South Carolina

1.0 Introduction

1.1 CERCLA's History and Objectives

Congress passed the Comprehensive Environmental Response, Compensation, and Liability Act,[1] commonly referred to as CERCLA or "Superfund," on December 11, 1980, in response to the perceived gap in environmental protection caused by inactive and abandoned hazardous waste sites. The events at Love Canal and other disposal sites across the nation had convinced Congress that public health and the environment were at peril because of releases of contaminants from uncontrolled dumps. CERCLA is a nationwide program designed to respond to situations involving the past disposal of hazardous substances. As such, it complements the Resource Conservation and Recovery Act (RCRA),[2] which regulates ongoing hazardous waste handling and disposal.

Throughout its history, CERCLA has been roundly criticized by industry as a rigorously strict system that hinders economic growth and penalizes individual companies by requiring them to perform extensive and costly cleanups without regard to when the original disposal took place or the fact that a company may have exercised due care in handling hazardous materials. At the same time, Congress and the American public have vented frustration over the slow pace of cleanup and the reported waste of taxpayer monies. To many on both sides of these issues, CERCLA has been an expensive failure.

In the fall of 2010, EPA published a five year strategic plan for fiscal years 2011-2015.[3] In the FY 2011-2015 EPA Strategic Plan, EPA sets forth its seven priorities and five strategic goals through fiscal year 2015. Among these goals, Goal 3 is "Cleaning Up Communities and Advancing Sustainable Development." One way EPA proposes to accomplish this goal is by "accelerating efforts through our Superfund program to confront significant local environmental challenges."[4] To do this, EPA began an Integrated Cleanup Initiative (ICI), which it defines as "a multi-year effort to better use the most appropriate assessment and cleanup authorities to address a greater number of sites, accelerate cleanups, and put sites back into productive use while protecting human health and the environment."[5] As part of the ICI, EPA is developing "performance measures to address the start, management and completion of the cleanup process."[6] In fact, from 2011 forward, EPA will not deem a cleanup a success when the construction of a remedy is complete, but rather when the site is actually "ready for anticipated use."[7]

EPA's measurable cleanup goals to be accomplished by 2015 include the following:

- Conduct environmental assessments at 20,600 (cumulative) brownfield properties from the 2009 baseline (2009 Baseline: 14,600 properties assessed);

- Make an additional 17,800 acres of brownfield properties ready for reuse from the 2009 baseline. (2009 Baseline: 11,800 acres made ready for reuse);

- Complete 93,400 assessments at potential hazardous waste sites to determine if they warrant CERCLA remedial response or other cleanup activities (2010 Baseline: cumulative total number of assessments completed was 88,000);

- Increase to 84 percent the number of Superfund final and deleted National Priority List (NPL) sites and RCRA facilities where human exposures to toxins from contaminated sites are under control. (As of October 2009 Baseline: 70 percent Superfund final and deleted NPL sites and RCRA facilities have human exposures under control out of a universe of 5,330); and,

- Ensure that 799 Superfund NPL sites are "sitewide ready for anticipated use." (Baseline as of October 2009: 409 final and deleted NPL sites had achieved this status.)[8]

This chapter will discuss CERCLA's most significant features. It is organized into nine major sections. The first section is an introductory overview of CERCLA. Subsequent sections will discuss CERCLA's primary terms and concepts, remedial provisions, liability provisions, settlement procedures, release reporting requirements, federal facility requirements, CERCLA's future, and additional sources of information.

1.2 Overview of CERCLA's Provisions

When originally enacted, CERCLA was far less complex than it is today. In 1986, CERCLA was extensively amended by the Superfund Amendments and Reauthorization Act (SARA).[9] SARA added many provisions to CERCLA and clarified much of what was unclear in the original act. CERCLA was amended again with the implementation of the Small Business Liability Relief and Brownfields Revitalization Act in 2002.[10] The second amendment created a new class of "innocent party" and attempted to make more clear the status of contiguous property owners (see *infra* section 4.5.2.1). However, even after the amendments, CERCLA's major emphasis has remained the cleanup of inactive hazardous waste sites and the distribution of cleanup costs among the parties who generated and handled hazardous substances at these sites.

CERCLA's major provisions are designed to address comprehensively the problems associated with hazardous waste sites. CERCLA provides EPA the authority to clean up these sites under what may be generically called its response or remedial provisions. In doing so, it details the procedures and standards that must be followed in remediating these sites. CERCLA, like most environmental statutes, also contains enforcement provisions. These provisions identify the classes of parties liable under CERCLA, detail the causes of action that will lie under the statute, and provide guidance on settlements with EPA. In addition, CERCLA contains provisions specifying when releases of hazardous substances must be reported and the procedures to be followed for the cleanup of federal installations.

1.3 The Superfund

One of the most important features of CERCLA is the creation of the Hazardous Substance Superfund to be used by EPA in cleaning up hazardous waste sites. It is to this fund that CERCLA owes its "Superfund" nickname. The Superfund is created by taxes imposed upon the petroleum and chemical industries as well as by an environmental tax on corporations. In addition, general tax revenue is contributed to the Superfund.[11]

The Superfund may be used not only to pay EPA's cleanup and enforcement costs and certain natural resource damages but also to pay for certain claims of private parties. Private parties are entitled to payment from the Superfund for EPA-approved cleanups that they have performed.[12] In addition, private parties may file claims for reimbursement when they have performed a cleanup but have been unable to obtain payment from the facility owner or operator[13] or when EPA has administratively required them to conduct a cleanup that is deemed to be arbitrary and capricious or for which they are not liable.[14] However, the Superfund may not be used to finance the remediation of federal facilities.[15]

1.4 Sources of CERCLA Law

For those unfamiliar with CERCLA law and lore, finding, let alone understanding, CERCLA's provisions can often be difficult. Many of the procedures that apply in the typical CERCLA matter are set forth in layers of statutory, regulatory, and policymaking documents. While it is true that the foundation for CERCLA is the statute itself, forecasting the government's actions is possible only when one understands the myriad regulations, policy letters, and papers issued by EPA. These materials detail everything from EPA procedures for remediating contaminated groundwater to collecting stipulated penalties in settlements. Often, EPA staff-level employees are not aware of many of these policy statements.

2.0 Important CERCLA Terms

An understanding of CERCLA's key terms and phrases is essential in interpreting both the remedial and the liability features of CERCLA. Among the most critical terms are those discussed below.

2.1 Hazardous Substance and Pollutant or Contaminant

CERCLA is designed to address problems and redress complaints associated with hazardous substances. With the single exception relating to pollutants or contaminants, discussed below, if a matter does not involve a CERCLA hazardous substance, it does not fall within the scope of CERCLA. Understanding what constitutes a CERCLA hazardous substance is therefore critical.

2.1.1 Definition of Hazardous Substance

Hazardous substances are defined in CERCLA Section 101(14). They are defined by reference to substances that are listed or designated under other environmental statutes. They include hazardous wastes under RCRA, hazardous substances defined in Section 311 of the Clean Water Act, toxic pollutants designated under Section 307 of the Clean Water Act, hazardous air pollutants listed under Section 112 of the Clean Air Act, substances designated under Section 102 of CERCLA that "may present substantial danger to public health or welfare or the environment," characteristic hazardous wastes under Section 3001 of RCRA, and imminently hazardous chemical substances or mixtures that EPA has addressed under Section 7 of the Toxic Substances Control Act.

In order to facilitate the identification of CERCLA hazardous substances, EPA has prepared a list of these substances, which is located at 40 C.F.R. Part 302.

2.1.2 Quantity of Hazardous Substance

It is important to note that CERCLA, unlike most other environmental statutes, contains no requirement that a specified amount of a hazardous substance be present before a response action can be taken or a party found liable for a release or threat of release of such a substance.[16] This is true in spite of the fact that CERCLA's reporting requirements mandate reporting a release of hazardous substances only when a specified quantity is released[17] (see *infra* section 6.0). This so-called reportable quantity has no effect on a party's liability.[18] The release of any quantity of a hazardous substance is sufficient to establish liability. The rationale for the distinction is that CERCLA's response and enforcement provisions are designed to deal with a release, which is defined as "any spilling, leaking . . ."[19] while CERCLA's reporting requirements specifically require a minimum quantity be discharged before a report need be filed.[20]

2.1.3 Petroleum Exclusion

Excluded from the definition of hazardous substance is "petroleum, including crude oil or any fraction thereof."[21] This exception, which has become known as the petroleum exclusion, plays a significant role in CERCLA since many sites contain petroleum contamination. In many cases, the companies responsible for the petroleum contamination are not liable for CERCLA cleanup costs.[22] This is true even though petroleum contamination is addressed under RCRA. The result has been situations in which sites, particularly former gasoline service stations, cannot be the subject of CERCLA actions but can be the subject of actions brought under RCRA.[23]

The meaning of the petroleum exclusion has been the subject of considerable debate as petroleum frequently contains other listed hazardous substances. The most common of these are the so-called BTEX compounds—benzene, ethylbenzene, toluene, and xylene. Whether these substances, when present in petroleum, are hazardous substances has been the source of controversy. In 1987, EPA's general counsel issued an opinion addressing when such substances, if present in petroleum, are considered hazardous. The opinion states that such substances are not hazardous as long as they are found in refined petroleum fractions or they are not present at levels that exceed those normally found in such fractions.[24] In short, indigenous, refinery-added hazardous substances are exempted. The opinion indicates that substances added to petroleum as a result of contamination during use are not within the petroleum exclusion and that in such cases the substances are considered CERCLA hazardous substances. This test has met favorable reaction from several courts considering the issue.[25]

2.1.4 Pollutant or Contaminant

While the vast majority of actions taken under CERCLA relate to CERCLA hazardous substances, CERCLA also provides authority for EPA to respond to "a release or substantial threat of release . . . of any pollutant or contaminant which may present an imminent and substantial danger to public health or welfare."[26] Under CERCLA, pollutants or contaminants encompasses just about anything. By definition, such substances include compounds that upon exposure "will or may reasonably be anticipated to cause" certain specified harmful health effects.[27] While EPA can respond to and clean up a site polluted by either a hazardous substance or a pollutant or contaminant, the statute does not authorize EPA to recover its cleanup costs from private parties or to issue an order directing the parties to perform a cleanup when the substance involved is only a pollutant or contaminant. Only sites contaminated with hazardous substances are subject to such actions.[28] Consequently, while the definition of a pollutant or contaminant is broad, this breadth of coverage has no practical impact on private parties.

2.2 Release or Threat of Release

In order for EPA to undertake a response action under CERCLA and for liability to attach, there must be a release or substantial threat of a release of a hazardous substance into the environment. The discharge of a certain quantity of a hazardous substance need not occur for a release or substantial threat of release to exist. Any quantity, however small, is adequate to trigger CERCLA.[29]

Under CERCLA, the term "release" is defined broadly to include virtually any situation leading to a hazardous substance being freed from its normal container. A release thus occurs whenever there is "any spilling, leaking, pumping, pouring, emitting, emptying, discharging, injecting, escaping, leaching, dumping, or disposing into the environment (including the abandonment or discarding of barrels, containers, and other closed receptacles containing any hazardous substance or pollutant or contaminant)."[30]

Excluded from the definition of release are releases occurring in the workplace covered by employer claims procedures; emissions from the exhausts of motor vehicles, rolling stock, aircraft, vessels, or pipeline pumping station engines; certain nuclear releases; and the normal application of fertilizer.[31] These exceptions are designed to ensure that workplace-related incidents, nuclear incidents, and exhaust emissions remain regulated by laws other than CERCLA and to avoid interference with agricultural activities. While not specifically excluded from the definition of release, federally permitted releases (such as releases pursuant to an NPDES permit under the Clean Water Act) are treated differently than other releases.[32] The only remedy provided under CERCLA for such a release is that under existing law relating to the permit issued.[33]

As with a release, the term "substantial threat" of a release is interpreted broadly. Cases that have determined whether such a threat exists have had little difficulty agreeing with the subjective appraisal of EPA. Corroding tanks, the presence of a hazardous substance in a location where it might freely move in the environment, and abandoned tanks have all been deemed examples of threatened releases.[34]

2.3 Facility or Vessel

Before a party can be liable under CERCLA's cost recovery and abatement sections, there must first be a release or threatened release from a facility or vessel.[35] Interestingly enough, there is no corresponding requirement for EPA response actions.[36] While this would appear to create situations where EPA might perform a cleanup and be unable to recover its costs, court decisions have so broadly interpreted the definition of facility that there is virtually no possibility that such a situation could arise.

CERCLA defines a facility in two parts. First, it lists a variety of things that constitute facilities (e.g., building, structure, installation, equipment, pipe or pipeline, or well),[37] and, second, it provides that a facility is also "any site or area where a hazardous substance has . . . come to be located."[38] Perhaps it is easier to consider what is not a facility. Specifically excluded are consumer products in consumer use and vessels. A private passenger car has been held to meet the consumer product in consumer use exclusion.[39] However, a commercial tractor trailer that leaked hazardous substance during a delivery has been held not to qualify for the "consumer products" exemption.[40] Under CERCLA, the term vessel means any craft used as a means of transportation on water.[41]

While "facility" includes any site where a hazardous substance has come to be located, one district court has held that where there has been migration of contaminants to an adjacent tract of land under separate ownership, there must be some connection among the properties besides proximity (such as a single area of waste disposal or manufacturing facility) for the adjacent land to be considered part of the "facility."[42] However, where you have a large site with pervasive contamination, the United States Court of Appeals for the Fourth Circuit ("Fourth Circuit") has held that: a lessee of a very small portion of the larger site can't split the site into smaller sub-sites based on geographic ownership or operation to avoid liability altogether or to avoid joint and several liability since "facility" is defined as anywhere hazardous substances have come to be located.[43]

2.4 Environment

The term "environment" under CERCLA is important because a release requires the freeing of a hazardous substance into the environment. Absent this, CERCLA's response and enforcement provisions are not triggered. Like all other CERCLA terms, environment is defined broadly to include any surface water, groundwater, drinking water supply, land surface, subsurface strata, and ambient air.[44]

2.5 National Priorities List

The National Priorities List, otherwise known as the NPL, is an important facet of CERCLA's response procedures. First established in 1981 under Section 105(a)(8)(B) of CERCLA, the NPL is part of the National Contingency Plan (NCP) and must be updated annually. CERCLA requires that EPA develop criteria for determining priorities among the various releases or threatened releases throughout the nation. These criteria are to be based on risks to public health, welfare, or the environment, taking into account a variety of factors, including the extent of population at risk, the hazard potential of the facility's hazardous substances, the potential for contamination of drinking water supplies, and the threat to ambient air.[45] Applying these criteria, EPA scores and ranks the various sites for possible listing on the NPL.

EPA's original scoring system was issued in 1980. In 1990, EPA revised its hazardous ranking scoring system pursuant to the 1986 SARA amendments.[46]

EPA's decision to list a site on the NPL is considered an action pursuant to the Administrative Procedure Act[47] and subject to notice and public comment. Parties challenging a site listing by EPA must do so within 90 days after EPA's final decision.[48] The failure to challenge a listing during this period operates as a bar to any subsequent challenges.[49]

It is important to recognize that only sites listed on the NPL qualify for long-term remedial actions financed by the Superfund.[50] A site not listed on the NPL may still be the subject of a more short-term removal action.[51]

2.6 National Contingency Plan

The primary guidance document for CERCLA response actions is the National Oil and Hazardous Substances Pollution Contingency Plan, commonly called the National Contingency Plan (NCP). The NCP sets forth the procedures that must be followed by EPA and private parties in selecting and conducting CERCLA response actions.

The NCP has been present in various forms since it was first promulgated in 1973. At that time, it was prepared pursuant to the Federal Water Pollution Control Act[52] and designed to address the removal of oil and other hazardous substances. With CERCLA's passage in 1980, EPA was required to expand the NCP to place greater emphasis on the procedures for responding to releases of hazardous substances.[53] The NCP has been revised several times. The current version of the NCP is far more comprehensive than all of its predecessors.[54]

The NCP sets forth the responsibilities of the various organizations (e.g., national response teams, regional response teams, on-scene coordinators, remedial project managers) that take part in responses to releases, describes how coordination among these various organizations is to occur, establishes methods and criteria for determining the appropriate extent of response, outlines the procedures to be followed in performing cleanups (remedial actions or removals), and establishes the method by which EPA is to prepare an administrative record to support its actions. What the NCP fails to do is tell EPA the specific type of remedy to employ in each situation. This is largely a matter left to the discretion of EPA in each instance. The vagueness of the NCP on this issue means that the subject of remedy selection is sometimes hotly contested in CERCLA proceedings.

3.0 CERCLA's Remedial Provisions

Whenever confronting a situation involving the need to conduct a cleanup, EPA has two basic options under CERCLA. It may conduct the cleanup itself and later seek to recover its costs from potentially responsible parties (PRPs) in a subsequent cost recovery action, or it can compel the PRPs to perform the cleanup (either voluntarily or involuntarily) through administrative or judicial proceedings.

3.1 EPA's Authority to Act

At CERCLA's core are its provisions setting forth EPA's authority and the procedures EPA must follow in responding to releases. Section 104(a)(1) sets forth the authority to act. Under this section, EPA is authorized, consistent with the NCP, to remove and provide for remedial actions relating to hazardous substances or pollutants or contaminants whenever either of these conditions exists:

- Any hazardous substance is released or there is a substantial threat of such release into the environment, or

- There is a release or substantial threat of release into the environment of any pollutant or contaminant that may present an imminent and substantial danger to the public health or welfare.

Thus, this section sets forth the two broad categories of response actions available—remedial actions and removals.

3.2 Categories of Response Actions

3.2.1 Removal

Under CERCLA, removal actions are undertaken to deal with environmental emergencies.[55] Such actions could include the providing of alternate water supplies to persons whose groundwater has been polluted, the immediate cleanup of hazardous waste spilled from a container, or the erection of a fence around a hazardous waste site. In short, just about any action that tends to diminish the threat of a hazardous waste site and that can be done promptly qualifies as a removal.

Removal actions can occur at a site not listed on the NPL, or they can occur as part of the initial response to a seriously contaminated NPL site that will later be the subject of a more formal and extensive remedial action. For example, investigations of a site that will be the subject of a more extensive remedial action are considered removal actions.[56]

Because the administrative requirements imposed on an EPA removal action are far less than those for a remedial action, removals are frequently done in conjunction with more formal remedial actions.

There are, however, some limitations on removals. Ordinarily a removal action must be capable of being completed within one year and cost no more than $2 million.[57] Exceptions are allowed when any of these situations exist:

- Continued action is necessary to respond to an emergency.

- There is an immediate risk to public health or the environment.

- The action is part of a larger approved remedial action.

- Continuation of the removal is consistent with the proposed remedial action.[58]

The breadth of these exceptions generally means that in situations where EPA wants to continue a removal action beyond one year or above $2 million, it can find a basis for doing so.

3.2.2 Remedial Actions

Unlike removals, remedial actions are long-term, permanent cleanups. Thus, while a removal may alleviate an immediate threat to human health or the environment, a remedial action is designed to permanently eliminate any threat that a site might pose. While a removal can be accomplished in a matter of weeks, remedial actions take years or, in some cases, decades to complete. Examples of remedial actions include constructing dikes, trenches, or clay covers; excavations; and the permanent destruction or neutralization of hazardous substances.[59]

3.3 Steps in the Remedial Process

Because remedial actions are significantly more complex and costly, more detailed requirements are set forth in CERCLA and the NCP for such actions than for removals. Not surprisingly, PRPs are also very concerned with the process by which remedial actions are selected and conducted by EPA and will often seek to participate in the process used to select such remedies.

3.3.1 Site Identification and Initial Evaluation

Sites are brought to EPA's attention in numerous ways. Site information may be contained in reports of releases submitted either under Section 103(a) of CERCLA (see *infra* section 6.0) or under other federal reporting requirements. Citizens' complaints, investigations by government agencies, and submissions by state agencies are also potential sources of information.[60]

Once brought to EPA's attention, sites with releases or threatened releases are listed in the Comprehensive Environmental Response and Liability Information System (CERCLIS) for subsequent evaluation. CERCLIS contains the official inventory of CERCLA sites and supports EPA's site planning and tracking process.[61]

EPA then assembles information on the site and conducts a preliminary assessment (PA) to determine the scope of the potential environmental problem. The PA, which provides the initial screening of sites, focuses on determining whether the site presents a risk of a release of hazardous substances. A PA may be performed merely by reviewing existing data on the site; if appropriate, a site inspection may also be conducted. The PA may or may not result in a recommendation that further investigation be done.

If, after the performance of a PA, it appears that the site presents a threat and that it will score high enough to be listed on the NPL, EPA conducts additional site investigations to gather more data about the hazardous substances at the site, possible human and environmental receptors, and migration pathways. This information is then combined with the information developed in the PA to score the site in accordance with the NPL's hazardous ranking system.

3.3.2 NPL Listing

Formal site scoring is conducted using EPA criteria and scoring procedures set forth in the hazardous ranking system.[62] Among the criteria applied are toxicity of the substances, the location of potential receptors, exposure pathways, threats to the human food chain, and threats to ambient air and groundwaters. Site listing occurs when a score greater than 28.5 is achieved.[63]

Once listed on the NPL, CERCLA's expensive remedial process is committed. Because NPL listing guarantees prolonged and expensive government response actions, challenges to site listing occasionally occur. They have largely been unsuccessful.[64]

3.3.3 Planning Remedial Actions—SCAP

EPA's remedial action timing is tied not only to the nature of each individual site but also to EPA's concern with meeting congressionally mandated cleanup numbers.[65] This so-called bean counting is an integral part of the overall CERCLA process and explains in part why certain sites appear to languish for years and then suddenly generate a great deal of EPA activity.

EPA's nationwide strategic plan for addressing hazardous waste sites is set forth in its Superfund Comprehensive Accomplishments Plan (SCAP). This document provides details on each site in a computer printout format and specifies those activities that are expected to occur during each fiscal quarter. Analysis of the SCAP can provide any party concerned with a particular site a preview of EPA's long-term planning for the site. In many cases, information will appear in the SCAP before it is widely known to the public.

3.3.4 Remedial Investigation/Feasibility Study

The first major event in the remedial action process after NPL listing is the performance of the Remedial Investigation/Feasibility Study (RI/FS). The RI/FS is the most important facet of any remedial action because it determines the scope of remedial action to be undertaken. The purpose of the RI/FS is to assess site conditions and evaluate alternatives to the extent necessary to select a remedy.[66] EPA then selects one of the alternatives discussed in the RI/FS as the remedy for the site.

As the name implies, the RI/FS consists of two phases, although in practice they are often very interrelated. The first phase is the remedial investigation (RI).[67] The RI, which in many cases can take years to perform, is designed to assess the nature and extent of releases of hazardous substances and determine those areas of a site where releases have created damage or the threat of damage to public health or the environment.

It is during the RI process that extensive soil and groundwater sampling is performed and voluminous reports detailing the results of these investigations are prepared. The purposes of these investigations include determining the nature of the site's geology and hydrogeology, locating the sources of contamination, identifying the type and mobility of contaminants present, and defining the nature of any threat to human health and the environment. In short, the overall purpose of the RI is to collect data necessary to adequately characterize the site for the purpose of developing and evaluating effective remedial alternatives. At the conclusion of the RI, it is expected that EPA will have a reasonably good idea of the sources of contamination, the nature and extent of contamination, and the actual and potential exposure routes.

When enough technical information about the site is available to analyze potential remedies, EPA will then prepare a feasibility study (FS).[68] The objective of the FS is to develop a range of remedial alternatives for consideration. As such, the FS evaluates in detail potential remedies for the site, taking into account the findings of the RI. In evaluating options, EPA considers the extent to which each complies with the cleanup criteria specified in CERCLA Section 121.[69] (See *infra* section 3.3.5.2.)

The entire RI/FS process can be extremely costly and time consuming. Costs, which can range as high as several million dollars, may increase if EPA elects to remediate a site in what are known as operable units. The use of operable units—which represents nothing more than a phased approach to site clean-ups—began in the mid-1980s. It is now rare that a major site cleanup does not include the use of operable units. When operable units are used, they ordinarily represent the remediation of a segment of the site. For example, a single site may include three operable units: one operable unit may be designed to address the cleanup and isolation of the sources of contamination at the site, a second operable unit may pertain to remediation of groundwater at the site, and a third operable unit may relate to the remediation of areas adjoining the site. EPA prefers this approach in order to begin remediation of certain portions of the site while other portions are undergoing study and evaluation.[70]

3.3.5 Determining the Appropriate Level of Cleanup

3.3.5.1 General Considerations

One of the most controversial issues at any CERCLA site is the level or degree of cleanup that must be achieved before the site is considered clean. At each site, the scope and variety of contamination vary. Moreover, each site's relationship to the public and the environment differs. The bottom line questions are whether the site must be cleaned up to pristine predisposal conditions and, if not, what levels of cleanup are adequate.

The issues that arise with regard to cleanup standards include the level of groundwater remediation required, the level of residual soil contamination that will be permitted to remain, and the extent to which site remediation will require excavation of contaminated soils and debris. At the crux of these issues is the question, what levels of risk are acceptable? Since cleanups resulting in the removal of all or nearly all risks are more costly and take longer to complete, all parties with a stake in the CERCLA process have concern about how cleanup standards are established.

3.3.5.2 CERCLA Section 121

History shows that CERCLA cleanups have become significantly more expensive with each passing year. Costs have been driven upward by the discarding of many formerly acceptable procedures for remediating sites and the substitution of remedies that are designed to achieve far greater permanence and far less residual risk. This trend continued with the 1986 SARA amendments, which set forth much stricter requirements, making cleanups more conservative and costly. As these costs have risen, many have questioned the need for such expensive cleanups in situations where the risk factors applied are stricter in some cases than risks people encounter every day.

Section 121 of CERCLA sets forth the statutory requirements for cleanup standards. It provides that CERCLA-based remedial actions be in accordance with its precepts and, to the extent practicable, with the NCP.[71] Section 121 also requires remedial actions to be cost-effective. This latter requirement appears to have become a secondary factor applied by EPA in selecting remedies.

In setting forth the factors to be applied, Section 121 evidences a clear preference for remedies that are permanent and involve the treatment of hazardous substances to reduce their volume, toxicity, or mobility.[72] This has meant that remedies involving the construction of man-made barriers to contain contamination within a designated area are disfavored. At the same time, Section 121 clearly indicates that the off-site transport and disposal of hazardous substances without treatment should be EPA's least-favored remedial approach. Reading Section 121 as a whole, it is clear that Congress's preferred approach is the permanent destruction of hazardous substances through treatment. Various procedures are set forth that drive EPA's remedial decisions in that direction. For example, when hazardous substances are left on-site, Section 121 requires that EPA review the adequacy of the remedy every five years. If the review indicates that the remedy is inadequate, EPA must select a new remedy.[73]

CERCLA's greatest impetus toward permanent treatment is the requirement that a remedy achieve all Applicable or Relevant and Appropriate Requirements (ARARs) where hazardous substances are left on-site. Section 121 states that the following are ARARs for the hazardous substance, pollutant, or contaminant concerned:

- Any standard, requirement, criteria, or limitation under any federal environmental law;

- Any promulgated standard, requirement, criteria, or limitation under a state environmental or facility siting law that is more stringent than any federal standard.[74]

Application of ARARs at CERCLA sites has meant that remedies must achieve the highest cleanup levels established by other federal and state standards. By incorporating requirements from other state and federal environmental statutes and regulations into CERCLA, Section 121 ensures that CERCLA remedies will be extremely conservative and costly. Section 121, however, does not specify just what ARARs pertain to a specific site. As a result, the selection of ARARs has become a part of the RI/FS process.

3.3.5.3 Remedy Selection Criteria and ARARs under the NCP

The NCP attempts to fill in some of the gaps left by Section 121 and provide more detail regarding the criteria to be used in both selecting remedies and applying ARARs.

The NCP provisions regarding remedy selection clearly diminish Section 121's mandate that selected remedies be cost-effective. While Section 121(a) emphasizes that remedies be cost-effective and does not suggest that cost-effectiveness be less of a factor than other considerations, the NCP relegates cost-effectiveness to merely a measure by which certain other factors are to be evaluated.

The NCP sets forth nine criteria that must be applied in evaluating remedies. These nine criteria are in turn divided into three major categories. The first of these three major categories is labeled threshold criteria.[75] There are two threshold criteria: (1) overall protection of human health and the environment and (2) compliance with ARARs.

Should a proposed remedy fail to meet both threshold criteria, it will not be selected. If the proposed remedy does meet the criteria, it is then evaluated by application of the second major category of criteria, which is known as primary balancing criteria. Primary balancing criteria consist of the following:

- long-term effectiveness and permanence;

- reduction of toxicity, mobility, or volume through treatment;

- short-term effectiveness;

- implementability; and

- cost.

It is during the application of the primary balancing criteria that the NCP provides for the consideration of cost-effectiveness. Cost-effectiveness is determined by evaluating the first three primary balancing criteria to assess overall effectiveness of the remedy. A remedy is deemed cost-effective if its costs are proportional to its overall effectiveness as established by these three criteria.[76] Obviously, this appraisal is very subjective, and results can vary widely from site to site.

The final major category of criteria is modifying criteria. Two criteria fall within this category. They are state acceptance and community acceptance. Both modifying criteria are clearly of limited importance since they are merely required to be considered by EPA in selecting a remedy.[77] Since that consideration occurs at the very end of the evaluation process—presumably after EPA has a reasonably firm idea of what it desires based upon the other criteria—it can be expected that very strong public and state disapproval would have to exist for a remedy to be discarded.

Since compliance with ARARs is a threshold criterion, determining what ARARs are and whether a remedy will comply with them assumes critical importance. The NCP therefore attempts to expand on the discussion of ARARs contained in Section 121. As the phrase implies, ARARs consist of both applicable and relevant and appropriate standards or requirements. The NCP states that an applicable requirement is one which "specifically addresses a hazardous substance, pollutant, contaminant, remedial action, location, or other circumstance found at a CERCLA site."[78] Thus, applicable requirements at a site with releases into the air or surface water would include those standards addressing air emissions or surface water discharges.

Determining what constitutes a relevant and appropriate standard is more difficult. This is largely because of the greater subjectivity involved. The NCP lists several factors to apply in determining whether a standard is relevant and appropriate:

- The purpose of the requirement being considered and the purpose of the CERCLA action.

- The medium (groundwater, surface water, soil, etc.) regulated or affected by the requirement and the medium contaminated at the site.

- The substances regulated by the requirement and the substances at the site.

- The activities regulated by the requirement and the remedial action contemplated.

- Any variances, waivers, or exemptions of the requirement and their availability for the circumstances at the site.

- The type of place regulated and the type of place affected by the release or CERCLA action.

- The type and size of the structure or facility regulated and the type and size of the structure affected by the release or contemplated by the CERCLA action.

- Any consideration of use or potential use of the affected resources in the requirement and the use or potential use of the affected resource at the site.[79]

Once determined to apply, an ARAR must be met unless it is waived. CERCLA contains a list of the limited circumstances in which EPA may select a remedy not meeting an ARAR but still permitting hazardous substances to remain on-site.[80] These circumstances are as follows:

- The selected remedy is only part of a total remedy that will attain the ARAR.

- Compliance with the ARAR will lead to greater risk to human health or the environment than alternative actions.

- Compliance is technologically impracticable from an engineering perspective.

- The remedy will attain an equivalent standard of performance to the ARAR through use of another approach.

- With respect to state standards, the state has not consistently applied the standard itself under similar circumstances.

- With respect to situations involving Superfund-financed remedies, the need to retain sufficient monies in the Superfund to respond to other sites overrides application of the ARAR to protect public health, welfare, and the environment.

3.3.6 Record of Decision

After completion of the RI/FS, EPA issues a Record of Decision (ROD), which sets forth EPA's selected remedy as well as the factors that led to its selection. The ROD must set forth all facts, analyses of facts, and site-specific policy determinations in sufficient detail for the situation. It must explain how the remedy is protective of human health and the environment, detail applicable ARARs and how they will be attained (or why they are waived), and set forth how the remedy is cost-effective and uses permanent solutions to the maximum extent possible.[81] The ROD must also respond to any public comments on the remedy selected by EPA. Once issued, the ROD must be placed in the administrative record supporting EPA's action at the site.

3.3.7 Administrative Record

The entire remedial process is subject to public notice and comment. In addition, EPA must compile an administrative record. The public,[82] as well as the state,[83] may review and comment on EPA's proposed remedial actions; such comments must be included in the administrative record. The administrative record must also contain EPA's responses to all public comments received[84] and all documents considered and relied upon by EPA in selecting its remedy.

The administrative record is critical, not only to the decision-making process but also to any subsequent judicial review of EPA's preferred remedy. Judicial review of EPA's remedy selection decision is limited to the administrative record.[85] Unless review of the administrative record shows EPA's decision to be arbitrary and capricious, the decision will be upheld.[86]

3.3.8 Implementation of the Cleanup Decision

After issuance of the ROD, EPA completes a remedial design (RD). It is through the RD that the ROD's conceptual remedy is reduced to a detailed design permitting its construction and operation. The remedial action phase involves the construction and operation of the remedy in accordance with the RD. Costs to implement a remedy at a CERCLA site can vary considerably. Seldom will they be less than $1 million. Not infrequently they can exceed $50 million. More costly remedies are likely in situations of extensive groundwater contamination where long-term aquifer restoration is attempted.

3.3.9 State Involvement: Prerequisite to EPA Remedial Action

As indicated earlier, CERCLA requires that EPA consult with affected states before selecting an appropriate remedial action.[87] EPA continues to develop a comprehensive plan enabling it to share Superfund responsibilities with interested and capable states to allow cleanup of more sites.[88] CERCLA also provides that EPA cannot proceed with a remedial action using Superfund monies unless EPA first receives certain assurances from the state involved. These required assurances are set forth in CERCLA Section 104(c)(3). This section provides that EPA shall not undertake a remedial action unless the state in which the release has occurred first enters into a contract or cooperative agreement with EPA providing that the state will provide future maintenance of the remedial action, ensure the availability of a hazardous waste disposal facility for any necessary off-site disposal, and pay or ensure payment of 10 percent of the cost of the remedial action, including all future maintenance.[89] A state's inability or unwillingness to meet the 10 percent funding requirement can pose a significant barrier to EPA's ability to conduct a Superfund-financed remedial action.

4.0 CERCLA's Liability Provisions

4.1 Overview

CERCLA contains two basic liability provisions:

1. A provision permitting EPA and private parties to recover their cleanup costs.[90]

2. A provision permitting EPA to seek a judicial order requiring a liable party to abate an endangerment to public health, welfare, or the environment.[91]

In addition to its two major liability provisions, CERCLA also includes provisions (1) permitting EPA to take certain administrative actions to compel private parties to undertake actions necessary to protect public health, welfare, or the environment; (2) permitting private parties to bring citizen suits to enforce CERCLA's provisions; and (3) providing authority for natural resource trustees to bring actions for damages to natural resources.

4.2 CERCLA's Operative Concepts

It is important to understand that there are certain key operative concepts that permeate CERCLA's liability provisions. These concepts, while most directly applicable to CERCLA's cost recovery provisions (Section 107), have also been found applicable to CERCLA's abatement provisions (Section 106).

4.2.1 Strict, Joint and Several, and Retroactive Liability

Courts have found that CERCLA imposes strict and, in most cases involving multiparty sites, joint and several liability with no requirement that a party's hazardous substances have been the cause for the cleanup or response action.

CERCLA's strict liability scheme has been uniformly endorsed by the courts.[92] The basis for CERCLA's strict liability is found in its requirement that liability be construed in accordance with the liability standard for Section 311 of the Clean Water Act. Because the courts have interpreted Clean Water Act Section 311 as imposing strict liability, they have had little problem reaching a similar result under CERCLA.[93] Consequently, claims that a party was not negligent or that its activities were consistent with standard industry practices provide no defense to liability.[94]

While CERCLA contains no statutory mandate that liability be joint and several, courts in practice have freely found such liability. In many cases, this has occurred despite the existence of a strong basis for apportionment and despite Congress having deleted provisions imposing joint and several liability from CERCLA before its enactment. The deletion, however, has not been viewed as removing the possibility of joint and several liability on a case-by-case basis but instead as not mandating joint and several liability in all instances.[95] Nevertheless, courts have for the most part readily found joint and several liability whenever there is any evidence of the commingling of hazardous substances by different parties[96] (see *infra* section 4.8.4).

The practical result of this presumptive joint and several liability has been EPA's ability to sue a few PRPs at major Superfund sites and obtain judicial decisions that each is individually responsible for all cleanup costs at the site. While this stance has greatly simplified EPA's task, it has burdened defendants not only with total cleanup costs but also with the prospect of pursuing costly contribution actions against parties EPA has elected not to sue (see *infra* section 4.11).

CERCLA's standard of causation is minimal. In fact, based on some decisions, there is arguably no causation requirement with regard to individual defendants at multiparty sites where there has been a release.[97] In CERCLA Section 107 cost recovery actions, for example, the issue of causation has been reduced to whether a release or threatened release has caused a plaintiff to incur response costs. It has been stated that a "causal link between a defendant's release and the plaintiff's response" must be established for liability to attach.[98] However, at multiparty sites it has typically not mattered whether a party's own waste was released or threatened to have been released as long as some hazardous substance at the site has been discharged.[99] Thus, the government need not track or fingerprint a PRP's waste in order to recover under CERCLA.[100]

Finally, the vast majority of courts addressing the issue have found that CERCLA liability is retroactive. Under these decisions, parties may be found liable as a result of actions they took long before CERCLA's enactment.[101] However, a Supreme Court decision addressing the Coal Industry Retiree Health Benefits Act gave rise to new arguments addressing CERCLA's retroactivity. The Supreme Court held that a law violates the Fifth Amendment if "[1] it imposes retroactive liability [2] on a limited class of parties that could not have anticipated the liability, and [3] the extent of the liability is substantially disproportionate to the parties' experience."[102] Despite the decision in *Eastern Enterprises,* defendants have found courts unwilling to scrap the retroactive application of CERCLA.[103]

4.2.2 Individual and Corporate Liability

One of the unique features of CERCLA's liability scheme is that liability has been found in situations where application of traditional notions of corporate law, such as concepts of limited liability, would exempt individual corporate officers and parent corporations. This breadth of coverage is attributable in part to the flexibility of CERCLA's liability language. In other respects, it is due to the willingness of the courts to use this language to cast the liability net widely in order to achieve what they view as CERCLA's remedial purpose.[104]

CERCLA Section 101(20)(A) provided the initial impetus for the courts to discard traditional concepts of individual and corporate liability. This section defines the term "owner or operator" under CERCLA. In so doing, it indicates that the term "does not include a person, who without participating in the management of a vessel or facility, holds indicia of ownership primarily to protect his security interest in the vessel or facility."[105] Courts have derived from this provision the affirmative implication that a person who does participate in management and owns an interest in a business is liable under CERCLA for his company's waste disposal practices.[106] Conversely, liability as an operator does not attach to a person who inadvertently comes into contact with a hazardous substance at a CERCLA site.[107]

Based on Sections 101(20)(A) and 107(a)(3), which render liable "[a]ny person who . . . arranged for disposal . . . of hazardous substances owned or possessed by such person," courts have evolved what is termed the control test. The control test has been used in determining to what extent individual corporate officers and parent corporations may be found liable. This control test has come to mean that an individual corporate officer or a parent corporation can be found liable if either has exercised control over a corporation's hazardous waste handling and disposal activities.[108] In some cases, courts have held that direct control over waste handling need not be shown as long as control over the overall business operations, including environmental matters, of the corporation is shown.[109] Most disturbing, from the perspective of the individual corporate officer and parent corporations, has been the suggestion, in at least one case, that simply having the authority to control waste disposal activities may be sufficient to create liability—even though such ability to control was never exercised.[110] Other decisions have found this authority to control test to be too expensive and to require an actual nexus with disposal activities.[111]

While some courts have continued to follow traditional notions of corporate law in assessing the liability of parent corporations or individual officers,[112] the

605 of Environmental Law Handbook

clear trend has been to determine liability based on CERCLA's developing control test.

However, the Supreme Court has indicated that trial courts should concentrate on the traditional corporate concept of "piercing the corporate veil" to find liability.[113] An analysis of the parent's direct liability must rest on the relationship between the parent and the facility rather than the parent and the subsidiary. Active participation in, and the exercise of control over, the operations of a subsidiary may not subject a parent to derivative liability without a piercing of the corporate veil.[114]

Similar judicial leanings are evident in decisions relative to successor corporations.[115] Argument can be made that liability should not attach where there is no continuity of ownership even though the successor company undertook most of the seller's business.[116] Similarly, a district court held recently that the substantial continuity test was no longer a valid theory of successor liability under CERCLA.[117] Furthermore, an asset-only purchase transaction can result in CERCLA liability on the party or corporate successor who purchases substantially all the assets where the acquisition documents are ambiguous and there is evidence that the intent of the purchaser of the assets was to take them "as is," including liabilities.[118]

Arguably, the environmental liability of a company and its shareholders is extinguished once the company is dissolved and its assets distributed to its shareholders.[119] Recently a circuit court of appeals rejected the argument that CERCLA preempts state law as to capacity to be sued and was unwilling to adopt an equitable trust doctrine as federal common law.

4.2.3 Bar against Pre-enforcement Review

As indicated above, the process of selecting a remedial action is lengthy and tremendously expensive. Frequently, PRPs, persons living near a site, and environmental groups disagree with EPA's method of performing its studies or with the cleanup plan EPA has selected. For this reason, before EPA incurs the tremendous costs of implementing the remedial action it has selected, one or more of these groups may wish to challenge the action selected by filing a civil suit to enjoin performance of the remedy. CERCLA's provisions facilitating EPA's ability to obtain liability determinations against PRPs are complemented by provisions that, quite literally, make it impossible for these same PRPs, as well as citizens or environmental groups, to challenge EPA's remedial actions until a time of EPA's own choosing.

Section 113(h) limits the jurisdiction of courts to hear challenges to EPA response actions or administrative orders requiring PRPs to perform cleanups (see *infra* section 4.7). Courts have jurisdiction to hear such matters only in the following situations:

1. Section 107 cost recovery actions or actions for contribution;

2. Actions to enforce a CERCLA Section 106 administrative order or to seek penalties for violation of such an order;

3. Actions for reimbursement under Section 106(b)(2) (actions for private party reimbursement from the Superfund);

4. Citizen suits under Section 310 alleging that a removal action or remedial action violated CERCLA's provisions after such actions have been completed, except where a removal action is to be followed by a remedial action, in which case the action may not be heard until the remedial action is concluded; and

5. Actions brought by EPA under Section 106 in which EPA is seeking an order compelling a party to perform a cleanup.

The courts have typically held that Section 113(h) removes from their jurisdiction any cases seeking to challenge EPA's actions in situations other than those listed above.[120] Indeed, some courts have suggested that any judicial action that might interfere with EPA's ongoing cleanup actions cannot be heard, even if such actions do not directly challenge the remedial action selected.[121]

4.3 EPA's Enforcement Policy

EPA has always used its enforcement authority to pursue the recovery of cleanup costs and to seek judicial orders (consensual or involuntary) requiring PRPs to perform cleanups. However, within the past several years, EPA has adhered to a more aggressive enforcement policy. This policy evolved from a 1989 management review of the CERCLA program conducted by EPA.[122] In essence, EPA's announced policy is one of enforcement first for all phases of response actions at CERCLA sites.[123] Accordingly, when a site requires remediation and PRPs are identified, it is EPA's stated policy to require the PRPs to clean up the site rather than conduct the cleanup with Superfund monies. EPA's policy is to issue administrative orders under CERCLA Section 106 to PRPs prior to the performance of a cleanup by EPA (see *infra* section 4.7).

Due to the economic downturn that the United States has experienced in the last few years, EPA has had to adjust the way it approaches enforcement for contaminated properties. Specifically, EPA has stated that in FY 2013, its National Enforcement and Compliance Assurance program will see an overall reduction of 45.0 full time employees.[124] EPA has said that it is therefore devoting less time and money to PRP searches, settlement activities, compliance assistance and oversight activities at Superfund sites, including federal facilities.[125] This is a noticeable change from FY 2010, when Administrator Lisa Jackson stated that EPA's $10.5 billion budget, the largest level of funding in EPA's history, represented "a strong commitment to enforcing our nation's environmental laws and ensur[ing] that EPA has the resources necessary to maintain a robust and effective criminal and civil enforcement program."[126]

4.4 Identifying Responsible Parties

4.4.1 PRP Search

Before it can initiate an enforcement action, EPA must first identify those parties responsible for a site's cleanup. Because many CERCLA sites are the result of disposal activities by hundreds of companies, EPA has developed a highly structured procedure for identifying these companies. EPA initially conducts what is referred to as a PRP search. This search is ordinarily performed by an EPA contractor. The process involves obtaining and organizing all available documents associated with the site's operation (e.g., invoices, manifests, trip tickets) to determine which entity sent a certain substance to the site.[127] A computer database, reflecting the quantity and nature of wastes contributed by each responsible party, is often created as a result of this process.

4.4.2 CERCLA Section 104(e)

EPA is aided in its ability to identify PRPs by Section 104(e) of CERCLA. This section authorizes EPA to issue information requests requiring a party to provide information to EPA concerning the nature and quantity of materials it may have disposed of at a site, the nature and extent of any release of a hazardous substance at the site, and information concerning its ability to pay for the cleanup.[128] Section 104(e) also gives EPA the authority to obtain access to vessels and facilities to inspect and copy documents,[129] to enter and conduct sampling at such locations,[130] and to issue orders directing compliance with such requests.[131] Penalties for failure to comply with any request made pursuant to CERCLA Section 104(e) can amount to $37,500 per day.[132]

EPA's use of CERCLA Section 104(e) information requests is a routine step in the investigative process. Section 104(e) responses form a significant basis for EPA's judgment as to the relative liability of parties. Moreover, since responses to these requests are publicly available, the information they contain may be used by PRPs at multiparty sites to institute contribution actions or allocate damages in cost recovery actions brought by the government.[133]

EPA has been successful in obtaining sizable penalties from parties who have failed to respond to Section 104(e) requests for information.[134] The failure of a party to allow access or properly respond to a CERCLA Section 104(e) request for information can result in significant penalties regardless of whether the denial was willful.[135]

4.5 Response Cost Recovery Actions

4.5.1 Overview

The vast majority of litigation under CERCLA is brought pursuant to Section 107. This section permits the United States, individual states, or private parties to bring an action to recover costs they have incurred in responding to a release or a threatened release of a hazardous substance. At the same time, Section 107 has been recognized as setting forth the basic liability scheme applicable to all causes of action under CERCLA. Traditionally, courts have found that the categories of parties liable under Section 107 are also liable under CERCLA's other liability provisions.[136]

4.5.2 Categories of Liable Parties under CERCLA

A liable party under CERCLA Section 107(a) can generally be viewed as any party having some involvement with the creation, handling, or disposal of a hazardous substance at a site. The categories of liable parties include these:

1. Current owners and operators of the facility or vessel involved.

2. Former owners and operators of a facility who were involved with the facility during the time any hazardous substance was disposed at the facility.

3. Persons who arranged for disposal or treatment of hazardous substances that they owned or possessed at a facility.

4. Persons who accepted hazardous substances for transport to disposal or treatment facilities or sites that they selected.[137]

Since CERCLA 107(a) does little more than generally identify the categories of liable parties, it has been left to the courts to address in detail how a party may fit within each category.

4.5.2.1 Current Owners and Operators

The first category of liable parties, current facility owners and operators,[138] is the easiest type of liable party to identify. A current owner or operator is the owner or operator at the time a cleanup is performed or at the time litigation is initiated.[139] A current owner or operator is statutorily liable regardless of whether it had any involvement in the handling, disposal, or treatment of hazardous wastes at the facility or whether hazardous substances were disposed of at the facility during its period of ownership or operation.[140] Where statutory liability is broad, EPA has issued enforcement guidance narrowing the scope of liability in certain instances.[141]

There are few statutory exceptions to current owner/operator liability under CERCLA. One exception exists for state or local governments. Unless they have caused a release or threatened release, state and local governments are not liable as owners or operators where they acquire ownership or control of property involuntarily through bankruptcy, tax delinquency, abandonment, or other circumstances associated with their function as sovereign.[142]

An additional exception exists to protect the banking industry. Under the exception, those parties "who, without participating in the management of a vessel or facility, [hold] indicia of ownership primarily to protect [their] security interest" are exempted from owner/operator liability.[143]

Because in some cases it is inequitable to find current owners and operators liable where they have merely acquired a facility after all disposal activities have ceased, Congress created in the 1986 SARA amendments what is known as the innocent purchaser defense. This defense is available when a current owner or operator can establish that it did not know or have reason to know at the time of purchase that any hazardous substance had been disposed of at the facility. In establishing this lack of knowledge, the current owner or operator must show that, before buying the property, it undertook "all appropriate inquiry into the previous ownership and uses of the property consistent with good commercial or customary practice."[144] The defense becomes unavailable if the property is later transferred to another party without the owner/operator disclosing any knowledge of on-site waste disposal gained during his ownership or possession.[145]

As one might imagine, the innocent purchaser defense has created a windfall for environmental consulting firms. An entire industry has been built around the defense as corporations have increasingly called upon these firms to conduct the due diligence investigations necessary to establish the appropriate inquiry required by the defense.

The innocent purchaser defense was amended in January 2002 to provide clearer guidance on what constitutes appropriate inquiry.[146] To meet its statutory charge to promulgate regulations covering standards and practices for when a landowner has reason to know of prior contamination,[147] EPA proposed federal standards and practices for conducting all appropriate inquiries as required under CERCLA Sections 101(35)(B)(ii) and (iii).[148]

In the final rule published on November 1, 2005, EPA established specific regulatory requirements for conducting all appropriate inquiries into the previous ownership, uses, and environmental condition of a property for purposes of qualifying for certain landowner liability protections under CERCLA.[149] The final rule became effective on November 1, 2006.

Until November 1, 2006, parties could have met the appropriate inquiry standard by following the procedures of the American Society for Testing and Materials (ASTM) published in the interim standard.[150] EPA clarified that persons who purchased property on or after May 31, 1997, could have used either ASTM E1527-00 titled "Standard Practice for Environmental Site Assessments: Phase I Environmental Site Assessment Process" or the earlier standard ASTM E1527-97 cited by Congress in the Brownfields amendments.[151] Further, until November 1, 2006, parties could have satisfied the statutory requirements for all appropriate inquiries by complying with ASTM E1527-05 or the standards set out in the final rule.[152]

Make no mistake that beginning November 1, 2006, the only operative standard for conducting all appropriate inquiries is the requirements set out in the final rule and, as allowed by the final rule, the procedures of ASTM International Standard 1527-05.[153] The all appropriate inquiry final rule broadens the scope of environmental inquiry and envisions that an "environmental professional" will, among other things:

- conduct interviews with individuals knowledgeable about the subject property, for example, current and past owners, operators, and occupants of the subject property and owners or occupants of neighboring or nearby properties;[154]

- perform visual on-site inspections of the subject property and, from the subject property, visual inspections of adjourning properties;[155]

- review historical sources of documents and records, search recorded environmental liens, and review federal, state, tribal, and local government records;[156] and

- draft a report identifying conditions indicative of releases or threatened releases, identifying data gaps, and setting out the environmental professional's qualifications.[157]

ASTM published a new standard in 2013: ASTM E1527–13. The revised standard clarifies the steps a prospective purchaser must take to satisfy "all appropriate inquiry."[158] Keep in mind that parties seeking to obtain liability protection by conducting all appropriate inquiry must also comply with after-purchase obligations such as taking reasonable steps to stop any continuing releases, providing full cooperation to persons conducting response actions on the subject property, and complying with information requests or subpoenas.[159]

The innocent purchaser defense is of limited use, however, because the defense fails if the site assessment provides information that furnishes the prospective purchaser knowledge that contamination exists on the property.[160]

With the passage of the Small Business Liability Relief Act,[161] a new class of "innocent" party was created—the bona fide prospective purchaser.[162] A bona fide prospective purchaser is defined as a person (or a tenant of a person) who acquires ownership of property after January 11, 2002,[163] and, among other things:

- who made all appropriate inquiries into the previous ownership and uses of the property in accordance with good commercial and customary standards and practices;

- where all disposal of hazardous substances at the property occurred before the bona fide prospective purchaser acquired the property;

- who provides all legally required notices concerning the discovery or release of any hazardous substances at the property;

- who exercises appropriate care regarding hazardous substances at the property by taking reasonable steps to stop any continuing releases, prevent any threatened future release, and prevent or limit human, environmental, or natural resource exposure to any previously released hazardous substances;

- who provides full cooperation to persons conducting response action at the property;

- who does not impede the effectiveness or integrity of any institutional control employed at the property in connection with the response action;

- who complies with any request for information or administrative subpoena;[164] and

- who is not potentially liable or affiliated with any person that is potentially liable for response cost at the property through familial relationship or any contractual, corporate, or financial relationship other than that by which title to the property is conveyed.

It may appear from the language above that a party that purchases a piece of contaminated property and does "all appropriate inquiry" pre-purchase investigation of past environmental conditions would clearly be safe from liability.

However, in the *Ashley II* case, the Fourth Circuit has recently held that the purchaser's practice of allowing old sumps that it knew contained contaminated water to remain on the property voided its innocent purchaser status.[165] The Court held that this failure to stop a continuing release violated the post-purchase "due care" or "reasonable steps" requirements of the bona fide prospective purchaser defense.[166]

The Small Business Liability Relief Act amended the definition of owner or operator by excluding a person who owns property that is "contiguous to or otherwise similarly situated with respect to, and that is or may be contaminated by a release of a hazardous substance from, real property that is not owned by that person."[167] Congress intended this provision to protect so-called contiguous property owners who are "essentially victims of pollution incidents caused by their neighbor's actions."[168] The mantle of contiguous property owner is not without some peril since such owners must meet certain standards and requirements[169] just as an innocent landowner and a bona fide prospective purchaser must. Protection for a contiguous property owner is unavailable if the contiguous property owner knows or has reason to know at the time of purchase that any hazardous substance had been disposed of on the property. Thus, the contiguous property owner must show it conducted all appropriate inquiry before purchasing the property.

If the federal government conducts a response action at the property and the response action increases the fair market value of the property, the federal government may recover, as a windfall lien, the increase in the fair market value of the property owned by the bona fide prospective purchaser.[170]

The expansive nature of current owner and operator liability is best reflected in CERCLA's case law. Courts have found lessees liable as owners[171] and as operators.[172] In recent years, courts have stretched owner and operator liability to include mining companies where the defendants historically mined the site and caused releases and where they allegedly deposited mine tailings on the land and these tailings were transported by wind to nearby streams being cleaned up.[173] Courts also have found corporate officials who actively participated in their companies' management and disposal activities to be operators under CERCLA.[174] In some cases, this liability has been found merely when the corporate official had the authority to control disposal of hazardous wastes.[175] Parent corporations have been found liable as operators at sites held by subsidiaries where it has been shown that the parents exercised influence over the subsidiaries' management and waste disposal.[176] It has been held that a lender who actively participates in the business of its borrower or whose "involvement with the management of the borrower's facility is sufficiently broad to support the inference that it could affect hazardous waste-disposal decisions" can be an owner or operator of the borrower's facility.[177] While some courts have found that state agencies may be liable as owner/operators when they have actively engaged in activities at sites that have made site conditions worse or led to further releases,[178] the Supreme Court has found that, absent their consent, states may not be sued by private plaintiffs.[179]

4.5.2.2 Former Owners and Operators

CERCLA's liability provisions addressing former owners and operators are ostensibly designed to reach former owners and operators who owned the facility when the disposal of hazardous substances occurred.[180] Unless disposal occurred while these parties owned or operated the site, the courts have found them not liable.[181]

Logically one might conclude that a former owner or operator cannot be liable unless there has actually been waste handling and discharge of hazardous substances into the environment during its period of ownership or operation. However, such has not always been the case, in part because the courts have disagreed on what constitutes disposal.

Some courts have given the term disposal a broad meaning. They have suggested that disposal can occur in situations where previously discharged hazardous substances continue to migrate at a site or where that past owner engaged in earth moving and construction activities at a previously contaminated site.[182] This interpretation is based upon the fact that, under CERCLA, disposal is defined by reference to its definition under RCRA and includes "the discharge, deposit, injection, dumping, spilling, leaking or placing of any solid waste or hazardous waste into or on any land or water."[183] Under this definition, courts have found that continued migration of hazardous substances constitutes disposal.[184] Thus, under this concept, former owners/operators can be liable regardless of whether they had any role in disposal activities or even knew that hazardous substances were migrating while they owned the property.

Other courts have taken a more restrictive view of disposal for purposes of former owner/operator liability. They have found that continued migration of hazardous substances alone is not adequate. Rather, liability attaches, in their view, only if hazardous substances were introduced into the environment during the former owner's or operator's association with the site.[185]

4.5.2.3 Generators or Arrangers

At most CERCLA sites, the "deepest pockets" fall within the third category of liable parties: generators or arrangers. This is because, at most major CERCLA sites, many of these parties are Fortune 500 companies.

This category of liable parties encompasses more than those who have merely produced or generated hazardous substances. By definition, it includes "any person who by contract, agreement, or otherwise arranged for disposal or treatment . . . of hazardous substances owned or possessed by such person."[186] Thus, the major issues associated with this category of liable parties involve what constitutes (1) an arrangement for disposal and (2) ownership or possession of hazardous substances. Courts have broadly interpreted an arrangement for disposal or treatment to reach practically any situation where there has been a relationship between two entities involving the handling and ultimate disposal of a waste containing hazardous substances.

Aside from the traditional situation where the generator of a hazardous substance has arranged for its disposal, arrangements deemed sufficient to trigger liability have included the following:

1. Selling a waste material containing hazardous substances to another party for its use in its business.[187]

2. Contracting for the disposal of hazardous substances as fill at a construction site.[188]

3. Entering into an agreement for the production of chemicals from furnished raw materials while knowing that the second party's production would lead to the disposal of hazardous substances.[189]

4. Historical knowledge and continuation of disposal practices resulting in a hazardous substances release from a mining tailings pile.[190]

5. Performing cleanup after demolition of a manufacturing facility.[191]

In 2009, the Supreme Court rendered a decision of critical importance to parties facing CERCLA liability as arrangers.[192] Addressing the expanse of cases, the Supreme Court found at one end are cases where a party entered into a transaction "for the sole purpose of discarding a used and no longer useful hazardous substance."[193] In such cases, there is a clear intent to dispose of a hazardous substance, and liability arises under Section 107(a)(3). At the other end are cases as mentioned earlier in this section involving the sale of a useful product and "the purchaser of that product later, and unbeknownst to the seller, disposed of the product in a way that led to contamination."[194] No liability would attach in such a situation. Cases falling between these two ends are varied, but the Supreme Court, based on a plain reading of CERCLA, held "an entity may qualify as an arranger when it takes intentional steps to dispose of a hazardous substance."[195] Generally courts faced with arranger liability since the Supreme Court's decision have conducted a fact-intensive inquiry into a defendant's purported intent to dispose of a hazardous substance.[196]

There have been few situations where courts have not found an arrangement to exist where the ultimate disposal of a hazardous substance has occurred. One situation where an arrangement has not been found is the sale by one company to another of a useful product (as opposed to a waste) containing hazardous substances.[197] Thus, it appears that characterizing the material sold as a waste is important in determining liability under this aspect of the generator or arranger provision. Another situation where an arrangement has not been found is one where the company that arranged for the removal of materials containing hazardous substance did not make the decision to dispose of the materials at a CERCLA site.[198] Where a third party makes the crucial decision to send the materials to a disposal site and the company had no knowledge of the third party's arrangement with the disposal site, arranger liability will not attach.[199]

To promote the use and reuse of scrap materials to minimize waste and conserve natural resources, Congress created an exemption to liability as an arranger under CERCLA when it passed the Superfund Recycling Equity Act (SREA).[200] SREA specifically exempts a person who arranged for recycling of recyclable materials such as scrap metal, scrap rubber (other than whole tires), spent batteries, and other such scrap materials.[201] The courts are now grappling with diverse issues relating to SREA such as retroactivity, burden of proof, attorney fees, and contractor liability.[202]

Generally, courts have tended to ignore CERCLA's apparent requirement that a generator or arranger must have owned or possessed the hazardous substance for which there has been an arrangement for disposal. In order to find liability, courts have relied on concepts such as constructive possession. Constructive possession exists when a party has the authority to control the handling and disposal of hazardous substances. Consequently, a waste broker who arranges for disposal can be liable as a generator or arranger despite the lack of actual ownership or possession.[203]

Another extension of liability can be found in situations where a company provides a product such as a chemical to a company and the company's use of the product results in a release. In this scenario, "arranging" for a transaction in which there necessarily would be leakage or some other form of disposal is sufficient to impose arranger liability. Such liability would attach even though the product manufacturer had no direct contact with the company using the product.[204]

Plaintiffs have tried to broaden the arranger liability provision. In one case, the district court refused to extend arranger liability to the seller of dry cleaning machinery.[205] In that case, the dry cleaner sued the seller of the machine as an "arranger" because the dry cleaner relied on the instruction manual which directed it to discharge its wastewater down the drain, resulting in a release of hazardous substances. The court held that manual instructions were not steps to dispose of hazardous materials.[206]

Responding to the nearly impossible burdens of proof which would arise if they had to do so, courts have universally held that plaintiffs need not "finger-print" a generator's or arranger's hazardous substances at a site. It is sufficient to show that there are hazardous substances like those of the generator or arranger at the site and that there is evidence showing that the generator's or arranger's hazardous substances were sent to the site.[207]

4.5.2.4 Transporters

The final category of liable parties under CERCLA encompasses those who have transported a hazardous substance to a site from which there has been a release or threatened release.[208] Parties in this category are typically commercial waste haulers.

Section 107(a)(4), which addresses transporter liability, defines a liable party as one "who accepts or accepted any hazardous substances for transport to dis-posal or treatment facilities or sites selected by such person from which there is a release or a threatened release." Thus, under this section, a transporter is liable only if it selected the disposal or treatment site.[209]

Determining whether transporter site selection has occurred is largely a case-by-case analysis. Any involvement in helping a generator select where to dispose its waste may be sufficient.[210] The mere fact that a transporter has taken waste to the only state-licensed disposal facility available does not necessarily mean that a transporter did not participate in site selection, particularly when the transporter helped smaller generators identify the facility.[211] Both private haulers and com-mon carriers can be found liable as transporters if they participated in site selec-tion.[212] However, if a transporter's actions involved recyclable materials such as scrap metal, scrap paper, scrap glass, and spent batteries, his conduct as a trans-porter under CERCLA Section 107(a)(4) is exempted from liability.[213]

4.5.3 Elements of CERCLA Cost Recovery

In addition to establishing that a party fits within one of the categories of liable parties, the elements of liability in CERCLA Section 107 cost recovery action include the following:

1. a release or threatened release

2. of a hazardous substance

3. from a vessel or facility

4. which has led to the incurrence of response costs.

Elements 1, 2, and 3 have been discussed in depth earlier in this chapter. The fourth element—incurrence of response costs—warrants greater discussion at this point.

4.5.3.1 What Constitutes Recoverable Response Costs?

What constitutes a recoverable response cost is largely determined with reference to CERCLA's definition of response. CERCLA Section 101(25) defines response as meaning "remove, removal, remedy, and remedial action, [where] all such terms (including the terms removal and remedial action) include enforcement activities related thereto."[214] Response costs thus incorporate any costs associated with a removal or remedial action.

Specific examples of recoverable response costs include investigative costs even where actual and real threat to human health and the environment are not proven;[215] costs associated with sampling and monitoring to assess and evaluate the extent of a release or threatened release;[216] costs associated with detecting, identifying, controlling, and disposing of hazardous substances;[217] and costs associated with investigating the extent of danger to the public or environment.[218] While some courts have found otherwise,[219] the majority have also held that EPA's indirect costs (e.g., administrative and overhead) are also recoverable response costs.[220] Certain costs have been found not to be recoverable response costs. They include, among other things, medical monitoring costs,[221] road repair and snow removal costs,[222] lost profits and general damages,[223] routine firefighting costs,[224] increased future monitoring costs due to redevelopment,[225] and longer-term remedial costs that were not necessary after a short-term removal action was done until the developer wanted to redevelop the property and needed a more stringent standard.[226]

Whether attorney fees are recoverable as response costs in a CERCLA 107 action will depend, to some extent, on whether a private party or the government is seeking to recover these costs. Since the definition of response includes costs associated with enforcement, courts have universally held that Department of Justice and EPA attorney fees and litigation costs associated with bringing a CERCLA action are recoverable response costs.[227]

On the other hand, attorney fees are not recoverable by a private party when they are incurred while negotiating with EPA or during litigation.[228] A private party may recover attorney fees for work that is "closely tied to the actual cleanup."[229]

The government may not necessarily recover all costs it incurs regarding the cleanup of a contaminated site. For example, courts disagree over whether EPA is entitled to recover costs associated with monitoring a PRP's cleanup performed under the authority of a settlement with EPA.[230]

As indicated in section 4.5.3, before any response cost is recoverable under Section 107, it must be shown that the release or threatened release caused the incurrence of the costs. For example, a landowner whose land adjoins a site with a threatened release would not be entitled to response costs for the installation of monitoring wells if the wells were installed in response to another unrelated event.[231] This causation requirement is particularly applicable to private cost recovery actions since the CERCLA section authorizing such actions limits recovery to "necessary costs of response."[232] Presumably, unnecessary costs are not recoverable; in fact, some courts have suggested that if an action after objective evaluation is not reasonable, the costs should not be recoverable.[233]

4.5.3.2 Compliance with the NCP

In both private and EPA cost recovery actions, an essential element is that the party seeking such costs must have complied with the provisions of the NCP in incurring such costs. While both EPA and private parties must comply with the NCP, courts have interpreted CERCLA to create a different burden of proof with regard to establishing NCP compliance in each instance. CERCLA provides that EPA is entitled to all costs not inconsistent with the NCP,[234] while in private actions such costs must be consistent with the NCP.[235] This statutory difference has meant that a defendant must prove response costs were inconsistent with the NCP in EPA's cost recovery actions,[236] while the plaintiff seeking response costs in private actions bears the burden of establishing that its costs were consistent with the NCP.[237]

While courts have uniformly found that the failure to comply with the NCP is a barrier to the recovery of response costs,[238] the extent of compliance necessary has been subject to differing interpretations. Since the government is accorded a presumption of consistency, and challenges to its actions are limited to an administrative record—reversible only when arbitrary and capricious[239]—it is not surprising that cases addressing the issue of NCP consistency have largely been in the context of private cost recovery actions.[240] Two approaches for assessing the degree of necessary compliance have evolved. One approach holds that a private party must strictly comply with the NCP in order to recover its response costs.[241] Other courts have taken a less restrictive view. They have held that only substantial compliance with the NCP is required.[242] This more reasonable approach is likely to be the standard of review in the future, particularly because the NCP sets forth a substantial compliance requirement for private response actions.[243] For example, courts have held recently that the NCP requirements were "not intended to be a checklist of required actions for private remediations"[244] and that "the standard of compliance for all versions of the NCP is substantial compliance."[245]

Resourceful private parties who have incurred response costs cannot use state tort law to recover costs of a remediation that failed to comply with the NCP.[246] Failure to submit a plan of remediation for public notice and comment as required by the NCP was fatal to a private party's cost recovery action despite CERCLA's savings clause.[247]

It should be noted the NCP creates a presumption that private party costs incurred in complying with a cleanup mandate from EPA are consistent with the NCP.[248] This presumption has been accepted by some courts.[249]

4.6 CERCLA Section 106 Abatement Actions

The second major cause of action available under CERCLA arises under CERCLA Section 106.[250] This section authorizes EPA to seek judicial relief requiring a PRP to abate an imminent and substantial endangerment to the public health or welfare or to the environment because of an actual or threatened release of a hazardous substance from a facility. Such an action may be maintained only by EPA and is not available to private parties.[251] The purpose of a CERCLA Section 106 action for judicial relief is to require liable parties at a site to pay for a cleanup, thus avoiding commitment of Superfund monies for the cleanup.

Most courts have found the general classes of liable parties and elements of proof under CERCLA Section 106 the same as those under Section 107.[252] The most significant difference is that under Section 106 there must also be a situation which may present an "imminent and substantial endangerment." To date, this difference between the two causes of action has had little apparent impact. EPA has routinely filed suits containing both causes of action. While paying lip service to the imminent and substantial endangerment requirement of Section 106, courts have had little difficulty finding that such an endangerment exists since the standard necessary to establish an imminent and substantial endangerment is minimal. Case law has construed imminent to mean not that the harm must be immediate but that it could arise in the future if unabated.[253] Similarly, endangerment has been construed to mean not actual harm but only a threat of a potential harm.[254] It is therefore difficult to imagine a situation with a release or threatened release without there also being an imminent and substantial endangerment.

Notwithstanding the above, there are differences between CERCLA Sections 106 and 107 that can lead to different results. Section 106 provides for equitable relief and states that district courts "shall have jurisdiction to grant such relief as the public interest and the equities of the case may require." As a result, some courts have held that certain equitable defenses not available in a Section 107 action are available in Section 106 cases.[255] A minority of courts have also refused to limit their review of a remedy in a CERCLA Section 106 action to EPA's administrative record. In doing so, they have stressed the equitable nature of a Section 106 action and the fact that CERCLA Section 113's language prohibiting pre-enforcement review limits the scope of judicial review to EPA's administrative record only in situations "concerning the adequacy of any response action taken or ordered" by EPA.[256] On the other hand, courts have held that EPA may seek judicial enforcement of a 106 order by injunction and not exclusively by penalties and, in so doing, the Court need not look at equities since it is simply enforcing an administrative order based on the record.[257]

Finally, the type of cleanup available under Section 106 is arguably different from that available under Section 107. Section 106 is designed to abate an endangerment, while Section 107 is designed to obtain costs associated with responding to a release or threatened release. Full site remediation, which is clearly available under Section 107, may not be warranted to abate an endangerment in every case. Some courts have noted this limitation.[258] Thus, despite the fact that EPA has indicated it can use Section 106 to obtain the same types of cleanups available under Section 107, the scope of cleanup under Section 106 remains at issue.[259]

4.7 CERCLA Section 106 Administrative Orders

4.7.1 Recent Popularity of Administrative Orders

In addition to authorizing the injunctive relief mechanism (see *supra* section 4.6), Section 106 of CERCLA authorizes EPA to issue a unilateral administrative order to compel a private party to undertake a response action.[260] This enforcement tool was seldom used before SARA's enactment. By 1989, however, in response to criticism that its enforcement program was not sufficiently aggressive and a clearly expressed congressional desire to encourage settlement of lawsuits and private funding of cleanup work, EPA began to use Section 106 orders routinely as part of its enforcement-first policy.

The Section 106 order is EPA's most potent enforcement tool and a powerful settlement incentive. CERCLA authorizes EPA to impose stiff penalties for a party's failure to comply with an order, including potential treble damages. Moreover, judicial review is unavailable until EPA decides to initiate an enforcement or cost recovery action. EPA will normally issue Section 106 administrative orders only to those parties that are the largest contributors of waste to a site, are financially viable, and against which there is substantial evidence of liability.

4.7.2 Authority to Issue Administrative Orders

Authority for the issuance of a unilateral administrative order is contained in Section 106. This section sets forth the following legal prerequisites for issuance of an order:

622 ❖ Environmental Law Handbook

a. The existence of
   i.   an actual or threatened release
   ii. of a hazardous substance
   iii. from a facility;

b. An administrative finding that there is or may be an imminent or substantial endangerment; and

c. Relief that "may be necessary" to abate the imminent hazard.

EPA's finding of imminent and substantial endangerment and its determination of necessary relief required to abate the endangerment may well be in dispute. However, PRPs have little opportunity to challenge the existence of these requirements until after the recipient fulfills its obligation under the order or EPA seeks enforcement of the order against a non-complying party.

4.7.3 Judicial Review of Administrative Orders

A party believing it may have good cause for its refusal to comply with a Section 106 order cannot immediately obtain judicial relief to set aside the order. Under CERCLA, the timing of judicial review is essentially determined by EPA. As indicated, Section 113 provides that no federal court shall have jurisdiction to review any order issued under Section 106 until EPA seeks to enforce its order or sues to recover the costs of undertaking the response action directed in the order (see *supra* section 4.6).

In addition, CERCLA does not provide a party with a formal opportunity to file public comments that criticize findings made in the order. Instead, it is EPA's policy to offer the respondent a limited opportunity to meet with the agency to discuss the order. The scope of this conference is very narrow. According to an EPA policy statement, the conference is "not intended to be a forum for discussing liability issues or whether the order should have been issued. Instead, the conference is designed to ensure that the order is based on complete and accurate information, and to facilitate understanding of implementation."[261]

Once a party is able to obtain judicial review, the district court will use a deferential standard of review in considering any arguments the recipient might have about the merit of or necessity for EPA's selected response action. The court's review will be limited to material in the administrative record, and the selected response action will be upheld unless the court finds it to be arbitrary, capricious, or not in accordance with law.[262] If not already determined, issues of liability would be tried de novo. To the extent they are not connected to the merits or adequacy of EPA's chosen response action, issues relating to the existence of sufficient cause should also be tried de novo (see *infra* section 4.7.5). It is unclear under what standard issues relating to EPA's legal authority to issue the order—the existence of an imminent and substantial endangerment, for instance—would be determined.

4.7.4 Reimbursement from the Superfund

In an attempt to encourage expeditious compliance with Section 106 orders, CERCLA provides that a party who complies with a cleanup order may file a claim against the Superfund to recover costs of complying with the order. However, a party may recover only if that party can show that it was not a liable party under Section 107 or that the response action ordered was arbitrary, capricious, or contrary to law. EPA has established procedures for filing, evaluating, and resolving claims against the Superfund.[263]

4.7.5 Penalties for Failure to Comply; Defenses

A party that refuses or fails to comply with a Section 106 order may be assessed up to $37,500 per day of the violation.[264] In addition, an unjustified failure or refusal to comply may also result in punitive damages equal to, but not more than, three times the amount of costs incurred as a result of the party's failure to take the action required by the order.[265] Passages in CERCLA's legislative history indicate that the amount of punitive damages will be set by the court exercising its equitable discretion.[266]

A party may avoid the imposition of penalties by establishing that it had sufficient cause for its failure to comply with the order.[267] Only a few cases to date have had occasion to construe the term sufficient cause; those that have rely heavily upon statements contained in CERCLA's legislative history.[268] Under these decisions, the party which has failed to comply with the order bears the burden of demonstrating that it has a reasonable, objectively grounded belief that:

- it was not a liable party (as defined in Section 107) under CERCLA or that it had a defense to such liability under Section 107(b);

- it was a de minimis contributor to the release or threatened release;

- the order was legally invalid for some reason (e.g., no evidence of an imminent or substantial endangerment);

- financial, technical, or other inability prevented compliance with the order;[269] and

- the response action ordered was not cost-effective as required by CERCLA Section 121(b), or was otherwise inconsistent with the NCP.[270]

Recently, arguments were made that the administrative orders regimen of CERCLA Sections 106, 107(c)(3), and 113(h) violates the Due Process Clause of the Fifth Amendment to the United States Constitution. The appellate court found that a due process challenge to this regimen was not a challenge to the way in which EPA was administering the statute. Since the challenge did not question a removal or remedial action selected under CERCLA Section 104 or an order issued under CERCLA Section 106, it was not barred by pre-enforcement review limitations.[271]

Consequently, in order to challenge a Section 106 order, "a party must show that the applicable provisions of CERCLA, EPA regulations and policy statements, and any formal or informal hearings or guidance EPA may provide, give rise to an objectively reasonable belief in the invalidity or inapplicability of the cleanup order."[272]

Given the provisions described above, parties who receive a 106 administrative order have few options under the statute. A party may either comply with the order or face judicial action by EPA. If a party chooses to comply with the order, he may, after fulfilling his obligations under the order, seek reimbursement under Section 106(b)(2)(A). The major advantage of this approach is the avoidance of penalties. However, this advantage may be offset by unpredictability about the size of the financial commitment necessary to comply and the lengthy period that funds will be tied up before a reimbursement claim is considered. In the event of noncompliance, the issues would be addressed in a later district court action by EPA to enforce the order or, if EPA funds and implements the response action itself, to recover its response costs plus penalties and punitive damages.

4.8 Defenses to Liability

Generally speaking, there are few affirmative defenses available in a CERCLA action. This is particularly true with regard to CERCLA Section 107 cost recovery actions. While the defenses available in a Section 106 abatement action appear to be broader and may include certain equitable defenses, the case law in the area is unsettled.

4.8.1 Statutory Defenses

CERCLA Section 107 limits affirmative defenses to situations where a release was caused solely by one of the following:

- An act of God.
- An act of war.

- An act or omission of a third party (other than an employee, agent, or party with whom there is a contractual relationship) as long as the defendant exercised due care and took precautions against foreseeable acts of the third party.[273]

Many courts have found that these are the only affirmative defenses available in a CERCLA Section 107 action.[274] For this reason, EPA has often been successful in having any other defenses raised by a defendant struck early during enforcement proceedings.[275] Nevertheless, in most CERCLA actions, a variety of defenses, including many equitable defenses (e.g., due care, compliance with existing standards, estoppel), have been raised. In some cases, the courts have appeared willing to go beyond CERCLA's three statutory defenses and consider these additional defenses on the theory that they raise issues relating to apportionment.[276] Thus, despite CERCLA's limited statutory defenses, it is always to a defendant's advantage to raise additional defenses.

The necessity of asserting other equitable defenses is more apparent when one considers the limited instances in which the statutory defenses are available. Each defense is narrowly written and has been narrowly construed by the courts.

There is little case law interpreting the act of God defense. What case law exists suggests that it is to be interpreted narrowly. The defense requires more than mere natural occurrences but rather exceptional events.[277] For example, a federal court recently held that a current mine site owner was not entitled to the act of God defense because heavy rains were not enough of an "exceptional natural phenomena" to which the defense applies.[278] Also, the defense will not apply where the presence of the hazardous substance that led to the expenditure of response costs was "not [solely] a 'natural phenomenon' of an exceptional, inevitable, and irresistible character."[279]

There has also been little discussion of the act of war defense by the courts. It remains unclear whether the defense will be limited to releases caused by combat or whether it may extend to releases caused by increased production demands resulting from a war. Consistent with the narrow interpretation given other defenses, it can be expected that the act of war defense will be limited to releases caused by combat.[280] For example, a recent decision allocated to the federal government 100 percent of the cost of cleaning up a site where oil companies had disposed of by-products of aviation gas manufactured in World War II.[281] The court reasoned the cleanup costs were costs of World War II and that the American public should bear the burden of a cost directly created by the war effort.[282] Not surprisingly, terrorist attacks like the ones of 9/11 have been held to qualify as an "act of war" affirmative defense in a CERCLA strict liability case involving a contaminated building near the World Trade Center.

Most litigation concerning these defenses has focused on the third-party defense. Since the defense is available only when the third party "solely" caused the release, any involvement, however slight, that the defendant may have had in contributing to the release will make the defense unavailable.[283] In addition, few situations will arise in which the third party will not have had a direct or indirect[284] contractual relationship with the defendant in some way. Leases, employment contracts, waste hauling contracts, and real estate sales contracts can each constitute a connection to the third party that will nullify the defense.[285] The third-party defense's most useful application appears to arise in the innocent purchaser[286] and bona fide prospective purchaser situations (see *supra* section 4.5.2.1).

4.8.2 Equitable and Other Defenses

As indicated, defendants frequently will raise many defenses in addition to the three statutory defenses. Some of these defenses have been based upon alleged procedural violations by EPA. Others could be generically categorized as equitable defenses. Courts have divided over the availability of these additional defenses. Generally, defenses raising procedural omissions (e.g., failure to provide a private party the opportunity to perform a cleanup, failure to notify responsible parties, failure to list a site on the NPL) have been unsuccessful.[287]

Defendants have had more success in raising equitable defenses such as estoppel, unclean hands, and laches. While some courts have ruled that these defenses are unavailable in a CERCLA Section 107 action,[288] others have suggested that they may be asserted.[289] Regardless, equitable defenses are more likely to be available in a CERCLA Section 106 proceeding since the court is required to render its decision based on the equities of the case.[290]

4.8.3 Statute of Limitations

CERCLA contained no specific statute of limitations provision prior to the 1986 SARA amendments. This omission was remedied with the addition of Section 113(g), which contains limitation periods for cost recovery actions, natural resource damages, and contribution actions.

With regard to cost recovery actions, Section 113(g)(2) sets forth two limitation periods—one for removals and another for remedial actions. It also contains a tacking provision which extends the limitation period for removals when they are followed by a remedial action.[291] Response cost claims flowing from a removal action must ordinarily be brought within three years after completion of the removal.[292] However, the government may extend this period by finding that a waiver for continued response is needed. Claims flowing from a remedial action must be brought within six years "after initiation of physical onsite construction of the remedial action."[293] The tacking provision arises when a remedial action is initiated within three years after completion of the removal action. In such a case, costs associated with the removal can be recovered with the remedial action costs. Thus, it is theoretically possible that the period to recover removal costs may extend up to nine years. Because the limitations periods are tied to whether an event is a removal or remedial action, correctly categorizing an action becomes critical to evaluating the appropriate limitations period.[294]

The limitations period for natural resource damage claims (see *infra* section 4.10) is three years after the later of either (1) the "date of the discovery of the loss and its connection with the release" or (2) the date of promulgation of natural resource damage assessment regulations.[295] Since the government's initial effort at promulgating final natural resource damage assessment regulations has been struck by the courts, there has been debate over when the limitations period actually begins to run.[296] In the most important decision on the subject to date, the Circuit Court for the District of Columbia has held that, notwithstanding their later nullification, for purposes of the limitations period prescribed in the statute, natural resource damage assessment regulations were promulgated when originally published.[297]

With regard to contribution actions for response costs or damages, Section 113(g)(3) provides such actions must be brought no more than three years after (1) the date of judgment in any action under CERCLA for recovery of such costs or damages or (2) the date of an administrative order or entry of a judicially approved settlement with respect to such costs or damages.[298] There have been a string of recent federal cases analyzing when the three year period begins to run.[299]

4.8.4 Divisibility/Apportionment

Traditionally, joint and several liability does not exist where the harm is divisible or reasonably capable of apportionment.[300] Divisibility is a defense to joint and several liability in which a party makes "a causation-based argument that the cleanup costs . . . should be divided between [a defendant] and another responsible party."[301] In such cases, each tortfeasor is liable only for the harm or portion of harm that it individually caused. A party alleging damages are divisible ordinarily has the burden to prove the damages are divisible.[302]

At most multiparty sites, responsible parties have had little success in avoiding joint and several liability by arguing that the harm caused is divisible or capable of apportionment.[303] Rather than hear a defendant's arguments on divisibility of harm during the liability phase of the case, many courts have tended to accept EPA's argument that the commingling of wastes renders the harm indivisible. Accordingly, in most cases involving multiparty sites, defendants have been unable to raise divisibility of harm as a partial or total defense to liability.[304] Instead, they have been forced to raise the issue during secondary proceedings to allocate costs among those parties deemed jointly and severally liable. Thus, at sites where several parties have contributed high levels of a hazardous substance and others contributed de minimis levels of a far less hazardous substance, each is jointly and severally liable irrespective of its actual contribution.

This approach was recently affirmed by the Fourth Circuit. In that case, the Court held: 1) when a site with pervasive phosphate fertilizer contamination undergoes redevelopment and secondary disposal through construction activities, divisibility can't be used to avoid liability under CERCLA; a current owner PRP who neither caused the initial contamination nor engaged in secondary disposal through construction activities can't avoid strict liability solely by arguing "zero share" through a divisibility of harm argument; and lessee cannot avoid joint and strict liability on a large parcel by arguing that it has only leased a small portion of the site.[305] The Court did give some relief, however, in holding that even if these PRPs cannot seek apportionment as a way to avoid joint and strict liability in a CERCLA Section 107 cost recovery case, they can ask a court for equitable allocation in a Section 113 contribution action.[306]

Some courts have demonstrated disapproval of the above approach. One federal circuit court found that commingled waste is not synonymous with indivisible harm and suggested that a PRP should be permitted a hearing during the liability phase of a proceeding to establish that the harm was divisible and that its waste could not have contributed to the release because of its relative toxicity, migratory potential, and synergistic capacity.[307] Another federal circuit court held that the imposition of joint and several liability was improper when the defendants had demonstrated that "a reasonable and rational approximation of each defendant's individual contribution to the contamination [could] be made."[308] Some courts have allowed defendants a real opportunity in CERCLA litigation involving multiparty sites to avoid the imposition of joint and several liability.[309] In some cases, they may be able to avoid liability altogether.

The United States Supreme Court in *Burlington Northern* implicitly acknowledged a method of escaping joint and several liability.[310] As explained by the Supreme Court, a single harm is divisible when there is a reasonable basis to discern the degree to which different parties contribute to the damage.[311] A party may prove divisibility even where its wastes have become commingled with wastes of other parties.[312] The Supreme Court affirmed the district court's approach, holding the evidence supporting apportionment need not be specific and detailed, but must be "facts contained in the record reasonably support[ing] the apportionment of liability."[313] Thus a "rough calculation" based on percentages of land area, time of ownership, and types and amounts of hazardous materials requiring remediation, including a 50 percent margin of error, was supported by the record as sufficiently reasonable to provide a reasonable basis for apportionment.[314] There has been a lot of case law since *Burlington Northern* split on how to apply the case in different circumstances.[315] Needless to say, EPA is quite concerned about the impact of these decisions on its enforcement efforts since more liability hearings to assess divisibility are anticipated.

4.9 Citizen Suit Provisions

CERCLA, as other environmental statutes,[316] contains a citizen suit provision. This provision permits any person to initiate a civil action in two instances: (1) against any other person (including the United States) for violations of any standard, regulation, condition, requirement, or order effective under CERCLA; and (2) against any officer of the United States for failure to perform a nondiscretionary act under CERCLA.[317] With respect to the first type of action, a United States district court may enforce the standard, regulation, condition, requirement, or order and impose civil penalties for such a violation. In the second type of action, the appropriate district court may order the officer to perform the act or duty.[318]

Prior to initiating a citizen suit, one must first provide 60 days' notice of the intended action to EPA, the alleged violator, and, in certain instances, the state involved.[319] This requirement is jurisdictional.[320]

Both responsible parties and environmental groups have attempted to use the citizen suit provisions to obtain, either directly or indirectly, review of EPA's remedial action process. These attempts have consistently failed. CERCLA and decisions from the courts make clear that the provisions of CERCLA Section 113(h), which limit judicial review of EPA's remedial actions, take precedence over the citizen suit provisions, even when the challenge is only to EPA's procedures in selecting a remedy and not to the remedy itself.[321]

Furthermore, private citizens may not only file a citizens suit under CERCLA to review EPA's remedial actions, they also may not pursue a claim for civil penalties incurred because of non-compliance with an EPA-issued Unilateral Order.[322]

Decisions by the Supreme Court and the Fourth Circuit Court of Appeals have raised the issue of the viability of citizen suits under environmental laws in general.[323] In *Steel Company*, the Supreme Court held that the citizen group did not have Article III standing on the grounds that the complaint failed the redressability component of standing. In *Laidlaw*, the Fourth Circuit dismissed as moot a citizen suit under the Clean Water Act because the citizen group's injury was not redressable by the relief sought. However, the Supreme Court ruled that the plaintiffs in *Laidlaw* had standing to sue. As to redressability, the

Supreme Court found that "to the extent that [civil penalties] encourage defendants to discontinue current violations and deter them from committing future ones, [civil penalties] afford redress to citizen plaintiffs who are injured or threatened with injury as a consequence of ongoing unlawful conduct."[324]

4.10 Natural Resources Damages

The majority of CERCLA actions to date have involved the assessment of liability and damages for costs related to response actions associated with a release. However, the government is increasingly invoking claims under CERCLA's natural resources damages provision to recover costs associated with the loss of a contaminated area's natural resources.

4.10.1 Statutory Provision

Section 107(a)(4)(C) of CERCLA provides that responsible parties may be held liable for "damages for injury to, destruction of, or loss of natural resources, including the reasonable costs of assessing such injury, destruction, or loss resulting from such a release."[325] While the definition of natural resources is broad in scope and encompasses not only more commonly considered resources such as land, wildlife, fish, and biota but also air, water, groundwater, drinking water supplies, and any other resources, it is limited to those resources owned, held in trust, or otherwise controlled by a state, the federal government, or an Indian tribe. Hence, damages to private property where no government interest is involved are not recoverable.[326]

Monies recovered for natural resources damages are to be used for restoration or replacement of the resource or for acquisition of an equivalent resource.[327] Regulations interpreting CERCLA's natural resource provisions clearly indicate that natural resource damages are compensatory rather than punitive in nature.[328]

Although the government is not required to provide notice to a private party when it initiates a claim against the Superfund for natural resources,[329] CERCLA does contain further limitations on the recovery of natural resources damages. Section 107(f) prohibits recovery for natural resource losses identified in an environmental assessment and thus authorized by permit or license.[330] Moreover, unlike response actions, actions for the recovery of natural resources damages have limited retroactivity; under the act, "[t]here shall be no recovery . . . where such damages and the release of a hazardous substance from which such damages resulted have occurred wholly before [December 11, 1980, the date of CERCLA's enactment]."[331]

4.10.2 Potential Plaintiffs

CERCLA identifies those parties that may assert natural resource damages claims. Specifically, CERCLA provides for designation of federal or state trustees who are authorized to assess natural resource damages and bring actions for recovery of damages.[332] Although certain courts have extended trusteeship to include those municipalities specifically designated by a state, a municipality's ability to pursue natural resource damages remains questionable.[333] Double recovery is not permitted either where there are multiple trustees or where both cleanup and resources restoration costs are claimed.[334] In fact, a trustee's failure to join co-trustees can be grounds for dismissal in certain situations.[335]

4.10.3 Historical Inactivity

Throughout the 1980s, the federal and the state governments initiated few actions to recover natural resource damages. This lack of activity resulted in part from Section 107's prescription against retroactive application (see *supra* section 4.8). Moreover, until enactment of SARA, the federal and state governments had relatively easy access to Superfund monies to resolve natural resource damage claims. The monies could be used both to assess the injury to the natural resources as a result of a release and to restore or replace such resources.[336] However, as amended by SARA, CERCLA currently provides that "[n]o natural resource claim may be paid from the Superfund unless the President determines that the claimant has exhausted all administrative and judicial remedies to recover the amount of such claim from the person who may be liable under Section 107."[337]

Further contributing to the limited use of CERCLA's natural resource provisions was the difficulty in characterizing the value of natural resources damaged or lost as a result of a release. Although CERCLA included provisions requiring assessment regulations at its enactment, the first of such regulations were not promulgated until 1986.

4.10.4 Assessment Regulations

Section 111 of CERCLA indicates that natural resource damages shall be assessed by those individuals indicated in the NCP.[338] In keeping with this mandate, regulations governing such assessments were to be promulgated, including the following: "identify[ing] the best available procedures to determine such damages, including both direct and indirect injury, destruction or loss and . . . tak[ing] into account consideration of factors, including, but not limited to, replacement value, use value, and the ability of the ecosystem or resource to recover."[339]

In 1986 and 1987, the Department of Interior (DOI)[340] promulgated two types of assessment regulations dependent upon the associated release:

- Type A regulations ostensibly for assessing damages resulting from minor releases but actually limited to coastal and marine environment damage;[341] and

- Type B regulations for individual cases whose damages have been caused by more serious discharges.[342]

Both sets of regulations became the subject of intense litigation, resulting in their being struck down and remanded to the DOI for revision.[343]

On March 25, 1994, the DOI issued a final rule revising the Type B rule to comply with all but one aspect of the court's order. The rule establishes a procedure for calculating natural resource damages based on costs of restoring, replacing, or acquiring the equivalent of injured resources. It also allows for the assessment of all use values of injured resources that are lost to the public pending completion of restoration of equivalent resources.[344] The DOI proposed revisions to Type A assessments in coastal/marine areas later in 1994.[345] EPA's 1994 Type B rule was also subjected to judicial challenge. In the resulting court decision, the majority of the rule was upheld.[346]

4.10.5 Prospect of Increased Use

Coupled with the stricter natural resource provisions enacted by SARA, the promulgation of the assessment regulations has substantially increased the likelihood of natural resource damage litigation. Individuals identified as trustees in the NCP are required to assess natural resources damage, and restoration costs cannot be borne by the Superfund until all administrative and judicial remedies are exhausted (see *supra* section 4.10.3). Moreover, assessments conducted in compliance with the assessments regulations are entitled to a rebuttable presumption in proceedings to recover damages from responsible parties.[347] A party incurring costs to assess natural resource damages can further recover those costs, even where the government did not ultimately use that assessment work and it did not strictly follow the DOI assessment regulations.[348] Given these powerful incentives, the federal government or its state counterpart has little reason not to initiate a natural resource action against responsible parties. Moreover, as technical studies increasingly indicate that once-hailed remedial practices such as pump-and-treat technologies cannot return a resource to its original condition or that such restoration is technically impracticable, litigation for lost use of natural resources will probably increase.

4.10.6 Proof Issues

The standard for natural resource litigation is significantly different than that for response actions. Under Section 107(a) of CERCLA, liability for release of a hazardous substance is based in strict liability and requires no element of causation. The DOI, however, has interpreted natural resources damage actions as requiring a traditional causation analysis typical of tort actions. This interpretation has been affirmed by the courts.[349] Consequently, to prevail on a claim for injury to a natural resource, the trustee must show by a preponderance of the evidence[350] that the defendant's hazardous substance release "was the sole or substantially contributing cause of each alleged injury to natural resources."[351] In so doing, the trustee must show the following:

- what resource was injured;
- at what specific locations of the natural resource the injury occurred;
- when the injury occurred;
- which release of what substance caused the injury; and
- by what pathway the natural resource was exposed to the substance.[352]

Conversely, defendants carry the burden of proof when asserting as a defense that damages being sought are exempt.[353]

4.11 Contribution Actions

In view of CERCLA's liability scheme, including strict liability, joint and several liability (in most cases), and few defenses, it is not surprising that contribution actions assume a major role in CERCLA litigation.

Prior to the 1986 SARA amendments, some question existed whether a right of contribution existed under CERCLA. The 1986 SARA amendments resolved the matter by adding Section 113(f). This section specifically provides for contribution actions among jointly and severally liable parties and states that in resolving such claims, courts should apply such equitable factors as they deem appropriate. This language gives the courts broad discretion in determining cost allocation among jointly and severally liable parties in a contribution action. The factors that appear to be relevant include these:

- The volume of hazardous substances contributed by each party.
- The relative degree of toxicity of each party's wastes.
- The extent to which each party was involved in the generation, transportation, treatment, storage, or disposal of the substances involved.
- The degree of care exercised in handling the hazardous substances.
- The degree of cooperation by the parties with government officials in order to prevent any harm to public health or the environment.[354]

While courts are free to apply any other equitable factors they deem appropriate, most allocations derive from applying the above factors.

Contribution actions may be brought either during or following a CERCLA Section 107 cost recovery action or CERCLA Section 106 abatement action.[355] However, in most government enforcement actions, contribution actions are set for hearing after the government's liability case against the primary defendants is resolved.[356] But what of situations where a PRP seeks contribution from other PRPs for environmental cleanup costs when no civil action has been brought under CERCLA Section 106 or 107(a)? Most courts of appeals interpreted Section 113(f)(1) broadly and allowed PRPs to sue other PRPs to recover cleanup costs at any time after cleanup costs were incurred. PRPs initiated voluntary cleanups with the encouragement of EPA and then sought cleanup costs from other PRPs. The Supreme Court reversed long-standing practice across much of the nation by holding that a private party who has not been sued under Section 106 or Section 107 may not bring a claim for contribution under Section 113(f)(1) against other PRPs to recover cleanup costs incurred voluntarily.[357] The decision in *Aviall Services* drastically narrowed the ability of PRPs to bring contribution claims against recalcitrant PRPs.

At many multiparty sites, certain PRPs desire to settle with EPA, while others, for whatever reasons, feel that a settlement is not in their best interests. In these cases, EPA may see fit to settle with the first group for less than the full amount of its claim while reserving the remainder of its claim for an action against the nonsettlors. In such instances, CERCLA provides what is known as contribution protection for the settlors. It does so by stating that a party "[which] has resolved its liability to the United States or a State in an administrative or judicially approved settlement shall not be liable for claims for contribution regarding matters addressed in the settlement."[358] A settling party may be liable, however, for costs outside the scope of "matters addressed in the settlement."[359]

After *Aviall Services*, PRPs were faced still with the question unanswered by the Supreme Court—whether a PRP could bring a direct cost recovery action against another PRP at the same site. Some appellate courts after *Aviall Services* began to overturn or modify earlier decisions limiting CERCLA Section 107 to certain PRPs.[360]

In 2007, the Supreme Court in a unanimous decision expanded its decision in *Aviall Services* and restored some certainty to cost recovery and contribution litigation that followed the *Aviall Services* decision in 2004.[361] The *Atlantic Research* decision by the Supreme Court provided that a PRP could bring a cost recovery action against other PRPs based upon CERCLA Section 107(a) and is not limited exclusively to a cause of action for contribution under CERCLA Section 113(f). The Supreme Court concluded that the phrase "any other person" in CERCLA Section 107(a)(4)(B) must be read so that "cost recovery actions by any private party, including PRPs" are authorized.[362]

The Supreme Court's efforts to clarify the relationship between CERCLA Section 107(a) and Section 113(f) and the use of each provided much-needed guidance to PRPs. Uncertainties remain after *Atlantic Research*, however. The federal circuit courts remain divided as to whether cost recovery claims can be brought by a private party who is doing a cleanup pursuant to a settlement with EPA.[363] Furthermore, there is still confusion as to the impacts of joint and several liability under Section 107(a) versus equitable division counterclaims under Section 113(f); the recovery of remediation costs incurred because of a CERCLA Section 106 order; whether a CERCLA administrative order qualifies as a "civil action"; and the interaction of previously precluded state law claims for contribution and restitution with claims under Section 107(a) and Section 113(f). Nonetheless, *Atlantic Research* did much to encourage parties to implement voluntary cleanup activities with the hope of recovering some or all of the cleanup costs.

5.0 Settlements with EPA

5.1 Overview

Although certain CERCLA cases have proceeded through trial, these cases are the exception rather than the rule. Settlement is the norm in CERCLA cases, and this preference can be explained for several reasons. From EPA's perspective, settlement is preferable because it conserves Superfund monies as well as EPA's limited resources. Settlements also free EPA's personnel to work on other cleanups. From the perspective of PRPs, settlement is often preferred because it permits them to exercise greater control over the selection and implementation of remedial actions, presumably minimizing costs. PRPs also often prefer settlement to avoid the tremendous costs of litigating a CERCLA case.

This is not to say that the settlement process is smooth or produces results uniformly acceptable to PRPs. Indeed, negotiations can be protracted, contentious, and extremely costly. This scenario is particularly likely at multiparty sites where PRPs must negotiate not only with EPA but also with each other and, in some cases, with the state where a site is located. While it is EPA's policy to settle, increasingly it has demonstrated inflexibility both with regard to the remedial action selected and with the terms of the settlement agreement. Consequently, many PRPs have begun to question whether settlement is necessarily the best course. Some PRPs have decided to perform cleanups under Section 106 administrative orders rather than under a settlement agreement.

5.2 Controlling Authority

Parties attempting to negotiate a CERCLA settlement with EPA often find that the flexibility of EPA negotiators is constrained both by CERCLA's settlement provisions and by a variety of guidance documents issued by EPA. Moreover, EPA has prepared model settlement documents for use by its staff-level negotiators. Because of these constraints, truly negotiated settlements are not likely to occur.

The SARA amendments added Section 122, titled "Settlements." This section sets forth procedures that EPA may follow if it attempts to settle a CERCLA case. EPA's decision whether to invoke the procedures under CERCLA Section 122 is discretionary and not subject to judicial review.[364] However, Section 122 codifies many of the settlement policies that EPA had followed prior to the SARA amendments. The section should therefore be consulted in detail by any party attempting to settle a CERCLA case because in many instances it provides specific instructions for when and how various settlement provisions may be used. For example, Section 122(f) provides detailed requirements addressing the circumstances in which EPA can provide a covenant not to sue in a settlement agreement. Other sections address such issues as partial funding by the Superfund (mixed funding), de minimis settlements, and public participation in settlements.

Section 122 also contains extensive discussion of special notice procedures that EPA may follow when it determines that a period of negotiation would "facilitate an agreement."[365] These procedures provide that if EPA elects to pursue settlement under Section 122, it must provide PRPs notice including the names and addresses of all other PRPs, the volume and nature of substances each party contributed to the site (if known), and a ranking of the responsible parties by volume contributed. These special notice procedures also contain provisions authorizing EPA to prepare a nonbinding preliminary allocation of responsibility for the PRPs to use in their attempts to allocate costs among themselves. To date, however, EPA has not seen fit to use this provision extensively. This agency reluctance is probably due to the fact that EPA would prefer not to be bound by the notice provision's requirements or lose its flexibility in dealing with potential settlors.

Throughout CERCLA's history, EPA has from time to time issued guidance documents on various issues associated with settlements. In 1985, EPA issued what continues to be its primary settlement policy.[366] This document, which predates the SARA amendments, is generally consistent with CERCLA Section 122. It remains the only comprehensive treatment of overall CERCLA settlement policy by EPA. Since 1986, EPA has issued a variety of guidance documents addressing individual settlement topics. Among the topics these guidance documents address are the following: covenants not to sue,[367] de minimis party settlements,[368] stipulated penalties in consent decrees,[369] and mixed funding.[370] In any negotiation it can be expected that EPA's negotiators will attempt to comply with any applicable guidance document.

5.3 Consent Decrees and Consent Orders

Settlements with EPA are ordinarily memorialized in a consent decree or an administrative order on consent (consent order). The difference between the two forms of agreement is that a consent decree is filed with and signed by a federal court, while a consent order does not involve any judicial action. Moreover, any settlement and consent order involving total response costs greater than $500,000 requires approval by the U.S. Department of Justice.[371] Not surprisingly, most parties prefer to have a settlement memorialized through a consent decree, as there is a neutral third party—the judge—available to resolve disputes.

Section 122(d)(2)(a) provides the proposed consent decree must be filed with the federal district court at least 30 days before a final judgment is entered.[372] Further, the federal government must provide an opportunity to persons who are not named as parties to the action to comment on the terms of the proposed consent decree.[373] Some federal courts have allowed non-settling PRPs to intervene in CERCLA litigation brought by the federal government seeking court approval of a consent decree.[374] The question was whether a non-settling PRP's potential loss of its contribution rights under Section 113(f)(2) (see *infra* section 4.11) presented an interest significant enough to support intervention in a CERCLA settlement proceeding. The appellate court concluded a non-settling PRP had an interest worthy of protection in CERCLA litigation because entry of the consent decree would bar its contribution rights against the settling PRPs.[375] Further, the appellate court held a non-settling PRP had an interest in the amount of the judicially approved settlement because it might be liable for the remaining costs.[376]

The terms and conditions of consent orders and consent decrees were the source of extensive negotiations between EPA and potential settlors at one time. The issuance of model consent orders and consent decrees by EPA has hindered the opportunity for meaningful negotiations.[377] Experience to date with these model documents suggests that staff-level negotiators will be unwilling to vary from most of their provisions.

5.4 Major Settlement Issues

While no two CERCLA settlement negotiations involve precisely the same issues, there are several issues that commonly arise. The frequency with which these issues occur is reflected in the fact that they are the subject of discussion in both Section 122 and EPA guidance documents.

5.4.1 Mixed Funding and Carve Outs

As discussed earlier, at every multiparty CERCLA site there are parties that wish to settle with EPA and those that cannot or do not. At the same time, there may be a vast quantity of wastes at the site that came from defunct or bankrupt companies. Wastes from these defunct or bankrupt companies have traditionally been referred to as a site's orphan share. Thus, at most sites, those parties that settle will ordinarily account for less than 100 percent of the volume of hazardous substances at the site. In fact, it is not uncommon for many settlements to involve settlors whose cumulative volume of waste represents less than 50 percent of that present at the site.

Settlors in the situations described above are quite naturally interested in avoiding 100 percent of the liability for site remediation and EPA's past response costs. Consequently, they have often sought EPA's payment for a portion (usually the orphan share) of these costs through use of Superfund monies—a process referred to as mixed funding.[378] At the same time, these settlors will seek to have EPA carve out part of its remedial action or costs from their liability and proceed against the nonsettlors for the portion carved out.

Section 122(b)(1) gives EPA the authority to enter into mixed funding agreements whereby EPA agrees to use the Superfund to reimburse settlors a portion of the costs they incur in performing an agreed-upon remedial action. EPA's guidance on mixed funding acknowledges that Congress recognized the need to consider settlements for less than 100 percent and to use Superfund monies for shares of parties "unknown, insolvent, similarly unavailable, or [which have] refuse[d] to settle." The guidance, which encourages the use of mixed funding in appropriate situations, lists the following factors as considerations in evaluating mixed funding settlements:

- The strength of the liability case against both nonsettlors and settlors.
- Those options the government may have if a settlement is not reached.
- The size of the share to be covered by the Superfund.
- The good faith of the settlors.[379]

The guidance identifies the best situations for mixed funding as those where the settlors offer a substantial portion of remediation costs and where the government has a strong case against financially viable nonsettlors.

EPA's use of mixed funding has been uneven. Nonetheless, mixed funding has been available to deal with the problems of orphan shares and nonsettlors at some sites.[380] However, EPA has been more receptive to carving out a portion of its costs for the remedial action for nonsettling parties to absorb.

5.4.2 De Minimis Parties

At most multiparty sites there are a large number of companies that disposed of relatively small quantities of hazardous substances. Section 122(g) addresses these so-called de minimis parties. It encourages EPA to "as promptly as possible" reach a final settlement with such parties and identifies the following types of situations in which a de minimis settlement is appropriate:

- Situations where both the amount and toxicity of hazardous substances contributed by a party are minimal compared with other hazardous substances at the facility; and

- Situations where a party is the owner of the property where the facility is located but did not conduct or permit the generation, handling, or disposal of hazardous substances at the facility; contribute to the release or threatened release from the facility; or acquire the facility with knowledge that it had been used to store, handle, or dispose of hazardous substances.[381]

Aside from the opportunity of an early settlement, de minimis parties are ordinarily offered a settlement with real finality. In return for what is known as a "premium payment," EPA will ordinarily provide de minimis parties a complete covenant not to sue, which is revocable only if subsequent information reveals that the party's waste contribution was not truly de minimis. This guarantee means that, should future problems develop at a site, these de minimis parties will not be required to participate in or fund future remediation efforts.[382] Of course, as stated above, de minimis settlements must be judicially approved and can be challenged by other PRPs or interested parties.[383]

5.4.3 De Micromis Contributors

EPA defines a de micromis party as someone "whose contribution of waste is extremely small, even less than a de minimis party's contribution."[384] With the passage of the Small Business Liability Act (see *supra* section 4.5.2.1), Congress created an exemption for de micromis contributors by adding a Subsection (o) to CERCLA Section 107 (42 U.S.C. § 9607). Subsection (o) provides that a person shall not be liable, with respect to response costs at a facility on the NPL, if liability is based solely on the person being an arranger or transporter under CERCLA.[385] Such person must demonstrate that the total amount of material containing hazardous substances was less than 110 gallons of liquid materials or less than 200 pounds of solid materials.[386] As to be expected, there are exceptions to the exemption, such as materials that contain hazardous substances that contribute significantly to the cost of the response action.[387]

In response to the Small Business Liability Act, EPA amended its guidance and now uses the term "de micromis contributor" to apply only to statutorily exempt de micromis parties under CERCLA Section 107(o).[388] EPA considers settlements with nonexempt de micromis settlements under CERCLA Section 122(g).[389]

5.4.4 Covenants Not to Sue and Reopeners

For most settlors, a settlement with EPA that entails subsequent remediation actions does not represent finality. Because there is great uncertainty at most sites whether the remedial action selected will prove effective, neither CERCLA nor EPA guidance provides a complete release from future liability.

CERCLA Section 122(f) provides that settlements may contain a covenant not to sue. There is no provision for the use of a release. In considering whether to issue a covenant not to sue, EPA is to consider whether such a covenant is in the public interest, whether it would expedite a response action, whether the settlor is in compliance with the consent decree, and whether the response action has been approved by EPA.

In most cases, however, EPA's covenant not to sue is illusory. CERCLA provides that, except in certain designated instances, a covenant not to sue must be accompanied by an additional provision—known as a reopener—which allows EPA to sue for future liability resulting from unknown conditions.[390] EPA guidance on covenants not to sue also requires that the reopener provision permit a subsequent suit in situations where additional information reveals that the remedy is "no longer protective of public health or the environment." This reopener is required in all settlements except those involving the following situations:

1. De minimis parties.

2. "Extraordinary circumstances" where reasonable assurances exist that public health and the environment will be protected from future releases and where certain enumerated factors (e.g., nature of risks, toxicity, strength of evidence, ability to pay, litigation risks, etc.) are considered.

3. Portions of a remedial action that entail:

   • the off-site transport of hazardous substances to RCRA-approved disposal facilities where EPA has required off-site disposal after rejecting an alternative permitting on-site or other disposal; or

- the treatment of hazardous substances "so as to destroy, eliminate, or permanently immobilize the hazardous constituents of such substances" such that they no longer present a significant threat.[391]

5.4.5 Stipulated Penalties

CERCLA settlements, whether consent orders or consent decrees, routinely contain provisions for stipulated penalties in the event that a settlor fails to meet certain designated milestone events. The use and amount of these penalties are the subjects of negotiation, but generally EPA seeks to extract a penalty amount deemed sufficient to motivate the settlor to meet the deadline set by the agreement.

CERCLA Section 121(e)(2) provides for the use of stipulated penalties in consent decrees. EPA's guidance on the use of stipulated penalties in consent decrees has interpreted this provision to require that all consent decrees involving a remedial action contain provisions for stipulated penalties.[392] It is EPA's policy to tie stipulated penalties to compliance schedules, performance standards, and reporting requirements. However, stipulated penalties do not arise if delay is occasioned by a force majeure event or, in some situations, where an interim deadline is missed but a final deadline is met.

One of the policy's more disturbing features to settlors is EPA's insistence that stipulated penalties continue to accrue during any delay caused by a dispute under the consent decree. Where the dispute is resolved in EPA's favor, a settlor forfeits the accrued amount. Thus, the policy hinders settling parties from effectively using a consent decree's dispute provisions.

6.0 Release Reporting Requirements

CERCLA Sections 102 and 103 provide the basis for requiring certain parties to give notice of a release of hazardous substances. Section 103(a) requires that any person in charge of a vessel or facility notify the National Response Center (*see* 33 U.S.C. § 1251 *et seq.*) as soon as that person has knowledge of any release from the vessel or facility of a hazardous substance equal to or greater than the reportable quantity for that substance. As indicated in section 2.2, a release is defined broadly to include the escape of a hazardous substance into the environment.[393]

The crux of CERCLA's reporting requirements is the concept of reportable quantities. Simply stated, a reportable quantity is the amount of a substance which must be reported if released. Reportable quantities for hazardous substances are established by EPA pursuant to Section 102. Where EPA has not indicated a listed substance's reportable quantity, Section 102 further specifies that the quantity shall be one pound, unless the hazardous substance has a reportable quantity under the Clean Water Act, in which case the latter will be used.

EPA has promulgated regulations listing the various hazardous substances regulated under CERCLA and specifying their reportable quantities.[394] These regulations should be consulted in detail when determining whether a release must be reported because the reportable quantities for hazardous substances vary significantly. The regulations also provide detailed guidance on assorted issues that arise in determining whether a report must be filed, including the calculations for a reportable release. As a general rule, to ascertain whether a substance's release has equaled or exceeded its reportable quantity, the person in charge of the facility or vessel must calculate the total amount released during any 24-hour period. If the total amount equals or exceeds the reportable quantity during that 24-hour period, it must be reported.[395]

Failure to report a release involving a reportable quantity of a hazardous substance can result in both civil and criminal penalties. The maximum criminal penalty is three years in prison for a first conviction and five years for a subsequent conviction.[396] Fines may also be imposed. Civil penalties equal to $32,500 per day for failure to report may be assessed.[397]

Since there are more listed hazardous substances under CERCLA than under other environmental laws, it is important that parties do not assume a report need not be filed merely because it is not required under another statute.

Notwithstanding the above discussion, certain types of releases are exempted from CERCLA's notice requirements, irrespective of the quantity released. Pursuant to CERCLA Section 103(a), the following types of releases need not be reported:

- Releases resulting from application, handling, or storage of pesticides registered under the Federal Insecticide, Fungicide, and Rodenticide Act.[398]

- Federally permitted releases.[399]

- Releases regulated under Subtitle C of RCRA that have been or need not be reported pursuant to RCRA.[400]

- Continuous releases from a facility for which notification has been given previously.[401]

7.0 Federal Facilities

As with the private sector, years of inattention to the environmental harm posed by certain activities have caused many federal facilities serious environmental problems. The greatest problems exist for facilities associated with the massive military-industrial complex—Department of Energy and Department of Defense facilities—which was constructed in response to World War II and the Cold War. Past disposal practices contributing to pollution at these facilities include the use of unlined pits, holding ponds, drying beds, landfills, discharge to the ground, and on-site burning of wastes. The estimated costs of cleanup are staggering. Citizens, states, and environmental groups have expressed outrage at the conditions of many of these facilities and have sought to have input in determining appropriate cleanups.

CERCLA contains broad waivers of sovereign immunity that permit individuals and states to bring cost recovery actions against federal facilities[402] and to bring citizen suits for the facilities' compliance with the statute.[403] The authority of citizens and states to bring action against these facilities has been a spur toward their cleanup.

The 1986 SARA amendments reflected Congress's great concern for federal facilities by creating an entire section—Section 120—devoted to their cleanup. Section 120(a) provides for federal facility compliance, both substantively and procedurally, to the same extent as any private entity.[404] This compliance includes requirements related to listing on the NPL (e.g., site assessments, hazardous ranking, and evaluation procedures).

Section 120 also addresses hazardous waste cleanup at federal facilities and establishes requirements that are unique to federal facilities. These requirements include the creation of a Federal Agency Hazardous Waste Compliance Docket listing facilities that manage hazardous waste or have potential hazardous waste problems. This list is then used to provide timetables for addressing the problems at each facility. A preliminary assessment and, as needed, site inspection are required within 18 months of the listing of a facility. Subsequently, the facility is scored under the hazardous ranking system to determine whether it should be placed on the NPL. If listed on the NPL, the facility must begin a RI/FS within six months of its NPL listing. While performing the RI/FS, consultation with EPA and the state must occur. Within 180 days of EPA's review of the RI/FS, an interagency agreement must be entered into with EPA for the performance of the selected remedy.[405]

In response to the various hazardous waste problems at their facilities, both the Department of Defense (DOD) and the Department of Energy have formulated extensive long-term cleanup plans. DOD's plan—the Defense Environmental Restoration Program—is funded by monies set aside by Congress under the Defense Environmental Restoration Account (DERA). The 1984 Defense Appropriations Act created DERA as a set-aside fund to pay for DOD response actions under CERCLA and the NCP. The use of DERA funds is limited to addressing past disposal problems, not correcting currently usable facilities.

8.0 Superfund's Future

The Love Canal site in Niagara County, New York, has been removed from the NPL. All cleanup work at the site has been completed, and monitoring conducted at the site over the past 15 years confirms that the cleanup goals have been achieved.[406] Throughout the time of Love Canal's investigation and cleanup, many aspects of Superfund have been controversial. Nearly everyone finds fault with at least part of it. Few find all of its features acceptable. For this reason, future modifications to Superfund can be expected. It is also why there is constant pressure on EPA to develop policies that ameliorate some of Superfund's most counterproductive features.

EPA is over two years into implementation of the FY 2011–2015 Strategic Plan. EPA recently put out a summary of its "Superfund National Accomplishments" for Fiscal Year 2012. In that document, EPA stated that in 2012 EPA accomplished the following:

- Increased the total number of sites where EPA actions controlled a potential or actual exposure risk to humans by 13, increasing the cumulative total to 1,361 NPL sites where exposure is under control;

- Increased the total number of sites where EPA actions controlled the migration of contaminated groundwater through engineered remedies or natural processes by 18, bringing the program's cumulative total to 1,069 NPL sites where contaminated groundwater migration is under control;

- Obligated nearly $389 million in appropriated funds, state cost-share contributions, and PRP settlement resources for conducting on-the-ground work to clean up contaminated sites;

- Obligated more than $240 million in appropriated funds, state cost-share contributions, and PRP settlement resources to conduct and oversee site assessments and investigations, selection and design of cleanup plans, and support for state, tribal, community involvement activities, and other activities;

- Completed and provided oversight at 428 removal actions to address immediate and substantial threats to communities;

- Started 46 new remedial construction projects, including 12 EPA-funded projects and 34 PRP-funded projects through EPA's Superfund remedial program;

- Continued to conduct or provide oversight at more than 400 remedial construction projects started in prior fiscal years;

- Completed all physical construction of the cleanup remedy at 22 sites across the country for a total of 1,142 sites, or approximately 68 percent of the sites on the NPL;

- Completed 142 remedial action projects;

- Ensured 66 NPL sites have all long-term protections, including institutional controls, in place necessary for anticipated use, bring the cumulative total of sites ready for anticipated use to 606;

- Completed 1,151 remedial site assessments, for a cumulative total of 91,067 remedial assessments completed since 1980;

- Placed 24 new sites and proposed 18 additional sites to the NPL; deleted 11 sites from the NPL;

- Conducted 230 five-year reviews, including 39 reviews at federal facility sites; and,

- Secured private party commitments of nearly $900 million to fund cleanup work.[407]

However, as stated in its FY 2013 EPA Budget in Brief, due to the "fiscally constrained environment, the EPA will reduce the resources that support program activities, including PRP searches, cleanup settlements, and cost recovery."[408] To save money, EPA will continue to strive to ensure that responsible parties take the lead in cleaning up sites. To do this, it is likely that EPA will continue its trend of issuing more unilateral orders to a select group of solvent PRPs to fund upfront the assessment and cleanup process.

9.0 Research Sources

To learn more about CERCLA or Superfund, visit the following sites:

- U.S. EPA Superfund Home Page: http://www.epa.gov/superfund/

- U.S. EPA FY 2009 Annual Plan: http://www.epa.gov/budget/2010/fy_2010_annual_plan.pdf

- Superfund FAQS: http://cfpub.epa.gov/superapps/index.cfm?fuseaction =faqs.default

- Locate Hazardous Waste Sites: http://www.epa.gov/enviro/sf/

- Superfund Information Systems—RODs: http://www.epa.gov/super fund/sites/rods/index.htm

- Superfund Information Systems—CERCLIS Database: http://www.epa .gov/superfund/sites/cursites/index.htm

- Superfund Information Systems—Data Elements Dictionary: http:// www.epa.gov/superfund/sites/ded/index.htm

- Superfund Information Systems—Sites: http://www.epa.gov/superfund/ sites/index.htm

- Superfund Information Systems—Superfund Cleanup Policies and Guid-ance: http://cfpub.epa.gov/compliance/resources/policies/cleanup/super fund/

- Superfund Information Systems—Reportable Quantities: http://www .epa.gov/oem/content/reporting/rqover.htm

- Superfund Information Systems—RD/RA: http://epa.gov/superfund/ cleanup/rdra.htm

- Superfund Information Systems—Site Redevelopment: http://epa.gov/ superfund/programs/recycle

- Superfund Information Systems—Remedy Selection: http://epa.gov/ superfund/policy/remedy/sfremedy/remedies.htm

- Superfund Laws and Regulations: http://www.epa.gov/superfund/policy/ index.htm

- U.S. EPA Brownfields: http://www.epa.gov/brownfields/

- Brownfields—Related Law and Regulations: http://www.epa.gov/brown fields/laws/index.htm

- Brownfields—All Appropriate Inquiries Fact Sheet: http://www.epa.gov/ brownfields/aai/aai_final_factsheet.pdf

- Brownfields Funding and Financing: http://epa.gov/brownfields/mmat ters.htm

- Brownfields—Tools and Technical Information: http://epa.gov/brown fields/tools/index.htm

- Guidance on Prospective Purchaser Agreements: http://www.epa.gov/ swerosps/bf/laws/liability/#ap

- Policy on the Issuance of Comfort Letters: http://www.epa.gov/brown fields/liab.htm#ci

- Lender and Fiduciary Protection: http://www.epa.gov/brownfields/liab .htm#la

- Small Business Liability Relief and Brownfields Revitalization Act: http://www.epa.gov/brownfields/sblrbra.htm

- Lender Liability Exemption: Updated Questions and Answers: http://www.epa.gov/compliance/resources/publications/cleanup/superfund/factsheet/lender-liab-07-fs.pdf

- FindLaw—Environmental News: http://news.findlaw.com/legalnews/environment/

- ASTM Standards: http://www.astm.org

- U.S. EPA—Search for Guidance: http://www.epa.gov/nscep/

Notes

[1] 42 U.S.C. §§ 9601 *et seq.*

[2] 2 U.S.C. §§ 6901 *et seq.*

[3] US. EPA, *FY 2011-2015 EPA Strategic Plan.*

[4] *Id.*, page 2.

[5] *Id.*, page 17.

[6] *Id.*

[7] *Id.*, at 38.

[8] *Id.*, at 49-51.

[9] Pub. L. No. 99-499, Oct. 17, 1986; 126 Cong. Rec. S13112 *et seq.* (daily ed. Sept. 19, 1986).

[10] H.R. 2869, 107th Cong. (2001) (hereinafter Small Business Liability Act).

[11] *See* Title V of the Superfund Amendments and Reauthorization Act of 1986.

[12] 42 U.S.C. § 9611(a)(2).

[13] 42 U.S.C. § 9612.

[14] 42 U.S.C. § 9606(b)(2).

[15] 42 U.S.C. § 9611(e)(3).

[16] *But see United States v. Alcan Aluminum Corp.*, 964 F.2d 252 (3d Cir. 1992) (suggesting concentration might affect apportionment of liability). *See also Acushnet Co. v. Coaters, Inc.*, 937 F. Supp. 988 (D. Mass. 1996) (individual company not liable as its waste could not have leached out of groundwater at higher than background levels).

[17] 42 U.S.C. § 9602.

[18] *United States v. Wade*, 577 F. Supp. 1326 (E.D. Pa. 1983).

[19] 42 U.S.C. § 9601(22).

[20] 42 U.S.C. § 9603.

[21] 42 U.S.C. § 9601(14). *See Cariddi v. Consol. Alum. Corp.*, 478 F. Supp. 2d 510 (D. Mass. 2007) (petroleum exclusion includes mineral spirits distilled from petroleum).

[22] *Wilshire Westwood Assoc. v. Atlantic Richfield Corp.*, 881 F.2d 801 (9th Cir. 1989).

[23] *Compare Wilshire Westwood Assoc.*, 881 F.2d at 801 (9th Cir. 1989) (CERCLA) with *Zands v. Nelson*, 779 F. Supp. 1254 (S.D. Cal. 1991) (RCRA).

[24] U.S. EPA, memorandum from Francis S. Blake to J. Winston Porter, "Scope of the CERCLA Petroleum Exclusion under Sections 101(14) and 104(a)(2)" (July 31, 1987) (on file at EPA).

25 *E.g., Wilshire Westwood Assocs. v. Atlantic Richfield Corp.*, 881 F.2d 801 (9th Cir. 1989); *Washington v. Time Oil Co.*, 687 F. Supp. 529 (W.D. Wash. 1988).

26 42 U.S.C. § 9604.

27 42 U.S.C. § 9601(33).

28 *See* 42 U.S.C. §§ 9606, 9607.

29 *United States v. Conservation Chem. Co.*, 619 F. Supp. 162, 233 (W.D. Mo. 1985). *But see Amoco Oil Co. v. Borden, Inc.*, 889 F.2d 664, 670 (5th Cir. 1989) (release of any quantity not sufficient to create liability unless hazard justified response action).

30 42 U.S.C. § 9601(22); 67 Fed. Reg. 45321 (July 9, 2002). *See United States v. Dico, Inc.*, 266 F.3d 864 (8th Cir. 2001) (filling of drums, leaking through cracks in vat, routine dumping).

31 *Id. See City of Tulsa v. Tyson Foods, Inc*, 258 F. Supp. 2d 1263 (N.D. Okla. 2003).

32 *See, e.g.,* U.S. EPA, Guidance on CERCLA Section 101(10)(H) Federally Permitted Release Definition for Certain Air Emissions, 67 Fed. Reg. 18899 (Apr. 17, 2002).

33 42 U.S.C. § 9607(j).

34 *United States v. Metate Asbestos Corp.*, 584 F. Supp. 1143 (D. Ariz. 1984) (asbestos lying on ground); *New York v. Shore Realty Corp.*, 759 F.2d 1032, 1045 (2d Cir. 1985) (corroding tanks, failure to license facility); *United States v. Northernaire Plating Co.*, 670 F. Supp. 742, 747 (W.D. Mich. 1987) (abandoned drums), *aff'd sub nom.*; *United States v. R.W. Meyer, Inc.*, 889 F.2d 1497 (6th Cir. 1989), *cert. denied*, 494 U.S. 1057 (1990).

35 42 U.S.C. § 9607.

36 42 U.S.C. § 9604.

37 *Tetra Technologies, Inc. v. Kansas City Southern Ry. Co.*, 122 Fed. Appx. 99 (5th Cir. 2005) (pipeline); *United States v. Union Corp.*, 277 F. Supp. 2d 478 (E.D. Pa. 2003) (sewer system); *Louisiana v. Braselman Corp.*, 78 F. Supp. 2d 543 (E.D. La. 1999) (railroad track).

38 42 U.S.C. § 9601(9). *See, e.g., United States v. General Electric Co.*, 460 F. Supp. 2d 395 (N.D.N.Y. Nov. 2, 2006) (facility in "very close proximity" to contamination is "onsite"); *Otay Land Co. v. U.E. Ltd., L.P.*, 440 F. Supp. 2d 1152 (S.D. Cal. July 18, 2006) (shooting range not a facility because shotgun shells and clay pigeons were consumer products in consumer use and exempted from definition of "facility").

39 *Emergency Services Billing Corp (ESBC) v. Allstate Insurance Co.*, 668 F.3d 459 (7th Cir. 2012).

40 *Emergency Services Billing Corp. v. Vitran Express Inc.*, No. 11-CV-0492 (S.D. Ind., December 7, 2011).

41 42 U.S.C. § 9601.

42 *Alprof Realty LLC v. Corp. of Presiding Biship the Church of Jesus Christ of Latterday Saints*, No. 09-cv-5190, 2012 WL 4049800, at *8-11 (E.D.N.Y. Sept. 13, 2012).

43 *PCS Nitrogen v. Ashley II of Charleston, LLC*, No. 11-2087, * 27-28 (4th Cir. April 4, 2013); See also *EPEC Polymers, Inc. v. NL Industries Inc.*, CA No. 12-3842 (D.N.J. May 24, 2013) (owner of property across the river from the Superfund site can be held liable because "facility" includes not only where the cleanup is taking place, but where the hazardous substances came from, even if the Corps dredging operations spread the contamination).

44 42 U.S.C. § 9601(8).

45 42 U.S.C. § 9605(a)(8)(A).

46 55 Fed. Reg. 51532 (1990).

47 *See* 5 U.S.C. § 553.

48 *See* 42 U.S.C. § 9613(a).

49 *See Washington State Dep't of Transp. v. United States Envtl. Protection Agency*, 917 F.2d 1309 (D.C. Cir. 1990), *cert. denied*, 501 U.S. 1230 (1991).

50 40 C.F.R. § 300.425(b)(1).

51 *Id.*

[52] 33 U.S.C. §§ 1251 *et seq.*

[53] 42 U.S.C. § 9605(a).

[54] 40 C.F.R. Part 300. The NCP was last amended in 1994. 59 Fed. Reg. 47384 (1994).

[55] 42 U.S.C. § 9601(23).

[56] *Id.*

[57] 42 U.S.C. § 9604(c)(1).

[58] *Id. See, e.g., United States v. W. R. Grace & Co.*, 429 F.3d 1224 (9th Cir. 2005).

[59] 42 U.S.C. § 9601(24).

[60] 40 C.F.R. § 300.405.

[61] 40 C.F.R. § 300.5.

[62] *See* U.S. EPA, The Hazard Ranking System Guidance Manual; Interim Final (Nov. 1992); Hazardous Ranking System, Final Rule, 55 Fed. Reg. 51532 (1990).

[63] 40 C.F.R. Part 300 (Appendix A).

[64] *See Stoughton v. United States Envtl. Protection Agency*, 858 F.2d 747 (D.C. Cir. 1988) (unsuccessful challenge); *but see Tex Tin Corp. v. United States Envtl. Protection Agency*, 992 F.2d 353 (D.C. Cir. 1993) (successful challenge).

[65] *See* 42 U.S.C. § 9616(d),(e).

[66] 40 C.F.R. § 300.430(a)(2).

[67] *See generally* 40 C.F.R. § 300.430(d).

[68] *See generally* 40 C.F.R. § 300.430(e).

[69] 42 U.S.C. § 9621.

[70] 40 C.F.R. § 300.430(a)(1)(ii)(A).

[71] 42 U.S.C. § 9621(a). While Section 121 lists general factors to be applied, the NCP attempts, consistent with the factors listed in Section 121, to provide more detailed cleanup requirements. *See* 40 C.F.R. Part 300.

[72] 42 U.S.C. § 9621(b).

[73] 42 U.S.C. § 9621(c).

[74] 42 U.S.C. § 9621(d)(2)(A).

[75] *See generally* 40 C.F.R. § 300.430(f).

[76] 40 C.F.R. § 300.430(f)(1)(ii)(D).

[77] 40 C.F.R. § 300.430(f)(1)(ii)(E).

[78] 40 C.F.R. § 300.400(g)(1).

[79] 40 C.F.R. § 300.400(g)(2).

[80] 42 U.S.C. § 9621(d)(4).

[81] 40 C.F.R. § 300.430(f)(5).

[82] 42 U.S.C. §§ 9613(k) and 9617.

[83] 42 U.S.C. § 9621(f)(1)(E), (H).

[84] 42 U.S.C. § 9617(b).

[85] 42 U.S.C. § 9613(j)(1).

[86] *City of Colton v. American Promotional Events, et al.*, 2010 WL 2991399 (9th Cir. Aug. 2, 2010) (a city that admittedly did not follow the NCP to investigate and remedy groundwater contamination was not entitled to a declaratory judgment that defendants are liable for future cleanup costs).

[87] 42 U.S.C. § 9604(c)(2).

[88] Memorandum from Elaine F. Davis, acting director, Office of Emergency and Remedial Response, Regarding Enhancing State and Tribal Role Directive, OSWER Directive No. 9375.3-06P (Jan. 17, 2001).

[89] 42 U.S.C. § 9604(c)(3).

[90] 42 U.S.C. § 9607.

[91] 42 U.S.C. § 9606.

[92] *E.g.*, *Levin Metals Corp. v. Parr-Richmond Terminal Co.*, 799 F.2d 1312 (9th Cir. 1986); *United States v. Northeastern Pharmaceutical & Chem. Co.* (NEPACCO), 810 F.2d 726 (8th Cir. 1986), *cert. denied*, 484 U.S. 848 (1987).

[93] *Substances v. Burlington Northern*, 479 F.3d 1113 (9th Cir. 2007); *New York v. Shore Realty Corp.*, 759 F.2d 1032 (2d Cir. 1985). *But see Elementis Chromium L.P. v. Coastal States Petroleum Co.*, 450 F.3d 607 (5th Cir. 2006).

[94] *United States v. Conservation Chem. Co.*, 619 F. Supp. 162, 204 (W.D. Mo. 1985).

[95] *United States v. Chem-Dyne Corp.*, 572 F. Supp. 802 (S.D. Ohio 1983).

[96] *E.g.*, *United States v. Monsanto Co.*, 858 F.2d 160, 171 (4th Cir. 1988); *O'Neil v. Picillo*, 682 F. Supp. 706 (D.R.I. 1988), *aff'd*, 883 F.2d 176 (1st Cir. 1989), *cert. denied sub nom.*, *American Cyanamid Co. v. O'Neil*, 493 U.S. 1071 (1990); *United States v. NCR Corp et al.*, 688 F.3d 833 (7th Cir. 2012); *Pakootas v. Teck Cominco Metals, Ltd.*, 868 F.Supp. 2d 1106 (E.D. Wash. 2012); *Litgo N.J., Inc. v. Martin*, No. 06-cv-2891, 2012 WL 32200, at *11 (D.N.J. Jan. 5, 2012). Several federal circuit courts have found that commingled waste may, nevertheless, be divisible. *See United States v. Alcan Aluminum Corp.*, 964 F.2d 252 (3d Cir. 1992); *In re Bell Petroleum Servs, Inc.*, 3 F.3d 889 (5th Cir. 1993).

[97] *But see* discussion regarding causation in Natural Resource Damage Claims, *infra* section 4.10.

[98] *See Boeing Co. v. Cascade Corp.*, 207 F.3d 1177 (9th Cir. 2000); *Dedham Water Co. v. Cumberland Farms, Inc.*, 689 F. Supp. 1223, 1224 (D. Mass. 1988), *rev'd on other grounds*, 889 F.2d 1146, 1151-1154 (1st Cir. 1989).

[99] *United States v. South Carolina Recycling & Disposal, Inc.* (SCRDI), 653 F. Supp. 984, 992 (D.S.C. 1984), *aff'd in part and vacated in part sub nom.*, *United States v. Monsanto Co.*, 858 F.2d 160 (4th Cir. 1988), *cert. denied*, 490 U.S. 1106 (1989). *See also Acme Printing Ink Co. v. Menard, Inc.*, 870 F. Supp. 1465 (E.D. Wis. 1994) (proper test for causation is whether release or threatened release caused incurrence of response costs, not whether defendant's hazardous waste caused response cost).

[100] *United States v. Hercules*, 165 F. Supp. 2d 253 (N.D. N.Y. 2001). *See also Sherwin-Williams Co. v. ARTRAGroup, Inc.*, 125 F. Supp. 2d 739 (D. Md. 2001) (causation is relevant when assessing damages, not when determining liability).

[101] *United States v. NEPACCO*, 810 F.2d 726, 732-733 (8th Cir. 1986), *cert. denied*, 484 U.S. 848 (1987); *United States v. Olin Corp.*, 927 F. Supp. 1506 (S.D. Ala. 1996), *rev'd*, 107 F.3d 1506 (11th Cir. 1997).

[102] *Eastern Enterprises v. Apfel*, 118 S. Ct. 2131, 2149 (1998).

[103] *Franklin County Convention Facilities Authority v. American Premier Underwriters*, 240 F.3d 534 (6th Cir. 2001); *United States v. Dico, Inc.*, 266 F.3d 864 (8th Cir. 2001).

[104] *See United States v. Mottolo*, 695 F. Supp. 615, 624 (D.N.H. 1988), *aff'd*, 26 F.3d 261 (1st Cir. 1994).

[105] 42 U.S.C. § 9601(20)(A).

[106] *United States v. NEPACCO*, 810 F.2d 726, 742 (8th Cir. 1986), *cert. denied*, 484 U.S. 848 (1987); *United States v. Tarrant*, No. 03-3899 (D.N.J. Jan. 25, 2007); *United States v. Bliss*, 20 Envtl. L. Rep. 20879 (E.D. Mo. 1988).

[107] *United States v. Qwest Corp.*, 353 F. Supp. 2d 1048 (D. Minn. 2005).

[108] *United States v. NEPACCO*, 810 F.2d 726 (8th Cir. 1986), *cert. denied*, 484 U.S. 848 (1987); *New York v. Shore Realty Corp.*, 759 F.2d 1032 (2d Cir. 1985).

[109] *Vermont v. Staco Inc.*, 684 F. Supp. 822, 831-832 (D. Vt. 1988); *United States v. Kayser-Roth Corp.*, 910 F.2d 24 (1st Cir. 1990), *cert. denied*, 498 U.S. 1084 (1991).

[110] *See United States v. Fleet Factors Corp.*, 901 F.2d 1550, 1556 (11th Cir. 1990), *cert. denied*, 498 U.S. 1046 (1991). *See also United States v. Nicolet*, 712 F. Supp. 1193 (E.D. Pa. 1989) (familiarity with and

capacity to control subsidiary's waste disposal practices). *But see BP Amoco Chem. Co. v. Sun Oil Co.*, No. A.00-82-KAJ (D. Del. May 5, 2004) (no evidence of unusual level of control).

[111] *United States v. TIC Inv. Corp.*, 68 F.3d 1082 (8th Cir. 1995), *reh'g denied* (8th Cir 1996) (nexus test applied in "arranger" liability case); *South Carolina Electric & Gas Co. v. UGI Utilities, Inc.*, No. 2:06-CV-02627, 2012 WL 1432543 (D.S.C. Apr. 11, 2012) (mere existence of dual board members between parent and subsidiary not enough to impose liability where no evidence that parent managed, directed or conducted operations specifically related to leakage or disposal of hazardous waste).

[112] *E.g., United States v. Cordova Chem. Co.*, 59 F.3d 584 (6th Cir. 1995); *Joslyn Corp. v. T.L. James & Co.*, 696 F. Supp. 222 (W.D. La. 1988), *aff'd*, 893 F.2d 80 (5th Cir. 1990), *cert. denied*, 498 U.S. 1108 (1991).

[113] *United States v. Bestfoods*, 524 U.S. 51, 118 S. Ct. 1876, 141 L. Ed. 2d 43 (1998).

[114] *See United States v. Kayser-Roth Corp., Inc.*, 2001 WL 150469 (1st Cir. Dec. 3, 2001) (parent's exercise of substantial control warranted piercing the corporate veil); *Schiavone v. Pearce*, 77 F. Supp. 2d 284 (D. Conn. 1999) (overlapping and intertwining management officers could not establish liability alone); *Cyprus Amax Minerals Co. v. TCI Pacific Communications, Inc.*; No. 11-CV-252, 2012 WL 4006122, at *4-6 (N.D. Okla. Sept. 12, 2012) (law of the state of incorporation governs claims seeking to pierce the corporate veil in CERCLA cases).

[115] *United States v. Marmon Holdings, Inc. et al.*, No. 2:10-CV-00526, 2011 WL 4381893 (D. Idaho, September 19, 2011); *Precision Brand Products Inc. v. Downers Grove Sanitary Dist.*, No. 1:08-cv-05549 (N.D. Ill. August 8, 2011).

[116] *New York v. Nat'l Serv. Indus., Inc.*, 380 F. Supp. 2d 122 (E.D.N.Y. 2005); *International Flavors & Fragrances, Inc. v. St. Paul Protective Insurance Co.*, 98 A.D.3d 854 (N.Y. App. Div. 2012); *Atwell v. DJO, Inc.*, 803 F. Supp. 2d 369 (E.D.N.C. 2011). But see *United States v. General Battery*, 423 F.3d 294 (3d Cir. 2005).

[117] *Action Mfg. Co. v. Simon Wrecking Co.*, 387 F. Supp. 2d 439 (E.D. Pa. 2005).

[118] *PCS Nitrogen v. Ashley II of Charleston LLC*, No. 11-2087, *21-21 (4th Cir. April 4, 2013); See also *United States v. Sterling Centrecorp, Inc.*, 2011 WL 6749801 (E.D. Cal. Dec. 22, 2011); *United States v. NCR Corp et al.*, No. 1:10-cv-00910-(E.D. Wis. December 19, 2011).

[119] *Marsh v. Rosenblum*, 499 F.3d 165 (2d Cir. 2007).

[120] *E.g., Alabama v. United States Envtl. Protection Agency*, 871 F.2d 1548 (11th Cir.), *cert. denied sub nom., Alabama ex rel. Siegelman v. United States EPA*, 493 U.S. 991 (1989); *Barmet Aluminum Corp. v. Thomas*, 730 F. Supp. 771 (W.D. Ky. 1990), *aff'd sub nom., Barmet Aluminum Corp. v. Reilly*, 927 F.2d 289 (6th Cir. 1991); *Anactostia Riverkeeper v. Washington Gas Light Co.*, No. 11-1453, 2012 WL 4336243, at *4-6 (D.D.C. Sept. 24, 2012) (district court dismissed RCRA claim against site owner where the federal government had lodged a consent degree providing for a CERCLA remedy at the site); *Sackett v. EPA*, 132 S.Ct. 1367, 1374 (2012) (Supreme Court avoided deciding if there is a due process right to pre-enforcement review of EPA Unilateral Orders by deciding the case on Clean Water Act grounds). *But see United States v. Princeton Gamma-Tech, Inc.*, 31 F.3d 138 (3d Cir. 1994) (review and injunctive relief may be available when a property owner asserts bona fide allegations that an EPA cleanup will cause irreparable harm to public health or environment).

[121] *North Shore Gas Co. v. United States Envtl. Protection Agency*, 753 F. Supp. 1413 (N.D. Ill. 1990), *aff'd*, 930 F.2d 1239 (7th Cir. 1991); *United States v. Cordova Chem. Co. of Michigan*, 750 F. Supp. 832 (W.D. Mich. 1990). *But see Frey v. United States Envtl. Protection Agency*, 403 F.3d 828 (7th Cir. 2005) (EPA cannot preclude review by pointing to ongoing investigation with no clear end in sight); *Oil, Chemical & Atomic Workers Int'l Union v. Pena*, 18 F. Supp. 2d 6 (D.D.C. 1998) (court allowed review of plans to recycle radioactive materials because recycling is not an integral part of the cleanup).

[122] U.S. EPA, *Superfund Facts—The Program at Work* at http://www.epahome/other2-1017.htm.

123   U.S. EPA Memorandum from Susan E. Brown, director, Office of Site Remediation Enforcement, U.S. EPA to Superfund National Policy Managers and others (March 17, 2006) (on file at EPA).

124   *FY 2013 EPA Budget in Brief* (Feb. 2012) at http://www2.epa.gov/planandbudget/fy2013.

125   *Id.* at 71.

126   Lisa P. Jackson, EPA administrator *Testimony before the S. Comm. on Env't & Public Works*, 111th Cong. 8 (May 12, 2009).

127   *See* U.S. EPA, OSWER Directive 9834.6, Potentially Responsible Party Search Manual (1987).

128   42 U.S.C. § 9604(e)(2). *See United States v. Martin*, No. 99C1130 (N.D. Ill. July 26, 2000).

129   *Id.*

130   42 U.S.C. § 9604(e)(4).

131   42 U.S.C. § 9604(e)(5). EPA issued its final Civil Monetary Penalty Inflation Adjustment Rule as mandated by the Debt Collection Improvement Act of 1996 to adjust EPA's civil monetary penalties for inflation, 69 Fed. Reg. 7121 (Feb. 13, 2004) (codified at 40 C.F.R. pt. 19).

132   *Id.*

133   42 U.S.C. § 9604(e)(7).

134   *United States v. Crown Roll Leaf, Inc.*, 29 Env't Rep. Cas. (BNA) 2025 (D.N.J. 1989) ($142,000 penalty).

135   *See, e.g., United States v. Ponderosa Fibers of America, Inc.*, 2001 U.S. Dist. LEXIS 16151 (N.D.N.Y. Sept. 27, 2001) (97-day delay unreasonable when based on general excuses); *B.F. Goodrich Co. v. Murtha*, 697 F. Supp. 89 (D. Conn 1988).

136   *United States v. Bliss*, 667 F. Supp. 1298, 1313 (E.D. Mo. 1987).

137   42 U.S.C. § 9607(a)(1)–(a)(4).

138   Although Section 107(a)(1) is written in the conjunctive, courts have interpreted it in the disjunctive. *See, e.g., Long Beach Unified Sch. Dist. v. Dorothy B. Godwin California Living Trust*, 32 F.3d 1364, 1367 (9th Cir. 1994); *Commander Oil Corp. v. Barlo Equip. Corp.*, 215 F.3d 321, 328 (2d Cir. 2000).

139   *California Dep't of Toxic Substances v. Hearthside Residential Corp.*, No. 09-55 389 (9th Cir. July 22, 2010); *Sherwin-Williams Co. v. ARTA Grp. Co.*, 125 F. Supp. 2d 739.745 (D.Md. 2001); *Philadelphia v. Stepan Chem. Co.*, 1987 U.S. Dist. LEXIS 7058 (E.D. Pa. 1987).

140   *Ashley 11 of Charleston, LLC v. PCS Nitrogen, Inc.*, 2010 WL 4025885 (D.S.C. Oct. 13, 2010); *United States v. Tyson*, 1986 U.S. Dist. LEXIS 21325 (E.D. Pa. 1986).

141   *E.g.,* EPA Lender Liability Policy, 60 Fed. Reg. 63517 (Dec. 11, 1995); EPA Guidance on Agreements with prospective Purchasers of Contaminated Property, 60 Fed. Reg. 34792 (July 3, 1995); EPA Supplemental Guidance: Support of Regional Efforts to Negotiate Prospective Purchaser Agreements (PPAs) at Superfund Sites and Clarification of PPA Guidance, http://www.epa.gov/region4/ead/legal/ppa.htm (Jan. 1, 2001). EPA's Lender Liability Policy was enacted into law by Congress in the Asset Conservation, Lender Liability and Deposit Insurance Protection Act of 1996, Pub. L. No. 104-208 (1996); U.S. EPA Memorandum from Cynthia Giles, Assistant Administrator, and Mathy Stainislaus, Assistant Administrator, Office of Enforcement and Compliance, "Revised Enforcement Guidance Regarding the Treatment of Tenants Under the CERCLA Bona Fide Prospective Purchaser Provision" (Dec. 5, 2012).

142   42 U.S.C. § 9601(20)(D).

143   42 U.S.C. § 9601(20)(A). *See United States v. Posses*, 1998 U.S. Dist. LEXIS 7902 (No. 90-0654, May 6, 1998).

144   *See* 42 U.S.C. § 9601(35).

145   42 U.S.C. § 9601(35)(C).

146   Small Business Liability Act, *supra. See generally* Ben A. Hagood Jr., *The New Prospective Purchaser Exception to Environmental Liability*, South Carolina Lawyer, May/June 2002, at 35.

147   42 U.S.C. § 9601(35).

148   69 Fed. Reg. 52542 (Aug. 26, 2004).

149   70 Fed. Reg. 66070 (Nov. 1, 2005) (codified at 40 C.F.R. pt. 312).

150 U.S. EPA, All Appropriate Inquiries (Nov. 2005) at http://www.epa.gov/brownfields/regneg.html. *See also* 68 Fed. Reg. 24888 (May 9, 2003).

151 Fed. Reg. 66070, 66072 (Nov. 1, 2005).

152 *Id.*

153 70 Fed. Reg. 66070, 66108 (Nov. 1, 2005).

154 70 Fed. Reg. 66070, 66082–66083 (Nov. 1, 2005).

155 70 Fed. Reg. 66070, 66095–66097 (Nov. 1, 2005).

156 70 Fed. Reg. 66070, 66091–66095 (Nov. 1, 2005).

157 70 Fed. Reg. 66070, 66077–66078 (Nov. 1, 2005).

158 *Regulations governing ASTM Technical Committees,* ASTM International (April 2012); Work Item: ASTM WK34591 – Revision of E1527-05 Standard Practice for Environmental Site Assessments; Phase I Environmental Site Assessment Process, ASTM Int'l, http://www.astm.org/DATABASE.CART/WORK ITEMS/WK34591.htm.

159 *Ashley 11 of Charleston,* WL4025885 at 53–54.

160 42 U.S.C. § 9601(35)(A). *See Hidden Lakes Development, LP v. Allina Health System,* No. 02-406 (June/July) (D. Minn. Sept. 27, 2004).

161 H.R. 2869, 107th Cong. (2001), *supra.*

162 42 U.S.C. § 9601(35)(C).

163 The requirement that the property be purchased after January 11, 2002, was recently affirmed in the case of *Haskins v. Cherokee Grand Avenue, LLC,* No. C-11-05142, 2012 WL 1110014, at *3-4 (N.D. Cal. Apr. 2, 2012).

164 42 U.S.C. § 9601(40).

165 *PCS Nitrogen v. Ashley II of Charleston LLC,* No. 11-2087 (4th Cir. April 4, 2013).

166 *Id.* at *31.

167 42 U.S.C. § 9607(q).

168 U.S. EPA, *Interim Enforcement Discretion Guidance regarding Contiguous Property Owners* (Jan. 13, 2004) at http://www.epa.gov/compliance/resources/policies/cleanup/superfun d/contig-prop.pdf.

169 42 U.S.C. § 9607(q)(1)(A).

170 42 U.S.C. § 9607(r).

171 *United States v. South Carolina Recycling & Disposal Inc. (SCRDI),* 653 F. Supp. 984, 1003 (D.S.C. 1984), *aff'd in part and vacated in part sub nom.; United States v. Monsanto Co.,* 858 F.2d 160 (4th Cir. 1988), *cert. denied,* 490 U.S. 1186 (1989). *But cf. Commander Oil Corp v. Barlo Equipment Corp.,* 215 F.3d 321 (2d Cir. 2000) (party had no control over site operations and bore no responsibility for contamination); *Long Beach Unified Sch. Dist. v. Dorothy B. Godwin Living Trust,* 32 F.3d 1364 (9th Cir. 1994) (owning an easement alone, with no more of an active role, does not render the easement holder an owner or operator under CERCLA); *City of Los Angeles v. San Pedro Boat Works,* 635 F.3d 400 (9th Cir. 2011) (a company holding a permit from the City to use a ship repair berth was not liable as an "owner" or "operator" under CERLCA where it did not operate the boat works facility).

172 *United States v. Best Foods,* 524 U.S. 51, 118 S. Ct. 1876, 141 L. Ed. 2d 43 (1998); *PCS Nitrogen v. Ashley II of Charleston LLC,* No. 11-2087, * 27-28 (4th Cir. April 4, 2013).

173 *ASARCO, LLC v. Hecla Mining Co.,* No. 12-CV-0381, 2012 WL 5929962, at *3-4 (E.D. Wash. Nov. 27, 2012); *ASARCO, LLC v. NL Indus., Inc.,* No. 4:11-CV-00864, 2012 WL 4480738, at *3-4 (E.D. Mo. Sept. 28, 2012).

174 *New York v. Shore Realty Corp.,* 759 F.2d 1032 (2d Cir. 1985); *United States v. Union Corp.,* 259 F. Supp. 2d 356 (E.D. Pa. 2003).

175 *United States v. Carolina Transformer Co.,* 978 F.2d 832 (4th Cir. 1992).

176   *United States v. Best Foods*, 524 U.S. 51, 118 S. Ct. 1876, 141 L. Ed. 2d 43 (1998); *United States v. Kayser-Roth Corporation*, 2001 WL 150469 (1st Cir. Dec. 3, 2001). But see *Joslyn Mfg. Co. v. T. L. James & Co.*, 893 F.2d 80, 83 (5th Cir. 1990), *cert. denied*, 490 U.S. 1108 (1991).

177   *United States v. Fleet Factors Corp.*, 901 F.2d 1550, 1557 (11th Cir. 1990); *Bancorpsouth Bank v. Envtl. Operations*, No. 4:11CV9, 2012 U.S. Dist. Lexis 159466, at *32-33 (E.D. Mo. Nov. 7, 2012) (lender denied motion to dismiss CERCLA liability where allegations of enough post-foreclosure control over the contaminated site resulting in releases of hazardous substances). But see EPA Lender Liability Policy, 60 Fed. Reg. 63517 (Dec. 11, 1995) (requiring actual participation instead of mere influence).

178   *CPC Int'l Inc. v. Aerojet-General Corp.*, 731 F. Supp. 783, 788 (W.D. Mich. 1989). But see *United States v. Dart Indus.*, 847 F.2d 144 (4th Cir. 1988) (government entity not liable under CERCLA for activities related to regulatory function).

179   *Seminole Indian Tribe of Florida v. Florida*, 517 U.S. 44, 116 S. Ct. 1114, 134 L. Ed. 2d 252 (1996). But see *Pennsylvania v. Lockheed Martin Corp.*, 681 F.3d 503 (3d. Cir. 2012) (private party may file a counter-claim against the state in a CERCLA cost recovery action on a recoupment theory—up to the amount of any state judgment against a private party).

180   42 U.S.C. § 9607(a)(2).

181   *E.g., New York v. Shore Realty Corp.*, 759 F.2d 1032, 1044 (2d Cir. 1985).

182   *Carson Harbor Village, Ltd. v. UNOCAL Corp.*, 227 F.3d 1196 (9th Cir. 2000), *overruled by Clean HarborVillage, Ltd. v. UNOCAL Corp.*, 270 F.3d 863 (9th Cir. 2001) (*en banc*); *Nurad, Inc. v. William E. Hooper & Sons Co.*, 966 F.2d 837 (4th Cir.), *cert. denied sub nom., Mumaw v. Nurad, Inc.*, 113 S. Ct. 377 (1992); *PCS Nitrogen v. Ashley II of Charleston LLC*, No. 11-2087, * 27-28 (4th Cir. April 4, 2013).

183   42 U.S.C. § 6903(3).

184   *See, e.g., United States v. Waste Indus.*, 734 F.2d 159, 164 (4th Cir. 1984); *In re Tutu Wells*, 994 F. Supp. 638 (D.V.I. 1998). But see *United States v. 150 Acres of Land*, 204 F.3d 698 (6th Cir. 2000).

185   *See, e.g., Bob's Beverage, Inc. v. Acme, Inc.*, 264 F.3d 692 (6th Cir. 2001); *United States v. CDMG Realty*, 96 F.3d 706 (3d Cir. 1996).

186   42 U.S.C. § 9607(a)(3).

187   *United States v. A & F Materials Co.*, 582 F. Supp. 842 (S.D. Ill. 1984); *United States v. General Electric Co.*, 670 F.3d 377, 391 (1st Cir. 2012). But see *Appleton Papers, Inc. v. George A. Whiting Paper Co.*, No. 08-C-16, 2012 WL 2704920 (E.D. Wis. July 3, 2012) (generalized knowledge that paper recycling would lead to discharges of waste products from the paper coatings was not enough to make the scrap paper seller an "arranger" for disposal).

188   *Jersey City Redevelopment Auth. v. PPG Indus.*, 655 F. Supp. 1257 (D.N.J. 1987).

189   *United States v. Aceto Agricultural Chem. Corp.*, 699 F. Supp. 1384 (S.D. Iowa), *aff'd in part and rev'd in part*, 872 F.2d 1373 (8th Cir. 1988).

190   *ASARCO, LLC v. NL Indus.*, No. 4:11-CV-00864, 2012 WL 4480738 (E.D. Mo. Sept. 28, 2012); but see *Pakootas v. Teck Cominco Metals Ltd.*, No. CV-04-256-LRS (E.D. Wash. Nov. 29, 2011).

191   *Ford Motor Co. v. Edgewood Props.*, No. 06-cv-1278, 2012 WL 4172133, at *14-18 (D.N.J. Aug. 21, 2012) (arranger liability of cleanup contractor at manufacturing facility demolition site depends on degree of control over contaminated debris and intent to dispose of hazardous substances).

192   *See generally, Burlington Northern and Santa Fe Railway Co. v. United States*, 129 S. Ct. 1870 (2009).

193   *Id.* at 1878.

194   *Id.*

195   *Id.* at 1879. *See also Amcast Indus. Corp. v. Detrex Corp.*, 2 F.3d 746 (7th Cir. 1993), *cert. denied*, 114 S. Ct. 691 (1994); *United States v. Cello-Foil Prods., Inc.*, 848 F. Supp. 1352 (W.D. Mich. 1994).

196   *See Celanese Corp. v. Martin K. Eby Const. Co., Inc.*, 2010 WL 362031 (5th Cir. Sept. 20, 2010) (no liability where defendant did not know actions caused disposal). *See generally, Hinds Investments, L.P. v. Team Enterprises, Inc.*, 2010 WL 922416 (E.D. Cal. Mar. 12, 2010) (plaintiff failed to show intentional

disposal); *Appleton Papers, Inc. v. George A. Whiting Paper Co.*, Slip. Op., 2009 WL 5064049 (E.D. Wis. Dec. 16, 2009) (defendants had little or no knowledge of disposal).

[197] *Pneumo Abex Corp. v. High Point, Thomasville and Denton Railroad Co.*, 142 F.3d 769 (4th Cir. 1998); *Florida Power & Light Co. v. Allis Chalmers Corp.*, 893 F.2d 1313 (11th Cir. 1990). *But cf. Morton International, Inc., v. A. E. Staley Mfg. Co.*, 343 F.3d 669 (3rd Cir. 2003) (pipeline company owned mercury that during processing produced waste); *California Dept. of Toxic Substances Control v. Alco Pacific, Inc.*, No. 05-55962 (9th Cir. Nov. 28, 2007) (material sold constituted "waste" rather than "useful product"); *In re Voluntary Purchasing Groups, Inc. Litigation*, 2002 WL 203088, No. CIV A 3:94-CV-2477-H (N.D. Tex. Sept. 3, 2002) (sale of commercial product not exempt where it resulted in leaking); *Team Enterprises, LLC v. Western Investment Real Estate Trust*, 2011 WL 3075759 (9th Cir. July 26, 2011) (manufacturer and seller of useful product lacked requisite intent to qualify as "arranger" simply because it didn't instruct buyer on proper disposal techniques).

[198] *United States v. North Landing Line Cont. Co.*, 3 F. Supp. 2d 694 (E.D.Va. 1998).

[199] *See Chesapeake & Potomac Telephone Co. v. Peck Iron & Metal Co., Inc.*, 814 F. Supp. 1293 (E.D.Va. 1993).

[200] 42 U.S.C. § 9627(a).

[201] 42 U.S.C. § 9627(b).

[202] *See generally United States v. Mountain Metal Co.*, 137 F. Supp. 2d 1267 (N.D. Ala. 2001) (retroactive application); *Gould, Inc. v. A&M Battery & Tire Service*, 176 F. Supp. 324 (M.D. Pa. 2001) (burden of proof).

[203] *United States v. Bliss*, 667 F. Supp. 1298 (E.D. Mo. 1987).

[204] *United States v. Lyon*, No. 07-0491, 2007 U.S. Dist. LEXIS 94329 (E.D. Cal. Dec. 14, 2007). *But cf. Team Enterprises LLC v. Western Inv. Ins. Trust*, No. CV F 08-0872 (E.D. Cal. June 11, 2010).

[205] *KFD Enterprises, Inc. v. City of Eureka*, No. C 08-4571, 2012 WL 6554097 (N.D. Cal. Dec. 14, 2012).

[206] *Id.* at * 1.

[207] *E.g., United States v. Hercules*, 165 Fed. Supp. 2d 253 (N.D. N.Y. 2001); *United States v. Cantrell*, 92 F. Supp. 2d 704 (S.D. Ohio 2000) (disposal of trace amounts of hazardous substance can support liability).

[208] 42 U.S.C. § 9607(a)(4).

[209] *E.g., The Port of Redwood City v. Gibson Envtl Inc.*, No. 03-15662 (9th Cir. Feb. 25, 2005); *United States v. Hardage*, 761 F. Supp. 1501 (W.D. Okla. 1990). *See also* U.S. EPA, *Policy for Enforcement Actions against Transporters under CERCLA* (Dec. 23, 1985).

[210] *Action Mfg. Co., Inc. v. Simon Wrecking Co.*, No. 06-3679 (3d Cir. July 28, 2008).

[211] *See generally United States v. Hardage*, 750 F. Supp. 1444 (W.D. Okla. 1990).

[212] *Id.*

[213] 42 U.S.C. § 9607(a)(4); 42 U.S.C. § 9627(a)(1).

[214] 42 U.S.C. § 9601(25).

[215] *Forest Park National Bank & Trust v. Ditchfield*, No. 10 C 3166, 2012 WL 3028342, at *23 (N.D. Ill. July 24, 2012); *CNH America, LLC v. Champion Environmental Services, Inc.*, 863 F. Supp. 2d 793, 809 (E.D. Wis. 2012).

[216] *E.g., California v. George Besone dba Truck Sales Co.*, 141 F.3d 1179 (9th Cir. 1998); *Cadillac Fairview/ California, Inc. v. Dow Chem. Co.*, 840 F.2d 691, 695 (9th Cir. 1988).

[217] *NL Indus. v. Kaplan*, 792 F.2d 896, 898 (9th Cir. 1986).

[218] *Brewer v. Ravan*, 680 F. Supp. 1176 (M.D. Tenn. 1988).

[219] *United States v. Ottati & Goss*, 694 F. Supp. 977, 994-994 (D.N.H. 1988), *aff'd in part and vacated in part, remanded*, 900 F.2d 429 (1st Cir. 1990).

[220] *United States v. E.I. Dupont De Nemours and Co.*, 432 F.3d 161 (3d Cir. 2005) *reversing en banc, United States v. Rohm & Haas*, 2 F.3d 1265 (3d Cir. 1993); *United States v. Hardage*, 733 F. Supp. 1424, 1438-1439 (W.D. Okla. 1989) *aff'd in part, rev'd in part*, 982 F.2d 1436 (10th Cir. 1992), *cert. denied*, 114

S. Ct. 300 (1993); *United States v. R.W. Meyer, Inc.*, 889 F.2d 1497, 1503 (6th Cir. 1989), *cert. denied*, 110 S. Ct. 1527 (1990).

221 *Struhar v. City of Cleveland*, 7 F. Supp. 2d 948 (N.D. Ohio 1998); *Coburn v. Sun Chem. Corp.*, 1988 U.S. Dist. LEXIS 12548 (E.D. Pa. 1988). *But see United States v. W.R. Grace & Co.*, 280 F. Supp. 2d 1149 (D. Mont. 2003) (costs of health effects study are recoverable).

222 *Syms v. Olin Corp.*, 408 F.3d 95 (2d Cir. 2005).

223 *Mola Dev. Corp. v. United States*, 1985 U.S. Dist. LEXIS 22674 (C.D. Cal. 1985). *But see Jaasma v. Shell Oil Co.*, 412 F.3d 501 (3d Cir. 2005).

224 *American Alternative Insurance CO. v. Moon Nurseries, Inc.*, No. 11-cv-2267, 2012 WL 892620 (D.Md. Mar. 14, 2012).

225 *Saline River Props., LLC v. Johnson Controls, Inc.*, No. 10-cv-10507, 2012 WL 3308114, at *15-16 (E.D. Mich. Aug. 13, 2012); but see *Forest Park Nat'l Bank & Trust v. Ditchfield*, No. 10 C 3166, 2012 WL 30283242 at *23 (N.D. Ill. July 24, 2012) (future monitoring costs are recoverable and give rise to issuance of a declaratory judgment where substantial cleanup work remained to be conducted).

226 *Minnesota ex rel Northern Pacific Center, Inc. v. BNSF Railway Co.*, 686 F.3d 567, 572-575 (8th Cir. 2012).

227 *E.g., United States v. South Carolina Recycling & Disposal, Inc. (SCRDI)*, 653 F. Supp. 984, 1009 (D.S.C. 1984), *aff'd in part and rev'd in part sub nom., United States v. Monsanto*, 858 F.2d 160 (4th Cir. 1988), *cert. denied*, 490 U.S. 1106 (1989).

228 *Key Tronic Corp. v. United States*, 511 U.S. 809 (1994).

229 *Franklin County Convention Facilities Authority v. American Premier Underwriters*, 240 F.3d 534 (6th Cir. 2001).

230 *Compare United States v. Rohm & Haas Co.*, 2 F.3d 1265 (3d Cir. 1993) (costs not recoverable) *with United States v. Lowe*, No. H-91-830, 1994 WL 518025 (S.D. Tex. Sept. 20, 1994) (costs recoverable). *See also United States v. E.I. Dupont De Nemours and Co.*, 432 F.3d 161 (3d Cir. 2005) (EPA can recover oversight costs of response actions performed by a private party); *Lenox Inc. v. James Langley Operating Co.*, 91 F. Supp. 2d 743 (D.N.J. 2000) (EPA cannot recover oversight costs of remedial activity performed by private party).

231 *See Dedham Water Co. v. Cumberland Farms, Inc.*, 770 F. Supp. 41 (D. Mass. 1991).

232 42 U.S.C. § 9607(a)(4)(B).

233 *Amoco Oil Co. v. Borden, Inc.*, 889 F.2d 664 (5th Cir. 1989); *Stratford Holding LLC v. Fog Cap Retail Investors, LLC et al.*, CA No. 1:11-cv-03463 (N.D. Ga., Atlanta Div. Sept. 2012).

234 42 U.S.C. § 9607(a)(4)(A).

235 42 U.S.C. § 9607(a)(4)(B).

236 *See United States v. NEPACCO*, 810 F.2d 726 (8th Cir. 1986), *cert. denied*, 484 U.S. 848 (1987).

237 *Amland Prop. Corp. v. ALCOA*, 711 F. Supp. 784, 801 (D.N.J. 1989).

238 *E.g., Carroll v. Litton Sys, Inc.*, 1995 U.S. App. LEXIS 691 (4th Cir. Jan. 13, 1995) *cert. denied*, 516 U.S. 816, 116 S. Ct. 70, 133 L. Ed. 2d 31 (1995).

239 *United States v. Akzo Nobel Coatings, Inc.*, 990 F. Supp. 892 (E.D. Mich. 1998) (EPA has no obligation to minimize response costs and NCP does not require response costs to be reasonable, proper, or cost-effective).

240 *See Voggenthaler v. Maryland Square, LLC*, No. 2:08-cv-1618, 2012 WL 1815651, at *9 (D.Nev. May 17, 2012) (State of Nevada's failure to make removal action plan available for public comment dod not render its costs unrecoverable even though NCP requires it).

241 *Amland Prop. Corp. v. ALCOA*, 711 F. Supp. 784 (D.N.J. 1989).

242 *Wickland Oil Terminals v. ASARCO, Inc.*, 792 F.2d 887 (9th Cir. 1986); *Sealy Connecticut, Inc. v. Litton Industries, Inc.* (D. Conn. 2000) (substantial compliance with NCP even though no RI/FS prepared). *But*

cf. Raytheon Constructors, Inc. v. ASARCO Inc., 2000 U.S. Dist. LEXIS 6069 (D. Colo. 2000) (failure to prepare RI/FS for remedial action not compliance with NCP).

[243] 40 C.F.R. § 300.700(c)(3)(i).

[244] *Franklin County Convention Facilities Authority v. American Premier Underwriters*, 240 F.3d 534 (6th Cir. 2001).

[245] *Sherwin-Williams Co. v. ARTRA Group, Inc.*, 125 F. Supp. 2d 739 (D. Md. 2001).

[246] *PMC, Inc. v. Sherwin-Williams Co.*, 151 F.3d 610 (7th Cir. 1998).

[247] 42 U.S.C. § 9652(d) (CERCLA will not "affect or modify in any way the obligations or liabilities of any person under other . . . State law"); *Union Pacific Railroad Co. v. Reilly Industries, Inc.*, 215 F.3d 830 (8th Cir. 2000) (insubstantial compliance because public participation occurred only after remedy had been chosen and work had begun); *Bedford Affiliates v. Sills*, 156 F.3d 416 (2d Cir. 1998) (extensive state environmental agency involvement sufficed for public comment).

[248] 40 C.F.R. § 300.700(c)(3)(i).

[249] *United States v. Western Processing Co.*, 1991 U.S. Dist. LEXIS 16021 (W.D. Wash. July 31, 1991).

[250] 42 U.S.C. § 9606.

[251] *Velsicol Chem. Corp. v. Reilly Tar & Chem. Corp.*, 1984 U.S. Dist. LEXIS 24317 (E.D. Tenn. 1984).

[252] *E.g., United States v. Price*, 577 F. Supp. 1103, 1113 (D.N.J. 1983). *But see United States v. Wade*, 546 F. Supp. 785, 794 (E.D. Pa. 1982), *appeal dismissed*, 713 F.2d 49 (3d Cir. 1983).

[253] *B.F. Goodrich v. Murtha*, 697 F. Supp. 89, 95 (D. Conn. 1988).

[254] *United States v. Conservation Chem. Co.*, 619 F. Supp. 162, 175 (W.D. Mo. 1985).

[255] *United States v. Hardage*, 663 F. Supp. 1280 (W.D. Okla. 1987).

[256] *Id.* at 1284.

[257] *United States v. NCR Corp.*, No. 10-C-910, 2012 WL 5831201 (E.D. Wis. Nov. 16, 2012).

[258] *E.g., United States v. NEPACCO*, 579 F. Supp. 823, 840 n.17 (W.D. Mo. 1984), *aff'd in part and rev'd in part*, 810 F.2d 726 (8th Cir. 1986), *cert. denied*, 484 U.S. 848 (1987).

[259] *See* U.S. EPA, "Memorandum on Use and Issuance of Administrative Orders under Section 106(a) of CERCLA" (Sept. 8, 1983), reprinted in 41 *Env't Rep.* 2931, 2935.

[260] *See generally General Electric Co. v. Jackson*, No. 09-5092 (D.C. Cir. June 29, 2010).

[261] U.S. EPA, *Guidance on CERCLA Section 106(a) Unilateral Administrative Orders for Remedial Design and Remedial Action*, OSWER Dir. # 9833.01-a (Mar. 13, 1990).

[262] *See* 42 U.S.C. §§ 9613(j), 9621(a).

[263] 58 Fed. Reg. 5460 (1993) (to be codified at 40 C.F.R. pt. 307).

[264] 42 U.S.C. § 9606(b)(1). EPA issued its final Civil Monetary Penalty Inflation Adjustment Rule as mandated by the Debt Collection Improvement Act of 1996 to adjust EPA's civil monetary penalties for inflation. 69 Fed. Reg. 7121 (Feb. 13, 2004) (codified at 40 C.F.R. pt. 19).

[265] 42 U.S.C. § 9607(c)(3). *See also United States v. Lecarreaux*, 1992 U.S. LEXIS 9365 (D.N.J. Feb. 18, 1992); "EPA Policy on Civil Penalties," 17 *Env't L. Rep.* 35083 (Feb. 16, 1984).

[266] *See Solid State Circuits v. United States Envtl. Protection Agency*, 812 F.2d 383 (8th Cir. 1987).

[267] 42 U.S.C. §§ 9606(b)(1), 9607(c)(3).

[268] *See Solid State Circuits v. United States Envtl. Protection Agency*, 812 F.2d 383 (8th Cir. 1987) (providing extensive discussion of defense).

[269] *See, e.g., United States v. Parsons*, 723 F. Supp. 757, 763 (N.D. Ga. 1989), vacated, 936 F.2d 526 (11th Cir. 1991).

[270] *Solid State Circuits v. United States Envtl. Protection Agency*, 812 F.2d 383, 391 n.11 (8th Cir. 1987).

[271] *General Electric Co. v. Environmental Protection Agency*, 360 F.3d 188 (D.C. Cir. Mar. 2, 2004).

[272] *Solid State Circuits v. United States Envtl. Protection Agency*, 812 F.2d 383, 392 (8th Cir. 1987).

[273] 42 U.S.C. § 9607(b).

274 *E.g., United States v. Rohm & Haas Co.*, 669 F. Supp. 672, 675 (D.N.J. 1987).

275 *E.g., United States v. Dickerson*, 640 F. Supp. 448, 450–451 (D. Md. 1986).

276 *United States v. Hardage*, 116 F.R.D. 460, 463 (W.D. Okla. 1987).

277 *United States v. Barrier Industries*, 991 F. Supp. 678 (S.D.N.Y. 1998); *United States v. Alcan Aluminum, Corp.*, 892 F. Supp. 648 (M.D. Pa. 1995); *United States v. Stringfellow*, 661 F. Supp. 1053, 1061 (C.D. Cal. 1987).

278 *United States v. Sterling Centrecorp Inc.*, No. 08-2556 (E.D. Cal., Dec. 8, 2011); citing *United States v. Stringfellow*, 661 F. Supp. 1053, 1059 (C.D. Cal. 1987).

279 *United States v. W. R. Grace & Co.-Conn.*, 280 F. Supp. 2d 1149, 1174 (D. Mont. 2003).

280 See *FMC Corp. v. United States Dep't of Commerce*, 786 F. Supp. 471 (E.D. Pa. 1992), *aff'd* 10 F.3d 987 (3d Cir. 1993), *vacated, reh'g granted en banc* 10 F.3d 987 (3d Cir. 1994), *aff'd* 29 F.3d 833 (3d Cir. 1994).

281 *In re Sept. 11 Litigation*, Nos. 21 MC 101 and 08 Civ. 9146, 2013 WL 1137320 (S.D.N.Y. Mar. 20, 2013).

282 *Cadillac Fairview/Cal., Inc. v. Dow Chemical*, 299 F.3d 1019 (9th Cir. 2002).

283 42 U.S.C. § 9607(b).

284 *United States v. Hooker Chems. & Plastics Corp.*, 680 F. Supp. 546 (W.D.N.Y. 1988) (suggesting indirect relationship sufficient to bar third-party defense).

285 *E.g., United States v. Tyson*, 25 Env't Rep. Cas. (BNA) 1897 (E.D. Pa. 1986).

286 See generally *United States v. Domenic Lombardi Realty, Inc.*, 290 F. Supp. 2d 198 (D.R.I. 2003) (must show contamination was caused solely by third party); *Interfaith Community Organization v. Honeywell International, Inc.*, 263 F. Supp. 796 (D.N.J. 2003) (current property owner exercised due care with regard to contamination).

287 *E.g., New York v. Shore Realty Corp.*, 759 F.2d 1032, 1046 (2d Cir. 1985). But see *Bulk Distribution Ctrs. v. Monsanto Co.*, 589 F. Supp. 1437, 1448 (S.D. Fla. 1984).

288 *Kelley v. Thomas Solvent Co.*, 714 F. Supp. 1439, 1451 (W.D. Mich. 1989).

289 *Mardan Corp. v. C.G.C. Music, Ltd.*, 600 F. Supp. 1049 (D. Ariz. 1984), *aff'd*, 804 F.2d 1454 (9th Cir. 1986); *Bergmann v. Michigan State Transportation Commission*, No. 10-1708/1770 (6th Cir. 2011) (court held that the doctrine of laches, not the state statute of limitations, governs the timeliness of motions to enforce Superfund consent decrees).

290 *United States v. Hardage*, 1987 U.S. Dist. LEXIS 13977 (W.D. Okla. 1987).

291 See generally *United States v. Nalco Chemical Co.*, No. 91 4482 (N.D. Ill. Apr. 10, 2002) (one continuous removal action allowed opportunity to recover 20 years of removal costs).

292 *E.g., United States v. Nalco Chem. Co.*, 2002 U.S. Dist. LEXIS 6679 (N.D. Ill. 2002); *Sherwin-Williams Co. v. ARTRA Group, Inc.*, 125 F. Supp. 2d 739 (D. Md. 2001); *United States v. General Electric Co.*, 670 F.3d 377, 394 (1st Cir. 2012).

293 *United States v. Navistar Int'l. Tran. Corp.*, 152 F.3d 702 (7th Cir. 1998); *OBG Technical Services, Inc. v. Northrop Grumman Space & Missions Systems Corp.*, 503 F. Supp. 2d 490 (D. Conn. 2007).

294 *E.g., State of California v. Hyampton Lumber Co.*, 903 F. Supp. 1389 (E.D. Cal. 1995) (installation of lumber pole, electrical hardware, and water pipe was initiation of construction as remedial action); *Kelley v. E. I. du Pont de Nemours and Co.*, 17 F.3d 836 (6th Cir. 1994) (surface drum and soil removal followed by RI/FS and remedy selection was one removal action).

295 42 U.S.C. § 9613(g)(1).

296 *Ohio v. United States Dep't of Interior*, 880 F.2d 432 (D.C. Cir. 1989).

297 *Kennecott Utah Copper Corp. v. United States Dept of Interior*, 88 F.3d 1191 (D.C. Cir 1996). See also *United States v. Montrose Chem. Corp.*, 883 F. Supp. 1396 (C.D. Cal. 1995) (same holding).

298 See generally *Chitayat v. Vanderbilt Associates*, No. 03-5314 (E.D.N.Y. Mar. 23, 2010); *Cytec Industries v. B.F. Goodrich*, C2-00-1398 (S.D. Ohio Jan. 23, 2003); *Union Carbide Corp. v. Thiokol*, 890 F. Supp. 1035 (S.D. Ga. 1994).

299 *ASARCO, LLC v. Shore Terminals, LLC*, No. 3:11-cv-01384, 2012 WL 2050253, at *8-9 (N.D. Cal. June 6, 2012 (a judicially approved settlement among private parties triggered the statue of limitations period at a site); *American Premier Underwriters, Inc. v. General Electric Co*, 866 F.Supp. 2d 883, 890,

892-897 (S.D. Ohio 2012); *ASARCO, LLC v. Atl. Richfield Co.*, No. CV 12-53-H, 2012 WL 5995662, at *1-3 (D. Mont. Nov. 30, 2012); *ASARCO v. Hecla Min. Co.*, No. CV-12-0381, 2012 WL 5929962, at *5 (E.D. Wash. Nov. 27, 2012).

300   Restatement (Second) of Torts, Sections 433A, 433B.

301   *ITT Indus., Inc. v. Borg Warner, Inc.*, 2010 WL 1172533 at 24 (W.D. Mich. Mar. 24, 2010).

302   Restatement (Third) of Torts, Section 26. *See Raytheon Aircraft Co. v. United States*, 532 F. Supp. 2d 1306, 1310 (D. Kan. 2007).

303   *E.g., United States v. Vertac Chem. Corp.*, 453 F.3d 1031 (8th Cir. 2006); *United States v. Chem-Dyne Corp.*, 572 F. Supp. 802 (S.D. Ohio 1983). *But see United States v. Alcan Aluminum Corp.*, 2006WL5278224. *Materials Co.*, 578 F. Supp. 1249 (S.D. Ill. 1984); *United States v. NCR Corp.*, 688 F.3d 833 (7th Cir. 2012); *Pakootas v. Teck Cominco Metals, Ltd.*, 868 F.Supp. 2d 1106 (E.D. Wash. 2012); *Litgo N.J., Inc. v. Martin*, No. 06-cv-2891, 2012 WL 32200, at *11 (D.N.J. Jan. 5, 2012).

304   *State of New York v. Solvent Chemcial*, CA No. 10-2026-cv (2nd Cir. Dec. 2011) (even if Dupont and Olin may have limited contribution to the site, they could not escape liability for ongoing and future cleanup costs at the early stages of the cleanup).

305   *PCS Nitrogen Inc. v. Ashley II of Charleston, LLC*, No. 11-2087, at *25, 27-28, and 36-37 (4th Cir. April 4, 2013).

306   *PCS Nitrogen Inc. v. Ashley II of Charleston, LLC*, No. 11-2087, at *40 (4th Cir. April 4, 2013); *see also United States v. NCR.*

307   *United States v. Alcan Aluminum Corp.*, 964 F.2d 252 (3d Cir. 1992), *reh'g granted, United States v. Alcan Aluminum Corp.* (N.D.N.Y. 2000) (defendant's wastes contributing to need for overall cleanup not divisible).

308   *In re Bell Petroleum Servs., Inc.*, 3 F.3d 889, 903 (5th Cir. 1993).

309   *See United States v. Hercules*, 247 F.3d 706 (8th Cir. 2001); *United States v. Manzo*, No. Civ. A. 97-289 (MLC), 2001 WL 980554 (D.N.J. Aug. 15, 2001).

310   *Burlington Northern*, 129 S. Ct. at 1882–1884.

311   *Id.* at 1881.

312   *Hercules*, 247 F.3d at 718, cited in *Burlington Northern*, 129 S. Ct. at 1881.

313   *Id.* at 1882.

314   *Id.* at 1882–1883.

315   *Team Enterprises, LLC v. West Investment Real Estate Trust*, 647 F.3d 901, 910 (9th Cir. 2011); *Celanese Corp. v. Martin K. Eby*, 620 F.3d 529, 533 (5th Cir.); *United States v. General Electric Co.*, No. 11-1034, 2012 WL 639189 (1st Cir., Feb. 29, 2012).

316   *See* 42 U.S.C. § 7604 (Clean Air Act); 33 U.S.C. § 1365 (Clean Water Act).

317   42 U.S.C. § 9659.

318   42 U.S.C. § 9659(c).

319   42 U.S.C. § 9659(a), (d)(1), (e).

320   *Rennie v. T&L Oil, Inc.*, No. 06-CV-0506 (N.D. Okla. Dec. 11, 2007); *Roe v. Wert*, 706 F. Supp. 788, 792 (W.D. Okla. 1989).

321   *Oil Chemical and Atomic Workers International Union, AFL-CIO v. Richardson*, 214 F.3d 274 (3d Cir. 2000); *Broward Garden Tenants Ass'n. v. EPA*, 157 F. Supp. 1329 (S.D. Fla. 2001). *See, e.g., Schalk v. Reilly*, 900 F.2d 1091 (7th Cir.), *cert. denied sub nom., Frey v. Reilly*, 498 U.S. 981 (1990).

322   *Patokas et al. v. Teck Cominco Metals, Ltd. et al.* No. 08-35951, No. 10-35045 (9th Cir. June 1, 2011).

323   *See The Steel Company v. Citizens for a Better Tomorrow*, 523 U.S. 83, 118 S. Ct. 10003 (1998); *Friends of the Earth, Inc. v. Laidlaw Environmental Services, Inc.*, 149 F.3d 303 (4th Cir. 1998), *cert. granted*, 67 U.S.L.W. 3541 (No. 98-822).

324   *Friends of the Earth, Inc. v. Laidlaw Environmental Services, Inc.*, 528 U.S. 167, 145 L. Ed. 2d 610, 630 (2000).

325   42 U.S.C. § 9607(a)(4)(C).

326   42 U.S.C. § 9601(16). *See also Lutz v. Chromatex, Inc.*, 718 F. Supp. 413, 419 (M.D. Pa. 1989); *Ohio v. United States Dep't of Interior*, 880 F.2d 432, 460–461 (D.C. Cir. 1989).

327 42 U.S.C. § 9607(f)(1).

328 *See* 51 Fed. Reg. 27674, at 52127–52128 (1986); *see also Ohio v. United States Dep't of Interior*, 880 F.2d 432, 474 (D.C. Cir. 1989).

329 42 U.S.C. § 9612(a). *See also Idaho v. Howmet Turbine Component Co.*, 814 F.2d 1376, 1377 (9th Cir. 1987).

330 42 U.S.C. § 9607(f). *See also Idaho v. Hanna Mining Co.*, 882 F.2d 392, 395 (9th Cir. 1989).

331 42 U.S.C. § 9607(f). *See also United States v. NEPACCO*, 579 F. Supp. 823, 839 (W.D. Mo. 1984), *aff'd in part and rev'd in part*, 810 F.2d 726 (8th Cir. 1986) (pre-CERCLA costs are not recoverable); *United States v. Wade*, 577 F. Supp. 1326 (E.D. Pa. 1983). *But see United States v. Shell Oil Co.*, 605 F. Supp. 1064 (D. Colo. 1985) (retroactivity permitted where damages continued after enactment).

332 42 U.S.C. § 9607(f)(2).

333 *See, e.g., Fireman's Fund Insurance Co. v. City of Lodi*, 271 F.3d 911 (3d Cir. 2001). *Compare New York v. Exxon Corp.*, 633 F. Supp. 609, 619 (S.D.N.Y. 1986) (permitting municipal trusteeship); *Boonton v. Drew Chem. Corp.*, 621 F. Supp. 663, 667 (D.N.J. 1985) (same) *with Bedford v. Raytheon Co.*, 755 F. Supp. 469 (D. Mass. 1991) (disallowing municipal trusteeship).

334 42 U.S.C. § 9607(f)(1).

335 *Oklahoma v. Tyson Foods, Inc.*, 258 F.R.D. 472, 483 (N.D. Okla. 2009); but see *United States v. Asarco, Inc.*, 471 F.Supp. 2d 1063, 1068 (D. Idaho 2005).

336 42 U.S.C. § 9611(c)(1)(2).

337 42 U.S.C. § 9611(b)(2)(A).

338 42 U.S.C. § 9611.

339 42 U.S.C. § 9651(c)(2).

340 *See* Exec. Order No. 12,316, 46 Fed. Reg. 42237, 42240 (1981) (designating the DOI as party to promulgate assessment regulations), *superseded by* Exec. Order No. 12,580, 52 Fed. Reg. 2923 (1987). *See also* 42 U.S.C. § 9651(c).

341 52 Fed. Reg. 9042 (1987), *amended* at 53 Fed. Reg. 9769 (1988); 53 Fed. Reg. 20143 (1988); 54 Fed. Reg. 39015 (1989). *See also Colorado v. United States Dep't of Interior*, 880 F.2d 481, 490 (D.C. Cir. 1989) (limited application of Type A regulations to marine and coastal environments not arbitrary or capricious).

342 51 Fed. Reg. 27674 (1986), *amended* at 53 Fed. Reg. 5166 (1988).

343 *See Ohio v. United States Dep't of the Interior*, 880 F.2d 432 (D.C. Cir. 1989); *Colorado v. United States Dep't of Interior*, 880 F.2d 481, 490–491 (D.C. Cir. 1989).

344 59 Fed. Reg. 14262 (Mar. 25, 1994).

345 59 Fed. Reg. 63300 (Dec. 8, 1994).

346 *Kennecott Utah Copper Corp. v. United States Dep't of Interior*, 88 F.3d 1191 (D.C. Cir. 1996).

347 42 U.S.C. § 9607(f)(2)(C).

348 *Appleton Papers, Inc. v. George A. Whiting Paper Co.*, 2012 WL 2704920, at * 13.

349 *Ohio v. United States Dep't of Interior*, 880 F.2d 432, 470–472 (D.C. Cir. 1989); *Coeur d'Alene Tribe v. Asarco, Inc.* 280 F.Supp. 2d 1094, 1124 (S.D. Idaho 2003); *N.J. Dep't of Envtl. Prot. V. Dimant*, No A-3180-09T2, at *19 (N.J. Super. Ct. App. Div. Mar. 18, 2011).

350 *Idaho v. Southern Refrigerated Transport, Inc.*, 1991 U.S. Dist. LEXIS 1869 (D. Idaho Jan. 24, 1991) (natural resource damages must be proved by preponderance of the evidence).

351 *United States v. Montrose Chem. Corp. of California*, 1991 U.S. Dist. LEXIS 10128 (C.D. Cal. 1991); *Commissioner of the Dept. of Planning & Natural Resources v. Century Alumina Co.*, D.V.I. No. 05-62 (D.V.I., November 30, 2011) (failure of the Virgin Islands environment department to establish an aluminum company's liability as a parent corporation in a Superfund cost recovery case bars its nature resource damage claim against the same defendant).

352 *Id.*

353 *In re Acushnet River & New Bedford Harbor: Proceedings re Alleged PCB Pollution*, 716 F. Supp. 676, 686 (D. Mass. 1989).

354 *See* H.R. Rep. No. 253, 99th Cong., 1st Sess., pt. 3, 19, *reprinted in* 1986 U.S. Code Cong. & Admin. News 3038, 3042.

355 42 U.S.C. § 9613(f)(1).

356 *E.g., United States v. Bell Petroleum Serv.*, 1989 U.S. Dist. LEXIS 16238 (W.D. Tex. Nov. 9, 1989).

357 *Cooper Industries, Inc. v. Aviall Services, Inc.*, 157 U.S. 157 (2004), 125 S. Ct. 577, 2004 U.S. Lexis 8271.

358 42 U.S.C. § 9613(f)(2).

359 *See Akzo Coatings v. Aigner Corp.*, 30 F.3d 761 (7th Cir. 1994); *Advanced Technology Corp. v. Eliskim, Inc.*, 96 F. Supp. 2d 715 (N.D. Ohio 2000) (contribution protection extends only to future claims unless consent decree unambiguously included past claims).

360 *Metro Water Reclamation Dist. v. North Am. Galvanizing & Coatings, Inc.*, 473 F.3d 824 (7th Cir. 2007); *Atl. Research Corp. v. United States*, 459 F.3d 827 (8th Cir. 2006) *reversing Dico, Inc. v. Amoco Oil Co.*, 340 F.3d 525 (8th Cir. 2003); *Consol. Edison Co. of N.Y. v. UGI Util., Inc.*, 423 F.3d 90 (2d Cir. 2005).

361 *United States v. Atl. Research Corp.*, 551 U.S. 128, 127 S. Ct. 2331 (2007).

362 *Id.* at 2336.

363 *Bernstein v. Bankert*, Nos. 11-1501, 11-1523, 2012 WL 6601218 (7th Cir., Dec. 19, 2012) (parties performing cleanup work under an administrative order on consent were not limited to a contribution claim under 113); *Emhart Industries Inc. v. United States, D.R.I.*, No. 11-023 (Dist. R.I., October 31, 2011) (citing *Atlantic Research* and holding that a party that has entered into an administrative settlement with EPA can pursue a Section 107(a) cost-recovery action against the federal government). But see *Solutia, Inc. v. McWane, Inc.*, 672 F.3d 1230, 1236-37 (11th Cir. 2012) (per curiam) (no section 107 cost recovery claim was available to private parties carrying out cleanup work pursuant to a consent decree with the United States where the defendants to the 107 action had also entered into a settlement with EPA barring contribution claims under 113(f)(2)); *Morrison Enterprises LLC v. Dravo Corp.*, No. 10-1468, No. 10-1469 (8th Cir. April 5, 2011) (Section 113(f) is the sole remedy for a liable party that had incurred response costs pursuant to an administrative or judicially approved settlement under Section 107).

364 42 U.S.C. § 9622(a).

365 42 U.S.C. § 9622(e).

366 50 Fed. Reg. 5034 (1985).

367 52 Fed. Reg. 28038 (1987).

368 57 Fed. Reg. 29313 (June 2, 1992); U.S. EPA, Streamlined Approach for Settlement with De Minimis Waste Contributors under CERCLA Section 122(g)(1)(A), OSWER Directive No. 9834.7-1D (July 30, 1993).

369 U.S. EPA, Office of Enforcement and Compliance Monitoring, *Guidance on the Use of Stipulated Penalties in Hazardous Waste Consent Decrees*, OSWER Directive No. 9835.2b (1987) at http://www.epa.gov/compliance/resources/policies/cleanup/superfund/stip-hazwst-mem.pdf.

370 53 Fed. Reg. 8279 (1988).

371 42 U.S.C. § 9622(h)(1).

372 42 U.S.C. § 9622(d)(2)(a).

373 42 U.S.C. § 9622(d)(2)(b).

374 *United States v. Aerojet Gen. Corp.*, 2010 WL 2179169 (9th Cir. June 2, 2010); *United States v. Albert Inv. Co.*, 585 F.3d 1386 (10th Cir. 2009); *United States v. Union Elec. Co.*, 64 F.3d 1152 (8th Cir. 1995). *But see United States v. Alcan Aluminum, Inc.*, 25 F.3d 1174, 1184 (3d Cir. 1994).

375 *Aerojet*, 2010 WL 2179169, at 4.

376 *Id.* at 4-5.

377 *See* U.S. EPA, Revised Model Administrative Order on Consent for CERCLA Remedial Investigation/Feasibility Study at http://www.epa.gov/compliance/resources/policies/cleanup/superfund/rev-aoc-rifs-mod-04-mem.pdf, OSWER Directive No. 9835.3-1A (Jan. 30, 1990); U.S. EPA, Superfund Program, "Model CERCLA RD/RA Consent Decree," 56 Fed. Reg. 30996–31012 (July 8, 1991).

378 *See* U.S. EPA, Interim Guidance on Orphan Share Compensation for Settlors of Remedial Design/Remedial Action and Non-Time-Critical Removals (June 3, 1993). http://www.epa.gov/compliance/resources/policies/cleanup/superfund/orphan-share-rpt.pdf.

379 *See* 53 Fed. Reg. 8279 (1988).

380 EPA has offered $235 million in orphan share compensation at 160 sites across the nation as of September 30, 2003. U.S. EPA, Superfund Reforms Overview Mid-year FY 2004, at http://www.epa.gov/superfund/programs/reforms/docs/reforms_overview04.pdf.

381 42 U.S.C. § 9622(g)(1).

382 EPA has completed 530 de minimis settlements with 28,000 small waste contributors at numerous CERCLA sites over the years. U.S. EPA, Superfund Reforms Overview Mid-year FY 2004, at http://www.epa.gov/superfund/programs/reforms/_overview04.pdf.

383 *United States v. George A. Whiting Paper Co.*; No. 10-2480 (7th Cir. May 4, 2011) (de minimis settlement allowed over objection of intervening PRPs).

384 U.S. EPA, Superfund Facts FAQ: Superfund Enforcement at http://www.epa.gov/compliance/resources/faqs/cleanup/superfund/enf-faqs.htmlgetdone/settlements.html (last updated Nov. 12, 2008).

385 Small Business Liability Act, H.R. 2869, 107th Cong. (2001); 42 U.S.C. § 9607(o).

386 *Id.*

387 *Id.*

388 U.S. EPA, memorandum, "Revised Settlement Policy and Contribution Waiver Language Regarding Exempt De Micromis and Non-Exempt De Micromis Parties" (Nov. 6, 2002). http://www.epa.gov.compliance/resources/policies/cleanup/superfund/wv-exmpt-dmicro-mem.pdf.

389 *See, e.g., United States v. Keystone Sanitation Co., Inc.*, No. 1: CV-93-1482 (M.D. Pa. Sept. 10, 1999).

390 42 U.S.C. § 9622(f)(6).

391 42 U.S.C. § 9622(f)(2).

392 *Guidance on the Use of Stipulated Penalties in Hazardous Waste Consent Decrees* (1987).

393 *See supra* section 2.4 for definition of environment.

394 40 C.F.R. § 302, updated at 67 Fed. Reg. 45134 (July 9, 2002) (codified at 40 C.F.R. § 302).

395 40 C.F.R. § 302.5(b).

396 42 U.S.C. § 9603(b).

397 42 U.S.C. § 9609(b), (c).

398 42 U.S.C. § 9603(e).

399 42 U.S.C. § 9603(a).

400 42 U.S.C. § 9603(f)(1).

401 42 U.S.C. § 9603(f)(2).

402 42 U.S.C. § 9620(a).

403 42 U.S.C. § 9659(a).

404 42 U.S.C. § 9620(a).

405 42 U.S.C. § 9620(c), (d), (e).

406 U.S. EPA, *EPA Removes Love Canal from Superfund List* at http://www.epa.gov/superfund/news/lovecanal.htm (Sept. 30, 2004).

407 U.S. EPA, *Superfund National Accomplishments Summary Fiscal Year 2012.*

408 *FY 2013 EPA Budget in Brief,* at 70 (Feb. 2012).

Chapter 10

National Environmental Policy Act

James W. Spensley
Spensley & Associates
Denver, Colorado

1.0 Overview

The National Environmental Policy Act of 1969 (NEPA)[1] has been heralded as the Magna Carta of the country's environmental movement. It was signed into law on January 1, 1970, to address the need for a national environmental policy to guide the growing environmental consciousness and to shape a national response.

NEPA contains three important elements:

1. The declaration of national environmental policies and goals.

2. The establishment of action-forcing provisions for federal agencies to implement those policies and goals.

3. The establishment of a Council on Environmental Quality (CEQ) in the executive office of the president.

The essential purpose of NEPA is to ensure that environmental factors are given the same consideration as other factors in decision-making by the federal agencies. The effectiveness of NEPA has stemmed from its environmental impact statement (EIS) requirement that federal agencies must consider the environmental effects of, and any alternatives to, all proposals for major federal actions that significantly affect the quality of the human environment.

Although CEQ published early guidelines for federal agencies to implement NEPA, it was the federal courts in the early 1970s that had the most influence on shaping NEPA's action-forcing provision, section 102(2)(C).[2] Because this provision was virtually ignored during its legislative formulation, judicial interpretations established the basic definitions for section 102(2)(C) concerning who must comply with NEPA, what level of federal involvement triggers an EIS, what constitutes a major action that significantly affects the environment, and other fundamental issues. This EIS requirement has become the heart of NEPA and has had a profound impact on federal agency decision-making.

During this early period, the threat of litigation over the EIS requirement caused many federal agencies to overreact by including in their statements every possible environmental reference that could be found. This resulted in lengthy EISs that neither decision-makers nor the public would read. Today, CEQ regulations emphasize the need to reduce excessive paperwork and focus on the essential information that is needed by decision-makers and the public. NEPA's emphasis and importance have evolved from a procedural lever used by project opponents to stop or delay proposed federal projects to a more comprehensive framework for documenting and integrating essential environmental information into the federal decision-making process.

The current trend in NEPA compliance has focused on the use of an environmental assessment (EA) to conduct a threshold analysis of whether a full EIS is required. CEQ is placing new emphasis on the use of the EA in order to avoid extensive and duplicative documentation while more effectively integrating key environmental factors in the federal decision-making process and opening up the process to outside parties.[3]

2.0 NEPA's Development

NEPA was enacted at a time when the Congress heard testimony from many quarters of society warning of impending environmental degradation and even disaster.[4] Members of the Congress competed for the popular leadership of this new environmental movement. More than 2,000 legislative proposals having a bearing on environmental matters were introduced into the 91st Congress that preceded NEPA.[5] Few congressional members understood or expected that this brief, idealistic NEPA statute would be so successful in reforming federal agency decision-making and bringing the public into the process.

2.1 Legislative History

The legislative formulation of NEPA principles began years before the statute was enacted.[6] In 1959, Senator James E. Murray (D-Montana) attempted to legislate a national environmental policy when he introduced the Resources and Conservation Act of 1960, which included the creation of a high-level council of environmental advisers.[7] However, it was not until the late 1960s that Senator Henry Jackson (D-Washington) and Congressman John Dingell (D-Michigan) collaborated to enact the present statute. Early versions of the legislation contained neither policy and goals nor an action-forcing provision. It was not until the legislation had passed both houses of Congress and been amended by a House-Senate Conference Committee that the present policy and reporting provisions were included. Although the legislative history is unclear in many respects, Senator Jackson clearly felt that it was the federal government's failures and unresponsiveness that had led to much of the country's environmental degradation. "The most important feature of the act," according to Senator Jackson, "is that it establishes new decision-making procedures for all agencies of the federal government."[8]

2.2 Policy and Goals

NEPA's policies are broad and general and its goals lofty. Indeed, section 101 of the act was written as if to inspire rather than to regulate. It emphasizes the need to recognize "the profound impact of man's activity on the interrelations of all components of the natural environment"[9] and to recognize that "each person should enjoy a healthful environment . . . and to contribute to the preservation and enhancement of the environment."[10] It recognizes the balancing of trade-offs that must occur in the decision-making process by promoting the "use [of] all practicable means and measures . . . [to] fulfill the social, economic, and other requirements of present and future generations of Americans."[11] It goes on to recognize six more specific goals as a guide to the federal government to implement this new policy.[12]

2.3 Council on Environmental Quality

The Council on Environmental Quality (CEQ) was created by Title II of NEPA[13] and modeled after the Council of Economic Advisors created by the Employment Act of 1946.[14] The CEQ was placed in the executive office of the president and composed of three members appointed by the president and confirmed by the Senate. Under the statute, CEQ is to assist and advise the president in the preparation of an annual environmental quality report on the progress of federal agencies in implementing the act, on national policies to foster and promote the improvement of environmental quality, and on the state of the environment. Shortly after signing NEPA into law, President Nixon expanded CEQ's mandate by Executive Order No. 11514, directing it to issue guidelines to federal agencies for the preparation of EISs and to coordinate federal programs related to environmental quality.[15]

This executive order further directed federal agencies to develop procedures to ensure timely dissemination of public information concerning federal plans and programs with environmental impacts in order to obtain the views of all interested parties. This public participation mandate, combined with the disclosure requirements of NEPA, has in large part been responsible for the significant and lasting effectiveness of NEPA.

CEQ has played a central role in the development of the EIS process. Its first guidelines were issued in April 1971 and required each department and agency of the federal government to adopt its own guidelines consistent with those from CEQ.[16] Although the guidelines did not have the status of formal agency regulations, the courts often recognized them with considerable deference.[17] Subsequently, President Carter, by Executive Order 11991, authorized CEQ to adopt regulations rather than guidelines on EIS preparation.[18] In 1978, CEQ adopted regulations that reflected its earlier guidelines and the numerous court decisions that had created NEPA's early common law.[19]

CEQ has no authority to enforce its regulations. However, it has played a major role in advising agencies on compliance matters. Federal agencies have not availed themselves of CEQ's advice as often as they should to avoid problems and litigation.

3.0 Requirements for Federal Agencies

The requirements of NEPA are mandatory for federal agencies and over the years have been a major force in reforming agency decision-making processes. NEPA contains largely "procedural" requirements that are supplemental to existing statutory responsibilities of the federal agencies.[20] In *Calvert Cliffs' Coordinating Comm. Inc. v. United States Atomic Energy Comm'n*,[21] Judge Skelly Wright, writing for the court, notes:

> NEPA, first of all, makes environmental protection a part of the mandate of every federal agency and department. . . . It [the agency] is not only permitted, but compelled, to take environmental values into account. Perhaps the greatest importance of NEPA is to require . . . agencies to consider environmental issues just as they consider other matters within their mandates.[22]

Although NEPA's provisions apply only to federal agencies, the pervasiveness of federal decisions affecting state and local matters as well as private actions makes NEPA an issue for many. An applicant should have a direct interest in the successful completion of an agency's EIS so as to avoid potentially time-consuming and expensive litigation. Moreover, agencies increasingly are finding ways to shift the costs of NEPA compliance to those requesting some federal action or decision.[23] Therefore, an applicant will want to ensure that the environmental studies and documents are prepared in a cost-effective manner and in accordance with the procedural requirements of NEPA.

The only agency that the courts have recognized as having a limited exemption from NEPA is the Environmental Protection Agency (EPA). Although there is no reference to an exemption for EPA in the statute, EPA has argued that it should be exempt for the reason that it has statutory responsibility for protection of the environment. Some legislation has specifically exempted EPA from NEPA compliance. Under the Energy Supply and Environmental Coordination Act of 1974, an exemption is provided to EPA for its actions under the Clean Air Act.[24] Similarly, under the Clean Water Act, EPA is exempted from the obligation to prepare an EIS on some actions such as discharge permits for existing sources of water pollution.[25] Other EPA nonregulatory actions require NEPA compliance, such as the issuance of construction grants for water treatment facilities.

3.1 CEQ Regulations

The CEQ regulations begin by calling for agencies to integrate NEPA requirements with other planning requirements at the earliest possible time to ensure that plans and decisions reflect environmental values, avoid delays later in the process, and head off potential conflicts.[26] Agencies are to use a "systematic, interdisciplinary approach" as required by section 102(2)(A) and to study and develop appropriate alternatives to recommended courses of action for unresolved conflicts in the use of available resources as provided in section 102(2)(E).[27]

NEPA's action-forcing provision, section 102(2)(C), requires that an EIS shall be "include[d] in every recommendation or report on proposals for legislation and other major Federal actions significantly affecting the quality of the human environment."[28] The key terms in this statement are defined in the CEQ regulations and have been the most judicially interpreted words of NEPA.

CEQ states its intention that judicial review of agency compliance with these regulations should not occur before an agency has filed a final EIS or has made an appropriate finding of no significant impact, or takes action that will result in irreparable injury.[29] Furthermore, CEQ suggests that a trivial violation of these regulations should not give rise to an independent cause of action.

The regulations require each agency to adopt procedures consistent with these regulations for implementing NEPA's provisions. Specifically, the agencies are to identify typical classes of action

1. which normally require an EIS;

2. which normally do not require either an EIS or an environmental assessment (categorical exclusions [§ 1508.4]); and

3. which normally require environmental assessments but not necessarily an EIS.[30]

Agency procedures may provide specific criteria for limited exceptions to classified proposals.[31]

The first question is whether a federal agency must prepare an EIS. As noted earlier, each of the key words in section 102(2)(C) has been the subject of judicial interpretation in answering that question. Is there an agency proposal for an action? Is the action federal? Is it major? Is it significant? Does the action affect the human environment? The CEQ regulations define each of these statutory terms.[32]

The EIS requirement is not triggered unless there is a proposal for action by a federal agency.[33] Because agencies are constantly involved in planning and program formulation, it is not always easy to determine when a proposal has been made. If a proposal is made too early in the planning process, it will contain insufficient information to provide the necessary environmental disclosure.[34] On the other hand, if the agency prepares an EIS too late in the planning process, it becomes simply a post hoc justification for a decision already made. The regulations have addressed this timing question by defining the term proposal as that which

exists at the stage in the development of an action when an agency subject to the Act has a goal and is actively preparing to make a decision on one or more alternative means of accomplishing that goal and the effects can be meaningfully evaluated. Preparation of an environmental impact statement on a proposal should be timed (§ 1502.5) so that the final statement may be completed in time . . . to be included in any recommendation or report on the proposal.[35]

If there is a proposal, it must be a federal proposal in order for an EIS to be required. Clearly policies, plans, programs, and projects proposed by federal agencies meet this definition.[36] CEQ regulations also address actions with effects that may be major and which are potentially subject to federal control and responsibility.[37] Further, private, state, and local actions which have sufficient federal involvement may also require an EIS. Such nonfederal actions that are regulated, licensed, permitted, or approved by federal agencies generally are considered federal for NEPA purposes.[38] The need for federal permits, licenses, and other approvals from a federal agency program are examples in which seemingly nonfederal actions have triggered NEPA compliance.

Federal assistance to a nonfederal project or action may also trigger NEPA. The primary determinant in these cases is the extent to which the federal control is or may be exercised. Generally, there have been three forms of federal assistance: categorical grants, block grants, and some form of revenue sharing. Federal categorical grants to nonfederal projects usually require NEPA compliance. Block grants and revenue-sharing arrangements are typically exempt from NEPA when there is limited federal involvement in these programs.[39]

On the other hand, there are two situations that generally will not constitute major federal actions under NEPA. The first situation is governmental inaction, where that failure to act is not otherwise subject to review by the courts or administrative agencies under the Administrative Procedure Act or other laws.[40] The second situation is mere approval by the federal government of action by a private party where that approval is not required for the private party to go forward.[41] Most circuits have focused on the indicia of control over the private actors by the federal agency.

There are two other key words that require definition in the threshold determination of NEPA application—one must determine whether the federal action is major and significantly affects the quality of the human environment. These two terms have been the subject of considerable judicial discussion without establishing a universally accepted definition. CEQ regulations provide that the term major reinforces but does not have a meaning independent of the term significantly.[42] Agencies have defined major actions in their program-specific regulations. CEQ regulations have attempted to define significantly by suggesting consideration of both the context and the intensity of the specific circumstances.[43] The context refers to the surrounding circumstances where the action is proposed and its impact upon society as a whole, the affected region, the affected interests, and the locality. The term intensity refers to the severity of the impact. The regulations refer to a list of considerations which an agency should take into account when weighing the significance of the impacts.[44]

The last key term is quality of the human environment. At the time Congress enacted NEPA, primary attention was focused on improving and preserving the natural environment as reflected in the policies and goals section of NEPA. However, this phrase has been given broad definition.[45] In *Hanly v. Mitchell,*[46] where the plaintiffs were concerned about a detention center planned for downtown Manhattan, the court recognized that NEPA applied to protection of the urban quality of life as well. Although other cases have supported this broad definition of impacts upon the human environment, at least one case has concluded that "pure economic impacts" without other accompanying physical impacts do not trigger NEPA's application.[47] In one case, aesthetic impacts on the urban environment were sufficient to trigger a NEPA review.[48] The CEQ regulations advise that economic and social effects are not intended by themselves to require preparation of an EIS, but when they are interrelated with natural or physical environmental effects, then they must be discussed.[49]

3.2 Relationship to Other Federal Laws

NEPA is a policy and procedural statute that has been interpreted by the courts to make environmental protection a part of the mandate of every federal agency and department.[50] The court in *Calvert Cliffs* cites Senator Jackson, NEPA's principal sponsor, as stating that "no agency will be able to maintain that it has no mandate or no requirement to consider the environmental consequences of its actions."[51] Further, the court interpreted the congressional intent of NEPA to indicate that environmental factors must be considered throughout agency review processes. It went on to underscore the act's requirement that environmental consideration be given "to the fullest extent possible," finding that this language set a high standard for agencies to meet.

Courts have also recognized that, in some limited circumstances, federal actions may be wholly or partially exempt from compliance with NEPA due to statutory conflicts. These conflicts may arise from explicit statutory exemptions as well as implied conflicts. As noted previously, EPA has been expressly exempted from NEPA compliance for all of its actions under the Clean Air Act and specific actions under the Clean Water Act.[52] Congress has also expressly exempted specific agency projects or programs from NEPA compliance, such as the Alaska Pipeline.[53]

A more controversial situation arises where NEPA is determined to be inapplicable because of agency statutory duties that preclude compliance with NEPA's procedural requirements. In *Flint Ridge Dev. Co. v. Scenic Rivers Ass'n of Oklahoma*,[54] the Supreme Court held that an agency's specific statutory directive to review a matter within 30 days was mandatory and that compliance with NEPA would frustrate this legislative directive. However, the Court did not relieve the agency of all NEPA duties under this conflicting legislation. It specifically noted that the agency had the authority and obligation to require additional environmental information and to consider environmental factors in its decision-making process.

The courts have recognized a closely related situation when an agency is not given discretion in making a decision. In *Atlanta Coalition on Transpor. Crisis, Inc. v. Atlanta Regional Comm'n*,[55] the U.S. Department of Transportation had made an interpretation of a federal law that it was required to adopt under the relevant statutes, and the court held that the agency decisions which "do not entail the exercise of significant discretion" do not require an EIS. Other circuits have also held that when an agency has no discretion to consider environmental values implementing a statutory requirement, its actions are ministerial and not subject to NEPA.[56]

Some federal agencies have claimed an implied exemption from NEPA for actions taken under the cloak of national security or national defense. Although such an implied exemption has not been recognized, the Supreme Court has upheld a Freedom of Information Act exception to disclosure in the EIS process.[57] The Court specifically noted that public disclosure under NEPA is governed by the Freedom of Information Act while agencies must prepare NEPA documentation even for classified proposals. Agencies may include specific criteria for providing limited exceptions to the disclosure provisions of the CEQ regulations for classified proposals.[58]

Perhaps the most important relationship of NEPA to other environmental laws is the role the EIS plays as the public repository of the combined environmental assessment of all applicable environmental laws. Most agency regulations require the EIS to identify and discuss possible violations of the standards established by other more substantive environmental statutes.

3.3 Functional Equivalency

The courts have been asked, in several cases, to determine whether compliance with other environmental laws which require environmental analyses similar to NEPA constitutes the functional equivalent of the NEPA process. In a few cases, the courts have recognized such an exception to NEPA compliance for the EPA only.

For a court to apply the functional equivalency exception, it must find that the statute creating the agency, as well as the specific statute being applied, together provide sufficient substantive and procedural standards to ensure a full and adequate consideration of all pertinent environmental issues by the agency.[59] The key is the consideration of the issues by the agency; thus courts have rejected arguments for applying the exception where the environmental consequences of the actions were, or were not, considered by agency outsiders.

The functional equivalency exception is "not . . . a broad exemption from NEPA for all environmental agencies or even for all environmentally protective regulatory actions of such agencies. Instead, [it is] a narrow exemption from the literal requirements for those actions which are undertaken pursuant to sufficient safeguards so that the purpose and policies behind NEPA will necessarily be fulfilled."[60]

Courts have held that the functional equivalency exception to NEPA has been met with respect to EPA actions under the Clean Air Act,[61] the Federal Insecticide, Fungicide and Rodenticide Act,[62] the Resource Conservation and Recovery Act,[63] the Toxic Substances Control Act,[64] the Safe Drinking Water Act,[65] and the Ocean Dumping Act.[66] Courts have not yet addressed whether EPA Superfund cleanup actions under the Comprehensive Environmental Response, Compensation and Liability Act (CERCLA) fall within the functional equivalency exception.

One of the primary arguments against applying the exception to CERCLA is that often the agency which caused the contamination is the one which is cleaning it up, albeit under EPA supervision. In such a case, the agency with primary responsibility does not have the mandate in its organic statute to protect the environment. Indeed, courts have not yet applied the exception to agencies other than EPA, even where the agency arguably has substantial environmental responsibilities,[67] and have rejected arguments to extend the exception to actions by the Forest Service,[68] the National Marine Fisheries Service,[69] the National Institutes of Health,[70] and the Bureau of Land Management,[71] among others.

However, it has been suggested that NEPA procedures could be easily melded with the early remedial investigation and feasibility study (RI/FS) required by CERCLA,[72] perhaps, in view of the importance CERCLA places on prompt remedial actions, by using the expedited process allowed by NEPA in cases of emergency.[73] Indeed, this is the approach taken by the Department of Energy, which has decided to prepare a programmatic EIS to address the agency-wide implications of its CERCLA cleanup efforts, which can be tiered to sitewide EISs which analyze the environmental impacts of treatment, storage, and disposal facilities and the cumulative impacts of DOE cleanup actions.[74] NEPA compliance for individual DOE/CERCLA projects will be accomplished through the use of categorical exclusions or EA/FONSIs[75] (FONSI: finding of no significant impact) drafted during the RI/FS process.[76]

4.0 Strategic Approaches to NEPA Compliance

The strategy for successful compliance with NEPA's provisions is achieved by integrating environmental awareness and environmental factors early in the planning and decision-making process. Recognizing that NEPA is largely a procedural statute, compliance with its provisions calls for planning and analysis which fully considers and documents on a timely basis the environmental considerations and alternatives to the proposed action. Sound environmental planning provides opportunities for the federal agency to design proposals early in the process that meet both the agency's programmatic and environmental objectives and help ensure successful NEPA compliance.

4.1 Nonmajor Actions (Categorical Exclusions)

The first step in planning for an agency proposal or private action is to determine whether that proposal or action will be subject to NEPA documentation. Agency regulations developed in accordance with CEQ directives should assist in defining the kind of NEPA documentation required. The least amount of documentation is required for actions that fit into a categorical exclusion. A categorical exclusion, sometimes referred to as a "CatEx," "CE," or "CX," is an agency-identified category of actions which "do not individually or cumulatively have a significant effect on the human environment" and which have been found to have had no such effect in past instances.[77] Proposals or actions that fit these exclusion categories do not require an EA, an EIS, or other extensive documentation unless unique circumstances create the possibility those significant impacts could occur. However, a categorical exclusion is not an exemption from compliance with NEPA but merely an administrative tool to avoid paperwork for those actions without significant environmental effects.[78]

Ninety to ninety-five percent of most federal agency actions are classified as categorical exclusions not requiring an EA or EIS. As mentioned earlier, CEQ regulations require that every federal agency adopt procedures to implement those actions which normally do not require either an environmental impact statement or an environmental assessment.[79] Many federal agencies use three classifications of category exclusions for proposed actions: (1) those actions that are specifically listed in the federal agency's NEPA implementing regulations as exclusions requiring little or no documentation or federal approval if determined by a state agency; (2) those actions that are not listed but still qualify for an exclusion and need documentation and federal approval; and (3) those actions that would otherwise qualify as categorical exclusions but involve some unique circumstances requiring some study and analysis to ensure that they do not involve significant impacts and federal approval.[80]

Typically, unique circumstances might include an action where there is substantial controversy on environmental grounds or inconsistencies with any federal, state, or local law, requirement, or administrative determination relating to the environmental aspects of the action.

If a nonfederal action has some minor federal involvement, a court may determine that the federal action is a minor action not subject to NEPA. To be subject to NEPA, the action must be one over which the federal agency has sufficient discretion and control to make NEPA application meaningful.[81] This "small handle" problem is addressed in some cases by having the federal agency prepare a NEPA analysis on those portions of the project over which it has "sufficient control and responsibility" in lieu of federalizing the entire project.[82] Some courts have found insufficient federal control or approval when it is marginal to the project.[83]

4.2 Formulating the Proposal

It is important in the early planning stages to clearly define the need to be addressed by the proposed action. The definition of need is often closely aligned with the definition of the required no-action alternative which must be discussed in the EIS. If the need is ill-defined or vague, the proposed action and any alternatives may also suffer and will likely be difficult to assess. This result may weaken the proposal and increase its vulnerability to a potential challenge in the EIS process.

If early scoping and consultation with affected parties is accomplished, a notion of the environmental concerns will be known. To the extent that the proposed action can be designed or formulated to incorporate mitigation measures which address these concerns, it is more likely that the proposed action will have a sound footing for acceptance and will avoid significant impacts. This fulfills NEPA's intent.

In formulating the proposed action, the agency must be careful to include all of the actions related to the proposed action that constitutes the proposal.[84] The problem of segmentation or piece-mealing has arisen in projects which involve various stages of development or where agencies have attempted in the past to avoid major actions by splitting up a proposed action. The proposed action must include all of these connected actions as part of the proposal. CEQ provides guidance in the definition of the scope of the EIS on such connected actions which are closely related and should be considered together in a single EIS.[85] The regulations state the following points:

Actions are connected if they

1. automatically trigger other actions which may require EISs;

2. cannot or will not proceed unless other actions are taken previously or simultaneously;

3. are interdependent parts of a larger action and depend on the larger action for their justification.[86]

For example, in highway cases, where this issue originally arose,[87] a project planned between two points may involve the construction of several highway segments over time. Under the Federal Highway Administration NEPA regulations, in order to avoid segmentation, a project must (1) connect logical termini, (2) have independent utility or independent significance, and (3) not restrict future transportation improvement alternatives.[88]

4.3 Purpose and Need

Closely aligned with the formulation of the proposal is the statement of the "purpose and need" for that proposal. The "purpose and need" statement provides the basis for defining the proper scope of the project, identifying "reasonable alternatives" to consider, and selecting the criteria used to evaluate the alternative choices. It may also manifest the community's desires for action and thereby justify the agency's proposal.

The U.S. Environmental Protection Agency and other resource agencies have been critical of NEPA documents for not providing sufficient justification or explanation for the proposed action. In 2003, the CEQ chairman provided some guidance to the secretary of transportation on the preparation of a "purpose and need" statement.[89] In his letter, Chairman Connaughton cites the CEQ regulations that state the purpose and need is to "briefly specify the underlying purpose and need to which the agency is responding in proposing alternatives including the proposed action."[90] He further clarifies that this discussion is typically one or two paragraphs long and provides an important general context, understanding, and framework in which "reasonable alternatives" to the proposed action will be identified.

Chairman Connaughton also notes that the lead agency—the federal agency proposing to take the action—has the authority and responsibility to define the purpose and need for purposes of NEPA analysis which is consistent with its overall responsibilities for the "scope, objectivity, and content of the entire statement or of any other responsibility" under NEPA.[91]

Although federal courts generally have been deferential in their review of a lead agency's "purpose and need" statements, absent a finding that an agency acted in an arbitrary or capricious manner, courts have cautioned agencies not to put forward a purpose and need statement that is so narrow as to define competing "reasonable alternatives" out of consideration (and even out of existence).[92] In one case, the Bureau of Land Management had adopted as its own the purposes of a developer which had requested a land use exchange with the agency.[93] The court held that the statement of purpose and need was so narrow that it foreordained approval of the exchange.

Several agencies, such as the Federal Highway Administration and Federal Transit Administration, have provided further guidance on "purpose and need" formulations for state departments of transportation, local transit agencies, and other joint lead agencies involved in preparation or review of NEPA documents.[94]

The purpose and need statement should be as quantitative as possible to facilitate the evaluation of alternatives in the NEPA document. Further, it should be as concise and understandable as possible. Relevant information on factors considered during the metropolitan or statewide planning process[95] should be included or incorporated by reference, as appropriate. As noted below, this helps to integrate the long-range planning performed with the specific NEPA actions proposed to implement that planning.

4.4 Integrating Long-Range Planning and NEPA

The preparation of NEPA documents should consider incorporating the applicable long-range planning decisions made by local, state, and regional bodies as they relate to the "purpose and need" for agency actions. By so doing, the project-level NEPA document may not need to reproduce the consideration of alternatives earlier evaluated and discarded during the long-range planning processes. For example, in the transportation planning process, the Congress has mandated procedures for developing long-range transportation plans and shorter range transportation improvement programs.[96] In order to be eligible for federal funding, projects must come from this process. NEPA and the government-wide regulations that implement NEPA clearly contemplate the integration of the NEPA process with planning processes.[97]

Several court cases have challenged the use of planning studies and decisions that limit the scope of reasonable alternatives in the NEPA project-level document.[98] Recent guidance from the Chief Counsels of FHWA and FTA has addressed this issue by stating that studies, analyses, or conclusions from the transportation planning process to be incorporated into the NEPA process must meet certain standards established by NEPA.[99] Those standards for a planning process include a transportation planning process that has (1) complied with current transportation planning requirements (e.g., provided an opportunity for public involvement and considered relevant planning factors); (2) involved state and federal agencies with an opportunity to comment upon the long-range transportation plan and improvement program; and (3) documented the products from the process that were made available for public review during the planning process.

4.5 Tiering

There are various levels in the planning and decision-making process where an EIS may be required. Federal decisions made at the national level among competing programmatic alternatives and policies which affect the entire federal effort may require the preparation of a programmatic EIS (PEIS). Proposals for federal actions may also be made at a regional level, requiring an EIS which is focused on regional considerations and which must be more specific than the national PEIS. Finally, a proposed project at a specific site may require an EIS more detailed than the regional EIS or national PEIS.

Tiering is an approach whereby the very site-specific project EIS can incorporate by reference and without repetition the broader considerations of a regionwide EIS, or even a national PEIS, if they are relevant. CEQ regulations note that tiering is appropriate when the sequence of EISs is from a program, plan, or policy EIS to a site-specific statement or from an EIS on a specific action at an early stage (such as a need and site selection) to a subsequent statement at a later stage. Tiering in such cases is appropriate when it helps the responsible federal agency focus on the issues which are ripe for discussion and exclude from consideration issues already decided or not yet ripe.[100]

An example is the Federal Aviation Administration (FAA), which might prepare a programmatic EIS on its nationwide systems airport plan to evaluate choices and alternatives to providing national aviation services. On a regional or statewide basis, the FAA may focus on providing air service improvements within that region, using a regionwide or statewide EIS. Finally, for a specific airport proposal, a project EIS would be developed which could incorporate by reference any relevant information from the regionwide or statewide EIS, or information from the nationwide PEIS.

Tiering is a useful tool when new federal programs are initiated which must later be delegated to regional programs and finally become site-specific activities. Tiering can be used in the NEPA compliance process to avoid duplication and provide the appropriate detail required for the level of action under consideration. Using the tiered system, a project-specific EA or EIS need only focus on potential environmental impacts of the project that are not covered by earlier, broader statements.

4.6 Environmental Assessments

An environmental assessment (EA) is used as a screening document to determine whether an agency must prepare an EIS or make a finding of no significant impact (FONSI). CEQ regulations describe an EA as a concise public document that also serves to aid an agency's compliance with NEPA when no EIS is necessary, and to facilitate preparation of an EIS when one is necessary.[101] An EA should include a brief discussion of the need for the proposal; of alternatives, as required by section 102(2)(E); of the environmental impacts of the proposed action and alternatives; and a listing of agencies and persons consulted.

Although most agency procedures do not require public involvement prior to finalizing an EA document, it is advisable for agencies to consider facilitating public comment at the draft EA stage. Early public input will help the agency prepare a final EA which addresses adequately and completely the environmental issues likely to be raised by opponents of an agency action. Moreover, it will assist the agency in preparing the FONSI, which becomes the record for review by a court if challenged.

A FONSI briefly presents the reasons why an action, not otherwise categorically excluded, will not have a significant effect on the human environment. It must include the EA or a summary of the EA in supporting the FONSI determination.[102] Although EAs and FONSIs are public documents, they are not filed in a central location like EISs.

CEQ regulations require that, in certain limited circumstances, the agency must make the FONSI determination available for public review by some means, including state and area-wide clearinghouses, for 30 days before the agency makes its final determination of whether to prepare an EIS, and before any action may begin.[103] Those circumstances are as follows:

- The proposed action is, or is closely similar to, one which normally requires the preparation of an EIS under the procedures adopted by the agency.

- The nature of the proposed action is one without precedent.

EAs need to be of sufficient length to ensure that the underlying decision about whether to prepare an EIS is sound, but it should not attempt to be a substitute for an EIS.[104] A thorough EA provides a good information base early in the process for both agency and public consideration.

5.0 EIS Preparation

If it is determined that a proposed federal action, or nonfederal action having sufficient federal involvement, does not fall within a designated categorical exclusion or does not qualify for a FONSI, then the responsible federal agency or agencies must prepare an EIS.

5.1 Lead Agency

The proposed action may be one where several agencies have some responsibility and all must comply with NEPA. CEQ regulations provide for a lead agency to take primary responsibility for the preparation of the EIS and to supervise the process.[105] Other agencies which have a responsibility by law for the joint action then become cooperating agencies.[106] If a disagreement should arise among the agencies as to who should be the lead, CEQ regulations provide guidance based upon the magnitude of the agency's involvement; its project approval authority, expertise, and duration of involvement; and the sequence of the agency's involvement.[107] If a determination cannot be made on these factors, the CEQ can be asked to make the necessary determination.

The lead agency concept avoids duplication and enhances cooperation among the agencies. In addition, where there are state or local environmental reporting requirements, the lead agency can team with state or local agencies in the preparation of one EIS or environmental document to satisfy all requirements, thereby reducing duplication.[108]

At this stage in the process, sufficient environmental planning should have been completed to clearly identify the proposed action and reasonable alternatives thereto. Further, if an EA has been prepared for this proposed action, some early coordination with affected agencies and interest groups will have already occurred. Thus, the agency should be prepared to publish a notice of intent to prepare an EIS and initiate the first step—the scoping process.[109]

5.2 Scoping and Early Coordination

The scoping process is the first opportunity for the agency to involve the public by describing the agency's planning efforts to address the needs identified and to solicit comments on the scope of actions, alternatives, and impacts which need to be considered. The CEQ regulations require that this be an early and open process conducted as soon as practicable after its decision to prepare an EIS.[110] The lead agency must invite the participation of affected federal, state, and local agencies; any affected Indian tribes; the proponents of the action; and other interested persons (including those who might not be in accord with the action on environmental grounds).[111]

This scoping process is used to identify the significant issues requiring in-depth analysis in the EIS and to eliminate from detailed study those issues which are not significant or have been covered by prior environmental reviews. The scoping process is also used by the agency to make preliminary assignments between the lead agency and cooperating agencies concerning the EIS preparation, to identify other public EAs or EISs which are being or will be prepared that are related to the EIS under consideration, to identify other environmental review and consultation requirements that need to be integrated into this process, and finally, to establish a schedule for the timing of the EIS and the ultimate decision on the proposed action.

The CEQ regulations allow the agencies flexibility in several other areas, such as setting page limits on environmental documents, setting time limits, adopting procedures to combine the EA process with the scoping process, and holding early scoping meetings or meetings which may be integrated with other early planning meetings.[112]

The scoping process is important because it sends a signal to the public about both the agency's attitude toward public involvement and its planning for the proposal at hand. It also provides an opportunity for the agency to set reasonable boundaries on the timing, content, and process that will be used for the

EIS. It may also be used to restrict new subjects from being introduced later to challenge the agency's decision.[113]

The scoping process also offers an opportunity for the agency to investigate the criteria which commenting agencies will use in determining the environmental factors that are important and what impacts are likely to be considered significant.

5.3 Use of the EA and Applicant's Information

After the scoping process is completed, the lead agency must begin to prepare for collecting and assimilating the environmental information needed for the EIS. A starting point for this process is to review the material prepared for the EA or supplied by the applicant.

CEQ regulations provide that an agency may require an applicant to submit environmental information for possible use by the agency in preparing an EIS. The agency must assist the applicant in outlining the types of information required and must independently evaluate the information submitted in order to take responsibility for its accuracy.[114] Similarly, if an agency permits an applicant to prepare an EA, the agency must undertake a similar evaluation of its own and assume responsibility for the scope and content of the EA.[115]

5.4 Delegation

The responsibility for preparing the EIS belongs to the lead federal agency pursuant to section 102(2)(C). Under many federal programs, delegation to the states has been a common practice, particularly where the state acts as an applicant for federal funding. The Federal Highway Administration is one agency that delegated to the states many of the responsibilities under the Federal Aid Highway program. In 1975, this practice was challenged by an environmental group in *Conservation Soc'y of S. Vermont v. Secretary of Transportation*.[116]

In holding that the Federal Highway Administration could not delegate its NEPA responsibility to the state, the court noted:

A state agency is established to pursue defined state goals. In attempting to serve federal approval of a project, "self-serving assumptions" may ineluctably color a state agency's presentation of the environmental data or influence its final recommendation. Transposing the federal duty to prepare the EIS to a state agency is thus unlikely to result in as dispassionate an appraisal of environmental considerations as the federal agency itself could produce.[117]

The surrounding states interpreted this decision as prohibiting any delegation to state highway agencies and thus stopped all highway construction in the Northeast. Congress responded in 1975 with the only substantive amendment to NEPA since its enactment by adding a new section to address the delegation issue, section 102(2)(D).[118]

This section provides that an EIS may be prepared by a state agency having statewide jurisdiction so long as the responsible federal official furnishes guidance, participates in the preparation, and independently evaluates the EIS prior to its approval and adoption. Further, the amendment provides that if the proposed action has any impacts on an adjoining state or federal land management entity, the responsible federal official must solicit that state's or entity's views on potential impacts.[119]

An earlier court case had disapproved the preparation of an EIS by a private applicant on account of the potential self-serving interest of the applicant in receiving an approval from the agency.[120] However, this decision did not prevent an applicant from assisting the agency by submitting environmental information or by participating in environmental studies that form the basis for an EIS.[121]

Similarly, the use of consultants in the preparation of an EIS is a common practice and is acceptable so long as the federal agency retains sufficient control of their work product.[122] The CEQ regulations state that the agency should avoid conflicts of interest and require a disclosure statement from the contractor indicating that it has no financial or other interest in the project. Further, the federal agency is to provide guidance and participate in the preparation of the EIS, evaluate it independently, and take responsibility for its scope and content.[123]

5.5 Content of EIS

The purpose of an EIS is to help public officials make informed decisions that are based on an understanding of environmental consequences and the reasonable alternatives available to them. "[EISs] shall be concise, clear, and to the point, and shall be supported by evidence that agencies have made the necessary environmental analyses."[124]

Section 102(2)(C) requires an EIS to describe

- the environmental impacts of the proposed action;

- any adverse environmental impacts which cannot be avoided should the proposal be implemented;

- the reasonable alternatives to the proposed action;

- the relationship between local short-term uses of man's environment and the maintenance and enhancement of long-term productivity; and

- any irreversible and irretrievable commitments of resources which would be involved in the proposed action should it be implemented.

EISs have evolved so that they place more emphasis on a description of the affected environment, the alternatives to the proposed action, and possible mitigation measures than on what is outlined in the statute. The CEQ regulations outline a recommended format for EIS preparation.[125]

The alternatives section of the EIS is the heart of the EIS.[126] Once the affected environment and environmental consequences are described, the discussion of the proposed action and alternatives should be presented in a comparative form in order to sharply define the issues and provide a clear basis for the choice among options by the decision-maker and the public. CEQ regulations require that all reasonable alternatives, within or outside the jurisdiction of the lead agency, including the no-action alternative, be discussed.[127] CEQ has provided guidance on the range of alternatives agencies must consider.[128] Further, the courts have held that a "reasonable alternative" is defined by reference to a project's objectives or purpose and need statement.[129] In one case where a coordinated effort was undertaken to solve a problem of national scope, it was held that a solution that lies outside of an agency's jurisdiction might be a "reasonable alternative" and so might an alternative within that agency's jurisdiction that solves only a portion of the problem, given that other agencies might be able to provide the remainder of the solution.[130] A discussion in the alternatives section should also include appropriate mitigation measures not already included in the proposed action.

The environmental consequences section of the EIS provides the scientific and analytic basis for the comparison of alternatives. It must include a discussion of direct effects of the proposed action and alternatives; indirect effects; possible conflicts with objectives of federal, regional, state, and local (including Indian tribes) land use plans; policies and controls of the area concerned; and other key areas outlined in the CEQ regulations.[131]

When evaluating reasonably foreseeable significant adverse effects in the EIS, if there is incomplete or unavailable information on account of the costs of obtaining such information, the agency is directed to include within the EIS a statement that such information is incomplete or unavailable, the relevance of such information, a summary of existing credible scientific evidence which is relevant to evaluating the reasonably foreseeable adverse impacts, and the agency's evaluation of such impacts based upon theoretical approaches or research methods generally accepted in the scientific community.[132] Earlier CEQ regulation had required a worst-case analysis in such situations but revoked this analysis requirement with a 1986 amendment to the regulations after considerable debate.[133] The Supreme Court later approved this revocation of the CEQ regulation, noting that it was not a prior codification of any judicial determination and thus the Court should give substantial deference to CEQ's revocation amendment.[134] Several courts have held that a NEPA document that fails to disclose and analyze differing scientific opinions is defective.[135]

The discussion of indirect effects or impacts has been the most vulnerable to challenge. Indirect effects include economic growth-inducing effects of the proposed action, changes in land use patterns induced by the action, anticipated changes in population density or growth areas, and related impacts on air, water, and other natural systems, including ecosystems. Effects also include those resulting from actions which may have both beneficial and detrimental effects, even if, on balance, the agency believes that the effect will be beneficial.

Finally, cumulative impacts must also be covered in an EA or EIS which requires analysis of the "incremental impact of the action when added to other past, present, and reasonably foreseeable future actions, regardless of what agency (federal or nonfederal) or person undertakes such other actions. Cumulative impacts can result from individually minor but collectively significant actions taking place over a period of time."[136] This language from the CEQ regulations substantially expands the discussion of impacts in the EIS but allows considerable discretion by the agency in defining some of the key terms in its definition. Further, the regulation defining significantly requires the federal agency to consider "actions related to other actions with individually insignificant, but cumulatively significant, impacts."[137] The courts have scrutinized closely cumulative impact analyses in EAs and EISs and appear willing to find them inadequate on this basis.[138] (See 5.9 for more discussion of cumulative impacts.)

5.6 Commenting and Public Involvement

The NEPA statute makes public involvement in the process an essential element in ensuring informed decision-making at the federal level. Section 102(2)(C) requires that "[c]opies of [the EIS] and the comments and views of the appropriate Federal, state and local agencies, which are authorized to develop and enforce environmental standards, shall be made available to the President, the Council on Environmental Quality and to the public as provided by [the Freedom of Information Act]."[139] Further, section 102(2)(G) requires that the federal agencies must make available to the states, counties, municipalities, institutions, and individuals, advice and information useful in restoring, maintaining, and enhancing the quality of the environment.[140]

Public involvement was expanded by both Executive Order 11514[141] and the CEQ Guidelines[142] (now regulations). The CEQ regulations provide for involvement by requiring "public notice of NEPA-related hearings, public meetings, and the availability of environmental documents" so that interested persons and agencies can be informed.[143]

Public involvement can occur at three stages in the EIS process: initial scoping, commenting on the draft EIS, and commenting on the final EIS prior to a record of decision. At the scoping stage, public involvement is valuable to identify the potential environmental impacts, to judge the breadth of potential controversial issues, and to observe the public's reaction to the need for action and the alternatives that may exist to satisfy the need. Effective public involvement can also assist the agency in prioritizing the issues that need to be addressed in the EIS. At the draft EIS comment stage, the public can provide valuable feedback to the agency in identifying both the impacts which have not been adequately addressed and areas where gaps of information or analysis may exist. Comments regarding potential mitigation measures from the public may also be helpful to the agency at this juncture. Lastly, public comments on the final EIS assist the agency in making its final decision and preparing a formal record of decision. This is the last opportunity the public has to ensure that the agency has all the relevant information and analyses before it, and that significant issues have been properly addressed.

The CEQ regulations direct the agency, after preparing a draft EIS and before preparing a final EIS, to obtain the comments of any federal agency which has jurisdiction by law or special expertise with respect to environmental impacts involved or which is authorized to develop and enforce environmental standards.[144] Further, the agency must request the comments of appropriate state and local agencies which are authorized to develop and enforce environmental standards; Indian tribes, when effects may occur on a reservation; and any agency which has requested that it receive comments on actions of the kind proposed.[145] Finally, the agency must request comments from the applicant, if any, and from the public, affirmatively soliciting comments from those persons or organizations who may be interested or affected.[146]

The lead agency preparing the final EIS must then assess and consider the comments both individually and collectively and respond by making necessary changes in the EIS, making factual corrections, or explaining why the comments do not warrant further agency response.[147] All of the substantive comments received on the draft EIS must be attached to the final EIS whether or not the comment is thought to merit individual discussion by the agency.

The CEQ regulations require agencies to make diligent efforts to involve the public in the NEPA process by providing public notice of NEPA-related hearings, public meetings, and the availability of environmental documents, and by holding or sponsoring public hearings or public meetings whenever appropriate or in accordance with statutory requirements applicable to the agency.[148]

Although the form of public involvement is within the discretion of the lead agency, some recent challenges have been made to the use of an "open house" format for receiving public input. In *Sierra Club v. U.S. DOT*,[149] the plaintiffs argued that the Federal Highway Administration (FHWA) violated its public hearing requirement by using an "open house" format in lieu of the more traditional public hearing. The language of the CEQ regulations which refer to "public hearings or public meetings" was incorporated into FHWA regulations.[150] The Court recognized that the term "public hearing" is ambiguous in the sense that no definition of the term is given either in CEQ or FHWA regulations. However, it went on to note that the term "public hearing" does not preclude an open house format. Although the court upheld the FHWA position in giving substantial deference to FHWA's interpretation that the open house format satisfied the public hearing requirements, the Court observed that the open house format "limits the opportunity for citizens to directly and publicly confront agency decision-makers with opposing views."[151] The Court further stated that the purpose of providing a record from which informed agency decision-making can be made is weakened by the open house format. No verbatim recording of the proceedings is typically made under this procedure. Consequently, neither the public nor agency decision-makers acquires a complete picture of the interaction between the public and the agency.

5.7 Mitigation of Impacts

Appropriate mitigation measures must be included in the EIS.[152] Once an agency decision is made, any mitigation measures or other conditions established in the EIS or during its review and committed as part of the decision must be implemented by the lead agency or other appropriate consenting agency.[153] CEQ lists five generic mitigation measures in its regulatory definition of mitigation.[154]

Whether NEPA requires agencies to commit to mitigation measures in the first instance was addressed by the Supreme Court in *Robertson v. Methow Valley Citizens*.[155] The Court of Appeals had held that NEPA imposes a substantive duty on agencies to take action to mitigate the adverse effects of major federal actions, which entails the further duty to include in every EIS a detailed explanation of specific actions that will be employed to mitigate the adverse effects.[156] The Supreme Court reversed the finding, noting the difference between a requirement that mitigation be discussed and a substantive requirement that a complete mitigation plan be formulated and adopted. "[I]t would be inconsistent with NEPA's reliance on procedural mechanisms—as opposed to substantive, result-based standards—to demand the presence of a fully developed plan that will mitigate environmental harm before an agency can act."[157] The Court found no substantive requirement or duty to include in an EIS a detailed explanation of specific measures which will be employed to mitigate adverse impacts of a proposed action.

5.8 Proposals for Legislation

Section 102(2)(C) requires the preparation of an EIS for proposals for legislation as well as for major federal actions.[158] CEQ regulations require that a legislative EIS be transmitted to Congress within 30 days of the formal transmittal of a legislative proposal to Congress.[159] The intent is to provide a document that can serve as the basis for public and congressional debate. A scoping process is not required as part of a legislative EIS, and normally only a draft EIS will be required.[160]

Very little attention has been given to proposals for legislation under NEPA, primarily because most legislative proposals come from the president or the executive office of the president, which are not included in the definition of federal agency.[161] Further, in the extensive communication which occurs between the Congress and the executive branch, it is often very difficult to determine when a proposal will trigger the need for an EIS.

The Supreme Court has addressed the question of whether an EIS is required for an appropriations request from an agency. In *Andrus v. Sierra Club*,[162] the Court held that an EIS was not required when the Office of Management and Budget proposed a significant reduction in the Fish and Wildlife Service appropriation for the operation of the National Wildlife Refuge System. The Court referenced CEQ regulations, which define legislation as "a bill or legislative proposal" and omit any reference to "appropriation requests."[163] Therefore, the Court held that an EIS was not required, and further, that requiring an EIS on appropriation proposals would circumvent and eliminate "the careful distinction Congress had maintained between appropriations and legislation."[164]

5.9 Cumulative Effects

One of the unique aspects of NEPA is its recognition of the need to understand the "interrelationships of all components of the natural environment" and the importance of meeting the needs of "present and future generations of Americans." This recognition was reflected in early CEQ guidance[165] and now in its regulations[166] as in part the requirement to consider cumulative effects.

The CEQ regulations define three types of effects: (1) direct, (2) indirect, and (3) cumulative. While federal agencies routinely address direct and indirect effects, they have difficulty in addressing the cumulative effects.[167] A cumulative impact is defined as the "impact on the environment which results from the incremental impact of the action when added to other past, present, and reasonably foreseeable future actions regardless of what agency (federal or nonfederal) or person undertakes such other actions."[168] The regulations note that cumulative impacts can result from individually minor but collectively significant actions taking place over time. One court has declared that "the purpose of this requirement is to prevent agencies from dividing one project into multiple individual actions 'each of which individually has an insignificant environmental impact, but which collectively have a substantial impact.'"[169]

The term reasonably foreseeable has been limited in several cases to those actions which are not speculative or too far off in the distant future.[170] Most circuits have followed this rule except for the Tenth Circuit, which uses an independent utility test that requires a discussion of cumulative impacts of action only if the actions are "so interdependent that it would be unwise or irrational to complete one without the other."[171]

In addition, federal agencies are required to consider together in the same EIS connected, cumulative, and similar actions.[172] Connected actions are those that automatically trigger other actions that may require EISs, cannot proceed unless other actions are taken previously or simultaneously, or are interdependent parts of a larger action and depend on the larger action for justification. Cumulative actions are those that when viewed with other actions proposed by the agency have cumulatively significant impacts and therefore should be discussed in the same EIS. Similar actions are those that when viewed with other reasonably foreseeable or proposed agency actions have similarities that provide a basis for evaluating their environmental impacts together, such as common timing or geography. Although CEQ's regulations do not specifically direct agencies to consider connected actions, cumulative actions, and similar actions in defining the scope of an Environmental Assessment (EA), the impacts from such actions should be considered together in a single EA.

The courts have also struggled with judging the extent of the obligation of federal agencies to consider cumulative impacts. The difficulty with enforcing the requirement for cumulative impact analysis stems in part from the agency's decision regarding the appropriate scope of its proposed action and its ability to foresee and measure the effects of other related actions. In *Fritiofson v. Alexander*,[173] the court held that when the U.S. Corps of Engineers approved a permit to construct a canal system for a housing development on an island in Galveston Bay, Texas, it should have considered the effects, not only of the housing project, for which approval was sought, but also of the cumulative impacts of other past and future development on the island. The court cited the CEQ regulations which requires connected, cumulative, and similar actions be considered together in the same EIS when the proposals are functionally or economically related. However, the court also noted that the Supreme Court in *Sierra Club v. Kleppe*[174] limited the extent to which agencies had to consider the effects of related actions to those actually proposed, not simply contemplated. Nevertheless, many courts have addressed the cumulative effects analysis requirement.[175]

CEQ began a cumulative effects analysis in late 1992 to find ways to improve approaches to cumulative effects analysis. In 1994, the CEQ published a handbook on cumulative effects titled *Cumulative Effects Analysis Handbook for NEPA Practitioners.*

There has been considerable writing about how best to meet this cumulative effects analysis requirement. It appears, however, that no single, best approach has yet been identified. The scoping process is helpful to establish the proper scope of the proposed action and the temporal and spatial boundaries of the cumulative impacts to be considered. Input from other federal, state, and local agencies and the interested public can help identify a reasonable basis for the EIS analysis.

5.10 Supplemental Statements

The duty to supplement an EIS after it has been prepared is prescribed by the CEQ regulations.[176] This regulation requires an agency prepare supplemental environmental impact statements (1) if the agency makes substantial changes in the proposed action that are relevant to environmental concerns, or (2) if there are significant new circumstances or information relevant to environmental concerns and bearing on the proposed action or its impacts.

Courts have applied the same standard of "significance" as used in the determination of when an EIS is required when examining "substantial changes" and "significant new circumstances." The inquiry is whether changes will affect the quality of the human environment "in a significant manner or to a significant extent not already considered by a federal agency."[177] These same requirements have been applied by the courts to the supplementation of an environmental assessment when no EIS is prepared.[178]

If a supplementary EIS is required, the agency must prepare, circulate, and file a supplement to a statement in the same fashion (exclusive of scoping) as a draft and final statement unless alternative procedures are approved by the CEQ.[179]

6.0 NEPA's Extraterritorial Application

International application of NEPA has been a matter of controversy since the statute does not explicitly indicate whether it applies outside the United States.

Courts have found that there is a presumption against the extraterritorial application of laws absent an express congressional mandate. Further, some agencies have argued that compliance with NEPA could present obstacles to meeting certain foreign policy objectives. While section 102(2)(F) requires that "all agencies of the federal government shall . . . recognize the worldwide and long-range character of environmental problems and . . . lend appropriate support . . . to maximize international cooperation," it appears to impose a duty on federal agencies only to recognize worldwide environmental problems.

Nevertheless, a D.C. Court of Appeals decision, reversing an early District Court decision, held that the operation of an incinerator in the Antarctic by the National Science Foundation required an EIS, holding explicitly that "the presumption against extraterritorial application does not apply where the effect will occur in Antarctica, as Antarctica has no sovereign, and the United States has a measure of legislative control over the continent."[180] In a more recent case,[181] the court found that the presumption against the extraterritorial application of U.S. laws does not apply because the planning for the challenged agency action occurred entirely within the boundaries of the United States (following the holding in *Environmental Defense Fund v. Massey*, 986 F.2d 528 [D.C. Cir. 1994]). According to the court, the federal activity regulated by NEPA is the decision-making process of the agencies, not the underlying project.

In 1979, President Carter issued Executive Order No. 12114 on the environmental effects abroad of major federal actions, based on his independent executive authority rather than on NEPA. Nevertheless, the objective of the executive order was to further the purposes of NEPA by providing procedures for ensuring that pertinent environmental considerations were given to actions having effects outside the geographical boundaries of the United States.[182] Although it does not create a cause of action in the courts, it provides for environmental analysis and documentation for actions affecting the global commons or for actions in which foreign nations are not participating with the United States and for certain actions which could create a serious public health risk.[183]

In February 1991, the United States signed a Convention on Environmental Impact Assessment with European countries obligating the signatories to consult when an activity is likely to cause adverse transboundary environmental impacts. The Department of State, EPA, and CEQ are designing the implementation strategy for the convention.[184]

7.0 Environmental Justice

Environmental justice is a NEPA consideration that was introduced by President Clinton on February 11, 1994, in Executive Order (E.O.) 12898 titled "Federal

Actions to Address Environmental Justice in Minority Populations and Low-Income Populations." This E.O. was designed to focus the attention of federal agencies on the human health and environmental conditions in minority communities and low-income communities. The president emphasized that existing laws, including the National Environmental Policy Act, provide opportunities for federal agencies to address environmental hazards in minority and low-income communities. Thus, the E.O. requires federal agencies to adopt strategies to address environmental justice concerns within the context of agency operations.

In July 1996, the EPA published draft guidance[185] to implement its environmental justice goals in EPA's preparation of environmental impact statements and environmental assessments under NEPA. In this draft guidance, EPA's Office of Environmental Justice offers the following definition of environmental justice:

The fair treatment and meaningful involvement of all people regardless of race, color, national origin, or income with respect to the development, implementation, and enforcement of environmental laws, regulations, and policies. Fair treatment means that no group of people, including racial, ethnic, or socioeconomic group, should bear a disproportionate share of the negative environmental consequences resulting from industrial, municipal, and commercial operations or the execution of federal, state, local, and tribal programs and policies.

The presidential memorandum accompanying the E.O. calls for a variety of actions. Four specific actions were directed to NEPA-related activities:

1. Each federal agency must analyze environmental effects, including human health, economic, and social effects, of federal actions, including effects on minority communities and low-income communities, when such analysis is required by NEPA.

2. Mitigation measures outlined or analyzed in EAs, EISs, or Records of Decision, whenever feasible, should address significant and adverse environmental effects of proposed federal actions on minority communities and low-income communities.

3. Each federal agency must provide opportunities for community input in the NEPA process, including identifying potential effects and mitigation measures in consultation with affected communities and improving accessibility of public meetings, official documents, and notices to affected communities.

4. In reviewing other agencies' proposed actions under Section 309 of the Clean Air Act, EPA must ensure that the agencies have fully analyzed environmental effects on minority communities and low-income communities, including human health, social, and economic effects.

8.0 EPA Review and Comment

The EPA has specific authority and responsibility under Section 309 of the Clean Air Act[186] to review and comment in writing on the environmental impact of any matter relating to the duties and responsibilities granted pursuant to the act or other provisions of the authority of the administrator. Such review and comment authority relates to the following:

Legislation proposed by a federal department or agency.

Newly authorized federal projects for construction and any major federal action subject to section 102(2)(C) of the National Environmental Policy Act.

Proposed regulations published in any department or agency of the federal government.

Such written comments must be made public at the conclusion of any review.

EPA adopted an Environmental Review Process to implement this authority and responsibility in a set of policies and procedures.[187] These policies and procedures define the review process, assign internal responsibilities, and outline mechanisms for resolving problems that arise in the Environmental Review Process.

As part of its Environmental Review Process, EPA has developed a rating system for draft EISs which summarizes EPA's level of concern about the adequacy of the document. The rating system is alpha-numeric. The alphabetical categories, which signify EPA's evaluation of the environmental impacts of the proposal, are these:

LO: lack of objections

EC: environmental concerns

EO: environmental objections

EU: environmentally unsatisfactory

The numerical categories, which signify an evaluation of the adequacy of the information and assessment in the EIS, are these:

1. Adequate

2. Insufficient information

3. Inadequate

Depending upon the ratings, EPA may initiate follow-up discussions with the lead agency. If the EIS receives an Unsatisfactory rating and significant issues are not resolved with the lead agency, EPA may refer the proposed regulation or major action to the Council on Environmental Quality, along with its assessment for resolution. CEQ has only received some 26 referrals in its history from all agencies including EPA. In such cases, if CEQ cannot resolve the issue, it may refer the matter to the president, although that has never been done.[188]

EPA should provide comments to the lead agency within 45 days from the start of the official review period. In general, EPA's comments should be focused on the proposal but may also review the complete range of alternatives, identifying those that are environmentally unacceptable to EPA and identifying EPA's preferred alternative. EPA's comment letter on the draft EIS should reflect all of EPA's responsibilities that may bear on the action, including measures to avoid or mitigate damage to the environment or to protect, restore, and enhance the environment.

Finally, EPA's policy is to conduct detailed reviews of final EISs which have had significant issues raised by EPA at the draft EIS stage. The detailed review and submission of comments will be done for those actions rated EO, EU, or 3 at the draft stage. These EPA reviews and comments are almost always important indicators to the public of what the acceptability of the proposed action should be in the community.

9.0 Judicial Review of NEPA

The courts have played a crucial role in enforcing NEPA's environmental mandates. Judicial review is not expressly provided for in the statute, but federal agencies have held that judicial review of agency decisions is implied under NEPA.[189] Judicial review usually occurs when the agency either decides not to file an EIS or makes a final decision after completing the EIS process. Generally, the courts review an agency's EIS to determine whether it is adequate under NEPA's statutory provisions.

The court case most often cited in setting the standard of review for agency decisions under NEPA is *Citizens to Preserve Overton Park, Inc. v. Volpe*.[190] Although this case was not a NEPA case, the Supreme Court indicated that courts must conduct a substantial inquiry into agency decisions to determine whether the agency has taken a hard look at the issues. This hard look doctrine has become the hallmark of judicial review in environmental law.

However, this hard look does not mean that a court can substitute its own judgment for that of the agency. Under NEPA, as in administrative law generally, once a court is satisfied that the agency has given fair and adequate consideration to the relevant evidence, the agency decision will not be set aside absent a finding that the decision was "arbitrary, capricious, an abuse of discretion, or otherwise not in accordance with law."[191] In essence, this means that the agency decision will not be set aside unless the court is convinced there has been a clear error of judgment by the agency.[192] The reason for this deferential standard of review is that the agency's decision turns on the resolution of factual disputes—an inquiry which the agency, by virtue of its substantial technical expertise, is more qualified to conduct than the court. Thus, the Supreme Court in 1989 held that an agency's decision not to prepare a supplemental EIS based on new information was not a clear error of judgment, inasmuch as there were conflicting views in the scientific community with respect to the significance of that information, and the agency could only decide which side to believe based on its own scientific expertise.[193]

By contrast, where the outcome of the dispute turns on the agency's legal interpretation of applicable statutes or regulations, a court will conduct a less deferential review and may substitute its own judgment for that of the agency. The reason for this is clear: in matters of legal interpretation, as opposed to matters of fact, the agency has no special expertise that makes its decision preferable to that of a court. There is one important qualification to this rule, however. A court will give effect to an agency's interpretation of its own organic statute or regulations, as long as that interpretation is a reasonable one.[194] In addition, the courts have accorded substantial deference to CEQ's regulations regarding the implementation of NEPA.

An important issue in obtaining judicial review is standing. Most environmental challenges under NEPA are brought by environmental organizations or third parties who may not have participated in the agency decision that is the subject of litigation. Their standing or access to the courts has been routinely granted under NEPA, although it may become more difficult to do so in the future.

While the courts apply the basic significant injury test for standing under the Constitution and the Administrative Procedure Act (APA),[195] at least one court has suggested that when this test is applied to NEPA litigation, there is perhaps a lower threshold for standing than is typically required.[196] This is because the nature of rights created by NEPA may compel an unusually broad definition of the act's zone of interest, thus making it easier to obtain standing under NEPA than under most statutes.

In general, plaintiffs have successfully maintained standing by alleging their use of areas that may be affected by an agency's failure to prepare an EIS, or areas in close proximity to those areas.

In 1990, however, the Supreme Court held that plaintiffs failed to satisfy the specific injury requirement if they could only allege that they use certain lands "in the vicinity of" the potentially affected areas.[197] The Supreme Court acknowledged that NEPA does not provide a private right of action for violations of its provisions, but rather that an injured party must seek relief under the APA.

To demonstrate standing under the APA, a plaintiff must identify some final agency action that affects him or her and must show that he or she has suffered a legal wrong because of the agency action or has been adversely affected by that action within the meaning of the relevant statute. To be "adversely affected within the meaning of the statute," a plaintiff must be within a zone of interest sought to be protected by the statutory provision that forms the basis of the complaint. Using this test of standing, the court found that the plaintiffs' interests were within the zone of interest to be protected by NEPA but that the plaintiffs' claiming use "in the vicinity" of the agency action was not enough to render them adversely affected. Given these findings, the court ruled that the plaintiffs had not set forth "specific facts" in their affidavit sufficient to survive the agency's motion for summary judgment.

While proving significant injury is certainly the most difficult part of establishing standing, a plaintiff must also show that the alleged significant injury will occur as a result of the agency's action. By characterizing the threatened injury as a chance that the agency, by failing to comply with NEPA, would overlook serious environmental harm, courts have found the causation element to be easily met. For example, in *City of Los Angeles v. Nat'l Highway Traffic Safety Admin.*,[198] the Federal Court of Appeals for the District of Columbia granted standing to an environmental group that claimed the government, by failing to prepare an EIS, risked overlooking the impact of proposed federal fuel economy standards on global warming. The court held that as long as there is a "real possibility" that the agency would have reached a different decision if it had complied with the requirements of NEPA, standing should be granted. One judge disagreed, focusing instead on the alleged injury in the form of the "environmental nightmare" that would result from global warming. Because the agency's activity would, at most, have only an insignificant impact on global warming, the judge would have denied standing on the grounds that the agency's failure to prepare an EIS "appears to be but an insignificant tributary to the causal stream leading to the overall harm that petitioners have alleged."[199]

Another important Supreme Court decision was handed down in 2007 in *Massachusetts v. EPA*.[200] Various state and local governments and environmental organizations sued the federal EPA challenging its denial of their petition requesting that the agency regulate greenhouse gases under the federal Clean Air Act. EPA had denied the petition claiming that it lacked the authority to regulate greenhouse gas emissions because they did not qualify as "air pollutants" under the Clean Air Act. Although EPA argued that plaintiffs lacked standing to sue, the Supreme Court disagreed in a 5-4 decision holding that standing did not prevent the Court from reaching the merits, and also holding the "special position and interest" of Massachusetts to be of considerable relevance as a sovereign state rather than as a private individual as in the 1992 Defenders of Wildlife case.[201] This decision appeared to expand the standing for plaintiffs.

However, a recent Supreme Court decision in *Summers v. Earth Island Institute*[202] issued another restrictive standing interpretation. In this case, the U.S. Forest Service had approved a salvage timber sale in a large portion of the Sequoia National Forest following a fire. The Forest Service did not provide public notice or allow an appeal for the proposed project since it has exempted such requirements for categorically excluded actions under their NEPA regulations. After an environmental group challenged the absence of notice and the unavailability of the appeals process, a settlement was reached. The Forest Service then argued that this group lacked standing to sue to challenge the validity of the regulation exempting the notice and appeals provision. The Supreme Court held that the settlement remedied any injury suffered by the group and that the group now lacked standing since they had no sufficient evidence of firm intentions to visit those forest locations in the future. This decision reinforces the earlier Court decisions that require the plaintiffs to demonstrate a precise geographical nexus between the challenged actions and the alleged injuries (see note 197).

10.0 CEQ Study of NEPA's Effectiveness

To bring attention to NEPA's 25th anniversary, the Council on Environmental Quality (CEQ) initiated a NEPA Effectiveness Study to evaluate its successes and failures. The study solicited input from a wide range of participants, including some of the original framers of NEPA, members of Congress, state and local agencies, those who drafted the CEQ regulations, and federal agencies with experience in implementing the act. A special effort was made to include opinions of the public. The study focused on identifying limitations to the effective and efficient implementation of the act.

Overall, the study found that NEPA's most enduring legacy is as a framework for collaboration between federal agencies and those who will bear the environmental, social, and economic impacts of agency decisions. As a result, the federal agencies today are more open and responsible for the consequences of their actions than they were before NEPA was enacted. However, the study participants also noted that frequently NEPA takes too long and costs too much, agencies make decisions before hearing from the public, documents are too long and technical for many people to use, and training for agency officials, at times, is inadequate.

The NEPA Effectiveness Study identified five elements of the NEPA process that are critical to its effective and efficient implementation. The following is a summary of the study findings.

Strategic planning: the extent to which agencies integrate NEPA's goals into their internal planning processes at an early stage.

The study found that the "NEPA process" is often triggered too late to be fully effective. At the same time, agency managers who have learned to use NEPA have discovered it helps them do their jobs. NEPA's requirements to consider alternatives and involve the public and other agencies with expertise can make it easier to discourage poor proposals, reduce the amount of documentation down the road, and support innovation. NEPA helps managers make better decisions, produce better results, and build trust in surrounding communities. Fortunately, many agencies are making progress by taking a more comprehensive and strategic approach to decision-making.

Public information and input: the extent to which an agency provides information to and takes into account the views of the surrounding community and other interested members of the public during its planning and decision-making process.

NEPA was credited for opening the federal process to public input, which has improved the effectiveness of project design and implementation. Nonetheless, the success of a NEPA process heavily depends on whether an agency has systematically reached out to those who will be most affected by a proposal, gathered information and ideas from them, and responded to the input by modifying or adding alternatives. This desired level of public involvement is not always achieved. Citizens sometimes feel frustrated because they are being treated as adversaries rather than welcome participants in the NEPA process. Increased public involvement in the common, but less comprehensive, environmental analysis process leading to EA can help overcome these difficulties and help forge true partnerships with other agencies and the surrounding communities.

Interagency coordination: how well and how early agencies share information and integrate planning responsibilities with other agencies.

NEPA's requirement for interagency coordination has avoided or resolved many conflicts, reduced duplication of effort, and improved the environmental permitting process. Uncoordinated processes, on the contrary, put agencies—and the public—in adversarial positions and delay federal actions that are important to local and regional economies, as well as actions that are intended to improve the environment. Interagency coordination is hampered because agencies often have different timetables, requirements, and modes of public participation. Federal, state, and local agencies are increasingly using tools such as interagency agreements at the start of a planning process to coordinate timetables and resolve disputes.

Interdisciplinary place-based approach to decision-making: focuses the knowledge and values from a variety of sources on a specific place.

Experience with the NEPA process has shown that better decisions—those that meet the needs of the community and minimize adverse impacts on the environment—require the integrated perspective that can only be obtained by incorporating expertise and information from many fields and sources, including state and local agencies. The keys to implementing an interdisciplinary place-based approach and addressing the full range of cumulative effects are obtaining adequate environmental data and finding the tools to use it. Although the current lack of quality environmental baseline data can hamper the requisite comparison of alternatives, federal agencies are employing or developing new environmental indicators (comparable to economic indicators) to provide more consistent information on the status of resources over time and geography. At the same time, new methods and tools, such as geographic information systems (GIS), are beginning to help agencies consider cumulative effects and focus analyses.

Science-based and flexible management approaches: once projects are approved.

Most of the study participants believed that agencies should monitor actual impacts once a project is begun, both to ensure that mitigation measures are effective and to verify predictions of impact. Agencies can improve environmental protection, get projects underway earlier, and dramatically reduce costs by monitoring actual impacts and modifying project management, rather than aiming to answer every potential question with certainty before a project is approved. Several agencies are already using the experience gained from monitoring to improve analyses of similar projects in the future. Most study participants felt that, where resources are not likely to be damaged permanently and there is an opportunity to repair past environmental damage, an adaptive environmental management approach may be the best means for an agency to meet its specific and NEPA missions.

After President George W. Bush took office, he established another NEPA task force to review the National Environmental Policy Act and examine opportunities to modernize NEPA analyses and documentation and improve the coordination of NEPA processes between all levels of government and the public.

11.0 NEPA Task Force

The NEPA Task Force was established in April 2002 to review the current NEPA implementing practices and procedures in the following areas: technology and information management and security; federal and intergovernmental collaboration; programmatic analyses and subsequent tiered documents; and adaptive management and monitoring.[203] In addition, the NEPA Task Force reviewed other NEPA implementation issues such as the level of detail included in agencies' procedures and documentation for promulgating categorical exclusions; the structure and documentation of environmental assessments; and implementation practices that would benefit other agencies.

The task force interviewed federal agencies; reviewed public comments, literature, reports, and case studies; and spoke with individuals and representatives from state and local governments, tribes, and interest groups. The task force received comments from more than 650 respondents representing federal, state, and local governments, tribes, organizations, and individuals.

The NEPA Task Force presented its Report Modernizing NEPA Implementation to CEQ in September 2003.[204] It included extensive recommendations to promote the development and use of new technologies for information sharing and to enhance public involvement; formation of a Federal Advisory Committee of diverse individuals, with a variety of experiences in the NEPA process, which can contribute to the development of collaborative guidance and training for agencies; to promote consistent, clear, cost-effective programmatic NEPA analyses, documents, and tiering that meet agency and stakeholder needs; and to convene an adaptive management work group to consider revising existing regulations or establishing new guidance to facilitate agencies' ability to exercise the option of incorporating adaptive management into their NEPA process.

The task force also focused its efforts on documenting the basis and process for establishing categorical exclusions, the categorical exclusion approval process, and documenting the use of categorical exclusions. Among its recommendations, the task force recommended that CEQ expeditiously issue clarifying guidance to address the kind of documentation needed at the time a categorical exclusion is used to ensure more consistent use.

With respect to Environmental Assessments (EAs), the task force stated that new CEQ guidance is needed to specify existing minimum EA requirements for all EAs in one guidance document. This guidance should explain:

- appropriate analysis of alternatives, including the no action alternative;

- when mitigation measures must be considered;

- appropriate public involvement; and

- suitable use of an EA standardized analysis form.

Further, the task force recommended that CEQ address what should be included in an EA and FONSI to demonstrate that agencies have comprehensively considered the potential environmental consequences of the proposed action before taking the action (i.e., taken a "hard look") and emphasized that EAs and FONSIs should focus on issues or resources that might be significantly affected or are a public concern.

Finally, the task force recommended that CEQ, in consultation with the Environmental Protection Agency, Advisory Council on Historic Preservation, Fish and Wildlife Service, the National Oceanic and Atmospheric Administration's National Marine Fisheries Service, and other agencies, as appropriate, develop a handbook to effectively integrate the NEPA process with Endangered Species Act Section 7 consultation, National Historic Preservation Act Section 106 coordination, Clean Air Act conformity requirements, and Clean Water Act total maximum daily load and Section 404 requirements.

12.0 Adaptive Management

One of the criticisms of NEPA is the lack of follow-through once the NEPA document is completed and the agency has taken action. As noted above, the Council on Environmental Quality Task Force identified "adaptive management" as one way to address this concern. One definition of "adaptive management" is "a structured, iterative process of optimal decision making in the face of uncertainty, with an aim to reducing uncertainty by system monitoring."[205] Because of the difficulty in accurately predicting or forecasting environmental impacts to our complex natural systems, the use of adaptive management provides a mechanism to monitor potential impacts identified in the NEPA document and make appropriate adjustments. Although NEPA does not require post-ROD monitoring of impacts, neither does it prevent an agency from committing to such monitoring or urging a third party to conduct such monitoring if potential impacts could be significant.

13.0 NEPA and Transportation

The Congress reauthorized the U.S. Department of Transportation (USDOT) surface transportation programs in the Safe, Accountable, Flexible, Efficient Transportation Equity Act—A Legacy for Users (SAFETEA-LU).[206] This new act contains many new provisions addressing planning and environmental issues.[207] However, it also makes changes to the USDOT NEPA procedures by adding some streamlining provisions to the NEPA process.[208] Congress has on past occasions amended NEPA through "backdoor" amendments like these which apply only to specific projects or programs.[209] Thus, the changes to NEPA procedures and applicability contained in the SAFETEA-LU legislation only apply to USDOT programs.

These SAFETEA-LU amendments do reflect a congressional approach to addressing some of the more generic NEPA issues which many agencies have recognized as being troublesome. It may also represent a trend in how other agencies may propose to modify their NEPA procedures. Section 6002 of SAFETEA-LU adds a new section 139 to the federal highway statutory provisions outlining a streamlined environmental review process.

13.1 Participating Agencies

Present CEQ regulations recognize the roles of a "lead" agency and "cooperating" agencies in the NEPA process.[210] One new SAFETEA-LU provision amending the FHWA environmental review process gives special recognition to governmental stakeholders in the NEPA process—for example, all federal, state, tribal, regional, and local government agencies that may have an interest in the project, by designating them as "participating agencies."[211] The concept of this new "participating agency" is intended to be distinct from, and more inclusive than, the concept of "cooperating agency."[212] The status of a "cooperating agency" generally has been assigned only to those agencies that are expected to play an extensive role—that is, an agency that has a permitting responsibility with respect to the project. Participating agencies encompass cooperating agencies as well as any other agencies that submit comments, participate in interagency review meetings, or otherwise are engaged in the environmental review process. Another distinction is that, pursuant to CEQ regulations, a cooperating agency may adopt without recirculation the environmental impact statement of a lead agency when, after an independent review of the statement, the cooperating agency concludes that its comments and suggestions have been satisfied. This provision is particularly important to permitting agencies, such as the U.S. Army Corps of Engineers, who, as cooperating agencies, routinely adopt USDOT documents.[213]

The roles and responsibilities of participating agencies include, but are not limited to: [214]

• Participating in the NEPA process starting at the earliest possible time, especially with regard to the development of the purpose and need statement, range of alternatives, methodologies, and the level of detail for the analysis of alternatives.

- Identifying, as early as practicable, any issues of concern regarding the project's potential environmental or socioeconomic impacts. Participating agencies also may participate in the issue resolution process described later in this guidance.

- Providing meaningful and timely input on unresolved issues.

- Participating in the scoping process.

Accepting the designation as a participating agency does not indicate project support and does not provide an agency with increased oversight or approval authority beyond its statutory limits, if applicable. Nongovernmental organizations and private entities cannot serve as participating agencies.

Although the project sponsor may initially identify potential participating agencies, the lead agency decides which agencies to invite to serve as participating agencies as early as practicable in the environmental review process.

If a federal agency chooses to decline to be a participating agency, its response letter to an invitation must state that the agency (1) has no jurisdiction or authority with respect to the project, (2) has no expertise or information relevant to the project, and (3) does not intend to submit comments on the project. If the federal agency's response does not state the agency's position in these terms, then the agency should be treated as a participating agency.[215]

A state, tribal, or local agency must respond affirmatively to the invitation to be designated as a participating agency. If the state, tribal, or local agency fails to respond or declines the invitation, regardless of the reasons for declining, the agency will not be considered a participating agency.[216]

13.2 Coordination Plan Required

Another change in the USDOT NEPA procedures is the requirement for a coordination plan. SAFETEA-LU requires that the lead agencies establish a plan for coordinating public and agency participation and comment during the environmental review process. The coordination plan should outline (1) how the lead agencies have divided the responsibilities for compliance with the various aspects of the environmental review process, such as the issuance of invitations to participating agencies; and (2) how the lead agencies will provide the opportunities for input from the public and other agencies, in accordance with applicable laws, regulations, and policies. In addition, the coordination plan may establish a schedule of regular meetings and may identify which persons, organizations, or agencies should be included for each coordination point, as well as time frames for input by those persons, organizations, and agencies.

13.3 Purpose and Need Statement

SAFETEA-LU does not substantively change the concept of purpose and need that was established by CEQ. However, SAFETEA-LU requires that the development of the project's purpose and need should be a collaborative process in which the lead agencies must provide opportunities for the involvement of participating agencies and the public and must consider the input provided by these groups. Per previous guidance issued by CEQ, which was affirmed by Congress in its conference report on SAFETEA-LU, participating agencies should afford substantial deference to the USDOT's articulation of the purpose and need for a transportation action. After considering this input, the lead federal agency, in consultation with the other lead agencies, is ultimately responsible for making the decision regarding the purpose and need used in the NEPA evaluation.

Importantly, the new provisions reaffirm the appropriateness of including local and state objectives in the purpose and need statement. For example, the statement of objectives might include goals and objectives obtained from federal, state, or local planning documents that describe land use, growth, or other targets or limits. These planning objectives might indicate that high density land use is planned for the study area and would require improved infrastructure. In such a case, it would be appropriate for travel demand forecasting or other modeling to consider the future land use as long as the land use forecast was obtained from an official federal, state, or local planning document and was determined appropriate for use during NEPA.[217]

13.4 Environmental Review Process

Other provisions of SAFETEA-LU outlining a new environmental review process for transportation projects added other new requirements. First, one of the significant factors creating long delays in the project development process is waiting for the NEPA process to be completed. The new law requires federal agencies, to the maximum extent practicable, to carry out its obligations under other applicable law concurrently, and in conjunction, with the review required under NEPA, unless doing so would impair the ability of the federal agency to carry out those obligations and to formulate and implement administrative, policy, and procedural mechanisms to enable the agency to ensure completion of the environmental review process in a timely, coordinated, and environmentally responsible manner.

SAFETEA-LU also mandated that the DEIS comment period not exceed 60 days, unless a different comment period is established by agreement of the lead agencies, the project sponsor, and all participating agencies. The previous FHWA regulations allowed 30 days for a comment period unless the administration determined, for good cause, that a different period is warranted.[218] An extension did not require the agreement of the project sponsor or all participating agencies. The DEIS comment period begins on the date that EPA publishes the notice of availability of the DEIS in the *Federal Register*. All other comment periods remain at 30 days.

13.5 Statute of Limitations on Challenges

SAFETEA-LU established a 180-day statute of limitations (SOL) on claims against USDOT and other federal agencies for certain environmental and other approval actions.[219] The SOL established by SAFETEA-LU applies to a permit, license, or approval action by a federal agency if:

1. the action relates to a transportation project; and

2. an SOL notification is published in the *Federal Register* (FR) announcing that a federal agency has taken an action on a transportation project that is final under the federal law pursuant to which the action was taken.

If no SOL notice is published, the period for filing claims is not shortened from what is provided by other parts of federal law. If other federal laws do not specify a statute of limitations, then a six-year claims period applies.

13.6 Delegation of Categorical Exclusions

After entering into a Memorandum of Understanding with the secretary, each state may assume responsibility for categorical exclusions, with FHWA in a programmatic monitoring role.[220] Another provision calls for the secretary to establish a categorical exclusion, to the extent appropriate, for activities that support the deployment of intelligent transportation infrastructure and systems.[221]

SAFETEA-LU establishes a project delivery pilot program for five states (specified as Alaska, Ohio, Oklahoma, Texas, and California), allowing them to apply to USDOT to assume all USDOT environmental responsibilities under NEPA and other environmental laws (excluding the Clean Air Act and transportation planning requirements). This delegation authority is limited to highway projects, and it could be for specific projects within a state or a programmatic delegation.[222]

A pilot program is established under which, during the first three years after enactment, the secretary may allow up to five states to assume environmental responsibilities (including NEPA and 4(f)) for Recreational Trails and Transportation Enhancement projects.

14.0 Proposed CEQ Guidance

The Council on Environmental Quality (CEQ) recently prepared three draft guidance memoranda for public review and comment that address the use of categorical exclusions, the consideration of greenhouse gas emissions in NEPA documents, and on mitigation and monitoring. Only one of these guidance documents dealing with categorical exclusions has been issued in final form. The other two draft guidance documents will not become effective until issued by CEQ in final form. No deadline for their finalization has been set. Nevertheless, this draft guidance is a harbinger of potential future regulation.

14.1 Establishing Categorical Exclusions

The CEQ has issued this guidance in order to assist agencies in establishing and applying categorical exclusions that are the most frequently used method of compliance with NEPA. It states that this guidance does not create any new requirements and that CEQ's interpretation of NEPA is entitled to deference. CEQ acknowledges that "inappropriate reliance on categorical exclusions may thwart the purposes of NEPA, compromising the quality and transparency of agency decision-making as well as the opportunity for meaningful public participation and review." As noted earlier, the CEQ NEPA Task Force recommended that CEQ issue clarifying guidance in 2003. This new guidance only addressed categorical exclusions established by federal agencies and not those established by Congress.

The guidance addresses how agencies should: establish categorical exclusions by outlining the process required, use of public involvement and documentation to help define and substantiate a proposed categorical exclusion; apply established categorical exclusions and identify when to prepare documentation; and finally, conduct periodic reviews of categorical exclusions to assure their continued appropriate use and usefulness.

Some of the new CEQ interpretations in this guidance on categorical exclusions worth noting are the following:

14.1.1 Regional Variations

CEQ notes that some activities may be more variable in their environmental effects and therefore require "a more detailed description to ensure the category is limited to actions that have been shown not to have individual or cumulatively significant effects. For example, the status and sensitivity of environmental resources vary across the nation; consequently, it may be appropriate to categorically exclude a category of actions in one area or region rather than across the nation as a whole." This new flexibility to the application of categorical exclusions to specific contexts may more accurately reflect the real environmental impacts expected from these excluded activities. On the other hand, it may open up the need for more CEQ interpretive guidance on how different these applications may be without creating new and unintended exemptions from the NEPA 102 process.

14.1.2 Defining Categorical Exclusion Conditions

The council encourages the agencies to consider broadly defined criteria that characterize types of actions that, based on the agency's experience, do not cause significant environmental effects. If this technique is adopted, it encourages them to offer several examples of activities frequently performed by agency personnel which would normally fall in these categories. Agencies also need to consider whether the cumulative effects of several small actions would cause sufficient environmental impact to take the actions out of the categorically excluded class.

The guidance also advises agencies to avoid categorical exclusions that divide a proposed action into smaller elements or segments that do not have independent utility to the agency.

Finally, CEQ encourages agencies responsible for NEPA compliance to develop and maintain the capacity to monitor actions approved as categorical exclusions to ensure the prediction that there will not be significant impacts is borne out in practice.

14.1.3 Substantiating a New Categorical Exclusion

This area of the guidance provides suggestions on how to evaluate whether a new categorical exclusion is appropriate and how to support the determination that the proposed categorical exclusion describes a category of actions that does not individually or cumulatively have a significant effect on the human environment.

Aside from the normal process of gathering information, evaluating that information, and making findings to explain how the agency determined the category of actions avoids illegal segmentation, the guidance suggests the use of an "impact demonstration project." That is a project consisting of an EA or EIS prepared for a proposed action for which the agency lacks experience with its implementation or effects. This NEPA documentation for the impact demonstration project should explain how the results of the analysis will be used to evaluate the merits of a proposed categorical exclusion. The demonstration project should have a similar scope as well as operational and environmental context as the category of actions being proposed as a categorical exclusion.

14.1.4 Public Engagement and Disclosure

Although agencies using a categorical exclusion are not required to consult with the public, this guidance encourages federal agencies in appropriate circumstances to engage the public in some way (e.g., through notification or disclosure) before using the categorical exclusion. Involving the public may assist the agency in identifying any extraordinary circumstances or cumulative impacts that might disqualify the use of a categorical exclusion.

CEQ also advises the agencies to use current technologies to provide the public with access to information on how the agency has complied with NEPA. Specifically, it recommends agencies provide access to the status of NEPA compliance (e.g., completing environmental review by using a categorical exclusion) on agency websites, particularly in those situations where there is a high public interest in a proposed action. A recent initiative by the Department of Energy to post categorical exclusion determinations provides an example of how agencies can effectively increase transparency in their decision-making when using categorical exclusions.

14.2 Consideration of the Effects of Climate Change and Greenhouse Gas Emissions

One of the current concerns that has vexed NEPA document preparers is how to account for greenhouse gas emissions generated by their proposed actions. Many proposed agency actions involve relatively small projects that directly or indirectly may generate CO_2 emissions, but are wholly insignificant when compared to major proposed programmatic actions. This new draft guidance is intended to help explain how federal agencies should analyze the environmental effects of greenhouse gas (GHG) emissions and climate change when they describe the environmental effects of a proposed agency action in accordance with section 102 of NEPA and the CEQ regulations. The hallmark of this guidance is for agencies to use their "rule of reason" judgment in first deciding if GHG emissions need to be considered, then how to consider them and to evaluate their significance for proposed actions.

CEQ advises federal agencies to consider, in scoping their NEPA analyses, whether analysis of the direct and indirect GHG emissions from their proposed actions may provide meaningful information to decision-makers and the public. Specifically, if a proposed action would be reasonably anticipated to cause direct emissions of 25,000 metric tons or more of CO_2-equivalent GHG emissions on an annual basis, agencies should consider this an indicator that a quantitative and qualitative assessment may be meaningful to decision-makers and the public. CEQ does not propose this as an indicator of a threshold of significant effects, but rather as an indicator of a minimum level of GHG emissions that may warrant some description in the appropriate NEPA analysis for agency actions involving direct emissions of GHGs.

The draft guidance recognizes that there are more sources and actions emitting GHGs (in terms of both absolute numbers and types) than are typically encountered when evaluating the emissions of other pollutants. From a quantitative perspective, there are no dominating sources and fewer sources that would be even close to dominating total GHG emissions. The global climate change problem is much more the result of numerous and varied sources, each of which might seem to make a relatively small addition to global atmospheric GHG concentrations.

Thus, under this proposed guidance, agencies are advised to use the scoping process to set reasonable spatial and temporal boundaries for this assessment and focus on aspects of climate change that may lead to changes in the impacts, sustainability, vulnerability, and design of the proposed action and alternative courses of action. At the same time, agencies should recognize the scientific limits of their ability to accurately predict climate change effects, especially of a short-term nature, and not devote effort to analyzing wholly speculative effects.

14.2.1 When to Evaluate GHG Emissions

Because the federal government by statute, executive orders, and agency policies is committed to the reduction of GHG emissions, a proposed federal action that generates CO_2 emissions should consider GHG emissions among alternatives if it is useful and relevant to the decision. Where the proposed activity is subject to GHG emissions accounting requirements, such as Clean Air Act reporting requirements that apply to stationary sources that directly emit 25,000 metric tons or more of CO_2-equivalent GHG on an annual basis, the agency should include this information in the NEPA documentation for consideration by decision-makers and the public.

CEQ does not propose this reference point for use as a measure of indirect effects, the analysis of which must be bounded by limits of feasibility in evaluating upstream and downstream effects of federal agency actions. In the agency's analysis of direct effects, it would be appropriate to: (1) quantify cumulative emissions over the life of the project; (2) discuss measures to reduce GHG emissions, including consideration of reasonable alternatives; and (3) qualitatively discuss the link between such GHG emissions and climate change. However, it is not currently useful for the NEPA analysis to attempt to link specific climatological changes, or the environmental impacts thereof, to the particular project or emissions, as such direct linkage is difficult to isolate and to understand. The estimated level of GHG emissions can serve as a reasonable proxy for assessing potential climate change impacts, and provide decision-makers and the public with useful information for a reasoned choice among alternatives.

14.2.2 How to Evaluate GHG Emissions

Once an agency has determined that it is appropriate to consider GHG emissions, the draft guidance recommends that agencies should consider quantifying those emissions using the following technical documents, to the extent that this information is useful and appropriate for the proposed action under NEPA:

- For quantification of emissions from large direct emitters: 40 CFR Parts 86, 87, 89, et al. Mandatory Reporting of Greenhouse Gases; Final Rule, U.S. Environmental Protection Agency (74 Fed. Reg. 56259-56308). Note that "applicability tools" are available (http://www.epa.gov/climate change/emissions/GHG-calculator/).

- For determining whether projects or actions exceed the 25,000 metric ton of CO_2-equivalent greenhouse gas emissions.

- For quantification of Scope 1 emissions at federal facilities: Greenhouse gas emissions accounting and reporting guidance that will be issued under Executive Order 13514 Sections 5(a) and 9(b) (http://www.ofee.gov).

- For quantification of emissions and removals from terrestrial carbon sequestration and various other project types: Technical Guidelines, Voluntary Reporting of Greenhouse Gases (1605(b) Program, U.S. Department of Energy) (http://www.eia.doe.gov/oiaf/1605/). CEQ notes that agencies may also find useful information in the following sources: Renewable Energy Requirements Guidance for EPACT 2005 and EO 13423 (http://www.ofee.gov/eo/epact05_fedrenewenergyguid_final_on _web.pdf), EPA Climate Leaders GHG Inventory Protocols (http:// www.epa.gov/climateleaders/resources/inventory-guidance.html).

For proposed actions that are not adequately addressed in the GHG emission reporting protocols listed above, agencies should use NEPA's provisions for interagency consultation with available expertise to identify and follow the best available procedures for evaluating comparable activities. Agencies are encouraged to consider the emissions source categories, measurement methodologies, and reporting criteria outlined in these documents, as applicable to the proposed action, and follow the relevant procedures for determining and reporting emissions. The NEPA process does not require submitting a formal report or participation in the reporting programs. Rather, under this proposed guidance, only the methodologies relevant to the emissions of the proposed project need to be considered and disclosed to decision-makers and the public.

The draft guidance recognizes that inherent in NEPA and the CEQ implementing regulations is a " 'rule of reason,' which ensures that agencies determine whether and to what extent to prepare an EIS based on the usefulness of any new potential information to the decision-making process." Where a proposed action is evaluated in either an EA or an EIS, the agency may look to reporting thresholds in the technical documents cited above as a point of reference for determining the extent of direct GHG emissions analysis that is appropriate to the proposed agency decision. As proposed in draft guidance above, for federal actions that require an EA or EIS the direct and indirect GHG emissions from the action should be considered in scoping and, to the extent that scoping indicates that GHG emissions warrant consideration by the decision-maker, quantified and disclosed in the environmental document.

In assessing direct emissions, an agency should look at the consequences of actions over which it has control or authority. When a proposed federal action meets an applicable threshold for quantification and reporting, CEQ proposes that the agency should also consider mitigation measures and reasonable alternatives to reduce action-related GHG emissions. Analysis of emissions sources should take account of all phases and elements of the proposed action over its expected life, subject to reasonable limits based on feasibility and practicality.

Agencies should apply the rule of reason to ensure that their discussion pertains to the issues that deserve study and de-emphasizes issues that are less useful to the decision regarding the proposal, its alternatives, and mitigation options. In addressing GHG emissions, consistent with this proposed guidance, CEQ expects agencies to ensure that such description is commensurate with the importance of the GHG emissions of the proposed action, avoiding useless bulk and boilerplate documentation, so that the NEPA document may concentrate attention on important issues.

To the extent that a federal agency evaluates proposed mitigation of GHG emissions, the quality of that mitigation—including its permanence, verifiability, enforceability, and additionality—must be carefully evaluated. Among the alternatives that may be considered for their ability to reduce or mitigate GHG emissions are enhanced energy efficiency, lower GHG-emitting technology, renewable energy, planning for carbon capture and sequestration, and capturing or beneficially using fugitive methane emissions. In some cases, such activities are part of the purpose and need for the proposed action; and the analysis will provide an assessment, in a comparative manner, of the alternatives and their relative ability to advance those objectives.

14.2.3 Consideration of Effects on Climate Change

The draft guidance calls for agencies to determine which climate change impacts warrant consideration in their EAs and EISs because of their impact on the analysis of the environmental effects of a proposed agency action. Through scoping of an environmental document, agencies determine whether climate change considerations warrant emphasis or de-emphasis. When scoping the impact of climate change on the proposal for agency action, the sensitivity, location, and time frame of a proposed action will determine the degree to which consideration of these predictions or projections is warranted. As with analysis of any other present or future environment or resource condition, the observed and projected effects of climate change that warrant consideration are most appropriately described as part of the current and future state of the proposed action's "affected environment."

CEQ notes that climate change can affect the environment of a proposed action in a variety of ways. For instance, climate change can affect the integrity of a development or structure by exposing it to a greater risk of floods, storm surges, or higher temperatures. Climate change can increase the vulnerability of a resource, ecosystem, or human community, causing a proposed action to result in consequences that are more damaging than prior experience with environmental impacts analysis might indicate. For example, an industrial process may draw cumulatively significant amounts of water from a stream that is dwindling because of decreased snowpack in the mountains or add significant heat to a water body that is exposed to increasing atmospheric temperatures. Finally, climate change can magnify the damaging strength of certain effects of a proposed action.

Using NEPA's "rule of reason" governing the level of detail in any environmental effects analysis, agencies should ensure that they keep in proportion the extent to which they document their assessment of the effects of climate change. Climate change effects should be considered in the analysis of projects that are designed for long-term utility and located in areas that are considered vulnerable to specific effects of climate change (such as increasing sea level or ecological change) within the project's time frame. For example, a proposal for long-term development of transportation infrastructure on a coastal barrier island will likely need to consider whether environmental effects or design parameters may be changed by the projected increase in the rate of sea level rise.

The guidance cites several sources for the best scientific information available on the reasonably foreseeable climate change impacts. Federal agencies may summarize and incorporate by reference the Synthesis and Assessment Products of the U.S. Global Change Research Program (USGCRP, http://www.global change.gov/publications/reports/scientific-asses sments/saps), and other major peer-reviewed assessments from USGCRP. Particularly relevant is the report on climate change impacts on water resources, ecosystems, agriculture and forestry, health, coastlines and arctic regions in the United States: Global Climate Change Impacts in the United States (http://www.globalchange.gov/publications/ reports/scientific-asse ssments/us-im pacts).

Finally, CEQ suggests that agencies should also consider the particular impacts of climate change on vulnerable communities where this may affect the design of the action or the selection among alternatives. Tribal and Alaska Native communities that maintain their close relationship with the cycles of nature have observed the changes that are already underway, including the melting of permafrost in Alaska, disappearance of important species of trees, shifting migration patterns of elk and fish, and drying of lakes and rivers. These effects affect the survival for both their livelihood and their culture. Further, sovereign tribal governments with legal rights to reservations and trust resources are affected by ecological changes on the landscape in ways that many Americans are not.

14.2.4 EPA Reactions to GHG and Climate Change Guidance

At least one controversial decision made by CEQ in this guidance is to exempt federal land and resource management actions from this guidance, but it seeks public comment on the appropriate means of assessing the GHG emissions and sequestration that are affected by federal land and resource management decisions. The only apparent reason for this exemption is the lack of any established federal protocol for assessing the effects on atmospheric carbon release and sequestration at a landscape scale from land use changes or management strategies.

The U.S. Environmental Protection Agency has commented to CEQ that this guidance should be made clearer and stronger and not exempt federal land and resource management actions. They point out that in fact methodologies are available and in current use and that there are additional methodologies under development. For example, in January 2010, the Oregon/Washington Office of the Bureau of Land Management (BLM) issued guidance (Instruction Memorandum OR-2010-012) that provides a framework for analysis of GHG emissions from BLM actions, and the consideration of changing climate conditions in BLM's NEPA documents. Also, the National Park Service (NPS) and the EPA have developed the Excel-based "Climate Leadership in Parks" tool (http://www.nps.gov/climatefriendlyparks) to assist national park managers in calculating the GHG emissions of park operations. EPA acknowledges that current methodologies in many cases are unrefined but that an exemption pertaining to federal land and resource management actions would be a setback for further refinement instead of providing the incentive for continued work toward more sensitive, precise, and quantitative methodologies.

Another EPA criticism of the draft guidance is the intended treatment of indirect emissions, in terms of both quantification and mitigation. They point out that the guidance as written is unclear on which indirect emissions should routinely be quantified and what resources are available for such quantification. EPA finds this particularly troublesome, as one of the key difficulties in NEPA analyses has to do with how to bound the analysis of indirect effects for GHG emissions and how to address cumulative impacts, an issue on which the guidance is largely silent. EPA recommends that CEQ consider using the criteria of whether indirect effects have a reasonably close causal connection with the proposed action and whether they provide useful information to a decision-maker and the public.

Finally, EPA notes that the draft guidance is largely silent on the issues of GHG emissions from the transportation sector that accounts for nearly a third of total GHG emissions in the United States. Moreover, the discussion of mitigation options is weak and doesn't provide clear direction to federal agencies. EPA recommends an approach used by the Commonwealth of Massachusetts in its Draft GHG Policy and Protocol which contains an appendix that lists a range of suggested mitigation measures for consideration.

14.3 NEPA Mitigation and Monitoring

This draft guidance recognizes mitigation as an important mechanism for agencies to use to avoid, minimize, rectify, reduce, or compensate the adverse environmental impacts associated with their actions. Federal agencies typically rely upon mitigation to reduce environmental impacts through modification of proposed actions and consideration and development of mitigation alternatives during the NEPA process. Planned mitigation at times can serve to reduce the projected impacts of agency actions to below a threshold of significance or to otherwise minimize the effects of agency action. However, as identified in several studies, ongoing agency implementation and monitoring of mitigation measures is limited and in need of improvement.

Through this draft guidance, CEQ proposes three central goals to help improve agency mitigation and monitoring. First, proposed mitigation should be considered throughout the NEPA process. Decisions to employ mitigation measures should be clearly stated, and those mitigation measures that are adopted by the agency should be identified as binding commitments to the extent consistent with agency authority, and reflected in the NEPA documentation and any agency decision documents. Second, a monitoring program should be created or strengthened to ensure mitigation measures are implemented and effective. Third, public participation and accountability should be supported through proactive disclosure of, and access to, agency mitigation monitoring reports and documents. Although these goals are broad in nature, CEQ recommends implementing agency NEPA procedures and guidance be employed to establish procedures that create systematic accountability and the mechanisms to accomplish those goals.

14.3.1 Mitigation in NEPA Analyses and Decisions

CEQ NEPA regulations identify mitigation in the NEPA process as measures to avoid, minimize, rectify, reduce, or compensate for environmental impacts. The CEQ regulations provide for mitigation in the form of alternatives, and NEPA itself requires agencies to "study, develop, and describe appropriate alternatives to recommended courses of action in any proposal which involves unresolved conflicts concerning alternative uses of available resources."

Mitigation measures that an agency is adopting should be discussed in an EIS and must be included in the Record of Decision. In an EA, mitigation measures adopted to avoid a significant impact must be included in the finding of no significant impact (FONSI). Thus, this guidance approves of the use of the "mitigated FONSI" when the NEPA process results in enforceable mitigation measures.

The new guidance encourages agencies to create internal processes to ensure that mitigation actions adopted in any NEPA process are documented and that monitoring and appropriate implementation plans are created to ensure that mitigation is carried out. For agency decisions based on an EIS, the regulations require that "a monitoring and enforcement program shall be adopted . . . where applicable for mitigation." It goes on to state that mitigation commitments should be structured to include adaptive management in order to minimize the possibility of mitigation failure.

Finally, CEQ reminds the agencies that engaging the public in the environmental aspects of federal decision-making is a key aspect of NEPA, and opportunities for public involvement in the development and implementation of monitoring plans and programs should be provided. Further, it is the responsibility of the lead agency to make the results of relevant monitoring available to the public.

The EPA is supportive of these new guidelines although it has recommended clarification in a few areas. For example, the term "mitigation alternatives" can be confusing in the NEPA context since the term alternatives usually refers to proposed action alternatives which may include mitigation.

14.4 Summary

The three new guidelines incorporate much of the informal guidance that CEQ has given in the past and that agencies have adopted in their administration of NEPA regulations. Only in a few areas does CEQ appear to introduce new ideas. For example, in the GHG guidelines, CEQ sets an expectation for the rigor of analyses required to consider the effects of GHG emissions. This expectation may create new burdens for agencies in preparing an EIS or EA and extend the cost and time for compliance.

15.0 Conclusion

NEPA continues to serve as the cornerstone environmental law, and its mandates have been more fully integrated into the decision-making process of federal agencies. The federal agencies continue to refine their individual NEPA regulations to fit new initiatives and concerns. For example, streamlining of environmental processes was the focus of executive orders by the Bush administration and the identification of best NEPA management practices.[223]

On January 22, 2009, President Obama's nominee for chairman of the Council on Environmental Quality, Nancy Helen Sutley, was confirmed by the Senate. Ms. Sutley received a master of public policy from the John F. Kennedy School of Government at Harvard University, and an undergraduate degree from Cornell University. She was an EPA official during the Clinton administration, and served as special assistant to the EPA administrator in Washington, D.C. The council continues to have a budget of approximately $3 million which supports 22 full-time employees.

16.0 Research Sources

To learn more about NEPA and agency regulations, check the following additional resources:

- Council on Environmental Quality Homepage: http://www.whitehouse.gov/ceq/
- CEQ Regulations for Implementing NEPA: http://ceq.eh.doe.gov/nepa/regs/ceq/toc_ceq.htm
- NEPANet—NEPA Statute, Regulations, and Reports from CEQ: http://ceq.eh.doe.gov/nepa/nepanet.htm
- Federal Agencies NEPA Procedures: http://ceq.eh.doe.gov/nepa/regs/agency/agencies.cfm
- NEPA Case Law Review: http://ceq.eh.doe.gov/nepa/caselaw.html
- EPA NEPA Site: http://www.epa.gov/Compliance/nepa/index.html
- USDA Forest Service NEPA Site: http://www.fs.fed.us/forum/nepa/welcome.htm
- Department of Energy NEPA Site: http://tis.eh.doe.gov/nepa/

- Federal Highway Administration NEPA Overview: http://www.fhwa.dot .gov/environment/00001.htm

- Bureau of Land Management NEPA Handbook: http://www.blm.gov/ nhp/efoia/wo/handbook/h1790-1.html

- U.S. Fish and Wildlife Service NEPA Compliance Procedures: http:// policy.fws.gov/550fw2.html

- NASA NEPA Review: http://www.hq.nasa.gov/office/codej/codeje/ je_site/nepa/aboutenepa.html

- FEMA Most Commonly Encountered Laws and Executive Orders: http://www.fema.gov/ep/laws.shtm

- Federal Transit Administration Environmental Process: http://www.fta .dot.gov/office/planning/ep/

- Department of Commerce NOAA NEPA Coordination: http://www .nepa.noaa.gov/

- Federal Communication Commission NEPA Rules: http://wireless.fcc .gov/siting/npaguid.html

- National Association of Environmental Professionals NEPA Working Group: http://www.naep.org/NEPAWG/NEPAWG.html

Notes

[1] 42 U.S.C. §§ 4321–4370c.

[2] 42 U.S.C. § 4332(2)(C); *see also* Frederick R. Anderson, *NEPA in the Courts: A Legal Analysis of the National Environmental Policy Act* (1973).

[3] Diana Bear, "NEPA at 19: A Primer on an 'Old Law' with Solutions to New Problems," 19 *Envtl. L. Rep.* (Envtl. L. Inst.) 10060 (1989).

[4] Environmental Quality: Hearings on H.R. 12143 before the Subcommittee on Fisheries and Wildlife Conservation, Committee on Merchant Marine and Fisheries, 91st Cong., 1st Sess. (1969).

[5] Library of Congress, C.R.S., Env. Policy Div., Congress and the Nation's Environment and Environmental Affairs of the 91st Congress (1971).

[6] Anderson, *supra* note 2, at 4-14.

[7] S.2549, 86th Cong., 2d Sess. (1960).

[8] Henry Jackson, "Environmental Quality, the Courts and Congress," 68 *Mich. L. Rev.* 1079 (1970).

[9] 42 U.S.C. § 4331(a).

[10] *Id.* § 4331(c).

[11] *Id.* § 4331(a).

[12] *Id.* § 4331(b).

[13] *Id.* §§ 4341–4347.

[14] 15 U.S.C. §§ 1021–1025.

[15] Exec. Order No. 11514, 3 C.F.R. 356 (1972).

[16]   36 Fed. Reg. 7723 (Apr. 23, 1971).

[17]   *See*, e.g., *Environmental Defense Fund, Inc. v. Hoffman*, 566 F.2d 1060 (8th Cir. 1977).

[18]   Exec. Order No. 11991, 3 C.F.R., 1966–1970 Comp., p. 902 (1977).

[19]   43 Fed. Reg. 55,978 (1978).

[20]   *See Vermont Yankee Nuclear Power Corp. v. Natural Resources Defense Coun.*, 435 U.S. 519 (1978), *cert. granted*, 459 U.S. 1034 (1982), *rev'd on other grounds*, 462 U.S. 87 (1983).

[21]   449 F.2d 1109 (D.C. Cir. 1971).

[22]   *Id.* at 1112.

[23]   *See Alumet v. Andrus*, 607 F.2d 911 (10th Cir. 1979); *see also* David Sive and Frank Friedman, *A Practical Guide to Environmental Law* §§ 7.01(a), 7.02(k) (1987).

[24]   15 U.S.C. § 793(c)(1).

[25]   33 U.S.C. § 1371(c)(1).

[26]   *Id.* § 1501.2.

[27]   *Id.*

[28]   42 U.S.C. § 4332(2)(C).

[29]   40 C.F.R. § 1500.3 (1991).

[30]   *Id.* § 1507.3(b)(2).

[31]   *Id.* § 1507.3(c).

[32]   *Id.* § 1508.

[33]   *Id.* § 1502.5; *see also Kleppe v. Sierra Club*, 427 U.S. 390 (1976).

[34]   *See Scientists' Inst. for Public Information, Inc. v. Atomic Energy Commission*, 481 F.2d 1079 (D.C. Cir. 1973) (for discussion of timing); *see also Aberdeen and Rockfish R.R. Co. v. Students Challenging Regulatory Agency Procedures (SCRAP)*, 422 U.S. 289 (1975).

[35]   40 C.F.R. § 1508.23 (1991).

[36]   *Id.* § 1508.18.

[37]   *Id.*

[38]   *Id.*; *see generally* D. Mandelker, *NEPA Law and Litigation* § 8.16 (1984).

[39]   *Carolina Action v. Simon*, 389 F. Supp. 1244 (M.D.N.C. 1975), *aff'd*, 522 F.2d 295 (4th Cir. 1975).

[40]   40 C.F.R. § 1508.18 (1991).

[41]   *See New Jersey Dept't of Envtl. Protection and Energy v. Long Island Power Auth.*, 30 F.3d 403, 415-416 (3d Cir. 1994).

[42]   40 C.F.R. § 1508.18.

[43]   *Id.* § 1508.27.

[44]   *Id.*

[45]   42 U.S.C. § 4331(a).

[46]   460 F.2d 640 (2d Cir. 1972), *cert. denied*, 409 U.S. 990 (1972).

[47]   *Breckinridge v. Rumsfeld*, 537 F.2d 864 (6th Cir. 1976), *cert. denied*, 429 U.S. 1061 (1977).

[48]   *Save the Courthouse Comm. v. Lynn*, 408 F. Supp. 1323 (S.D.N.Y. 1975).

[49]   40 C.F.R. § 1508.14 (1991).

[50]   *Calvert Cliffs Coordinating Committee Inc.*, 449 F.2d at 1112.

[51]   *Id.* at 1113.

[52]   *See supra*, section 3.0.

[53]   15 U.S.C. § 719H(c)(3).

[54]   426 U.S. 776 (1976); *see also cf. Jones v. Gordon*, 792 F.2d 821 (9th Cir. 1986).

[55]   599 F.2d 1333, 1344-45 (5th Cir. 1979).

56 *See Sugarloaf Citizens Ass'n v. FERC*, 959 F.2d 508, 513 (4th Cir. 1992); *Goos v. ICC*, 911 F.2d 1283, 1296 (8th Cir. 1990); and *Milo Community Hospital v. Weinberger*, 525 F.2d 144, 147 (1st Cir. 1975).

57 *Weinberger v. Catholic Action of Hawaii/Peace Education Project*, 454 U.S. 139 (1981); *see also*, F. L. McChesney, "Nuclear Weapons and 'Secret' Impact Statements: High Court Applies FOIA Exemptions to EIS Disclosure Rules," 12 *Envtl. L. Rep.* (Envtl. L. Inst.) 10007 (1982).

58 40 C.F.R. § 1507.3(c) (1991).

59 *See, e.g., Alabama v. United States Environmental Protection Agency*, 911 F.2d 499 (11th Cir. 1990); *Environmental Defense Fund v. Environmental Protection Agency*, 489 F.2d 1247 (D.C. Cir. 1973).

60 *EDF v. EPA*, 489 F.2d at 1257.

61 *Portland Cement Ass'n v. Ruckelshaus*, 486 F.2d 375 (D.C. Cir. 1973), *cert. denied*, 417 U.S. 921 (1974).

62 *EDF v. EPA*, 489 F.2d at 1256-57.

63 *Alabama v. EPA*, 911 F.2d at 504.

64 *Warren County v. State of North Carolina*, 528 F. Supp. 276, 286-87 (E.D.N.C. 1981).

65 *Western Nebraska Resources Coun. v. United States Environmental Protection Agency*, 943 F.2d 867, 871-72 (8th Cir. 1991).

66 *Maryland v. Train*, 415 F. Supp. 116, 121-22 (D. Md. 1976).

67 *Compare Wyoming v. Hathaway*, 525 F.2d 66, 71-72 (10th Cir. 1975) *cert. denied, sub nom. Wyoming v Kleppe*, 426 U.S. 906 (1976), *with Texas Comm. on Natural Resources v. Bergland*, 573 F.2d 201, 208 (5th Cir.), *cert. denied*, 439 U.S. 966 (1978) *and Jones v. Gordon*, 621 F. Supp. 7, 13 (D. Alaska 1985), *aff'd in part, rev'd in part*, 792 F.2d 821 (9th Cir. 1986).

68 *Texas Committee on Natural Resources*, 573 F.2d at 208.

69 *Jones*, 621 F. Supp. at 7.

70 *Foundation on Economic Trends v. Heckler*, 587 F. Supp. 753, 765-66 (D.D.C. 1984), *aff'd in part, vacated in part on other grounds*, 756 F.2d 143 (D.C. Cir. 1985).

71 *Sierra Club v. Hodel*, 848 F.2d 1068, 1094-95 (10th Cir. 1988).

72 42 U.S.C. § 9620(e)(1).

73 40 C.F.R. § 1506.11 (1991).

74 Dept. of Energy, Guidance on Implementation of the DOE NEPA/CERCLA Integration Policy (Nov. 15, 1991).

75 *See infra*, section 4.4.

76 *Id.* DOE expects only a relatively few projects will require the preparation of an EIS during the RI/FS for individual projects.

77 40 C.F.R. § 1508.4 (1991).

78 *See Bear, supra* note 3, at 10063.

79 40 C.F.R. §§ 1507.3 and 1508.4 (1991).

80 *See, e.g.,* FHWA NEPA implementing regulations, 23 C.F.R. § 771.117.

81 *See Macht v. Skinner*, 916 F.2d 13 (D.C. Cir. 1990); *see also* Daniel R. Mandelker, *NEPA Law and Litigation* § 8:16 (1984); *Winnebago Tribe of Nebraska v. Ray*, 621 F.2d 269, 272 (8th Cir.), *cert. denied*, 449 U.S. 836 (1980). *Citizens against Rails-to-Trails v. Surface Transportation Board*, 267 F.3d 1144 (D.C. Cir. 2001). *City of New York v. Mineta*, 262 F.3d 169 (2d Cir. 2001).

82 *E.g., see* U.S. Corps of Engineers regulations at 33 C.F.R. pt. 325, app. B, § 7(b).

83 *See Marbled Murrelet v. Babbitt*, 83 F.3d 1068 (9th Cir. 1996).

84 40 C.F.R. § 1502.4(a) (1991).

85 *Id.* § 1508.25(a).

86 *Id.* § 1508.25(a)(1).

87 *See Named Individual Members of the San Antonio Conservation Soc'y v. Texas Highway Dept.*, 446 F.2d 1013 (5th Cir. 1971), *cert. denied*, 406 U.S. 933 (1972).

88   23 C.F.R. § 771.111(f).

89   Letter from CEQ Chairman James L. Connaughton to Secretary of Transportation Norman Mineta, May 12, 2003. (*See* http://www.fhwa.dot.gov/stewardshipeo/connaughtonmay12.htm.)

90   40 C.F.R. § 1502.13.

91   40 C.F.R. §§ 1501.5, 1506.5.

92   *Simmons v. U.S. Army Corps of Engineers*, 120 F.3rd 664 (7th Cir. 1997).

93   *National Parks & Conservation Ass'n v. Bureau of Land Management*, 586 F.3d 735 (9th Cir. 2009).

94   FHWA/FTA Memorandum titled *Guidance on "Purpose and Need,"* from Mary Peters, FHWA administrator, and Jennifer Dorn, FTD administrator, July 23, 2003. (*See* http://nepa.fhwa.dot.gov/ReNepa/Re Nepa.nsf/All + Documents/EFE6B59BE347825685256D8900722F05/$FILE/FHWA_FTA%20Joint %20Guidance%20on%20Purpose%20and%20Need.pdf.) *See also Sylvester v. United States Army Corps of Eng'rs*, 882 F.2d 407 (9th Cir. 1989).

95   *See* "Integrating Long Range Planning and NEPA" in subsection 4.4.

96   23 U.S.C. §§ 134 and 135; and 49 U.S.C. §§ 5303-5306.

97   Examples are contained in 40 C.F.R. §§ 1501.1(a); 1501.1(b); 1501.1(d); and 1502.2.

98   *North Buckhead Civic Association v. Skinner*, 903 F.2d 1533 (11th Cir. 1990); *Simmons v. U.S. Army Corps of Engineers*, 120 F.3rd 664 (7th Cir. 1997); *Carmel-by-the-Sea v. U.S. DOT*, 123 F.3d 1142 (9th Cir. 1997); *Utahns for Better Transportation v. U.S. DOT*, 305 F.3d 1152 (10th Cir. 2002); *Sierra Club v. U.S. Department of Transportation*, 350 F. Supp. 2nd 1168 (D. Nev. 2004).

99   Memorandum re. *Integration of Planning and NEPA Process*, draft 9/20/04, D. J. Gribbin, chief counsel of FHWA, and William Sears, chief counsel of FTA.

100 *Id.* § 1508.28.

101 *Id.* § 1508.9.

102 *Id.* § 1508.13.

103 *Id.* § 1501.4(e)(2).

104 *See* Bear, *supra* note 3, at 10063.

105 40 C.F.R. § 1501.5 (1991).

106 *Id.* § 1501.6.

107 *Id.* § 1501.5(c).

108 *Id.* § 1506.2.

109 *Id.* § 1501.7. The "notice of intent" must (1) describe the proposed action and possible alternatives, (2) describe the proposed scoping process, and (3) provide the name and address of a person within the agency to contact concerning the EIS. *Id.* § 1508.22.

110 *Id.* § 1501.7.

111 *Id.* § 1501.7(a).

112 *Id.* § 1501.7(b).

113 *See Vermont Yankee Nuclear Power Corp.*, 435 U.S. at 551-54.

114 40 C.F.R. § 1506.5 (1991).

115 *Id.* § 1506.5(b).

116 508 F.2d 927 (2d Cir. 1974), *vacated*, 423 U.S. 809 (1975) (vacated as a result of subsequent legislation).

117 *Id.* at 931.

118 42 U.S.C. § 4332(2)(D).

119 *Id.* § 4332(2)(D)(iv).

120 *Green County Planning Bd. v. Federal Power Comm'n.*, 455 F.2d 412 (2d Cir.), *cert. denied*, 409 U.S. 849 (1972).

121 *Sierra Club v. Lynn*, 502 F.2d 43 (5th Cir. 1974), *cert. denied*, 421 U.S. 994, 422 U.S. 1049 (1975).

122 *Natural Resources Defense Coun. v. Callaway*, 524 F.2d 79 (2d Cir. 1975).

123   40 C.F.R. § 1506.5(c) (1991).

124   *Id.* § 1500.2(b).

125   *Id.* § 1502.10.

126   *Id.* § 1502.14.

127   *Id.* § 1502.14.

128   46 Fed. Reg. 18026, 18027 (1981) (Council on Environmental Quality, "Forty Most Asked Questions Concerning CEQ's National Environmental Policy Act Regulations," Question 1).

129   *See Natural Resources Defense Council, Inc. v. Morton,* 148 U.S. App. D.C. 5, 458 F.2d 827, 836 (D.C. Cir. 1972).

130   *Id.*

131   40 C.F.R. § 1502.16 (1991).

132   *Id.* § 1502.22.

133   51 Fed. Reg. 15625 (1986).

134   *Robertson v. Methow Valley Citizens,* 490 U.S. 332, 356 (1989).

135   *Sierra Club v. Bosworth,* 199 F. Supp. 2d 971 (N.D.Cal. 2002); *League of Wilderness Defenders-Blue Mountains Diversity Project v. Marquis-Brong,* not reported (D. Ore. 2003); and *League of Wilderness Defenders v. Zielinski,* 187 F. Supp. 2d 1263 (D. Ore. 2002).

136   40 C.F.R. § 1508.7 (1991).

137   *Id.* § 1508.27(b)(7).

138   *See Fritiofson v. Alexander,* 772 F.2d 1225 (5th Cir. 1985); *Thomas v. Peterson,* 753 F.2d 754 (9th Cir. 1985).

139   42 U.S.C. § 4332(2)(C).

140   *Id.* § 4332(2)(G).

141   *See supra,* note 15.

142   *See supra,* note 16.

143   40 C.F.R. § 1506.6(b) (1991).

144   *Id.* § 1503.1.

145   *Id.*

146   *Id.*

147   *Id.* § 1503.4.

148   *Id.* § 1506.6.

149   310 F. Supp. 2d 1168 (Nev. 2004).

150   23 C.F.R. § 771.111(h).

151   310 F. Supp. 2d 1168 at 1208.

152   *Id.* § 1502.14(f).

153   *Id.* § 1505.3.

154   *Id.* § 1508.20.

155   490 U.S. 332 (1989).

156   *Methow Valley Citizens Coun. v. Regional Forester,* 833 F.2d 810 (9th Cir. 1987), *cert. granted,* 47 U.S. 1217 (1988), *rev'd,* 490 U.S. 332 (1989).

157   *Robertson,* 490 U.S. at 353.

158   42 U.S.C. § 4332(2)(C).

159   40 C.F.R. § 1506.8 (1991).

160   *Id.* § 1506.8(b).

161   *Id.* § 1508.12. The presidential exemption applies only to the president and immediate staff, not to offices in the EOP like CEQ.

[162] 442 U.S. 347 (1979).

[163] *Id.* at 357.

[164] *Id.* at 364.

[165] The Council on Environmental Quality issued Interim Guidelines on April 30, 1970, for the preparation of environmental impact statements under Executive Order 11514 (1970). This guidance interpreted the statutory clause "major Federal actions significantly affecting the quality of the human environment" to be construed by agencies "with a view to the overall, *cumulative impact* of the action proposed (and of further actions contemplated)." (F.R. Doc. 70-5769.)

[166] 40 C.F.R. § 1508.25.

[167] In 1993, CEQ reviewed 116 Final EISs to determine the extent they addressed cumulative effects. Only 67 EISs mentioned cumulative impact analysis while 49 ignored it. Of the 67 EISs, only 31 EISs provided evidence of cumulative impact analysis for some or all affected resources discussed.

[168] 40 C.F.R. § 1508.7.

[169] *See Natural Resources Defense Council. v. Hodel,* 275 U.S. App. D.C. 69, 865 F.2d 288, 297 (D.C. Cir. 1988).

[170] *See C.A.R.E. Now, Inc. v. Federal Aviation Administration,* 844 F.2d 1569 (11th Cir. 1988); *Headwaters, Inc. v. Bureau of Land Management,* 914 F.2d 1174 (9th Cir. 1990).

[171] *See Wyoming Outdoor Council Power River Basin Res. Council v. United States Corps of Eng'rs,* 351 F. Supp. 2d 1232 (D. Wyo. 2005).

[172] 40 C.F.R. § 1508.25(a).

[173] 772 F.2d 1225 (5th Cir. 1985).

[174] 427 U.S. 390 (1976).

[175] *Daly v. Volpe,* 514 F.2d 1106 (1975); *Natural Resources Defense Council v. Callaway,* 524 F.2d 79 (2nd Cir. 1975); *Thomas v. Peterson,* 753 F.2d 754 (9th Cir. 1985); *Conner v. Dep't of Interior,* 27 ERC 1143 (9th Cir. 1988).

[176] 40 C.F.R. § 1502.9(c)(1) (1991).

[177] *See Marsh v. Oregon Natural Resources Council,* 490 U.S. 360, 374 (1989); *see also Price Road Neighborhood Ass'n, v. U.S. Dept of Transportation,* 113 F.3d 1505, 1509 (9th Cir. 1997).

[178] *See Idaho Sporting Congress v. Thomas,* 137 F.3d 1146, 1152 (9th Cir. 1998); also *Id.*

[179] 40 C.F.R. § 1502.9(c)(4) (1991).

[180] *Environmental Defense Fund v. Massey,* 986 F.2d 528, 529 (D.C. Cir. 1993).

[181] *Natural Resources Defense Council v. U.S. Department of the Navy,* unpublished (C.D. Cal. 2002).

[182] Executive Order No. 12114, 3 C.F.R. 356 (1980).

[183] *Id.* §§ 2–3.

[184] Council on Environmental Quality, 22nd Annual Report, p. 136 (1992).

[185] 61 FR 36727 (1996).

[186] 42 U.S.C. 7609, Public Law 91604 12(a), 84 Stat. 1709.

[187] *Policy and Procedures for the Review of Federal Actions Impacting the Environment,* U.S. EPA, Office of External Affairs, Office of Federal Activities, Washington, D.C.

[188] Elizabeth Blaug, General Counsel's Office, CEQ.

[189] *Calvert Cliffs Coordinating Committee, Inc.,* 449 F.2d at 1115; *see also Environmental Defense Fund v. Corps of Engineers of the United States Army,* 470 F.2d 289 (8th Cir. 1972), *cert. denied,* 412 U.S. 931 (1973).

[190] 401 U.S. 402 (1971).

[191] 5 U.S.C. § 706(2); *Marsh v. Oregon Natural Resources Coun.,* 490 U.S. 360 (1989).

[192] *Marsh,* 490 U.S. at 377-78, 385.

[193] *Id.*

194 *Robertson v. Methow Valley Citizens Council*, 490 U.S. at 358-59.

195 5 U.S.C. §§ 551–559.

196 *Public Citizen v. Nat'l Highway Traffic Safety Admin.*, 848 F.2d 256, 261 (D.C. Cir. 1988).

197 *Lujan v. National Wildlife Federation*, 487 U.S. 871 (1990).

198 912 F.2d 478, 498 (D.C. Cir. 1990).

199 *Id.* at 483-84.

200 127 S. Ct. 1438 (2007).

201 504 U.S. 555 (1992).

202 129 S. Ct. 1142 (2009).

203 *See* memorandum establishing Task Force at http://ceq.eh.doe.gov/ntf/20020410memo.html.

204 *See* Task Force Report at http://ceq.eh.doe.gov/ntf/report/pdftoc.html.

205 This approach was developed by the ecologists C. S. Holling and Carl J. Walters at the University of British Columbia, Canada, in the 1970s.

206 Public Law 109-59, August 10, 2005.

207 Sections of SAFETEA-LU address transportation planning (§ 6001), air quality transportation conformity (§ 6011), requirements of § 4(f) (§ 6009), and environmental review of activities that support deployment of intelligent transportation systems (§ 6010).

208 *Id.*, §§ 6002–6011.

209 *See* discussion of congressional exemptions from certain NEPA provision in Daniel R. Mandelker, *NEPA Law and Litigation*, 2nd ed., § 5:6.

210 40 C.F.R. §§ 1501.5 and 1501.6.

211 *See* footnote 1, § 6002(a).

212 Conference Report 109-203, SAFETEA-LU, July 28, 2005, at p. 1047.

213 40 C.F.R. § 1506.3.

214 FHWA Proposed Guidance for SAFETEA-LU Environmental Review Process, June 29, 2006.

215 23 U.S.C. § 139(d)(3) added by § 6002 of SAFETEA-LU.

216 *Id.*

217 *Supra* note 9.

218 23 C.F.R. § 771.119.

219 SAFETEA-LU, § 6002(l).

220 SAFETEA-LU, § 6004 adding new § 326 to 23 U.S.C.

221 SAFETEA-LU, § 6010.

222 SAFETEA-LU, § 6005 adding new § 327 to 23 U.S.C.

223 EO 13274 "Environmental Stewardship and Transportation Infrastructure Project Review," September 18, 2002 (67 FR 59449).

Chapter 11

Climate Change and Environmental Law

Richard Alonso and Michael Weller[1]
Bracewell LLP

1.0 Introduction

Regulation of greenhouse gases (GHGs) and the development of climate law to address the issues surrounding climate change are well on their way. Legislative efforts have started and stopped, but the Obama administration and the United States Environmental Protection Agency (EPA) have pushed forward with policies and regulations to curb the emissions of GHGs from many sectors of the U.S. economy and to show leadership within the international community. While Congressional action on climate change is not likely in the near future, climate law will continue to evolve through federal and state regulation, private party litigation, presidential directives, market forces, and other means. Climate law has achieved sufficient momentum to carry forward even if a future Presidential administration seeks to slow the pace of regulatory change. In short, climate law is here to stay, and it presents an exciting new area of law for the environmental practitioner.

This chapter examines the early history of climate law and summarizes key regulatory developments in the effort to control GHG emissions. It looks into several areas of existing law to identify how each is contributing to the portfolio of climate law. Of these, the Clean Air Act (CAA) has preeminent place, but we look also to corporate and securities law, energy law, and laws governing protected species and environmental impact assessment. Although our focus is federal, we also review the contributions of tort law and the prominent regional programs currently in place to reduce greenhouse gas emissions.

The chapter is arranged in two parts. The first part focuses on governing law—the actual stuff of compliance obligations. The second part offers observations about practical issues, such as permitting, emissions trading, corporate due diligence, and corporate governance.

2.0 Governing Law

It is a mistake to believe that, absent a federal climate-change statute, climate law is a barren field. Quite the contrary. Legal obligations with respect to climate issues exist in all sorts of areas, including federal and state regulations, corporate law, energy law, and natural resources law. Below we review the most interesting areas in which legal obligations are emerging in relation to climate change. Before doing so, we begin with a review of the Obama administration's stated intentions and policy objectives as well as Congress's previous efforts to pass a comprehensive climate bill.

2.1 The Obama Administration and the U.S. Congress

Elected in November 2008 on a cresting wave of Democratic urgency that included a dose of popular environmentalism and youthful optimism, Barack Obama wasted no time in setting nationwide greenhouse gas reduction as an objective of his administration. In fact, more than a year before the election, he gave early notice of his intentions in a speech in Portsmouth, New Hampshire.[2] The lengthy speech announced a manifesto on climate change and related energy issues. Calling climate change "the planet's greatest threat" and "one of the most urgent challenges of our generation," then Senator Obama described America as the "last, best hope of Earth" for determining "the very future of life on this Earth." He directly linked the nation's posture on climate change to the nation's excessive dependence on fossil energy generally and imported oil specifically, and to the nation's security challenges.

Casting global warming as "not a someday problem" but an immediate problem that drives storms, forest fires, famine, war, and strife around the world, Senator Obama used the speech to outline a comprehensive energy plan that, among other things, would include specific legal measures:

- setting mandatory increases in automotive fuel efficiency;

- implementing a "phase-out" of the "carbon economy that's causing our changing climate" by:
  - setting a hard cap on all carbon emissions to achieve an 80 percent reduction by 2050 with interim milestones in preceding decades; and
  - creating a cap-and-trade regime for greenhouse gas emissions in which tradable allowances are bought, not allocated, in order to "make dirty energy expensive";

- investing $150 billion over ten years to develop and deploy "clean, affordable energy," including "next generation" biofuels to the tune of 2 billion gallons by 2013;

- requiring 25 percent of all electricity to be fueled by renewable sources by 2025;

- using "the carbon cap and whatever tools are necessary to stop new dirty plants from being built in America—including a ban on new traditional coal facilities";

- setting the goal of 50 percent greater energy efficiency across the nation by 2030 by:

  o making new buildings 50 percent more efficient;

  o making all federal buildings carbon neutral by 2025;

  o installing a digital smart grid; and

  o mandating the phase-out of all incandescent lightbulbs in the United States.

These ambitious goals proved, in almost all instances, too challenging to achieve much progress during his first term. Two years and one month after his speech in Portsmouth, and in the immediate aftermath of losing the Democratic majority in the House of Representatives and narrowly retaining a Democratic majority in the Senate, now-President Obama gave a lengthy press conference in which the economy—not global warming—was front and center and in which his ambitions for fighting off "the planet's greatest threat" were significantly tempered by economic and political realities.[3] As for cap-and-trade legislation, that was "just one way of skinning the cat, it was not the only way."[4]

And while the economy was to be the primary focus, the president can point to several climate-related initiatives from his first term that deserve note. For example, the president installed former EPA Administrator Carol Browner as the "czarina" heading the new White House Office of Energy and Climate Change Policy.[5] Until she stepped aside in March 2011, Ms. Browner was widely seen as a skilled insider who wielded exceptional authority over the administration's climate policy, although EPA Administrator Lisa Jackson remained the cabinet-level official in charge of national environmental policy during President Obama's first term. Regulatory actions taken by EPA during President Obama's first term included: a crucial regulatory "finding" that greenhouse gases constitute a threat to public health and welfare, thereby paving the way for direct regulatory restrictions on emissions; a new rule requiring the collection of masses of information about the emission of greenhouse gases from many producing sectors of the economy; a new rule establishing greenhouse gas emission standards for light duty vehicles; and a new rule designed to establish thresholds for requiring a permit to emit greenhouse gases from power plants, refineries, cement plants, and other facilities.[6] Beyond these regulatory actions, a raft of nonregulatory initiatives stresses voluntary or cooperative efforts to reduce greenhouse gas emissions.[7]

Climate change was for the most part left off the table during the 2012 presidential campaign. However, within the first six months of his second inauguration, President Obama had already given two speeches that indicated action on climate change would be a top priority in his second term. In his second inaugural address on January 21, 2013 and with Hurricane Sandy still a fresh memory for those in the northeast, President Obama stated that "[w]e will respond to the threat of climate change, knowing that the failure to do so would betray our children and future generations. Some may still deny the overwhelming judgment of science, but none can avoid the devastating impact of raging fires, and crippling drought, and more powerful storms."[8] Six months later on June 25, 2013, President Obama introduced his "Climate Action Plan," a comprehensive plan that generally aims to cut carbon emissions in the United States, take steps to prepare for current impacts of climate change, and lead international efforts to address global climate change.[9]

Some of the major components of the Climate Action Plan include (1) directing EPA to establish carbon pollution standards for new and existing power plants; (2) making available up to $8 billion in loan guarantees for advanced fossil energy and efficiency projects; (3) directing DOI to permit enough renewables projects on public lands by 2020 to power more than 6 million homes; (4) setting a goal to reduce carbon pollution by at least 3 billion metric tons cumulatively by 2030 through efficiency standards for appliances and federal buildings; (5) piloting innovative strategies in the Hurricane Sandy–affected region to strengthen communities against future extreme weather and other climate impacts; and (6) committing to expand major new and existing international initiatives, including bilateral initiatives with China, India, and other major emitting countries.[10]

As described above, President Obama's multifaceted approach to crafting a national climate policy has been necessary considering the dim outlook for passing a cap-and-trade bill or any other comprehensive climate legislation. The chronology with regard to legislation is quickly told. In June 2009, the House of Representatives passed (by seven votes) the American Clean Energy and Security Act of 2009,[11] which Rep. Henry Waxman of California had developed with Rep. Edward Markey of Massachusetts. Called ACES or Waxman-Markey, the bill called for an economy-wide cap-and-trade system. Hailed as a bold measure that marked final climate legislation as an achievable goal, the bill was a bride without a groom in the Senate, which never considered a comprehensive climate bill on the floor. Various committees of the Senate took up the climate issue, and the Energy and Natural Resources Committee and the Environment and Public Works Committee each passed bills in June 2009[12] and November 2009,[13] respectively. But these efforts in the Senate lacked a unifying theme, a political champion, and a viable political future. Resuscitative efforts were attempted by Senators Kerry, Graham, and Lieberman[14] and later by Senators Cantwell and Collins,[15] but to no avail. By July 2010 it was clear even to Senate Majority Leader Harry Reid that no broad legislation to reduce greenhouse gas emissions was going to pass the 111th Congress.[16] In 2013, Senators Barbara Boxer and Bernie Sanders introduced the Climate Protection Act of 2013, a fairly comprehensive piece of legislation that includes, among other things, a fee on carbon emissions where revenues generated would be partially distributed to clean energy programs and as rebates for consumers to offset any increases in energy prices.

As in recent years, the prospects of significant climate legislation passing Congress in the near future are slim, at least in the broad format envisioned in bills like Waxman-Markey and Boxer-Sanders. The most significant Congressional actions from 2014 through 2016 were Congress's efforts to slow down or invalidate efforts by the Obama administration to implement its Climate Change Action Plan. However, none of those efforts has been successful to date.

2.2 Air Emissions Law

Until recently, the debate over climate change focused on whether it was actually occurring, and in some cases, whether the warming of the planet could be attributed to human behavior. While some may believe these issues are still up for debate, the consensus in the United States and in many other parts of the world is that anthropogenic climate change is real and dangerous. The quandary now is how to address a truly global phenomenon via domestic policy.

The primary options on the table for controlling greenhouse gas emissions in the United States include using the existing federal Clean Air Act or waiting for Congress to pass legislation specific to climate change. Despite administrative petitions, legal challenges, and threats to nullify legislatively, EPA's program for regulating greenhouse gas emissions under the existing Clean Air Act has begun in earnest. The following section provides a summary of efforts to control greenhouse gas emissions under the existing Clean Air Act.

2.2.1 *Massachusetts v. EPA*

In a petition for a writ of certiorari from the United States Supreme Court, several states and environmental groups queried whether EPA has the authority to regulate greenhouse gas emissions from new motor vehicles under Section 202 of the Clean Air Act. The Supreme Court answered definitively in *Massachusetts v. EPA*, issuing a decision that would pave the way for the first regulation of greenhouse gases under the Clean Air Act.[17]

Section 202(a)(1) of the Clean Air Act provides that EPA must promulgate "standards applicable to the emission of any air pollutant from any class or classes of new motor vehicles or new motor vehicle engines, which in [the EPA administrator's] judgment cause, or contribute to, air pollution which may reasonably be anticipated to endanger public health or welfare."[18] The petitioners in *Massachusetts v. EPA* sought to have EPA regulate greenhouse gases under Section 202. EPA argued that in enacting the Clean Air Act, Congress never intended to regulate substances such as greenhouse gases that contribute to a global phenomenon such as climate change. EPA further reasoned that, if Congress did not intend to regulate greenhouse gases, then these substances could not be considered "air pollutants" under the Clean Air Act.

The Supreme Court sided with the state and environmental group petitioners, finding that greenhouse gases "fit well" within the Clean Air Act's definition of "air pollutant" and that they could be regulated if EPA determines they cause or contribute to climate change.[19] The Supreme Court's decision did not mandate that EPA regulate greenhouse gases under the Clean Air Act. Instead, the Court's decision placed the onus on EPA to decide whether greenhouse gases, as air pollutants under the Clean Air Act, cause or contribute to air pollution that endangers public health or welfare. The administrator's determination whether an air pollutant endangers the public health or welfare is referred to as an "endangerment finding." After the Supreme Court's decision, it was only a matter of time—two years, as it happens—until such an endangerment finding was undertaken. In the meantime, several related developments created additional momentum and context.

2.2.2 EPA's Program to Regulate Greenhouse Gases under the Clean Air Act

On July 30, 2008, EPA released an advanced notice of proposed rulemaking (ANPR) specifically to solicit public comment on how the agency should respond to *Massachusetts v. EPA*.[20] The ANPR is an extraordinary document that addresses a wide range of issues. In it, EPA pores over not only the many sections of the Clean Air Act that could be implicated in regulating greenhouse gases, but also the potential technologies that could be employed in controlling emissions and the possible legislative proposals that might address climate change. The ANPR was issued to address the numerous climate-related actions pending before EPA, including the Supreme Court's remand of a rule applicable to new motor vehicles, several petitions for regulation of non-road vehicles, and petitions for regulation of electric utilities and industrial sources.

An important primary purpose of the ANPR was to highlight the interconnectedness of the various sections of the Clean Air Act and the difficulties of regulating greenhouse gases under the statute. Based on the structure of the Clean Air Act, regulation under one section could trigger requirements to regulate under another. EPA notes in the ANPR that regulation of greenhouse gases could result in an expansion of EPA's authority that could have a "profound effect on virtually every sector of the economy and touch every household in the land."[21] EPA's opinion, as outlined in the ANPR, is that regulation of greenhouse gases under the Clean Air Act presents "insurmountable obstacles" because the statute is better suited to address air pollution on a local or regional level than on a global scale.[22] Secretary Stephen L. Johnson stated his concerns clearly:

> I believe the ANPR demonstrates the Clean Air Act, an outdated law originally enacted to control regional pollutants that cause direct health effects, is ill-suited for the task of regulating global greenhouse gases. Based on the analysis to date, pursuing this course of action would inevitably result in a very complicated, time-consuming and, likely, convoluted set of regulations. These rules would largely pre-empt or overlay existing programs that help control greenhouse gas emissions and would be relatively ineffective at reducing greenhouse gas concentrations given the potentially damaging effect on jobs and the U.S. economy.[23]

It is evident in the ANPR that EPA feared promulgating regulations that would significantly increase the costs of energy and transportation in the United States, with "no assurance that the regulations would materially affect global greenhouse gas atmospheric concentrations or emissions."[24]

2.2.3 The Johnson Memorandum

As EPA discussed in the ANPR, one of the main issues with regulating greenhouse gases within the Clean Air Act framework is that regulation under one program can trigger regulation under others. For example, EPA could make a decision that it is appropriate to regulate greenhouse gases from mobile sources under Section 202 and then be compelled to regulate emissions from stationary sources regardless of whether it believed the same danger to public health or welfare existed. Following the Supreme Court's decision in *Massachusetts v. EPA*, environmental groups intervened in many permit proceedings based on this very premise, in attempts to force EPA to include greenhouse gas emission standards in certain stationary source permits.[25]

The relevant regulatory "trigger" involved the Clean Air Act Prevention of Significant Deterioration (PSD) permit program. The PSD program requires new and modified major stationary sources of "regulated" pollutants to comply with what many industries believe are expensive and burdensome preconstruction permitting requirements. Environmental groups believed PSD, including application of best available control technology, should apply to carbon dioxide because the PSD regulations provide in part that a "regulated" pollutant includes "[a]ny pollutant that otherwise is subject to regulation under the [Clean Air Act]."[26]

Environmental groups argued that the existing monitoring and reporting requirements for carbon dioxide under the Acid Rain program constitute "regulation" and that following the decision in *Massachusetts v. EPA*, carbon dioxide could be defined as a "pollutant" under the Clean Air Act. Taken together, carbon dioxide was now a Clean Air Act pollutant "subject to regulation" under the Acid Rain program and therefore subject to the PSD program. EPA disagreed, countering that the monitoring and reporting requirements of the Acid Rain program do not equate to being "subject to regulation" because they do not constitute the "actual control of emissions."

In 2008, the Environmental Appeals Board (EAB) issued a decision on one of the PSD permit challenges. The EAB determined that, while EPA was not required to treat carbon dioxide as "subject to regulation," it was in the agency's discretion to do so. This left it to EPA to interpret the meaning of the phrase. EPA Administrator Johnson provided the agency's interpretation in a December 18, 2008, memorandum, concluding that "subject to regulation" means a regulation requiring "actual control" of the pollutant. Administrator Johnson reasoned in the memorandum that "it is not sound policy to trigger mandatory emissions limitations under the PSD program on the basis of rules designed for information gathering."[27]

2.2.4 The EPA Greenhouse Gas Regulatory Saga

It was apparent from the earliest stages of the Obama presidency that, in one way or another, the United States would be taking action on climate change. Parallel efforts included listings under the Endangered Species Act, guidance from the Council on Environmental Quality on consideration of greenhouse gases during the National Environmental Policy Act (NEPA) process, and guidance from the Securities and Exchange Commission (SEC) on climate-related disclosures. With regard to emission control law, the Obama administration indicated that the preferred method for accomplishing the control of greenhouse gas emissions was via legislation, not through the existing Clean Air Act. However, the Obama administration was not going to wait for Congress to act, and EPA opened the regulatory floodgates in spring of 2009.

On April 20, 2009, EPA published in the *Federal Register* its proposed mandatory monitoring and reporting program for greenhouse gases. This was followed by the publication of a Section 202 endangerment finding on April 24,

2009; a proposal to regulate greenhouse gas emissions from mobile sources under Section 202 on September 28, 2009; a formal reconsideration of the Johnson Memorandum on October 7, 2009; and, finally, what has come to be known as the "Tailoring Rule" on October 27, 2009. Collectively, the regulatory proposals made manifest the complex issues laid out in the 2008 ANPR. Having made the decision to regulate greenhouse gases from mobile sources, the structure of the Clean Air Act then required the regulation of stationary sources as well.

2.2.5 The GHG Reporting Rule

The EPA GHG Reporting Rule, finalized in late 2009, created a national registry of greenhouse gas emissions for all sectors of the economy.[28] The GHG Reporting Rule requires industrial GHG sources, fuel suppliers, manufacturers, electric generating units, certain mobile sources, landfills, and even certain animal feeding operations to monitor and report their GHG emissions on an annual basis. The proposed rule covers the six primary greenhouse gases—carbon dioxide (CO_2), methane (CH_4), nitrous oxide (N_2O), hydrofluorocarbons (HFC), perfluorocarbons (PFC), and sulfur hexafluoride (SF_6)—as well as certain other fluorinated gases such as nitrogen trifluoride (NF_3) and hydrofluorinated ethers.

EPA crafted the rule as a means of collecting data in support of its agenda to control greenhouse gas emissions under the Clean Air Act, but it also was intended to inform climate-related legislative efforts.[29] The rule defines the sources that must report their GHG emissions annually, and it defines the methods of measurement or calculation to be used in reporting the emissions.

Shortly after EPA finalized its initial GHG reporting rule, the agency issued three additional proposals expanding reporting requirements to the oil and natural gas production industry and several other sectors.[30] Finalized on November 30, 2010, Subpart W adds GHG monitoring and reporting requirements for petroleum and natural gas systems, including natural gas pipeline transportation facilities, natural gas distribution facilities, crude petroleum and natural gas production, and natural gas liquid extraction facilities.[31] Various legal challenges are pending to address concerns regarding errors, inaccuracies, and the burden imposed by various requirements.

On March 18, 2011, EPA issued a final rule extending the deadline for submitting 2010 data from March 31, 2011, to September 30, 2011.[32] The delay was in part prompted by issues with EPA's electronic data reporting system. In January 2012, EPA began providing public access to the reported 2010 GHG emission data through its interactive Data Publication Tool, which is called the Facility Level Information on Greenhouse Gases Tool (FLIGHT). Source categories that were obligated to begin monitoring in calendar year 2011 (such as petroleum and natural gas systems) reported those annual emissions in September 2012. Altogether, 41 source categories report GHG emissions data to EPA, accounting for approximately 85–90% of the total U.S. GHG emissions.

2.2.6 The Endangerment Finding

On December 15, 2009, EPA issued an endangerment finding under Section 202 of the Clean Air Act, finding that "emissions of well-mixed greenhouse gases from the transportation sources covered under CAA section 202(a) contribute to the total greenhouse gas air pollution, and thus to the climate change problem, which is reasonably anticipated to endanger public health and welfare."[33]

EPA based its finding on scientific data collected by a variety of sources, including the U.S. Global Climate Research Program, the Intergovernmental Panel on Climate Change, and the National Research Council.[34] EPA found that the emission of greenhouse gases and the accompanying effects of climate change negatively impact air quality, increase temperatures, impact extreme weather events, and increase the potential for disease. Furthermore, EPA determined that mobile sources regulated under Section 202 were significant sources of greenhouse gases. In fact, EPA notes in the endangerment finding that "[Section 202] transportation sources are responsible for 23 percent of total annual U.S. greenhouse gas emissions, making [them] the second largest [source] in the United States behind electricity generation."[35]

2.2.7 The Light Duty Vehicle (LDV) Rule

On March 7, 2010, EPA finalized what would become the first program under the Clean Air Act designed specifically to control the emission of greenhouse gases. The rulemaking addresses the Section 202 endangerment finding, focusing on the greenhouse gas emissions from mobile sources, such as cars, sport utility vehicles, minivans, trucks, buses, and motorcycles.[36] The rule was released in tandem with the National Highway Traffic Safety Administration's corporate average fuel economy (CAFE) standards.

The "LDV Rule" establishes fleet-wide average carbon dioxide emission standards based on a vehicle's carbon dioxide footprint.[37] New standards will take effect with model year (MY) 2012 vehicles and increase through MY 2016. Covered vehicles must meet combined average emissions of 250 grams/mile of CO_2 in MY 2016.[38] If automobile manufacturers focus entirely on improvements to fuel economy, this limitation equates to approximately 35.5 miles per gallon (mpg). However, EPA's program allows manufacturers to obtain credits via improvements to vehicle air conditioning systems that reduce hydrofluorocarbon (HFC) emissions.[39] The LDV Rule also establishes a cap for nitrous oxide and methane tailpipe emissions.[40] The LDV Rule represents an important step in greenhouse gas regulation for two reasons. First, as previously mentioned, it is the first direct regulatory control of greenhouse gas emissions under the Clean Air Act. Second, given the interlinkages of the Clean Air Act, it implicates the regulation of a wide range of stationary sources of greenhouse gases.

2.2.8 The Interpretive Rule

In the waning days of the Bush administration, EPA received a petition for reconsideration of the agency's interpretation of the phrase "subject to regulation" set forth in the Johnson Memorandum.[41] The Obama administration's EPA granted the petition and announced that it would take public comment on the issues covered in the memorandum and those raised in the *In re Deseret* opinion. EPA solicited comment on five possible interpretations of the regulatory phrase "subject to regulation," including (1) the "actual control" interpretation; (2) the "monitoring and reporting" interpretation; (3) the inclusion of regulatory requirements for specific pollutants in state implementation plans; (4) an EPA finding of endangerment; and (5) the grant of a section 209 waiver interpretation.[42]

Aside from a few minor changes, EPA decided to maintain the "actual control" interpretation set forth in the Johnson Memorandum.[43] The only modification is that EPA established that "actual controls" occur when a regulatory requirement to control emissions "takes effect," instead of when the emissions controls are finalized as regulations.[44] Through this interpretation, EPA declared that the PSD program requirements will apply to greenhouse gases when the tailpipe standards contained in the LDV Rule take effect for MY 2012, which began on January 2, 2011.

2.2.9 The Tailoring Rule

Once EPA finalized the LDV Rule, it was apparent that greenhouse gases would soon be "subject to regulation," a scenario that would trigger the applicability of the PSD and Title V programs for stationary sources. Under the applicable sections of the Clean Air Act, these new requirements would now apply to sources that emit more than 100 or 250 tons per year of greenhouse gases. With "traditional" air pollutants such as sulfur dioxide (SO_2), nitrogen oxides (NOx), and volatile organic compounds (VOCs), these emissions thresholds and accompanying regulatory requirements are typically triggered only by large utilities, industrial facilities, and manufacturers. Carbon dioxide and greenhouse gases present a whole different scenario.

Greenhouse gases, carbon dioxide in particular, are emitted in much larger quantities from a diverse group of sources. In fact, thousands of sources, including small businesses, hospitals, and schools, may release more than 250 tons of GHG emissions per year. EPA estimates that "if PSD requirements were to apply to GHG sources at the 100/250 tons per year (tpy) statutory levels, 40,496 projects—consisting of 3,299 projects at industrial sources and 37,197 projects at commercial or residential sources—would need PSD permits each year."[45] Such a situation would lead to significant costs for many small sources and would necessitate a regulatory permitting program much larger than currently exists.

To avoid the consequences of a literal interpretation of the Clean Air Act applicability thresholds, EPA issued a rule (the Tailoring Rule) that simply sets the regulatory trigger higher, "tailoring" the PSD rule's applicability to the "largest" sources of greenhouse gas emissions. EPA justified its reading of the Clean Air Act based on two statutory interpretation doctrines: (1) the "absurd results" doctrine, by which the agency abandons a literal reading of the statute in order to effectuate congressional intent and avoid absurd results; and (2) the "administrative necessity" doctrine, under which EPA applies statutory requirements in a way that avoids "impossible administrative burdens."[46] The Tailoring Rule established emission thresholds for PSD and Title V permitting via a two-step phase-in process, referred to as "Step 1" and "Step 2." As described by EPA, the phase-in process under the Tailoring Rule is as follows:

- Under Step 1 of the Tailoring Rule, PSD permitting requirements applies to sources' GHG emissions if the sources were subject to PSD anyway because of their non-GHG regulated air pollutants ("anyway" sources), and emit (or had the potential to emit) at least 75,000 tpy carbon dioxide equivalent (CO_2e) if the source is a new major source, or increases emissions by this amount if the source is an existing source that proposes to undertake a modification. For Title V, existing sources with, or new sources obtaining, Title V permits are required to address GHG emissions in those permits as necessary.

- Under Step 2, PSD applies to the largest GHG-emitting sources that emit or have the potential to emit at least 100–250 tpy of GHGs on a mass basis, and that are either new sources that emit at least 100,000 tpy CO_2e, or existing sources that emit at that level and that undertake modifications that increase emissions by at least 75,000 tpy CO_2e. In addition, under Step 2, Title V applies to sources that emit or have the potential to emit 100 tpy GHG on a mass basis, and emit or have the potential to emit 100,000 tpy CO_2e.[47]

On July 3, 2012, EPA issued a final rule or "Step 3" of the Tailoring Rule, which maintained the GHG permitting thresholds at the levels set in the initial Tailoring Rule.[48] In considering whether to lower the threshold, EPA concluded that it was not administratively feasible to apply PSD and Title V permitting requirements to smaller sources.[49] EPA also included in that proposed rule improvements to the GHG permitting process, by (1) increasing flexibilities and the usefulness of plantwide applicability limitations (PALs) for GHGs; and (2) creating the regulatory authority for EPA to issue synthetic minor permits for GHGs in certain situations.[50]

Despite EPA's further tailoring of the applicability thresholds, many issues existed at the time the rule was finalized, including concerns over permitting delays, costs, the readiness of states to implement the program, what would constitute best available control technology for controlling GHG emissions, and whether EPA's approach was legally sound.

In October 2010, EPA issued two supplemental GHG-related regulations. The first was designed to ensure that states are prepared to issue PSD and Title V permits for sources that trigger the greenhouse gas thresholds set forth in the Tailoring Rule. The second created a means by which EPA can step in and issue those permits if a state fails to do so or is legally unable to. After completing a review of state programs, EPA determined that some State Implementation Programs (SIPs) explicitly preclude application of the PSD program to sources that emit greenhouse gases and that certain state constitutions or other state laws would limit the ability of the state to apply PSD to greenhouse gases.

EPA concluded that the SIPs for thirteen states are "substantially inadequate" and issued a SIP Call relying on its authority under CAA Section 110(k)(5). The SIP Call requires the thirteen affected states to submit a "corrective SIP revision that applies the PSD program to GHG sources." EPA requires the states to submit corrective SIP revisions by December 2011. If a state does not submit corrective SIP revisions by that time, EPA will immediately issue a finding of substantial inadequacy and will promulgate a Federal Implementation Plan (FIP) in lieu of a state plan. EPA indicated that the FIP will mirror the regulations found at 40 C.F.R. § 52.21, with minor adjustments so that it applies to the emission of greenhouse gases.

2.2.10 EPA's Clean Power Plan

As summarized above, President Obama released a Climate Action Plan to reduce emissions of CO_2 and other greenhouse gases. At the same time, he directed EPA to propose standards for CO_2 from existing power plants by June 2014 and to finalize them by June 2015. On June 2, 2014, EPA responded to the president's directive by proposing the Clean Power Plan (CPP or Plan), which set an emissions reduction target to decrease power plant CO_2 emissions to 30% below 2005 (historical peak) levels by 2030. EPA published the proposed rule in the June 18, 2014 *Federal Register*.[51] The rule received more than 2 million comments during its 165 day comment period (EPA extended the 120 day comment period by 45 days).

Since its issuance, the CPP has been a singularly controversial EPA regulation, and it is currently the subject of substantial multiparty litigation. The Plan lays out distinct approaches that states may implement to reduce CO_2 emissions from existing electric generating units. States must develop plans to reduce CO_2 emissions or emissions rates from existing fossil-fuel-fired power plants, and they must achieve interim CO_2 emissions performance rates between 2022 and 2029 and the final CO_2 emissions performance rates by 2030. Each state has discretion in determining how best to achieve its targeted CO_2 emissions reductions. The Plan provides for an array of tools for the states to reduce compliance costs, including source-by-source command-and-control measures, interstate cap-and-trade, renewable portfolio standards, and energy efficiency improvements, among others. Once a state determines the tools that will best achieve its emissions target, the state must submit an implementation plan for EPA approval.

The state goals were developed by examining 3 building blocks:

1. An average heat rate improvement of 2–3% for all existing coal-fired plants

2. Change dispatch to disfavor coal until combined cycle natural gas plants have average capacity factor of 75%

3. Requirements for construction and operation of additional wind and solar generation—23% of U.S. electric generation in 2030 (much smaller in proposal)

States may also implement end-user energy efficiency programs and provide incentives for energy efficiency and renewable energy projects within environmental justice communities.

2.2.11 EPA's Regulation of Methane Emissions

On May 12, 2016, EPA issued a final rule to reduce methane emissions from new, reconstructed, and modified oil and gas facilities. EPA's new rule finalized amendments to the New Source Performance Standards (NSPS), which previously focused on controlling VOC emissions, not methane.[52] First, the rule adds oil and gas sources to the list of those regulated under the previous 2012 VOC NSPS for new and modified sources.[53] Second, the rule establishes methane NSPS for new and modified sources in the oil and gas industry.[54] The new standards for the oil and natural gas source category set standards for both GHGs and VOCs.[55]

The rule expands the VOC standards to include sources and equipment not regulated under the 2012 NSPS.[56] Additionally, the rule establishes methane standards for equipment leaks at natural gas processing plants, hydraulically fractured gas well completions, and equipment downstream from the wellhead.[57]

The NSPS applies to new, modified, and reconstructed equipment, processes, and activities in the production, processing, transmission, and storage phases of oil and natural gas systems.[58] Sources now regulated include hydraulically fractured oil well completions, fugitive emissions from well sites, compressor stations, and pneumatic pumps.[59] The rule does not apply to distribution entities.

In addition to the oil and gas sector, EPA is focusing on landfills to control methane emissions. EPA sent its final rules regulating emissions of methane from landfills to the White House Office of Management and Budget (OMB) for review on June 14, 2016.[60] The rules consist of a NSPS rule for new and modified landfills as well as a rule revising emission guidelines for existing landfills.[61]

EPA developed the rules in response to a 2011 petition from the Environmental Defense Fund requesting that the agency update the NSPS for landfill methane emissions. EPA has a statutory duty to review and, if necessary, revise NSPS rules eight years after they are issued, but had not done so for the new and modified landfill NSPS, which was issued in 1996 and altered in later technical amendments.[62] Although EPA has no statutory duty to revise the emissions guidelines for existing sources, it has the discretion to do so when circumstances indicate that it is appropriate to do so.[63] The existing landfill emission guidelines were last set in 2000. Under the proposed rules, landfills would be required to capture landfill gases emitted above a threshold of 34 metric tons of methane, which is significantly lower than the existing 50 metric ton threshold.[64]

2.2.12 Legal Challenges to EPA's Actions under the Clean Air Act

EPA's greenhouse gas regulatory initiatives have met with stiff opposition from industry, from the U.S. Congress, and even from environmental groups claiming that the proposals are not as far-reaching as they should be. While litigation is ongoing, the rules remain in effect. On June 26, 2012, the U.S. Court of Appeals for the District of Columbia Circuit upheld the validity of the LDV Rule and the endangerment finding and dismissed the challenges to the Tailoring Rule.[65] Although some congressional efforts sought to strip EPA of its authority to regulate greenhouse gases using the Clean Air Act, none of the attempts has proved successful to date. So after a long period of uncertainty, the United States is poised to move forward, choosing to regulate greenhouse gases via the complex network of programs that is the Clean Air Act. Unfortunately, the uncertainty is just beginning, since many questions still remain.

On June 23, 2014, the U.S. Supreme Court released its opinion in *Utility Air Regulatory Group v. EPA (UARG)*, in which it struck down a portion of EPA's

Tailoring Rule for GHG emissions.[66] This was the Court's first decision to limit EPA's authority to regulate GHGs under the Clean Air Act.

At issue in *UARG* was EPA's Tailoring Rule, by which it sought to regulate certain stationary sources under the CAA's PSD and Title V permitting programs.[67] EPA argued that it was compelled by its regulation of GHGs from motor vehicles to regulate GHGs from large stationary sources under the PSD and Title V programs.[68] Problematically, the CAA's numerical threshold to trigger PSD and Title V is low—250 tons per year—and thousands of small sources would likely come within the scope of EPA's regulation.[69] To remedy this problem, EPA attempted to "tailor" the regulation to include only those sources with the potential to emit 100,000 tons of GHG per year.[70] In doing so, EPA essentially rewrote the statutory emissions thresholds for these portions of the CAA.

Rejecting EPA's approach, the Supreme Court held that EPA is not compelled to regulate greenhouse gases under the PSD and Title V programs and that EPA is not permitted to rewrite the applicable statutory emission thresholds.[71] A stationary source's GHG emissions alone cannot be the basis for subjecting it to PSD and Title V permitting requirements, and doing so amounted to an "enormous and transformative expansion in EPA's regulatory authority without clear congressional authorization."[72]

Instead, according to the Court, EPA may regulate any level of GHG emissions under PSD or Title V when a source is already subject to those programs by virtue of its emissions of conventional pollutants.[73] EPA may require those sources to use the Best Available Control Technology to address GHG emissions, so long as the source's GHG emissions are more than a *de minimis* amount.[74] If the source's conventional emissions alone do not trigger PSD or Title V, that source's GHG emissions alone will not suffice to trigger these regulations.[75]

While the *UARG* decision involved the scope of EPA's authority to require large stationary sources to control GHG emissions under CAA permitting provisions, it is important to note that this decision only covers specific portions of the CAA. The decision does not limit EPA's authority to proceed with GHG regulation under other portions of the Act. In other words, the decision would not, for example, prevent EPA from regulating GHGs from new or existing sources under Section 111 of the CAA.

On August 3, 2015, President Obama and EPA Administrator Gina McCarthy announced the final CPP rule to regulate carbon emissions from existing fossil-fuel-fired power plants. In the announcement, President Obama stated that the CPP includes the first standards on CO_2 emissions from power plants ever proposed by EPA. Ten days later, and before the final rule was published in the *Federal Register*, states filed an emergency petition for extraordinary relief in the

D.C. Circuit, seeking a stay of the final rule.[76] The emergency petition is unusual because the parties seeking it had not yet filed suit against EPA challenging the CPP. Typically, a petition for review would be filed before a court is asked to issue an order staying the implementation of a rule. These challenges were dismissed in September 2015, pending the final rule's publication in the *Federal Register*.

On October 23, 2015, EPA published its final CPP in the *Federal Register*.[77] That same day, nearly half of all the states filed a petition for review in the D.C. Circuit, arguing that the CPP is an illegal attempt to "reorganize the nation's energy grid" among other arguments.[78] Petitions by multiple other entities were subsequently filed. All petitions challenging the CPP were consolidated into one case.

While the litigation is ongoing at the appellate level, and after the appellate court denied a stay of the rule pending the litigation, an unusual interlocutory stay request was made to the U.S. Supreme Court. On February 9, 2016, the U.S. Supreme Court stayed CPP implementation pending judicial review, which was viewed as an extraordinary order in the context of the Clean Air Act. This is the first time the U.S. Supreme Court granted a stay of an EPA rule after the appeals court denied the same request. The order is viewed by many as an indication of how important the CPP is to the judicial system. The Court clearly wanted to opine on the CPP and was concerned that its opinion would not be significant if implementation were to have started without its direction.

Subsequently, in another extraordinary procedural twist, on May 16, 2016, the D.C. Circuit, on its own motion, ordered that the case be heard *en banc*, rather than by the three-judge panel originally scheduled to hear the case. Oral argument is scheduled for September 27, 2016. Once again, this is a rare occurrence within the D.C. Circuit and demonstrates that the judges want to carefully review the CPP.

2.2.13 Obama Administration International Efforts

Using the Clean Power Plan as evidence that the United States is serious about regulating CO_2 emissions and showing leadership in combating climate change, the Obama administration was instrumental in the development of the Paris Agreement,[79] adopted December 12, 2015. The Paris Agreement was developed within the framework of the United Nations Framework Convention on Climate Change (UNFCCC) dealing with GHG emissions reduction, mitigation, and finance, and it was the first time all nations addressed climate change as an issue impacting the entire international community.

Representatives of 195 states adopted the Paris Agreement by consensus at the 21st Conference of the Parties (COP21) of the UNFCCC. The document was opened for signature at the U.N. headquarters on April 22, 2016 (Earth Day), at which time 175 parties signed it (174 countries and the European Union) and 15 states deposited their instruments of ratification.[80] After signing the Paris Agreement, each participating country must unilaterally ratify it, which will involve passage by national legislatures in many cases.[81] The Paris Agreement will become effective 30 days after 55 countries, representing 55 percent of global emissions, have signed and ratified it.[82] A nation that ratifies and enters the Paris Agreement may not withdraw from it for three years, and then only after giving one year's notice.[83]

The Paris Agreement is designed to ensure that global temperatures increase by no more than 2°C by the end of the century, with the goal that global temperatures increase no more than 1.5°C during that time.[84] Towards that end, Parties to the Agreement are required to prepare and communicate successive nationally determined contributions (NDCs) and to pursue domestic mitigation measures with the aim of achieving such contributions.[85] This includes, for the first time, requirements that Parties regularly report on their emissions and implementation efforts.[86] Parties will also undergo international review—there will be a global "stocktake" every five years to assess progress towards achieving the purpose of the Paris Agreement and to inform further individual actions.[87] The Paris Agreement recognizes that Parties' efforts will represent a progression over time, and subsequent NDCs will reflect a country's highest possible ambition.[88]

2.3 Tort Law

In the absence of statutes or regulations controlling greenhouse gas emissions, a wide range of plaintiffs, including individuals, environmental groups, and states, are using common law tort actions to enjoin greenhouse gas emissions and even seek damages. Tort law claims provide a nonstatutory basis for apportioning liability for harms to person or property. They involve the "breach of a duty that the law imposes on persons who stand in a particular relation to one another."[89] In the context of climate change, plaintiffs have filed suits based on theories of nuisance, trespass, and negligence.[90] Climate-related nuisance claims involve allegations that the defendant's emission of greenhouse gases contributes to global warming and constitutes a significant and unreasonable interference with the public right to use, enjoy, and preserve the ecological values of the natural world. Plaintiffs may assert a nuisance claim where the defendant's emissions either constitute continuing conduct or produce a permanent long-lasting effect that has a significant effect on the public right. As for trespass claims, some plaintiffs have asserted that a defendant's emission of greenhouse gases has in turn caused debris and hazardous substances to enter and remain on the plaintiff's property. Climate-related negligence claims have centered on the defendant's duty to conduct its business without unreasonably endangering public health or the environment by emitting greenhouse gases.

The relief sought varies. Some plaintiffs attempt to use common law torts as a substitute for regulatory controls, seeking injunctive relief and asking courts to place specific limits on the emission of greenhouse gases from specific sources. Other plaintiffs seek compensation for damages, alleging that a defendant's greenhouse gas emissions have caused climate change, which in turn is damaging their health or property interests. Unlike legal challenges to rulemakings, which are conceptual and of general applicability, tort claims can target a facility, an industry sector, or a region; can directly compensate a plaintiff with money; and—by creating uneven effects in the marketplace—can stimulate congressional or EPA movement toward a national policy.

Tort claims have several advantages. As noted above, common law tort claims provide a means of airing grievances in court absent statutory or regulatory provisions for citizen suits. Thus, if federal or state government has not acted by implementing regulatory controls, a plaintiff can still seek a remedy for alleged harms. Furthermore, tort law is a bedrock common law principle on which such an extensive library of case law has been built that plaintiffs can pluck their preferred precedent from the shelf with ease. Tort causes of action also generally involve few elements, making it easier for plaintiffs to analogize their claims to favorable precedent across multiple jurisdictions.

But there are limitations, too. If climate change legislation is passed or regulatory programs are developed, defendants can argue that the plaintiff's claims are preempted or displaced. For claims based on state law, defendants could argue that the federal regulatory program preempts state common law.[91] In cases where a plaintiff's claims are based on the federal common law, a defendant could argue that the federal common law is displaced by the regulatory scheme developed by Congress or EPA.[92] Other limitations may become apparent if a plaintiff's claim is heard on the merits. For example, the burden of proving proximate causation is inherently difficult when trying to link a specific source's emissions to a specific injury that is (allegedly) caused not by the emissions themselves but by the emissions' generalized effect on the atmosphere and the atmosphere's specific effect on the plaintiff. The burden is especially great in the absence of consensus science about most of the links in the causal chain.

2.3.1 Recent Climate Change Tort Lawsuits

In the fall of 2009, just as public comment was winding down on the suite of EPA's proposed greenhouse gas regulations, federal courts issued the first round of decisions addressing whether plaintiffs could rely on tort claims to challenge the emission of greenhouse gases. While the U.S. Courts of Appeals for the Second Circuit and the Fifth Circuit overturned district court decisions, finding that plaintiffs had standing to proceed with their tort claims against greenhouse gas emitters,[93] a federal district court in California dismissed plaintiffs' federal tort claims for lack of subject matter jurisdiction.[94] Thus far, the court decisions have focused solely on whether the plaintiffs' claims can be heard; none of the decisions has reached the merits. While the court opinions provide insight into the issues that could arise should the cases be heard on the merits, some question whether recent decisions from the Fifth Circuit and the Supreme Court may have closed the door for such claims in federal court. The following summaries provide an overview of federal court cases in which plaintiffs have asserted common law tort claims in the context of climate change.

In *Connecticut v. American Electric Power Co.*, the Second Circuit issued the first decision by a federal appeals court finding that tort claims could proceed against greenhouse gas emitters.[95] The case began in 2004 when two groups of plaintiffs filed separate tort actions seeking to cap the carbon dioxide emissions of the same five electric generating utilities (EGUs). In one suit, Connecticut joined with California, Iowa, New York, New Jersey, Rhode Island, Vermont, Wisconsin, and the City of New York to file federal common law public nuisance claims against what it referred to as the "five largest emitters of carbon dioxide in the United States . . . among the largest in the world."[96] In addition, a group of three environmental land trusts filed both public and private nuisance claims against the EGU defendants.

The complaints asserted that global warming constitutes a public nuisance and that the defendants' "past, present, and future emissions will remain in the atmosphere and contribute to global warming for many decades and, possibly, centuries."[97] No monetary damages were sought. Instead, plaintiffs asked the court for injunctions that would force each defendant "to abate its contribution to the nuisance by capping its emissions by a specified percentage each year for at least a decade."[98] The defendants countered that the plaintiffs' claims should be dismissed based on the political question doctrine, which requires courts to refrain from resolving policy issues better left to political branches of government. The district court agreed with the defendants and dismissed the complaints, reasoning that the plaintiffs' claims presented a "non-justiciable political question . . . consigned to the political branches and not the judiciary" because resolution would require "identification and balancing of economic, environmental, foreign policy, and national security interests."[99]

On appeal, the Second Circuit held that the district court had erred in relying on the political question doctrine to dismiss the plaintiffs' complaints. In its analysis, the Second Circuit relied on political question formulations set forth in *Baker v. Carr*,[100] noting that the Supreme Court rarely finds that a political question will bar a court from hearing a case.[101] Under *Baker*, a case may involve a political question if there is: (1) a textually demonstrable constitutional commitment of the issue to a coordinate political department; (2) a lack of judicially discoverable and manageable standards for resolving it; (3) the impossibility of deciding without an initial policy determination of a kind clearly for nonjudicial discretion; or (4) the impossibility of a court's undertaking independent resolution without expressing lack of the respect due coordinate branches of government; (5) an unusual need for unquestioning adherence to a political decision already made; or (6) the potentiality of embarrassment from multifarious pronouncements by various departments on one question.[102] The Second Circuit concluded that none of the *Baker* factors were met, reasoning that while "the political implications of any decision involving possible limits on carbon emissions are important in the context of global warming . . . not every case with political overtones is non-justiciable."[103]

Because the district court treated the political question doctrine as a threshold jurisdictional determination, it never reached the issue of whether the plaintiffs failed to state a claim under the federal common law of nuisance. The Second Circuit exercised its discretion and considered this issue as well, concluding that all plaintiffs stated a claim under the federal common law of nuisance. The decision by the Second Circuit allows the plaintiffs to proceed with their federal common law claims in federal district court.

In August 2010, four utilities filed a petition for certiorari, asking the U.S. Supreme Court to consider the case. Shortly thereafter, twelve states, including Arkansas, Hawaii, Indiana, Kansas, Kentucky, Nebraska, North Dakota, Ohio, Pennsylvania, South Carolina, Utah, and Wyoming, filed an amicus brief asking the Supreme Court to overturn the Second Circuit's decision.

The Obama administration also filed a brief on behalf of the Tennessee Valley Authority requesting that the Supreme Court overturn the Second Circuit's decision. Arguing that EPA's recently promulgated greenhouse gas rules "displaced" the federal common law nuisance claims asserted by the plaintiffs, the solicitor general's brief asks the Supreme Court to grant certiorari, vacate the Second Circuit's judgments, and remand the case for consideration of prudential standing and whether EPA's regulatory actions have displaced the plaintiff's claims. The Supreme Court granted certiorari and heard oral arguments in *Connecticut v. American Electric Power Co.* on April 19, 2011. The questioning from justices on both ends of the political spectrum focused on issues of preemption, displacement, and standing. On June 20, 2011, a unanimous Supreme Court reversed the Second Circuit, holding that EPA's authority to regulate under the Clean Air Act "displace[s] any federal common law right to seek abatement of carbon-dioxide emissions from fossil-fuel fired power plants."[104] In its discussion regarding displacement, the Supreme Court noted that "[t]he test for whether congressional legislation excludes the declaration of federal common law is simply whether the statute 'speak[s] directly to [the] question' at issue." The court

744 ❖ Environmental Law Handbook

reasoned that "the [Clean Air Act] 'speaks directly' to emissions of carbon dioxide from the defendants' plants" because under the Act EPA is tasked with establishing emissions standards for stationary sources that cause or contribute to air pollution.[105] Considering this, the court concluded that "[t]he Act itself thus provides a means to seek limits on emissions of carbon dioxide from domestic power plants—the same relief the plaintiffs seek by invoking federal common law."[106] According to the Supreme Court, allowing the plaintiffs' common law claims would have equated to a "parallel track."[107]

Shortly after the Second Circuit's decision in *Connecticut v. American Electric Power Co.*, the Fifth Circuit reached a similar conclusion in *Comer v. Murphy Oil USA*, reversing a district court's determination that tort-based claims against greenhouse gas emitters were non-justiciable political questions.[108] In *Comer*, residents and landowners along the coast of Mississippi filed suit against members of the energy, manufacturing, and chemical industries, alleging that greenhouse gas emissions from defendants' businesses caused global warming, which in turn resulted in a sea-level rise that exacerbated the effects of Hurricane Katrina. Unlike *Connecticut v. American Electric Power Co.*, plaintiffs sought no injunctive relief and instead asserted claims for compensatory and punitive damages based on state common law actions of public and private nuisance, trespass, negligence, unjust enrichment, fraudulent misrepresentation, and civil conspiracy.[109]

The United States District Court for the Southern District of Mississippi dismissed the plaintiffs' case as presenting a non-justiciable political question and for lack of standing. A three-judge panel in the Fifth Circuit reversed, citing the district court's flawed political question analysis and its inability to elucidate how the plaintiffs' claims "have been committed by the Constitution or federal laws 'wholly or indivisibly' to a federal political branch."[110] Notably, the Fifth Circuit panel observed that "[c]ommon law tort claims are rarely thought to present non-justiciable political questions . . . [because] . . . the common law of tort provides clear and well-settled rules on which the district court can easily rely."[111] The Fifth Circuit panel compared the district court's decision to that of the district court in *Connecticut v. American Electric Power Co.*, which it declared "a serious error of law."[112] The plaintiffs' claims for public and private nuisance, trespass, and negligence survived on appeal; however, the panel dismissed the unjust enrichment, fraudulent misrepresentation, and civil conspiracy claims for lack of standing.[113]

For a brief moment it looked as if there was a consensus among the Second and Fifth Circuits that climate change nuisance cases could proceed in federal court. However, that all changed in early 2010 when the Fifth Circuit agreed to hear the appeal before the full court, and then because of multiple judge recusals declared it could not hear the case after all because it lacked a quorum. The interesting result of these events is that the Fifth Circuit declared that the earlier three-judge panel decision was vacated at the moment the full court agreed to hear the case. The court determined that neither the *en banc* court nor the panel could "conduct further judicial business" in the appeal and the case was dismissed. This chain of events allowed the district court's decision to stand. In August 2010, the plaintiffs filed a petition for writ of mandamus, asking the Supreme Court to address several procedural questions regarding their right to an appeal. On January 10, 2011, the Supreme Court denied the plaintiffs' mandamus petition.

Refusing to abandon their claims, the plaintiffs in *Comer* filed a second suit in the same district court against many of the same energy companies that had been named in the original complaint.[114] The plaintiffs again asserted nuisance, trespass, and negligence claims arising from Hurricane Katrina. The district court once more dismissed the case and on May 14, 2013, the Fifth Circuit affirmed dismissal of the case on the basis of *res judicata* alone, ignoring all other bases articulated by the district court.[115]

In late September 2009, yet another federal district court sided with defendants, dismissing plaintiffs' climate change nuisance claims as non-justiciable under the political question doctrine.[116] In *Kivalina*, the Native village of Kivalina, an Inupiat Eskimo village of approximately 400 people, alleged that the greenhouse gas emissions of several oil, energy, and utility companies were causing global warming, and by association, arctic ice melt. In a similar vein to the *Comer* case, the plaintiffs asserted that diminished sea ice left the Kivalina coast more susceptible to winter storms and erosion. The plaintiffs asserted the federal common law of nuisance to recover the costs associated with relocating the Kivalina residents.

The United States District Court for the Northern District of California concluded that application of the second and third *Baker* factors in the political question doctrine precluded its consideration of the plaintiffs' nuisance claim. In discussing the second *Baker* factor, the court concluded that no "judicially discoverable and manageable standard" was available to resolve the plaintiffs' claims, which were "on a scale unlike any prior environmental pollution case."[117] With regard to the third *Baker* factor, the court considered whether in adjudicating the plaintiffs' claims it would be required to make a policy judgment "of a legislative nature."[118] Because nuisance claims require consideration not only of the harm experienced, but also of the utility of a defendant's actions, the court would be left with the task of determining what would have been an acceptable level of greenhouse gas emissions. This, the court reasoned, would require the "judiciary to make a policy decision about who should bear the cost of global warming."[119]

In *Kivalina*, the district court also considered the issue of Article III standing, applying the standard set forth in *Lujan v. Defenders of Wildlife* requiring (1) an injury in fact; (2) causation; and (3) redressability.[120] The court in *Kivalina* focused on the causation factor, which requires "a fairly traceable connection between the alleged injury in fact and the alleged conduct of the defendant."[121] In finding that the plaintiffs lacked standing because of an inability to demonstrate a fairly traceable connection, the court noted that plaintiffs had merely alleged contribution without any demonstration that greenhouse gas emissions of defendants were responsible for the effects listed in the complaint.

In September 2012, a three-judge panel of the Ninth Circuit affirmed the dismissal of *Kivalina*, holding that the Clean Air Act and all regulatory actions taken under EPA's authority displaced federal common law claims over emissions.[122] Relying heavily on the Supreme Court's ruling in *Connecticut v. AEP*, the panel argued that even though the plaintiffs in *Kivalina* sought monetary damages as opposed to injunctive relief, it would be "incongruous to allow" a federal common law cause of action to proceed when it "has [already] been extinguished by Congressional displacement."[123] On May 20th, 2013, the Supreme Court declined the plaintiff's request to overturn the ruling issued by the lower courts.[124]

A recent case out of the Fourth Circuit could potentially limit plaintiffs' common law tort claims in the climate change context. In *North Carolina, ex rel. Cooper v. Tennessee Valley Authority*, the state of North Carolina filed suit against the Tennessee Valley Authority asking a federal district court to declare the air emissions from TVA's coal-fired power plants in Alabama and Tennessee a nuisance.[125] North Carolina asked the court to issue an injunction and impose emissions caps and control technologies. The district court agreed with the plaintiffs and issued the injunction. On appeal, the Fourth Circuit reversed the district court's opinion, finding it to be "flawed." The Fourth Circuit noted that if the district court's injunction were allowed to stand it would

> encourage courts to use vague public nuisance standards to scuttle the nation's carefully created system for accommodating the need for energy production and the need for clean air. The result would be a balkanization of the clean air regulations and a confused patchwork of standards, to the detriment of industry and the environment alike.[126]

The Fourth Circuit reasoned further that "TVA's plants cannot logically be public nuisances under Alabama and Tennessee law where TVA is in compliance with EPA NAAQS, the corresponding state SIPs, and the permits that implement them."[127] Under the Fourth Circuit's reasoning, it would appear that climate change tort suits could face an uphill battle when EPA's greenhouse gas regulatory program takes effect or if federal climate change legislation is enacted.

While the Supreme Court's decision in *Connecticut v. American Electric Power Co.* appears to have closed the door on plaintiffs' efforts to address climate change via common law claims in federal court, the decision does not foreclose the plaintiffs' option to file suit based on state common law.

2.4 Species Protection Law

The polar bear has become the poster animal for advocates of swift action on climate change. Images of the large arctic predator clinging to a small bobbing slab of ice have become a widely used trope in political discourse. Why the polar bear? The debate over "listing" the polar bear under the federal Endangered Species Act was one of the more publicized attempts by environmental groups to force consideration of climate change using an existing federal environmental statute. The Endangered Species Act (ESA) provides broad protection for both plant and animal species listed under the act.[128] While it is the species at issue that is listed as either "threatened" or "endangered," the ESA also includes protections for habitat associated with the species. The following overview helps explain how climate change and the ESA intersect.

The U.S. Fish and Wildlife Service (FWS) administers the ESA under the authority of the secretary of the Interior. Section 4 of the ESA provides that any interested person may petition the secretary of the Interior to compel the listing of a species under the act.[129] When a petition is received, the secretary must consider whether the subject species is an endangered or threatened species because of: (1) the present or threatened destruction, modification, or curtailment of its habitat or range; (2) the overuse of the species for commercial, recreational, scientific, or educational purposes; (3) disease or predation; (4) the inadequacy of existing regulatory mechanisms; or (5) any other natural or man-made factors affecting its continued existence.[130] Endangered species are species that are in danger of extinction.[131] Threatened species are likely to become endangered species in the foreseeable future.[132] The secretary must make a listing decision relying on the best available scientific and commercial data. The ESA does not allow consideration of economic factors during the species listing process.

The ESA also requires that the secretary designate the geographical area essential to the conservation of the listed species—that is, the "critical habitat."[133] In contrast to the species listing process, the secretary may consider economic factors when determining whether to designate critical habitat. The secretary may postpone designating critical habitat for up to 12 months after the final listing of a species as endangered—but only if it has a good reason for its inability to determine the species' critical habitat.[134]

Once a species is listed, the ESA regulates all public and private activity that has an impact on the listed species. Under Section 7 of the ESA, federal agencies must review all federal actions and may not undertake any action that jeopardizes the continued existence of any endangered or threatened species or that destroys or adversely affects these species' critical habitats.[135] Federal actions include actions authorized or funded by federal agencies.[136] The restriction on federal agencies even affects private individuals and corporations that are constructing projects jointly with federal agencies, receiving federal funds for a project, applying for a federal permit or license, leasing land or water rights from the federal government, or conducting activities on federal property, such as mineral exploration or development, real estate development, cutting timber, or even hunting.

In another section of the ESA that regulates private activity that occurs on private property, Section 9 prohibits any person from "taking" an endangered species.[137] Under the ESA, "take" means "to harass, harm, pursue, hunt, shoot, wound, kill, trap, capture, or collect, or to attempt to engage in such conduct."[138] "Harm" is defined by the Fish and Wildlife Service as "an act which actually kills or injures wildlife." Such a broad definition for harm means that significant habitat modification or degradation may result in take if wildlife is injured by "significantly impairing essential behavioral patterns, including breeding, feeding or sheltering."[139] Courts have held that the ESA prohibits activities on private land that modify the habitat of an endangered species in a way that either causes a decline in the total population of the species or completely prevents the species' recovery.[140] Therefore, the ESA prohibits far more than injuries to individual animals, birds, or fish; it proscribes the degradation of endangered species' habitats. The restrictions on altering or destroying critical habitat can essentially halt all development of land potentially within the species' habitat.

The structure of the ESA requires consideration of climate change in many different instances, including during the listing process under Section 4, the jeopardy consultations under Section 7, and the take prohibitions in Section 9.

Environmental groups such as the Center for Biological Diversity (CBD) and the Natural Resources Defense Council (NRDC) have filed numerous Section 4 petitions requesting the secretary to list species that are at risk from climate change. While there is a long list of species to choose from—petitions have been filed on behalf of the Pacific walrus, various species of caribou, the American pika, and two species of Caribbean coral—the polar bear remains an excellent case study for considering climate change in the context of the ESA.

In 2005, CBD submitted a petition under Section 4 requesting that the secretary list the polar bear as threatened. The CBD's polar bear petition provides that "changes in sea-ice extent, thickness, movement, fragmentation, location, duration, and timing will have significant and often adverse impacts on [the] polar bear [resulting in] population declines and extirpations, and possible global extinction of the species."[141] After several years with no action, CBD filed suit to force the FWS to make a listing decision.[142] On May 15, 2008, the FWS issued a final rule listing the polar bear as a threatened species under the ESA.[143] The polar bear listing was not the first species given protected status under the ESA because of climate change. In 2006, the United States National Marine Fisheries Service (NMFS) listed both elkhorn and staghorn coral species as threatened, citing documented "increases in global air and sea surface temperatures."[144] The FWS made the following findings with regard to the polar bear listing:

- Polar bears are sea ice–dependent species.

- Reductions in sea ice are occurring now and are very likely to continue to occur within the foreseeable future.

- The linkage between reduced sea ice and population reductions has been established.

- Impacts on polar bear populations will vary in their timing and magnitude, but all populations will be affected within the foreseeable future.

- The rate and magnitude of the predicted changes in sea ice will make adaptation by polar bears unrealistic.[145]

Opponents of listing the polar bear under the ESA feared project delays from the need for increased governmental coordination under Section 7 as well as the possible need for incidental take permits under Section 9 simply because a project results in GHG emissions. Other groups, including the federal government, feared that the listing might be used by environmental groups to force the United States to regulate greenhouse gases to protect species threatened by climate change. The logic behind this latter assessment is that the federal government could be forced to regulate greenhouse gas emissions, because greenhouse gases cause climate change, a phenomenon allegedly causing sea-ice melt, which in turn is negatively impacting protected polar bear populations. Considering that climate change is a global phenomenon, the Section 7 consultation process for climate-sensitive species like the polar bear could become extremely burdensome. Projects with high greenhouse gas emissions would need to consider impacts to the polar bear, regardless of their geographic location.

When the polar bear listing was announced, Interior Secretary Dirk Kempthorne stated in a press release that "[the listing] should not open the door to use of the ESA to regulate greenhouse gas emissions from automobiles, power plants, and other sources [because] the ESA is not the right tool to set U.S. climate policy."[146] To ensure this did not occur, the FWS issued a special rule under Section 4(d) limiting the application of the prohibition on take of the polar bear.[147] Essentially, the rule states that the ESA will not prohibit the incidental take of polar bears as a result of activities outside the bears' range. The

FWS also issued a final rule that amended interagency regulations that govern Section 7 consultations. While many thought the Obama administration would roll back the limitations on protections for polar bears, Interior Secretary Ken Salazar announced on May 8, 2009, that the Section 4(d) regulations would remain. Echoing the sentiments of his predecessor, Secretary Salazar stated that "[while] the greatest threat to the polar bear is the melting of the Arctic sea ice caused by climate change . . . the Endangered Species Act is not the proper mechanism for controlling our nation's carbon emissions."[148]

As a result of a suit filed by CBD and NRDC, on November 4, 2010, the U.S. District Court for the District of Columbia remanded the decision to list the polar bear back to FWS.[149] That court ruled that the FWS relied on an erroneous reading of the ESA when deciding to list the polar bear as threatened instead of endangered. In December 2010, the FWS filed a document with the U.S. District Court for the District of Columbia clarifying its legal reasoning and justifying the decision to list the polar bear as threatened.

On February 23, 2011, the district court granted summary judgment in favor of the FWS, concluding that the plaintiffs' claims that "FWS misapplied the statutory criteria for a listing decision by ignoring or misinterpreting the record before it and failing to articulate the grounds for its decision" were simply not sufficient to demonstrate that the listing decision was indeed "arbitrary and capricious" in nature.[150]

In March 2013, the D.C. Circuit determined that the Listing Rule was instead "the product of FWS's careful and comprehensive study and analysis" and that "[i]ts scientific conclusions are amply supported by data and well within the mainstream on climate science and polar bear biology."[151] The D.C. Circuit also found that the challenges brought forth by the State of Alaska "plainly lack[ed] merit," as the written justification provided by FWS fully satisfied its obligations under Section 4(i).[152] On April 29, 2013, the D.C. Circuit rejected without comment requests for a panel rehearing and rehearing en banc.[153] Less than a month later, on May 15, 2013, the Center for Biological Diversity issued a Notice of Intent to sue FWS for failure "to timely conduct a status review and complete a recovery plan for the ESA-listed polar bear," a violation of 16 U.S.C. § 1533(c)(2).

2.5 Environmental Impact Assessment Law

When it passed the National Environmental Policy Act (NEPA) in 1970, Congress set a monumental cornerstone in the nation's environmental edifice. As explained further in chapter 10, NEPA requires the federal government to evaluate the environmental impacts of its own decisions. Specifically, whenever a federal agency contemplates taking a major action—such as issuing a permit needed for a new bridge, highway, or pipeline—it must first prepare either an environmental impact statement (EIS) or an environmental assessment (EA) to help ensure that its decision is informed by an adequate understanding of the likely environmental effects of issuing the permit as well as the availability of alternative actions. Forty years later, NEPA continues to exert a powerful discipline over public and private activity in the United States. Interestingly, it does so by imposing procedural requirements, not substantive ones: federal agencies remain free to issue permits for environmentally unsound projects, so long as they have adequately analyzed the consequences of doing so.

In the legal debate over climate change, NEPA has become a preferred tool for challenging projects that arguably contribute to the emission of greenhouse gases or otherwise detract from efforts to combat global warming. The reason for the preference lies, in part, in NEPA's potent remedy: it allows the suspension or rescission of the challenged federal action, thereby halting or killing the proposed project that depended upon the federal action. Moreover, the decision whether to suspend the permit is generally made quickly, at a preliminary injunction hearing that may follow within weeks of filing a NEPA case. Finally, NEPA challenges are by their nature well suited to forcing more attention to the issue of global warming, whether or not the challenge succeeds on the merits.

The abundance of climate-related NEPA actions can also be explained by the relative inaction of the legislative and executive branches in passing new laws and promulgating new regulations that directly address the perils of global warming and mankind's contribution to it. Simply put, NEPA provides a means for drawing the judicial branch into the political discussion. And the courts have obliged.

But before turning to a summary of key appellate NEPA cases involving climate change, it is worthwhile to examine two actions by the White House Council on Environmental Quality (NEPA's governing body) to address climate change. These two actions are separated by thirteen years, and neither has been finalized. Nevertheless, they provide some insight into the nexus of NEPA and climate change.

2.5.1 CEQ's Draft Climate Change Guidance of 1997

Ten years before *Massachusetts v. EPA* galvanized attention to climate issues under the Clean Air Act, the Council on Environmental Quality (CEQ) recognized that a "growing body of scientific evidence supports the concern that global climate change will result from the continued build-up of greenhouse gases in the atmosphere."[154] Accordingly, CEQ prepared a draft guidance document that would direct federal agencies to take climate change into consideration in NEPA evaluations. The draft guidance was circulated within the executive branch but was not formally proposed to the public for comment.

Relying heavily on the IPCC's Second Assessment Report, CEQ proposed to determine that the "available scientific evidence . . . indicates that climate change is 'reasonably foreseeable' impacts of emissions of greenhouse gases, as that phrase is understood in the context of NEPA and the CEQ regulations."[155] The draft guidance reminded federal agencies that "reasonably foreseeable impacts" includes catastrophic impacts from improbable events that, despite their improbability, are supported by scientific evidence and not just conjecture. Consequently, federal agencies were admonished to "determine whether and to what extent their actions affect greenhouse gases."[156]

The draft guidance was never finalized, but it was also never withdrawn.

2.5.2 CEQ's Proposed Climate Change Guidance of 2010

On February 18, 2010, CEQ invited public comment on a proposed guidance document describing how and when climate change considerations should factor into environmental impact assessments by federal agencies under NEPA.[157] The proposed guidance recommends that federal agencies consider climate change if the proposed action (such as a federal permit) would lead to the release of at least 25,000 tons of greenhouse gases. However, the guidance intentionally does not define any standard—quantitative or qualitative—by which to measure the significance of a climate impact for purposes of NEPA. "Significant" effects on the environment are those that NEPA requires an agency to consider avoiding or mitigating before it approves a project. In contrast, the 25,000-ton threshold is proposed as a guideline for initiating consideration of climate change effects. Agencies would still be guided by a "rule of reason" when making a case-by-case assessment of the potential effects of their actions on the environment via climate change.

In considering climate change, agencies are cautioned to "be realistic" and to "ensure the scientific and professional integrity of their assessment," as well as to "recognize the scientific limits of their ability." Throughout the draft guidance, CEQ takes notable steps to emphasize that all climate-related impact assessments should be proportional to the importance of climate change to the decision-making process.

The energy sector, the transportation sector, and tribal and Native Alaskan communities are singled out for attention in the draft guidance. Likewise, the document highlights the importance of comparing the proposed action against alternatives on the basis of expected climate-change effects. In doing so, agencies are invited to consider not just federal but also state and local goals for energy conservation and reductions in greenhouse gas emissions, especially as associated with energy production. Furthermore, the proposed action is to be assessed against a "no action" alternative that is based on a projection of the reasonably foreseeable future condition of the affected environment subject to climate change.

CEQ has not finalized the proposed guidance, which will not become effective until finalized.

2.5.3 Selected Court Decisions

In the past twenty years, more than fifty cases—far too many to recount here—have asserted claims or arguments concerning climate change in the context of NEPA. A sampling of federal decisions will give a sense of the issues and their resolution. The cases are plucked from the areas of offshore energy development, automobile fuel efficiency, forest management, coal transportation, and energy issues in the Pacific Northwest.

In *Center for Biological Diversity v. Department of the Interior*,[158] plaintiffs challenged the Department of the Interior's initiation of the new five-year leasing program (2007–2012) for oil and gas development on the Outer Continental Shelf in the Beaufort, Bering, and Chukchi Seas of offshore Alaska. They asserted numerous arguments under NEPA and the Outer Continental Shelf Lands Act (OCSLA), including claims that the department failed to consider the leasing program's effects on climate change and the effects of climate change on the outer continental shelf (OCS). The appellate court ruled that the NEPA claim was not ripe for judicial review, but it considered and ultimately rejected the climate change arguments under OCSLA.

With respect to the NEPA claim, the court rejected the plaintiffs' substantive standing theory, which was that the department's approval of the leasing program causes climate change, in turn impacting species and habitat enjoyed by the plaintiffs. The court explained that the Supreme Court in *Massachusetts v. EPA* accepted standing because Massachusetts as a state was entitled to special solicitude, since it was asserting its sovereign rights with respect to a commonly shared threat, whereas in this case even the tribal government of Point Hope (arguendo a sovereign) was only asserting derivative rights of its citizens. Setting *Massachusetts v. EPA* aside, substantive standing was in any event lacking under *Defenders of Wildlife v. Lujan*: plaintiffs "rely on too tenuous a causal link between their allegations of climate change and Interior's action in the first stage of this Leasing Program." Nevertheless, the court held that plaintiffs did have procedural standing because their immediate, particularized interests (enjoyment of indigenous animals of Alaska) were threatened by the department's failure to observe procedural requirements.

Having breathed life into the NEPA claims by accepting procedural standing, the court then choked them off by ruling them unripe for judicial review. The court explained that a five-year plan is merely the first stage of a multistage process for a leasing program. No irreversible or irretrievable commitment of resources results from the plan until leases are sold in a subsequent stage. Interestingly, the court ruled the climate claims under OCSLA to be ripe for review—but rejected them on the merits. OCSLA does not require the department to consider the climate effects of consuming oil or gas produced under the leasing program; DOI need only consider environmental effects "on a localized area basis" around the drill/production site because OCSLA is focused on exploration and production, not on consumption. Moreover, OCSLA requires the department to have leasing programs for exploration and production, which inevitably produces oil and gas that is consumed, so climate effects from consumption are unavoidable under the statutory mandate.

In *North Slope Borough v. MMS*,[159] an Alaskan borough and the Alaska Eskimo Whaling Commission challenged MMS's[160] decision not to prepare a supplemental EIS as it prepared to lease a tract on the OCS in the Beaufort Sea for the purpose of oil and gas exploration by private industry. The agency had prepared an EA that led to a finding of no significant impact, which the plaintiffs asserted did not properly reflect the impact of oil and gas exploration on Inupiat subsistence activities. Moreover, plaintiffs argued that it was arbitrary and capricious of MMS to determine that the risks to polar bears from the cumulative impact of global warming were able to be mitigated. Even though the mitigation plan was neither complete nor legally enforceable, the appellate court rejected the plaintiffs' claims. In light of the subsequent blowout of the *Macondo* well in the Gulf of Mexico, it is interesting to consider whether the court would come to the same conclusions now. In any event, the blowout resulted in a suspension of federal leasing activity in Alaska and has prompted the federal government to redefine the NEPA requirements for offshore drilling.

The link between car emissions and global warming has been hotly discussed for many years, so it is not surprising to find that NEPA has been an important element in cases addressing corporate average fuel efficiency (CAFE) standards. For example, in the late 1980s, the City of Los Angeles and NRDC challenged the CAFE standard for model year 1989 in light of global warming concerns. The case, *City of Los Angeles v. NHTSA*,[161] fractured the three-judge panel and set in motion many years of struggle between the National Highway Transportation Safety Administration (NHTSA) and environmentalists. With respect to the MY 1989 standard, a majority consisting of Chief Judge Patricia Wald and Judge Ruth Bader Ginsburg held that NRDC had standing "to challenge the MY 1989 CAFE standard on global warming grounds." But only one judge—Chief Judge Wald—found NHTSA to have acted arbitrarily in concluding that the MY 1989 standard would have too insignificant an effect on global warming to merit an EIS. Accordingly, NRDC's global warming challenge was denied.

Chief Judge Wald (writing in the minority on this point) found arbitrary NHTSA's conclusion that the calculated increase in carbon dioxide emissions over the fleet's 20-year life span was less than 1 percent of the country's anticipated CO_2 emissions over that period and was therefore not likely to be significant (hence obviating an EIS). Nevertheless, in light of NHTSA's interim commitment to prepare a programmatic EIS that might in due course prove adequate, Chief Judge Wald noted that she would not have suspended the MY 1989 standard.

The issue did not lie dormant at the agency or in the courts. For example, in successive cases styled *Center for Biological Diversity v. National Highway Transportation Safety Administration*,[162] plaintiffs challenged the federal agency's decision to promulgate a CAFE standard that called for an increase in fuel efficiency that would yield only a modest decrease in greenhouse gas emissions from vehicles. The agency had prepared an EA that concluded that no significant adverse impact would result from the expected decrease in greenhouse gas emissions via greater fuel efficiency. This time the court disagreed, holding the decision to be arbitrary and capricious. The court explained that the agency had failed to monetize the value of carbon emissions, had failed to set a backstop (minimum fuel efficiency standard regardless of fleet makeup), and had failed to set fuel economy standards for vehicles in the 85,000–10,000 pound class. Accordingly, the court rejected the EA as insufficient to demonstrate no likely significant impact.

In the follow-up case in 2008, the court denied a request for rehearing en banc on the 2007 decision but chose to replace its 2007 decision with a modified opinion that ordered the agency to conduct either a revised EA or a new EIS (the 2007 opinion had ordered an EIS). The court determined that precedent distinguished circumstances when the remedy for a bad EA was to order an EIS (viz. when the record shows likelihood of significant impact) or a revision of the EA (viz. when the EA/FONSI is deficient in ways that obscure whether a significant impact is likely).

Like the automobile, coal production and combustion have been lightning rods for climate change litigation. For example, in *Mid States Coalition for Progress v. Surface Transportation Board*,[163] the Mayo Foundation joined the City of Rochester, Sierra Club, and others in claiming that the Surface Transportation Board (STB) violated NEPA in deciding to approve a new 280-mile rail line through Rochester to Wyoming's Powder River Basin[164] and to upgrade about 600 miles of existing rail. At issue was the likelihood that better options for transporting coal would lead to more coal consumption and more greenhouse gas emissions.

The STB had approved the new rail line, but the court reversed on NEPA grounds and remanded the decision to the STB. The court found that the STB had failed to adequately examine the reasonably foreseeable effects on the environment of making coal more readily available by the proposed rail improvement, especially the effects of greenhouse gases like carbon dioxide.[165] The court rejected the STB's contention that these effects were not reasonably foreseeable. The court explained that, so long as the nature of an effect is reasonably foreseeable, it should not be ignored even if the extent of the effect is uncertain. Instead, the agency must address the issue and follow the procedure outlined in 40 C.F.R. § 1502.22 for situations where information is incomplete or unavailable. Subsequently, the STB developed a more robust modeling analysis of impacts from the increased use of coal flowing from the decision to build a new rail line. This analysis was included in a final supplemental EIS, which was challenged by Sierra Club and others. The court rejected the challenge as meritless in *Mayo Foundation v. Surface Transportation Board.*[166]

Coal is not the only energy source facing challenges under NEPA—but the consideration of issues can be markedly different. For example, in *Association of Public Agency Customers, Inc. v. Bonneville Power Administration,*[167] the court gave only the briefest attention to climate issues. The court denied the plaintiffs' challenge to Bonneville Power Administration's[168] proposal to relieve certain entities of stranded cost liability and to change transmission access requirements in the Pacific Northwest. BPA had prepared an EIS in conjunction with its proposed new business plan. Plaintiffs argued that the EIS failed to discuss "global warming implications from the effects of greenhouse gases released from increased DSI [direct service industries, which obtain power from BPA] operations." The court dispensed with the argument in two sentences: "Petitioners are in error because the BP EIS sufficiently considered these issues. Table 4.3-1 examines the environmental impact to increased DSI operations, including CO_2 output."[169]

The glancing touch to climate issues was not simply a function of the case's 1997 vintage. For example, in *Northwest Environmental Advocates v. National Marine Fisheries Service,*[170] plaintiffs challenged the federal government's decision to deepen the Columbia River channel from 40 feet to 43 feet, thereby removing a significant constraint on shipping but also potentially endangering salmon and other species. The appellate court affirmed the district court's determination of NEPA adequacy, without any reference to climate change. The dissenting opinion, however, argued that the U.S. Army Corps of Engineers (Corps) had failed to take the requisite "hard look" under NEPA and noted that one of the NEPA inadequacies was the failure to consider how the "now-certain rising of sea level [will] impact salinity of the estuarine lower Columbia River." The dissent asserted that the impacts of climate change compounded the uncertainty in the accuracy and adequacy of the federal government's modeling of impacts from the channel deepening.

Two recent decisions deserve note as indicators of what is percolating up from the district court system. In *Hapner v. Tidwell*,[171] the court rejected the plaintiffs' contention that global warming should have been discussed in an EA for the United States Forest Service's proposed plan for reducing the risk of wildfire in the Gallatin National Forest. The court noted that, in light of the plan's small scale (forest thinning on 810 acres and prescribed burning on 300 more acres), the agency had given appropriately proportional consideration to the issue of global warming: it was sufficient to have addressed comments about climate change in the agency's notice of final decision.

In *Sierra Club v. Clinton*,[172] the court rejected Sierra Club's NEPA challenge to the secretary of state's EIS supporting a presidential permit for a proposed new pipeline from Alberta to North Dakota to carry heavy crude oil (bitumen) from Canadian tar sands. Sierra Club had challenged the narrowness of the proposal's purpose and need, the adequacy of the indirect and cumulative impacts analysis, the failure to address the impacts of another pipeline within the same EIS, and the failure to consider the impacts of abandoning the pipeline. Notable is the absence of any specific discussion in the opinion of global warming or climate change, even though the driver for the entire litigation is Sierra Club's implacable opposition to the extraction of tar sands, in part because of its global warming implications. The case demonstrates that NEPA, while often a preferred tool in fighting projects that allegedly contribute to global warming, will not always be the chosen instrument.

2.6 State and Regional Climate Change Regimes

Until recently, it was not clear whether the U.S. Congress or the EPA would act first to control greenhouse gas emissions via a national program. Acknowledging that the political will might not ever exist at the federal level, several states opted to move forward in developing their own greenhouse gas emissions control programs through collaborative regional efforts. The regional efforts extend across the United States, from the Regional Greenhouse Gas Initiative (RGGI) in the northeast, to the Midwestern Greenhouse Gas Accord (MGGA) in the central part of the country, California's cap-and-trade program AB-32, and out to other Western States and Canada with the Western Climate Initiative (WCI).

Regional programs generally involve a memorandum of understanding (MOU) by which the governors of participating states commit to a joint strategy for reducing greenhouse gas emissions.[173] The agreements read like a legislative resolution, first by recognizing the economic, environmental, and energy-related issues associated with climate change and then by including guiding principles for capping and then reducing greenhouse gases. While the details of the MOU may differ from one regional program to the next, all of the regional programs in the United States include a pledge to develop a market-based cap-and-trade system.

The MOU serves to memorialize the goals of participating states; however, the success of a regional initiative is entirely dependent on each state's adoption of statutory or regulatory rules necessary to create and enforce the program. To accomplish this, the regional initiatives develop model rules that detail the specific components of the program.[174] Once the model rule is complete, it is incumbent on each state to adopt the model rule by whatever legislative or regulatory process is appropriate. Currently, one greenhouse gas cap-and-trade scheme is actively operating in the United States.

The first regional effort within the United States to develop a cap-and-trade program began in the northeast. In 2003, governors from nine northeastern states outlined what would become the RGGI, a cap-and-trade program focusing on the control of carbon dioxide emissions from the utility sector—specifically, electric generators with a nameplate capacity of at least 25 megawatts.[175] By 2007, ten states had signed the RGGI MOU: Maryland, New Jersey, New York, Connecticut, Delaware, Massachusetts, Rhode Island, New Hampshire, Vermont, and Maine. The RGGI MOU includes commitments to regional- and state-specific carbon dioxide emission caps.

In 2006, RGGI released a draft model rule that incorporates provisions on applicability, exemptions, permitting requirements, allowance allocations and tracking, monitoring and reporting, and treatment of emissions offsets. The cap-and-trade program is based in part on EPA's NOx Budget Trading Program and CAIR NOx, and on the SO2 Trading Programs for State Implementation Plans.[176] Under the RGGI program, each electric generating unit must hold allowances equal to the amount of its CO_2 emissions, with one emission allowance equating to one ton of CO_2. The program caps the carbon dioxide emissions of the utility sector at 188 million (short) tons per year through 2014 and cuts carbon dioxide emissions to 10 percent below 2005 levels by 2018.[177] By the end of 2008, all ten participating states had adopted the RGGI Model Rule, setting the stage for the beginning of the trading program on January 1, 2009.

After two years of operation and several allowance auctions, one thing is clear—the RGGI program has generated substantial revenue for participating states. RGGI estimates it has recovered proceeds of nearly $730 million from the first nine auctions.[178] According to RGGI, nearly 80 percent of the auction proceeds are used by states for investment in energy efficiency and renewable energy. It appears that the RGGI states are on track to meet their carbon dioxide reduction targets; however, some question whether the RGGI cap was set too high in the first place.

A report prepared for RGGI indicates that carbon dioxide emissions have declined 33 percent, from 184.4 million tons in 2005 to 123.7 tons in 2009.[179] The report attributes the emission reductions largely to (1) lower electricity load because of weather and the economy; (2) fuel switching from coal to natural gas because of low gas prices; and (3) changes in capacity mix.[180] The report estimates that changes in weather accounted for approximately 25 percent of the decrease in carbon dioxide emissions from 2005 to 2009.[181]

The report did not assess the direct role played by the RGGI cap-and-trade program in reducing carbon dioxide emissions; however, it notes that the impact of RGGI compliance is embedded in some of its findings. Specifically, the report explains that the lower electricity load could be influenced by state energy efficiency programs and that fuel switching may occur as a result of "narrowing the fuel price differential between fuels with different carbon content."[182] One RGGI consultant estimates that carbon dioxide emissions in participating states will stay below the target cap through at least 2030 regardless of the additional reduction caused by the energy efficiency and renewable energy programs funded by RGGI.[183]

As required by the RGGI MOU, RGGI conducted a program review in 2012 that revealed (1) "[a] significant excess supply of allowances relative to actual emission levels in the region; and (2) [t]he current cost control measures in the program, which are based upon expansion of the percentage of offset allowances allowable for compliance, would likely be ineffective in controlling costs if the emissions cap is made binding."[184] Based on that program review, RGGI announced in February 2013 that it would tighten its allowable emissions from participating states at 91 million tons per year beginning in 2014 and declining 2.5 percent each year from 2015 through 2020.[185]

While RGGI continues to operate and adapt, other regional programs are still in the early stages of development. In 2007, the Midwestern Greenhouse Gas Accord (MGGA) was signed by the premier of Manitoba and the governors of Wisconsin, Michigan, Minnesota, Illinois, Iowa, and Kansas. While the MGGA Model Rule was finalized on May 7, 2010, the member states have been slow to adopt the rule, and the start date for the MGGA cap-and-trade program has not yet been determined.

Also in 2007, the governors of Arizona, California, New Mexico, Oregon, and Washington signed an agreement forming the Western Climate Initiative

(WCI). Since 2007, the states of Utah and Montana as well as four Canadian provinces have joined the WCI. The WCI unveiled a model rule on July 27, 2010. While similar to RGGI in most aspects, the WCI Model Rule is not just limited to carbon dioxide emissions from the utility sector. The WCI Model Rule calls for an economy-wide cap, addressing nearly 90 percent of carbon dioxide emissions in participating jurisdictions.[186] The WCI's goal is to reduce greenhouse gas emissions to 15 percent below 2005 levels by 2020. The WCI opted for a program that covers most sectors of the economy in order to achieve reductions at the least possible cost and to minimize emissions leakage.[187] Emissions leakage occurs if activities that generate greenhouse gas emissions shift from a jurisdiction participating in the WCI to a jurisdiction that does not participate and that does not have comparable greenhouse gas emission controls. While several jurisdictions participating in the WCI have adopted the necessary legal infrastructure to carry out the program, others have been slow to do so, and some states have withdrawn altogether.[188]

While still coordinating with other states through the WCI, California passed AB 32, the Global Warming Solutions Act of 2006, a statewide greenhouse gas emissions cap that includes penalties for noncompliance. On November 1, 2010, the California Air Resources Board (CARB) released the proposed regulations to implement the statewide cap-and-trade program set to take effect in 2012.[189] The California program covers the utility sector and large industrial sources with the goal of reducing the state's greenhouse gas emissions to 1990 levels by 2020.[190] Implementation of AB 32 has faced several setbacks along the way. Notably, CARB's GHG-related regulations developed in response to AB 32 were challenged in court, and on May 20, 2011, the Superior Court of California issued a stay of the cap-and-trade portion of the CARB program.[191] The court found that CARB failed to adequately describe and analyze alternatives to the cap-and-trade program, respond to comments, and comply with the California Environmental Quality Act (CEQA).

A California Court of Appeals decision allowed CARB to continue implementation of the cap-and-trade program while it worked on a revised alternatives analysis to its cap-and-trade program. The court was satisfied with CARB's revisions to the alternatives analysis and on November 14, 2012, CARB held its first auction under the cap-and-trade program.

Just one day prior to CARB's first auction, the California Chamber of Commerce filed a lawsuit challenging the auction portion of the cap-and-trade program, claiming that the "ARB's self-allocation and auctioning or selling-off of GHG allowances pursuant to [its] regulations are not authorized by the provisions of AB 32."[192] The Chamber alleged that auctioning allowances constituted an unauthorized, unconstitutional tax not approved by the state legislature. On

April 16, 2013, the Pacific Legal Foundation also filed suit on the same grounds. Despite continuing legal challenges, CARB has continued to move forward with its cap-and-trade program by holding another auction on May 16, 2013. CARB has also linked the cap-and-trade program with a similar climate change initiative in Quebec.

Moving forward, regional programs will need to address issues such as timely adoption of model rules, setting an accurate cap, appropriate expenditure of auction proceeds, integration of offsets, and adapting to new legal strictures if a federal program is ever adopted and implemented. Another issue critical to the success of the regional programs is an obvious one: participation. In 2011, RGGI experienced some unrest as individual states considered legislation to remove them from the program. While efforts were under way by state lawmakers in New Hampshire, New Jersey, and Delaware to limit, modify, or completely remove their respective states from the RGGI program, only New Jersey moved forward with officially ceasing participation in the program.[193]

Regional programs will likely present implementation issues for the Clean Power Plan if the CPP withstands judicial challenge and is implemented in its current state. The CPP imposes individual requirements on each state and encourages trading programs among states. The existing regional programs may form a base for compliance under the CPP, or they could be subsumed by a nationwide trading program if that is the course states want to take.

2.7 Corporate Securities Law

Whatever its status on Capitol Hill, climate change is certainly on the agenda in the corporate boardroom. Companies in many sectors are concerned about the potential effects on market position and market valuation from possible new greenhouse gas emission standards, tort liability for past emissions, and new requirements for developing land, natural resources, and industrial facilities. Some companies may also see business opportunities emerging from climate change itself or from the debates surrounding it. For publicly traded companies, the perceived risks and opportunities arising from climate change (and from the country's approach to it) are proper topics for internal consideration and may justify external communication in SEC filings and in voluntary reports such as triple-bottom-line or sustainability reports. Companies are also developing governance systems for managing the uncertainties of climate change risk while executing their corporate strategies.

As one considers the influx of climate change issues into corporate law and practice, the views of the SEC loom large. In early 2010, the SEC issued new guidance with respect to the corporate disclosure of climate change risk and in doing so signaled its interest in applying the Sarbanes-Oxley law to assess corporate governance of climate change risk. We discuss these federal developments below, in addition to reviewing an unusual effort by the New York attorney general to probe—under state law—the sufficiency of climate disclosures by certain companies that use or sell coal.

2.7.1 Background on Corporate Environmental Disclosure

Corporate environmental disclosure is governed by SEC Regulation S-K and various accounting rules.[194] Regulation S-K requires regular reporting (annually and quarterly), and it mandates specific content, including disclosure of environmental compliance and investment affecting the business (Item 101), environmental legal proceedings (Item 103), and known environmental trends and uncertainties that could reasonably prove material (Item 303).

Item 101 requires consideration of the compliance costs associated with existing and new environmental legal requirements dealing with climate change. The public company must recognize the material effects of compliance on expenditures, earnings and competitive position, and it must disclose the material capital expenditures for the current reporting year and for further years as the company deems material. In the case of climate change, no federal climate-change legislation has passed into law, although some new regulations (such as the GHG inventory rule) have been promulgated. The prevailing view is that the most expensive and complex climate change laws lie in the future (if at all) and are not yet a matter for material current expenditures.

Despite the absence of comprehensive climate change legislation, legal proceedings based on climate change have been coursing through the courts. As noted above, perhaps the most innovative are tort-law claims seeking monetary damages for the alleged effects of specific companies' emissions on the climate and the alleged consequent effect of the changing climate on the plaintiffs' protected interests. Other claims are being lodged under NEPA, ESA, and the Clean Air Act to challenge permits that allegedly do not adequately account for the permitted activity's effects on climate and consequent effect on protected habitat or air quality. For companies in these lawsuits, Item 103 comes into consideration. If legal proceedings are material, or if they are asserted by the government and involve monetary sanctions of $100,000 or more, disclosure is required.

Item 303 is likewise relevant to climate change. The management of the company must provide a narrative discussion of historical results and future prospects. The idea is that the investing public should have not only the facts and figures about the company in a snapshot but also the perspective of management on the trends and uncertainties that, in management's judgment, materially affect future liquidity, capital resources, and results of operations. There are two keys to Item 303: knowing what materiality means, and knowing when a trend or uncertainty is disclosable. A fact is material when—in the eyes of management—it is substantially likely that a reasonable investor would consider the total mix of available information to have been significantly altered by omitting the fact. The SEC has repeatedly confirmed that materiality is not merely a quantitative measure, and even as a quantitative measure there is no minimum threshold of significance.

The other key to Item 303 is knowing when a trend or uncertainty is disclosable. The established analytical framework is to ask, first, whether the trend or uncertainty is likely to come to pass; if it is not likely, the inquiry ceases, though the company may do well to track the trend or uncertainty in case its likelihood increases. If the trend or uncertainty is likely to come to pass, or if the likelihood is unknown, the company must disclose and discuss it, unless management concludes that a material effect is not reasonably likely even if the trend or uncertainty came to pass. In short, the test under Item 303 favors disclosure in the face of uncertainty and relies heavily on the judgment of management (subject always to the oversight of the SEC and the courts). Management's discussion and analysis under Item 303 has been the principal venue for consideration of climate change and its potential material effects on the business.

A final word on Sarbanes-Oxley is worthwhile in the context of climate change, though it is often omitted in discussions of climate disclosure. Sarbanes-Oxley imposes an obligation on companies and management to create "controls and procedures" to ensure integrity in disclosures and financial audits.[195] CEOs and CFOs must periodically certify that such controls and procedures are in place. Serious personal and corporate consequences follow from noncompliance. In essence, whereas Regulation S-K focuses on complete, relevant, and accurate descriptions of the company and its risks and opportunities, Sarbanes-Oxley focuses on the internal architecture of corporate governance to ensure the sustained integrity of the company's self-knowledge and disclosure. Given the multivariable complexities of climate change and its nexus with individual businesses, governance is a topic worth exploring more closely. As we will see, the SEC recently drew attention to this point.

2.7.2 Disclosure Guidance from the SEC

In September 2007, CERES and a broad array of co-petitioners filed a joint petition urging the SEC to address the topic of climate change disclosure.[196] In essence, the petition presented climate change as a physical phenomenon and discussed its potential to affect the financial health of companies through increased physical risks (e.g., sea-level rise, increased incidence and severity of storms, and water scarcity) and rising compliance expenditures, among other factors. The petition also recorded the urgent clamor among investors and investor groups for more and better information about how these risks affect specific companies. On this basis, the petitioners sought to justify the intercession of the SEC via an interpretive guidance that would reinforce the necessity for companies to consider climate change risks and to disclose them adequately.

The petition purportedly did not seek any change in disclosure law but rather guidance on how to ensure better disclosure.[197] However, lurking below the surface seemed to be the suggestion that the SEC should compel more (as well as more specific) climate change disclosure, as though climate change risks were per se material or carried a rebuttable presumption to that effect.

The SEC took the petition under advisement. Despite occasional efforts to nudge it forward, the petition threatened to slide into irrelevance as the months and years passed without action or interest by the commission. The petition's fortunes turned a corner with the appointment of Mary Schapiro as chairman of the SEC.[198] Within months, the commission's staff let it be known that the commission was interested in the petition and the topic of climate change.

Climate change disclosure eventually made it onto the commission's official agenda in January 2010. By a vote of 3 to 2, the SEC adopted[199] a new interpretive release that prompted jubilation among disclosure activists and measured concern from public companies—especially since the guidance would apply immediately to the annual reports being prepared around that time. Stripped to its essentials, the guidance identified four areas for particular evaluation when assessing corporate risks from climate change in the context of SEC-mandated disclosure, namely:

- the impact of existing as well as pending climate change legislation and regulation;

- the impact of international accords and treaties on climate change or greenhouse gas emissions;

- the actual and potential indirect consequences of climate change regulation or business trends (e.g., reduced demand for carbon-intensive products); and

- the actual and potential impacts of the physical effects of climate change.

With respect to the first item—new laws governing greenhouse gas emissions—the SEC stressed that, in its view, the traditional analysis under Item 303 required consideration of proposed climate change legislation as a trend or uncertainty if a company could not determine that the legislation was not likely to pass. Beyond these focal points, the commission devotes many pages of the guidance to laying out the existing structure of environmental disclosure under the SEC laws, as well as to surveying current knowledge about climate change.

The key question for reporting companies is whether the guidance changes the existing approach to evaluating climate change risks for purposes of disclosure under Regulation S-K. Even the commissioners who supported the guidance (perhaps especially these commissioners) acknowledged that the guidance does not—and legally cannot—modify the existing laws governing disclosure. Yet, as at least one commissioner pointed out, the SEC appears conflicted in its intention to change disclosure practice with respect to climate change while professing no change to the governing disclosure rules.[200]

Taking the commission at its word that no change in the existing disclosure rules is either intended or accomplished by the new guidance, it is useful to consider what the commission has not done.

- The SEC did not change the existing framework of disclosure laws.

- The traditional standard of materiality still applies to climate change disclosure.

- Climate change disclosure still requires a case-by-case evaluation of materiality.

- The SEC did not make a finding that existing climate change disclosures have been inadequate.

- The SEC is not making it mandatory to disclose carbon footprint or other measures taken to reduce greenhouse gas emissions.

- The SEC did not express an opinion about the existence of global warming (although Commissioner Aguilar did emphasize the threat of global warming as a justification for the SEC's action).

Is it then a surprise to find relatively few changes in the substance and detail of climate-related disclosures in the first round of annual reports on Form 10-K to appear since the guidance was issued?

Doubtless contributing to the relative stasis in disclosure practice in the immediate aftermath of the guidance was the dynamic nature of the legislative discussion about greenhouse gas emission limitations. In the four months following the new guidance, the fortunes of climate change legislation in Congress declined precipitously, before being eclipsed in the public's eye by the catastrophic blowout of the *Deepwater Horizon* in the Gulf of Mexico. With even less certainty surrounding what might be the chief factor in determining costs and strategies surrounding climate change, the application of the traditional analytical framework for assessing risk and materiality under Regulation S-K would not have resulted in more, nor more detailed, disclosure about climate change risks from proposed legislation. What is interesting to note is that the presence of the SEC's new guidance seemed not to alter substantially the result of this traditional analysis.

In the end what may prove the most important aspect of the guidance is buried in two footnotes.[201] There, the SEC noted that controls and procedures under Sarbanes-Oxley should encompass risks associated with climate change in all its relevant dimensions. In essence, the SEC pointed in the direction of a governance model for managing climate-related risks in business. The SEC expects companies to keep themselves well-informed about climate change, about the progress of climate legislation and international treaties, and about corporate facts such as carbon footprints. Accordingly, public companies have been refocusing on the adequacy of their governance systems with respect to climate change.

The significance of this point about governance is that the commission has tapped a powerful enforcement tool—Sarbanes-Oxley—to augment its oversight of environmental disclosures. While Sarbanes-Oxley has always encompassed environmental issues as much as other issues, the guidance is the first indication that the SEC intends to look expressly for environmental governance structures with respect to environmental issues, in particular climate change. Thus, regardless whether a company's traditional analysis of climate-related risks results in solid or flimsy disclosures, the SEC can and presumably will look into the governance structures that lie behind the company's understanding of climate-related risks. Whether the SEC feels that this deeper inquiry is worthwhile as a stand-alone basis for inquiry, or is largely an adjunct investigation if other matters at the company are already being investigated, remains to be seen.

2.7.3 State Investigation into Climate Disclosure

The same week that CERES filed its petition seeking guidance from the SEC on the disclosure of climate risks, New York Attorney General Andrew Cuomo (a co-petitioner with CERES) opened an investigation into five companies to explore whether the business risks associated with the companies' commitments to coal and coal-fired power plants (including plants outside of New York State) were adequately addressed in their corporate environmental disclosures filed with the SEC.[202]

The investigation was the first (and so far remains the only) public governmental investigation of a publicly traded company's climate-related disclosures—but it was not initiated by the SEC and was not premised on federal securities law. Instead, the New York attorney general proceeded under the 1921 Martin Act, a state statute that grants immense power to the New York attorney general to investigate companies whose stock trades in New York. It criminalizes any false statement by one who knew the truth, who could have known the truth with reasonable effort, or who made no reasonable effort to ascertain the truth of the statement.

Letters accompanying the subpoenas expressed concern about plans to build coal-fired power plants at a time when New York State was engaged in the Regional Greenhouse Gas Initiative designed to reduce regional carbon emissions. In speaking about the investigation, the New York attorney general explained, "[t]he concept here is using the securities laws to investigate whether the economic risks of these [coal-fired power plants] are being disclosed—the economic risks which are dovetailing with the environmental concerns."[203]

In time, the New York attorney general concluded a so-called "assurance of discontinuance" (AOD) with each of three of the five companies being investigated.[204] These AODs resolve the investigation without admissions or denials and with certain stipulations concerning climate-related disclosures to be made in the future. The gravamen of the stipulations is that disclosures are required to the extent the company's greenhouse gas emissions materially affect its financial exposure from climate change risk. While some heralded the AODs for setting a new standard for climate disclosure, others have pointed out that the stipulations do not require climate-related disclosure absent a determination of material effect on the company—which is the essence of the existing standard under Regulation S-K.

3.0 Practical Considerations

Having surveyed the evolving landscape of law governing climate change in the United States, it is fair to ask what the practical effect of all this is. Below we examine a few areas of special interest: permitting, emissions trading, corporate transactions, and corporate governance.

3.1 Emissions Trading

Climate change clearly has a financial dimension. By the end of 2010 the emission allowance auctions conducted by RGGI alone will have yielded nearly a billion dollars in proceeds for participating states. While auction proceeds are a substantial new source of revenue for some states in the northeastern United States, they represent only a small portion of the worldwide market in carbon, which was expected to grow to nearly $165 billion in 2010.[205] In 2008, the World Bank described the carbon market as "the most visible result of early regulatory efforts to mitigate climate change" and as responsible for "sending market signals for the price of mitigating carbon emissions [which] in turn, has stimulated innovation and carbon abatement worldwide."[206]

There are generally two types of carbon markets, mandatory and voluntary, and both generally involve the trading of emission allowances and carbon offsets. Mandatory carbon markets are the product of legislation or regulatory initiatives, as is the case with RGGI. In mandatory cap-and-trade programs like RGGI, a finite number of allowances are created every year, and the number declines over time as the cap tightens, forcing regulated entities to reduce emissions or purchase more of the ever-scarcer allowances. Programs like RGGI put a price on emission allowances that can be traded between regulated entities as they try to balance their projected needs for allowances. In 2009, it is estimated that nearly $2.18 billion worth of RGGI allowances were traded.[207]

Offsets are an important component of the carbon market in the United States. A carbon offset is a "unit of carbon dioxide-equivalent that is reduced, avoided, or sequestered to compensate for emissions occurring elsewhere."[208] "Elsewhere" means somewhere outside the reach of the program's cap. Cap-and-trade programs often allow a regulated entity to use a certain amount of offsets toward their compliance obligation, provided the reductions reflected in the offsets were not already mandated. RGGI allows regulated entities to use qualifying offsets to cover up to 3.3 percent of reported emissions; however, to date, none have been issued.[209]

Voluntary carbon markets, such as the Chicago Climate Exchange (CCX), lack regulatory drivers. Instead, they may be motivated by a variety of factors, including corporate responsibility, the desire to prepare for potential future regulation, and the attraction of investors.[210] The CCX was established in 2003 as a voluntary but legally binding trading system for reducing greenhouse gas emissions.[211] Those who chose to participate make a legally binding commitment to a target cap on their greenhouse gas emissions. Much like the mandatory markets, some members will have a surplus of "Carbon Financial Instruments" and others a deficit—thereby encouraging trading. Despite early successes, a fading "pre-compliance market" sealed the fate of the CCX allowance trading program, which CCX discontinued in December 2010.[212]

Offsets are traded more abundantly on the CCX voluntary market. "Offset providers" in the agricultural, forestry, waste management, and renewable energy sectors can register projects that in turn are traded on the CCX market.[213] Many of the projects that qualify as offsets under the CCX program are outside the reach of mandatory cap-and-trade programs. For example, landfill methane collection, agricultural best management practices, reforestation, and renewable energy systems can mitigate greenhouse gas emissions, and CCX attempts to capture this value via its offset registration and crediting system.[214] The overall offset market in the United States was estimated in 2009 to be approximately $74 million.[215] While CCX concluded its emissions reduction commitment program at the end of 2010, a new offsets program will run for 2011 and 2012.

The carbon market in the United States also includes derivatives trading. Derivatives are "financial instruments that are linked to a specific financial instrument or indicator or commodity . . . through which specific financial risks can be traded in financial markets."[216] In the United States, derivatives are traded as a means of hedging against price fluctuation in carbon emission allowances and offsets. The Chicago Climate Futures Exchange (CCFE) specializes in the trading of a wide range of environmental derivatives, including futures on RGGI allowances[217] and SO_2 and NOx allowances under EPA's Clean Air Interstate Rule (CAIR).[218]

After the financial collapse of 2008–2009, much focus was placed on poorly understood financial instruments, including derivatives. In 2010, Congress passed the Dodd-Frank Wall Street Reform and Consumer Protection Act.[219] Under Section 750 of Dodd-Frank, Congress directed the Commodity Futures Trading Commission (CFTC) to establish a working group to evaluate existing and future carbon derivative markets and to issue a report with recommendations "for the oversight of existing and prospective carbon markets to ensure an efficient, secure, and transparent carbon market, including oversight of spot markets and derivative markets."

On November 19, 2010, the CFTC began soliciting public comments on the proper oversight of carbon markets.[220] Although the current carbon derivative market in the United States is relatively small, the potential for expansion of that market as a result of future state and regional programs, or even a national cap-and-trade program, may be enough for the CFTC to recommend increased oversight.

3.2 Corporate Transactions

Corporate transactions are deals—deals to merge, deals to acquire, deals to borrow money or to sell stock or to create a joint venture or to do any of a multitude of things by which companies seek to expand their reach, leverage their assets, and build value. Deals involve risk. In fact, deals are about taking risk for advantage. Fundamental to any deal is understanding the risks well enough to make a shrewd decision about whether and on what terms to conclude it.

Climate change creates risks that, to varying extents, can and should be included in one's analysis of a contemplated corporate transaction. By no means are all transactions affected by climate risks, but some are—and probably more will be as time goes by. The panoply of risks that can arise from climate change includes the following:

- *Physical risk.* While much attention is given to sea-level rise, whose projected effects seem attenuated by its glacial pace, storms are not limited to shorelines. Global warming is understood to drive storm frequency and intensity, which correlate with physical damage, business interruption, and other financial detriments.

- *Compliance costs.* Greenhouse gas regulations create compliance obligations that cost money and must be factored into budgets, cash flow models, financial statements, and profitability assessments. For example, the Tailoring Rule establishes an emissions threshold above which many companies will need, for the first time, PSD permits that not only establish emissions limitations but also necessitate capital expenditures for multimillion-dollar pollution control equipment.

- *Development constraints.* Physical risks and permit limits may each create substantial constraints on an asset's amenability to development, expansion, rebuilding, and so forth.

- *Liability.* Tort liability for the effects of global warming on individuals and communities seemed unimaginable ten years ago but is now being tested in the courts in cases against specific companies. If these suits gain traction, a new dimension of risk will be defined for business sectors that contribute significantly to greenhouse gas emissions.

- *Supply chain.* A particular company is only as stable as its least stable supplier whose contributions are material to the company. To the extent climate risks affect these suppliers, the risks carry through to the company. Accordingly, it is not enough to understand the direct climate risks associated with the company; one must consider the indirect risks as well.

- *Brand and reputation.* In retail sectors, cash flow and business opportunity are defined significantly by branding and overall reputation. In discussing the new SEC guidance on climate risk disclosure, the SEC chairman drew attention to the possibility that societal perceptions about climate risk and environmental credentials may tarnish or burnish corporate brands and reputations. For a company that sells its products around the world, these societal perceptions (and associated risks) can vary widely by geography, much as retail manufacturers have learned that customers (and regulators) in California have different expectations for products than do residents of other states.

- *Raw materials and inputs.* As regulatory and other constraints are placed on certain basic industries (e.g., chemicals, electric power, cement, and petroleum refining) in order to reduce greenhouse gas emissions, these basic goods can become scarcer or pricier or both. For example, the cost structures of fertilizer manufacturers and aluminum smelters are heavily weighted by power costs, just as the vast array of plastic products are dependent on the chemicals and refining sectors.

This short list is merely indicative, not comprehensive, of the range of climate-related risks that can be relevant in a given transaction. In some sense, these risks are ordinary and commonsensical, but they can also be subtle. For example, Vladimir Stenek at the International Finance Corporation has prepared an interesting analysis of climate risks as actually and potentially reflected in projects supported by multilateral financing.[221] Among several insights in his report is this simple one: in 2003, a European heat wave killed 35,000 people, shut down 14 power plants (spiking power prices by 1,300 percent) and inflicted $15 billion in losses in the agricultural sector. This is bad enough, but more subtle is the recognition that the heat wave was a 1-in-500-year event in 2003, whereas by 2040 it will be a 1-in-2-year event.

How to tackle these risks in the context of a transaction? Ever since the advent of modern statutory environmental law, and certainly after the introduction of the Superfund law in 1980, businesses have developed ever more specific protocols for conducting environmental risk investigations that meet the market standard for "due diligence." These protocols vary by sector, by company, and by investigator, and they are not legal or otherwise enforceable norms, but they do represent benchmarks in the marketplace. What is interesting to note is how limited has been the evolution of these due-diligence protocols toward inclusion of climate risks over the past few years. In certain transactions, climate risks are indeed analyzed in detail—will a PSD permit be required? what are the water supply issues if the drought continues? and so on—but the run-of-the-mill transaction does not inquire deeply into climate risks whereas, for example, Superfund risks for off-site disposal are part and parcel of the great majority of environmental due-diligence investigations for corporate transactions.

Several reasons underlie the slow evolution of due-diligence standards for climate risks. One reason is the gap between the short investment horizon for a deal and the often long horizon for the climate risk to materialize. For example, a private equity fund will often intend to acquire a business and re-sell it within five years, which is too short an interval for the time-discounted risk of sea-level rise, for example, to have much bearing on the transaction. Another reason is that climate risks are to some extent subsumed within existing areas of due-diligence inquiry—for example, inquiries into the adequacy of permits, the cost of regulatory compliance, and the sufficiency of insurance coverage for storm damage. A third reason is that some climate risks are generic to a sector—that is, they are felt more or less equally across businesses in a sector—so the risk does not present a competitive issue. And some climate risks are simply too difficult to develop much hard information about, either because information is poorly organized or inaccessible (supply chain risks) or because the risks themselves are poorly understood by experts (weather effects).

Nevertheless, the nature of due-diligence inquiries is that they are adaptive, in the sense that they continually adapt to perceived shifts in risks, either because of skillful anticipation of new risks or because of painful lessons learned from the failure to do so.

3.3 Corporate Governance

Our discussion of climate laws and risks brings us inevitably to the topic of corporate governance. It would be hard to find a public company of any size in the United States that has not already confronted the complexity of corporate risks arising from climate change. The risks of regulatory compliance costs, physical damage, resource constraints, supply chain weakness, reputational risk, and so forth—all these are refracted in a kaleidoscope whose shifting colors challenge any management team striving for a clear view of the future. What is needed is corporate governance, which is a system that controls risk by coupling awareness of uncertainty and complexity with a method for defining and adhering to a strategy. It embodies directed rather than ad hoc analysis, systematic communication, and controlled decision-making. It provides a method for making optimal choices amid uncertainty and risk.[222]

Governance is not at all new in the corporate environmental arena. Company environmental policies, compliance systems, training programs, sustainability reporting, and auditing are a few of the programs that can contribute to good governance of environmental risk. What is different about climate risk, however, is that the uncertainties attached to the method and extent of a particular impact from climate change often overwhelm what is known. It is hard—if not impossible—to incorporate "climate risk measures" into, say, an environmental auditing program that is based on regulatory standards.

Practical considerations are not the only factor driving public companies toward a governance strategy for climate risks: so is Sarbanes-Oxley. As noted earlier, the SEC has already pointed to this statute as requiring corporate controls and procedures that encompass risks associated with climate change in all its relevant dimensions. Senior management must certify the accuracy and completeness of the financial reports, and the company must ensure that internal financial controls are regularly assessed—with outside expertise. The threat of criminal sanction only emphasizes the significance of these duties.

Public companies have responded accordingly. While every company has different mechanisms for governance of any issue, especially one as fraught with uncertainty as company-specific climate risk, five basic principles generally emerge:

- *Know the company's carbon metrics.* Too much is often made of basic indicators such as annual greenhouse gas emissions, Scope 1-3 emissions, emissions per revenues, and so forth. Even trend lines for these parameters can tell us almost nothing about the actual nature and extent of climate risk for a particular company. Nevertheless, they are a legitimate and necessary starting point for a more sophisticated analysis of corporate climate risk.

- *Know what you know about climate change.* Climate issues have been compelling, front-page reading for years, so it is no surprise that talented people within companies have tried to understand the issues and test how they affect or might affect the company. The difficulty is that these people may reside within marketing, legal, accounting, government affairs, and any number of other departments. The key is to ensure that these in-house aggregators of knowledge are properly connected, overseen, and directed: the organization as a whole must know what it knows about climate change.

- *Communicate and disclose with discipline.* Knowing what you say about climate risk is at least as important as being aware of what you already know about the subject. Corporate disclosure takes many forms, not just mandatory disclosure under the SEC laws. Public statements by management, sustainability reports, responses to international climate registry questionnaires, and many other vehicles for intentional and inadvertent discussion of climate issues abound. What is said should be as carefully coordinated as any earnings report to shareholders—indeed, for the same reasons.

- *Connect and control your internal efforts.* Especially in light of Sarbanes-Oxley, public companies can ill afford to undertake important analyses that are not linked to the proper sources of information and to the right decision-making processes. Cross-linking is essential. For example, financial modeling in the accounting department and emissions modeling based on dispatchability are two vital areas that deserve careful coordination within a power-generating company.

- *Benchmark performance against other companies.* Especially when confronting a complex risk involving many interrelated uncertainties, it is comforting—as well as instructive—to benchmark one's governance techniques against the patterns of performance of one's peers within the same sector and in unrelated sectors. Just beware of the herd mentality, which over the long run defines mediocrity.

4.0 Conclusion

Climate law is taking shape before our eyes. The actions by the Obama administration have set into motion concrete and enforceable programs to regulate greenhouse gases. Time will tell whether the courts will brake the momentum built by the Obama administration or allow it to roll forward with gathering speed. In either case, climate law is here to stay and will continue to develop, reaching into ever more areas of environmental law. In the absence of federal legislation that comprehensively addresses greenhouse gases, it has been the U.S. Environmental Protection Agency's regulatory initiatives as well as the law of the states, of torts, of species protection, of environmental impact assessment, and of other fields that has determined the outline of climate law. No student of environmental law and its evolution will doubt that, over time, environmental law bends to meet the challenges of the day, and it will be no different for the problem of climate change.

Notes

[1] The authors would like to thank Elizabeth P. Corey for her assistance in updating and improving this year's chapter.

[2] Barack Obama, "Remarks of Senator Barack Obama: Real Leadership for a Clean Energy Future" (Oct. 8, 2007), available at http://www.barackobama.com/2007/10/08/remarks_of_senator_barack_obam _28.php (last visited Nov. 29, 2010); see also Jeff Zeleny, "Obama Proposes Capping Greenhouse Gas Emissions and Making Polluters Pay," NY Times (Oct. 9, 2007), available at http://www.nytimes.com/ 2007/10/09/us/politics/09obama.html.

[3] The White House Office of the Press Secretary press release, "Press Conference by the President" (Nov. 3, 2010), available at http://www.whitehouse.gov/the-press-office/2010/11/03/press-conference-presi dent; see also St. Petersburg Times Politifact.com, "Create Cap-and-trade System with Interim Goals to Reduce Global Warming," available at http://politifact.com/truth-o-meter/promises/promise/456/create -cap-and-trade-system-with-interim-goals-to-/ (last visited on Nov. 29, 2010).

[4] Id.

[5] Lois Romano, "Transcript: The Post's Lois Romano Interviews Carol Browner," Washington Post (Jan. 14, 2009), available at http://www.washingtonpost.com/wpsrv/politics/documents/transcript_interview _carol_browner_011409.html.

[6] See U.S. EPA, Regulatory Initiatives, available at http://www.epa.gov/climatechange/initiatives/index.html (last visited on Nov. 29, 2010).

[7] See U.S. EPA, Current and Near-Term Greenhouse Gas Reduction Initiatives, available at http://www.epa .gov/climatechange/policy/neartermghgreduction.html (last visited on Nov. 29, 2010).

[8] President Barack H. Obama, speech, "Second Inaugural Address" (Jan. 21, 2013).

[9] Executive Office of the President, "The President's Climate Action Plan" (June 2013), available at http:// www.whitehouse.gov/sites/default/files/image/president27sclimateactionplan.pdf.

[10] Id.

[11] American Clean Energy and Security Act of 2009, H.R. 2454, 111th Cong. (2010).

[12] American Clean Energy Leadership Act of 2009, S. 1462, 111th Cong. (2009).

[13] Clean Energy Jobs and American Power Act, S. 1733, 111th Cong. (2009).

[14] American Power Act, S. 1733, 111th Cong. (2010).

[15] Carbon Limits and Energy for America's Renewal, S. 2877, 111th. Cong. (2010), available at http://www.govtrack.us/congress/bill.xpd?bill=s111-2877.

[16] Carl Hulse and David Herszenhorn, "Democrats Call Off Climate Bill Effort," *NY Times* (July 22, 2010), available at http://www.nytimes.com/2010/07/23/us/politics/23cong.html.

[17] *Massachusetts v. EPA*, 549 U.S. 497 (2007).

[18] 42 U.S.C. § 7521(a)(1).

[19] *Massachusetts v. EPA*, 549 U.S. at 532.

[20] 73 Fed. Reg. 44354 (July 30, 2008).

[21] *Id.* at 44355.

[22] *Id.* at 44362.

[23] *Id.* at 44355. Interestingly, EPA included in the ANPR release comments received from other federal agencies during the interagency review process, such as the Department of Agriculture, the Department of Commerce, the Department of Transportation, and the Department of Energy. Those comments generally reflect Secretary Johnson's view that the Clean Air Act is poorly suited to reducing greenhouse gas emissions.

[24] *Id.* at 44362.

[25] *See In re Deseret Power Elec. Coop.*, PSD Appeal No. 07-03 (EAB Nov. 13, 2008).

[26] 40 C.F.R. § 52.21(b)(50)(iv).

[27] *See* Memorandum from Stephen L. Johnson, administrator, U.S. EPA, to U.S. EPA regional administrators, "EPA's Interpretation of Regulations that Determine Pollutants Covered By Federal Prevention of Significant Deterioration (PSD) Permit Program" (Dec. 18, 2008).

[28] 74 Fed. Reg. 56260 (Oct. 30, 2009).

[29] *Id.* at 56265.

[30] 75 Fed. Reg. 18608 (Apr. 12, 2010) proposing GHG reporting for petroleum and natural gas systems; 75 Fed. Reg. 18576 (Apr. 12, 2010) proposing GHG reporting on carbon dioxide injection and geologic sequestration; and 75 Fed. Reg. 18652 (Apr. 12, 2010) proposing GHG reporting of fluorinated GHGs from certain source categories, including electronic manufacturing, the production of fluorinated gas, and the use of electrical transmission and distribution equipment.

[31] 75 Fed. Reg. 74458 (Nov. 30, 2010).

[32] 76 Fed. Reg. 14812 (Mar. 18, 2011).

[33] 75 Fed. Reg. 66496, 66499 (Dec. 15, 2009). Noting that Section 202(a) source categories include passenger cars; heavy-, medium-, and light-duty trucks; motorcycles; and buses.

[34] *Id.* at 66497.

[35] *Id.* at 66499; *see also* U.S. EPA, *Inventory of U.S. Greenhouse Gas Emissions and Sinks: 1990–2007.* EPA 430–R–09–004 (Apr. 15, 2009), available at http://epa.gov/climatechange/emissions/downloads09/GHG2007entire_report-508.pdf.

[36] 75 Fed. Reg. 25324 (Mar. 7, 2010).

[37] *Id.* at 25396.

[38] *Id.* at 25330.

[39] *Id.*

[40] *Id.*

[41] 73 Fed. Reg. 80300 (Dec. 31, 2008).

[42] 74 Fed. Reg. 51535 (Oct. 7, 2009).

43 75 Fed. Reg. 17004 (Apr. 2, 2010).

44 *Id.* at 17006.

45 75 Fed. Reg. 31514, 31537-38 (Jun. 3, 2010).

46 *Id.* at 31516.

47 U.S. EPA, *Final Step 3 for the GHG Tailoring Rule Continues to Focus Permitting on the Largest Emitters, Fact Sheet* (July 2013), available at http://www.epa.gov/NSR/documents/20121012fs.pdf.

48 77 Fed. Reg. 41051 (July 12, 2013).

49 *Id.*

50 U.S. EPA, *Final Step 3 for the GHG Tailoring Rule Continues to Focus Permitting on the Largest Emitters, Fact Sheet* (July 2013).

51 *Carbon Pollution Emission Guidelines for Existing Stationary Sources: Electric Utility Generating Units*, 79 Fed. Reg. 34830 (June 18, 2014) (to be codified at 40 C.F.R. Part 60).

52 *Oil and Natural Gas Sector: Emission Standards for New, Reconstructed, and Modified Sources*, 81 Fed. Reg. 35824 (June 3, 2016) (to be codified at 40 C.F.R. Part 60).

53 *Id.* at 35825.

54 *Id.* at 35827.

55 *Id.* at 35824.

56 *Id.* at 35827.

57 *Id.*

58 *Id.* at 35825, 35844.

59 *Id.* at 35825, 35845.

60 *Standards of Performance for Municipal Solid Waste Landfills*, 80 Fed. Reg. 52162 (August 27, 2015); *Emission Guidelines and Compliance Times for Municipal Solid Waste Landfills*, 80 Fed. Reg. 52100 (August 27, 2015).

61 *See generally* 80 Fed. Reg. 52162; 80 Fed. Reg. 52100.

62 80 Fed. Reg. at 52162.

63 80 Fed. Reg. 52162; 80 Fed. Reg. 52100.

64 80 Fed. Reg. at 52162.

65 *Coal. for Responsible Regulation v. EPA*, 684 F.3d 102 (D.C. Cir. 2012).

66 *Util. Air Regulatory Grp. v. EPA*, 134 S. Ct. 2427 (2014).

67 *Id.* at 2437.

68 *Id.* at 2436.

69 *Id.* at 2443.

70 *Id.* at 2437, 2444-45.

71 *Id.* at 2445.

72 *Id.* at 2444-45.

73 *Id.* at 2449.

74 *Id.* at 2447-48.

75 *Id.* at 2447-49.

76 Filed by the States of Alabama, Arkansas, Florida, Indiana, Kansas, the Commonwealth of Kentucky, Louisiana, Michigan, Nebraska, Ohio, Oklahoma, South Dakota, West Virginia, Wisconsin, and Wyoming.

77 *Carbon Pollution Emission Guidelines for Existing Stationary Sources: Electric Utility Generating Units*, 80 Fed. Reg. 64662 (Oct. 23, 2015) (to be codified at 40 C.F.R. Part 60).

78 Filed by the States of Texas, Alabama, Arkansas, Colorado, Florida, Georgia, Indiana, Kansas, Louisiana, Missouri, Montana, Nebraska, New Jersey, Ohio, South Carolina, South Dakota, Utah, West Virginia,

Wisconsin, Wyoming, the Commonwealth of Kentucky, the Arizona Corporation Commission, the State of Louisiana Department of Environmental Quality, the State of North Carolina Department of Environmental Quality, and Attorney General Bill Schuette on behalf of the People of Michigan.

79 UNFCCC: Paris Agreement, art. 2.1, Dec. 15, 2015. The Agreement has not yet entered into effect.

80 *Id.* at art. 20.1; *see also* UNFCC: Paris Agreement Signature Ceremony, List of Representatives to High-Level Signature Ceremony (April 22, 2016).

81 UNFCCC: Paris Agreement, art. 21, Dec. 15, 2015.

82 *Id.* at art. 21.1.

83 *Id.* at arts. 28.1 and 28.2.

84 *Id.* at art. 2.1(a)-(c).

85 *Id.* at art. 2.2.

86 *Id.* at art. 4.9.

87 *Id.*

88 *Id.* at art. 4.3.

89 *Black's Law Dictionary* 1626 (9th ed. 2009).

90 For a discussion of common law tort claims used in the environmental context, *see* chapter 1.

91 *See, e.g., Int'l Paper Co. v. Ouellette*, 479 U.S. 481, 494 (1987).

92 *See, e.g., City of Milwaukee v. Illinois*, 451 U.S. 304, 313, 315 (1981).

93 *Connecticut v. Am. Elec. Power Co.*, 582 F.3d 309 (2d Cir. 2009); *Comer v. Murphy Oil USA*, 585 F.3d 855 (5th Cir. 2009).

94 *Native Vill. of Kivalina v. ExxonMobil et al.*, 663 F. Supp. 2d 863 (N.D. Cal. 2009).

95 *Connecticut v. Am. Elec. Power Co.*, 582 F.3d 309.

96 *Connecticut v. Am. Elec. Power Co.*, 406 F. Supp. 2d 265, 268 (S.D.N.Y. 2005).

97 *Id.* at 265.

98 *Id.* at 270.

99 *Id.* at 274.

100 369 U.S. 186, 210 (1962).

101 *Connecticut v. Am. Elec. Power Co.*, 582 F.3d at 321.

102 *Baker*, 369 U.S. at 217.

103 *Connecticut v. Am. Elec. Power Co.*, 582 F.3d at 332.

104 *Am. Elec. Power Co. v. Connecticut*, 131 S. Ct. 2527, 2537 (2011).

105 *Id.* (internal citations omitted).

106 *Id.* at 2530–31.

107 *Id.* at 2531.

108 *Comer*, 585 F.3d 855 (5th Cir. 2009).

109 *Id.* at 860-861.

110 *Id.* at 879.

111 *Id.* at 880 (citation omitted).

112 *Id.* at 876.

113 *Id.* at 880.

114 *Comer v. Murphy Oil USA, Inc.*, 839 F. Supp. 2d 849 (S.D. Miss. 2012).

115 *Comer v. Murphy Oil USA, Inc.*, 718 F.3d 460 (5th Cir. 2013).

116 *Kivalina*, 663 F. Supp. 2d 863 (N.D. Cal. 2009).

117 *Id.* at 876.

118 *Id.*

119 *Id.*

120 *Lujan v. Defenders of Wildlife*, 504 U.S. 555, 559-60 (1992).

121 *Id.*

122 *Native Vill. of Kivalina v. ExxonMobil Corp.*, 696 F.3d 849 (9th Cir. 2012).

123 *Id.* at 15.

124 *Native Vill. of Kivalina v. ExxonMobil Corp.*, 133 S. Ct. 2390 (2013) (order denying certiorari).

125 *North Carolina, ex rel. Cooper v. Tennessee Valley Auth.*, 615 F.3d 291 (4th Cir. 2010).

126 *Id.* at 296.

127 *Id.* at 310.

128 16 U.S.C. §§ 1531-1544.

129 16 U.S.C. § 1533(b)(3)(A).

130 16 U.S.C. § 1533(a)(1).

131 16 U.S.C. § 1532(6).

132 16 U.S.C. § 1532(20).

133 16 U.S.C. § 1532(5).

134 *N. Spotted Owl v. Lujan*, 758 F. Supp. 621 (W.D. Wash. 1991).

135 16 U.S.C. § 1536(a).

136 16 U.S.C. § 1536(a)(2).

137 16 U.S.C. § 1538(a)(1)(B)-(C).

138 16 U.S.C. § 1532(19).

139 50 C.F.R. § 17.3; *Babbitt v. Sweet Home Chapter of Cmtys. for a Great Oregon*, 515 U.S. 687, 704 (1995).

140 *See, e.g., Palila v. Hawaii Dep't of Land & Natural Res.*, 639 F.2d 495 (9th Cir. 1981); *Palila v. Hawaii Dep't of Land & Natural Res.*, 852 F.2d 1106 (9th Cir. 1988).

141 *See* Center for Biological Diversity, *Petition to List the Polar Bear (Ursus maritimus) as a Threatened Species under the Endangered Species Act*, at vi (Feb. 16, 2005).

142 *See Ctr. for Biological Diversity v. Norton*, Case No. C-05-5191-JSW (N.D. Cal.) (filed Dec. 15, 2005); *Ctr. for Biological Diversity v. Kempthorne*, Case No. C-08-1339-CW (N.D. Cal.) (filed Mar. 10, 2008).

143 73 Fed. Reg. 28212 (May 15, 2008).

144 71 Fed. Reg. 26852, 26857 (May 9, 2006).

145 73 Fed. Reg. 28212, 28249 (May 15, 2008).

146 *See* U.S. Department of Interior press release, "Secretary Kempthorne Announces Decision to Protect Polar Bears under Endangered Species Act" (May 14, 2008).

147 16 U.S.C. § 1533.

148 *See* U.S. Fish and Wildlife Service press release, "Salazar Retains Conservation Rule for Polar Bears Underlines Need for Comprehensive Energy and Climate Change Legislation" (May 8, 2009), available at http://www.fws.gov/news/newsreleases/showNews.cfm?newsId = 20FB90B6-A188-DB01-04788E0 892D91701.

149 *In re Polar Bear Endangered Species Act Listing and 4(d) Rule Litig.*, D.D.C., No. 08-764 (Nov. 4, 2010).

150 *In re Polar Bear Endangered Species Act Listing & Section 4(d) Rule Litig.—MDL No. 1993*, 709 F.3d 1, 7 (D.C. Cir. 2013).

151 *Id.* at 8.

152 *Id.* at 17-18.

153 *In re Polar Bear Endangered Species Act Listing & Section 4(d) Rule Litig.—MDL No. 1993*, No. 1:08-mc-00764 (D.C. Cir. Apr. 29, 2013) (order denying petition for hearing *en banc*).

154 *See* Draft memorandum from Kathleen A. McGinty, chairman, Council on Environmental Quality, to heads of federal agencies, "Guidance regarding Consideration of Global Climatic Change in Environmental Documents Prepared Pursuant to the National Environmental Policy Act" (Oct. 8, 1997).

[155] *Id.* (awkward phrasing is original).

[156] *Id.*

[157] *See* Memorandum from Nancy H. Sutley, chair, Council on Environmental Quality, to heads of federal departments and agencies, "Draft NEPA Guidance on Consideration of the Effects of Climate Change and Greenhouse Gas Emissions" (Feb. 18, 2010).

[158] *Ctr. for Biological Diversity v. U.S. Dept. of Interior*, 563 F.3d 466 (D.C. Cir. 2009).

[159] *N. Slope Borough v. Minerals Mgmt. Serv.*, No. 08-35180, 2009 U.S. App. LEXIS 19321 (9th Cir. 2009).

[160] MMS is the federal Minerals Management Service, which was recently renamed the Bureau of Ocean Energy Management, Regulation, and Enforcement. The bureau resides within the U.S. Department of the Interior.

[161] *City of Los Angeles v. Nat'l Highway Traffic Safety Admin.*, 912 F.2d 478 (D.C. Cir. 1990).

[162] *Ctr. for Biological Diversity v. Nat'l Highway Traffic Safety Admin.*, 508 F.3d 508 (9th Cir. 2007), *opinion vacated and withdrawn*, *Ctr. for Biological Diversity v. Nat'l Highway Traffic Safety Admin.*, 538 F.3d 1172 (9th Cir. 2008).

[163] *Mid States Coal. for Progress v. Surface Transp. Bd.*, 345 F.3d 520 (8th Cir. 2003).

[164] In 2008, the Powder River Basin supplied more than 40 percent of the coal produced in the United States. U.S. Energy Information Administration, *Annual Coal Report 2008*, at 17 (Mar. 2010).

[165] The court noted as significant that sulfur dioxide emissions would not increase regardless of how much more coal was produced because the Clean Air Act capped sulfur emissions. In contrast, carbon dioxide emissions are uncapped.

[166] *Mayo Found. v. Surface Transp. Bd.*, 472 F.3d 545 (8th Cir. 2006).

[167] *Ass'n of Pub. Agency Customers, Inc. v. Bonneville Power Admin.*, 126 F.3d 1158 (9th Cir. 1997) [hereinafter *APAC*].

[168] Bonneville Power Administration (BPA) is a federal agency that markets predominantly hydropower from more than thirty generating plants in the Pacific Northwest. It also operates about three-quarters of the transmission system in the region.

[169] *APAC*, 126 F.3d at 1186.

[170] *Nw. Envtl. Advocates v. Nat'l Marine Fisheries Serv.*, 460 F.3d 1125 (9th Cir. 2006).

[171] *Hapner v. Tidwell*, 621 F.3d 1239 (9th Cir. 2010).

[172] *Sierra Club v. Clinton*, Civil No. 09-2622, 2010 WL 4117271 (D. Minn. Oct. 19, 2010).

[173] *See* Regional Greenhouse Gas Emissions Initiative Memorandum of Understanding (Dec. 20, 2005) (hereinafter RGGI MOU); Western Regional Climate Action Initiative (Feb. 26, 2007); Midwestern Greenhouse Gas Accord (Nov. 15, 2007).

[174] *See* Final Regional Greenhouse Gas Emissions Model Rule (Dec. 31, 2008) ("Final RGGI Model Rule"), available at http://www.rggi.org/docs/Model%20Rule%20Revised%2012.31.08.pdf; Final Model Rule for the Midwestern Greenhouse Gas Reduction Accord (Apr. 2010), available at http://www.midwesternaccord.org/Final_Model_Rule.pdf; Detailed Design for the WCI Regional Program (July 27, 2010), available at http://www.westernclimateinitative.org/component/remository/func-startdown/280/.

[175] Final RGGI Model Rule 1.4 at 20.

[176] 40 C.F.R Part 96.

[177] RGGI MOU at 3.

[178] RGGI press release, "Ten States Mark Second Anniversary of Regional Program to Reduce Greenhouse Gas Emissions" (Sept. 10, 2010).

[179] *See* New York State Energy Research and Development Authority, "Relative Effects of Various Factors on RGGI Electricity Sector CO_2 Emissions: 2009 Compared to 2005," Draft White Paper, at 3 (Nov. 3, 2010) (hereinafter 2010 RGGI Effects Report).

[180] *Id.*

181 *Id.* at 8. Noting that a summer with "above-average" temperatures will increase the need for air-conditioning, which requires additional electricity, and that 2005 was a relatively hot summer as compared to the summer of 2009.

182 *Id.* at 4.

183 *See* ICF Consulting, *RGGI Reference Case Results and Assumptions,* at 9 (Nov. 5, 2010), available at http://www.rggi.org/docs/RGGI_Reference_Case_110510.pdf.

184 RGGI 2012 Program Review: Summary of Recommendations to Accompany Model Rule Amendments, available at http://www.rggi.org/design/program_review.

185 *Id.*

186 Western Climate Initiative, Design Summary at 5.

187 *Id.*

188 *See* Governor Janice K. Brewer, Executive Order 2010-06, "Governor's Policy on Climate Change" (Feb. 2, 2010); *see also* statement by Dianne Nielson, energy adviser, State of Utah, as published in the Utah Petroleum Association, "Utah Won't Implement WCI Plan—At Least for Now" (May 5, 2010).

189 *See* California Air Resources Board Rulemaking Activity in 2010—California Cap-and-Trade Program, available at http://www.arb.ca.gov/regact/regact10.htm.

190 *See* California Office of the Governor Press Release, *Gov. Schwarzenegger Signs Landmark Legislation to Reduce Greenhouse Gas Emissions* (Sept. 27, 2006).

191 *See* May 20, 2011, judgment in the case of *Ass'n of Irritated Residents, et al. vs California Air Res. Bd.,* Superior Court of California, County of San Francisco. Case No. CPF-09-509562.

192 Petition for Writ of Mandate and Complaint for Declaratory Relief at 5, *California Chamber of Commerce v. California Air Res. Bd.,* No. 34-2012-80001313 (Cal. Sup. Ct. Nov. 13, 2012).

193 *See* New Hampshire House Bill 519, which passed the New Hampshire House in February 2011. *See also* Delaware House Bill 86, introduced April 6, 2011.

194 *See generally* 17 C.F.R. § 229.1 *et seq.*

195 *See generally* Sarbanes-Oxley Act of 2002, Pub. L. No. 107-204, 116 Stat. 756 (2002).

196 *CERES et al.,* Petition for Interpretive Guidance on Climate Change Disclosure, available at http://www.incr.com//Document.Doc?id=187.

197 *Id.* at 51.

198 *See* Westlaw News Room Clean Air Report, "Revised Petition to SEC For Climate Reporting Cites EPA Actions," 2009 WLNR 24811557 (Dec. 10, 2009). ("A source involved in the coalition's effort says that SEC members, including Chairwoman Mary Schapiro, in recent months have provided indications that a rulemaking regarding climate change risk disclosure is coming.")

199 U.S. Securities and Exchange Commission press release, "SEC Issues Interpretive Guidance on Disclosure Related to Business or Legal Developments Regarding Climate Change" (Jan. 27, 2010), available at http://www.sec.gov/news/press/2010/2010-15.htm; *see also* Jim Efstathiou, "SEC Sets Corporate Climate-Change Disclosure Standard," Bloomberg Businessweek (Jan. 27, 2010), available at http://www.businessweek.com/news/2010-01-27/sec-sets-climate-change-disclosure-standards-for-companies.html.

200 Troy A. Paredes, commissioner, Securities and Exchange Commission, speech, "Statement Regarding Commission Guidance Regarding Disclosure Related to Climate Change" (Jan. 27, 2010).

201 75 Fed. Reg. 6295 n.62, 6296 n.71.

202 Felicity Barringer and Danny Hakim, "New York Subpoenas 5 Energy Companies," *NY Times* (Sept. 16, 2007), available at http://www.nytimes.com/2007/09/16/nyregion/16greenhouse.html.

203 *Id.*

204 New York Office of the Attorney General press release, "Attorney General Cuomo Announces Agreement with AES to Disclose Climate Change Risk to Investors" (Nov. 19, 2009), available at http://www.ag.ny.gov/media_center/2009/nov/nov19a_09.html.

205 *See* Point Carbon, "Global Carbon Market Worth 121bn in 2010, Up 33%, Predicts Point Carbon" (Jan. 29, 2010), available at http://www.pointcarbon.com/aboutus/pressroom/pressreleases/1.1393070.

206 Philippe Ambrosi and Karan Capoor, *State and Trends of the Carbon Market 2008*, World Bank, Washington, D.C., at 1 (May 2008).

207 *See* U.S. Government Accountability Office, *Carbon Trading: Current Situation and Oversight Considerations for Policymakers*, at 12 (Aug. 19, 2010) (hereinafter GAO Carbon Trading Report).

208 World Resources Institute, *Bottom Line On . . .* , Issue 17, Offsets (Aug. 2010).

209 RGGI MOU at 5.

210 *Ecosystems Marketplace. Offsetting Emissions: A Business Brief on the Voluntary Carbon Market* at 2. 2nd ed. (Feb. 2008).

211 *See generally* Chicago Climate Exchange website, available at http://www.chicagoclimatex.com (last visited on Nov. 29, 2010).

212 CCX Fact Sheet, Chicago Climate Exchange: By the Numbers (Oct. 21, 2010).

213 *See generally* Chicago Climate Exchange website, available at http://www.chicagoclimatex.com (last visited on Nov. 29, 2010).

214 Chicago Climate Exchange, General Offset Program Provisions, at 6 (Aug. 20, 2009).

215 GAO Carbon Trading Report at 12.

216 *See* International Monetary Fund website available at http://www.imf.org/ external/np/sta/fd/index.htm (last visited on Nov. 29, 2010).

217 *See* CCFE, RGGI Futures and Options, available at http://www.ccfe.com/ccfe Content.jsf?id = 4565851 (last visited on Nov. 29, 2010).

218 *See* CCFE, SO$_2$ and NOx, available at http://www.ccfe.com/ccfeContent.jsf?id = 4565951 (last visited on Nov. 29, 2010).

219 Dodd-Frank Wall Street Reform and Consumer Protection Act, H.R. 4173 Sec. 750, 111th Cong. (2010).

220 CFTC press release, "CFTC Seeks Public Input for a Study regarding the Oversight of Existing and Prospective Carbon Markets" (Nov. 19, 2010), available at http://www.cftc.gov/PressRoom/Press Releases/pr5937-10.html.

221 Vladimir Stenek et al., *Climate Risks and Financial Institutions: Challenges and Opportunities*, World Bank Group International Finance Corporation (2010), available at http://www.ifc.org/ifcext/sustainability.nsf/ AttachmentsByTitle/p_ClimateRiskandFIsFullreport/$FILE/IFCClimate_RiskandFIs_FullReport.pdf.

222 *See generally* Kevin A. Ewing, "A Governance Strategy for Engaging Climate-Change Risk," *Executive Counsel* 5, no. 4 (July/Aug. 2008); Kevin A. Ewing, "Global Warming: The Director's Perspective," *NACD—Director's Monthly* (Aug. 2008).

Chapter 12

Toxic Substances Control Act[1]

Michael Boucher and Stanley W. Landfair
Dentons US LLP

1.0 Introduction

The Toxic Substances Control Act (TSCA, or the Act), 15 U.S.C. §§ 2601-2629, was enacted on October 11, 1976. The Act has been amended four times. The first three amendments resulted in an additional title to the Act, such that TSCA now contains four titles: Title I—the Control of Toxic Substances; Title II—the Asbestos Hazard Emergency Response Act; Title III—the Indoor Radon Abatement Act; and Title IV—the Lead-Based Paint Exposure Reduction Act. The scope of this chapter, however, is limited to Title I of the Act, the Control of Toxic Substances.

The fourth and most recent amendment is actually a long and elaborate series of amendments, embodied in a statute known as the "Frank R. Lautenberg Chemical Safety for the 21st Century Act" (H.R. 2576), which the President signed into law on June 22, 2016 as Public Law No. 114-182. This Act amends the "core" provisions of TSCA in many significant ways, and is described in many circles as a "comprehensive" revision to TSCA, and referred to as "TSCA Reform."

The breadth of the new amendments is indeed significant. Nevertheless, TSCA remains the same in its fundamental approach to the regulation of chemical substances that are not otherwise regulated under other federal laws (such as pesticides regulated under the Federal Insecticide, Fungicide and Rodenticide Act, or pharmaceutical products, regulated under the Federal Food, Drug and Cosmetic Act. TSCA continues to place on manufacturers of chemical substances and mixtures the responsibility to provide data on health and environmental effects, and gives EPA comprehensive authority to regulate their manufacture, use, distribution in commerce, and disposal.

To implement this authority, the amended TSCA continues to afford EPA the regulatory tools identified below providing EPA with:

- *Authority to require testing* of chemicals that may present a significant risk or that are produced in substantial quantities and result in substantial human or environmental exposure, established under TSCA § 4, and now enhanced to allow EPA to require testing to support a premanufacture notification ("PMN") or Significant New Use Notification ("SNUN"), to support EPA risk evaluations and for other reasons;

- *Premanufacture review* of new chemical substances prior to their commercial production and introduction into the marketplace in a PMN or prior to allowing a significant new use pursuant to a SNUN under TSCA § 5, now made more rigorous by requiring EPA affirmatively to make certain findings, most notably the finding whether a chemical presents an Unreasonable Risk, rather than by allowing expiration periods to lapse;

- *Authority to limit or prohibit* the manufacture, use, distribution, and disposal of existing chemical substances under TSCA § 6, now enhanced by requiring EPA to establish a risk evaluation process, under which the Agency will be required to identify chemicals that present an Unreasonable Risk;

- *Recordkeeping and reporting* requirements to ensure that the EPA administrator would continually have access to new information on chemical substances under TSCA § 8, which remain substantially unchanged;

- *Export notice* requirements that allow EPA to inform foreign governments of shipments of chemical substances into their countries, impose under TSCA § 12, substantially unchanged; and

- *Import certification* requirements under TSCA § 13, which ensure that all chemical substances imported into the United States comply with the Act, also substantially unchanged.

This is the twenty-fourth consecutive year in which we have published a summary of TSCA in this Handbook. In all of the previous years, we have incorporated our discussion of changes to the law and its implementing regulations in on integrated text that summarizes the requirements and prohibitions imposed by the Act. Given the number and complexity of the Amendments under the Lautenberg Act this year, and the need of a sophisticated reader to identify the changes distinctly form the preexisting provisions, we have taken a different approach in the text below: the remainder of the text discusses and summarizes TSCA, its requirements and prohibitions before the Amendments were enacted, and the supplement at the end of this chapter addresses only the changes. We believe the reader will find this approach useful this year, while the Amendments are new and before implementing regulations are promulgated. We anticipate that we will incorporate the Amendments into the text of the summary of TSCA next year, and elaborate upon them as implementing regulations are promulgated.

2.0 Activities Subject to TSCA

The varied requirements of TSCA apply to persons and companies that manufacture, process, distribute, use, or dispose of TSCA-regulated chemicals. Thus, it is necessary to determine, case by case, whether a particular activity constitutes regulated conduct. Unfortunately, TSCA defines neither "use" nor "dispose," and the definitions of "manufacture," "process," and "distribute" are worded too broadly to provide meaningful guidance. Moreover, EPA's implementing regulations generally define these terms more narrowly than the statute. Consequently, the scope of TSCA jurisdiction often remains unclear. The definition of these important jurisdictional terms and the duties of those who fall within them are discussed below.

2.1 Manufacture

TSCA § 3(7) defines "manufacture" to include not only the traditional notions of manufacture and production but also the importation of TSCA-regulated chemical substances or mixtures. Under TSCA, manufacturers of chemical substances generally must (1) sponsor tests and submit data to EPA regarding chemicals they manufacture; (2) submit a premanufacture notice (PMN) before manufacturing a chemical substance not on the TSCA Inventory or before manufacturing a chemical for a significant new use; (3) avoid manufacture of PCBs; (4) maintain records and submit reports as required by § 8; (5) submit to EPA inspections and subpoenas as authorized by § 11; and (6) certify compliance with TSCA upon importation as required by § 13.

EPA regulations implementing TSCA § 5 (Premanufacture Notification) and § 8 (Reporting and Recordkeeping) limit jurisdiction to persons who "manufacture for commercial purposes" and define "commercial purposes" as

the purpose of obtaining an immediate or eventual commercial advantage for the manufacturer, and includes, among other things,

- for distribution in commerce, including for test marketing, and

- for use by the manufacturer, including use for product research and development, or as an intermediate.

Further, this definition applies to substances that are produced coincidentally during the manufacture, processing, use, or disposal of another substance or mixture, including by-products that are separated from that other substance or mixture and impurities that remain in that substance or mixture.[2]

EPA has expanded the statutory definition of "manufacture" by including the act of "extracting" a chemical from another chemical substance or mixture of substances.[3] Importantly, a toll manufacturer also is considered a manufacturer under the premanufacture and significant new use notification regulations. The purchasing or contracting company also may be considered a manufacturer, however, if (1) the toll manufacturer produces the substance exclusively for that purchasing company and (2) the purchasing company specifies the identity of the substance and controls the amount produced and the basic technology for the plant processes.[4]

2.2 Process

TSCA § 3(10) defines "process" as the preparation of a chemical substance or mixture, after its manufacture, for distribution in commerce:

(A)   in the same form or physical state as, or in a different form or physical state from, that in which it was received by the persons so preparing such substance or mixture; or

(B)   as part of an article containing the chemical substance or mixture.

TSCA § 3(11) further defines the term "processor" as "any person who processes a chemical substance or mixture."

Processors of chemical substances must (1) provide EPA with data under test rules, in some circumstances; (2) notify EPA prior to processing a chemical for a significant new use; (3) comply with EPA orders issued under §§ 5(e), 5(f), or 6(b) or rules promulgated under § 6(a); (4) avoid processing PCBs except as permitted by EPA; (5) comply with the recordkeeping and reporting requirements of §§ 8(c), 8(d), and 8(e); and (6) submit to EPA inspections and subpoenas, as authorized by § 11.

If EPA's regulations implementing the various subsections of TSCA applied to everyone who fell within the literal language of these broad definitions, TSCA requirements would be imposed on thousands of businesses that Congress never intended the law to touch. To avoid such problems for some reporting requirements under TSCA § 8, EPA has passed implementing rules that apply only to some processors.

Recognizing the need to address this issue in a comprehensive and organized manner, several years ago EPA made available a package of all EPA guidance documents that address the definitions of "process" or "processor."[5] EPA also solicited written comments and held a one-day public meeting to allow interested persons an opportunity to present their views on EPA's interpretation of "process" under TSCA. Several commenters urged EPA to begin formal rulemaking to modify the definition of "processor" and to limit or eliminate application of the term to basic manufacturers and other companies that traditionally have not considered themselves chemical processors. At the time, the agency planned to review all written and oral comments received and to address, as appropriate, the issues identified, starting with those that seemed to be of the greatest concern to the regulated community and others. Since 1992, however, there has been no significant dialogue or further EPA action on this issue.

2.3 Use

TSCA does not provide a definition of "use," nor has EPA issued comprehensive guidance on the distinction between "use" and "process." Nonetheless, users of chemical substances (who are not also manufacturers, processors, or distributors) must (1) comply with regulations issued under § 6(a); (2) refrain from using PCBs, except as permitted by EPA; (3) refrain from using any chemical substance they know or have reason to know has been manufactured, produced, or distributed in violation of TSCA, as prohibited under TSCA § 15(2); and (4) submit to EPA inspections and subpoenas, as authorized by § 11.

2.4 Distribute

Under TSCA § 3(4), the terms "distribute in commerce" and "distribution in commerce" mean to sell, to introduce, or to deliver a chemical substance into commerce or to hold the mixture or article after its introduction into commerce. The term "commerce" is defined in TSCA § 3(3) to mean interstate trade, traffic, transportation, or other activity which affects interstate trade, traffic, transportation, or commerce.

The TSCA definition of "distribution" thus encompasses more than the usual concept of sales or transportation, but its scope is not clear. For example, if applied literally, the portion that defines "holding" a chemical after its introduction in commerce as "distribution" would make any purchaser of a chemical a distributor since the person would necessarily hold the substance briefly before using it. In practice, EPA interprets the term to apply to persons who purchase a chemical and hold it for purposes of later distribution.

Distributors of chemical substances (who are not also manufacturers or processors) must (1) comply with rules issued under § 6(a), (2) refrain from distributing PCBs except as permitted by EPA, (3) report "substantial risk information" to EPA under § 8(e), and (4) submit to EPA inspections and subpoenas, as authorized by § 11.

2.5 Dispose

Disposal is another activity not defined in TSCA. As a result, TSCA imposes no direct obligation on disposers of chemicals, but they may be subject to several types of rules or orders issued pursuant to the Act. Disposers of chemical substances (who are not also manufacturers, processors, distributors, or users) must (1) comply with regulations issued under § 6(a), (2) dispose of PCBs according to requirements of the PCB disposal regulations, and (3) submit to EPA inspections and subpoenas, as authorized by § 11.

3.0 The TSCA Inventory

TSCA § 8(b) requires EPA to compile, keep current, and publish a list of chemical substances manufactured or processed for commercial purposes in the United States. This "list," known as the TSCA Inventory, forms the basis for distinguishing between "existing" chemicals (those included on the TSCA Inventory) and "new" chemicals (substances that require premanufacture notification under TSCA § 5). Thus, it is critically important to understand the TSCA Inventory and how it is compiled, kept current, and used.

3.1 Initial Compilation of the Inventory

The Inventory was developed pursuant to EPA's Inventory Reporting Regulations in December 1977. To be eligible for inclusion in the Inventory, a substance had to be a "reportable chemical substance," defined under the regulations as (1) a chemical substance; (2) manufactured, imported, or processed for a commercial purpose in the United States between January 1, 1975, and the date of publication of the Initial Inventory (June 1, 1979); and (3) not specifically excluded from the Inventory.[6] These three criteria are discussed below.

3.1.1 Chemical Substance

The statutory definition of the term "chemical substance" was incorporated directly into the Inventory Reporting Regulations, and includes any organic or inorganic substance of a particular molecular identity, including any combination of such substances occurring in whole or in part as a result of a chemical reaction or occurring in nature, and any element or uncombined radical.[7]

The regulations also incorporate the statutory exclusions from the definition of "chemical substance" for (1) any mixture; (2) any commercial pesticide; (3)

tobacco and certain tobacco products; (4) any nuclear source material or by-product; (5) any pistol, firearm, revolver, shells, and cartridges; and (6) any commercial food, food additive, drug, cosmetic, or device.[8]

3.1.2 Manufactured or Imported for a "Commercial Purpose"

A chemical substance manufactured or imported "for a commercial purpose" is one manufactured or imported for distribution in commerce (including test marketing) or for use by the manufacturer or importer, including use as an intermediate.[9]

3.1.3 Specifically Excluded Substances

"Mixtures" and "chemicals manufactured for a non-commercial purpose" are explicitly excluded from the Inventory by virtue of the definition of "chemical substance" under TSCA § 3(2)(B). The following also are excluded pursuant to § 8(b) and implementing regulations.

3.1.3.1 Research and Development

Any chemical substance manufactured or processed only in small quantities for research and development (R&D) is excluded from the Inventory under TSCA § 8(b)(1). The R&D exemption is discussed in further detail *infra* at section 4.3.2.

3.1.3.2 Pesticides

Because pesticides, as defined in the Federal Insecticide, Fungicide, and Rodenticide Act (FIFRA), are specifically excluded from the definition of chemical substances under TSCA § 3(2)(B)(ii), such substances are excluded from the Inventory. If a substance has multiple uses, those uses that are not subject to FIFRA are subject to TSCA, and thus must be included on the Inventory.

3.1.3.3 Articles

EPA defines an "article," for TSCA purposes, as a manufactured item formed into a specific shape or design during manufacture which has an end-use function dependent upon its shape or design during end-use and which has no change of chemical composition during its end-use separate from the purpose of the article.[10] Articles were excluded from Inventory reporting.

3.1.3.4 Impurities

An impurity is defined as "a chemical substance which is unintentionally present in another chemical substance."[11] Impurities are specifically excluded from the Inventory by regulation.[12]

3.1.3.5 By-products

A by-product is a chemical substance produced without a specific commercial intent during the manufacture or processing of another chemical substance(s) or mixture(s).[13] EPA excluded from the Inventory by-products which have no commercial purpose. [14]

3.1.3.6 Chemicals Produced from Incidental Reactions

Chemical substances produced as a result of incidental reactions were excluded from the Inventory because they were not intentionally produced for commercial purposes.[15]

3.1.3.7 Non-isolated Intermediates

Intermediates, defined as chemicals that are both manufactured and partially or totally consumed in the chemical reaction process, or are intentionally present in order to affect the rate of chemical reactions by which other chemical substances or mixtures are being manufactured, are subject to Inventory reporting. Non-isolated intermediates, however, defined as those intermediates that are not intentionally removed from the equipment in which they are manufactured, are excluded from reporting.[16]

3.2 Inventory Corrections

In 1980, EPA, recognizing that companies sometimes made errors in reporting substances and that often these errors were not discovered for many years, began to accept corrections to Inventory submissions under the following limited circumstances. Corrections must be submitted by the company that currently owns the rights to the chemical, be accompanied by adequate documentation, and fall into one of the following three categories: (1) corrections of the chemical identity of previously reported materials, (2) corrections to identify previously unrecognized isolated intermediates, and (3) corrections made in response to communications from EPA which identify reporting errors.[17]

3.3 Maintaining and Updating the Inventory Database

EPA continuously adds to the Inventory new chemicals that have cleared TSCA § 5 PMN review and for which Notices of Commencement of Manufacture have been filed. The agency also periodically removes, or "delists," from the Inventory "orphan chemicals" that are not currently being manufactured or imported for commercial purposes.

Prior to delisting, the agency publishes a notice of its intent to delist in the *Federal Register* and in its quarterly, *Chemicals in Progress Bulletin*. As a result of this process, the Inventory is maintained as a list of chemicals currently in commerce, not just those that were in commercial use during the 1975–1979 reporting period for the initial Inventory.

In June 1986, EPA issued an Inventory Update Rule requiring manufacturers and importers of certain chemicals listed on the Inventory to report current data on production volume, plant site, and site-limited status.[18] This rule remained in effect through 2002, and required reporting every four years for all chemical substances listed on the Inventory, except for the following: (1) polymers, (2) microorganisms, (3) naturally occurring substances, and (4) inorganics.[19]

Under the 1986 rule, any company that manufactured or imported any "reportable substance" for commercial purposes in amounts of 10,000 pounds or more at any time during the most recent complete corporate fiscal year immediately preceding the reporting year was obligated to file the report.[20]

EPA amended the Inventory Update Rule significantly in 2003. The current IUR, which took effect in 2006, requires any company that manufactures a chemical substance in the United States, or imports a chemical substance into the United States, in excess of 25,000 pounds during the calendar year prior to the reporting year, to file an IUR Report identifying the site at which the chemical was manufactured and imported, and the amount. The current IUR further requires any company that manufactures or imports a chemical substance in excess of 300,000 pounds to complete and file a further report regarding the manufacture, processing, distribution, and use of that chemical, and exposure to persons that results from such manufacture, processing, distribution, and use. IUR Reports are now due every five years, rather than every four. Exemptions from reporting under the Inventory Update Rule are available to small manufacturers and for certain chemicals exempt from premanufacture notification requirements.[21]

The Inventory Update Rule requires each manufacturer or importer subject to the rule to maintain specific records documenting the information submitted to EPA.[22] Importantly, production records for substances manufactured at less than the reporting thresholds must be maintained to justify a decision not to report.

3.4 Proposed Amendments

On August 13, 2010, EPA proposed significant amendments to the IUR.[23] Among the proposed changes were the following: (1) requiring use of electronic reporting software to submit all IUR information; (2) beginning after the 2011 reporting period, requiring reporting if production volume of a chemical exceeded 25,000 pounds in any calendar year since the last principal reporting year; (3) requiring reporting of the production volume for each year since the last IUR reporting year; (4) requiring significantly more information regarding what is done with a chemical at the manufacturing or importation site; (5) requiring processing and use information on all reported chemicals, not just those manufactured or imported at volumes of 300,000 pounds or more, thereby requiring all reporters of non-excluded substances to report information in all parts of the IUR Form U; (6) requiring up-front substantiation of claims that processing or use information is confidential business information; and (7) reducing the reporting interval from five to four years.

At the time of this printing, the amendments had not become law, and there was significant question when, or whether, EPA would publish a final rule. On May 11, 2011, EPA suspended the requirement for any IUR submissions, pending completion of the rulemaking process (76 Fed. Reg. 27273 [May 11, 2011]).

3.5 How to Use the Inventory

The 1985 edition of the Inventory, with its 1990 Supplement, is the most current hard-copy version. In addition, companies may search online for a chemical substance on the public version of the TSCA Inventory at EPA's Chemical Registry System (CRS), http://www.epa.gov/srs. CD-ROM, diskette, and tape versions that include chemicals added to the Inventory since 1990 are also available. These public versions consist of nonconfidential identities and generic names for confidential substances. EPA maintains the master file that contains both the confidential and the nonconfidential identities.

There are five volumes in the 1985 TSCA Inventory, each indexed to categorize the TSCA list of chemical substances in different ways. Volume 1 lists chemical substances in ascending order by CAS registry number, the CAS Index, or by preferred names. Volumes 2 and 3 are an alphabetically ordered listing of all CAS Index or preferred names, EPA submitter names, and CAS synonyms for the substances in the Chemical Substance Identity section. Volume 4 lists all substances appearing in the Chemical Substance Identity section that have determinable molecular formulas. Volume 5 lists substances of unknown or variable composition, complex reaction products, and biological materials (UVCB) substances.

3.5.1 Searching the Inventory

Volume 1 of the 1985 Inventory contains instructions on how to use the Inventory. The appropriate procedure for searching the Inventory depends upon the amount of information known about the substance in question. The easiest way to determine if a substance is listed in the printed Inventory is to search for its

CAS registry number in Volume 1. If the CAS registry number for the substance is already known, then it is necessary only to determine if the substance was included in the Chemical Substance Identities section. If the CAS registry number is not known, indexes such as the Molecular Formula Index can assist in determining whether the chemical appears on the Inventory.

3.5.2 Searches for Confidential Identities: Bona Fide Request

Because confidential chemicals are not listed by specific chemical identity and new confidential chemicals are continually being added, the only way to determine if a substance is on the Inventory is to search the master file version of the Inventory. This version includes both confidential and nonconfidential chemical identities and is kept current by EPA. EPA will search the confidential Inventory only if the person requesting the search can demonstrate a bona fide intent to manufacture or import the substance for a commercial purpose. [24]

A notice of bona fide intent to manufacture or import must be submitted in writing and include the following information: (1) the specific chemical identity, (2) a signed statement of intent to manufacture or import for a commercial purpose, (3) a description of the research and development activities conducted, (4) the purpose of the manufacture or import, (5) an elemental analysis, and (6) either an X-ray diffraction pattern (for inorganic substances), a mass spectrum, or an infrared spectrum.[25]

4.0 New Chemical Review

Under TSCA § 5, any person intending to manufacture or import a chemical substance first must determine whether it is listed on the TSCA Inventory. If it is listed, then manufacture or importation may commence immediately. If the chemical substance is not listed on the Inventory, then the manufacturer or importer must determine whether the chemical substance is excluded altogether from regulation under TSCA or whether it is exempt from the requirements. If the chemical substance is neither excluded nor exempted, the prospective manufacturer or importer must comply with the premanufacture notice (PMN) requirements before commencing those activities.

4.1 PMN Requirements

The PMN must contain (1) information such as the identity of the chemical, categories of use, amounts manufactured, by-products, employees exposed, and the manner or method of disposal to the extent known or "reasonably ascertainable"; (2) any test data related to the chemical's effects on health or the environment in the submitter's possession or control; and (3) a description of any other data concerning the health and environmental effects of the chemical, insofar as they are known to or are "reasonably ascertainable" by the submitter.[26]

The policy underlying TSCA is that manufacturers and processors of chemical substances should bear the responsibility for developing adequate data regarding substances' effects on health and the environment. It is noteworthy that § 5 does not expressly authorize the administrator to require or obligate the PMN submitter to produce specific tests with a PMN, except where a chemical substance is subject to a rule promulgated under § 4. Thus, unlike comparable laws outside the United States, TSCA does not require a base set of premarket data on a new chemical.

Under § 5(a), EPA must review the PMN within 90 days of its submission. During its PMN review, EPA must assess the potential risks associated with the manufacture, processing, distribution, use, and disposal of the new substance based upon information supplied by the PMN submitter and available from various agency databases and the scientific literature, and, ultimately, based upon the agency's own professional judgment. If EPA takes no regulatory action on the PMN within the 90-day review period, the submitter may commence commercial manufacture or importation forthwith and without the need for prior agency approval. Within 30 days of commencing manufacture or importation, the manufacturer or importer must file a Notice of Commencement (NOC) of Manufacture or Import.[27] The NOC certifies that commercial manufacture or importation actually has occurred. After receiving an NOC, EPA will add the PMN substance to the Inventory, and the new chemical will then become an "existing" chemical under TSCA.

The statute provides EPA with three means to prevent, delay, or limit manufacture after the 90-day review period expires. First, under § 5(c), the agency may delay manufacture up to an additional 90 days for "good cause." Second, under § 5(e)(1)(A)(i), EPA may issue a proposed order to limit or prohibit manufacture if the agency determines that available information is "insufficient to permit a reasoned evaluation" of the health and environmental effects of the new chemical substance. Third, under § 5(f)(2), EPA may propose a § 6(a) rule limiting or conditioning manufacture or under § 5(f)(3)(B) may issue a proposed order totally banning manufacture, if there is a "reasonable basis to conclude that the manufacture . . . presents or will present an unreasonable risk of injury to health or the environment." Each of these agency actions is subject to judicial review, although the scope of review varies under each provision.

4.2 Exclusions from PMN Requirements

The PMN requirements apply to a "new chemical substance" and, once an applicable rule is promulgated, to a "significant new use" of an existing chemical substance. The statutory definition of "chemical substance" excludes any mixture; any pesticide as defined by the Federal Insecticide, Fungicide, and Rodenticide Act; any food, food additive, drug, cosmetic, or device as defined by the Federal Food, Drug, and Cosmetic Act; various nuclear materials regulated under the Atomic Energy Act; and any tobacco or tobacco product.[28] Thus, by definition, these substances are excluded from TSCA jurisdiction and, as such, are not subject to the PMN requirements. The PMN requirements nevertheless may apply to such "excluded" substances if they also are intended for a "TSCA use."

4.3 Exemptions from PMN Requirements

TSCA explicitly establishes two exemptions from the PMN requirements for test marketing and Research and Development (R&D), and grants EPA authority to establish additional exemptions by regulation where the agency determines that the manufacture, processing, distribution, or use of a chemical substance will not present an unreasonable risk to health or the environment. Pursuant to this authority, EPA has prescribed 15 exemptions to the PMN requirements. Several of the more important exemptions are discussed below.

4.3.1 Test Market Exemption

TSCA § 5(h)(1) authorizes the administrator to exempt a new chemical substance from the PMN requirements when it is manufactured for test marketing purposes if the administrator determines that the proposed test marketing activity will not present an unreasonable risk to human health or the environment. The Test Market Exemption (TME) permits a company to assess the commercial viability of a new chemical and to receive customer feedback on product performance before filing a PMN. Under TSCA § 5(h)(1), the test marketer must apply for this exemption and must demonstrate that the proposed activity is legitimate test marketing which will not present an unreasonable risk.

EPA reviews a TME application in essentially the same manner as it does a PMN. Yet, under TSCA § 5(h)(6), EPA must review a TME application within 45 days of its receipt. According to EPA, however, the agency's failure to complete its review of a TME application within 45 days does not constitute an automatic approval. Rather, unlike a PMN submitter, a TME applicant must await EPA approval prior to initiating activity.

4.3.2 Research and Development Exemption

TSCA § 5(h)(3) exempts from the PMN and "significant new use rule" (SNUR) requirements small quantities of new chemicals used solely for R&D under the supervision of a technically qualified individual if the manufacturer or importer notifies persons engaged in R&D of any health risks associated with the substance. Unlike the other exemptions under § 5(h), the manufacturer or importer need not apply for the R&D exemption. EPA regulations establishing requirements for the R&D exemption appear at 40 C.F.R. § 720.36. EPA requires that a technically qualified individual supervise the R&D activities and that the manufacturer or importer evaluate any potential risks associated with the R&D substance, notify persons involved in the R&D of those risks, and maintain certain records of their R&D activity. In evaluating risks, the manufacturer or importer must consider all health and environmental effects data in its "possession or control." This includes information in the files of agents and employees engaged in the R&D and marketing of the new chemical. When R&D activity is conducted in laboratories using prudent laboratory conditions, however, this risk assessment need not be performed.

4.3.3 Low-Volume Exemptions

Under TSCA § 5(h)(4), EPA has exempted certain low-volume and low-release, low-exposure chemicals from the full PMN requirements by providing an expedited 30-day review.[29] Although a low-volume exemption (LVE), in one form or another, has existed for some time, EPA significantly modified the low-volume exemption in 1995.[30] At the same time, EPA added a new exemption for low-release, low-exposure chemicals (LoREX). In order to grant an LVE or LoREX exemption, EPA must determine that the chemical substance will "not present an unreasonable risk of injury to health or the environment."[31]

Under the now existing LVE, any manufacturer or importer who intends to produce or import a new chemical substance in quantities of 10,000 kilograms or less per year may be eligible for the LVE. As long as EPA can determine that "the potential human exposure to, and environmental release of, the new chemical substance at the higher aggregate production volume will not present an unreasonable risk of injury to human health and the environment," it should grant multiple LVEs.[32] The application for exemption must be submitted on the standard PMN form.[33] As before, representations in the LVE application regarding human exposure or environmental release controls employed during the manufacture, processing, distribution in commerce, use, and disposal of the chemical, the location of manufacture, and the use to which the chemical will be put still are binding, and LVE chemicals still will not be included in the TSCA Inventory.

If new information causes the LVE chemical to become ineligible for the exemption, EPA will revoke it. Before revoking the LVE, however, EPA will notify the manufacturer or importer in writing of the agency's intent to revoke. After receiving notice of EPA's intent to revoke, the manufacturer or importer within 15 days may file objections or an explanation of its "diligence and good faith" in attempting to comply with the terms of the exemption.[34] Within 15 days of receiving the objections or explanation, EPA will make a final determination of whether the chemical remains eligible for the LVE.[35] If so, EPA will leave the LVE in effect. If not, and EPA also determines that the manufacturer or importer did not act in good faith to meet the terms of the exemption, then within seven days of notification by EPA, all activities involving the LVE chemical must cease.[36] Alternatively, if EPA determines that the manufacturer or importer of the LVE chemical did act in good faith, activities involving the LVE chemical may continue while a PMN for the chemical is prepared and reviewed.[37]

Under the former LVE, annual production or import volume was limited to 1,000 kgs and to a single manufacturer or importer. All exemptions previously granted under the former LVE will remain binding and effective under the superseded provisions, even though such provisions will no longer be contained in the Code of Federal Regulations.[38] If manufacturers or importers wish to upgrade their 1,000 kg-LVE to the new 10,000 kg-LVE, they must submit another exemption application.

The LoREX exemption is available for chemicals that meet stringent and binding release and exposure criteria, regardless of production volume.[39] Briefly, those criteria for consumers and the general population are (1) no dermal exposure, (2) no inhalation exposure (except that allowed as ambient air releases from incineration), and (3) no exposure in drinking water greater than 1 mg/year.[40] Criteria for workers during the manufacturing, processing, distribution in commerce, use, and disposal of the substance are (1) no dermal exposure and (2) no inhalation exposure. The ambient surface water criterion is 1 ppb, and the criterion for ambient air releases from incineration is 1 g/m^3 maximum annual average concentration.

LoREX chemicals are subject to the same administrative requirements as LVE chemicals, such as a 30-day review period and mandatory use of the PMN form for submission of the exemption application. In addition, representations in the LoREX application regarding human exposure or environmental release controls used during the manufacture, processing, distribution in commerce, use, and disposal of the chemical; the location of manufacture; and the use to which the chemical will be put are binding. Finally, LoREX chemicals will not be included in the TSCA Inventory.

4.3.4 Polymer Exemption

Under TSCA § 5(h)(4), EPA also provides a complete exemption from the PMN requirement for certain polymers. As with all exemptions under § 5(h)(4), EPA must find that the exempted polymers will not present an unreasonable risk of injury to human health or the environment. In order to be eligible for the polymer exemption, the new chemical substance must meet three criteria: (1) it must be a "polymer" as defined in 40 C.F.R. § 723.250(b), (2) it must not be specifically excluded by 40 C.F.R. § 723.250(d), and (3) it must meet certain exemption criteria (i.e., have a certain number-average molecular weight or be a polyester of a certain type) as set forth in 40 C.F.R. § 723.250(e).

As of May 30, 1995, the polymer exemption does not require an application. Persons may manufacture or import polymers pursuant to the exemption without prior notification to EPA.[41] All that EPA requires is an annual report, submitted by January 31, indicating the number of new polymers manufactured or imported pursuant to the exemption for the first time during the previous year and by whom they were manufactured or imported.[42] In addition to this annual report, parties that manufacture or import polymers pursuant to the exemption must maintain detailed records documenting that the new chemical substance meets the criteria for an exempt polymer and otherwise demonstrating compliance with the exemption.[43]

Under the new polymer exemption, polymers will no longer be placed on the TSCA Inventory unless manufacturers or importers elect to proceed under the PMN/NOC process.[44] EPA does not intend to remove polymers from the TSCA Inventory that already are listed.[45] Presumably, manufacturers or importers can submit a PMN for a new polymer at any time and need not cease manufacture of an otherwise exempt polymer during the pendency of the PMN review period. Manufacturers and importers will have the option, however, of continuing to manufacture or import the polymer pursuant to the former polymer exemption (which includes restrictions on residual monomer and low molecular weight species content) or of manufacturing or importing the polymer under the new exemption.[46]

4.3.5 "Polaroid" Exemption

In response to a petition from the Polaroid Corporation, EPA exempted new chemical substances used in or for instant photographic and "peel-apart" film articles.[47] Under the terms of the so-called "Polaroid" exemption, manufacturers of instant photographic materials may commence manufacture of new chemical substances for these products immediately upon submitting an exemption notice pursuant to 40 C.F.R. § 723.175. These new chemical substances, however, cannot be distributed in commerce until a PMN is filed and the review period has ended.

4.3.6 New Chemicals Imported in Articles

Under 40 C.F.R. § 720.22(b)(1), a manufacturer must file a PMN on any new chemical substances imported into the United States for commercial purposes "unless the substance is imported as part of an article." The term "article" is defined at 40 C.F.R. § 720.3(c). Although EPA's definition of article specifically excludes "fluids and particles . . . regardless of shape or design," importers of articles that contain fluids or particles that are not intended to be removed and that have no separate commercial purpose are excluded from the PMN requirements. Conversely, EPA considers that a substance cannot be "a part" of an article if it is released and, upon release, has a commercial purpose. Thus, according to EPA, articles that contain fluids designed to be used or released in order for the article to function, like ink in pens, are not encompassed by this exemption.

4.3.7 Impurities, By-products, Non-Isolated Intermediates

EPA has excluded from the PMN requirements impurities, by-products, non-isolated intermediates, and chemicals formed incidentally when exposed to the environment or to other chemicals.[48] These exemptions are essentially identical to exemptions from the initial Inventory, which are found at 40 C.F.R. § 710.4. In fact, EPA often uses its discussion of these exemptions in the Preamble and Response to Comments in its initial Inventory reporting rule to clarify the scope and applicability of these same exemptions from the PMN requirements.

4.3.8 Chemicals Formed during the Manufacture of an Article

EPA also exempts from the PMN requirements "any other chemical substance formed during the manufacture of an article destined for the marketplace without further chemical change of the chemical substance except for those chemical changes that occur as described elsewhere in this paragraph."[49] Thus, for example, EPA exempts new chemicals formed upon use of rubber molding or curable plastic compounds, inks, drying oils, adhesives or paints, and metal finishing compounds.[50]

4.3.9 Chemicals Formed Incidental to the Use of Certain Additives

Under 40 C.F.R. § 720.30(h)(7), EPA exempts from the PMN requirements new chemicals formed incidental to the use of certain additives intended solely to impart specific physiochemical characteristics when these additives function as intended. Thus, the agency exempts new chemical substances formed incidental to use of a specific additive—such as a pH neutralizer, stabilizer, or binder—if the additive is used only for the purposes of achieving a specific physiochemical characteristic, and it functions solely to achieve that characteristic. For example, EPA excludes a new chemical substance formed incidental to the addition of bleach to cotton if the manufacturer adds the bleach only to change a specific physiochemical characteristic of the cotton and not to make a major compositional change.[51]

In response to its belief that the regulated community largely misconstrued the so-called "additives" exemption, EPA disseminated to the regulated community, by letter dated June 29, 1994, guidance for applying this exemption to various manufacturing scenarios. In this letter, EPA states that a substance is excluded from the Inventory or PMN reporting requirements if:

1. The substance is formed from a chemical reaction that involves the use of a chemical substance of the type described under 40 C.F.R. § 710.4(d)(7) or § 720.30(h)(7).

2. The substance does not function to provide one or more primary properties that would determine the use of the product or product mixture distributed in commerce, even though it may impart certain physiochemical characteristics to the product, product mixture, or formulation of which it is a part.

3. The substance is not itself the one intended for distribution in commerce as a chemical substance per se. Although it may be a component of the product, product mixture, or formulation actually distributed in commerce, it has no commercial purpose separate from the product, product mixture, or formulation of which it is a component.

EPA's letter also applies the new guidance to a real-life manufacturing scenario in the following example:

Where an acid polymer is converted to its soluble amine salt during an ink formulation process in which other ingredients are added, the polymer salt formed as a result of a chemical reaction that brings the insoluble acid polymer into solution is exempt because (1) it does not itself contribute a primary property that is essential to the functioning of the ink as a viable commercial product, (2) it is not itself the product intended for distribution in commerce as a chemical substance per se, and (3) it has no commercial purpose separate from the ink formulation.

Nevertheless, even with this new guidance, determining whether a particular chemical substance is exempt can be challenging.

4.4 Nanotechnology

4.4.1 Background

Nanotechnology is the understanding and control of matter at dimensions of roughly 1 to 100 nanometers, where unique phenomena enable novel applications.[52] In its 2001 budget, the Clinton administration raised nanotechnology to the level of a federal initiative, referring to it as the National Nanotechnology Initiative (NNI).[53] In 2003, the importance of a coordinated federal program for nanotechnology R&D was recognized by enactment of the 21st Century Nanotechnology Research and Development Act.[54] EPA participates in the NNI and supports research on both the uses and potential risks of nanotechnology.[55]

Nanotechnology is currently used in a wide variety of commercial applications and consumer products[56] and was incorporated into more than $30 billion in manufactured goods in 2005, more than double the previous year.[57] The beneficial properties of nanoscale materials derive from their unusually small size and/or large ratio of surface area to mass relative to macroscale equivalents. These same qualities also raise human health and environmental concerns, however, because nanoparticles are more easily absorbed by inhalation and through the skin, move around more easily within living organisms and in the environment, and may pose different or worse hazards than their macroscale equivalents.

The current regulatory concern with nanotechnology arises primarily from a lack of information for assessing risks. There is, for example, no good database of the hazards presented by various nanoscale materials, and there are no established protocols for testing nanomaterials. Also, the Quantitative Structure-Activity Relationships (QSARs) used by EPA for risk assessments under TSCA currently lack any benchmarks for nanoscale materials. Consequently, assessing the risks of nanomaterials is an uncertain science at present. Furthermore, industry is just starting to develop strategies for safely handling nanomaterials.[58]

4.4.2 Regulation of Nanotechnology under TSCA

Nanoscale materials that otherwise qualify as "chemical substances"[59] are subject to EPA regulation under TSCA. Determining whether nanoscale versions of existing substances are new chemicals subject to PMN requirements can be problematic, however, because, historically, EPA has listed particular molecular identities[60] on the TSCA Inventory but not different physical forms of the same chemical composition.[61] Accordingly, while EPA has said, for example, that manufacturing titanium dioxide (an existing chemical) in different particle sizes does not create any new chemicals,[62] it is unclear whether the Inventory listing of titanium dioxide also includes nanoengineered forms of the substance, such as nanotubes, or whether the nanoengineered forms have particular molecular identities different from the substance listed on the TSCA Inventory and, therefore, are new chemicals subject to PMN requirements. To resolve this critical issue, EPA is preparing but has not yet published a paper explaining when the agency would consider a nanoscale chemical existing or new.[63]

In addition to requiring PMNs for new nanoscale chemicals, EPA has the option to regulate nanomaterials by declaring specific activities with the nanoengineered forms of existing substances "new uses" subject to Significant New Use Notice (SNUN) or other requirements under Significant New Use Rules

(SNURs). The agency also could seek to prohibit or control any nanomaterials that pose unreasonable risks of injury to health or the environment under TSCA § 6,[64] despite the procedural obstacles to rulemaking under this section.

Before taking such actions, however, EPA has invited stakeholders to collaborate with the agency to design a Nanoscale Materials Stewardship Program under TSCA, which could involve collecting existing data from manufacturers and processors of existing nanoscale chemicals, the voluntary development of test data needed for future policy and regulatory decisions, and/or creating a basic set of risk management practices for developing and commercializing nanoscale materials.[65] EPA plans to use information resulting from the stewardship program to support the further development of its TSCA program for nanoscale materials, including any regulatory actions that may be needed to protect human health and the environment.[66] In addition, EPA has issued a draft Nanotechnology White Paper, which describes why EPA is interested in nanotechnology across its programs, the agency's applicable statutory mandates, and risk assessment issues specific to nanotechnology across environmental media.[67]

5.0 Preparing the PMN and Seeing It through EPA

Although more than 30,000 new chemical substances have been reviewed through the PMN process and the process has become routine from EPA's perspective, the PMN remains a substantial hurdle to overcome for the manufacturer who wants to market a new chemical quickly and efficiently. The unwary manufacturer may encounter such problems as delays in the review process, or unexpected and costly restrictions on manufacture (which EPA may impose under TSCA § 5(e) or § 5(f)). As discussed below, a manufacturer can minimize many of these potential problems by recognizing them in advance and planning a PMN strategy that is specific to the chemical substance.

5.1 Manufacturer's PMN Selection Strategy

For purposes of this discussion, there are four types of PMNs: (1) the "standard" PMN for a single chemical substance; (2) the "consolidated" PMN for two or more substances sharing similar molecular structures and use patterns; (3) the "joint" PMN, for use when two companies must jointly submit data; and (4) the "exemption" PMN for substances that are manufactured in low volumes or have low release, low exposure, or are manufactured for test marketing purposes. Each of the four types of PMN offers specific advantages and poses special problems to the PMN submitter.

The standard PMN is appropriate where the PMN substance has a distinct molecular structure and a single company can provide the necessary data. Prior to May 1995, the standard PMN had been used historically in more than 75 percent of all submissions. With the changes in May 1995 to the low-volume and polymer exemptions and the addition of the low-release, low-exposure exemption, EPA expected this number to drop substantially.

A consolidated PMN is appropriate when a company wishes to manufacture several chemicals that are similar in molecular structure and similar in use. A consolidated PMN reduces the need for repetitive filing and requires only a single $2,500 filing fee. Prior to its submission, however, EPA must confirm that the agency will treat the new chemicals as similar in structure for PMN purposes. The manufacturer must be aware that each chemical so noticed will receive a separate PMN number and that the manufacturer must file a separate Notice of Commencement for each chemical substance subsequently manufactured. Historically, consolidated PMNs are filed most often for certain sodium, lithium, and potassium salts of the same acid.

Two or more companies may file a joint PMN where one manufacturer does not possess all the information necessary to complete the PMN form. Such a situation commonly arises in cases where one company develops a new chemical substance that incorporates a second company's proprietary product. Manufacturers also may find joint PMNs useful as a means of sharing or reducing administrative costs and filing fees.

An exemption PMN is appropriate when a chemical substance meets either the low-volume or low-release, low-exposure criteria set forth at 40 C.F.R. § 723.50 or the test marketing exemption criteria set forth at 40 C.F.R. § 720.38. The principal advantage of an exemption PMN is a shortened review period. A manufacturer who relies upon an exemption PMN, however, is bound to its restrictions. Because these limitations are targets of EPA inspection and enforcement activities, exemption PMNs generally are recommended only when time considerations make them especially attractive.

5.2 Minimizing Delays

The best means to avoid a delay in manufacturing operations arising from the PMN process is to submit the PMN far in advance of the production schedule. Although such a strategy can reduce production delays, it requires the manufacturer to initiate the PMN process rather early in the product development process. This presents a risk, of course, that some PMNs may be submitted for products that are not produced for intervening reasons.

Manufacturers frequently encounter delays in the PMN process due to the failure to submit required information. If any required information is missing or incomplete, EPA will return the PMN to the submitter. Delays also may result from the inconsistency of information from one section of the PMN to another. Another frequent source of delays arises when a submitter, in attempting to protect confidential business information, fails to supply a generic name for the new chemical or a generic description of its use. Such delays may be avoided only through coordination, planning, and experience.

5.3 Avoiding Unnecessary Regulation under TSCA § 5

New chemicals that are delayed during the PMN process or become subject to TSCA § 5(e) Consent Agreements and corresponding SNURs often lose much market value. It is most often the uncertainty arising from insufficient risk assessment data in the PMN that causes EPA to impose such restrictions.

If such restrictions are to be avoided, the PMN submitter must provide a risk assessment that is as comprehensive as possible. Risk is commonly derived by the simple equation: Risk Hazard Exposure. A manufacturer can demonstrate that the "risk" is low by furnishing information sufficient to show that either the "hazard" or "exposure" component of the equation is low.

Hazard information for a new chemical is best supplied as actual human and environmental toxicity information on the specific chemical. Exposure information, although more difficult to quantify, typically includes the expected production volume and uses of the new substance and, when available: (1) certain of the substance's physical properties that impact exposure potential; (2) the numbers and types of human exposure; and (3) the types of release.

Once hazard and exposure information are known, a risk assessment should be developed and included in the PMN. The manufacturer must follow up the risk assessment with a discussion in the PMN of a risk management program, the most common elements of which include routine hazard communication techniques such as appropriate labels and Material Safety Data Sheets.

5.4 EPA's Review of the PMN and Use of Checklists

EPA's PMN review process includes not only the elements of risk assessment but also many technical and administrative details. A submitter thus is well advised to develop a series of checklists for filing PMNs. These checklists should (1) ensure that all requested information is included and is consistent throughout the PMN; (2) mirror the items on EPA's own checklist, most of which can be obtained from EPA; and (3) address issues that continue after the PMN is submitted, including the obligation to file an NOC within 30 days after commercial manufacture begins, to adhere to any limitations that may apply in the case of exemption PMNs, and to ensure compliance with any TSCA § 5(e) restrictions.

6.0 Regulation of New Chemicals and Uses

Under TSCA § 5, once a manufacturer has submitted a PMN, it may commence commercial operations after waiting 90 days without specific EPA approval, unless the agency exercises one of three statutory options described below. First, under TSCA § 5(a), EPA may delay manufacture for one additional 90-day review period for "good cause." Second, under TSCA § 5(e), EPA may issue a proposed order limiting or prohibiting manufacture if the agency makes statutorily prescribed findings regarding risk. Third, under TSCA § 5(f), EPA may propose a § 6(a) rule which becomes immediately effective to limit or condition manufacture, or issue a proposed order totally banning manufacture if the Agency concludes that manufacture "presents or will present an unreasonable risk of injury to health or [the] environment."

6.1 EPA Regulation under TSCA § 5(e)

TSCA § 5(e) grants EPA authority to issue an administrative order regulating a new chemical substance if the agency finds that (1) there is insufficient information to evaluate the risk reasonably; and (2) either the chemical may present an unreasonable risk to health and the environment, or it will be produced in substantial quantities with the result that either substantial quantities will enter the environment or there will be substantial or significant human exposure to the substance. The purpose of a TSCA § 5(e) order is to ban or limit manufacture, distribution, use, or disposal of a chemical pending development of sufficient data for EPA to evaluate the risks the chemical poses to human health or the environment. Where EPA acts unilaterally to issue a § 5(e) order, it must be proposed at least 45 days before the end of the PMN review period. Such unilateral orders become effective on the day the review period ends.

6.1.1 EPA's Standard § 5(e) Consent Order

TSCA § 5(e) does not provide explicit authority for EPA to enter into "consent" orders. EPA developed the consent order concept to permit the introduction of new chemicals into the market while controlling any potential risk during the time needed to develop the required data by agreement with the prospective manufacturer, thus avoiding an adversary procedure. Under a § 5(e) consent order, the manufacturer is usually permitted to proceed with commercial manufacture and in return agrees to certain restrictions on the production, distribution, or disposal of the new chemical, pending development of information that EPA considers necessary to evaluate the potential hazards.

6.1.2 EPA Evaluation of § 5(e) Data

After receiving the required test data, EPA may determine that such data are (1) invalid; (2) equivocal; (3) valid and positive (the chemical poses an unreasonable risk); or (4) valid and negative (the chemical poses no unreasonable risk). EPA interprets § 5 as enabling the agency to take further action under its standard consent orders based on the submitted data without resorting to procedures required under TSCA §§ 4 or 6.

If EPA determines that the test results are scientifically invalid, the company must cease production or importation of the PMN substance when the aggregate volume reaches the production limit. The company may contest EPA's finding by submitting a report prepared by a "qualified person" (expert) explaining why the data are scientifically valid. If a specific event beyond the control of the company has prevented the development of scientifically valid data, the company may submit a report documenting this extenuating circumstance within several weeks of its occurrence. Upon EPA's concurrence, the company may continue to manufacture beyond the production limit provided a study is initiated, usually within three months, and that the data are submitted within a specified time.

Data are scientifically equivocal if insufficient for the agency to conduct a reasoned risk evaluation of the substance, when evaluated together with other available information. Upon a finding by EPA that the data are equivocal, a submitter has similar opportunities to refute the EPA finding or to negotiate for new conditions to allow for continued manufacture of the subject chemical.

A finding of valid, positive data indicates that the chemical poses an unreasonable risk. The company may challenge EPA's determination but may not manufacture the chemical until EPA is convinced that the chemical will not present an unreasonable risk, or a court reverses EPA's position.

EPA may determine that the data demonstrate the chemical will not present an unreasonable risk. Despite such negative data, however, the agency still may decline to modify or revoke the order if EPA finds that the risk may be unreasonable without continued use of engineering or other controls. Often the company must affirmatively petition for such a revocation of the consent order.

6.1.3 Preparation of the § 5(e) Consent Order

Because complex consent orders often take lengthy periods of time to negotiate and issue, EPA has created a "two-track" system of consent order preparation. The "fast track" is used where the PMN submitter agrees to certain standard terms. Such "fast-track" consent orders take an average of 70 working days, compared to 124 working days for a "standard" § 5(e) consent order.

A "standard" consent order is the product of several stages of draft, review, and comment. Once all parties sign the consent order, it becomes effective the day following the lapse of the PMN review period. If the review period has been suspended voluntarily beyond the statutory period, EPA and the submitter will revoke jointly any remaining time.

A party to a TSCA § 5(e) consent order may challenge an EPA decision that is based on the data submitted pursuant to the consent order. Companies that disagree with the agency's determination may challenge the decision by filing (1) a petition under TSCA § 21 for the "issuance, amendment, or repeal" of the § 5(e) order; (2) a petition under the terms of the consent order for modification or revocation of provisions of the consent order; or (3) an action for judicial review under the Administrative Procedure Act (APA).

6.1.4 Unilateral § 5(e) Orders

If EPA determines that the potential risk from a PMN substance cannot be reduced to acceptable levels through engineering controls or production limitations or that a mutually agreeable consent order cannot be negotiated, the agency will issue a proposed unilateral § 5(e) order. The agency generally uses these orders to ban a PMN substance outright. Because under § 5(e)(1)(B) a unilateral order must be issued no later than 45 days before the end of the review period, EPA will give priority to its development and issuance.

If the PMN submitter files "objections specifying with peculiarity" the provisions of the order deemed objectionable and stating the grounds therefore, the proposed order will not take effect.[68] A company must address EPA's findings of fact with respect to the PMN chemical and the agency's resulting conclusion that the issuance of a § 5(e) order is required. In this instance, the administrator must apply to a federal district court for an injunction to prohibit or limit the commercial manufacture, processing, distribution, use, or disposal.[69] If, after evaluating the objections, the administrator determines there is no basis to limit or ban the PMN substance under § 5(e), EPA will not act to finalize the unilateral order.

6.2 EPA Regulation under TSCA § 5(f)

If EPA determines that a new chemical substance presents or will present an unreasonable risk before the agency can issue a rule under § 6 to protect against such risks, the administrator may act under § 5(f) to control that risk. Under § 5(f), the administrator may issue either a proposed rule to limit or delay manufacture, production, use, or disposal, or a proposed order to ban all use of the substance and apply for a federal injunction to prohibit the chemical from entering commerce.

6.2.1 Proposed § 5(f) Rules

Section 5(f)(2) authorizes the administrator to issue an immediately effective proposed rule under § 6(a) that limits or delays manufacture of a chemical substance undergoing a PMN review. Under § 6(a), EPA has authority to (1) limit the amount; (2) prohibit particular uses; (3) limit the amount or concentration for a particular use; (4) require specific labels; (5) require recordkeeping; (6) prohibit or regulate commercial use; (7) prohibit or regulate disposal; and (8) give notice of the risk. Such a rule is effective immediately upon publication in the *Federal Register*.

To date, EPA has proposed only three § 5(f) rules covering four chemicals. EPA has not yet "finalized" these proposed rules because the agency never contemplated rulemaking under TSCA § 6. Nevertheless, the rules were effective as of the date they were published. They were recorded in the Code of Federal Regulations and, for all intents and purposes, function as final rules.

Judicial relief from a § 5(f) rule is probably unavailable because TSCA § 6(d)(2)(A) provides that "[s]uch a proposed rule which is made so effective shall not, for purposes of judicial review, be considered final agency action." Presumably, an affected party could challenge EPA's failure to complete the rulemaking in an expeditious manner as directed by TSCA § 6(d)(2)(B). Any challenge to the merits of the rule, however, would have to wait until the final rule was issued.

6.2.2 Proposed § 5(f) Orders

If EPA determines it necessary to ban a chemical from commercial manufacture, distribution, processing, use, and disposal, the agency must issue a proposed § 5(f) order and apply for an injunction. The proposed order takes effect upon the expiration of the review period unless the submitter files objections in accordance with TSCA § 5(e)(1)(C). If EPA issues a proposed order, the agency must apply to federal court for an injunction before the expiration of the review period, unless it determines on the basis of the objections filed that the substance does not or will not present an unreasonable risk.[70] To date, EPA has not proposed any orders under TSCA § 5(f).

6.3 Significant New Use Rules

Persons who submitted initial Inventory notices were required to describe the uses to which their chemicals were being put. Similarly, a PMN submitter must describe the intended uses of the new chemical. If EPA determines that a particular use of a chemical already on the Inventory constitutes a "significant new use," the agency can issue a Significant New Use Rule (SNUR). A SNUR requires anyone who wants to manufacture or process a chemical substance for a use that EPA has determined is a "significant new use" to give EPA 90 calendar days' prior notice.[71] This notice is referred to as a Significant New Use Notice, or SNUN.

If, after reviewing a SNUN, EPA fails to initiate any action under §§ 5, 6, or 7, then TSCA § 5(g) requires the administrator to publish a notice in the

Federal Register giving EPA's reasons for not initiating any action. As is the case with a PMN, a SNUN submitter may manufacture, import, or process the chemical for the "significant new use" without EPA approval or further notice to EPA upon expiration of the 90-day review period.

6.3.1 SNUR Standard

TSCA sets few criteria for determining when EPA may deem a new use "significant." EPA must consider "all relevant factors."[72] In accordance with the statutory criteria that are provided, EPA generally defines a "significant new use" broadly as a use that will result in increased production volume, a different or greater extent of exposure, a different disposal method, or even a different manufacturing site.

6.3.2 Who Must Report

All persons who intend to manufacture, import, or process for commercial purposes a chemical substance identified at 40 C.F.R. § 721, Subpart E, are required to report. In addition, any person who intends to distribute the substance to others must submit a SNUN unless he or she can document that (1) he or she has notified in writing each person who purchases or otherwise receives the chemical from him of the applicable SNUR, (2) each such recipient has knowledge of that specific section of Subpart E, or (3) each recipient cannot undertake any significant new use described in the specific section of Subpart E.[73] Finally, a person who processes a chemical substance listed in Subpart E for a "significant new use" must submit a SNUN unless he or she can document that: (1) the person does not know the specific chemical identity of the chemical substance being processed; and (2) the person is processing the chemical substance without knowledge of the applicable SNUR.[74]

EPA recognizes certain exemptions from the requirement to make a SNUN report which are identical to those applied to PMNs.[75] EPA has never required manufacturers of non-isolated intermediates to apply for exemptions. Presumably, manufacturers of SNUR-listed chemicals who produce them only as non-isolated intermediates are exempt from the SNUN requirements as well.

6.3.3 Alternative Measures to Control Exposure

EPA also has established a procedure whereby a manufacturer or processor may petition the agency to allow use of alternative measures to control exposure to or environmental release of a chemical substance without submitting a SNUN if EPA determines that the alternative measure provides substantially the same degree of protection as the methods specified in the SNUR. Persons intending to employ alternative control measures must submit a request to EPA for a determination of equivalency before commencing manufacture, importation, or processing activities with the alternative controls. EPA has 45 days to determine the equivalency of the proposal and will mail a notice of the results to the submitter, who may commence manufacture upon receipt.[76]

6.3.4 Obligations of Distributors

If a manufacturer, importer, or processor of a chemical acknowledges that someone who purchases or otherwise obtains the chemical from him is engaged in a significant new use without submitting a SNUN, the distributor must stop supplying the chemical substance and must submit the SNUN, unless the distributor can document that (1) he or she has notified the recipient and the EPA Office of Enforcement and Compliance Assurance (OECA) in writing within 15 days of the first time he or she has knowledge; (2) within 15 working days after notifying the recipient that the recipient has provided him with written assurance that the recipient is aware of the terms of Subpart E and will not engage in the significant new use; and (3) he or she has promptly provided OECA with a copy of the recipient's written assurances.[77]

6.3.5 Determining Inventory Status

The chemicals listed in 40 C.F.R. § 721, Subpart E, are often listed by generic names because the manufacturers have claimed the specific chemical identities as confidential. In order to determine whether a specific chemical is subject to a SNUN, a bona fide request may be filed with the agency.[78]

6.3.6 Use of SNURS to Support § 5(e) Consent Orders

When EPA has concerns about a new chemical substance but does not want to prohibit its manufacture completely, the agency will enter into a consent order with the PMN submitter, allowing limited production under carefully controlled conditions. Once the chemical is placed on the Inventory, however, other manufacturers can begin producing this substance without complying with the restrictions in the consent order, giving them a competitive advantage over the original manufacturer.

As a result, manufacturers subject to § 5(e) consent orders have urged EPA to designate as a "significant new use" any manufacture of such a substance that is not in compliance with the same restrictions placed upon the original manufacturers in the consent orders. Once EPA issues such a SNUR, any manufacturer who intends to depart from the conditions imposed under the SNUR must file a SNUN 90 days before doing so. Because development of even a relatively simple SNUR and its issuance concurrently with a § 5(e) consent order requires commitment of substantial agency resources, EPA rarely issues such SNURs.

6.3.7 Generic SNUR Rule

The agency's difficulties in developing SNURs to support the § 5(e) consent order program prompted the agency to develop the "Generic SNUR Rule." This rule establishes standardized significant new uses, recordkeeping requirements, and two procedures EPA can use to issue SNURs without the usual notice-and-comment rulemaking.[79] The Generic SNUR Rule has five subparts. Subpart A defines terms. Subpart B lists standardized significant new uses that EPA may, by rule, apply to any existing chemical. Subpart C establishes recordkeeping requirements that EPA may impose upon manufacturers, importers, or processors of any chemical subject to a SNUR. Subpart D establishes "expedited" rulemaking procedures that EPA may use to develop SNURs for chemical substances and creates a procedure by which persons affected by the SNUR may petition the agency to modify or revoke it. Subpart E is a list of chemicals subject to SNURs and their designated significant new uses. EPA may establish significant new uses other than those in Subpart B and can impose recordkeeping requirements other than those in Subpart C but only by notice-and-comment rulemaking.

The Generic SNUR Rule (Subpart B) establishes five categories of standardized significant new uses. These are (1) commercial activities where a program of appropriate protective equipment has not been established;[80] (2) commercial activities where a worker hazard communication program has not been established;[81] (3) disposal of a listed substance;[82] (4) release to water of a listed substance;[83] and (5) a broad "catchall" section, designating more than two dozen activities that, taken collectively, are so inclusive as to provide EPA the tools to regulate virtually any activity.[84]

Section 721.160 (Subpart D) establishes expedited procedures EPA can use to impose SNURs on chemicals that have been the subject of a final order issued under § 5(e). These procedures include (1) direct final rulemaking, (2) interim final rulemaking, and (3) notice-and-comment rulemaking.

When EPA uses direct final rulemaking procedures to issue a SNUR, it issues a final rule in the *Federal Register*. Unless EPA receives written notice within 30 days of publication that someone wishes to submit adverse or critical comments, the rule will be effective 60 days from the date of publication. If EPA receives such timely notice, however, the agency must provide for more formal rulemaking procedures.

EPA will use interim final rulemaking procedures when the agency believes that a significant new use is likely to take place before a direct final rule would become effective. In this case, the agency will issue an interim final rule in the final rule section of the *Federal Register*. The SNUR will take effect on the date of publication and persons will have 30 days to submit comments. However, such interim rules will cease to be effective 180 days after publication unless, within the 180-day period, EPA issues a final rule in the *Federal Register* that responds to any written comments received.

Although not an "expedited" procedure, EPA also may use traditional notice-and-comment procedures to issue a SNUR. In this case, EPA issues a proposal in the *Federal Register* and allows a 30-day comment period. EPA generally uses notice-and-comment rulemaking where the agency anticipates adverse comments.

6.3.8 Expedited SNURs for New Chemical Substances Not Subject to § 5(e) Orders

Section 721.170 of 40 C.F.R. establishes the procedures and criteria under which EPA may use expedited procedures to impose SNURs on a chemical that satisfied the PMN process but was not made subject to a § 5(e) consent order. EPA will promulgate a SNUR for such a chemical only if the substance meets one or more of the concern criteria listed in § 721.170(b). The concern criteria are basically the same criteria EPA uses when determining whether a new chemical substance should be subject to a § 5(e) consent order. Thus, the criteria call for a SNUR if exposure is likely to result from new uses not in the PMN or would have called for a § 5(e) order if they had been in the PMN.

Any person affected by a SNUR may request modification or revocation of any SNUR requirement that has been added to Subpart E by using the expedited procedures. The request must be accompanied by information sufficient to support the request.[85]

7.0 Biotechnology

EPA's biotechnology policy under TSCA is developing amid substantial controversy. The agency has asserted that it has broad authority under TSCA to regulate genetically engineered microorganisms. Because of the conflicting interests involved and the uncertainty surrounding biotechnology products, the agency only recently promulgated final comprehensive biotechnology regulations. Until these regulations became final, EPA was requiring certain researchers, manufacturers, processors, distributors, and importers to comply with selected TSCA reporting requirements.

7.1 1986 Framework for Regulation of Biotechnology Products

EPA first asserted TSCA authority over genetically engineered microorganisms in a 1984 proposed policy statement.[86] In 1986, EPA published the final version of the policy statement that established the reporting requirements that were in effect for genetically engineered microorganisms until the recent publication of the final rule.[87] Pursuant to the policy statement, EPA required compliance with PMN requirements for "new" microorganisms and § 8(e) reporting for all microorganisms. In addition, EPA requested voluntary compliance with other § 8 reporting requirements. The agency had not provided clear guidance on reporting requirements, however, leaving submitters to rely largely on informal guidance.

7.2 Guidance Documents on PMN Submissions for Biotechnology Products

Several sources of information provided guidance for PMN submitters. The basic reporting requirements for microorganisms were contained in EPA's 1986 policy statement. Also, to assist persons preparing PMNs for biotechnology products under the 1986 policy statement, EPA had prepared an information packet containing several draft guidelines. These guidelines were continuously evolving to reflect changes in policy and additional experience gained through reviewing PMNs on biotechnology products. Some of the guidelines were general and addressed the administrative details and informational requirements for completing a PMN. One dealt with substantiation of confidentiality claims, another with bona fide submissions for a search of the master Inventory file to determine if a microorganism is listed on the confidential portion of the Inventory, and a third with preparing PMNs for closed-system, large-scale fermentations. In addition, several 1986 and 1987 guidance documents addressed the full PMN submission, the sanitized version, and confidentiality claims.

7.3 The EPA Biotechnology PMN Review Process

While its policies were still in gestation, EPA was addressing PMN submissions on biotechnology products on a case-by-case basis. The submitter was advised to contact EPA as early as possible in the project development process for a pre-notice consultation. Nonetheless, EPA did have a process for reviewing these PMN submissions. In fact, to date, EPA has reviewed more than 30 PMNs for intergeneric microorganisms used in the manufacture of enzymes or pesticide intermediates, and more than 25 voluntary PMNs for R&D activities involving microorganisms.

Following receipt of the PMN, EPA publishes an announcement in the *Federal Register* describing the submission.[88] EPA then develops hazard and exposure assessments based on information submitted in the PMN, other available scientific information, and consultation with non-agency experts. These assessments are then combined to form a risk assessment. At this point, EPA may ask for assistance from a Biotechnology Science Advisory Committee (BSAC) Subcommittee containing scientists with expertise relevant to the PMN in question. At the conclusion of a PMN review the agency may reach one of three decisions: (1) there is sufficient information to determine that the risks are unreasonable; (2) there is sufficient information to determine that the risks are reasonable; or (3) there is insufficient information to make a reasoned evaluation of risk. Finally, the agency may issue a consent order under § 5(e) wherein it imposes certain restrictions on testing pending development by the PMN submitter of additional information.

7.4 EPA's Biotechnology Policy: The Final Rule

In 1988, EPA drafted a proposed biotechnology rule, but the White House Office of Management and Budget (OMB) returned it to EPA for reconsideration of several issues. In response to comments by OMB as well as other government agencies, industry, academia, and public interest groups, EPA continued to revise the draft, and finally, on September 1, 1994, EPA published proposed regulations for the manufacture and processing of microorganisms under TSCA § 5 (premanufacture notification).[89] On April 11, 1997, EPA published the final rule, which became effective June 10, 1997.[90]

7.4.1 Definition of New Microorganism

The final rule defines microorganism to mean an organism classified, using the five-kingdom classification system of Whittacker, in the kingdoms Monera (or Procaryotae), Protista, Fungi, and the Chlorophyta and the Rhodophyta of the Plantae, and a virus or virus-like particle. New microorganisms are those not listed on the TSCA Inventory and that result from deliberate, intergenetic combinations of genetic material from organisms in different genera. Consistent with its prior policy, EPA is excluding from the definition of "new microorganisms" those resulting from the addition of intergeneric material that is well characterized and contains only non-coding regulatory regions such as operators, promoters, origins of replication, terminators, and ribosome-binding regions. In addition, naturally occurring microorganisms are implicitly listed on the TSCA Inventory (as are all naturally occurring substances).

7.4.2 Premanufacture Notification

EPA requires premanufacture notification for new microorganisms using a microbial commercial activity notice (MCAN). The MCAN must be submitted 90 days prior to commercial manufacture or import of a new microorganism or prior to the manufacture, import, or processing of an existing microorganism for a significant new use. There is no specific submission form for an MCAN. The information required to be submitted with the MCAN is listed in the final rule at 40 C.F.R. § 725.155. EPA will add new microorganisms to the inventory upon receipt of a notice of commencement of manufacture or import (NOC). The timing of the NOC for microorganisms is the same as for traditional chemicals. EPA is proposing to identify and list microorganisms on the TSCA Inventory by a taxonomic designation and certain phenotypic and genotypic information.

7.4.3 Exemptions from MCAN

EPA exempts certain microorganisms from all or part of the MCAN requirement based on a finding that the microorganism does not present an unreasonable risk to human health or the environment. These exemptions differ from those available for traditional chemicals. For example, microorganisms will not be eligible for the low-volume exemption but will be eligible for a similar test marketing exemption (TME).

EPA also established tiered exemptions for certain microorganisms. The Tier I exemption is a complete exemption from the MCAN requirement. In order to qualify for the Tier I exemption, the recipient microorganism must be listed in 40 C.F.R. § 725.420, the introduced genetic material must be limited in size, of known function and associated nucleotide sequences, poorly mobilizable, and free of certain nucleotide sequences that encode toxins.[91] The site where the microorganism will be used must meet certain containment and control standards.[92] Although manufacturers and importers need not apply for Tier I exemptions, they are required to submit a certification to EPA at least ten days prior to commercial manufacture or import stating that the microorganism meets the Tier I exemption criteria.[93]

The Tier II exemption provides for expedited review of microorganisms that meet the recipient organism requirements of § 725.420 and genetic material requirements of § 725.421 but will not meet the containment and control requirements of § 725.422. The exemption application must be submitted 45 days prior to commencing manufacture or import.

7.4.4 Regulation of R&D Activities

EPA regulates microorganisms during commercial research and development (R&D) more closely than traditional chemicals due to the ability of microorganisms to multiply on their own once released into the environment. Provided the R&D takes place in a "contained structure," EPA exempts such activity from all but recordkeeping, containment and/or inactivation controls, and employee notification requirements.[94] In addition, the R&D must be supervised by a technically qualified individual. This exemption is very similar to the standard R&D

exemption for traditional chemicals. If the R&D activity is conducted under the supervision of another federal agency that requires compliance with NIH Guidelines for Research Involving Recombinant DNA Molecules, EPA exempts such R&D from all regulation under TSCA, even the recordkeeping, containment, and employee notification requirements.[95]

EPA exempts R&D activities involving intentional testing in the environment of specifically listed microorganisms deemed to be safe. At this time, EPA is listing two microorganisms eligible for this exemption.[96] Pursuant to this exemption, EPA will place restrictions on the recipient microorganisms, the introduced genetic material, and the conditions of use. In addition, persons who intend to conduct R&D activities pursuant to this exemption must submit a certification stating compliance with the provisions of the exemption prior to initiation of the activity.[97]

Persons engaged in R&D activities that do not qualify for the contained structure exemption or are not specifically exempted under § 725.239 must submit a TSCA experimental release application (TERA) 60 days prior to commencing such activities. Thus, the TERA process provides a shortened review period compared to the MCAN process, and the data requirements are somewhat less burdensome than the MCAN data requirements. EPA may extend the TERA review period by 60 days for "good cause." Unlike the MCAN or PMN, however, if EPA determines prior to expiration of the TERA review period that the activity does not pose an unreasonable risk to human health or the environment, EPA would allow the R&D activity to proceed prior to expiration of the review period.

8.0 Testing under TSCA

One of Congress's objectives in enacting TSCA was to require chemical manufacturers and processors to develop data on the health and environmental effects of their products.[98] Under the Act, EPA may require manufacturers and processors to develop safety and environmental data when (1) the chemical may present an unreasonable risk of injury or (2) substantial quantities of the chemical are produced with the potential for substantial environmental or human exposure.[99]

8.1 Selection of Chemicals for Testing

Congress created the Interagency Testing Committee (ITC) "to make recommendations to the Administrator respecting the chemical substances and mixtures to which the Administrator should give priority consideration."[100] The ITC consists of designees from eight agencies of the federal government. TSCA requires the ITC to give priority consideration to substances that are suspected of causing or contributing to cancer, gene mutations, or birth defects. Within 12 months after the ITC designates a chemical, the agency must initiate § 4 rulemaking or publish its reasons for not doing so.

In making its testing recommendations, the ITC must consider eight factors, including the quantities in which the substance is manufactured or enters the environment, the extent and duration of human exposure, whether the substance is closely related to a chemical substance known to present an unreasonable risk of injury, the existence of data concerning the effects of the substance, and the extent to which testing may aid the agency to predict the effects of a substance on health or the environment.[101]

The addition of a chemical substance to the TSCA § 4(e) Priority List triggers reporting requirements under TSCA §§ 8(a) and 8(d). Under the § 8(a) Preliminary Assessment Information Rule (PAIR), manufacturers must submit production and exposure data on ITC-listed chemicals within 90 days of publication in the *Federal Register* of the amendment adding the chemical. Under the § 8(d) Health and Safety Data Reporting Rule, manufacturers who fall within the North American Industry Classification System (NAICS) (in effect as of January 1, 1997) Subsector 325 (chemical manufacturing and allied products) or Industry Group 32411 (petroleum refineries) must submit to EPA unpublished health and safety studies within 60 days of the agency's listing.[102]

8.2 Testing Triggers

Whether a test rule is risk-based or exposure-based will influence the type of testing required. The testing "triggers" are discussed below.

8.2.1 TSCA § 4(a)(1)(A): Risk Trigger

EPA may require testing if the agency finds that (1) the chemical or mixture may present an unreasonable risk of injury to human health or the environment, (2) existing data on and experience with the chemical or mixture are insufficient to reasonably predict or determine the effects of the chemical substance, and (3) testing is necessary to obtain such data.[103] EPA's first step, therefore, is to make a risk determination. EPA must find that the chemical may present an unreasonable risk.

As EPA uses the term, "risk" is a function of both hazard (toxicity) and exposure. The agency considers several factors in assessing the possible unreasonable risk of a substance, including knowledge of a chemical's physical and chemical properties, structural relationships to other chemicals with demonstrated adverse effects, data from inconclusive tests, and case history data.[104] Moreover, EPA has advised manufacturers that risk may be significant, even when exposure is extremely low.

Even though a § 4(a)(1)(A) test rule is not exposure-based, the agency still must demonstrate some possibility of exposure before it may issue a test rule under the "unreasonable risk" rationale because exposure is a necessary component of risk analysis. In *CMA v. EPA*, however, the D.C. Circuit held that EPA could rely on inferences to establish exposure, "so long as all the evidence—including the industry evidence—indicates a more-than-theoretical probability of exposure."[105]

Not only must EPA determine that the chemical or mixture may present a risk, the agency also must find that the existing data and experience are insufficient to determine or predict the effects of concern.[106] Data may be insufficient if EPA determines that existing studies are too flawed to be relied upon or otherwise inadequate to determine risk. Additionally, the agency must affirm that testing is necessary to develop data under TSCA § 4(a)(1)(A)(iii). If the agency decides that ongoing studies will enable EPA to determine whether a substance presents an unreasonable risk, no further testing will be required. In addition, the agency will not require chemical testing if no testing methodology exists which would lead to the production of the necessary data.

8.2.2 TSCA § 4(a)(1)(B): Exposure Trigger

TSCA § 4(a)(1)(B) provides EPA with an alternative basis for requiring testing founded on an exposure trigger. Using an exposure trigger, EPA can require testing if (1) a chemical substance is produced in substantial quantities; (2) a substance is reasonably expected to be released into the environment in substantial quantities, or there is or may be significant or substantial human exposure; (3) there are insufficient data or experience upon which to reasonably predict the effects on human health or the environment; and (4) testing is necessary to develop the data.

By its express terms, § 4(a)(1)(B) requires both substantial production and substantial or significant exposure. This trigger requires an exposure finding much higher than that required to satisfy the exposure trigger under § 4(a)(1)(A).[107] This difference is based on the fact that less exposure is necessary when EPA has a scientific basis for suspecting potential toxicity under § 4(a)(1)(A).

Prior to 1993, EPA had declined to quantify "substantial," contending that it is "neither feasible nor desirable to make strict numerical definitions of substantial exposure or release," and that production and exposure determinations should be made individually for each chemical.[108] Then, on May 14, 1993, EPA published the final policy statement on TSCA § 4(a)(1)(B) findings in which it has quantified "substantial" production, release, and exposure.[109] The policy establishes quantitative thresholds to serve as guidance for determining "substantial" production, release, and human exposure (see table 12.1).

In addition to making a finding of substantial production volume or exposure under TSCA § 4(a)(1)(B), EPA also must determine that there are insufficient data and that testing is necessary to develop the needed information. These required findings are identical to those in TSCA § 4(a)(1)(A), discussed above.

8.3 Tests and Studies under TSCA § 4

After EPA determines that at least one of the regulatory triggers under TSCA § 4(a) has been met and after a public comment period, EPA publishes the test rule. A TSCA § 4 test rule must identify specifically the chemical substance or mixture to be tested; the standards for the development of test data; and, for existing chemicals, the time period during which the test data must be submitted.[110]

TSCA § 4 grants EPA wide latitude in deciding the types and amount of testing it may require. "The health and environmental effects for which standards . . . may be prescribed include carcinogenesis, mutagenesis, teratogenesis, behavioral disorders, cumulative or synergistic effects, and any other effect which may present an unreasonable risk of injury to health or the environment."[111] Generally, EPA requires studies on acute, subchronic, and chronic toxicity; oncogenicity; reproduction; teratogenicity; mutagenicity; neurotoxicity; environmental effects; and chemical fate.

8.3.1 Good Laboratory Practice Standards

Any study whose purpose is to satisfy a TSCA test rule must meet EPA Good Laboratory Practice (GLP) standards. TSCA GLP standards are codified at 40 C.F.R. § 792. TSCA GLP standards prescribe minimum requirements that the laboratory and sponsor must fulfill in areas such as organization and personnel, equipment, test facility operations, and study protocol. Any person who submits to EPA a test required by a § 4 test rule must submit a statement, signed by the submitter and the study director, to the effect that: (1) the study complies with GLP requirements; or (2) describes the differences between the practices used in the study and TSCA GLP requirements; or (3) the person was not the sponsor of the study, did not conduct the study, and does not know whether the study complies with TSCA GLP requirements.

8.3.2 Development and Implementation of Test Rules

EPA in 1985 issued guidelines and procedures for use of single-phase rulemaking and now uses this procedure almost exclusively.[112] In the single-phase test rule,

EPA proposes the pertinent Office of Pollution Prevention and Toxics (OPPT) (formerly the Office of Toxic Substances) test guideline as the required test standard in the initial notice of proposed rulemaking. Other methodologies may be proposed during the public comment period. The final rule promulgates as the test standard either the OPPT test guideline or other suitable guidelines. The agency uses single-phase rulemaking for most TSCA § 4 rules, reserving two-phase rulemaking only for testing where there are no well-accepted test methodologies.

8.3.3 Letters of Intent

Within 30 days after the effective date of a test rule, each person subject to the rule must either notify EPA by letter of intent to conduct testing or submit an application for exemption.[113] Manufacturers or processors who continue their activities and who do not submit either a letter of intent to test or a request for an exemption will be considered in violation of the rule.[114] Typically, where both manufacturers and processors are subject to the test rule, processors will only participate if specifically directed to do so or if no manufacturer has made known its intent to test. If no manufacturer notifies EPA within 30 days of receipt of EPA's notification, all manufacturers and processors will be in violation of the rule from the 31st day after receipt of notification.[115]

8.3.4 Test Standards

Each test rule must include standards that prescribe the manner in which data are to be developed and any test methodology or other requirements that are necessary to assure that the manufacturer produces reliable and adequate data.[116] EPA has codified guidelines that may be used to establish test standards in § 4 test rules.[117] These guidelines do not become mandatory test standards until they are promulgated as such in individual § 4 rulemakings.

8.4 Exemptions from Testing

Although TSCA § 4 requires any person who manufactures, imports, or processes a chemical subject to a test rule to conduct testing, such a person may seek an exemption. TSCA § 4(c)(2) authorizes EPA to exempt a manufacturer or processor from a test rule if it is determined that the applicant's substance "is equivalent to a chemical substance or mixture for which data has been submitted" or for which data are being developed in response to a test rule. Under the exemption, persons subject to a test rule have 30 days within which to either supply a letter of intent to comply or seek an exemption.[118]

EPA will conditionally grant an exemption if the agency has received and adopted a complete proposed study plan, has determined that the substance that is the subject of the exemption application is equivalent to the test substance for which the required data have been or will be submitted, and has concluded that submission of the required test data would be duplicative of data which have been or will be submitted under the test rule.[119]

EPA may deny an exemption application if (1) the applicant fails to demonstrate data equivalency, (2) the applicant fails to submit the information required under 40 C.F.R. §§ 790.82 or 790.85, (3) the agency has not received an adequate study plan for the test rule for which the exemption is sought, or (4) the study sponsor fails to submit the required data.[120] Although an applicant whose exemption has been denied can appeal the denial, the appeal does not stay the applicant's obligations under TSCA § 4.[121] Moreover, an exemption is only conditional and may be terminated if the agency determines that equivalent testing has not been initiated in a timely manner or that the equivalent testing did not comply with the test rules or good laboratory practices.[122]

Persons who manufacture less than 500 kilograms (1,100 pounds) of a chemical annually are exempt from the procedural requirements of a test rule unless the test rule directs them to comply with a rule's testing requirement.[123] As in the case of processors, such manufacturers still would be legally subject to test rules and would not be exempt from reimbursement claims.

8.5 Reimbursement Procedures

Any person receiving an exemption from a testing requirement must reimburse persons who perform required testing for a portion of costs expended in generating the data.[124] (Because processors are deemed to have fulfilled their testing and reimbursement obligation indirectly "through higher prices passed on by those directly responsible, the manufacturers," processors normally make no direct reimbursement payments.)[125] Although EPA strongly encourages the parties to reach a voluntary agreement on the amount of reimbursement, the administrator may issue a reimbursement order directing those who received an exemption "to provide fair and equitable reimbursement" to those who incurred the costs. Reimbursement orders are developed in consultation with the Department of Justice and the Federal Trade Commission. The administrator must take into account all relevant factors, including competitive position and market share of the persons providing and receiving reimbursement.[126]

If the parties are unable to agree, they may submit their dispute to arbitration and may request a hearing with the American Arbitration Association (AAA).[127] A hearing notice will be published in the *Federal Register*, after which any party may file a written answer in response or set forth additional claims. However, once a hearing officer is appointed, no additional or different claims can be asserted without the consent of the hearing officer.

After hearing, a proposed reimbursement order will be put forth which, based on a formula, provides that in general, each person's share of the test costs shall be in proportion to its share of the total production volume of the test chemical. EPA has recognized, however, that the allocation of test costs based on market share may not always be equitable. Therefore, any party may propose factors besides market share if their application produces a fair and equitable result.

Cooperative testing reduces costs and avoids duplicative testing. The most frequent form of organization used to conduct cooperative testing is the joint venture, which is being used with increasing frequency as a means to reduce the costs and risks of developing environmental and toxicological data required by a § 4 test rule. The joint venture is an unincorporated entity that operates much like a partnership but is limited to accomplishing the TSCA testing objectives of the group. Most joint ventures have a business group and a technical group. The latter develops protocols, monitors the studies, and reviews the results. The former typically decides when assessments will be made for expenses and decides if and when the scope of the testing program should be expanded beyond the original tests.

The most important provision in the agreement is the terms of sharing the costs and testing. Generally the costs can be apportioned on the basis of the market share of each participant, on an equal basis, or on some variant of these two. The joint venture can test only one substance "representative" of all of the members' products and that substance must meet all the requirements of the test rule.

8.6 Judicial Review

TSCA § 19 provides for appellate review of EPA test rules that are contested. A court may review, however, only the record of the rulemaking proceeding before the agency, and the agency's findings are conclusive, if supported by "substantial evidence."[128]

8.6.1 Jurisdiction, Standing, and Venue

A petition for judicial review must be filed within 60 days of the final rule. The standing provision of § 19 indicates that "any person" may file a petition seeking review of a final rule. "Any person" would include any producer of a substance or any interested organization, such as a trade association or environmental group; no injury need be shown. A petition may be filed in (1) the District of Columbia, (2) the circuit in which the petitioner resides, or (3) the circuit in which the petitioner has its principal place of business.[129]

8.6.2 The Rulemaking Record

TSCA test rules are promulgated on the basis of the rulemaking record, which the court of appeals will review to determine whether it is supported by substantial evidence. The court will not hold a new (de novo) hearing on whether and how a chemical substance or mixture should be tested. The reviewing court will consider only the evidence contained in the rulemaking record consisting of (1) the final test rule, (2) the necessary findings, (3) transcripts of oral presentations, and (4) written submissions of interested parties. The rulemaking record also includes any other information which EPA considers relevant to the test rule and "which the Administrator identified, on or before the date of the promulgation of such rule, in a notice published in the Federal Register."[130]

8.6.3 Standard of Review: "Substantial Evidence"

TSCA § 19(c)(1)(B) also prescribes the standard of judicial review: "[T]he court shall hold unlawful and set aside such rule if the court finds that the rule is not supported by substantial evidence in the rulemaking record . . . taken as a whole." In imposing the substantial evidence test, Congress cautioned that EPA need only demonstrate that the rule is "reasonably" supported.

In reviewing agency actions, however, courts give close scrutiny to the rulemaking record to assure that factual findings are supported by substantial evidence and that the rulemaking record adequately explains the agency's decisions. While a reviewing court may defer to EPA on scientific and policy issues, the court will examine the rulemaking record for a full explanation of the agency's rationale in its adopted approach. The courts agree that judicial review of § 4 test rules should be "demanding" and "fairly rigorous."[131]

8.7 TSCA § 4(f) Findings of Significant Risk

The agency's actions after receipt of test data that indicate a "significant risk" are governed by TSCA § 4(f). If the test data indicate to the administrator that there may be a "reasonable basis to conclude that a chemical substance or mixture presents or will present a significant risk of serious or widespread harm to human beings from cancer, gene mutations, or birth defects," the administrator must initiate appropriate rulemaking. If EPA chooses not to initiate rulemaking, the agency must publish in the *Federal Register* the reasons for not taking action.[132]

8.7.1 Criteria for Risk

Under TSCA § 4(f), EPA must take regulatory action when the chemical poses "a significant risk of serious or widespread harm to human beings." EPA considers this § 4(f) "significant risk" trigger to present a higher risk threshold than for those actions under TSCA § 6 which require a finding of "unreasonable risk."

EPA will determine that a significant risk of serious harm exists when there is a population whose members are at high individual risk from the substance. If the agency estimates that humans will be exposed to doses that produced an effect observed in animals or humans, the agency will make a § 4(f) finding. In addition, EPA will find a "significant risk of serious harm" where an exposed population does not enjoy an adequate margin of safety.

Significant risk of widespread harm is determined to exist when a large number of persons are exposed to the substance at a level on which a significant aggregate population risk is predicated. Although the individual risk may not be as high as that needed under the previous criterion, the harm associated with the risk must be widespread.

8.7.2 Review Period

Once EPA determines that the § 4(f) criteria have been met, the agency has 180 days to decide whether to initiate regulatory action. This 180-day period can be extended for an additional 90 days for "good cause" under TSCA § 4(f)(2). The agency will begin the 180-day review period when it receives sufficient information to make a § 4(f) finding. In general, EPA will not solicit public comments prior to making a § 4(f) finding, and the final § 4(f) finding will be made by the administrator.

9.0 Reporting and Retention of Information

TSCA § 8 establishes reporting and recordkeeping requirements to provide EPA with information on which to base regulatory and enforcement actions and to track patterns of adverse reactions to chemicals. EPA uses the information obtained under § 8 in other EPA programs to provide chemical information to industry and citizens, to evaluate existing data to determine their adequacy for risk assessment purposes, to identify data gaps, and to monitor ongoing activities with respect to specific chemicals.

9.1 TSCA § 8(a): Reports

Under TSCA § 8(a), EPA may require companies to maintain records and submit reports on their chemical manufacturing, importing, and processing activities. The agency has used its § 8(a) authority to impose recordkeeping and reporting requirements on specific listed chemicals. In implementing its § 8(a) authority, EPA has issued "model" rules that require submission of detailed production and exposure data on certain listed chemicals.

The first of these model rules, the Preliminary Assessment Information Rule (PAIR), issued in June 1982, automatically adds chemicals to the PAIR list 30 days after they are placed on the ITC Priority Testing List.[133] The rule requires manufacturers and importers to submit a two-page PAIR report for each plant site involved in manufacturing or importing a listed chemical substance within 60 days of the effective date of the listing of the chemical. Small manufacturers, manufacturers of less than 500 kilograms per site, and manufacturers of the substance solely for R&D or as an impurity, non-isolated intermediate, or by-product are exempt from PAIR reporting.[134]

The second model rule, the Comprehensive Assessment Information Rule (CAIR), issued on December 22, 1988, was intended to elicit far more detailed information about a more narrow group of chemical substances. CAIR was extremely controversial when promulgated, due to the lack of a low volume exemption or a de minimis concentration exemption, the amount of information required to be reported, the fact that processors were required to comply, and the requirement that manufacturers of mixtures incorporating CAIR-listed chemicals disclose this information so that processors of these mixtures would be aware of their reporting obligation or, alternatively, report for their customers. Initially, CAIR listed only 19 chemicals. Persons who manufactured or processed any of these 19 listed chemicals during the CAIR reporting period (February 1987 to February 1989) were required to prepare and file CAIR reports. Due to the controversy surrounding the rule, EPA has added no other chemicals to the original 19 on the CAIR list.

In 1993, EPA did publish proposed amendments to CAIR addressing those aspects of the rule that made it so controversial when promulgated.[135] EPA never finalized these amendments, however, and has indicated that it does not antici-pate taking any final action on this rule for some time as it "reassesses its TSCA information needs."[136] EPA made these statements in a *Federal Register* notice in which EPA withdrew the CAIR regulations from the C.F.R. Given the current "inactive" status of CAIR (i.e., no one has had to file any CAIR reports since the late 1980s), EPA reasoned that its presence in the C.F.R. is confusing to the public and regulated community and so removed the rule until such time as the CAIR amendments become final.

The Inventory Update Rule, issued in 1986 and amended in 2003, also was issued under authority of TSCA § 8(a). The Inventory Update Rule requires manufacturers and importers of certain chemicals listed on the Inventory to report current data on the production volume, plant site, and site-limited status of the substances, as well as use and exposure information for chemicals manufac-tured or imported in excess of certain volume thresholds.[137] The requirements under this rule are discussed *supra* in section 3.3, in conjunction with the TSCA Inventory.

9.2 TSCA § 8(c): Records of Significant Adverse Reactions

TSCA § 8(c) requires manufacturers, processors, and distributors to keep records of significant adverse reactions to health and the environment alleged to have been caused by a chemical substance or mixture they manufacture, process, or distribute. Allegations by employees must be kept on file for 30 years; allegations by others, for five years. These allegations do not have to be reported to EPA unless the agency specifically requests them. EPA may require submission of copies of the § 8(c) records to the agency, however, and employees can petition the agency to collect and release § 8(c) information.

EPA has defined "significant adverse reaction" to mean a reaction that may indicate a substantial impairment of normal activities, or long-lasting or irreversible damage to health or the environment.[138] In order to place some limitation on an otherwise open-ended recording obligation, EPA has provided a narrow exemption for known human health effects.[139] Those environmental reactions that must be recorded include gradual or sudden changes in the composition of animal life or plant life, abnormal numbers of deaths of organisms, reduction of the reproductive success of a species, reduction in agricultural productivity, and alterations in the behavior or distribution of a species.[140]

In order to constitute a recordable allegation under § 8(c), the statement must state clearly the alleged cause of the adverse reaction.[141] An "allegation" is defined as a statement, made without formal proof or regard for evidence, that a chemical substance or mixture has caused a significant adverse reaction to health or the environment. It is important to remember that a series of identical or very similar allegations about a particular substance may indicate a significant risk, which can trigger reporting requirements under § 8(e).

9.3 TSCA § 8(d): Health and Safety Studies

Section 8(d) requires that, upon request, a person who manufactures, processes, or distributes in commerce any chemical substance or mixture must submit to the administrator lists and copies of health and safety studies conducted by, known to, or ascertainable by that person.

In May 1996, EPA announced plans for the first major overhaul of the TSCA § 8(d) Model Reporting Rule, which was adopted in 1982 and then amended in 1986. The EPA's goal was to streamline the reporting requirements while maintaining the ability to protect human health and the environment through the collection of data regarding potential risks. On April 1, 1998, EPA published the revisions to the Model Reporting Rule as a direct final rule, without a proposal and prior opportunity for comment.[142] The agency viewed the action as noncontroversial because it substantially reduces existing reporting requirements, and the agency anticipated there would be no significant adverse comments. These revisions became effective on June 30, 1998.

Under the revised Model Reporting Rule, submission of unpublished health and safety studies continues to be required on certain specifically listed chemicals or mixtures. EPA has narrowed the categories of persons required to report. Only persons who fall within the North American Industry Classification System (NAICS) (in effect as of January 1, 1997) Subsector 325 (chemical manufacturing and allied products) or Industry Group 32411 (petroleum refineries), and who currently manufacture (including import) a chemical substance or a mixture listed at 40 C.F.R. § 716.120 (or propose to do so) or who manufactured (including imported) within the ten years preceding the effective date of the listing of the chemical are subject to the provisions of the Model Reporting Rule.

EPA may promulgate a rule under § 8(d) to subject to the provisions of the Model Reporting Rule any person who does not fall within NAICS Subsector 325 or Industry Group 32411, and who had proposed to manufacture (including import) or process, had manufactured (including imported) or processed, proposes to manufacture (including import) or process, or is manufacturing (including importing) or processing a chemical substance or a mixture listed at 40 C.F.R. § 716.120. Persons who process (or propose to do so) are not subject to the reporting requirements unless otherwise required in a specific rule. Although TSCA gives EPA the authority to impose this reporting requirement on persons who distribute listed chemical substances in commerce, EPA thus far has chosen not to exercise this authority.

There are two phases to § 8(d) reporting. First, persons are required to submit copies of all nonexempt, requested studies in their possession at the time they become subject to the rule. Second, EPA must be informed within 30 days of any study on a subject chemical initiated by or for such manufacturer or processor.[143]

Other streamlining revisions adopted by the EPA are as follows. In rulemaking proceedings that add substances or mixtures to § 716.120, EPA will narrow the focus of the reporting requirements to specifically identify the types of health and/or environmental effects studies that must be reported and the chemical grade/purity requirements that must be met or exceeded in individual studies. The reporting period for a listed substance or mixture has been shortened to terminate 60 days after the effective date on which a listed substance or mixture is added to 40 C.F.R. § 716.120. Because of this change in the reporting period, EPA will no longer conduct biennial review of the listed chemical substances and mixtures to determine whether to remove or retain each substance or mixture. Persons are required to conduct file searches only for reportable information dated on or after January 1, 1977, the effective date of TSCA, unless a subsequent section 8(d) rule requires a more extensive search. EPA shortened the sunset period for all current reporting requirements for all chemicals listed at 40 C.F.R. § 716.20 for which reporting was required, by amending the sunset date to June 30, 1998.

9.4 TSCA § 8(e): Substantial Risk Information

Section 8(e) requires any person who manufactures, processes, imports, or distributes a chemical substance to report to EPA any information concerning the substance that "reasonably supports the conclusion that the chemical substance or mixture presents a substantial risk of injury to health or the environment" unless the person knows that EPA has already been adequately informed. Although EPA has not issued regulations implementing § 8(e), the agency has issued other types of formal guidance.[144] EPA issued a TSCA Section 8(e) Reporting Guide in June of 1991 (available through the TSCA Hotline), and has provided some limited policy guidance through § 8(e) status reports, and occasionally through its monthly publication, *TSCA Chemicals in Progress*. The status reports are a summary of EPA's initial review of submitted § 8(e) reports, and—for your information—are available for public viewing in the OPPT Public Reading Room at EPA Headquarters in Washington, D.C. Moreover, in the course of the TSCA § 8(e) Compliance Audit Program (CAP), EPA publicly issued a number of responses to inquiries from CAP participants and trade associations.

On March 16, 1978, EPA published a "Statement of Interpretation and Enforcement Policy; Notification of Substantial Risk" concerning the Section 8(e) notification requirement.[145] Although the 1978 policy statement remains the fundamental source of specific guidance, EPA has revised its guidance provisions for reporting information regarding nonemergency releases of chemical substances into, or chemical contamination of, the environment. On June 13, 1993, and again on March 20, 1995, EPA issued proposed revisions to the 1978 policy statement.[146]

On June 3, 2003, EPA issued a new reporting guidance titled "TSCA Section 8(e); Notification of Substantial Risk; Policy Clarification and Reporting Guidance" to address public comments that were solicited in 1993 and 1995.[147] The 2003 "policy clarification" is aimed at explaining a statutory obligation, which became effective with the enactment of TSCA in 1977. Although § 8(e) is self-implementing and does not require regulations to become effective, the EPA guidance publications provide a roadmap of how a court is likely to view the corresponding responsibilities of those subject to § 8(e) regulation.

Specifically, the 2003 revisions addressed: (1) the reporting of information on the release of chemical substances to, and the detection of chemical substances in, environmental media; (2) the reporting deadline for written "substantial risk" information; and (3) the circumstances under which certain information need not be reported to EPA under § 8(e) of TSCA.[148]

The 2003 policy clarification explained that a "substantial risk of injury to health or the environment" means a risk of considerable concern because of "the seriousness of the effect and (b) the fact or probability of its occurrence."[149] In its evaluation, EPA looks at human health as well as environmental effects. The 2003 guidance also explained that the obligation to report is imposed on not only the top-ranking officers of a company or officers having authority for the organization's execution of its § 8(e) obligations, but also on employees "who are capable of appreciating the significance of pertinent information."[150] Internal safeguards may be taken to relieve these employees of the reporting obligation, but all corporate officials responsible for, and having authority for implementing, the organization's execution of an internal program retain personal liability for assuring that required information is submitted.

The 2003 guidance modifications changed the interpretation regarding the timing for submission of § 8(e) reporting—extending the reporting time from "within 15 working days" to 30 calendar days.[151] The exception is that for "emergency incidents of environmental contamination," immediate reporting is necessary.

EPA also determined that certain information is not necessary to report. The 2003 guidance clarification identified "non-reportable" information to include substantial risk information that is obtained from specified sources, generally official publications or databases or public media reports, and certain information that will be reported under other federal programs.

According to updated contact information, TSCA § 8(e) notices should be delivered to the document processing center for TSCA. Emergency incidents of environmental contamination, however, should be reported to the EPA administrator or the National Response Center by telephone as soon as the person has knowledge of the incident.

EPA has also provided a question and answer document available with respect to the 2003 Reporting Guidance. This Q&A document can be found on the OPPT's TSCA section 8(e) Internet site: http://www.epa.gov/oppt/tsca8e/.

10.0 Existing Chemical Regulation

TSCA § 6 grants EPA full authority to regulate existing chemicals that present unreasonable risks to health or the environment. Under TSCA § 6, EPA must place controls and restrictions, including outright bans if necessary, upon the manufacture, use, processing, disposal, or distribution of such chemicals. This is EPA's most extreme regulatory power.

10.1 Procedures and Standards for TSCA § 6 Regulation

EPA must initiate § 6 rulemaking to regulate a chemical substance when the agency finds "a reasonable basis to conclude that the manufacture . . . use, or disposal of a chemical . . . will present an unreasonable risk of injury to health or the environment," and that the risks cannot be addressed by EPA or any other agency under another statute.[152] In determining whether a perceived risk is "unreasonable," the agency must conduct a risk assessment of the chemical substance. The risk/benefit comparison required by § 6 must consider (1) the effects on health and the environment, (2) the magnitude of exposure to humans and the environment, (3) the benefits of the substance and the availability of substitutes, and (4) the reasonably ascertainable economic consequences of the rule.[153] Once having found an unreasonable risk, EPA must choose the least burdensome restrictions adequate to protect against the identified risk.[154] In addition to controls on the chemical itself, EPA can order a manufacturer or processor to use approved quality control procedures if EPA determines the chemical substance is manufactured or processed in a manner "which unintentionally causes" it to present an unreasonable risk.

10.2 Chemical-Specific Regulations

EPA has regulated only six chemical substances under this section since TSCA's inception: asbestos, chlorofluorocarbon, dioxins, hexavalent chromium, certain metalworking fluids, and polychlorinated biphenyls. In the case of asbestos, the regulations were ultimately overturned. In the case of polychlorinated biphenyls (PCB), the regulations may be the most widely applicable and best known of any TSCA regulations.

10.2.1 Asbestos

EPA's asbestos regulations serve to illustrate some of the difficulties the agency has experienced in implementing TSCA § 6 controls. In 1989, after more than ten years of effort, EPA issued a final rule to ban the manufacture, import, processing, and distribution of virtually all asbestos products. EPA issued the regulations because exposure to asbestos fibers is associated with pulmonary fibrosis (asbestosis), lung cancer, and other cancers and diseases both inside and outside the lungs and because millions of people are exposed to airborne asbestos fibers.[155]

After a bitterly fought challenge to the asbestos regulations brought by industry, the U.S. Court of Appeals for the Fifth Circuit overturned EPA's ban.[156] The court held that EPA failed to justify use of the ban. EPA did not demonstrate that some intermediate alternative action would not be adequate. Nor did the agency give notice that it intended to predict exposure by use of data on "analogous" substances. Moreover, said the court, EPA failed to consider evidence that available substitutes were toxic also. This failure demonstrates the regulatory hurdles facing EPA under § 6 and suggests why so few TSCA § 6 actions have been initiated.

10.2.2 Chlorofluorocarbons (CFCs)

Chlorofluorocarbons (CFCs) had been earmarked for regulation prior to the effective date of TSCA. In 1978, EPA promulgated final regulations prohibiting almost all propellant uses of chlorofluorocarbons (e.g., in aerosol sprays). Under the regulations, the manufacturing, processing, or distribution of fully halogenated chlorofluoroalkanes for aerosol propellant use is prohibited, except for enumerated "essential" uses.

EPA also has issued a rule to implement the Montreal Protocol on Substances That Deplete the Ozone Layer. This international agreement calls for a 50 percent reduction in production and consumption of CFCs. EPA did not issue this rule under TSCA, but rather under its Clean Air Act Authority.[157] Although the rule regulates production and consumption of CFCs through an allotment system, it did not modify or rescind the TSCA regulations regarding CFC use as a propellant. In 1995, however, in recognition of the fact that the Clean Air Act provisions have made the TSCA requirements obsolete, EPA withdrew the CFC regulations from the C.F.R.[158]

10.2.3 Tetrachlorodibenzo-P Dioxin (TCDD)

At one time, EPA regulated the treatment and disposal of wastes containing tetra-chlorodioxins (TCDD) (commonly referred to as "dioxin") under TSCA (see 40 C.F.R. § 775 [1984]). EPA later acknowledged that the regulation of hazardous waste disposal more logically belonged under RCRA. In 1985, EPA promulgated RCRA regulations that prescribe land disposal and treatment standards (i.e., incineration) of dioxin-contaminated wastes. As part of that rule, EPA revoked the TSCA regulation of dioxin-contaminated wastes.[159]

10.2.4 Hexavalent Chromium

EPA prohibits use of hexavalent chromium as a corrosion inhibitor in comfort cooling towers (CCTs) as part of air conditioning and refrigeration systems.[160] EPA determined that hexavalent chromium compounds are human carcinogens and that continued use in CCTs would pose an unreasonable risk to human health. Because the risk of human exposure posed by the use of hexavalent chromium chemicals in industrial cooling towers is low, the rule does not ban such use. To eliminate misuse, distributors of hexavalent chromium–based water treatment chemicals are required to place warning labels on containers and retain records of all shipments of hexavalent chromium–based chemicals intended for use in industrial cooling towers.

10.2.5 Metalworking Fluids

On three occasions, EPA has used its § 6(a) authority to address potential hazards that could arise from mixing nitrosating agents with certain amides and salts. The three rules involved PMN substances that were intended for use in metalworking fluids. In each case, EPA determined that, under common metalworking industry practices, use of the new substance would expose employees to incidentally created N-nitrosodiethanolamine. The rules EPA promulgated prohibit mixing nitrosating agents with metalworking fluids that contain the specific PMN substances and require distributors of the PMN substances to affix warning labels to containers of the substances and to send advance warning letters and copies of the regulations to customers.

10.2.6 Polychlorinated Biphenyls

TSCA § 6 specifically required EPA to regulate PCBs by establishing a legal presumption under § 6(e) that PCBs pose an unreasonable risk. In general, EPA's PCB regulations, set forth at 40 C.F.R. § 761, cover the following areas: (1) prohibited and authorized commercial activities, (2) marking requirements, (3) storage and disposal requirements, (4) exemptions from the general prohibitions, (5) spill cleanup policy, (6) recordkeeping requirements, (7) sampling requirements, and (8) decontamination requirements. These widely applicable regulations are discussed briefly below.

On December 6, 1994,[161] EPA published a proposed rule modifying the PCB disposal rules. On June 29, 1998,[162] EPA published the final rule promulgating significant amendments affecting the use, manufacture, processing, distribution in commerce, and disposal of PCBs. EPA believes that this rule will result in substantial cost savings to the regulated community while protecting against unreasonable risk of injury to health and the environment from exposure to PCBs. In August 2000, the United States Court of Appeals for the Fifth Circuit for the most part rejected a challenge to the 1998 PCB rule by industry and environmental groups.[163]

The manufacture, processing, or distribution of PCBs in commerce for use in the United States is prohibited unless conducted in a manner that EPA has determined is "totally enclosed" or has otherwise specifically authorized. A "totally enclosed" manner is defined as any manner which will ensure that exposure of human beings or the environment to PCBs as a result of the activity will be insignificant.[164]

Standardized PCB warning labels must be affixed to specific types of items such as electrical, hydraulic, and heat transfer equipment; containers; and vehicles.[165] There are formats for large and small PCB labels, and these labels must be used whenever PCB warning marks are required. Marking requirements extend to storage areas, as well as to particular PCB articles.

Existing PCBs and PCB articles are to be disposed of gradually through methods by which exposure is virtually eliminated. The regulations define "disposal" so that virtually any release of PCBs to the environment in concentrations of 50 ppm or greater is considered a prohibited act of disposal. Disposal standards exist that encompass the diversity of PCB contaminated waste, including liquids, electrical equipment, hydraulic machinery, other contaminated articles, dredge and sludge, research and development waste, PCB/radioactive waste, and containers that once held PCBs.

When PCBs and PCB-containing items are removed from use, they may be stored for up to one year while awaiting disposal. The EPA may grant requests for a one-year extension and for subsequent additional extensions provided certain conditions are met. All items stored must be marked to indicate the date the item was removed from service, and the storage facility must be constructed to contain spills. In addition, operators must inspect the stored PCBs every 30 days and follow specific recordkeeping requirements.

EPA has established decontamination standards and procedures for removing PCBs, which are regulated for disposal, from water, organic liquids, nonporous surfaces, concrete, and nonporous surfaces covered with a porous surface.[166] Decontamination in accordance with these requirements does not require a PCB disposal approval, but a person wishing to decontaminate material in a manner other than prescribed in the regulations must obtain permission from the EPA regional administrator.[167] Materials from which PCBs have been removed by decontamination may be distributed in commerce and used or reused. Materials meeting the applicable decontamination standards or procedures are unregulated for disposal.

EPA has issued a policy governing the reporting and cleanup of all spills resulting from the release of materials containing PCBs in concentrations greater than 50 parts per million (ppm).[168] The policy classifies PCB spills as either low-concentration spills or high-concentration spills. Low-concentration spills have a PCB concentration of less than 500 ppm and involve less than one pound of

PCBs. High-concentration spills have a PCB concentration of greater than 500 ppm or are low-concentration spills that either involve one pound or more of PCBs or 270 gallons or more of untested mineral oil.[169] Any spill that involves a release of more than ten pounds of PCBs must be reported immediately to the appropriate EPA regional office. (CERCLA also requires reporting of all spills involving one pound or more to the National Response Center.)

The level of cleanup required under the PCB cleanup policy is determined by the following facts: (1) the spill location, (2) the potential for exposure to residual PCBs remaining after the cleanup, (3) the concentration of PCBs initially spilled, and (4) the nature and size of the population potentially at risk from exposure.[170] In general, greater potential human exposure results in a more stringent cleanup standard.

Compliance with the PCB cleanup policy will "create a presumption against both enforcement action for penalties and the need for further cleanup under TSCA."[171] However, when cleanups are required under RCRA, CERCLA, or other statutes, they may have to meet standards different from those imposed by TSCA.

Operators of a facility must prepare and keep at hand an annual report for the previous calendar year if their facility contains 45 kilograms or more of PCBs in PCB containers, one or more PCB transformers, or 50 or more large PCB capacitors, or is used for PCB storage or disposal.[172] Persons engaged in activities involving PCBs must maintain other records described specifically in § 761.

EPA has promulgated a rule that creates a nationwide PCB manifesting system under TSCA.[173] This rule was amended recently by the 1998 amendments to provide clarification and incorporate provisions previously promulgated under RCRA regulations that seemed appropriate for inclusion. The rule requires all PCB disposal companies, transporters, commercial storers, and generators of PCB wastes who store their own wastes to notify EPA of their activities and identify their facilities. All companies that notify EPA receive an EPA registration number. EPA has attempted to use the least burdensome restrictions by integrating its federal PCB regulations with state regulations under RCRA and by allowing PCB operators to use the RCRA Uniform Manifest, which has space designated for additional information required under various state RCRA programs.

11.0 Relationship between TSCA and Other Laws

Pesticides regulated under the Federal Insecticide, Fungicide, and Rodenticide Act and substances regulated under the Federal Food, Drug, and Cosmetic Act are excluded from jurisdiction under TSCA. Moreover, other statutes administered by EPA, statutes administered by other federal agencies such as the Occupational Safety and Health Act and Consumer Product Safety Act, and toxic substances laws adopted by states or their political subdivisions also regulate chemical risks. The relationship between TSCA and these statutes is discussed below.

11.1 Federal Insecticide, Fungicide, and Rodenticide Act (FIFRA)

A chemical must satisfy a two-pronged test to meet the TSCA pesticide exclusion. First, the chemical must fall within the FIFRA definition of a "pesticide." Second, the chemical must be "manufactured, processed, or distributed in commerce for use as a pesticide."[174] Accordingly, EPA considers raw materials and inert ingredients to be subject to TSCA until they become components of a pesticide product, at which time the agency considers them to be subject to FIFRA.[175] EPA also contends that TSCA's provisions, including the TSCA § 8(e) notification of substantial risk requirements, apply to R&D candidate pesticides prior to the submission of an application for an Experimental Use Permit or a FIFRA § 3 registration, because under FIFRA these chemicals are not yet considered pesticides.[176] EPA also takes the position that a pesticide does not fall within the TSCA § 3(2)(B)(ii) pesticide exclusion during disposal because the chemical is not being "manufactured, processed, or distributed in commerce for use as a pesticide" during the disposal process.

11.2 Federal Food, Drug, and Cosmetic Act (FDCA)

TSCA § 3 also excludes foods, food additives, drugs, devices, and cosmetics subject to the FDCA from the TSCA definition of "chemical substance."[177] EPA's position is that a substance should be exempt from TSCA regulation at the point that the Food and Drug Administration (FDA) regulates the substance.[178]

11.3 TSCA's Relationship to Other Federal Laws

TSCA § 9 addresses EPA's authority to regulate those chemicals that fall within the purview of both TSCA and other federal statutes. Commonly called TSCA's "referral" provision, § 9 establishes procedures by which EPA can refer regulation of chemical risks to other agencies that have adequate statutory authority to regulate the risks. Referral is accomplished by means of a detailed report that describes EPA's findings. If the referral agency either issues an order declaring that the activities described in EPA's report "do not present the risk" that the administrator alleges, or initiates within 90 days of its response to EPA "action to protect against such risk," EPA is barred from using TSCA §§ 6 or 7 to regulate the risk.[179] If the referral agency determines, however, that it lacks adequate authority to regulate the risk "to a sufficient extent," explicitly defers the regulatory prerogative back to EPA, or fails to respond within the deadline set by EPA, then EPA remains free to act under TSCA to regulate the risk.

TSCA § 9(b), the intra-agency counterpart of § 9(a), requires the administrator to "coordinate" actions taken under TSCA with actions taken under other statutes administered "in whole or part" by EPA. If the administrator determines that a chemical risk "could be eliminated or reduced to a sufficient extent by actions taken under the authorities contained in such other federal laws, the administrator shall use such authorities to protect against such risk."[180] If, however, the administrator in her discretion determines that "it is in the public interest to protect against such risk" by actions taken under TSCA, she is not required to regulate the risk under the other statute.[181]

11.4 TSCA Preemption of State and Local Laws

TSCA § 18 governs the relationship between TSCA and state and local laws that regulate chemical risks. Section 18 states that TSCA does not "affect [i.e., preempt] the authority" of states or their political subdivisions to regulate the same chemicals covered by TSCA, subject to two exceptions. First, if EPA adopts a testing rule under TSCA § 4, state and local requirements for testing the same chemical are prohibited.[182] Second, if EPA adopts a rule or order under TSCA §§ 5 or 6, state and local regulations on the same chemical (other than disposal regulations) are prohibited, unless such regulations are identical to EPA's, carry out a federal law (such as the Clean Air Act), or ban the use of the chemical (other than its use in manufacturing or processing of other chemicals).[183]

Despite the foregoing, § 18(b) gives the administrator authority to allow (by rule) otherwise preempted state or local laws to be adopted or to continue in effect if they are consistent with EPA's actions under TSCA, afford a higher degree of protection than actions taken by EPA under TSCA, and do not unduly burden interstate commerce.

12.0 TSCA Inspections and Enforcement

TSCA §§ 11 and 16 authorize EPA to conduct inspections and subpoena documents to monitor for compliance with the Act and provide for the imposition of both civil and criminal penalties for TSCA violations. In addition, EPA may seize products under the authority of §§ 7 or 17(b). The agency usually limits seizure actions to those instances where a civil penalty action is insufficient to protect human health or the environment. Under § 7, EPA may conduct an "imminent hazard" seizure even absent a violation of TSCA.

12.1 Inspections

Under TSCA § 11 an EPA agent may inspect (1) any establishment in which chemical substances or mixtures are manufactured, processed, stored, or held before or after distribution in commerce; and (2) any conveyance being used to transport such materials in connection with distribution in commerce. An inspection may extend to all things within the premises or conveyances under inspection, including records, files, papers, processes, controls, and facilities, so long as they bear on compliance with the Act.[184] Although TSCA § 11 does not require EPA to obtain a search warrant prior to entry and inspection, independent constitutional considerations may make it necessary for EPA to obtain an administrative search warrant in order to enter the premises when permission is denied.[185] EPA policy presently calls for an inspector to obtain a warrant when lawful entry has been denied.

12.1.1 Types of Inspections

A company may undergo any of several "types" of inspections. For example, an inspection may be conducted for § 5 new chemical activity, for § 6(e) PCB violations, for § 8 reporting and recordkeeping compliance, or for any combination of the above. In addition, an inspection may be either "specific" (i.e., targeting specific chemicals or regulations) or "general" (i.e., assessing overall compliance).

Often the most extensive inspections are § 8 "verification" inspections. EPA will check to see if the targeted company has set up both a centralized system for tracking allegations of adverse effects concerning chemicals under § 8(c) and a well-publicized procedure for its employees to report significant risk information under § 8(e). The absence of such systems and procedures would raise suspicions about a company's TSCA compliance.

12.1.2 EPA Inspection Procedures

Inspection procedures fall into the following categories: (1) pre-inspection preparation, (2) notification and entry, (3) opening conference, (4) sampling and documentation, (5) closing conference, and (6) report preparation and follow-up.[186]

12.1.2.1 Pre-inspection Preparation

EPA's appropriate regional office will usually provide written notification to a facility several weeks prior to an actual inspection. The notice will specify the authority for the inspection and discuss what will be covered by the inspection. The inspector also will provide a declaration of confidential business information (CBI) form that the company must use to declare that certain information requested is CBI.

12.1.2.2 Notification and Entry

At the inspection, the investigator will identify himself and present official agency credentials. If the inspector does not have a search warrant he or she must obtain the consent of the facility officials. Although the company may at any time revoke its permission to enter, all information collected before permission is revoked remains in the possession of the inspector.

12.1.2.3 Opening Conference

The inspector will conduct an opening conference with facility officials where the purpose of the inspection, the parameters of the inspection, and the procedures to be followed are outlined. The inspector will discuss how questions will be handled during the inspection and at the closing conference, and should inform facility officials of their legal rights. If the facility officials have any objections as to how the inspection will be carried out, they should raise them during the opening conference.

12.1.2.4 Sampling and Documentation

In most cases, the inspector will know from pre-inspection preparation which records will be reviewed during the inspection. The investigator will always examine facility records and, when deemed necessary, will take physical samples in order to obtain documentation in support of any contemplated enforcement action.

12.1.2.5 Closing Conference

At the conclusion of the inspection, the EPA inspector will present the facility with a receipt itemizing all samples and documents taken during the inspection. Inspectors will not make statements as to the ultimate status of the facility or discuss the legal consequence of potential noncompliance. However, an inspector may discuss observed deviations from recommended procedures and inform facility personnel of problems that might require immediate attention. Inspectors may offer suggestions based on their preliminary findings. Inspectors also may request additional data and ask follow-up questions regarding their observations and measurements.

12.1.2.6 Report Preparation and Follow-Up

The inspection report is the compilation of factual information gathered at the compliance inspection. A copy of the final audit report may be obtained through the EPA office that initiated the audit. The regional office will use this report to determine whether follow-up action is appropriate and whether it should pursue criminal charges or civil enforcement.

12.1.3 EPA Authority to Issue Subpoenas

TSCA § 11(c) authorizes EPA to issue administrative subpoenas to require the attendance and testimony of witnesses and the production of reports, papers, documents, answers to questions, and such other information "that the Administrator deems necessary."[187] EPA interprets its § 11(c) power as an omnibus subpoena authority to support EPA's regulatory activities under other statutes that do not provide subpoena authority so long as a "chemical substance" is involved.

EPA has attempted to extend its TSCA § 11 subpoena power to activities conducted entirely outside the United States. On September 21, 1994, EPA issued subpoenas to 95 U.S. companies demanding information about the activities of their subsidiaries operating in Mexicali, Mexico. Several subpoena recipients voluntarily provided the requested data in exchange for EPA withdrawing the subpoena, thereby negating the need to challenge this use of EPA's subpoena power. Subpoena recipients and observers alike, however, remain concerned that this incident not serve as precedent for EPA to hereafter use TSCA § 11 in a similar manner.

12.2 Civil Penalties

EPA may impose civil penalties of up to $32,500 for each violation of TSCA, with each day that a violation continues constituting a separate violation.[188] In determining an appropriate civil penalty for a TSCA violation, the administrator must take into account nine specific factors that pertain to the nature, circumstances, extent, and gravity of the violation and also pertain to the violator's culpability, compliance history, financial position, and "other matters" as justice requires.[189] The agency's treatment of these factors is set forth in EPA's Guidelines for the Assessment of Civil Penalties under Section 16 of the Toxic Substances Control Act,[190] and other more specific policies, as discussed below.

12.2.1 TSCA Civil Penalty Policy

The TSCA Civil Penalty Policy requires a two-stage determination of a proposed civil penalty. First, a penalty matrix is used to calculate a gravity-based penalty (GBP). The GBP is based on the nature, extent, and circumstances of the violation. Second, the GBP may be adjusted upward or downward, taking into account several additional factors, including ability to pay, effect on ability to conduct business, any history of prior violations, culpability, and such other factors "as justice may require."

EPA considers two principal criteria for assessing a violator's culpability: (1) the person's knowledge of the TSCA requirement; and (2) the person's degree of control over the violation.[191] Where the violation is "willful" (i.e., the violator intentionally committed an act which he or she knew was a violation), the TSCA Civil Penalty Policy calls for a 25 percent increase in the civil penalty.[192] Criminal penalties may apply as well.[193] EPA considers the culpability of a violator to include the violator's "attitude" after the violation is discovered. Accordingly, the agency will adjust a proposed penalty upward or downward by up to 15 percent, depending on whether the violator is making "good faith" efforts to comply with the appropriate regulations, the promptness of the violator's corrective actions, and any assistance the violator gives EPA to minimize any harm to the environment that was caused by the violation.

The TSCA Civil Penalty Policy lists nine additional matters EPA will consider under its statutory mandate to consider "such other matters as justice may require." EPA takes the position that, regardless of other factors, proposed penalties should be increased when necessary to pay for government investigative and cleanup costs and, in appropriate cases, to ensure that the violator does not profit from noncompliance.[194] On the other hand, EPA will consider reducing proposed penalties where (1) the violator's cost of cleanup plus penalty seem excessive, (2) there is conflict or ambiguity vis-à-vis other federal regulations, (3) the violator makes voluntary environmentally beneficial expenditures above and beyond those required by law, (4) national defense or foreign policy issues intervene, (5) new owners are burdened with a prior owner's history of violations, and (6) the "extent" of the violation falls very close to the borderline between a significant or a minor violation, and, as a result, the penalty calculated seems disproportionately high.

The issue of whether and what statute of limitations may apply to TSCA enforcement actions can have a dramatic impact on the extent to which EPA may impose civil penalties on a noncompliant company. Until recently, EPA had asserted successfully that TSCA had no statute of limitations. Thus, EPA could bring an enforcement action and assess civil penalties for any violation of TSCA, no matter how stale. On March 4, 1994, however, the D.C. Circuit Court of Appeals issued an opinion holding that the general federal statute of limitations, 28 U.S.C. § 2462, for civil violations applies to TSCA enforcement actions.[195]

The *3M* Court found that 28 U.S.C. § 2462 applies to all administrative civil penalty actions brought before federal agencies, and cited four cases and two congressional reports supporting this finding.[196] The Court also found that a TSCA enforcement action constitutes a proceeding for the "enforcement of a civil penalty" consistent with the language of § 2462. EPA's contention that "enforcement" connotes only an action to collect a penalty already assessed was rejected.[197] The Court also rejected EPA's contention that the period of limitations did not begin to run until EPA first discovered the violation, not when the violation first occurred. An action, suit, or proceeding must be commenced within five years of the date of the violation giving rise to the penalty.[198]

The *3M* decision was significant in that it imposed a five-year statute of limitations where previously EPA asserted that none existed. However, the statute of limitations may not apply to cut off entirely the liability from "continuing" violations, such as the failure to report substantial risk information under TSCA § 8(e). The question remains as to which TSCA violations would be considered to be "continuing" violations and similarly protected from repose by action of the statute of limitations.

12.2.2 Regulation-Specific Penalty Policies

The TSCA § 5 Enforcement Response Policy prescribes administrative penalties for noncompliance with TSCA § 5(e) or 5(f) orders, rules, or injunctions, and significant new-use rules; for failure to submit PMNs; for submission of false or misleading information; and for commercial use of a substance that was produced without a PMN or valid exemption. The § 5 Policy also addresses violations of the regulations governing NOCs although those regulations were promulgated under § 8.

The TSCA § 5 Enforcement Response assigns each type of potential violation to one of three categories, as follows: (1) Chemical Control Violations, (2) Control-Associated Data-Gathering Violations, and (3) Hazard Assessment Violations (TSCA § 5 Penalty Policy at 7). These categories are then used in conjunction with facts pertaining to the specific case to calculate the GBP. After the GBP is calculated, the penalty may be increased or decreased due to the various factors listed in the TSCA Civil Penalty Policy. In a like manner, the TSCA §§ 8, 12, and 13 Penalty Policy addresses § 8 reporting and recordkeeping violations; § 12(b) export notification violations; and § 13 import certification violations.

Both the TSCA § 5 Enforcement Response and the TSCA §§ 8, 12, and 13 Enforcement Response Policy allow violators to reduce penalties by up to 80 percent as a result of confessing and cooperating. The agency has shown great reluctance, however, to reduce the base penalty by more than 80 percent, even if the self-confessor can show the best of attitudes and substantial steps taken to rectify the violation and to bring itself into full compliance with TSCA.

A strict application by EPA of the Civil Penalty Policy is not appropriate in every instance, however. In one appeal before EPA's chief judicial officer, a company prevailed against the agency's position that the civil penalty to be assessed must be determined by strict adherence to the Penalty Policy.[199] On appeal by EPA, the hearing officer's downward adjustment of the penalty for "good attitude" and appropriate mitigating steps taken by 3M was upheld. More importantly, however, the appeals officer departed entirely from the

Civil Penalty Policy and reduced the penalty by an additional 15 percent pursuant to TSCA § 16(a)(2)(B), which allows for an increase in the downward adjustment to account for "such other matters as justice may require." The total penalty was thereby reduced by 95 percent from that originally proposed. This aspect of the 3M case has since been used successfully by other companies seeking reduced penalties.

Before initiating civil penalty procedures under TSCA, the agency sometimes will issue a notice of noncompliance (NON), advising a company that a violation of TSCA has been detected or that the agency is keeping track of the company's actions with respect to correcting a violation. The issuance of an NON is discretionary and may occur when the violation is a minor one, not posing a significant threat to human health, and when other positive factors are present.[200]

12.2.3 EPA Self-Policing Policy

On December 22, 1995, EPA issued its "Self-Policing Policy," which took effect on January 22, 1996.[201] EPA issued a revised Self-Policing Policy on April 11, 2000, which took effect on May 11, 2000, and superseded the previous policy.[202] Through the policy, EPA promises to eliminate all gravity-based penalties for violations of federal environmental laws voluntarily discovered and promptly reported to EPA. In order to qualify for full penalty reduction, a company must satisfy each of the nine conditions outlined in the policy. In addition, the policy states that EPA will eliminate 75 percent of the gravity-based penalties for violations that were not "systematically discovered," provided the company meets the policy's other eight conditions. The agency, however, reserves the right to impose fines to eliminate any economic benefit a company may have obtained through noncompliance.

EPA also states that the agency will not recommend criminal prosecution for a company that discovers violations and discloses them under the policy, though the responsible individuals could still be charged. Consistent with its long-held view, the final policy expresses EPA's strong opposition to a statutory evidentiary privilege for environmental audits but indicates that EPA will not routinely request or use an environmental audit report to initiate a civil or criminal investigation.

In order to effectively use the policy, a company must be prepared to quickly demonstrate compliance with all nine conditions. For some conditions, this is more easily accomplished with advanced planning.

The policy's nine conditions are as follows:

Systematic Discovery	To receive mitigation of *all* gravity-based penalties, a company must discover violations through an environmental audit or through due diligence.
Voluntary Discovery	The discovery of violations must be voluntary and not required by order or permit. EPA examples of involuntary discoveries include emissions detected in accordance with a permit's monitoring requirements or emissions detected in accordance with the terms of a judicial or administrative consent order.
Prompt Disclosure	Violations (or potential violations) must be reported to EPA within 21 calendar days of their discovery.
Independent Discovery	Violations must be discovered *and* disclosed before the commencement of a government inspection, investigation, or request for information; notice of a citizen suit; filing of a third-party complaint; filing of a report by a "whistle-blower" employee; or the imminent discovery of the violation by a regulatory agency.
Correction and Remediation	Violations must be certified as being corrected within 60 days, and the company must take steps identified by EPA to remedy the violation.
Prevent Recurrence	A company must agree to take steps to prevent recurrence of the violation. This may include improving audits and implementing a compliance management system.
No Repeat Violations	No identical or closely related violations can have occurred at the same facility within the past three years, and the violation cannot be part of a parent's pattern of violation within the past five years.

Other Violations Excluded	The violations did not result in serious actual harm or present an imminent and substantial endangerment; or the violations are not ones for which the company previously received penalty mitigation.
Cooperation	The company cooperates with EPA in its investigation of the violation and any related noncompliance issues.

Systematic Discovery is the critical condition for full penalty reduction, and is the condition that requires the most forethought and preparation to satisfy. The Self-Policing Policy affords the regulated entity a choice in how it will satisfy this condition—discovery through an "environmental audit" or through "an objective, documented, systematic practice or procedure reflecting the regulated entity's due diligence in preventing, detecting and correcting violations."

The policy defines an environmental audit as "a systematic, documented, periodic, and objective review by regulated entities of facility operations and practices related to meeting environmental requirements." In order to show "due diligence," the regulated entity must develop "compliance policies, standards, and procedures that identify how employees and agents are to meet the requirements of laws, regulations, permits, and other sources of authority for environmental requirements." The policy sets out several additional criteria for due diligence, all of which flow from this fundamental starting point. Beyond compliance policies and procedures, a qualifying compliance program also must include the following:

- Assignment of overall responsibility for overseeing compliance for the entire company and assignment of specific responsibility for assuring compliance at each facility.

- Mechanisms for assuring that compliance policies are carried out, including monitoring and auditing systems reasonably designed to detect and correct violations.

- Efforts to communicate the regulated entity's compliance program to its employees.

- Incentives to managers and employees to perform consistent with the compliance program.

- Procedures for the prompt and appropriate correction of any violations and modification of the compliance program to prevent future violations.

In addition, EPA has published a model protocol for auditing a facility's compliance with TSCA requirements for PCBs, asbestos, and lead-based paint, but the audit protocol does not address the requirements for non-PCB commercial chemical substances in Title I of TSCA and, therefore, will be of limited use to many facilities.[203]

Given the choice, a company probably should not rely solely on audits to uncover TSCA violations. While a company may choose to conduct periodic TSCA audits to cleanse itself of liability for past violations, most entities discover at least some TSCA violations in a less structured way, usually in the course of ordinary business. A comprehensive compliance program that meets the policy's criteria for due diligence can establish and maintain a high level of compliance and simultaneously set the stage for penalty-free disclosure of the occasional violation that may "slip through the cracks."

Although the Self-Policing Policy provides incentives to audit for environmental compliance, confessing a violation of environmental law to EPA in the hope of paying no, or a significantly reduced, civil penalty requires a certain amount of faith that the agency will apply consistently and fairly the somewhat subjective criteria of the Self-Policing Policy. Similarly, EPA officials have acknowledged in public statements that the success of the policy in encouraging auditing will depend in large part on the consistency of its decisions, because consistency provides regulated entities with greater assurance that they can accurately predict the enforcement consequences in advance of a decision to audit or confess. Still, certain areas of ambiguity remain. Companies should be aware at a minimum of the following issues.

12.2.3.1 EPA Discretion to Recover Economic Benefit

EPA has stated that the agency "reserves the right to collect any economic benefit that may have been realized as a result of noncompliance, even where the entity meets all other policy conditions."[204] For PMN violations, for example, EPA has sought to recover economic benefit based upon the savings associated with delayed preparation or avoidance of the PMN. EPA uses the BEN computer model to calculate the economic benefit that regulated entities obtain as a result of violating environmental requirements.

12.2.3.2 Criminal Liability Issues

EPA states that its policy "in general" is not to recommend criminal prosecution of a self-disclosing company.[205] Nevertheless, this assurance does not extend, for example, to cases where corporate officials were consciously involved in or willfully blind to violations, or concealed or condoned them. EPA also has declined to extend its "no criminal referral" policy to individual company employees, where the company has reported violations under the policy.[206] Thus, individual officers or employees could face criminal charges for egregious conduct uncovered by an audit. Finally, ultimate prosecutorial discretion resides with the U.S. Department of Justice.[207]

12.2.3.3 Public Access to Audit Information

The Self-Policing Policy, as a condition of penalty mitigation, requires that a regulated entity cooperate "as requested by EPA and provides such information as is necessary and requested by EPA to determine applicability of [the] policy."[208] Once documents are provided to EPA, there always is some potential that the agency will not be able to protect them from disclosure under the Freedom of Information Act (FOIA). Confidential business information is exempt from release under FOIA, but nonconfidential information in audit documents still might be subject to release.[209] Moreover, waiving the attorney-client privilege to allow EPA to allow the company's entitlement to the benefits of the Self-Policing Policy could be an issue.

These issues aside, TSCA offenses generally, by their very nature, will easily meet several of the nine conditions that might prove problematic when reporting violations under other statutes. For example, many TSCA violations are paperwork problems that are easily corrected (Condition No. 4) and create no actual harm or endangerment (Condition No. 7). In addition, companies receive little, if any, quantifiable economic benefit from many types of TSCA violations and therefore could avoid having penalties calculated on that basis.

12.3 Settlement Procedures

EPA encourages negotiated settlements of civil penalty proceedings.[210] Thus, a settlement conference may be requested at any time during civil enforcement proceedings. A negotiated settlement agreement often will provide for two types of activities. First, it might include a mandatory audit provision, requiring the violator to conduct a self-audit to uncover and report additional TSCA violations and to initiate remedial measures. Second, a negotiated settlement may provide for additional compliance measures designed to further the agency's policies, for example, a commitment by the defendant to conduct a series of TSCA educational seminars or to prepare a TSCA guidance manual for employees. Generally, a provision is included which places a cap on the total amount of fines.

In certain circumstances, a settlement in an administrative action may be reached that assesses a civil penalty but also provides for the respondent to undertake remedial action as a means of remitting the entire assessed penalty. Such a settlement is referred to as a settlement with conditions (SWC). The purpose of an SWC is to enhance the level of compliance where violations require complex remedies.

12.4 Administrative Hearings

If the agency considers a violation serious enough or if settlement negotiations are unsuccessful, EPA will institute civil penalty actions leading to an administrative hearing. During the action, EPA will follow the procedures set forth in the Consolidated Rules of Practice (CROP), which govern these administrative actions.[211] Usually a prehearing conference intended to facilitate and expedite the proceedings is held where the parties discuss settlement of the case, consolidation of issues, evidence and witnesses to be presented, and any potential method to expedite the hearing.[212]

The administrative hearing is a full evidentiary hearing conducted under the CROP and the Administrative Procedure Act. Witnesses usually are examined orally under oath, but may submit a written statement if the testimony is complicated.[213] The presiding officer may issue a subpoena to compel the attendance of witnesses or the production of documentary evidence.[214]

At the conclusion of the hearing, the parties may detail their position in proposed findings of fact and law and proposed orders submitted to the presiding officer for consideration in issuing the initial decision. The initial decision becomes a final order within 45 days unless an adversely affected party makes an appeal to the administrator, the administrator determines *sua sponte* that a review of the initial decision is appropriate, or the party files within 20 days a motion to reopen the hearing.[215]

TSCA § 16(a)(3) provides that any person may seek judicial review in the court of appeals of an order assessing a civil penalty. Judicial review under TSCA § 16 is appellate review; that is, the court reviews the record of the civil penalty proceeding before the agency, and the agency's findings of fact are conclusive if supported by "substantial evidence."

12.5 Criminal Liability

It is a misdemeanor punishable by up to one year's imprisonment and up to $25,000 for each day of violation for any person "knowingly or willfully" to violate any provision of § 15.[216] To obtain a conviction against a company or an individual under § 16(b), the government must prove beyond a reasonable doubt that the defendant violated a requirement of TSCA and that the violation was committed "knowingly or willfully."

Case law indicates that specific knowledge of a TSCA requirement may not be necessary to establish a "knowing and willful" violation when the probability of regulation is so great that anyone handling the substance should be presumed to be aware that it is regulated.[217]

A corporation generally may be found liable for violations of regulations and statutes such as TSCA when such violations are committed by any of its employees, regardless of their position within the company, so long as those employees are acting within the scope of their authority and for the benefit of the corporation. In addition, courts generally will not permit a corporation to assert lack of corporate knowledge as a defense when any one individual who comprehended its full import obtained information; a corporation is considered to have acquired the collective knowledge of its employees. Moreover, it makes no difference whether a corporation has instructed its lower-level employees to obey the law in performance of their duties. If such an employee disobeys company instructions and violates the law, the corporation is not shielded from criminal liability.[218]

12.6 Citizen Actions and Petitions

TSCA contains "private attorney general" provisions, whereby any person may commence a civil action against any other person who is alleged to be in violation of TSCA. In addition, any person may sue to force the administrator to compel the performance of any nondiscretionary act under TSCA.[219] Attorneys' fees and other court costs may be awarded if a court determines that such an award is appropriate.

TSCA § 21 likewise permits any person to petition the administrator to initiate proceedings for the issuance, amendment, or repeal of certain rules.[220] EPA may hold a public proceeding in order to determine the merit of a citizen's petition but must act on the petition within 90 days of its filing.[221] If the petition is granted, the administrator must promptly commence an appropriate proceeding under §§ 4, 5, 6, or 8.[222] If the petition is denied, the administrator must publish the reasons for such denial in the *Federal Register.*[223]

An unsuccessful petitioner may seek judicial review by filing an action in a U.S. district court.[224] The type of agency action sought in the citizen's petition will determine the legal standard a court will apply to EPA's petition denial. If the subject petition sought the initiation of rulemaking, the petitioner is entitled to de novo review.[225] By contrast, if the administrator denies or fails to act upon a § 21 petition to amend or repeal an existing rule the court will apply the APA's arbitrary and capricious standard.

EPA has issued guidance, including a TSCA checklist for preparing citizen petitions under TSCA § 21.[226] With this guidance petitioners should be able to present their requests in a comprehensive and persuasive manner and to facilitate the agency's review and response.

13.0 Importation and Exportation

Importers of any chemical substance must comply not only with the same obligations imposed on domestic manufacturers, but also with a certification requirement pursuant to TSCA § 13. Similarly, exporters of chemicals may be subject to export notification obligations pursuant to TSCA § 12.

13.1 Import Regulation: TSCA § 13

TSCA § 13 requires the secretary of the treasury (the executive branch with authority over the U.S. Customs Service) to refuse entry into U.S. customs territory for a shipment of any chemical substance or mixture, if: (1) it fails to comply with any TSCA rule or regulation; or (2) it is offered for entry in violation of a § 5, 6, or 7 rule order, or action (TSCA § 13(a)(1)). The U.S. customs territory includes the 50 states, the District of Columbia, and Puerto Rico.[227] Thus, Customs Service regulations require an importer to certify at the port of entry that either (1) any chemical substance in the shipment is subject to TSCA and complies with all applicable rules and orders thereunder or (2) is not subject to TSCA.[228] Customs has established approximately 90 ports where entry documents may be filed.[229] In February 2000, the Customs Service amended the importation requirements and reduced the regulatory burden by permitting use of a blanket certification for multiple shipments in lieu of a separate certification for each individual shipment.[230]

Customs Service regulations establish precise requirements regarding the form of the required certification, including sample statements. According to the regulations, the importer must use one of the statements as worded; no other language may be substituted. The certification may appear either on the appropriate entry document or commercial invoice, or on an attachment to the entry document or invoice. The importer, or its agent, must keep a copy of the import certification along with other Customs entry documentation for five years.[231]

13.1.1 Importer Defined

Under Customs regulations, an "importer" is the "person primarily liable for the payment of any duties on the merchandise, or an authorized agent acting on his behalf." Thus, the importer may be a consignee, the importer of record, or the actual owner of the merchandise.[232] Generally, the consignee will make the certification.

13.1.2 Determining TSCA Status of Imported Substance

The importer is responsible for determining whether a chemical substance is on the TSCA Inventory. If the importer does not know whether the chemical substance to be imported is on the Inventory, the importer can file a bona fide intent to import request in order to have EPA search the master Inventory.[233]

If the chemical is not on the Inventory and is being imported for a commercial purpose, the importer must comply with the TSCA § 5 premanufacture notification requirements before importation. If the chemical product is not on the Inventory but is being imported solely for research and development purposes governed by TSCA, the importer still must make a positive certification that the chemical substance is imported in compliance with TSCA.

13.1.3 Exclusions

If a chemical substance is excluded from TSCA jurisdiction under TSCA § 3(2)(B), it is subject to a negative certification or to no certification at all, depending on which exclusion applies. EPA takes the position that in order to be excluded from all certification requirements, a chemical substance must be imported solely for an excluded purpose. If, subsequent to importation, the importer uses a substance for a TSCA purpose, then such use could constitute a TSCA violation. If a shipment is being imported for both a non-TSCA and a TSCA purpose, the importer must identify that portion of the shipment that is subject to TSCA and that which is not. For the former, the importer must certify that it complies with TSCA and for the latter the importer must certify that it is not subject to TSCA.

13.1.4 Articles, Samples, and Wastes

A manufacturer of any new chemical substance imported into the United States for commercial purposes must file a PMN "unless the substance is imported as part of an article."[234] EPA interprets this to exempt from the PMN requirement articles containing chemical substances that (1) are not intended to be removed from the article and (2) have no separate commercial purpose. Articles containing chemical substances intended to be used or released, such as ink in pens, are not encompassed by this exemption.

Companies occasionally receive unsolicited free samples of chemicals from offshore vendors for R&D purposes. Such samples are subject to TSCA § 13, as well as other TSCA provisions, such as § 5, even though they are unsolicited. To avoid potential liability, many companies refuse to accept such samples and return them to the shipper.

Imported wastes, both hazardous and nonhazardous, are also subject to TSCA because they are "chemical substances" within the meaning of the Act. As such, they require a positive certification, even if accompanied by a hazardous waste manifest pursuant to the Resource Conservation and Recovery Act of 1976 (RCRA).[235]

13.1.5 Detention of Shipments by Customs

A shipment may be detained by Customs whenever there exists a reasonable belief that the shipment is not in compliance with TSCA or no certification is filed. When Customs detains a shipment, it must give prompt notice of the detention and specify the reasons therefore to both EPA and the importer.[236] If reasonable grounds exist to believe that the shipment may be brought into compliance with TSCA, the shipment may be released under bond. If released under bond, the shipment must not be used or disposed of until EPA makes a final determination on its entry into the United States.[237]

An importer whose shipment has been detained may submit a written explanation to EPA as to why the shipment should be permitted entry. EPA then, within 30 days of the date of notice of detention, will make a decision on whether to allow entry.[238] Only if EPA determines that the shipment is in compliance with TSCA will it be released.[239] If the shipment is not in compliance, however, entry will be refused, or if the shipment has been released on bond, its redelivery will be demanded.[240] Under such circumstances, the importer must bring the shipment into compliance or export the shipment.[241] If the importer decides to export the noncomplying shipment the importer must provide written notice of the exportation.[242]

13.2 Export Regulation: TSCA § 12

TSCA § 12(a) exempts from most provisions of the Act any chemical substance, mixture, or article manufactured, processed, or distributed solely for export from the United States.[243] In order to qualify for this export exemption, the substance, mixture, or article must bear a stamp or label stating that it is intended solely for export.[244] The recordkeeping and reporting requirements of TSCA § 8, however, continue to apply to such chemical exports.

TSCA § 12(b) requires exporters to notify EPA before exporting any substance for which test data are required under §§ 4 or 5(b), when regulatory action has been proposed or taken under §§ 5 or 6, or when an action is pending or relief has been granted under §§ 5 or 7. Export notification is required regardless of the intended foreign use of the regulated chemical. EPA does not consider it relevant whether the chemical is being exported for use in a manner that is not regulated domestically under an action, rule, or order.[245] In addition to the export notices required under § 12(b), special notices are required in the case of PCBs.[246]

13.2.1 Export Notification Requirement

For chemical substances regulated under TSCA § 4, EPA requires submission of an export notice for the first shipment to each country.[247] EPA recently amended

its export notification requirements with respect to chemicals subject to TSCA §
5(e) consent orders, § 5(a)(2) SNURs, and § 5(b) test data requirements.[248] The
amended regulations require submission of an export notice for the first shipment to each country instead of an annual notification of the first shipment to
each country. For all other chemical substances subject to TSCA § 5(f), § 6, or
§ 7, EPA requires notification of the first shipment each year to each country.[249]
The notice must be postmarked on the date of export or within seven days of
forming the "intent to export," whichever is earlier.[250] Intent to export regulated
substances "must be based on a definite contractual obligation, or an equivalent
intra-company agreement, to export the regulated chemical."[251]

EPA's Export Notification Rule defines an "exporter" as the "person who,
as the principal party in interest in the export transaction, has the power and
responsibility for determining and controlling the sending of the chemical substance or mixture to a destination out of the customs territory of the United
States."[252]

Within five days of receiving a TSCA § 12(b) export notice, EPA must
transmit the following information to the importing country: (1) the name of
the regulated chemical, (2) a summary of the regulatory action the agency has
taken, (3) the name of an EPA official to contact for further information, and
(4) a copy of the relevant *Federal Register* notice.[253]

13.2.2 New Chemicals

A new chemical substance is subject to export notification only if it is subject to
a § 4 test rule, is included on the § 5(b)(4) "risk" list, is subject to an order
under § 5(e) or 5(f), or is subject to a proposed or final significant new-use
rule.[254] In the absence of such specific action, the export notification provisions
do not apply to new chemical substances intended solely for export. Moreover,
export notification need not accompany export of a chemical substance contained in an article unless the agency specifically requires export notification for
such articles in the context of individual rulemakings.[255]

13.2.3 De Minimis Exception

EPA's recent amendments to its export notification requirements established de
minimis concentration levels that exempt from export notification products containing most reportable chemicals at concentrations of less than 1 percent by
weight or volume.[256] Known or potential human carcinogens, however, have a
de minimis concentration level of 0.1 percent by weight or volume, and PCBs
have a de minimis concentration level of 50 ppm.

13.2.4 Confidentiality

Exporters may assert confidentiality claims for any information contained in export notices at the time such notices are submitted.[257] No proof of the confidentiality claim is required at the time of submission, but each page must be marked "confidential business information," "proprietary," or "trade secret."[258] Such information is treated by EPA as confidential and may be disclosed to the public only through the procedures set forth at 40 C.F.R. § 2.[259]

14.0 TSCA Reform

Although, or perhaps because, TSCA existed without major amendment for more than thirty years, increasing support for chemical regulatory reform in the United States developed over the past decade. Advocates of reform pointed to several factors that allegedly showed that TSCA's regulatory scheme was outdated, or that it never worked at all. Most notably, the U.S. Government Accountability Office (GAO) was highly critical of TSCA's ability to adequately protect health and environment in the United States. Specifically, the GAO noted that EPA often lacked sufficient data to ensure that potential health risks associated with new and existing chemicals are identified;[260] that EPA did not routinely assess existing chemicals and issued few regulations controlling such chemicals;[261] and that EPA's ability to share data collected under TSCA was limited.[262]

In addition legislation in the European Union (EU) and in Canada has significantly altered international chemical regulation and ostensibly provided models for TSCA reform in the United States. Both the Registration, Evaluation, and Authorization of Chemicals (REACH) Regulation, adopted by the EU in December 2006,[263] and the Canadian Environmental Protection Act (CEPA), adopted by Canada in 1999,[264] represented a significant shift away from the regulatory approach embodied in TSCA. Both REACH and CEPA mandate that manufacturers develop and submit basic health and safety data for new chemicals; require regulatory review and scientific assessment of human health and environmental risks associated with new chemicals;[265] require a regulatory body to categorize and prioritize all existing chemical substances for toxicity assessment;[266] and require screening assessments for chemicals deemed to present a threat to health.[267] In addition, REACH requires chemical companies to develop basic data regarding the physical chemical properties of existing chemicals, shifts responsibility for demonstrating a chemical's safety from regulators to chemical manufacturers, and allows regulators to take precautionary action before all relevant studies become available.

Finally, state and local governments have been stepping in to fill perceived gaps in TSCA. For example, California has passed a bill requiring identification and prioritization of existing hazardous chemicals, and allowing regulators to take action restricting, or banning, troublesome chemicals.[268] This type of state legislation not only could provide a framework for TSCA reform but also could force federal action, as state and local laws create a patchwork of regulations and place an additional regulatory burden on industry.

14.1 Reform Models That Were Proposed and Not Enacted

One program that appeared to provide a basis for TSCA reform in recent years was known as the Chemical Assessment and Management Program (ChAMP). ChAMP addressed the central complaint against TSCA, namely, EPA's inability to collect sufficient information regarding existing chemicals for the purposes of conducting risk assessments and implementing appropriate risk management actions. Under ChAMP, by 2012, EPA would have collected data voluntarily provided by manufacturers and importers of existing chemicals, completed screening-level assessments, produced risk-based prioritizations, and initiated any needed regulatory action on about 6,750 chemicals manufactured or imported into the United States in quantities greater than 25,000 pounds per year. As of March 2009, EPA had developed and posted risk-based prioritizations for 220 high-production volume chemicals and had posted hazard-based prioritizations for 83 chemicals.

Although reform measures consistent with ChAMP appeared to be gaining support from both EPA and industry, anti-chemical pressure groups that sought drastic regulatory change advanced the Kid-Safe Chemicals Act (KSCA) as a preferable reform mechanism. KSCA, which had some similarities to REACH, was on the congressional radar as long ago as 2005 and was reintroduced in 2008 by Senator Frank Lautenberg (D-NJ).[269]

The 2008 version of KSCA (KSCA 2008), which eventually stalled in Congress, shifted the burden of producing health and safety data for affected chemical substances from EPA to manufacturers and importers. Under the original version of KSCA, chemicals could not be manufactured, used, or imported into the United States prior to EPA review of such data and a determination with "reasonable certainty" that the chemical posed no threat to human health or the environment.[270]

In addition, KSCA 2008 would have required EPA to create a priority list categorizing all chemical substances distributed in commerce in the United States. EPA then would have been required to make a safety determination pursuant to a new safety standard established by KSCA and take appropriate action within three years of each chemical's addition to the priority list. Under the KSCA safety standard, existing data would have "provided reasonable certainty that no harm will be caused by aggregate exposure of a fetus, infant, child, worker, or member of any other sensitive group to the chemical substance" and would have been "requisite to protect the public welfare from any known or anticipated adverse effects" in order for the chemical to be deemed "safe."[271] If EPA failed to make a safety determination in a timely fashion, manufacturers would have been required to notify the public that the agency's safety review of the chemical in question was pending. If EPA failed to make a safety determination within five years, the chemical would have been automatically banned.[272]

On April 15, 2010, Senator Frank Lautenberg introduced the Safe Chemicals Act of 2010 in the United States Senate.[273] On July 22, 2010, following stakeholder comments and meetings, Representatives Bobby Rush and Henry Waxman introduced the Toxic Chemicals Safety Act of 2010 in the House of Representatives.[274] Neither bill garnered enough congressional support to get out of committee before the 111th Congress ended on January 3, 2011.

14.2 Passage of the Frank R. Lautenberg Chemical Safety for the 21st Century Act (H.R. 2576)

As indicated in the introduction to this chapter, the Frank R. Lautenberg Chemical Safety for the 21st Century Act (H.R. 2576) became law on June 22, 2016. Its provisions and their effect are discussed in the supplement to this chapter.

15.0 Research Sources

To learn more about the TSCA, here are some additional resources:

- TSCA Hotline: 202-554-1404, 202-554-5603 (fax); E-mail address: tsca-hotline@epa.gov
- Toxic Substances Control Act: http://www4.law.cornell.edu/uscode/15/ch53.html
- Office of Pollution Prevention and Toxics (OPPT) Homepage: http://www.epa.gov/opptintr/index.html
- EPA Asbestos Homepage: http://www.epa.gov/opptintr/asbestos/index.html
- EPA PCB Homepage: http://www.epa.gov/pcb/
- Interagency Testing Committee (includes links to member agencies and published reports): http://www.epa.gov/opptintr/itc/info.htm
- OPPT Microbial Biotechnology Program: http://www.epa.gov/opptintr/biotech/biorule.htm
- OPPT Nonconfidential Information Center (also referred to as the public docket). Open from 8:30 A.M. to 4:30 P.M. Monday through Friday

EST, excluding legal holidays; located in Room B102, EPA West, 1301 Constitution Avenue NW, Washington, DC 20004; E-mail address: oppt.ncic@epa.gov

- OPPT TSCA Test Submissions (TSCATS) Database: http://www.epa .gov/opptintr/chemtest/accsmain.htm

- The TSCA Inventory: http://www.epa.gov/opptintr/chemtest/index.htm

- TSCA Import/Export Requirements: http://www.epa.gov/opptintr/chem test/imex.htm

- TSCA Section 5 Significant New Use Rules: http://www.epa.gov/op ptintr/chemtest/pdflist5.htm

- TSCA Sections 8, 12(b), and 13 data-gathering activities: http://www.epa .gov/opptintr/chemtest/sct8main.htm

- 2002 TSCA Inventory Update Rule: http://www.epa.gov/oppt/iur/iur02/ index.htm

Notes

[1] This chapter is condensed from the *TSCA Handbook* (Government Institutes, 2006, 4th ed.), which was coauthored by the many partners and associates of Dentons US LLP (formerly McKenna Long & Aldridge LLP) who practice in this area. Mr. Landfair, a partner in the firm's San Francisco office, and Mr. Boucher, a partner in the firm's Washington, D.C. office, edited and updated this material.

[2] 40 C.F.R. §§ 717.3(e), 712.3(h), 704.3, 716.3, and 720.3(r).

[3] 40 C.F.R. §§ 704.3, 716.3 and 720.3(t).

[4] 40 C.F.R. § 720.3(t).

[5] 57 Fed. Reg. 38832 (1992).

[6] 40 C.F.R. § 710.4.

[7] TSCA § 3(2)(A). *See also* 40 C.F.R. § 710.2(h).

[8] *See* TSCA § 3(2)(A); 40 C.F.R. § 710.2(h).

[9] 40 C.F.R § 710.2(p).

[10] 40 C.F.R. § 710.2(f).

[11] 40 C.F.R. § 710.2(m).

[12] 40 C.F.R. § 710.4(d)(1).

[13] 40 C.F.R. § 710.2(g).

[14] 40 C.F.R. § 710.4(d)(2).

[15] 40 C.F.R. § 710.4(d)(3)-(7).

[16] 40 C.F.R. § 710.4(d)(8).

[17] 45 Fed. Reg. 50544 (1980).

[18] 51 Fed. Reg. 21438 (1986).

[19] 40 C.F.R. § 710.26.

[20] 40 C.F.R. § 710.28.

[21] 40 C.F.R. § 710, Subpart C.

22 40 C.F.R. § 710.57.
23 75 Fed. Reg. 49656.
24 40 C.F.R. § 720.25(b)(1).
25 40 C.F.R. § 720.25(b)(2).
26 TSCA § 5(d).
27 40 C.F.R. § 720.102.
28 *See* TSCA § 3(2)(B).
29 40 C.F.R. § 723.50.
30 60 Fed. Reg. 16336 (1995).
31 TSCA § 5(h)(4).
32 40 C.F.R. § 723.50(f).
33 40 C.F.R. § 723.50(e)(1).
34 40 C.F.R. § 723.50(h)(2)(ii).
35 40 C.F.R. § 723.50(h)(2)(iii).
36 40 C.F.R. § 723.50(h)(2)(v).
37 40 C.F.R. § 723.50(h)(2)(vi).
38 40 C.F.R. § 723.50(m).
39 60 Fed. Reg. at 16337.
40 40 C.F.R. § 723.50(c)(2).
41 40 C.F.R. § 723.250.
42 40 C.F.R. § 723.250(f).
43 40 C.F.R. § 723.250(g) and (j).
44 60 Fed. Reg. 16326 (1995).
45 *Id.*
46 40 C.F.R. § 723.250(i).
47 40 C.F.R. § 723.175.
48 40 C.F.R. § 720.30(h).
49 40 C.F.R. § 720.36(h)(6).
50 *Id.*
51 43 Fed. Reg. 9256 (1978).
52 National Nanotechnology Initiative, "What Is Nanotechnology?" http://www.nano.gov/html/facts/what IsNano.html (last visited Dec. 1, 2006).
53 NNI, History, http://www.nano.gov/html/about/history.html.
54 15 U.S.C. §§ 7501–7509.
55 NNI, Government Departments and Agencies, http://www.nano.gov/html/about/nniparticipants.html; EPA, Nanotechnology: Research Projects, http://es.epa.gov/ncer/nano/research/index.html.
56 *See, e.g.,* NNI, Applications/Products, http://www.nano.gov/html/facts/appsprod.html; Project on Emerging Nanotechnologies, A Nanotechnology Consumer Products Inventory, http://www.nanotech project.org/44.
57 Lux Research, The Nanotech Report, at iii (4th ed. 2006), available at http://www.luxresearchinc.com/ TNR4_TOC.pdf.
58 *See, e.g.,* Andrew Maynard, *et al.*, "Nature.com, Safe Handling of Nanotechnology" (Nov. 15, 2006), http://www.nature.com/news/2006/061113/full/444267a.html.
59 15 U.S.C. § 2602(2).
60 TSCA defines "chemical substance" as any organic or inorganic substance of a "particular molecular identity," but the latter term is not otherwise defined. 15 U.S.C. § 2602(2)(A). An industry lawyer has

proposed that "particular molecular identity" includes chemical name, molecular formula, and chemical structure. Mark Duvall, "Regulating Nanomaterials under Section 5 of the Toxic Substances Control Act," *Daily Environment Report* 209 at B-1, B-5 (Oct. 30, 2006).

[61] Notable exceptions include carbon, graphite, and diamond (all elemental carbon) and silica, quartz, and cristobalite (all silicon dioxide).

[62] Bureau of National Affairs, "Nanoscale Manufacture of Existing Chemical Does Not Make It 'New,' EPA Official Says," *Daily Environment Report*, No. 224 at A-5, A-6 (Nov. 21, 2006).

[63] *Id.*

[64] 15 U.S.C. § 2605.

[65] EPA, Nanoscale Materials Stewardship Program, http://www.epa.gov/oppt/nano/.

[66] *Id.*

[67] EPA, Nanotechnology Work Group, Nanotechnology White Paper (Dec. 2, 2005 external review draft), available at http://www.epa.gov/osa/pdfs/EPA_nanotechnology_white_paper_external_review_draft_12 -02-2005.pdf.

[68] TSCA § 5(e)(1)(C).

[69] TSCA § 5(e)(2)(A)(i).

[70] TSCA § 5(f)(3)(D).

[71] TSCA §§ 5(a)(1)(B) and 5(a)(2); 40 C.F.R. § 721.

[72] TSCA § 5(a)(2).

[73] 40 C.F.R. § 721.5.

[74] *Id.*

[75] 40 C.F.R. § 721.45.

[76] 40 C.F.R. § 721.30.

[77] 40 C.F.R. § 721.5.

[78] 40 C.F.R. § 721.11. *See supra* at Section 3.4.2.

[79] *See* 40 C.F.R. § 721 *et seq.*

[80] 40 C.F.R. § 721.63.

[81] 40 C.F.R. § 721.72.

[82] 40 C.F.R. § 721.85.

[83] 40 C.F.R. § 721.90.

[84] 40 C.F.R. § 721.80.

[85] 40 C.F.R. § 721.185.

[86] 49 Fed. Reg. 50886 (1984).

[87] 51 Fed. Reg. 23324 (1986).

[88] TSCA § 5(d)(2).

[89] 59 Fed. Reg. 45526 (1994).

[90] 62 Fed. Reg. 17909 (1997); 40 C.F.R. § 725.100.

[91] 40 C.F.R. § 725.421.

[92] 40 C.F.R. § 725.422.

[93] 40 C.F.R. § 725.424.

[94] *See* 40 C.F.R. §§ 725.234 and 235.

[95] 40 C.F.R. § 725.232.

[96] 40 C.F.R. § 725.239.

[97] 40 C.F.R. § 725.238.

[98] TSCA § 2(b)(1).

[99] TSCA § 4(a)(1).

100   TSCA § 4(e).

101   TSCA § 4(e)(1)(A).

102   *See* 40 C.F.R. §§ 712, 716.

103   TSCA § 4(a)(1)(A).

104   *Id.*

105   859 F.2d 977, 989 (D.C. Cir. 1988).

106   TSCA § 4(a)(1)(A)(ii).

107   45 Fed. Reg. 48528 (1980).

108   50 Fed. Reg. 20664 (1985).

109   58 Fed. Reg. 28735 (1993).

110   TSCA § 4(b)(1).

111   TSCA § 4(b)(2)(A).

112   50 Fed. Reg. 20652 (1985).

113   40 C.F.R. § 790.45.

114   40 C.F.R. § 790.45(e), (f).

115   40 C.F.R. § 790.48(a)(3).

116   TSCA § 4(b)(1)(B).

117   40 C.F.R. §§ 796 (Chemical Fate), 797 (Environmental Effects), and 798 (Health Effects).

118   40 C.F.R. § 790.80(b)(1).

119   40 C.F.R. § 790.87.

120   40 C.F.R. § 790.88.

121   40 C.F.R. § 790.90.

122   40 C.F.R. § 790.93(a).

123   54 Fed. Reg. 21237 (1989).

124   TSCA § 4.

125   40 C.F.R. § 791.45(a).

126   TSCA § 4(c)(4)(A).

127   40 C.F.R. § 791.20(a).

128   TSCA § 19(c)(1)(B)(i).

129   *See* 28 U.S.C.A. § 1391(c).

130   TSCA § 19(a)(3)(E).

131   *CMA v. EPA*, 859 F.2d 977, 992 (D.C. Cir. 1988); *Ausimont U.S.A. Inc. v. EPA*, 838 F.2d 93, 96 (3d Cir. 1988); *Shell Chemical Co. v. EPA*, 826 F.2d 295, 297 (5th Cir. 1987).

132   TSCA § 4(f)(2).

133   40 C.F.R. § 712.

134   40 C.F.R. § 712.25.

135   58 Fed. Reg. 63134 (1993).

136   60 Fed. Reg. 31918 (1995).

137   *See* 40 C.F.R. § 710.

138   40 C.F.R. § 717.3(i).

139   40 C.F.R. § 717.12(b).

140   40 C.F.R. § 717.12(c).

141   40 C.F.R. § 717.10(b)(2).

142   63 Fed. Reg. 15765 (1998).

143   40 C.F.R. §§ 716.60, 716.65.

144 Statement of Interpretation and Enforcement Policy, 43 Fed. Reg. 11110 (1978) ("1978 Policy Statement").

145 43 Fed. Reg. 11110-16 (1978).

146 58 Fed. Reg. 37735 (1993) and 60 Fed. Reg. 14756 (1995), respectively.

147 68 Fed. Reg. 33129 (2003).

148 On February 12, 2005, EPA clarified the effective date of the 2003 Reporting Guidance document. As the June 3, 2003, *Federal Register* notice did not include a specific statement regarding the effective date, by standard EPA practice, the Reporting Guidance became effective and applicable on the publication date (June 3, 2003). 70 Fed. Reg. 2162, at 2163 (2005).

149 68 Fed. Reg. 33129, at 33138 (2003).

150 68 Fed. Reg. 33129, at 33137 (2003).

151 68 Fed. Reg. 33129, at 33130 (2003).

152 TSCA § 6(a).

153 TSCA § 6(c)(1)(A)–(D).

154 TSCA § 6(a).

155 40 C.F.R. § 763.

156 *Corrosion Proof Fittings v. EPA*, 987 F.2d 1201 (5th Cir. 1991).

157 53 Fed. Reg. 30566 (1988).

158 60 Fed. Reg. 31919 (1995).

159 50 Fed. Reg. 2006 (1985).

160 40 C.F.R. § 749.68.

161 59 Fed. Reg. 62788 (1994).

162 63 Fed. Reg. 35383 (1998).

163 *Central & Southwest Services, Inc. v. United States EPA*, 220 F.3d 683 (5th Cir. 2000).

164 TSCA § 6(e)(2).

165 40 C.F.R. § 761.

166 40 C.F.R. § 761.79.

167 40 C.F.R. § 761.79.

168 40 C.F.R. § 761.120-135.

169 52 Fed. Reg. 10692 (1987).

170 *Id.* at 10688-90.

171 *Id.* at 10694.

172 40 C.F.R. § 761.180.

173 "Polychlorinated Biphenyls: Notification and Manifesting for PCB Waste Activities," 53 Fed. Reg. 37436 (1988).

174 TSCA § 3(2)(B)(ii).

175 42 Fed. Reg. 64586 (1977).

176 51 Fed. Reg. 15098 (1986).

177 TSCA § 3(2)(B)(vi).

178 42 Fed. Reg. 64586 (1977).

179 TSCA § 9(a)(2).

180 TSCA § 9(b).

181 *Id.*

182 TSCA § 18(a)(2)(A).

183 TSCA § 18(a)(2)(B).

184 TSCA § 11(b).

[185] *See Marshall v. Barlow's, Inc.*, 436 U.S. 307, 325 (1978).

[186] EPA, TSCA Inspection Manual 3-1 to 3-62 (1980).

[187] *See EPA v. Alyeska Pipeline Service Co.*, 836 F.2d 443 (9th Cir. 1988) (holding that EPA is required only to show that the documents or testimony sought by the subpoena are relevant to determining whether there is a problem that may be remedied under TSCA).

[188] As enacted, TSCA provides for civil penalties of up to $25,000 per violation. Beginning March 15, 2004, EPA increased the maximum civil penalty to $32,500 under authority granted by the Debt Collection Improvement Act of 1996, Pub. L. No. 104-134, sec. 31001, 110 Stat. 1321-358 (1996) (31 U.S.C. §§ 3270B-D). 69 Fed. Reg. 7121 (Feb. 13, 2004). This increase applies to violations that occur after March 15, 2004. For violations that occurred between January 30, 1997, and March 15, 2004, the maximum civil penalty is $27,500. *See* 61 Fed. Reg. 69360 (Dec. 31, 1996).

[189] TSCA § 16(a)(2)(B).

[190] 45 Fed. Reg. 59770 (1980).

[191] 45 Fed. Reg. 59773 (1980).

[192] *Id.*

[193] *See* Criminal Liability section below.

[194] 45 Fed. Reg. 59774 (1980).

[195] *3M v. Environmental Protection Agency*, 17 F.3d 1453 (D.C. Cir. 1994).

[196] *Id.* at 1456.

[197] *Id.* at 1458.

[198] *Id.* at 1462.

[199] In the Matter of 3M Company (Minnesota Mining and Mfg.), Docket No. TSCA-88-H-06, TSCA Appeal No. 90-3 (Feb. 28, 1992).

[200] EPA, TSCA Compliance/Enforcement Guidance Manual at 6-3 (July 21, 1984).

[201] 60 Fed. Reg. 66706 (1995) ("Incentives for Self-Policing: Discovery, Disclosure, Correction and Prevention of Violations").

[202] 65 Fed. Reg. 19618.

[203] EPA, Office of Enforcement and Compliance Assurance, Protocol for Conducting Environmental Compliance Audits of Facilities with PCBs, Asbestos, and Lead-based Paint Regulated under TSCA (March 2000).

[204] 65 Fed. Reg. at 19620, 19626.

[205] *Id.* at 19621.

[206] *Id.* at 1925.

[207] *Id.* at 19620.

[208] *Id.* at 19626.

[209] *Id.* at 19624.

[210] 40 C.F.R. § 22.18(a).

[211] 40 C.F.R. § 22.

[212] 40 C.F.R. § 22.19(a).

[213] 40 C.F.R. § 22.22(b).

[214] 40 C.F.R. § 22.33(b).

[215] 40 C.F.R. §§ 22.27, 22.28.

[216] TSCA § 16(b).

[217] *See United States v. International Minerals & Chemical Corp.*, 402 U.S. 558 (1971) (concluding that no actual knowledge of a restrictive shipping regulation was necessary when the shipper was aware that he was shipping sulfuric acid).

218 *See, e.g.*, Hilton Hotels Corp., 467 F.2d 1000 (9th Cir. 1972), *cert. denied,* 409 U.S. 1125 (1973); but cf. *United States v. Beusch,* 596 F.2d 871 (9th Cir. 1979) (existence of company instructions and policies may be considered by the jury in determining whether the employee in fact acted to benefit the corporation).

219 TSCA § 20.

220 *See* 40 C.F.R. § 702.

221 *See* TSCA § 21(b)(2) and (3).

222 TSCA § 21(b)(3).

223 *Id.*

224 TSCA § 21(b)(4)(A).

225 TSCA § 21(b)(4)(B).

226 *See* 50 Fed. Reg. 46825 (1985).

227 19 C.F.R. § 101.1(e).

228 19 C.F.R. § 12.121(a).

229 19 C.F.R. § 101.3(b).

230 65 Fed. Reg. 10701 (2000); 19 C.F.R. § 12.121.

231 19 C.F.R. § 162.1a(a)(2), .1b, .1c.

232 *See* 19 C.F.R. § 101.1(1).

233 40 C.F.R. § 720.25(b).

234 40 C.F.R. § 720.22(b)(1).

235 42 U.S.C. § 6901–6992k.

236 19 C.F.R. § 12.122(c).

237 19 C.F.R. § 12.123(b).

238 19 C.F.R. § 12.123(a).

239 19 C.F.R. § 12.123(c).

240 *Id.*

241 19 C.F.R. § 12.124(a).

242 19 C.F.R. § 12.125.

243 TSCA § 12(a)(1).

244 TSCA § 12(a)(1)(B).

245 45 Fed. Reg. 82844 (1980).

246 *See* 40 C.F.R. § 707.60(c).

247 40 C.F.R. § 707.65(a)(2)(ii).

248 71 Fed. Reg. 66244 (Nov. 14, 2005) (to be codified at 40 C.F.R. Parts 707 and 799), technical correction issued at 71 Fed. Reg. 68750 (Nov. 28, 2006).

249 40 C.F.R. § 707.65(a)(2)(i).

250 40 C.F.R. § 707.65(a)(1)–(3).

251 40 C.F.R. § 707.65(a)(3).

252 40 C.F.R. § 707.63(b).

253 40 C.F.R. § 707.70(a), (b).

254 45 Fed. Reg. 82844 (1980).

255 40 C.F.R. § 707.60(b).

256 71 Fed. Reg. 66244 (Nov. 14, 2005), technical correction issued at 71 Fed. Reg. 68750 (Nov. 28, 2006).

257 40 C.F.R. § 707.75(a), (b).

258 40 C.F.R. § 707.75(b).

259 40 C.F.R. § 707.75(c).

260 Government Accountability Office, GAO No. 05-458, "Chemical Regulation: Options Exist to Improve EPA's Ability to Assess Health Risks and Manage Its Chemical Review Program" (June 2005), pp. 10–18, available at http://www.gao.gov/new.items/d05458.pdf.

261 *Id.* at 18–31.

262 *Id.* at 31–34.

263 Parliament and Council Regulation 1907/2006, 2006 O.J. (L 396) 1, *available at* http://eur-lex.europa.eu/LexUriServ/LexUriServ.do?uri = CONSLEG:2006R1907:20081012:EN:PDF.

264 Canadian Environmental Protection Act, S.C. 1999, c. 33 (CEPA), *available at* http://laws.justice.gc.ca/en/C-15.31/index.html.

265 *Id.* at § 68.

266 *Id.* at §§ 73, 76.

267 *Id.* at § 74.

268 California Green Chemistry Initiative, SB 509, AB 189.

269 Kid-Safe Chemicals Act of 2008, S. 3040, 110th Cong. (2008).

270 *Id.* at §§ 2(b)(2)(B), 2(b)(2)(C).

271 *Id.* at § 501(5).

272 *Id.* at § 504(b)(1).

273 S. 3209, 111th Cong. (2010).

274 H.R. 5820, 111th Cong. (2010).

Summary of H.R. 2576

Frank R. Lautenberg Chemical Safety for the 21st Century Act

Michael D. Boucher and Stanley W. Landfair

Current Status

On May 24, 2016, the House of Representatives passed the Frank R. Lautenberg Chemical Safety for the 21st Century Act (H.R. 2576) by a vote of 403 yeas to 12 nays. The Senate passed the bill by voice vote on June 7. On the same day, Senate Republicans and Democrats entered separate bill analyses into the June 7, 2016, Congressional Record, to shape interpretation of Congress's intent. The President signed the bill into law on June 22, 2016, as Public Law No. 114-182.

On June 29, EPA posted a First Year Implementation Plan. On June 30, EPA hosted a webinar to provide an overview. The EPA webinar materials continue to be available on the Agency's website at https://www.epa.gov/assessing-and-managing-chemicals-under-tsca/frank-r-lautenberg-chemical-safety-21st-century-act. Also available at the site are a summary of the amendments and a printout of the amended Toxic Substances Control Act, as it now appears in the United States Code at 50 U.S.C. Chapter 53.

A summary of the changes to TSCA follows. In describing the changes, we use the terms "Toxic Substances Control Act" or "TSCA" to refer to the Toxic Substances Control Act, as enacted in 1976; "Act" or the "amendments" to refer to the legislative vehicle that effects the amendments; and the term "amended TSCA" or "amended law" or to refer to the Toxic Substances Control Act, as amended.

It is important to note that most of the changes are not self-implementing, but rather will require EPA to promulgate regulations under a notice-and-comment rulemaking process. Thus, many of the amendments may not take effect for several years.

Major Changes to TSCA

Changes to TSCA Section 4, Testing of Chemical Substances and Mixtures.
The Act adds to the authority conferred to EPA under TSCA to issue test rules,
providing additional new authority to require testing of a chemical substance or
mixture by rule, by order (which is new), or by consent agreement, as needed, in
the following cases:

(1) to review a pre-manufacture notice ("PMN") or significant new use
notice ("SNUN") submitted by an importer or manufacturer for a new
chemical or a new use, respectively, under section 5 of TSCA;

(2) to implement a requirement in a rule, order, or consent agreement for a
PMN or SNUN substance under section 5(e) or 5(f);

(3) to perform a risk evaluation of any substance that EPA has designated as
a "high priority" for risk evaluation under new section 6(b);

(4) to implement a requirement contained in a rule under new section 6(a)
for a high-priority substance that has undergone risk evaluation under
new section 6(b);

(5) to prioritize a substance for risk evaluation under new section 6(b), with
limitations;

(6) at the request of another federal agency under another federal law to
meet regulatory testing needs regarding toxicity and exposure; and

(7) to determine whether a chemical substance, mixture, or article imported
or manufactured for export only presents an unreasonable risk of injury
to health or the environment while in the United States.

When exercising its new authority to require testing by order, EPA must
prepare a "statement of need" that explains, among other things, why the Agency
is using an order instead of a rule or consent agreement. EPA may issue test rules
and orders to current and prospective importers, manufacturers, and processors,
as appropriate.

The amendments provide that EPA must employ a tiered screening and
testing process, unless the Agency can justify advanced testing without screening-
level testing. The Act similarly requires EPA to establish a new TSCA program
to develop and implement alternative test methods and strategies to reduce,
refine, or replace vertebrate animal testing.

Changes to Section 5, Manufacturing and Processing Notification. The
Act does not change the requirement to for a manufacturer to submit a pre-
manufacturing notification ("PMN") prior to importing or manufacturing a new

chemical, the requirement to submit a Significant New Use Notification ("SNUN") prior to importing, manufacturing, or processing a chemical for a significant new use; the applicable EPA review period for PMNs and SNUNs; or the current PMN and SNUN exemptions. The amended law does add a requirement, however, for EPA to make one of the following affirmative determinations, with respect to every PMN and SNUN, that:

(1) the PMN or SNUN substance "presents" an unreasonable risk of injury to health or the environment, ignoring costs and other non-risk factors and including any unreasonable risk to potentially exposed or susceptible subpopulation that EPA identifies as relevant ("Unreasonable Risk"), in which case EPA must propose an immediately effective section 6 rule under section 5(f) or issue an order under section 5(f);

(2) EPA cannot perform a "reasoned evaluation" of health and environmental effects based on the available information, in which case EPA must impose a section 5(e) order;

(3) in the absence of sufficient information to make a "reasoned evaluation" of health and environmental effects, the PMN or SNUN substance "may present" an Unreasonable Risk, in which case EPA also must impose a section 5(e) order;

(4) the PMN or SNUN substance will have substantial production with substantial environmental releases or with significant or substantial human exposure, in which case EPA again must impose a section 5(e) order; or

(5) the PMN or SNUN substance will not present an Unreasonable Risk, in which case the submitter may commence importation, manufacturing, or processing, as appropriate.

To implement the new PMN and SNUN determinations required of EPA, the Act makes significant changes to section 5(e) orders, which will, however, continue to broadly prohibit or limit any combination of TSCA-regulated activities (importing, manufacturing, processing, distributing, using, or disposing of) of PMN and SNUN substances. The amendments take away EPA's discretion to use section 5(e) orders, and requires instead that the Agency impose section 5(e) orders in three specific cases, and eliminates both proposed section 5(e) orders and the related procedures for submitters who object to them. The end result is that EPA is likely to issue many more section 5(e) orders than it does under the current TSCA.

Similarly, the Act makes significant changes to section 5(f), to ensure that EPA uses it when the Agency finds that a PMN or SNUN substance presents an

Unreasonable Risk. Under the new section 5(f), EPA retains the current option to propose an immediately effectively section 6 rule, but the current proposed orders are replaced with directly applicable ones, and gone are procedures for submitters who object to proposed orders. Also, new section 5(f) orders can restrict activities with a PMN or SNUN substance and are not limited to prohibitions. The end result is that EPA is likely to propose more immediately effective section 6 rules and issue more orders under section 5(f), but this is not hard to do, since EPA has not acted under section 5(f) since the 1980s.

Within 90 days after taking action against a PMN or SNUN substance under section 5(e) or 5(f), the amended law also requires EPA to initiate a significant new use rule ("SNUR") or publish the reasons for not doing so. This is a new deadline and supersedes the one in EPA's current SNUR regulations. 40 C.F.R. § 721.160(d). In addition, before EPA takes action under section 5(e) or 5(f) to address workplace exposures, the Agency is to consult with the U.S. Occupational Safety and Health Administration ("OSHA") "to the extent practicable." Given the deadlines for EPA to review PMNs and SNUNs and to act under sections 5(e) and 5(f) in specific cases, it is not clear how much time the Agency will have to consult with OSHA as a practical matter.

If EPA makes either of the determinations in item (5) and (6) listed above (that the PMN or SNUN substance will not present an Unreasonable Risk or is a "low-hazard substance") before the end of the PMN or SNUN review period, then the submitter may commence importation, manufacturing, or processing, as appropriate, upon EPA's determination and before the end of the review period. If EPA fails to make a required PMN or SNUN determination on time, the Agency must refund the fee paid by the submitter. In addition, although 40 C.F.R. § 721.45 already allows EPA to require a SNUN for a substance imported or processed in an article or category of articles, the bill expressly authorizes the Agency to do so upon an affirmative finding in a SNUR that "reasonable potential for exposure to the substance through the article or category of articles" justifies a SNUN.

Changes to Section 6, Prioritization, Risk Evaluation, and Regulation of Chemical Substances and Mixtures. The Act requires EPA to establish by rule a risk evaluation process, under which the Agency will determine whether chemical substances present an Unreasonable Risk. The amended law also requires EPA to establish by rule a separate risk-based screening process, under which the Agency will designate chemical substances as "high-priority substances" for risk evaluations or "low-priority substances" for which risk evaluations are not warranted at the time. EPA will publish and take public comments on all proposed designations.

Initially, EPA will conduct and publish risk evaluations for ten chemical substances drawn from the 2014 update of the TSCA Work Plan for Chemical

Assessments. Thereafter, EPA will conduct and publish risk evaluations for chemical substances that EPA has designated as high-priority substances. In addition, an importer or manufacturer of a substance may ask EPA at any time to evaluate the risks of the substance, if the requester agrees to cover the costs. Industry-requested evaluations must be at least 25 percent of EPA's caseload if industry makes a sufficient number of requests and cannot exceed 50 percent of EPA's caseload, excluding industry requests to evaluate the risks of substances drawn from the 2014 update of the TSCA Work Plan for Chemical Assessments.

By three and half years following the Act's enactment into law, EPA must be conducting risk evaluations for at least 20 high-priority substances and must have designated at least 20 chemicals as low-priority substances. Subsequently, EPA must designate high-priority substances and conduct risk evaluations at a pace consistent with its ability to meet the applicable deadlines for risk evaluations. EPA will publish and take public comments on the scope of all prospective risk evaluations and all draft risk evaluations prior to their finalization.

If EPA determines that a substance presents an Unreasonable Risk following a risk evaluation, the Act requires EPA to promulgate a rule that applies requirements to the substance until it no longer presents an Unreasonable Risk. The requirements do not need to be the "least burdensome" ones available. Nevertheless, the rule must consider (1) benefits of the substance, (2) reasonably ascertainable economic consequences of the rule, and (3) the availability of technically and economically feasible alternatives.

The rule must exempt replacement parts for complex durable goods and complex consumer goods that are designed prior to publication of the rule, unless the replacement parts contribute significantly to the unreasonable risks. In addition, the rule must prohibit or restrict articles or categories of articles containing the substance only to the extent necessary to address the identified risks from exposure to the substance through the article or category of articles.

The rule can exempt specific uses of a substance that meets specific criteria: the use is critical and has no technically and economically feasible safer alternatives; compliance with a requirement of the rule would significantly disrupt the national economy, national security, or critical infrastructure; or the use as compared to reasonably available alternatives provides a substantial benefit to health, the environment, or public safety. All exemptions will be time-limited.

Finally, the amended section 6 now mandates fast-track regulation by rule, without any risk evaluation, of substances drawn from the 2014 update of the TSCA Work Plan for Chemical Assessments that are persistent, bio-accumulative, and toxic; are not metals or metal compounds; and for which EPA has not completed a Work Plan Problem Formulation, initiated a review under section

5, or entered into a testing consent agreement under section 4. The covered substances must satisfy criteria for general population, susceptible subpopulation, or environmental exposure. Fast-track regulation of covered substances must reduce exposure "to the extent possible." A substance that otherwise requires fast-track regulation by rule can escape it within the first 90 days following enactment of the Act into law if EPA designates the substance as a high-priority substance for risk evaluation or an importer or manufacturer of the substance asks EPA to perform a risk evaluation of it, except that any rule prohibiting or restricting the substance following EPA's risk evaluation still must reduce exposure to the substance to the extent possible.

Changes to Section 8 Requirements for Reporting and Retaining Information. The Act makes no changes to sections 8(c) (records of allegations of significant adverse reactions), 8(d) (health and safety study reporting), or 8(e) (substantial risk reporting). The Act does make significant changes, however, to sections 8(a) (reporting) and 8(b) (inventory), as follows.

The amended TSCA slightly alters EPA's rulemaking authority in section 8(a), under which the Agency currently administers the Preliminary Assessment Information Rule and the Chemical Data Reporting Rule. The Act allows section 8(a) rules to impose differing requirements on manufacturers (including importers) and processors and requires rules to include the necessary level of detail for reporting and the proper manner for reporting exposure and use information. The Act discourages "unnecessary and duplicative" reporting, seeks to minimize compliance costs for small businesses, and directs reporting obligations to those most likely to have relevant information. In addition, the amended TSCA now requires EPA to propose a rule to limit reporting for importers and manufacturers of inorganic byproducts that are recycled, reprocessed, or reused.

In amended section 8(b), the Act codifies several historical conventions used to name chemicals for the TSCA Chemical Substance Inventory ("Inventory"). In addition, the amendments require EPA to promulgate a rule under which importers, manufacturers, and processors will notify the Agency about substances that the companies have imported, manufactured, or processed for a non-exempt commercial purpose during the 10-year period immediately preceding the enactment of the Act into law. EPA will then designate as "active substances" all substances on the Inventory for which the Agency receives notices. EPA will designate the remaining substances on the Inventory as "inactive substances." EPA will not remove any substances from the Inventory.

Before EPA requires reporting of active substances, the Agency will establish an interim list of active substances "for the purpose of section 6(b)," although the risk evaluation process in new section 6(b) does not mention active substances, interim or otherwise. Under earlier versions of the Act, EPA would have selected substances for risk evaluation from the universe of active substances. Therefore, we infer from the reference to section 6(b) in new section 8 that Congress intends EPA to perform risk evaluations on active substances, even though new section 6(b) itself says nothing at all about such requirements for active substances.

After EPA has required reporting of active substances, the Agency will establish, publish, and maintain separate active and inactive substance lists (and presumably get rid of the interim active substance list). EPA will continue to maintain the Inventory in two parts, with a confidential portion and a non-confidential portion available to the public. As part of the rulemaking for reporting on active substances, however, the Act directs EPA to require importers, manufacturers, and processors to assert and substantiate any claims of confidentiality for substances on the confidential portion of the Inventory. In addition, the Agency will establish an elaborate program to review claims of confidentiality made by importers, manufacturers, and processors. The amended section 8(b) is unusually focused on claims of confidentiality for chemical identities.

The Act establishes a new notice requirement for persons who want to import, manufacture, or process an inactive substance for a non-exempt commercial purpose. Upon receiving notice, EPA will designate the substance as an active substance, review any claim of confidentiality for the chemical identity, and prioritize the substance for a risk evaluation under new section 6(b) as EPA "determines to be necessary."

Changes to 14, Confidential Information. The Act replaces section 14 of TSCA with an entirely new text. New section 14 protects trade secrets and other confidential business information from disclosure, provided that such information is submitted to EPA for reasons pursuant to TSCA and satisfy new procedural requirements.

New section 14(b) identifies information that is never protected from disclosure: information from health and safety studies; aggregated production volumes or, alternatively, production volumes expressed as ranges; general process descriptions; and otherwise confidential information about a substance or mixture that EPA will ban or phase out under a new section 6(a) rule, with exceptions.

New section 14(c) also requires claims of confidentiality to be asserted, to include a supporting certification statement, and, ultimately, to be substantiated in accordance with new or existing EPA rules. *See, e.g.,* 40 C.F.R. § 2.208. For claims of confidentiality for chemical identities, a structurally descriptive generic name is required, and it must comply with new guidance that EPA will develop.

New section 14(c) further identifies information that is presumed to be confidential and is not subject to substantiation requirements (but must still be claimed as confidential and include the supporting certification statement): specific information about processes; marketing and sales information; supplier and customer identities; detailed formulas for mixtures; specific information about uses of substances and mixtures; specific production volumes; and the specific chemical identity of substances claimed as confidential in a PMN, before the substance is first offered for commercial distribution.

In addition, new section 14(d) identifies many circumstances under which EPA shall disclose otherwise confidential information to specific people for specific purposes: to officers and employees of the United States for law enforcement purposes or to carry out federal health or environmental laws; to contractors of the United States and their employees to perform work related to TSCA and subject to conditions specified by the Agency; to anyone to protect health or the environment against an unreasonable risk; to state and local governments, on request, to administer or enforce a law, if the requester has an agreement with EPA to adequately protect the confidential information; to federal or state health or environmental professionals or to treating physicians or nurses in non-emergency situations, if the recipient provides a statement of need and signs a confidentiality agreement with EPA that satisfies certain conditions; to a variety of people in emergency situations, and the submitter of the confidential information may ask the recipient to provide a statement of need, sign a confidentiality agreement, and provide both documents to EPA as soon as practicable; to anyone in connection with a proceeding under TSCA, provide that disclosure protects confidentiality to the extent practicable without impairing the proceeding; and to anyone if any other federal law requires disclosure.

For confidential information that is exempt from substantiation requirements, confidentiality lasts until the submitter withdraws the claim or until EPA becomes aware that the information no longer qualifies for confidential treatment. All other confidential information is protected for ten years, unless the submitter withdraws the claim or EPA discovers that the information no longer qualifies for protection. Before the initial ten-year protection period ends, the submitter may request a ten-year "extension" (a renewal), and there is no limit on the number of consecutive extensions that a submitter may request.

EPA can ask a submitter to re-substantiate a claim of confidentiality made before or after the Act has become law after a substance is designated as a high-priority substance under new section 6(b), when an inactive substances becomes an active substances under section 8(b), or if EPA determines that disclosure of confidential information would help the Agency to conduct a risk evaluation or issue a rule for a substance that presents an unreasonable risk under section 6. In addition, EPA must request re-substantiation when the public requests a copy of confidential information, if the Agency believes that the information no longer qualifies for protection, or when EPA determines that any substances presents an unreasonable risk under new section 6(b).

Changes to Section 18, Preemption. The approach toward preemption of state action is addressed under the Act in four ways: (1) *Permanent preemption*, where state action in the regulation of a chemical is permanently preempted either based on the type of state action or because EPA finds through a risk evaluation that the chemical is safe or takes final action to address the chemical's risks; (2) *Pause,* where state action is paused when EPA's risk evaluation is underway, but lifted when EPA completes the evaluation or misses a deadline for its completion; (3) *Exemptions*, whereby states can apply for and obtain waivers from both permanent and "pause" preemption, allowing states to regulate chemicals in a manner that would otherwise be preempted or when EPA is in the process of evaluating the chemical or has regulated the chemical, if certain conditions are met; and (4) *Enforcement*, whereby states may effectively "co-enforce" in certain circumstances, and are prohibited from enforcing state laws under other circumstances. These approaches are addressed in more detail below.

Permanent Preemption. As a general matter, the Act prohibits states from requiring study data already required by EPA. The Act further prohibits states from restricting the manufacture, processing, distribution, or use of a chemical, if EPA considered that manufacture, processing, distribution, or use in a risk evaluation, and EPA concluded that the chemical is safe or established a rule to address the chemical's risks and such rule is effective. The Act permits states to regulate other manufacturing, processing, distribution or use, however, if they are not covered by the scope of the risk evaluation. Similarly, states cannot require notification of a significant new use for which a SNUN is required. On the other hand, the Act allows EPA to waive this preemption, allowing states to impose such regulations if, among other factors, peer-reviewed scientific evidence supports regulation and regulation would not burden interstate commerce.

Pause. The Act prohibits states from establishing new restrictions on the manufacture, processing, distribution, or use of a "high-priority" substance during the period that EPA is conducting a risk evaluation. This "high-priority pause" applies only to the manufacturing, processing, distribution, and uses included in the scope of EPA's risk evaluation. The Act allows states to impose restrictions on low-priority substances, and to continue to enforce regulations that are in effect at the time that EPA begins an evaluation. EPA must waive this preemption, allowing states to impose new regulations, if the state enacts its statute or proposes or finalizes an administrative action within 18 months after EPA initiated the prioritization or by the date EPA publishes the scope of the risk evaluation (whichever is first) or if, among other factors, peer-reviewed scientific evidence supports the state's restriction and the restriction would not burden interstate commerce.

Enforcement. The Act allows state governments to adopt certain requirements and prohibitions, including requirements for reporting, monitoring, and "other information obligations," that differ from those imposed by EPA. States may also enact certain requirements and prohibitions related to water or air quality or waste treatment or disposal. The Act also allows states to impose regulatory requirements identical to those imposed by EPA, but the total of penalties imposed by EPA and a state may not exceed those that EPA could have imposed under TSCA. Where EPA imposes a penalty, a state may not assess a penalty for the same violation. States can, however, enforce any chemical restrictions imposed by April 22, 2016, and may take any action under state laws in effect on August 31, 2003. The Act's preemption provisions do not preempt any civil cause of action, such as for personal injury, wrongful death, negligence, strict liability, or failure to warn.

Changes to 26, Administration. The amended law allows EPA to collect up to $25 million in fees each year, in addition to congressional appropriations, to defray the costs of carrying out activities under TSCA sections 4, 5, 6, and 14. Fees are no longer capped at $2,500, or $100 for small businesses, and instead may increase over time to ensure that they cover up to 25 percent of EPA's relevant costs. Fees must nonetheless be "sufficient and not more than reasonably necessary" to defray costs. Congressional appropriations cannot fall below 2014 levels, to prevent fees from being used to replace appropriations.

For purposes of carrying out TSCA sections 4, 5, and 6, the amendments require EPA to follow minimum scientific standards, make decisions based on the weight of scientific evidence, and consider "reasonably available" information about substances and mixtures. In addition, the amended law now requires EPA to develop many news policies, procedures, and guidance that the Agency will need to carry out TSCA, as amended.

The Act requires EPA to report to Congress on the Agency's ability to carry out amended section 6 and to publish annual plans that inform the public of the schedule and resources necessary to complete risk evaluations under that provision. Lastly, the Act establishes a new Science Advisory Committee on Chemicals to provide independent advice to the Agency about implementing the amended TSCA.

Minor Changes to TSCA

Changes to Section 3, Definitions. The Act adds to TSCA three new terms: "conditions of use," guidance," and "potentially exposed or susceptible subpopulation."

Changes to Section 12, Exports. The Act adds to current section 12(c) regarding exports of elemental mercury, prohibiting the export of certain mercury compounds.

Changes to Section 16, Penalties. The Act updates civil penalties for violations of TSCA, increases criminal penalties, and establishes a new category of criminal penalties for "knowing and willful" violations when a person knows at the time of the violation that it will place any person in "imminent danger of death or serious bodily injury."

Changes to Section 19, Judicial Review. The Act adds deadlines to seek judicial review of low-priority designations under new section 6(b) and makes the U.S. Courts of Appeals for the District of Columbia the exclusive venue for such an action.

Insignificant Changes

The following provisions of TSCA were amended in minor ways, but not in ways that affect operational requirements: Section 2 Findings, Policy, and Intent; Section 7, Imminent Hazards; Section 9, Relationship to Other Federal Laws; Section 20, Citizens' Civil Actions; Section 25, Studies (repealed); Section 28, State Programs.

Provisions with No Changes

The following provisions were not changed: Section 10, Research, Development, Collection, Dissemination, and Utilization of Data; Section 11, Inspections and Subpoenas; Section 13, Entry into Customs Territory of the United States [Imports]; Section 15, Prohibited Acts; Section 17, Specific Enforcement and Seizure; Section 21 Citizens' Petitions; Section 22, National Defense Waiver; Section 23, Employee Protection; Section 24, Employment Effects; Section 27, Development and Evaluation of Test Methods; Section 29, Authorization of Appropriations; and Section 30, Annual Report.

Chapter 13

Pesticides

Marshall Lee Miller
Baise & Miller
Washington, D.C.

1.0 Background to the Federal Regulation of Pesticides

The benefits of pesticides, herbicides, rodenticides, and other economic poisons are well known. They have done much to spare us from the ravages of disease, crop infestations, noxious animals, and choking weeds. They have been a major reason why U.S. agriculture has grown to feed the world. Over the past half century, however, beginning with Rachel Carson's book *Silent Spring* in 1962,[1] there has been a growing awareness of the hazards as well as the benefits of these chemicals, which may be harmful to man and the balance of nature. Pesticides are poisons; they are intended to be.

The ability to balance these often conflicting effects is hampered by continuing scientific uncertainties. We still lack full understanding of environmental side effects, the subcellular mechanism of human carcinogens, and a host of other factors that are important for a proper evaluation of pesticide suitability. Yet scientific progress, especially in the genetic area, has been so rapid over the past several decades that we are now realizing that many of our previous assumptions have been wrong, or at least oversimplified. The best scientific knowledge is now more important than ever.[2]

The nature of pesticides is itself changing. Where once the term was almost synonymous with "agricultural chemicals," now many pesticides are not chemicals at all. One listing of pesticide data from the U.S. Environmental Protection Agency (EPA) on 19 active ingredients registered revealed only eight conventional chemicals, while 11 were biopesticides.[3] Moreover, agriculture is yielding to public health as the center of pesticide controversy, with debates on West Nile virus and malaria even leading some commentators to call for bringing back DDT.

This is not primarily a chapter about pesticides, or even methods of pest-control; it is a chapter about the regulation of pesticides.

1.1 Overview

Public concern regarding pesticides was a principal cause of the rise of the environmental movement in the United States in the late 1960s and early 1970s. Rachel Carson's slim opus was compared in revolutionary impact to Harriet Beecher Stowe's *Uncle Tom's Cabin* a century before. It was therefore probably the most important reason for the creation of the EPA.[4] In the first couple of years of the agency, I can personally attest, pesticide issues dominated the EPA priority agenda, more than any other subject, maybe more than all the others put together.[5]

While public attention since then has shifted to various other environmental media, the pesticide issue—with its implications for the safety of the food supply and of people in the agricultural area—is still central to the public's notion of environmental protection. Indeed, the fluctuation of interest in this topic is often an accurate barometer of public distrust in the official environmental agencies.[6]

In the past few years this distrust has taken a new and different form. EPA is now being criticized not only by the environmentalists for not doing enough, but also by others for ordering unnecessarily costly tests or extreme limitations. At the heart of both views is the belief that the agency's actions are not always firmly based on good science—a skepticism that is, of course, by no means limited to EPA's pesticide program.

I believe the best way to understand an organization or a law is to trace how it evolves. For some readers or the "just tell me what I have to do to comply" ilk, feel free to skip over this history and go straight to section 3.0 following.

1.2 Early Efforts at Pesticide Regulations

Chemical pesticides have been subject to some degree of federal control since the Insecticide Act of 1910.[7] This law was concerned primarily with protecting pesticide purchasers, usually farmers, from ineffective products and deceptive labeling. It contained neither a federal registration requirement nor any significant safety standards. The relatively insignificant usage of pesticides before World War II made regulation a matter of low priority.

The war dramatically stimulated both the use and the development of pesticides. DDT became a world hero and undoubtedly saved millions of lives. Pesticide use in farm production made the agrochemical industry a key sector in the economy. The resulting effects on public health and farm production made pesticides a virtual necessity.

In 1947, Congress enacted a more comprehensive statute, the Federal Insecticide, Fungicide, and Rodenticide Act (FIFRA).[8] This law required that pesticides distributed in interstate commerce be registered with the U.S. Department of Agriculture (USDA). It also established rudimentary labeling requirements. This act, like its predecessor, was concerned mostly with product effectiveness; the statute did, however, declare pesticides *misbranded* if they were necessarily harmful to man, animals, or vegetation (except weeds) even when properly used.[9]

Three major defects in the new law soon became evident. First, the registration process was largely an empty formality since the secretary of agriculture could not refuse registration even to a chemical he deemed highly dangerous. He could register "under protest," but this had no legal effect on the registrant's ability to manufacture or distribute the product. Second, there was no regulatory control over the use of a pesticide contrary to its label, as long as the label itself complied with the statutory requirements.[10] Third, the secretary's only remedy against a hazardous product was a legal action for misbranding or adulteration, and—this was crucial—the difficult burden of proof was on the government.

The statute nevertheless remained unchanged for almost two decades. Pesticides were not then a matter of public concern, and the USDA was under little pressure to tighten regulatory control. Only a handful of registrations under protest were made during that period, and virtually all of these actions involved minor companies with ineffective products. The one notable lawsuit involving a fraudulently ineffective product was lost by the USDA at the district court level and mooted by the court of appeals.[11]

In 1964 the USDA persuaded Congress to remedy two of these three perceived defects: The registration system was revised to permit the secretary to refuse to register a new product or to cancel an existing registration, and the burden of proof for safety and effectiveness was shifted to the registrant.[12] These changes considerably strengthened the act, in theory, but made little difference in practice. The Pesticide Registration Division, a section of USDA's Agricultural Research Service, was understaffed—in 1966 the only toxicologist on the staff was the division's director—and the division was buried deep in a bureaucracy concerned primarily with promoting agriculture and facilitating the registration of pesticides. The cancellation procedure was seldom if ever used,[13] and there was still no legal sanction against a consumer applying the chemical for an unapproved or delisted use.

The growth of the environmental movement in the late 1960s, with its concern about the widespread use of agricultural chemicals, overwhelmed the meager resources of the Pesticide Division. Environmental groups filed a barrage of lawsuits demanding the cancellation or suspension of a host of major pesticides, such as DDT, aldrin-dieldrin, mirex, and the herbicide 2,4,5-T. This demanding situation required a new approach to pesticide regulations. (These cases will be discussed more fully in section 8 of this chapter.)

1.3 Pesticide Regulation Transferred to the Environmental Protection Agency

On December 2, 1970, President Richard Nixon signed Reorganization Order No. 3 creating the EPA.[14] Note carefully this often-forgotten point—the EPA was created not by Congress, as many assume, but by a presidential ukase from Nixon. This order assigned to EPA the functions and many of the personnel previously under Interior, Agriculture, and other government departments. EPA thereby inherited from USDA not only the Pesticides Division but also a host of environmental lawsuits against the secretary of agriculture.

Thus, within the first two or three months of its inception, the new agency was compelled to make a number of tough regulatory decisions. EPA's outlook was considerably influenced by judicial decisions in several of the cases it had inherited from USDA.[15] These court decisions consistently held that the responsible federal agencies had not sufficiently examined the health and environmental problems associated with pesticide use. These cases helped to shape, indeed force, EPA's pesticide policy during its formative period and ever since.[16]

2.0 Overview of FIFRA and Amendments

FIFRA is one of the most federal of the environmental laws. Unlike the air, water, and some other statutes that defer or delegate considerable responsibility to the states, at least in theory, under FIFRA states and localities are given little scope. This is deliberate; from the beginning, pesticide regulation has rested on a national system of registration and labeling. Nevertheless, there is a limited state role in registration and an ongoing, heated legal controversy over the authority of localities (and tort plaintiffs suing under state law) to impose conditions on pesticides beyond those set forth by EPA.[17] This issue of the extent of federal preemption has become the central focus of FIFRA litigation over the past several decades and, as we shall see, has been raised all the way to the Supreme Court.

FIFRA also interacts with the Food and Drug Administration (FDA) in the areas of pesticide residues and disinfectants and with the Occupational Safety and Health Administration as it applies to manufacturing and field workers using or exposed to pesticides.[18]

2.1 Organization of the Pesticide Program within EPA

Within EPA the pesticide program is under an assistant administrator, one of about a dozen (the number varies from time to time) in the agency. In this case it is the assistant administrator for Chemical Safety and Pollution Prevention (OCSPP). If this sounds unfamiliar, it is because the office was renamed in April

2010 from the prior and more descriptive Office of Prevention, Pesticides, and Toxic Substances (OPPTS).

The assistant administrator for OCSPP is a presidential appointee, subject to Senate confirmation, on par with the heads of EPA's air, water, hazardous waste, and other programs, as well as with the head of OSHA in the Department of Labor.

In the Obama administration, the first AA for the OCSPP was Steve Owens, a lawyer who served for many years as head of the state of Arizona's environmental program. In January 2012 the president nominated Jim Jones, a long-time EPA economist, to replace him. He has an M.A. from the University of California at Santa Barbara and a B.A. from the University of Maryland, both in economics. For an extraordinarily long 19 months the Senate failed to act on his nomination, so he was in a somewhat crippled acting capacity. It is worth noting that for a short time Jones had been head of the pesticide office that now comes under him.

The previous director of the Pesticide Program itself was Steven Bradbury, a Ph.D. in toxicology and entomology. Since 2014 the director has been Jack Housenger. The pesticide office has an annual budget of approximately $150 million and 850 employees, making it the largest EPA headquarters' program office. The "umbrella" organization OCSPP has another $110 million and 350 employees in its other programs.[19]

2.2 Background to FIFRA and the 1972 FEPCA

FIFRA,[20] as amended by the Federal Environmental Pesticide Control Act (FEPCA) of October 1972 and the series of FIFRA amendments since then,[21] is a complex statute. Terms sometimes have a meaning different from, or even directly contrary to, normal English usage. For example, the term "suspension" really means an immediate ban on a pesticide, while the harsher-sounding term "cancellation" indicates only the initiation of administrative proceedings that can drag on for many years. The repeated amending of FIFRA reflects congressional, industry, and environmentalist conflicts and often discontent about the federal control of pesticide distribution, sale, and use.

The amendments to FIFRA in 1972, known as FEPCA,[22] amounted to a virtual rewriting of the law. FEPCA, not the 1947 FIFRA, is the real pesticide law today. A personal note: We at the EPA debated in 1972 whether to continue calling the law FIFRA or to refer to it, more accurately, as FEPCA. We opted for "FIFRA" to preserve the sense of continuity in pesticide regulation. The changes were considered necessary to

- strengthen the enforcement provisions of FIFRA,

- shift the legal emphasis from labeling and efficacy to health and environment,

- provide for greater flexibility in controlling dangerous chemicals,

- extend the scope of federal law to cover intrastate registrations and the specific uses of a given pesticide, and

- streamline the administrative appeals process.

EPA was given expanded authority over the field use of pesticides, and several categories of registration were created that give EPA more flexibility in fashioning appropriate control over pesticides.

2.3 Subsequent FIFRA Amendments: An Overview

Amendments to FIFRA since 1972 have been a battleground between environmentalists and various farmer and agricultural chemical interests. The fight has been virtually a stalemate; the outcome has oscillated back and forth between one group and the other, while the actual amount of change has been relatively small.[23]

The 1975 amendments are typical. They are significant not for what they actually changed but for the motivations that prompted them—a counterattack by the agricultural and agrochemical industries. Not surprisingly, EPA viewed these amendments as, at best, unnecessary and, at worst, a further encumbrance upon an already complicated administrative procedure. EPA was required to consult with the Department of Agriculture and the agricultural committees of Congress before issuing proposed or final standards regarding pesticides. On the other hand, environmentalists were pleased that EPA got the authority to require that farmers take (largely meaningless) exams before being certified as pesticide applicators.

By 1978 Congress had to address the near collapse of EPA's pesticide registration program. EPA was given the authority to conditionally register a pesticide pending study of the product's safety and was authorized to perform generic reviews without requiring compensation for use of a company's data. The 1980 amendments provided for a (again, largely meaningless) two-house veto over EPA rules and regulations, and they required the administrator to obtain scientific advisory review of suspension actions after they were initiated.

The 1988 legislation was a minor victory for the environmentalists in that it called for accelerated review of pre-1970 registrations and removed most of the indemnification requirements for canceled pesticides. However, it was derided as "FIFRA Lite" for all the proposed changes it did not include, and the "accelerated review" never got out of first gear.[24]

The enormous 1990 Food and Agricultural Act made a few small changes to FIFRA, principally a recordkeeping requirement for certified applicators, but the pesticide provisions were limited to one subtitle of Title XIV of the act.[25] It did make one important change: The 1996 amendments finally repealed the controversial Delaney amendments—this change was not trivial, as we'll discuss later—and also extended the validity of registrations from five years to fifteen, as will be discussed in greater detail in section 11 of this text.

The Pesticide Registration Improvement Act (PRIA) of 2003 is more technical than substantive, important mainly to registrants. It sets fees and decision timetables for the agency's evaluation of pesticide registration applications.[26]

3.0 Pesticide Registration

The heart of FIFRA is the pesticide registration program.[27] Before a pesticide can be manufactured, distributed, or imported, it must be approved by EPA. The data to support registration can take years and millions of dollars of testing, and the submittal to and approval by EPA can require several additional years. Registration is thus an expensive and complicated process, more akin to FDA drug registration than the simple notification required for nonpesticidal chemicals under the Toxic Substances Control Act (TSCA).

3.1 Definition of Pesticides, Pests, and Devices

What is a pesticide? According to the statute, a pesticide is any substance intended for "preventing, destroying, repelling or mitigating any pest." It also includes substances intended for "use as a plant regulator, defoliant, or desiccant."[28] Note that the definition depends upon a use that is intended or claimed.[29] A substance that does not have claims, labels, or advertisements calling it a pesticide, even though it may be very effective as one, is not a pesticide under FIFRA The line can be a narrow one, however, as the California "worm poop" case in 2012 has shown. (Curious? Then please read the footnote.)[30]

Pests are defined as "insects, rodents, worms, fungus, weeds, plants, virus, bacteria, micro-organisms, and other animal life."[31]

A pesticide device is an object used for "trapping, destroying, repelling, or mitigating any pest or any other form of plant or animal life."[32] Firearms are excluded by statute, and the agency has also exempted instruments that depend upon the skill of the person using it. Specifically mentioned in the exemption are flyswatters and traps for vertebrate animals, such as mousetraps. Presumably, EPA would also exclude spears, baseball bats, and large rocks, although the regulations do not so state.[33]

3.2 Pesticide Registration Procedures

All new pesticide products used in the United States, with minor exceptions, must first be registered with EPA. This involves the submittal of the complete formula, a proposed label, and "full description of the tests made and the results thereof upon which the claims are based." The registration is very specific; it is not valid for all formulations or uses of a particular chemical. That is, a separate registration is required for each specific crop or insect on which the pesticide product may be applied as well as for different dosages of application, and each use must be supported by research data on safety and efficacy. The term "pesticide product" itself, however, is surprisingly ambiguous. It can mean the active ingredients alone, or the combination of active and inert ingredients, or perhaps even a related device.[34]

The administrator must approve the registration if the following conditions are met:

- its composition is such as to warrant the proposed claim for it;

- its labeling and other materials required to be submitted comply with the requirements of this act;

- it will perform its intended function without unreasonable adverse effects on the environment; and

- when used in accordance with widespread and commonly recognized practice, it will not generally cause unreasonable adverse effects on the environment.[35]

The operative phrase in the above criteria is "unreasonable adverse effects on the environment," which was added to the act in 1972. This phrase is defined elsewhere in FIFRA as meaning "any unreasonable risk to man or the environment, taking into account the economic, social, and environmental costs and benefits of the use of the pesticide."[36] In fact, as economic poisons, pesticides often cause adverse effects beyond their target species; balancing this collateral damage against the benefits of pesticide use is a major, continuing EPA policy function. Congress thus clearly did not envisage FIFRA as a "strict liability" statute or presume that there would be no negative effects of pesticide use on unintended parties.[37]

Registrations are for a limited period; thereafter, they automatically expire unless an interested party petitions for renewal and, if requested by EPA, provides additional data indicating the safety of the product.[38] Throughout most of its history this period of validity was only five years. The 1996 amendments changed this to fifteen years.

For the past few years, pre-EPA registrations have been coming up for renewal under much stricter standards than when originally issued.[39] The agricultural chemical companies have complained that the increased burden of registration is discouraging the development of new pesticides, but there seems to be no responsible alternative.

Information required for registration includes not only the standard chemical descriptions and specific identification of pests and hosts but also extensive testing data. Where EPA deems this insufficient, it can and does demand additional testing. This registration procedure, we note, is in marked contrast to TSCA's far less rigorous notification process. Petitioners can also rely on public information or, by providing compensation, on data already generated by other companies for the same or similar products.

The 1988 amendments set a timetable for the completion of the studies needed for reregistration. These deadlines parallel the time requirements in Section 3(c) of FIFRA titled "Additional Data to Support Existing Registration."[40] These timetables may be extended only in such extraordinary circumstances as a major loss of experimental animals, the unintended loss of laboratory results, or the destruction of laboratory equipment and facilities.

In addition, the 1996 amendments require EPA, when registering pesticides for uses on food or animal feed, to consider available information and reasonable assumptions concerning the dietary exposure levels of different consumer groups, especially children.

After the administrator's review is completed, he may either ask for additional data to support the reregistration or declare the pesticide canceled or suspended. Otherwise, he is to approve the reregistration.

Even if the pesticide has some negative effects, as many do, these may be balanced against the benefits of usage, such as avoiding the economic damage by insects to crops or the possible threats to public health. (The latter benefit has an enhanced status under the 1996 amendments to FIFRA, discussed below.) A new pesticide may also be beneficial by being less harmful to nontarget species than existing pesticides.

3.3 Conditional Registration

The near collapse of EPA's pesticide registration process in the mid-1970s, when almost no pesticides were registered or reregistered for several years, prompted the creation of a system of conditional registration or reregistration. This could be applied when certain data on a product's safety had either not yet been supplied to EPA or had not yet been analyzed to ensure, according to FIFRA Section 3(c)(5)(D), that "it will perform its intended function without unreasonable adverse effects on the environment."[41] While this was intended as a temporary measure, conditional registrations for new pesticides continued for years to be almost the rule rather than the exception.

Three kinds of conditional registrations are authorized by Section 6 of the 1978 law, which amended FIFRA Section 3(c) with a new section, titled "Registration under Special Circumstances":

1. Pesticides identical or very similar to currently registered products.

2. New uses to existing pesticide registrations.

3. Pesticides containing active ingredients not contained in any currently registered pesticide for which data need be obtained for registration.[42]

These conditional registrations must be conducted on a case-by-case basis, with the last type of conditional registration further limited both by duration and by the requirement that the "use of the pesticide is in the public interest." Conditional registration is prohibited if a Notice of Rebuttable Presumption against Registration (RPAR) has been issued for the pesticide, and the proposed new use involves use on a minor food or feed crop for which there is an effective registered pesticide not subject to an RPAR proceeding.

Cancellation of conditional registrations must be followed by a public hearing, if requested, within 75 days of the request but must be limited to the issue of whether the registrant has fulfilled its conditions for the registration.[43]

3.4 Streamlining of Reregistration

EPA's reregistration of pesticides, even though extended from five years to the present fifteen-year period, has always been plagued by both a slow regulatory pace and the feeling that much of the safety data underlying the registrations were inadequate by contemporary scientific standards. The 1988 amendments added an entire section, which was renumbered as FIFRA Section 4, covering this topic.[44] This section provided that the data submitted in support of registrations before EPA's creation in 1970 would no longer be considered adequate for reregistration unless the applicant bears the burden of proof otherwise.[45]

The section set a 48-month timetable for the completion of the studies needed for reregistration. These deadlines were to parallel the time requirements in FIFRA Section 3(c)(2)(B), titled "Additional Data to Support Existing Registration." These timetables are virtually absolute; they may be extended only in such extraordinary circumstances as a major animal loss, the unintentional loss of laboratory results, or the destruction of laboratory equipment and facilities.

After the administrator's review is completed, he may ask for additional data to support the reregistration or declare the pesticide canceled or suspended.

Otherwise, he is to approve the reregistration. Under the previous version of FIFRA, no consequences were set for failure of a registrant to provide compensation to the original provider of any data relied upon or to share in the payments. The 1988 amendments specified that the administrator, in such a case, must issue a notice of intent to suspend that registrant's registration.

The reregistration continues to lag, despite years of criticism from Congress and environmentalists, and one can safely anticipate these complaints will persist for years to come.[46]

3.5 Registration of "Me-Too" Pesticides

For those pesticides that are identical or very similar to other registered products, the 1988 amendments provided that EPA should expedite approvals of these registrations.[47] (These are akin to generic or "me too" drugs at the FDA.) If proprietary data prepared by competitors are used, financial compensation (indemnification) must be given to the generator, as will be discussed below. To assist the acceleration process, the administrator is to use up to $2 million of the fees collected.[48]

3.6 Registration Fees

A one-time registration fee per active ingredient is authorized by the 1988 amendments.[49] The formula is complex, providing for an initial fee of $50,000, a final fee that may be two or three times that amount, and a bulk discount for categories of more than 50 and 200 registrations. Recall that there must be a registration for each formulation or each specific use. This could therefore add up to real money.

In addition, registrants had to pay an annual fee through the year 2000 to supplement EPA's pesticide reregistration budget. The legislation emphasized, however, that no other fee can be imposed by EPA other than the above. Moreover, the administrator is empowered to reduce or waive the fees for minor use pesticides where their availability would otherwise be in question. He is to report annually to Congress on the application of this authority.

3.7 Categorical Pesticide Review

EPA had long complained that registration, and especially reregistration reviews, should be conducted for entire classes of chemicals rather than be limited to examining each particular registration as it comes up for renewal. This authority has always existed under FIFRA, but a district court decision in 1975[50] on compensation for data made this so complicated that the plan was dropped pending a legislative solution.

The amendment that finally emerged under this label in Section 4 of the 1978 act, however, was considerably different in scope: "No applicant for registration of a pesticide who proposes to purchase a registered pesticide from another producer in order to formulate such purchased pesticide into an end-use product shall be required to (i) submit or cite data pertaining to the safety of such purchased product; or (ii) offer to pay reasonable compensation . . . for the use of any such data."[51]

3.8 Efficacy

The requirements for submission of test data on a pesticide's efficacy are now discretionary for EPA. Registrants are still expected to conduct all the standard tests. EPA may occasionally ask to review the data, but this is no longer routine except for antimicrobials and rodenticides.[52] This provision is interesting because it marks a complete reversal from the original purpose of federal pesticide legislation earlier in the twentieth century, which was to protect farmers from ineffective products and "snake oil" pesticide claims.

Another irony is that courts are now citing EPA's disinterest in efficacy to erode federal preemption of tort lawsuits. In other words, EPA's cherished exclusive authority over pesticide labels (see section 7.3 of this chapter) is weakened as to the label claims that EPA admits it no longer looks at seriously.[53]

3.9 Modifications and Transfers of Registrations

Minor changes in the pesticide formulation need only be reported to EPA. In this context, however, "minor" means extremely minor changes, such as different sources for inert ingredients or very small changes in labeling. Anything more significant must be submitted to EPA for approval as an amended registration.[54]

Registrations may not be transferred to another entity without EPA's approval. This also applies whenever a company is acquired by another or broken up.[55] However, approval is routinely given, and a third party may acquire rights to sell or distribute a pesticide product merely by filing a supplemental notice of registration.[56]

3.10 Trade Secrets

The issue in FIFRA registration that generated more controversy than any other in the first few years after the post-1972 FEPCA (FIFRA) amendments involved the treatment of the trade secrets in data submitted to EPA for registration.[57] The judicial protection of commercial trade secrets has gradually eroded during the past few years. Many so-called trade secrets were in fact widely known throughout the industry and did not merit confidential status. Section 10 of

FIFRA, added in the 1972 amendments, provides that trade secrets should not be released, but if the administrator proposes to release them, he should provide notice to the company to enable it to seek a declaratory judgment in the appropriate district court.

Section 10 provides that "when necessary to carry out the provisions of this Act, information relating to formulas of products acquired by authorization of this Act may be revealed to any federal agency consulted and may be revealed at a public hearing or in findings of fact issued by the Administrator."[58] Consequently, if the public interest requires, a registrant must assume that the formula for his product can be made available, although in practice this may not occur very often.

It is, of course, desirable that scientists and others outside industry and government should be able to conduct tests on the effects of various pesticides. For example, in one case debated by the agency for several years, a professor needed to know the chemical composition of a particular pesticide to conduct certain medical experiments. The question of whether EPA or a court should furnish this information to a bona fide researcher, with or without appropriate safeguards to preserve confidentiality, was resolved in the experimenter's favor after an investigation revealed that the chemical composition in fact was not really a trade secret within the industry.[59]

Because of the controversy surrounding the disclosure of trade secrets, Congress amended FIFRA in 1975 and 1978. The 1975 amendments[60] cleared up an ambiguity created by the 1972 amendments by specifying that the new use restrictions applied only to data submitted on or after January 1, 1970. The definition of trade secrets was left to the administrator.

EPA took the position that the 1972 and 1975 amendments restricted use and disclosure of only a narrow range of data, such as formulas and manufacturing processes, but not hazard and efficacy data. However, the industry challenged this view with some initial success.[61] In 1978, Congress again amended Section 10 to limit trade secrets protection to formulas and manufacturing processes, thus reflecting EPA's position. This was a significant change and has spawned a host of litigation.[62]

In *Ruckelshaus v. Monsanto*,[63] the Supreme Court held almost unanimously (7½ to ½) that while a company did have a property right to the data under state law, the key question was whether it had a reasonable expectation that it would not be disclosed or used by other companies, albeit with adequate compensation. This expectation, the Court found, could only be for the period between the 1972 FIFRA amendments and the 1978 amendments, when the interim change in Section 10 of the act first promised strict confidentiality.[64] For this period, compensation is available through the federal Tucker Act and probably through the statutory arbitration process too. For the periods on either side of those dates, there need be no compensation.

3.11 "Featherbedding" or "Me-Too" Registrants

The second most contested provision in EPA's initial FIFRA registration was the issue of "featherbedding" on registration. The original version in the House stated that "data submitted in support of an application shall not, without permission of the applicant, be considered by the Administrator in the support of any other application for registration."[65] Supporters of the provision, basically the larger manufacturers, claimed that it prevented one company from "freeloading" on the expensive scientific data produced by another company. Environmentalists dubbed this the "mice extermination amendment" for requiring subsequent registrants to needlessly duplicate the laboratory experiments of the first registrant.

The groups finally found an acceptable compromise allowing subsequent registrants to reimburse the initial registrant for reliance on its data, adding to the above language the words "unless such other applicant shall first offer to pay reasonable compensation for producing the test data to be relied upon."

The section originally provided that disputes over the amount of compensation should be decided by the administrator. The 1975 amendments deleted this unfortunate clause, which ensured that the original registrant would have nothing to lose by appealing to a district court since "in no event shall the amount of payment determined by the court be less than that determined by the Administrator." The 1978 amendments finally removed the unwelcome task from the administrator entirely by providing for mediation by the Federal Mediation and Conciliation Service.[66]

The 1975 amendments also pushed back the effective date of the compensation provision from October 1972, the date of the enactment of the FEPCA amendments, to an arbitrary date of January 1, 1970.[67]

The data compensation provision created many problems in the registration process. Pesticide manufacturers brought several lawsuits to determine the breadth of this provision, the proper use of the data, and the amount of compensation to which a manufacturer is entitled for use of its data.[68]

In the case *In re Ciba-Geigy Corp. v. Farmland Industries, Inc.*,[69] EPA set out criteria to be applied in determining what constitutes reasonable compensation under Section 3(c). Plaintiff Ciba-Geigy claimed that it was entitled to $8.11 million in compensation from Farmland Industries for the latter's use of test data to register three pesticides. The defendant argued that it should pay only a proportional share of the actual cost of producing the data based on its share of the market for the products, approximately $49,000. The plaintiff contended that reasonable compensation should be based on the standards used in licensing technical knowledge: an amount equal to the cost of reproducing the data plus a royalty on gross sales for three years.

The administrative law judge hearing the case ruled that a latter, cost-royalty formula was closer to Congress's intent to avoid unnecessary testing expenses. He concluded that the reasonable compensation provision was not intended to provide reward for research and development as the plaintiff's formula would do. The fairest compensatory formula, according to the judge, was using the data producer's cost adjusted for inflation and the defendant's market share two or three years after initial registration. Although no reward for research and development was created, this compensation formula does create an incentive to research because the benefits gained from decreased costs of subsequent registrants outweigh the disadvantages of decreasing the original data producer's projects.

In 1984, the U.S. Supreme Court ruled in *Ruckelshaus v. Monsanto Co.*[70] that pesticide health and safety data were property under Missouri law and thus were protected under the Fifth Amendment of the Constitution. However, as noted above, this was the case in which the Court overruled a lower court in finding that use of data submitted prior to 1972 and after 1978 was not a taking under the Constitution since the registrant had no expectation of confidentiality, except during the ambiguous period between the 1972 and 1978 amendments. The Supreme Court ingeniously decided the remedy was not to find FIFRA unconstitutional, as the lower court had done, but to allow a claim against the government for compensation under the Tucker Act.[71]

By statute, EPA is supposed to review and approve or deny a me-too application within 90 days.[72] This compares favorably with the 180-day time period for FDA's me-too generic drug reviews, which, in any case, are rarely completed in even twice that time.

3.12 Essentiality in Registration

Another registration change strongly supported by the pesticide industry was a prohibition against EPA's refusing to register a substance because it served no additional useful or necessary purpose. This is not the same as efficacy, above, nor was this a dispute as to whether a registration application must demonstrate that a product would "perform its intended function." Some chemical companies were apprehensive that EPA might refuse to register a new product because an old one satisfactorily performed its intended function. EPA's best interest and that of the public, however, lies in having as much duplication of pesticide applications as reasonably possible since the existence of a similar but safer chemical facilitates the removal of a hazardous pesticide from the market.

The companies were correct, however, in recognizing that the availability of alternative products could have an important bearing on the cancellation-suspension process, as we will see below.

4.0 Control over Pesticide Usage

Until the 1972 FEPCA reforms, the government had no control over the actual use of a pesticide once it had left a manufacturer or distributor properly labeled. Thus, for example, a chemical that would be perfectly safe for use on a dry field might be environmentally hazardous if applied in a marshy area, and a chemical acceptable for use on one crop might leave dangerous residues on another. The label could of course have spelled out these conditions, but what if the pesticide was frequently misused? EPA's only recourse (other than occasional subtle hints to the producer) was to cancel the entire registration—obviously too unwieldy a weapon to constitute a normal means of enforcement.

A second problem was that a potential chemical might be too dangerous for general use but could be used safely by trained personnel. There was, however, no legal mechanism for limiting its use only to qualified individuals. Because of these problems, both environmentalists and the industry agreed that EPA should be given more flexibility than merely the choice between canceling or approving a pesticide.

4.1 Statutory Basis for Control over Pesticide Usage through Certification

In 1972, Congress provided for the classification of pesticides into general and restricted categories, with the latter group available only to certified applicators.[73] There are several categories of applicators, including private applicators and commercial applicators, who use or supervise the application of pesticides on property other than their own. A pesticide label permitting use only "under the direct supervision of a certified applicator" means, of course, that the chemical is to be applied under the instructions and control of a certified applicator who, however, curiously is not required to be physically present when and where the pesticide is applied.

The additional flexibility of the certification program was a principal reason the agrochemical industry eventually supported the 1972 amendments to FIFRA, but some environmentalists were concerned that the program might become a farce, especially when administered by certain states. Certification standards are prescribed by EPA, but any state desiring to establish its own certification program may do so if the administrator determines that it satisfies the guidelines and statutory criteria (see section 4.3 of this chapter).

Since 1972, it has been unlawful either "to make available for use, or to use, any registered pesticide classified for restricted use for some or all purposes other than in accordance with" the registration and applicable regulations. Stiff penalties for violations of these restrictions include fines up to $25,000 and imprisonment for up to a year.

The validity of the certification program, however, was considerably undermined by the 1975 amendments to FIFRA. The amendments relaxed the procedures for certification by forbidding EPA to demand any examinations of an applicant's knowledge.[74] Some states may license anyone who applies, but EPA requirements for periodic reporting and inspection provide some degree of control.

The Food Quality Protection Act of 1996 (FQPA) established two new categories of pesticide applicators—maintenance applicators, who use or supervise structural or lawn care pesticides; and service technicians, who use or supervise these pesticides on someone else's property for a fee. States are authorized to set minimum training requirements for these new categories.[75]

4.2 Self-Certification of Private Applicators

The clearest illustration of Congress's altered view toward FIFRA is its treatment of the certification program, which had been a major reason for the enactment of the FIFRA overhaul back in 1972. The amendments provided that the pesticides that might be too harmful to the applicators or to the environment if indiscriminately used could continue to be applied by farmers and pesticide operators who had received special training in avoiding these problems.

The program had run into resistance from the beginning from farmers who resented the requirement that they be trained to use chemicals on their own property. The changed law does not remove the examination requirement from commercial applicators, who apply pesticides to property other than their own.[76] It does create an exemption, however, that covers not only the farmer who is applying pesticides to his own land but also his employees. And it must be remembered that the hazards are not necessarily limited to the applicator; organophosphates, which are nerve gases, may be highly toxic to the applicators, but many other substances if improperly used may run off to threaten neighboring farms or the environment in general. The amended law does not seem to recognize this latter problem.

The 1975 amendments also removed the authority of the administrator to require, under state plans submitted for his approval, that farmers take exams before being certified. In other words, EPA may require a training program but may not require any examination to determine if the information has been learned.[77] In the opinion of the House Agriculture Committee, "The farmer would be more aware of the dangers of restricted use pesticides if each time he makes a purchase he is given a self-certification form to read and sign."[78] One wonders if a similar arrangement for airline pilot self-certification would be considered acceptable.

4.3 Experimental Use Permits

FIFRA provides for experimental use permits for registered pesticides.[79] The purpose of this seemingly innocuous section is to permit a registration applicant to conduct tests and "accumulate information necessary to register a pesticide under Section 3."[80] This provision, however, has already been used in at least one successful effort to evade a FIFRA cancellation-suspension order. Under strong political pressure from western sheep interests and their congressional spokesmen, EPA granted a Section 5 permit for the limited use of certain banned predacides and devices, including the "coyote getter" using thallium sulfate.

On July 18, 1979, EPA issued final regulations under which a state may develop its own experimental permits program.[81] A state, by submitting a plan that meets the requirements of EPA's regulations, may receive authorization to issue experimental use permits to potential registrants under 24(c) of FIFRA (restricted use registration), agricultural or educational research agencies, and certified applicators for use of a restricted use pesticide.

Permits cannot be issued by a state for a pesticide containing ingredients subject to an EPA cancellation or suspension order, or to a notice of intent to cancel or suspend, or which are not found in any EPA registered product.[82] The regulations also contain strict limitations on the production and use of a pesticide. Periodic reports must be submitted by the permittee to the state detailing the progress of the research or restricted use. In addition, permits cannot be issued for more than three years.

4.4 Two-House Congressional Veto over EPA Regulations

The 1980 amendments changed Section 25(a) to provide for a two-house veto (i.e., both House and Senate), not the prior unconstitutional one-house, congressional veto over EPA rules or regulations.[83] Under the amendments, the administrator is required to submit to each house of Congress new FIFRA regulations. If Congress adopts a concurrent resolution disapproving the new regulation within 90 days of its promulgation, it will not become effective. However, if neither house disapproves the regulation after 60 days and the appropriate committee of neither house has reported out a disapproving regulation, the regulation becomes effective.[84]

This amendment may be good, popular politics in theory but has not been an effective restraint on EPA rulemaking. For good or ill, Congress is rarely capable of such prompt and concerted action.

5.0 Removal of Pesticides from the Market

FIFRA is not merely concerned with the registration or reregistration of pesticides coming on the market. It also has mechanisms for taking action against products considered to pose a risk to man and the environment.

5.1 Cancellation

While the registration process may be the heart of FIFRA, cancellation represents the cutting edge of the law and attracts the most public attention. Cancellation is used to initiate review of a substance suspected of posing a "substantial question of safety" to man or the environment.[85]

Note that definition: cancellation does not ban the product. Contrary to public assumptions, during the pendency of the proceedings the product may be freely manufactured and shipped in commerce. A cancellation order, although final if not challenged within 30 days, usually leads to a public hearing or scientific review committee or both and can be quite protracted; it can last for a matter of months or even years. A recommended decision from the agency hearing examiner (now called the administrative law judge, or ALJ) goes to the administrator or to his delegated representative, the chief agency judicial officer, or the three-member agency appeals panel for a final determination on the cancellation. (The agency has varied the internal appeal process from time to time.) Only if the decision is upheld, the product would finally be banned from shipment or use in the United States.[86]

There are several quite different types of action covered under the single term "cancellation."[87] First, there is a cancellation when EPA believes a substance is a highly probable threat to man or the environment but for which there is not yet sufficient evidence or urgency to warrant immediate suspension. This is the usual meaning. Second, there can be a cancellation when scientific tests indicate some cause for concern and a public hearing or scientific advisory committee is desired to explore the issue more thoroughly. And third, there could be a cancellation issued in response to a citizens' suit to enable both critics and defenders of the pesticide to present their arguments.

These distinctions are quite important. State authorities, for example, often recommend that farmers cease using a canceled product that they thought had been declared unsafe, although EPA may have considered the action in the second and third categories above. Conversely, there were occasions when EPA wanted to communicate its great concern over the continued use of a product without resorting to the more immediate and drastic remedy of suspension. This problem is not resolved completely by the amended FIFRA, but at least two levels of action are distinguished, essentially combining the second and third categories, above, into one.

The administrator may issue a notice of his intent either (1) to cancel a registration or to change its classification, together with the reasons (including the factual basis) for his action; or (2) to hold a hearing to determine whether its registration should be canceled or its classification changed.[88] This revision of the law may not have solved EPA's communications problem with local officials, but it did provide a basis for a distinction that EPA sometimes needed to make.

5.2 Suspension

A suspension order, despite its misleading name, is an immediate ban on the production and distribution of a pesticide. It is mandated when a product constitutes an *imminent hazard* to man or the environment and may be invoked at any stage of the cancellation proceeding or even before a cancellation procedure has been initiated. According to the "18th of March Statement," a seminal 1971 EPA pronouncement, "an imminent hazard may be declared at any point in the chain of events which may ultimately result in harm to the public."[89] A suspension order must ordinarily be accompanied by the issuance of a cancellation order if one is not already outstanding.

5.2.1 Ordinary Suspension

The purpose of an ordinary suspension is to prevent an imminent hazard during the time required for cancellation or change in classification proceedings. An ordinary suspension proceeding is initiated when the administrator issues notice to the registrant that he is suspending use of the pesticide and includes the requisite findings as to imminent hazard. The registrant may request an expedited hearing within five days of receipt of the administrator's notice. If no hearing is requested, the suspension order can take effect immediately thereafter, and the order is not reviewable by a court.

The original notion was that suspension procedurally "resembles . . . the judicial proceedings on a contested motion for a preliminary injunction"[90] and that it remains in effect until the cancellation hearing is completed and a final decision is issued by the administrator.[91] This connotation of temporariness does not actually accord with reality but has been the consistent theme of judicial decisions since the agency's inception. According to this view, the function of a suspension order is not to reach a definitive decision on the registration of a pesticide but to grant temporary, interim relief.[92]

The Court of Appeals for the District of Columbia has repeatedly stated this view: "The function of the suspension decision is to make a preliminary assessment of evidence and probabilities, not an ultimate resolution of difficult issues,"[93] and "the suspension order thus operates to afford interim relief during the course of the lengthy administrative proceedings."[94]

The courts have specifically noted that imminent hazard does not refer only to the danger of an immediate disaster: "We must caution against any approach to the term 'imminent hazard' used in the statute, that restricts it to a concept of crises."[95] In another early case, the court declared that the secretary of agriculture has concluded that the most important element of an "imminent hazard to the public" is a serious threat to public health, that a hazard may be imminent even if its impact will not be apparent for many years, and that the public protected by the suspension provision includes fish and wildlife. These interpretations all seem consistent with the statutory language and purpose.[96]

5.2.2 Emergency Suspension

The emergency suspension is the strongest environmental action EPA can take under FIFRA. It immediately halts all uses, sales, and distribution of the pesticide.[97] An emergency suspension differs from an ordinary suspension in that it is *ex parte*. That is, the registrant is not given notice or the opportunity for an expedited hearing prior to the suspension order taking effect. The registrant is, however, entitled to an expedited hearing thereafter to determine the propriety of the emergency suspension. The administrator can use this procedure only when he determines that an emergency exists that does not allow him to hold a hearing before suspending use of a pesticide. This authority has only rarely been invoked.

EPA first used the emergency suspension procedure in 1979 when it suspended the sale and use of the herbicides 2,4,5-T and Silvex for specified uses. EPA issued the suspension orders based on its judgment that exposure to the pesticides created an immediate and unreasonable risk to human health. EPA's action was reviewed by a Michigan district court in *Dow Chemical Co. v. Blum*,[98] where the plaintiffs petitioned for judicial review of EPA's decision and a stay of the emergency suspension orders. In upholding EPA's order, the court analogized the emergency suspension order to a temporary restraining order and defined the term emergency as a "substantial likelihood that serious harm will be experienced during the three or four months required in any realistic projection of the administrative suspension process."[99]

The court held that this standard required the administrator to examine five factors:

1. the seriousness of the threatened harm;

2. the immediacy of the threatened harm;

3. the probability that the threatened harm would result;

4. the benefits to the public of the continued use of the pesticides in question during the suspension process; and

5. the nature and extent of the information before the administrator at the time he makes his decision.

The court also held that an emergency suspension order may be overturned only if it was arbitrary, capricious, or an abuse of discretion, or if it was not "issued in accordance with the procedures established by law."[100] This is a high hurdle for an aggrieved party to overcome.

The FQPA of 1996 amending FIFRA (see section 11 of this chapter) made one major change in the emergency suspension process, allowing a suspension to be issued for no more than 90 days without a simultaneous notice of intent to cancel.[101]

5.3 Misbranding and Stop-Sale Orders

EPA has traditionally used the bare charge of misbranding for certain unambiguous offenses, notably instances where the pesticide made claims unsupported by the registration. The violation was usually obvious, the appeals uncommon, and the remedy simple—namely, to order the sales of the pesticide halted.

In the early 1990s, however, EPA began for the first time to use the charge of misbranding in cases where the agency questioned the effectiveness of the registered formulation. This is a dubious practice. If the product does not work, it should not be reregistered, or it should be canceled under Section 6. By using the misbranding approach rather than cancellation, the agency circumvents the procedural safeguards, including the public hearings and scientific advisory committees provided in the statute. For that very reason, this approach should be strongly disfavored.[102]

Ironically, while less procedural protection is afforded by the misbranding approach, the legal consequences can be more severe: Unlike with cancellation or even suspension, EPA can prevent a misbranded product from being exported or sold abroad.

5.4 International Effect of EPA Cancellations

EPA cancellation and suspension decisions, as agency administrators have repeatedly noted, are meant to apply only to the United States. The reason is that the risk-benefit calculations applied to challenged pesticides are based on conditions in this country and would not necessarily be valid for different risks and different benefits abroad.

This interpretation has not been without its critics. Because of its potential significance, an entire separate part of this chapter is devoted to this topic (see section 9).

EPA has also been working with foreign governments and international organizations toward a unified approach to certain pesticides. This will undoubtedly expand. On the other hand, it has faced criticism for U.S.-based decisions that might not fit circumstances abroad. The current DDT–malaria debate has turned on this pivotal point.

5.5 Disposal and Recall

An important question following a cancellation or suspension action is whether to recall those products already in commerce. Misbranded pesticides may be confiscated, and on several occasions EPA has ordered manufacturers to recall a pesticide when the hazard so warranted. But for both practical and administrative reasons cancellation-suspension orders have generally provided that banned pesticides may be used until supplies are exhausted, without being subject to recall.[103] It may seem inconsistent to ban a substance as an imminent hazard, yet allow quantities already on the market to be sold, but repeated challenges by environmental groups have been unsuccessful.[104]

This policy was thought necessary, for example, in the mercury pesticides case in which EPA scientists concluded that the recall and collection of certain mercuric compounds would result in a concentration more harmful to the environment than permitting the remaining supplies to be thinly spread around the country. In the DDT case in the early 1970s, the administrator decided that his final cancellation order would not go into effect for six months to enable the transition to alternative products, by ensuring the availability of adequate supplies of alternative pesticides (namely, organophosphates, which can be very hazardous to untrained applicators), and to allow time for training and educational programs to prevent misuse of the new chemicals.

EPA first promulgated regulations for the storage and disposal of pesticides back in May 1974.[105] These detailed the appropriate conditions for incineration, soil injection, and other means of disposal; established procedures for shipment back to the manufacturers or to the federal government; directed that transportation costs should be borne by the owner of the pesticide; and provided standards for storage. The regulations devoted considerable attention to the disposal problem of pesticide containers, which have caused a significant proportion of accidental poisonings.

5.6 Compensation for Canceled Pesticides

Under FIFRA Section 15, EPA must pay compensation to registrants and applicators for pesticides canceled or suspended. This section was the single most controversial issue in the passage of FEPCA back in 1972. The amendment's industry supporters threatened to block passage of the entire 1972 legislation if this section was not attached. Public interest groups complained that it would force taxpayers to indemnify manufacturers for inadequate testing and would encourage the production of unsafe chemicals.[106] To the extent that this provision was intended not so much for indemnification as to deter EPA from issuing costly cancellations,[107] it served to undermine the purposes of this act.

As a partial compromise, a clause was added to bar indemnification to any person who "had knowledge of facts which, in themselves, would have shown that such pesticide did not meet the requirements" for registration and continued thereafter to produce such pesticide without giving notice of such facts to the administrator. If properly applied, even under the most expedited agency procedures, that saving clause could have disqualified registrants and manufacturers from compensation in virtually all cancellation and suspension actions.

Under this provision, EPA paid out $20 millon to manufacturers of the two pesticides, 2,4,5-T and ethylene dibromide, and an additional $40 million indemnification for a third canceled pesticide, dinoseb. These sums came directly from the budget of EPA's Pesticide Office, which then totaled only about $40 million.[108] Obviously this constituted an enormous disincentive for EPA to cancel pesticides, and everyone knew it.

This indemnities provision was eventually recognized as a mistake. In the 1988 legislation on FIFRA, the House and Senate both voted to remove the section, except for the indemnification of end users (i.e., farmers and applicators), so chemical manufacturers would no longer be covered.[109] Farmers and other users are still eligible for compensation through the federal government's regular Judgment Fund.[110] This reflects the philosophy of an earlier congressional prohibition, contained in the appropriations bill for fiscal year 1988, which provided that any sums should be paid from the general U.S. Treasury, not from

EPA's budget, so the agency would not be penalized for taking measures it deemed proper.[111]

5.7 Balancing Test in FIFRA

Risk assessment is an integral part of FIFRA.[112] After all, pesticides are poisons, useful because they are harmful to some disfavored forms of life.

Some commentators feel that certain types of pesticides, particularly carcinogens, should be forbidden *per se* as was done under the now-repealed Delaney Amendment to the Food, Drug, and Cosmetics Act.[113] FIFRA does not require this inflexibility, although the courts have cautioned that the law "places a heavy burden on any administrative officer to explain the basis for his decision to permit the continued use of a chemical known to produce cancer in experimental animals."[114]

The balancing that is applied during the registration process and, more formally, during the cancellation proceedings is to determine whether there are "unreasonable adverse effects on the environment," taking into consideration the "economic, social, and environmental costs and benefits of the use of any pesticide."

In a suspension proceeding, however, which is based on the threat of imminent hazard, FIFRA does not require a balancing of environmental risks and benefits. It has nevertheless been EPA's declared policy since its inception to conduct such an analysis, although in practice the benefits would obviously need to be considerable to balance a finding of imminent hazard. One administrator noted that "the Agency traditionally has considered benefits as well as risks . . . and, in his opinion, should continue to do so."[115]

5.8 Requirements of Consultation by EPA with USDA

Congress decided in the 1975 amendments to require that EPA engage in formal consultation with USDA and with the agriculture committees of the House and Senate before issuing proposals or final standards regarding pesticides. This amended Section 6(b) of FIFRA to provide that EPA should give 60 days' notice to the secretary of agriculture before a notice is made public. The secretary then must respond within 30 days, and these comments, along with the response of the EPA administrator, are published in the *Federal Register*.[116] These consultations, however, are not required in the event of an imminent hazard to human health for which a suspension order under Section 6(c) is warranted.

At the same time that the administrator provides a copy of any proposed regulations to the secretary of agriculture, he is also required to provide copies to the respective House and Senate agricultural committees. The practical impact of this requirement is that Congress is provided an opportunity to communicate displeasure to the administrator before a proposal is issued without necessarily having to subject these comments to scrutiny in the public record.[117] The effect of these requirements on EPA has been slight, in part because the agency pays little heed to comments from the USDA.

5.9 Economic Impact on Agriculture Statement

The 1975 amendments also reflected the increasing trend in government toward requiring impact statements before regulations can be issued. Congress, borrowing from the environmental impact statement process[118] and the economic impact statement requirements,[119] mandated that the administrator, when deciding to issue a proposal, "shall include among those factors to be taken into account the impact of the action proposed in such notice on production and prices of agricultural commodities, retail food prices, and otherwise on the agricultural economy."[120]

The necessity for this legal provision is technically questionable since the balancing of risks and benefits is at the heart of FIFRA. The committees themselves were vague about the actual need for this legislation. Nevertheless, Congress felt that something was lacking. As the Senate report declared, it "concurs in the House position that EPA has not always given adequate consideration to agriculture in its decisions."[121]

5.10 Scientific Advisory Committees

Because the Scientific Advisory Committees play such an important role in the cancellation-suspension process, they deserve special attention in this section.

According to the old FIFRA, prior to 1972, a registrant challenging a cancellation order could request either a public hearing or a scientific advisory committee; and, in practice, cases involving several registrants usually resulted in both. EPA was also strongly dissatisfied with the vague and often contradictory reports of the advisory committees.

In the 1972 amendments to FIFRA, the advisory committee was transformed into an adjunct of the hearing process, resolving those scientific questions which the administrative law judge or the parties determined were essential to the final decision by the administrator. The amendments streamlined the process so that committee deliberations could proceed simultaneously with the administrative hearings, thereby saving time and making them a part of the fact-finding and evaluation system rather than a separate proceeding with long delays and divisions of responsibility. By meeting outside of the public hearing, the scientists could also avoid being subject to cross-examination and other legal burdens they consider unappealing.

The advisory process, however, was again made more formalistic by the 1975 amendments. The use of a scientific advisory committee was mandated both for cancellation actions (where they are usually requested anyway) and for any general pesticide regulations.[122] The amendments required that the administrator submit proposed and final regulations to a specially constituted scientific advisory panel, separate from the agency's regular Scientific Advisory Committees, at the same time that he provides copies to the secretary of agriculture and to the two agricultural committees of Congress. The advisory committee then has 30 days in which to respond. Membership on this committee is prescribed in unusual detail. The administrator can select seven members from a group of twelve nominees—six nominated by the National Science Foundation and six by the National Institutes of Health.[123]

In 1980, Section 25(d) was amended to allow the chairman of a Scientific Advisory Committee to create temporary subpanels on specific projects.[124] One would have thought he had this authority anyhow. Section 25(d) was also amended to require the administrator to submit any decision to suspend the registration of a pesticide to a scientific advisory panel (SAP) for its comment.[125]

The amendment did not alter the administrator's authority to issue a suspension notice prior to the SAP review; it only requires him to obtain SAP review after the suspension is initiated. The 1980 amendments also required the administrator to issue written procedures for independent peer review of the design, protocol, and conduct of major studies carried out under FIFRA.[126]

This is micro legislation at its policy nadir. One might question the value of ever more advisory committees when, as EPA Administrator Russell Train pointed out years ago, "EPA is already awash in scientific advisory panels."[127]

6.0 Administrative and Judicial Review

EPA enforcement actions and other administrative actions usually follow a clearly specified series of internal appeals. The action first goes to an administrative law judge (ALJ). After discovery and hearings, a process that can take a year or two, the judge renders a decision that can then be appealed within the agency. The next level used to be the administrator or the special assistant acting in his name; then for two decades this role was institutionalized in the chief judicial officer. Later, this office was expanded into a formal three-member Environmental Appeals Board (EAB).[128] After this, the administrator can personally intervene but now rarely does. Thereafter, the aggrieved party can appeal to the federal courts.

6.1 Scope of the Administrator's Flexibility

The EPA administrator renders the final agency judgment on administrative actions and appeals. Since issues reach him only after passing through a series of committees—lower-level enforcement officials, administrative law judges, and other officials—the question is how much discretion he has to reach a decision at variance with those rendered below.

6.1.1 Concerning the Scientific Advisory Committee

In emphasizing the administrator's regulatory flexibility, the courts have rejected the contention that he must "rubber-stamp" the findings of the Scientific Advisory Committee or the administrative law judge. This is illustrated by *Dow Chemical v. Ruckelshaus* concerning the herbicide 2,4,5-T. In 1970, even before the creation of EPA, the USDA suspended some uses of the chemical and canceled others because of the high risk that it, or a dioxin contaminant known as TCDD, had proved a potent teratogen in laboratory tests. Most of these uses were not challenged, but Dow did contest the cancellation of its use on rice. A Scientific Advisory Committee convoked by EPA concluded that the "confused aggregate of observations indicated registrations should be maintained" but that there remained serious questions needing further extensive research. The administrator reviewed the report in considerable detail and concluded that a "substantial question of safety" existed sufficient to justify an administrative hearing; in the meantime, the cancellation was maintained.[129] Dow appealed, but the Court of Appeals for the Eighth Circuit held that the administrator was not compelled to follow the recommendations of the advisory committee if—and this is, of course, crucial—he had a justifiable basis for doing otherwise.[130]

6.1.2 Concerning the Administrative Law Judge

The administrator is also not bound by findings of the ALJs. This conclusion follows the longtime general principle of administrative law that a hearing examiner's decision should be accorded only the deference it merits. As the Supreme Court said long ago in the *Universal Camera* case, "we do not require that the examiner's findings be given more weight than in reason and in light of judicial experience they deserve."[131] Only if the decision-maker arbitrarily and capriciously ignored the findings of an examiner, or if the credibility of witnesses was crucial to the case—an infrequent situation in a pesticide administrative hearing—might a different conclusion be indicated.

6.2 Standing for Registration, Appeals, and Subpoenas

FIFRA originally assumed that only registrants would be interested in the continuation of a product's registration or the setting of public hearings and scientific advisory committees. It was increasingly evident, however, that this unintended exclusion of both users and environmentalists needed revision.

Whereas a registrant, when faced with cancellation, might prefer not to contest those minor categories of use that it regarded as financially insignificant, a pesticide user might regard them as essential for the protection of his crops.

The law was therefore amended in 1972 by FEPCA to allow not only registrants but any "other interested person with the concurrence of the registrant" to request continuation of the registration.[132] While this amendment remedies the problem of legal standing, it does not provide the resources and data which users, particularly small farmers or organizations, would need to support a renewal application.[133] Note that the registration holder must agree, which he might not do in instances where an environmental group was opposed or where a use was relatively unimportant to him but could be crucial for some user group.

Another problem of standing relates to the right of environmental and consumer groups to use the administrative procedures under cancellation-suspension. The act does not specifically give citizens' groups the right to request a public hearing, but the administrator himself is now empowered to call a hearing that he might do at the request of such a group. Furthermore, as already discussed, all interested parties may request consent of the administrative law judge to refer scientific questions to a special committee of the National Academy of Sciences for determination, a right which did not exist before.

The issue of standing came up in the troubling case *Environmental Defense Fund v. Costle*[134] when the D.C. Circuit upheld EPA's denial of standing for an environmental group that requested a Section 6(d) cancellation hearing on the continued use of chlorobenzilate in four states. The Environmental Defense Fund (EDF) requested the hearing after the administrator issued a Notice of Intent to Cancel the registration of chlorobenzilate for all uses other than citrus spraying in four states. The administrator denied the hearing, holding that FIFRA was not structured for the purpose of entertaining objections by persons having no real interest in stopping the cancellation from going into effect but who object to the agency's refusal to propose actions.[135]

On appeal, the D.C. Circuit upheld the administrator's decision that EDF was not an adversely affected party under Section 6(d), stating that a 6(d) hearing may be used only to stop a cancellation proceeding, not initiate one. The proper procedure for EDF, the court said, in seeking review of EPA's decision to retain the registration for citrus users was to challenge, in district court, the notice provisions permitting the limited use under Section 16(a) of FIFRA.[136]

Considering that the users of a minor application may have a bigger stake in the pesticide than the chemical manufacturer, it was regrettable that the two circuit courts, the Ninth in 1989 and the D.C. Circuit in 1996, have held that nonregistrant users have no right to prevent a settlement and force further proceedings. Congress still needs to address this important issue.[137]

6.3 Judicial Appeals

Under the old version of FIFRA,[138] appeals from decisions of the administrator went to the U.S. Court of Appeals. According to Section 16 of the amended FIFRA, however, appeals under some circumstances may go to a federal district court.[139] Other appeals go to the court of appeals.

This change provoked considerable controversy in EPA during the legislative process. The rationale for change was that courts of appeals are not designed to develop a factual record if none existed from the proceeding below. It thus seemed logical that in those instances where a record was developed, after public hearing or otherwise, the appeal should be to the court of appeals, whereas in cases where there was no record for the court to review, the matter should go to a district court for findings of fact.

Section 16 has been the focus of several appeals court decisions that reached contrary holdings on the issue of whether the federal courts or the courts of appeals have jurisdiction to review the denial of a request for a FIFRA Section 6(d) hearing on a notice of cancellation. In *Environmental Defense Fund v. Costle*,[140] the D.C. Circuit Court held that if an administrative record exists in support of a denial of a hearing request, jurisdiction lies exclusively with the courts of appeals. In *AMVAC Chemical Corp. v. EPA*,[141] a divided Ninth Circuit panel rejected the D.C. Circuit's analysis and held that a denial of a hearing was a procedural action and not an order following a public hearing within the meaning of Section 16(b). Hence, the court held that judicial review of hearing request denials lies in the district courts.

In 1996 the D.C. Circuit Court of Appeals clarified that a public hearing was not always required. Since the distinction between district and appellate jurisdiction turned on whether there was an adequate record for review, the court declared, a pesticide case in which there was a voluminous record was properly before the court of appeals even though there might not actually have been a hearing.[142]

6.4 The Role of Public Hearings

On a related point, there has been a growing tendency at EPA to dilute the FIFRA requirements for public hearing to include those situations in which only written public comments were submitted. That was clearly not the intention of Congress in enacting FIFRA; it denies to the parties a fundamental right to be heard by agency decision-makers and to react in front of them to the comments of other parties. A public hearing is a public session allowing testimony and confrontation with a recorded transcript. It should not be allowed to become anything less.[143]

One legal commentator caustically characterized EPA's record on this issue under President Clinton's administrator, Carol Browner, thusly: "Browner's abandonment of sound science and her Administration's wholesale repudiation of traditional notice-and-comment rulemaking dealt a serious blow to accepted notions of fair play and due process."[144]

7.0 Role of States and Localities

As the name declares, FIFRA is obviously a federal statute. For all pesticides, nationwide, it is EPA that controls the registration, labeling, cancellation proceedings, and other regulatory activities. States and local communities, however, are often under strong political pressure from constituents who feel that EPA's regulation is inadequate. This feeling may be the result either of skepticism about the agency's motives or competence, or of a belief that specific local conditions exist beyond the scope of federal regulation or interest.

On the other hand, pesticide manufacturers and applicators fear that hundreds of conflicting local pesticide ordinances would create a regulatory nightmare. Resolution of this conflict requires a political determination by Congress. Unfortunately, Congress has largely avoided the issue of federal preemption. Without adequate guidance, therefore, the courts have had to struggle to guess from existing legislation what Congress intended. For that reason, the various inconsistent judicial decisions have created more confusion.[145] (This issue of preemption is discussed more fully below in section 7.3, below.)

7.1 Intrastate Registrations

Under the old FIFRA[146] federal authority did not extend to intrastate use and shipment of pesticides with state registrations. This meant that federal authority could be avoided simply by having manufacturing plants in the principal agricultural states. The 1972 FEPCA amendments broadened the registration requirement to include any person in any state who sells or distributes pesticides.

The states do retain some authority under Section 24 "to regulate the sale or use of any pesticide or device in the state, but only if and to the extent that the regulation does not permit any sale or use prohibited by this Act." States, furthermore, cannot have labeling and packaging requirements different from those required by the act—a measure that was popular among some chemical manufacturers who feared that each state might have different labeling requirements. It excludes a feature common to several of the other environmental laws whereby states may impose stricter requirements than the federal ones on pesticide use within their jurisdiction.

Finally, the section gives a state the authority, subject to certification by EPA, to register pesticides for limited local use in treating sudden and limited pest infestations, without the time and administrative burden required by a full EPA certification.

7.2 Greater State Authority

Several sections of the 1978 amendments reflect Congress's intent to give the states greater responsibility in regulating pesticides. This includes not only training and cooperative agreements but also increasing federal delegation to the states over such matters as intrastate registrations and enforcement. The EPA administrator, however, retains overall supervisory responsibility and ultimate veto authority.

Because some states, such as California, have promulgated stringent guidelines for pesticide regulations, there has been proposed legislation to limit state authority under Section 24 to gather data about a pesticide for state registration.[147] Pesticide manufacturers have complained for years that state registration procedures, which may require additional studies and data gathering, are time consuming and costly. State officials, on the other hand, believe that EPA pays too little attention to valid local needs and therefore wish for more autonomy.

7.3 Federal Preemption and State Authority

During the past several decades, no FIFRA subject has inspired more litigation and court appeals than the question of federal preemption. The cause, for the most part, has not been an attempt by states to infringe upon federal prerogatives; rather, the issue has arisen in private tort suits by injured litigants seeking to sue pesticide manufacturers and applicators.[148]

A similar problem has arisen for FDA's drug labels and other areas, including food, where state tort actions have challenged the agencies' federal exclusivity.[149]

First, though, the state efforts at regulation will be considered. There was some justification for the fears of pesticide manufacturers that the states would impose more stringent labeling requirements despite the FEPCA amendments. According to Section 24(b), states "shall not impose or continue in effect any requirements for labeling or packaging in addition to or different from those required under this subchapter."[150]

California imposed additional data requirements under its restricted-use registration. In *National Agricultural Chemicals Association v. Rominger,*[151] a federal district court declined to issue a preliminary injunction against the state's regulations on the grounds that there was no congressional mandate to occupy the field when Section 24 was enacted; thus, there was no federal preemption of restricted-use registrations.[152]

The U.S. Supreme Court attempted to clarify this muddle. In *Wisconsin Public Intervenor v. Mortier*,[153] the court considered a small-town ordinance requiring 60 days' notice and a permit for applying pesticides on public and some private lands. Warning signs were required 24 hours before spraying. A pesticide sprayer who was denied a permit sued, contending that the ordinance violated both federal and state laws regulating pesticides. The Wisconsin Supreme Court agreed.

However, the U.S. Supreme Court held unanimously that the local ordinance was not preempted by federal law. Since the local restrictions related to usage of a pesticide, not to FIFRA-regulated label claims, states were authorized by FIFRA to regulate certain aspects of pesticide use. These, said the Court, may be delegated by the states to their political subdivisions, towns, and municipalities. Significantly, EPA and the Justice Department, which had traditionally opposed a multiplicity of local regulations on pesticides, in this case felt there was no infringement of FIFRA's federal preemption.

The second, more complicated issue has involved the preemption of private tort suits. In short, the question was whether state or local courts could rule that EPA-approved labels provided the public with inadequate warning of pesticide hazards. This is not a trivial matter. If a judge or jury could decide that a FIFRA label was somehow misleading or inadequate, they could in effect assume EPA's authority over pesticides. After all, states do not have the direct authority to order label changes. Why should they be allowed to do so indirectly by the threat of tort litigation?

In 1992 the Supreme Court had decided a seemingly similar preemption case involving health warnings on cigarette packs, the famous *Cipollone v. Liggett Group* decision.[154] When the *Papas v. Zoecon Corp.* case on FIFRA preemption reached the high court, the justices signaled that they wanted it to follow that precedent by unanimously remanding the case to the Eleventh Circuit to decide in light of *Cipollone*.[155]

Since then, a deluge of FIFRA cases raised the same questions and, for the most part, got more or less the same answers, namely, that preemption does bar tort suits claiming possible inadequacy of EPA-approved pesticide labels, but it does not prevent claims regarding product defects, faulty tests, or warranties.[156]

In the *Bates v. Dow Agrosciences LLC*[157] case in 2005, the U.S. Supreme Court took a further step restricting the preemption defense against tort claims. In overturning the Fifth Circuit, the Court found first that FIFRA barred only state law "requirements," which the justices defined as "a rule of law that must be obeyed." Jury verdicts, even those with multimillion-dollar awards, were merely an option for the manufacturer and did not necessarily require the pesticide manufacturer to change its EPA-approved labeling.

Second, the Court said while negligent-failure-to-warn rule claims are based on common law rules and thus can be said to be legal requirements and thus subject to FIFRA, they too are not preempted because they are, unlike *Cipollone*, "in addition or different from" FIFRA requirements; rather, the two can be read in parallel.[158]

These views gathered a majority of the Court (7–2, with dissents in part) but the reasoning is strained and unconvincing; moreover, they hardly reflect an understanding of realities. No manufacturer can afford to consider large jury verdicts merely "options," so juries can, in effect, rewrite the FIFRA labels.[159]

Here is where it gets interesting. The dissent (Thomas, with Scalia) displayed a much better understanding of the complexities of the issue than the majority. Three years later, in an almost identical preemption case but this time involving interpretation of the FDA statute, Justice Scalia led an 8-1 majority the other way in finding that there was in fact federal preemption of a tort suit. With such margins, the often-contentious liberal-conservative split on the Court was obviously not a factor.

With these wide vote swings indicating that not even the Supreme Court has figured out this issue, lower courts in subsequent FIFRA cases have naturally just followed the 2005 FIFRA precedent, with little attempt to resolve the logical impasse. Some clarification from Congress would be useful, either to abandon the pretense of preemption or to restate it more definitively, but unfortunately this is unlikely.

8.0 Litigation Issues

Preemption, discussed above, is clearly the leading litigation issue. Prior to that, during the first decade or so of the new FIFRA, attention shifted from being concerned with product safety to focusing on data confidentiality and the financial compensation for its use by other companies.[160] That does not necessarily mean that safety is ignored or that all sides have reached consensus on what constitutes a health risk, but that the environmental safety issue is now contested more at the staff level within EPA's pesticide office than at the administrator's level or in the courts. The pesticide industry has focused instead on allocating the tremendously expensive costs of developing and registering the few products that survive the testing process and can be marketed. But for that reason, the judicial doctrines on health and risk set forth in EPA's first half-dozen years remain the basis for pesticide regulation.

The extensive litigation about federal preemption has already been summarized in section 7.3, above, of this chapter. The challenges to the implementation of FQPA are discussed in section 11.6, below.

8.1 Basic Cases

The early pesticides cases, originating in the period before EPA's creation, generally resulted in court determinations that the responsible federal agency, usually meaning USDA, had not sufficiently examined the health and environmental problems.

A leading case in this respect is the landmark 1970 court of appeals decision by Judge Bazelon in *Environmental Defense Fund v. Hardin,*[161] which not only gave legal standing to environmental groups under the FIFRA but also determined that the secretary of agriculture's failure to take prompt action on a request for suspension of the registration of DDT was tantamount to a denial of suspension and therefore was suitable for judicial review.[162]

That same year the Seventh Circuit Court of Appeals held *en banc* in *Nor-Am v. Hardin*[163] that a pesticide registrant could not enjoin a suspension order by the secretary of agriculture since the administrative remedies, namely, the full cancellation proceedings, had not been exhausted: "The emergency suspension becomes final only if unopposed or affirmed in whole or in part, by subsequent decisions based upon a full and formal consideration."[164]

An underlying reason for the court's action, which took the unusual step of reversing a three-judge court of appeals panel in the same circuit,[165] was the realization that the suspension procedure, which had been designed to deal with imminent hazards to the public, could effectively be short-circuited by injunctions. In the court's view, therefore, a suspension decision is only equivalent to a temporary injunction that shall hold until the full cancellation proceedings are completed.[166]

One of the most important of the earlier cases was decided under the name *EDF v. Ruckelshaus.*[167] The court, in another opinion by Judge Bazelon, found that the secretary of agriculture had earlier failed to take prompt action on a request for the interim suspension of DDT registration but that the secretary's findings of fact, such as the risk of cancer and its toxic effect on certain animals, implicitly constituted a finding of "substantial question concerning the safety of DDT," which the court declared warranted a cancellation decision. The suspension issue was remanded (to the administrator of the newly created EPA, William Ruckelshaus) once again for further consideration.

The decision is worthy of attention on two additional points. First, Judge Bazelon made the sweeping statement that "the FIFRA requires the secretary to issue notices and thereby initiate the administrative process whenever there is a substantial question about the safety of the registered pesticide. The statutory scheme contemplates that these questions will be explored in the full light of a public hearing and not resolved behind the closed doors of the secretary."[168]

Second, the court approved the findings of the secretary that a hazard may be imminent even if its effect would not become realized for many years, as is the case with most carcinogens, and that the "public" protected by the suspension provision includes fish and wildlife in the environment as well as any narrow threat to human health.

8.2 Labels in Theory and Practice

FIFRA is based on labeling. Yet EPA has realized for decades that most people pay little heed to label warnings or directions. As one prominent pesticide official tersely admitted, "Labeling is almost worthless." Another, a former head of EPA's pesticide office, Daniel Barolo, voiced an even stronger view on the label issue: "We all agree that the label stinks."[169] Yet the system is so integral to FIFRA and so engrained now as not to be changed easily.

One of the most interesting early pesticide cases, *In re Stearns*,[170] raised the question of whether a chemical that was too toxic to be safely used around the home could be banned even though it was labeled properly with cautionary statements and symbols such as the skull and crossbones. "Stearn's Electric Paste," a phosphorous rat and roach killer, was so potent that even a small portion of a tube could kill a child, and a larger dose would be fatal to an adult. There was no known antidote. An incomplete survey of state health officials indicated several dozen deaths and many serious accidents, most involving young children. (It looked like toothpaste.)

Because of this hazard and the existence of safer substitutes, the USDA canceled the registration of the paste in May 1969, before the creation of EPA, and a USDA judicial officer upheld this action in January 1971 by relying on the provision in the old FIFRA that "the term misbranded shall apply . . . to any economic poison . . . if the labeling accompanying it does not contain directions for use which are necessary and, if complied with, adequate for the protection of the public."[171]

A year and a half later, however, the Seventh Circuit Court of Appeals concluded that the statutory test for misbranding was whether a product was safe when used in conformity with the label directions, not whether abuse or misuse was inevitable. The court was impressed with the conspicuous poison markings and contended that "disregard of such a simple warning would constitute gross negligence."[172] The hazard to young children left the court chillingly unmoved:

"such tragedies are a common occurrence in today's complex society and must be appraised as discompassionately as possible." The cancellation order was set aside.

Clearly, this 1972 decision placed much too much emphasis on the label and not enough on the environmental safety of the product.

The issue was confronted more decisively by the Eighth Circuit a year later in another Lindane case, *Southern National v. EPA*.[173] The registrants challenged a proposed EPA label reading in part, "Not for use or sale to drug stores, super-markets, or hardware stores or other establishments that sell insecticides to consumers. Not for sale to or use in food handling, processing or serving establishments." In EPA's opinion, acceptance of such a label would avoid the necessity of canceling the entire registration. The court questioned whether EPA was within the scope of its powers under the (old) FIFRA in placing the burden on the manufacturer to discourage distribution to homes but nevertheless sustained the agency action in all respects.

EPA's policy position, both then and now, is that if there are safer alternatives to a product that arguably constitutes a substantial question of safety, the hazardous product should be removed from the market.[174]

8.3 Fraudulent Registrations

A pesticide registered using indisputably fraudulent or misrepresented data should be invalid. This seems obvious and axiomatic. Yet for many years some commentators assumed that there was no clear regulatory mechanism for invalidating a registration once issued, except by a full-blown cancellation process. This was not quite the case, for EPA had previously revoked rather than canceled at least two registrations for misrepresentation.[175] Nevertheless, in *In re Termilind*[176] the deceptive registrant argued that FIFRA did not provide any procedure except cancellation-suspension for removing a pesticide from the market once the registration had been issued. EPA relied on the inherent authority of an agency to correct its own error and found the fraudulent registration void *ab initio*, that is, invalid from the beginning.[177]

EPA's decision seems simple enough, but it had three other consequences worth noting. First, since it took the agency 20 months to come to this conclusion, the deceitful registrants reportedly scored a sizable number of sales. Moreover, EPA made a controversial decision to allow continued sales of existing stocks until they were depleted. Second, the agency read into the statute a "fitness" provision. "If the Agency knows that a registrant has a history of willful misrepresentation, the reliability of the materials submitted by the applicant is subject to question." Therefore, the agency could not make the required determination under FIFRA Section 3(c) that the pesticide will not "generally cause unreasonable adverse effects on the environment."[178]

Third, this innocuous-seeming decision unleashed a flood of petitions that other pesticide registrations were fraudulent for one reason or other. EPA responded with a series of *ad hoc* procedural decisions that were not based on legally issued regulations, while long delays served to reward any miscreants if they existed.[179]

8.4 Possible Future Litigation Issues

There are several FIFRA areas where litigation or at least considerable controversy may be expected in the future. These include whether Clean Water Act permits are required for pesticide releases in or near water. (This is discussed briefly below, in section 12.3.) Second, possibly, would be the ramifications of spray drift: what is normal and acceptable extent of unintentional deviation of some applied pesticides to the property of others, and even the definition of spray. Third, the plea for reinstatement of DDT for antimalarial uses abroad is being widely debated now (see sections 5.4 and 9.0), and some allowance might be made.

9.0 Exports and Imports

Section 17 of FIFRA, in addition to maintaining the provision that imports should be subject to the same requirements of testing and registration as domestic products, also retained the controversial provision excluding U.S. exports from coverage under the act, other than for certain recordkeeping requirements.[180] The equating of manufacturing and imports is logical since potential harm to the environment is not dependent on the origin of the pesticides. The exemption of exports is more controversial.[181]

There were two reasons for this treatment of exports. First, the agricultural chemical producers, seeing the market for some of their pesticide products, such as the chlorinated hydrocarbons, drying up in this country, wished to continue exporting the products abroad. They argued that foreign producers would not be stopped from manufacturing these chemicals, and they wished to continue to compete as well as to keep in operation profitable product lines.

A secondary but more compelling reason was that cancellation decisions made in the United States are based upon a risk-benefit analysis that might have little relevance to conditions abroad. For example, the oft-mentioned DDT is neither needed nor, because of insect resistance, very useful for the control of malaria in the United States. However, the situation in, say, Ceylon (Sri Lanka), might be quite different and should thus be considered differently there.[182]

One objection to this latter argument is that persistent pesticides may be distributed by oceans and the atmosphere in a worldwide circulation pattern that does not stop at national boundaries. A second problem is that there is no requirement that foreign purchasers relying on EPA registration as proof of a product's safety be notified of cancellation-suspension proceedings. Only after a final agency decision—which may take years—is the State Department legally required to inform foreign governments. The 1978 amendments did add a requirement that such exports be labeled that they are "not registered for use in the U.S."[183]

In 1980, EPA issued a final policy statement on labeling requirements.[184] Under the 1978 amendments, pesticides that are manufactured for export must have appropriate bilingual labeling that identifies the product and protects the persons who come into contact with it. If the pesticide is not registered for use in the United States, the exporter must obtain a statement from the foreign purchaser acknowledging its unregistered status.[185]

The policy statement implements these new requirements by requiring exported products to bear labels containing an EPA establishment number, a use classification statement, and the identity of the producer, as well as information about whether the pesticide is registered for use in the United States. In the case of highly toxic pesticides, a skull and crossbones must appear and the word poison, along with a statement of practical treatment written bilingually.[186] What the term bilingual would mean in a multilingual country, such as India, is not clear.

The policy statement also requires that a foreign purchaser of an unregistered pesticide sign a statement showing that he understands that the pesticide is not registered for use in the United States. The exporter must receive the acknowledgment before the product is released for shipment and submit it to EPA within seven days of receipt. EPA then transmits the acknowledgments to the appropriate foreign officials via the State Department. The acknowledgment procedure applies only to the first annual shipment of an unregistered pesticide to a producer; subsequent shipments of the product to the same producer need not repeat the acknowledgment process.[187]

10.0 Amendments to FIFRA

The changes in a law over time may not be exciting, but they do show those provisions that have become most controversial. They can also illuminate the political trends, which show the future course of the law. (This evolution has cursorily been described in section 2 of this chapter.)

10.1 Need for FIFRA Renewal

The authorization for FIFRA under the 1972 act was limited to three years.[188] Congress was therefore provided the opportunity in 1975 and periodically thereafter to review the strengths and shortcomings of the 1972 legislation, even though some portions of that law were not scheduled to go into effect until four years after enactment.[189] This review, however, also provided a chance to redress the balance for those, both within and without Congress, who believed that EPA had been given too much authority.[190]

Three decades of amendments to FIFRA have produced no coherent pattern of improvements to the basic statute. Unlike most other environmental statutes, there has been no clear progression toward greater environmental protection (some amendments, in the 1970s, even went the other way). And those that were more protective, in theory, have not proved very effective.

10.2 Hogtie the EPA: 1975 Amendments to FIFRA

Congress's 1975 amendments to FIFRA were significant, not for what they actually changed but for the motivations that prompted them. The amendments themselves were viewed by many as, at best, unnecessary and, at worst, a further encumbrance upon an already complicated administrative procedure. They did, however, indicate a strong desire on the part of Congress—or at least the respective agriculture committees of the House and Senate—to restrict EPA's authority to regulate pesticides. The situation was summarized by an editorial in a Washington, D.C., newspaper captioned, "Trying to Hogtie the EPA."[191]

10.3 Data Compensation Changed: 1978 Amendments to FIFRA

The 1978 amendments made changes in a number of areas. Studies showing pesticide efficacy were made optional, relieving EPA of the chore of determining whether a pesticide actually worked for the purposes claimed. The data compensation provisions of the act were made even more complex, although the EPA administrator was removed from his role as arbitrator of the financial settlement.

10.4 Two-House Veto: 1980 Amendments to FIFRA

FIFRA was amended again in 1980, but the amendments made only minor changes in Section 25 of the act to provide for a two-house congressional veto of EPA rules and regulations and some additional tampering with the Scientific Advisory Committee.

10.5 FIFRA Lite: 1988 Amendments to FIFRA

FIFRA was amended again in October 1988. Dubbed "FIFRA Lite," the amendments were notable mostly for what they did not contain; namely, they lacked the hotly debated provisions sought by environmentalists for protection of the nation's groundwater supplies from contamination by pesticides. The bill also lacked the section sought by the grocery manufacturers to preempt stricter state standards like those under California's Proposition 65 right-to-know law. The legislation did correct a long-standing flaw in the act involving compensation for canceled pesticides and streamlined the pesticide reregistration process, but it also imposed a substantial fee.

10.6 Minor Pesticide Uses: 1990 Amendments to FIFRA

The 1990 Food and Agriculture Act, part of a larger farm bill, made small changes to FIFRA. It provided recordkeeping requirements for certified applicators, and it allowed the administrator to waive the maintenance fee for minor agricultural use pesticides under certain conditions.

10.7 Bye-Bye Delaney: 1996 Amendments to FIFRA

Prodded by the courts, Congress finally undertook the long-overdue revision of the Delaney Clause. Because of the immediacy and the importance of these amendments, they will be given a special discussion in section 11, below.

10.8 Fees and Timetables: 2003 PRIA Amendments to FIFRA

The PRIA sought to reduce the time frames for registration decisions, as well as to make those decisions more predictable, in exchange for enhanced fees from the pesticide industry ($116 million over five years). Small businesses, defined as fewer than 500 employees (previously 150) get a waiver of half the fee; if annual global gross sales are less than $10 million, all the fee is waived. The PRIA amendments mostly update the fee structure for various EPA pesticide activities.

11.0 Food Quality Protection Act (FQPA) of 1996

The Delaney Clause was a well-intentioned 1958 amendment to the Food, Drug, and Cosmetic Act (FDCA) that barred any cancer-causing food additive. It seemed to make sense at the time, for who would want to put carcinogenic additives into food? The problem, however, was twofold. First, pesticide residues were considered food additives. Second, the increasing sophistication in analytical chemical techniques meant that pesticides could be detected at lower and lower levels. EPA was faced with the prospect of having to ban many common pesticides, under FDCA's complex residue-tolerance process (described below in section 12.1), because trace amounts could now be detected in foods.[192]

11.1 Regulatory Dilemma under the Delaney Clause

EPA tried to follow a reasonable approach. For two decades the agency tried repeatedly to persuade Congress to correct the situation. Environmentalists opposed this attempt, not because they did not recognize the increasing scientific absurdity, but because they feared allowing a regulatory dike to be breached. In any case, EPA's effort failed because, one suspects, congressmen were reluctant to be seen as "soft on cancer."

In October 1988, EPA tried a new approach. It issued a new interpretation of the Delaney Clause with regulations permitting use of four pesticides that were known carcinogens—benomyl, mancozeb, phosmet, and trifluralin—under circumstances that the agency concluded would pose only a *de minimis* risk of causing cancer.[193] However, a federal appellate court held in *Les v. Reilly*[194] that EPA had no discretion to permit use of carcinogenic food additives, including pesticides, regardless of the minimal degree of risk. The court thereby refused to allow EPA to expunge the clause by administrative fiat, even if it might be obsolete. That determination was left to Congress. As the court explained, "once the finding of carcinogenicity is made, the EPA has no discretion."[195]

11.2 Demise of Delaney

The *Les v. Reilly* case finally prodded Congress into doing what it had long hesitated to do—update the tolerance-residue provisions in FDCA. The result was the passage of FQPA.[196]

According to FQPA Section 405, any pesticide residue on a food is considered unsafe unless the agency has set a tolerance for the substance and the residue is below that level. However, EPA is no longer bound to ban insignificant residues of pesticides just because they might be classified as carcinogens. Instead, the agency can grant a tolerance if the product is determined to be safe. As defined in the amendments, safe means that "there is a reasonable certainty that no harm will result from the aggregate exposure to the pesticide chemical residue," including both dietary and nondietary total exposure.[197]

Despite the controversy over whether a distinction should be made between residues in raw and in processed foods, in this section FQPA applied this rule of safety to both types of food.[198]

Even if the administrator does decide that a particular pesticide is not safe, he is allowed under FQPA to grant a tolerance, provided that the pesticide (1) has public health benefits greater than the risk from the dietary residue or (2) if the tolerance was "necessary to avoid a significant disruption in domestic production of an adequate, wholesome, and economical food supply."[199] This could be done if the yearly risk from exposure is no more than 10 times the yearly risk that the administrator had found to be safe.

Under the amendment, the operative standard has moved from Delaney's unrealistic "zero risk" to a "negligible" risk standard, based on a lifetime increased cancer risk of one in a million.[200] This, of course, presumes that such risks can be calculated or even determined, which is questionable, but the change nevertheless is a major step forward toward regulatory sanity.

11.3 Public Health Pesticides

With the growing concern over insect-vectored threats to human health, such as Lyme disease, Congress included Subtitle C in FQPA.[201] This amended the definition of unreasonable adverse effects on the environment by requiring risk assessment for public health pesticides separately from other pesticides. The intent was to ensure that pesticides necessary for controlling disease be given a more sympathetic review. In addition, Subtitle C defines public health pesticide as any minor use pesticide product registered for use and used for vector control in public health programs. Finally, at registration, the administrator is required to set standards considering the degree of potential beneficial or adverse effect on humans and the environment.

11.4 Infants and Children

Whether infants and children are more (or less) susceptible to the harmful effects of pesticides is not known, but the National Research Council had earlier recommended that this possibility be studied. The FQPA added a requirement for special studies of the issue, and this was used as part of the pro-environmental public relations trade-off for the law that gutted the hitherto untouchable Delaney Clause. In signing the law on the eve of the 1996 Democratic Convention, President Clinton surrounded himself with children and proclaimed, "I call this the Peace of Mind Act because parents will know that the fruits, grains and vegetables children eat are safe."[202]

11.5 Human Test Data

One of the unintended consequences of FQPA's emphasis on studying the effect of pesticides on children is to raise the whole question of human testing. While no one is deliberately dosing children with pesticides, so far as is known, a dozen or more known tests involving adults have been submitted to EPA over the past few years. While there has long been a debate about the accuracy of animal testing data, especially with carcinogens, the renewed interest in human testing is driven by a new factor. Because the FQPA protocols have led toward sharply lower levels of allowed pesticides in food, some chemical manufacturers have sought to show that humans might be less susceptible to certain pesticides. Either the human reaction is less sensitive than that of the animal models or the effects might not exist at all.

The debate is now whether it is ethical to accept such data from paid volunteers. In 1998 EPA declared a moratorium on using such tests. In 2002 this led one trade association to sue EPA in federal court to compel acceptance. The plaintiffs contended that EPA had a statutory obligation to consider all relevant and reliable data.[203] The Court of Appeals for the D.C. Circuit struck down the EPA ban, albeit on procedural grounds for lack of proper rulemaking notice.[204]

A scientific panel of manufacturers, environmentalists, and researchers met in January 2003 to attempt to resolve this highly emotional impasse.[205] Historians may recall a similar debate decades ago about whether to use the results of Nazi medical experiments in World War II concentration camps. This controversy never came to a head, however, because the quality of the German experiments was so poor that there was little information to use.

11.6 Other Provisions of FQPA

The FQPA consisted of four other titles which made changes in FIFRA. The most significant, Title I, allows an emergency suspension for 90 days without a simultaneous notice of intent to cancel.[206] Other changes establish a standing Science Review Board of 60 scientists that would assist the Science Advisory Panel for FIFRA,[207] set a goal of evaluating the data supporting pesticide registrations every fifteen years,[208] and establish two new categories of pesticide applicators for those handling routine lawn and maintenance work.[209]

Title II deals with special treatment for minor crop uses, which have historically gotten short shrift from both EPA and the leading pesticide companies.[210] This is a welcome addition, though we will have to see how it works in practice. The title also provides special arrangements for antimicrobial pesticide registrations, that is, disinfectants and sterilants, which are very different from general agricultural pesticides but have hitherto been treated little differently under the law.[211]

Title III establishes a data-collection program to assure the safety of infants and children, whose consumption of or vulnerability to pesticides might possibly require extra measures. Title IV sets pesticide registration fees.

This legislation, despite its controversial abolishing of Delaney, received unprecedented bipartisan support. It passed the House of Representatives unanimously. Yet, ironically, the belated complaints from some chemical companies about certain provisions, notably the data-collection requirements, have reportedly been so acerbic that some believe the bill might not have passed if the complaints had been registered earlier.

12.0 Pesticide Regulation under Other Federal Statutes

Pesticides are not regulated solely under FIFRA. They may also involve regulatory authority under FDCA, under the statutes of several other federal agencies, and under other environmental laws administered by EPA.

12.1 Pesticides under the Food, Drug and Cosmetics Act (FDCA)

One important function of EPA regarding pesticides is not derived from FIFRA: the setting of tolerances for pesticide residues in food. This authority, originally granted to the FDA under FDCA,[212] was transferred to EPA by the 1970 Reorganization Plan establishing the agency and, more specifically, by subsequent detailed memorandums of agreement between EPA and FDA.

The reorganization plan provided that EPA should set tolerances and "monitor compliance," while the secretary of health, education, and welfare, predecessor to today's health and human services (HHS), would continue to enforce compliance.[213] The amendments to FIFRA in 1972 also invested EPA with authority to prevent misuse of registered pesticides. Under Section 408 of FDCA, the administrator issues regulations exempting any pesticides for which a tolerance is unnecessary to protect the public health. Otherwise, he "shall promulgate regulations establishing tolerances with respect to . . . pesticide chemicals which are not generally recognized among experts . . . as safe for use . . . to the extent necessary to protect the public health." This is the GRAS list.

Pesticide residues are present in (mostly) negligible levels in most meats, fruits, and vegetables whether or not chemicals are applied to them. Using the most advanced analytical chemical techniques, DDT, for example, is still detectable in most foods, even in mothers' milk. As analytical methods continue to improve, detection of pesticides in anything can become universal.

Before registration of a pesticide, a residue tolerance must be set for the maximum level at which that chemical can be safely ingested. The process has been described as quasi-scientific, or even pseudoscientific, since no one really knows what levels are safe, if any, and how to calculate for the different sensitivities of individuals. Therefore, regulatory levels are usually set at two or three orders of magnitude (100 or 1,000 times) below the level at which the pesticide has demonstrated no effect on experimental animals.[214] Some particularly hazardous chemicals are set at "zero residue," but this is causing an increasing problem as the detection capability of analytical equipment is improved.[215]

EPA's pesticide jurisdiction is supposed to cover only residues resulting from a chemical's use as a pesticide but not exposure resulting from, say, dust blowing from a factory (this may be covered by EPA's Clean Air Act) or a truck carrying the chemicals. In two major cases involving HCB (hexachlorobenzene) contamination of cattle in Louisiana and sheep in the Rocky Mountains, the HCB was blown from open trucks onto pastureland while being transported from one point to another. EPA assumed responsibility for these cases because the tolerance problems regarding health are really the same whether the chemical entered the food as a result of agricultural use or in some other manner, and FDA was only too glad to oblige.

The question of whether DDT was an unintentional food additive in fish within the meaning of FDCA was raised long ago in *U.S. v. Ewing Bros.*[216] The Seventh Circuit explained that prior to the Delaney Amendment, which banned all additives "found to induce cancer when ingested by man or animal," the term did not cover substances present in the raw product and unchanged by processing. However, after 1958 the definition was expanded so that a single tolerance could cover both raw and processed foods. Since DDT was an additive and EPA had not issued a tolerance, DDT was theoretically a food adulterant and contaminated items were liable to seizure.[217]

This could mean, however, that most foods could be seized as adulterated, including the Great Lakes fish at issue in Ewing. Realizing this in 1969, FDA had established an interim action level of 5 parts per million DDT in fish, thereby excluding all but the most contaminated samples.[218] This procedure was approved by the Seventh Circuit Court of Appeals in *U.S. v. Goodman,*[219] which held that the commissioner of FDA had "specific statutory authority in the Act empowering him to refrain from prosecuting minor violations"[220] and that this permitted him to set and enforce action levels in lieu of totally prohibiting the distribution of any food containing DDT at any level.

The FDA has expanded the presumed scope of its authority under the Medical Devices Act of 1976 so as to include disinfectants as medical devices. These pesticides, which have always been regulated as registered pesticides under FIFRA, are now subjected to dual jurisdiction. A memorandum of understanding between the two agencies endeavors to divide the field between medical and nonmedical application.

12.2 Clean Air Act of 1970 and Its Progeny

Pesticides in the air may be regulated under Section 112 of the Clean Air Act pertaining to hazardous air pollutants. A hazardous pollutant is defined as one for which "no ambient air quality standard is applicable and which in the judgment of the Administrator may cause, or contribute to, an increase in mortality or an increase in severe irreversible, or incapacitating reversible illness."[221] EPA publishes a list of hazardous air pollutants from time to time, and once a pollutant is listed, proposed regulations establishing stationary source emission standards must be issued unless the substance is conclusively shown to be safe. This section has so far not been applied to pesticides but could acquire more significance in the future.

12.3 Federal Water Pollution Control Act of 1972

The Clean Water Act—historically the Federal Water Pollution Control Act (FWPCA)—has collided with FIFRA in a most unexpected way. In March 2001, a federal appeals court on the West Coast decided that a water discharge permit was required for the spraying of aquatic pesticides to control algae and weeds in an irrigation canal. This NPDES (National Pollution Discharge Elimination System) was designed to control industrial and other effluents from factories and other usually stationary sources.[222] It had never before been held that a pesticide being applied exactly as intended was a "pollutant," a definition that could have serious implications for thousands of other products besides pesticides. Moreover, the ruling imposed a significant administrative burden; the permit system is a slow and ponderous one, yet a new permit would presumably be required each time a farmer or applicator wanted to spray a different portion of his holding.

Lest anyone think that the permit requirement was limited to aquatic applications to a few ponds or canal banks, the following year the same appeals court extended this ruling to the Forest Service's aerial spraying of insecticides in Washington and Oregon.[223] The court held that the area-wide spraying of national forests constituted a "point source" of pollutants, and a permit was thus required because some of the pesticides being sprayed might get into streams and lakes.

Both EPA and the states have attempted to work around this problem to provide some limited regulatory relief or exemption from enforcement actions.[224] Then, in late November 2006, the George W. Bush administration issued a final rule, replacing an earlier one, that an NPDES permit is not required in two instances: (1) when the pesticide is made to control pests in the water itself and (2) when the application is to control pests that are "over, including near, waters" in question.[225]

The Clean Water Act of 1972, as amended, has at least three provisions applicable to pesticides. Under Section 301, pesticide manufacturers and formulators, like all other industrial enterprises, must apply for discharge permits if they release effluent into any body of water. These point sources of pollution had to apply the best practicable control technology by 1977 and by 1983 had to use the best available control technology.[226]

Hazardous and ubiquitous pesticides may be controlled under Section 307 governing toxic substances.[227] Within one year of the listing of a chemical as a toxic substance, the special discharge standards set for it must be achieved. There was originally some dispute over whether pesticides should properly be regulated under this section because, unless they are part of a discharge from an industrial concern, they generally derive from nonpoint sources such as runoff from fields and therefore could be controlled under a third provision, Section 208, which is largely under the jurisdiction of the states.[228] The requirement of an NPDES discharge permit not just for manufacturing effluent but also for actual pesticide applications has been very controversial since the Ninth Circuit's 2002 decision against Forsgren in *League of Wilderness Defenders v. Forsgren* in 2002.[229]

EPA's principal function under Section 208 is to identify and oversee problems of agricultural pollution, regulated at the state and local levels. By 1977, according to the statute, state authorities were to have formulated control programs for the protection of water quality from pesticides and other agricultural pollutants such as feedlots.

In January 1991, EPA issued regulations requiring operators of 80,000 drinking water systems to monitor for the presence of 60 contaminants, including a number of pesticides, and remove those in excess of permitted levels.[230]

12.4 Solid Waste Disposal Acts

EPA had very limited authority under Section 204 of the Solid Waste Disposal Act, as amended by the Resource Recovery Act of 1970,[231] to conduct research, training, demonstrations, and other activities regarding pesticide storage and disposal.[232] Enactment of the Resource Conservation and Recovery Act (RCRA) in October 1976 gave EPA an important tool for controlling the disposal of pesticides, particularly the waste from pesticide manufacture.

12.5 Occupational Safety and Health Act

The EPA and the Department of Labor share somewhat overlapping authority under FIFRA and the Occupational Safety and Health Act (OSHA) for the protection of agricultural workers from pesticide hazards. This produced a heated interagency conflict during 1973, although FIFRA and its legislative history clearly indicated that EPA had primary responsibility for promulgating reentry and other protective standards in this area and that OSHA must yield to existing standards by other federal agencies.[233] The question was finally settled by the White House in EPA's favor after a court had enjoined labor's own proposed standards.[234]

Since then, the two agencies have cooperated on development of the federal cancer policy in the late 1970s, which grew out of EPA's suspension of the pesticides aldrin and dieldrin. In 1990, they concluded a memorandum of understanding to facilitate joint enforcement of their laws.

12.6 Federal Hazardous Substances Act

The Federal Hazardous Substances Act of 1970 regulates hazardous substances in interstate commerce. However, pesticides subject to FIFRA and FDCA have been specifically exempted by regulation[235] from the definition of the term hazardous substance. This statute is administered by the mostly moribund Consumer Product Safety Commission (CPSC), an independent federal agency that also administers the Poison Prevention Packaging Control Act of 1970, designed to protect children from pesticides and other harmful substances. It is not yet clear how EPA and the CPSC will divide their overlapping authority in this area or whether EPA will deign to notice CPSC at all.

12.7 Federal Pesticide Monitoring Programs

The FDA and USDA assist EPA in monitoring pesticide residues in food. The FDA conducts frequent spot checks and publishes an annual Market Basket Survey, in which pesticide residues are analyzed in a representative sampling of grocery items. The FDA's Poison Control Center also compiles current statistics on chemical poisoning. The USDA's Animal and Plant Health Inspection Service conducts spot checks on pesticides in meats and poultry based on samples taken at slaughterhouses throughout the country.

The Department of Interior samples pesticide residues in fish and performs experiments to determine the effects of pesticides that may be introduced into the aquatic environment. The Geological Survey Division of the Interior also conducts periodic nationwide water sampling for pesticides and other contaminants. The National Oceanic and Atmospheric Administration under the Department of Commerce monitors aquatic areas for pesticide levels, and the Department of Transportation's Office of Hazardous Substances records accidents involving pesticides in shipment and distribution.

Several of the FIFRA amendments considered in the early 1990s have been directed toward remedying perceived shortcomings in the pesticide residue system. Unless there is some new evidence of a real need for such legislative protection, this seems to be a solution looking for a problem.

12.8 National Environmental Policy Act

EPA is not bound by the National Environmental Policy Act (NEPA) to file environmental impact statements on its pesticide decisions. The procedures under FIFRA are an adequate substitute. Although the strict language of NEPA states that all agencies of the federal government should file impact statements, this law was enacted before EPA existed. The courts almost unanimously have found that there is little logic in requiring an agency whose sole function is protection of the environment to file a statement obliging it to take into consideration environmental factors.[236]

Courts nevertheless hesitated to grant a blanket exemption to EPA, preferring to stress that EPA actions are mandated by a particular statute (although this justification has not exempted certain non-environmental agencies), or they have noted that EPA procedures for explanation and public comment were an adequate substitute for the same procedures under NEPA.[237] This "functional equivalence" argument has also been applied to state environmental agencies.[238]

13.0 Biotechnology

The field of biotechnology promises great advances in human well-being, being more important in the twenty-first century than computers were in the last half of the twentieth. In the environmental area, it offers innovations, such as the creation of industrial enzymes that would be capable of, among other things, purifying water and degrading toxic chemical wastes. However, because genetic engineering is so new, still being developed, and little understood, it has been surrounded by controversy over both its safety and who should regulate it.

13.1 The Promise and Fear of Biotechnology

Biotechnology's relevance for pesticides is that scientists have already succeeded in inserting genes with insecticidal effects into a few crops. This inhibits or kills pests seeking to munch on these plants. At first glance one would expect environmentalists to welcome such "natural" pesticides because this means the crops require little or no chemical spraying. After all, most plants have developed their own defense systems over the millennia, resulting in such products as caffeine, nicotine, capsicum (hot peppers), and even chocolate. Instead, however, environmentalists have led the opposition to this new technology.

There are at least three reasons for these objections. First, there are fears that these products can have unintended dire effects on nontarget species. For example, several years ago some studies raised the concern that genes spliced into corn to protect it from noxious caterpillars could also be lethal to the lovely monarch butterfly.[239]

Second, there is a vaguer but more alarming concern that these "frankenfoods" can harm man and the environment by proliferating into other crops, mutating into other forms, or turning out to have other harmful traits. In this view, biotechnology could be akin to the kudzu vine, water hyacinth, or scores of other plants and animals that were initially fostered but for some reason got out of control.

The debate over "frankenfood" reached an absurd point in August 2002 when the African country of Zambia refused shipments of genetically modified corn despite widespread famine in the country. People died from this decision; the question is, for what? European nations denied that they had encouraged African nations to refuse the grain. In January 2003 then–U.S. Trade Representative Robert B. Zoellick declared that the antiscientific European position was contributing to starvation in the developing world. "I find it immoral that people are not being able to be supplied food to live in Africa because people have invented dangers about biotechnology."[240]

Third—and here this author shows a bit of cynicism—European countries and others that have fallen far behind the United States in bioengineering want to reduce competition from U.S. agricultural and other products. Using boycotts and governmental decrees, the opposition to biotechnology has thus become a novel form of "nontariff barrier" in world trade.

Without dismissing these concerns, one must note that all of our important food crops have undergone centuries of genetic manipulation. This is evident from looking at the tiny husks that became modern corn or the harsh grass that became our wheat. Our ancestors may not have understood Mendelian principles and gene splicing, but they nevertheless turned weeds into feed. Therefore, the bucolic dream of all-natural foods is a myth.

13.2 The Initial Controversy over Regulating Biotechnology

Some groups want tighter regulation of the biotechnology industry. Jeremy Rifkin, head of an environmental group called Foundation for Economic Trends, is one of the most determined opponents of biotechnology. In fact, he believes it should be banned altogether. Most of his attention has focused on biotechnology developments and efforts in the pesticides field.[241]

In 1980, however, Rifkin lost the landmark case of *Diamond v. Chakrobarty*[242] when the Supreme Court ruled that genetically altered organisms may be patented. Now when individuals and firms put time and money into biotechnology research, they can be assured of earning economic rewards, but the ruling also stretched considerably the definition of patentability.

In May 1986, EPA authorized the first permits for the release of a genetically engineered pesticide to a professor from the University of California at Berkeley. The genetically altered bacteria strain, known as "ice-minus" or "Frostban," was developed by the university and licensed by Advanced Genetic Sciences Inc.[243]

On June 18, 1986, President Reagan signed the Coordinated Framework for Regulation of Biotechnology, which sets out specific agency roles and statutory authority and ensures the industry's environmental safety and economic viability. Legislation has also been proposed in Congress to set up a regulatory structure for reviewing the safety of genetically engineered products under TSCA.

In August 1990, a blue-ribbon panel under the direction of then Vice President Dan Quayle concluded that biotech products should be treated no differently from those produced by conventional chemical methods. These risk-based principles, for use by EPA, USDA, FDA, and others, were not much different from those currently in use for FIFRA. In other words, only the end product is relevant; how it was produced, whether by biochemists or by bacteria, should be irrelevant.

The principles were as follows:

1. Federal government regulatory oversight should focus on the characteristics and risks of the biotechnology product, not the process by which it is created.

2. For biotechnology products that require review, regulatory review should be designed to minimize regulatory burden while ensuring the protection of public health and welfare.

3. Regulatory programs should be designed to accommodate the rapid advances in biotechnology. Performance-based standards are, therefore, generally preferred over design standards.

4. In order to create opportunities for the application of innovative new biotechnology products, all regulations in environmental and health areas, whether or not they address biotechnology, should use performance standards rather than specifying rigid controls or specific designs for compliance.[244]

13.3 "Frankenfood" Enforcement

Biologically modified food must receive federal regulatory approval before marketing. In 2000 biomodified "Starburst" corn that had not been approved for human consumption was found in taco shells and many other foodstuffs. A hurried attempt was made to withdraw hundreds of these products from the market, as if they were a serious health risk. EPA's expressed concern was that the corn might provoke an allergic reaction in some people and therefore needed to be tested. This incident revealed the difficulty of keeping food products separate from non-approved products. In December 2000 the USDA announced plans to issue rules needed to prevent contamination and to monitor gene-spliced crops.[245]

This distinction between the techniques for producing better plants is contrary to the earlier federal guidelines that looked only at the effects of the final product, not how it was produced. And if each plant variation is to be tested for its effects, then that should logically be required for each new graft or crossbred variety.

Admittedly there is at least one difference with genetic engineered crops. As the late Nobel Prize winner Norman Borlaug pointed out,

> In the past conventional plant breeders were forced to bring unwanted genes along with desirable ones when incorporating insect or disease resistance in a new crop variety. The extra genes often had negative effects, and it took years of crossbreeding and selection to oust them. Conventional plant breeding is crude in comparison to the methods being used in genetic engineering, where we move one or a few genes that we know are useful.[246]

14.0 Research Sources

- Pesticide.net; Agchemicals.info; Biopesticides.info; Antimicrobials.info: http://www.pestlaw.com

- National Pesticide Information Center (NPIC): 1-800-858-7378; npic@ace.orst.edu

- EPA's Antimicrobial Information Hotline: 1-703-308-0127 or 1-703-308-6467; Info_Antimicrobial@epa.gov

- OPPTS (Office of Prevention, Pesticides, and Toxic Substances) Chemical Library: 202-566-0800; http://www.epa.gov/opptintr/library

- Fact Sheets for Health and Safety, Regulatory Action, and Specific Chemical Facts: http://www.epa.gov/pesticides/factsheets/index.htm

Notes

[1] Rachel Carson, *Silent Spring* (New York: Houghton Mifflin, 1962). See also the extensive biography of her in Linda Lear, *Rachel Carson: The Life of the Author of Silent Spring* (N.Y.: Henry Holt, 1997).

[2] A reader wishing more detail on pesticides generally is referred to the book by Marshall Lee Miller, ed., *Pesticides Law Handbook* (Rockville, MD: Government Institutes, 1999).

[3] EPA Pesticide Program Annual Report for 2003, "Promoting Safety for America's Future," p. 4.

[4] One environmentalist, Audubon's Roland Clement, has tried to put this adulation in perspective: "It's a fabrication to say that she's the founder of the environmental movement. She stirred the pot. That's all." (Quoted in Eliza Griswold's "How 'Silent Spring' Ignited the Environmental Movement," Reuters, 21 September 2012.) He is right, of course, in that there were many environmentalists toiling in the vineyards decades before Carson, but the title of Griswold's article sums it up best.

5   The author was special assistant to the first admiminstrator of EPA and also chief judicial officer.

6   There is voluminous literature on accusations that pesticides approved by EPA can cause considerable, perhaps to particularly sensitive individuals. For example, Jessie MacLeod, *Canary in the Courtroom: How Pesticide Poisoning Changed a Woman's Life and Forced Her into Civil Action* (New York: Universe, 2006).

7   36 Stat. 331 (1910).

8   61 Stat. 190 (1947). The present act is still known as FIFRA, although there have been major changes, especially with the FEPCA amendments in 1972, in the law since then. For convenience, we will refer to the pre-1972 version as the "Old FIFRA."

9   Old FIFRA (pre-1972) § 2(z)(2)(d). *See* H. Rep. 313 (80th Cong., 1st Sess.). 1947 U.S. Code Cong. Serv. 1200, 1201.

10 Under Food, Drug, and Cosmetic Act (FDCA) practice, doctors may prescribe pharmaceuticals for "off indication" purposes not mentioned on the labels—a practice that has survived repeated onslaughts by the drug regulators at the Food and Drug Administration.

11 *Victrylite Candle Co. v. Brannan*, 201 F.2d 206 (D.C. Cir., 1952).

12 Act of May 12, 1964, Pub. L. No. 88-30S, 78 Stat. 190. There were other, less significant, amendments in 1959 (73 Stat. 286) and 1961 (75 Stat. 18, 42).

13 Instead, a Pesticide Registration Notice would be sent ordering the removal of one or more listed uses from the registration.

14 Reorganization Order No. 3 of 1970, § 2(a)(1), 1970 U.S. Code Cong. Ad. News 2996, 2998, 91st Cong. 2nd Sess. The EPA was thus not created by an act of Congress, as most people assume, but by the supposed "anti-environmentalist" president Richard Nixon.

15 It also inherited cases concerning pesticide residues from the Food and Drug Administration of the Department of Health, Education, and Welfare (HEW), now the Department of Health and Human Services (HHS).

16 These cases will be discussed later in section 8 of this chapter.

17 *See* section 6 of this chapter.

18 *See* section 11 of this chapter.

19 EPA official figures for FY 2010 and later, available at www.epa.gov.

20 7 U.S.C. § 135, *et seq.*

21 Pub. L. No. 96-516, 86 Stat. 973, October 21, 1972; Pub. L. No. 94-140, November 28, 1975; Pub. L. No. 95-396, 92 Stat. 819, September 30, 1978; Pub. L. No. 96-539, 94 Stat. 3194; December 17, 1980; Pub. L. No. 100-532, October 25, 1988; 104 Stat. 3627 (1990); Pub. L. No. 104-170, August 2, 1996.

22 Pub. L. No. 92-516, 86 Stat. 973, October 21, 1972.

23 Details of the various amendments are provided in section 10 of this chapter.

24 The amendments to FIFRA are reviewed in somewhat more detail in section 10 of this chapter.

25 Food, Agriculture, Conservation, and Trade Act of 1990, Title XIV, Subtitle H.

26 PRIA became effective on March 23, 2003; there have been several periodic updates since then.

27 This topic is discussed more fully in chapters 2 and 3 of Miller, *Pesticide Law Handbook*, cited above.

28 FIFRA § 2(u), 7 U.S.C. § 136(u).

29 40 C.F.R. § 152.15. Note that this definition under FIFRA is not consistent with the EPA's interpretation of intent in pesticidal exemptions from TSCA, Section 3(2)(B).

30 The EPA has attempted from time to time to challenge this principle, declaring that a substance that makes no pesticidal claims may nevertheless be a pesticide if "everybody knows" it affects pests. The most notable attempt, involving citronella candles, was rebuffed by the courts. *Gulf Oil Corp. v. EPA*, 548 F.2d 1228, 9 ERC 1989 (5th Cir. 1977). In California, however, in the famous "worm poop" case, state environmental regulators fined a producer of worm-generated fertilizer over $100 thousand as a pesticide for claiming it made plants healthier and thus better able to resist pests. The fine was upheld on appeal

but, despite its possible importance, the decision was ordered withheld from official publicationby the nervous court so it cannot be cited as a legal precedent. *Hahn v. Department of Pesticide Regulation* (California Court of Appeals, Third District, C066493, 2012).

31 FIFRA § 2(t), 7 U.S.C. § 136(t). Lest that list leave something out, the EPA has declared it has the authority to declare almost anything else a pest subject to FIFRA. 40 C.F.R. § 152.5.

32 FIFRA § 2(h), 7 U.S.C. § 136(h).

33 41 Fed. Reg. 51065 (Nov. 19, 1976).

34 49 Fed. Reg. 37916 (Sept. 26, 1984).

35 FIFRA § 2(bb), 7 U.S.C. § 136(bb). Courts have sometimes simplified the statutory test by combining it into two parts, grouping the A with B and C with D. *Montana Pole Treating Plant v. I.F. Laucks*, 775 F. Supp. 1399 (D. Mont. 1991), *aff'd*, 993 F.2d 676 (9th Cir. 1993).

36 *Id.* The 1975 amendments, as will be discussed, added the specific requirement that decisions also include consideration of their impact on various aspects of the agricultural economy.

37 The debate over spray drift to neighboring fields is currently one arena for this principle. See EPA, Pesticide Registration Notice, 2001 draft, "Spray and Dust Drift Label Statements for Pesticide Products."

38 FIFRA § 6(a), 7 U.S.C. § 136d(a).

39 The 1988 amendments, in fact, provided that data submitted in support of registration before the EPA's creation in 1970 would no longer be considered adequate for reregistration, unless the applicant bears the burden of proof otherwise.

40 FIFRA § 3(c)(2)(B); 7 U.S.C. § 136a(c)(2)(B).

41 FIFRA § 3(c)(5)(D); 7 U.S.C. § 136a(c)(5)(D).

42 FIFRA § 3(c)(7); 7 U.S.C. § 136a(c)(7).

43 Section 12 of 1978 amendments, amending FIFRA § 6; 7 U.S.C. § 136d. Final regulations were issued in 1979: 44 Fed. Reg. 27932 (May 11, 1979).

44 Section 102 of the 1988 amendments, redesignated as Section 4 of FIFRA by Section 801(q) of the 1988 law.

45 The actual cutoff date is given as January 1, 1970, although the EPA was not created until December 2, 1970.

46 Two commentators predicted that the 1988 reregistration changes would cause the demise of "as much as one third of current registrations." Ferguson & Gray, 19 *ELR* 10070, 10080 (Feb. 1989). Half a decade later congressional hearings revealed that only 250 of the 20,000 older pesticides had been reregistered. Testimony of Peter F. Guerraro, U.S. Government Accounting Office, October, 29 1993, before House Subcomm. on Environment.

47 FIFRA, Section 3(c)(3); 7 U.S.C. § 136a(c)(3).

48 FIFRA, Section 4(k)(3); 7 U.S.C. § 136a-1(k)(3).

49 FIFRA, Section 4(I); 7 U.S.C. § 136a-1(I).

50 *Mobay Chemical Corp. v. Train*, 392 F. Supp. 1342, 8 ERC 1227 (W.D. Mo. 1975).

51 1978 act, amending FIFRA § 3(c)(2); 7 U.S.C. § 136a(c)(2).

52 40 C.F.R. § 158.640.

53 EPA *amicus curiae* brief (submitted Mar. 1999); *Etcheverry v. Tri-Ag Service Inc.*, 993 P.2d 366 (Cal. 2000); *American Cyanamid Co. v. Geye*, 79 S.W. 3d 21 (Tex. 2002); *Lowe's Home Centers v. Olin Corp.*, 313 F.3d 1307 (11th Cir. 2002).

54 40 C.F.R. § 152.44-46.

55 40 C.F.R. § 152.135.

56 FIFRA § 3(e), 7 U.S.C. § 136d(e), and 40 C.F.R. § 152.135.

[57] FIFRA § 10, 7 U.S.C. § 136h. Trade secrets are also a source of contention in the implementation of TSCA.

[58] FIFRA § 10(b), 7 U.S.C. § 136h(b). Note that state agencies are not mentioned.

[59] The reverse situation, where a chemical company sought an administrative subpoena of the testing files of two university researchers on pesticides, was raised in *Dow Chemical Co. v. Allen*, 672 F.2d 1262, 17 ERC 1013 (7th Cir., 1982). The request was rejected as unduly burdensome and not particularly probative since the EPA had not relied on their data in studies still uncompleted.

[60] Pub. L. No. 94-140, 89 Stat. 75 (1975).

[61] *Mobay Chemical Corp. v. Costle*, 447 F. Supp. 811, 12 ERC 1228 (W.D. Mo. 1978), appeal dismissed 439 U.S. 320, *reh. denied*, 440 U.S. 940 (1979); *Chevron Chemical Co. v. Costle*, 443 F. Supp. 1024 (N.D. Cal. 1978).

[62] Pub. L. No. 95-396, 92 Stat. 812.

[63] 104 S. Ct. 2862, 21 ERC 1062 (1984).

[64] 28 U.S.C. § 1491.

[65] FIFRA, § 3(C)(1)(D), 7 U.S.C. § 136a(C)(1)(D).

[66] Pub. L. No. 95-396 § 2(2), 92 Stat. 819.

[67] Pub. L. No. 94-140, § 12, amending FIFRA § 3(c)(1)(D); 7 U.S.C. § 136a(c)(1)(D). The 1972 amendments had not actually specified an effective date, but most authorities assumed it was the date of enactment.

[68] *See Amchem Products Inc. v. GAF Corp.*, 594 F.2d 470 (5th Cir., 1979), *reh. den.*, 602 F.2d 724 (5th Cir. 1979); *Mobay Chemical v. EPA*, 447 F. Supp. 811, 12 ERC 1572 (W.D. Mo., 1975), 439 U.S. 320, 12 ERC 1581 (*per curiam*) (1979).

[69] Initial Decision, FIFRA Comp. Dockets Nos. 33, 34, and 41 (Aug. 19, 1980).

[70] *Ruckelshaus v. Monsanto Co.*, 104 S. Ct. 2862 (1984).

[71] 28 U.S.C. § 1491.

[72] FIFRA § 3(c)(3)(B), 7 U.S.C. § 136a(c)(3)(B).

[73] The original title, certified pesticide applicator (CPA), was changed because of possible confusion with certified public accountants.

[74] Pub. L. No. 94-140 § 5, amending FIFRA § 4(a)(1); 7 U.S.C. § 136a-1(a)(1).

[75] FQPA § 120.

[76] *See* the definition of commercial applicator in FIFRA § 2(e); 7 U.S.C. § 136(e).

[77] States may themselves require an examination of certified applicators, but under the amended FIFRA, the EPA could not make this a prerequisite for state plan approval. *See* Pub. L. 94-140 § 5, amending FIFRA § 4, 7 U.S.C. 136b. *See also* Senate Report No. 94-452, pp. 7–8.

[78] House Report No. 94-497, p. 9.

[79] FIFRA § 5, 7 U.S.C. § 136c. The 1975 amendments added a specific provision for agricultural research agencies, public or private.

[80] FIFRA § 5(a), 7 U.S.C. § 136c(a).

[81] 44 Fed. Reg. at 41783 (July 18, 1978); 40 C.F.R. § 172.20.

[82] 44 Fed. Reg. at 41788. States may, however, issue permits for products containing ingredients subject to the RPAR process.

[83] Pub. L. No. 96-539, 94 Stat. 3194, 3195 amending 7 U.S.C. § 136w(4).

[84] The constitutionality of congressional vetoes of administrative rules has been challenged. The Supreme Court in 1983 held that one-house vetoes are unconstitutional. Since then legislation has had to be revised to conform to the legislative mode: *both* houses must pass legislation, which is then presented to the president for his approval or disapproval. *Immigration and Naturalization Service v. Chadha*, 462 U.S. 919, 103 S. Ct. 2764 (1983), affirming, 634 F.2d 408 (9th Cir., 1980).

85   *EDF v. Ruckelshaus*, 439 F.2d 584, 591-92, 2 ERC 1114, 1119 (D.C. Cir., 1971).

86   The scientific review committee and other features of this process will be discussed in sections 5.10 and 6.1 of this chapter.

87   The cancellation-suspension section of the old act was § 4(c); it is § 6 in the post-1972 FIFRA.

88   FIFRA § 6(b), 7 U.S.C. § 136d(b). Note that the administrator himself may request a hearing, a power that he did not have under the old FIFRA, although in fact he assumed this authority in his August 1971 cancellation order on the herbicide 2,4,5-T.

89   *See* EPA's March 18, 1971, Statement, p. 6, prepared by then special assistant to the administrator Richard Fairbanks, later an ambassador and assistant secretary of state.

90   *EDF v. EPA* 465 F.2d 538, 4 ERC 1523, 1530 (D.C. Cir., 1972).

91   *Nor-Am v. Hardin*, 435 F.2d 1151, 2 ERC 1016 (7th Cir., 1970), *cert. denied*, 402 U.S. 935 (1971).

92   *See In re Shell Chemical*, Opinion of the Administrator, pp. 8–11, 6 ERC 2047 at 2050 (1974).

93   *EDF v. EPA, supra*, 465 F.2d at 537, 4 ERC at 1529.

94   *EDF v. Ruckelshaus, supra*, 439 F.2d at 589, 2 ERC at 1115.

95   *EDF v. EPA, supra*, 465 F.2d at 540, 4 ERC at 1531.

96   *EDF v. Ruckelshaus, supra*, 439 F.2d at 597, 2 ERC at 1121–1122.

97   Its counterpart in TSCA is Section 7, but that provision has remained virtually unused since inception in 1976.

98   469 F. Supp. 892, 13 ERC 1129 (E.D. Mich., 1979).

99   *Id.* at 902, 13 ERC at 1135.

100 *Id.* The court stated that it arrived at its decision to uphold the EPA's order "with great reluctance" and would not have ordered the emergency suspension on the basis of the information before the EPA but was not empowered to substitute its judgment for that of the EPA. 469 F. Supp. at 907, 13 ERC at 1140.

101 FQPA § 102.

102 The agency suffered a setback in the first case using this theory, *Metrex v. EPA* in federal district court in Denver, although on the narrower grounds that the EPA's test data were invalid. The federal EPA was not alone in wanting to circumvent the lengthy cancellation process, as shown by a New York state court decision back in 1995. There the state banned by regulatory rulemaking rather than by cancellation certain high concentrations of the anti-tick pesticide DEET. The court upheld the practice (*Chemical Specialties Mfgrs. Ass'n v. Jorling*, 85 N.Y. 2d 382, 626 N.Y.S. 2d 1, 649 N.E.2d 1145 [1995]). FIFRA §§ 19 and 25, 7 U.S.C. §§ 136q and 136w. *See also* the previous discussion of indemnities.

103 *Compare* the recall authority of the Consumer Product Safety Commission under Section 15 of its Hazardous Substance Act, 15 U.S.C. § 1274, Pub. L. No. 91-113, which makes recall almost mandatory. The Consumer Product Safety Act, Section 15, on the other hand, provides several options, 15 U.S.C. 2064, Pub. L. No. 92-573.

104 *See, e.g., EDF v. EPA*, 510 F.2d 1292, 7 ERC 1689 (D.C. Cir., 1975).

105 39 Fed. Reg. 15236 (May 1, 1974), 40 C.F.R. § 165.

106 FIFRA § 15, Pub. L. No. 92-516.

107 *See* section 4.1, "Indemnities," in this chapter.

108 *Washington Post*, September 15, 1988.

109 *See* the fuller discussion of the FIFRA Amendments of 1988, *infra*.

110 Section 501 of the 1988 amendments.

111 FY 1988 Continuing Appropriation Act, Pub. L. No. 100-202.

112 *See* the chapter on risk assessment by Joseph Rodericks et al., in Miller, *Pesticides Law Handbook*, p. 113ff.

113 FDCA § 409(c)(3)(A), 21 U.S.C. § 348(c)(3)(A). The relationship between the FIFRA and the FDCA will be discussed later in more detail.

[114] *EDF v. Ruckelshaus, supra*, 439 F.2d at 596, 2 ERC at 1121.

[115] *In re Shell Chemical, supra.*, p. 11, 6 ERC 2047 at 2050–2051, the Aldrin-Dieldrin case, upheld unanimously by the D.C. Court of Appeals in *EDF v. EPA*, 510 F.2d 1292, 7 ERC 1689 (1975).

[116] These time deadlines may be by agreement between the administrator and the secretary, Pub. L. No. 94140, § 1.

[117] The EPA has often required that congressional communications after the issuance of a proposal be placed on the public record; where this was not done, as in the DDT proceedings, environmental groups successfully sued to ensure that these contacts and written comments were made public.

[118] National Environmental Policy Act (NEPA), § 102(2)(c), U.S.C. §§ 4321 *et seq.* (1969); *see also* 36 Fed. Reg. 7724 (1971) and 38 Fed. Reg. 20549 (1973).

[119] Presidential Executive Order No. 11821, November 29, 1974.

[120] Pub. L. No. 94-104, § 1, amending FIFRA § 6(b), 7 U.S.C. § 136d.

[121] Senate Report No. 94-452, p. 9.

[122] Pub. L. No. 94-140, § 7, amending FIFRA § 25. A more detailed analysis of the 1975 changes appears in section 5.0 of this chapter.

[123] Pub. L. No. 94-140, § 7, amending FIFRA § 25(d), 7 U.S.C. § 136w.

[124] Pub. L. No. 96-539, 94 Stat. 3195.

[125] *Id.*

[126] No. 96-1020, 96th Cong., 2d Sess. (1980) p. 4.

[127] Statement of then-EPA Administrator Russell Train to the Senate Agricultural Committee, reprinted in Senate Report No. 94-452, p. 18.

[128] EPA, "A Critical Guide to the EPA's Environmental Appeals Board," in EPA.gov/eab.

[129] The deficiencies in the advisory report, which was poorly reasoned and internally inconsistent, contributed to the agency's skepticism toward this system of information collection and analysis.

[130] This case is better remembered for its unconscionable delay of the administrative process. Dow appealed first to a district court in Arkansas and obtained an injunction against further EPA action on 2,4,5-T, although FIFRA explicitly excluded district courts from jurisdiction. The Eighth Circuit reversed, noting that the court below lacked jurisdiction and that in any case Dow was not entitled to an injunction during a period when "the cancellation orders have no effect on Dow's right to ship and market its product until the administration cancellation process has been completed." *Id.*, at 1326, 5 ERC at 1250.

[131] *Universal Camera Corp. v. NLRB*, 340 U.S. 474 (1951).

[132] FIFRA § 6(a)(1), 7 U.S.C. § 136d(a)(1). *See also McGill v. EPA*, 593 F.2d 631, 13 ERC 1156 (5th Cir., 1979).

[133] A good example is the Aldrin-Dieldrin suspension proceeding, in which the registrant was almost solely interested in the use for certain crops, while the USDA had to join the proceeding to ensure that other, minor registrations were properly represented. This USDA action under the new FIFRA, however, was necessary not because the users now lacked legal standing, but presumably because they lacked adequate resources. *In re Shell Chemical, supra.*, 6 ERC 2047.

[134] 631 F.2d 922, 15 ERC 1217 (D.C. Cir., 1980), *cert. denied*, 449 U.S. 1112.

[135] Final Decision, FIFRA Docket No. 411 (Aug. 20, 1979) at 12–22.

[136] 631 F.2d at 935, 15 ERC at 1229. This case is also noteworthy for its treatment of judicial review under Section 16(b): *see* discussion of Judicial Review in section 4.2 of this chapter.

[137] *Northwest Food Processors Ass'n v. Reilly*, 886 F.2d 1075 (9th Cir. 1989), *cert. denied*, 497 U.S. 1004 (1990). A similar result was reached by the D.C. Circuit in *National Grain Sorghum Producers Association, Inc. v. EPA*, 84 F.3d 1452 (CADC 1996).

[138] Old FIFRA § 4(d).

[139] FIFRA § 16(a)–(c), 7 U.S.C. § 136n(a)–(c).

140 631 F.2d 922, 15 ERC 1217 (D.C. Cir., 1980) *cert. denied*, 449 U.S. 1112. This case is also important for its treatment of standing, discussed in the previous subsection.

141 653 F.2d 1260, 15 ERC 1467 (9th Cir., 1980), as amended February 5, 1981, *reh. denied*, April 10, 1981.

142 *National Grain Sorghum Producers Association, Inc. v. EPA*, 84 F.3d 1452 (CADC 1996).

143 The author of this chapter, while assistant to the administrator of the EPA, and advised by Charles Fabrikant, helped draft, among others, the hearing and jurisdictional sections of FIFRA in 1971–1972 and worked closely with Congress on FEPCA's enactment. Public hearings meant public hearings.

144 Lynn L. Bergson, "Browner's Legacy, Whitman's Challenge: An Overview," *Pollution Prevention Review*, Summer 2001.

145 *See* chapter 9 on state and local regulations in Miller, *Pesticides Law Handbook*.

146 Old (pre-1972) FIFRA § 4(a).

147 *See* "Hearings Before the House Agricultural Committee, Federal Insecticide, Fungicide, and Rodenticide Act Amendments," H.R. 5203, Serial No. 97-R (1982).

148 Ian M. Hughes, "Does FIFRA Label State Tort Claims for Inadequate Warning 'Preempted?'" 7 *Vill. Envtl. L. J.* 313 (1996); Celeste Marie Steen, "FIFRA's Preemption of Common Law Tort Actions Involving Genetically Engineered Pesticides," 38 *Ariz. L. Rev.* 763 (1996); Kyle W. Lathrop, "Environmental Law—FIFRA After 'Wisconsin Public Intervenor v. Mortier': What Next?" 17 *J. Corp. L.* 887 (1993).

149 Leonard H. Glantz, George J. Annas, "The FDA, Preemption, and the Supreme Court," *New England Journal of Medicine*, May 1, 2008, 358:1883-1885; "Supreme Court Asked to Hear Preemption Case Involving Methylmercury. . . ." Food Liability Laws Blog, Jan. 30, 2009.

150 7 U.S.C. § 136v(b).

151 500 F. Supp. 465, 15 ERC 1039 (E.D. Cal. 1980).

152 The court also dismissed challenges to two other provisions of the California laws for lack of ripeness. These challenges were claims that the statute improperly allowed the state to set residue tolerances different from EPA tolerances and that certain labeling requirements for insecticides were improperly imposed.

153 501 U.S. 597, 111 S. Ct. 2476 (1991).

154 *Cipollone v. Liggett Group*, 505 U.S., 504, 112 S. Ct. 2608 (1992). This case, and its relation to pesticides, received extensive legal commentary; see, for example, Stephen D. Otero, *The Case Against FIFRA Preemption: Reconciling Cipollone's Preemption Approach with Both the Supremacy Clause and Basic Notions of Federalism*, 36 Wm. & Mary L. Rev. 783 (1995).

155 *Papas v. Zoecon Corp.*, 505 U.S., 1215, 112 S. Ct. 3020 (1992).

156 *See, e.g.*, EPA amicus curiae brief (submitted Mar. 1999) in *Monique Etcheverry v. Tri-Ag Service Inc.*, 993 P.2d 366 (Cal. 2000); *but see Lowe's Home Centers, Inc. v. Olin Corp.*, 313 F.3d 1307 (11th Cir. 2002).

157 544 U.S. 431, 125 S. Ct. 1788 (2005). The first appellate court to consider preemption after *Bates* reversed a district court decision granting summary judgment to defendants and allowed a trial for personal injury was *Wuebker v. Wilbur-Ellis Co.*, 418 F.3d 883 (8th Cir. 2005).

158 The "parallel requirements" reading is based on *Medtronic, Inc. v. Lohr*, 518 U.S. 470, 116 S. Ct. 2240 (1996), an FDA medical devices case.

159 Although every appellate court that has addressed the issue of inadequate labeling has held that FIFRA expressly preempts state law, there has nevertheless been a perceptible difference between the circuits in the degree to which they will extend the doctrine. The Tenth and Eleventh Circuits have been most protective of the EPA's authority, the Fourth and Fifth have given more latitude to state law, and the others have come out somewhere in the middle. *See, e.g., Arkansas-Platte & Gulf Partnership v. Van Waters & Rogers, Inc.*, 981 F.2d 1177 (10th Cir. 1993); *Papas v. Upjohn Co.*, 985 F.2d 516 (11th Cir. 1993) (Papas II); *Lowe's Home Centers, Inc. v. Olin Corp., supra, Lowe v. Sporicidin International*, 47 F.3d

124 (4th Cir. 1995); *Worm v. American Cyanamid Co.*, 5 F.3d 744 (4th Cir. 1993) (Worm II); *Mac-Donald v. Monsanto*, 27 F.3d 1021 (5th Cir. 1994); *Dow Agro Sciences v. Bates*, F.3d (5th Cir. 2003) (preemption, upheld warranty disclaimer); *King v. E. I. duPont de Nemours & Co.*, 996 F.2d 1346 (1st Cir. 1993); *Shaw v. Dow Brands, Inc.*, 994 F.2d 364 (7th Cir. 1993); *Bice v. Leslie's Poolmart, Inc.*, 39 F.3d 887 (8th Cir. 1994).

[160] *See, e.g.*, Rosemary O'Leary, *Environmental Change: Federal Courts and the EPA* (Philadelphia: Temple University Press, 1994), p. 46 *et seq.*

[161] 428 F.2d 1083, 1 ERC 1347 (D.C. Cir., 1970).

[162] As there was no administrative record underlying the secretary's inaction, however, the court remanded the issue to the USDA "to provide the court with a record necessary for meaningful appellate review." This concept that a nondecision can in fact itself be a decision after an unduly long delay has regretfully not been repeated very often in later years. *See, e.g., Beyond Pesticides/National Coalition Against the Misuse of Pesticides v. EPA*, Memorandum Opinion, 407 F. Supp. 2d 38 (D.C.D.C. 2005).

[163] 435 F.2d 1151, 2 ERC 1016 (7th Cir., *en banc*, 1970).

[164] *Id.*, at 1157, 2 ERC at 1019.

[165] 435 F.2d 1133, 1 ERC 1460 (7th Cir., 1970).

[166] 435 F.2d at 1160–1161.

[167] *EDF v. Ruckelshaus*, 439 F.2d 584, 2 ERC 1114 (D.C. Cir., 1971). This was a sequel to the earlier *EDF v. Hardin* case, *supra*, but the name of the administrator of the EPA was substituted for the secretary of agriculture since the authority of USDA had been transferred to the EPA the month before.

[168] *Id.*, at 594, 2 ERC at 1119. Because there may be a "substantial question of safety" about most pesticides, administrative necessity has forced the EPA to interpret this as requiring cancellation of only the most harmful chemicals.

[169] *Pesticide and Toxic Chemical News*, Nov. 20, 1996, p. 11.

[170] 2 ERC 1364 (Opinion of Judicial Officer, USDA, 1971); *Stearns Electric Paste Company v. EPA*, 461 F.2d 293, 4 ERC 1164 (7th Cir., 1972).

[171] Old FIFRA § 2(z)2(c).

[172] *Stearns Electric Paste, supra.*, 461 F.2d at 310, 4 ERC at 1175.

[173] 470 F.2d 194, 4 ERC 1881 (8th Cir., 1972). This case was decided about a month after the enactment of the new FIFRA on October 21, 1972, but that law was not yet applied there. Presumably a different result would have ensued.

[174] *See In re King Paint*, 2 ERC 1819 (Opinion of EPA Judicial Officer, 1971).

[175] *In re Alfred Waldner Co.*, 59 Fed. Reg. 49395 (Sept. 28, 1994); and *In re Accufilter Int'l Inc.*, 59 Fed. Reg. 60013 (Nov. 21, 1994).

[176] 62 Fed. Reg. 61890 (Nov. 19, 1997).

[177] See *Alberta Gas Chems., Ltd. v. Celanese Corp.*, 650 F.2d 9, 13 (2nd Cir. 1981) ("It is a well established principle that an administrative agency may reconsider its own decisions . . ."). Ironically, the EPA's Pesticide Office borrowed this Latin doctrine, I believe, from the plaintiff's brief in the earlier carbofuran case where the plaintiffs claimed that an agency settlement decision was unsupported by hard evidence and therefore should be held invalid from the very beginning. *National Grain Sorghum Producers Ass'n, Inc. v. EPA*, 84 F.3d 1453 (1996).

[178] *Termilind* at 61893; 7 U.S.C. § 136a(c)(5).

[179] *See* Lynn L. Bergeson and Lisa M. Campbell, "Leveling the FIFRA Playing Field: Life Beyond *Termilind*," 30 ELR 10125 (1999).

[180] FIFRA § 8, 17(c), 7 U.S.C. § 1360(c). The old FIFRA provisions on exports was § 3(a)(5)(b); FIFRA § 8, 7 U.S.C. § 136 f.

[181] *See* an entire chapter on this important subject in Miller, *Pesticides Law Handbook*, chapter 10.

[182] A campaign has recently arisen in favor of DDT, either to exonerate it in this country or to push for its use abroad against malaria because of special local conditions. The literature on this issue is absolutely voluminous. See, for example, "SA praised for fight against malaria," in SouthAfrica.info, 29 January 2013 (pro-DDT); "Malaria, Mosquitoes, and DDT," WorldWatch Institute, May-June 2002 (anti-DDT).

[183] FIFRA § 17(a)(2), 7 U.S.C. § 136o(e)(f). *See also* 44 Fed. Reg. 4358 (Jan. 19, 1979).

[184] 45 Fed. Reg. 50274 (July 28, 1980).

[185] Pub. L. No. 95-396, 92 Stat 833; codified at 7 U.S.C. § 136(o).

[186] 45 Fed. Reg. at 50274, 50278 (July 28, 1980).

[187] *Id.*, at 50276–50277.

[188] FIFRA § 27. Actually the term for the act was less than three years since the act finally went into effect in October 1972 and the authorization expired June 30, 1975.

[189] One such example was the EPA's authority under § 27 to require that a pesticide be registered for use only by a certified applicator.

[190] House Report No. 94-497, "Extension and Amendment of the FIFRA, as Amended," September 19, 1975, for H.R. 8841, p. 5.

[191] *Washington Star*, October 8, 1975.

[192] A good discussion of the residue-tolerance procedure is found in Linda J. Fisher et al., "A Practitioner's Guide to the FIFRA: Part III," 24 *ELR* 10629 (Nov. 1994), Sec. XIII, p. 10646 *et seq.*

[193] 53 Fed. Reg. 41110. An ancient legal maxim is the "*lex non curat de minimus*"—the law does not concern itself with trifles.

[194] 968 F.2d 985 (9th Cir. 1992).

[195] *Id.* at 988.

[196] Title IV of the FQPA. *See* the chapter on this topic in Miller, *Pesticides Law Handbook*, p. 83ff.

[197] FQPA of 1996, § 405, amending FDCA § 408 as § 408(b)(2)(A)(ii).

[198] Raw foods are called "raw agricultural commodities," or RAC, in the jargon-filled act.

[199] FQPA, § 405, for FDCA § 408(b)(2)(B).

[200] FQPA § 405.

[201] Pub. L. 104-170 § 230.

[202] William H. Rodgers Jr., *Environmental Law: Vol. 3, Pesticides and Toxic Substances* (St. Paul, Minn.: West Group, 1998), Spring 1998 Pocket Part, p. 17.

[203] "Human test data ban violates FIFRA and FFDCA, say CropLife," *Pesticide and Toxic Chemical News*, April 29, 2002, pp. 9–10.

[204] *CropLife America v. EPA*, 329 F.3d 876 (D.C. Cir. 2003).

[205] Denise Grady, "Debate Erupts Over Testing Pesticides on Humans," *New York Times*, Jan. 9, 2003.

[206] FQPA § 102, amending FIFRA § 6(c)(3), 7 U.S.C. § 136d(c)(3).

[207] FQPA § 104.

[208] FQPA § 106.

[209] FQPA § 120.

[210] FQPA § 210. The 1996 amendments expanded the 10-year period of exclusive use for minor use pesticides one additional year for each registered within seven years, up to a total of 13 years. P.6. L. 101-624 § 1493, 7 U.S.C. § 136a-1(i)(5)(A).

[211] FQPA § 221, *et seq.*

[212] FDCA § 408, 21 U.S.C. § 346a, *et seq.*

[213] Health, Education, and Welfare (HEW), the cabinet department, later divided into the present Department of Health and Human Services (HHS) and the Department of Education.

214 This is an oversimplification. The tolerance margin depends on the particular effects of the chemical. Also, it presumes that animals will exhibit the same effects as humans and at approximately the same doses, neither of which is certain.

215 The Acceptable Daily Intake (ADI) is two or three magnitudes (100 to 1,000 times) below the level at which no observable effect was found in rats or mice over a lifetime. The Theoretical Maximum Residue Contribution (TMRC), the sum of all tolerances for each commodity, must not exceed the ADI. *See* Marguerite L. Leng, "Pesticide Residues in Food and Water: Public Perception and Reality," in American Institute of Chemists, *The Chemist* (Jan./Feb. 1997, pp. 11–16).

216 502 F.2d 715, 6 ERC 2073 (7th Cir., 1974).

217 Under FDCA § 402(a)(2)(C), 21 U.S.C. § 342(a)(2)(C), this affects only a substance that "is not generally recognized among experts . . . as having been adequately shown . . . to be safe under the conditions of its intended use. . . ." This category is usually called GRAS, for "generally recognized as safe." *See* FDCA § 201(s), 21 U.S.C. § 321(s). Without a tolerance, "the presence of the DDT causes fish to be adulterated without any proof that it is actually unfit as food." 6 ERC 2073, 2077.

218 Action levels and enforcement, unlike tolerance setting, remain a prerogative of FDA under Section 306 of FDCA, 21 U.S.C. § 336.

219 486 F.2d 847, 5 ERC 1969 (7th Cir., 1973).

220 *Id.*, at 855, 5 ERC at 1974; FDCA § 306, 21 U.S.C. § 336; *U.S. v. 1500 Cases*, 245 F.2d 208, 210–211 (7th Cir., 1956); *U.S. v. 484 Bags*, 423 F.2d 839, 841 (5th Cir., 1970).

221 Clean Air Act, § 112(a)(1), 42 U.S.C. § 1857c-7(a)(1) (1970).

222 *Headwaters Inc., v. Talent Irrigation District*, 243 F.3d 526 (9th Cir., 2001).

223 *League of Wilderness Defenders/Blue Mountains Biodiversity Project v. Forsgren*, 309 F.3d 1181 (9th Cir., 2002).

224 For example, "Agency Weighs Permit, Enforcement Relief for Aquatic Pesticide Use: Stakeholders Call Measures Insufficient," *Inside EPA*, May 11, 2001.

225 "Application of Pesticides to Waters of the United States in Compliance with FIFRA," 71 Fed. Reg. 2271 (Nov. 27, 2006), amending 40 C.F.R. Part 122, Final Rule. The earlier interpretation was published Feb. 1, 2005. See the authoritative report by the U.S. government's Congressional Research Service, Claudia Copeland, "Pesticide Use and Water Quality: Are the Laws Complementary or in Conflict?" 13 July 2012.

226 FWPCA § 301, 33 U.S.C. § 1311.

227 FWPCA § 307, 33 U.S.C. § 1317. The criteria for this list are given in 38 Fed. Reg. 18044 (1973).

228 The EPA, however, has not followed this reasoning. The § 307 list of approximately 300 toxic pollutants contains many of the major pesticides. *See NRDC v. Train* (D.C. Cir., 1976) 8 ERC 2120.

229 309 F.3d 1181 (9th Cir. 2002); *No Spray Coalition, Inc. v. City of New York*, 252 F.3d 148 (2d. Cir. 2001).

230 40 C.F.R. § 141, National Primary Drinking Water Regulations.

231 42 U.S.C. § 3251 *et seq.*, 79 Stat. 997 (1965), 84 Stat. 1227 (1970); Resource Conservation and Recovery Act (RCRA) § 204, 42 U.S.C. § 3253.

232 RCRA § 212, 42 U.S.C. 3241. *See also* RCRA § 209, 42 U.S.C. § 3254c.

233 OSHA § 6, 29 U.S.C. § 655.

234 *Florida Peach Growers Assn. v. Dept. of Labor*, 489 F.2d 120 (5th Cir., 1974).

235 16 C.F.R. § 1500 3(b)(4)(ii).

236 *E.g., Essex Chemical Corp. v. Ruckelshaus*, 486 F.2d 427, 5 ERC 1820 (D.C. Cir., 1973); *Portland Cement Assn. v. Ruckelshaus*, 486 F.2d at 375, 5 ERC 1593 (D.C. Cir. 1973).

237 *EDF v. EPA*, 489 F.2d at 1257, 6 ERC at 1119.

238 *In the Matter of Chemical Specialties Mfgrs. Ass'n v. Jorling*, 85 N.Y. 2d 382, 649 N.E. 2d 1145 ("hard look" by state agency at pesticide DEET for Lyme disease justified finding of no adverse environmental effects).

239 Fortunately, the latest studies suggest that this particular concern is unfounded, at least for monarch butterflies, but the debate isn't over.

240 Elizabeth Becker, "U.S. Threatens to Act Against Europeans Over Modified Foods," *New York Times*, Jan. 10, 2003. Mr. Zoellick became the deputy secretary of state in 2005 and head of the international organization, the World Bank, in 2007.

241 Rifkin is not taken very seriously in the United States, but his book became the number-one seller in Italy and number three in Germany. Italian Prime Minister Massimo D'Alema devoted most of an hour-long press conference to his 1998 book *The Biotech Century*. "Thinkers on the Left Get a Hearing Everywhere but at Home," *New York Times*, Nov. 11, 2000, p. B7.

242 447 U.S. 303, 100 S. Ct. 2204.

243 *Id.* at 902, 13 ERC at 1135.

244 *BNA Chemical Reporter*, Aug. 17, 1990, 788.

245 Reuters news service, Dec. 1, 2000.

246 Norman Borlaug, "We Need Biotech to Feed the World," *Wall Street Journal*, Dec. 6, 2000. A good overview of the political controversy is found in Andrew Curry, "Seeds of Conflict," *Discover*, April 2013, pp. 38-46.

Chapter 14

Pollution Prevention Act

John M. Scagnelli
Scarinci Hollenbeck, Lyndhurst, New Jersey

1.0 Overview

The Federal Pollution Prevention Act of 1990, following the lead of many state statutes in the 1980s, made pollution prevention national environmental policy. The U.S. Environmental Protection Agency (EPA), following the Act's mandate, has sought to integrate pollution prevention as an ethic throughout its activities. EPA's efforts have occurred in phases since the Act's passage. During the first phase, which occurred during the early to mid-1990s, EPA established a series of pollution prevention related programs, such as the Common Sense Initiative and the Excellence in Leadership Program, better known as Project XL. A part of Project XL, Project XLC or eXcellence and Leadership for Communities, was used to facilitate integrated environmental management and redevelopment of geographical areas and communities. During the second phase, beginning in the mid-1990s, EPA moved toward greater institutionalization of pollution prevention programs into its mainstream activities, including regulations, permitting, technical assistance, compliance, and enforcement. EPA's Persistent, Bioaccumulative, and Toxic (PBT) Chemical Initiative and Environmentally Preferable Purchasing Program for federal agencies illustrated its move toward institutionalization.

The third phase occurred during the Bush Administration between 2001-2008. EPA moved its pollution prevention efforts away from the major multimedia pollution prevention programs begun during the Clinton Administration, such as the Common Sense Initiative and Project XL, and from specific pollution prevention subject area programs, such as EPA's Persistent, Bioaccumulative, and Toxic (PBT) Strategy, which focused on reducing risks from highly toxic substances in the food chain. EPA refocused its pollution prevention activities on voluntary initiatives, labeling programs, pollution prevention partnering with business, and pollution prevention information clearinghouse functions.

Under the Obama Administration, beginning in 2009, EPA has continued to focus on voluntary initiatives, labeling programs, pollution prevention partnering with business, and pollution prevention information clearing house functions. This chapter reviews EPA's pollution prevention programs since the adoption of the Pollution Prevention Act in 1990 and the direction of state pollution prevention programs.

2.0 Federal Pollution Prevention Strategy

2.1 Background

The Federal Pollution Prevention Act of 1990[1] (PPA) establishes pollution prevention as a national objective. The PPA required EPA to develop and implement a strategy to promote source reduction.[2] In the Act, Congress declared pollution prevention to be the highest level of acceptable environmental practice. The Act states that pollution which cannot be prevented should be recycled. If it is not feasible to prevent or recycle pollution, pollution should be treated; the Act mandates that disposal or other release of pollution into the environment is a last resort.

The PPA defines pollution prevention as source reduction and other practices that reduce or eliminate the creation of pollutants through increased efficiency in the use of raw materials, energy, water, or other resources or the protection of natural resources by conservation.[3]

The Act required EPA to identify measurable pollution prevention goals and to consider the effect of agency programs on source reduction.[4] The Act also amended the reporting requirements of the Emergency Planning and Community Right-to-Know Act (EPCRA)[5] through its Toxic Chemical Release Inventory (TRI). Under the Act, facilities required to file an annual toxic chemical release form under Section 313 for any toxic chemical are required to provide information on pollution prevention and recycling for each facility and for each toxic chemical.[6] The PPA required the Administrator of EPA to submit biennial reports to Congress detailing the steps EPA has taken to implement the strategy to promote pollution prevention.[7]

2.2 EPA's Pollution Prevention Strategy

EPA published its Pollution Prevention Strategy to incorporate pollution prevention into every aspect of its existing programs beginning in February 1991.[8] The Strategy was designed to respond to the PPA's requirement that measurable source reduction goals be established. Although not an official rulemaking, the

Strategy sets forth a national pollution prevention model and a voluntary program for companies to reduce aggregate environmental releases of specific chemicals. EPA uses the data from the TRI established under the EPCRA to track industrial pollution prevention efforts.

2.3 EPA's Pollution Prevention Programs in the 1990s

2.3.1 EPA's Environmental Leadership Program

EPA's Environmental Leadership Program (ELP) was designed by EPA to test alternative compliance approaches. The ELP allowed facilities to use environmental management techniques to streamline reporting requirements and reduce compliance inspections. The goal was to achieve improvements in environmental quality while working within the framework of existing environmental laws.

The ELP Program was designed to recognize and provide incentives to facilities that were willing to develop and demonstrate accountability for compliance with existing laws. The Program focused on encouraging, not directing, companies to develop and implement pollution prevention management practices and to establish environmental goals beyond those set for regulatory compliance. The ELP sought to reward companies, through public recognition and other incentives, for voluntarily incorporating pollution prevention into high level corporate decisions and facility practices and systems. The ELP also included an element of public accountability to encourage companies' progress toward meeting the ELP's goals.

2.3.1.1 Scope of the ELP Program

EPA established national risk reduction goals for participation in the ELP. The TRI provided the basis for setting national goals and measuring progress at the source. However, the TRI varied in the quality of reported data and did not include reporting of all significant pollutants or sources. EPA therefore sought to gather additional pertinent information through the two components of the ELP: (1) the Corporate Statement of Environmental Principles and (2) the Model Facility Program.

Corporate Statement of Environmental Principles. In cooperation with corporations and industry, EPA developed environmental principles to govern the way corporations design, manufacture, market, and distribute products. Companies were required to conduct their operations in accordance with those principles and commit to specific pollution prevention goals by subscribing to a written commitment to abide by the principles. The Corporate Statements of Environmental Principles were to be maintained in a public docket to allow members of the public access to examine the contents.

The facilities subscribing to the Corporate Statement of Environmental Principles were required to observe disclosure, testing, and reporting principles concerning substances required to be listed on the TRI; publish a plan for pollution prevention in accordance with the method prescribed under the PPA; provide information to employees and the public concerning pollution prevention practices; and commit to assessing environmental factors and incorporating pollution prevention strategies at each stage of a product's life cycle. The facilities were required to pledge to institute facility-wide environmental compliance management systems to promote and monitor environmental compliance.

The Model Facility Program. The second component of the ELP provided for public recognition of facilities that met strict environmental criteria as "Model Facilities." Participation in the Model Facilities Program differed from the Corporate Statement of Environmental Principles because in the Program EPA certified that the facility met stringent environmental compliance standards. Facilities participating in the Model Facilities Program were required to subscribe to a Statement of Environmental Principles and provide EPA with comprehensive data regarding all facility activities with a potentially significant impact on the environment, including sources not covered by the TRI or PPA reporting requirements.

The enhanced reporting requirements included supplying data related to EPA's national risk reduction goals regarding a facility's consumption of energy, water, and other raw materials. Facilities also had to develop a plan for achieving the national risk reduction goals by emphasizing measures that reduced waste through pollution prevention practices, perform a product life cycle assessment, and enact an environmental cost accounting approach which reflected the impact of pollution activities. Worker participation and facility compliance through the implementation of a comprehensive environmental compliance management system was required and the facility's compliance record stringently screened for acceptance into the Model Facility Program.

The major incentive for ELP participation was public recognition. EPA announced the Model Facilities and provided a flag or seal bearing the Model Facility Program logo. Other incentives included a commitment by EPA to accelerate the permit and product registration process, reduce monitoring and reporting requirements, issue multimedia permits, and allow companies to offset voluntary actions against future regulatory requirements.

2.3.1.2 Criteria for Participation in the ELP Program

To participate in the ELP Program, facilities needed to have a mature environmental management system (EMS) and auditing program in place. Facilities needed to be willing to disclose the results of any facility-wide audit, although this information could be submitted to EPA on a confidential basis. Facilities were required to demonstrate that their employees and their communities were involved in developing and implementing the facility's EMS program. Facilities also were required to have plans for environmental enhancement activities in their operations and a good history of compliance with environmental laws and regulations.

If selected for participation in the ELP Program, the facility was required to submit annual performance reports for each of the six years of participation. The performance reports (1) discussed in detail the facility's EMS goals and activities, (2) contained information on the formal audits that were required to be conducted at the facility in years two and five of the program, (3) included an EMS performance evaluation, and (4) discussed any EPA compliance inspections. The annual performance reports on ELP facilities were required to be available for public inspection.

EPA had estimated that once the ELP Program was up and running, at least 75 facilities would apply to the ELP annually.

2.3.1.3 Benefits of the ELP Program

EPA believed the ELP would benefit the public because it encouraged industry to monitor itself, which would lead to improved compliance, pollution prevention, and environmental protection. Industry would benefit because its leaders would have an opportunity to be recognized by EPA for their outstanding environmental management practices. The program was designed to give industry a chance to reform barriers to self-monitoring and compliance efforts. Further, the program was designed to benefit government by allowing federal–state partnerships to prosper while also giving EPA the ability to gather empirical data on environmental compliance measures and methodology.

2.3.1.4 Status of the ELP Program

In 1994, EPA initiated a pilot project to test parts of the ELP and explore ways both EPA and the states could encourage facilities to develop innovative auditing and compliance programs and reduce the risk of noncompliance through pollution prevention practices.

In 1996, EPA completed a one-year pilot project. The pilot program involved the participation of ten private sector facilities and two federal facilities. EPA's Office of Compliance, within the reorganized Office of Enforcement and Compliance Assurance, coordinated the pilot projects with regional and state partner involvement.

The pilot project was to have been utilized by EPA to develop the full-scale Environmental Leadership Program. EPA issued a proposed framework for the

Program in late 1996. Under the proposed framework, facilities would have to commit to six years of ELP participation. Participation would be renewed every six years.

In March 1998, EPA put implementation of the full-scale ELP Program on hold while the Agency reviewed its strategy for coordination of EPA's voluntary programs. The Agency attempted to define a framework to ensure that the ELP Program made the best use of limited resources to promote improvements in environmental compliance and performance, was consistent in its approach to voluntary partnership programs, and clearly defined the need and purpose for each program. The Agency did not roll out implementation of the full-scale ELP Program before the Bush Administration came into office in 2001, however.

2.3.2 EPA's Common Sense Initiative

A major pollution prevention development in the 1990s was the Common Sense Initiative (CSI). On July 20, 1994, EPA began CSI as a way to protect human health and the environment by application of an industry-by-industry approach to environmental policy.

CSI replaced the pollutant-by-pollutant approach with an industry-by-industry approach. The CSI brought together different levels of government officials, environmentalists, and industry leaders to create strategies to work cleaner, cheaper, and smarter to protect the health of people of this country and its natural resources. EPA believed CSI would have a cleaner effect because participating industries would achieve true environmental protection. EPA thought that CSI would be cheaper because tailoring environmental protection on an industry-by-industry basis would save billions of dollars. EPA also believed that CSI would be smarter because the program utilized people who had a stake in the outcome working together to protect the environment.

CSI examined environmental protection in industries from top to bottom and created a blueprint for achieving environmental protection. Six industries that the focus of CSI's first phase: auto manufacturing, computers and electronics, iron and steel, metal plating and finishing, oil refining, and printing.

CSI was based on the premise that the environment is best protected when tough environmental goals are set using flexibility and innovation to reach those goals. EPA assembled teams of industry executives, environmental and community representatives, and federal, state, and local officials to improve the environmental regulation and performance of the six pilot industries. By using teams working together, EPA sought to avoid an adversarial approach to environmental protection. Additionally, the teams consisted of individuals with a stake in the outcome. By utilizing the expertise of industry, environmental leaders and grassroots activists and local, state, and federal government officials, EPA believed that CSI would improve the environmental regulation and performance of the six pilot industries.

2.3.2.1 Blueprint to Achieve Real Environmental Protection

Each CSI team was responsible for examining how EPA and its state partners interacted with an industry and to define areas for improvement. There were six key areas for improvement, and they made up EPA's blueprint for achieving real environmental protection:

- Alternative Flexible Regulatory Systems: Each team conducted a review of every major regulation applicable to their industry and improved new regulations through increased coordination. The CSI marked the first time in EPA history that such a comprehensive review was took place.

- Pollution Prevention: The CSI wanted to avoid the mistakes of the past that shifted pollution from one area to another. In its place, the CSI's objective was to make pollution prevention a part of normal business practices in every industry. The CSI's goal was to encourage industry to exceed pollution prevention standards as opposed to simply meeting minimum standards.

- Reporting: Each team was tasked to make environmental information collection easier for industry and to allow the public greater access.

- Compliance: With the help of the reorganized Office of Enforcement and Compliance Assurance, each team offered those companies motivated to achieve real environmental protection a more flexible way to obtain this goal. Significantly, those companies not so motivated were made to understand the consequences that would occur from a strong enforcement program. EPA believed that a strong environmental enforcement program would prevent companies that were complying with the law from suffering a competitive disadvantage to companies not complying.

- Permitting: The permit process was improved so that it was responsive to the needs of the public and industry.

- Environmental Technology: Industry needed to have the incentives and flexibility necessary to create new technology to meet and exceed environmental standards and cut costs.

2.3.2.2 Achievements and Actions

The CSI six-sector subcommittees began work in January 1995 and initiated more than 40 projects involving more than 150 stakeholders who actively participated in work groups. Some of the highlights of the subcommittees' work were the following:

- Automotive Manufacturing: This sector focused on assessing life-cycle management in the automobile industry. This included an evaluation of every step of a car's production, starting from the design and collection of raw materials through disposal at the end of a car's useful life. The sector assessed the automobile regulatory system so that recommendations could be made for regulatory systems which would help communities understand and participate in environmental quality.

- Computers and Electronics: This sector focused on evaluating issues related to the disposal of end-of-life electronic equipment. The sector undertook pilot projects to determine the viability of residential collection and recycling programs. It also evaluated the composition of waste streams and worked on removing federal regulatory barriers to recycling through the development of "commonsense" hazardous waste requirements. It also worked on reinvention of environmental reporting to remove regulatory burdens.

- Iron and Steel: The iron and steel subcommittee focused on monitoring and improved environmental performance. This included pilot projects on multimedia permitting and work on promoting new and cleaner technologies within the industry. The subcommittee also worked on projects to redevelop iron and steel brownfields.

- Printing: This sector worked on two innovative projects. One project was a comprehensive outreach program to printers, suppliers, and the community about opportunities for pollution prevention in the printing process. The second project was a new permitting system developed specifically for printers, with the initial focus on small printers, followed by customers and suppliers.

- Metals Finishing: The sector developed a set of voluntary performance goals to promote pollution prevention and environmental management. Some of the projects worked on included auditing of firms to assess source reduction options and related regulatory barriers; an evaluation and improvement of regulatory reporting requirements; the establishment of a National Metal Finishing Resource Center; the development of low-cost, efficient technologies for controlling emissions; and solid waste definition issues.

- Petroleum Refining: The sector worked on a project to evaluate equipment leaks and to recommend efficient ways to reduce the loss of fluids and vapors through such leaks. The sector also sought to improve duplication in regulatory reporting, which impacted the industry.

2.3.2.3 CSI's Final Status

The CSI signaled a new approach for EPA to protect the environment. It removed an adversarial system and instead brought together people with the knowledge to find environmental solutions. The CSI moved beyond media-specific regulations to view an industry as a whole. EPA at the time believed the CSI could produce greater environmental protection for the public at lower cost.

The CSI program participants agreed that the CSI approach had significant value and should be added as another tool to improve environmental policy and management. In February 1998, EPA reaffirmed its commitment to the CSI by requesting the CSI Council to share its "lessons" and provide the Agency with an action plan to integrate those lessons into the Agency's core processes so that the Agency could build the ability and capacity to act on sector-based opportunities.

On December 17, 1998, the CSI Council conducted its final meeting. The six active CSI sector subcommittees also conducted their final meetings in December 1998. The completion of those meeting was the conclusion of the CSI process, which began in 1994. Based upon the CSI work, an Agency-wide sector action plan was approved in the fall of 1998 by the CSI Council and EPA management. The sector action plan called for continued external stakeholder advice and consultation to the Agency on sector-related environmental issues. Accordingly, a new Committee on Sectors was created under the auspices of the National Advisory Committee on Environmental Policy Technology to provide this external stakeholder forum. A Fiscal Year 2000 Sector-Based Action Plan was prepared to further the continued integration of sector-based approaches into EPA activities. EPA, in September 2000, presented a draft five-year plan for regulating environmental performance by industrial sectors rather than by environmental media, such as air or water.

When the Bush Administration took office in 2001, EPA shifted its attention away from the CSI to other pollution prevention programs.

2.3.3 EPA's Excellence in Leadership (XL) Program

In 1995, EPA announced a set of actions directed toward giving regulated sources greater flexibility to develop alternative strategies for environmental compliance. The program, called eXcellence in Leadership (XL), was part of the Clinton Administration's "Reinventing Environmental Regulation" initiative, announced in March 1995. In his report, President Clinton announced 25 high-priority actions to improve the environmental regulatory system. The most notable of these was Project XL. The XL Program was another example of EPA's commitment to incorporating pollution prevention strategies into its policies.

The XL Program went beyond command and control regulatory systems by granting industrial participants flexibility in meeting regulatory requirements in exchange for an enforceable commitment by the participants to attain greater environmental results than what would have been achieved through full compliance. The first eight participants in the XL Pilot Project were approved by President Clinton in December 1995. EPA targeted 50 XL projects for eventual selection.

The XL Pilot Projects tested potential avenues for facilities to achieve environmental compliance by implementing technologically innovative and cost-effective alternatives to regulatory requirements. Project XL established a process for individual companies to develop unique environmental strategies for their particular facilities through collaboration with governmental officials and the interested public and other stakeholders.

2.3.3.1 Criteria for Participation in the XL Program

To be selected for participation in Project XL, projects were required to meet specific criteria. The criteria, as published by EPA in May 1995, included the following:[9]

- Environmental Results: Projects were required to achieve "cleaner results" than what would be achieved through compliance with current and reasonable anticipated future regulations. The results could be achieved directly through the environmental performance of the project or through the reinvestment of the cost savings from the project in activities that produce greater environmental results. Explicit measures for achieving the cleaner results were included in the project agreement negotiated among stakeholders.

- Stakeholder Support: Applicants were required to gain the support of parties that had a stake in the environmental impacts of the project. Stakeholders included communities near a project, local or state governments, and business, environmental, and other public interest groups.

- Innovative Strategies: The project was required to test innovative alternatives, including processes, technologies, or management practices, for achieving environmental results and pollution prevention. Projects were set up to systematically test these alternatives against several regulatory requirements and to involve more than one environmental medium. Pilot projects were required to reflect EPA's pollution prevention objectives for protecting the environment by preventing the generation of pollution rather than controlling pollution once it has been created.

- Transferability: The pilots were required to be transferable or amenable to implementation into EPA's programs or in other industries or facilities in the same industry.

2.3.3.2 Status of the XL Program

In December 1995, eight pilot projects were selected for participation in Project XL. Since 1995, additional projects were selected to participate in the program, while some of the original participants have dropped out. By August 1998, nine pilots were implemented, and 20 additional projects were developed. The corporate participants included Berry Corporation, Weyerhauser, Intel Corporation, HADCO Corporation, Merck & Co., Inc., Osi Specialists, Inc., Molex Incorporated, and Lucent Technologies. The project proposals selected included emissions trading, facility emissions caps, multimedia permitting, and elimination of obsolete requirements.

The first project approved by EPA for the XL pilot program was the Berry project. This project focused on preparing a comprehensive multimedia operating permit that encompassed all of the facility's emissions. In return for its operating flexibility, Berry committed to reduce water consumption, increase the use of nonhazardous pest controls, reserve acreage for habitat conservation, and use process wastewater for irrigation.

The XL Project, however, experienced some growing pains. Two of the initial corporate participants, Anheuser-Busch and 3M Company, after negotiation with EPA, withdrew their project proposals. Both companies were unwilling to provide EPA with an up-front guarantee that their facilities would achieve superior environmental performance standards in exchange for regulatory flexibility. According to 3M Company, whose XL project involved a multimedia permit with emissions caps and below regulatory levels, EPA's restriction would have been burdensome and would have allowed the failure of a single superior environmental performance standard to constitute grounds for permit amendment or revocation before the end of the permit's five-year term.

Despite varying expectations concerning the purpose of the Project, Project XL gained widespread support from the business community. EPA intended to learn from the pilot projects and promote cooperation and forge closer ties among the regulators and the regulated community. EPA's goal was to establish at least 50 partnerships with the XL participants. With the change in federal administration in 2001, EPA shifted its attention away from Project XL to other pollution prevention programs.

2.3.4 Project XLC

A part of Project XL, Project XLC, or eXcellence and Leadership for Communities, was used to facilitate integrated environmental management and redevelopment of geographical areas and communities. EPA used the Project XL approach to deal with environmental issues on an integrated basis in ecologically defined areas and communities. Included areas could encompass watersheds, politically defined jurisdictions such as a city or tribal land, or a community identified area such as a neighborhood. Like Project XL, all XLC projects were required to address specific selection criteria in order to qualify as an XLC project. In addition to the project XL criteria, XLC projects were also required to develop strategies that presented economic opportunity in conjunction with improved environmental quality and that incorporated new or existing community goals and plans.

2.3.5 Mainstreaming Pollution Prevention

Beginning in the mid-1990s, EPA has moved toward greater institutionalization of pollution prevention programs into its mainstream activities, including regulations, permitting, technical assistance, and compliance and enforcement.

An example of EPA's movement toward pollution prevention institutionalization is its Priority Persistent, Bioaccumulative, and Toxic (PBT) Pollutant Strategy. The adverse health and ecological effects from these pollutants—particularly mercury, PCBs, and dioxin—make them candidates for risk reduction and pollution prevention on a cross-media basis.

Another example of EPA's move toward pollution prevention institutionalization was its Environmentally Preferable Purchasing Program (EPP). The EPP is a federal-wide program that encouraged and assisted federal agencies in the purchasing of environmentally preferable products and services under the mandate of Executive Order 13101, which directed all federal procurement officials to assess and give preference to those products and services which are environmentally preferable. The EPP has been continued under the Obama Administration, with renewed emphasis on federal agencies making purchasing decisions with the environment in mind. On October 8, 2009, President Obama signed Executive Order No. 13514 "Federal Leadership in Environmental Energy and Economic Performance" which mandates that federal agencies eliminate waste, recycle, prevent pollution, and foster markets for sustainable technologies and environmentally preferable markets, among other objectives. Executive Order No. 13514 provided renewed support for EPA's Environmentally Preferable Purchasing Program (EPP).

2.3.6 Multimedia Permitting

Another important pollution prevention initiative during the 1990s was multimedia permitting. Launched as part of President Clinton's "Reinventing Environmental Regulation" initiative, multimedia permitting provided an opportunity for selected industries to submit one application for one permit.

EPA organized a Permits Improvement Team (PIT) to meet with the regulated community, regulators, and the public to develop strategies for the program. The PIT process involved obtaining detailed input from the public and the regulated community and developing a permitting program that (1) incorporated performance-based standards rather than command and control requirements, (2) improved methods of data collection, and (3) streamlined permitting techniques, such as group permits and de minimis exemptions.

Permittees at pilot facilities could submit a single application for a single permit, setting forth all the pollution control and cleanup requirements for that facility. EPA believed this approach promoted "commonsense" solutions to multimedia pollution problems and encouraged the use of pollution prevention.

2.3.7 The National Environmental Performance Partnership System

In an effort to provide more flexibility to states, EPA and state officials in the 1990s launched a program called the National Environmental Performance Partnership System (NEPPS). The NEPPS represented a new era of environmental protection by allowing states to step out of EPA's shadow and establish their own environmental goals and indicators and address local needs and problems.

Under the program, states negotiated annual agreements with their regional EPA office instead of submitting traditional work plans and set consensus-based environmental goals and mechanisms for measuring their success in meeting these goals. The program was intended to assist states and EPA in understanding the nature of environmental problems and think more broadly about how to address them as well as providing the states with the necessary flexibility to develop innovative environmental programs which responded to local needs and problems.

Over 30 states entered into Performance Partnership Agreements (PPAs) with EPA. For the regulated community, the NEPPS provided a mechanism for implementing new environmental approaches that offered flexibility in return for increased performance. For example, EPA intended at the time that states would be authorized to implement innovative regulatory programs under the PPAs, such as the XL and XLC Projects and the CSI.

2.3.8 The Joint EPA/State Innovations Agreement

Building on the NEPPS, EPA and state officials launched in the 1990s an initiative to allow states even more flexibility to implement innovative environmental programs such as pollution prevention. The program was established by the Joint EPA/State Agreement to Pursue Regulatory Innovations (the Regulatory Innovation Agreement), signed by EPA and senior state environmental officials in 1998. The purpose of the Regulatory Innovation Agreement was to allow EPA and the states to improve environmental protection and environmental management practices and to provide timely decision making.

The Regulatory Innovation Agreement was intended to permit states to pursue their regulatory reinvention ideas unimpeded. To do this, EPA and the states agreed that innovation activities that did not require a change in federal guidances, regulations, or statutes could proceed without EPA review. EPA's role consisted of giving support and advice, if requested. If an idea was outside of the existing federal regulatory scheme, the Regulatory Innovation Agreement established a process which required that EPA provide improved oversight and review of state proposals so that EPA and the state could jointly review and evaluate environmental and efficiency benefits derived from the proposed innovation. This process was intended to foster cooperative exploration of innovative approaches that could lead to substantial improvements in regulatory policy and environmental protection.

2.4 EPA's Pollution Prevention Programs After 2000

After the Bush Administration took office in 2001, EPA refocused its pollution prevention efforts away from major multimedia pollution prevention programs, such as the CSI and Project XL, and from specific pollution prevention subject area programs such as EPA's Persistent, Bioaccumulative, and Toxic (PBT) Strategy. EPA's pollution prevention efforts were redirected to voluntary initiatives designed to encourage the incorporation of pollution prevention concepts into the daily operations of government agencies and businesses. EPA's voluntary pollution prevention initiatives are listed on EPA's pollution prevention website at http://www.epa.gov/ebtpages/pollutionpreventionprograms.html. EPA's website lists initiatives in the areas of best management practices, conservation, energy, pollution prevention programs, recycling, smart growth, sustainable development, transportation alternatives, voluntary partnerships, and waste reduction.

EPA continued its emphasis upon pollution prevention partnering between EPA and businesses, with such efforts as EPA's WasteWise Program, Clean Diesel Campaign, and Coal Combustion Products Partnership (C2P2), a joint government/industry program to increase the beneficial use of coal combustion products to reduce energy consumption and greenhouse gas emissions and incentivize industrial recycling. Examples include the use of coal ash in concrete manufacture as a replacement for Portland cement, and the Smart Way Transport Partnership, a program designed to improve performance and fuel efficiency of

U.S. truck and rail freight transport through the use of a voluntary market incentive system.

EPA has also reemphasized its role as a pollution prevention information clearinghouse through its Pollution Prevention Information Clearinghouse (PPIC) Program.

2.4.1 EPA's Green Products Efforts

EPA has promoted a Green Products effort to encourage consumers and companies to incorporate environmental factors into their purchasing process.

EPA's Green Products effort comprised several initiatives. During the Clinton administration, EPA had promoted a Consumer Labeling Initiative (CLI) under which EPA and industrial task force partners conducted consumer research on the green labeling of household pesticide and cleaning products. On March 6, 2000, at the Philadelphia Flower Show, EPA and its partners launched the "Read the Label First!" Campaign to educate consumers concerning the importance of reading product labels. The CLI task force created Phase I and II Reports, which summarized its work, which focused primarily on indoor and outdoor insecticides and household hard surface cleaners.

A Green Products initiative begun under the Clinton Administration and continued under the Bush and Obama Administrations is EPA's Environmentally Preferable Purchasing (EPP) Program designed to encourage and assist federal agencies to integrate environmental concerns into their purchasing decisions. EPA's EPP website (http://www.epa.gov/epp/) contains information sources, guidances and case studies to assist federal agencies in procuring environmentally preferable products and services.

EPA maintains a website (http://www.epa.gov/epawaste/partnership/conserve/tools/stewardship/index.htm) which serves as a resource for companies interested in reducing the life cycle environmental effects of products. The website contains information relating to the reduction of environmental impacts of products and green servicing.

EPA's Sustainable Futures (SF) Initiative promotes the use of EPA's models and methods to screen new chemicals for potential risks. Companies such as PPG Industries, Eastman Kodak, Inc., Cytac Industries, Inc. and International Flavors and Fragrances, Inc. have participated in the program. EPA's June 2005 P2 Framework Manual describes how EPA's models can be used to estimate and screen potential hazards and risks of chemicals. Information relating to EPA's

Sustainable Futures (SF) Initiative is maintained on EPA's website at http://www.epa.gov/oppt/sf/.

2.4.2 EPA's Voluntary Standards Network

EPA has emphasized the use of voluntary standards to support its rulemaking compliance activities and partnership programs with industry, such as the Environmental Leadership Program (ELP) and the Common Sense Initiative (CSI). EPA maintains a Voluntary Standards Network which provides sources of voluntary standards, such as ISO 14000 standards and information relating to standards setting private organizations. EPA's Voluntary Standards Network website is maintained at http://www.epa.gov/oppt/p2home/pubs/programs/voluntary.htm.

2.4.3 Pesticide Environmental Stewardship Program (PestWise)

EPA initiated the Pesticide Environmental Stewardship Program (PestWise) to reduce pesticide risks in agricultural and nonagricultural settings through a public/private partnership. The PestWise Program is a voluntary program that forms partnerships with pesticide users to reduce potential health and environmental risks associated with pesticide use and to implement pollution prevention strategies for addressing those risks. EPA's PestWise Program is coordinated by EPA's Office of Pesticide Programs. Information about EPA's PestWise Program is maintained on EPA's website at http://www.epa.gov/pestwise/about.htm.

2.4.4 Design for the Environment (DFE) and Green Chemistry Programs

EPA's Office of Pollution Prevention and Toxics (OPPT) maintains a Design for the Environment (DFE) Program. Under the DFE Program, companies submit their products to EPA for review and EPA evaluates every product ingredient against a set of health and environmental criteria and determines whether the product as a whole meets safety criteria and is packaged in an environmentally friendly manner. All product ingredients must be disclosed either on the product or on the manufacturer's website. If the product passes EPA's review, the manufacturer is approved to use EPA's Design for the Environment (DFE) label on the product. As of December 2011, more than 2,500 products carried the DFE label. A description of EPA's Design for the Environment (DFE) Program is maintained on EPA's website at http://www.epa.gov/dfe/faqs.html.

EPA has also supported the use of green chemistry in the design of chemical products and process to reduce or eliminate the use and generation of hazardous substances. EPA promotes green chemistry through the Presidential

Green Chemistry Challenge Awards and through educational activities, publications, grants and fellowships. Information about EPA's green chemistry projects and programs is maintained on EPA's website at http://www.epa.gov/greenchemistry/.

2.4.5 EPA's Pollution Prevention Information Clearinghouse

EPA has emphasized its role as a pollution prevention clearinghouse role since the advent of the Bush administration in 2001. EPA maintains a Pollution Prevention Information Clearinghouse (PPIC) as an information source designed to support pollution prevention activities. EPA's PPIC website contains pollution prevention archives and data bases and can be accessed at http://www.epa.gov/oppt/ppic/.

2.4.6 National Partnership for Environmental Priorities

EPA's National Partnership for Environmental Priorities (NPEP) encourages public and private organizations to form voluntary partnerships with EPA to reduce the use and release of any of 31 priority chemicals, such as 1,2,4 trichlorobenzene, dioxins/furans, naphthalene, PAH group chemicals, cadmium, lead, and mercury. As of August 8, 2012, EPA suspended active participation in the National Partnership for Environmental Priorities (NPEP) Program. See, http://www.epa.gov/osw/partnerships/npep/.

2.4.7 EPA's WasteWise Program

WasteWise is a voluntary EPA program targeting the reduction of municipal solid waste and certain types of industrial waste. EPA WasteWise partners include local governments, nonprofit organizations, and multinational corporations. Partners conduct waste assessments to identify waste reduction opportunities and to establish baselines to measure progress in reaching waste reduction goals. Information about the WasteWise Program can be found on the WasteWise website at http:/www.epa.gov/epawaste/conserve/smm/wastewise/index.htm.

2.4.8 Executive Order No. 13514

On October 8, 2009, President Obama signed Executive Order No. 13514 "Federal Leadership in Environmental, Energy, and Economic Performance." The Order requires federal agencies to eliminate waste, recycle, prevent pollution, and foster markets for sustainable technologies and environmentally preferable markets, as well as reducing their greenhouse gas emissions from direct and indirect activities, conserve and protect water resources and design, construct, maintain and operate high-performance, sustainable buildings.

Executive Order No. 13514 can be found on EPA's website at http/www.epa
.gov/p2/pubs/laws.htm.

2.4.9 EPA 2010-2014 Pollution Prevention (P2) Program Strategic Plan

In February 2010, EPA released a Pollution Prevention (P2) Program Strategic
Plan for the years 2010-2014. Under the Plan, EPA announced the following
five goals:

1. Reducing the generation of greenhouse gas (GHG) emissions to mitigate
    climate changes. Strategic target: By 2014, reduce, conserve, or offset 115
    MMT CO_2e cumulatively, compared to the 2006 baseline amount of
    1.2 MMT CO_2e reduced, conserved, or offset.

2. Reducing the manufacture and use of hazardous materials to improve
    human and ecological health. Strategic target: By 2014, reduce 20 billion
    pounds of hazardous materials cumulatively, compared to the 2006 base-
    line of 0.46 billion pounds.

3. Reducing the use of water and conserving other natural resources to pro-
    tect ecosystems. Strategic target: By 2014, reduce water use by 190 billion
    gallons cumulatively, compared to the 2006 baseline amount of 2.3 bil-
    lion gallons reduced.

4. Creating business efficiencies that derive economic benefits and improve
    environmental performance. Strategic target: By 2014, save $14 billion
    through pollution prevention improvements in business, institutional,
    and government costs cumulatively, compared to the 2006 baseline of
    $2.1 billion dollars saved.

5. Institutionalize and integrate pollution prevention practices through gov-
    ernment services, policies, and initiatives.

EPA's 2010-2014 Pollution Prevention (P2) Plan can be found on EPA's
website at http://www.epa.gov/p2/pubs/laws.htm.

2.4.10 EPA's Economy, Energy and Environment Initiative (E3)

EPA has developed a technical assistance framework to assist federal agencies,
states, and local communities in integrating sustainability considerations into
their activities. On the federal level, EPA on September 25, 2010, entered into a
Memorandum of Understanding (MOU) with the U.S. Departments of Commerce, Energy and Labor and the U.S. Small Business Administration for the
Economy, Energy and Environment Initiative (E3) to Support Sustainable Manufacturing. The E3 MOU is designed to foster local public-private partnerships

to coordinate and target federal resources to assist manufacturers on becoming more efficient, competitive and sustainable. E3 projects are designed to provide small and medium enterprises (SMEs) with a single point of contact to coordinate federal resources to support manufacturers in becoming more sustainable.

Information about EPA's E3 Initiative can be found on EPA's website at http://www.e3.gov/.

3.0 State Pollution Prevention Programs

Almost all states now have pollution prevention programs in place. These programs accomplish waste reduction through regulatory and nonregulatory initiatives and promote pollution prevention through technical assistance and public recognition. The history of certain of the state programs is discussed below. An excellent source of information of state pollution prevention programs on the Internet is found through the website of the Massachusetts Toxics Use Reduction Institute at http://www.p2gems.org.

3.1 Mandatory Waste Reduction Programs

A number of states have passed mandatory waste reduction statutes requiring companies to reduce the generation of hazardous waste. In Iowa, for example, the legislature passed the Waste Minimization Act in 1989 requiring reductions in the generation of hazardous wastes through recycling and source reduction.[10] Massachusetts[11] and Tennessee[12] have passed similar waste reduction programs mandating significant reductions in statewide hazardous waste. In 1991, Iowa's pollution prevention activities were strengthened by the passage of the Toxics Pollution Prevention Program.[13] The statute encourages, not requires, certain toxic users[14] to develop a facility-wide multimedia toxics pollution prevention plan.

In 1991, the Arizona legislature passed its Amendments to Hazardous Waste Management Statutes.[15] The statute requires a person who owns or operates a facility that meets certain conditions to prepare and implement a pollution prevention plan that addresses a reduction in the use of toxic substances and the generation of hazardous wastes.[16] On July 25, 1994, the Director of the Arizona Department of Environmental Quality announced a statewide goal of reducing hazardous waste by 25 percent by 2000. This announcement fulfilled the mandate of Section 963, requiring the Director to establish a numeric goal for the state for waste minimization by January 1, 1994.[17] The Director had until January 1, 1999, to establish a numeric goal for the state for toxic use reduction.[18]

New York has a statewide goal for hazardous waste reduction of 50 percent by 1999.[19] In 1992, New York State's Department of Environmental Conservation (DEC) published its Multimedia Pollution Prevention Initiative (M2P2).[20]

M2P2 marked a new approach to environmental quality management in New York State. The program sought to help facilities use multimedia pollution prevention through source reduction.

Other states have passed mandatory waste reduction planning and reporting statutes. The Alabama Hazardous Waste Management Act[21] requires waste generators to report annually on efforts to reduce the volume and toxicity of wastes generated. In 1989, California enacted the Hazardous Waste Reduction and Management Review Act requiring industries that generate 12,000 kilograms or more of hazardous wastes to annually review their operations for potential waste reduction measures and to prepare an implementation schedule.[22] A similar statute was passed in Louisiana.[23]

3.2 Multimedia Permit Programs and Other Regulatory Innovations

New Jersey passed its Pollution Prevention Act (NJPPA)[24] to focus the state's approach to waste minimization and pollution prevention. The NJPPA established an Office of Pollution Prevention in the New Jersey Department of Environmental Protection (NJDEP) and authorized regulations that encouraged voluntary pollution prevention. New Jersey established a statewide goal of a 50 percent reduction in the use, discharge, or generation of hazardous substances over a five-year period. Covered industrial facilities must prepare Pollution Prevention Plans to be kept at the facility and Pollution Prevention Plan Summaries and Progress Reports for submittal to the NJDEP.[25] Pollution Prevention Plans and Plan Summaries must address the use and discharge of New Jersey Right-to-Know substances, New Jersey Toxic Catastrophe Prevention Act substances, EPCRA Section 313, and Superfund substances.

In December 1993, under a pilot program, the NJDEP selected priority industrial facilities to test multimedia permits. Each selected priority industrial facility received facility-wide permits that incorporated all formerly held facility permits[26] under the Solid Waste Management Act,[27] the Air Pollution Control Act,[28] the Water Pollution Control Act,[29] and the NJPPA. The facility-wide permit program was designed to incorporate pollution prevention planning into all NJDEP permit programs integrating use, output, release, and compliance data for facilities.

Other states have developed similar innovative regulatory programs to encourage pollution prevention. For instance, since 1995, Minnesota has been authorized by EPA to take the lead in the selection and implementation of the XL Program at the state level. Massachusetts launched a pilot self-certification program intended to replace low-risk environmental permits at the state level.

Companies involved in this program, called the "Environmental Results Program," are asked to commit to meeting environmental performance standards and to provide annual certifications of compliance with such standards in exchange for suspended permit requirements. California environmental officials also prepared to implement a pilot program to test the idea of replacing environmental permits with facility-wide compliance plans.

3.3 Voluntary Technical Assistance Programs

A majority of states that have considered pollution prevention but have not enacted regulatory programs utilize some form of technical assistance. These programs include establishing technology centers through a consortium of local colleges and research institutions, source reduction programs, and generator seminars or multimedia waste reduction programs and include both public and private participation and funding. The states that have enacted such programs include Florida,[30] Illinois,[31] and Ohio.[32]

4.0 Conclusion

EPA's pollution prevention approach has undergone several changes in emphasis and direction since the adoption of the Pollution Prevention Act in 1990. EPA initially established a series of pollution prevention programs, such as the Common Sense Initiative (CSI) and the Excellence in Leadership Program, better known as Project XL. The CSI and XL programs reflected EPA's intention in the early and mid-1990s to promote pollution prevention on a broad multimedia and industry scale. In the mid-1990s, EPA moved toward institutionalization of pollution prevention programs into its mainstream activities in regulations, permitting, technical assistance, and compliance and enforcement.

Under the Bush administration, beginning in 2001, EPA refocused its pollution prevention efforts away from multimedia and specific pollution prevention programs toward voluntary initiatives, pollution prevention partnering between EPA and businesses, and EPA pollution prevention information clearinghouse functions. Under the Obama administration, beginning in 2009, EPA has focused on voluntary initiatives, labeling programs, and pollution prevention partnering with businesses, and pollution prevention information clearinghouse functions.

5.0 Research Sources

To learn more about pollution prevention, here is a list of helpful websites:

- EPA's Pollution Prevention website: http://www.epa.gov/opptintr/p2 home.

- EPA's Green Chemistry Initiatives website: http://www.epa.gov/green chemistry/pubs/programs.html.

- EPA's Sustainable Futures (SF) Initiative website: http://www.epa.gov/ oppt/sf/pubs/basic.htm.

- EPA's Green Products website: http://www.epa.gov/epawaste/index.htm.

- EPA's Voluntary Standards Network website: http://www.epa.gov/oppt/ p2home/pubs/programs/voluntary.htm.

- EPA's Pesticide Environmental Stewardship Program (PestWise) website: http://www.epa.gov/pestwise/about/index.htm.

- EPA's Pollution Prevention Information Clearinghouse (PPIC) website: http://www.epa.gov/oppt/ppic/.

- EPA's Pollution Prevention and Toxics website: http://www.epa.gov/oppt.

- Massachusetts Toxics Use Reduction Institute website: http://www.turi .org/about.

Notes

1. The Pollution Prevention Act of 1990, Omnibus Budget Reconciliation Act of 1990, 42 U.S.C.A. 13101 *et seq.*, Pub. L. 101-508 (November 5, 1990), section 6601 *et seq.*
2. Source reduction means any practice that (1) reduces the amount of any hazardous substance, pollutant, or contaminant entering any waste stream or otherwise released into the environment (including fugitive emissions) prior to recycling, treatment, or disposal, and (2) reduces the hazards to public health and the environment associated with the release of such substances, pollutants, or contaminants. 42 U.S.C.A. 13101(b).
3. 42 U.S.C.A. 13102(5)(A).
4. 42 U.S.C.A. 13103 (b).
5. 42 U.S.C.A. 11001 *et seq.* Section 11023 requires facilities subject to EPCRA to complete a toxic chemical release form.
6. 42 U.S.C.A. 13106.
7. 42 U.S.C.A. 13107(a).
8. 56 *Fed. Reg.* 7849 (February 26, 1991).
9. *See* 60 *Fed. Reg.* 27282 (May 15, 1995).
10. Iowa Code 455B.481.
11. Toxics Use Reduction Act, Mass. Gen. Laws, Chapter 21 I. The act mandates a 50 percent reduction in toxic and hazardous by-products by 1997.
12. Tennessee Hazardous Waste Reduction Act of 1990, House Bill No. 2217. The act mandates a 25 percent reduction in hazardous waste by June 30, 1995.
13. Iowa Code 455B.518.
14. Toxic user means a large quantity generator as defined pursuant to the Federal Resource Conservation and Recovery Act, 42 U.S.C. 6901 *et seq.* or a person required to report pursuant to Title III of the Federal Superfund Amendments and Reauthorization Act of 1986. Iowa Code 455 B. 516.

[15] House Bill 2121.

[16] 49 Az Rev. Statutes §963.

[17] The July announcement refined the director's January 1994 announcement calling for a reduction of waste by 25 to 50 percent by 2000.

[18] 49 Az. Rev. Statutes §963.

[19] 27 N.Y. ECL Section 27-908.

[20] The Multimedia Pollution Prevention Initiative is the result of two Department of Environmental Conservation Organization and Delegation Memoranda. The first memorandum was the Reduction and Integrated Facility Management, DEC O&D Memo 92-13. The second was the Pollution Prevention Initiative, DEC O&D Memo 92-24.

[21] Alabama Code Section 22-30 *et seq.*

[22] 1989 Hazardous Waste Reduction and Management Review Act. (Senate Bill 14); 1992 Amendments to the Hazardous Waste Source Reduction and Management Review Act of 1989. (Senate Bill 1726).

[23] 1987 Louisiana Waste Reduction Law, Act No. 657.

[24] N.J.S.A. 13:1D-35 *et seq.* (1991). Pollution Prevention Rules, N.J.A.C. 7:1K-1.1 *et seq.* (1993).

[25] *See* Pollution Prevention Program Rules, N.J.A.C. 7:1K *et seq.* (March 1, 1993).

[26] N.J.S.A. 13:1D-4 *et seq.* and N.J.A.C. 7:1K-7 *et seq.*

[27] N.J.S.A. 13:1E-1 *et seq.*

[28] N.J.S.A. 26:2C-1 *et seq.*

[29] N.J.S.A. 58:10A-1 *et seq.*

[30] The Florida Department of Environmental Regulation has received one of 14 Federal Resource Conservation and Recovery Act grants to develop a State Training Action Plan for Florida state personnel and hazardous waste generators.

[31] The 1989 Illinois Toxic Pollution Prevention Act (SB 1044) established a voluntary toxic pollution prevention program within the Illinois EPA.

[32] The Ohio Technology Transfer Organization and the Fisher/Troy Toxic Use Bill establish the funding for a hazardous waste assistance center.

Chapter 15

Emergency Planning and Community Right-to-Know Act

Rolf R. von Oppenfeld
TESTLaw Practice Group

1.0 Background

The federal Emergency Planning and Community Right-to-Know Act (EPCRA), 42 U.S.C. Section 11001 et seq., was signed into law on October 17, 1986, as part (Title III) of the much broader Superfund Amendments and Reauthorization Act, which amended the Comprehensive Environmental Response, Compensation, and Liability Act (CERCLA). Under EPCRA's provisions, certain businesses must submit information about a broad spectrum of potentially hazardous chemicals used in their facilities to state and local authorities and to the public upon request.

The primary goals of EPCRA are to provide the public access to information concerning hazardous chemicals present in the community and to use this information in order to adopt local emergency response plans in the event of a hazardous chemical release. EPCRA aims to achieve these goals through two mechanisms. First, it compels the establishment of state and local emergency planning bodies as well as the development and implementation of local emergency plans. Second, it requires certain facilities to provide detailed reports concerning the presence and health effects of specified chemicals and releases. If an emergency or accident occurs, emergency personnel will be able to properly assess the magnitude of the situation and adopt necessary measures in order to protect the public from any danger.

EPCRA is divided into three subchapters. Subchapter I (Sections 301–305) establishes the framework for state and local emergency planning. Subchapter II (Sections 311–313) sets forth reporting requirements for the submission of information concerning the type and quantity of hazardous chemicals maintained at certain facilities to federal, state, and local agencies. Subchapter III (Sections 321–330) contains miscellaneous provisions concerning trade-secret protection, enforcement, and public availability of information. The first two subchapters contain four basic programs. Sections 301 to 303 concern emergency planning, Section 304 deals with emergency release notification, sections 311 and 312 relate to hazardous chemical storage and reporting requirements, and Section 313 sets forth the Toxic Chemical Release Inventory. Each of these programs have different but overlapping chemical lists, reporting threshold quantities, and notification periods.

EPCRA is administered at the federal level by the U.S. Environmental Protection Agency (EPA), which, among other things, receives Toxic Chemical Release Inventory (Form R) Section 313 reports, oversees Title III implementation nationwide, establishes and revises the lists of hazardous chemicals, and fines companies (up to $37,500 per day) for noncompliance.

2.0 Emergency Planning and Notification

2.1 State Commissions, Planning Districts, and Local Committees (Section 301)

2.1.1 State Emergency Response Commissions

Under the provisions of EPCRA, the governor of each state is required to appoint a state emergency response commission (SERC). In the event that he or she fails to do so, the governor must act as the emergency response commission until one is appointed. The SERC must designate local emergency planning districts and appoint and organize the activities of local emergency planning commissions (LEPCs). LEPCs must be appointed within one month after a district is designated. The SERC is responsible for supervising and coordinating LEPCs, processing requests from the general public for EPCRA information, and reviewing local emergency plans.

2.1.2 Emergency Planning Districts

The SERC has the duty to designate emergency planning districts in order to expedite the preparation and implementation of emergency plans and strategies. The emergency planning district may consist of existing political subdivisions or multijurisdictional planning commissions.

2.1.3 Local Emergency Planning Committees

The SERC must appoint members of an LEPC for each emergency planning district. The LEPC must include elected state and local officials; police, fire, civil defense, and public health professionals; environmental, hospital, and transportation officials, as well as representatives of facilities subject to Subchapter I requirements; community groups; and the media. Facilities subject to the emergency planning requirements must notify the LEPC of a representative who will participate in the planning process as a facility emergency coordinator. The LEPC's primary responsibility is to develop an emergency response plan, discussed below, and evaluate available resources for preparing for and responding to a potential chemical accident. Furthermore, the LEPC must establish rules, give public notice of its activities, establish procedures for handling public requests for information, and allow public comment on the plan. The extent of the required emergency plan is outlined in Section 303, discussed below.

2.1.4 Tribal Emergency Response Commissions

Under Sections 301 to 303 of EPCRA, states form SERCs. Similarly, tribal chief executive officers appoint tribal emergency response commissions (TERCs) to accomplish the following: (1) designate local emergency planning districts as needed; (2) appoint an LEPC to serve each of the districts; (3) coordinate and supervise LEPC activities; (4) coordinate proposals for and distribution of federal grant funds for TERCs and/or tribal LEPCs; (5) review LEPC plans, recommending any needed changes; (6) establish procedures for receiving and processing public requests for information collected under EPCRA; and (7) obtain further information about a particular chemical or facility, when needed.

There are several options that tribes can turn to when implementing the EPCRA programs. The tribe may enter into a cooperative agreement with another tribe or the state within which its lands are located. The tribe may also choose to implement the program directly within Indian Country. The tribe can also choose to implement some of EPCRA's requirements while delegating the rest to a SERC through a cooperative agreement. These options would allow the tribe to develop an EPCRA program that meets the specific needs of the tribe. If a TERC is not established or a cooperative agreement is not reached, the tribal chief executive officer will operate as the TERC. Once the TERC or the cooperative agreement is reached, they must meet all the requirements imposed upon LEPCs and SERCs.[1]

2.2 Substances and Facilities Covered and Notification (Section 302)

2.2.1 Substances Covered

EPCRA's Subchapter I requirements apply only to those substances designated as "extremely hazardous substances" (EHSs). (By contrast, reporting requirements under Sections 311 to 313 apply to a much broader range of substances.) The list of EHSs is defined in Section 302(a)(2) as "the list of substances published in November 1985 by the Administrator in Appendix A of the Chemical Emergency Preparedness Program Interim Guidance." This list was established by EPA in order to identify chemical substances which could cause serious irreversible health effects from accidental releases. The list is based primarily on the inherent acute toxicity of each substance and may be revised by EPA (although revisions to the list are based on acute and chronic toxicity, reactivity, volatility, dispersibility, and combustibility or flammability). At the present time, there are 356 EHSs. The list of EHSs may be found in 40 C.F.R. Part 355, Appendix A.

2.2.2 Threshold Planning Quantities

A facility must engage in emergency planning based on the presence of an EHS only if that substance exists at the facility in an amount exceeding its TPQ. Each EHS's TPQ is listed in 40 C.F.R. Part 355, Appendix A. Any facility that produces, uses, or stores any of the listed chemicals in a quantity greater than the TPQ must meet all emergency planning requirements. In determining whether the TPQ of an EHS is present, it is necessary to determine whether, at any given instant, a facility has on-site, in all forms where the substance exists in concentrations greater than 1 percent by weight, an amount of an EHS exceeding its TPQ. If the EHS exists in forms where it is less than 1 percent by weight of a compound or mixture, it is regarded as de minimis (i.e., not significant), and its volume is not considered in determining whether the TPQ level of the substance is present.[2] EHSs that are solids are subject to either of two threshold planning quantities separated by a slash (e.g., 500/10,000 pounds). The lower quantity applies only if the solid exists in powdered form and has a particle size less than 100 microns, is handled in solution or in molten form, or meets the criteria for National Fire Protection Association rating of 2, 3, or 4 for reactivity. If the solid does not meet any of these criteria, it is subject to the upper (10,000 pound) TPQ.[3] In 2012, EPA revised the manner in which TPQs are applied to EHSs that are non-reactive solid chemicals in solution in order to reflect less potential for airborne releases beyond the fenceline.[4] As with substances covered by the emergency planning and notification provisions, EPA may revise the TPQs by considering the same criteria (toxicity, reactivity, volatility, dispersibility, combustibility, or flammability).

2.2.3 Facilities Covered

Facilities at which EHSs are present in amounts exceeding the TPQ are subject to Subchapter I requirements. EPCRA defines facility expansively as "all buildings, equipment, structures, and other stationary items which are located on a single site or on contiguous or adjacent sites and which are owned or operated by the same person (or by any person which controls, is controlled by, or under common control with, such person)."[5] In addition, the term includes natural structures serving as containment structures for human use, including subsurface structures, if chemicals are purposefully placed in or removed from such structures by human means. EPCRA generally does not apply to the transportation (including storage incident to transportation) of substances otherwise subject to EPCRA except for Section 304 emergency notification requirements.[6]

The owner/operator of a facility subject to this section must provide notice to the SERC that the facility is governed by the emergency planning requirements of Subchapter I within 60 days after the facility becomes subject to the requirements of this section.[7] In addition, the facility owner/operator must appoint an emergency response coordinator and notify the LEPC of that person's identity within 60 days after a facility first becomes subject to these emergency planning provisions.[8] Finally, the owner/operator must notify the LEPC (within 30 days) of any changes occurring at the facility that may affect community planning.[9]

2.3 Comprehensive Emergency Response Plans (Section 303)

2.3.1 Emergency Plan Requirements

Each LEPC is required to prepare (and annually update) an emergency plan. At a minimum this plan must include the following information: (1) identification of facilities covered under Subchapter I, identification of routes likely to be used to transport EHSs, and identification of facilities contributing to or subjected to additional risk because of their proximity to facilities covered under Subchapter I; (2) methods and procedures to be followed by facility owners and operators and medical personnel in responding to a release of EHSs; (3) designation of a community emergency coordinator and facility emergency coordinators; (4) procedures providing for effective and timely notification by the facility emergency coordinator and the community emergency coordinator to persons specified in the emergency response plan and to the general public when a release has occurred; (5) methods for determining the occurrence of a release and the likely affected area or population; (6) identification of emergency equipment and facilities available in the community and at each covered facility; (7) evacuation plans; (8) training programs, including schedules for training emergency response and medical personnel; and (9) methods and schedules for exercising the emergency plan. The LEPC may request from covered facilities whatever information is necessary to facile Tate implementation of the emergency plan. The SERC then reviews the proposed plan to ensure that it is consistent with the plans adopted by other LEPCs in the state. EPA has published general guidance documents for preparing and implementing emergency plans. If desired by the LEPC, its plan will be reviewed by regional response teams established pursuant to CERCLA.

2.4 Emergency Notification in the Event of a Release (Section 304)

2.4.1 Reportable Releases

A facility owner/operator may be required to notify federal, state, or local authorities upon the release of specified substances from a facility (which for purposes of release notification includes means of transportation, such as motor vehicles, rolling stock, and aircraft) at which hazardous chemicals are produced, used, or stored.

A "release" is defined as any spilling, leaking, pumping, pouring, emitting, emptying, discharging, injecting, escaping, leaching, dumping, or disposing of something to the environment.[10] If a release is fully contained and only persons within the site or sites belonging to the facility are exposed, a notification is not required.[11] If the release is not confined or has the potential of escaping containment, notification must be made when air, land surface, surface water, groundwater, or subsurface strata are or may be affected.

A facility must meet the EPCRA reporting requirements set forth below if the release is (1) of an EHS in excess of its EPCRA reportable quantity (RQ) (located in 40 C.F.R. Part 355, Appendix A and not the same as that substance's TPQ) or (2) is of a "hazardous substance" as defined by CERCLA whose release would have to be reported under Section 103(a) of CERCLA (i.e., where the release exceeds the substance's CERCLA reportable quantity, found at 40 C.F.R. Part 302, Table 302.4).[12] Per Executive Order 12856, federal facilities are also subject to Section 304 reporting requirements as owners or operators.[13]

Many of the CERCLA and EPCRA reporting requirements are the same, and the substance lists often overlap. Notably, however, the petroleum exclusion in the definition of hazardous substances under CERCLA is inapplicable under EPCRA. Section 304 reporting requirements are in addition to any possible CERCLA reporting requirements and do not take the place of such requirements. In other words, release of a "hazardous substance" in an amount exceeding its CERCLA RQ could trigger reporting requirements under both CERCLA and EPCRA. Therefore, the release of a hazardous substance that could go off-site means a facility may have to report to the LEPC and SERC under EPCRA and the NRC under CERCLA.

2.4.2 Exemptions to the Reporting Requirements

The following are exempt from Section 304 reporting requirements: (1) releases resulting in exposure solely to persons within the boundaries of the facility; (2) "continuous" (i.e., stable in quantity and rate) releases under Section 103(f) of CERCLA, for which similar notification has already been given to EPA (except for "statistically significant increases" as defined in Section 103[e] of CERCLA);

(3) releases exempt from CERCLA reporting under Section 101(22) of CERCLA (i.e., when the release is from certain engine exhaust, certain nuclear incidents, or the normal application of fertilizer); (4) "federally permitted releases" under Section 101(10) of CERCLA (essentially, a release allowed, through permit or otherwise, by a federal statute more narrowly addressed to the type of release at issue; e.g., releases permitted under the Clean Water Act or the Clean Air Act); (5) releases of pesticide products exempted from CERCLA reporting by Section 103(e) of CERCLA; (6) releases not meeting the technical definition of "release" in Section 101(22) of CERCLA; and (7) certain air releases from animal wastes; and (8) certain releases of radionuclides.[14]

On December 21, 1999, EPA published interim guidance regarding the federally permitted release exception under CERCLA/EPCRA that limited the exception for hazardous substances.[15] However, on May 19, 2000, this interim guidance was suspended indefinitely pending revisions.[16] On April 17, 2002, EPA released its final general guidance,[17] with some further changes made to exempt certain animal waste releases, on December 18, 2008.[18]

2.4.3 The Federally Permitted Release Exemption

Under EPCRA Section 304(a)(2), federally permitted releases under CERCLA Section 103(a) are exempt from reporting requirements.[19] Section 101(10) of CERCLA contains 11 definitions of "federally permitted releases." These exemptions include federally permitted releases in compliance with: (1) a National Pollutant Discharge Elimination System (NPDES) permit; (2) a Clean Water Act (CWA) 404 dredge and fill Army Corps of Engineers permit; (3) a final Resource Conservation and Recovery Act (RCRA) Treatment Storage and Disposal facility permit; (4) a permit under the Marine Protection, Research, and Sanctuaries Act; (5) injections authorized under federal or EPA-approved state underground injection control programs; (6) Clean Air Act (CAA) permits or control regulations; (7) discharges to publicly owned treatment works (POTWs); and (8) permits under the Atomic Energy Act.[20] However, determining the applicability of the exemption has proved difficult. In *In re Mobil Oil Corp.*, the court stated that the "federally permitted release exception applies only in those situations where the release is in compliance with its permit."[21] EPA issued its latest guidance on EPCRA Section 304 and CERCLA Section 101(1)(H), Federally Permitted Release Definition for Certain Air Emissions, on April 17, 2002.[22] On October 4, 2006, EPA amended its regulations to resolve a discrepancy between the guidance and its regulations (formally increasing the reportable quantities for nitrogen oxide and dioxide due to combustion-related activities).[23]

The federally permitted release exemption exempts from notification certain air emissions of hazardous substances and EHSs when the release is subject to a permit or control regulation issued pursuant to CAA Sections 111 and 112, Title I part C, Title I part D, or a Section 110 State Implementation Plan (SIP).[24] Whether a particular air release of a hazardous substance or EHS is exempt from the reporting requirements requires a case-by-case determination based on the specific permit language or applicable control requirement. To help clarify some common questions concerning which permitted releases are exempt from reporting, EPA published the "Guidance on the CERCLA Section 101(10)(H) Federally Permitted Release Definition for Certain Air Emissions."[25] The guidance covers the following issues: emission exceedances of permit limits and control regulations, criteria pollutants (VOCs, PM, and NOx), minor sources, waivers, accidents and malfunctions, and start-up and shutdown.[26] The guidance is structured in question-and-answer form and includes the following:

1. A release is not federally permitted if it exceeds permit limits or limits contained in the regulations.

2. If a source is in compliance with a permit or regulation limiting VOC or PM emissions and the limits have the net effect of controlling the release of constituent hazardous substances, such releases would likely qualify as federally permitted releases.

3. Releases in compliance with a federally enforceable threshold as well as releases that comply with any federally enforceable technology requirements, operational requirements, work practices, or other control practices would generally meet the definition of "federally permitted release" when the emission threshold limits or eliminates the release of the designated hazardous substance or EHS at issue.

4. If a source has been granted a waiver from otherwise applicable control requirements, releases of hazardous substances that would have been controlled by the otherwise applicable regulations are federally permitted releases.

5. Accidental releases and malfunctions that may result in the release of a hazardous substance above its CERCLA RQ do not qualify for the federally permitted release exemption, even if you are operating consistent with your facility's accident and malfunction plan.

6. If a release is in compliance with the requirements of an approved plan for start-up or shutdown that contains federally enforceable procedures that limit or control the releases, then the release would generally qualify for the federally permitted release exemption. However, if a release is exempt from CAA regulation or is otherwise not subject to emission limits or other controls during start-up or shutdown, then these uncontrolled releases do not qualify for the exemption.[27]

Under Section 101(10)(H) of CERCLA, "federally permitted release" includes "any emission into the air subject to a permit or control regulation" from any new stationary source or hazardous air pollutant source, emissions controlled under the new source review program, and emissions regulated by a SIP submitted in accordance with Section 110 of the CAA.[28] The Environmental Appeals Board upheld EPA's interpretation of the language "subject to a permit or control regulation" to require that the facility be in compliance with the permit or control regulation in order to take advantage of the exemption.[29]

EPA distinguished between regulations governing the operation of a facility and those governing the emissions limitations. In *In re Borden Chemicals and Plastics Co.*, the regulations applicable to the facility exempted "unpreventable emergency relief valve releases from constituting operations violations subject to EPA enforcement."[30] The administrative law judge held that the question of whether the release was "unpreventable" and therefore exempt from EPA enforcement is distinct from the determination of whether the release exceeds the relevant emission standard.[31]

EPA applies the federally permitted release exemption to RCRA releases where (1) the facility has a final permit for "treatment, storage or disposal" of a RCRA hazardous waste; (2) the permit specifically identifies and controls for the substances released; and (3) the release is in compliance with the terms of the permit.[32] Also, releases reported to the NRC under RCRA subtitle C are exempt from the Section 103 reporting requirements of CERCLA.[33]

Federally permitted releases to water in compliance with the CWA are defined as (1) discharges in compliance with an NPDES permit under Section 402, (2) discharges resulting from circumstances identified and reviewed and part of the public record with respect to a permit issued or modified under Section 402, (3) continuous or anticipated intermittent discharges from a point source identified in a permit or permit application under Section 402, and (4) discharges in compliance with a legally enforceable permit under Section 404.[34]

Some releases into POTWs are also exempted; however, some require reporting, depending on whether the POTW is required to have a pretreatment program. If a facility releases a hazardous substance that exceeds its RQ to a POTW without a pretreatment program, the release is considered a "release into the environment" and requires reporting.[35] This is based on EPA's determination that a POTW is not a totally enclosed structure.[36] If the POTW does have a federally approved pretreatment program, the release is permitted unless it exceeds the pretreatment standard.[37]

2.4.4 Notification Requirements

The owner/operator of a facility must immediately notify the community emergency coordinator of the LEPC and the SERC of any reportable release.[38] By contrast, notice of a release under CERCLA, which may be required in addition to Section 304 reporting for releases of certain substances, is made on the national level to the NRC. If the release occurs during transportation, then notification should be made through the 911 system, or if one is not present, then through an operator.[39]

Notification must include, to the extent known at the time notice is given:[40] (1) the chemical name or identity of any released substance; (2) whether the chemical is an extremely hazardous substance; (3) an estimate of the quantity released into the environment; (4) the time and duration of the release; (5) the medium into which the release occurred; (6) any known or anticipated acute or chronic health risks and, where appropriate, advice regarding necessary medical attention; (7) proper precautions to take as a result of the release; and (8) the names and telephone numbers of persons to be contacted for further information.

As soon as possible following a release, the owner or operator must provide written follow-up notice, updating the above information and including additional information on (1) actions taken to respond to and contain the release, (2) any known or anticipated acute or chronic health risks associated with the release, and (3), where appropriate, advice regarding medical attention required for those exposed.[41]

Follow-up notice should be within 30 days of the release.[42]

2.4.5 Penalties for Violating Notice Requirements

Violations of the emergency release notification requirements may result in civil penalties of up to $37,500 for each violation.

The "knowing and willful" failure to provide emergency notice of a release as required by Section 304 may result in criminal penalties of up to $25,000 and/or two years' imprisonment. Criminal penalties will increase to $50,000 and/or five years imprisonment for a second "knowing and willful" failure to provide emergency notice of a release.

Penalties are based on the guidance issued by EPA on September 30, 1999, titled "Interim Final Enforcement Response Policy for Sections 304, 311, and 312 of the Emergency Planning and Community Right-To-Know Act and Section 103 of the Comprehensive Environmental Response, Compensation and Liability Act."[43] The policy is used by EPA to calculate penalties for civil and administrative actions, and for settlements. There are two parts to a penalty under the policy. The first part is the base penalty.[44] The base penalty takes into consideration the (1) nature, (2) circumstances, (3) extent, and (4) gravity of the violation.

The "nature" of the violation simply refers to whether the violation is of an EPCRA or a CERCLA reporting requirement.[45] The "circumstances" factor considers the actual or potential harm to human health and the environment as a result of the failure to notify.[46] The "extent" of the violation refers to the timeliness of the notification. For example, for CERCLA Section 103, there are three levels. A violation is a Level 1 violation if the notice was not made within two hours of acquiring knowledge of the release. The violation is Level 2 if the report is made more than one but less than two hours after acquiring knowledge of a release, and Level 3 is for delays of less than an hour but more than 15 minutes.[47] The "gravity" of the violation refers to the amount of the substance released relative to the reportable quantity for that substance. There are three gravity levels. Level A refers to releases greater than ten times the reportable quantity. Level B is for releases greater than five times but less than ten times the reportable quantity. Level C refers to releases greater than the reportable quantity but less than or equal to five times the reportable quantity.[48] EPA uses the extent and gravity levels to assign a range for the base penalty using a matrix. After the penalty range is assigned, the circumstances factor is used to come to a precise dollar for the base penalty.[49]

After the base penalty is determined, it is adjusted up or down based on adjustment factors. These adjustment factors include (1) ability to pay, (2) prior history of violations, (3) degree of culpability, (4) economic benefit or savings, and (5) such other factors as justice may require.[50] For the ability to pay factor, the policy lists information that must be submitted to qualify for such an adjustment, including tax returns.[51] EPA has a computer model (ABEL) that it often uses to analyze ability to pay questions.[52] The base penalty may be increased by up to three times based on repeat violations that have occurred within five years. Evidence of a prior violation may include a judgment, consent agreement, consent decree, or order. Violations at different facilities of the same corporation are considered unless the facilities are in substantially different lines of business or are substantially independent in their management.[53]

Other factors that EPA will consider are size of the business (base penalty may be reduced by 15 percent for first-time violators employing fewer than 100 people), attitude of the violator (base penalty may be reduced 35 percent based on this factor), willingness to undertake a Supplemental Environmental Project, and whether notification was voluntary (those who conduct an audit and self-disclose may receive up to a 100 percent reduction in the gravity component of the base penalty, assuming the other criteria are met).

Penalties may be adjusted further as follows. There are three levels of culpability. Level 1 involves a willful violation, and the penalty may be adjusted upward by 25 percent.[54] Level 2 applies where the violator had sufficient knowledge to recognize the hazard or significant control over the situation, but the failure to report was not willful. This is no adjustment to the base penalty for a Level 2 violation.[55] Level 3 refers to a situation where the violator lacked sufficient knowledge of the hazard or lacked significant control over the situation. The base penalty may be adjusted down by 25 percent for a Level 3 violation.[56]

2.5 Emergency Training and Review of Emergency Systems (Section 305)

Section 305 authorizes federal officials involved in emergency training to provide training for federal, state, and local personnel in hazard mitigation, emergency preparedness, and other aspects of responding to hazardous chemicals.

Additionally, Section 305(b) requires EPA to initiate a study assessing the ability of current technology to prevent the release of EHSs, measure the threat of any such releases, and identify specific substances, their chemical composition, and the relative concentration of the constituent sub-stance. EPA is also required to examine and suggest ways to improve public emergency alert devices in the event of a release of EHSs.

3.0 Reporting Requirements

3.1 Material Safety Data Sheet Reporting Requirements (Section 311)

3.1.1 Reporting Requirements

Approximately 550,000 facilities are subject to Section 311 and 312 requirements. Owners and operators of facilities to which Section 311 applies are required to submit information to specified authorities regarding the presence of hazardous chemicals at their facilities. The required information was due on or before October 17, 1990 (or within three months after a facility first becomes subject to Section 311). This is a one-time only reporting requirement (unless supplemental reporting requirements are triggered, as discussed below).[57]

Section 311 applies to any facility (1) that is required under the Occupational Safety and Health Act (OSHA) and its regulations to prepare or have available a material safety data sheet (MSDS) for a hazardous chemical[58] and (2) that keeps such a chemical present at the facility in an amount greater than the minimum threshold levels established by Section 311's regulations (discussed below).[59] If Section 311 requires an owner or operator to provide information on hazardous chemicals present at a facility, the owner or operator may submit the chemicals' MSDSs or a list of chemicals for which the facility is required to maintain an MSDS (grouped by hazard category).[60] The owner/operator must submit the required information to the SERC, the LEPC, and the local fire department with jurisdiction over the facility.[61] These bodies prefer submission of a list rather than a series of MSDSs but will accept either. The MSDS itself must include the permissible exposure limits under OSHA and the threshold limit value as prescribed by the American Congress of Governmental Industrial Hygienists and any other exposure limits, if applicable.

3.1.2 Minimum Threshold Levels

The reporting requirements of Section 311 will be triggered only by the presence of a hazardous substance at a facility above specified threshold amounts. The applicable thresholds differ depending upon whether a chemical is considered just a "hazardous chemical" or also an "EHS." In calculating the amounts of individual hazardous chemicals present in mixtures, any quantities of the chemical where it constitutes less than 1 percent (or 0.1 percent if carcinogenic) by weight of the mixture need not be included. If the mixture is reported as a whole (rather than by individual hazardous components), then the total quantity of the mixture should be reported.[62]

3.1.2.1 Hazardous Chemicals

Section 311 adopts the OSHA definition of "hazardous chemicals," as set forth in 29 C.F.R. Section 1910.1200(c).[63] Under OSHA's definition, a "hazardous chemical" is any element, chemical, or compound that is a physical or health hazard. Although OSHA does not provide a specific list of chemicals it considers to be hazardous, it provides the criteria for determining whether a chemical constitutes a physical or health hazard.[64] However, EPA excludes some substances that would otherwise be included in OSHA's definition.[65] These include (1) food additives, drugs, and cosmetics regulated by the Food and Drug Administration; (2) solid substances in manufactured items as long as exposure to the substance does not occur under normal working conditions; (3) consumer products; (4) chemicals used in research labs, hospitals, and medical facilities; and (5) any substance used routinely in agricultural operations or fertilizer for consumer sale.

If a hazardous chemical for which an owner/operator is required to prepare or have available an MSDS is present at a facility at any one time in an amount equal to or greater than 10,000 pounds (4,540 kg), the owner or operator is required to submit an MSDS or list meeting the requirements of Section 311 within three months after the facility first becomes subject to Section 311.[66]

3.1.2.2 Extremely Hazardous Substances

An EHS is any substance that is listed in 40 C.F.R. Part 355, Appendix A, as discussed above. The owner/operator of a facility must submit an MSDS or other information concerning an EHS if such substance is present at the facility at any one time in an amount equal to or greater than 500 pounds (227 kg, or approximately 55 gallons) or the TPQ for that chemical, whichever is less.[67] If the amount of an extremely hazardous substance at a facility exceeds the lesser of 500 pounds or its TPQ, the required documents must be submitted within three months after the facility first becomes subject to Section 311. In determining whether the reporting threshold for an EHS has been exceeded, a facility should aggregate all quantities of the substance present in mixtures and all other quantities present elsewhere in the facility.[68]

One example of a reportable EHS that is commonly overlooked by industry is the industrial lead-acid battery containing sulfuric acid.[69] These types of batteries are found in emergency power backup systems used for communication equipment, computers, and lighting. Appendix A of 40 C.F.R. Part 355 lists sulfuric acid as an EHS with 500 pounds as its threshold reportable quantity. Therefore, facilities with such a quantity are subject to EPCRA Sections 302, 311, and 312 reporting requirements, even though the facilities believe that the industrial batteries fall under the "article" exemption.[70] However, EPA stated that since batteries are likely to leak, spill, or break during regular operations of use and foreseeable emergencies, then they are not "articles" and are required to be reported under EPCRA.[71]

3.1.3 Supplemental Reporting

The owner/operator of a facility that has not previously submitted MSDSs may be required to submit MSDSs for hazardous chemicals to the LEPC within 30 days of the request, even if the owner or operator prefers to submit (or already has submitted) a list of those chemicals.[72] There is no minimum threshold for reporting in response to such a request.

The public may obtain MSDSs filed with the designated authorities by submitting a written request to the LEPC. If someone requests an MSDS and the committee does not have the requested MSDS in its possession, the committee is required to request the MSDS from the facility.[73]

Once an MSDS is submitted, even as the result of a request made by an appropriate authority, a revised MSDS must be submitted within three months after the discovery of significant new information.[74]

3.1.4 Alternate Reporting by List

As noted above, an owner/operator may submit either an MSDS for each chemical required to be reported under Section 311 or a list of such chemicals.[75]

3.2 Hazardous Chemical Inventory Form Reporting Requirements (Section 312)

3.2.1 Regulated Activities

Section 312 requires facilities that accumulate specified quantities of hazardous chemicals or EHSs on-site to submit hazardous chemical inventory forms to specified authorities (the SERC, the LEPCs, and the fire department with jurisdiction over the facility). The initial report, which covers the prior calendar year, is due by March 1 of the year after the facility first becomes subject to Section 312 and annually thereafter.[76]

3.2.2 Reporting Requirements

Reporting on a Tier I or Tier II inventory form (provided by EPA) or on a state or local form containing identical information is mandatory if the owner or operator of a facility is required under OSHA to prepare or have available an MSDS for a hazardous chemical and if such a chemical is present in the facility in an amount greater than the minimum levels established by the Section 312 regulations.

The thresholds for determining whether Section 312 reporting is required are identical to thresholds under Section 311. For hazardous chemicals, the threshold is 10,000 pounds (4,550 kg). For EHSs, the threshold is 500 pounds (227 kg, or approximately 55 gallons) or the TPQ for that substance, whichever quantity is less.[77]

For individual hazardous chemicals present in mixtures, quantities of that chemical constituting less than 1 percent by weight (0.1 percent if a carcinogen) of the mixture need not be included.[78] However, if the mixture is reported as a whole rather than by individual hazardous components, then the total quantity of the mixture should be reported, and there is no analogous de minimis exception.[79]

To determine if the reporting threshold for an EHS has been exceeded, a facility should aggregate all quantities of the substance present in mixtures and all other quantities present elsewhere in the facility (there is no 1 percent de minimis exception).[80]

When calculating whether a threshold has been exceeded, a facility must determine whether the threshold quantity was present at the facility at any given time during the preceding calendar year. If so, both Tier I and Tier II require estimates of the average and maximum daily amounts present at the facility but allow that estimate to be reported in ranges (e.g., 0 to 99 pounds, 100 to 999 pounds, 1,000 to 9,999 pounds, etc.).

3.2.2.1 Tier I

A Tier I report provides information on the maximum and average daily amounts and general location of hazardous chemicals at a facility. Reporting is not required for individual chemicals. Rather, a facility simply reports the amounts and general location of all chemicals posing a particular type of hazard, which correspond to the physical and health hazards identified by OSHA in its regulations governing hazardous chemicals.[81] Tier I reports are due annually by March 1.[82] If the SERC or LEPC requests further information, then a Tier II inventory form must be completed.

3.2.2.2 Tier II

A Tier II report is chemical-specific and more detailed with respect to location and manner of storage of the chemical than a Tier I report. A Tier II report must contain (1) the chemical or common name as provided on the MSDS, (2) an indication whether the substance is extremely hazardous, (3) the form of hazardous chemical (solid, gas, etc.), (4) applicable health and physical hazard categories, (5) an estimated maximum amount of the chemical present at the facility during the preceding year, (6) an estimated average daily amount of the chemical present at the facility during the preceding year in each category, (7) the number of days the chemical was on-site, (8) a description of the manner of storage of the hazardous chemical, (9) the location of the chemical at the facility, and (10) an indication whether the owner or operator elects to withhold location of a specific chemical from public exposure pursuant to EPCRA Section 324.[83] The submission of a Tier II report is not automatically required under Section 312 but must be submitted if requested by the SERC, the LEPC, or the local fire department, by March 1.[84] Today, most states require Tier II. Several states have specific additional requirements that must be met in addition to the federal Tier II requirements. A Tier II report may also be required if there is a citizen request on a hazardous chemical at a facility in a quantity greater than 10,000 pounds. The SERC and the LEPC must then request a Tier II report from that facility.[85] However, most companies prefer to submit Tier II forms because Tier I information is readily available to the public by the SERC or LEPC upon submission.[86] Tier II forms contain restrictions on public disclosure, which is dependent upon who is requesting the information: the SERC, the LEPC, local fire department, state or local officials, or the public.[87] On July 13, 2012, EPA made a number of changes to the Tier I and II programs, effective January 1, 2014.[88] The Tier I and Tier II reporting forms were revised, and must be complied with for reports due on March 1, 2014 (for reporting year 2013).

3.2.2.3 Tier II Software

EPA has available on its website the Tier II Submit Software,[89] a software program developed by EPA for use by facilities to enter and submit EPCRA Section

312 chemical information, also known as Tier II reports. The software allows users to enter multiple facilities, chemicals, and contacts. The program also includes many of the state's additional data requirements that need to be submitted. Many states have more specific Tier II reporting procedures and requirements for which EPA maintains a website with linked information.[90]

3.2.3 Public Requests for Information

Any person may request Tier II information for a facility by writing to the SERC or LEPC.[91] If the request for information is made by a state or local official acting in her official capacity or the request (regardless of who makes it) concerns hazardous chemicals being kept at the facility in excess of 10,000 pounds and the commission or committee does not already have the requested information, the commission or committee must ask the owner or operator of the facility to submit such information.[92] If the original request for information is not made by a public official acting in her official capacity and if the request concerns chemicals at the facility in amounts below the 10,000-pound threshold, the committee or commission may still request the information from the owner or operator of the facility.

3.2.4 Penalties

A violation of the Section 312 reporting requirements may result in a fine of up to $37,500 per violation.[93] Each day a violation continues is considered a separate violation. Penalties are based on the Enforcement Response Policy issued by EPA on September 30, 1999, as previously mentioned.[94]

3.3 Toxic Chemical Release Reporting Requirements (Section 313)

For assistance in completing and submitting Section 313 reports, EPA has developed extensive EPCRA/TRI Training Materials.[95] EPA has proposed mandating electronic submission of Section 313 reports.[96]

3.3.1 Regulated Activities

Owners and operators of regulated facilities must complete and submit an EPA Form R report summarizing any "releases" of certain toxic chemicals into the environment. For purposes of Section 313, reporting is not limited to unpermitted or accidental spills into the environment. Rather, it includes any method by which the facility allows a toxic chemical to enter an environmental medium such as air, water, or soil. Releases include transfers to off-site landfills or other treatment facilities, discharges to municipal sewer systems, direct additions of a toxic chemical to the environment through air emissions (including fugitive emissions), direct discharges to surface water or underground injection wells, and on-site landfilling or placement in other forms of impoundments.

Reports must be submitted annually to EPA by July 1 for the preceding calendar year.[97] Now, reports can be submitted to EPA electronically using the TRI CD-ROM. The software can also be downloaded from the EPA website at http://www.epa.gov/tri/report.htm. Although it is no longer published in the Code of Federal Regulations, Form R is available directly from EPA. A broad list of required reporting elements is set forth at 40 C.F.R. Section 372.85(b).[98] These include (1) the name, location, and type of business; (2) whether the chemical is manufactured, imported, processed, or otherwise used and to what chemical category it belongs; (3) a range of estimates of the maximum amount of the toxic chemical present at any time during the preceding year; (4) the amount of the toxic chemical annually released into the air, water, and land; (5) off-site locations where the facility transfers the toxic chemicals for disposal, recovery, recycling, or treatment; and (6) waste treatment or disposal methods for and their efficiency for each waste stream.[99]

3.3.2 Reporting Requirements

The owner or operator of a plant, factory, or other facility must submit a report on all releases of a hazardous chemical during a calendar year if, during that calendar year,[100]

(a) The facility has ten or more full-time employees.

(b) The facility is in a Standard Industrial Classification (SIC) (as in effect on January 1, 1987) major group or industry code listed in § 372.23(a), for which the corresponding North American Industry Classification System (NAICS) (as in effect on January 1, 2007, for reporting year 2008 and thereafter) subsector and industry codes are listed in § 372.23(b) and (c) by virtue of the fact that it meets one of the following criteria:

   (1) The facility is an establishment with a primary SIC major group or industry code listed in § 372.23(a), or a primary NAICS subsector or industry code listed in § 372.23(b) or § 372.23(c).

   (2) The facility is a multi-establishment complex where all establishments have primary SIC major group or industry codes listed in § 372.23(a), or primary NAICS subsector or industry codes listed in § 372.23(b) or § 372.23(c).

   (3) The facility is a multi-establishment complex in which one of the following is true:

      (i) The sum of the value of services provided and/or products shipped and/or produced from those establishments that have primary SIC major group or industry codes listed in § 372.23(a), or primary NAICS subsector or industry codes listed in § 372.23(b) or § 372.23(c) is greater than 50 percent of the total value of all services provided and/or products shipped from and/or produced by all establishments at the facility.

(ii) One establishment having a primary SIC major group or industry code listed in § 372.23(a), or a primary NAICS subsector or industry code listed in § 372.23(b) or § 372.23(c) contributes more in terms of value of services provided and/or products shipped from and/or produced at the facility than any other establishment within the facility.

(c) The facility manufactured (including imported), processed, or otherwise used a toxic chemical in excess of an applicable threshold quantity of that chemical set forth in § 372.25, § 372.27, or § 372.28.

EPA may apply the requirements of Section 313 to facilities in addition to those designated under the statute if such application is warranted based on factors that include, but are not limited to, the toxicity of a chemical handled by the facility, that facility's proximity to population centers or to other facilities releasing the chemical, and the facility's chemical release history.

3.3.2.1 Requirements for Manufacturing and Processing of Toxic Chemicals

"Manufacture" means to produce, prepare, import, or compound a toxic chemical. It also includes the incidental production of a listed toxic chemical as a byproduct or impurity in the manufacturing, processing, or use of other chemicals.[101] "Processing" refers to the separation of a toxic chemical, after its manufacture, for distribution in commerce in any form as part of an article.[102] EPA clarifies in the instructions to Form R that "process" encompasses "incorporative activities" such as the use of a reactant (feedstock, raw material, intermediate, or initiator) or formulation component (e.g., additives, dyes, solvents, lubricants, and flame retardants).

Beginning with the July 1, 1990 report, Section 313 reports have had to be submitted annually where the manufacturing and processing of listed chemicals exceeds 25,000 pounds per year for the previous year.[103] Thresholds for earlier reporting years were higher (75,000 pounds for the report due in 1988 and 50,000 pounds for the report due in 1989).

3.3.2.2 Requirements for Toxic Chemicals "Otherwise Used"

Section 313 also applies to any use of a listed toxic chemical not covered by the terms "manufacture" or "process." Within the meaning of Section 313, "use" includes the use of a toxic chemical contained in a mixture or trade-name product.[104] In the May 1, 1997, *Federal Register*, EPA modified its definition of activities considered "otherwise used" as it applies to EPCRA Section 313 activity thresholds to include on-site treatment for destruction, disposal, and stabilization when the covered facility engaged in these activities receives materials containing any chemical from off-site for the purposes of further waste management activities.

Any use of a toxic chemical, other than in "manufacturing" or "processing," exceeding 10,000 pounds per year requires the annual submission of a toxic chemical release report.[105]

3.3.2.3 Determining Whether a Reporting Threshold Has Been Exceeded

Owners or operators of facilities manufacturing, processing, or otherwise using chemicals listed in Section 313 must evaluate the amounts of such chemicals manufactured, processed, or otherwise used for the purpose of determining whether a threshold has been exceeded. In making that determination, Section 313 permits owners or operators to rely on readily available data and reasonable estimates.

3.3.2.4 Exemptions

Certain amounts of chemicals need not be factored into the threshold calculations. In calculating a facility's chemical consumption to determine whether a threshold has been exceeded, the following are not included:

1. Amounts of toxic chemicals present in mixtures and trade-name products in concentrations of less than 1 percent (or in concentrations of less than 0.1 percent if the chemical is defined by OSHA as a carcinogen);[106]

2. Amounts of toxic chemicals used

    a.   as a structural component of a facility;

    b.   in routine janitorial or facility grounds maintenance;

    c.   in foods, drugs, cosmetics, or other items for personal use;

    d.   in motor vehicle maintenance; or

e. in process water or noncontact cooling water as drawn from the environment or municipal sources or in air used either as compressed air or as part of combustion;[107]

3. Amounts of toxic chemicals that are manufactured, processed, or used in a laboratory under the supervision of a technically qualified individual, except that this does not apply to specialty chemical production or to production processing or use of toxic chemicals in pilot plant scale operations;[108] and

4. Amounts of toxic chemicals present in "articles" at a facility.[109] An "article" is a manufactured item that

a. does not release a toxic chemical under normal processing and use conditions,

b. is shaped into a specific design during manufacture, and

c. has end-use functions dependent on its shape or design.[110]

3.3.2.5 Allocation of Responsibility between Owners and Lessees

A person who owns the land on which a facility subject to Section 313 regulation is located but who has no other business interest in the operation of the regulated facility is not subject to Section 313 reporting requirements.[111] If two or more persons that do not have any common corporate or business interests operate separate establishments within a single facility (e.g., multiple businesses operating in one industrial park), each person must treat his own establishment as a facility for purposes of Section 313.[112]

3.3.2.6 Mixtures and Trade-Name Products

If the owner or operator of a facility knows that a toxic chemical is present as a component of a mixture or trade-name product and knows the concentration of the chemical in the product, he or she must determine the weight of the chemical imported, processed, or otherwise used as part of the mixture and combine that weight with other amounts of the same chemical manufactured, processed, or used at the facility in order to determine whether a threshold has been exceeded.[113] If the owner or operator knows the identity of the chemical and the upper bound of its concentration in the mixture but is unaware of its specific concentration, the owner or operator must presume that the chemical is present in the mixture at the upper bound of the concentration.[114] If the owner or operator knows the identity of the chemical but has no other information, that chemical need not be included in determining whether the threshold has been exceeded.[115] If the owner or operator knows the concentration or the upper bound concentration but not the specific identity of a toxic chemical present in a mixture, the owner or operator must determine the amount of the chemical imported, processed, or otherwise used as a part of the mixture in order to determine whether a threshold has been exceeded using either the specific concentration or the upper limit. If a threshold has been exceeded, the owner or operator must report this by identifying the chemical with its generic or trade name.[116]

3.3.2.7 Range Reporting for Relatively Small Releases

For most toxic chemicals, Form R requires facilities to submit total annual estimates of the amount of the chemical released to various environmental media. However, Form R allows facilities to report annual releases of less than 1,000 pounds of a toxic chemical to an environmental medium in one of three reporting ranges: 1 to 10 pounds, 11 to 499 pounds, and 500 to 999 pounds.

3.3.2.8 Recordkeeping

If the owner or operator of a facility is required to report under Section 313, he or she must retain a copy of the report, all documents and materials used in determining that the report was required, and all supporting documents for three years from the date of submission of the report.[117]

3.3.2.9 Additions of Chemicals and Threshold Adjustments

Section 313 of EPCRA established an initial list of more than 300 chemicals and 20 chemical categories. However, Congress has given EPA authority to modify release reporting in various ways, including adding or deleting toxic chemicals subject to reporting and modifying thresholds triggering reporting requirements. In order for a chemical (or category of chemicals) to be added to the list of toxic chemicals, EPA must determine that there is sufficient evidence to establish any one of the following:[118]

1. The chemical is known to cause or can reasonably be anticipated to cause significant adverse acute human health effects at concentration levels that are reasonably likely to exist beyond facility site boundaries as a result of continuous, or frequently recurring, releases.

2. The chemical is known to cause or can reasonably be anticipated to cause in humans

   a. cancer or teratogenic effects or

   b. serious or irreversible

      i. reproductive dysfunctions,

      ii. neurological disorders,

iii. heritable genetic mutations, or

iv. other chronic health effects.

3. The chemical is known to cause or can reasonably be anticipated to cause, because of

a. its toxicity,

b. its toxicity and persistence in the environment, or

c. its toxicity and tendency to bioaccumulate in the environment, a significant adverse effect on the environment of sufficient seriousness, in the judgment of the administrator, to warrant reporting under this section.

While Section 313(f)(1) contains default reporting thresholds, Section 313(f)(2) allows EPA to "establish a threshold amount for a toxic chemical different from the amount established by [Section 313(f)(1)]."[119]

As an illustration of these authorities, on October 29, 1999, EPA finalized a rule under EPCRA Section 313 that lowered the threshold reporting requirement for persistent bioaccumulative toxic chemicals (PBTs).[120] For example, the reporting requirement for polychlorinated biphenyl is now 10 pounds for those classified as highly persistent and highly bioaccumulative. The rule also added seven chemicals and two chemical compounds, bringing the total number of Section 313–regulated PBT chemical and chemical compounds to eighteen. The most significant addition was the dioxin and dioxin-like compounds category.

The typical reporting thresholds under EPCRA are 10,000 and 25,000 pounds. The thresholds for PBTs has been reduced to 10 and 100 pounds, with the lone exception of dioxin and dioxin-like compounds, whose threshold is 0.1 grams. EPA also excluded PBTs from the de minimis exception. The dioxin and dioxin-like compounds category is reported as a single chemical category but consists of seventeen specific compounds. These compounds are primarily polychlorinated dibenzo-para (p)-dioxins and polychlorinated dibenzofurans. EPA has also identified several chemicals that have the potential to contain dioxin and/or dioxin-like compounds, including vinyl chloride and polyvinyl chloride. A facility must report for this category if it manufactures, processes, or otherwise uses 0.1 grams of dioxin or dioxin-like compounds. Definitions for "manufacture, process, and otherwise use" can be found at 40 C.F.R. Section 372.3. In May 2000, EPA issued draft guidance for reporting under the dioxin and dioxin-like category.[121] In this rule, EPA deferred making decisions on listing dicofol, cobalt, and cobalt compounds to further investigate and study their bioaccumulative effects.

Additionally, the June 1999 EPA guidance has clarified that facilities generating "water dissociable nitrate compounds as by-products during wastewater treatment processes" are subject to reporting requirements.[122] Nitrate compounds triggering reporting requirements may include ammonia, sodium nitrate, and nitric acid, and a list of chemical names and compounds covered can be found in the guidance document.

Another example of the use of the Section 313(f)(2) authority is the lowering of the lead reporting threshold on January 17, 2001, affecting a wide range of facilities and industries. This decision was based on evidence that lead was a PBT. The current thresholds for lead reporting are typical—10,000 and 25,000 pounds. However, the new final rule lowers the reporting threshold to 100 pounds for those facilities that manufacture, process, or otherwise use lead or lead compounds.[123] "However, lead contained in stainless steel, brass, and bronze allows remains reportable under the 25,000 pound manufacture and process reporting threshold."[124] As with the other PBTs, lead is no longer eligible for de minimis exemptions. Initially, the Bush administration postponed the rule's effective date. However, the administration relented, and the first reports at the lower thresholds were due on or before July 1, 2002, for the 2001 calendar year. For assistance in completing and submitting Section 313 release reports under the new lead and lead compound rule, EPA has developed a guidance document detailing what facilities must file release reports and what forms of lead are not affected by the new rule.[125] On November 26, 2010, EPA added sixteen new chemicals to the TRI list because they were "reasonably anticipated to cause cancer in humans."[126]

3.3.3 Annual Certification Statement—Form A

The "Toxic Chemical Release Inventory Alternate Threshold for Facilities with Low Annual Reportable Amounts" provides facilities otherwise meeting EPCRA Section 313 reporting thresholds the option of reporting on the Form A, provided that their amounts manufactured or processed or otherwise used do not exceed 1 million pounds per year and additional requirements set forth at 40 C.F.R. § 327.27 are met. Form A, which is described as the "certification statement" in 59 Federal Register 61488 (Nov. 30, 1994), is intended as a means to reduce the compliance burden associated with EPCRA Section 313. In lieu of submitting a Form R, the Form A must be submitted on an annual basis for each eligible chemical. As with the Form R, the Form A is toxic chemical–specific. Thus, in some instances, a facility may submit the Form A for some chemicals and the Form R for other chemicals.

3.3.4 Supplier Notification Requirement

With certain exceptions discussed in the regulations, Section 313 requires owners who operate facilities that (1) are in SIC codes 20 to 39 (or a corresponding

NAICS code); (2) manufacture a toxic chemical; and (3) sell or otherwise supply a mixture or trade-name product containing the chemical to a facility covered by Section 313 or to someone who will ultimately supply such a facility with the chemical, to provide written notification to each person to whom the mixture is supplied.[127]

3.3.4.1 Notification Content

Notification must include the name of each toxic chemical present in the mixture, the percentage by weight of each toxic chemical in the product, and a statement that the mixture contains a chemical subject to the reporting requirements of Section 313. If OSHA requires a supplier to provide an MSDS with the mixture, such notification must be attached or incorporated into the MSDS. If the notification is attached, clear instructions must be provided stating the effect that copying of the MSDS shall include copying of the notification.[128]

3.3.4.2 Notification Deadlines

In the event that the mixture contains a toxic chemical listed in the regulations as having an effective date of January 1, 1987, notification must be provided with the first shipment to each consumer beginning January 1, 1989.[129] However, if the mixture contains a toxic chemical listed in the regulations with an effective date of January 1, 1989, or later, each recipient must be notified with the first shipment of the mixture or trade-name product in the first calendar year of the chemical's effective date.

3.3.5 Penalties

EPA is responsible for enforcing the requirements of Section 313 and any rules promulgated pursuant to EPCRA. Section 325(c) of EPCRA authorizes the administrator to assess civil administrative penalties for Section 313 violations. An owner or operator, other than a government entity, who violates Section 313 is liable for a penalty of up to $37,500 per day per violation.[130] Each day the violation continues may constitute a separate violation. There is no cap on the total penalty amount a facility may be assessed. The penalty may be assessed by administrative order or by an action in a federal district court for the district where the violator resides or maintains his or her principal place of business.

In a consolidated action in 1993, EPA filed administrative complaints against 37 companies seeking civil penalties of almost $2.8 million for alleged failure to file Section 313 reports in a timely fashion.[131] EPCRA Section 313 is a strict liability provision, and ignorance of the law is no excuse.[132] EPCRA's enforcement policy provides for the filing of civil administrative complaints for a first violation of the following: (1) late filing of Form R, (2) failure to comply with EPCRA requirements, (3) failure to maintain records documenting Form R filings, and (4) failure to notify customers when required.[133] Any person in violation of Section 313 is subject to the maximum penalty of $37,500 per day for each violation.

EPA also uses a gravity-based penalty matrix with eighteen different penalties ranging up to $37,500 for each chemical per facility per year in violation.[134] The gravity-based penalty is based on "extent" inputs and on inputs for "circumstance" levels. Extent inputs include (1) whether the amount of chemicals at issue is more or less than 10 times the threshold, (2) whether sales are more or less than $10 million per year, and (3) whether total employment is more or less than 50 employees and on inputs for "circumstance" levels.[135] There are six "circumstance" levels that reflect "the seriousness of the violation as it relates to the accuracy and availability of the information to the community, states and the federal government."[136] The EPCRA Section 313 Enforcement Response Policy allows EPA to adjust the gravity-based penalty. Facilities may receive an adjustment under two circumstances: (1) up to 30 percent good attitude adjustment for correcting violations after an EPA inspection (up to 15 percent for cooperating with EPA during compliance evaluation and enforcement processes and up to 15 percent reduction for good-faith effort at prompt compliance) and (2) 25 percent reduction for voluntary disclosure plus up to an additional 25 percent reduction if disclosure is within 30 days, accompanied by appropriate steps to ensure future compliance, so long as the facility did not have a violation in the past two years.[137] In addition, EPA does consider "attitude" and "voluntary disclosure" to be mutually exclusive, so a facility can get a reduction for both.[138]

Another type of penalty offset is a Supplemental Environmental Project (SEP). However, SEPs are subject to a case-by-case determination and negotiation process.[139] A typical SEP for an EPCRA violation might include an emergency planning and preparedness project providing assistance, such as computers and software, communication systems, chemical emission detection and inactivation equipment, HAZMAT equipment, or training, to a responsible state or local emergency planning or response entity. Such SEPs are acceptable where the primary impact of the project is within the same emergency planning district or state affected by the violations.

The last type of penalty offset is inability to pay. A company may qualify for a reduced fine if it can prove that it is unable to pay.[140] However, EPA has stated that companies are required to borrow money, sell assets, cut expenses, and take other measures before EPA will reduce the fine under the inability to pay theory.[141]

EPCRA does not provide criminal sanctions for Section 313 violations. However, pursuant to 18 U.S.C. Section 1001, it is a criminal offense to falsify information submitted to the federal government. This would apply to Section 313 records intentionally generated with false or misleading information. Knowing failure to file a Section 313 report may also be prosecuted under 18 U.S.C. Section 1001, as a concealment of required information.

Administrative penalties for Section 313 violations are determined in two stages: (1) determination of a "gravity-based" penalty and (2) adjustments to the gravity-based penalty.[142] The gravity-based penalty is determined by the circumstances and extent of the violation. Once the gravity-based penalty has been determined, upward or downward adjustments may be made in consideration of voluntary disclosure, history of prior violations, delisted chemicals, attitude, other factors as justice may require, SEPs, and ability to pay. The penalty matrix for Section 313 violations includes eighteen possible penalties ranging up to $37,500.

EPA has stated that it will pursue a policy of strict liability in penalizing Section 313 violations. The court in *Steeltech, Ltd. v. U.S. EPA* stated that a lack of knowledge will not reduce culpability as EPA does not wish to encourage ignorance of EPCRA and its requirements among the regulated community (*Steeltech, Ltd. v. U.S. EPA*, 273 F.3d 652 [6th Cir. 2001]).

3.3.6 Challenges to Section 313 TRI Reporting

In *Dayton Power and Light v. Browner*,[143] the court upheld EPA's authority to extend Section 313 requirements to electric generating facilities that combust oil and coal. The court determined that EPA is allowed to broaden TRI reporting if it furthers the purpose of the reporting. The mining industry filed a similar challenge, challenging EPA's application of TRI to the mining industry by the use of the rules preamble and guidance documents. The district court, however, dismissed the action as not yet ripe. The D.C. Circuit Court found that the case was ripe because it subjected companies to enforcement actions and fines for noncompliance.

While adding the mining industry to the list of covered industries was not generally controversial, EPA's application of fundamental TRI concepts to the industry was more troublesome. In a recent court decision, the mining industry successfully challenged EPA's interpretation of the terms "manufacture" and "process" as applied to the activities of ore extraction and beneficiation.[144] EPCRA defines "process" as

> the preparation of a toxic chemical, after its manufacture, for distribution in commerce—(1) in the same form or physical state as, or in a different form or physical state, from that in which it was received by the person so preparing such chemical, or (2) as part of an article containing the toxic chemical.[145]

In the final rule adding the mining industry to the TRI program, EPA interpreted the term "manufacture" to include manufacture by natural processes.[146] Under this interpretation, the preparation of toxic chemicals (i.e., metals) contained in ores for distribution in commerce occurs after the chemicals have been "manufactured." Hence, EPA claimed that extraction and beneficiation activities were TRI "processing," and as a result, the listed TRI chemicals found in waste rock—the material remaining after coal and ores are removed—at mining sites would have to be counted toward "processing" thresholds and considered TRI releases.

As recognized by the court in National Mining Association, "EPA's interpretation of the definition of 'manufacture' means that all materials in existence have been manufactured." The court rejected this interpretation by finding that "manufacture" requires "human involvement in the creation of a thing." Accordingly, the court ruled that extraction and beneficiation activities could not qualify as "processing" and that the TRI chemicals in waste rock at mining sites were not reportable.

The court's holding is supported by common sense. Mining inherently involves the movement of large quantities of earth, which naturally contains numerous listed TRI substances, particularly metals, as well as the sought-after coal and ore. Simply moving earth is not the same as using a chemical to manufacture another product or preparing a substance for distribution in commerce. The TRI chemicals in waste rock remain in the environment in which they were naturally produced and do not represent the introduction of new substances into the environment.

In *Barrick Goldstrike Mines, Inc. v. Whitman*,[147] the court addressed additional applications of EPCRA requirements to mining operations in a 25-page opinion. Among its findings. the court said that waste rock, which EPA defines as "the consolidated material of the rock that surrounds the ore," is eligible for the de minimis exemption but also upheld EPA's interpretation that tailings and other by-products were to be reported in the annual TRI. EPA subsequently issued its analysis of the decision and how it would affect reporting obligations.[148]

3.4 Common EPCRA Compliance Errors

EPCRA release reporting requirements are extremely difficult to interpret and can lead to a multitude of errors and misinterpretations. This section discusses the ten most common EPCRA compliance errors:

1. Unnecessary reporting of historical contamination to federal or state authorities. It is important to note that emergency release reporting rarely applies to historical contamination involving a site's past operations.

2. Reporting of oil releases. An oil release must create a "sheen" on the surface of waters of the United States in order to be reportable under the CWA.

3. Failure to provide a timely written follow-up report under Section 304(c).

4. Misunderstanding the intent of "release into the environment" under CERCLA versus off-site impact under EPCRA. To clarify, CERCLA requires that the release be "into the environment," whereas EPCRA requires the presence of a potential or actual off-site impact before reporting requirements are triggered.

5. Inconsistent release reporting versus CAA reports. Certain manufacturing operations need to ensure that their release reports are consistent with CAA reports.

6. Failure to notify LEPCs of EPCRA releases. LEPCs must be notified of a chemical release, in addition to the NRC and SERC.

7. Overlooking unique state/local release reporting statutes. Many state/local governments have additional release reporting requirements that must be met.

8. Comprehensive compliance with Section 313 Form R. Current guidance must be followed, and off-site releases must be properly documented.

9. Failure to designate appropriate releases as "continuous." If a release qualifies as continuous, it should be reported as such to avoid unnecessary repeat reporting, which draws attention to the facility.

10. The inability to recognize Section 311/312 obligations in nonchemical industries. Sections 311 and 312 apply regardless of the type of facility or business involved. For instance, they apply to such common items as ammonia in refrigeration units or sulfuric acids in industrial batteries.[149]

4.0 Relationship to Other Laws (Section 321)

Section 321 provides that no EPCRA provision shall preempt or otherwise affect any state or local law. There is one exception: any state or local law requiring submission of an MSDS requires it to be in identical form to that specified in Section 311. However, the state or locality may require supplemental or additional information to be submitted through the use of additional sheets attached to the MSDS or by some other appropriate means.

4.1 Pollution Prevention Act of 1990

The federal Pollution Prevention Act (PPA) of 1990[150] requires each owner or operator of a facility required to file an annual toxic chemical release form under Section 313 of EPCRA to also file a toxic chemical source reduction and recycling report for the preceding calendar year. Owners and operators of facilities manufacturing, processing, or otherwise using chemicals listed in Section 313 must evaluate the amounts of such chemicals manufactured, processed, or otherwise used for the purpose of determining whether a threshold has been exceeded. Section 313 allows facilities to rely on readily available data and reasonable estimates in making that determination.

Once it is determined that a Section 313 report is required for a facility, the PPA requires the filing of an additional toxic chemical source reduction and recycling report, which must include, on a facility-by-facility basis for each toxic chemical, (1) the quantity of chemical entering any waste stream (or otherwise released into the environment) prior to recycling, treatment, or disposal and the percentage change from the preceding year, without accounting for episodic releases; (2) the amount of chemical recycled, the percentage change from the previous year, and the process used (recycling may be either on- or off-site); (3) source-reduction measures used with respect to each chemical reported by the following categories: equipment or procedure modification, reformulation or redesign of product, substitution of raw materials, and improved housekeeping measures (management, training, inventory control, materials handling, other general operational measures); (4) an estimate of the amount of toxic chemicals to be used and recycled for the next two years, plus an estimate of percentage change from reporting year; (5) the ratio of production this past year to the previous year; (6) techniques used to identify source reduction opportunities; (7) amount of any toxic chemicals released due to a catastrophic event, remedial action, or other episodic release not associated with the production process; and (8) amount of chemical treated (at the facility or elsewhere) plus the percentage change from the previous year.[151]

These combined EPCRA/PPA reporting requirements establish a relatively easy way to measure each facility's progress toward source reduction and waste minimization.

5.0 Trade Secrets (Sections 322 and 323)

According to Section 322, a person required to submit information under Section 303, 311, 312, or 313 may withhold from any such submission a specific chemical's identity if he or she claims that the information constitutes a trade secret and explains the basis for this belief. The person must include on a separate sheet submitted to EPA the information that he or she seeks to have withheld from the required submission in order that EPA may make a determination as to whether the information truly constitutes a trade secret. A person seeking trade-secret protection must demonstrate the following:

1. That the person has not disclosed the information to anyone else, unless under a guarantee of confidentiality, and that he or she has taken reasonable measures to protect the confidentiality of the information.

2. That federal or state law does not mandate that the information be disclosed.

3. That disclosure of the information is likely to cause substantial harm to the competitive position of the disclosing party.

4. That the chemical identity is not readily discoverable through reverse engineering.

Both the party claiming trade-secret protection and a member of the public seeking access to the withheld information may petition for judicial review of EPA's decision. Section 323 creates one exception to the confidentiality of trade secrets: a specific chemical identity must be disclosed where it is necessary for diagnosis or treatment of an individual by a health professional.

6.0 Public Access to Information (Section 324)

The public has access to every emergency response plan, MSDS, list, inventory form, toxic chemical release form, and follow-up emergency notice except for that information protected as a trade secret. Each emergency planning committee must designate a location where such information may be reviewed during normal working hours.

7.0 Enforcement (Section 325)

7.1 Emergency Planning Violations

Should a facility fail to notify the SERC that it is subject to Subchapter A or fail to notify the LEPC of its designated facility emergency coordinator (or fail to provide other relevant information), the administrator may order the facility to comply with these requirements. The failure to comply with such an order exposes the facility to a civil penalty of up to $37,500 per day for as long as the failure to comply continues.[152]

7.2 Emergency Notification Violations

In the event of a release, the administrator may assess a Class I administrative penalty of up to $37,500 per day per violation for failure to provide emergency notification under Section 304. Before such a penalty will be assessed, the accused must be given notice and the opportunity for a hearing. For a first violation, the administrator may also assess a Class II administrative penalty of up to $37,500 per day. In addition, the administrator may bring a civil action in U.S. district court asking the court to assess a penalty of up to $37,500 per day per violation for a first violation. Criminal penalties may be sought for a knowing and willful failure to provide notice under Section 304. The court may impose a fine of up to $25,000 and/or two years' imprisonment for the first violation; for a second violation, the penalties imposed may include a fine of up to $50,000 and/or five years' imprisonment.

7.3 Section 311 Reporting Violations

Any person (other than a governmental entity) who violates the reporting requirements of Section 311 is liable for a civil penalty of $16,000 per day per violation. Each day a violation continues is considered to be a separate violation. These same penalties apply to those claiming trade-secret protection who fail to separately submit to the administrator the information for which trade-secret protection is claimed or who refuse to divulge trade secrets to a health professional when they are needed for diagnosis or treatment (pursuant to Section 323).

7.4 Section 312 and 313 Reporting Violations

EPA is responsible for enforcing the requirements of Section 313 and any rules promulgated pursuant to EPCRA. Section 325(c) of EPCRA authorizes the administrator to assess civil administrative penalties for Section 313 violations. An owner or operator, other than a government entity, who violates Section 313 is liable for a penalty of up to $37,500 per day for each violation. Each day the violation continues may constitute a separate violation. There is no cap on the total penalty amount a facility may be assessed. The penalty may be assessed by administrative order or by an action in the U.S. district court for the district where the violator resides or maintains his or her principal place of business. For example, in a consolidated action in 1993, EPA filed administrative complaints against 37 companies seeking civil penalties of almost $2.8 million for alleged failure to file Section 313 reports in a timely fashion (for 1991 and earlier years).[153]

7.5 Section 322 and 323 Trade-Secret Violations

Frivolous trade-secret claims may be punished by administrative penalties or court actions with fines of up to $37,500 for each such claim. Knowing and willful disclosure of information entitled to protection as a trade secret shall be subjected to criminal penalties of $20,000 and/or one year imprisonment. Health professionals may bring an action in U.S. district court to compel the facility owner to disclose the necessary information for diagnosis and treatment in addition to the monetary penalties mentioned above.

8.0 Civil Actions (Section 326)

8.1 Citizen Suits

Any person may commence a civil action against a facility owner or operator for (1) failure to submit a follow-up emergency notice under Section 304, (2) failure to submit an MSDS or list under Section 311, (3) failure to complete and submit an inventory form under Section 312, or (4) failure to complete and submit a toxic chemical release form under Section 313. Such a suit may not be commenced prior to 60 days after the plaintiff has given notice of the alleged violation to EPA, the state, and the alleged violator. No citizen suit may be maintained against a facility owner or operator if the administrator has commenced and is diligently pursuing an administrative order or civil action to enforce the requirement concerned or to impose a civil penalty with respect to a violation of the requirement.

Any person may bring a civil action against the administrator of EPA for (1) failure to publish inventory forms under Section 312, (2) failure to respond to a petition to add a chemical to or delete a chemical from the Section 313 list of toxic chemicals, (3) failure to publish a toxic chemical release form under Section 313, (4) failure to establish a computer database of toxic chemicals in accordance with Section 313, (5) failure to promulgate the trade-secret regulations required by Section 322, or (6) failure to render a decision within nine months in response to a petition by a member of the public to review the classification of information as trade secrets.

In addition, a citizen may sue EPA, a state governor, or SERC for failure to provide a mechanism for public availability of information under Section 324. Finally, a citizen may sue a state governor or SERC for failure to respond to a request for Tier II information within 120 days after the date of the request.

No citizen suit may be commenced against EPA on the six grounds listed above or against EPA, state governor, or SERC for failure to provide public access to information until 60 days after the plaintiff gives notice to the defendant that the plaintiff intends to commence the action.

In *Steel Co. v. Citizens for a Better Environment*, 118 S. Ct. 1003 (March 4, 1998), the U.S. Supreme Court handed down a ruling that limits the number of citizen suits brought under EPCRA. The Court vacated and remanded the Seventh Circuit's decision in *Citizens for a Better Environment v. Steel Company*, 90 F.3d 1237 (7th Cir. 1996), and held that the plaintiffs lacked standing to sue because the requested relief would not redress the plaintiff's injury, and therefore the case did not present an Article III case or controversy.

The defendants in the suit, Steel Company, a.k.a. Chicago Steel and Pickling Company, had, since 1988, the first year of EPCRA's filing deadlines, failed to complete and submit the required hazardous chemical inventory and toxic-chemical release forms under EPCRA Sections 312 and 313. In 1995, the environmental group Citizens for a Better Environment sent notice to the company that it would file a citizen suit under EPCRA to seek an injunction and penalties for the reporting violations pursuant to EPCRA Section 326. As mentioned above, EPCRA allows citizens to file a suit, but only after giving notice and waiting 60 days. In this case, Steel Company completed and submitted the overdue forms prior to the end of the 60-day period. It then filed a motion to dismiss, arguing that EPCRA does not authorize suits for purely past violations.

The U.S. Supreme Court vacated the Seventh Circuit's decision, which in 1996 held that the environmental organization could bring its citizen suit for wholly past violations. On review, the Supreme Court did not decide whether EPCRA authorizes citizen suits for wholly past violations. The Court instead held that the environmental group lacked standing to sue. Because the group failed to allege a continuing violation or imminent future violation, the relief they requested would not help to redress any injury they suffered, and thus the group lacked standing to sue. The group sought $25,000 per day in fines, attorney and expert witness fees, an injunction that would require the company to give the environmental group duplicate reports, and the right to inspect the facilities. Analyzing each of their requests, the Court found none were likely to remove the effects of past violations.

Although the majority did not reach the question of whether EPCRA authorizes suits for wholly past violations, the Court's ruling on redressability makes such a suit difficult to bring. The Court's ruling requires a party to at least allege that violations are continuing or that there is a likelihood of future violations, not just past violations, to have standing. One remaining issue may be what supporting facts are needed to cure the pleading defect identified by the Court or, in other words, what circumstances are needed to aver that violations are likely to occur in the future. If the threshold is low, such that past violations provide the necessary likelihood of future violations, then a plaintiff may be able to overcome the redressability and standing issue needed to maintain an EPCRA suit quite easily. If the threshold is high, such that it is necessary to show a history of violations, the number of citizen suits will diminish substantially.

The effect of the Supreme Court decision was mitigated by the U.S. Supreme Court in *Friends of the Earth v. Laidlaw Envtl. Servs. (TOC), Inc.*[154] In that case, the efficacy of citizen suit standing was upheld for past violations that are likely to reoccur. The Supreme Court attempts to harmonize the Laidlaw and Steel decisions by stating that "Steel Co. held that private plaintiffs, unlike the Federal Government, may not sue to assess penalties for wholly past violations, but our decision in that case did not reach the issue of standing to seek penalties for violations that are ongoing at the time of the complaint and that could continue into the future if undeterred."[155] The impact of both Steel and Laidlaw remains unclear. However, under EPCRA, because first-time offenders should be able to escape a citizen suit merely by submitting the missing forms, citizen groups may be less inclined to waste their scarce resources going after facilities that have a clean record and target repeat offenders instead. Ironically, coincident with the Supreme Court's recent decisions regarding standing, EPA has released data that make it less difficult for citizen groups to determine which facilities have a history of noncompliance.

8.2 State or Local Government Suits

A state or local government may sue a facility owner or operator for failure to (1) notify the emergency response commission of its being covered under Subchapter A of EPCRA, (2) submit an MSDS or list under Section 311, (3) make available information requested under Section 311, or (4) submit an inventory form under Section 312. A SERC or LEPC may sue a facility owner or operator for failure to provide information requested under Sections 303 or 312. No such suit may be brought if EPA is diligently pursuing an administrative order or civil action to remedy the alleged violation.

8.3 Costs

In any litigation commenced under Section 326, the court may award the prevailing or substantially prevailing party its costs of litigation, including reasonable attorneys' and expert witness fees. Such an award is completely at the court's discretion.

9.0 Federal Acquisition and Community Right to Know

On August 3, 1993, President Clinton signed Executive Order (EO) 12856, requiring all federal agencies to comply with EPCRA and the PPA.[156] This was an important requirement for federal agencies because in 1995, federal facilities were responsible for releasing 6,730,862 pounds of toxics; by 1997, they achieved a reduction of almost 45 percent, down to 3,707,932 pounds.[157]

On August 8, 1995, President Clinton signed EO 12969, mandating that each federal agency include in contract solicitations, as an eligibility criterion for competitive acquisition contracts expected to exceed $100,000, the requirement that federal contractors ensure that Toxic Chemical Release Inventory Forms (Form R) are filed by their covered facilities for the life of the contract.[158] The EO does not expand the types of facilities required to provide information for the Toxic Release Inventory. Nor does the EO's $100,000 applicability threshold replace or obviate the obligation of facilities to comply with the reporting and recordkeeping requirements of Section 313 (which has no $100,000 applicability threshold).[159] Rather, the EO simply requires contractors to include in their bid a certification that they (if awarded the contract) will ensure that their covered facilities file a Form R for the life of the contract for covered activities unless an exemption provided by the EO applies. In addition, the EO requires the contract between the federal agency and contractor to have a clause to this effect.

On April 22, 2000, EO 13148 was signed by President Clinton, requiring all federal agencies to reduce their reported TRI releases and off-site transfers of toxic chemicals for treatment and disposal by 10 percent annually or by 40 percent overall by December 31, 2006.[160] The EO further mandated that all federal agencies reduce their use of selected toxic chemicals, hazardous substances, and pollutants, or their generation of hazardous and radioactive wastes at their facilities by 50 percent by December 31, 2006.[161] Finally, each agency was required to develop a plan to phase out Class I ozone-depleting substances for all nonexcepted uses by December 31, 2010.[162]

10.0 Internet Development and TRI Reporting

The Environmental Defense Fund has established an Internet site to track toxic chemical releases at http://www.scorecard.org. The following are major features of the site:

1. Pollution Locator—reports are available on toxic chemical releases from manufacturing plants.

2. Chemical Information—information available on whether chemicals have been tested for health effects and how harmful they may be to the environment.

3. Health Effects—addresses what chemicals are suspected causes of adverse health effects.

4. Regulatory Control—addresses various regulatory programs that govern chemicals.

5. Discussion Forums—allows persons to discuss views on pollution problems in communities, chemicals in consumer products, and the health effects of various chemicals.

6. Facility Contact—allows users to contact facility representatives via fax; also provides e-mail service to contact state and federal decision-makers.

11.0 Research Sources

Listed below are some helpful EPCRA resources:

EPA Office of Emergency Management

http://www.epa.gov/oem/

EPA EPCRA Requirements Webpage

http://www.epa.gov/oem/content/epcra/index.htm

EPA Federal Register Notices on Various EPCRA Programs

http://www.epa.gov/osweroe1/lawsregs.htm#frhaz

EPCRA Frequent Questions

http://www.epa.gov/osweroe1/content/epcra/epcra-qa.htm

EPA List of Lists (includes chemicals regulated under various EPCRA programs)

http://www.epa.gov/emergencies/tools.htm#lol

Tier II Chemical Inventory Reports / Tier2 Submit

http://www.epa.gov/osweroe1/content/epcra/tier2.htm

TRI-Listed Chemicals

http://www.epa.gov/tri/trichemicals/index.htm

TRI Threshold Screening Tool

http://www.epa.gov/tri/reporting_materials/threshold/index.htm

TRI Reporting Forms and Instructions

http://www.epa.gov/tri/reporting_materials/forms/index.html

TRI-MEweb Tutorials

Online EPA Webinar Training Modules on TRI Basic & Advanced Reporting Issues

http://www.epa.gov/tri/training/RY12/EPA_RY12_Basic/index.html

http://www.epa.gov/tri/training/RY12/EPA_RY12_Advanced/index.html

http://www.epa.gov/tri/reporting_materials/tutorials/tutorialindex.html

TRI Guidance Documents

http://www.epa.gov/tri/reporting_materials/guidance_docs/index.htm

Enforcement Response Policy for EPCRA Sections 304, 311, 312

http://www.epa.gov/enforcement/waste/documents/policies/epcra304.pdf

Enforcement Response Policy for EPCRA Sections 313

http://www.epa.gov/compliance/resources/policies/civil/epcra/
epcra313erp.pdf

Notes

[1] *See* EPA Fact Sheet: "Chemical Emergency Preparedness and Prevention in Indian Country," http://www.epa.gov/osweroe1/docs/tribalalert.pdf.

[2] *See* 40 C.F.R. § 355.13.

[3] *See* 40 C.F.R. § 355.15.

[4] *See* 40 C.F.R. § 372.16(b); 77 Fed. Reg. 16679 (March 22, 2012).

[5] 40 C.F.R. § 355.61.

[6] *See* 42 U.S.C. § 11047.

[7] *See* 40 C.F.R. § 355.20(a).

[8] *See* 40 C.F.R. § 355.20(b).

[9] *See* 40 C.F.R. § 355.20(c).

[10] *See* 40 C.F.R. § 355.61.

[11] *See* 40 C.F.R. § 355.31.

[12] *See* 40 C.F.R. § 355.33.

[13] *See* "Guidance for Implementing Executive Order 12856," EPA 300-B-95-005, April 1995; www.epa.gov/Compliance/resources/policies/civil/federal/12856guidance.pdf.

[14] *See* 40 C.F.R. § 355.31.

[15] *See* 64 Fed. Reg. 71614 (1999).

[16] *See* Arizona State Bar ENRLS Update, October 2000, at 13.

[17] *See* 67 Fed. Reg. 18899 (2002).

[18] *See* 73 Fed. Reg. 76960 (2008).

[19] U.S.C. § 11004(a)(2).

[20] *See* 42 U.S.C. § 9601(10).

[21] *In re Mobil Oil Corp.*, 5 E.A.D. 490 (Environmental Appeals Board 1994).

[22] *See* 67 Fed. Reg. 18899 (April 17, 2002).

[23] *See* 71 Fed. Reg. 58525 (2006).

[24] *See* 67 Fed. Reg. 18899 (April 17, 2002).

[25] *See id.*

[26] *See id.*

[27] *See id.*

28 42 U.S.C. § 9601(10)(H).

29 *See In re Mobil Oil Corp.*, at 505.

30 *In re Borden Chemicals & Plastics*, 1993 WL 70228 at 4–6 (EPA Feb. 18, 1993).

31 *See Borden* at 5–6.

32 *See* 40 C.F.R. § 202.3(f)(5).

33 *See* 42 U.S.C. § 9603(f)(1).

34 *See* 42 U.S.C. §§ 9601(10)(A)-(D).

35 *See* 40 C.F.R. § 302.6(a).

36 *See* EPA Hotline, February 1986.

37 *See id.*

38 *See* 40 C.F.R. §§ 355.40(b)(1), 355.42(a).

39 *See* 40 C.F.R. § 355.42(b).

40 *See* 40 C.F.R. § 355.40(a).

41 *See* 40 C.F.R. § 355.40(b).

42 75 Fed. Reg. 39852, 39857 (July 13, 2010).

43 *See* U.S. EPA, Office of Regulatory Enforcement, Enforcement Response Policy for Sections 304, 311, and 312 of the Emergency Planning and Community Right to Know Act and Section 103 of the Comprehensive Environmental Response, Compensation and Liability Act (1999) (Enforcement Response Policy), available at http://www.epa.gov/enforcement/waste/documents/policies/epcra304.pdf.

44 *See id.* at 9.

45 *See id.* at 10.

46 *See id.* at 17.

47 *See id.* at 12–13.

48 *See id.* at 15–16.

49 *See id.* at 17–18.

50 *See id.* at 9.

51 *See id.* at 24.

52 *See id.*

53 *See id.* at 26.

54 *See id.* at 26.

55 *See id.* at 28.

56 *See id.*

57 *See* 40 C.F.R. § 370.33.

58 *See* 58 Fed. Reg. 17574 (March 26, 2012).

59 *See* 40 C.F.R. § 370.10.

60 *See* 40 C.F.R. § 370.30.

61 *See* 40 C.F.R. § 370.32.

62 *See* 40 C.F.R. § 370.14.

63 *See* 40 C.F.R. § 370.66.

64 *See* 29 C.F.R. § 1910.1200(c) and Appendix A.

65 *See* 40 C.F.R. § 370.13.

66 *See* 40 C.F.R. § 370.33.

67 *See* 40 C.F.R. § 370.10.

68 *See* 40 C.F.R. § 370.14.

69 *See* Keller and Heckman, *Batteries and EPCRA: Don't Wait Until an Enforcement Initiative Leaves You Powerless to Correct a Commonly Overlooked Reporting Requirement* (2001), 3.

70   *See id.*

71   *See id.*

72   *See* 40 C.F.R. § 370.30(c).

73   *See* 40 C.F.R. § 370.60.

74   *See* 40 C.F.R. §§ 370.31(a), 370.33(b).

75   *See* 40 C.F.R. § 370.30(a)(2).

76   *See* 40 C.F.R. § 370.45.

77   *See* 40 C.F.R. § 370.10.

78   *See* 40 C.F.R. § 370.14(c).

79   *See* 40 C.F.R. § 370.14(b).

80   *See* 40 C.F.R. § 370.14(a).

81   *See* 40 C.F.R. § 370.14(c).

82   *See* 40 C.F.R. § 370.45.

83   *See* EPCRA § 312(d)(2); 42 U.S.C. § 11022(d)(2); 40 C.F.R. § 370.42.

84   *See* 40 C.F.R. § 370.45(b).

85   *See* 40 C.F.R. § 372.61(a)(ii).

86   42 U.S.C. § 11044(a).

87   *See* Sidney M. Wolf, "Fear and Loathing about the Public Right to Know: The Surprising Success of EPCRA," 11 *J. Land Use & Envtl. L.* 217 (Spring 1996).

88   77 Fed. Reg. 41300 (July 13, 2012).

89   *See* http://www.yosemite.epa.gov/osweroe1/content/epcra/tier2.htm.

90   *Id.*

91   *See* 40 C.F.R. § 370.61.

92   *See* 40 C.F.R. § 370.61(a) (2).

93   *See* 40 C.F.R. § 19.4.

94   *See* The Enforcement Response Policy at http://www.epa.gov/compliance/resources/policies/civil/epcra/epcra304.pdf.

95   http://www.epa.gov/tri/training/index/index.htm; http://www.epa.gov/tri/reporting_materials/guidance_docs/index.htm.

96   *See* 77 Fed. Reg. 13061 (March 5, 2012).

97   *See* 40 C.F.R. § 372.30(d).

98   *See* USEPA, *EPCRA Section 313 Questions and Answers*, November 1997, EPA 745-B-97-008; USEPA, *Toxic Chemical Release Inventory Reporting Forms and Instructions*, February 1998, EPA 745-K-98-001; USEPA *Title III List of Lists*, November 1998, EPA 550-B-98-017.

99   *See* U.S. Envtl. Protection Agency, Emergency Planning and Community Right-to-Know Act 2, 3 (2000) (EPA 550-F-00-004).

100   *See* 40 C.F.R. § 372.22.

101   *See* 40 C.F.R. § 372.3.

102   *Id.*

103   *See* 40 C.F.R. § 372.25.

104   *See* 40 C.F.R. § 372.3.

105   *See* 40 C.F.R. § 372.25.

106   *See* 40 C.F.R. § 372.38(a).

107   *See* 40 C.F.R. § 372.38(c).

108   *See* 40 C.F.R. § 372.38(d).

109   *See* 40 C.F.R. § 372.38(b).

110 *See* 40 C.F.R. § 372.3.

111 *See* 40 C.F.R. § 372.38(e).

112 *See* 40 C.F.R. § 372.38(f).

113 *See* 40 C.F.R. § 372.30(b)(3)(i).

114 *See* 40 C.F.R. § 372.30(b)(3)(ii).

115 *See* 40 C.F.R. § 372.30(b)(3)(iii).

116 *See* 40 C.F.R. § 372.30(b)(3)(iv) and (v).

117 *See* 40 C.F.R. § 372.10.

118 *See* 42 U.S.C. 11023.

119 *See* also 40 C.F.R. § 372.28.

120 *See* 64 Fed. Reg. 58666 (1999).

121 *See* U.S. EPA, Emergency Planning and Community Right-to-Know Act—Section 313: Guidance for Reporting Toxic Chemicals within the Dioxin and Dioxin-like Compounds Category (May 2000).

122 *See* U.S. EPA, The Toxic Release Inventory: List of Toxic Chemicals within the Water Dissociable Nitrate Compounds Category and Guidance for Reporting (1999); U.S. Envtl. Protection Agency, Enforcement Alert, March 2000.

123 *See* 66 Fed. Reg. 4499, 4505 (2001).

124 *Id.*

125 EPA EPCRA Section 313: Guidance for Reporting Releases and Other Waste Management Quantities of Toxic Chemicals: Lead and Lead Compounds, EPA 260-B-01-027 (Dec. 2001).

126 75 Fed. Reg. 72727 (Nov. 26, 2010).

127 *See* 40 C.F.R. § 372.45.

128 *Id.*

129 *Id.*

130 *See* 40 C.F.R § 372.18; 4 C.F.R. § 19.4.

131 *See* 24 Envt'l Rep. (BNA) 263 (June 11, 1993).

132 *See* EPCRA § 313 Enforcement Response Policy at 14 (1992).

133 *See* EPCRA § 313 Enforcement Response Policy at 4–7.

134 *See* Rodney F. Lorang, 23 Env't Rep. (BNA) 2736, 2737 (1993).

135 *See* EPCRA § 313 Enforcement Response Policy at 9–11.

136 *See id.*

137 *See id.* at 14–16.

138 *See id.* at 16.

139 *See id.* at 19.

140 *See id.* at 19–20.

141 *See* Lorang at 2739.

142 *See id.*

143 *See* 44 F. Supp. 2d 356 (D.D.C. 1999). *See also* Christie Ingram, *Dayton Power v. Browner*, 21 *Energy L. J.* 159 (2000).

144 *See National Mining Assoc., et al. v. EPA*, No. 97-N-2655 (D. Col. Jan. 16, 2001) (*NMA*).

145 EPCRA § 313(b) (1) (B).

146 *See* 62 Fed. Reg. 23934 (May 1, 1997).

147 *Barrick Goldstrike Mines, Inc. v. Whitman*, Civil Action No. 99-958 (TJP), 2003 WL1919310 (D.D.C. Apr. 2, 2003); http://www.nma.org/pdf/tri/barrick_decision040203.pdf.

148 http://www.epa.gov/tri/lawsandregs/barrick_lawsuit_epa_analysis.htm; 68 Fed. Reg. 62579 (Nov. 5, 2003).

149 E. Lynn Grayson, "EPCRA Basics, Do's and Don'ts," *Natural Resources & Environment* 16, no. 1, at 302 (Summer 2001).

150 *See* 42 U.S.C. §§ 13101–13109.

151 *See* 42 U.S.C. § 13106.

152 *See* Enforcement Response Policy at 4–9.

153 *See* 24 Env't Rep. (BNA) 263 (June 11, 1993).

154 528 U.S. 127, 120 S. Ct. 693 (2000).

155 120 S. Ct. at 708.

156 *See* 58 Fed. Reg. 41981 (Aug. 6, 1993).

157 1997 TRI Report at 4–6 (1997).

158 Executive Order 12969, *Federal Acquisition and Community Right-To-Know*, 60 Fed. Reg. 40989 (Aug. 8, 1995).

159 *See* USEPA, *Guidance Implementing Executive Order 12969*, 60 Fed. Reg. 50738 (Sept. 29, 1995).

160 *See* Executive Order 13148, Part 2, Section 204.

161 *See* Executive Order 13148, Part 2, Section 205.

162 *See* Executive Order 13148, Part 2, Section 206.

Chapter 16

Occupational Safety and Health Act

Marshall Lee Miller
Baise & Miller
Washington, D.C.

1.0 Overview

It is not often recognized that the Occupational Safety and Health Administration (OSHA) is also perhaps the most important environmental health agency in the government. Even EPA, with far greater resources and public attention, deals with a smaller range of much less hazardous exposures than does OSHA. After all, individuals are more likely to be exposed to high concentrations of dangerous chemicals in their workplaces than in their backyards.

OSHA was once called the most unpopular agency in the federal government. It was criticized for its confusing regulations, chronic mismanagement, and picayune enforcement. With somewhat less accuracy, business groups likened it to an American Gestapo, while labor unions denounced it as ineffective, unresponsive, and bureaucratic.

Most damning of all, OSHA was often simply ignored. It no longer is. Although OSHA still has its weaknesses and most of its standards are sadly outmoded, its penalties have sharply increased in severity. This has caught the attention of labor and management alike. Moreover, the agency has gradually improved its general reputation.

This led the prestigious Maxwell School of Government at Syracuse, a few years ago, to grade OSHA a B-minus, the same mark it gave the U.S. EPA.[1] Sadly, this grade is far too generous. While OSHA does deserve considerable credit for shaking off an initially dreadful image, its failure to expand or even update its 45-year-old health standards is indefensible. Enforcement cannot be effective if there is nothing to enforce.

OSHA's response is that the workplace fatality rates have dropped sharply in the over four decades since the agency's creation, even though the U.S. workforce has doubled. In a piece called "OSHA Is Making a Difference," the agency reckoned that deaths have declined from 38 per day in 1970 to 13 a day in 2011.[2] That assumes of course that OSHA alone made all the difference, which it didn't, but it was an significant part of the national change in perceptions of occupational and environmental problems. So, OSHA, take a bow.

1.1 Comparison of OSHA and EPA

There are several distinct differences between OSHA and EPA besides the obvious occupational jurisdiction.

First, OSHA has major responsibility over safety in the workplace as well as health.

Second, OSHA is essentially an enforcement organization, with a majority of its employees as inspectors, performing tens of thousands of inspections a year. This "highway patrol" function, inspecting and penalizing thousands of businesses large and small, has been the major reason for OSHA's traditional unpopularity. At EPA, on the other hand, inspections and enforcement are seen as a relatively smaller part of the operation.

Third, whereas EPA functions as an independent regulatory agency, albeit headed by a presidential appointee, OSHA is a division of the Department of Labor. This organizational arrangement not only provides less prestige and less independence for OSHA but also has posed an internal conflict of whether OSHA should be primarily a health (and safety) or a labor-oriented agency. Nevertheless, OSHA and EPA regulate different aspects of so many health issues—asbestos, vinyl chloride, carcinogens, hazard labeling, and others—that it is reasonable to regard them both as overlapping environmental organizations.[3]

1.2 OSHA, the Organization

OSHA has a staff of 2,200 throughout the country in ten regional offices and scores of area offices. Almost exactly half of the personnel are safety and health inspectors. Around 600 workers are located at OSHA headquarters in Washington, D.C., near Capitol Hill. The annual budget exceeds half a billion dollars, a significant increase over the $350 million level of only a few years ago, though interestingly the number of employees and inspections remain almost the same.[4]

The organization is headed by the assistant secretary of labor for occupational safety and health, a presidential appointee. All recent appointees have had considerable experience in the field. Under the Barack Obama administration, the OSHA administrator has been David Michaels, a former professor at George

Washington University who previously served in the Bill Clinton administration as head of the environmental and occupational safety program at the Department of Energy.

There's a delightful irony here. Shortly before Michaels was appointed administrator, he published a book, *Doubt Is Their Product: How Industry's Assault on Science Threatens Your Health*, blaming industry lobbyists for undermining agency rulemaking. Now, in this respect, OSHA is no different from every other regulatory agency. One wonders if he now realizes that the standard-setting process is much more complicated than mere industry resistance.[5]

The previous appointee, under the George W. Bush administration, was (from February 2006) Edwin G. Foulke, Jr., a South Carolina labor lawyer who earlier had been chairman of the quasi-judicial Occupational Safety and Health Review Commission in the 1990s. His predecessor until the end of 2004 was John L. Henshaw, an official in the North Carolina Department of Labor and the department's chief lobbyist on occupational safety and health matters with the state legislature.

The head of OSHA has traditionally been aided by one to three deputy assistant secretaries (DASs), also often political appointees, as well as by a number of other senior personnel who head offices such as health standards, safety standards, enforcement, policy planning, and federal programs.[6]

This chapter emphasizes the health aspects of OSHA because much press attention and the agency's own public emphasis since the mid-1970s has been on toxic hazards. Nevertheless, OSHA is predominantly an occupational *safety* organization. The two parts of the organization are quite distinct: there are separate inspectors and standards offices for each, and the two groups are different in terms of background, education, and outlook. There are also far more safety inspectors than health inspectors.

The agency lately conducts an average of around 40,000 inspections a year. Despite the popular view that shifting politics determines how strict inspections and penalties are in any given period, the statistics do not bear this out. Inspections, for example, are remarkably consistent over the years: in 2012 there were 40,961 inspections, compared with 38,700 back in 2005, 39,000 in 2009, and in 2010 almost 41,000. Proposed penalties average around $100 million.[7]

More than half of the inspections are in the construction area, and a quarter are in manufacturing.

The number of inspections is only about half of what it was in some earlier years, but this fact alone is not necessarily a reliable indicator of agency effectiveness. Remember, an "inspection" is one visit to one workplace, whether that visit involved one or a dozen inspectors and was at a giant chemical plant or a mom-and-pop grocery. You can see how you can make the numbers come out any way you want. Importantly, this definition of an inspection may now be changing to reflect these differences.

The 40,000 or so OSHA inspections[8] each year find an almost unvarying total number of 87,000 violations each year (e.g., 2004—86,708; compared with 2009—87,663), of which about 65,000 (2004—61,666; compared with 2008—67,052—and 2009—67,663) are deemed serious.[9]

State OSHA inspections average a little less than 60,000 a year, but with only around $50 million in proposed penalties. Approximately half of the states have their own state OSHA programs, as discussed below.

2.0 Legislative Framework

OSHA was created in December 1970—the same month as EPA—with the enactment of the Occupational Safety and Health Act (OSH Act)[10] and officially began operation in April 1971. When compared with other environmental acts, the OSH Act is very simple and well drafted. This does not mean that one necessarily agrees with the provisions of every section, but it is clearly and concisely written so that details can be worked out in implementing regulations. And unlike the other environmental laws that have been amended several times, becoming longer and more tangled each time, the OSH Act has scarcely been amended or modified since its original passage.[11] This is both a positive and a negative.[12]

2.1 Purpose of the Act

The act sets an admirable but impossible goal: namely, to ensure that "no employee will suffer material impairment of health or functional capacity" from a lifetime of occupational exposure.[13] It does not require—or even seem to allow—a balancing test or a risk-benefit determination.[14] The supplementary phrase in the OSH Act, "to the extent feasible," was not meant to alter this. This absolutist position, comparable only to one provision in the Clean Air Act,[15] reflects Congress's displeasure at previous overly permissive state standards, which traditionally seemed always to be resolved against workers' health. In fact, the concession to feasibility was added almost as an afterthought.

Business groups did obtain two provisions in the law as their price for support. First, industry insisted that states should be encouraged to assume primary responsibility for implementation, in order to minimize the role of the federal OSHA. Second, because of their distrust for the allegedly pro-union bias of the Department of Labor, responsibility for first-level adjudication of violations would be vested in an independent Occupational Health and Safety Review Commission with a three-member panel of judges named by the president and approved by the Senate. There is no comparable provision in any of EPA's environmental laws.

Congress did reject an industry effort to separate entirely the standard-setting authority from the enforcement powers of the new organization, but it created the National Institute for Occupational Safety and Health (NIOSH), located in another government department, the Department of Health and Human Services (HHS), to play a significant role in the standard-setting process. Thus, the three main functions of OSHA are these:

1. setting of safety and health standards;

2. their enforcement through federal and state inspectors; and

3. employer and employee education and consultation.

2.2 Coverage of the Act

In general, coverage of the act extends to all employers and their employees in the 50 states and all territories under U.S. jurisdiction.[16] An employer is defined as any "person engaged in a business affecting commerce who has employees; significantly, this does not include the United States or any State or political subdivision of a State."[17] Coverage of the act was clarified by regulations published in the *Federal Register* in January 1972.[18] These regulations, already summarized above, interpret coverage as follows:

1. The term employer excludes the United States and states and political subdivisions.

2. Any employer employing one or more employees is under its jurisdiction, including professionals, such as physicians and lawyers; agricultural employers; and nonprofit and charitable organizations.

3. Self-employed persons are not covered.

4. Family members operating a farm are not regarded as employees.

5. To the extent that religious groups employ workers for secular purposes, they are included in the coverage.

6. Domestic household employment activities for private residences are not subject to the requirements of the act.

7. Workplaces already protected by other federal agencies under other federal statutes (discussed later) are also excluded.

In total, OSHA directly or indirectly covers more than 100 million workers in six million workplaces.

2.3 Exemptions from the Act

The OSH Act and regulations exempt a number of different categories of employees. The most important exemption is for workplaces employing 10 or fewer workers. What often is not recognized is that this exemption is only partial; these smaller establishments are still subject to accident and worker complaint investigations and the hazard communication requirements These are all discussed in detail below.

Federal and state employees are also exempted from direct coverage by OSHA. As discussed below, however, the former are subject to OSHA rules under OSH Act Section 19 and several presidential executive orders, and most states having their own state OSHA plans also cover their state and local government workers.

Workers are also exempted if they are covered under other federal agencies, such as railroad workers under the Federal Railroad Administration or maritime workers subject to Coast Guard regulations. This exemption has sometimes generated intergovernmental friction where the other agency has general safety and health regulations but not the full coverage of OSHA regulations. In other words, is the exemption absolute or only proportional? Under the OSH Act Section 9, OSHA is supposed to defer to the other agency if it can better protect the workers, and, similarly, the other agency is expected to recede when the situation is reversed. Of course, considerations of turf and politics are often paramount.[19]

2.4 Mine Safety and Health Administration

One occupational exemption is so significant that it deserves special mention, as many laymen may assume that coal and other mining industries are also regulated under OSHA. They are not. They are regulated by the Mine Safety and Health Administration (MSHA), which is also under the Department of Labor, to where it was transferred from the Interior Department in 1978. MSHA is actually slightly larger than OSHA (about 2,400 employees compared with 2,200), though with a substantially smaller budget (roughly $350 million compared with $550 million) because of its different functions. MSHA currently has one inspector for every four mines, and mines are supposed to be inspected a number of times a year to deal with the much greater hazards in mining operations than in most other workplaces.[20]

From time to time there has been a debate about whether OSHA and MSHA should be merged, but each time there has been unanimous consensus that they should not be.

2.5 Telecommuting and Home Workplaces

Workplaces are workplaces, even if they are in a private home. That was at least the principle OSHA relied on in 1999 to attempt to exert its authority over the growing number of white-collar workers who use their modems rather than their motor cars to commute to work. This is a good example of the type of political furor OSHA can create, often unintentionally, and is worth examining briefly as illustrating a clash of regulatory factors.

Of course, OSHA had always claimed (if rarely exercised) jurisdiction over "sweatshops" and other industries even if operated from someone's home. Therefore, when OSHA was asked for a simple interpretation about its coverage of home office workers, it applied the same logic. In an interpretative ruling from the Office of Compliance Programs in November 1999, the agency stated that OSHA would hold employers responsible for injuries to employees at home.[21] This triggered a political explosion.

The National Association of Manufacturers declared, "We see this as the long arm of OSHA coming into people's homes."[22] The chairman of a powerful congressional committee warned that the policy would put "home workers in the position of having to comply with thousands of pages of OSHA regulations."[23]

What OSHA had failed to realize was these new workers were not someone's employees needing protection from exploitative bosses. They were their own bosses, or they certainly saw themselves as such. And they saw OSHA intervention not as protective but intrusive.

On January 5, 2000, the secretary of labor, Alexis Herman, announced the cancellation of the short-lived OSHA policy.

2.6 Multiemployer Workplaces[24]

Workers commonly find themselves in settings where a general contractor oversees a group of subcontractors who themselves are on the premises of a third party. This is especially true of the construction realm which makes up to half of all OSHA citations. If someone gets injured, which party bears primary responsibility?

Because of the multitude of possible scenarios, there is no one constant answer. However, the first question to ask is which party had real control over the workplace? The second question is whether something inherent in the property caused the hazard? And third, if equipment is at fault, whose responsibility was it to provide and maintain it? There may be a lot of blame to go around, including on the worker himself.

As you can imagine, this has been a contentious, much litigated area. As a rule of thumb, OSHA tends to seek one responsible party and to push liability as far up the chain of responsibility as possible. The important thing to note is that this issue is a problem, so even before starting operations in a multiemployer setting, you should make the delineations of authority clear, or at least to your best advantage.

3.0 Scope of OSHA Standards

To give the reader an idea of the areas covered by the standards, the following is a subpart listing from the Code of Federal Regulations, Part 1910, Occupational Safety and Health Standards. Note that the listing comprises mostly safety standards. The health standards are all contained in Subpart Z, except for some provisions in Subparts A, C, G, I, K, and R, which can cover both categories.

3.1 Areas Covered by the OSHA Standards

- Subpart A: General (purpose and scope, definitions, applicability of standards, etc.)

- Subpart B: Adoption and Extension of Established Federal Standards (construction work, ship repairing, longshoring, etc.)

- Subpart C: General Safety and Health Provisions (preservation of records)

- Subpart D: Walking-Working Surfaces (guarding floor and wall openings, portable ladders, requirements for scaffolding, etc.)

- Subpart E: Means of Egress (definitions, specific means by occupancy, sources of standards, etc.)

- Subpart F: Powered Platforms, Manlifts, and Vehicle-Mounted Work Platforms (elevating and rotating work platforms, standards, organizations, etc.)

- Subpart G: Occupational Health and Environmental Control (ventilation, noise exposure, radiation, etc.)

- Subpart H: Hazardous Materials (compressed gases, flammables, storage of petroleum gases, effective dates, etc.)

- Subpart I: Personal Protective Equipment (eye/face, respiratory, electrical devices, etc.)

- Subpart J: General Environmental Controls (sanitation, labor camps, safety color code for hazards, etc.)

- Subpart K: Medical and First Aid (medical services, sources of standards)

- Subpart L: Fire Protection (fire-suppression equipment, hose and sprinkler systems, fire brigades, etc.)

- Subpart M: Compressed Gas and Compressed Air Equipment (inspection of gas cylinders, safety relief devices, etc.)

- Subpart N: Materials Handling/Storage (powered industrial trucks, cranes, helicopters, etc.)

- Subpart O: Machinery and Machine Guarding (requirements for all machines, woodworking machinery, wheels, mills, etc.)

- Subpart P: Hand and Portable Powered Tools and Other Hand-Held Equipment (guarding of portable power tools)

- Subpart Q: Welding, Cutting, and Brazing (definitions, sources of standards, etc.)

- Subpart R: Special Industries (pulp, paper and paperboard mills, textiles, laundry machinery, telecommunications, etc.)

- Subpart S: Electrical (application, National Electrical Code)

- Subpart T: Commercial Diving Operations (qualification of team, pre- and postdive procedures, equipment, etc.)

- Subparts U–Y: [Reserved]

- Subpart Z: Toxic and Hazardous Substances (air contaminants, asbestos, vinyl chloride, lead, benzene, etc.)

3.2 Overview of Standards

When OSHA was created, Congress realized that the new agency would require years to promulgate a comprehensive corps of health and safety standards. The OSH Act therefore provided that for a two-year period ending in April 1972, the agency could adopt as its own the standards of respected professional and trade groups. These are the consensus standards issued under Section 6(a) of the statute.[25] Nobody could have imagined that four decades later these imperfect and outdated standards would still form the overwhelming majority of OSHA regulations.

3.3 Overview of Health Standards

Health issues, notably environmental contaminants in the workplace, have increasingly become a national concern over the past several decades. Health hazards are much more complex, more difficult to define, and, because of the delay in detection, perhaps more dangerous to a larger number of employees.

Unlike safety hazards, the effects of health hazards may be slow, cumulative, irreversible, and complicated by nonoccupational factors.

If a machine is unequipped with safety devices and maims a worker, the danger is clearly and easily identified and the solution usually obvious. However, if workers are exposed for several years to a chemical that is later found to be carcinogenic, there may be little help for those exposed.

In the nation's workplaces there are tens of thousands of toxic chemicals, many of which are significant enough to warrant regulation. Yet OSHA only has a list of fewer than 500 substances, and these are mostly simple threshold limits adopted under Section 6(a) from the recommended lists of private industrial hygiene organizations back in the 1960s and early 1970s. This list is being updated now, but with glacial slowness.

The promulgation of health standards involves many complex concepts. To be complete, each standard needs not only exposure limits but medical surveillance requirements, recordkeeping, monitoring, and multiple physical reviews, just to mention a few factors. At the present rate, promulgation of standards on every existing toxic substance could take many thousands of years even if no new chemicals were invented.

Ironically, an attempt to update the health standards for hundreds of substances in one regulatory action by borrowing newer figures from respected health professional organizations was opposed by the labor unions (and industry) and struck down by an appellate court in 1992. A sad story.[26]

3.4 Overview of Safety Standards

Safety hazards are those aspects of the work environment that, in general, cause harm of an immediate and sometimes violent nature, such as burns, electrical shock, cuts, broken bones, loss of limbs or eyesight, and even death. The distinction from health hazards is usually obvious; mechanical and electrical are considered safety problems, while chemicals are considered health problems. Noise is difficult to categorize; it is somewhat arbitrarily classified as a health problem.

The Section 6(a) adoption of national consensus and other federal agency standards created chaos in the safety area. It was one thing for companies to follow industry or association guidelines that, in many cases, had themselves not been modified in years; it was another thing for those guidelines actually to be codified and enforced as law. In the two years the act provided for OSHA to produce standards derived from these existing rules, the agency should have examined these closely, simplified them, deleted the ridiculous and unnecessary ones, and promulgated final regulations that actually identified and eliminated hazards to workers. But in the commotion of organizing an agency from scratch, it did not happen that way.

Nor did affected industry groups register their objections until later. During the entire two-year comment period, not a single company or association filed an objection with OSHA.

Almost all of the so-called "Mickey Mouse" standards (yes, that's what the agency calls them) were safety regulations, such as the requirements that fire extinguishers be attached to the wall exactly so many inches above the floor. The requirement for "split" toilet seats acquired almost legendary significance. Undertrained OSHA inspectors often failed to recognize major hazards while citing industries for minor violations "which were highly visible, but not necessarily related to serious hazards to workers' safety and health."[27]

Section 6(g) of the OSH Act directs OSHA to establish priorities based on the needs of specific "industries, trades, crafts, occupations, businesses, workplaces, or work environments." The Senate report accompanying the OSH Act stated that the agency's emphasis initially should be put on industries where the need was determined to be most compelling.[28] OSHA's early attempts to target inspections, however, were sporadic and, for the most part, unsuccessful. The situation has improved somewhat in the following years, for both health and safety, in part because of the recent requirement that some priority scheme be used that could justify search warrants.[29] But, as we shall see, that has brought its own problems.

4.0 Standard Setting

Setting standards can be a complex and protracted process. There are thousands of chemical substances, electrical problems, fire hazards, and many other dangerous situations prevalent in the workplace for which standards needed to be developed.

To meet the objectives defined in the act, three different standard-setting procedures were established:

1. Consensus Standards, under Section 6(a);

2. Permanent Standards, under Section 6(b); and

3. Emergency Temporary Standards, under Section 6(c).

4.1 Consensus Standards: Section 6(a)

Congress realized that OSHA would need standards to enforce while it was developing its own. Section 6(a) allowed the agency, for a two-year period that ended on April 25, 1973, to adopt standards developed by other federal agencies or to adopt consensus standards of various industry or private associations.[30] This resulted in a list of around 420 common toxic chemicals with maximum permitted air concentrations specified in parts per million (ppm) or in milligrams per cubic meters (mg/m^3).

There are several problems inherent in these standards. First, these threshold values are the only elements to the standard. There are no required warning labels, monitoring, or medical recordkeeping, nor do they generally distinguish between the quite different health effects in eight-hour, 15-minute, peak, annual average, and other periods of exposure. Second, being thresholds, they are based on the implicit assumption that there are universal no-effect levels below which a worker is safe. For carcinogens, this assumption is quite controversial.

Third, most of the consensus standards were originally established not on the basis of firm scientific evidence but, as the name implies, from existing guidelines and limits of various industry, association, and governmental groups. Before OSHA's creation, these were naturally very informal, were intended to be general, nonbinding guidelines, and had been in circulation for a number of years with no urgency to keep them current. Consequently, neither industry nor labor bothered to comment when OSHA first proposed the consensus standards. Many of these "interim" standards were already out of date by the time they were adopted by OSHA, and they are now legally frozen in time until OSHA goes through the full Section 6(b) administrative rulemaking process.

Fourth, OSHA consensus standards often involve "incorporation by reference," especially in the safety area. This raises the above deficiencies to a logarithmic plateau. In some cases, these pre-1972 publications were not standards or even formal association guidelines but mere private association pamphlets that are no longer in print and not easily obtainable. For example, OSHA's general regulation on compressed gases merely states that the cylinders should be in safe condition and maintained "in accordance with Compressed Gas Association pamphlet P-1-1965" and several similar documents, often unobtainable now.[31]

Fifth, not all of these "toxics" are on the list because they really pose a health hazard. Although that has been the unquestioned assumption of certain later rulemakings, such as the requirement for Material Safety Data Sheets, it is not correct. For example, some chemicals such as carbon black were listed because of "good housekeeping" practices—a facility with even a small amount of this intrusive black substance will look filthy—and not because it was considered hazardous at the levels set.

Nevertheless, Congress was undoubtedly correct in requiring the compilation of such a list. Otherwise, there would have been no OSHA health standards at the beginning. There are virtually no others even now.

4.2 Standards Completion and Deletion Processes

The agency has attempted to deal with one of the shortcomings of the consensus standards by what is called the Standards Completion Process. Over a number of years, OSHA has taken some threshold standards and added various medical, monitoring, and other requirements.[32] At least a broader range of protection is offered to exposed workers.

The agency has also sought to reduce the number of safety standards. This is done by eliminating those so-called "Mickey Mouse" standards that have little bearing on worker protection but impose voluminous requirements. More often, the simplification has come by removing redundant sections and cross-references. This eliminates pages but not a lot more.

Nevertheless, OSHA is proud of its compliance with the presidential directive that federal agencies review and remove duplicative or repetitive regulations.[33]

4.3 Permanent Standards: Section 6(b)

Permanent standards must now be developed pursuant to Section 6(b). This is the familiar standard-setting and rulemaking process followed by most other federal agencies under the Administrative Procedure Act.[34]

Permanent standards may be initiated by a well-publicized tragedy, court action, new scientific studies, or the receipt of a criteria document from the National Institute for Occupational Safety and Health (NIOSH), an organization described later in this chapter. The criteria document is a compilation of all the scientific reports on a particular chemical, including epidemiological and animal studies, along with a recommendation to OSHA for a standard. The recommendation, based supposedly only on scientific health considerations, includes suggested exposure limits (eight-hour average, peaks, etc.) and appropriate medical monitoring, labeling, and other proscriptions.

Congress assumed that NIOSH would be the primary standard-setting arm of OSHA, although the two are in different government departments—Health and Human Services (HHS) and Labor, respectively. According to this model, OSHA would presumably take the scientific recommendations from NIOSH, factor in engineering and technical feasibility, and then promulgate as similar a standard as possible. However, the system has never worked this way. Instead, OSHA's own standards office has generally regarded NIOSH's contribution as just one step in the process—and not one entitled to a great deal of deference.[35]

Following receipt of the criteria document or some other initiating action, OSHA will study the evidence and then possibly publish a proposed standard.

In reality, most candidate standards never get this far: the hundreds of NIOSH documents, labor union petitions, and other serious recommendations have resulted in only a few new health standards since 1970.[36]

The proposed standard is then subjected to public comment for (typically) a 90-day period, often extended, after which the reactions are analyzed and informal public hearings are scheduled. In a few controversial instances, there may be more than one series of hearings and comments. Then come the post-hearing comments, which can perhaps be the most important presentations by the parties. After considerable further study, a final standard is eventually promulgated. The entire process might theoretically be accomplished in under a year, but in practice it takes a minimum of several years or, as with asbestos, even decades.

The following is a list of some of the final health standards that OSHA has promulgated to date:

1. Asbestos

2. Fourteen carcinogens

   —4-Nitrobiphenyl   —benzidine

   —alpha-nephthylamine   —ethyleneimine

   —methyl chloromethyl ether   —beta-propiolactone

   —3,3'-dichlorobenzidine   —2-acetylaminofluorene

   —bis-chloromethyl ether   —4-dimethylaminoazobenzene

   —beta-naphthylamine   —N-nitrosodimethylamine

   —4-aminodiphenyl   —(MOCA stayed by court action).

3. Vinyl chloride

4. Inorganic arsenic

5. Lead

6. Coke-oven emissions

7. Cotton dust

8. 1,2-dibromo-3-chloropropane (DBCP)

9. Acrylonitrile

10. Ethylene oxide

11. Benzene

12. Field sanitation

13. Hexavalent chromium, back in February 2006

14. Crystalline silica, effective June 2016

The list is obviously incredibly short for almost four decades of OSHA standard setting.

4.4 Emergency Temporary Standards

The statute also provides for a third standard-setting approach, specified for emergency circumstances where the normal, ponderous rulemaking procedure would be too slow. Section 6(c) gives the agency authority to issue an emergency temporary standard (ETS) if necessary to protect workers from exposure to grave danger posed by substances "determined to be toxic or physically harmful or from new hazards."[37]

Such standards are effective immediately upon publication in the *Federal Register*. An ETS is valid, however, for only six months. OSHA is thus under considerable pressure to conduct an expedited section 6(b) rulemaking for a permanent standard before the ETS lapses. For this reason, a quest for an emergency standard has been the preferred route for labor unions or other groups seeking a new OSHA standard. These ETSs have not fared well. When challenged in the courts; virtually all have been struck down as insufficiently justified, however.

4.5 General Duty Clause, 5(a)(1)

There is actually a fourth type of enforceable standard, one that covers situations for which no standards currently exist.

Since OSHA has standards for only a few hundred of the many thousands of potentially dangerous chemicals and workplace safety hazards, there are far more potentially dangerous situations than the rules cover. Therefore, inspectors have authority under the General Duty Clause to cite violations for unsafe conditions even where specific standards do not exist.[38] Agency policy has shifted back and forth between encouraging the use of "Section 5(a)(1)," as the clause is often termed, since this ensures that unsafe conditions will be addressed, and discouraging its use on the theory that, in fairness, employers should be liable only for compliance with specific standards of which they are given knowledge.

However, the agency has acknowledged that many of the standards that do exist are woefully out of date and thus cannot be relied upon for adequate protection of worker safety and health. The traditional notion was that compliance with an existing specific standard—even if demonstrably unsafe—precluded an OSHA citation.[39] This has been called into question by the courts. In April 1988, a federal appellate court allowed OSHA to cite for violations of the General Duty Clause even where a company was in full compliance with a specific numerical standard on the precise point in question.[40] Bare compliance with the standards on the books, therefore, might not be responsible management. This decision was expected to trigger a host of similar court rulings on other antiquated standards, or even to goad the agency into revising its regulations, but the case remains a singularity.

4.6 Feasibility and the Balancing Debate

There has been a continuing debate over feasibility and balancing in OSHA enforcement. The important issues include the following:

- Can OSHA legally consider economic factors in setting health or safety standards levels?

- If so, is this consideration limited only to extreme circumstances?

- Does the OSH Act provide for a balancing of costs and benefits in setting standards?

- Can OSHA mandate engineering controls although they alone would still not attain the standard?

- And, can OSHA require engineering controls even if personal protective equipment (such as earplugs) could effectively, if often only theoretically, reduce hazards to a safe level and at a much lower cost?

These questions have been extensively litigated before the Occupational Safety and Health Review Commission (OSHRC) and the courts. Most of the debate has been over the interpretation of feasibility in Section 6(b)(5) of the act.

One must remember that OSHA legislation was originally seen by Congress in rather absolutist terms: any standard promulgated should be one "which most adequately assumes . . . that no employee will suffer material impairment of health." Only late in the congressional debate was the Department of Labor able to insert the phrase "to the extent feasible" into the text. This was intended to prevent companies having to close because unattainable standards were imposed on them, but it was not spelled out to what extent economic as well as technical feasibility was included.[41]

Since the term feasibility was not clearly defined, there has been much confusion over how to interpret what Congress intended, as the earlier cases show. In

Industrial Union Department, AFL v. Hodgson, the D.C. Circuit accepted that economic realities affected the meaning of feasible, but only to the extent that "a standard that is prohibitively expensive is not 'feasible.' "[42] It was Congress's intent, the court added, that this term would prevent a standard unreasonably "requiring protective devices unavailable under existing technology or by making financial viability generally impossible." The court warned, however, that this doctrine should not be used by companies to avoid needed improvements in their workplaces: Standards may be economically feasible even though, from the standpoint of employers, they are financially burdensome and affect profit margins adversely. Nor does the concept of economic feasibility necessarily guarantee the continued existence of individual employers.[43]

A similar view was adopted in 1975 by the Second Circuit in *The Society of the Plastics Industry v. OSHA,* written by Justice Clark, who cited approvingly the case above.[44] He held that feasible meant not only that which is attainable technologically and economically now but also that which might reasonably be achievable in the future. In this case, which concerned strict emissions controls on vinyl chloride, he declared that OSHA may impose "standards which require improvements in existing technologies or which require the development of new technology, and . . . is not limited to issuing standards based solely on devices already fully developed."[45]

Neither court undertook any risk-benefit analysis, such as attempting to compare the hundreds of millions of dollars needed to control vinyl chloride with the lives lost to angiosarcoma of the liver. Those who have attempted to develop such equations have generally concluded the task is undoable, at least for most such chronic health effects.[46]

A third federal appeals court, however, took a strongly contrary position in a case involving noise. In *Turner Co. v. Secretary of Labor,* the Seventh Circuit Court of Appeals decided that the $30,000 cost of abating a noise hazard should be weighed against the health damage to the affected workers, taking into consideration the availability of personal protective equipment to mitigate the risk.[47]

This holding is not unreasonable, but the logic is based on a highly tenuous interpretation of the law. The court, without providing any clear rationale for its view, held that "the word 'feasible' as contained in 29 CFR § 1910.95(6)(1) must be given its ordinary and common sense meaning of 'practicable.' " (This may be so, but this semantic tool is of no analytical value.) From this the court concluded,

> Accordingly, the Commission erred when it failed to consider the relative cost of implementing engineering controls . . . versus the effectiveness of an existing personal protective equipment program utilizing fitted earplugs.[48]

This interpretation does not follow from the analysis. In fact, since the Turner Company had both the financial resources and the technical capability to abate the noise problem, compliance with the regulation would appear to be "practicable." The court, however, considered this term to mean that a cost-benefit computation should be made.

In 1982, the U.S. Court of Appeals for the Ninth Circuit, in the case of *Donovan v. Castle & Cooke Foods and OSHRC*,[49] also held that the Noise Act and the regulations permit consideration of relative costs and benefits to determine what noise controls are feasible.

OSHA gave the plant a citation on the grounds that, although Castle & Cooke required its employees to wear personal protective equipment, its failure to install technologically feasible engineering and administrative controls[50] constituted a violation of the noise standard and that the violation could be abated only by the implementation of such controls. OSHA argued that engineering and administrative controls should be considered economically infeasible only if their implementation would so seriously jeopardize the employer's economic condition as to threaten continued operation.

On appeal, OSHA argued that neither the OSHRC nor the courts are free to interpret economic feasibility because its definition is controlled by the Supreme Court's decision in *American Textile Manufacturers Institute, Inc. v. Donovan*.[51] The appeals court, however, decided that the Supreme Court's interpretation of the term feasible made in *American Textile* was not deemed controlling for the noise standards. It also affirmed that economic feasibility should be determined through a cost-benefit analysis and that in the case of Castle & Cooke the costs of economic controls did not justify the benefit that would accrue to employees. Thus, the decision to vacate the citation was upheld.

4.7 Struggling for Standards: Popcorn Lungs and Cranes

Two cases, one health and one safety, illustrate the difficulty of setting OSHA standards.

The agency has been struggling for nearly a decade to regulate diacetyl (2,3-butadione), a chemical used to give popcorn salt a buttery flavor and in certain beers and wines to improve their texture. Manufacture of this substance has been blamed for a rare but serious and untreatable lung disease in workers, namely bronchitis obliterans. There is also suggestive evidence that it may play a role in Alzheimer's disease.

In the early and mid-2000s, several juries awarded multimillion-dollar verdicts to victims of this condition. EPA has had an investigation underway since 2004. In 2006 the Teamsters Union filed with OSHA a formal request for a rulemaking to protect workers exposed to diacetyl. Only in 2009 was an advanced notice of proposed rulemaking issued, merely asking for information to be used in a possible future rulemaking. So far, nothing more has happened.[52]

On the other hand, the agency has finally been able to issue a new safety for construction cranes and derricks. In 2003 OSHA collected a group of union and industry representatives to solicit their views on improving the archaic 1971 standard and preventing the average 30 to 50 deaths a year from accidents from collapse, electrocution, and falls. After several years, other interested parties, owners, insurance companies, and experts reached consensus on a 120-page draft. By 2008 it was ready for release as a proposal, and after several years of well-publicized and tragic deaths from collapsed devices in New York, Houston, and elsewhere, OSHA issued the final standard in July 2010. Granted this was "only" an update of an existing standard, but at least something emerged from the regulatory process.[53]

5.0 Variances

Companies that complain that OSHA standards are unrealistic are often not aware that they might be able to create their own version of the standards. The alternative proposed has to be at least as effective as the regular standard, but it can be different.

5.1 Temporary Variances

Section 6(b)(6)(A) of the OSH Act establishes a procedure by which any employer may apply for a "temporary order granting a variance from a standard or any provision thereof." According to the act, the variance will be approved when OSHA determines that the requirements have been met and establishes

- that the employer is unable to meet the standard "because of unavailability of professional or technical personnel or of materials and equipment" or because alterations of facilities cannot be completed in time;

- that he is "taking all available steps to safeguard" his workers against the hazard covered by the standard for which he is applying for a variance; and

- that he has an "effective program for coming into compliance with the standard as quickly as practicable."[54]

This temporary order may be granted only after employees have been notified and, if requested, there has been sufficient opportunity for a hearing. The variance may not remain in effect for more than one year, with the possibility of only two six-month renewals.[55] The overriding factor for a temporary variance is the employer's demonstration of good faith.[56]

5.2 Permanent Variances

Permanent variances can be issued under Section 6(d) of the OSH Act. A permanent variance may be granted to an employer who has demonstrated "by a preponderance" of evidence that the "conditions, practices, means, methods, operations or processes used or proposed to be used" will provide a safe and healthful workplace as effectively as would compliance with the standard. This is a high burden of proof but not an insurmountable one.

6.0 Compliance and Inspections

OSHA is primarily an enforcement organization. In its early years both the competence of its inspections and the size of the assessed fines were pitifully inadequate; they were the primary reason OSHA was not taken seriously by either labor unions or the business community. That picture has now changed significantly.

6.1 Field Structure

The Department of Labor has divided the territory subject to the OSH Act into ten federal regions, the same boundaries that EPA also uses. Each region contains from four to nine area offices. When an area office is not considered necessary because of a lack of industrial activity, a district office or field station may be established. Each region is headed by a regional administrator, each area by an area director. In the field, compliance officers represent area offices and inspect work sites in their vicinity, except in situations where a specialist or team from outside might be required.

6.2 Role of Inspections

The only way to determine compliance by employers is inspections, but inspecting all the workplaces covered by the OSH Act would require many decades. Each year there are tens of thousands of federal inspections and as many or more state inspections, but there are several million workplaces. Obviously, a priority system for high-hazard occupations is necessary, along with random inspections just to keep everyone "on their toes."

Inspections are supposed to be surprises; indeed, there are criminal penalties for anyone giving advance notice to the sites beforehand.[57] The inspections may occur in several ways: they may be targeted at random, triggered by worker complaints; set by a priority system based on hazardous probabilities; or set by events such as a fatality or explosion. Inspectors expect admittance without search warrants, but a company has the constitutional right to refuse admittance until OSHA obtains a search warrant from a federal district court.[58] Such refusal is frankly not a good idea except in very special circumstances, such as when the additional delay would allow a quick cleanup of the workplace to bring it into compliance.

6.3 Training and Competence of Inspectors

There has been a major problem with OSHA inspectors in the past, namely, the training program did not adequately prepare them for their tasks, and the quality of the hiring was uneven. In the early days there was tremendous pressure from the unions to get an inspection force on the job as soon as possible, so recruitment was often hurried and training was minimal. Inspectors would walk into a plant where, for example, pesticide dust was so thick workers could not see across the room, yet, because there was no standard as such, the inspectors would not think there was a problem. This is a real example.[59] But had there been a fire extinguisher in the wrong place and had the inspector been able to see it through the haze, he would have cited the plant for a safety violation. This early bumbling was the source of much of the animus against OSHA that persists even today.

Competence among staff has markedly improved since the early days of the program. Both in-house training efforts by OSHA and increased numbers of professional training programs conducted by colleges and universities have contributed to these improvements. There is also a greater sensitivity toward workers and their representatives.[60]

6.4 Citations, Fines, and Penalties

If the inspector discovers a hazard in the workplace, a citation and a proposed fine may be issued. In the law, citations can be serious, nonserious, willful, or repeated. In fact, by one count, there are at least nine types of penalty findings under the OSH Act. They are as follows:

- De minimis—A technical violation but one posing insignificant risk and for which no monetary penalty is warranted.

- Nonserious—The basic type of penalty. No risk of death or serious injury is posed, but the violation might still cause some harm. This is the first major category.

- Serious—The hazard could lead to death or serious injury. This is the second major category.

- Failure to correct—Violations when found must be remediated within a certain period of time. If a subsequent reinspection finds this has not been done or has been allowed to recur, this fairly serious citation is in order.

- Repeated—Continuous violations, discussed below.

- Willful—Intentional violations, discussed below.

- Criminal—Applicable under the OSH Act only for cases involving death.

- Egregious—Supposedly heinous situations, discussed below.

- Section 11(c)—Penalties for company retaliation against complainers and whistle-blowers, also discussed at length below.

6.5 OSHA Citation and Penalty Patterns

OSHA now averages around 40,000 inspections a year.[61] These result in around 88,000 violations, of which 67,000 are ranked as serious. This is amazingly consistent each year, though lately the "other than serious" category has declined somewhat while serious violations have risen. So-called willful violations, which for a while seemed to be growing disproportionately, have settled down to around 400–700 a year. Repeat violations, which might reflect a company's failure to learn from experience, average around 2,500 a year.[62]

These inspections are focused on the industries and sectors where statistics indicate greater potential hazards. Contrary to the common assumption that most inspections are in manufacturing, in fact that sector accounts for only about one-fourth of the inspections. More than half are in the construction industry, with another quarter distributed over all other types of workplaces.

OSHA's Enhanced Enforcement Program (EEP), launched in 2004 and since updated, provides the following industry areas of emphasis:

- Landscaping

- Oil and gas field services

- Residential building construction

- Commercial and institution building construction

- Highway, street, and bridge construction

Notice how the overwhelming emphasis of this program seems to be on construction activities, contrary to the usual stereotype. The landscaping target may be surprising, but a large number of chemicals are used in this profession. Manufacturing is not ignored by OSHA, however.

Specially targeted sectors in the manufacturing area, with four-digit SIC codes, have most recently been designated:

- Plastic products (3089)

- Sheet metalwork (3444)

- Fabricated structural metal (3441)

- Metal stampings (3469)

- Fabricated metal products (3499)

- Motor vehicle parts (3714)

- Construction machinery (3431)

- Shipbuilding and repair (3731)[63]

The National Emphasis Program (NEP) from time to time designates certain sectors or hazards for special agency scrutiny. As of 2016, these include the following:

COMBUSTIBLE DUST

OSHA Instruction CPL 03-00-008—National Emphasis Program on Combustible Dust (Reissued) (Date: 03/11/2008)

FEDERAL AGENCIES

OSHA Notice FAP 01 15-01—Federal Agency Targeting Inspection Program for 2015 (FEDTARG15) (Date: 04/28/2015)

HAZARDOUS MACHINERY

OSHA Instruction CPL 03-00-019—National Emphasis Program on Amputations (Date: 08/13/2015)

HEXAVALENT CHROMIUM

OSHA Instruction CPL 02-02-076—National Emphasis Program—Hexavalent Chromium (Date: 02/23/2010)

ISOCYANATES

OSHA Instruction CPL 03-00-017—National Emphasis Program—Occupational Exposure to Isocyanates (Date: 06/20/2013)

LEAD

OSHA Instruction CPL 03-00-009—National Emphasis Program on Lead (Date: 08/14/2008)

PRIMARY METAL INDUSTRIES

OSHA Instruction CPL 03-00-018—National Emphasis Program—Primary Metal Industries (Date: 10/20/2014)

PROCESS SAFETY MANAGEMENT

OSHA Instruction CPL 03-00-014—PSM Covered Chemical Facilities National Emphasis Program (Date:11/29/2011)

OSHA Instruction CPL 03-00-010—Petroleum Refinery Process Safety Management National Emphasis Program (Date: 08/18/2009) [PDF*]

Note: This NEP is still in effect, but Federal inspections of all refineries have been completed and there are no inspections currently programmed. However, this NEP may still provide guidance for State Plan Offices which program refinery inspections within their jurisdictions.

SHIPBREAKING

OSHA Instruction CPL 03-00-020—National Emphasis Program on Shipbreaking (Date: 03/07/2016)

SILICA

OSHA Instruction CPL 03-00-007—National Emphasis Program on Crystalline Silica (Date: 01/24/2008)

TRENCHING & EXCAVATION

OSHA Instruction CPL 02-00-069—Special Emphasis Program on Trenching and Excavation (Date: 9/19/1985)

6.6 Communicating and Enforcing Company Rules

Many, arguably even most, accidents are due to human negligence, often involving an act that is contrary to company policy. Merely claiming a company policy, however, is not enough, for OSHA does not look very favorably upon this defense. For employers to plead employee misconduct as a defense to an OSHA citation, the company must first demonstrate three things:

- First, of course, is to prove the existence of such rules.[64]

- Second, an employer must prove that these rules were effectively communicated to the employees. Proof can include written instructions, evidence of required attendance at education sessions, the curriculum of training programs, and other forms that should be documented.[65]

- Third, many companies that can demonstrate the above two principles fall short on the third, namely, that there should be evidence the policies are effectively enforced.[66] For this, evidence of disciplinary action taken against infractions of the rules, though not necessarily the precise rule that would have prevented the accident under investigation, is necessary. The closer to the actual circumstance, of course, the more that proof of active company enforcement is dispositive.[67]

If the above three principles can all be demonstrated, they constitute a reasonable defense to charges of violating the regulations, even in cases of death or serious injury.

Note that this defense is not limited to the misconduct of a low-ranking employee. Misconduct of a supervisor, although it may suggest inadequate company policy and direction, can also be shown as an isolated and personal failing. According to an appellate court, the proper focus of a court is on the effectiveness of the employer's implementation of his safety program and not on whether the unforeseeable conduct was by an employee or supervisory personnel.[68]

6.7 Warrantless Inspections: The Barlow Case

Litigants have challenged OSHA's constitutionality on virtually every conceivable grounds from the First Amendment to the Fourteenth.[69] The one case that has succeeded has led to the requirement of a search warrant, if demanded, for OSHA inspectors.

The Supreme Court in *Marshall v. Barlow's Inc.*[70] decided that the Fourth Amendment to the Constitution, providing for search warrants, was applicable to OSHA, thereby declaring unconstitutional Section 8(a) of the act, in which Congress had authorized warrantless searches.[71]

While the Court held that OSHA inspectors are required to obtain search warrants if denied entry to inspect, it added that OSHA must meet only a very minimal probable cause requirement under the Fourth Amendment in order to obtain them. As Justice White explained,

Probable cause in the criminal sense is not required. For purposes of an administrative search such as this, probable cause justifying the issuance of a warrant may be based not only on specific evidence of an existing violation but also on a showing that "reasonable legislative or administrative standards for conducting an . . . inspection are satisfied with respect to a particular [establishment]."[72]

Moreover, if so many companies demanded warrants that the inspection program was seriously impaired, the Court indicated it might reconsider its ruling. This ironically would make enjoyment of a constitutional right partly contingent on few attempting to exercise it. It is therefore not surprising that commentators, both liberals and conservatives, were critical of the decision. Conservative columnist James J. Kilpatrick declared flatly,

> If the Supreme Court's decision in the Barlow case was a "great victory," as Congressman George Hansen proclaims it, let us ask heaven to protect us from another such victory anytime soon.[73]

As a practical matter, there are relatively few denials of entry to OSHA, and hence OSHA requests few search warrants from the courts. In most circumstances, companies know it is not a good idea to demand a warrant from an OSHA inspector.

7.0 Recordkeeping

For an agency that seems grounded in practical workplace realities, OSHA's regulations increasingly emphasize recordkeeping and paperwork requirements. Moreover, recent OSHA enforcement efforts have been directed heavily toward paperwork violations.

7.1 Accident Reports

Any workplace accident requiring treatment or resulting in lost work time must be recorded within six working days on an OSHA Form 300. This is officially entitled the Log and Summary of Recordable Occupational Injuries and Illnesses, although no one uses that longer term. This document is supposed to provide insight into accident types and causes for both the company and OSHA inspectors. It must be retained for five years. Criminal penalties apply to any "knowing false representation" on these and other required records.[74]

There is a newer document, Form 300A, which provides additional information and supposedly makes it easier for employers to calculate injury incidence rates.

A third document is the OSHA Form 301, which describes in detail the nature of each of the recorded accidents. All the supporting information does not have to be on this one form, provided that the material is available in the file. This form is officially called the Supplementary Record of Occupational Injuries and Illnesses.

A fourth required document is the Annual Summary of accidents and illnesses, statistics based on the Form 300 data. This summary must be signed by a responsible corporate official and posted in some conspicuous place by the following first day of February each year.[75]

7.2 Monitoring and Medical Records

OSHA's health standards increasingly contain provisions calling for medical records, monitoring of pollution, and other information. Safety, as well as health standards, may also require periodic inspections of workplaces or equipment, and these inspections must be recorded. These medical and exposure records must be retained for a staggering 30 years. A company going out of business or liquidating must transfer these records to NIOSH.[76]

For example, the OSHA noise standards mandate baseline and periodic hearing tests,[77] the lead standard requires measuring of blood-lead levels and other data that can be the basis for removal from the workplace until the levels go down, and the ionizing radiation regulation requires careful recording of exposure and absorption information.

A host of safety (and some health) regulations requires (1) written safety programs, (2) specified training, (3) documented routine inspections, or combinations of all three.

There is no clear pattern to these requirements; they must be checked separately for each regulation. For example, the safety standard on derricks does not require the first but does require the second and third, while cranes require only the third.[78] Some safety standards, such as fire protection, lockout/tagout, process safety management, and employee alarms, require all three.[79] The health standards tend to require all three as well, including those for bloodborne pathogens and for hazard communications.[80]

OSHA has increasingly levied substantial fines for failure to comply with these recordkeeping regulations. For example, a Texas steelmaker was fined $1.7 million, much of it for "purposefully" not recording workplace injuries and illnesses.[81]

7.3 Hazard Communication

The OSHA hazard communication (hazcom) program, which is described more fully later in this chapter, requires companies making or using hazardous chemicals to provide information to their workers on possible exposure risks. The program provides for these measures:

1. Labeling of toxic chemicals;

2. Warning signs and posters;

3. Material safety data sheets (MSDSs) on hazardous chemicals;

4. A written policy setting forth the company's handling of issues under the hazcom program; and

5. A list of hazardous chemicals on the premises.[82]

7.4 Access to Records

Employees and their designated legal or union representatives have the right to obtain access to their records within 15 working days. They may not be charged for duplication or other costs. Former employees are also given this access.

There are certain limited exceptions to disclosure for highly sensitive personal information, such as psychiatric evaluation, terminal illness, and confidential informants. Otherwise the view is that even the most secret chemical formulas and business information must be revealed to the employees or former employees if they are relevant to exposure and toxicity. This could be a godsend for industrial espionage, but so far there have been few claims that this is a practical problem.

OSHA inspectors also have access to these records. From time to time some company challenges this access as a violation of the Fourth Amendment, but an inspector has little difficulty in obtaining a search warrant.

7.5 Programmatic Standards

OSHA is giving more attention to programmatic standards. Those are standards that deal with broad categories of occupational problems rather than a special chemical or safety issue. The controversial ergonomics proposed standard was such an example. Moreover, it was based on companies providing evidence that they have set up a specific program rather than having OSHA dictate what the detailed content of that program should be. Although these are perhaps not recordkeeping in the absolute sense, their reliance on paperwork and documentation merits their mention in this recordkeeping section.

8.0 Refusal to Work and Whistle-Blowing

Employees have a right to refuse to work when they beieve conditions are unsafe. OSHA rules protect them from discrimination based on this refusal. And if employees see unsafe or unhealthy workplace conditions, they have a right to report them to OSHA without fear of reprisals or discrimination.

8.1 Refusal to Work

OSHA has ruled, and the Supreme Court has unanimously upheld, the OSHA principle that workers have the right to refuse to work in the face of serious injury or death.[83] The leading case was a simple one. Two workers refused to go on some wire mesh screens through which several workers had fallen partway and, two weeks before, another worker had fallen to his death. When reprimanded, the workers complained to OSHA. The Supreme Court in the *Whirlpool* case had no difficulty in finding that the workers had been improperly discriminated against by their employer in this case.

How a court would rule in less glaring circumstances is harder to predict. Interestingly, there has not been a swarm of such cases in the decades since this decision, despite dire predictions of wholesale refusal and consequent litigation.

8.2 Protection of Whistle-Blowing

If a worker is fired or disciplined for complaining to governmental officials about unsafe work conditions, he has a legal remedy under the OSH Act for restoration of his job or loss of pay.[84] Similar provisions, administered also by OSHA's "11(c)" staff, have been inserted into over 20 other federal statutes, including EPA's Emergency Planning and Community Right-to-Know Act in the Superfund legislation, as well as ones that have little to do with environmental or occupational protection.[85]

Congress assumed that the employees in a given workplace would be best acquainted with the hazards there. It therefore statutorily encouraged prompt OSHA response to worker complaints of violations.[86] Since this system could be undermined if employers penalized complaining employees, the act in Section 11(c) provides sanctions against such retaliation or discrimination: "No person may discharge or in any manner discriminate against any employee because such employee has filed any complaint or instituted or caused to be instituted any proceeding under or related to this Act or has testified or is about to testify in any such proceeding or because of the exercise by such employee on behalf of himself or others of any right afforded by this Act."[87]

If discrimination occurs, particularly if an employee is fired, a special OSHA team intervenes to obtain reinstatement, back wages, or—if return to the company is undesirable—a cash settlement for the worker. If agreement cannot be reached, the agency resorts to litigation.

This entire system has not worked quite as expected. First, worker complaints have surprisingly not been a very fruitful source of health and safety information. Far too many of the complaints came in bunches, coinciding with labor disputes in a particular plant.[88] OSHA therefore finally had to abandon its policy of trying to investigate every single complaint.[89]

Second, the Section 11(c) process has worked slowly and uncertainly, so even though an employee may receive vindication, the months (or even years) of delay and anguish are a strong disincentive for workers to report hazards.

Third, it is often difficult to determine whether a malcontented worker was fired for informing OSHA or for a number of other issues which might cloud the employer–employee relationship. Does the complaint have to be the sole cause of dismissal or discrimination, or can some (fairly arbitrary) allocation be made?

Fourth, there is continuing controversy over whether 11(c) should protect workers complaining of hazards to those other than OSHA, such as to newspapers or other governmental authorities, even if the direct or indirect result is an OSHA inspection.

In the famous Kepone tragedy of 1975, in Virginia an employee complained of hazardous chemicals to his supervisor, was fired, and only then went to OSHA. Not only was he declared unprotected by the act, but his complaint, no longer a worker complaint, was not even investigated at the time. Although agency officials have sworn not to repeat that mistake, the issue of what triggers 11(c) protection—a complaint of unsafe workplace conditions or reporting that matter to OSHA—can be a confusing one.

A related current issue is whether an employee who reports a hazard to the press, whose ensuing publicity triggers an OSHA investigation, is protected by 11(c). In one notable instance, OSHA regional officials decided in favor of the worker and won the subsequent litigation in federal district court. The solicitor of labor, however, disagreed and attempted to withdraw the agency from a winning position.[90]

Still, in another case, a Brooklyn bookstore worker supposedly dismissed for whistle-blowing was reinstated with an $18,000 cash settlement within only four months. More typical was an airline worker in Puerto Rico who took four years to litigate through the district court and court of appeals before being awarded a somewhat larger amount.[91] So a worker can never really be sure how he might fare if he does complain.

In FY 2012 a record total of 2,787 whistle-blower complaints were filed with OSHA. Many of those, however, concerned not occupational issues but 22 statutes ranging from corporate financial irregularities under Sarbanes-Oxley (SOX) to the newly enacted Affordable Care Law (ObamaCare). So, from an occupational point of view, these numbers have become increasingly meaningless.[92] According to earlier OSHA investigators, about 20 percent had some merit.[93]

9.0 Federal and State Employees

The exclusion of federal and state employees in the Act has been the topic of much discussion and debate.

9.1 Federal Agencies

Federal employees are not covered directly by OSHA, at least not to the extent that federal agencies are subject to fines and other penalties. However, the presumption was that the agencies would follow OSHA regulations in implementing their own programs. Section 19 of the OSH Act designates the responsibility for providing safe and healthful working conditions to the head of each agency. A series of presidential executive orders has emphasized that this role should be taken seriously. Nevertheless, many commentators feel the individual agencies' programs are inadequate and inconsistent.

In 1980 the leading presidential executive order[94] was issued, broadening the responsibility of federal agencies for protecting their workers, expanding employee participation in health and safety programs, and designating circumstances under which OSHA will inspect federal facilities. In the operation of their internal OSHA programs, agency heads have to meet requirements of basic program elements issued by the Department of Labor and comply with OSHA standards for the private sector unless they can justify alternatives.

Contrary to common belief, the U.S. Postal Service, as a quasi-private corporation, is no longer immune to OSHA penalties. For example, one post office in Ohio was assessed $225,000 in fines, including several citations for "willful" violations.[95]

9.2 State Employees

The OSH Act excludes the employees of state governments. However, in those states that have their own OSHA programs, the majority also cover their own state and local employees. Some labor unions believe this exclusion of state workers is one of the most serious gaps in the OSH Act, and several congressional bills have sought in vain to remedy the perceived omission. In light of Supreme Court decisions, however, such bills even if enacted might not be constitutional as "unfunded mandates" under the Tenth Amendment.[96]

10.0 State OSHA Programs

The federal OSHA program was intended by many legislators and businesses only to fill the gaps where state programs were lacking. The states were to be the primary regulatory control. It has not happened that way, of course, but approximately two dozen state programs are still important.[97]

10.1 Concept

The OSH Act requires OSHA to encourage the states to develop and operate their own job safety and health programs, which must be "at least as effective as" the federal program.[98] Until effective state programs were approved, federal enforcement of standards promulgated by OSHA preempted state enforcement[99] and continue to do so where state laws have major gaps. Conversely, state laws and regulations remain in effect when no federal standard exists.

Before approving a submitted state plan, OSHA must make certain that the state can meet criteria established in the act.[100] Once a plan is in effect, the secretary may exercise "authority . . . until he determines, on the basis of actual operations under the State plan, that the criteria set forth are being applied."[101] But he cannot make such a determination for three years after the plan's approval. OSHA may continue to evaluate the state's performance in carrying out the program even after a state plan has been approved. If a state fails to comply, the approval can be withdrawn, but only after the agency has given due notice and opportunity for a hearing.

10.2 Critiques

The program has not developed as anticipated into an essentially state-oriented system, although almost half the states have their own system.

Organized labor has never liked the state concept, both because of its poor experience with state enforcement in the past and because it realized that its strength could more easily be exercised in one location—Washington, D.C.—than in all 50 states and the territorial capitals, many of which are traditionally hostile to labor unions. This has meant, ironically, that some of the better state programs, in areas where unions had the most influence, were among the first rejected by state legislators under strong union pressure.

Industry has cooled to the local concept because it requires multistate companies to contend with a variety of state laws and regulations instead of a uniform federal plan. Furthermore, at least in the past, state OSHAs have often been considerably larger than the local federal force, so there could be more inspections, if much lower average fines.

It was therefore never clear what incentive a state had to maintain its own program since a governor could always terminate his state's plan and save the budgetary expenses, knowing that the federal government would take up the slack. California's Governor Deukmejian, for example, came to this conclusion in 1987 and terminated the well-regarded state Cal-OSHA program. However, the idea did not stick; California's state program was soon reestablished, and, surprisingly, the notion did not spread.

Organized labor and industry are not alone in their criticism of the state programs. Health research organizations, OSHA's own national advisory committee, and some of the states themselves have also voiced disapproval of the state program policy. Ineffective operations at the state level, disparity in federal funding, and the lack of the necessary research capability are just a few of the criticisms lodged.[102]

There is some defense of state control, however. "To the extent that local control increases the responsiveness of programs to the specific needs of people in that area, this [a state plan] is a potentially good policy."[103] But reevaluation and revision will be necessary in the next several years if OSHA's policy for state programs is to be accepted by all the factions involved.

11.0 Consultation

Employers subject to OSHA regulation, particularly small employers, would benefit from on-site consultation to determine what must be done to bring their workplaces into compliance with the requirements of the OSH Act. This was particularly true during the agency's formative years, but the need is a continuing one. Although OSHA's manpower and resources are limited, this assistance, where rendered, should be free from citations or penalties.

In a recent year the agency recorded 31,500 consultative visits to smaller businesses, and almost 900 (mostly larger) companies were recognized in the Safety and Health Achievement Recognition Program.[104]

As in so many other areas of OSHA regulation, there has been much controversy surrounding the consultation process. Union leaders have always feared that OSHA could become merely a toothless educational institution rather than one with effective enforcement. But Section 21(c) of the act does mandate consultation with employers and employees "as to effective means of preventing occupational injuries and illnesses."[105]

11.1 Education

Along with the consultation provisions, the statute provides for "programs for the education and training of employers and employees in the recognition, avoidance, and prevention of unsafe or unhealthful working conditions in employments covered" by the act.[106] OSHA produces brochures and films to educate employees about possible hazards in their workplaces. But there are problems at every stage of the information process, from generation to utilization.

Back in 1979, OSHA began experimenting with a New Directions Training and Education Program, which made available millions in grants to support the development and strengthening of occupational safety and health competence in business, employee, and educational organizations. This program supported a broad range of activities, such as training in hazard identification and control, workplace risk assessment, medical screening and recordkeeping, and liaison work with OSHA, NIOSH, and other agencies. "The goal of the program was to allow unions and other groups to become financially self-sufficient in supporting comprehensive health and safety programs."[107] This program, criticized by some as a payoff to constituent groups, especially labor unions, was a natural target of the budget cutters during the Reagan administration, but the concept of increased consultation has been given even greater emphasis.

There was also a provision that state plans may include on-site consultation with employers and employees to encourage voluntary compliance.[108] The personnel engaged in these activities must be separate from the inspection personnel, and their existence must not detract from the federal enforcement effort. These consultants not only point out violations but also give abatement advice.

11.2 Alliances

Much of OSHA's focus over the past several decades has been in arranging "alliances" with trade associations, businesses, professional groups, and even universities. The present program, initiated in March 2002, attempts to enlist other organizations in the safety fight and also serves to make the public image of OSHA less confrontational. Whether this will result in better workplace safety and health than, say, reviving the near-dead standard-setting effort remains to be seen.

12.0 Overlapping Jurisdiction

There are other agencies involved with statutory responsibilities that affect occupational safety and health in their particular spheres. These agencies indirectly regulate safety and health matters in their attempt to protect public safety.

One example of an overlapping agency is the Department of Transportation and its constituent agencies, such as the Federal Railroad Administration and the Federal Aviation Administration. These agencies promulgate rules concerned with the safety of transportation crews and maintenance personnel as well as the traveling public and consequently overlap similar responsibilities of OSHA.

Section 4(b)(1) of the OSH Act states that when other federal agencies "exercise statutory authority to prescribe or enforce standards or regulations affecting occupational safety or health," the OSH Act will not apply to the working conditions addressed by those standards. Memorandums of understanding (MOUs) between these agencies and OSHA have eliminated much of the earlier conflict.

EPA is the organization that overlaps most frequently with OSHA. When a toxic substance regulation is issued by EPA, OSHA is affected if that substance is one that also appears in the workplace. For instance, both agencies are concerned with pesticides, EPA with the general environmental issues surrounding the pesticides and OSHA with some aspects of the agricultural workers who use them. During the early 1970s, there was a heated interagency conflict over field reentry standards for pesticides (see the chapter on pesticides), a struggle that spilled over into the courts and eventually had to be settled by the White House in EPA's favor.[109] It is hoped that the OSHA–EPA MOU of 1990 and similar such agreements with other agencies will prevent the repetition of such problems.

Thus, although the health regulatory agencies generally function in a well-defined area, overlap does occur. As another example, there are toxic regulations under Section 307 of the Clean Water Act (historically, the Federal Water Pollution Control Act), Section 112 of the Clean Air Act, and under statutes of the Food and Drug Administration (FDA) and the Consumer Product Safety Commission (CPSC). These regulatory agencies realized the need for coordination, particularly when dealing with something as pervasive as toxic substances; back in the Carter administration they combined their efforts into a cross-disciplinary working group called the Interagency Regulatory Liaison Group (IRLG). Although the IRLG was abolished at the beginning of the Reagan administration, the concept of interagency working groups is a good one. The federal agencies involved in regulation should rid themselves of the antagonism and rivalry of the past and cooperate with one another to meet the needs of the public. Unvortunately it has not happened that often.

13.0 OSHRC

The OSH Act established the OSHRC as "an independent quasi-judicial review board"[110] consisting of three members appointed by the president to six-year terms. It is not a part of OSHA or even of the department of labor. Any enforcement actions of OSHA that are challenged must be reviewed and ruled upon by the commission.[111]

13.1 OSHRC Appeal Process

Any failure to challenge a citation within 15 days of issuance automatically results in an action of the OSHRC to uphold the citation. This is much too short a time in practical terms, particularly when involving small, inexperienced businesses, but the limit is not discretionary under the law. This decision by default is "jurisdictional," that the commission lacks authority even to consider an appeal, and it is not subject to review by any other forum, court, or agency. This is patently unfair.

When an employer challenges a citation, the abatement period, or the penalty proposed, the commission then designates a hearing examiner, an administrative law judge, who hears the case; makes a determination to affirm, modify, or vacate the citation or penalty; and reports his finding to the commission.[112] This report becomes final within 30 days unless a commission member requests that the commission itself review it. The employer or agency may then seek a review of the decision in a federal appeals court.

13.2 Limitations of the Commission

One of the major problems with the OSHRC is the issue of its very nature. "The question has arisen of the extent to which the Commission should conduct itself as though it were a court rather than a more traditional administrative agency."[113] The commission cannot look to other independent agencies in the government for a resolution of this problem "because its duties and its legislative history have little in common with the others."[114] It cannot conduct investigations, initiate suits, or prosecute; therefore, it is best understood as an administrative agency with the limited duty of "adjudicating those cases brought before it by employers and employees who seek review of the enforcement actions taken by OSHA and the Secretary of Labor."[115]

Another problem inherent in the organization of the commission is the separation from the president's administration. There has been a question of where the authority of the administration ends and the authority of the commission begins. Because of the autonomous nature of the commission, it cannot always count on the support of the executive agencies. In fact, OSHA has generally ignored commission precedents, and few inspectors are even aware of the commission interpretations on various regulations. That did not appear to change even when a former chairman of the commission, Edwin Foulke (1990–1995), became the head of OSHA a decade later.

14.0 NIOSH

As mentioned earlier, the standard-recommending arm of OSHA is actually in a totally separate government department. This procedure has never worked well, even at best during the late 1970s, and has now ceased to work at all.

14.1 In Theory

Under the OSH Act, the Bureau of Safety and Health Services in the Health Services and Mental Health Administration was restructured to become the National Institute for Occupational Safety and Health (NIOSH) so as to carry out the responsibilities of the Department of Health, Education, and Welfare (now the Department of Health and Human Services, HHS) under the act.[116] For more than four decades NIOSH has reported, illogically, to the Centers for Disease Control, and the two organizations have headquarters in Atlanta, Georgia.

Since mid-1971, NIOSH has claimed the training and research functions of the act, along with its primary function of recommending standards. For this latter task, NIOSH provides recommended standards to OSHA in the form of criteria documents for particular hazards. These are compilations and evaluations of all available relevant information from scientific, medical, and (occasionally) engineering research.

The order of hazards selected for criteria development is determined several years in advance by a NIOSH priority system based on severity of response, population at risk, existence of a current standard, and advice from federal agencies (including OSHA) as well as involved professional groups.[117]

These criteria documents may actually have some value apart from their role in standards making. Even though they do not have the force of law, they are widely distributed to industry, organized labor, universities, and private research groups as a basis to control hazards. The criteria documents may also serve as a "basis for setting international permissible limits for occupational exposures."[118]

14.2 In Practice

To the extent that certain criteria documents may be deficient, as discussed earlier, this expansive role for them among laymen poses a real problem. This problem may unfortunately continue to worsen if NIOSH declines in both funds and morale. Nevertheless, there is arguably some small benefit in having the two organizations separate. NIOSH has on occasion criticized OSHA for regulatory decisions that the former believed were scientifically untenable.

A review of NIOSH criteria projects shows that virtually all date from the 1970s and most still await OSHA action. Almost no new documents have emerged in the past several decades. That is not years—that is decades.

Since OSHA does not react to NIOSH's recommendations, the agency has tried to reinvent itself as a guide to the public. For example, in 2006, the U.S. Chemical Safety and Hazard Investigation Board (CSB) proposed that NIOSH include research on chemical production safety in the National Occupational Research Agenda. This suggestion would focus the organization on ways to prevent, for example, the series of deadly explosions at oil refineries in Texas and elsewhere.[119]

In May 2010, at a joint appearance before the American Industrial Hygiene Association (AIHA), the heads of OSHA and NIOSH, David Michaels and John

Howard, pledged to revitalize the relationship with "an unprecedented level of cooperation."[120] It has been more than three decades since a close working relationship existed between the two agencies, and this would indeed be welcome. However, cynics may note that the previous episode of good feeling did not result in an outpouring of new standards either, and so far neither has this one.[121]

15.0 Hazard Communication Regulation

OSHA's output of health standards has never been impressive. In past years, it has tried three imaginative approaches to get around this bottleneck. The first was the interagency"federal" cancer policy designed to create a template for dealing in an expedited fashion with a number of hazardous chemicals. That was shut down, as mentioned before, by a change in the White House in the 1980s. The second was the wholesale review initiated in 1988 of all the Z-1 list consensus standards—an effort strongly opposed by the unions, was struck down by the courts in the 1990s. The third, characterized by one OSHA official as the agency's most important rulemaking ever, is the hazard communication (hazcom) regulation issued in November 1983.[122]

15.1 Reason for the Regulation

This standard, sometimes known as the "worker right-to-know" rule, provides that hazardous chemicals must be labeled, Material Safety Data Sheets (MSDSs) on hazards must be prepared, and workers and customers should be informed of potential chemical risks.

How could a rule with such far-reaching consequences be issued from the Reagan administration, which so stressed deregulation and deliberately avoided issuing other protective regulations? The answer lies in an almost unprecedented grassroots movement at the state and municipal levels to enact their own "worker right-to-know" laws, which, many businessmen felt, could be a considerable burden on interstate commerce. They therefore lent their support to OSHA in its confrontation with the Office of Management and Budget at the White House. A federal regulation on this subject would arguably preempt the multiplicity of local laws.

The rule was originally presumed to apply only to a few hundred, perhaps a thousand, particularly hazardous chemicals. The individual employers would evaluate the risk and then decide for themselves which products merited coverage. Most employers were unable or unwilling to make such scientific determinations. Within a year or two, this limited program expanded into universal coverage.

15.2 Scope and Components

Published on November 25, 1983, OSHA's Hazard Communication or "Right-to-Know" Standard[123] went into effect two years later, in November 1985, for chemical manufacturers, distributors, and importers, and in May 1994 for manufacturers that use chemicals. It required that employees be provided with information concerning hazardous chemicals through labels, MSDSs, training and education, and lists of hazardous chemicals in each work area. Originally it covered only manufacturing industries classified in SIC codes 20 to 39, but by court order in 1987 it was extended to virtually all employers.[124]

Every employer must assess the toxicity of chemicals it makes, distributes, or uses based on guidelines set forth in the rule. Then it must provide this material downstream to those who purchase the chemicals through MSDSs.[125] The employers are then required to assemble a list of the hazardous materials in the workplace, label all chemicals, provide employees with access to the MSDSs, and provide training and education. While all chemicals must be evaluated, the "communication" provisions apply—in theory—only to those chemicals known to be present in the workplace in such a way as to potentially expose employees to physical or health hazards.

Special provisions apply to the listing of mixtures that constitute health hazards. Each component that is itself hazardous to health and that makes up 1 percent or more of a mixture must be listed. Carcinogens must be listed if present in quantities of 0.1 percent or greater.

The Hazard Communication Standard is a performance-oriented rule. While it states the objectives to be achieved, the specific methods to achieve those objectives are at the discretion of the employer. Thus, in theory, employers have considerable flexibility to design programs suitable for their own workplaces. However, this may mean the employers will be uncertain about how to comply with the standard.

The purpose of labeling is to give employees an immediate warning of hazardous chemicals and a reminder that more detailed information is available. Containers must be labeled with chemical identity, appropriate hazard warnings, and the name and address of the manufacturer. The hazard warnings must be specific, even as to the endangered body organs. For example, if inhalation of a chemical causes lung cancer, the label must specify that and cannot simply say "harmful if inhaled" or even "causes cancer." Pipes and piping systems are exempt from labeling, as are those substances required to be labeled by another federal agency.

MSDSs, used in combination with labels, are the primary tools for transmitting detailed information on hazardous chemicals. An MSDS is a technical document that summarizes the known information about a chemical. Chemical manufacturers and importers must develop an MSDS for each hazardous chemical produced or imported and pass it on to the purchaser at the time of the first shipment. The employer must keep these sheets where employees will have access to them at all times.

The purpose of employee information and training programs is to inform employees of the labels and MSDSs and to make them aware of the actions required to avoid or minimize exposure to hazardous chemicals. The format of these programs is left to the discretion of the individual employer. Training programs must be provided at the time of initial assignment and whenever a new hazard is introduced into the workplace.

15.3 Hazard Evaluation

Chemical manufacturers are required to evaluate all chemicals they sell for potential health and physical hazards to exposed workers. Purchasers of these chemicals may rely on the supplier's determination or may perform their own evaluations.

There are really no specific procedures to follow in determining a hazard. Testing of chemicals is not required, and the extent of the evaluation is left to the manufacturers and importers of hazardous chemicals. However, all available scientific evidence must be identified and considered. A chemical is considered hazardous if it is found so by even a single "valid" study. Chemicals found on the following master lists are automatically deemed hazardous under the standard:

- The International Agency for Research on Cancer monograph;

- The Annual Report on Carcinogens published by the National Toxicology Program;

- OSHA's "Subpart Z" list, found in Title 29 of the Code of Federal Regulations, Part 1910; and

- Threshold Limit Values for Chemical Substances and Physical Agents in the Work Environment, published by the American Conference of Governmental Industrial Hygienists.

If a substance meets any of the health definitions in Appendix A of the standard, it is also to be considered hazardous. The definitions given are for a carcinogen, a corrosive, a chemical that is highly toxic, an irritant, a sensitizer, a chemical that is toxic, and target organ effects.

Appendix B of the standard gives the principal criteria to be applied in complying with the hazard determination requirement. First, animal as well as human data must be evaluated. Second, if a scientific study finds a chemical to be hazardous, the effects must be reported whether or not the manufacturers or importers agree with the findings.

Appendix C of the standard gives a lengthy list of sources that may assist in the evaluation process. The list includes company data from testing and reports on hazards, supplier data, MSDSs or product safety bulletins, scholarly textbooks, and government health publications.

In practice, as noted above, companies have begun requiring MSDSs from manufacturers for all chemicals they purchase, so the evaluation aspect of the standard has become unimportant.

15.4 Trade Secrets

Although there is agreement that there must be a delicate balance between the employee's right to be free of exposure to unknown chemicals and the employer's right to maintain reasonable trade secrets, the exact method of protection has been considerably disputed.

Under the standard, a trade secret is considered to be defined as in the *Restatement of Torts*, that is, something that is not known or used by a competitor. However, as noted above, OSHA had to revise its definition to conform with a court ruling that said that a trade secret may not include information that is readily discoverable through reverse engineering.[126]

Although the trade-secret identity may be omitted from the MSDS, the manufacturer must still disclose the health effects and other properties about the chemical. A chemical's identity must immediately be disclosed to a treating physician or nurse who determines that a medical emergency exists.

In nonemergency situations, any employee can request disclosure of the chemical's identity if he demonstrates through a written statement a need to know the precise chemical name and signs a confidentiality agreement. The standard specifies all purposes that OSHA considers demonstrate a need to know a specific chemical identity.

The standard initially limited this access to health professionals, but in 1985, the U.S. Court of Appeals for the Third Circuit ruled that trade-secret protections must be narrowed greatly, allowing not only health professionals but also workers and their designated representatives (meaning union officials) the same access as long as they follow the required procedures.[127] In response, OSHA issued a final rule on trade secrets in September 1986[128] that narrows the definition of trade secret. It denies protection to chemical identity information that is readily discoverable through reverse engineering. It also permits employees, their collective bargaining representatives, and occupational nurses access to trade-secret information.

Upon request, the employer must either disclose the information or provide written denial to the requester within 30 days. If the request is denied, the matter may be referred to OSHA.

15.5 Federal Preemption Controversy

Several states and labor groups have filed suits challenging state laws that are more protective. New Jersey, for example, has enacted the toughest labeling law in the nation, requiring industry to label all its chemical substances, whether or not they are hazardous, and supply the information to community groups and health officials as well as to workers.

These groups were also concerned that, because the original OSHA standard only covered the manufacturing sector. More than 50 percent of the workers (such as those workers in the agricultural and construction fields) would thus be unprotected, and OSHA did not cover (and still does not) such groups as state employees and consumers. Moreover, they argued that OSHA would be incapable of enforcing worker protection because of the staff cuts made by hostile administrations.

The chemical industry, on the other hand, favored a uniform federal regulation because it believed it would be less costly and easier to comply with one federal rule as opposed to several state and local rules that would often conflict or be confusing.

In October 1985, the U.S. Court of Appeals for the Third Circuit ruled that the federal Hazard Communication Standard does not preempt all sections of New Jersey's right-to-know laws designed to protect workers and the public from chemical exposure—only those that apply to groups the agency's rules covered, which were then only in the manufacturing sector.[129] Thus, while some parts of a state law may be preempted, other provisions may not be.

In September 1986, the same Third Circuit also found that the federal Hazard Communication Standard did not entirely preempt requirements under Pennsylvania's right-to-know act pertaining to worker protection in the manufacturing industry where the state rules relate to public safety generally and for protection of local government officials with police and fire departments. However, five days later, also in September 1986, the U.S. Court of Appeals for the Sixth Circuit ruled that a right-to-know ordinance enacted by the city of Akron, Ohio, is preempted by the federal standard in manufacturing sector workplaces.

In 1992, the Supreme Court came down strongly on the side of preemption. The *Gade v. National Solid Waste Management Association* case, although it involved OSHA's so-called HAZWOPER regulations[130] rather than hazard communication, involved a state law requiring additional training for heavy equipment operators on hazardous waste sites. The high court found that the OSHA regulations preempted the state despite arguments that the federal rules only set a minimum that the state could exceed—the situation in most environmental laws—and the more transparent claim that the state laws had a dual purpose in protecting the public as well as workers.[131]

In 1997 a unanimous federal appeals court, relying on *Gade*, held that the OSHA hazard communication rule preempted California's famous Proposition 65 requirements (the public must be warned of carcinogens and other harmful substances, including buildings).

However, a word of caution—the attitude of the U.S. Supreme Court toward federal preemption in general continues to be confused and contradictory. The high court has tended to limit the claims of federal preemption, whether in drug regulation, pesticides, or tort liability, so beware of situations where federal and state rules—including common law jury decisions—seem to overlap. This is discussed more fully in the pesticides chapter of this book.[132]

16.0 Ergonomics Issues

The ergonomics issue has been one of the few championed by OSHA in recent years. Ironically, when the standard finally emerged, it ran into a buzz saw of hostility that forced OSHA to retreat. Opposition ranged from criticism of it as a defective standard to the concern that ergonomic issues were so highly particular to a given workplace that universal rules made no sense.

16.1 Background

For more than three decades OSHA officials have worked toward developing a standard on ergonomics. The original impetus was a series of reports from Midwest poultry and meatpacking plants that workers were developing "carpal tunnel syndrome" (CTS). This is a condition that develops from repetitive motion of the hand and wrist that irritates the nerve running through a bone channel near the thumb. Because similar conditions can develop from repetitive motion or strain in other parts of the body, such as with "tennis elbow," the malady was relabeled "cumulative trauma syndrome," also conveniently abbreviated CTS, then changed to "repetitive motion syndrome" and so on until the more sweeping term "ergonomics" was adopted.

Along the way, OSHA was hitting offending companies with fines in the millions of dollars, some of the biggest in the agency's history. All of this had to be done under OSHA's "general duty clause," the famous Section 5(a)(1) of the act, because there was no specific standard that addressed this particular condition. With the congressional rejection of OSHA's Ergonomic Standard, OSHA may again fall back to the general duty clause to deal with clear cases of abuse.

16.2 Scope of the Problem

Ergonomics was not a new word or a new concept. It had long been used in Europe to denote arrangements of workers and tools that maximized productivity with a minimum of wasted effort. This was based on, ironically, the American-developed "time and motion studies" in the manufacturing industry a century ago. The "erg" in "ergonomics," after all, is from the Greek word meaning "work." The term also came to be used in furniture and office design with the connotation of comfortable and well laid out.

The workplace collision came when the concept of mass production—that each worker repeat a number of simple steps all day—clashed with the physical irritation that might cause to certain parts of the body. The better companies sought to deal with the problem, though most were concerned with the boredom and carelessness aspects of endless repetition rather than with possible deleterious effects on the body. The remedies, however, tended to be very specific to each work-site or even each job. So how could a general standard be developed?

A very different problem was raised for OSHA priorities. Considering the host of unregulated chemicals, life-threatening workplace hazards, and a pathetically slow agency pace for dealing with them, is this where OSHA should be putting its priorities for at least a decade?

Congress did not think so and for a number of years put a "rider" on OSHA's appropriation bills that such an omnibus ergonomic standard should not be developed. Because of a congressional slipup, however, and the confusion in the year right before the 2000 presidential elections, OSHA was able to slide out a proposal in November 2000, due to take effect just days before the new president and Congress took office and could do anything about it. Once in effect, it was legally much more difficult to overturn it, except for denying appropriations for enforcement, and a closely divided House and Senate had more pressing issues.[133]

16.3 Scope of the Standard

Since the ergonomics standard was finally overturned by Congress, it might seem pointless to note how the regulation was intended to work. However, the ergonomics issue itself has not gone away; the general duty clause may still be invoked, and companies have to deal with it quite apart from OSHA.

The 2000 standard was designed to reduce the incidence of musculoskeletal disorders (MSDs) by requiring that companies establish programs to prevent them. In other words, the standard is not prescriptive but procedural.

The standard applied to all general industry workplaces under OSHA but not, for technical legal reasons, to the construction, maritime, agricultural, or most railroad operations. They were eventually supposed to have their own standards once the legal steps were completed. Being subject to the standard, however, did not mean that it automatically applies in its entirety. Some actions have to be taken, and others need occur only after an action trigger. The trigger was, in Western parlance, a hair trigger that would go off very easily. Therefore, most workplaces expected to fall under its provision sooner rather than later.

Certain specified initial actions had to be taken by every employer: every employee must be given, first, basic information about MSDs, including symptoms and reporting obligations; second, a summary of the requirements of the act; and, third, a written notice in a conspicuous place or by electronic communication.

An action trigger occurs when an employee reports a work-related MSD that rises above a certain threshold, namely, when (1) it requires days away from work, restricted work, or medical treatment beyond first aid; or (2) the symptoms last for more than seven consecutive days. The trigger is then met if the employee's job "routinely involves, on one or more days a week, exposure to one or more relevant risk factors at the levels described in the Basic Screening Tool in Table W-1." In making this determination an employer could seek assistance from a health care professional, who plays a key role in implementation of the subsequent program.

The enormous OSHA attention devoted to developing this standard was, in this author's opinion, not worth the diversion from more serious health standards. However, since the failure of the standard-setting process was due to lack of will and not resources, arguably there was no real diversion. Since it is already developed now, it was a test of the Obama administration whether we would see the "Son of Ergonomics" emerge, and it did not. It is safe to predict that it will not emerge in the next decade either.

17.0 Legislation

The OSH Act has remained virtually untouched since its passage in 1970. With the inauguration of a Democratic president, Bill Clinton, in 1993 and Democratic control of both houses of Congress, the expectation was that the labor unions would secure the passage of the first significant revisions in the law.

Under the circumstances, the proposed legislation was surprisingly innocuous. It included verbose and often unnecessary sections on enforcement, refusal to work, and other issues. Among them was a seemingly innocuous section providing for labor–management safety committees in the workplace. Both employers and employees have found these committees quite useful, but some manufacturers' organizations criticized the language as forcing a much greater role for labor unions.

With the Republican election victories in the House and Senate in late 1994, not only did these Democratic legislative plans collapse, but the victors prepared their own onslaught on the OSH Act. To the surprise of many, the draconian Republican plans to curtail or even eliminate OSHA got no further than the previous Democratic plans to expand it. "Organized labor counted its victories in this year's Congress by the number of bills defeated rather than enacted."[134]

Congressional oversight has been most intense regarding OSHA's proposed ergonomics standard back in 2000. As discussed above, Congress used the appropriations process to order the agency not to issue the standard. The Clinton administration eventually refused to sign the legislation that included these prohibitions on the eve of the 2000 presidential elections. However, legislation was also introduced to direct OSHA to encourage safer medical needles, give small businesses more input into agency regulatory proceedings, bar home office inspections, and (signed into law) expand federal compensation for radiation-related exposure.[135]

With the election of the Democratic presidential candidate in 2008 and overwhelming Democratic majorities in both House and Senate during the first two years of the first Obama administration, one would have perhaps expected that long pent-up plans for legislative strengthening of OSHA would finally occur. However, as I predicted then, "that is unlikely to happen. Congress is already swamped with some of the most ambitious bills in history. . . . In this heated atmosphere, OSHA enjoys no priority."

Part of the reason is the major change in the labor unions, traditionally OSHA's strongest supporters. Although the Democrats are heavily indebted to the labor unions for their electoral role, that no longer means what it used to. The steel workers, manufacturing crafts, and other OSHA-related guilds have steadily declined. The unions in the ascent are teachers' unions and government employees, and they have never cared much about OSHA.

With the Republican "shellacking" of the Obama administration in the later congressional elections, and a stumbling economy preoccupying political leaders of both parties, there was little interest in legislative changes in the OSHA law.

So barring some really major industrial accident that fans the embers of legislative reform, perhaps toward more criminalization, or an unlikely but barely possible concerted push for restoration of OSHA's convoluted ergonomics standard, the OSHA law that will exist two years or even two decades from now will probably be little changed from the one that exists today.

Notes

¹ "Report Card on Government Agencies," AP, Feb. 2, 1999. Nevertheless, in another study, OSHA tied with the Internal Revenue Service for the lowest ranking among federal agencies in terms of "customer approval." University of Michigan Business School, "American Customer Satisfaction Report," Dec. 15, 1999. Not everything has improved. A detailed critique of OSHA prepared by an outgoing senior official a quarter century ago could regrettably be reissued today with relatively few changes. *See* "Report on OSHA: Regulatory and Administrative Efforts to Protect Industrial Health," January 1977, 108 pp., by the author of this chapter.

² OSHA, "Commonly Used Statistics," webpage, June 2013.

³ To prevent this overlap from causing jurisdictional confusion, the two agencies developed a Memorandum of Understanding (MOU) in 1990 to delineate and coordinate their respective activities. OSHA-EPA MOU, Nov. 23, 1990.

⁴ Department of Labor Budget for FY2009. NIOSH, in the Department of Health and Human Services, receives $326 million. These numbers, as well as the small amount for the quasi-judiciary OSH Review Commission, an independent agency, should really be added together to give the total picture of federal resources devoted to occupational safety and health, comparable to the effort for EPA where all these functions are consolidated in one organization and one budget.

⁵ David Michaels, *Doubt Is Their Product: How Industry's Assault on Science Threatens Your Health* (Oxford: Oxford University Press, 2008).

⁶ In the 15-month interval between Henshaw and Foulke, a DAS, Jonathan Snare, a Texas lawyer, served as acting assistant secretary.

⁷ The official statistics are from OSHA, at www.osha.gov.

⁸ OSHA, "Enforcement—Ensuring Safe and Healthy Workplaces," updated Dec. 19, 2008.

⁹ In 2015 there were 35,820 federal inspections, plus another 43,471 inspections by state-run OSHA programs.

¹⁰ Occupational Safety and Health Act of 1970, PL 91-596, 84 Stat. 1590.

¹¹ This lack of change could obviously also be considered a negative factor, but a comparison with some of EPA's ponderously detailed legislation shows the benefits of keeping the basic statute simple. OSHA annual appropriations legislation, however, has been modified several times to restrict OSHA authority over small businesses, farming, hunting, and other subjects.

¹² OSH Act § 6(b)(5), emphasis added.

¹³ I'm reconsidering my own position on this point. While the relatively sleek format of the OSHA certainly makes it easier to administer and is vastly preferable to the 2000-page monstrosities that Congress has lately been enacting that no one has time to read before passage, the delegation of sweeping powers from the legislative branch to the myriad faceless bureaucrats in executive branch agencies raises serious policy and constitutional concerns. See, for example, Philip Hamburger, *Is Administrative Law Unlawful?* (Chicago: University of Chicago Press, 2014).

¹⁴ This issue will be discussed in detail in section 4.6 of this chapter.

¹⁵ Clean Air Act § 112, 42 U.S.C. § 1857, the National Emission Standards for Hazardous Air Pollutants (NESHAP).

¹⁶ OSH Act § 4(a)–4(b)(2).

¹⁷ OSH Act § 3(5). Congress's annual appropriations language has excluded several "peripheral" categories of employers in the past few years.

¹⁸ 37 FR 929, Jan. 21, 1972, codified at 29 C.F.R. § 1975.

¹⁹ EPA learned this lesson back in 1984 when Deputy Administrator James Barnes quite properly deferred to OSHA on certain asbestos workplace matters. Congressional critics, who believed OSHA would not treat the matter seriously or competently, raised such furor that EPA retained jurisdiction. Even earlier,

in 1973, OSHA and EPA had an acrimonious dispute over which agency should have primary jurisdiction over protecting farm workers from pesticides. EPA won.

[20] The Mine Safety and Health Act of 1978, as amended most recently in 2006. See the official webpage for the agency at www.msha.gov and the article "Mine Safety and Health Administration" in Wikipedia.

[21] Richard Fairfax, director of the Office of Compliance Programs, Opinion letter to CSC Credit Services of Houston, Texas, November 15, 1999. Lest one think this was merely a hasty OSHA response, note that the company's request for an opinion was submitted in August 1997, 27 months before.

[22] Jenny Krese, director of the association's employment policy, BNA, *OSHA Reporter*, January 6, 2000, p. 5.

[23] On elementary questions such as this you may want to note the online Kindle book by Mark Moran, *The OSHA Answer Book*, 10th ed., 2015.

[24] Representative Pete Hoekstra (R-Mich.), chairman of the House Oversight and Investigations Subcommittee of the House Education and Workforce Committee, *id.*, January 13, 2000, p. 22.

[25] These consensus standards are discussed below in sections 3.4 and 4.1 of this chapter.

[26] *AFL-CIO v. OSHA*, 965 F.2d 962 (11th Cir. 1992).

[27] Statement of Basil Whiting, deputy assistant secretary of labor for OSHA, before the Committee on Labor and Human Resources, U.S. Senate, Mar. 21, 1980, pp. 5–6.

[28] For the legislative history of the act, *see especially* the Conference Report 91-1765 of Dec. 16, 1970, as well as H.R. 91-1291 and S.R. 91-1282.

[29] *See Marshall v. Barlow's Inc.*, 436 U.S. 307 (1978), which will be discussed later in this chapter.

[30] 39 FR 23502, June 27, 1974.

[31] 29 C.F.R. § 1910.101.

[32] Since the 6(a) process ended in April 1972, the standards promulgated thereunder cannot be modified or revised without going through the notice and comment administrative procedures under Section 6(b).

[33] *See, e.g.*, the OSHA press release of June 19, 1998: "OSHA Eliminates Over 1,000 Pages of Regulations to Save Employers Money, Reduce Paperwork, and Maintain Protection."

[34] 5 U.S.C. § 553 *et seq.*

[35] NIOSH criteria documents vary considerably in quality, depending in part on whom they were subcontracted to, but another problem is that too often they are insufficiently discriminating in evaluating questionable studies. That is, one scientific study is regarded as good as any other study, without regard to the quality of the data or the validity of the protocols. Of course, another factor in OSHA's attitude just might be the "not invented here" syndrome. This is discussed in detail in section 14 of this chapter.

[36] This meager number of chemicals does *not* reflect OSHA's scientific judgment that the other candidates are unworthy or that the agency has sharply different priorities, although these may be partial factors. More important reasons are poor leadership, technical inexperience, and a bit of politics.

[37] OSH Act § 6(c)(1).

[38] OSH Act § 5(a)(1); 29 U.S.C. § 654(a)(1).

[39] This is exemplified by *Phelps Dodge Corporation* (OSHRC Final Order, 1980), 9 OSHC 1222, which found no violation of the act to expose workers to "massive amounts of sulphur dioxide for short periods of time" since there was no maximum ceiling value in the standard and the employer was complying with the eight-hour average value required in the specific sulfur dioxide regulation. The citation for violation of § 5(a)(1) was therefore vacated.

[40] *International Union, UAW v. General Dynamics Land System Division*, 815 F.2d 1570, 13 OSHC 1201 (CADC 1988). The court held that employer's knowledge was the crucial element; if he knew that the OSHA standard was not adequate to protect workers from a hazard, he could not claim he was maintaining a safe workplace within the meaning of § 5(a)(1), even if he were adhering to a standard he knew was outmoded. The court thereby dismissed the argument that the employer would not know what is legally expected of him; he was expected to maintain a safe workplace, specific regulations notwithstanding.

There was no specific provision in the statute that prevented a general duty citation when a specific standard existed. Note, however, that no other court has since used this rationale.

41 This account of the behind-the-scenes machinations is based on this author's personal discussions with the late Congressman William Steiger (R-Wis.), a principal author of the act, and Judge Lawrence Silberman, now of the Court of Appeals for the District of Columbia Circuit, who was then solicitor of labor. The legislative history is relatively unhelpful on this subject. *See, e.g.,* hearings before the Select Subcommittee on Labor, Committee on Education and Labor, "Occupational Safety and Health Act of 1969," 2 vols., 1969.

42 499 F.2d 467, 1 OSHC 1631 (D.C. Cir., 1974).

43 1 OSHC 1631 at 1639.

44 509 F.2d 1301, 2 OSHC 1496 (2nd Cir., 1975), *cert. den.* 421 U.S. 922.

45 509 F.2d at 1309, 2 OSHC at 1502 (2nd Cir., 1975).

46 *See, e.g.,* the conclusions of the National Academy of Sciences report, "Government Regulation of Chemicals in the Environment," 1975.

47 561 F.2d 82, 5 OSHC 1970 (7th Cir., 1977). The OSHRC decisions on *Turner* and the related *Continental Can* case can be found at 4 OSHC 1554 (1976) and 4 OSHC 1541 (1976), respectively.

48 5 OSHC 1790 at 1791.

49 692 F.2d 641, 10 OSHC 2169 (1982).

50 Engineering controls are those that reduce the sound intensity at the source of that noise. This is achieved by insulation of the machine, by substituting quieter machines and processes, or by isolating the machine or its operator. Administrative controls attempt to reduce workers' exposure to excess noise through use of variable work schedules, variable assignments, or limiting machine use. Personal protective equipment includes such devices as earplugs and ear muffs provided by the employer and fitted to individual workers.

51 452 U.S. 490, 101 S. Ct. 2478, 9 OSHC 1913 (June 17, 1981). In this case, representatives of the cotton dust industry challenged proposed regulations limiting permissible exposure levels to cotton dust. Section 6(b)(5) of the act requires OSHA to "set the standard which most adequately assures, to the extent feasible . . . that no employee will suffer material impairment of health. . . ." The industry contended that OSHA had not shown that the proposed standards were economically feasible. However, the Supreme Court upheld the cotton dust regulations, holding that the "plain meaning of the word 'feasible' is capable of being done, executed, or effected" and that a cost-benefit analysis by OSHA is not required.

52 Well, not quite nothing. In 2010 OSHA did issue a Worker Alert to warn against exposure to diacetyl, but that's pretty close to nothing.

53 Susan Podziba, "Safety Starts at the Top," *New York Times,* June 12, 2008; OSHA Release, "OSHA Issues Final Rule on Cranes and Derricks in Construction," July 28, 2010.

54 OSH Act § 7(b)(6)(A).

55 *Id.*

56 E. Klein, Variances, in *Proceedings of the Occupational Health and Safety Regulations Seminar* (Washington, D.C.: Government Institutes, 1978), p. 74.

57 OSH Act Section 17(f0).

58 *See* a later section in this chapter on the Supreme Court's *Barlow's* decision interpreting the Fourth Amendment to the U.S. Constitution.

59 This happened with Kepone in the notorious Hopewell, Virginia, incident in 1975 and with asbestos for many years at a plant in Tyler, Texas.

60 Statement of Lane Kirkland, president, AFL-CIO, before the Senate Committee on Labor and Human Resources on Oversight of the Occupational Safety and Health Act, April 1, 1980.

61 In fiscal year 2012 there were 40,961 inspections. Compare this with 39,167 inspection almost a decade earlier in 2004. Of the latter, 57 percent were in the construction sector, 22 percent in manufacturing, and 1 percent in maritime.

[62] OSHA, "Enforcement—Ensuring Safe and Healthy Workplaces," updated Dec. 19, 2009.

[63] "Top Ten Federal OSHA Targeted SIC Codes," *Manufacturing Sector*, 4th Quarter 1998, OSHA.

[64] *The Carborundum Company* (OSHRC Judge, 1982), 10 OSHC 1979.

[65] *Schnabel Associates, Inc.* (OSHRC Judge, 1982), 10 OSHC 2109. Moreover, employers should retain copies of training curriculum, tests, and other evidence of the educational program, recommends Susan M. Olander, counsel for the Federated Rural Electric Insurance Exchange. BNA, *OSHA Reporter*, Oct. 19, 2000, pp. 933-34.

[66] *Galloway Enterprises, Inc.* (OSAHRC Judge, 1984), 11 OSHC 2071.

[67] *Bethlehem Steel Corporation, Inc.* (OSAHRC Judge, 1985), 12 OSHC 1606. *Dover Electric Company, Inc.* (OSAHRC Judge, 1984), 11 OSHC 2175.

[68] *Brock v. L. E. Myers Company*, 818 F.2d 1270, 13 OSHC 1289 (6th Cir., 1987).

[69] A good, if dated, summary of these early challenges is found in volume I of Walter B. Connolly and David R. Cromwell II, *A Practical Guide to the Occupational Safety and Health Act* (New York: New York Law Journal Press, 1977).

[70] 436 U.S. 307 (1978).

[71] There are non-OSHA circumstances in which warrants are not required, such as federal inspection of liquor dealers, gun dealers, and automobiles near international borders, and in other matters with a long history of federal involvement.

[72] *Marshall v. Barlow's Inc., supra*, quoting *Camara v. Municipal Court*, 387 U.S. 523 at 538 (1967).

[73] *Washington Star*, June 2, 1978.

[74] OSH Act § 17(g).

[75] Recordkeeping requirements are set forth generally in 29 C.F.R. § 1904.

[76] 29 C.F.R. § 1910.20.

[77] OSHA's noise monitoring and recordkeeping requirements for hearing loss and *standard threshold shift* (STS, previously "significant threshold shift") are particularly complex and have been subject to considerable litigation.

[78] 29 C.F.R. § 1910.181, and § 1910.178–179.

[79] 29 C.F.R. §§ 1910.156 *et seq.*, 1910.147, 1910.119, and 1910.165.

[80] 29 C.F.R. § 1910.1030, and 29 C.F.R. § 1200.

[81] BNA, *OSHA Reporter*, Oct. 26. 2000, p. 951.

[82] 29 C.F.R. § 1910.1200.

[83] 29 C.F.R. § 1977.12 (1979); *Whirlpool Corp. v. Marshall*, 445 U.S. 1, 8 OSHC 1001 (1980). This case also stands as a textbook example of when it is unwise to appeal a lower court's ruling.

[84] OSH Act § 11(c), 29 U.S.C. § 660; 29 C.F.R. § 1977.

[85] Title III of the Superfund Amendment and Reauthorization Act of 1986 (SARA). These amendments are designed to "prevent future Bhopals" (the chemical disaster that killed thousands of residents of the city of Bhopal, India) by informing community fire and emergency centers what chemicals a company has on-site.

[86] OSH Act § 8(f)(1).

[87] OSH Act § 11(c)(1).

[88] A contrary union view by Peg Seminario, AFL-CIO's director of health and safety, is that "[h]istorically OSHA inspections conducted as a result of a complaint produce just as significant results in identifying serious violations and uncovering hazards as the general scheduled inspections." Quoted in BNA, *OSHA Reporter*, Mar. 16, 2000, p. 202.

[89] OSHA has nevertheless strengthened the workers' role in the on-site consultation process. 29 C.F.R. § 1908 (December 2000).

[90] *Washington Post*, "About Face Considered in OSHA Suit," Oct. 20, 1982.

91 *Occupational Hazard*, news for Aug. 2, 2006, and Mar. 10, 2006, respectively, at http://www.occupa tionalhazard.com.

92 OSHA webpage, statistics, FY 2012.

93 Based on investigations in FY 2008. OSHA, "Enforcement—Ensuring Safe and Healthy Workplaces," update 19 December 2008.

94 Executive Order 12196, signed Feb. 26, 1980, 45 *FR* 12769, superseding Executive Order 11807 of Sept. 28, 1974.

95 "OSHA Slaps $225K fine on main post office," in *Dayton Daily News*, 19 August 2010.

96 *Printz v. United States*, 521 U.S. 898 (1997); *New York v. United States*, 505 U.S. 144 (1992).

97 There are 21 states and one territory with complete state plans for the private and public sectors and three states and one territory that cover only public employees. Around 10 others have withdrawn their pro- grams over the past few decades, but the number has never been more than half the states.

98 OSH Act §§ 2(b)(11) and 18(c)(2).

99 OSH Act § 18(a).

100 OSH Act § 18(c)(1)–(c)(8).

101 OSH Act § 18(c).

102 Robert Hayden, "Federal and State Rules" in *Proceedings of the Occupational Health and Safety Regulation Seminar* (Washington, D.C.: Government Institutes, 1978), pp. 9–10.

103 Nicholas A. Ashford, *Crisis in the Workplace: Occupational Disease and Inquiry* (Boston: MIT Press, 1976), p. 231.

104 "OSHA: 2005, 2006 and Beyond," in *Occupational Hazards*, news, Jan. 26, 2006, at http://www.occupa tionalhazards.com.

105 OSH Act § 21(c)(2).

106 OSH Act § 21(c)(1).

107 U.S. Department of Labor, "OSHA News," Apr. 12, 1978.

108 29 C.F.R. § 1902.4(c)(2)(xiii).

109 *Florida Peach Growers Assn. v. Dept. of Labor*, 489 F.2d 120 (5th Cir., 1974). To avoid this type of confrontation, in 1976 Congress provided in Section 9 of the Toxic Substances Control Act for detailed coordination procedures to be followed when jurisdictional overlap occurs.

110 Ashford, *Crisis*, p. 145.

111 OSH Act § 12(a)–(b).

112 OSH Act § 12(j).

113 Ashford, *Crisis*, p. 145.

114 *Id.*, pp. 281–82.

115 *Id.*

116 OSH Act § 22(a).

117 John F. Finklea, "The Role of NIOSH in the Standards Process," in *Proceedings of the Occupational Health and Safety Regulation Seminar*, p. 38.

118 *Id.*, p. 39.

119 "CSB Proposes New Ideas for Updated NIOSH Agenda," in *Occupational Hazards*, news, Mar. 7, 2006, at http://www.occupationalhazards.com.

120 AIHA press release, "OSHA, NIOSH Pledge Cooperation on PELs and Other Health Issues," May 26, 2010.

121 This halcyon period in the late 1970s occurred when Eula Bingham was head of OSHA and Jack Finklea headed NIOSH.

122 49 FR 52380, Nov. 25, 1983.

123 48 FR 53280; 29 C.F.R. § 1200.

124 52 FR 31852, Aug. 24, 1987, in response to *United Steelworkers of America, AFL-CIO v. Pendergrass*, 819 F.2d 1263 (3rd Cir., 1987).

125 There is some legal question whether OSHA, which has jurisdiction over employer–employee health and safety relations, has authority over the relationship between a company and its downstream customers.

126 Restatement of Torts, section 757: "Liability for Disclosure or Use of Another's Trade Secret."

127 *United Steelworkers of America, AFL-CIO-CLC v. Auchter, et al.*, 763 F.2d 728; 12 OSHC 1337 (3rd Cir., 1985).

128 51 FR 34590.

129 *New Jersey State Chamber of Commerce v. Hughey*, 774 F.2d 587, 12 OSHC 1589 (3rd Cir., 1985).

130 Hazardous Waste Operations and Emergency Response (HAZWOPER) regulations in 29 C.F.R. § 1910.120.

131 *Gade v. National Solid Wastes Management Ass'n*, 505 U.S. 88, 112 S. Ct. 2374 (1992).

132 *Wyeth v. Levine*, 555 U.S. 555 (2009); Robert Barnes, "Justices Rule Against Drug Company in Injury Case," *Washington Post*, Mar. 5, 2009; compare *Geier v. American Honda*, 529 U.S. 861 (2000) on automobile safety.

133 OSHA ergonomics program standard final rule, 65 FR 68261 (Nov. 14, 2000), taking effect 60 days later.

134 "GOP Labor Bills Make Little Headway," AP, Oct. 28, 1998.

135 In the 106th Congress, H.R. 987, H.R. 4577, and S. 1070 restricting OSHA on issuing an ergonomics standard; H.R. 5178 on needlestick prevention, S. 1156 amending the Small Business Regulatory Enforcement Fairness Act (SBREFA) of 1996; H.R. 4098 barring home office inspections; and S. 1515 signed into law by President Clinton on July 10, 2000, as P.L. 106-245.

Chapter 17

Environmental Management Systems and Environmental Law

Christopher L. Bell
Greenburg Traurig LLP
Houston, Texas

1.0 Overview

Environmental management systems (EMSs) are used to accomplish many goals, including complying with the law, identifying and managing risks, satisfying customer demands, gaining competitive advantage, enhancing brand image, increasing efficiency, and serving as a foundation for initiatives such as sustainable development, product stewardship, and value-chain management. Although the law does not typically explicitly require EMSs, their popularity and inextricable linkage with compliance have given EMSs a permanent place in the environmental legal landscape. EMSs are also part of overall corporate governance, and are not solely the province of environmental professionals.

EMSs assist organizations to systematically and consistently identify, meet, and manage their environmental obligations. The effectiveness of EMSs is measured by performance, not certificates, high-flying phrases, or glossy annual environmental reports. The fundamental goal of an effective EMS is deceptively simple: provide the necessary tools, resources, information, and direction so that when people show up for work, they will do the right thing, at the right time, every time.

The common building blocks of an effective EMS include (1) top management leadership, participation, and policy setting; (2) identifying environmental issues (or risks) and legal requirements; (3) establishing objectives to successfully manage those issues and requirements in line with policy; (4) creating programs and procedures that establish how, by whom, and when the objectives will be met; (5) training people so that they know their roles and responsibilities in the system; (6) monitoring, measuring, and auditing to track performance and verify implementation; and (7) taking preventive and corrective action. Stakeholder engagement is increasingly seen by leading companies as an essential component of an effect EMS.

The popularity of EMSs is reflected in the rapid and widespread acceptance of the International Organization for Standardization's (ISO) ISO 14001 EMS standard that was first published in September 1996, underwent a modest revision in late 2004, and received its first significant rewrite in 2015.[1] By the end of 2014, approximately 325,000 organizations worldwide had implemented EMSs that were certified by third parties as conforming to the ISO 14001 EMS standard, including thousands of organizations in the United States.[2] In addition, countless other organizations have been using the standard to guide their EMS programs without certification. ISO 14001 has also been widely used as a foundation for EMS models in the public sector (e.g., by the U.S. Environmental Protection Agency [EPA] and in Executive Order 13148 issued by the White House) and the private sector (e.g., the American Chemistry Council's RC 14001).[3] Further, many companies have successfully developed and implemented their own EMS designs.

An effective EMS enhances the traditional and largely technical compliance assurance approach to include the business-oriented "plan-do-check-act" concept well understood by most business people. The importance of effective management systems and corporate culture in meeting environmental and safety obligations and preventing incidents has been highlighted in the post-event analyses of the *Deepwater Horizon* incident in the Gulf of Mexico.[4]

Section 2 of this chapter discusses the general relationship between EMSs, compliance assurance, and the law. Section 3 sets forth the basic elements of an effective EMS.

2.0 Legal Relevance of Environmental Management Systems

2.1 Overview

There are several reasons why environmental lawyers should understand and be involved in the design and implementation of EMSs. An effective EMS:

- decreases the likelihood that noncompliance will occur;

- increases the likelihood of early detection of noncompliance should it occur;

- enhances the opportunity for prevention, early mitigation, and corrective action; and

- may lead to more lenient enforcement responses by regulators should non-compliance occur.

Therefore, an EMS is directly relevant to an organization's ability to have an effective compliance assurance system that successfully prevents and detects noncompliance. EMS should be part of the organization's overall risk management and compliance assurance efforts, including codes of ethics/conduct and corporate governance. Therefore, it is not only prudent, but also falls within the traditional functions of an attorney, to be directly involved in the design, implementation, and oversight of an EMS. A good EMS is an essential element of "preventive lawyering" rather than bringing in counsel only after a problem surfaces. Counsel should also guard against viewing their primary role in EMSs as process-oriented "privilege watchdogs," and should be involved in the substantive design, implementation, and oversight functions.

2.2 EMSs, Enforcement Discretion, and Penalty Mitigation

Regulators and enforcers have long taken into account a company's compliance assurance program in determining the type and intensity of enforcement response in the event of noncompliance. EPA's first formal foray into environmental management was its 1986 audit policy, setting forth general guidelines for auditing programs.[5] EPA revised its audit policy in 1995, 2000, and 2008, suggesting that companies that discover, promptly disclose, and correct noncompliance may, under certain circumstances, qualify for significant penalty mitigation or even complete enforcement discretion.[6] Among the criteria that EPA will consider is whether a company has discovered noncompliance through the operation of a "compliance management system," the elements of which are consistent with basic EMS principles.

In 1991, the U.S. Department of Justice (DOJ) issued a policy titled "Factors in Decisions on Criminal Policy Prosecutions for Environmental Violations in the Context of Significant Voluntary Compliance or Disclosure Efforts by the Violator" (July 1, 1991).[7] This policy, which has been updated in 1999, 2003, 2006, 2008, and 2015, views compliance programs, auditing, self-policing, and the voluntary disclosure of violations as "mitigating factors" when DOJ is deciding whether to bring criminal enforcement actions against business organizations.[8]

Also in 1991, the U.S. Sentencing Commission issued the Organizational Sentencing Guidelines, which established (initially mandatory) criteria for courts to follow when imposing criminal penalties on companies. These criteria included incentives that encouraged companies to implement systematic compliance assurance programs.[9] The Sentencing Commission's criteria were largely the application of common sense: organizations should develop and implement standards for complying with the law, train their employees to comply with them, establish an organizational structure to implement the program (including a process for internal reporting without fear of retribution), and verify that the program is working (along with imposing discipline where standards are violated).

The Sentencing Commission significantly revised these criteria in 2004. The Commission broadened the scope of the criteria, increasing the emphasis on board of directors and senior management responsibility; highlighted ethical as well as compliant conduct; and suggested that organizations should design their programs around regular assessments of their risks of noncompliance.[10] The Sentencing Commission made further adjustments to the guidelines in 2010, including enhancing the prominence of those responsible for implementing compliance programs.[11] Therefore, EMSs should be viewed as part of overall corporate governance for which boards of directors and senior management are responsible, and are not solely the responsibility of environmental staff and attorneys.

The Department of Justice's and the Sentencing Guidelines' criteria were instrumental in spurring the "first wave" of compliance management programs in the early 1990s, programs that typically included environmental as well as other legal requirements.[12] These federal policies, along with EPA's auditing policy, have created an expectation among many enforcement agencies and regulators that "good" companies will have a defined environmental compliance system or EMS.

It is commonplace for enforcers to demand information about a company's EMS at the early stages of an enforcement matter. What is frequently at issue in enforcement matters is whether alleged noncompliance was caused by a "bad apple" employee acting on his or her own in violation of company policy (or perhaps an unusual or unexpected sequence of events), or was the outcome of systemic organizational noncompliance. Any organization that raises the "bad apple" or "unexpected event" defenses should be prepared to demonstrate that it had an effective EMS/compliance program in place that was designed to address reasonably expected risks, and was being implemented and enforced.

However, implementing an effective compliance management system does not guarantee that the government will not press an enforcement case, or that it will immunize a company against criminal liability for the actions of its employees. See, for example, *U.S. v. Ionia Mgmt. S.A.*, 555 F.3d 303 (2d Cir. 2009) (in affirming the conviction of a shipping company under the Act to Prevent Pollution From Ships, 33 U.S.C. § 1901, the court noted that compliance programs do not immunize a corporation from liability when employees, acting within the scope of their authority, violate the law, citing *U.S. v. Twentieth Century Fox Film Corp.*, 882 F.2d 656 [2d. Cir. 1989]).

Once an enforcement action is taken, regulators frequently demand that defendants implement an EMS as a condition of settling the government's claims (whether settling a civil matter or including an EMS as a condition of a criminal plea agreement or an associated agreement to not bar a company from government contracts).[13] EPA has issued guidance on how and when to include an EMS as an element in settling enforcement matters.[14] EPA's National Enforcement Investigations Center has developed guidance on incorporating "compliance-focused" EMSs into consent decrees.[15]

2.3 EMS and Regulatory Initiatives

While EPA has not explicitly required EMSs in regulations aimed at the private sector, the agency has made encouraging EMSs a major initiative.[16] EPA issued a "position statement" promoting EMS on May 15, 2002, which was updated on December 13, 2005; launched "EPA's Strategy for Determining the Role of Environmental Management Systems in Regulatory Program" on April 12, 2004; and has committed to implementing EMSs within EPA, and reaffirmed that committment in a formal statement on April 8, 2014. EPA has implemented EMSs at more than 30 of its own locations.[17] EPA's EMS-related goals include supporting the wider adoption of EMSs across a range of organizations and situations, promoting excellence in the practice of EMSs inside and outside of EPA, and more fully integrating EMSs into agency programs and activities.

There are also environmental, health and safety regulatory requirements that directly incorporate or are structured around compliance management systems concepts. The most obvious examples are the Clean Air Act risk management planning ("RMP") and related OSHA process safety management programs, both of which employ management systems principles to prevent catastrophic accidents. Perhaps taking a page from the ISO 14001 third-party certification paradigm, EPA's proposed revisions to the RMP regulations in 2016 include provisions for mandatory third-party auditing for certain categories of facilities.[18] The Bureau of Safety and Environmental Enforcement has made the implementation of safety and environmental management systems a requirement for offshore oil and gas operations.[19]

The federal government is also encouraging the implementation of EMS through its procurement policies. For example, the Federal Acquisition Regulations ("FAR") that apply to government contracting, were recently amended to include EMS requirements in government contracts, as well as a number of mandates regarding "sustainable acquisition" (76 Fed. Reg. 31395 [May 31, 2011]). The revisions to the FAR reflect an ongoing effort by the federal government to put its purchasing power to work to encourage improved environmental performance, both in services and products.[20] They also require that contracts include provisions for conforming with EMSs at federal facilities.[21]

The federal government's efforts to encourage EMS implementation have not been limited to the private sector. In 2000, Executive Order 13,148, Greening the Government Through Leadership in Environmental Management, established the goal of making EMSs a "fundamental and integral component" of federal government policies.[22] Executive Order 13,148 required all federal facilities to have EMSs in place by the end of 2005, based on the U.S. EPA's Code of Environmental Management Principles for Federal Agencies (1997) or another framework such as ISO 14001. Since then, EO 13,148 has been updated with EO 13,423 (January 24, 2007), EO 13,514 (October 5, 2009), and EB 13,693 (March 19, 2015), which increased the emphasis on EMSs in federal government operations and also established a number of explicit goals regarding energy and water conservation, pollution prevention, and reduction of greenhouse gas emissions.[23] There are also efforts underway to explore the use of EMSs by federal agencies to facilitate and improve compliance with the National Environmental Policy Act.[24]

EPA has also been encouraging state and local governments to implement EMSs. For example, in 2000 EPA launched its Local Government Environmental Management Systems Initiative, aimed at promoting EMSs by municipalities. EPA also has several grant programs supporting the implementation of EMSs at the state level.[25] EPA also established a "compliance assistance policy," aimed at encouraging small governments to improve their environmental performance, which includes deferring penalties and encouraging the implementation of EMSs.[26]

Many states have launched pilot projects to encourage EMS implementation and to determine how, if at all, EMSs improve environmental performance and protection. Several states have gone a step further and passed legislation authorizing the development of regulatory incentive programs to reward organizations that have successfully integrated EMSs into their facilities.[27] Some of these states, such as Connecticut and Maine, specifically require participating organizations to use an ISO 14001–certified EMS. In Texas, a facility's EMS is explicitly taken into account when "scoring" that facility's compliance history, which is then a factor in permitting and enforcement decisions.[28]

These federal and state programs compel the conclusion that effective EMSs play a role in shaping public policy on compliance and environmental performance. The advantages that attach to organizations implementing effective EMSs are likely to increase as the trend favoring alternatives to the traditional model of environmental regulation continues to flourish.

2.4 The Broader Context

General compliance and ethics programs have become a central feature of corporate governance. This was highlighted in the seminal *Caremark* case, in which the Delaware Court of Chancery (one of the most influential courts on corporate law) concluded that individual members of boards of directors have a fiduciary duty to ensure that a corporation acts in compliance with applicable laws and has a compliance program to meet this obligation (*In re Caremark Inc. Derivative Litigation* 698 A.2d 959 [1996]). The *Caremark* court expressly discussed the Sentencing Guidelines, noting that "any rational person attempting in good faith to meet an organizational governance responsibility would be bound to take into account this development [the criteria for compliance programs in the Sentencing Guidelines] and the enhanced penalties and the opportunities for reduced sanctions that it offers." The Delaware Supreme Court has since confirmed the reasoning in *Caremark*, holding that directors may be liable for failure to exercise appropriate oversight if the directors failed utterly to implement any reporting system or controls or, having implemented such a system, consciously failed to monitor or oversee its operations and thus prevented themselves from being informed of risks or problems requiring their attention. See, for example, *Stone v. Ritter*, 911 A.2d 362 (Del. 2006); *In re Walt Disney Co. Deriv. Litig.*, 906 A.2d 27 (Del. 2006).

There has been an explosion of interest in compliance and ethics programs, driven largely by the rash of financial scandals that have come to light since the turn of the century and the economic crash of 2007–2009, as well as the increasingly vigorous enforcement of anti-corruption laws. The Sarbanes-Oxley Act of 2002 established a series of requirements associated with financial control, including codes of conduct, internal controls, and reporting requirements that are being implemented by the SEC.[29] It was a provision of Sarbanes-Oxley that directed the Sentencing Commission to review and revise its criteria for compliance programs in 2004. More pressure to improve compliance programs and internal controls was generated by the Dodd-Frank Wall Street Reform and Consumer Protection Act of 2010, P.L. 111-203.

In response to these developments, organizations in the United States have been putting tremendous resources into comprehensive compliance and ethics programs that control activities that are relevant to how financial performance is recorded, analyzed, and reported. Organizations are reviewing and revising their overall corporate governance and compliance programs in response to the revised Sentencing Guidelines provisions on compliance and ethics programs. In addition to these general compliance program initiatives, a myriad of sector-specific compliance program criteria have been established by agencies such as the Food and Drug Administration, the Department of Health and Human Services, and the Customs Service.

The increased interest in compliance assurance systems and ethics programs has not been limited to the United States. In addition to ISO 14001, international initiatives have been characterized by broader forays into general topics such as anti-corruption, social responsibility, and sustainable development. For example, in 2000, the Organization of Economic Cooperation and Development (OECD), to which the United States belongs, published its revised OECD Guidelines for Multi-national Organizations, which establish a "code of conduct" on a range of issues, including labor, bribery, occupational safety, and environment, and just issued *Good Practice Guidance on Internal Controls, Ethics, and Compliance* (2010). A coalition of private sector and nongovernmental organizations has created Social Accountability 8000, which applies management systems principles to labor and social issues and is typically implemented in conjunction with accredited third-party auditors to verify conformance. ISO published ISO 26000 in 2010, a guidance document aimed at assisting private and public sector organizations on the topic of "social responsibility." ISO has also just published a standard on anti-bribery management systems (ISO 37001:2016), using the same management systems structure as ISO 9001 and 14001.

Specific legal requirements are also driving transnational compliance programs. For example, compliance with (and the enforcement of) the U.S. Foreign Corrupt Practices Act ("FCPA") by DOJ and the SEC has led many multinationals to implement worldwide programs aimed at preventing corruption, sometimes under the compulsion of consent or deferred prosecution agreements.[30] In 2012, DOJ and the SEC published guidance on FCPA compliance programs.[31] The presence of an effective anti-corruption program played a central role in a well-publicized decision by the government to decline to prosecute a high-profile FCPA case.[32] Such guidance, though on a different subject matter than environmental compliance, nonetheless provides insight into what, in the government's view, constitutes an effective compliance program.

The development of global value chains and worldwide "just-in-time" manufacturing systems, combined with increasing requirements on environmental- and safety-related product content and performance, are also posing complex challenges that are typically best addressed through effective EMSs. For example, the European Union's Directives "On the Restriction of the Use of Certain Hazardous Substances in Electrical and Electronic Equipment" ("RoHS") and "End of Life Vehicles" ("ELV") restrict the presence of certain hazardous materials in electronics and vehicles.[33] These directives have resulted in global supply-chain management and product stewardship compliance strategies that demand integrating environmental compliance into product design, outsourcing, inventory control, manufacture, distribution, and product end-of-life.

The importance of the environmental aspects of systematic global value-chain management has been dramatically increased with the implementation of the EU's Regulation (EC) No. 1907/2006 concerning the Registration, Evaluation, Authorisation and Restriction of Chemicals ("REACH"), which imposes significant technical and information-sharing requirements on the manufacture, distribution, and use of most chemicals on the EU market and, effectively, on the world market. The efforts necessary to comply with REACH are reverberating through the global supply chain, as companies struggle to consistently and accurately answer basic questions about raw materials sourcing, material, and product content. Developments in the United States raise similar issues, ranging from the newly amended Toxic Substances Control Act[34] increasingly stringent energy consumption requirements for appliances to tougher restrictions on the presence of hazardous substances in consumer products and toys that might be produced anywhere in the world to the SEC's reporting rules relating to the use of so-called "conflict minerals" promulgated pursuant to the Dodd-Frank Act. These challenges will only increase as governments and companies grapple with the even more complex issues associated with energy management and climate change.

EMSs should be designed and implemented in a manner that is integrated and consistent with organizations' overall compliance and ethics programs. Companies are designing their compliance programs around a complex and diverse set of instructions, from the wide-ranging policies of the Department of Justice, the Sentencing Commission, and Sarbanes-Oxley to the numerous sector-specific guidelines that have been established by regulatory bodies or market pressures. In addition, many companies that are subject to these requirements do not operate in the United States alone and are looking to implement comprehensive and consistent programs that cover their non-U.S. as well as U.S. operations. For example, multinationals whose shares are listed in the U.S. markets that are implementing a worldwide environmental reporting program based on the Global Reporting Initiative's (GRI) G4 Sustainability Reporting Guidelines[35] must coordinate such an effort with increasingly complex SEC financial controls and disclosure requirements, including those related to environmental issues such as climate change, the SEC's regulations on conflict minerals, and even novel state disclosure requirements.[36]

Finally, there is increasing pressure to implement more holistic strategies based on ethical considerations or broad concepts such as sustainable development or social responsibility that do not rely solely on specific legal obligations. For example, the series of fatal accidents in factories in Southeast Asia in 2012 and 2013 has led to private-sector commitments by major Western retailers regarding the safety of facilities in their value chain.[37] The private sector has responded to these pressures in a variety of ways. Thousands of companies have developed high-level compliance and ethics programs and codes of conduct modeled after the Sentencing Guidelines criteria. In addition, many companies have created subject matter–specific compliance programs (e.g., environmental, antitrust, customs, FDA, anticorruption), whose design and implementation may vary widely within the same company. These subject matter–specific programs sometimes are not integrated into companies' high-level compliance programs based on the Sentencing Guidelines or their Sarbanes-Oxley internal controls. "Silo" approaches to compliance assurance can result in wasted resources and inconsistent programs that are difficult to effectively and efficiently implement. Organizations implementing EMSs and their counsel should seriously evaluate how the EMS will be integrated and be consistent with their other compliance and ethics programs.

2.5 International Considerations

EMSs generally and ISO 14001 in particular carry significant weight in the international arena. There is little doubt that EMSs are an important part of public and corporate policy around the world. EMSs are viewed as one of the building blocks or implementation strategies for sustainable development.

International bodies are increasingly viewing ISO 14001 certification as an indication of corporate social responsibility.[38] For example, the implementation plan of the 2002 World Summit on Sustainable Development included the proposal that corporations consider ISO 14001 certification an integral element for ensuring accountability in overseas operations, particularly in developing countries.[39] Many multinational corporations are making implementing effective EMSs worldwide a central component of their public sustainable development strategies. The World Bank is also incorporating EMSs in its review of projects. The United States has promoted EMSs at the international level, as reflected in a 2000 guidance document on EMSs generated by the Commission for Environmental Cooperation, an arm of the North American Free Trade Agreement.[40]

Many regions and countries are already implementing environmental policies that include EMSs. Perhaps the most prominent example is the EU's Eco-Management and Audit Scheme ("EMAS"), which is an EMS-based program to which organizations may seek third-party registration. Further, EMSs may be useful in countries with less developed environmental protection regimes. Multinationals are increasingly using EMSs to implement consistent approaches to environmental protection, regardless of the degree to which local laws exist or are enforced. Effective EMSs can also assist companies to better identify and manage environmental concerns that are increasingly being expressed by local communities around the world through "extralegal," sometimes even violent, methods.[41] In some countries, the mere fact that a company has obtained formal legal authorizations for a project or that the project complies with official legal requirements does not mean that the project will be unopposed. This opposition can also make its way into U.S. courts, as non-U.S. plaintiffs are making more aggressive and creative use of statutes such as the Alien Tort Claims Act to seek redress in the United States for the actions of U.S. companies overseas.[42] Prudent liability and risk management suggests taking into account environmental issues through a more comprehensive EMS approach rather than relying solely on formal legal documents.

3.0 Environmental Management Systems

EMSs are the application of widely accepted business principles to environmental protection.

- Identify your key environmental risks, issues and obligations, taking into account the context and nature of your business.

- Establish what you want to do (policy and objectives).

- Determine how you want to do it (programs, procedures, and instructions).

- Tell people what you want them to do (communication and training).

- Make sure they do it (implementation, measurement, and auditing).

- Periodically review the entire process to identify opportunities to improve.

For decades, management has been applying these "plan, do, check, act" principles to business functions such as inventory, finance, quality, and production.

EMSs focus on establishing programs and procedures to integrate environmental performance into everyday operations so that organizations "do it right the first time." This is a shift away from the traditional approach of attempting to audit environmental performance into organizations. In the traditional model, detailed technical requirements are established by environmental professionals, and facilities are commanded to meet them. Facilities are then periodically audited/inspected/bludgeoned to the desired level of performance. That approach substitutes auditing for a real implementation plan and system.

The traditional model is reactive: using auditing as the primary control mechanism identifies shortcomings after they have occurred rather than focusing on preventing them from occurring in the first instance. One cannot audit a facility into compliance any more than one can inspect quality into an already manufactured part. Decades ago, the emphasis in the quality arena shifted to integrating quality into design and production so that fewer deficiencies were detected at the inspection phase. ISO 14001 and other EMS models reflect a similar approach to environmental protection and compliance.

In an EMS, organizations conduct their environmental affairs through a structured management system. The basic tenet of ISO 14001 is: "Say what you do, do what you say, and be able to demonstrate that you did it." In the event of unwanted attention by the enforcement authorities, having implemented an EMS should help in demonstrating the presence of a credible and implemented compliance assurance system. The failure to fully implement (and to demonstrate such implementation with evidence) an EMS can reduce the credibility of a company in the eyes of regulators or other stakeholders.

EMSs assist organizations to systematically identify and manage their environmental obligations. Some of these obligations are established by law, making the identification of and compliance with legal requirements an integral element of an EMS. However, an organization's most important environmental issues might not involve specific legal requirements. For example, reducing greenhouse gas emissions, implementing product stewardship programs, assisting local communities, or committing to sustainable development might not be legal requirements in many jurisdictions but nonetheless be important goals for some companies.

The Sentencing Guidelines criteria also reflect such an "extralegal" perspective, directing that organizations should have "compliance assurance and ethics programs," with commentary noting that ethics (i.e., "do the right thing"), not just a formal emphasis on the law (i.e., do solely what is required), is an important element of effective compliance programs.

What follows is a summary of key elements of a typical EMS. This summary is structured around certain (but not all) provisions of ISO 14001 because of its widespread acceptance and because it contains most of the common components found in EMS models (to be clear, however, this section is not intended as a detailed recitation of every element of ISO 14001:2015, nor does it outline EMS elements in the order of the standard).

ISO 14001 was revised in 2015, in accordance with the ISO policy that ISO standards be periodically reviewed to identify opportunities for improvement.

ISO 14001:2015 reflects an increased emphasis on top management commitment, tailoring the EMS to an understanding of the organization's overall context and risks, sustainable development, stakeholder engagement and value chain responsibility. ISO 14001:2015 has also been re-designed around a common management system structure that ISO intends to use for all of its management systems standards in an effort to establish consistency among those standards. However, the standard does retain the basic "plan-do-check-act" approach (though using different terminology). It remains to be seen what the market reaction to ISO 14001:2015 will be, given that the market is much more sophisticated regarding EMS than it was when ISO 14001 was first published in 1996, and elements of the generic management systems language imposed on ISO 14001:2015 are not necessarily a good fit with the environmental risk management and regulatory context.

It is important, however, to emphasize that ISO 14001 is not the only or necessarily the best EMS model for any particular organization. Accordingly, this discussion also takes into account certain elements of other prominent models, such as the Sentencing Commission's or DOJ's criteria.[43] This summary highlights issues likely to be of interest to environmental counsel, and does not address every step of EMS (or compliance and ethics program) design and implementation.

3.1 Review of Selected Provisions of an Effective EMS from a Legal Perspective

3.1.1 Scope and Context[44]

There are a number of initial decisions that must be made regarding the scope and structure of the EMS. These include:

- Whether to approach EMS design on a facility-by-facility basis, or to adopt a broader business unit or corporate approach. For multinationals, should there be a consistent framework for the EMS worldwide, or should there be a tailored approach for each region or country?

- If subsidiaries or joint ventures will be covered by the EMS, how will it be structured to decrease the risk that the "corporate veil" will be "pierced" in the event that these entities incur liability (while maintaining the system's effectiveness)?

- What activities will be covered by the EMS? For example, will the EMS cover just manufacturing activities, or will it also cover product and packaging content, design and performance, services, or value-chain management? If any of these activities is omitted, is there a credible justification, and might it create risk-management issues, since a company's biggest environmental, health, and safety ("EHS") risks might lie outside of its facilities and "traditional" EHS issues?

- Should the EMS be integrated with the organization's other relevant business or operational systems? If so, how? For example, should the organization create an integrated EHS management system, or will occupational safety be managed separately? How will the EMS relate to the organization's corporate governance, enterprise risk management, ethics, value-chain management, and other controls?

- Who will be responsible for implementing, maintaining, and supervising the EMS? Note that there can be a difference between administering and implementing an EMS. Administration might be a staff function (e.g., professional assistance, document and record management), while implementation might be a line function (e.g., top management at a plant taking responsibility for implementing the EMS).

- What EMS model should the organization use? ISO 14001? Sentencing Guidelines? EMAS? A custom-designed approach that combines a variety of existing models and that is tailored to the specific needs of the organization? If the organization decides to use ISO 14001, should it bother getting "certified" by a third-party "registrar"? Outside of situations where it is demanded by customers, the value of third-party certification is controversial. Some argue that registration provides needed discipline and credibility, while critics argue that registrars do not look at performance and that registration can give the incorrect impression that "everything is OK." Whatever decision is made, it is important to understand that third-party certifications are not a guarantee of compliance or an automatic shield against enforcement.

- What are the overall objectives of the EMS? Compliance only? Sustainable development? Managing value-chain risks? Are there "public facing" factors that need to be taken into account or important views of interested parties?

These are only some of the initial scoping questions that should be considered in the formative steps of EMS development. Though some of these were presented in an "either-or" format, most are susceptible to being resolved in a variety of ways.

The context in which the EMS is being developed can have a significant impact on how the EMS is designed. For example, developing and implementing an EMS as part of a civil consent decree or criminal plea agreement is typically a very different process than doing so in the context of implementing a global sustainable development strategy. ISO 14001:2015 includes provisions on identifying and evaluating the overall context of the organization as an initial step in the EMS design and scoping process.

It is prudent to have counsel as part of the EMS design and implementation team from the outset as these questions are being asked and answered, since the choices regarding which questions to ask (and not ask) will often have significant risk management implications, and the ultimate answers will frequently set the course for the balance of the EMS.

3.1.2 Leadership and Policy[45]

The revised ISO 14001 adds detail on the responsibilities of top management to oversee and supervise the implementation of the EMS. Among other things, top management should establish, document, communicate to employees, and implement a policy that includes a commitment to comply with the law and other agreements the organization has made (e.g., trade association codes of practice). In ISO 14001, this policy must also be made available to the public (in the EU's EMAS model, the policy must be affirmatively published).

Because an effective EMS must implement the commitments made by top management and the policy must include a commitment to compliance, compliance assurance is thus a major function of an EMS based on ISO 14001. This is consistent with the Sentencing Guidelines, which direct that an effective compliance assurance system must be designed to prevent and detect noncompliance. Accordingly, the organization must, through the EMS, systematically identify and comply with its legal obligations. Systemic noncompliance is evidence that the policy commitment is not being met and that the EMS is not working.

Under ISO 14001, top management must also commit to continual improvement and the prevention of pollution. This is arguably a more explicit appeal to the importance of extralegal issues than the Sentencing Guidelines' increased emphasis on ethical conduct. ISO 14001 encourages organizations to achieve a reasonable balance between managing regulated and nonregulated environmental issues (e.g., it is increasingly common for top-level policies to include broad commitments to sustainable development, to becoming more energy efficient, or to reducing greenhouse gas emissions, though the latter are becoming increasingly regulated).

One challenge in formulating top-level policies is reaching a balance between inspirational (or aspirational) exhortations setting the direction for the future and aggressive commitments that, if they are not met, might expose the organization to reputational and even legal harm (e.g., allegations of "greenwash" if a company's public pronouncements are not matched by its environmental performance). Policies should be carefully scrutinized to ensure that the EMS will be designed and implemented to achieve the commitments that are made in the policy, and that this achievement can be credibly demonstrated. Indeed, a company's policy can arguably be used as an audit checklist, "running to ground" each of the high-flying phrases to verify, with demonstrable evidence, that it is being concretely implemented. If questions about how a specific provision of a company's environmental policy is being implemented (including evidence of that implementation) are met with puzzled looks, that is a signal that the company's system and performance are not in line with the policy.

3.1.3 Roles and Responsibilities[46]

Roles and responsibilities in the EMS should be documented at the various levels of the organization. This allows one to understand, at an organizational level, who is responsible for what, and creates a structure so that individuals know what their responsibilities are. Therefore, the EMS must identify those responsible and accountable for implementing the EMS and meeting environmental obligations, including the compliance-related activities (e.g., identifying legal requirements, compliance assurance procedures, and monitoring/measuring). Further, the leadership of the EMS (whether an individual or a committee) must be identified.

Top management must also provide the resources necessary to effectively implement the EMS (i.e., no "unfunded mandates"). This last point is critical: enforcement agencies might review an organization's commitment of resources (personnel and financial) during civil and criminal investigations of significant environmental or safety incidents as part of an evaluation of how serious the organization (and top management) is about environmental performance and compliance.

While the revised ISO 14001 is more explicit about the responsibilities of "top management," the Sentencing Guidelines place greater emphasis on structure and responsibility at the senior levels, establishing roles and training requirements for the board of directors (or the "governing authority"), "high-level" managers, and managers with specific responsibilities for compliance assurance.[47] Therefore, in order for an EMS to be consistent with the Sentencing Guidelines, it must include explicit oversight roles and responsibilities all the way to the board of directors or "governing authority" level.

The 2010 amendments to the Sentencing Guidelines further emphasize this point, stating that to achieve full "credit" for having an effective program, "the individual or individuals with operational responsibility for the compliance and ethics program [must] have direct reporting obligations to the governing authority or an appropriate subgroup thereof (e.g., an audit committee of the board of directors)."[48] The Commission goes on to specify that "direct reporting obligations" means that the person responsible for the compliance program must have the "express authority to communicate directly with the governing authority or an appropriate subgroup thereof (A) promptly on any matter involving criminal or potential criminal conduct, and (B) no less than annually on the implementation and effectiveness of the compliance and ethics program."

The Sentencing Guidelines criteria also emphasize responsibility by providing that organizations should guard against giving authority to individuals who might violate the law, and discipline those who violate the compliance program requirements, while also considering incentives to encourage compliance.[49] A system that is not consistently enforced might not be taken seriously internally (e.g., by managers or other employees) or externally (e.g., by regulators or enforcers).

The Sentencing Guidelines' emphasis on ethics, not just compliance, highlights the role of the governing authority and management in establishing, executing and demonstrating a "culture" of ethical and compliant conduct. A purely rules-based approach is typically an inadequate foundation for an effective EMS.

It is important to consider the relative roles of EHS professionals, line management, and counsel in establishing roles and responsibilities. A traditional approach has been to pronounce that EHS professionals are "responsible for compliance." However, EHS professionals are typically staff who have no authority over the people or operations that create the compliance obligations. Further, most organizations typically have only a small number of EHS professionals who cannot be everywhere at once.

A more balanced, and typically more effective, approach is for line management to be responsible for compliance, with EHS professionals providing staff support (e.g., technical/regulatory expertise in writing procedures, training, answering questions, etc.). Similarly, oversight can be exercised by senior management and the appropriate committee(s) of the board of directors, again supported as appropriate by EHS professionals (including lawyers). This approach makes it clear that environmental compliance and performance is a serious management priority, and not just something that the "environmentalist" worries about.

3.1.4 Significant Environmental Aspects[50]

Organizations must identify what ISO 14001 calls the "environmental aspects" of their activities, products, and services that have or may have a significant environmental impact. These "significant environmental aspects" are the factual backbone of the EMS, comprising the important environmental issues or risks that the organization will manage with its EMS. Put in non-ISO terms, an effective EMS should include a disciplined process for identifying, and keeping current, the organization's environmental (or EHS) "risk footprint."

The organization's understanding of its overall strategic context and related risks and opportunities, along with the defined the scope of its EMS, will in turn establish the scope of the process of defining environmental issues or aspects. For example, will the evaluation be limited to the environmental issues directly associated with manufacturing operations or include the value-chain and product stewardship elements of operations as well? Under ISO 14001, there is an expectation that such environmental issues will be addressed. Of course, from a risk-management perspective, it would be prudent to understand how any excluded issues are going to be managed. For example, if compliance with product content or performance regulations is not going to be explicitly managed in the EMS, how (and by whom) are these obligations going to be addressed?

Under ISO 14001, organizations are not required to perfectly align their concept of "significance" with that of the regulators. For example, an organization may decide that certain issues are environmentally significant even if they are comparatively unregulated.

As a practical matter, however, organizations should not ignore regulatory requirements when determining which environmental aspects will be identified or deemed significant. Indeed, an organization whose EMS is not tied to ISO 14001 might decide to focus solely on regulatory requirements. Regulations are judgments by representatives of the public (i.e., the regulators) about the activities (and products and services) that pose potential or actual risks to human health or the environment. Therefore, it is reasonable to take the regulatory status of an environmental aspect into account when determining its significance. Otherwise, one would be effectively ignoring the judgment reflected in the law and perhaps inviting the attention of regulators.

It would be prudent to think carefully before declaring that an issue that is important to regulators is not significant to the organization. A conscious and documented decision that a regulated activity is "insignificant" for EMS purposes and thus does not need to be actively managed could come back to haunt an organization if there is an enforcement action related to that activity. For all these reasons, counsel should be involved in identifying the significant environmental issues that will be the focus of the EMS.

The Sentencing Guidelines criteria have an analogous step, directing that an organization conduct and regularly update an assessment of its legal risks, including the risks of noncompliance, taking into account the nature of the organization's business and how it conducts that business.[51] However, the Guidelines have a more explicit regulatory perspective, since the focus is on the risk of noncompliance, and, of course, have a broader scope than just environmental matters. Taking ISO 14001 and the Sentencing Guidelines together, an effective EMS will systematically identify the organization's significant environmental compliance and risk issues so that they will be appropriately managed through the balance of the EMS.[52]

3.1.5 Identifying and Evaluating Compliance Obligations[53]

The cornerstone of an effective compliance program is knowing what the law is and how it applies to the organization. It is well-established that ignorance of the law is rarely a defense to alleged violations of the law. Therefore, an effective compliance system must have a process for identifying and having access to legal requirements, and keeping this information current.[54]

This should be more than an identification process: just creating a catalog of legal requirements is of limited value. Companies should determine how these legal requirements apply to their specific activities and environmental issues. For example, it is not enough to know that the Clean Air Act applies to your operations: you should understand how and where it applies, and what must be done to comply. Complex legal requirements should be "translated" into practical processes that will make compliance more likely. For example, facilities that have Clean Air Act Title V permits should have processes for complying with the deviation and certification reporting requirements that are something more than circulating the permit to operations with the instruction to let the EHS department know if there have been any deviations. In addition, change management and capital expenditure procedures should include an evaluation of whether a particular project triggers permitting or other requirements.

Legal requirements may range from traditional facility-oriented regulations aimed at controlling wastes, air emissions, and water discharges to the growing number of product content, performance, packaging, marketing, and "end-of-life" regulations that are appearing in markets throughout the world, such as ROHS, REACH and the conflict minerals reporting requirements, to the emerging requirements associated with the carbon-constrained economy and climate change. Further, contracts that include environmental requirements are also common. Such requirements address a variety of issues, from product content to the environmental performance of suppliers' manufacturing facilities to more general issues related to sustainable development.

ISO 14001 also requires organizations to take the "other requirements" to which they voluntarily subscribe as seriously as their legal requirements. If a company volunteers to do something (e.g., joins a trade association that requires conformance to certain environmental requirements or publicly commits to a code of conduct), it should meet that commitment.[55] Again, this reflects the effort of ISO 14001 to have organizations "say what they do and do what they say." The revised ISO 14001:2015 arguably creates opportunities for misunderstanding by including such voluntarily subscribed to "other requirements" in the definition of "compliance obligations."

The Sentencing Guidelines criteria arguably go even further, asserting in commentary that an organization's "failure to incorporate and follow applicable industry practice or the standards called for in any applicable governmental regulation weighs against the finding of an effective compliance and ethics program."[56] Thus, an organization might find itself having to explain why it did not adopt and implement industry practices or standards relevant to the enforcement issue at hand.

ISO 14001 also includes provisions on identifying potential "interested parties" and determining what their "needs and expectations" might be, so that the EMS will take these into account as well.[57]

The role of counsel with respect to this element of an EMS is obvious: identifying, interpreting, and determining how to comply with legal requirements is what lawyers do. This also reflects the active and preventive nature of an effective EMS. Rather than waiting to call an attorney after the enforcement problem arises or the litigation is threatened, it is prudent to systematically include counsel up front in the procedure for identifying, tracking, interpreting, and communicating about legal and other requirements, as well as designing and implementing the procedures intended to achieve compliance.

3.1.6 Objectives, Planning and Programs[58]

Measurable objectives must be established that, among other things, take into account top management's commitments to compliance, continual improvement and prevention of pollution, its significant environmental aspects and compliance obligations, as well as, in the 2015 version of ISO 14001, the "requirements" of interested parties.[59] An organization that does not have objectives that address compliance will be hard-pressed to demonstrate that it is following through on the commitment to comply. The absence of any compliance-related objectives will also be difficult to explain from a Sentencing Guidelines perspective.

Wholly apart from ISO 14001, one would question the prudence of an organization that would ignore compliance in setting its environmental objectives, given the potential organizational and personal liability consequences associated with such a decision. The measurable objectives represent what senior management wants the organization to achieve and enable employees to focus on clear, articulated goals. Employees, regulators, and the public might conclude that compliance is not a management priority in the absence of measurable compliance objectives.[60]

Since the objectives must also take into account the organization's policy commitments and any other requirements to which it subscribes, it is usually not sufficient to settle for objectives that are based solely on compliance. For example, it is common for organizations to establish goals aimed at reducing waste, increasing recycling, or using less energy (ISO published a standard on energy management, ISO 5001, in June 2011). Further, as a practical matter, many compliance goals are usually "trailing indicators" that are less effective at preventing noncompliance and improving environmental performance than "leading indicators" that set the "trigger" before noncompliance or environmental harm occurs (this is a well-understood concept in occupational safety, where tracking and investigating events such as "near misses" is commonly viewed as an effective "leading indicator" technique to decrease the likelihood of injuries).

Organizations must also create and execute plans that identify the "who, what, how, and when" with respect to achieving their objectives and monitoring results and performance. The objectives cannot simply be a "wish list" without a defined way to achieve them. The organization should not rest solely on vague declarations that it will act in a sustainable manner, that it will "comply with all applicable laws," that "every employee is responsible for compliance," or that the environmental professional is responsible for compliance (particularly since, as noted above, EHS professionals typically have no authority over many of the activities to which the compliance requirements apply).

Effective EMSs will typically distribute compliance and other responsibilities throughout the organization, placing responsibilities on the functions and management responsible for creating the compliance obligations in the first instance. Compliance obligations must be translated into specific programs and actions (including those for preventing and responding to emergency situations) that will be taken by those with defined responsibility and accountability pursuant to a specific schedule. This is easy to check from an auditing perspective: one can pick a handful of key compliance obligations and track them through the entire organization to identify how compliance is achieved on a practical and systematic basis.

3.1.7 Operational Planning, Controls and Procedures[61]

The organization must establish processes for controlling its activities in order to meet the requirements of the EMS, including managing the significant environmental aspects, achieving the objective and executing the plans, and meeting compliance obligations. This is the component of an EMS that typically deals with the details of environmental management and compliance (i.e., the "how" part of the programs discussed in the preceding section), and may range from eliminating a risk entirely to managing it through engineering controls, specific operating criteria, or procedures that provide direction to those who work on the organization's behalf. This does not mean that there has to be a control for every single legal requirement or that the controls have to be expressed in legal terms or even mention compliance.

Reflecting the broader scope of the revised ISO 14001, the EMS must address "outsourced processes" and "ensure" that they are "controlled or influenced." While the goals behind this new text are understandable, implementing them may raise challenging issues for companies who seek to manage their liability risks by avoiding even the appearance of exercising control over other entities. In addition, consistent with an increased emphasis on life-cycle thinking, the revised ISO 14001 directs organizations to address environmental issues associated with product design and services, accompanied by a suggestion that organizations consider providing information to downstream users about the significant environmental impacts associated with the use of end-of-life of products and services. These procedures and controls may extend the reach of the EMS into the realm of product designers, procurement managers who deal with suppliers, and marketing and advertising, and may have far-reaching implications on design and value-chain management and contractual controls.[62]

Organizations must also communicate relevant environmental requirements to "external providers" (e.g., suppliers or contractors). For example, an organization may direct suppliers to provide only chemicals that are on EPA's TSCA Chemical Inventory, to exclude any materials that are on California's Proposition 65 list, or to certify that CFCs are not contained in or used in the manufacture of any components.

These procedures include those associated with preventing and responding to emergencies. This element of the EMS encompasses a number of emergency prevention/response-related compliance requirements, such as CAA § 112(r) risk management planning (and the related OSHA process safety management program) or SPCC plans.

The concept is straightforward: when people (including contractors) show up for work, they must have instructions telling them what to do so that the organization can meet its legal (and other) obligations, including its measurable compliance objectives and targets. Simply having binders of legal requirements and permits in the environmental professional's office or buried on the organization's website will not suffice. Nor will circulating complex and detailed legal documents or memoranda to busy operational personnel with a curt command to "comply" or "call if you have any questions" be particularly useful.

This information should be translated into practical instructions relevant to people's jobs that they can understand and then consistently implement. One strategy is to integrate environmentally relevant instructions into everyday business or operational practices and procedures rather than having a "green binder" that is separate from the "regular job instructions." To the extent that an organization has identified and set goals regarding nonregulated issues (e.g., a recycling goal), procedures for those issues will also be expected.

Maintenance procedures play a critical role in implementing an effective EMS, particularly with respect to the proper operation and monitoring of pollution control equipment. Computer-based information and task management software provide opportunities to enhance the integration of EHS requirements into operational, business, and maintenance procedures. There is similar software dedicated to the environmental profession, though caution must be exercised to avoid creating "silos," where the bulk of the information related to the management of the EMS is on the "environmental software" and not on the software used by the rest of the organization. Procedures can also be communicated simply through posters or pictures, which can be particularly effective in facilities where many languages are spoken.

Management of change is also a central element of operational control. Many environmental incidents arise out of inadequate planning for changed circumstances, or not even being aware that circumstances have changed. An effective EMS will include procedures that remind users to look for and be aware of changed procedures and take appropriate steps to properly manage them, and management of change procedures that will evaluate the potential environmental consequences of planned changes and the mitigating or preventive measures that should be taken to address those consequences. Sophisticated organizations include knowledge management and transfer systems to capture accumulated experience as personnel change positions, retire, etc.

It is also important to recognize the limits of formal procedures. It is difficult to create and implement rules for every potential circumstance.[63] Further, establishing a purely rules-oriented culture may create the implication that actions are allowed unless expressly prohibited or controlled (i.e., "I thought it was OK because there were not any rules against what I did"). The Sentencing Guidelines recognize this challenge by directing that management establish a culture of ethical and compliant conduct. In other words, even in the absence of specific rules or direct supervision, the culture of the organization should encourage everyone to "do the right thing" and not create an environment where ethics or regulations are viewed as unfortunate irritants that have to be worked around (reflecting the concept that ethics deals with what people do when no one is watching).

3.1.8 Competence and Awareness[64]

The EMS and its related controls and procedures will not be very effective unless the right people know about and understand them. Therefore, training and awareness are core elements of an EMS. People (including on-site contractors, temporary employees, visitors, etc.) whose work affects the organization's environmental performance and its ability to achieve its compliance obligations must be competent, based on appropriate education, training or experience. The revised ISO 14001 has placed the focus on actual competence rather than the rote assembly of training records that may, or may not, produce the desired and necessary competence. A key element of competence is the ability to perform work in line with the applicable controls and procedures, including those related to managing environmental risk and compliance.

Further, all employees (and on-site contractors, temporary employees, visitors, etc.) must be made aware of the importance of conforming with the policy (including the commitment to comply), procedures (including those necessary to comply), significant environmental impacts associated with their work (which may include regulated items), their roles and responsibilities in conforming with the policy and procedures (both of which have compliance-related elements), and the potential consequences of departure from the procedures (which may include noncompliance). Therefore, compliance assurance is an important element of EMS training and awareness.

Thus, when conducting EMS audits it will be necessary to verify not only that appropriate training has occurred or that job qualifications have been met, but to check on the competence of the individuals being reviewed. Merely looking at training records and materials is not enough. An effective EMS audit should include asking people questions aimed not simply at verifying that they received training, but that they understood it and know what they are doing (and what they are supposed to know). It also should not be assumed that periodic training is an adequate replacement for readily available practical procedures or instructions. Information buried in a company's computer-based training system may not be an effective procedure.

A frequent shortcoming of training programs is an assumption that managers (particularly senior managers) do not need training. Nothing could be further from the truth, since frequently it is the decisions by senior managers that might have the most significant impact on a company's environmental or risk "footprint." The Sentencing Guidelines criteria address this shortcoming by emphasizing the importance of training the board of directors (or "governing authority") and senior management about the compliance and ethics program.[65]

3.1.9 Performance Evaluation, Monitoring and Measurement[66]

"What gets measured gets done" is a fundamental management principle. If environmental performance generally, and compliance performance in particular, are not being frequently and consistently measured and internally reported, the signal conveyed to employees is that these issues may not be important to top management (at least in comparison to what is measured). If the key performance indicators (KPIs) are all about production, quality, delivery, and finance, and EHS metrics are nowhere to be seen, periodic top-management pronouncements that EHS issues are important might not be taken seriously.

Therefore, an effective EMS includes procedures to regularly measure the organization's environmental performance. Where those operations and activities are regulated, those key characteristics will typically include monitoring required by law (e.g., monitoring air emissions or water discharges are required by permit), which are growing increasingly complicated not only at the facility level, but as requirements related to products and services increase as well. Organizations should also track performance, conformance with objectives (including the compliance-related ones), and operational controls. Thus, an effective EMS will include procedures that define "what, how, when and who" of monitoring, including how and by whom any results should be evaluated. This should include defined procedures for regularly measuring the performance of the compliance-assurance elements of the EMS.[67]

ISO 14001 contemplates more than the traditional compliance audit that checks EHS performance maybe annually or even less often. Organizations measure their financial performance on an ongoing basis, supplemented by a periodic audit of their books and financial systems to verify that the data generated by the systems are accurate. Similarly, ISO 14001 pushes organizations to measure environmental performance on an ongoing basis, so that management knows on a "real-time" basis how the organization is performing, complemented by periodic auditing to verify that the system is producing reliable data.

This is a departure from the traditional approach of "reporting by exception," where senior management gets to know (or wants to know) about environmental issues only if there is a problem (which is frequently too late). One effective non-quantitative monitoring technique is frequent questions asked by senior management during the course of everyday business: having the boss ask his or her direct reports (i.e., not EHS staff) pointed questions about EHS performance during regular business or operational meetings can go a long way toward ensuring the ongoing effective implementation of the EMS.

3.1.10 Evaluation of Compliance[68]

The organization must have procedures to periodically evaluate its compliance performance. This is typically done through a compliance auditing program that includes auditing frequency, criteria, etc. However, most organizations have other compliance evaluation activities, such as required or voluntary inspections, "walk-arounds," trend analyses, and so on, the result of which should be taken into account in addition to traditional audits. It is important to compile and evaluate all of this information to get a more complete picture of compliance. For example, if a facility is regularly finding (and perhaps fixing) noncompliance through regular inspections, but the formal annual audit does not pick this up because the facility has been "scrubbed" to prepare for the audit, relying solely on the formal audit results might give one an inaccurate picture of what is going on. Further, particularly at larger companies, formal compliance audits at individual facilities might only take place on a relatively long cycle (e.g., 3 years), creating a risk for gaps in information if such audits are the sole basis upon which compliance performance is evaluated and managed.

Compliance evaluation activities should also not be limited to what many practitioners view as "traditional" environmental legal requirements associated with manufacturing. Compliance evaluation should cover contractual requirements, requirements related to products, packaging, and services, and other obligations. This is particularly important given the significant increase in product regulations: if problems in these areas are caught for the first time by the value chain (e.g., customers) or regulators, the economic and reputational consequences could be quite significant (e.g., business interruptions). In addition, the auditing program should cover compliance with "other requirements" that the organization has committed to meet, even if those requirements are voluntary (e.g., verifying that the company has implemented an obligation that is a condition of membership in the trade association to which it belongs). If such obligations are taken so lightly as to not be checked, then perhaps they should be dropped.

Effective auditing and compliance verification activities are particularly important to enforcement and regulatory authorities. An organization with a weak compliance auditing and inspection program will be in a very difficult position to convince the authorities, the public, or even its own employees that it has an effective EMS. This is evident in the focus of the Sentencing Guidelines criteria on "preventing and detecting" noncompliance (which were enhanced in the 2010 amendments) and the DOJ prosecutorial criteria.[69]

3.1.11 Communication[70]

An effective EMS includes internal communications procedures. Compliance problems, systems failures and major environmental incidents can often be traced to communications failures. The increasing complexity of legal requirements has increased the emphasis on effective internal communications procedures and effective information management systems. For example, it is difficult to comply with complex Title V Clean Air permits, including the annual certification requirement, without good internal systems to collect and manage the volumes of information necessary for timely compliance. Some compliance obligations are spread across many functions in an organization, recommending procedures to ensure that the right people have the right information at the right time. For example, the chemical regulations of TSCA and REACH implicate everything from product design and manufacture to import and export and global value-chain information. In that vein, the revised ISO 14001 directs that organizations must have an internal communications plan that includes the "what, when, to whom and how" with respect to communications, and that takes into account its compliance obligations. Transparency and accuracy is also important: the information being communicated should be consistent with the information that is being generated by the EMS.

The Sentencing Guidelines criteria go beyond most EMS models with respect to internal communications, directing organizations to implement "whistle-blowing" procedures that allow employees to report compliance concerns or ask questions without fear of retaliation. Such programs raise a number of issues, including how to manage investigations and corrective action, encourage cooperation and prevent retaliation, and, particularly for multinationals, comply with the privacy requirements of various jurisdictions (especially the EU).[71] Further, in order to fully benefit from the EPA, DOJ, and Sentencing Guidelines policies related to effective compliance systems, one must typically disclose potential violations to the government.

Organizations implementing ISO 14001 must also communicate, as appropriate, externally about it EMS. These communications may be required by law (e.g., various regulatory reporting requirements) or they may involve general communications with the public and customers about environmental or sustainability issues, or more focused communications with specific interested parties. ISO 14001 does not require formal annual environmental or sustainability reports, though many companies with EMSs do publish such reports.

Although external communication is largely voluntary from an ISO 14001 perspective, federal and state law in the United States already requires that a large volume of environmental information about many facilities be made available to the public. This information includes permit applications, hazardous waste and permit discharge reports, chemical use and release information under the "right-to-know" laws, and release reporting in the event of chemical spills or accidents, much of which is increasingly available on the internet, not just through freedom of information act requests.

Corporate disclosures for publicly traded companies must also include certain information about environmental liabilities, including disclosures related to the potential impacts of climate change on a company's operations, and conflict minerals have been added to the SEC reporting requirements.[72] Much of this information is now available in a variety of electronic databases that can be viewed on the Internet. How an organization complies with these legal disclosure requirements should be integrated into its EMS. Organizations should also consider external communications in the development and implementation of their emergency prevention and response plans.

Other EMS models have sought to increase the emphasis on public participation and communication. For example, the ISO 14001–based EMS that was a requirement for participating in EPA's now defunct Performance Track program required regular public reporting (beyond what is required by law). The Multi-State Working Group's External Value Environmental Management System Voluntary Guidance (March 2004) encourages the implementation of EMS to include far more public participation and communication than is required by ISO 14001 or the law.[73] In addition, the U.S. government has included public communications elements in plea agreements and other settlements of environmental enforcement actions, requiring the settling company to put more detailed environmental performance information on publicly accessible websites than would otherwise be required by law.

Many proponents of sustainable development believe that external communications with stakeholders are an essential element, with many championing comprehensive annual reports.[74] This "stakeholder facing" approach is reflected in the ISO 26000 guidance document on social responsibility, as well as the popular Global Reporting Initiative. Of course, prudence dictates that organizations should be sure that they have built the underlying systems to achieve sustained environmental performance before launching communications initiatives and annual reports aimed at establishing a "green" reputation.[75] It is a risk indeed to start with the "public face" of sustainability reporting in the hopes that it will "drive" the company so that the facts and reality will eventually catch up with the publicity.

The external communications element of an effective EMS might also be integrated with an organization's financial reporting system, including internal financial controls. As publicly traded companies implement their internal controls to meet the requirements of Sarbanes-Oxley and Dodd-Frank, EMS procedures that are related to tracking and managing environmental issues with financial consequences (e.g., remediation, transactions, climate change) should be integrated with (or at least be consistent with) SEC-mandated procedures.

3.1.12 EMS Auditing[76]

The organization must audit its EMS to verify that the system conforms to the organization's requirements and ISO 14001 (or whatever EMS model is being used) and that it has been implemented and maintained.[77] This is related but not identical to the compliance evaluation/auditing discussed above. This auditing process is aimed at (1) verifying that the system has been properly designed in light of the applicable criteria and (2) that it is being effectively implemented. EMS audits have some similarities to financial audits that focus on verifying the adequacy of the financial system and its controls (i.e., which is a different, though related, task than measuring and communicating financial performance on an ongoing basis). Thus, an effective EMS will check compliance from at least three perspectives: regular monitoring and measuring, periodic evaluations of compliance (e.g., compliance auditing), and EMS auditing.

An EMS audit is not merely a "paperwork" audit that reviews procedures; it is an audit verifying effective implementation. That includes verification that the compliance assurance system is working. The applicable measure is whether the system is working, not whether perfection (e.g., 100 percent compliance) has been achieved.[78] This is done by verifying (1) that the necessary and adequate procedures are in place; (2) that these procedures are actually being implemented; and (3) that they are effective.

The evidence can be collected from a number of sources, including observations, interviews, and reviewing procedures and records. Verifying that the necessary procedures exist is only the beginning. There must also be objective evidence that the procedures are being implemented as planned and that the procedures are achieving the desired result. This is frequently a commonsense inquiry that seeks to verify that what is written in the procedures reflects what actually happens on the ground; that relevant managers, employees, and contractors are aware of and trained on the procedure; that there is objective evidence that the procedure has indeed been implemented; and that the implementation has produced the desired performance.

EMS audits that pay inordinate attention to the paperwork at the expense of "real-world" implementation and verification are inadequate. EMS auditors should not spend all of their time sitting in windowless rooms looking at paper or computer screens: they have to walk around, looking, listening, and talking, to get an understanding of whether and how the system is actually working.[79]

When designing an EMS auditing program (and when conducting EMS audits), it may be prudent to consider the following passage from DOJ's Principles of Prosecuting Business Organizations.

> The Department has no formulaic requirements regarding corporate compliance programs. The fundamental questions any prosecutor should ask are: Is the corporation's compliance program well designed? Is the program being applied earnestly and in good faith? Does the corporation's compliance program work? In answering these questions,

the prosecutor should consider the comprehensiveness of the compliance program; the extent and pervasiveness of the criminal misconduct; the number and level of the corporate employees involved; the seriousness, duration, and frequency of the misconduct; and any remedial actions taken by the corporation, including, for example, disciplinary action against past violators uncovered by the prior compliance program, and revisions to corporate compliance programs in light of lessons learned. Prosecutors should also consider the promptness of any disclosure of wrongdoing to the government. In evaluating compliance programs, prosecutors may consider whether the corporation has established corporate governance mechanisms that can effectively detect and prevent misconduct. For example, do the corporation's directors exercise independent review over proposed corporate actions rather than unquestioningly ratifying officers' recommendations; are internal audit functions conducted at a level sufficient to ensure their independence and accuracy; and have the directors established an information and reporting system in the organization reasonably designed to provide management and directors with timely and accurate information sufficient to allow them to reach an informed decision regarding the organization's compliance with the law.

Prosecutors should therefore attempt to determine whether a corporation's compliance program is merely a "paper program" or whether it was designed, implemented, reviewed, and revised, as appropriate, in an effective manner. In addition, prosecutors should determine whether the corporation has provided for a staff sufficient to audit, document, analyze, and utilize the results of the corporation's compliance efforts. Prosecutors also should determine whether the corporation's employees are adequately informed about the compliance program and are convinced of the corporation's commitment to it. This will enable the prosecutor to make an informed decision as to whether the corporation has adopted and implemented a truly effective compliance program that, when consistent with other federal law enforcement policies, may result in a decision to charge only the corporation's employees and agents or to mitigate charges or sanctions against the corporation.[80]

Good EMS audits can be effective in providing early warnings of potential problems before they ripen into dangerous incidents or significant noncompliance. For example, an EMS audit might uncover deficiencies in the design or implementation of training programs before the inadequate training leads to problems. Or it might identify "soft" issues such as inadequate top management participation or weak mid-level management commitment to EHS issues that, if unchecked, could eventually result in major problems or incidents.

Companies sometimes combine EMS and compliance audits into a single process. EMS audits can also be combined with other systems audits, such as of safety management systems, quality management systems audits (ISO 9001), or audits of compliance and ethics programs conducted pursuant to the Sentencing Guidelines.[81]

3.1.13 Corrective Action[82]

This is the "fix what you find" element of any effective EMS, including ISO 14001. Organizations must have a procedure for preventing and correcting detected nonconformities, including noncompliance. Corrective action should be taken regardless of the source of the information: it is not limited to responding to audit findings. Some of the most important information about noncompliance and systems deficiencies does not come up during formal audits. Rather, it may surface during informal inspections, management reviews, walk-arounds, or internal communications or e-mails. Such information should not be kept out of the preventive/corrective action procedures just because it did not come from an auditor.

Where appropriate, the corrective action must also include changes to the underlying system to prevent future nonconformities. This is a continuation of the fundamental point that systems deficiencies can be as critical as or even more important than specific instances of regulatory noncompliance. This is so even if there is not a specific regulatory requirement tied to the systems deficiency. For example, systems deficiencies in areas such as training, management commitment, or sufficiency of resources could all lead to serious incidents or noncompliance if not corrected. It is a serious error to reserve for preventive and corrective action only instances of "real noncompliance," and treat the correction of systems defects as optional.

Preventive action is not limited to preventing the recurrence of nonconformities that have already occurred (e.g., through root cause analysis). The EMS should be designed to prevent nonconformities from occurring in the first instance. This may be done through other elements of the system (e.g., identifying environmental aspects, programs and operational controls, training, monitoring and measuring) rather than creating a discrete preventive action program (as well as through the operation of systems that may be required by law, such as CAA § 112(r) risk management planning or OSHA process safety management).

As with auditing, preventive/corrective action is a very important factor when enforcers or regulators are reviewing a company's EMS. The government will not be sympathetic, and indeed will typically be quite harsh, toward companies that are not seriously looking for problems, and then do not promptly and effectively fix detected problems.[83] This is one of the underlying premises of the

EPA, DOJ, and Sentencing Guidelines criteria: companies that have effective systems that detect, promptly correct, and voluntarily report noncompliance to the appropriate regulators may qualify for a reduced enforcement response. On the other hand, if significant noncompliance is first detected by the government (or reported by a whistle-blower), and there is little or no evidence that the company has been taking the noncompliance seriously, the enforcement consequences can be quite serious.

3.1.14 Management Review And Continual Improvement[84]

Top management must periodically review the EMS to "ensure its continuing suitability, adequacy, and effectiveness." The review must include an evaluation of a wide range of information, including input about business risks and opportunities, the results of audits, the status of corrective action, performance against objectives, follow-up from previous reviews, inputs from interested parties, and recommendations for improvement. An effective approach to management review is to integrate it into regular management meetings (e.g., weekly and monthly business and operational sessions) rather than conducting less frequent "environmental" meetings. This approach is consistent with the principle of integrating environmental management into operational management and also creates a platform for regular and visible management participation in the EMS.

The Sentencing Guidelines emphasize that this is not merely an obligation of top operational management; rather, in addition, the board of directors (or "governing authority") must oversee the operation of the compliance system and periodically review information on the performance of the system. Therefore, the design and implementation of the EMS should take into account how both senior operational management and the board (or the "governing authority") will exercise oversight.

The failure of regular, visible, and direct participation by senior management is frequently a root cause in instances of environmental noncompliance and incidents. This is also often an important issue in enforcement investigations. This is the "what were they thinking?" or "how could they not know?" inquiry that comes up after a major incident. For these reasons, "passive" management reviews during which middle or senior managers (or the board) are simply presented with a slide show by the EHS professionals, are typically not effective. The point is not to "check the box" that a management review has occurred: rather, it is for management, on a regular basis, to actively participate in and exercise oversight over the EMS, and not just leave it up to the EHS professionals. Being able to demonstrate the active engagement of senior management, and not just the periodic and passive reception of information, is central to the effectiveness, as well as the internal and external credibility, of the EMS.

3.1.15 Documentation and Records[85]

The recent revisions in ISO 14001:2015 reflect an effort to decrease the documentation requirements, perhaps in response to a common criticism that the ISO management standards focused too much on the paperwork. However, it makes sense that necessary and important procedures (e.g., operational controls and instructions) should be documented and controlled (including electronically), including those necessary to manage compliance. This enhances the shift from an "oral tradition" that can result in performance lapses as people move in and out of jobs to a more disciplined and structured compliance assurance strategy. "Document control" adds further discipline to compliance assurance by requiring that the correct versions of the necessary procedures be available to the right people at the right time at the right place so that they will do the right thing. Neither the organization's employees nor the enforcers will be impressed with inaccurate or out-of-date procedures (i.e., uncontrolled documents, whether paper or electronic) that do not reflect actual or expected practice.

The organization should also create and maintain records sufficient to demonstrate that it is "doing what it says it is doing." The commitment to compliance, as reflected through the various elements of the EMS and the underlying procedures, must be actually implemented. The records are a significant element of the evidence of this implementation. Therefore, the organization must maintain records of the implementation of the compliance assurance elements of the EMS and have a system for managing and maintaining those records (and, of course, comply with any legally mandated record creation and retention requirements).

While the details and complexities of attorney-client privilege are beyond the scope of this chapter, privilege is an important issue to consider in the design and implementation of an EMS. Some attorneys are concerned that formal EMSs will lead to the creation of documents that will effectively be a "path to liability/conviction" because it is difficult to protect many EMS documents under the attorney–client privilege protection. This legitimate concern should be balanced with the understanding that an effective EMS should lead to better performance and hence decrease the likelihood of enforcement actions in the first instance. It would not make sense to recommend not having an EMS (or an undocumented EMS) just because the system might someday be subject to discovery. The liability concerns about EMS documentation also should not be overstated: organizations that do not have formal EMSs typically have more than their fair share of "smoking-gun" documents (e.g., "flaming e-mails" between managers or paper documents with unfortunate handwritten notes on them).

Many companies distinguish, for privilege purposes, between their "normal" EMS procedures and activities more likely to deal with enforcement-sensitive information, such as audits and incident investigations, which might be conducted under privilege. However, some companies have found that running an entire audit and corrective action program under privilege can be cumbersome and sometimes inhibit rapid and effective communications, and reserve the use of privilege for enforcement-sensitive investigations. Privilege issues should be addressed up front in the design of the EMS, with the involvement of counsel (including the potential applicability of federal or state audit privilege and disclosure policies).

A well-designed EMS might make the need to claim privilege less likely (i.e., by improving performance) and can include prudent document and records management practices that allow the EMS to function efficiently while still providing appropriate privilege protection (e.g., when conducting investigations).[86] Perhaps the most vital element of prudent document management is making sure that the EMS documentation accurately reflects reality: one of the biggest liability threats posed by a documented EMS is not doing what was documented (or relying on inaccurate or obsolete documents). Counsel's regular participation in the EMS can increase the likelihood that accurate documents will be created.

The privilege issues associated with EMS are complicated by the fact that getting full "credit" for having a compliance assurance system under DOJ's prosecutorial policy and the Sentencing Guidelines for enforcement discretion or penalty mitigation purposes is conditioned upon the organization "cooperating" with the enforcers. DOJ (based largely on the 2003 Thompson Memorandum) historically took the position that "full cooperation" meant waiving the attorney-client privilege at the government's demand, a position that was not fully accepted by the Sentencing Commission during the recent round of revisions to the Sentencing Guidelines.

The Sentencing Commission had previously been silent on this issue. However, in the 2004 revisions to the guidelines, the Sentencing Commission opined that a full waiver of privilege was not a prerequisite to a determination of full cooperation "unless such waiver is necessary in order to provide timely and thorough disclosure of all pertinent information known to the organization."[87] In April 2006, the Sentencing Commission voted to eliminate the reference to the waiver of attorney-client privilege as a condition of a finding of cooperation with the government (though the 2010 amendments did add a provision regarding voluntary disclosure).[88]

In December 2006, DOJ revised its position on what constitutes "cooperation" and arguably softened its position on waiving the attorney-client privilege in the so-called McNulty Memorandum, which replaced the Thompson Memorandum. The department subsequently and apparently retreated even more in the Filip Memorandum in 2008, claiming that it would no longer demand non-factual privileged information as a condition of cooperation, though there remain serious doubts among the defense bar as to whether this represents real change in the department's position.

The 2015 Yates Memorandum has little explicit to say about the topic of privilege (the term appears only once, in a general statement that cooperation should be "within the bounds of law and legal privileges"), but forcefully states that for a corporation to get "any consideration" for cooperation, it must identify "all" individuals involved in or responsible for the alleged misconduct (regardless of seniority) and turn over "all facts" related to the misconduct. This is a highly charged topic that has been and will continue to be a controversial issue.

Counsel for companies with operations or relationships outside the United States should not assume that U.S. privilege rules apply worldwide. For example, the European Court of Justice (the EU's highest court) held in 2010 that communications between in-house counsel and their internal clients were not protected by attorney-client privilege, finding that in-house counsel were not sufficiently independent (at least in the competition law context) to justify the protection.[89] This raises interesting challenges not only for communications within the EU, but also between in-house counsel based in the United States (or other non-EU locations) and their EU colleagues and clients.

Counsel can play a valuable role in creating and reviewing documented procedures. Counsel can evaluate the legal accuracy of documents and also ask the hard questions to determine if the procedures are wishful thinking or an accurate reflection of what really happens. However, counsel should also avoid "over-lawyering" document management by pushing the privilege issue at the expense of the communication necessary for the effective and credible implementation of the EMS or filling documents with dense legal jargon. While privilege is an important topic to attorneys, it should not dominate counsel's participation in the EMS design and implementation process (or the perception of counsel by the non-lawyers). Other EMS issues, such as policy, identifying environmental aspects/issues, identifying, tracking, and communicating about legal requirements, auditing, and management review, are all equally, perhaps even more, important issues from a legal perspective.

4.0 Conclusion

EMSs are an accepted and expected part of the business and environmental compliance landscape, applying well-accepted management principles to assist organizations in identifying and meeting their environmental obligations and commitments, including their legal ones. EMSs are based on the logical concept that better environmental performance can be achieved when environmental obligations are systematically identified and managed rather than randomly, reactively, and episodically addressed. ISO 14001 has become the domestically and internationally accepted framework for this approach, though this is not to suggest it is the only model or that third-party certification to ISO 14001 is necessary to an effective EMS.

EMSs have significant legal implications. Not having an EMS likely increases an organization's exposure to public and private liability. Any organization implementing an effective EMS will be necessarily implementing a comprehensive environmental compliance assurance system. EMSs are a framework for affirmatively and successfully identifying and managing legal obligations and liabilities rather than simply waiting for audits and lawsuits to first identify legal "problems." Regulatory requirements, whether RCRA hazardous waste programs, Clean Air Act Title V permits, or chemical or product requlations can be managed through EMSs. EMSs are also being called upon to manage compliance with transnational legal requirements. EMSs play an important role in determining whether enforcement discretion or penalty mitigation will be exercised where potential noncompliance has occurred, and are an element of organization-wide compliance and ethics programs. Federal and state governments are also looking to EMS as an element of innovative regulatory strategies aimed at cost-effectively improving environmental performance and public participation. Lastly, EMSs are a foundation for implementing broader strategies such as sustainable development, social responsibility, product stewardship, and and can form a component of overall enterprise risk management. Therefore, environmental lawyers should understand and be prepared to participate in the design, implementation, and review of EMSs.

5.0 Research Sources

The following sources provide additional information about EMSs:

- ABA Section of Environment, Energy and Natural Resources, Special Committee on Second Generation Issues: http://www.abanet.org/envi ron/committees/secondgeneration/home

- International Organization for Standardization: http://www.iso.ch

- U.S. EPA Environmental Management Systems site: http://www.epa.gov/ ems/

- U.S. Sentencing Commission: http://www.ussc.gov

Notes

[1] ISO 14001: 2015, *Environmental Management Systems-Specification with Guidance for Use*, may be obtained from the American National Standards Institute (ANSI). ISO standards reflect the consensus

(defined as at least a two-thirds positive vote) of the national standards bodies from more than 100 participating nations. ANSI is the U.S. representative to ISO. The delegations typically include representatives of standards organizations and private industry and, in some cases, public interest groups. In many countries, the national standards organizations are governmental entities. Public interest groups representing environmental and consumer concerns have been encouraged and, in some instances, subsidized to participate, and ISO is currently considering revisions to its procedures to increase the participation of nongovernmental organizations. Federal agencies are required by the National Technology Transfer and Advancement Act of 1995 to participate in the standards development process and to consider standards when developing and implementing public policy. In part based on this mandate, the EPA has been a vigorous participant in the U.S. ISO delegations working on international environmental standards. OMB Circular A-119, *Federal Participation in the Development and Use of Voluntary Consensus Standards and in Conformity Assessment Activities* (Feb. 10, 1998), revised in 2016 (81 Fed. Reg. 4673 (Jan. 27, 2016) provides guidance on implementing these requirements.

2   *See ISO Survey of Certifications 20014 (ISO 2015).* Third-party certification (also known as registration) involves an audit of the organization's EMS by an accredited, independent auditor that verifies that the EMS meets the requirements of ISO 14001 and that the EMS has actually been implemented. ISO 14001 does not require third-party certification, and certification is not certification to a defined level of environmental performance or compliance. To maintain their certifications, organizations are subject to annual or semiannual "surveillance" audits by the third party, and the certification must be renewed every three years. Most of the countries that participate in ISO have a national accreditation body that manages the certification process, including registrar accreditation and auditor qualifications.

3   One of the first formal U.S. government statements regarding management systems came in the area of occupational safety with the Occupational Health and Safety Administration's Voluntary Protection Program in 1982. *See* 47 Fed. Reg. 29025; 50 Fed. Reg. 43804; 51 Fed. Reg. 33669; 52 Fed. Reg. 7337. While this chapter focuses on environmental management systems, occupational health and safety management systems are also widely implemented, often integrated with EMS. There is considerable national standards activity on this subject, including in the United States (ANSI published ANSI Z10, a standard on safety management systems in 2005 and revised it in 2012). ISO is working on an occupational safety standard that, if completed, will be titled ISO 45001. In the meantime, a non-ISO standard called OHSAS 18001 has been widely used.

4   *See, e.g., Deepwater: The Gulf Oil Disaster and the Future of Offshore Drilling*, Report to the President, National Commission on the BP Deepwater Horizon Oil Spill and Offshore Drilling (Jan. 11, 2011); *Report of Investigation into the Circumstances Surrounding the Fire, Explosion, Sinking and Loss of Eleven Crew Members Aboard the Mobile Offshore Drilling Unit Deepwater Horizon*, U.S. Coast Guard (MISLE Activity No. 3721503) (Apr. 2011); *Deepwater Accident Investigation Report*, BP (Sept. 8, 2010).

5   51 Fed. Reg. 25004.

6   Incentives for Self-Policing: Discovery, Disclosure, Correction and Prevention of Violations, 60 Fed. Reg. 66705 (Dec. 22, 1995); 60 Fed. Reg. 16875 (Apr. 3, 1995); 65 Fed. Reg. 19618 (Apr. 11, 2000); 73 Fed. Reg. 44991 (Aug. 1, 2008); 80 Fed. Reg. 7647 (Dec. 9, 2015). More than a dozen states have also adopted self-disclosure policies.

7   Factors in Decisions on Criminal Prosecutions for Environmental Violations in the Context of Significant Voluntary Compliance (U.S. Department of Justice, July 1991); Federal Prosecution of Corporations (U.S. Department of Justice, June 16, 1999); *Principles of Federal Prosecution of Business Organizations* (U.S. Department of Justice, Jan. 20, 2003; Dec. 12, 2006; and Aug. 28, 2008); Individual Accountability for Corporate Wrongdoing (U.S. Department of Justice, Sept. 9, 2015). These factors are embodied in Section 9-28.000 of the U.S. Attorney's Manual.

8   The New Jersey Prosecutor's Office has also issued Voluntary Environmental Audit/Compliance Guidelines (May 15, 1992), which resemble Department of Justice policy. The New Jersey Guidelines provide great detail about what a compliance program must look like. Such programs will be viewed as "mitigating

factors" in the exercise of the prosecutor's criminal environmental enforcement discretion. Massachusetts Department of Environmental Protection's Guidance on Incorporating Environmental Management Systems into Enforcement Negotiations and Settlements (Jan. 2001) states at p. 2 that "DEP considers the adoption and implementation of an EMS to be *part of the activity necessary* for a regulated entity that routinely engages in activity regulated by DEP to return to, achieve, maintain and/or improve overall environmental compliance" (emphasis in the original).

9   56 Fed. Reg. 22762, Section 8A1.2–8B2.1. Although the Organizational Sentencing Guidelines do not formally apply to companies convicted of environmental crimes, they have nonetheless been commonly used by companies as a guide in the development of compliance assurance programs in the environmental area.

10   The revised criteria were published in the *Federal Register* on May 19, 2004 (69 Fed. Reg. 28994-29028) and can also be found on the Sentencing Commission's website at http://www.ussc.gov. For more background on the Sentencing Guidelines and the issues raised during the revisions process, see *Report of the Ad Hoc Advisory Group on the Organizational Sentencing Guidelines* (Oct. 7, 2003). The importance of the Sentencing Guidelines' Criteria was not decreased by the U.S. Supreme Court holding that the Guidelines were unconstitutional to the extent that they were mandatory and that criminal sentences could not be enhanced based on facts not found by the jury. *United States v. Booker*, 543 U.S. 220 (2005) (a result reinforced in a decision holding that even though the Guidelines are advisory, an amended and more stringent version of the Guidelines cannot be applied retroactively, *U.S. v. Peugh*, No. No. 12-62 (U.S. June 10, 2013)). The Supreme Court held that sentencing courts may still use the Guidelines in an advisory fashion, signaling their continued viability, a signal courts have taken to heart. *See Report on the Continuing Impact of United States v. Booker on Federal Sentencing* (U.S. Sentencing Commission 2012). Further, prosecutors and regulators will still take compliance systems into account when making enforcement decisions, and organizations will still find the adequacy of such systems important when defending themselves against charges of wrongdoing. Finally, implementing effective compliance programs is good corporate governance and risk management.

11   The amendments were proposed in May 2010 and became effective November 1, 2010. *See* 75 Fed. Reg. 27388 (May 14, 2010).

12   The fact that these programs typically focused on compliance does not mean that they were not "legitimate" EMS. There is a mistaken view among some commentators that the only "real" EMS are those that "assume" and "go beyond" compliance. This view denigrates compliance with the law, which represents meeting an entity's obligations to the public as defined by the public's representatives through legislation and regulations. Minimizing the key role of compliance in an EMS ignores the liability, financial, and reputational consequences of noncompliance. Ambitious commitments to sustainable development and social responsibility can be rapidly and potentially irreversibly undercut by significant or sustained noncompliance.

13   For example, detailed provisions about environmental management and compliance systems, including oversight of such systems, were included in the probation and debarment agreements resolving an enforcement case against the Duke Energy Company alleging criminal violations of the Clean Water Act. *U.S. v. Duke Energy Bus. Servs., LLC, et al.,* Case Nos. 5:15-CR-00062, 5:15-CR-00067, 5:15-CR-00068 (E.D. N.C., May 14, 2015). *See also U.S. v. BP Exploration* (D. Alaska Sept. 1999); *U.S. v. ASARCO* (D. Mont. May 5, 1998) and (D. Ariz. June 2, 1998); *U.S. v. Koppers Industries, Inc.* (N.D. Alabama, Dec. 13, 2002); *U.S. v. Massachusetts Bay Transportation Authority*, C.A. No. 04CV10481-MEL (D. Ma), 69 Fed. Reg. 15381 (Mar. 25, 2004); *The Clean Air Council v. Sunoco, Inc.*, C.A. No. 02-1553 GMS (D. Del. Apr. 2, 2003) (noting an EMS requirement in an enforcement agreement between the company and state regulators); *U.S. v. National Railroad Passenger Corporation*, C.A. No. 01-11121-RWZ (D. Ma.), 66 Fed. Reg. 37706 (July 19, 2001); *U.S. v. Alcoa, Inc.*, C.A. No. 4:99CV61 AS (N.D. Indiana), 67 Fed. Reg. 3735 (Jan. 25, 2002); *U.S. v. Ferro Corp.*, C.A. No. 2:02 CV 115 (N.D. Indiana), 67 Fed. Reg. 16123 (Apr. 4, 2002); *U.S. v. Boston Sand and Gravel Co.*, C.A. No. 02-109999-JLT (D. Ma.), 67 Fed.

Reg. 40750 (June 13, 2002); *U.S. v. Nucor* (D. S.C. Dec. 19, 2000). EPA's compliance initiatives aimed at universities and hospitals have also produced a number of settlement agreements mandating implementation of EMS.

14 *Guidance on the use of Environmental Management Systems in Enforcement Settlements as Injunctive Relief and Supplemental Environmental Projects* (U.S. EPA, June 2005).

15 Compliance-Focused Environmental Management Systems–Enforcement Agreement Guidance (U.S. EPA, Aug. 1997. Revised Jan. 2005). While this guidance is consistent with ISO 14001, it is much more focused on compliance issues and does not reflect the balance contained in ISO 14001 regarding nonregulated environmental issues.

16 The widespread acceptance and implementation of ISO 14001 could have additional legal implications if it is viewed by the courts as an "industry standard." Consensus standards have been used as a factor in demonstrating the applicable standard of care in civil litigation. *See, e.g., Hansen v. Abrasive Engineering & Manufacturing, Inc.,* 856 P.2d 625 (S. Ct. Br. 1993); *Kent Village Assoc. v. Smith* 657 A.2d 330 (Md. App. 1995); *Gilden v. U.S.,* F. Supp. 2d 168 (D.D.C. 2015).

17 EPA has established an EMS website describing its policies and providing links to related information. http://www.epa.gov/ems/ (last visited Nov. 8, 2016). EPA has implemented EMS at more than 30 of its own locations.

18 89 Fed. Reg. 13, 638, 13654–13662 (Mar. 14, 2016).

19 30 C.F.R. Part 250, Subpart S.

20 *See, e.g., Department of Defense Green Procurement Strategy—Promoting Environmental Stewardship Throughout The Department Of Defense* (Nov. 2008).

21 48 C.F.R. Subpart 23.9.

22 65 Fed. Reg. 24593 (Apr. 26, 2000).

23 *See* www.fedcenter.gov/programs/EMS for further information on EMS initiatives within the executive branch (last visited Nov. 8, 2016). Implementation of EMSs throughout the federal government is facilitated by the Office of the Chief Sustainability Officer.

24 67 Fed. Reg. 45510 (July 9, 2002). *See* "Aligning National Policy Act Processes with Environmental Management Systems—A Guide for NEPA and EMS Practitioners" (CEQ 2007); Boling, *Environmental Management Systems and NEPA: A Framework For Productive Harmony,* 35 ELR 10022 (2005).

25 *See, e.g.,* 69 Fed. Reg. 60861 (Oct. 13, 2004).

26 *Agency Policy and Guidance: Small Local Governments Compliance Assistance Policy,* 69 Fed. Reg. 31278 (June 2, 2004). The EMS portion of this policy outlines 17 elements of an EMS that are consistent with ISO 14001.

27 They include Colorado, Connecticut, Florida, Illinois, Maine, Oregon, Texas, and Wisconsin. *See* Colo. Rev. Stat. §§ 25-6.7-101–110; Conn. Gen. Stat. § 22a-6y; Fla. Stat. Ann. § 403.0752; Ill. Comp. Stat. 5/52.3-1–4; Me. Rev. Stat. Ann. tit. 38, § 343-G; Or. Rev. Stat. §§ 468.501–.521; Tex. Water Code Ann. § 5.127; Wis. Stat. § 299.80.

28 30 TAC Ch. 90. 30 TAC § 90.30, which became effective in July 2012, also provides regulatory incentives to companies that implement EMS, including a 10% "compliance history credit."

29 Even before Sarbanes-Oxley, the SEC established a list of factors, including the existence of internal compliance programs and procedures, that it would take into account in deciding whether to prosecute a matter. *Report of Investigation Pursuant to Section 21(a) of the Securities Exchange Act of 1934 and Commission Statement on the Relationship of Cooperation to Agency Enforcement Decisions* (SEC, Oct. 23, 2001).

30 The FCPA requires companies to implement internal controls to prevent bribery. 15 U.S.C. § 78m(b)(2)(A)-(B). The SEC and DOJ have brought FCPA enforcement actions alleging the absence or failure of internal controls, and have imposed compliance management system requirements as part of settling FCPA claims. *See, e.g., U.S. v. Panalpina World Transport* (S.D. Tex., Nov. 4, 2010); *SEC v. Veraz*

Networks, Inc., CV-10-2849 (PVT) (N.D. Cal., June 29, 2010); *SEC v. Halliburton Co. and KBR, Inc.*, 4:09-CV-399 (S.D. Tex, Feb. 11, 2009); *SEC v. Titan Corp.*, CV-05-0411 (D.D.C., Mar. 1, 2005).

31 FCPA—A Reference Guide to the U.S. Foreign Corrupt Practices Act (USDOJ/SEC 2012, revised 2015).

32 In a highly publicized case, a major corporation avoided enforcement under the FCPA due in large measure to a comprehensive anti-corruption compliance system that was described in some detail by the government in its pleadings relating to criminal allegations against an individual employee. *U.S. v. Peterson*, Cr. No. 12—224 (E.D. N.Y.).

33 Directive 2002/95/EC of the European Parliament and of the Council of 27 Jan. 2003; Directive 2000/53/EC of the European Parliament and of the Council of Sept. 18, 2000. In 2013, ISO published a standard aimed at enhancing product safety throughout the value chain: ISO 10377, "Consumer Product Safety—Guidelines for Suppliers" standard.

34 15 U.S.C. § 2601 et seq., as amended by the Frank R. Lautenberg Chemical Safety for the 21st Century Act, P.L. 114–82 (June 22, 2106).

35 See http://www.globalreporting.org/standards/G4/ (last visited June 5, 2016).

36 75 Fed. Reg. 6290 (Feb. 8, 2010) (announcing the SEC's guidance regarding disclosure of climate change information). According to the California Transparency in Supply Chains Act of 2010, all retail sellers doing business in California and having $100 million or more in annual worldwide gross receipts must make certain disclosures on their websites about labor and environmental issues related to their global supply chains.

37 *See, e.g.,* U.S. Retailers Offer Plan For Safety at Factories, *New York Times* (July 10, 2013); Retailers Take Bangladesh Safety Into Their Own Hands, *Wall Street Journal* (July 7, 2013).

38 One survey indicated that implementing EMS is one of the most commonly employed sustainable development activities (88 percent of respondents). *2002 Sustainability Report*, PriceWaterhouseCoopers (Aug. 2002).

39 World Summit on Sustainable Development, Plan of Implementation (2002).

40 *See Improving Environmental Performance and Compliance: 10 Elements of Effective Environmental Management Systems*, Commission for Environmental Cooperation, June 2000. The elements set forth in the guidance are based largely on ISO 14001.

41 For a more detailed discussion of this issue, *see* C. Bell, *International Environmental Standards and Industrial Codes of Conduct: Toward Sustainable Environmentalism*, 47 Rocky Mt. Min. L. Inst. § 25 (2001).

42 25 U.S.C. § 1350. The Supreme Court has restricted the use of the Alien Tort Claims Act in cases involving allegations of violations of international law occurring wholly outside of the U.S., applying the presumption against the extra-territorial application of U.S. law. *Kiobel v. Royal Dutch Shell*, 133 S. Ct. 1659 (2013).

43 Additional guidance on implementing EMS in general and ISO 14001 in particular can be found in a companion guidance document, ISO 14004. ISO 14004 is not intended for use in the third-party certification process.

44 ISO 14001:2015, Clause 4.

45 ISO 14001: 2015, Clause 5.

46 ISO 14001: 2015, Clauses 5.1 and 5.3.

47 Guidelines at § 8B2.1(b)(2). The importance of the board of directors' role in compliance programs was highlighted in the seminal *Caremark* case, in which the Delaware Court of Chancery (one of the most influential courts on corporate law) concluded that individual members of boards of directors have a fiduciary duty to ensure that a corporation acts in compliance with applicable laws and has a compliance program to meet this obligation. *In re Caremark Inc. Derivative Litigation* 698 A.2d 959 (1996). The *Caremark* court expressly discussed the Sentencing Guidelines criteria, noting that "any rational person at attempting in good faith to meet an organizational governance responsibility would be bound to take into account this development [the criteria in the Sentencing Guidelines] and the enhanced penalties and

the opportunities for reduced sanctions that it offers." The Delaware Supreme Court has since confirmed the reasoning in *Caremark*, holding that directors may be liable for failure to exercise appropriate oversight if the directors failed utterly to implement any reporting system or controls or, having implemented such a system, consciously failed to monitor or oversee its operations and thus prevented themselves from being informed of risks or problems requiring their attention. *Stone v. Ritter*, 911 A.2d 362 (Del. 2006); *In re Walt Disney Co. Deriv. Litig.*, 906 A.2d 27 (Del. 2006).

48 Meeting these criteria may allow a company to avoid an enhanced criminal sentence where a "high level" or "substantial authority" individual is implicated in a crime. In addition to the direct line of communication to the board, the organization must also have detected the violation before discovery outside the organization was likely and have voluntarily reported the issue to the authorities. Also no person with operational authority for the compliance/ethics program can be implicated in the matter.

49 Guidelines at § 8B2.1(b)(6).

50 ISO 14001: 2015, Clause 6.1.2.

51 Guidelines at § 8B2.1(c).

52 Organizations should also take other risk management programs into account when evaluating their environmental issues. For example, organizations that are implementing enterprise risk management (ERM) initiatives should ensure that the evaluation of environmental issues is consistently addressed under both the EMS and ERM (and that environmental issues from the EMS are incorporated into the ERM analysis).

53 ISO 14001: 2015, Clause 6.1.3.

54 A puzzling theme of certain critics of ISO 14001 is that it does not contain any performance standards and is therefore somehow deficient. This criticism misses the point because ISO 14001 was from the outset designed to assist organizations to identify and meet their obligations, not establish new ones or replace existing ones. An effort by ISO to establish such performance standards would no doubt have been criticized as an effort to subvert local, national, and regional environmental requirements.

55 Many private-sector programs pre-date ISO 14001. These include the American Chemistry Council's "Responsible Care" program in 1988 (and which has been enhanced several times since), the American Petroleum Institute's "STEP" initiative in 1990, the International Chamber of Commerce's "Business Charter on Sustainable Development" in 1991, and guidance documents produced by organizations such as the Global Environmental Management Initiative, Public Environmental Reporting Initiative, and the Global Reporting Initiative. Some trade associations, including the American Chemistry Council and the American Forest and Paper Association, make implementation of the trade association programs a condition of membership.

56 Guidelines at § 8B2.1, Commentary Application Notes 2 (A) and (B). The Guidelines' discussion of industry standards and practices highlights the possibility that such voluntary standards might nonetheless be transformed into legal requirements, whether by a court in a negligence or product liability case, or by the government if it concludes that the failure to follow such standards demonstrates the absence of an effective compliance and ethics program.

57 ISO 14001:2015, Clause 4.2.

58 ISO 14001: 2015, Clauses 6.1.4–6.2.2.

59 ISO 14001:2015, Clause 3.21, defines a "requirement" as a "need or expectation that is stated, generally implied, or obligatory." This is a rather unusual definition, since it arguably transforms a unilateral expectation of, for example, an interested party (which can include those who perceive themselves as affected by the organization), into a "requirement." This construction may make sense in the quality management context, where the "expectation" of a customer might fairly be viewed as a "requirement" by the supplier, but it has very different implications in the environmental management context, where the difference between the "expectations" of interested parties and legally binding obligations can be quite large. It will be interesting to see how this issue plays out as the revised standard is being implemented.

[60] This is an example of the value that counsel might add by being part of the EMS design and implementation team. Those who might be less sensitive to the legal implications of EMS might advise companies that it is inappropriate to set objectives aimed at maintaining compliance with legal requirements, arguing that compliance should be assumed and that the EMS objectives should focus solely on continual improvement. It is not logical to assume compliance has already been achieved when compliance is one of the key themes of an EMS. Further, it is not prudent risk or liability management to devalue the importance of maintaining compliance in an EMS. One should also consider the credibility of explaining the absence of clear compliance goals to enforcers or the public with the simple assertion that compliance "is assumed" or that a "real EMS" has more important matters than compliance to focus on.

[61] ISO 14001: 2015, Clauses 6.1.4, 6.22 and 8.1.

[62] *See, e.g.,* 75 Fed. Reg. 62122 (Oct. 11, 2012) (FTC's revision of its "Green Guides" governing environmental marketing claims); www.energystar.gov (home page for the Federal Energy Star program).

[63] Procedures do not have to be lengthy written narratives. Procedures can be web-based, expressed through posters on a wall, or demonstrated using pictures. For example, a waste management procedure might largely comprise pictures illustrating what types of wastes go in which containers.

[64] ISO 14001: 2015, Clauses 7.2 and 7.3.

[65] Guidelines at § 8B2.1(b)(4).

[66] ISO 14001: 2015, Clause 9.

[67] ISO has published a standard that provides guidance on measuring environmental performance: ISO 14031. ISO 14001 does not require conformance to ISO 14031.

[68] ISO 14001: 2015, Clause 9.1.2.

[69] Many states have various forms of "audit privilege" or "audit immunity" laws that vary considerably in their requirements (e.g., some require prior notification that an audit is being conducted) and the enforcement consequences of identifying noncompliance during audits.

[70] ISO 14001: 2015, Clause 7.4.

[71] The requirements associated with whistle-blowing have become widespread and increasingly complex. Most of the major environmental statutes have whistle-blower protection provisions, and the whistle-blowing provisions of the Sentencing Guidelines criteria and Sarbanes-Oxley have resulted in many companies establishing company-wide whistle-blower programs, described as everything from "hotlines" to "helplines." OSHA's Office of the Whistleblower Protection Program enforces most of the anti-retaliation protections for whistle-blowers, and is a good source of information (www.whistleblowers.gov, last visited Nov. 8, 2016). Whistle-blower programs will continue to get attention. On May 25, 2011, the SEC adopted additional regulations on whistle-blowing as part of the implementation of Section 922 of the Dodd-Frank Wall Street Reform and Consumer Protection Act of 2010. "Implementation of the Whistleblower Provisions of Section 21F of the Securities Exchange Act of 1934" (SEC Release No. 34-64545); see www.sec.gov/whistleblower.

[72] 75 Fed. Reg. 6290 (Feb. 8, 2010) (SEC guidance on climatge change disclosures). The SEC published a draft "concept release" in 2016 regarding corporate disclosures, including on matters such as climate change and sustainability. 81 Fed. Reg. 23916 (April 22, 2016). Portions of the SEC's conflict minerals regulations promulgated in 2012 (77 Fed. Reg. 56,274 (Sept. 12, 2012) were successfully challenged in court. *National Assoc. of Mfrs. v. SEC,* 800 F.3d 518 (D.C. Cir. 2015).

[73] The European Union's EMAS directive, which includes an EMS element, requires independently verified annual environmental reports. ISO 14001 has proven far more popular an EMS model in the European Union than has EMAS.

[74] ISO has created guidance on external communication that is designated as ISO 14063:2006. The starting point of this work is that there is no one superior form of external communication and that the appropriate method of communication depends on the intended audience, the sociocultural/economic context in which the communication will take place, and the subject matter and objectives of the communication.

It does not assume formal annual environmental reports are always an appropriate or the best form of environmental communication.

75 One of the more prominent models for reporting about sustainable development has been developed by the Global Reporting Initiative. *See* http://www.globalreporting.org/Home.

76 ISO 14001: 2015, Clause 9.2.

77 ISO 14001:2015 describes EMS auditing as "internal auditing." This may create ambiguities, since compliance auditing may also be "internal auditing." Further, the "internal" EMS auditing contemplated by ISO 14001 does not always have to be performed "internally"; rather, third-parties may be used to assist in conducting internal audits. It appears that the term "internal audits" was used in part to distinguish the internal auditing program from the optional "external" third-party certification process, which also involves auditing. For those companies seeking such certifications, they must have their own internal auditing program that cannot be satisfied by the "external" certification audits.

78 The ANSI-ASB National Accreditaton Board ("ANAB"), the entity responsible for managing the ISO 14001 registration process in the United States, has issued an advisory stating that an organization may be registered despite detected noncompliance when the organization has taken corrective action to address the noncompliance and the noncompliance does not indicate a major systems nonconformity. ANAB Advisory 14 (2005).

79 An extreme version of the inadequate "paperwork EMS audit" is when the auditor focuses primarily on the "official EMS paperwork" such that the target company effectively has two systems: the one that is audited and the one that is actually used in practice. This situation has obvious civil, criminal, and reputational risks.

80 U.S. Attorney's Manual at 9-28.800.B (2016).

81 ISO 14001 does not require that EMS audits be conducted in accordance with the ISO 19011 auditing standard.

82 ISO 14001: 2015, Clause 10.2.

83 *See, e.g.,* The Exercise of Investigative Discretion (EPA, Jan. 12, 1994) ("Devaney Memorandum").

84 ISO 14001: 2015 Clauses 9.3 and 10.3.

85 ISO 14001:2015, Clause 7.5. The revised ISO 14001 uses the term "documented information" to include both documented procedures and records. Organizations that maintain record retention systems for regulatory or risk management purposes might choose to retain a distinction between records and other forms of documentation.

86 Organizations should also determine whether there are any potentially applicable state audit-privilege laws or policies that should be taken into account when designing and implementing their EMS. For example, if state law provides for liability shields if a company notifies the state before an audit is conducted and the audit report is submitted to the state, the company should consider whether to include the appropriate steps in its audit procedure.

87 Guidelines at § 8C2.5, Commentary Application Note 12.

88 71 Fed. Reg. 28063 (May 15, 2006). Further, a federal court declared unconstitutional certain elements of government demands for cooperation pursuant to the Thompson Memorandum. *U.S. v. Jeffrey Stein, et al.*, 541 F.3d 130 (2d Cir. 2008).

89 *Akzo Nobel Chemicals Ltd. v. EU* (Case-550/07, Sept. 14, 2010).

Index

Small Business Liability Relief and Brownfields Revitalization Act, 23–24, 204, 232, 587
small system variances, 540–42
Smart Way Transport Partnership, 952
The Society of the Plastics Industry v. OSHA, 1021
soil, contaminated, 164–65
solid waste: definition of, 156–59; exclusions from, 156–58; recycled materials, 158–59; SWMU, 185–86
Solid Waste Agency of Northern Cook County v. U.S. Army Corps of Engineers (SWANCC), 29
Solid Waste Disposal Act, 434, 922
solid waste management units (SWMUs), 185–86
source water protection, 565–66
Southeast Alaska Conservation Council v. U.S. Army Corps of Engineers, 367
Southern National v. EPA, 911
Southview Associates Ltd. v. Bongartz, 52–53
sovereign immunity, waiver of, 191
species protection law, 747–50
specific intent, 104–5
Spill Prevention Control and Countermeasure (SPCC) Plans, 371–72, 452
spills: control of, 221; CWA and, 370–74; PCBs, 832–34; prevention equipment, 217–18, 220, 221, 223; prevention of, 370–74; reporting and cleanup of, 212, 214, 221, 229–30; response and liability, 372–74, 411
Stacy v. VEPCO, 19
Standardized Analytical Methods (SAMs), 553
standardized permits, 184–85
standards: agreed-upon, 91–93; causation, CERCLA and, 619, 627; consensus, 1015–16; ETS, 1019; financial accounting, 127–29; GLP, 819; health, 1013–14, 1016; mobile source emission, 281, 296–97; performance, for underground storage tank systems, 221–22; permanent, 1017–19; residual risk, CAA and, 284–86; safety, 1014–15; statutory of conduct, 88
Standards Completion Process, 1017
standard setting, OSHA and, 1012–14, 1020–23; consensus standards, 1015–16; ETS, 1019; permanent standards, 1017–19
standing, 41–43, 694, 902–3
Staples v. United States, 105
State Emergency Response Commissions (SERC), 964, 972, 978

state employees, 1035
state government, 2–3, 6–9, 28–33; CAA permit applications, 311; CERCLA and, 602–3; climate change and, 757–61; corporate climate disclosure and, 766–67; CWA and, 374–82; EMS and, 1062; enforcement and, 25–26, 131–32; EPCRA and, 964, 997; FIFRA and, 905–8; NPDES permit program, 342–43, 971; OPA and, 427, 434; OSHA and, 1035–37; pollution prevention and, 957–59; Regulatory Innovation Agreement, 951–52; SDWA and, 496, 545–46; TSCA and, 836; UST cleanup funds, 235–36
state implementation plans (SIPs): CAA and, 251, 254–58, 261–66, 735; EPA call authority, 256, 263–64; failure to develop sanctions for, 265; nonattainment, 257–58
statute of limitations (SOL), 626–27, 703
statutory immunity, 115
statutory standard of conduct, 88
statutory standing, 41–43, 87–88
Steel Company v. Citizens for a Better Environment, 629, 995–96
Steeltech, Ltd. v. U.S. EPA, 989
Sterling v. Velsicol Chemical Corp., 19
stipulated penalties, 641
Stockholm Declaration, 3
Stone v. Ritter, 1063
stop-sale orders, 896–97
storage facility, definition of, 175–76
storm water: definition of, 357–58; discharges of, 357–60
Strategic Plan, of EPA, 586–87
stratospheric ozone protection, 296–97
strict liability, 21–24, 421, 603–5
subject, of investigation, 114
submerged oil, 458
subrogation, OPA and, 433
subsistence, definition of, 412
substantial risk, reporting on, 787–88, 823
Subtitle D, under RCRA, 158–59, 168–69, 190–91
sue and settle strategy, 43
sulfur dioxide (SO_2), 252, 253, 309
sulfur hexafluoride. *See* greenhouse gas emissions
Summers v. Earth Island Institute, 695
Superfund, 587–88, 623, 644–45. *See also* Comprehensive Environmental Response, Compensation, and Liability Act